T0137282

Lecture Notes in Computer Science   **13668**

More information about this series at https://link.springer.com/bookseries/558

Shai Avidan · Gabriel Brostow ·
Moustapha Cissé · Giovanni Maria Farinella ·
Tal Hassner (Eds.)

Computer Vision – ECCV 2022

17th European Conference
Tel Aviv, Israel, October 23–27, 2022
Proceedings, Part VIII

 Springer

Editors
Shai Avidan
Tel Aviv University
Tel Aviv, Israel

Gabriel Brostow
University College London
London, UK

Moustapha Cissé
Google AI
Accra, Ghana

Giovanni Maria Farinella
University of Catania
Catania, Italy

Tal Hassner
Facebook (United States)
Menlo Park, CA, USA

ISSN 0302-9743   ISSN 1611-3349 (electronic)
Lecture Notes in Computer Science
ISBN 978-3-031-20073-1   ISBN 978-3-031-20074-8 (eBook)
https://doi.org/10.1007/978-3-031-20074-8

This Springer imprint is published by the registered company Springer Nature Switzerland AG
The registered company address is: Gewerbestrasse 11, 6330 Cham, Switzerland

Foreword

Organizing the European Conference on Computer Vision (ECCV 2022) in Tel-Aviv during a global pandemic was no easy feat. The uncertainty level was extremely high, and decisions had to be postponed to the last minute. Still, we managed to plan things just in time for ECCV 2022 to be held in person. Participation in physical events is crucial to stimulating collaborations and nurturing the culture of the Computer Vision community.

There were many people who worked hard to ensure attendees enjoyed the best science at the 16th edition of ECCV. We are grateful to the Program Chairs Gabriel Brostow and Tal Hassner, who went above and beyond to ensure the ECCV reviewing process ran smoothly. The scientific program includes dozens of workshops and tutorials in addition to the main conference and we would like to thank Leonid Karlinsky and Tomer Michaeli for their hard work. Finally, special thanks to the web chairs Lorenzo Baraldi and Kosta Derpanis, who put in extra hours to transfer information fast and efficiently to the ECCV community.

We would like to express gratitude to our generous sponsors and the Industry Chairs, Dimosthenis Karatzas and Chen Sagiv, who oversaw industry relations and proposed new ways for academia-industry collaboration and technology transfer. It's great to see so much industrial interest in what we're doing!

Authors' draft versions of the papers appeared online with open access on both the Computer Vision Foundation (CVF) and the European Computer Vision Association (ECVA) websites as with previous ECCVs. Springer, the publisher of the proceedings, has arranged for archival publication. The final version of the papers is hosted by SpringerLink, with active references and supplementary materials. It benefits all potential readers that we offer both a free and citeable version for all researchers, as well as an authoritative, citeable version for SpringerLink readers. Our thanks go to Ronan Nugent from Springer, who helped us negotiate this agreement. Last but not least, we wish to thank Eric Mortensen, our publication chair, whose expertise made the process smooth.

October 2022

Rita Cucchiara
Jiří Matas
Amnon Shashua
Lihi Zelnik-Manor

Preface

Welcome to the proceedings of the European Conference on Computer Vision (ECCV 2022). This was a hybrid edition of ECCV as we made our way out of the COVID-19 pandemic. The conference received 5804 valid paper submissions, compared to 5150 submissions to ECCV 2020 (a 12.7% increase) and 2439 in ECCV 2018. 1645 submissions were accepted for publication (28%) and, of those, 157 (2.7% overall) as orals.

846 of the submissions were desk-rejected for various reasons. Many of them because they revealed author identity, thus violating the double-blind policy. This violation came in many forms: some had author names with the title, others added acknowledgments to specific grants, yet others had links to their github account where their name was visible. Tampering with the LaTeX template was another reason for automatic desk rejection.

ECCV 2022 used the traditional CMT system to manage the entire double-blind reviewing process. Authors did not know the names of the reviewers and vice versa. Each paper received at least 3 reviews (except 6 papers that received only 2 reviews), totalling more than 15,000 reviews.

Handling the review process at this scale was a significant challenge. To ensure that each submission received as fair and high-quality reviews as possible, we recruited more than 4719 reviewers (in the end, 4719 reviewers did at least one review). Similarly we recruited more than 276 area chairs (eventually, only 276 area chairs handled a batch of papers). The area chairs were selected based on their technical expertise and reputation, largely among people who served as area chairs in previous top computer vision and machine learning conferences (ECCV, ICCV, CVPR, NeurIPS, etc.).

Reviewers were similarly invited from previous conferences, and also from the pool of authors. We also encouraged experienced area chairs to suggest additional chairs and reviewers in the initial phase of recruiting. The median reviewer load was five papers per reviewer, while the average load was about four papers, because of the emergency reviewers. The area chair load was 35 papers, on average.

Conflicts of interest between authors, area chairs, and reviewers were handled largely automatically by the CMT platform, with some manual help from the Program Chairs. Reviewers were allowed to describe themselves as senior reviewer (load of 8 papers to review) or junior reviewers (load of 4 papers). Papers were matched to area chairs based on a subject-area affinity score computed in CMT and an affinity score computed by the Toronto Paper Matching System (TPMS). TPMS is based on the paper's full text. An area chair handling each submission would bid for preferred expert reviewers, and we balanced load and prevented conflicts.

The assignment of submissions to area chairs was relatively smooth, as was the assignment of submissions to reviewers. A small percentage of reviewers were not happy with their assignments in terms of subjects and self-reported expertise. This is an area for improvement, although it's interesting that many of these cases were reviewers hand-picked by AC's. We made a later round of reviewer recruiting, targeted at the list of authors of papers submitted to the conference, and had an excellent response which helped provide enough emergency reviewers. In the end, all but six papers received at least 3 reviews.

The challenges of the reviewing process are in line with past experiences at ECCV 2020. As the community grows, and the number of submissions increases, it becomes ever more challenging to recruit enough reviewers and ensure a high enough quality of reviews. Enlisting authors by default as reviewers might be one step to address this challenge.

Authors were given a week to rebut the initial reviews, and address reviewers' concerns. Each rebuttal was limited to a single pdf page with a fixed template.

The Area Chairs then led discussions with the reviewers on the merits of each submission. The goal was to reach consensus, but, ultimately, it was up to the Area Chair to make a decision. The decision was then discussed with a buddy Area Chair to make sure decisions were fair and informative. The entire process was conducted virtually with no in-person meetings taking place.

The Program Chairs were informed in cases where the Area Chairs overturned a decisive consensus reached by the reviewers, and pushed for the meta-reviews to contain details that explained the reasoning for such decisions. Obviously these were the most contentious cases, where reviewer inexperience was the most common reported factor.

Once the list of accepted papers was finalized and released, we went through the laborious process of plagiarism (including self-plagiarism) detection. A total of 4 accepted papers were rejected because of that.

Finally, we would like to thank our Technical Program Chair, Pavel Lifshits, who did tremendous work behind the scenes, and we thank the tireless CMT team.

October 2022

Gabriel Brostow
Giovanni Maria Farinella
Moustapha Cissé
Shai Avidan
Tal Hassner

Organization

General Chairs

Rita Cucchiara	University of Modena and Reggio Emilia, Italy
Jiří Matas	Czech Technical University in Prague, Czech Republic
Amnon Shashua	Hebrew University of Jerusalem, Israel
Lihi Zelnik-Manor	Technion – Israel Institute of Technology, Israel

Program Chairs

Shai Avidan	Tel-Aviv University, Israel
Gabriel Brostow	University College London, UK
Moustapha Cissé	Google AI, Ghana
Giovanni Maria Farinella	University of Catania, Italy
Tal Hassner	Facebook AI, USA

Program Technical Chair

Pavel Lifshits	Technion – Israel Institute of Technology, Israel

Workshops Chairs

Leonid Karlinsky	IBM Research, Israel
Tomer Michaeli	Technion – Israel Institute of Technology, Israel
Ko Nishino	Kyoto University, Japan

Tutorial Chairs

Thomas Pock	Graz University of Technology, Austria
Natalia Neverova	Facebook AI Research, UK

Demo Chair

Bohyung Han	Seoul National University, Korea

Social and Student Activities Chairs

Tatiana Tommasi   Italian Institute of Technology, Italy
Sagie Benaim   University of Copenhagen, Denmark

Diversity and Inclusion Chairs

Xi Yin   Facebook AI Research, USA
Bryan Russell   Adobe, USA

Communications Chairs

Lorenzo Baraldi   University of Modena and Reggio Emilia, Italy
Kosta Derpanis   York University & Samsung AI Centre Toronto,
                                 Canada

Industrial Liaison Chairs

Dimosthenis Karatzas   Universitat Autònoma de Barcelona, Spain
Chen Sagiv   SagivTech, Israel

Finance Chair

Gerard Medioni   University of Southern California & Amazon,
                                 USA

Publication Chair

Eric Mortensen   MiCROTEC, USA

Area Chairs

Lourdes Agapito   University College London, UK
Zeynep Akata   University of Tübingen, Germany
Naveed Akhtar   University of Western Australia, Australia
Karteek Alahari   Inria Grenoble Rhône-Alpes, France
Alexandre Alahi   École polytechnique fédérale de Lausanne,
                                 Switzerland
Pablo Arbelaez   Universidad de Los Andes, Columbia
Antonis A. Argyros   University of Crete & Foundation for Research
                                 and Technology-Hellas, Crete
Yuki M. Asano   University of Amsterdam, The Netherlands
Kalle Åström   Lund University, Sweden
Hadar Averbuch-Elor   Cornell University, USA

Hossein Azizpour	KTH Royal Institute of Technology, Sweden
Vineeth N. Balasubramanian	Indian Institute of Technology, Hyderabad, India
Lamberto Ballan	University of Padova, Italy
Adrien Bartoli	Université Clermont Auvergne, France
Horst Bischof	Graz University of Technology, Austria
Matthew B. Blaschko	KU Leuven, Belgium
Federica Bogo	Meta Reality Labs Research, Switzerland
Katherine Bouman	California Institute of Technology, USA
Edmond Boyer	Inria Grenoble Rhône-Alpes, France
Michael S. Brown	York University, Canada
Vittorio Caggiano	Meta AI Research, USA
Neill Campbell	University of Bath, UK
Octavia Camps	Northeastern University, USA
Duygu Ceylan	Adobe Research, USA
Ayan Chakrabarti	Google Research, USA
Tat-Jen Cham	Nanyang Technological University, Singapore
Antoni Chan	City University of Hong Kong, Hong Kong, China
Manmohan Chandraker	NEC Labs America, USA
Xinlei Chen	Facebook AI Research, USA
Xilin Chen	Institute of Computing Technology, Chinese Academy of Sciences, China
Dongdong Chen	Microsoft Cloud AI, USA
Chen Chen	University of Central Florida, USA
Ondrej Chum	Vision Recognition Group, Czech Technical University in Prague, Czech Republic
John Collomosse	Adobe Research & University of Surrey, UK
Camille Couprie	Facebook, France
David Crandall	Indiana University, USA
Daniel Cremers	Technical University of Munich, Germany
Marco Cristani	University of Verona, Italy
Canton Cristian	Facebook AI Research, USA
Dengxin Dai	ETH Zurich, Switzerland
Dima Damen	University of Bristol, UK
Kostas Daniilidis	University of Pennsylvania, USA
Trevor Darrell	University of California, Berkeley, USA
Andrew Davison	Imperial College London, UK
Tali Dekel	Weizmann Institute of Science, Israel
Alessio Del Bue	Istituto Italiano di Tecnologia, Italy
Weihong Deng	Beijing University of Posts and Telecommunications, China
Konstantinos Derpanis	Ryerson University, Canada
Carl Doersch	DeepMind, UK

Matthijs Douze   Facebook AI Research, USA
Mohamed Elhoseiny   King Abdullah University of Science and
                                Technology, Saudi Arabia
Sergio Escalera   University of Barcelona, Spain
Yi Fang   New York University, USA
Ryan Farrell   Brigham Young University, USA
Alireza Fathi   Google, USA
Christoph Feichtenhofer   Facebook AI Research, USA
Basura Fernando   Agency for Science, Technology and Research
                                (A*STAR), Singapore
Vittorio Ferrari   Google Research, Switzerland
Andrew W. Fitzgibbon   Graphcore, UK
David J. Fleet   University of Toronto, Canada
David Forsyth   University of Illinois at Urbana-Champaign, USA
David Fouhey   University of Michigan, USA
Katerina Fragkiadaki   Carnegie Mellon University, USA
Friedrich Fraundorfer   Graz University of Technology, Austria
Oren Freifeld   Ben-Gurion University, Israel
Thomas Funkhouser   Google Research & Princeton University, USA
Yasutaka Furukawa   Simon Fraser University, Canada
Fabio Galasso   Sapienza University of Rome, Italy
Jürgen Gall   University of Bonn, Germany
Chuang Gan   Massachusetts Institute of Technology, USA
Zhe Gan   Microsoft, USA
Animesh Garg   University of Toronto, Vector Institute, Nvidia,
                                Canada
Efstratios Gavves   University of Amsterdam, The Netherlands
Peter Gehler   Amazon, Germany
Theo Gevers   University of Amsterdam, The Netherlands
Bernard Ghanem   King Abdullah University of Science and
                                Technology, Saudi Arabia
Ross B. Girshick   Facebook AI Research, USA
Georgia Gkioxari   Facebook AI Research, USA
Albert Gordo   Facebook, USA
Stephen Gould   Australian National University, Australia
Venu Madhav Govindu   Indian Institute of Science, India
Kristen Grauman   Facebook AI Research & UT Austin, USA
Abhinav Gupta   Carnegie Mellon University & Facebook AI
                                Research, USA
Mohit Gupta   University of Wisconsin-Madison, USA
Hu Han   Institute of Computing Technology, Chinese
                                Academy of Sciences, China

Bohyung Han	Seoul National University, Korea
Tian Han	Stevens Institute of Technology, USA
Emily Hand	University of Nevada, Reno, USA
Bharath Hariharan	Cornell University, USA
Ran He	Institute of Automation, Chinese Academy of Sciences, China
Otmar Hilliges	ETH Zurich, Switzerland
Adrian Hilton	University of Surrey, UK
Minh Hoai	Stony Brook University, USA
Yedid Hoshen	Hebrew University of Jerusalem, Israel
Timothy Hospedales	University of Edinburgh, UK
Gang Hua	Wormpex AI Research, USA
Di Huang	Beihang University, China
Jing Huang	Facebook, USA
Jia-Bin Huang	Facebook, USA
Nathan Jacobs	Washington University in St. Louis, USA
C. V. Jawahar	International Institute of Information Technology, Hyderabad, India
Herve Jegou	Facebook AI Research, France
Neel Joshi	Microsoft Research, USA
Armand Joulin	Facebook AI Research, France
Frederic Jurie	University of Caen Normandie, France
Fredrik Kahl	Chalmers University of Technology, Sweden
Yannis Kalantidis	NAVER LABS Europe, France
Evangelos Kalogerakis	University of Massachusetts, Amherst, USA
Sing Bing Kang	Zillow Group, USA
Yosi Keller	Bar Ilan University, Israel
Margret Keuper	University of Mannheim, Germany
Tae-Kyun Kim	Imperial College London, UK
Benjamin Kimia	Brown University, USA
Alexander Kirillov	Facebook AI Research, USA
Kris Kitani	Carnegie Mellon University, USA
Iasonas Kokkinos	Snap Inc. & University College London, UK
Vladlen Koltun	Apple, USA
Nikos Komodakis	University of Crete, Crete
Piotr Koniusz	Australian National University, Australia
Philipp Kraehenbuehl	University of Texas at Austin, USA
Dilip Krishnan	Google, USA
Ajay Kumar	Hong Kong Polytechnic University, Hong Kong, China
Junseok Kwon	Chung-Ang University, Korea
Jean-Francois Lalonde	Université Laval, Canada

Ivan Laptev	Inria Paris, France
Laura Leal-Taixé	Technical University of Munich, Germany
Erik Learned-Miller	University of Massachusetts, Amherst, USA
Gim Hee Lee	National University of Singapore, Singapore
Seungyong Lee	Pohang University of Science and Technology, Korea
Zhen Lei	Institute of Automation, Chinese Academy of Sciences, China
Bastian Leibe	RWTH Aachen University, Germany
Hongdong Li	Australian National University, Australia
Fuxin Li	Oregon State University, USA
Bo Li	University of Illinois at Urbana-Champaign, USA
Yin Li	University of Wisconsin-Madison, USA
Ser-Nam Lim	Meta AI Research, USA
Joseph Lim	University of Southern California, USA
Stephen Lin	Microsoft Research Asia, China
Dahua Lin	The Chinese University of Hong Kong, Hong Kong, China
Si Liu	Beihang University, China
Xiaoming Liu	Michigan State University, USA
Ce Liu	Microsoft, USA
Zicheng Liu	Microsoft, USA
Yanxi Liu	Pennsylvania State University, USA
Feng Liu	Portland State University, USA
Yebin Liu	Tsinghua University, China
Chen Change Loy	Nanyang Technological University, Singapore
Huchuan Lu	Dalian University of Technology, China
Cewu Lu	Shanghai Jiao Tong University, China
Oisin Mac Aodha	University of Edinburgh, UK
Dhruv Mahajan	Facebook, USA
Subhransu Maji	University of Massachusetts, Amherst, USA
Atsuto Maki	KTH Royal Institute of Technology, Sweden
Arun Mallya	NVIDIA, USA
R. Manmatha	Amazon, USA
Iacopo Masi	Sapienza University of Rome, Italy
Dimitris N. Metaxas	Rutgers University, USA
Ajmal Mian	University of Western Australia, Australia
Christian Micheloni	University of Udine, Italy
Krystian Mikolajczyk	Imperial College London, UK
Anurag Mittal	Indian Institute of Technology, Madras, India
Philippos Mordohai	Stevens Institute of Technology, USA
Greg Mori	Simon Fraser University & Borealis AI, Canada

Mathieu Salzmann	École polytechnique fédérale de Lausanne, Switzerland
Dimitris Samaras	Stony Brook University, USA
Aswin Sankaranarayanan	Carnegie Mellon University, USA
Imari Sato	National Institute of Informatics, Japan
Yoichi Sato	University of Tokyo, Japan
Shin'ichi Satoh	National Institute of Informatics, Japan
Walter Scheirer	University of Notre Dame, USA
Bernt Schiele	Max Planck Institute for Informatics, Germany
Konrad Schindler	ETH Zurich, Switzerland
Cordelia Schmid	Inria & Google, France
Alexander Schwing	University of Illinois at Urbana-Champaign, USA
Nicu Sebe	University of Trento, Italy
Greg Shakhnarovich	Toyota Technological Institute at Chicago, USA
Eli Shechtman	Adobe Research, USA
Humphrey Shi	University of Oregon & University of Illinois at Urbana-Champaign & Picsart AI Research, USA
Jianbo Shi	University of Pennsylvania, USA
Roy Shilkrot	Massachusetts Institute of Technology, USA
Mike Zheng Shou	National University of Singapore, Singapore
Kaleem Siddiqi	McGill University, Canada
Richa Singh	Indian Institute of Technology Jodhpur, India
Greg Slabaugh	Queen Mary University of London, UK
Cees Snoek	University of Amsterdam, The Netherlands
Yale Song	Facebook AI Research, USA
Yi-Zhe Song	University of Surrey, UK
Bjorn Stenger	Rakuten Institute of Technology
Abby Stylianou	Saint Louis University, USA
Akihiro Sugimoto	National Institute of Informatics, Japan
Chen Sun	Brown University, USA
Deqing Sun	Google, USA
Kalyan Sunkavalli	Adobe Research, USA
Ying Tai	Tencent YouTu Lab, China
Ayellet Tal	Technion – Israel Institute of Technology, Israel
Ping Tan	Simon Fraser University, Canada
Siyu Tang	ETH Zurich, Switzerland
Chi-Keung Tang	Hong Kong University of Science and Technology, Hong Kong, China
Radu Timofte	University of Würzburg, Germany & ETH Zurich, Switzerland
Federico Tombari	Google, Switzerland & Technical University of Munich, Germany

James Tompkin — Brown University, USA
Lorenzo Torresani — Dartmouth College, USA
Alexander Toshev — Apple, USA
Du Tran — Facebook AI Research, USA
Anh T. Tran — VinAI, Vietnam
Zhuowen Tu — University of California, San Diego, USA
Georgios Tzimiropoulos — Queen Mary University of London, UK
Jasper Uijlings — Google Research, Switzerland
Jan C. van Gemert — Delft University of Technology, The Netherlands
Gul Varol — Ecole des Ponts ParisTech, France
Nuno Vasconcelos — University of California, San Diego, USA
Mayank Vatsa — Indian Institute of Technology Jodhpur, India
Ashok Veeraraghavan — Rice University, USA
Jakob Verbeek — Facebook AI Research, France
Carl Vondrick — Columbia University, USA
Ruiping Wang — Institute of Computing Technology, Chinese Academy of Sciences, China
Xinchao Wang — National University of Singapore, Singapore
Liwei Wang — The Chinese University of Hong Kong, Hong Kong, China
Chaohui Wang — Université Paris-Est, France
Xiaolong Wang — University of California, San Diego, USA
Christian Wolf — NAVER LABS Europe, France
Tao Xiang — University of Surrey, UK
Saining Xie — Facebook AI Research, USA
Cihang Xie — University of California, Santa Cruz, USA
Zeki Yalniz — Facebook, USA
Ming-Hsuan Yang — University of California, Merced, USA
Angela Yao — National University of Singapore, Singapore
Shaodi You — University of Amsterdam, The Netherlands
Stella X. Yu — University of California, Berkeley, USA
Junsong Yuan — State University of New York at Buffalo, USA
Stefanos Zafeiriou — Imperial College London, UK
Amir Zamir — École polytechnique fédérale de Lausanne, Switzerland
Lei Zhang — Alibaba & Hong Kong Polytechnic University, Hong Kong, China
Lei Zhang — International Digital Economy Academy (IDEA), China
Pengchuan Zhang — Meta AI, USA
Bolei Zhou — University of California, Los Angeles, USA
Yuke Zhu — University of Texas at Austin, USA

Todd Zickler   Harvard University, USA
Wangmeng Zuo   Harbin Institute of Technology, China

Technical Program Committee

Davide Abati
Soroush Abbasi
  Koohpayegani
Amos L. Abbott
Rameen Abdal
Rabab Abdelfattah
Sahar Abdelnabi
Hassan Abu Alhaija
Abulikemu Abuduweili
Ron Abutbul
Hanno Ackermann
Aikaterini Adam
Kamil Adamczewski
Ehsan Adeli
Vida Adeli
Donald Adjeroh
Arman Afrasiyabi
Akshay Agarwal
Sameer Agarwal
Abhinav Agarwalla
Vaibhav Aggarwal
Sara Aghajanzadeh
Susmit Agrawal
Antonio Agudo
Touqeer Ahmad
Sk Miraj Ahmed
Chaitanya Ahuja
Nilesh A. Ahuja
Abhishek Aich
Shubhra Aich
Noam Aigerman
Arash Akbarinia
Peri Akiva
Derya Akkaynak
Emre Aksan
Arjun R. Akula
Yuval Alaluf
Stephan Alaniz
Paul Albert
Cenek Albl

Filippo Aleotti
Konstantinos P.
  Alexandridis
Motasem Alfarra
Mohsen Ali
Thiemo Alldieck
Hadi Alzayer
Liang An
Shan An
Yi An
Zhulin An
Dongsheng An
Jie An
Xiang An
Saket Anand
Cosmin Ancuti
Juan Andrade-Cetto
Alexander Andreopoulos
Bjoern Andres
Jerone T. A. Andrews
Shivangi Aneja
Anelia Angelova
Dragomir Anguelov
Rushil Anirudh
Oron Anschel
Rao Muhammad Anwer
Djamila Aouada
Evlampios Apostolidis
Srikar Appalaraju
Nikita Araslanov
Andre Araujo
Eric Arazo
Dawit Mureja Argaw
Anurag Arnab
Aditya Arora
Chetan Arora
Sunpreet S. Arora
Alexey Artemov
Muhammad Asad
Kumar Ashutosh

Sinem Aslan
Vishal Asnani
Mahmoud Assran
Amir Atapour-Abarghouei
Nikos Athanasiou
Ali Athar
ShahRukh Athar
Sara Atito
Souhaib Attaiki
Matan Atzmon
Mathieu Aubry
Nicolas Audebert
Tristan T.
  Aumentado-Armstrong
Melinos Averkiou
Yannis Avrithis
Stephane Ayache
Mehmet Aygün
Seyed Mehdi
  Ayyoubzadeh
Hossein Azizpour
George Azzopardi
Mallikarjun B. R.
Yunhao Ba
Abhishek Badki
Seung-Hwan Bae
Seung-Hwan Baek
Seungryul Baek
Piyush Nitin Bagad
Shai Bagon
Gaetan Bahl
Shikhar Bahl
Sherwin Bahmani
Haoran Bai
Lei Bai
Jiawang Bai
Haoyue Bai
Jinbin Bai
Xiang Bai
Xuyang Bai

Bowen Cai
Mu Cai
Qin Cai
Ruojin Cai
Weidong Cai
Weiwei Cai
Yi Cai
Yujun Cai
Zhiping Cai
Akin Caliskan
Lilian Calvet
Baris Can Cam
Necati Cihan Camgoz
Tommaso Campari
Dylan Campbell
Ziang Cao
Ang Cao
Xu Cao
Zhiwen Cao
Shengcao Cao
Song Cao
Weipeng Cao
Xiangyong Cao
Xiaochun Cao
Yue Cao
Yunhao Cao
Zhangjie Cao
Jiale Cao
Yang Cao
Jiajiong Cao
Jie Cao
Jinkun Cao
Lele Cao
Yulong Cao
Zhiguo Cao
Chen Cao
Razvan Caramalau
Marlène Careil
Gustavo Carneiro
Joao Carreira
Dan Casas
Paola Cascante-Bonilla
Angela Castillo
Francisco M. Castro
Pedro Castro

Luca Cavalli
George J. Cazenavette
Oya Celiktutan
Hakan Cevikalp
Sri Harsha C. H.
Sungmin Cha
Geonho Cha
Menglei Chai
Lucy Chai
Yuning Chai
Zenghao Chai
Anirban Chakraborty
Deep Chakraborty
Rudrasis Chakraborty
Souradeep Chakraborty
Kelvin C. K. Chan
Chee Seng Chan
Paramanand Chandramouli
Arjun Chandrasekaran
Kenneth Chaney
Dongliang Chang
Huiwen Chang
Peng Chang
Xiaojun Chang
Jia-Ren Chang
Hyung Jin Chang
Hyun Sung Chang
Ju Yong Chang
Li-Jen Chang
Qi Chang
Wei-Yi Chang
Yi Chang
Nadine Chang
Hanqing Chao
Pradyumna Chari
Dibyadip Chatterjee
Chiranjoy Chattopadhyay
Siddhartha Chaudhuri
Zhengping Che
Gal Chechik
Lianggangxu Chen
Qi Alfred Chen
Brian Chen
Bor-Chun Chen
Bo-Hao Chen

Bohong Chen
Bin Chen
Ziliang Chen
Cheng Chen
Chen Chen
Chaofeng Chen
Xi Chen
Haoyu Chen
Xuanhong Chen
Wei Chen
Qiang Chen
Shi Chen
Xianyu Chen
Chang Chen
Changhuai Chen
Hao Chen
Jie Chen
Jianbo Chen
Jingjing Chen
Jun Chen
Kejiang Chen
Mingcai Chen
Nenglun Chen
Qifeng Chen
Ruoyu Chen
Shu-Yu Chen
Weidong Chen
Weijie Chen
Weikai Chen
Xiang Chen
Xiuyi Chen
Xingyu Chen
Yaofo Chen
Yueting Chen
Yu Chen
Yunjin Chen
Yuntao Chen
Yun Chen
Zhenfang Chen
Zhuangzhuang Chen
Chu-Song Chen
Xiangyu Chen
Zhuo Chen
Chaoqi Chen
Shizhe Chen

Xiaotong Chen
Xiaozhi Chen
Dian Chen
Defang Chen
Dingfan Chen
Ding-Jie Chen
Ee Heng Chen
Tao Chen
Yixin Chen
Wei-Ting Chen
Lin Chen
Guang Chen
Guangyi Chen
Guanying Chen
Guangyao Chen
Hwann-Tzong Chen
Junwen Chen
Jiacheng Chen
Jianxu Chen
Hui Chen
Kai Chen
Kan Chen
Kevin Chen
Kuan-Wen Chen
Weihua Chen
Zhang Chen
Liang-Chieh Chen
Lele Chen
Liang Chen
Fanglin Chen
Zehui Chen
Minghui Chen
Minghao Chen
Xiaokang Chen
Qian Chen
Jun-Cheng Chen
Qi Chen
Qingcai Chen
Richard J. Chen
Runnan Chen
Rui Chen
Shuo Chen
Sentao Chen
Shaoyu Chen
Shixing Chen

Shuai Chen
Shuya Chen
Sizhe Chen
Simin Chen
Shaoxiang Chen
Zitian Chen
Tianlong Chen
Tianshui Chen
Min-Hung Chen
Xiangning Chen
Xin Chen
Xinghao Chen
Xuejin Chen
Xu Chen
Xuxi Chen
Yunlu Chen
Yanbei Chen
Yuxiao Chen
Yun-Chun Chen
Yi-Ting Chen
Yi-Wen Chen
Yinbo Chen
Yiran Chen
Yuanhong Chen
Yubei Chen
Yuefeng Chen
Yuhua Chen
Yukang Chen
Zerui Chen
Zhaoyu Chen
Zhen Chen
Zhenyu Chen
Zhi Chen
Zhiwei Chen
Zhixiang Chen
Long Chen
Bowen Cheng
Jun Cheng
Yi Cheng
Jingchun Cheng
Lechao Cheng
Xi Cheng
Yuan Cheng
Ho Kei Cheng
Kevin Ho Man Cheng

Jiacheng Cheng
Kelvin B. Cheng
Li Cheng
Mengjun Cheng
Zhen Cheng
Qingrong Cheng
Tianheng Cheng
Harry Cheng
Yihua Cheng
Yu Cheng
Ziheng Cheng
Soon Yau Cheong
Anoop Cherian
Manuela Chessa
Zhixiang Chi
Naoki Chiba
Julian Chibane
Kashyap Chitta
Tai-Yin Chiu
Hsu-kuang Chiu
Wei-Chen Chiu
Sungmin Cho
Donghyeon Cho
Hyeon Cho
Yooshin Cho
Gyusang Cho
Jang Hyun Cho
Seungju Cho
Nam Ik Cho
Sunghyun Cho
Hanbyel Cho
Jaesung Choe
Jooyoung Choi
Chiho Choi
Changwoon Choi
Jongwon Choi
Myungsub Choi
Dooseop Choi
Jonghyun Choi
Jinwoo Choi
Jun Won Choi
Min-Kook Choi
Hongsuk Choi
Janghoon Choi
Yoon-Ho Choi

Yukyung Choi
Jaegul Choo
Ayush Chopra
Siddharth Choudhary
Subhabrata Choudhury
Vasileios Choutas
Ka-Ho Chow
Pinaki Nath Chowdhury
Sammy Christen
Anders Christensen
Grigorios Chrysos
Hang Chu
Wen-Hsuan Chu
Peng Chu
Qi Chu
Ruihang Chu
Wei-Ta Chu
Yung-Yu Chuang
Sanghyuk Chun
Se Young Chun
Antonio Cinà
Ramazan Gokberk Cinbis
Javier Civera
Albert Clapés
Ronald Clark
Brian S. Clipp
Felipe Codevilla
Daniel Coelho de Castro
Niv Cohen
Forrester Cole
Maxwell D. Collins
Robert T. Collins
Marc Comino Trinidad
Runmin Cong
Wenyan Cong
Maxime Cordy
Marcella Cornia
Enric Corona
Huseyin Coskun
Luca Cosmo
Dragos Costea
Davide Cozzolino
Arun C. S. Kumar
Aiyu Cui
Qiongjie Cui

Quan Cui
Shuhao Cui
Yiming Cui
Ying Cui
Zijun Cui
Jiali Cui
Jiequan Cui
Yawen Cui
Zhen Cui
Zhaopeng Cui
Jack Culpepper
Xiaodong Cun
Ross Cutler
Adam Czajka
Ali Dabouei
Konstantinos M. Dafnis
Manuel Dahnert
Tao Dai
Yuchao Dai
Bo Dai
Mengyu Dai
Hang Dai
Haixing Dai
Peng Dai
Pingyang Dai
Qi Dai
Qiyu Dai
Yutong Dai
Naser Damer
Zhiyuan Dang
Mohamed Daoudi
Ayan Das
Abir Das
Debasmit Das
Deepayan Das
Partha Das
Sagnik Das
Soumi Das
Srijan Das
Swagatam Das
Avijit Dasgupta
Jim Davis
Adrian K. Davison
Homa Davoudi
Laura Daza

Matthias De Lange
Shalini De Mello
Marco De Nadai
Christophe De
    Vleeschouwer
Alp Dener
Boyang Deng
Congyue Deng
Bailin Deng
Yong Deng
Ye Deng
Zhuo Deng
Zhijie Deng
Xiaoming Deng
Jiankang Deng
Jinhong Deng
Jingjing Deng
Liang-Jian Deng
Siqi Deng
Xiang Deng
Xueqing Deng
Zhongying Deng
Karan Desai
Jean-Emmanuel Deschaud
Aniket Anand Deshmukh
Neel Dey
Helisa Dhamo
Prithviraj Dhar
Amaya Dharmasiri
Yan Di
Xing Di
Ousmane A. Dia
Haiwen Diao
Xiaolei Diao
Gonçalo José Dias Pais
Abdallah Dib
Anastasios Dimou
Changxing Ding
Henghui Ding
Guodong Ding
Yaqing Ding
Shuangrui Ding
Yuhang Ding
Yikang Ding
Shouhong Ding

Haisong Ding
Hui Ding
Jiahao Ding
Jian Ding
Jian-Jiun Ding
Shuxiao Ding
Tianyu Ding
Wenhao Ding
Yuqi Ding
Yi Ding
Yuzhen Ding
Zhengming Ding
Tan Minh Dinh
Vu Dinh
Christos Diou
Mandar Dixit
Bao Gia Doan
Khoa D. Doan
Dzung Anh Doan
Debi Prosad Dogra
Nehal Doiphode
Chengdong Dong
Bowen Dong
Zhenxing Dong
Hang Dong
Xiaoyi Dong
Haoye Dong
Jiangxin Dong
Shichao Dong
Xuan Dong
Zhen Dong
Shuting Dong
Jing Dong
Li Dong
Ming Dong
Nanqing Dong
Qiulei Dong
Runpei Dong
Siyan Dong
Tian Dong
Wei Dong
Xiaomeng Dong
Xin Dong
Xingbo Dong
Yuan Dong

Samuel Dooley
Gianfranco Doretto
Michael Dorkenwald
Keval Doshi
Zhaopeng Dou
Xiaotian Dou
Hazel Doughty
Ahmad Droby
Iddo Drori
Jie Du
Yong Du
Dawei Du
Dong Du
Ruoyi Du
Yuntao Du
Xuefeng Du
Yilun Du
Yuming Du
Radhika Dua
Haodong Duan
Jiafei Duan
Kaiwen Duan
Peiqi Duan
Ye Duan
Haoran Duan
Jiali Duan
Amanda Duarte
Abhimanyu Dubey
Shiv Ram Dubey
Florian Dubost
Lukasz Dudziak
Shivam Duggal
Justin M. Dulay
Matteo Dunnhofer
Chi Nhan Duong
Thibaut Durand
Mihai Dusmanu
Ujjal Kr Dutta
Debidatta Dwibedi
Isht Dwivedi
Sai Kumar Dwivedi
Takeharu Eda
Mark Edmonds
Alexei A. Efros
Thibaud Ehret

Max Ehrlich
Mahsa Ehsanpour
Iván Eichhardt
Farshad Einabadi
Marvin Eisenberger
Hazim Kemal Ekenel
Mohamed El Banani
Ismail Elezi
Moshe Eliasof
Alaa El-Nouby
Ian Endres
Francis Engelmann
Deniz Engin
Chanho Eom
Dave Epstein
Maria C. Escobar
Victor A. Escorcia
Carlos Esteves
Sungmin Eum
Bernard J. E. Evans
Ivan Evtimov
Fevziye Irem Eyiokur
    Yaman
Matteo Fabbri
Sébastien Fabbro
Gabriele Facciolo
Masud Fahim
Bin Fan
Hehe Fan
Deng-Ping Fan
Aoxiang Fan
Chen-Chen Fan
Qi Fan
Zhaoxin Fan
Haoqi Fan
Heng Fan
Hongyi Fan
Linxi Fan
Baojie Fan
Jiayuan Fan
Lei Fan
Quanfu Fan
Yonghui Fan
Yingruo Fan
Zhiwen Fan

Zicong Fan
Sean Fanello
Jiansheng Fang
Chaowei Fang
Yuming Fang
Jianwu Fang
Jin Fang
Qi Fang
Shancheng Fang
Tian Fang
Xianyong Fang
Gongfan Fang
Zhen Fang
Hui Fang
Jiemin Fang
Le Fang
Pengfei Fang
Xiaolin Fang
Yuxin Fang
Zhaoyuan Fang
Ammarah Farooq
Azade Farshad
Zhengcong Fei
Michael Felsberg
Wei Feng
Chen Feng
Fan Feng
Andrew Feng
Xin Feng
Zheyun Feng
Ruicheng Feng
Mingtao Feng
Qianyu Feng
Shangbin Feng
Chun-Mei Feng
Zunlei Feng
Zhiyong Feng
Martin Fergie
Mustansar Fiaz
Marco Fiorucci
Michael Firman
Hamed Firooz
Volker Fischer
Corneliu O. Florea
Georgios Floros

Wolfgang Foerstner
Gianni Franchi
Jean-Sebastien Franco
Simone Frintrop
Anna Fruehstueck
Changhong Fu
Chaoyou Fu
Cheng-Yang Fu
Chi-Wing Fu
Deqing Fu
Huan Fu
Jun Fu
Kexue Fu
Ying Fu
Jianlong Fu
Jingjing Fu
Qichen Fu
Tsu-Jui Fu
Xueyang Fu
Yang Fu
Yanwei Fu
Yonggan Fu
Wolfgang Fuhl
Yasuhisa Fujii
Kent Fujiwara
Marco Fumero
Takuya Funatomi
Isabel Funke
Dario Fuoli
Antonino Furnari
Matheus A. Gadelha
Akshay Gadi Patil
Adrian Galdran
Guillermo Gallego
Silvano Galliani
Orazio Gallo
Leonardo Galteri
Matteo Gamba
Yiming Gan
Sujoy Ganguly
Harald Ganster
Boyan Gao
Changxin Gao
Daiheng Gao
Difei Gao

Chen Gao
Fei Gao
Lin Gao
Wei Gao
Yiming Gao
Junyu Gao
Guangyu Ryan Gao
Haichang Gao
Hongchang Gao
Jialin Gao
Jin Gao
Jun Gao
Katelyn Gao
Mingchen Gao
Mingfei Gao
Pan Gao
Shangqian Gao
Shanghua Gao
Xitong Gao
Yunhe Gao
Zhanning Gao
Elena Garces
Nuno Cruz Garcia
Noa Garcia
Guillermo
    Garcia-Hernando
Isha Garg
Rahul Garg
Sourav Garg
Quentin Garrido
Stefano Gasperini
Kent Gauen
Chandan Gautam
Shivam Gautam
Paul Gay
Chunjiang Ge
Shiming Ge
Wenhang Ge
Yanhao Ge
Zheng Ge
Songwei Ge
Weifeng Ge
Yixiao Ge
Yuying Ge
Shijie Geng

Zhengyang Geng
Kyle A. Genova
Georgios Georgakis
Markos Georgopoulos
Marcel Geppert
Shabnam Ghadar
Mina Ghadimi Atigh
Deepti Ghadiyaram
Maani Ghaffari Jadidi
Sedigh Ghamari
Zahra Gharaee
Michaël Gharbi
Golnaz Ghiasi
Reza Ghoddoosian
Soumya Suvra Ghosal
Adhiraj Ghosh
Arthita Ghosh
Pallabi Ghosh
Soumyadeep Ghosh
Andrew Gilbert
Igor Gilitschenski
Jhony H. Giraldo
Andreu Girbau Xalabarder
Rohit Girdhar
Sharath Girish
Xavier Giro-i-Nieto
Raja Giryes
Thomas Gittings
Nikolaos Gkanatsios
Ioannis Gkioulekas
Abhiram
   Gnanasambandam
Aurele T. Gnanha
Clement L. J. C. Godard
Arushi Goel
Vidit Goel
Shubham Goel
Zan Gojcic
Aaron K. Gokaslan
Tejas Gokhale
S. Alireza Golestaneh
Thiago L. Gomes
Nuno Goncalves
Boqing Gong
Chen Gong

Yuanhao Gong
Guoqiang Gong
Jingyu Gong
Rui Gong
Yu Gong
Mingming Gong
Neil Zhenqiang Gong
Xun Gong
Yunye Gong
Yihong Gong
Cristina I. González
Nithin Gopalakrishnan
   Nair
Gaurav Goswami
Jianping Gou
Shreyank N. Gowda
Ankit Goyal
Helmut Grabner
Patrick L. Grady
Ben Graham
Eric Granger
Douglas R. Gray
Matej Grcić
David Griffiths
Jinjin Gu
Yun Gu
Shuyang Gu
Jianyang Gu
Fuqiang Gu
Jiatao Gu
Jindong Gu
Jiaqi Gu
Jinwei Gu
Jiaxin Gu
Geonmo Gu
Xiao Gu
Xinqian Gu
Xiuye Gu
Yuming Gu
Zhangxuan Gu
Dayan Guan
Junfeng Guan
Qingji Guan
Tianrui Guan
Shanyan Guan

Denis A. Gudovskiy
Ricardo Guerrero
Pierre-Louis Guhur
Jie Gui
Liangyan Gui
Liangke Gui
Benoit Guillard
Erhan Gundogdu
Manuel Günther
Jingcai Guo
Yuanfang Guo
Junfeng Guo
Chenqi Guo
Dan Guo
Hongji Guo
Jia Guo
Jie Guo
Minghao Guo
Shi Guo
Yanhui Guo
Yangyang Guo
Yuan-Chen Guo
Yilu Guo
Yiluan Guo
Yong Guo
Guangyu Guo
Haiyun Guo
Jinyang Guo
Jianyuan Guo
Pengsheng Guo
Pengfei Guo
Shuxuan Guo
Song Guo
Tianyu Guo
Qing Guo
Qiushan Guo
Wen Guo
Xiefan Guo
Xiaohu Guo
Xiaoqing Guo
Yufei Guo
Yuhui Guo
Yuliang Guo
Yunhui Guo
Yanwen Guo

Akshita Gupta
Ankush Gupta
Kamal Gupta
Kartik Gupta
Ritwik Gupta
Rohit Gupta
Siddharth Gururani
Fredrik K. Gustafsson
Abner Guzman Rivera
Vladimir Guzov
Matthew A. Gwilliam
Jung-Woo Ha
Marc Habermann
Isma Hadji
Christian Haene
Martin Hahner
Levente Hajder
Alexandros Haliassos
Emanuela Haller
Bumsub Ham
Abdullah J. Hamdi
Shreyas Hampali
Dongyoon Han
Chunrui Han
Dong-Jun Han
Dong-Sig Han
Guangxing Han
Zhizhong Han
Ruize Han
Jiaming Han
Jin Han
Ligong Han
Xian-Hua Han
Xiaoguang Han
Yizeng Han
Zhi Han
Zhenjun Han
Zhongyi Han
Jungong Han
Junlin Han
Kai Han
Kun Han
Sungwon Han
Songfang Han
Wei Han

Xiao Han
Xintong Han
Xinzhe Han
Yahong Han
Yan Han
Zongbo Han
Nicolai Hani
Rana Hanocka
Niklas Hanselmann
Nicklas A. Hansen
Hong Hanyu
Fusheng Hao
Yanbin Hao
Shijie Hao
Udith Haputhanthri
Mehrtash Harandi
Josh Harguess
Adam Harley
David M. Hart
Atsushi Hashimoto
Ali Hassani
Mohammed Hassanin
Yana Hasson
Joakim Bruslund Haurum
Bo He
Kun He
Chen He
Xin He
Fazhi He
Gaoqi He
Hao He
Haoyu He
Jiangpeng He
Hongliang He
Qian He
Xiangteng He
Xuming He
Yannan He
Yuhang He
Yang He
Xiangyu He
Nanjun He
Pan He
Sen He
Shengfeng He

Songtao He
Tao He
Tong He
Wei He
Xuehai He
Xiaoxiao He
Ying He
Yisheng He
Ziwen He
Peter Hedman
Felix Heide
Yacov Hel-Or
Paul Henderson
Philipp Henzler
Byeongho Heo
Jae-Pil Heo
Miran Heo
Sachini A. Herath
Stephane Herbin
Pedro Hermosilla Casajus
Monica Hernandez
Charles Herrmann
Roei Herzig
Mauricio Hess-Flores
Carlos Hinojosa
Tobias Hinz
Tsubasa Hirakawa
Chih-Hui Ho
Lam Si Tung Ho
Jennifer Hobbs
Derek Hoiem
Yannick Hold-Geoffroy
Aleksander Holynski
Cheeun Hong
Fa-Ting Hong
Hanbin Hong
Guan Zhe Hong
Danfeng Hong
Lanqing Hong
Xiaopeng Hong
Xin Hong
Jie Hong
Seungbum Hong
Cheng-Yao Hong
Seunghoon Hong

Yi Hong
Yuan Hong
Yuchen Hong
Anthony Hoogs
Maxwell C. Horton
Kazuhiro Hotta
Qibin Hou
Tingbo Hou
Junhui Hou
Ji Hou
Qiqi Hou
Rui Hou
Ruibing Hou
Zhi Hou
Henry Howard-Jenkins
Lukas Hoyer
Wei-Lin Hsiao
Chiou-Ting Hsu
Anthony Hu
Brian Hu
Yusong Hu
Hexiang Hu
Haoji Hu
Di Hu
Hengtong Hu
Haigen Hu
Lianyu Hu
Hanzhe Hu
Jie Hu
Junlin Hu
Shizhe Hu
Jian Hu
Zhiming Hu
Juhua Hu
Peng Hu
Ping Hu
Ronghang Hu
MengShun Hu
Tao Hu
Vincent Tao Hu
Xiaoling Hu
Xinting Hu
Xiaolin Hu
Xuefeng Hu
Xiaowei Hu

Yang Hu
Yueyu Hu
Zeyu Hu
Zhongyun Hu
Binh-Son Hua
Guoliang Hua
Yi Hua
Linzhi Huang
Qiusheng Huang
Bo Huang
Chen Huang
Hsin-Ping Huang
Ye Huang
Shuangping Huang
Zeng Huang
Buzhen Huang
Cong Huang
Heng Huang
Hao Huang
Qidong Huang
Huaibo Huang
Chaoqin Huang
Feihu Huang
Jiahui Huang
Jingjia Huang
Kun Huang
Lei Huang
Sheng Huang
Shuaiyi Huang
Siyu Huang
Xiaoshui Huang
Xiaoyang Huang
Yan Huang
Yihao Huang
Ying Huang
Ziling Huang
Xiaoke Huang
Yifei Huang
Haiyang Huang
Zhewei Huang
Jin Huang
Haibin Huang
Jiaxing Huang
Junjie Huang
Keli Huang

Lang Huang
Lin Huang
Luojie Huang
Mingzhen Huang
Shijia Huang
Shengyu Huang
Siyuan Huang
He Huang
Xiuyu Huang
Lianghua Huang
Yue Huang
Yaping Huang
Yuge Huang
Zehao Huang
Zeyi Huang
Zhiqi Huang
Zhongzhan Huang
Zilong Huang
Ziyuan Huang
Tianrui Hui
Zhuo Hui
Le Hui
Jing Huo
Junhwa Hur
Shehzeen S. Hussain
Chuong Minh Huynh
Seunghyun Hwang
Jaehui Hwang
Jyh-Jing Hwang
Sukjun Hwang
Soonmin Hwang
Wonjun Hwang
Rakib Hyder
Sangeek Hyun
Sarah Ibrahimi
Tomoki Ichikawa
Yerlan Idelbayev
A. S. M. Iftekhar
Masaaki Iiyama
Satoshi Ikehata
Sunghoon Im
Atul N. Ingle
Eldar Insafutdinov
Yani A. Ioannou
Radu Tudor Ionescu

Umar Iqbal
Go Irie
Muhammad Zubair Irshad
Ahmet Iscen
Berivan Isik
Ashraful Islam
Md Amirul Islam
Syed Islam
Mariko Isogawa
Vamsi Krishna K. Ithapu
Boris Ivanovic
Darshan Iyer
Sarah Jabbour
Ayush Jain
Nishant Jain
Samyak Jain
Vidit Jain
Vineet Jain
Priyank Jaini
Tomas Jakab
Mohammad A. A. K.
    Jalwana
Muhammad Abdullah
    Jamal
Hadi Jamali-Rad
Stuart James
Varun Jampani
Young Kyun Jang
YeongJun Jang
Yunseok Jang
Ronnachai Jaroensri
Bhavan Jasani
Krishna Murthy
    Jatavallabhula
Mojan Javaheripi
Syed A. Javed
Guillaume Jeanneret
Pranav Jeevan
Herve Jegou
Rohit Jena
Tomas Jenicek
Porter Jenkins
Simon Jenni
Hae-Gon Jeon
Sangryul Jeon

Boseung Jeong
Yoonwoo Jeong
Seong-Gyun Jeong
Jisoo Jeong
Allan D. Jepson
Ankit Jha
Sumit K. Jha
I-Hong Jhuo
Ge-Peng Ji
Chaonan Ji
Deyi Ji
Jingwei Ji
Wei Ji
Zhong Ji
Jiayi Ji
Pengliang Ji
Hui Ji
Mingi Ji
Xiaopeng Ji
Yuzhu Ji
Baoxiong Jia
Songhao Jia
Dan Jia
Shan Jia
Xiaojun Jia
Xiuyi Jia
Xu Jia
Menglin Jia
Wenqi Jia
Boyuan Jiang
Wenhao Jiang
Huaizu Jiang
Hanwen Jiang
Haiyong Jiang
Hao Jiang
Huajie Jiang
Huiqin Jiang
Haojun Jiang
Haobo Jiang
Junjun Jiang
Xingyu Jiang
Yangbangyan Jiang
Yu Jiang
Jianmin Jiang
Jiaxi Jiang

Jing Jiang
Kui Jiang
Li Jiang
Liming Jiang
Chiyu Jiang
Meirui Jiang
Chen Jiang
Peng Jiang
Tai-Xiang Jiang
Wen Jiang
Xinyang Jiang
Yifan Jiang
Yuming Jiang
Yingying Jiang
Zeren Jiang
ZhengKai Jiang
Zhenyu Jiang
Shuming Jiao
Jianbo Jiao
Licheng Jiao
Dongkwon Jin
Yeying Jin
Cheng Jin
Linyi Jin
Qing Jin
Taisong Jin
Xiao Jin
Xin Jin
Sheng Jin
Kyong Hwan Jin
Ruibing Jin
SouYoung Jin
Yueming Jin
Chenchen Jing
Longlong Jing
Taotao Jing
Yongcheng Jing
Younghyun Jo
Joakim Johnander
Jeff Johnson
Michael J. Jones
R. Kenny Jones
Rico Jonschkowski
Ameya Joshi
Sunghun Joung

Felix Juefei-Xu
Claudio R. Jung
Steffen Jung
Hari Chandana K.
Rahul Vigneswaran K.
Prajwal K. R.
Abhishek Kadian
Jhony Kaesemodel Pontes
Kumara Kahatapitiya
Anmol Kalia
Sinan Kalkan
Tarun Kalluri
Jaewon Kam
Sandesh Kamath
Meina Kan
Menelaos Kanakis
Takuhiro Kaneko
Di Kang
Guoliang Kang
Hao Kang
Jaeyeon Kang
Kyoungkook Kang
Li-Wei Kang
MinGuk Kang
Suk-Ju Kang
Zhao Kang
Yash Mukund Kant
Yueying Kao
Aupendu Kar
Konstantinos Karantzalos
Sezer Karaoglu
Navid Kardan
Sanjay Kariyappa
Leonid Karlinsky
Animesh Karnewar
Shyamgopal Karthik
Hirak J. Kashyap
Marc A. Kastner
Hirokatsu Kataoka
Angelos Katharopoulos
Hiroharu Kato
Kai Katsumata
Manuel Kaufmann
Chaitanya Kaul
Prakhar Kaushik

Yuki Kawana
Lei Ke
Lipeng Ke
Tsung-Wei Ke
Wei Ke
Petr Kellnhofer
Aniruddha Kembhavi
John Kender
Corentin Kervadec
Leonid Keselman
Daniel Keysers
Nima Khademi Kalantari
Taras Khakhulin
Samir Khaki
Muhammad Haris Khan
Qadeer Khan
Salman Khan
Subash Khanal
Vaishnavi M. Khindkar
Rawal Khirodkar
Saeed Khorram
Pirazh Khorramshahi
Kourosh Khoshelham
Ansh Khurana
Benjamin Kiefer
Jae Myung Kim
Junho Kim
Boah Kim
Hyeonseong Kim
Dong-Jin Kim
Dongwan Kim
Donghyun Kim
Doyeon Kim
Yonghyun Kim
Hyung-Il Kim
Hyunwoo Kim
Hyeongwoo Kim
Hyo Jin Kim
Hyunwoo J. Kim
Taehoon Kim
Jaeha Kim
Jiwon Kim
Jung Uk Kim
Kangyeol Kim
Eunji Kim

Daeha Kim
Dongwon Kim
Kunhee Kim
Kyungmin Kim
Junsik Kim
Min H. Kim
Namil Kim
Kookhoi Kim
Sanghyun Kim
Seongyeop Kim
Seungryong Kim
Saehoon Kim
Euyoung Kim
Guisik Kim
Sungyeon Kim
Sunnie S. Y. Kim
Taehun Kim
Tae Oh Kim
Won Hwa Kim
Seungwook Kim
YoungBin Kim
Youngeun Kim
Akisato Kimura
Furkan Osman Kınlı
Zsolt Kira
Hedvig Kjellström
Florian Kleber
Jan P. Klopp
Florian Kluger
Laurent Kneip
Byungsoo Ko
Muhammed Kocabas
A. Sophia Koepke
Kevin Koeser
Nick Kolkin
Nikos Kolotouros
Wai-Kin Adams Kong
Deying Kong
Caihua Kong
Youyong Kong
Shuyu Kong
Shu Kong
Tao Kong
Yajing Kong
Yu Kong

Zishang Kong
Theodora Kontogianni
Anton S. Konushin
Julian F. P. Kooij
Bruno Korbar
Giorgos Kordopatis-Zilos
Jari Korhonen
Adam Kortylewski
Denis Korzhenkov
Divya Kothandaraman
Suraj Kothawade
Iuliia Kotseruba
Satwik Kottur
Shashank Kotyan
Alexandros Kouris
Petros Koutras
Anna Kreshuk
Ranjay Krishna
Dilip Krishnan
Andrey Kuehlkamp
Hilde Kuehne
Jason Kuen
David Kügler
Arjan Kuijper
Anna Kukleva
Sumith Kulal
Viveka Kulharia
Akshay R. Kulkarni
Nilesh Kulkarni
Dominik Kulon
Abhinav Kumar
Akash Kumar
Suryansh Kumar
B. V. K. Vijaya Kumar
Pulkit Kumar
Ratnesh Kumar
Sateesh Kumar
Satish Kumar
Vijay Kumar B. G.
Nupur Kumari
Sudhakar Kumawat
Jogendra Nath Kundu
Hsien-Kai Kuo
Meng-Yu Jennifer Kuo
Vinod Kumar Kurmi

Yusuke Kurose
Keerthy Kusumam
Alina Kuznetsova
Henry Kvinge
Ho Man Kwan
Hyeokjun Kweon
Heeseung Kwon
Gihyun Kwon
Myung-Joon Kwon
Taesung Kwon
YoungJoong Kwon
Christos Kyrkou
Jorma Laaksonen
Yann Labbe
Zorah Laehner
Florent Lafarge
Hamid Laga
Manuel Lagunas
Shenqi Lai
Jian-Huang Lai
Zihang Lai
Mohamed I. Lakhal
Mohit Lamba
Meng Lan
Loic Landrieu
Zhiqiang Lang
Natalie Lang
Dong Lao
Yizhen Lao
Yingjie Lao
Issam Hadj Laradji
Gustav Larsson
Viktor Larsson
Zakaria Laskar
Stéphane Lathuilière
Chun Pong Lau
Rynson W. H. Lau
Hei Law
Justin Lazarow
Verica Lazova
Eric-Tuan Le
Hieu Le
Trung-Nghia Le
Mathias Lechner
Byeong-Uk Lee

Chen-Yu Lee
Che-Rung Lee
Chul Lee
Hong Joo Lee
Dongsoo Lee
Jiyoung Lee
Eugene Eu Tzuan Lee
Daeun Lee
Saehyung Lee
Jewook Lee
Hyungtae Lee
Hyunmin Lee
Jungbeom Lee
Joon-Young Lee
Jong-Seok Lee
Joonseok Lee
Junha Lee
Kibok Lee
Byung-Kwan Lee
Jangwon Lee
Jinho Lee
Jongmin Lee
Seunghyun Lee
Sohyun Lee
Minsik Lee
Dogyoon Lee
Seungmin Lee
Min Jun Lee
Sangho Lee
Sangmin Lee
Seungeun Lee
Seon-Ho Lee
Sungmin Lee
Sungho Lee
Sangyoun Lee
Vincent C. S. S. Lee
Jaeseong Lee
Yong Jae Lee
Chenyang Lei
Chenyi Lei
Jiahui Lei
Xinyu Lei
Yinjie Lei
Jiaxu Leng
Luziwei Leng

Jan E. Lenssen
Vincent Lepetit
Thomas Leung
María Leyva-Vallina
Xin Li
Yikang Li
Baoxin Li
Bin Li
Bing Li
Bowen Li
Changlin Li
Chao Li
Chongyi Li
Guanyue Li
Shuai Li
Jin Li
Dingquan Li
Dongxu Li
Yiting Li
Gang Li
Dian Li
Guohao Li
Haoang Li
Haoliang Li
Haoran Li
Hengduo Li
Huafeng Li
Xiaoming Li
Hanao Li
Hongwei Li
Ziqiang Li
Jisheng Li
Jiacheng Li
Jia Li
Jiachen Li
Jiahao Li
Jianwei Li
Jiazhi Li
Jie Li
Jing Li
Jingjing Li
Jingtao Li
Jun Li
Junxuan Li
Kai Li

Kailin Li
Kenneth Li
Kun Li
Kunpeng Li
Aoxue Li
Chenglong Li
Chenglin Li
Changsheng Li
Zhichao Li
Qiang Li
Yanyu Li
Zuoyue Li
Xiang Li
Xuelong Li
Fangda Li
Ailin Li
Liang Li
Chun-Guang Li
Daiqing Li
Dong Li
Guanbin Li
Guorong Li
Haifeng Li
Jianan Li
Jianing Li
Jiaxin Li
Ke Li
Lei Li
Lincheng Li
Liulei Li
Lujun Li
Linjie Li
Lin Li
Pengyu Li
Ping Li
Qiufu Li
Qingyong Li
Rui Li
Siyuan Li
Wei Li
Wenbin Li
Xiangyang Li
Xinyu Li
Xiujun Li
Xiu Li

Xu Li
Ya-Li Li
Yao Li
Yongjie Li
Yijun Li
Yiming Li
Yuezun Li
Yu Li
Yunheng Li
Yuqi Li
Zhe Li
Zeming Li
Zhen Li
Zhengqin Li
Zhimin Li
Jiefeng Li
Jinpeng Li
Chengze Li
Jianwu Li
Lerenhan Li
Shan Li
Suichan Li
Xiangtai Li
Yanjie Li
Yandong Li
Zhuoling Li
Zhenqiang Li
Manyi Li
Maosen Li
Ji Li
Minjun Li
Mingrui Li
Mengtian Li
Junyi Li
Nianyi Li
Bo Li
Xiao Li
Peihua Li
Peike Li
Peizhao Li
Peiliang Li
Qi Li
Ren Li
Runze Li
Shile Li

Sheng Li
Shigang Li
Shiyu Li
Shuang Li
Shasha Li
Shichao Li
Tianye Li
Yuexiang Li
Wei-Hong Li
Wanhua Li
Weihao Li
Weiming Li
Weixin Li
Wenbo Li
Wenshuo Li
Weijian Li
Yunan Li
Xirong Li
Xianhang Li
Xiaoyu Li
Xueqian Li
Xuanlin Li
Xianzhi Li
Yunqiang Li
Yanjing Li
Yansheng Li
Yawei Li
Yi Li
Yong Li
Yong-Lu Li
Yuhang Li
Yu-Jhe Li
Yuxi Li
Yunsheng Li
Yanwei Li
Zechao Li
Zejian Li
Zeju Li
Zekun Li
Zhaowen Li
Zheng Li
Zhenyu Li
Zhiheng Li
Zhi Li
Zhong Li

Zhuowei Li
Zhuowan Li
Zhuohang Li
Zizhang Li
Chen Li
Yuan-Fang Li
Dongze Lian
Xiaochen Lian
Zhouhui Lian
Long Lian
Qing Lian
Jin Lianbao
Jinxiu S. Liang
Dingkang Liang
Jiahao Liang
Jianming Liang
Jingyun Liang
Kevin J. Liang
Kaizhao Liang
Chen Liang
Jie Liang
Senwei Liang
Ding Liang
Jiajun Liang
Jian Liang
Kongming Liang
Siyuan Liang
Yuanzhi Liang
Zhengfa Liang
Mingfu Liang
Xiaodan Liang
Xuefeng Liang
Yuxuan Liang
Kang Liao
Liang Liao
Hong-Yuan Mark Liao
Wentong Liao
Haofu Liao
Yue Liao
Minghui Liao
Shengcai Liao
Ting-Hsuan Liao
Xin Liao
Yinghong Liao
Teck Yian Lim

Che-Tsung Lin
Chung-Ching Lin
Chen-Hsuan Lin
Cheng Lin
Chuming Lin
Chunyu Lin
Dahua Lin
Wei Lin
Zheng Lin
Huaijia Lin
Jason Lin
Jierui Lin
Jiaying Lin
Jie Lin
Kai-En Lin
Kevin Lin
Guangfeng Lin
Jiehong Lin
Feng Lin
Hang Lin
Kwan-Yee Lin
Ke Lin
Luojun Lin
Qinghong Lin
Xiangbo Lin
Yi Lin
Zudi Lin
Shijie Lin
Yiqun Lin
Tzu-Heng Lin
Ming Lin
Shaohui Lin
SongNan Lin
Ji Lin
Tsung-Yu Lin
Xudong Lin
Yancong Lin
Yen-Chen Lin
Yiming Lin
Yuewei Lin
Zhiqiu Lin
Zinan Lin
Zhe Lin
David B. Lindell
Zhixin Ling

Zhan Ling
Alexander Liniger
Venice Erin B. Liong
Joey Litalien
Or Litany
Roee Litman
Ron Litman
Jim Little
Dor Litvak
Shaoteng Liu
Shuaicheng Liu
Andrew Liu
Xian Liu
Shaohui Liu
Bei Liu
Bo Liu
Yong Liu
Ming Liu
Yanbin Liu
Chenxi Liu
Daqi Liu
Di Liu
Difan Liu
Dong Liu
Dongfang Liu
Daizong Liu
Xiao Liu
Fangyi Liu
Fengbei Liu
Fenglin Liu
Bin Liu
Yuang Liu
Ao Liu
Hong Liu
Hongfu Liu
Huidong Liu
Ziyi Liu
Feng Liu
Hao Liu
Jie Liu
Jialun Liu
Jiang Liu
Jing Liu
Jingya Liu
Jiaming Liu

Jun Liu
Juncheng Liu
Jiawei Liu
Hongyu Liu
Chuanbin Liu
Haotian Liu
Lingqiao Liu
Chang Liu
Han Liu
Liu Liu
Min Liu
Yingqi Liu
Aishan Liu
Bingyu Liu
Benlin Liu
Boxiao Liu
Chenchen Liu
Chuanjian Liu
Daqing Liu
Huan Liu
Haozhe Liu
Jiaheng Liu
Wei Liu
Jingzhou Liu
Jiyuan Liu
Lingbo Liu
Nian Liu
Peiye Liu
Qiankun Liu
Shenglan Liu
Shilong Liu
Wen Liu
Wenyu Liu
Weifeng Liu
Wu Liu
Xiaolong Liu
Yang Liu
Yanwei Liu
Yingcheng Liu
Yongfei Liu
Yihao Liu
Yu Liu
Yunze Liu
Ze Liu
Zhenhua Liu

Zhenguang Liu
Lin Liu
Lihao Liu
Pengju Liu
Xinhai Liu
Yunfei Liu
Meng Liu
Minghua Liu
Mingyuan Liu
Miao Liu
Peirong Liu
Ping Liu
Qingjie Liu
Ruoshi Liu
Risheng Liu
Songtao Liu
Xing Liu
Shikun Liu
Shuming Liu
Sheng Liu
Songhua Liu
Tongliang Liu
Weibo Liu
Weide Liu
Weizhe Liu
Wenxi Liu
Weiyang Liu
Xin Liu
Xiaobin Liu
Xudong Liu
Xiaoyi Liu
Xihui Liu
Xinchen Liu
Xingtong Liu
Xinpeng Liu
Xinyu Liu
Xianpeng Liu
Xu Liu
Xingyu Liu
Yongtuo Liu
Yahui Liu
Yangxin Liu
Yaoyao Liu
Yaojie Liu
Yuliang Liu

Yongcheng Liu
Yuan Liu
Yufan Liu
Yu-Lun Liu
Yun Liu
Yunfan Liu
Yuanzhong Liu
Zhuoran Liu
Zhen Liu
Zheng Liu
Zhijian Liu
Zhisong Liu
Ziquan Liu
Ziyu Liu
Zhihua Liu
Zechun Liu
Zhaoyang Liu
Zhengzhe Liu
Stephan Liwicki
Shao-Yuan Lo
Sylvain Lobry
Suhas Lohit
Vishnu Suresh Lokhande
Vincenzo Lomonaco
Chengjiang Long
Guodong Long
Fuchen Long
Shangbang Long
Yang Long
Zijun Long
Vasco Lopes
Antonio M. Lopez
Roberto Javier
    Lopez-Sastre
Tobias Lorenz
Javier Lorenzo-Navarro
Yujing Lou
Qian Lou
Xiankai Lu
Changsheng Lu
Huimin Lu
Yongxi Lu
Hao Lu
Hong Lu
Jiasen Lu

Juwei Lu
Fan Lu
Guangming Lu
Jiwen Lu
Shun Lu
Tao Lu
Xiaonan Lu
Yang Lu
Yao Lu
Yongchun Lu
Zhiwu Lu
Cheng Lu
Liying Lu
Guo Lu
Xuequan Lu
Yanye Lu
Yantao Lu
Yuhang Lu
Fujun Luan
Jonathon Luiten
Jovita Lukasik
Alan Lukezic
Jonathan Samuel Lumentut
Mayank Lunayach
Ao Luo
Canjie Luo
Chong Luo
Xu Luo
Grace Luo
Jun Luo
Katie Z. Luo
Tao Luo
Cheng Luo
Fangzhou Luo
Gen Luo
Lei Luo
Sihui Luo
Weixin Luo
Yan Luo
Xiaoyan Luo
Yong Luo
Yadan Luo
Hao Luo
Ruotian Luo
Mi Luo

Tiange Luo
Wenjie Luo
Wenhan Luo
Xiao Luo
Zhiming Luo
Zhipeng Luo
Zhengyi Luo
Diogo C. Luvizon
Zhaoyang Lv
Gengyu Lyu
Lingjuan Lyu
Jun Lyu
Yuanyuan Lyu
Youwei Lyu
Yueming Lyu
Bingpeng Ma
Chao Ma
Chongyang Ma
Congbo Ma
Chih-Yao Ma
Fan Ma
Lin Ma
Haoyu Ma
Hengbo Ma
Jianqi Ma
Jiawei Ma
Jiayi Ma
Kede Ma
Kai Ma
Lingni Ma
Lei Ma
Xu Ma
Ning Ma
Benteng Ma
Cheng Ma
Andy J. Ma
Long Ma
Zhanyu Ma
Zhiheng Ma
Qianli Ma
Shiqiang Ma
Sizhuo Ma
Shiqing Ma
Xiaolong Ma
Xinzhu Ma

Gautam B. Machiraju
Spandan Madan
Mathew Magimai-Doss
Luca Magri
Behrooz Mahasseni
Upal Mahbub
Siddharth Mahendran
Paridhi Maheshwari
Rishabh Maheshwary
Mohammed Mahmoud
Shishira R. R. Maiya
Sylwia Majchrowska
Arjun Majumdar
Puspita Majumdar
Orchid Majumder
Sagnik Majumder
Ilya Makarov
Farkhod F. Makhmudkhujaev
Yasushi Makihara
Ankur Mali
Mateusz Malinowski
Utkarsh Mall
Srikanth Malla
Clement Mallet
Dimitrios Mallis
Yunze Man
Dipu Manandhar
Massimiliano Mancini
Murari Mandal
Raunak Manekar
Karttikeya Mangalam
Puneet Mangla
Fabian Manhardt
Sivabalan Manivasagam
Fahim Mannan
Chengzhi Mao
Hanzi Mao
Jiayuan Mao
Junhua Mao
Zhiyuan Mao
Jiageng Mao
Yunyao Mao
Zhendong Mao
Alberto Marchisio

Diego Marcos
Riccardo Marin
Aram Markosyan
Renaud Marlet
Ricardo Marques
Miquel Martí i Rabadán
Diego Martin Arroyo
Niki Martinel
Brais Martinez
Julieta Martinez
Marc Masana
Tomohiro Mashita
Timothée Masquelier
Minesh Mathew
Tetsu Matsukawa
Marwan Mattar
Bruce A. Maxwell
Christoph Mayer
Mantas Mazeika
Pratik Mazumder
Scott McCloskey
Steven McDonagh
Ishit Mehta
Jie Mei
Kangfu Mei
Jieru Mei
Xiaoguang Mei
Givi Meishvili
Luke Melas-Kyriazi
Iaroslav Melekhov
Andres Mendez-Vazquez
Heydi Mendez-Vazquez
Matias Mendieta
Ricardo A. Mendoza-León
Chenlin Meng
Depu Meng
Rang Meng
Zibo Meng
Qingjie Meng
Qier Meng
Yanda Meng
Zihang Meng
Thomas Mensink
Fabian Mentzer
Christopher Metzler

Gregory P. Meyer
Vasileios Mezaris
Liang Mi
Lu Mi
Bo Miao
Changtao Miao
Zichen Miao
Qiguang Miao
Xin Miao
Zhongqi Miao
Frank Michel
Simone Milani
Ben Mildenhall
Roy V. Miles
Juhong Min
Kyle Min
Hyun-Seok Min
Weiqing Min
Yuecong Min
Zhixiang Min
Qi Ming
David Minnen
Aymen Mir
Deepak Mishra
Anand Mishra
Shlok K. Mishra
Niluthpol Mithun
Gaurav Mittal
Trisha Mittal
Daisuke Miyazaki
Kaichun Mo
Hong Mo
Zhipeng Mo
Davide Modolo
Abduallah A. Mohamed
Mohamed Afham
Mohamed Aflal
Ron Mokady
Pavlo Molchanov
Davide Moltisanti
Liliane Momeni
Gianluca Monaci
Pascal Monasse
Ajoy Mondal
Tom Monnier

Aron Monszpart
Gyeongsik Moon
Suhong Moon
Taesup Moon
Sean Moran
Daniel Moreira
Pietro Morerio
Alexandre Morgand
Lia Morra
Ali Mosleh
Inbar Mosseri
Sayed Mohammad
    Mostafavi Isfahani
Saman Motamed
Ramy A. Mounir
Fangzhou Mu
Jiteng Mu
Norman Mu
Yasuhiro Mukaigawa
Ryan Mukherjee
Tanmoy Mukherjee
Yusuke Mukuta
Ravi Teja Mullapudi
Lea Müller
Matthias Müller
Martin Mundt
Nils Murrugarra-Llerena
Damien Muselet
Armin Mustafa
Muhammad Ferjad Naeem
Sauradip Nag
Hajime Nagahara
Pravin Nagar
Rajendra Nagar
Naveen Shankar Nagaraja
Varun Nagaraja
Tushar Nagarajan
Seungjun Nah
Gaku Nakano
Yuta Nakashima
Giljoo Nam
Seonghyeon Nam
Liangliang Nan
Yuesong Nan
Yeshwanth Napolean

Dinesh Reddy
    Narapureddy
Medhini Narasimhan
Supreeth
    Narasimhaswamy
Sriram Narayanan
Erickson R. Nascimento
Varun Nasery
K. L. Navaneet
Pablo Navarrete Michelini
Shant Navasardyan
Shah Nawaz
Nihal Nayak
Farhood Negin
Lukáš Neumann
Alejandro Newell
Evonne Ng
Kam Woh Ng
Tony Ng
Anh Nguyen
Tuan Anh Nguyen
Cuong Cao Nguyen
Ngoc Cuong Nguyen
Thanh Nguyen
Khoi Nguyen
Phi Le Nguyen
Phong Ha Nguyen
Tam Nguyen
Truong Nguyen
Anh Tuan Nguyen
Rang Nguyen
Thao Thi Phuong Nguyen
Van Nguyen Nguyen
Zhen-Liang Ni
Yao Ni
Shijie Nie
Xuecheng Nie
Yongwei Nie
Weizhi Nie
Ying Nie
Yinyu Nie
Kshitij N. Nikhal
Simon Niklaus
Xuefei Ning
Jifeng Ning

Yotam Nitzan
Di Niu
Shuaicheng Niu
Li Niu
Wei Niu
Yulei Niu
Zhenxing Niu
Albert No
Shohei Nobuhara
Nicoletta Noceti
Junhyug Noh
Sotiris Nousias
Slawomir Nowaczyk
Ewa M. Nowara
Valsamis Ntouskos
Gilberto Ochoa-Ruiz
Ferda Ofli
Jihyong Oh
Sangyun Oh
Youngtaek Oh
Hiroki Ohashi
Takahiro Okabe
Kemal Oksuz
Fumio Okura
Daniel Olmeda Reino
Matthew Olson
Carl Olsson
Roy Or-El
Alessandro Ortis
Guillermo Ortiz-Jimenez
Magnus Oskarsson
Ahmed A. A. Osman
Martin R. Oswald
Mayu Otani
Naima Otberdout
Cheng Ouyang
Jiahong Ouyang
Wanli Ouyang
Andrew Owens
Poojan B. Oza
Mete Ozay
A. Cengiz Oztireli
Gautam Pai
Tomas Pajdla
Umapada Pal

Simone Palazzo
Luca Palmieri
Bowen Pan
Hao Pan
Lili Pan
Tai-Yu Pan
Liang Pan
Chengwei Pan
Yingwei Pan
Xuran Pan
Jinshan Pan
Xinyu Pan
Liyuan Pan
Xingang Pan
Xingjia Pan
Zhihong Pan
Zizheng Pan
Priyadarshini Panda
Rameswar Panda
Rohit Pandey
Kaiyue Pang
Bo Pang
Guansong Pang
Jiangmiao Pang
Meng Pang
Tianyu Pang
Ziqi Pang
Omiros Pantazis
Andreas Panteli
Maja Pantic
Marina Paolanti
Joao P. Papa
Samuele Papa
Mike Papadakis
Dim P. Papadopoulos
George Papandreou
Constantin Pape
Toufiq Parag
Chethan Parameshwara
Shaifali Parashar
Alejandro Pardo
Rishubh Parihar
Sarah Parisot
JaeYoo Park
Gyeong-Moon Park

Hyojin Park
Hyoungseob Park
Jongchan Park
Jae Sung Park
Kiru Park
Chunghyun Park
Kwanyong Park
Sunghyun Park
Sungrae Park
Seongsik Park
Sanghyun Park
Sungjune Park
Taesung Park
Gaurav Parmar
Paritosh Parmar
Alvaro Parra
Despoina Paschalidou
Or Patashnik
Shivansh Patel
Pushpak Pati
Prashant W. Patil
Vaishakh Patil
Suvam Patra
Jay Patravali
Badri Narayana Patro
Angshuman Paul
Sudipta Paul
Rémi Pautrat
Nick E. Pears
Adithya Pediredla
Wenjie Pei
Shmuel Peleg
Latha Pemula
Bo Peng
Houwen Peng
Yue Peng
Liangzu Peng
Baoyun Peng
Jun Peng
Pai Peng
Sida Peng
Xi Peng
Yuxin Peng
Songyou Peng
Wei Peng

Weiqi Peng
Wen-Hsiao Peng
Pramuditha Perera
Juan C. Perez
Eduardo Pérez Pellitero
Juan-Manuel Perez-Rua
Federico Pernici
Marco Pesavento
Stavros Petridis
Ilya A. Petrov
Vladan Petrovic
Mathis Petrovich
Suzanne Petryk
Hieu Pham
Quang Pham
Khoi Pham
Tung Pham
Huy Phan
Stephen Phillips
Cheng Perng Phoo
David Picard
Marco Piccirilli
Georg Pichler
A. J. Piergiovanni
Vipin Pillai
Silvia L. Pintea
Giovanni Pintore
Robinson Piramuthu
Fiora Pirri
Theodoros Pissas
Fabio Pizzati
Benjamin Planche
Bryan Plummer
Matteo Poggi
Ashwini Pokle
Georgy E. Ponimatkin
Adrian Popescu
Stefan Popov
Nikola Popović
Ronald Poppe
Angelo Porrello
Michael Potter
Charalambos Poullis
Hadi Pouransari
Omid Poursaeed

Shraman Pramanick
Mantini Pranav
Dilip K. Prasad
Meghshyam Prasad
B. H. Pawan Prasad
Shitala Prasad
Prateek Prasanna
Ekta Prashnani
Derek S. Prijatelj
Luke Y. Prince
Véronique Prinet
Victor Adrian Prisacariu
James Pritts
Thomas Probst
Sergey Prokudin
Rita Pucci
Chi-Man Pun
Matthew Purri
Haozhi Qi
Lu Qi
Lei Qi
Xianbiao Qi
Yonggang Qi
Yuankai Qi
Siyuan Qi
Guocheng Qian
Hangwei Qian
Qi Qian
Deheng Qian
Shengsheng Qian
Wen Qian
Rui Qian
Yiming Qian
Shengju Qian
Shengyi Qian
Xuelin Qian
Zhenxing Qian
Nan Qiao
Xiaotian Qiao
Jing Qin
Can Qin
Siyang Qin
Hongwei Qin
Jie Qin
Minghai Qin

Yipeng Qin
Yongqiang Qin
Wenda Qin
Xuebin Qin
Yuzhe Qin
Yao Qin
Zhenyue Qin
Zhiwu Qing
Heqian Qiu
Jiayan Qiu
Jielin Qiu
Yue Qiu
Jiaxiong Qiu
Zhongxi Qiu
Shi Qiu
Zhaofan Qiu
Zhongnan Qu
Yanyun Qu
Kha Gia Quach
Yuhui Quan
Ruijie Quan
Mike Rabbat
Rahul Shekhar Rade
Filip Radenovic
Gorjan Radevski
Bogdan Raducanu
Francesco Ragusa
Shafin Rahman
Md Mahfuzur Rahman
   Siddiquee
Hossein Rahmani
Kiran Raja
Sivaramakrishnan
   Rajaraman
Jathushan Rajasegaran
Adnan Siraj Rakin
Michaël Ramamonjisoa
Chirag A. Raman
Shanmuganathan Raman
Vignesh Ramanathan
Vasili Ramanishka
Vikram V. Ramaswamy
Merey Ramazanova
Jason Rambach
Sai Saketh Rambhatla

Clément Rambour
Ashwin Ramesh Babu
Adín Ramírez Rivera
Arianna Rampini
Haoxi Ran
Aakanksha Rana
Aayush Jung Bahadur
   Rana
Kanchana N. Ranasinghe
Aneesh Rangnekar
Samrudhdhi B. Rangrej
Harsh Rangwani
Viresh Ranjan
Anyi Rao
Yongming Rao
Carolina Raposo
Michalis Raptis
Amir Rasouli
Vivek Rathod
Adepu Ravi Sankar
Avinash Ravichandran
Bharadwaj Ravichandran
Dripta S. Raychaudhuri
Adria Recasens
Simon Reiß
Davis Rempe
Daxuan Ren
Jiawei Ren
Jimmy Ren
Sucheng Ren
Dayong Ren
Zhile Ren
Dongwei Ren
Qibing Ren
Pengfei Ren
Zhenwen Ren
Xuqian Ren
Yixuan Ren
Zhongzheng Ren
Ambareesh Revanur
Hamed Rezazadegan
   Tavakoli
Rafael S. Rezende
Wonjong Rhee
Alexander Richard

Christian Richardt
Stephan R. Richter
Benjamin Riggan
Dominik Rivoir
Mamshad Nayeem Rizve
Joshua D. Robinson
Joseph Robinson
Chris Rockwell
Ranga Rodrigo
Andres C. Rodriguez
Carlos Rodriguez-Pardo
Marcus Rohrbach
Gemma Roig
Yu Rong
David A. Ross
Mohammad Rostami
Edward Rosten
Karsten Roth
Anirban Roy
Debaditya Roy
Shuvendu Roy
Ahana Roy Choudhury
Aruni Roy Chowdhury
Denys Rozumnyi
Shulan Ruan
Wenjie Ruan
Patrick Ruhkamp
Danila Rukhovich
Anian Ruoss
Chris Russell
Dan Ruta
Dawid Damian Rymarczyk
DongHun Ryu
Hyeonggon Ryu
Kwonyoung Ryu
Balasubramanian S.
Alexandre Sablayrolles
Mohammad Sabokrou
Arka Sadhu
Aniruddha Saha
Oindrila Saha
Pritish Sahu
Aneeshan Sain
Nirat Saini
Saurabh Saini

Takeshi Saitoh
Christos Sakaridis
Fumihiko Sakaue
Dimitrios Sakkos
Ken Sakurada
Parikshit V. Sakurikar
Rohit Saluja
Nermin Samet
Leo Sampaio Ferraz
    Ribeiro
Jorge Sanchez
Enrique Sanchez
Shengtian Sang
Anush Sankaran
Soubhik Sanyal
Nikolaos Sarafianos
Vishwanath Saragadam
István Sárándi
Saquib Sarfraz
Mert Bulent Sariyildiz
Anindya Sarkar
Pritam Sarkar
Paul-Edouard Sarlin
Hiroshi Sasaki
Takami Sato
Torsten Sattler
Ravi Kumar Satzoda
Axel Sauer
Stefano Savian
Artem Savkin
Manolis Savva
Gerald Schaefer
Simone Schaub-Meyer
Yoni Schirris
Samuel Schulter
Katja Schwarz
Jesse Scott
Sinisa Segvic
Constantin Marc Seibold
Lorenzo Seidenari
Matan Sela
Fadime Sener
Paul Hongsuck Seo
Kwanggyoon Seo
Hongje Seong

Dario Serez
Francesco Setti
Bryan Seybold
Mohamad Shahbazi
Shima Shahfar
Xinxin Shan
Caifeng Shan
Dandan Shan
Shawn Shan
Wei Shang
Jinghuan Shang
Jiaxiang Shang
Lei Shang
Sukrit Shankar
Ken Shao
Rui Shao
Jie Shao
Mingwen Shao
Aashish Sharma
Gaurav Sharma
Vivek Sharma
Abhishek Sharma
Yoli Shavit
Shashank Shekhar
Sumit Shekhar
Zhijie Shen
Fengyi Shen
Furao Shen
Jialie Shen
Jingjing Shen
Ziyi Shen
Linlin Shen
Guangyu Shen
Biluo Shen
Falong Shen
Jiajun Shen
Qiu Shen
Qiuhong Shen
Shuai Shen
Wang Shen
Yiqing Shen
Yunhang Shen
Siqi Shen
Bin Shen
Tianwei Shen

Xi Shen
Yilin Shen
Yuming Shen
Yucong Shen
Zhiqiang Shen
Lu Sheng
Yichen Sheng
Shivanand Venkanna
  Sheshappanavar
Shelly Sheynin
Baifeng Shi
Ruoxi Shi
Botian Shi
Hailin Shi
Jia Shi
Jing Shi
Shaoshuai Shi
Baoguang Shi
Boxin Shi
Hengcan Shi
Tianyang Shi
Xiaodan Shi
Yongjie Shi
Zhensheng Shi
Yinghuan Shi
Weiqi Shi
Wu Shi
Xuepeng Shi
Xiaoshuang Shi
Yujiao Shi
Zenglin Shi
Zhenmei Shi
Takashi Shibata
Meng-Li Shih
Yichang Shih
Hyunjung Shim
Dongseok Shim
Soshi Shimada
Inkyu Shin
Jinwoo Shin
Seungjoo Shin
Seungjae Shin
Koichi Shinoda
Suprosanna Shit

Palaiahnakote
  Shivakumara
Eli Shlizerman
Gaurav Shrivastava
Xiao Shu
Xiangbo Shu
Xiujun Shu
Yang Shu
Tianmin Shu
Jun Shu
Zhixin Shu
Bing Shuai
Maria Shugrina
Ivan Shugurov
Satya Narayan Shukla
Pranjay Shyam
Jianlou Si
Yawar Siddiqui
Alberto Signoroni
Pedro Silva
Jae-Young Sim
Oriane Siméoni
Martin Simon
Andrea Simonelli
Abhishek Singh
Ashish Singh
Dinesh Singh
Gurkirt Singh
Krishna Kumar Singh
Mannat Singh
Pravendra Singh
Rajat Vikram Singh
Utkarsh Singhal
Dipika Singhania
Vasu Singla
Harsh Sinha
Sudipta Sinha
Josef Sivic
Elena Sizikova
Geri Skenderi
Ivan Skorokhodov
Dmitriy Smirnov
Cameron Y. Smith
James S. Smith
Patrick Snape

Mattia Soldan
Hyeongseok Son
Sanghyun Son
Chuanbiao Song
Chen Song
Chunfeng Song
Dan Song
Dongjin Song
Hwanjun Song
Guoxian Song
Jiaming Song
Jie Song
Liangchen Song
Ran Song
Luchuan Song
Xibin Song
Li Song
Fenglong Song
Guoli Song
Guanglu Song
Zhenbo Song
Lin Song
Xinhang Song
Yang Song
Yibing Song
Rajiv Soundararajan
Hossein Souri
Cristovao Sousa
Riccardo Spezialetti
Leonidas Spinoulas
Michael W. Spratling
Deepak Sridhar
Srinath Sridhar
Gaurang Sriramanan
Vinkle Kumar Srivastav
Themos Stafylakis
Serban Stan
Anastasis Stathopoulos
Markus Steinberger
Jan Steinbrener
Sinisa Stekovic
Alexandros Stergiou
Gleb Sterkin
Rainer Stiefelhagen
Pierre Stock

Ombretta Strafforello
Julian Straub
Yannick Strümpler
Joerg Stueckler
Hang Su
Weijie Su
Jong-Chyi Su
Bing Su
Haisheng Su
Jinming Su
Yiyang Su
Yukun Su
Yuxin Su
Zhuo Su
Zhaoqi Su
Xiu Su
Yu-Chuan Su
Zhixun Su
Arulkumar Subramaniam
Akshayvarun Subramanya
A. Subramanyam
Swathikiran Sudhakaran
Yusuke Sugano
Masanori Suganuma
Yumin Suh
Yang Sui
Baochen Sun
Cheng Sun
Long Sun
Guolei Sun
Haoliang Sun
Haomiao Sun
He Sun
Hanqing Sun
Hao Sun
Lichao Sun
Jiachen Sun
Jiaming Sun
Jian Sun
Jin Sun
Jennifer J. Sun
Tiancheng Sun
Libo Sun
Peize Sun
Qianru Sun

Shanlin Sun
Yu Sun
Zhun Sun
Che Sun
Lin Sun
Tao Sun
Yiyou Sun
Chunyi Sun
Chong Sun
Weiwei Sun
Weixuan Sun
Xiuyu Sun
Yanan Sun
Zeren Sun
Zhaodong Sun
Zhiqing Sun
Minhyuk Sung
Jinli Suo
Simon Suo
Abhijit Suprem
Anshuman Suri
Saksham Suri
Joshua M. Susskind
Roman Suvorov
Gurumurthy Swaminathan
Robin Swanson
Paul Swoboda
Tabish A. Syed
Richard Szeliski
Fariborz Taherkhani
Yu-Wing Tai
Keita Takahashi
Walter Talbott
Gary Tam
Masato Tamura
Feitong Tan
Fuwen Tan
Shuhan Tan
Andong Tan
Bin Tan
Cheng Tan
Jianchao Tan
Lei Tan
Mingxing Tan
Xin Tan

Zichang Tan
Zhentao Tan
Kenichiro Tanaka
Masayuki Tanaka
Yushun Tang
Hao Tang
Jingqun Tang
Jinhui Tang
Kaihua Tang
Luming Tang
Lv Tang
Sheyang Tang
Shitao Tang
Siliang Tang
Shixiang Tang
Yansong Tang
Keke Tang
Chang Tang
Chenwei Tang
Jie Tang
Junshu Tang
Ming Tang
Peng Tang
Xu Tang
Yao Tang
Chen Tang
Fan Tang
Haoran Tang
Shengeng Tang
Yehui Tang
Zhipeng Tang
Ugo Tanielian
Chaofan Tao
Jiale Tao
Junli Tao
Renshuai Tao
An Tao
Guanhong Tao
Zhiqiang Tao
Makarand Tapaswi
Jean-Philippe G. Tarel
Juan J. Tarrio
Enzo Tartaglione
Keisuke Tateno
Zachary Teed

Ajinkya B. Tejankar
Bugra Tekin
Purva Tendulkar
Damien Teney
Minggui Teng
Chris Tensmeyer
Andrew Beng Jin Teoh
Philipp Terhörst
Kartik Thakral
Nupur Thakur
Kevin Thandiackal
Spyridon Thermos
Diego Thomas
William Thong
Yuesong Tian
Guanzhong Tian
Lin Tian
Shiqi Tian
Kai Tian
Meng Tian
Tai-Peng Tian
Zhuotao Tian
Shangxuan Tian
Tian Tian
Yapeng Tian
Yu Tian
Yuxin Tian
Leslie Ching Ow Tiong
Praveen Tirupattur
Garvita Tiwari
George Toderici
Antoine Toisoul
Aysim Toker
Tatiana Tommasi
Zhan Tong
Alessio Tonioni
Alessandro Torcinovich
Fabio Tosi
Matteo Toso
Hugo Touvron
Quan Hung Tran
Son Tran
Hung Tran
Ngoc-Trung Tran
Vinh Tran

Phong Tran
Giovanni Trappolini
Edith Tretschk
Subarna Tripathi
Shubhendu Trivedi
Eduard Trulls
Prune Truong
Thanh-Dat Truong
Tomasz Trzcinski
Sam Tsai
Yi-Hsuan Tsai
Ethan Tseng
Yu-Chee Tseng
Shahar Tsiper
Stavros Tsogkas
Shikui Tu
Zhigang Tu
Zhengzhong Tu
Richard Tucker
Sergey Tulyakov
Cigdem Turan
Daniyar Turmukhambetov
Victor G. Turrisi da Costa
Bartlomiej Twardowski
Christopher D. Twigg
Radim Tylecek
Mostofa Rafid Uddin
Md. Zasim Uddin
Kohei Uehara
Nicolas Ugrinovic
Youngjung Uh
Norimichi Ukita
Anwaar Ulhaq
Devesh Upadhyay
Paul Upchurch
Yoshitaka Ushiku
Yuzuko Utsumi
Mikaela Angelina Uy
Mohit Vaishnav
Pratik Vaishnavi
Jeya Maria Jose Valanarasu
Matias A. Valdenegro Toro
Diego Valsesia
Wouter Van Gansbeke
Nanne van Noord

Simon Vandenhende
Farshid Varno
Cristina Vasconcelos
Francisco Vasconcelos
Alex Vasilescu
Subeesh Vasu
Arun Balajee Vasudevan
Kanav Vats
Vaibhav S. Vavilala
Sagar Vaze
Javier Vazquez-Corral
Andrea Vedaldi
Olga Veksler
Andreas Velten
Sai H. Vemprala
Raviteja Vemulapalli
Shashanka
    Venkataramanan
Dor Verbin
Luisa Verdoliva
Manisha Verma
Yashaswi Verma
Constantin Vertan
Eli Verwimp
Deepak Vijaykeerthy
Pablo Villanueva
Ruben Villegas
Markus Vincze
Vibhav Vineet
Minh P. Vo
Huy V. Vo
Duc Minh Vo
Tomas Vojir
Igor Vozniak
Nicholas Vretos
Vibashan VS
Tuan-Anh Vu
Thang Vu
Mårten Wadenbäck
Neal Wadhwa
Aaron T. Walsman
Steven Walton
Jin Wan
Alvin Wan
Jia Wan

Jun Wan
Xiaoyue Wan
Fang Wan
Guowei Wan
Renjie Wan
Zhiqiang Wan
Ziyu Wan
Bastian Wandt
Dongdong Wang
Limin Wang
Haiyang Wang
Xiaobing Wang
Angtian Wang
Angelina Wang
Bing Wang
Bo Wang
Boyu Wang
Binghui Wang
Chen Wang
Chien-Yi Wang
Congli Wang
Qi Wang
Chengrui Wang
Rui Wang
Yiqun Wang
Cong Wang
Wenjing Wang
Dongkai Wang
Di Wang
Xiaogang Wang
Kai Wang
Zhizhong Wang
Fangjinhua Wang
Feng Wang
Hang Wang
Gaoang Wang
Guoqing Wang
Guangcong Wang
Guangzhi Wang
Hanqing Wang
Hao Wang
Haohan Wang
Haoran Wang
Hong Wang
Haotao Wang

Hu Wang
Huan Wang
Hua Wang
Hui-Po Wang
Hengli Wang
Hanyu Wang
Hongxing Wang
Jingwen Wang
Jialiang Wang
Jian Wang
Jianyi Wang
Jiashun Wang
Jiahao Wang
Tsun-Hsuan Wang
Xiaoqian Wang
Jinqiao Wang
Jun Wang
Jianzong Wang
Kaihong Wang
Ke Wang
Lei Wang
Lingjing Wang
Linnan Wang
Lin Wang
Liansheng Wang
Mengjiao Wang
Manning Wang
Nannan Wang
Peihao Wang
Jiayun Wang
Pu Wang
Qiang Wang
Qiufeng Wang
Qilong Wang
Qiangchang Wang
Qin Wang
Qing Wang
Ruocheng Wang
Ruibin Wang
Ruisheng Wang
Ruizhe Wang
Runqi Wang
Runzhong Wang
Wenxuan Wang
Sen Wang

Shangfei Wang
Shaofei Wang
Shijie Wang
Shiqi Wang
Zhibo Wang
Song Wang
Xinjiang Wang
Tai Wang
Tao Wang
Teng Wang
Xiang Wang
Tianren Wang
Tiantian Wang
Tianyi Wang
Fengjiao Wang
Wei Wang
Miaohui Wang
Suchen Wang
Siyue Wang
Yaoming Wang
Xiao Wang
Ze Wang
Biao Wang
Chaofei Wang
Dong Wang
Gu Wang
Guangrun Wang
Guangming Wang
Guo-Hua Wang
Haoqing Wang
Hesheng Wang
Huafeng Wang
Jinghua Wang
Jingdong Wang
Jingjing Wang
Jingya Wang
Jingkang Wang
Jiakai Wang
Junke Wang
Kuo Wang
Lichen Wang
Lizhi Wang
Longguang Wang
Mang Wang
Mei Wang

Min Wang
Peng-Shuai Wang
Run Wang
Shaoru Wang
Shuhui Wang
Tan Wang
Tiancai Wang
Tianqi Wang
Wenhai Wang
Wenzhe Wang
Xiaobo Wang
Xiudong Wang
Xu Wang
Yajie Wang
Yan Wang
Yuan-Gen Wang
Yingqian Wang
Yizhi Wang
Yulin Wang
Yu Wang
Yujie Wang
Yunhe Wang
Yuxi Wang
Yaowei Wang
Yiwei Wang
Zezheng Wang
Hongzhi Wang
Zhiqiang Wang
Ziteng Wang
Ziwei Wang
Zheng Wang
Zhenyu Wang
Binglu Wang
Zhongdao Wang
Ce Wang
Weining Wang
Weiyao Wang
Wenbin Wang
Wenguan Wang
Guangting Wang
Haolin Wang
Haiyan Wang
Huiyu Wang
Naiyan Wang
Jingbo Wang

Jinpeng Wang
Jiaqi Wang
Liyuan Wang
Lizhen Wang
Ning Wang
Wenqian Wang
Sheng-Yu Wang
Weimin Wang
Xiaohan Wang
Yifan Wang
Yi Wang
Yongtao Wang
Yizhou Wang
Zhuo Wang
Zhe Wang
Xudong Wang
Xiaofang Wang
Xinggang Wang
Xiaosen Wang
Xiaosong Wang
Xiaoyang Wang
Lijun Wang
Xinlong Wang
Xuan Wang
Xue Wang
Yangang Wang
Yaohui Wang
Yu-Chiang Frank Wang
Yida Wang
Yilin Wang
Yi Ru Wang
Yali Wang
Yinglong Wang
Yufu Wang
Yujiang Wang
Yuwang Wang
Yuting Wang
Yang Wang
Yu-Xiong Wang
Yixu Wang
Ziqi Wang
Zhicheng Wang
Zeyu Wang
Zhaowen Wang
Zhenyi Wang

Zhenzhi Wang
Zhijie Wang
Zhiyong Wang
Zhongling Wang
Zhuowei Wang
Zian Wang
Zifu Wang
Zihao Wang
Zirui Wang
Ziyan Wang
Wenxiao Wang
Zhen Wang
Zhepeng Wang
Zi Wang
Zihao W. Wang
Steven L. Waslander
Olivia Watkins
Daniel Watson
Silvan Weder
Dongyoon Wee
Dongming Wei
Tianyi Wei
Jia Wei
Dong Wei
Fangyun Wei
Longhui Wei
Mingqiang Wei
Xinyue Wei
Chen Wei
Donglai Wei
Pengxu Wei
Xing Wei
Xiu-Shen Wei
Wenqi Wei
Guoqiang Wei
Wei Wei
XingKui Wei
Xian Wei
Xingxing Wei
Yake Wei
Yuxiang Wei
Yi Wei
Luca Weihs
Michael Weinmann
Martin Weinmann

Congcong Wen
Chuan Wen
Jie Wen
Sijia Wen
Song Wen
Chao Wen
Xiang Wen
Zeyi Wen
Xin Wen
Yilin Wen
Yijia Weng
Shuchen Weng
Junwu Weng
Wenming Weng
Renliang Weng
Zhenyu Weng
Xinshuo Weng
Nicholas J. Westlake
Gordon Wetzstein
Lena M. Widin Klasén
Rick Wildes
Bryan M. Williams
Williem Williem
Ole Winther
Scott Wisdom
Alex Wong
Chau-Wai Wong
Kwan-Yee K. Wong
Yongkang Wong
Scott Workman
Marcel Worring
Michael Wray
Safwan Wshah
Xiang Wu
Aming Wu
Chongruo Wu
Cho-Ying Wu
Chunpeng Wu
Chenyan Wu
Ziyi Wu
Fuxiang Wu
Gang Wu
Haiping Wu
Huisi Wu
Jane Wu

Jialian Wu
Jing Wu
Jinjian Wu
Jianlong Wu
Xian Wu
Lifang Wu
Lifan Wu
Minye Wu
Qianyi Wu
Rongliang Wu
Rui Wu
Shiqian Wu
Shuzhe Wu
Shangzhe Wu
Tsung-Han Wu
Tz-Ying Wu
Ting-Wei Wu
Jiannan Wu
Zhiliang Wu
Yu Wu
Chenyun Wu
Dayan Wu
Dongxian Wu
Fei Wu
Hefeng Wu
Jianxin Wu
Weibin Wu
Wenxuan Wu
Wenhao Wu
Xiao Wu
Yicheng Wu
Yuanwei Wu
Yu-Huan Wu
Zhenxin Wu
Zhenyu Wu
Wei Wu
Peng Wu
Xiaohe Wu
Xindi Wu
Xinxing Wu
Xinyi Wu
Xingjiao Wu
Xiongwei Wu
Yangzheng Wu
Yanzhao Wu

Yawen Wu
Yong Wu
Yi Wu
Ying Nian Wu
Zhenyao Wu
Zhonghua Wu
Zongze Wu
Zuxuan Wu
Stefanie Wuhrer
Teng Xi
Jianing Xi
Fei Xia
Haifeng Xia
Menghan Xia
Yuanqing Xia
Zhihua Xia
Xiaobo Xia
Weihao Xia
Shihong Xia
Yan Xia
Yong Xia
Zhaoyang Xia
Zhihao Xia
Chuhua Xian
Yongqin Xian
Wangmeng Xiang
Fanbo Xiang
Tiange Xiang
Tao Xiang
Liuyu Xiang
Xiaoyu Xiang
Zhiyu Xiang
Aoran Xiao
Chunxia Xiao
Fanyi Xiao
Jimin Xiao
Jun Xiao
Taihong Xiao
Anqi Xiao
Junfei Xiao
Jing Xiao
Liang Xiao
Yang Xiao
Yuting Xiao
Yijun Xiao

Yao Xiao
Zeyu Xiao
Zhisheng Xiao
Zihao Xiao
Binhui Xie
Christopher Xie
Haozhe Xie
Jin Xie
Guo-Sen Xie
Hongtao Xie
Ming-Kun Xie
Tingting Xie
Chaohao Xie
Weicheng Xie
Xudong Xie
Jiyang Xie
Xiaohua Xie
Yuan Xie
Zhenyu Xie
Ning Xie
Xianghui Xie
Xiufeng Xie
You Xie
Yutong Xie
Fuyong Xing
Yifan Xing
Zhen Xing
Yuanjun Xiong
Jinhui Xiong
Weihua Xiong
Hongkai Xiong
Zhitong Xiong
Yuanhao Xiong
Yunyang Xiong
Yuwen Xiong
Zhiwei Xiong
Yuliang Xiu
An Xu
Chang Xu
Chenliang Xu
Chengming Xu
Chenshu Xu
Xiang Xu
Huijuan Xu
Zhe Xu

Jie Xu
Jingyi Xu
Jiarui Xu
Yinghao Xu
Kele Xu
Ke Xu
Li Xu
Linchuan Xu
Linning Xu
Mengde Xu
Mengmeng Frost Xu
Min Xu
Mingye Xu
Jun Xu
Ning Xu
Peng Xu
Runsheng Xu
Sheng Xu
Wenqiang Xu
Xiaogang Xu
Renzhe Xu
Kaidi Xu
Yi Xu
Chi Xu
Qiuling Xu
Baobei Xu
Feng Xu
Haohang Xu
Haofei Xu
Lan Xu
Mingze Xu
Songcen Xu
Weipeng Xu
Wenjia Xu
Wenju Xu
Xiangyu Xu
Xin Xu
Yinshuang Xu
Yixing Xu
Yuting Xu
Yanyu Xu
Zhenbo Xu
Zhiliang Xu
Zhiyuan Xu
Xiaohao Xu

Yanwu Xu
Yan Xu
Yiran Xu
Yifan Xu
Yufei Xu
Yong Xu
Zichuan Xu
Zenglin Xu
Zexiang Xu
Zhan Xu
Zheng Xu
Zhiwei Xu
Ziyue Xu
Shiyu Xuan
Hanyu Xuan
Fei Xue
Jianru Xue
Mingfu Xue
Qinghan Xue
Tianfan Xue
Chao Xue
Chuhui Xue
Nan Xue
Zhou Xue
Xiangyang Xue
Yuan Xue
Abhay Yadav
Ravindra Yadav
Kota Yamaguchi
Toshihiko Yamasaki
Kohei Yamashita
Chaochao Yan
Feng Yan
Kun Yan
Qingsen Yan
Qixin Yan
Rui Yan
Siming Yan
Xinchen Yan
Yaping Yan
Bin Yan
Qingan Yan
Shen Yan
Shipeng Yan
Xu Yan

Yan Yan
Yichao Yan
Zhaoyi Yan
Zike Yan
Zhiqiang Yan
Hongliang Yan
Zizheng Yan
Jiewen Yang
Anqi Joyce Yang
Shan Yang
Anqi Yang
Antoine Yang
Bo Yang
Baoyao Yang
Chenhongyi Yang
Dingkang Yang
De-Nian Yang
Dong Yang
David Yang
Fan Yang
Fengyu Yang
Fengting Yang
Fei Yang
Gengshan Yang
Heng Yang
Han Yang
Huan Yang
Yibo Yang
Jiancheng Yang
Jihan Yang
Jiawei Yang
Jiayu Yang
Jie Yang
Jinfa Yang
Jingkang Yang
Jinyu Yang
Cheng-Fu Yang
Ji Yang
Jianyu Yang
Kailun Yang
Tian Yang
Luyu Yang
Liang Yang
Li Yang
Michael Ying Yang

Yang Yang
Muli Yang
Le Yang
Qiushi Yang
Ren Yang
Ruihan Yang
Shuang Yang
Siyuan Yang
Su Yang
Shiqi Yang
Taojiannan Yang
Tianyu Yang
Lei Yang
Wanzhao Yang
Shuai Yang
William Yang
Wei Yang
Xiaofeng Yang
Xiaoshan Yang
Xin Yang
Xuan Yang
Xu Yang
Xingyi Yang
Xitong Yang
Jing Yang
Yanchao Yang
Wenming Yang
Yujiu Yang
Herb Yang
Jianfei Yang
Jinhui Yang
Chuanguang Yang
Guanglei Yang
Haitao Yang
Kewei Yang
Linlin Yang
Lijin Yang
Longrong Yang
Meng Yang
MingKun Yang
Sibei Yang
Shicai Yang
Tong Yang
Wen Yang
Xi Yang

Xiaolong Yang
Xue Yang
Yubin Yang
Ze Yang
Ziyi Yang
Yi Yang
Linjie Yang
Yuzhe Yang
Yiding Yang
Zhenpei Yang
Zhaohui Yang
Zhengyuan Yang
Zhibo Yang
Zongxin Yang
Hantao Yao
Mingde Yao
Rui Yao
Taiping Yao
Ting Yao
Cong Yao
Qingsong Yao
Quanming Yao
Xu Yao
Yuan Yao
Yao Yao
Yazhou Yao
Jiawen Yao
Shunyu Yao
Pew-Thian Yap
Sudhir Yarram
Rajeev Yasarla
Peng Ye
Botao Ye
Mao Ye
Fei Ye
Hanrong Ye
Jingwen Ye
Jinwei Ye
Jiarong Ye
Mang Ye
Meng Ye
Qi Ye
Qian Ye
Qixiang Ye
Junjie Ye

Sheng Ye
Nanyang Ye
Yufei Ye
Xiaoqing Ye
Ruolin Ye
Yousef Yeganeh
Chun-Hsiao Yeh
Raymond A. Yeh
Yu-Ying Yeh
Kai Yi
Chang Yi
Renjiao Yi
Xinping Yi
Peng Yi
Alper Yilmaz
Junho Yim
Hui Yin
Bangjie Yin
Jia-Li Yin
Miao Yin
Wenzhe Yin
Xuwang Yin
Ming Yin
Yu Yin
Aoxiong Yin
Kangxue Yin
Tianwei Yin
Wei Yin
Xianghua Ying
Rio Yokota
Tatsuya Yokota
Naoto Yokoya
Ryo Yonetani
Ki Yoon Yoo
Jinsu Yoo
Sunjae Yoon
Jae Shin Yoon
Jihun Yoon
Sung-Hoon Yoon
Ryota Yoshihashi
Yusuke Yoshiyasu
Chenyu You
Haoran You
Haoxuan You
Yang You

Quanzeng You
Tackgeun You
Kaichao You
Shan You
Xinge You
Yurong You
Baosheng Yu
Bei Yu
Haichao Yu
Hao Yu
Chaohui Yu
Fisher Yu
Jin-Gang Yu
Jiyang Yu
Jason J. Yu
Jiashuo Yu
Hong-Xing Yu
Lei Yu
Mulin Yu
Ning Yu
Peilin Yu
Qi Yu
Qian Yu
Rui Yu
Shuzhi Yu
Gang Yu
Tan Yu
Weijiang Yu
Xin Yu
Bingyao Yu
Ye Yu
Hanchao Yu
Yingchen Yu
Tao Yu
Xiaotian Yu
Qing Yu
Houjian Yu
Changqian Yu
Jing Yu
Jun Yu
Shujian Yu
Xiang Yu
Zhaofei Yu
Zhenbo Yu
Yinfeng Yu

Zhuoran Yu
Zitong Yu
Bo Yuan
Jiangbo Yuan
Liangzhe Yuan
Weihao Yuan
Jianbo Yuan
Xiaoyun Yuan
Ye Yuan
Li Yuan
Geng Yuan
Jialin Yuan
Maoxun Yuan
Peng Yuan
Xin Yuan
Yuan Yuan
Yuhui Yuan
Yixuan Yuan
Zheng Yuan
Mehmet Kerim Yücel
Kaiyu Yue
Haixiao Yue
Heeseung Yun
Sangdoo Yun
Tian Yun
Mahmut Yurt
Ekim Yurtsever
Ahmet Yüzügüler
Edouard Yvinec
Eloi Zablocki
Christopher Zach
Muhammad Zaigham
    Zaheer
Pierluigi Zama Ramirez
Yuhang Zang
Pietro Zanuttigh
Alexey Zaytsev
Bernhard Zeisl
Haitian Zeng
Pengpeng Zeng
Jiabei Zeng
Runhao Zeng
Wei Zeng
Yawen Zeng
Yi Zeng

Yiming Zeng
Tieyong Zeng
Huanqiang Zeng
Dan Zeng
Yu Zeng
Wei Zhai
Yuanhao Zhai
Fangneng Zhan
Kun Zhan
Xiong Zhang
Jingdong Zhang
Jiangning Zhang
Zhilu Zhang
Gengwei Zhang
Dongsu Zhang
Hui Zhang
Binjie Zhang
Bo Zhang
Tianhao Zhang
Cecilia Zhang
Jing Zhang
Chaoning Zhang
Chenxu Zhang
Chi Zhang
Chris Zhang
Yabin Zhang
Zhao Zhang
Rufeng Zhang
Chaoyi Zhang
Zheng Zhang
Da Zhang
Yi Zhang
Edward Zhang
Xin Zhang
Feifei Zhang
Feilong Zhang
Yuqi Zhang
GuiXuan Zhang
Hanlin Zhang
Hanwang Zhang
Hanzhen Zhang
Haotian Zhang
He Zhang
Haokui Zhang
Hongyuan Zhang

Hengrui Zhang
Hongming Zhang
Mingfang Zhang
Jianpeng Zhang
Jiaming Zhang
Jichao Zhang
Jie Zhang
Jingfeng Zhang
Jingyi Zhang
Jinnian Zhang
David Junhao Zhang
Junjie Zhang
Junzhe Zhang
Jiawan Zhang
Jingyang Zhang
Kai Zhang
Lei Zhang
Lihua Zhang
Lu Zhang
Miao Zhang
Minjia Zhang
Mingjin Zhang
Qi Zhang
Qian Zhang
Qilong Zhang
Qiming Zhang
Qiang Zhang
Richard Zhang
Ruimao Zhang
Ruisi Zhang
Ruixin Zhang
Runze Zhang
Qilin Zhang
Shan Zhang
Shanshan Zhang
Xi Sheryl Zhang
Song-Hai Zhang
Chongyang Zhang
Kaihao Zhang
Songyang Zhang
Shu Zhang
Siwei Zhang
Shujian Zhang
Tianyun Zhang
Tong Zhang

Tao Zhang
Wenwei Zhang
Wenqiang Zhang
Wen Zhang
Xiaolin Zhang
Xingchen Zhang
Xingxuan Zhang
Xiuming Zhang
Xiaoshuai Zhang
Xuanmeng Zhang
Xuanyang Zhang
Xucong Zhang
Xingxing Zhang
Xikun Zhang
Xiaohan Zhang
Yahui Zhang
Yunhua Zhang
Yan Zhang
Yanghao Zhang
Yifei Zhang
Yifan Zhang
Yi-Fan Zhang
Yihao Zhang
Yingliang Zhang
Youshan Zhang
Yulun Zhang
Yushu Zhang
Yixiao Zhang
Yide Zhang
Zhongwen Zhang
Bowen Zhang
Chen-Lin Zhang
Zehua Zhang
Zekun Zhang
Zeyu Zhang
Xiaowei Zhang
Yifeng Zhang
Cheng Zhang
Hongguang Zhang
Yuexi Zhang
Fa Zhang
Guofeng Zhang
Hao Zhang
Haofeng Zhang
Hongwen Zhang

Hua Zhang	Zhizhong Zhang	Bowen Zhao
Jiaxin Zhang	Qilong Zhangli	Pu Zhao
Zhenyu Zhang	Bingyin Zhao	Bingchen Zhao
Jian Zhang	Bin Zhao	Borui Zhao
Jianfeng Zhang	Chenglong Zhao	Fuqiang Zhao
Jiao Zhang	Lei Zhao	Hanbin Zhao
Jiakai Zhang	Feng Zhao	Jian Zhao
Lefei Zhang	Gangming Zhao	Mingyang Zhao
Le Zhang	Haiyan Zhao	Na Zhao
Mi Zhang	Hao Zhao	Rongchang Zhao
Min Zhang	Handong Zhao	Ruiqi Zhao
Ning Zhang	Hengshuang Zhao	Shuai Zhao
Pan Zhang	Yinan Zhao	Wenda Zhao
Pu Zhang	Jiaojiao Zhao	Wenliang Zhao
Qing Zhang	Jiaqi Zhao	Xiangyun Zhao
Renrui Zhang	Jing Zhao	Yifan Zhao
Shifeng Zhang	Kaili Zhao	Yaping Zhao
Shuo Zhang	Haojie Zhao	Zhou Zhao
Shaoxiong Zhang	Yucheng Zhao	He Zhao
Weizhong Zhang	Longjiao Zhao	Jie Zhao
Xi Zhang	Long Zhao	Xibin Zhao
Xiaomei Zhang	Qingsong Zhao	Xiaoqi Zhao
Xinyu Zhang	Qingyu Zhao	Zhengyu Zhao
Yin Zhang	Rui Zhao	Jin Zhe
Zicheng Zhang	Rui-Wei Zhao	Chuanxia Zheng
Zihao Zhang	Sicheng Zhao	Huan Zheng
Ziqi Zhang	Shuang Zhao	Hao Zheng
Zhaoxiang Zhang	Siyan Zhao	Jia Zheng
Zhen Zhang	Zelin Zhao	Jian-Qing Zheng
Zhipeng Zhang	Shiyu Zhao	Shuai Zheng
Zhixing Zhang	Wang Zhao	Meng Zheng
Zhizheng Zhang	Tiesong Zhao	Mingkai Zheng
Jiawei Zhang	Qian Zhao	Qian Zheng
Zhong Zhang	Wangbo Zhao	Qi Zheng
Pingping Zhang	Xi-Le Zhao	Wu Zheng
Yixin Zhang	Xu Zhao	Yinqiang Zheng
Kui Zhang	Yajie Zhao	Yufeng Zheng
Lingzhi Zhang	Yang Zhao	Yutong Zheng
Huaiwen Zhang	Ying Zhao	Yalin Zheng
Quanshi Zhang	Yin Zhao	Yu Zheng
Zhoutong Zhang	Yizhou Zhao	Feng Zheng
Yuhang Zhang	Yunhan Zhao	Zhaoheng Zheng
Yuting Zhang	Yuyang Zhao	Haitian Zheng
Zhang Zhang	Yue Zhao	Kang Zheng
Ziming Zhang	Yuzhi Zhao	Bolun Zheng

Haiyong Zheng
Mingwu Zheng
Sipeng Zheng
Tu Zheng
Wenzhao Zheng
Xiawu Zheng
Yinglin Zheng
Zhuo Zheng
Zilong Zheng
Kecheng Zheng
Zerong Zheng
Shuaifeng Zhi
Tiancheng Zhi
Jia-Xing Zhong
Yiwu Zhong
Fangwei Zhong
Zhihang Zhong
Yaoyao Zhong
Yiran Zhong
Zhun Zhong
Zichun Zhong
Bo Zhou
Boyao Zhou
Brady Zhou
Mo Zhou
Chunluan Zhou
Dingfu Zhou
Fan Zhou
Jingkai Zhou
Honglu Zhou
Jiaming Zhou
Jiahuan Zhou
Jun Zhou
Kaiyang Zhou
Keyang Zhou
Kuangqi Zhou
Lei Zhou
Lihua Zhou
Man Zhou
Mingyi Zhou
Mingyuan Zhou
Ning Zhou
Peng Zhou
Penghao Zhou
Qianyi Zhou

Shuigeng Zhou
Shangchen Zhou
Huayi Zhou
Zhize Zhou
Sanping Zhou
Qin Zhou
Tao Zhou
Wenbo Zhou
Xiangdong Zhou
Xiao-Yun Zhou
Xiao Zhou
Yang Zhou
Yipin Zhou
Zhenyu Zhou
Hao Zhou
Chu Zhou
Daquan Zhou
Da-Wei Zhou
Hang Zhou
Kang Zhou
Qianyu Zhou
Sheng Zhou
Wenhui Zhou
Xingyi Zhou
Yan-Jie Zhou
Yiyi Zhou
Yu Zhou
Yuan Zhou
Yuqian Zhou
Yuxuan Zhou
Zixiang Zhou
Wengang Zhou
Shuchang Zhou
Tianfei Zhou
Yichao Zhou
Alex Zhu
Chenchen Zhu
Deyao Zhu
Xiatian Zhu
Guibo Zhu
Haidong Zhu
Hao Zhu
Hongzi Zhu
Rui Zhu
Jing Zhu

Jianke Zhu
Junchen Zhu
Lei Zhu
Lingyu Zhu
Luyang Zhu
Menglong Zhu
Peihao Zhu
Hui Zhu
Xiaofeng Zhu
Tyler (Lixuan) Zhu
Wentao Zhu
Xiangyu Zhu
Xinqi Zhu
Xinxin Zhu
Xinliang Zhu
Yangguang Zhu
Yichen Zhu
Yixin Zhu
Yanjun Zhu
Yousong Zhu
Yuhao Zhu
Ye Zhu
Feng Zhu
Zhen Zhu
Fangrui Zhu
Jinjing Zhu
Linchao Zhu
Pengfei Zhu
Sijie Zhu
Xiaobin Zhu
Xiaoguang Zhu
Zezhou Zhu
Zhenyao Zhu
Kai Zhu
Pengkai Zhu
Bingbing Zhuang
Chengyuan Zhuang
Liansheng Zhuang
Peiye Zhuang
Yixin Zhuang
Yihong Zhuang
Junbao Zhuo
Andrea Ziani
Bartosz Zieliński
Primo Zingaretti

Nikolaos Zioulis
Andrew Zisserman
Yael Ziv
Liu Ziyin
Xingxing Zou
Danping Zou
Qi Zou

Shihao Zou
Xueyan Zou
Yang Zou
Yuliang Zou
Zihang Zou
Chuhang Zou
Dongqing Zou

Xu Zou
Zhiming Zou
Maria A. Zuluaga
Xinxin Zuo
Zhiwen Zuo
Reyer Zwiggelaar

Contents – Part VIII

ECCV Caption: Correcting False Negatives by Collecting
Machine-and-Human-verified Image-Caption Associations for MS-COCO 1
*Sanghyuk Chun, Wonjae Kim, Song Park, Minsuk Chang,
and Seong Joon Oh*

MOTCOM: The Multi-Object Tracking Dataset Complexity Metric 20
*Malte Pedersen, Joakim Bruslund Haurum, Patrick Dendorfer,
and Thomas B. Moeslund*

How to Synthesize a Large-Scale and Trainable Micro-Expression Dataset? 38
Yuchi Liu, Zhongdao Wang, Tom Gedeon, and Liang Zheng

A Real World Dataset for Multi-view 3D Reconstruction 56
Rakesh Shrestha, Siqi Hu, Minghao Gou, Ziyuan Liu, and Ping Tan

REALY: Rethinking the Evaluation of 3D Face Reconstruction 74
*Zenghao Chai, Haoxian Zhang, Jing Ren, Di Kang, Zhengzhuo Xu,
Xuefei Zhe, Chun Yuan, and Linchao Bao*

Capturing, Reconstructing, and Simulating: The UrbanScene3D Dataset 93
Liqiang Lin, Yilin Liu, Yue Hu, Xingguang Yan, Ke Xie, and Hui Huang

3D CoMPaT: Composition of Materials on Parts of 3D Things 110
*Yuchen Li, Ujjwal Upadhyay, Habib Slim, Ahmed Abdelreheem,
Arpit Prajapati, Suhail Pothigara, Peter Wonka, and Mohamed Elhoseiny*

PartImageNet: A Large, High-Quality Dataset of Parts 128
*Ju He, Shuo Yang, Shaokang Yang, Adam Kortylewski, Xiaoding Yuan,
Jie-Neng Chen, Shuai Liu, Cheng Yang, Qihang Yu, and Alan Yuille*

A-OKVQA: A Benchmark for Visual Question Answering Using World
Knowledge 146
*Dustin Schwenk, Apoorv Khandelwal, Christopher Clark,
Kenneth Marino, and Roozbeh Mottaghi*

OOD-CV: A Benchmark for Robustness to Out-of-Distribution Shifts
of Individual Nuisances in Natural Images 163
*Bingchen Zhao, Shaozuo Yu, Wufei Ma, Mingxin Yu, Shenxiao Mei,
Angtian Wang, Ju He, Alan Yuille, and Adam Kortylewski*

Facial Depth and Normal Estimation Using Single Dual-Pixel Camera 181
  Minjun Kang, Jaesung Choe, Hyowon Ha, Hae-Gon Jeon,
  Sunghoon Im, In So Kweon, and Kuk-Jin Yoon

The Anatomy of Video Editing: A Dataset and Benchmark Suite
for AI-Assisted Video Editing 201
  Dawit Mureja Argaw, Fabian Caba Heilbron, Joon-Young Lee,
  Markus Woodson, and In So Kweon

StyleBabel: Artistic Style Tagging and Captioning 219
  Dan Ruta, Andrew Gilbert, Pranav Aggarwal, Naveen Marri,
  Ajinkya Kale, Jo Briggs, Chris Speed, Hailin Jin, Baldo Faieta,
  Alex Filipkowski, Zhe Lin, and John Collomosse

PANDORA: A Panoramic Detection Dataset for Object with Orientation 237
  Hang Xu, Qiang Zhao, Yike Ma, Xiaodong Li, Peng Yuan, Bailan Feng,
  Chenggang Yan, and Feng Dai

FS-COCO: Towards Understanding of Freehand Sketches of Common
Objects in Context 253
  Pinaki Nath Chowdhury, Aneeshan Sain, Ayan Kumar Bhunia,
  Tao Xiang, Yulia Gryaditskaya, and Yi-Zhe Song

Exploring Fine-Grained Audiovisual Categorization with the SSW60
Dataset 271
  Grant Van Horn, Rui Qian, Kimberly Wilber, Hartwig Adam,
  Oisin Mac Aodha, and Serge Belongie

The Caltech Fish Counting Dataset: A Benchmark for Multiple-Object
Tracking and Counting 290
  Justin Kay, Peter Kulits, Suzanne Stathatos, Siqi Deng, Erik Young,
  Sara Beery, Grant Van Horn, and Pietro Perona

A Dataset for Interactive Vision-Language Navigation with Unknown
Command Feasibility 312
  Andrea Burns, Deniz Arsan, Sanjna Agrawal, Ranjitha Kumar,
  Kate Saenko, and Bryan A. Plummer

BRACE: The Breakdancing Competition Dataset for Dance Motion
Synthesis 329
  Davide Moltisanti, Jinyi Wu, Bo Dai, and Chen Change Loy

Dress Code: High-Resolution Multi-category Virtual Try-On 345
  Davide Morelli, Matteo Fincato, Marcella Cornia, Federico Landi,
  Fabio Cesari, and Rita Cucchiara

A Data-Centric Approach for Improving Ambiguous Labels
with Combined Semi-supervised Classification and Clustering 363
Lars Schmarje, Monty Santarossa, Simon-Martin Schröder,
Claudius Zelenka, Rainer Kiko, Jenny Stracke, Nina Volkmann,
and Reinhard Koch

ClearPose: Large-scale Transparent Object Dataset and Benchmark 381
Xiaotong Chen, Huijie Zhang, Zeren Yu, Anthony Opipari,
and Odest Chadwicke Jenkins

When Deep Classifiers Agree: Analyzing Correlations Between Learning
Order and Image Statistics 397
Iuliia Pliushch, Martin Mundt, Nicolas Lupp, and Visvanathan Ramesh

AnimeCeleb: Large-Scale Animation CelebHeads Dataset for Head
Reenactment 414
Kangyeol Kim, Sunghyun Park, Jaeseong Lee, Sunghyo Chung,
Junsoo Lee, and Jaegul Choo

MUGEN: A Playground for Video-Audio-Text Multimodal Understanding
and GENeration 431
Thomas Hayes, Songyang Zhang, Xi Yin, Guan Pang, Sasha Sheng,
Harry Yang, Songwei Ge, Qiyuan Hu, and Devi Parikh

A Dense Material Segmentation Dataset for Indoor and Outdoor Scene
Parsing 450
Paul Upchurch and Ransen Niu

MimicME: A Large Scale Diverse 4D Database for Facial Expression
Analysis 467
Athanasios Papaioannou, Baris Gecer, Shiyang Cheng,
Grigorios Chrysos, Jiankang Deng, Eftychia Fotiadou,
Christos Kampouris, Dimitrios Kollias, Stylianos Moschoglou,
Kritaphat Songsri-In, Stylianos Ploumpis, George Trigeorgis,
Panagiotis Tzirakis, Evangelos Ververas, Yuxiang Zhou, Allan Ponniah,
Anastasios Roussos, and Stefanos Zafeiriou

Delving into Universal Lesion Segmentation: Method, Dataset,
and Benchmark 485
Yu Qiu and Jing Xu

Large Scale Real-World Multi-person Tracking 504
Bing Shuai, Alessandro Bergamo, Uta Büchler, Andrew Berneshawi,
Alyssa Boden, and Joseph Tighe

D2-TPred: Discontinuous Dependency for Trajectory Prediction Under
Traffic Lights 522
  *Yuzhen Zhang, Wentong Wang, Weizhi Guo, Pei Lv, Mingliang Xu,
  Wei Chen, and Dinesh Manocha*

The Missing Link: Finding Label Relations Across Datasets 540
  Jasper Uijlings, Thomas Mensink, and Vittorio Ferrari

Learning Omnidirectional Flow in 360° Video via Siamese Representation 557
  *Keshav Bhandari, Bin Duan, Gaowen Liu, Hugo Latapie, Ziliang Zong,
  and Yan Yan*

VizWiz-FewShot: Locating Objects in Images Taken by People with Visual
Impairments 575
  Yu-Yun Tseng, Alexander Bell, and Danna Gurari

TRoVE: Transforming Road Scene Datasets into Photorealistic Virtual
Environments 592
  *Shubham Dokania, Anbumani Subramanian, Manmohan Chandraker,
  and C. V. Jawahar*

Trapped in Texture Bias? A Large Scale Comparison of Deep Instance
Segmentation 609
  *Johannes Theodoridis, Jessica Hofmann, Johannes Maucher,
  and Andreas Schilling*

Deformable Feature Aggregation for Dynamic Multi-modal 3D Object
Detection 628
  *Zehui Chen, Zhenyu Li, Shiquan Zhang, Liangji Fang, Qinhong Jiang,
  and Feng Zhao*

WeLSA: Learning to Predict 6D Pose from Weakly Labeled Data Using
Shape Alignment 645
  *Shishir Reddy Vutukur, Ivan Shugurov, Benjamin Busam,
  Andreas Hutter, and Slobodan Ilic*

Graph R-CNN: Towards Accurate 3D Object Detection
with Semantic-Decorated Local Graph 662
  *Honghui Yang, Zili Liu, Xiaopei Wu, Wenxiao Wang, Wei Qian,
  Xiaofei He, and Deng Cai*

MPPNet: Multi-frame Feature Intertwining with Proxy Points for 3D
Temporal Object Detection 680
  *Xuesong Chen, Shaoshuai Shi, Benjin Zhu, Ka Chun Cheung, Hang Xu,
  and Hongsheng Li*

Long-tail Detection with Effective Class-Margins 698
   Jang Hyun Cho and Philipp Krähenbühl

Semi-supervised Monocular 3D Object Detection by Multi-view
Consistency 715
   Qing Lian, Yanbo Xu, Weilong Yao, Yingcong Chen, and Tong Zhang

PTSEFormer: Progressive Temporal-Spatial Enhanced TransFormer
Towards Video Object Detection 732
   *Han Wang, Jun Tang, Xiaodong Liu, Shanyan Guan, Rong Xie,
   and Li Song*

Author Index 749

ECCV Caption: Correcting False Negatives by Collecting Machine-and-Human-verified Image-Caption Associations for MS-COCO

Sanghyuk Chun[✉], Wonjae Kim, Song Park, Minsuk Chang, and Seong Joon Oh

NAVER AI Lab, Meylan, France
sanghyuk.c@navercorp.com

Abstract. Image-Text matching (ITM) is a common task for evaluating the quality of Vision and Language (VL) models. However, existing ITM benchmarks have a significant limitation. They have many missing correspondences, originating from the data construction process itself. For example, a caption is only matched with one image although the caption can be matched with other similar images and vice versa. To correct the massive false negatives, we construct the Extended COCO Validation (ECCV) Caption dataset by supplying the missing associations with machine and human annotators. We employ five state-of-the-art ITM models with diverse properties for our annotation process. Our dataset provides ×3.6 positive image-to-caption associations and ×8.5 caption-to-image associations compared to the original MS-COCO. We also propose to use an informative ranking-based metric mAP@R, rather than the popular Recall@K (R@K). We re-evaluate the existing 25 VL models on existing and proposed benchmarks. Our findings are that the existing benchmarks, such as COCO 1K R@K, COCO 5K R@K, CxC R@1 are highly correlated with each other, while the rankings change when we shift to the ECCV mAP@R. Lastly, we delve into the effect of the bias introduced by the choice of machine annotator. Source code and dataset are available at https://github.com/naver-ai/eccv-caption

1 Introduction

Image-caption aligned datasets (*e.g.*, MS-COCO Caption [13,40], Flickr30k [49], Conceptual Caption [10,56]) have become *de-facto* standard datasets for

---

M. Chang—Now at Google Research.
S. J. Oh—Now at University of Tübingen.

Supplementary Information The online version contains supplementary material available at https://doi.org/10.1007/978-3-031-20074-8_1.

S. Avidan et al. (Eds.): ECCV 2022, LNCS 13668, pp. 1–19, 2022.
https://doi.org/10.1007/978-3-031-20074-8_1

The man is playing tennis with a racket
A man taking a swing at a tennis ball
A man on a court swinging a tennis racket
A tennis player swinging a racket at a ball
A person hitting a tennis ball with a tennis racket
The man is playing tennis on the court
A man with a tennis racket swings at a tennis ball

Fig. 1. Inherent multiplicity of correspondences in MS-COCO Caption. While any image-caption pair above makes sense (positive pair), only red and blue image-caption pairs are marked as positive in MS-COCO Caption. (Color figure online)

training and evaluating Vision-Language (VL) models. Particularly, Image-to-Text Matching (ITM) tasks [5,11,12,15,18,20–22,25,26,33,37,39,59,64–66,69] are widely used benchmarks for evaluating a VL model. The existing ITM benchmark datasets are built by annotating captions (by alt-texts [10,50,56], web crawling [17], or human annotators [13]) for each image without considering possible associations with other images in the dataset. The collected image-caption pairs are treated as the only positives in the dataset, while other pairs are considered the negatives. However, in practice, there exists more than one caption to describe one image. For example, the description "The man is playing tennis with a racket" may describe multiple images with tennis players equally well (Fig. 1). We have observed that the number of missing positives is tremendous; there exist ×3.6 positive image-to-caption correspondences and ×8.5 caption-to-image correspondences than the original MS-COCO dataset.

While the huge number of false negatives (FNs) in VL datasets is potentially sub-optimal for training VL models, it is downright detrimental for evaluation. For example, the small number of positive correspondences of image-caption-aligned datasets limits the evaluation metrics.[1] In other tasks, such as image retrieval [34,41,46,63], the positives and negatives are defined by class labels; hence, the number of possible matched items is large enough to measure precision or mean average precision (mAP) metrics. On the other hand, because existing ITM benchmarks only have one positive correspondence for each item, they are only able to use recall-based metrics (*e.g.*, Recall@k) that are known to be less informative than the precision- or ranking-based evaluation metrics [44]. In this paper, we focus on correcting the FNs in the evaluation dataset and the recall-based evaluation metrics to make a fair comparison of VL models.

As our first contribution, we correct the FNs in MS-COCO Caption by constructing Extended COCO Validation (ECCV) Caption dataset. We annotate whether each MS-COCO image-caption pair is positive with human workers. The labor cost for this process scales quadratically with the size of the dataset (*e.g.*, MS-COCO has 76B possible image-caption pairs, while the number of images is only 123K). Since verifying every possible image-text pair is not scalable, we sub-sample the queries in the dataset and reduce the number of candidates for positive matches with the machine-in-the-loop (MITL) annotation process. MITL

---

[1] In MS-COCO Caption, a caption is only matched to one image, and an image is matched to five captions. Other datasets usually have one caption for each image.

lets a model reduce the number of candidate positives; then human annotators evaluate the machine-selected candidates. We employ five state-of-the-art ITM models with distinct properties as machine annotators; CLIP [50], ViLT [32], VSRN [39], PVSE [59], and PCME [15]. After post-processing, ECCV Caption contains 1,261 image queries (originally 5,000) but with 17.9 positive captions per image query on average (originally 5). It also contains 1,332 caption queries (originally 25,000) with 8.5 positive images per caption (originally 1).

While the use of a machine annotator is inevitable for the sake of scalability, the choice of a particular model may bias the dataset towards the specifics of the model. This can be problematic because different models show different filtered results to the human annotators, which brings the impartialness of the annotated dataset towards any particular model to the surface. In other words, the MITL annotations are not stable across model choices. Our studies show that the underlying ML model conditions the annotated dataset towards favoring certain models over the others. Therefore, this practice could lead to the danger of biased evaluation results using such datasets. We show that the rankings among the VL models can be arbitrarily shifted by modifying the underlying ML model. Our study also shows that using multiple machine annotators can alleviate machine bias in dataset construction. We note that the findings are applicable to a wide range of tasks in which users put labels on samples from a long list of candidate classes; our task is a special case of such a framework.

A similar MITL approach for expanding the positive matches was also employed by Parekh *et al.* [47], resulting in the dataset CrissCrossed Caption (CxC). However, CxC focuses on scoring the text-to-text similarities, resulting in many missing positives in the text-to-image relationship. Furthermore, CxC only employs one language-based machine annotator, which can lead to a biased dataset as our observation. Our ECCV Caption focuses on the inter-modality relationship and utilizes five ITM methods to avoid biased dataset construction. As another attempt to correct COCO benchmark, Chun *et al.* [15] annotate pseudo-positives by using the COCO instance classes, called Plausible Match (PM). For example, both images in Fig. 1 contain the same object class, "tennis racket". Hence, the red and blue captions are considered positives for both red and blue images. Although PM items can detect most of the false negatives, it also introduces many false positives. Compared to PM [15] which relies on noisy proxies for correspondence, we correct the missing false negatives with "human ground truths" with the help of machine annotations. All in all, our dataset results in a higher recall than CxC and high precision than PM.

We not only fix FNs but also evaluation metrics. We argue that R@1 can overestimate the model performance by focusing only on the accuracy of the top-1 item rather than the rest of the items. Instead, we propose to use better ranking-based evaluation metrics, mAP@R [44]. Our human study shows that mAP@R is more aligned to humans than Recall@k. Now that the FNs are corrected in the evaluation sets and the evaluation metric is fixed, we re-examine the known ranking of 25 state-of-the-art VL models evaluated in the COCO Caption. We have observed that COCO 5K R@1 & R@5, and CxC R@1 are highly correlated (larger than 0.87 Kendall's rank correlation τ). On the other hand, we observe that the rankings across methods measured by mAP@R on ECCV

Caption and COCO 1K R@1 are less well-correlated (τ=0.47). This confirms the observation by Musgrave *et al.* [44] and Chun *et al.* [15] on class-based datasets.

Our contributions are as follows. (1) We discover the false negative (FN) problem and quantify the exact number of wrong labels in MS-COCO. There exist ×3.6 positive image-to-caption associations and ×8.5 caption-to-image associations compared to the original MS-COCO. (2) We construct a corrected ITM test dataset, **ECCV Caption**, to avoid a wrong evaluation by FNs. We employ the machine-in-the-loop (MITL) annotation process to reduce the amount of human verification, resulting in saving 99.9% cost compared to the full exhaustive verification. ECCV Caption shares the same images and captions as the original MS-COCO; therefore, the existing methods can be evaluated on our dataset without additional training. We fix not only the annotations but also the evaluation metric. We propose to use mAP@R, a more human-aligned metric than R@1 for comparing model performances as shown in our human study. (3) We re-evaluate 25 state-of-the-art VL models on our ECCV Caption dataset based on mAP@R instead of Recall@k. In Table 4 and Fig. 4, we can observe that focusing on MS-COCO R@1 will mislead the true ranking between the models (MS-COCO R@1 and ECCV mAP@R show a low correlation). Our observation aligns with Musgrave *et al.* [44] and Chun *et al.* [15]; focusing on R@1 can mislead the true rankings between models. (4) We provide a detailed analysis of the constructed dataset and the model bias. In particular, we focus on avoiding potential model biases in the proposed dataset by employing multiple models. Our analysis shows that our design choice is effective in solving the model bias.

2   Related Works

2.1   Noisy Many-to-Many Correspondences of Image-Caption Datasets

There have been a few attempts to introduce many-to-many or noisy correspondences for VL datasets. Parekh *et al.* [47] construct a CrissCrossed Caption (CxC) dataset by employing a similar MITL approach to ours. However, CxC focuses on intra-modality similarity, particularly text-to-text. They employed the Universal Sentence Encoder [8] and average bag-of-words (BoW) based on GloVe embeddings [48], while we directly focus on the inter-modality relationships and utilizes powerful ITM methods [15,32,39,50,59] to select candidates for validation by humans. CxC contains human ratings for 89,555 image-to-caption associations, among which 35,585 are positive, ×1.4 more positive relationships than 25,000 in COCO Caption. We show that the additional positives by CxC are precise, but their annotations still have many missing positives (*i.e.*, high precision but low recall), resulting that R@1 on CxC perfectly preserves the rankings of VL models on COCO 5K R@1. On the other hand, our ECCV Caption has ×4.4 positives (×3.6 image-to-caption correspondences and ×8.5 caption-to-image correspondences) compared to COCO Captions and roughly three times more positives compared to CxC. Furthermore, it is possible to measure mAP on our dataset due to the abundance of positive pairs, unlike for CxC.

Another attempt by Chun *et al.* [15] focused on precision rather than R@1 by annotating the pseudo-positives in a fully algorithmic approach. The authors defined "plausible matching (PM)" items that have the same instance classes with the query image (or the image corresponding to the query caption) to annotate pseudo-positives. For example, both images in Fig. 1 contain the same instance class, "tennis racket", leading to the conclusion that the red and blue captions are marked as positives for both red and blue images. More precisely, two instances are PM if $y_1, y_2 \in \{0, 1\}^d$ differ at most ζ positions, where d is the number of instance classes (*e.g.*, for COCO, $d = 80$). Using the class-based pseudo-positives, Chun *et al.* propose Plausible-Match R-Precision (PMRP) metric, an R-Precision [44] metric based on the PM policy. The authors propose to use multiple ζ (*e.g.*, $\zeta \in \{0, 1, 2\}$) and report the average precision value. PM items can detect many missing false positives in the dataset, but we observe that most PM pseudo-positives are not actual positives (*i.e.*, high recall but low precision) — See Table 2. We also observe that PMRP shows a low correlation to other evaluation metrics; PMRP is a noisy metric compared to others.

2.2 Machine-in-the-Loop (MITL) Annotation

Humans and machines complement each other in the annotation process as they have different comparative advantages. Humans are the ultimate source of true labels, but they are slow and prone to errors and biases [27,57,60]. Machines are highly scalable, but their generalizability to unseen samples is limited. Machines are also prone to their own versions of errors and biases [43,54]. MITL annotations have been designed to take the best of both worlds [3,6,55,68].

Depending on the required trade-off between annotation quality and efficiency, one may opt for either single-turn or multi-turn annotation pipeline. The latter serves for the maximal demand for annotation quality: humans and machines alternate to correct and learn from each other's annotations [3,55]. This is a widely used technique, the applications ranging from building a dictionary of cooking vocabularies [9], to supporting real-time screen-reading for blind people [23] and characterizing system failures [45]. Here, we focus on *single-turn MITL annotations* to focus on the atomic building block for MITL pipelines in general. There are two types of the single-turn paradigm: machine-verified human annotations [62,67] or human-verified machine annotations. We focus on the latter, which are highly relevant for dealing with huge sources of data.

Under the human-verification framework, machines make label proposals for each image, focusing more on recall than precision [2,36]. Previous crowdsourcing research in human-computer interaction (HCI) had mainly focused on the annotation interface and its effects on the annotation [16,28,58], or building a crowdsourcing workflow that leverages microtask pipelines [4,31]. We investigate the side effects of the model choice in the MITL annotation paradigm where machines provide candidate label proposals.

3   ECCV Caption Dataset Construction

In this section, we describe ECCV Caption construction details. We annotate image-caption pairs in MS-COCO to solve the multiplicity of MS-COCO. However, the number of candidates is too huge for an exhaustive verification by humans: 76B for the whole dataset and 125M for the test split only. To reduce the amount of judgment by humans, we employ a single-turn machine-in-the-loop (MITL) annotation pipeline, containing three stages: (1) Filtering by machine annotators. (2) Judging the filtered relationships by MTurkers and additional verification by internal workers. (3) Post-processing and merging with CxC.

Table 1. Overview of the machine annotators. Differences among five ITM models in terms of architectures and training objectives are shown. ViLT and CLIP are trained on a massive amount of aligned VL data, while other methods only use COCO Caption.

Model	Text backbone	Visual backbone	Objective function
PVSE [59]	Bi-GRU [14]	ResNet-152 [24]	Multiple instance learning
VSRN [39]	Bi-GRU	Faster R-CNN [52]	Semantic reasoning matching
PCME [15]	Bi-GRU	ResNet-152	Probabilistic matching
ViLT [32]	Vision Transformer (ViT-B/32) [19]		Vision-language pre-training
CLIP [50]	Transformer [51]	ViT-B/32	Contrastive learning

3.1   Model Candidates for Machine Annotators

We choose five VL models with diverse properties to cover both diversity and practical relevance. The models use different text backbones (Bi-GRU [14], Transformer [61]), visual backbones (ResNet-152 [24], Faster R-CNN [52], ViT [19]), training objective functions, and training datasets as shown in Table 1. We use the officially released pre-trained weights by the authors. Specifically, we use the CutMix [70] pre-trained version for PCME to match the retrieval performances with others, and CLIP ViT-B/32, the largest model at the time of our data construction. We describe more details of each method in Appendix A.1.

We quantify the diversity of the models by measuring the differences in their retrieved items. We first retrieve the top 25 images for each model on the captions of the COCO Caption test split. We measure the similarities of the models in two different metrics. First, for every pair of models, we measure the Kendall rank correlation [30] between the two rankings of the retrieved items by the models. We observe that the models usually have low similarity ($\tau < 0.3$), except for PVSE and PCME. We additionally measure, for each pair of model i and j, the average ranking of model i's top-1 ranked item by model j. The top-1 items retrieved by the models are usually not included in the top-3 items by the others. These analyses show that the chosen models are diverse and the retrieved items do not correlate that much. The full results are shown in Appendix A.2.

3.2   Crowdsourcing on Amazon Mechanical Turk

We crowdsource image-caption matches on Amazon Mechanical Turk (MTurk) platform. For the sake of scalability, we subsample 1,333 caption queries and 1,261 image queries from the COCO Caption test split. Since the number of all possible matches is still prohibitive (40M), we employ the filtering strategy to reduce the number of candidates for human verification. We pre-select top-5 captions and images retrieved by the five models. After we remove the duplicate pairs from the (1,261 + 1,333) × 5 × 5 = 64,850 pairs, 46,424 pairs remain.

Table 2. Precision and recall of the existing benchmarks measured by our human verified positive pairs. A low Prec means that many positives are actually negatives, and a low Recall means that there exist many missing positives.

Dataset	I2T Prec	I2T Recall	T2I Prec	T2I Recall
Original MS-COCO Caption	47.3	20.0	89.4	12.8
CxC [47]	39.6	22.0	81.4	15.0
Plausible Match [15]	8.3	74.6	10.5	69.0

Table 3. The number of positive images and captions for each dataset. We show the number of positive items for the subset of the COCO Caption test split. The number of query captions and images are 1,332 and 1,261, respectively.

Dataset	# positive images	# positive captions
Original MS-COCO Caption	1,332	6,305 (=1,261×5)
CxC [47]	1,895 (×1.42)	8,906 (×1.41)
Human-verified positives	10,814 (×8.12)	16,990 (×2.69)
ECCV Caption	11,279 (×8.47)	22,550 (×3.58)

We package the task for human annotators into a series of Human Intelligence Tasks (HITs). Each HIT contains 18 machine-retrieved pairs, consisting of 1 true positive (*i.e.*, an *original positive pair*), 1 true negative (random pair, not in the top-25 of any model), and 16 pairs to be annotated. The golden examples are used for the qualification process; if a submitted HIT contains wrong answers to the golden examples, we manually verify the HIT. For each image-caption pair candidate, workers can choose an answer among the choices "100% YES", "Partially YES, but", "Mostly NO, because", and "100% NO". We use four choices instead three-level ("YES", "Not Sure", and "NO") to discourage workers from selecting "Not Sure" for all the questions. We have assigned 2,160 HITs, consisting of 43,200 pairs to be verified, to 970 MTurk workers. The crowdsourcing details, including an example HIT, compensation details, worker statistics, and detailed statistics for each machine annotator are in Appendix B.

3.3 Postprocessing MTurk Annotations

We observe that 21,995 associations among 43,200 associations are annotated as positives ("Yes" or "Weak Yes"). We then filter out 18 meaningless captions (*e.g.*, "I am unable to see an image above"), 14 wrong captions found by workers (*e.g.*, "A group of birds flying above the beach" for the image with many kites), and 1 duplicate image found in the training set. The full list is in Appendix C.1.

Using the 21,995 human-verified positives, we report precision and recall of the existing benchmarks. Let t_i be the set of human-annotated positives for the query i in Sect. 3.2 and r_i be the set of positives for i in the target dataset. We define precision and recall of a dataset as $Prec = \frac{1}{N} \sum_{i=1}^{N} \frac{|r_i \cap t_i|}{|r_i|}$ and $Recall = \frac{1}{N} \sum_{i=1}^{N} 1 - \frac{|t_i \setminus r_i|}{|t_i|}$. Table 2 shows precision and recall of COCO Caption, CxC [47], and Plausible Match (PM) pseudo-positives [15]. While COCO and CxC show high precisions, we observe that their recall is significantly low, around or less than 20%. Evaluating models on such a low-recall dataset with the R@1 metric can be highly misleading. A model may be able to retrieve good enough positive items which are not captured in the dataset, resulting in erroneously low R@1 scores. On the other hand, more than 70% of the positives can be captured by PM, but only about 10% of pseudo-positives are correct.

Fig. 2. ECCV Caption examples. The given caption query: "A herd of zebras standing together in the field". Red: original positive. Green: annotated as "100% Yes". Blue: annotated as "Weak Yes". More examples are in Appendix C.2. (Color figure online)

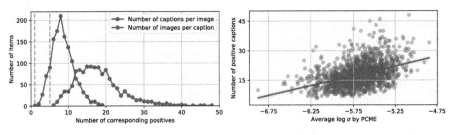

(a) Number of positive pairs.   (b) Multiplicity by positive items.

Fig. 3. Multiplicity in ECCV Caption. (a) The number of positive pairs in ECCV Caption. Dashed lines denote the number of the original COCO positives (1 image for each caption, and 5 captions for each image). ECCV Caption contains plenty of positive items per each modality. (b) PCME-predicted multiplicity against the number of positive captions for each image. There exists a positive correlation.

We consider the CxC positives as the additional sixth machine-human verified annotations, and extend our human-verified positives with CxC positives to construct the final ECCV Caption. Table 3 shows the detailed statistics of CxC, human-verified positives, and our ECCV Caption. Overall, ECCV Caption has ×8.47 positive images and ×3.58 positive captions than the original dataset. Figure 3a shows the number of positive images and captions per each item; there exist many positives beyond the original COCO associations. We illustrate example image-caption pairs from ECCV Caption in Fig. 2 and Appendix C.2.

We additionally analyze the multiplicity of ECCV Caption by PCME [15] that produces a degree of multiplicity (uncertainty) for each query. Figure 3b shows that more uncertain images correspond to more captions in our dataset. In other words, our new annotations capture the hidden FNs in COCO well.

4   Re-evaluation of ITM Models on ECCV Caption

In this section, we re-evaluate the existing VL models on our new dataset and previous benchmarks. We first introduce the evaluation metrics and comparison methods (Sect. 4.1). We compare the performances and analyze the results (Sect. 4.2).

4.1   Evaluation Metrics and Comparison Methods

Evaluation Metrics. The existing ITM benchmarks (*e.g.*, COCO Caption) use Recall@k metrics, particularly Recall@1 (R@1). Specifically, previous works measure R@1 for 5-fold validation splits (*i.e.*, each split has 1K images), and for the full test split [29]. The former is called COCO 1K R@k and the latter is called COCO 5K R@k, respectively. Previous studies separately report image-to-text, text-to-image retrieval R@1, R@5 and R@10 scores. However, as shown by Musgrave *et al.* [44], R@k is not an informative metric; embedding spaces with nearly 100% R@1 can have different properties. The problem becomes even worse for the ITM benchmarks, whose queries only have very few (usually only one) references: Even if a model correctly retrieves plausible items that are not among the set of original positives, the current benchmark cannot evaluate the model correctly. It is common to use larger values of k to less penalize wrong yet plausible predictions. However, as shown in Fig. 3a, the actual number of plausible positives can be larger than the typical choice of k (*e.g.*, 5 or 10). Instead, we suggest using mAP@R [44], a modified mAP measured by retrieving R items where R is the number of positives for the query. Previous ITM benchmarks cannot employ mAP@R because R is too small (*i.e.*, 1). Thanks to our human-verified ground-truth positives, we can reliably measure mAP@R on ECCV Caption.

We additionally conduct a human study to confirm that mAP@R is more aligned to humans than R@k. We collect 3,200 pairwise preferences of human annotators among (A) only top-1 is wrong (B) only top-1 is correct (C) top-1 to 5 are wrong (D) only top-5 is correct, and (E) all items are wrong. For example, if the number of positives is 8, then (A) shows 0 R@1, 100 R@5 and 66.0 mAP@R, (B) shows 100 R@k and 12.5 mAP@R, (C) shows 0 R@k and

Table 4. Re-evaluating VL models. ECCV Caption mAP@R, R-Precision (R-P), Recall@1 (R@1), CxC R@1, COCO 1K R@1, 5K R@1, and PMRP are shown. The numbers are the average between the image-to-text retrieval and text-to-image retrieval results. Full numbers for each modality and COCO R@5, R@10 results are in Appendix D.3. [†] denotes our re-implementation and "zero-shot" for VinVL and ViLT denotes VL pre-trained models without fine-tuning on the COCO Caption for the retrieval task.

	ECCV caption			CxC	COCO		
	mAP@R	R-P	R@1	R@1	1K R@1	5K R@1	PMRP
ResNet-152 [24] image encoder + Bi-GRU [14] text encoder							
VSE0[†] [20]	22.67	33.27	55.55	24.24	34.14	22.27	46.95
VSE++[†] [20]	35.01	45.50	73.11	37.95	48.46	35.79	54.26
PVSE K=1 [59]	33.98	44.49	73.25	38.38	48.67	36.20	53.56
PVSE K=2 [59]	40.26	49.92	76.74	40.18	50.29	38.13	55.52
PCME [15]	37.11	47.82	74.79	40.09	50.29	38.03	56.71
PCME (CutMix [70] pre-trained)[†] [15]	41.74	51.45	78.67	41.70	51.35	39.51	57.65
Region features based on Bottom-up Attention [1] and SCAN [37]							
VSRN [39]	42.28	51.84	81.51	48.85	58.33	46.74	55.44
VSRN + AOQ [12]	40.94	50.65	81.53	50.10	59.32	48.14	56.41
CVSE [64]	37.35	47.51	76.70	45.82	55.37	43.80	56.49
SGR [18]	35.80	46.04	78.77	50.60	58.87	48.86	56.91
SAF [18]	35.96	46.19	78.36	49.58	59.09	47.80	57.21
VSE infty (BUTD region) [11]	40.46	49.97	82.52	52.40	61.03	50.38	56.64
VSE infty (BUTD grid) [11]	40.40	50.09	83.01	53.47	62.26	51.60	56.87
VSE infty (WSL grid) [11]	42.41	51.43	86.44	60.79	68.07	59.01	57.65
Large-scale Vision-Language pre-training							
CLIP ViT-B/32 [50]	26.75	36.91	67.08	41.97	49.84	40.28	55.32
CLIP ViT-B/16 [50]	29.25	38.99	71.05	44.26	52.32	42.69	56.58
CLIP ViT-L/14 [50]	27.98	37.80	72.17	48.14	55.38	46.44	57.70
VinVL (zero-shot) [71]	22.18	32.93	55.19	33.74	43.51	32.07	47.26
VinVL [71]	40.81	49.55	87.77	67.76	82.38	66.39	54.72
ViLT (zero-shot) [32]	26.84	36.81	69.00	50.35	58.83	48.63	57.38
ViLT [32]	34.58	44.27	77.81	53.72	61.81	52.18	57.63
BLIP [38]	40.52	48.43	90.99	74.30	78.30	73.11	57.17
Different negative mining (NM) strategies							
PVSE K=1, No NM[†]	33.34	44.44	67.99	32.69	43.28	30.65	56.67
PVSE K=1, Semi-hard NM[†] [53]	36.63	47.36	73.97	38.17	48.49	36.00	55.15
PVSE K=1, Hardest NM[†] [20]	35.76	46.50	73.68	39.02	49.12	36.88	54.37

10.3 mAP@R, and (D) shows 0 R@1, 100 R@5 and 2.5 mAP@R. We compute user preference scores using Bradley-Terry model [7]. We observe that mAP@R is exactly aligned to the human preference score: (A: 70.85, B: 10.66, C: 13.15, D: 4.89, E: 0.44). We provide the details of the human study in Appendix D.1.

We also report modified Plausible Match R-Precision (PMRP) scores by changing R to $\min(R, 50)$, because the number of pseudo-positives R can be very large (e.g., larger than 10,000) but most of them are not actual positive (Table 2). While Chun et al. [15] proposed to use the average R-Precision for

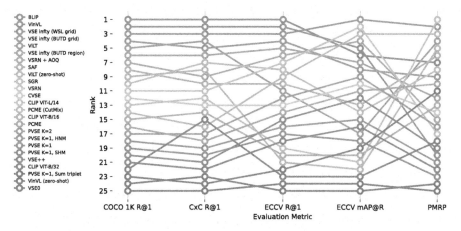

(a) Comparison of COCO, CxC, ECCV and PMRP.

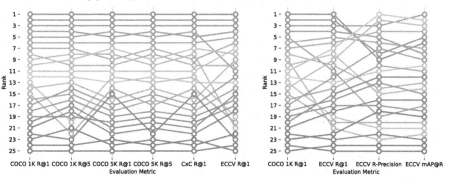

(b) Comparison of Recall@1 metrics.   (c) Comparison of ECCV metrics.

Fig. 4. Ranking correlation between different evaluation metrics. Ranking of methods is largely perserved between COCO and CxC Recall@1, while it is rarely preserved among COCO Recall@1, ECCV mAP@R and PMRP.

three different thresholds, (*e.g.*, $\zeta = \{0, 1, 2\}$), we only report PMRP when $\zeta = 0$. We additionally compute R@1, R@5, and PMRP scores on the original COCO Caption, R@1 on CxC, and R@1 and.R-Precision on ECCV Caption to analyze the correlation between each evaluation metric to ECCV mAP@R.

Evaluated Methods. We compare 25 state-of-the-art VL models, whose trained weights are publicly accessible, categorized into four groups: (1) visual semantic embedding (VSE) methods with the ResNet-152 [24] image encoder, and Bi-GRU [14] text encoder, including VSE0, VSE++ [20], PVSE [59] (K = 1 & K = 2), and PCME [15] (the official model and the CutMix pre-trained version); (2) VSE methods with region features extracted by Visual Genome [35] pre-trained Faster R-CNN [52] based on the implementation by Anderson *et al.* [1] and Lee *et al.* [37], including VSRN [39], VSRN + AOQ [12], CVSE [64], SGR,

Table 5. Rank correlations between evaluation metrics. Higher τ denotes two rankings are highly correlated, while τ values near zero denotes two rankings are barely correlated. We highlight the highly correlated pairs ($\tau > 0.8$) with red text.

	COCO 1K			COCO 5K			CxC	ECCV			COCO
	R@1	R@5	R@10	R@1	R@5	R@10	R@1	R@1	R-P	mAP@R	PMRP
COCO 1K R@1	–	0.87	0.86	0.89	0.97	0.92	0.89	0.72	0.39	0.47	0.45
COCO 1K R@5	0.87	–	0.97	0.79	0.88	0.93	0.79	0.81	0.49	0.58	0.39
COCO 1K R@10	0.86	0.97	–	0.77	0.86	0.91	0.77	0.79	0.49	0.57	0.43
COCO 5K R@1	0.89	0.79	0.77	–	0.89	0.83	1.00	0.65	0.30	0.39	0.45
COCO 5K R@5	0.97	0.88	0.86	0.89	–	0.95	0.89	0.75	0.41	0.50	0.43
COCO 5K R@10	0.92	0.93	0.91	0.83	0.95	–	0.83	0.80	0.47	0.55	0.38
CxC R@1	0.89	0.79	0.77	1.00	0.89	0.83	–	0.65	0.30	0.39	0.45
ECCV R@1	0.72	0.81	0.79	0.65	0.75	0.80	0.65	–	0.65	0.74	0.29
ECCV R-P	0.39	0.49	0.49	0.30	0.41	0.47	0.30	0.65	–	0.90	0.17
ECCV mAP@R	0.47	0.58	0.57	0.39	0.50	0.55	0.39	0.74	0.90	–	0.20
PMRP	0.45	0.39	0.43	0.45	0.43	0.38	0.45	0.29	0.17	0.20	–

SAF [18], and VSE∞ with BUTD region, grid and WSL grid features [11][2]. (3) Large-scale VL pre-training (VLP) methods, including pre-trained CLIP with ViT-B/32, ViT-B/16, and ViT/L14 backbones [50], pre-trained and fine-tuned ViLT [32], pre-trained and fine-tuned VinVL [71], and fine-tuned BLIP [38]. Here, "pre-trained" signifies that the model is trained with a massive image-text aligned dataset, but is not specifically trained for COCO Caption; "fine-tuned" signifies that the model is fine-tuned on COCO Caption for the ITM task. We note that VL transformers except CLIP need $O(|C| \times |I|)$ forward operations to compute the full pairwise ranks between $|C|$ number of captions and $|I|$ number of images, while other methods only need $O(|I|) + O(|C|)$ forward operations to compute the full pairwise ranks based on the cosine similarity. For example, VinVL takes 25 h to compute the full pairwise ranks for the COCO Caption test split by a single A100 GPU core, while VSE++ only takes 1 min in the same environment. (4) PVSE models with different negative mining (NM) methods, including no NM, semi-hard NM (SHM) [53], and hardest NM (HNM) [20].

We use the official trained weights for each model with a few exceptions. We re-implement VSE0, VSE++, PCME with CutMix pre-trained ResNet, and PVSE models with various NM strategies. The training details are in Appendix D.2

4.2   Re-evaluation of ITM Methods

Table 4 and Fig. 4 shows the full comparisons of 25 VL models with different evaluation metrics. We report the Kendall's rank correlations (tau-b) between

---

[2] Techinally speaking, VSE∞ (WSL grid) does not use region features, but CNN features extracted from Instagram-trained ResNext [42]. This study treats all VSE∞ variants as region feature-based models for convenience.

metrics in Table 5; larger τ denotes two metrics are more correlated. We report the full table including modality-wise results, R@5 and R@10 scores in Appendix D.3. We first observe that R@k scores across different datasets have high correlations among themselves (Fig. 4b and Appendix D.3). In terms of the ranking correlation, we observe that COCO 1K R@1 shows almost $\tau=0.9$ with the ranking yielded by R@5 (0.87), COCO 5K R@1 (0.89) and R@5 (0.97), or CxC R@1 (0.89). This implies that measuring Recall@k on different benchmarks, such as the original COCO Caption, CxC, and ECCV Caption are not more informative than only measuring Recall@k on COCO 1K or 5K. On the other hand, the rankings by COCO 1K are not preserved well to PMRP (0.45), ECCV R@1 (0.72), ECCV R-Precision (0.39) and ECCV mAP@R (0.47) in Kendall's τ. This implies that enlarging K of R@k (e.g., using R@5, R@10 instead of R@1) cannot be an alternative of mAP@R because R@k metrics are highly correlated each other as shown in Table 5. We also observe that the rankings by PMRP are relatively less correlated to the other metrics, such as COCO R@1 (0.45), ECCV R@1 (0.29) or ECCV mAP@R (0.20) in Kendall's τ.

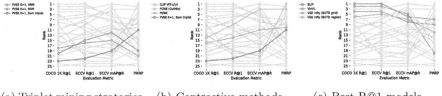

(a) Triplet mining strategies.   (b) Contrastive methods.   (c) Best R@1 models.

Fig. 5. Rankings of different VL models. Ranking of (a) PVSE models with diverse triplet mining strategies (b) contrastive methods (c) the best models are shown.

Our re-evaluation shows that existing ITM evaluation benchmarks can overestimate the VL model performance by focusing only on COCO R@1, where the rankings between COCO R@1 and ECCV mAP@R are not largely preserved. For example, we observe that the hardest negative mining technique [20], previously deemed useful for ITM tasks, is actually selectively effective for R@1, rather than for the actual task itself. Under our new metrics like ECCV mAP@R, we observe that the milder strategy of semi-hard negative mining is more effective – See Fig. 5a. Chun et al. [15] also observed a similar pattern in the CUB Caption dataset [63] by using the class-defined positives. Our finding is the first observation in the practical large-scale VL dataset. Similarly, we observe that many large-scale VL pre-training methods with high R@1 scores show inferior ECCV mAP@R scores compared to other visual semantic embedding techniques. For example, CLIP ViT-L/14 shows superior COCO 1K R@1 than PCME (55.4% and 40.1%, respectively). However, in terms of ECCV mAP@R, CLIP shows inferior performances than PCME (28.0% and 37.1%, respectively).

Similarly, we observe that PMRP shows different behaviors compared to other metrics. Especially, we observe that the contrastive models without a negative mining strategy are specialized to PMRP metric – Fig. 5b. We presume that it is because the contrastive learning strategy enforces the features with similar objects to be mapped to a similar embedding space. In contrastive the best models on COCO and ECCV (*e.g.*, BLIP, VinVL, and VSE∞) show inferior PMRP scores – Fig. 5c. We presume that it is because PMRP only captures the existence or absence of the objects, while an optimal retrieval also should consider the plausibility between matched image-caption pairs.

5 Discussion and Limitations

Potential Machine Biases in Our Dataset. Our dataset construction process contains the MITL annotation process, where the choice of machine annotators can potentially harm the dataset quality. The positives in our dataset are the retrieved items by the machine annotators. If the machines are biased towards undesired patterns (*e.g.* favoring certain items over the others), future methods built on our benchmark will overfit those patterns. In this work, we employ five diverse machine annotators to reduce the potential biases by models. In Appendix E, we explore and quantify the effect of the choice of multiple machine annotators on the dataset quality. From the study, we can conclude that our strategy (using more models) is effective to mitigate biases by a specific model.

Scale of ECCV Caption. In this work, we subsample 1,333 caption queries (5.3% of the full caption queries) and 1,261 image queries (25.2% of the full image queries) to reduce the scale of annotations. Note that without subsampling, we need to verify $(25,000 + 5,000) \times 5 \times 5 = 750K$ pairs, which costs 16 times more than our current version, almost $60K. Because we only subsample queries, not limiting the gallery samples, our dataset is an unbiased subset of the original COCO Caption. To scale up ECCV Caption, we have to reduce the human verification costs by reducing the total number of human verification. This can be achievable by applying a multi-turn MITL annotation process that alternatively repeats training machine annotators with human-annotated associations and verifying machine annotations by human workers. After enough iterations of the multi-turn MITL annotation process, we can automatically scale up our annotations by using the high-quality machine annotators while only low confident associations are verified by humans.

Noisy Annotations. Despite our additional verification process to keep the quality of the annotations, there can be noisy annotations (*i.e.*, false positives) in ECCV Caption due to the noisy nature of crowdsourcing annotations. The noisy annotations can also occur because we use both "100% YES" and "Partially YES" to build positive pairs. However, we still encourage to use ECCV Caption for evaluating VL models, because the existing datasets are noisier; they usually have only one positive item per each query and they have tremendously many FNs. On the other hand, noisy annotations of our dataset are still "plausible" rather than "wrong". We provide more discussion in Appendix F. Finally, we expect that a multi-turn MITL process can improve not only the labeling cost but also the annotation quality as shown by Benenson *et al.* [3].

6 Conclusion

MS-COCO Caption is a popular dataset for evaluating image-text matching (ITM) methods. Despite its popularity, it suffers from a large number of missing positive matches between images and captions. Fully annotating the missing positives with human labor incurs prohibitive costs. We thus rely on machine annotators to propose candidate positive matches and let crowdsourced human annotators verify the matches. The resulting ITM evaluation benchmark, Extended COCO Validation (ECCV) Caption dataset, contains $\times 8.47$ positive images and $\times 3.58$ positive captions compared to the original MS-COCO Caption. We have re-evaluated 25 ITM methods on ECCV Caption with mAP@R, resulting in certain changes in the ranking of methods. We encourage future studies on ITM to evaluate their models on ECCV mAP@R that not only focuses on the correctness but also on the diversity of top-k retrieved items.

References

1. Anderson, P., et al.: Bottom-up and top-down attention for image captioning and visual question answering. In: Proceedings of CVPR (2018)
2. Andriluka, M., Uijlings, J.R., Ferrari, V.: Fluid annotation: a human-machine collaboration interface for full image annotation. In: Proceedings of the 26th ACM International Conference on Multimedia, pp. 1957–1966 (2018)
3. Benenson, R., Popov, S., Ferrari, V.: Large-scale interactive object segmentation with human annotators. In: Proceedings of CVPR, pp. 11700–11709 (2019)
4. Bernstein, M.S., et al.: Soylent: a word processor with a crowd inside. In: Proceedings of the 23nd Annual ACM Symposium on User Interface Software and Technology, pp. 313–322 (2010)
5. Biten, A.F., Mafla, A., Gómez, L., Karatzas, D.: Is an image worth five sentences? a new look into semantics for image-text matching. In: Proceedings of the IEEE/CVF Winter Conference on Applications of Computer Vision, pp. 1391–1400 (2022)
6. Boykov, Y.Y., Jolly, M.P.: Interactive graph cuts for optimal boundary & region segmentation of objects in nd images. In: Proceedings of ICCV, vol. 1, pp. 105–112. IEEE (2001)
7. Bradley, R.A., Terry, M.E.: Rank analysis of incomplete block designs: I. the method of paired comparisons. Biometrika **39**(3/4), 324–345 (1952)
8. Cer, D., et al.: Universal sentence encoder. In: Proceedings of EMNLP (2018)
9. Chang, M., Guillain, L.V., Jung, H., Hare, V.M., Kim, J., Agrawala, M.: Recipescape: an interactive tool for analyzing cooking instructions at scale. In: Proceedings of the 2018 CHI Conference on Human Factors in Computing Systems, pp. 1–12 (2018)
10. Changpinyo, S., Sharma, P., Ding, N., Soricut, R.: Conceptual 12m: pushing web-scale image-text pre-training to recognize long-tail visual concepts. In: Proceedings of CVPR, pp. 3558–3568 (2021)

11. Chen, J., Hu, H., Wu, H., Jiang, Y., Wang, C.: Learning the best pooling strategy for visual semantic embedding. In: Proceedings of CVPR (2021)

12. Chen, T., Deng, J., Luo, J.: Adaptive offline quintuplet loss for image-text matching. In: Vedaldi, A., Bischof, H., Brox, T., Frahm, J.-M. (eds.) ECCV 2020. LNCS, vol. 12358, pp. 549–565. Springer, Cham (2020). https://doi.org/10.1007/978-3-030-58601-0_33

13. Chen, X., et al.: Microsoft coco captions: data collection and evaluation server. arXiv preprint arXiv:1504.00325 (2015)

14. Cho, K., Van Merriënboer, B., Bahdanau, D., Bengio, Y.: On the properties of neural machine translation: encoder-decoder approaches. arXiv preprint arXiv:1409.1259 (2014)

15. Chun, S., Oh, S.J., De Rezende, R.S., Kalantidis, Y., Larlus, D.: Probabilistic embeddings for cross-modal retrieval. In: Proceedings of CVPR (2021)

16. Chung, J.J.Y., Song, J.Y., Kutty, S., Hong, S., Kim, J., Lasecki, W.S.: Efficient elicitation approaches to estimate collective crowd answers. Proc. ACM Hum.-Comput. Interact. 3, 1–25 (2019)

17. Desai, K., Kaul, G., Aysola, Z., Johnson, J.: RedCaps: web-curated image-text data created by the people, for the people. In: NeurIPS Datasets and Benchmarks (2021)

18. Diao, H., Zhang, Y., Ma, L., Lu, H.: Similarity reasoning and filtration for image-text matching. In: Proceedings of AAAI (2021)

19. Dosovitskiy, A., et al.: An image is worth 16×16 words: transformers for image recognition at scale. In: Proceedinngs of ICLR (2021). https://openreview.net/forum?id=YicbFdNTTy

20. Faghri, F., Fleet, D.J., Kiros, J.R., Fidler, S.: VSE++: Improving visual-semantic embeddings with hard negatives. In: Proceedings of BMVC (2018)

21. Frome, A., et al.: Devise: a deep visual-semantic embedding model. In: Proceedings of NeurIPS, pp. 2121–2129 (2013)

22. Gu, J., Cai, J., Joty, S.R., Niu, L., Wang, G.: Look, imagine and match: improving textual-visual cross-modal retrieval with generative models. In: Proceedings of the IEEE Conference on Computer Vision and Pattern Recognition, pp. 7181–7189 (2018)

23. Guo, A., et al.: Vizlens: a robust and interactive screen reader for interfaces in the real world. Proceedings of the 29th Annual Symposium on User Interface Software and Technology (2016)

24. He, K., Zhang, X., Ren, S., Sun, J.: Deep residual learning for image recognition. In: Proceedings of CVPR (2016)

25. Huang, Y., Wu, Q., Song, C., Wang, L.: Learning semantic concepts and order for image and sentence matching. In: Proceedings of the IEEE Conference on Computer Vision and Pattern Recognition, pp. 6163–6171 (2018)

26. Huang, Z., et al.: Learning with noisy correspondence for cross-modal matching. In: Beygelzimer, A., Dauphin, Y., Liang, P., Vaughan, J.W. (eds.) Proceedings of NeurIPS (2021). https://openreview.net/forum?id=S9ZyhWC17wJ

27. Ipeirotis, P.G., Provost, F., Wang, J.: Quality management on amazon mechanical turk. In: Proceedings of the ACM SIGKDD Workshop on Human Computation, pp. 64–67 (2010)

28. Kaplan, T., Saito, S., Hara, K., Bigham, J.P.: Striving to earn more: a survey of work strategies and tool use among crowd workers. In: HCOMP (2018)

29. Karpathy, A., Fei-Fei, L.: Deep visual-semantic alignments for generating image descriptions. In: Proceedings of CVPR, pp. 3128–3137 (2015)

30. Kendall, M.G.: A new measure of rank correlation. Biometrika **30**(1/2), 81–93 (1938)
31. Kim, J., Nguyen, P., Weir, S.A., Guo, P.J., Miller, R., Gajos, K.Z.: Crowdsourcing step-by-step information extraction to enhance existing how-to videos. In: Proceedings of the SIGCHI Conference on Human Factors in Computing Systems (2014)
32. Kim, W., Son, B., Kim, I.: Vilt: vision-and-language transformer without convolution or region supervision. In: Proceedings of ICML (2021)
33. Kiros, R., Salakhutdinov, R., Zemel, R.S.: Unifying visual-semantic embeddings with multimodal neural language models. arXiv preprint arXiv:1411.2539 (2014)
34. Krause, J., Stark, M., Deng, J., Fei-Fei, L.: 3D object representations for fine-grained categorization. In: Proceedings of CVPR Worshops, pp. 554–561 (2013)
35. Krishna, R., et al.: Visual genome: connecting language and vision using crowdsourced dense image annotations. IJCV **123**(1), 32–73 (2017)
36. Kuznetsova, A., et al.: The open images dataset v4. IJCV **128**(7), 1956–1981 (2020)
37. Lee, K.H., Chen, X., Hua, G., Hu, H., He, X.: Stacked cross attention for image-text matching. In: Proceedings of ECCV (2018)
38. Li, J., Li, D., Xiong, C., Hoi, S.: Blip: bootstrapping language-image pre-training for unified vision-language understanding and generation (2022)
39. Li, K., Zhang, Y., Li, K., Li, Y., Fu, Y.: Visual semantic reasoning for image-text matching. In: Proceedings of ICCV, pp. 4654–4662 (2019)
40. Lin, T.-Y., et al.: Microsoft COCO: common objects in context. In: Fleet, D., Pajdla, T., Schiele, B., Tuytelaars, T. (eds.) ECCV 2014. LNCS, vol. 8693, pp. 740–755. Springer, Cham (2014). https://doi.org/10.1007/978-3-319-10602-1_48
41. Liu, Z., Luo, P., Qiu, S., Wang, X., Tang, X.: Deepfashion: powering robust clothes recognition and retrieval with rich annotations. In: Proceedings of CVPR, pp. 1096–1104 (2016)
42. Mahajan, D.K., et al.: Exploring the limits of weakly supervised pretraining. In: Proceedings of ECCV (2018)
43. Mehrabi, N., Morstatter, F., Saxena, N., Lerman, K., Galstyan, A.: A survey on bias and fairness in machine learning. ACM Comput. Surv. **54**(6) (2021). https://doi.org/10.1145/3457607
44. Musgrave, K., Belongie, S., Lim, S.N.: A metric learning reality check. In: Proceedings of ECCV (2020)
45. Nushi, B., Kamar, E., Horvitz, E.: Towards accountable ai: Hybrid human-machine analyses for characterizing system failure. In: HCOMP (2018)
46. Oh Song, H., Xiang, Y., Jegelka, S., Savarese, S.: Deep metric learning via lifted structured feature embedding. In: Proceedings of CVPR, pp. 4004–4012 (2016)
47. Parekh, Z., Baldridge, J., Cer, D., Waters, A., Yang, Y.: Crisscrossed captions: extended intramodal and intermodal semantic similarity judgments for ms-coco. arXiv preprint arXiv:2004.15020 (2020)
48. Pennington, J., Socher, R., Manning, C.D.: Glove: global vectors for word representation. In: Proceedings of EMNLP, pp. 1532–1543 (2014)
49. Plummer, B.A., Wang, L., Cervantes, C.M., Caicedo, J.C., Hockenmaier, J., Lazebnik, S.: Flickr30k entities: collecting region-to-phrase correspondences for richer image-to-sentence models. In: Proceedings of the IEEE International Conference on Computer Vision, pp. 2641–2649 (2015)
50. Radford, A., et al.: Learning transferable visual models from natural language supervision. In: Meila, M., Zhang, T. (eds.) Proceedings of ICML. Proceedings of Machine Learning Research, 18–24 July 2021, vol. 139, pp. 8748–8763. PMLR (2021). http://proceedings.mlr.press/v139/radford21a.html

51. Radford, A., Wu, J., Child, R., Luan, D., Amodei, D., Sutskever, I., et al.: Language models are unsupervised multitask learners. OpenAI blog **1**(8), 9 (2019)
52. Ren, S., He, K., Girshick, R., Sun, J.: Faster r-cnn: towards real-time object detection with region proposal networks. In: Proceedings of NeurIPS, pp. 91–99 (2015)
53. Schroff, F., Kalenichenko, D., Philbin, J.: Facenet: a unified embedding for face recognition and clustering. In: Proceedings of CVPR, pp. 815–823 (2015)
54. Scimeca, L., Oh, S.J., Chun, S., Poli, M., Yun, S.: Which shortcut cues will dnns choose? a study from the parameter-space perspective. In: International Conference on Learning Representations (ICLR) (2022)
55. Settles, B.: Active learning literature survey (2009)
56. Sharma, P., Ding, N., Goodman, S., Soricut, R.: Conceptual captions: a cleaned, hypernymed, image alt-text dataset for automatic image captioning. In: ACL, pp. 2556–2565 (2018)
57. Snow, R., O'Connor, B., Jurafsky, D., Ng, A.: Cheap and fast - but is it good? evaluating non-expert annotations for natural language tasks. In: Proceedings of the 2008 Conference on Empirical Methods in Natural Language Processing, pp. 254–263. Association for Computational Linguistics, Honolulu (2008). https://aclanthology.org/D08-1027
58. Song, J.Y., Fok, R., Lundgard, A., Yang, F., Kim, J., Lasecki, W.S.: Two tools are better than one: tool diversity as a means of improving aggregate crowd performance. In: 23rd International Conference on Intelligent User Interfaces (2018)
59. Song, Y., Soleymani, M.: Polysemous visual-semantic embedding for cross-modal retrieval. In: Proceedings of CVPR, pp. 1979–1988 (2019)
60. Sorokin, A., Forsyth, D.: Utility data annotation with amazon mechanical turk. In: 2008 IEEE Computer Society Conference on Computer Vision and Pattern Recognition Workshops, pp. 1–8 (2008). https://doi.org/10.1109/CVPRW.2008.4562953
61. Vaswani, A., et al.: Attention is all you need. In: Proceedings of NeurIPS, pp. 5998–6008 (2017)
62. Verma, Y., Jawahar, C.: Image annotation by propagating labels from semantic neighbourhoods. IJCV **121**(1), 126–148 (2017)
63. Wah, C., Branson, S., Welinder, P., Perona, P., Belongie, S.: The caltech-ucsd birds-200-2011 dataset (2011)
64. Wang, H., Zhang, Y., Ji, Z., Pang, Y., Ma, L.: Consensus-aware visual-semantic embedding for image-text matching. In: Proceedings of ECCV (2020)
65. Wehrmann, J., Souza, D.M., Lopes, M.A., Barros, R.C.: Language-agnostic visual-semantic embeddings. In: Proceedings of the IEEE/CVF International Conference on Computer Vision, pp. 5804–5813 (2019)
66. Wu, H., et al.: Unified visual-semantic embeddings: bridging vision and language with structured meaning representations. In: Proceedings of the IEEE/CVF Conference on Computer Vision and Pattern Recognition, pp. 6609–6618 (2019)
67. Wu, W., Yang, J.: Smartlabel: an object labeling tool using iterated harmonic energy minimization. In: Proceedings of the 14th ACM International Conference on Multimedia, pp. 891–900 (2006)
68. Xu, N., Price, B., Cohen, S., Yang, J., Huang, T.S.: Deep interactive object selection. In: Proceedings of CVPR, pp. 373–381 (2016)
69. Young, P., Lai, A., Hodosh, M., Hockenmaier, J.: From image descriptions to visual denotations: new similarity metrics for semantic inference over event descriptions. ACL **2**, 67–78 (2014)

70. Yun, S., Han, D., Oh, S.J., Chun, S., Choe, J., Yoo, Y.: Cutmix: regularization strategy to train strong classifiers with localizable features. In: Proceedings of ICCV (2019)
71. Zhang, P., et al.: Vinvl: making visual representations matter in vision-language models. In: Proceedings of CVPR (2021)

MOTCOM: The Multi-Object Tracking Dataset Complexity Metric

Malte Pedersen[1]([⊠]) , Joakim Bruslund Haurum[1,2] , Patrick Dendorfer[3] ,
and Thomas B. Moeslund[1,2]

[1] Aalborg University, Aalborg, Denmark
mape@create.aau.dk
[2] Pioneer Center for AI, Copenhagen, Denmark
[3] Technical University of Munich, Munich, Germany

Abstract. There exists no comprehensive metric for describing the complexity of Multi-Object Tracking (MOT) sequences. This lack of metrics decreases explainability, complicates comparison of datasets, and reduces the conversation on tracker performance to a matter of leader board position. As a remedy, we present the novel MOT dataset complexity metric (MOTCOM), which is a combination of three sub-metrics inspired by key problems in MOT: occlusion, erratic motion, and visual similarity. The insights of MOTCOM can open nuanced discussions on tracker performance and may lead to a wider acknowledgement of novel contributions developed for either less known datasets or those aimed at solving sub-problems.

We evaluate MOTCOM on the comprehensive MOT17, MOT20, and MOTSynth datasets and show that MOTCOM is far better at describing the complexity of MOT sequences compared to the conventional *density* and *number of tracks*. Project page at https://vap.aau.dk/motcom.

1 Introduction

Tracking has been an important research topic for decades with applications ranging from autonomous driving to fish behavior analysis [13,26,34,41]. The aim is to acquire the full spatio-temporal trajectory of an object of interest, but missing or inaccurate detections can make this a complicated task. When more objects are present in the scene simultaneously it is termed a multi-object tracking (MOT) problem and an additional task is to keep the correct identities of all objects throughout the sequence.

During the previous decade there has been an increase in the development of publicly available MOT datasets [7,9,14,27,40]. However, there has been no attempt to objectively describe the complexity of a dataset or its sequences except for using simple statistics like *density* and *number of tracks*, which are neither adequate nor explanatory, see Fig. 1. When a new dataset emerges, the community

---

Supplementary Information The online version contains supplementary material available at https://doi.org/10.1007/978-3-031-20074-8_2.

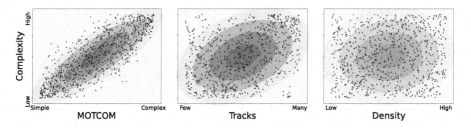

Fig. 1. Comparing the capability of the proposed MOTCOM metric against the conventional metrics (*number of tracks* and *density*) for describing MOT sequence complexity. The shared y-axis shows a HOTA [24] rank-based proxy for the ground truth complexity of the MOTSynth sequences [12]. The x-axes show the corresponding rank determined by each of the three metrics. The correlation between the complexity and MOTCOM is clearly stronger compared to both *tracks* and *density*. More details can be found in Sect. 5.

needs objective metrics to be able to characterize and discuss the dataset with respect to existing datasets, otherwise, 'gut feeling' and 'popularity vote' will rule. Furthermore, the absence of an objective MOT sequence complexity metric hinders an informed conversation on the capabilities of trackers developed for different datasets. Nowadays, it is important to rank high on popular MOT benchmark leaderboads in order to gain the attention of the community. This may hinder the acknowledgement of novel solutions that solve sub-problems of MOT particularly well and underrate solutions developed on less popular datasets. We expect that a descriptive and explanatory metric can help remedy these issues.

The literature suggests that there are three main factors that make MOT tasks difficult to solve [1–3, 26, 31]; namely, occlusion, erratic motion, and visual similarity. We hypothesize that the complexity of MOT sequences can be expressed by a combination of the aforementioned three factors for which we need to construct explicit metrics. Therefore, in this paper we propose the first-ever individual sub-metrics for describing the complexity of the three sub-problems and a unified quantitative MOT dataset complexity metric (MOTCOM) as a combination of these sub-metrics. In Fig. 1, we illustrate that MOTCOM is far better at estimating the complexity of the sequences of the recent MOTSynth dataset [12] compared to the commonly used *number of tracks* and *density*.

The main contributions of our paper are as follows:

1. The novel metric MOTCOM for describing the complexity of MOT sequences.
2. Three sub-metrics for describing the complexity of MOT sequences with respect to occlusion, erratic motion, and visual similarity.
3. We show that the conventional metrics *number of tracks* and *density* are not strong indicators for the complexity of MOT sequences.
4. We evaluate the capability of MOTCOM and demonstrate its superiority against *number of tracks* and *density*.

In the next section, we describe and analyse the three sub-problems followed by a presentation of the proposed metrics. In the remainder of the paper, we demonstrate and discuss how the metrics can describe and explain the complexity of MOT sequences.

2   Related Work

The majority of recent trackers utilize the strong performance of deep learning based detectors, e.g., by following the tracking-by-detection paradigm [4,43,45], tracking-by-regression [3], through joint training of the detection and tracking steps [33,49], or as part of an association step [23,30,48]. Trackers like Tracktor [3], Chained-Tracker [33], and CenterTrack [49] rely on spatial proximity which makes them vulnerable to sequences with extreme motion and heavy occlusion. At the other end of the spectrum are trackers like QDTrack [30], RetinaTrack [23], and FairMOT [48] which use visual cues for tracking. They are optimized toward tracking visually distinct objects and are not to the same degree limited by erratic motion or vanishing objects but instead sensitive to weak visual features. This indicates that the design of trackers is centered around three core problems: occlusion, erratic motion, and visual similarity. Below, we dive into the literature regarding these problems followed by insights on dataset complexity.

Occlusion. Occlusions can be difficult to handle and they are often simply treated as missing data [2]. However, in scenes were the objects have weak or similar visual features this can be harmful for the tracking performance [1,28,38].

Most authors state that a higher occlusion rate makes tracking harder [6,22, 25], but they seldom quantify such statements. An exception is the work proposed by Bergmann et al. [3] where they analyzed the tracking results with respect to object visibility, the size of the objects, and missing detections. Moreover, Pedersen et al. [31] argued that the number of objects is less critical than the amount and level of occlusion when it comes to multi-object tracking of fish. They described the complexity of their sequences based on occlusions alone.

Erratic Motion. Prior information can be used to predict the next state of an object which minimizes the search space and hence reduces the impact of noisy or missing detections. A linear motion model assuming constant velocity is a simple, but effective method for predicting the movement of non-erratic objects like pedestrians [26,28]. In scenes that include camera motion or complex movement more advanced models may improve tracker performance. Pellegrini et al. [32] proposed incorporating human social behavior into their motion model and Kratz et al. [19] proposed utilizing the movement of a crowd to enhance the tracking of individuals. A downside of many advanced motion models is an often poor ability to generalize to other types of objects or environments.

Visual Similarity. Visual cues are commonly used in tracklet association and re-identification and are well studied for persons [46], vehicles [18], and animals [37] such as zebrafish [15] and tigers [36]. Modern trackers often solve the association step using CNNs, like Siamese networks, based on a visual affinity model [3,21,44,47]. Such methods rely on visual dissimilarity between the objects. However, tracklet association becomes more difficult when objects are hard to distinguish purely by their appearance.

Dataset Complexity. Determining the complexity of a dataset is a non-trivial task. One may have a "feeling" or intuition about which datasets are harder than others, but this is subjective and can differ depending on who you ask, as well as differ depending on the task at hand. In order to objectively determine the complexity of a dataset, one has to develop a task-specific framework. An early attempt at this was the suite of 12 complexity measures (c-measures) by Ho and Basu [17], based on concepts such as inter-class overlap and linear separability. However, these c-measures are not suitable for image datasets due to unrealistic assumptions, such as the data being linearly separable. Therefore, Branchaud-Charron et al. [5] developed a complexity measure based on spectral clustering, where the inter-class overlap is quantified through the eigenvalues of an approximated adjacency matrix. This approach was shown to correlate well with the CNN performance on several image datasets. Similarly, Cui et al. [8] presented a framework for evaluating the fine-grainedness of image datasets, by measuring the average distance from data examples to the class centers. Both of these approaches rely on embedding the input images into a feature space by using, e.g., a CNN, and determining the dataset complexity without any indication of what makes the dataset difficult.

In contrast, dataset complexity in the MOT field has so far been determined through simple statistics such as the number of tracks and density. These quantities are currently displayed for every sequence alongside other stats such as resolution and frame rate for the MOTChallenge benchmark datasets [9]. The preliminary works of Bergmann et al. [3] and Pedersen et al. [31] have attempted to further explain what makes a MOT sequence difficult by investigating the effect of occlusions. However, there is no clear way of describing the complexity of MOT sequences and the current methods have not been verified.

3   Challenges in Multi-object Tracking

MOT covers the task of obtaining the spatio-temporal trajectories of multiple objects in a sequence of consecutive frames. Depending on the specific task, the objects may be represented as 3D points [31], pixel-level segmentation masks [42], or bounding boxes [29]. Despite the different representation forms, the concepts of occlusion, erratic motion, and visual similarity apply to all of them and add to the complexity of the sequences.

Occlusion. Occlusion describes situations where the visual information of an object within the camera view is partially or fully hidden. There are three types of occlusion: *self-occlusion*, *scene-occlusion*, and *inter-object-occlusion* [1]. Self-occlusion can reduce the visibility of parts of an object, e.g., if a hand is placed in front of a face, but defining the level of self-occlusion is non-trivial and depends on the type of object. Scene-occlusion occurs when a static object is located in the line of sight between the camera and the target object, thereby decreasing the visual information of the target. A scene-occlusion is marked by the red box in Fig. 2a, where flowers partially occlude a sitting person.

Inter-object-occlusion is typically the most difficult to handle, especially if the objects are of the same type, as the trajectories of multiple objects cross. An example can be seen in Fig. 2a, where the blue box marks a person that partially occludes another person.

Erratic Motion. We use motion as a term for an object's spatial displacement between frames. This is typically caused by the locomotive behavior of the object itself, camera motion, or a combination. As the number of factors that influence the observed motion increases, the motion becomes harder to predict. An example of two objects exhibiting different types of motion is presented in Fig. 2b. The blue object moves with approximately the same direction and speed between the time steps. Predicting the next state of the object seems trivial and the search space is correspondingly small. On the other hand, the red object behaves erratically and unpredictably while the motion model is less confident as illustrated by the larger search space.

Visual Similarity. The visual appearance of objects can vary widely depending on the type of object and type of scene. Appearance is especially important when tracking is lost, for example, due to occlusion, and re-identification is a common tool for associating broken tracklets. The complexity of this process depends on the visual similarity between objects, but intra-object similarity also plays a role. As an object moves through a scene, its appearance can change from the perspective of the viewer. The object may turn around, increase its distance to the camera, or the illumination conditions may change. Aside from the visual cues, the object's position is also critical. Intuitively, it becomes less likely to confuse objects as the spatial distance between them increases.

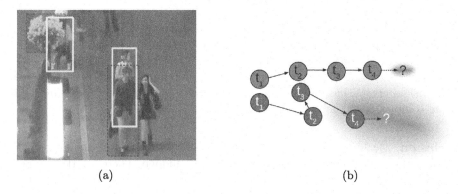

(a)   (b)

Fig. 2. a) Sample from MOT17-04 [27]. The yellow boxes illustrate objects partly occluded by scene-occlusion (red) and inter-object-occlusion (blue). b) The blue object displays nearly linear motion, whereas the red object is behaving erratically. The ellipsoids symbolize the confidence of an artificial underlying motion model. (Color figure online)

4   The MOTCOM Metrics

We propose individual metrics to describe the level of occlusion, erratic motion, and visual similarity for MOT sequences. Subsequently, we combine these three sub-metrics into a higher-level metric that describes the overall complexity of the sequences.

Preliminaries. We define a MOT sequence as a set of frames $F = \{1, 2, \dots\}$ containing a set of objects $K = \{k_1, k_2, \dots\}$. The objects do not have to be present in every frame, therefore, we define the set of frames where a given object is present by $F^k = \{t_1, t_2, \dots\}$. The objects present in a given frame t are defined as the set $K^t = \{k | k \in K \wedge t \in F^k\}$. At each frame t an object k is represented by its center-position in image coordinates and the height and width of the surrounding bounding box $k_t = (x, y, h, w)$.

4.1   Occlusion Metric

As mentioned in Sect. 3, occlusion can be divided into three types: self-, scene- and inter-object occlusion. In order to quantify the occlusion rate in a sequence, one should ideally account for all three types. However, it is most often non-trivial to determine the level of self-occlusion and it is commonly not taken into account in MOT. Pedersen et al. [31] used the ratio of intersecting object bounding boxes to determine the inter-object occlusion rate. Similarly, the MOT16, MOT17, and MOT20 datasets include a visibility score based on the intersection over area (IoA) of both inter- and scene-objects [9], where IoA is formulated as the area of intersection over the area of the target.

Following this trend, we omit self-occlusion and base the occlusion metric, OCOM, on the IoA and compute it as

$$\text{OCOM} = \frac{1}{|K|} \sum_{k}^{K} \bar{\nu}^k, \tag{1}$$

where $\bar{\nu}^k$ is the mean level of occlusion of object k. ν_t^k is in the interval $[0, 1]$ where 0 is fully visible and 1 is fully occluded. It is assumed that terrestrial objects move on a ground plane which allows us to interpret their y-values as pseudo-depth and decide on the ordering. Annotations are needed to calculate the occlusion level for objects moving in 3D. OCOM is defined in the interval $[0, 1]$ where a higher value means more occlusion and a harder problem to solve.

4.2   Motion Metric

The proposed motion metric, MCOM, is based on the assumption that objects move linearly when observed at small time steps. If this assumption is not upheld, it is a sign of erratic motion and thereby a more complex MOT sequence.

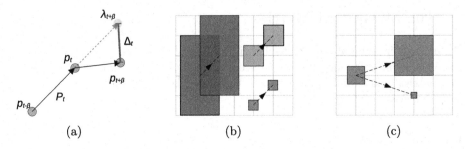

Fig. 3. a) Illustrative example of how the positional error Δ_t is calculated as the distance between the true position $p_{t+\beta}$ and estimated position $\lambda_{t+\beta}$. b) The three objects have traveled an equal distance. Relative to their size, the two smaller objects are displaced by a larger amount and the bounding box overlap disappears. c) If the size of an object increases between two time steps the displacement is relatively less important, compared to when the size of the object decreases.

Initially, the displacement vector, P_t^k, between the object's position in the current and past time step is calculated as

$$P_t^k = p_t^k - p_{t-\beta}^k, \tag{2}$$

where p_t is the position of object k at time t, defined by its x- and y-coordinates, and β describes the temporal step size. When calculating the displacement between two consecutive frames $\beta = 1$. The displacement vector in the first frame of a trajectory is set to zero and β is capped by the first and last frame of a trajectory when the object is not present at time $t \pm \beta$.

The position in the next time step is predicted using a linear motion model with constant velocity based on the current position and the calculated displacement vector. The position is predicted by

$$\lambda_{t+\beta}^k = P_t^k + p_t^k. \tag{3}$$

The error between the predicted and true position of the object is calculated by

$$\Delta_t^k = \ell_2(p_{t+\beta}^k, \lambda_{t+\beta}^k) \tag{4}$$

where ℓ_2 is the Euclidean distance function and a larger Δ_t^k indicates a more complex motion. See Fig. 3a for an illustration of how the displacement error is calculated. This approach may seem overly simplified, but it encapsulates changes in both direction and velocity. Furthermore, it is deliberately sensitive to low frame rates and camera motion, as both factors add to the complexity of tracking sequences.

Inspired by the analysis of decreasing tracking performance with respect to smaller object sizes by Bergmann et al. [3], the size is also taken into consideration. The combination of size and movement affects the difficulty of predicting the next state of the object. In Fig. 3b, the rectangles are equally displaced but do not experience the same displacement relative to their size. Intuitively, if a set of objects are moving at similar speeds, it is harder to track the smaller objects due to their lower spatio-temporal overlap.

Accordingly, the motion-based complexity measure is based on the displacement relative to the size of the object. As illustrated in Fig. 3c, the size of the object may change between two time steps. The direction of the change is critical as the displacement is less distinct if the size of the object is increasing, compared to the opposite situation. Therefore, we multiply the current size of the object with the change in object size to get the transformed object size

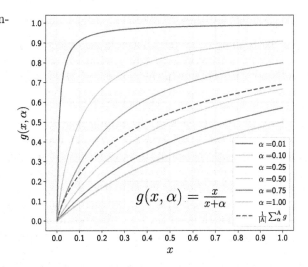

Fig. 4. α controls the growth of the function $g(x, \alpha)$ and decides when an output value of 0.5 is reached. The dashed line illustrates $g(x, \alpha)$ when using the average of a set of α values.

$$\rho_t^k = s_t^k \cdot \frac{s_{t+\beta}^k}{s_t^k} = s_{t+\beta}^k, \tag{5}$$

where $s_t^k = \sqrt{w_t^k \cdot h_t^k}$ and h_t^k and w_t^k are the height and width of object k at time step t, respectively. The motion complexity measure is then calculated as the mean size-compensated displacement across all frames, F, and all objects at each frame, K^t, and weighted by the log-sigmoid function $g(x, \alpha)$

$$\text{MCOM} = \frac{1}{|A|} \sum_\alpha^A g \left(\frac{1}{\sum_k^K |F^k|} \sum_k^K \sum_t^{F^k} \frac{\Delta_t^k}{\rho_t^k}, \alpha \right), \tag{6}$$

where the average of $A = \{0.01, 0.02, ..., 1.0\}$ is used to avoid manually deciding on a specific value for α. The use of the function $g(x, \alpha)$ is motivated by the aim of having an output in the range $[0, 1]$, where a higher number describes a more complex motion. The function $g(x, \alpha)$ is given by

$$g(x, \alpha) = \frac{1}{1 + e^{-\log(x)\alpha}} = \frac{1}{1 + \frac{\alpha}{x}} = \frac{x}{x + \alpha}, \tag{7}$$

where α affects the gradient of the monotonically increasing function and indicates the point where the output of the function will reach 0.5 as illustrated in Fig. 4. The function is designed such that displacements in the lower ranges are weighted higher. The argument for this choice is based on the assumption that minor increments to an extraordinarily erratic locomotive behavior have less impact on the complexity.

4.3   Visual Similarity Metric

In order to define a metric that links an object's visual appearance with tracking complexity, we investigate how similar an object in one frame is compared to itself and other objects in the next frame. Two objects may look similar, but they cannot occupy the same spatial position. Therefore, we propose a spatial-aware visual similarity metric called VCOM.

VCOM consists of a preprocessing, feature extraction, and distance evaluation step. For every object $k \in K$ in every frame $t \in F$ an image I_t^k is produced with the object's bounding box in focus and a heavy blurred background. We blur the image using a discrete Gaussian function, except in the region of the object's bounding box as visualized in Fig. 5a.

A feature embedding is then extracted from each of the preprocessed images. As opposed to looking at the bounding box alone, using the entire image allows us to retain and embed spatial information in the feature vector. The object's location is especially valuable in scenes with similarly looking objects and the blurred background contributes with low frequency information of the surroundings.

We blur the image with a Gaussian kernel with a fixed size of 201 and a sigma of 38 and extract the image features using an ImageNet [10] pre-trained ResNet-18 [16] model. We measure the similarity between the feature vector of the target object in frame t and the feature vectors of all the objects in frame $t + 1$ by computing the Euclidean distance. The uncertainty increases if more objects are located within the proximity of the target. Therefore, we do not only look for the nearest neighbor, but rather the number of objects within a given distance, $d(r)$, from the target feature vector

$$d(r) = d_{\mathrm{NN}} + d_{\mathrm{NN}} \cdot r \tag{8}$$

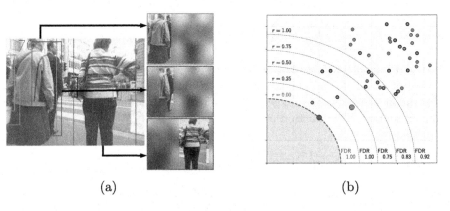

(a)	(b)

Fig. 5. a) Example showing three images with the object in focus and a blurred background produced from a frame from the MOT17-05 sequence. b) The distance ratio, r, affects the FDR when other objects are in the proximity of the target. The red dot is the nearest neighbor, the green dot is the true positive match, and the remaining dots are other objects. (Color figure online)

where d_{NN} is the distance to the nearest neighbor and r is a distance ratio. The ratio is multiplied by the distance to the nearest neighbor in order to account for the variance in scale, e.g., as induced by object resolution or distinctiveness.

An object within the distance boundary that shares the same identity as the target object is considered a true positive (TP) and all other objects are considered false positives (FP). By measuring the complexity based on the false discovery rate, $FDR = \frac{FP}{FP+TP}$, we get an output in the range $[0, 1]$ where a higher number indicates a more complex task. An illustrative example of how the FDR is determined based on the distance ratio r can be seen in Fig. 5b. It is ambiguous to choose a single optimal distance ratio r. Therefore, we calculate VCOM based on the average of distance ratios from the set $R = \{0.01, 0.02, ..., 1.0\}$

$$\text{VCOM} = \frac{1}{|R|} \sum_r^R \frac{1}{|F|} \sum_t^F \frac{1}{|K^t|} \sum_k^{K^t} FDR_{d(r)}(k) \tag{9}$$

4.4   MOTCOM

Occlusion alone does not necessarily indicate an overwhelming problem if the object follows a known motion model or if it is visually distinct. The same is true for erratic motion and visual similarity when viewed in isolation. However, the combination of occlusion, erratic motion, and visual similarity becomes increasingly difficult to handle.

Therefore, we combine the occlusion, erratic motion, and visual similarity metrics into a single MOTCOM metric that describes the overall complexity of a sequence. MOTCOM is computed as the weighted arithmetic mean of the three sub-metrics and is given by

$$\text{MOTCOM} = \frac{w_{\text{OCOM}} \cdot \text{OCOM} + w_{\text{MCOM}} \cdot \text{MCOM} + w_{\text{VCOM}} \cdot \text{VCOM}}{w_{\text{OCOM}} + w_{\text{MCOM}} + w_{\text{VCOM}}} \tag{10}$$

where w_{OCOM}, w_{MCOM}, and w_{VCOM} are the weights for the three sub-metrics. Equal weighting can be obtained by setting $w_{\text{OCOM}} = w_{\text{MCOM}} = w_{\text{VCOM}}$, while custom weights may be suitable for specific applications. During evaluation we weight the sub-metrics equally as we deem each of the sub-problems equally difficult to handle.

5   Evaluation

In the following experimental section, we demonstrate that MOTCOM is able to describe the complexity of MOT sequences and is superior to *density* and *number of tracks*. In order to do this, we compare the estimated complexity levels with ground truth representations. Such ground truths are not readily available, but a strong proxy can be obtained by ranking the sequences based on the performance of state-of-the-art trackers [20]. There exist many performance metrics with two of the most popular being MOTA [39] and IDF1 [35]. However, we apply the recent HOTA metric [24], which was proposed in response to the imbalance between detection, association, and localization within traditional metrics. Additionally, HOTA is the tracker performance metric that correlates the strongest with MOT complexity based on human assessment [24]. In the remainder of this section, we present the datasets and evaluation metrics we use to experimentally verify the applicability of MOTCOM.

5.1   Ground Truth

In order to create a strong foundation for the evaluation, we are in need of benchmark datasets with consistent annotation standards and leader boards with a wide range of state-of-the-art trackers. Therefore, we evaluate MOTCOM on the popular MOT17 [27] and MOT20 [9] datasets[1]. There are seven sequences in the test split of MOT17 and four sequences in the test split of MOT20, some of which are presented in Fig. 6. Furthermore, leader boards are provided for both benchmarks with results from 212 trackers for MOT17 and 80 trackers for MOT20. We use the results from the top-30 ranked trackers[2] based on the average HOTA score, so as to limit unstable and fluctuating performances.

In order to strengthen and support the evaluation, we include the training split of the fully synthetic MOTSynth dataset [12] which contains 764 varied sequences of pedestrians. A few samples from the dataset can be seen in Fig. 7. In order to obtain ground truth tracker performance for MOTSynth, we train and test a CenterTrack model [49] on the data. We have chosen CenterTrack as it has been shown to perform well when trained on synthetic data [12].

(a)   (b)

Fig. 6. Sample images from a) MOT17 [27] and b) MOT20 [9]. MOT17 contains varied urban scenes with and without camera motion. MOT20 contains crowded scenes captured from an elevated point of view and without camera motion.

Fig. 7. Sample images from the MOTSynth dataset [12]. The sequences vary in camera motion and perspective, environment, and lighting.

---

[1] With permission from the MOTChallenge benchmark authors.
[2] Leader board results obtained on March 4, 2022.

5.2   Evaluation Metrics

We evaluate and compare the dataset complexity metrics by their ability to rank the MOT sequences according to the HOTA score of the trackers. We rank the sequences from simple to complex by their *density, number of tracks* (abbr. *tracks*), MOTCOM score, and HOTA score. Depending on the metric, the ranking is in decreasing (HOTA) or increasing order (*density, tracks,* MOTCOM). The absolute difference between the ranks, known as Spearman's Footrule Distance (FD) [11], gives the distance between the ground truth and estimated ranks

$$\text{FD} = \sum_{i=1}^{n} |\text{rank}(x_i) - \text{rank}(\text{HOTA}_i)|, \tag{11}$$

where n is the number of sequences and x is *density, tracks,* or MOTCOM. In order to directly compare results of sets of different lengths, we normalize the FD by the maximal possible distance FD_{max} which is computed as

$$\text{FD}_{\text{max}} = \begin{cases} \sum_{i=1}^{n} i - \frac{n}{2} & \{n \mid 2m \,,\, m \in \mathbb{Z}^+\} \\ \sum_{i=1}^{n} i - \frac{n+1}{2} & \{n \mid 2m - 1 \,,\, m \in \mathbb{Z}^+\} \end{cases} . \tag{12}$$

Finally, we compute the normalized FD, $\text{NFD} = \frac{\text{FD}}{\text{FD}_{\text{max}}}$.

6   Results

In Table 1, we present the mean FD of the ranks of *density, tracks,* and MOTCOM against the ground truth ranks dictated by the average top-30 HOTA performance on the MOT17 and MOT20 test splits (individually and in combination). The numbers in parentheses are the normalized FD. Generally, MOTCOM has a considerably lower FD compared to *density* and *tracks*. This suggests that MOTCOM is better at ranking the sequences according to the HOTA performance.

A similar tendency can be seen for the CenterTrack-based results presented in Table 2. In order to increase the number of samples, we have evaluated CenterTrack on both the train and test splits of the MOT17 and MOT20 datasets. $\text{MOTChl}_{\text{test}}$ and $\text{MOTChl}_{\text{train}}$ are the test and train sequences, respectively, of

Table 1. Ground truth ranks are based on the average top-30 HOTA performance. The results are presented as the mean FD and the NFD in parentheses. A lower score is better and the results in bold are the lowest

Top-30	MOT17$_{\text{test}}$	MOT20$_{\text{test}}$	Combined
Density	1.71 (0.50)	1.00 (0.50)	3.82 (0.70)
Tracks	2.57 (0.75)	1.50 (0.75)	3.82 (0.70)
MOTCOM	**0.86 (0.25)**	**0.00 (0.00)**	**1.45 (0.27)**

Table 2. Ground truth ranks are based on the CenterTrack HOTA performance. The results are presented as the mean FD and the NFD in parentheses. A lower score is better and the results in bold are the lowest

CenterTrack	MOTChl$_{test}$	MOTChl$_{train}$	MOTChl$_{both}$	MOTSynth
Density	3.27 (0.60)	4.18 (0.77)	7.36 (0.67)	238.71 (0.63)
Tracks	2.73 (0.50)	3.64 (0.67)	6.64 (0.60)	193.50 (0.51)
MOTCOM	**2.36 (0.43)**	**2.18 (0.40)**	**4.82 (0.44)**	**100.17 (0.26)**

MOT17 *and* MOT20. MOTChl$_{both}$ includes *all* the sequences from MOT17 and MOT20. These results support our claim that MOTCOM is better at estimating the complexity of MOT sequences compared to *density* and *tracks*.

We present a Spearman's correlation matrix in Fig. 8 based on the top-30 trackers evaluated for the combined MOT17 and MOT20 test splits. It indicates that the *density* and *tracks* do not correlate with HOTA, MOTA, or IDF1, whereas MOTCOM has a strong negative correlation with all the performance metrics. Trackers evaluated on sequences with high MOTCOM scores tend to have lower performance

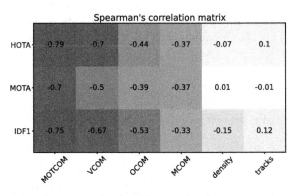

Fig. 8. Spearman's correlation matrix based on the performance of the top-30 trackers on MOT17 and MOT20.

while sequences with low MOTCOM scores gives higher performance. This underlines that MOTCOM can indeed be used to understand the complexity of MOT sequences.

7   Discussion

Our complexity metric MOTCOM provides tracker researchers and dataset developers a comprehensive score to investigate and describe the complexity of MOT sequences without the need for multiple baseline evaluations of different tracking methods. This allows for an objective comparison of different datasets without introducing potential training bias. Currently, the assessment of tracker performance is roughly speaking reduced to a placement on a benchmark leader board. This underrates novel solutions developed for less popular datasets or methods designed explicitly to solve sub-tasks such as occlusion or erratic motion.

Supplemented by the sub-metrics, MOTCOM provides a deeper understanding and more informed discussions on dataset composition and tracker performance, which will increase the explanability of MOT. In order to illustrate this,

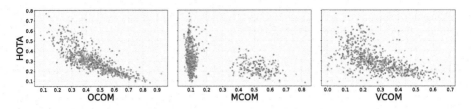

Fig. 9. The CenterTrack-based HOTA scores of the MOTSynth sequences plotted against the sub-metrics OCOM, MCOM, and VCOM, respectively.

we discuss the performance of CenterTrack on the MOTSynth dataset with respect to MOTCOM. Here we see that the occlusion level (OCOM) in Fig. 9 has a strong negative correlation with the HOTA score and the visual similarity metric (VCOM) has a relatively weak correlation with HOTA. Both cases expose the design of CenterTrack, which does not contain a module to handle lost tracks and is not dependent on visual cues for tracking. For the motion metric (MCOM) we see two distributions; one in the lower end and one in the upper end of the MCOM range. The objects are expected to behave similarly, so this indicates that parts of the MOTSynth sequences include heavy camera motion which is difficult for CenterTrack to handle. In Fig. 10, we show that MOTCOM is far better at estimating the complexity level compared to *tracks* and *density*.

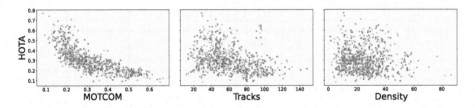

Fig. 10. The CenterTrack-based HOTA scores of the MOTSynth sequences plotted against MOTCOM, *tracks*, and *density*.

8   Conclusion

We propose MOTCOM, the first meaningful and descriptive MOT dataset complexity metric, and show that it is preferable for describing the complexity of MOT sequences compared to the conventional methods of *number of tracks* and *density*. MOTCOM is a combination of three individual sub-metrics that describe the complexity of MOT sequences with respect to key obstacles in MOT: occlusion, erratic motion, and visual similarity. The information provided by MOTCOM can assist tracking researchers and dataset developers in acquiring a deeper understanding of MOT sequences and trackers. We strongly suggest that the community uses MOTCOM as the prevalent complexity measure for increasing the explainability of MOT trackers and datasets.

Acknowledgements. This work has been funded by the Independent Research Fund Denmark under case number 9131-00128B.

References

1. Andriyenko, A., Roth, S., Schindler, K.: An analytical formulation of global occlusion reasoning for multi-target tracking. In: 2011 IEEE International Conference on Computer Vision Workshops (ICCV Workshops), pp. 1839–1846. IEEE (2011). https://doi.org/10.1109/ICCVW.2011.6130472
2. Andriyenko, A., Schindler, K.: Multi-target tracking by continuous energy minimization. In: 2011 IEEE Conference on Computer Vision and Pattern Recognition (CVPR), pp. 1265–1272 (2011). https://doi.org/10.1109/CVPR.2011.5995311
3. Bergmann, P., Meinhardt, T., Leal-Taixé, L.: Tracking without bells and whistles. In: 2019 IEEE/CVF International Conference on Computer Vision (ICCV), pp. 941–951 (2019). https://doi.org/10.1109/ICCV.2019.00103
4. Bewley, A., Ge, Z., Ott, L., Ramos, F., Upcroft, B.: Simple online and realtime tracking. In: 2016 IEEE International Conference on Image Processing (ICIP), pp. 3464–3468 (2016). https://doi.org/10.1109/ICIP.2016.7533003
5. Branchaud-Charron, F., Achkar, A., Jodoin, P.M.: Spectral metric for dataset complexity assessment. In: 2019 IEEE/CVF Conference on Computer Vision and Pattern Recognition (CVPR), pp. 3210–3219 (2019). https://doi.org/10.1109/CVPR.2019.00333
6. Cao, X., Guo, S., Lin, J., Zhang, W., Liao, M.: Online tracking of ants based on deep association metrics: method, dataset and evaluation. Pattern Recogn. **103** (2020). https://doi.org/10.1016/j.patcog.2020.107233
7. Chang, M.F., et al.: Argoverse: 3D tracking and forecasting with rich maps. In: 2019 IEEE/CVF Conference on Computer Vision and Pattern Recognition (CVPR), pp. 8740–8749 (2019). https://doi.org/10.1109/CVPR.2019.00895
8. Cui, Y., Gu, Z., Mahajan, D., van der Maaten, L., Belongie, S., Lim, S.N.: Measuring dataset granularity (2019). https://doi.org/10.48550/ARXIV.1912.10154
9. Dendorfer, P., et al.: MOTChallenge: a benchmark for single-camera multiple target tracking. Int. J. Comput. Vision **129**(4), 845–881 (2020). https://doi.org/10.1007/s11263-020-01393-0
10. Deng, J., Dong, W., Socher, R., Li, L.J., Li, K., Fei-Fei, L.: Imagenet: a large-scale hierarchical image database. In: 2009 IEEE Conference on Computer Vision and Pattern Recognition (CVPR), pp. 248–255 (2009). https://doi.org/10.1109/CVPR.2009.5206848
11. Diaconis, P., Graham, R.L.: Spearman's footrule as a measure of disarray. J. Roy. Stat. Soc.: Ser. B (Methodol.) **39**(2), 262–268 (1977). https://doi.org/10.1111/j.2517-6161.1977.tb01624.x
12. Fabbri, M., et al.: Motsynth: how can synthetic data help pedestrian detection and tracking? In: 2021 IEEE/CVF International Conference on Computer Vision (ICCV), pp. 10829–10839 (2021). https://doi.org/10.1109/ICCV48922.2021.01067
13. Gade, R., Moeslund, T.B.: Constrained multi-target tracking for team sports activities. IPSJ Trans. Comput. Vision Appl. **10**(1), 1–11 (2018). https://doi.org/10.1186/s41074-017-0038-z
14. Geiger, A., Lenz, P., Urtasun, R.: Are we ready for autonomous driving? The kitti vision benchmark suite. In: 2012 IEEE Conference on Computer Vision and Pattern Recognition (CVPR), pp. 3354–3361 (2012). https://doi.org/10.1109/CVPR.2012.6248074

15. Haurum, J.B., Karpova, A., Pedersen, M., Bengtson, S.H., Moeslund, T.B.: Re-identification of zebrafish using metric learning. In: 2020 IEEE Winter Applications of Computer Vision Workshops (WACVW), pp. 1–11 (2020). https://doi.org/10.1109/WACVW50321.2020.9096922
16. He, K., Zhang, X., Ren, S., Sun, J.: Deep residual learning for image recognition. In: 2016 IEEE Conference on Computer Vision and Pattern Recognition (CVPR), pp. 770–778 (2016). https://doi.org/10.1109/CVPR.2016.90
17. Ho, T.K., Basu, M.: Complexity measures of supervised classification problems. IEEE Trans. Pattern Anal. Mach. Intell. (PAMI) 24(3), 289–300 (2002). https://doi.org/10.1109/34.990132
18. Khan, S.D., Ullah, H.: A survey of advances in vision-based vehicle re-identification. Comput. Vis. Image Underst. 182, 50–63 (2019). https://doi.org/10.1016/j.cviu.2019.03.001
19. Kratz, L., Nishino, K.: Tracking with local spatio-temporal motion patterns in extremely crowded scenes. In: 2010 IEEE Computer Society Conference on Computer Vision and Pattern Recognition (CVPR), pp. 693–700 (2010). https://doi.org/10.1109/CVPR.2010.5540149
20. Leal-Taixé, L., Milan, A., Schindler, K., Cremers, D., Reid, I., Roth, S.: Tracking the trackers: an analysis of the state of the art in multiple object tracking. arXiv (2017). https://doi.org/10.48550/ARXIV.1704.02781
21. Leal-Taixé, L., Canton-Ferrer, C., Schindler, K.: Learning by tracking: Siamese cnn for robust target association. In: 2016 IEEE Conference on Computer Vision and Pattern Recognition Workshops (CVPRW), pp. 418–425 (2016). https://doi.org/10.1109/CVPRW.2016.59
22. Liu, C., Yao, R., Rezatofighi, S.H., Reid, I., Shi, Q.: Model-free tracker for multiple objects using joint appearance and motion inference. IEEE Trans. Image Process. 29, 277–288 (2020). https://doi.org/10.1109/TIP.2019.2928123
23. Lu, Z., Rathod, V., Votel, R., Huang, J.: Retinatrack: online single stage joint detection and tracking. In: 2020 IEEE/CVF Conference on Computer Vision and Pattern Recognition (CVPR), pp. 14656–14666 (2020). https://doi.org/10.1109/CVPR42600.2020.01468
24. Luiten, J., Osep, A., Dendorfer, P., Torr, P., Geiger, A., Leal-Taixé, L., Leibe, B.: Hota: a higher order metric for evaluating multi-object tracking. International Journal of Computer Vision (IJCV), pp. 548–578 (2021). https://doi.org/10.1007/s11263-020-01375-2
25. Luo, W., Kim, T.K., Stenger, B., Zhao, X., Cipolla, R.: Bi-label propagation for generic multiple object tracking. In: 2014 IEEE Conference on Computer Vision and Pattern Recognition (CVPR), pp. 1290–1297 (2014). https://doi.org/10.1109/CVPR.2014.168
26. Luo, W., Xing, J., Milan, A., Zhang, X., Liu, W., Kim, T.K.: Multiple object tracking: a literature review. Artif. Intell. 293, 103448 (2021). https://doi.org/10.1016/j.artint.2020.103448
27. Milan, A., Leal-Taixé, L., Reid, I., Roth, S., Schindler, K.: Mot16: a benchmark for multi-object tracking. arXiv (2016).https://doi.org/10.48550/ARXIV.1603.00831
28. Milan, A., Roth, S., Schindler, K.: Continuous energy minimization for multitarget tracking. IEEE Trans. Pattern Anal. Mach. Intell. (PAMI) 36(1), 58–72 (2014). https://doi.org/10.1109/TPAMI.2013.103
29. Milan, A., Schindler, K., Roth, S.: Challenges of ground truth evaluation of multi-target tracking. In: 2013 IEEE Conference on Computer Vision and Pattern Recognition Workshops (CVPRW), pp. 735–742 (2013). https://doi.org/10.1109/CVPRW.2013.111

30. Pang, J., et al.: Quasi-dense similarity learning for multiple object tracking. In: 2021 IEEE/CVF Conference on Computer Vision and Pattern Recognition (CVPR), pp. 164–173 (2021). https://doi.org/10.1109/CVPR46437.2021.00023
31. Pedersen, M., Haurum, J.B., Hein Bengtson, S., Moeslund, T.B.: 3D-ZEF: a 3D zebrafish tracking benchmark dataset. In: 2020 IEEE/CVF Conference on Computer Vision and Pattern Recognition (CVPR). pp. 2423–2433 (2020). https://doi.org/10.1109/CVPR42600.2020.00250
32. Pellegrini, S., Ess, A., Schindler, K., van Gool, L.: You'll never walk alone: modeling social behavior for multi-target tracking. In: 2009 IEEE 12th International Conference on Computer Vision (ICCV), pp. 261–268 (2009). https://doi.org/10.1109/ICCV.2009.5459260
33. Peng, J., et al.: Chained-tracker: chaining paired attentive regression results for end-to-end joint multiple-object detection and tracking. In: Vedaldi, A., Bischof, H., Brox, T., Frahm, J.-M. (eds.) ECCV 2020. LNCS, vol. 12349, pp. 145–161. Springer, Cham (2020). https://doi.org/10.1007/978-3-030-58548-8_9
34. Pérez-Escudero, A., Vicente-Page, J., Hinz, R.C., Arganda, S., De Polavieja, G.G.: idtracker: tracking individuals in a group by automatic identification of unmarked animals. Nat. Methods 11(7), 743–748 (2014). https://doi.org/10.1038/nmeth.2994
35. Ristani, E., Solera, F., Zou, R., Cucchiara, R., Tomasi, C.: Performance measures and a data set for multi-target, multi-camera tracking. In: Hua, G., Jégou, H. (eds.) ECCV 2016. LNCS, vol. 9914, pp. 17–35. Springer, Cham (2016). https://doi.org/10.1007/978-3-319-48881-3_2
36. Schneider, S., Taylor, G.W., Kremer, S.C.: Similarity learning networks for animal individual re-identification - beyond the capabilities of a human observer. In: 2020 IEEE Winter Applications of Computer Vision Workshops (WACVW), pp. 44–52 (2020). https://doi.org/10.1109/WACVW50321.2020.9096925
37. Schneider, S., Taylor, G.W., Linquist, S., Kremer, S.C.: Past, present and future approaches using computer vision for animal re-identification from camera trap data. Methods Ecol. Evol. 10(4), 461–470 (2019). https://doi.org/10.1111/2041-210X.13133
38. Stadler, D., Beyerer, J.: Improving multiple pedestrian tracking by track management and occlusion handling. In: 2021 IEEE/CVF Conference on Computer Vision and Pattern Recognition (CVPR), pp. 10953–10962 (2021). https://doi.org/10.1109/CVPR46437.2021.01081
39. Stiefelhagen, R., Bernardin, K., Bowers, R., Garofolo, J., Mostefa, D., Soundararajan, P.: The CLEAR 2006 evaluation. In: Stiefelhagen, R., Garofolo, J. (eds.) CLEAR 2006. LNCS, vol. 4122, pp. 1–44. Springer, Heidelberg (2007). https://doi.org/10.1007/978-3-540-69568-4_1
40. Sun, P., et al.: Scalability in perception for autonomous driving: waymo open dataset. In: 2020 IEEE/CVF Conference on Computer Vision and Pattern Recognition (CVPR), pp. 2443–2451 (2020). https://doi.org/10.1109/CVPR42600.2020.00252
41. Uhlmann, J.K.: Algorithms for multiple-target tracking. Am. Sci. 80(2), 128–141 (1992)
42. Voigtlaender, P., et al.: Mots: multi-object tracking and segmentation. In: 2019 IEEE/CVF Conference on Computer Vision and Pattern Recognition (CVPR), pp. 7934–7943 (2019). https://doi.org/10.1109/CVPR.2019.00813
43. Wojke, N., Bewley, A., Paulus, D.: Simple online and realtime tracking with a deep association metric. In: 2017 IEEE International Conference on Image Processing (ICIP), pp. 3645–3649 (2017). https://doi.org/10.1109/ICIP.2017.8296962

44. Xiang, Y., Alahi, A., Savarese, S.: Learning to track: online multi-object tracking by decision making. In: 2015 IEEE International Conference on Computer Vision (ICCV), pp. 4705–4713 (2015). https://doi.org/10.1109/ICCV.2015.534
45. Xu, J., Cao, Y., Zhang, Z., Hu, H.: Spatial-temporal relation networks for multi-object tracking. In: 2019 IEEE/CVF International Conference on Computer Vision (ICCV), pp. 3987–3997 (2019). https://doi.org/10.1109/ICCV.2019.00409
46. Ye, M., Shen, J., Lin, G., Xiang, T., Shao, L., Hoi, S.C.H.: Deep learning for person re-identification: a survey and outlook. IEEE Trans. Pattern Anal. Mach. Intell. (PAMI) **44**(6), 2872–2893 (2022). https://doi.org/10.1109/TPAMI.2021.3054775
47. Yin, J., Wang, W., Meng, Q., Yang, R., Shen, J.: A unified object motion and affinity model for online multi-object tracking. In: 2020 IEEE/CVF Conference on Computer Vision and Pattern Recognition (CVPR), pp. 6767–6776 (2020). https://doi.org/10.1109/CVPR42600.2020.00680
48. Zhang, Y., Wang, C., Wang, X., Zeng, W., Liu, W.: FairMOT: on the fairness of detection and re-identification in multiple object tracking. Int. J. Comput. Vision **129**(11), 3069–3087 (2021). https://doi.org/10.1007/s11263-021-01513-4
49. Zhou, X., Koltun, V., Krähenbühl, P.: Tracking objects as points. In: Vedaldi, A., Bischof, H., Brox, T., Frahm, J.-M. (eds.) ECCV 2020. LNCS, vol. 12349, pp. 474–490. Springer, Cham (2020). https://doi.org/10.1007/978-3-030-58548-8_28

How to Synthesize a Large-Scale and Trainable Micro-Expression Dataset?

Yuchi Liu[1]([✉]) [iD], Zhongdao Wang[2] [iD], Tom Gedeon[1] [iD], and Liang Zheng[1] [iD]

[1] Australian National University, Canberra, Australia
{yuchi.liu,tom.gedeon,liang.zheng}@anu.edu.au
[2] Tsinghua University, Beijing, China
wcd17@mails.tsinghua.edu.cn
https://github.com/liuyvchi/MiE-X

Abstract. This paper does not contain technical novelty but introduces our key discoveries in a data generation protocol, a database and insights. We aim to address the lack of large-scale datasets in micro-expression (MiE) recognition due to the prohibitive cost of data collection, which renders large-scale training less feasible. To this end, we develop a protocol to automatically synthesize large scale MiE training data that allow us to train improved recognition models for real-world test data. Specifically, we discover three types of Action Units (AUs) that can constitute trainable MiEs. These AUs come from real-world MiEs, early frames of macro-expression videos, and the relationship between AUs and expression categories defined by human expert knowledge. With these AUs, our protocol then employs large numbers of face images of various identities and an off-the-shelf face generator for MiE synthesis, yielding the MiE-X dataset. MiE recognition models are trained or pre-trained on MiE-X and evaluated on real-world test sets, where very competitive accuracy is obtained. Experimental results not only validate the effectiveness of the discovered AUs and MiE-X dataset but also reveal some interesting properties of MiEs: they generalize across faces, are close to early-stage macro-expressions, and can be manually defined. (This work was supported by the ARC Discovery Early Career Researcher Award (DE200101283) and the ARC Discovery Project (DP210102801).)

Keywords: Micro-expression · Action units · Facial expression generation

1 Introduction

Micro-Expressions (MiEs) are transient facial expressions that typically last for 0.04 to 0.2 s [9,23]. Unlike conventional facial expressions (or Macro-Expressions, MaEs) that last for longer than 0.2 seconds, MiEs are involuntary. They are difficult to be pretended, and thus more capable of revealing people's genuine

---

Supplementary Information The online version contains supplementary material available at https://doi.org/10.1007/978-3-031-20074-8_3.

S. Avidan et al. (Eds.): ECCV 2022, LNCS 13668, pp. 38–55, 2022.
https://doi.org/10.1007/978-3-031-20074-8_3

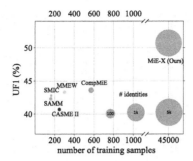

Fig. 1. We present a large-scale synthetic MiE training dataset, MiE-X, created by the proposed protocol. It is two magnitudes larger than existing real MiE recognition datasets in terms of number of MiE samples and number of identities. Compared with existing real-world MiE datasets, MiE-X allows the MiE classifier [21] to achieve consistently higher accuracy evaluated on the real-world MiE dataset CompMiE [33].

emotions. MiE recognition underpins various valuable applications such as lie detection, criminal justice and psychological consultation.

The difficulty in collecting and labeling MiEs poses huge challenges in building MiE recognition datasets [3]. First, collecting *involuntary* MiEs is strenuous, even in a controlled environment [3]. Unlike MaEs, which participants can easily "perform", MiEs are too vague and subtle to precisely interpret. Second, correctly labeling MiEs is difficult. It usually requires domain knowledge from psychology experts, and oftentimes even experts cannot guarantee a high accuracy of annotations. As a consequence, scales of existing MiE recognition datasets are severely limited: they typically consist of a few hundreds of samples from dozens of identities (refer Fig. 1 for an illustrative summary). Shortage of training data would compromise the development of MiE recognition algorithms.

In this work, we aim to address the data shortage issue by proposing a useful protocol for *synthesizing* MiEs. This protocol has three steps. First, we conveniently obtain a large number of faces from existing face datasets. Second, we compute sensible AUs. Third, we employ a conditional generative model to "add" MiEs onto these faces. Conditional facial expression generation is a well-studied problem, and we adopt an off-the-shelf algorithm, GANimation [29], which employs coefficients of Action Units (AUs) as the generative conditions.

At the core of this synthesis protocol, we contribute in finding three types of AUs helpful in the second step. The **first** type, intuitively, are AUs extracted from real-world, annotated MiE datasets. Specifically, we extract AU coefficients of annotated MiE samples and use these AU coefficients as conditions to transfer corresponding MiEs to faces of other identities. The **second** type are AUs extracted from early-stage MaEs. The formation of macro-expressions consists of a process of facial muscle movements, and we find early stages of these movements usually share similar values of AUs to those of MiEs. The **third** type are AU combinations given by expert knowledge. For example, human observations suggest that AU12 (`Lip Corner Puller`) is often activated when the subject is "happy", so we set AU12 to be slightly greater than 0 when synthesizing a "happy" MiE. In this regard, this work is an early attempt to explore the underlying *computational* mechanism of micro-expressions, and it would be of value for the community facilitating the understanding of micro-expressions and the design of learning algorithms.

Using the proposed three types of AUs, our protocol allows us to create a large-scale synthetic dataset, **MiE-X**, to improve the accuracy of data-driven MiE recognition algorithms. As shown in Fig. 1, MiE-X is two orders of magnitude larger than existing real-world datasets. Notably, despite being synthetic, MiE-X can be effectively used to train MiE recognition models. When the target application has the same label space as MiE-X, we can directly use MiE-X to train a recognition model, achieving competitive results to those trained on real-world data. Otherwise, MiE-X can be used for pre-training, and its pre-training quality outperforms ImageNet [6]. Our experiment shows that MiE-X consistently improves the accuracy of frame-based MiE recognition methods and a state-of-the-art video-based method.

- We introduce a large-scale MiE training dataset created by a useful protocol, for training MiE recognition models. The database will be released.
- We identify three types of AUs that allow for synthesizing trainable MiEs in the protocol. They are: AUs extracted from real MiEs, mined from early-stage of MaEs and provided by human experts of facial expressions.
- Our experiments reveal interesting properties of MiEs: they generalize across identities, are close to early-stage MaEs, and can be manually defined.

2   Related Work

Facial Micro-expression Recognition. Many MiE recognition systems use handcrafted features, such as 3DHOG [27], FDM [38] and LBP-TOP [42] descriptors. They describe facial texture patterns. Variants and extensions of LBP-TOP have also been proposed [13,14,37]. Afterwards, deep learning based solutions were proposed [11,16,17,20,24,25]. Petal *et al.* [24] use the VGG model pretrained on ImageNet [6] and perform fine-tuning for MiE recognition. In ELRCN [16], the network input is enriched by the concatenation of the RGB image, optical flow and derivatives of optical flow [34]. To reduce computation cost and prevent overfitting, it is common to use representative frames as model input. For example, Peng *et al.* [26] and Li *et al.* [19] select the onset frame, apex frame and offset frame in each micro-expression video. Branches [21] uses the onset and apex frame as model input. Following this practice, we focus on synthesising representative frames for MiEs.

Deep Learning From Synthetic Data. Deep learning using synthetic data has drawn recent attention. Many works use graphic engines to generate virtual data and corresponding ground truths. Richter *et al.* [30] use a 3D game engine to simulate training images with pixel-level label maps for semantic segmentation. In [32], prior human knowledge is used to constrain the distribution of synthetic target data. Tremblay *et al.* [35] randomize the parameters of

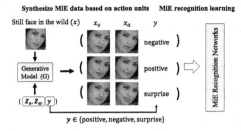

Fig. 2. Overview of the proposed protocol for synthesizing our MiE recognition dataset. We generate MiE samples (a triplet containing onset frame $\mathbf{x_o}$, apex frame $\mathbf{x_a}$ and the emotion label y) with a pretrained GANimation [29] model G, faces in the wild and AU vectors $(\mathbf{z}_o, \mathbf{z}_a)$ introduced in Sect. 4.2.

the simulator to force the model to handle large variations in object detection. Learning-based approaches [15,31,40] try to find the best parameter ranges in simulators so that the domain gap between generated content and the real-world data is minimized. Another line of works uses generative adversarial networks (GANs) to generate images for learning. For example, the label smoothing regularization technique is adopted for generated images [43]. Camstyle [44] trains camera-to-camera person appearance translation to generate new training data. CYCADA [12] reconstructs images and introduces semantic segmentation loss on these generated images to maintain consistent semantics.

Action Units (AUs) in Facial Analysis. Action Units are defined according to the Facial Action Coding System (FACS) [8], which categorizes the fundamental facial muscles movements by their appearance on the face. Correlations between Action Units and emotions are widely discussed in literature [7,9,28]. This work uses such correlations where we look for and validate effective AUs as generative conditions to synthesis realistic and trainable MiEs.

3 Preliminaries

MiE recognition aims to classify emotion categories of a given face video clip. In practice, the video clips should be first processed by a *spotting* algorithm to determine the onset (starting time), apex (time of the highest expression intensity) and offset (ending time) frames. In this work, we assume all data have been processed by spotting algorithms [3,33] and focus on the recognition task.

Emotion labels in existing datasets are usually different, ranging from 3 to 8 categories. In this work, we use a unified and balanced label space to synthesize MiE-X. Specifically, during synthesis, we choose the most basic categories (`positive`, `negative`, `surprise`, as defined in MEGC) and merge other emotion labels into these three categories. If the label space in the target dataset is different from MiE-X, we need to fine-tune the model further.

In the following sections, when mentioning action units (AUs), we by default refer to the AU coefficient vector $\mathbf{z} \in [0,1]^d$. Each dimension in vector $\mathbf{z}$ indicates the intensity of a specific action unit. There are usually $d = 17$ dimensions [1,29].

4   Synthesizing Micro-Expressions

4.1   The Proposed Protocol

Given a face image, an emotion label $y \in \{\texttt{positive}, \texttt{negative}, \texttt{surprise}\}$, and an onset-apex AU pair $(\mathbf{z_o}, \mathbf{z_a})$, our protocol uses GANimation [29] to generate an MiE sample consisting of two representative frames (refer Fig. 2).

First, we randomly select an "in-the-wild" face image $\mathbf{x}$ from a large pool of identities (we use the EmotionNet [10] dataset) as the template face upon which we add MiEs. Then, we find an onset AU $\mathbf{z_o}$, an apex AU $\mathbf{z_a}$, and the corresponding emotion label y. A triplet of $(\mathbf{z_o}, \mathbf{z_a}, y)$ could be computed from three different sources, which are elaborated in Sect. 4.2. Finally, a conditional generative model G is employed to transfer the onset and apex AUs to the template face $\mathbf{x}$, producing an onset frame $\mathbf{x_o} = G(\mathbf{x}, \mathbf{z_o})$ and an apex frame $\mathbf{x_a} = G(\mathbf{x}, \mathbf{z_a})$, whose emotion label is y (same as the label of $\mathbf{x}$). Here, we adopt GANimation [29] as G, which identity-preserving and only changes facial muscle movements. Training details of GANimation are provided in supp. materials.

Please note that the protocol uses existing techniques and that we do not claim it as our main finding. Also note that we do not synthesize entire video sequences of MiEs, but only the onset (the beginning) and apex (most intensive) frames. The motivation is three-fold. First, a full MiE clip may contain up to 50 frames, so a dataset of full MiEs can be 25 times as large as a dataset of representative frames (2 frames per MiE). Second, recent literature on MiE recognition (*e.g.*, [19,21,26]) indicate that using representative frames suffice to obtain very competitive accuracy. Last, synthesizing video sequences in a realistic way is much more challenging than static frames, requiring smooth motions and consistency over time. We leave video-level MiE generation to future work.

4.2   Major Finding: Action Units that Constitute Trainable MiEs

In the protocol, we make the major contribution in finding three sources of AUs that are most helpful to define the onset and apex AUs, to be described below.

AUs Extracted From Real MiEs. An intuitive source of MiE AUs are, of course, real-world MiE data. Assume we have a real-world MiE dataset with M MiE videos, where each video is annotated with the onset and apex frames. For each video, we extract the onset and apex AUs and record the emotion label, forming a set of AUs $\mathcal{Z}^{\mathrm{MiE}} = \{(\mathbf{z_o}^{(m)}, \mathbf{z_a}^{(m)}\}_{m=1}^M$ and labels $\mathcal{Y}^{\mathrm{MiE}} = \{y^{(m)}\}_{m=1}^M$. Here, AU coefficients are extracted with the OpenFace toolkit [1]. When synthesizing MiEs with a certain emotion category based on $\mathbf{z}^{\mathrm{MiE}}$, we randomly draw a pair of AUs from $\mathcal{Z}^{\mathrm{MiE}}$ that have the desired emotion label.

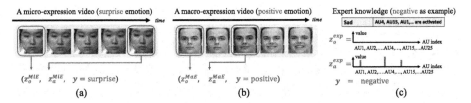

Fig. 3. Examples of how to compute $\mathbf{z}^{\mathrm{MiE}}$, $\mathbf{z}^{\mathrm{MaE}}$ and $\mathbf{z}^{\mathrm{exp}}$. **(a)** We compute $\mathbf{z}^{\mathrm{MiE}}$ from representative frames (*i.e.*, the onset frame and the apex frame) of real-world MiE videos. **(b)** Early frames in real-world macro-expression videos are used to obtain $\mathbf{z}^{\mathrm{MaE}}$. The hyperparameters of choosing the frame indices are selected in Sect. 5.3. **(c)** We specify an emotion type (*e.g.*, sad) and then the AU distribution from the Expert Mapping table [7], which determine the activated AU entries. Then we assign activated AU entries with intensity values (red bars) and others with 0. The hyperparameters of constraining intensity values are experimented in Sect. 5.3.

Discussion. Despite being a valuable source of MiEs AUs, existing real-world MiE data are severely limited in size, so $\mathcal{Z}^{\mathrm{MiE}}$ is far from being sufficient. If we had more MiE data, it would be interesting to further study whether our method can synthesize a better dataset. At this point, to include more MiE samples in our synthetic training set, we find another two AU sources below.

AUs Extracted From Early-Stage of Real MaEs. Abundant MaE videos exist in the community, which have a similar set of emotion labels with MiE datasets. These MaE videos usually start from a neutral expression, leak subtle muscle movements in early frames, and present obvious expressions later. In our preliminary experiments, we observe that AUs extracted from early frames of MaE videos have similar values as those of MiE clips. This suggests that MiEs and *early-stage* of MaEs have similar intensities in muscle movements, rendering the latter a potential source to simulate MiEs.

In leveraging MaE videos as an AU source, we regard the first frame of MaE clips, which usually has a neutral expression, as our onset frame. The selection of the apex frame is more challenging. However, we empirically observe that existing MaE clips usually present MiE-liked AU intensities in the first half of the video. Therefore, we use two hyperparameters to find the apex frame approximately. Suppose an MaE clip has n frames. An apex frame is randomly drawn from frame index $\lfloor \alpha \times n \rfloor$, where $\lfloor \cdot \rfloor$ rounds a number down to the nearest integer. The selections of α and β are briefly discussed in Sect. 5.3.

Discussion. Different MaE datasets may be different in the frame index of the onset and apex frames, so in practice we need to do a rapid scanning to roughly know them. But this process is usually quick, and importantly reliable, because 1) a certain dataset usually follows a stable pattern in terms of the onset and apex positions and 2) onset and apex states usually last for a while. As such, while this procedure requires a bit manual work, it is still very valuable considering the gain it brings (large-scale MiE data).

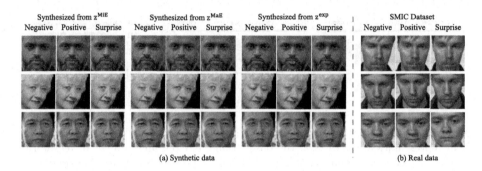

| Synthesized from z^MiE | Synthesized from z^MaE | Synthesized from z^exp | SMIC Dataset |
| Negative Positive Surprise | Negative Positive Surprise | Negative Positive Surprise | Negative Positive Surprise |

(a) Synthetic data   (b) Real data

Fig. 4. Examples of MiE apex frames from **(a)** synthetic (MiE-X) and **(b)** real-world (the SMIC dataset [18]) micro-expression data. In (a), we show three columns of synthesized MiE apex frames corresponding to three types of Action Units (AUs), *i.e.*, $\mathbf{z}^{\mathrm{MiE}}, \mathbf{z}^{\mathrm{MaE}}, \mathbf{z}^{\mathrm{exp}}$ described in Sect. 4.2. Both real-world data and synthetic data the shown under classes labels `positive`, `negative`, and `surprise`.

AUs Defined by Expert Knowledge. Studies reveal strong relationships between AUs and emotions [7,9,28]. Some explicitly summarize the posterior probability of each AU entry being activated for each emotion label: $P(z_i > 0|y)$, where z_i indicates the i-th entry of AU vector $\mathbf{z}$. The posterior probabilities, for simplicity, are usually modeled with a Bernoulli distribution [7], *i.e.*, $P(z_i > 0|y) = p$ and $P(z_i = 0|y) = 1 - p$. We find the AU distribution summarized by experts another effective source of AUs for synthesizing trainable MiEs.

We use the expert knowledge mainly to find the apex AUs, where we resort to a mapping table [7] that describes the aforementioned posterior probabilities. Given an emotion label, when generating the apex AUs $\mathbf{z}_a^{\mathrm{exp}}$, we first decide which entries in $\mathbf{z}_a^{\mathrm{exp}}$ should be activated (> 0) by drawing samples from the Bernoulli distribution. We then determine the intensities of the activated entries by randomly sampling from a uniform distribution with a fixed interval $[\mu, \nu]$. The selection of hyperparameters μ, ν is briefly discussed in Sect. 5.3. On the other hand, for the onset AUs $\mathbf{z}_o^{\mathrm{exp}}$, we set them to zero vectors, which means that no action unit is activated, thus representing a neutral face. Examples of how to compute the above three types of AUs are provided in Fig. 3.

Discussion. We use three basic expression categories (`positive`, `negative`, `surprise`) when synthesizing MiE-X, because these three classes form the largest common intersection between the label sets from the three sources. If we could have more fine-grained label space, it would be interesting to further explore how the label space affects the training quality of MiE-X.

4.3   The MiE-X Dataset

With the above three types of AUs and a large pool of in-the-wild faces, we eventually are able to synthesize a large-scale MiE recognition dataset, coined

MiE-X. MiE-X contains 5,000 identities, each with 9 MiE samples[1] , resulting in 45,000 samples in total. To our knowledge, MiE-X is the first large-scale MiE dataset and is more than two orders of magnitude larger than existing real-world MiE datasets. Visualization of the generated apex frames in MiE-X is provided in Fig. 4; comparisons with existing MiE datasets are illustrated in Fig. 1.

The strength of MiE-X as training data comes from its diversity in identity and MiE patterns[2]. For instance, it contains 5,000 human identities, encouraging models to learn identity-invariant expression features. At the same time, the three sources of AUs are complementary, provide a wide range of AU values, and sometimes have random AU perturbations. MiE-X alleviates overfitting risks and allows algorithms to consistently improve their accuracy.

5 Experiment

5.1 Experimental Setups

Baseline Classifiers. Two image-based MiE recognition methods are mainly evaluated in this paper: the **Branches** [21] and **ApexME** [19]. Both are trained for 80 epochs. More details are provided in supplementary materials.

Real-World Datasets. We report experimental results on commonly-used real-world datasets: **CompMiE** [33], **MMEW** and **SAMM**. CompMiE is proposed by the MiE recognition challenge MEGC2019 [33] which merges three existing real MiE datasets into one. The three component datasets are CASME II [39], SAMM [4,5], and SMIC [18], respectively. CompMiE has the same label space (Sect. 4.2) as MiE-X and consists of 442 samples from 68 subjects in total. MMEW and SAMM have 234 and 72 samples, respectively, and their label spaces are different with MiE-X[3]. The MaE dataset **CK+** [22] is a commonly used real-world MaE dataset containing 327 videos. Its label space is also merged into the same one as CompMiE. When generating MiE-X (see Sect. 4), we extract $\mathbf{z}^{\mathrm{MiE}}$ and $\mathbf{z}^{\mathrm{MaE}}$ from CompMiE and CK+, respectively.

Evaluation Protocols. We use subject-wise k-fold cross-validation, commonly performed in the community [3,16,19]. Specifically, when real-world data are used in testing, we split them into k subsets. Each time, we use $k-1$ subsets for training and the rest 1 subset for testing. The average accuracy of the k tests is reported. For CompMiE, $k = 3$; for MMEW and SAMM, $k = 5$. To evaluate the effectiveness of MiE-X, we replace real training sets (*i.e.*, $k-1$ subsets) with MiE-X when MiE-X is used for direct deployment. Note that, for each fold, MiE-X samples whose AUs (*i.e.*, $\mathbf{z}^{\mathrm{MiE}}$) are computed from real MiE samples in the

---

[1] For each ID and each of the three classes `positive`, `negative`, and `surprise`, we generate three MiE samples corresponding to three types of AUs. Each sample has an onset and an apex frames, totaling 9 MiE samples and 18 frames per ID.

[2] We also acknowledge GANimation that provides us with realistic facial images.

[3] Label space of MMEW: `happiness`, `surprise`, `anger`, `disgust`, `fear`, `sadness`; Label space of SAMM: `happiness`, `surprise`, `anger`, `disgust`, `fear`.

Table 1. Effectiveness of MiE-X in model (pre-)training. Models are pre-trained using MiE-X or other real-world datasets and then fine-tuned on real-world training data *i.e.*, CompMiE, or the combination of CompMiE and CK+ [22]. UF1 (%) and UAR (%) are reported on the CompMiE dataset after three-fold cross-validation. ApexME [19] and Branches [21] are used as baselines. We observe consistent accuracy improvement when models are pre-trained with MiE-X. In addition, when directly deploying the MiE-X pretrained model, the accuracy is also competitive.

| Pre-training | Fine-tuning | | ApexME [19] | | Branches [21] | |
MiE data	CompMiE	CK+	UF1	UAR	UF1	UAR
–	✓		41.8 ± 0.7	41.9 ± 0.7	43.6 ± 0.5	44.6 ± 0.6
–	✓	✓	45.0 ± 0.5	45.5 ± 1.0	45.2 ± 0.5	47.0 ± 0.6
SMIC [18]	✓		45.0 ± 1.7	44.8 ± 1.9	42.8 ± 0.8	41.4 ± 0.9
CASME [39]	✓		44.0 ± 1.2	45.1 ± 0.5	40.7 ± 0.9	41.4 ± 0.9
SAMM [5]	✓		43.7 ± 0.7	42.8 ± 0.5	42.3 ± 1.4	42.9 ± 1.7
MMEW [3]	✓		43.3 ± 0.8	44.4 ± 1.2	43.3 ± 1.3	44.1 ± 1.5
MiE-X			45.2 ± 0.5	46.3 ± 0.5	47.7 ± 0.5	48.9 ± 0.8
MiE-X	✓		46.9 ± 0.9	**48.3 ± 0.9**	50.7 ± 0.9	52.1 ± 1.4
MiE-X	✓	✓	**47.0 ± 0.8**	48.2 ± 0.4	**52.3 ± 0.7**	**52.3 ± 0.4**

test subset will not be used in training. If MiE-X is used for pre-training, where a fine-tuning stage is required, the $k - 1$ subsets will be used for fine-tuning. Other real-world datasets (*e.g.*, MMEW, SMIC) are also used for pre-training to form comparisons with MiE-X[4] Experiment is categorized as follows.

- Pre-training with MiE-X (or other competing datasets) and fine-tuning on target training set. We adopt this setting especially when the source domain has a different label space from the target domain.
- Training (or fine-tuning) with MiE-X (or other competing datasets) followed by direct model deployment. If the target domain and training dataset share the same label space, models obtained from the training set can be directly used for inference on the target test set.

Metrics. We mainly use unweighted F1-score (UF1) and unweighted average recall (UAR) [33]. UF1 and UAR indicate the average F1-score and recall, respectively, over all classes. We also report the conventional recognition rate on the MMEW [3] and SAMM [4] datasets to compare with the state of the art. By default, we run each experiment (k-fold cross-validation) 3 times and report the mean and standard variance of the results in the last epoch. Moreover, we provide the best accuracy among all epochs for reference (Table 2).

---

[4] We discard those samples in real-world datasets that overlap with the test subset.

5.2   Effectiveness of the Synthetic Database

Effectiveness of MiE-X in Training Models for Direct Deployment.
MiE-X has the same label space with CompMiE. So models trained with MiE-X can be directly evaluated on the CompMiE. In Table 1, ApexME and Branches trained with MiE-X alone produce an UF1 of 45.2% and 47.7%, respectively, which outperforms the training set composed of CompMiE and CK+.

Effectiveness of MiE-X in Model Pre-training. First, when using MiE-X for model pre-training, we observe consistent improvement over not using it (Table 1). For example, when we perform fine-tuning on CompMiE using the ApexME method, pre-training with MiE-X brings 5.1% and 7.1% improvement in UF1 and UAR, respectively, over not using MIE-X. Second, we compare MiE-X with existing datasets (*i.e.*, SMIC, CASME, SAMM, and MMEW) of their effectiveness as a pre-training set, on which we train the baseline MiE classifiers (*i.e.*, ApexME, Branches). We do three-fold cross-validation on CompMiE. For each fold, we use the dataset (e.g., SMIC) we would like to evaluate as the pre-training data. Samples are removed from the training set if they also appear in the test subset of CompMiE in the current fold. Then we fine-tune the model on the training subset of CompMiE. Results are shown in both Table 1 and Fig. 1. We observe that the model pre-trained on MiE-X significantly outperforms those pre-trained on other datasets. For instance, when we pre-train Branches on MiE-X, the final fine-tuning results on CompMiE in UF1 and UAR are 7.4% and 8.0% higher than using MMEW as the pre-training data. This phenomenon validates the effectiveness of our dataset and the proposed synthesis procedure.

Positioning Within the State of the Art. We follow a recent survey [3] and compare with the state of the art on two datasets, MMEW [3] and SAMM [4], all under 5-fold cross validation. Results are summarized in Table 2. We re-implemented three baselines (ApexME, Branches and DTSCNN), pretrained on either ImageNet or MiE-X. To pretrain the video-base method DTSCNN, we use a simple variant of MiE-X where each sample has multiple frames. Specifically, when computing z^{MiE} and z^{MaE}, we extract AUs for all the frames between the onset and apex frames. All these extracted AUs are used for frame generation. For z^{exp}, we linearly interpolate 8 AU vectors between the onset and apex AU vectors, thus generating 10 frames per sample.

Table 2 clearly informs us that MiE-X pre-training improves the accuracy of all the three methods. Importantly, when MiE-X is used for pre-training, MiE recognition accuracy is very competitive: DTSCNN achieves accuracy (best epoch) of 74.3 ± 0.5 % and 73.9 ± 0.9 % on MMEW and SAMM, respectively.

Table 2. Comparison with the state-of-the-art MiE recognition methods on MMEW and SAMM datasets. We re-implement ApexME, Branches and DTSCNN, which are pretrained with either ImageNet or MiE-X (grey). We report the mean recognition accuracy (%) and standard variance. † donates vide-based methods. "Last" means test result in the last epoch, and "Best" refers to the best accuracy among all epochs.

Methods	MMEW		SAMM	
	Last	Best	Last	Best
FDM [38]	34.6	–	34.1	–
LBP-TOP [42]	38.9	–	37.0	–
DCP-TOP [2]	42.5	–	36.8	–
ApexME [19]	48.5 ± 0.6	58.3 ± 0.9	41.3 ± 0.6	54.9 ± 0.7
ApexME + **MiE-X**	55.9 ± 2.0	61.4 ± 0.8	46.4 ± 0.7	60.3 ± 1.1
Branches [21]	50.1 ± 0.6	58.3 ± 0.6	44.5 ± 0.7	53.3 ± 0.5
Branches + **MiE-X**	56.8 ± 1.1	61.5 ± 1.0	48.7 ± 1.0	56.3 ± 0.8
TLCNN† [36]	–	69.4	–	73.5
DTSCNN† [25]	60.9 ± 1.3	71.1 ± 1.1	51.6 ± 1.8	60.6 ± 1.1
DTSCNN† + **MiE-X**	63.1 ± 1.0	74.3 ± 0.5	55.5 ± 1.4	73.9 ± 0.9

5.3   Further Analysis

All experiments in this section are performed on the Branches baseline [21].

Comparisons of Various AU Combinations. Figure 5 evaluates various AU combinations on CompMiE. We have the following observations. **First**, none of the three types of AUs are dispensable. We observe that the best recognition accuracy is obtained when all three types of AUs are used, which outperforms training with CompMiE+CK+ by 1.7% and 2.0% in UF1 and UAR, respectively. Importantly, if we remove any single type of AUs, the UF1 and UAR scores decrease. For example, when removing z^{MiE}, z^{MaE}, z^{exp} one at a time, the decrease in UF1 score is 1.6%, 1.0% and 1.6%, respectively.

Second, using two types of AUs outperforms using only a single type with statistical significance. For example, when using z^{MiE} and z^{MaE}, UF1 is higher than using z^{MaE} alone by 2.15%. In fact, the three AU types come from distinct and trustful sources, allowing them to be complementary and effective. This also explains why all three AU types are better than any combination of two.

Third, when using a single type of AUs, we find z^{MaE} or z^{exp} produces much higher UF1 and UAR than z^{MiE}. Their superiority could be explained by their diversity. Compared with z^{MiE}, MiEs generated from z^{MaE} and z^{exp} are much more diverse. Specifically, when constructing z^{MaE}, the index of apex frame is randomly drawn from a range $\lfloor \alpha \times n \rfloor$ and $\lfloor \beta \times n \rfloor$. Similarly, the randomness of AU intensities is also introduce by hyperparameter μ and ν when generating z^{exp}. In contrast, the index of the apex frame is fixed when constructing z^{MiE}.

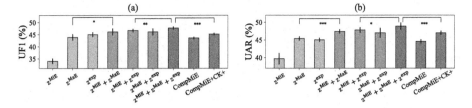

Fig. 5. Comparing training effectiveness of real-world data and various synthetic datasets sourced from different combinations of AUs. We compare UF1 **(a)** and UAR **(b)** on CompMiE. "n.s." means the difference is not statistically significant (*i.e.*, p-value > 0.05). $*$ denotes statistically significant (*i.e.*, $0.01 < p$-value < 0.05). $**$ and $***$ mean statistically very significant (*i.e.*, $0.001 < p$-value < 0.01) and statistically extremely significant (*i.e.*, p-value < 0.001), respectively. We observe decreased accuracy if we remove any of the three types of AUs. When all the three types are used for database creation, both UF1 and UAR exceed results obtained by training on real-world data, with very high statistical confidence.

Lastly, we compare results that employ two real-world training datasets. The first is CompMiE, described as in Sect. 5.1, and the second is a combination of CompMiE and CK+. It is shown that CompMiE + CK+ outperforms CompMiE by an obvious margin, suggesting that *early-stage of MaEs highly correlate with MiEs*. These results motivated us to mine effective AUs ($\mathbf{z}^{\text{MaE}}$) from MaEs.

Impact of the Number of AUs, IDs and MiE Samples in MiE-X. For MiE-X, the IDs, AUs and MiE samples are all important, and we now investigate how their quantities influence MiE recognition accuracy by creating MiE-X variants with different numbers of IDs, AU triplets and samples. Here, please note that the diversity is highly relevant to the number of distinct IDs/AUs/samples, so sometimes we use number and diversity interchangeably. When studying AU and ID diversity, we set the AU combination to be $\mathbf{z}^{\text{MaE}} + \mathbf{z}^{\text{exp}}$ because their diversity can be easily changed by specifying the number of sampling times from the uniform distributions (refer Sect. 4.2). When investigating the number of MiE samples, we use all three types of AUs.

To evaluate the influence of **AU** diversity, we set the number of MiE samples and IDs to 30,000 and 5,000 (6 samples per ID), respectively in all the dataset variations. The AU diversity can be customized by allowing multiple identities to share the same AU triple. Specifically, the number of AU triplets is set to 4,000, 6,000, 10,000, 30,000 and From the experimental results in Fig. 6 (a), we observe the effectiveness of synthetic data generally increases when AU diversity is improved. For example, the UF1 score increases by 1.8%, when the number of distinct AU triplets increases from 4,000 to 10,000. When the number of AUs is greater than 10,000, the curve reaches saturation.

To study the diversity of **IDs**, we fix the number of MiE samples and AU triplets in MiE-X to be 30,000. We set the ID number as 700, 1,000, 1,700, and 5,000, achieved by randomly selecting face images from the EmotionNet [10]

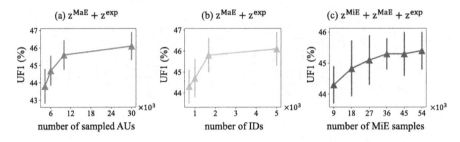

Fig. 6. (a)-(b): Impact of the number of AU triplets (a), IDs (b) and MiE samples (c). In (a)-(b), we use $\mathbf{z}^{\mathrm{MaE}}$ and $\mathbf{z}^{\mathrm{exp}}$ for database synthesis, while in (c) all three types AUs are used. We employ the Branches method [21]. When we gradually increase the numbers, the three-fold cross validation accuracy (UF1, %) on CompMiE first improves and then remains stable in all the three subfigures.

dataset[5]. In this experiment, an ID generates more than 6 MiE samples using AU triplets randomly drawn from the pool of 30,000. Results in Fig. 6 (b) show that more IDs leads to a higher recognition accuracy. For example, UF1 of synthetic dataset increases from 44.4% to 45.8% when the number of IDs increases from 700 to 1,700. When the number of IDs exceeds 1,700, the curve becomes stable.

To study the impact of the number of **MiE samples**, we fix the number of AU triplets to 9,000 and the number of IDs to 1,000. We then gradually increase the generated samples from 9,000 to 54,000 by reusing more AU triplets on each ID. Experimental results are shown in Fig. 6 (c). We find the effectiveness of the synthetic training set generally increases when more samples are included and that curve becomes flat when the number of samples are greater than 36k. For example, the UF1 is improved by 1.0%, when the number of samples increases from 9k to 36k. When the number of samples increases from 36k to 54k, there is a slight UF1 improvement of 0.2%. This observation is expected because when the number of IDs and AUs are fixed, the total information contained in the dataset is constrained. From the above experiments, we conclude that MiE-X benefits from more AUs, IDs and samples within a certain range.

Impact of Face Poses. We use 5,000 IDs with frontal faces to synthesize a training set variant which is compared with MiE-X composed of faces of various poses. To find the frontal faces, we manually select 10 frontal faces in the EmotionNet dataset as queries and for each search for 500 faces with similar facial landmarks detected by a pretrained MTCNN landmark detector [41].

Table 3. Performance comparison between training with and without side faces. Evaluation is on the CompMiE dataset.

	$w/$ side	w/o side
UF1 (%)	47.7 ± 0.5	47.4 ± 0.8

Table 3 summarizes the results on CompMiE, where we do not observe obvious difference between the two training sets. This can possibly be explained by

---

[5] Note that each image in EmotionNet usually denotes a different identity.

the fact that real-world MiE datasets mostly contain frontal faces collected in laboratory environments. Therefore, pose variance in MiE-X may not significantly influence performance on existingtests. Nevertheless, we speculate using various poses to generate MiE-X would benefit MiE recognition in uncontrolled environments.

Analysis of Other Hyperparameters. Due to the lack of validation data in real-world MiE datasets, we mostly used prior knowledge and intuition to choose the hyperparameters. Specifically, we chose $\alpha = 0.3$, $\beta = 0.5$ and $\mu = 0.1$, $\nu = 0.3$ in experiments. Here, we briefly analyze these two sets of hyperparameters involved in the AU computation on CompMiE using cross-validation. $[\alpha, \beta]$ is the interval from which the apex frames for computing $\mathbf{z}^{\mathrm{MaE}}$ are randomly selected. Specifically, we analyze three options: ($\alpha = 0.1$, $\beta = 0.3$), ($\alpha = 0.3$, $\beta = 0.5$) and ($\alpha = 0.5$, $\beta = 0.7$). The number of identities is 5,000. Recognition accuracy of the three options is given by Fig. 7 (a), where $\alpha = 0.3$, $\beta = 0.5$ produces the highest UF1 score. This result is in accordance with our intuition: the first 30% to 50% frames of an MaE would be more similar to an MiE.

$[\mu, \nu]$ is the interval from which the intensities of expert-defined AUs are uniformly sampled. Similarly, we analyze three options, *i.e.*, ($\mu = 0.1$, $\nu = 0.3$), ($\mu = 0.3$, $\nu = 0.5$) and ($\mu = 0.5$, $\nu = 0.7$). This is inspired by observing AU coefficients of real MiEs: the intensity of each action unit is not large, *i.e.*, < 0.7 in most cases, because micro-expressions have subtle facial muscle movements. Results are shown in Fig. 7 (b): the intensity range $[0.1, 0.3]$ is superior. Because the highest value of an MaE AU is 1.0, the value of $[\mu, \nu]$ delivers another intuitive message: facial AU intensities of MiEs are around 10% to 30% those of MaEs.

5.4 Understanding of MiEs: A Discussion

MiEs Generalize Across Faces. AUs extracted from real MiEs provide closest resemblance to true MiEs and are thus indispensable. These AUs $\mathbf{z}^{\mathrm{MiE}}$ are generalizable because they can be transplanted to faces of different identities. The fact that a higher number of face identities generally leads to a higher accuracy indicates the benefit of adding AUs $\mathbf{z}^{\mathrm{MiE}}$ to sufficiently many faces to improve MiE recognition towards identity invariance.

Early-Stage MaEs Resemble Real MiEs. To our knowledge, we make very early attempt to leverage MaEs for MiE generation. Although the two types of facial expressions differ significantly in their magnitude of facial movement, we find AUs in initial stages of MaEs are effective approximations to those in MiEs.

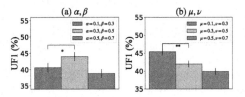

Fig. 7. Impact of hyperparameters in computing $\mathbf{z}^{\mathrm{MaE}}$ and $\mathbf{z}^{\mathrm{exp}}$. UF1 (%) on the CompMiE dataset is reported in each sub-figure. **(a):** MiE-X is composed by $\mathbf{z}^{\mathrm{MaE}}$ only. Three groups of α and β values are tested. **(b):** MiE-X is made from $\mathbf{z}^{\mathrm{exp}}$ only. Three groups of μ and ν are investigated. * and ** have the same meaning as Fig. 5.

Expert Knowledge is Transferable to MiEs. While AUs annotated by experts are used to describe MaEs, we find expert AUs with reduced magnitude are effective in synthesizing MiEs. We therefore infer from a computer vision viewpoint that MiEs are related to normal expressions but with lower intensity. Moreover, by examining the complementary nature of the three types of AUs, we infer that expert knowledge adds some useful computational cues, which do not appear in MaEs and real MiEs but can be humanly defined. Nevertheless, our work is limited in that the psychological aspects of MiEs are not considered, which will be studied in future with cross-disciplinary collaborations.

6   Conclusion

This paper addresses the data lacking problem in MiE recognition. An important contribution is the introduction of a large-scale synthetic dataset, MiE-X, with standard emotion labels to improve MiE model training. In the synthesis protocol, we feed faces in the wild, desired emotion labels and AU triplets (our focus) to a generation model. Specifically, sourced from real MiEs, early-stage MaEs, and expert knowledge, three types of AUs are identified as useful and complementary to endorse an effective protocol. This understanding of the role of AUs in effective MiE synthesis is another contribution of this work. Experiment on real-world MiE datasets indicates MiE-X is a very useful training set: models (pre-)trained with MiE-X consistently outperform those (pre-)trained on real-world MiE data. In addition, this paper reveals some interesting computational properties of MiEs, which would be of value for further investigation.

References

1. Baltrusaitis, T., Zadeh, A., Lim, Y.C., Morency, L.P.: Openface 2.0: facial behavior analysis toolkit. In: 2018 13th IEEE International Conference on Automatic Face & Gesture Recognition (FG 2018), pp. 59–66. IEEE (2018)
2. Ben, X., Jia, X., Yan, R., Zhang, X., Meng, W.: Learning effective binary descriptors for micro-expression recognition transferred by macro-information. Pattern Recogn. Lett. **107**, 50–58 (2018)
3. Ben, X., et al.: Video-based facial micro-expression analysis: a survey of datasets, features and algorithms. IEEE Trans. Pattern Anal. Mach. Intell. **44**, 5826–5846 (2021)
4. Davison, A., Merghani, W., Yap, M.: Objective classes for micro-facial expression recognition. J. Imaging **4**(10), 119 (2018)
5. Davison, A.K., Lansley, C., Costen, N., Tan, K., Yap, M.H.: SAMM: a spontaneous micro-facial movement dataset. IEEE Trans. Affect. Comput. **9**(1), 116–129 (2016)
6. Deng, J., Dong, W., Socher, R., Li, L.J., Li, K., Fei-Fei, L.: Imagenet: a large-scale hierarchical image database. In: 2009 IEEE Conference on Computer Vision and Pattern Recognition, pp. 248–255. IEEE (2009)
7. Du, S., Tao, Y., Martinez, A.M.: Compound facial expressions of emotion. Proc. Natl. Acad. Sci. **111**(15), E1454–E1462 (2014)
8. Eckman, P., Friesen, W.: Facial action coding system (facs): a technique for the measurement of facial action. A8@ 5 **3**, 56–75 (1978)

9. Ekman, P., Rosenberg, E.L.: What the face reveals: Basic and applied studies of spontaneous expression using the Facial Action Coding System (FACS). Oxford University Press, USA (1997)
10. Fabian Benitez-Quiroz, C., Srinivasan, R., Martinez, A.M.: Emotionet: an accurate, real-time algorithm for the automatic annotation of a million facial expressions in the wild. In: Proceedings of the IEEE Conference on Computer Vision and Pattern Recognition, pp. 5562–5570 (2016)
11. Hao, X., Tian, M.: Deep belief network based on double weber local descriptor in micro-expression recognition. In: Park, J.J.J.H., Chen, S.-C., Raymond Choo, K.-K. (eds.) MUE/FutureTech -2017. LNEE, vol. 448, pp. 419–425. Springer, Singapore (2017). https://doi.org/10.1007/978-981-10-5041-1_68
12. Hoffman, J., et al.: Cycada: cycle-consistent adversarial domain adaptation. arXiv preprint arXiv:1711.03213 (2017)
13. Huang, X., Wang, S.J., Zhao, G., Piteikainen, M.: Facial micro-expression recognition using spatiotemporal local binary pattern with integral projection. In: Proceedings of the IEEE International Conference on Computer Vision Workshops, pp. 1–9 (2015)
14. Huang, X., Zhao, G., Hong, X., Zheng, W., Pietikäinen, M.: Spontaneous facial micro-expression analysis using spatiotemporal completed local quantized patterns. Neurocomputing **175**, 564–578 (2016)
15. Kar, A., et al.: Meta-sim: learning to generate synthetic datasets. arXiv preprint arXiv:1904.11621 (2019)
16. Khor, H.Q., See, J., Phan, R.C.W., Lin, W.: Enriched long-term recurrent convolutional network for facial micro-expression recognition. In: 2018 13th IEEE International Conference on Automatic Face & Gesture Recognition (FG 2018), pp. 667–674. IEEE (2018)
17. Kim, D.H., Baddar, W.J., Ro, Y.M.: Micro-expression recognition with expression-state constrained spatio-temporal feature representations. In: Proceedings of the 24th ACM international conference on Multimedia, pp. 382–386. ACM (2016)
18. Li, X., Pfister, T., Huang, X., Zhao, G., Pietikäinen, M.: A spontaneous micro-expression database: inducement, collection and baseline. In: 2013 10th IEEE International Conference and Workshops on Automatic Face and Gesture Recognition (FG), pp. 1–6. IEEE (2013)
19. Li, Y., Huang, X., Zhao, G.: Can micro-expression be recognized based on single apex frame? In: 2018 25th IEEE International Conference on Image Processing (ICIP), pp. 3094–3098. IEEE (2018)
20. Liong, S.T., Gan, Y., Yau, W.C., Huang, Y.C., Ken, T.L.: Off-apexnet on micro-expression recognition system. arXiv preprint arXiv:1805.08699 (2018)
21. Liu, Y., Du, H., Liang, Z., Gedeon, T.: A neural micro-expression recognizer. In: 2019 14th IEEE International Conference on Automatic Face & Gesture Recognition (FG 2019). IEEE (2019)
22. Lucey, P., Cohn, J.F., Kanade, T., Saragih, J., Ambadar, Z., Matthews, I.: The extended cohn-kanade dataset (ck+): A complete dataset for action unit and emotion-specified expression. In: 2010 IEEE Computer Society Conference on Computer Vision and Pattern Recognition-Workshops, pp. 94–101. IEEE (2010)
23. Matsumoto, D., Yoo, S.H., Nakagawa, S.: Culture, emotion regulation, and adjustment. J. Pers. Soc. Psychol. **94**(6), 925 (2008)
24. Patel, D., Hong, X., Zhao, G.: Selective deep features for micro-expression recognition. In: 2016 23rd International Conference on Pattern Recognition (ICPR), pp. 2258–2263. IEEE (2016)

25. Peng, M., Wang, C., Chen, T., Liu, G., Fu, X.: Dual temporal scale convolutional neural network for micro-expression recognition. Front. Psychol. **8**, 1745 (2017)

26. Peng, M., Wu, Z., Zhang, Z., Chen, T.: From macro to micro expression recognition: Deep learning on small datasets using transfer learning. In: 2018 13th IEEE International Conference on Automatic Face & Gesture Recognition (FG 2018), pp. 657–661. IEEE (2018)

27. Polikovsky, S., Kameda, Y., Ohta, Y.: Facial micro-expressions recognition using high speed camera and 3d-gradient descriptor (2009)

28. Polikovsky, S., Kameda, Y., Ohta, Y.: Facial micro-expression detection in hi-speed video based on facial action coding system (FACS). IEICE Trans. Inf. Syst. **96**(1), 81–92 (2013)

29. Pumarola, A., Agudo, A., Martinez, A.M., Sanfeliu, A., Moreno-Noguer, F.: GAN-imation: anatomically-aware facial animation from a single image. In: Ferrari, V., Hebert, M., Sminchisescu, C., Weiss, Y. (eds.) ECCV 2018. LNCS, vol. 11214, pp. 835–851. Springer, Cham (2018). https://doi.org/10.1007/978-3-030-01249-6_50

30. Richter, S.R., Vineet, V., Roth, S., Koltun, V.: Playing for data: ground truth from computer games. In: Leibe, B., Matas, J., Sebe, N., Welling, M. (eds.) ECCV 2016. LNCS, vol. 9906, pp. 102–118. Springer, Cham (2016). https://doi.org/10.1007/978-3-319-46475-6_7

31. Ruiz, N., Schulter, S., Chandraker, M.: Learning to simulate. arXiv preprint arXiv:1810.02513 (2018)

32. Sakaridis, C., Dai, D., Van Gool, L.: Semantic foggy scene understanding with synthetic data. Int. J. Comput. Vision **126**(9), 973–992 (2018)

33. See, J., Yap, M.H., Li, J., Hong, X., Wang, S.J.: Megc 2019-the second facial micro-expressions grand challenge. In: 2019 14th IEEE International Conference on Automatic Face & Gesture Recognition (FG 2019), pp. 1–5. IEEE (2019)

34. Shreve, M., Godavarthy, S., Goldgof, D., Sarkar, S.: Macro-and micro-expression spotting in long videos using spatio-temporal strain. In: Face and Gesture 2011, pp. 51–56. IEEE (2011)

35. Tremblay, J., et al.: Training deep networks with synthetic data: Bridging the reality gap by domain randomization. In: Proceedings of the IEEE Conference on Computer Vision and Pattern Recognition Workshops, pp. 969–977 (2018)

36. Wang, S.J., et al.: Micro-expression recognition with small sample size by transferring long-term convolutional neural network. Neurocomputing **312**, 251–262 (2018)

37. Wang, Y., See, J., Phan, R.C.-W., Oh, Y.-H.: LBP with six intersection points: reducing redundant information in LBP-TOP for micro-expression recognition. In: Cremers, D., Reid, I., Saito, H., Yang, M.-H. (eds.) ACCV 2014. LNCS, vol. 9003, pp. 525–537. Springer, Cham (2015). https://doi.org/10.1007/978-3-319-16865-4_34

38. Xu, F., Zhang, J., Wang, J.Z.: Microexpression identification and categorization using a facial dynamics map. IEEE Trans. Affect. Comput. **8**(2), 254–267 (2017)

39. Yan, W.J., et al.: Casme II: an improved spontaneous micro-expression database and the baseline evaluation. PLoS ONE **9**(1), e86041 (2014)

40. Yao, Y., Zheng, L., Yang, X., Naphade, M., Gedeon, T.: Simulating content consistent vehicle datasets with attribute descent. In: Vedaldi, A., Bischof, H., Brox, T., Frahm, J.-M. (eds.) ECCV 2020. LNCS, vol. 12351, pp. 775–791. Springer, Cham (2020). https://doi.org/10.1007/978-3-030-58539-6_46

41. Zhang, K., Zhang, Z., Li, Z., Qiao, Y.: Joint face detection and alignment using multitask cascaded convolutional networks. IEEE Signal Process. Lett. **23**(10), 1499–1503 (2016). https://doi.org/10.1109/LSP.2016.2603342

42. Zhao, G., Pietikainen, M.: Dynamic texture recognition using local binary patterns with an application to facial expressions. IEEE Trans. Pattern Anal. Mach. Intell. **29**(6), 915–928 (2007)
43. Zheng, Z., Zheng, L., Yang, Y.: Unlabeled samples generated by GAN improve the person re-identification baseline in vitro. In: Proceedings of the IEEE International Conference on Computer Vision, pp. 3754–3762 (2017)
44. Zhong, Z., Zheng, L., Zheng, Z., Li, S., Yang, Y.: Camera style adaptation for person re-identification. In: Proceedings of the IEEE Conference on Computer Vision and Pattern Recognition, pp. 5157–5166 (2018)

A Real World Dataset for Multi-view 3D Reconstruction

Rakesh Shrestha[1(✉)], Siqi Hu[2], Minghao Gou[2,3], Ziyuan Liu[2], and Ping Tan[1,2]

[1] Simon Fraser University, Burnaby, Canada
{rakeshs,pingtan}@sfu.ca
[2] Alibaba XR Lab, Hangzhou, China
[3] Shanghai Jiao Tong University, Shanghai, China
gmh2015@sjtu.edu.cn

Abstract. We present a dataset of 998 3D models of everyday tabletop objects along with their 847,000 real world RGB and depth images. Accurate annotation of camera pose and object pose for each image is performed in a semi-automated fashion to facilitate the use of the dataset in a myriad 3D applications like shape reconstruction, object pose estimation, shape retrieval *etc*. We primarily focus on learned multi-view 3D reconstruction due to the lack of appropriate real world benchmark for the task and demonstrate that our dataset can fill that gap. The entire annotated dataset along with the source code for the annotation tools and evaluation baselines is available at http://www.ocrtoc.org/3d-reconstruction.html.

Keywords: Dataset · Multi-view 3D reconstruction

1 Introduction

Deep learning has shown immense potential in the field of 3D vision in recent years, advancing challenging tasks such as 3D object reconstruction, pose estimation, shape retrieval, robotic grasping etc. But unlike for 2D tasks [10,23,28], large scale real world datasets for 3D object understanding is scarce. Hence, to allow for further advancement of state-of-the-art in 3D object understanding we introduce our dataset which consists of 998 high resolution, textured 3D models of everyday tabletop objects along with their 847K real world RGB-D images. Accurate annotation of camera pose and object pose is performed for each image. Figure 1 shows some sample data from our dataset.

We primarily focus on learned multi-view 3D reconstruction due to the lack of real world datasets for the task. 3D reconstruction methods [15,38,43,48,50] learn to predict 3D model of an object from its color images with known camera and object poses. They require large amount of training examples to be able to generalize to unseen images. While datasets like Pix3D [44], PASCAL3D+ [52]

Supplementary Information The online version contains supplementary material available at https://doi.org/10.1007/978-3-031-20074-8_4.

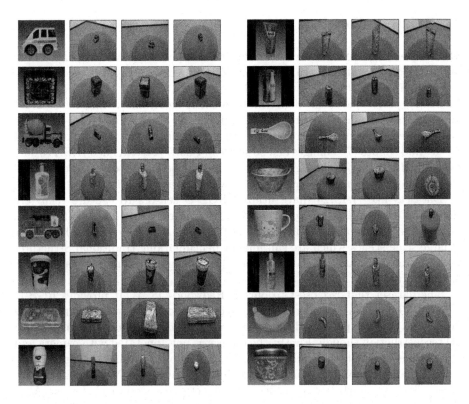

Fig. 1. Sample data from our dataset. From left to right, shown are visualization of textured 3D model, three sample multi-view images with wireframe object model superimposed based on annotated camera and object poses.

and ObjectNet3D [51] provide 3D models and real world images, they are mostly limited to a single image per model.

Existing multi-view 3D reconstruction methods [8,21,38,43,50] rely heavily on synthetic datasets, especially ShapeNet [6], for training and evaluation. There are a few works [25,38] utilizing real world datasets [7], but only for qualitative evaluation purpose, not for training or quantitative evaluation. To remedy this, we present our dataset and validate its usefulness by performing training as well as qualitative/quantitative evaluation with various state-of-the-art multi-view 3D reconstruction baselines.

The contributions of our work are as follows:

1. To the best our knowledge, our dataset is the first real world dataset that can be used for training and quantitative evaluation of learning-based multi-view 3D reconstruction algorithms.
2. We present two novel methods for automatic/semi-automatic data annotation. We will make the annotation tools publicly available to allow future extensions to the dataset.

2   Related Work

3D Shapes Dataset: Datasets like Princeton shape benchmark [42], FAUST [2], ShapeNet [6] provide a large collection of 3D CAD models of diverse objects, but without associated real world RGB images. PASCAL3D+ [52] and Object-Net3D [51] performed rough alignment between images from existing datasets and 3D models from online shape repositories. IKEA [27] also performed 2D-3D alignment between existing datasets but with finer alignment results on a smaller set of images and shapes (759 images and 90 shapes). Pix3D [44] extended IKEA to 10K images and 395 shapes through crowdsourcing and scanning some objects manually. These datasets mostly have single-view images associated with the shapes.

Datasets like [4,19,24] have utilized RGB-D sensors to capture relatively small number of objects and are mostly geared towards robot manipulation tasks rather than 3D reconstruction. Knapitsch *et al.* [22] provided a small number of large scale scenes which are suitable for benchmarking traditional Structure-from-Motion (SfM) and Multi-view Stereo (MVS) algorithms rather than learned 3D reconstruction.

The dataset that is closest to ours is Redwood-OS [7]. It provides RGB-D videos of 398 objects and their 3D scene reconstructions. There are several crucial limitations that has prevented widespread adoption of this dataset for multi-view 3D reconstruction though. Firstly, the dataset is not annotated with camera and object pose information. While the camera pose can be obtained using Simultaneous Localization and Mapping (SLAM) or Structure-from-Motion (SfM) techniques [3,11,32,40,41], obtaining accurate object poses is relatively harder. Also, the 3D reconstructions were performed on scene level rather than object level, making it difficult to directly use it for supervision of object reconstruction.

More recently, Objectron [1] and CO3D [37] have provided large scale video sequences of real world objects along with point clouds and object poses but without precise dense 3D models. We aim to tackle the shortcomings of the existing datasets and create a dataset that can effectively serve as a real world benchmark for learning-based multi-view 3D reconstruction models. Table 1 shows the comparison between the relevant datasets.

Table 1. Comparison between different datasets. Objectron and CO3D only provide point cloud models of the objects. Pix3D contains a mixture of scanned and CAD 3D models. PASCAL3D+ and ObjectNet3D only have rough object pose annotation, while the annotation is not provided in Redwood-OS. Only our dataset provides precisely scanned texture-mapped 3D models that are further registered to multi-view RGB images.

	Ours	Objectron	CO3D	Redwood-OS	Pix3D	IKEA	PASCAL3D+	ObjectNet3D
Multi-view images	✓	✓	✓	✓	✗	✗	✗	✗
Dense 3D models	✓	✗	✗	✓	✓	✓	✓	✓
Scanned 3D models	✓	✓	✓	✓	*	✗	✗	✗
Object pose annotation	✓	✓	✓	✗	✓	✓	*	*
Textured 3D models	✓	✗	✗	✗	✗	✗	✗	✗

3D Reconstruction: The methods in [15,16,34,45,48,54] predict 3D models from single-view color images. Since a single-view image can only provide a limited coverage of a target object, multi-view input is preferred in many applications. SLAM and Structure-from-Motion methods [3,11,32,40,41] are popular ways of performing 3D reconstruction but they struggle with poorly textured and non-Lambertian surfaces and require careful input view selection. Deep learning has emerged as a potential solution to tackle these issues. Early works like [8,17,21] used Recurrent Neural Networks (RNN) to perform multi-view 3D reconstruction. Pixel2Mesh++ [50] introduced cross-view perceptual feature pooling and multi-view deformation reasoning to refine an initial shape. MeshMVS [43] predicted a coarse volume from Multi-view Stereo depths first and then applied deformations on it to get a finer shape. All of these works were trained and evaluated exclusively on synthetic datasets due to the lack of proper real world datasets.

Some recent works like DVR [33], IDR [55], Neus [49], Geo-Neus [13] have focused on unsupervised 3D reconstruction with expensive per-scene optimization for each object. These methods encode each scene into separate Multi-layer Perceptron (MLP) that implicitly represents the scene as Signed Distance Function (SDF) or Occupancy Field. These works have obtained impressive results on small scale datasets of real world objects [20,53]. Our dataset can be further applied to evaluate these methods quantitatively on a much larger scale dataset.

3 Data Acquisition

Our data acquisition takes place in two steps. First, a detailed and textured 3D model of an object is generated using Shining3D® EinScan-SE 3D scanner. The scanner uses a calibrated turntable, a 1.3 Megapixel camera and visible light sources to obtain the 3D model of an object. Then, an Intel® RealSense™ LiDAR Camera L515 is used to record a RGB-D video sequence of the object on a round ottoman chair, capturing 360° view around the object. The video is recorded at 30 frames per second in HD resolution (1280 × 720). Figure 1 shows a number of 3D models and some sample color images from our dataset.

Datasets like [7,24] perform 3D model generation and video recording in one step by reconstructing the 3D scene captured by the images. The quality of the 3D models generated this way depends heavily on the trajectory of the camera and requires some level of expertise for data collection. Furthermore, these datasets use consumer grade cameras which cannot reconstruct fine details in the 3D geometry. We therefore use specialized hardware designed for high quality 3D scanning.

Another approach is to utilize 3D CAD models from online repositories and match them with real world 2D images, which are also mostly collected online [9, 27,51,52]. The downside of this approach is that it is difficult to ensure exact instance-level match between 3D models and 2D images. According to a survey conducted by Sun *et al.* [44], test subjects reported that only a small fraction of the images matched the corresponding shapes in datasets [51,52].

4 Data Annotation

The most challenging aspect of creating a large scale real world dataset for object reconstruction is generating ground truth annotations. Most learning-based 3D reconstruction methods require accurate camera poses as well as consistent object poses in the camera coordinate frame. While it is fairly easy to obtain the camera poses, obtaining accurate object poses is more challenging.

The methods in [44,52] perform object pose estimation by manually annotating corresponding keypoints in the 3D models and 2D images, and then performing 2D-3D alignment with the Perspective-n-Point (PnP) [14,26] and Levenberg-Marquardt algorithms [31]. Note that these datasets mostly contain a single image for each 3D model, which makes this kind of annotation feasible. In comparison, we aim to do this for video sequences with up to 1000 images, which could be manual intensive. Additionally, estimating object pose that is consistent over multi-view images will require keypoint matches at sub-pixel accuracy which is impossible by manual annotation.

On the other hand, the methods in [9,51] manually annotate the object pose directly by either trying to align the 3D model with the scene reconstruction [9] or the re-projected 3D model with 2D image [51]. We found these techniques to be inadequate for producing multi-view consistent object poses and therefore develop our own annotation systems.

4.1 Notations

We represent an object pose by $\xi \in SE(3)$ where $SE(3)$ is the 3D Special Euclidean Lie group [47] of 4×4 rigid body transformation matrix:

$$\xi = \begin{bmatrix} R & t \\ 0 & 1 \end{bmatrix} \tag{1}$$

where R is the 3×3 rotation matrix and t is the 3D translation vector.

We define object pose $_w\xi_{obj}$ as the transformation from canonical object frame (obj) to world frame (w). Similarly, the pose of the ith camera $_w\xi_{cam_i}$ represents the transformation from camera to world frame. The canonical object frame is centered at the object with z-axis pointing upwards along the gravity direction while the world frame is arbitrary (e.g. pose of the first camera).

We use pinhole camera model with camera intrinsics matrix K:

$$K = \begin{bmatrix} f_x & 0 & c_x \\ 0 & f_y & c_y \\ 0 & 0 & 1 \end{bmatrix} \tag{2}$$

where f_x and f_y are focal lengths and c_x and c_y principal points. These parameters are provided by the camera manufacturers.

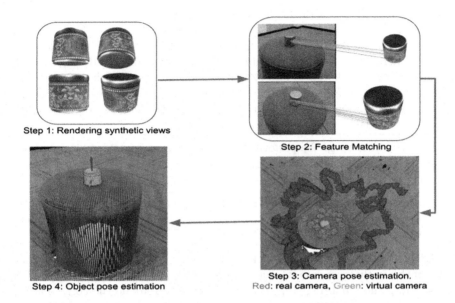

Step 1: Rendering synthetic views

Step 2: Feature Matching

Step 4: Object pose estimation

Step 3: Camera pose estimation.
Red: real camera, Green: virtual camera

Fig. 2. Texture-rich Object Annotation. *Step 1*: Synthetic views of the 3D model are rendered. *Step 2*: Feature matching is performed between/across real and synthetic images. *Step 3*: Pose of the real and virtual cameras are estimated. *Step 4*: Object pose is estimated by 7-DOF alignment between estimated and ground truth virtual camera poses.

The image coordinates p of a 3D point P_w in homogeneous world coordinate can be computed as:

$$p = K \left[R_i^T \ -R_i^T t_i \right] P_w \tag{3}$$

where R_i and t_i are the rotation and translation components of the camera pose.

The images taken from our RGB-D camera suffer from radial and tangential distortion. But for the purpose of annotation, we undistort the images so that the pinhole camera model holds.

We now present two methods for annotating our dataset depending on the texture-richness of the object being scanned: **Texture-rich Object Annotation** and **Textureless Object Annotation**.

4.2   Texture-rich Object Annotation

Since our 3D models have high-fidelity textures from our 3D scanner, we can utilize it to annotate the object pose in the recorded video sequence. We perform joint camera and object pose estimation by matching keypoints between images and 3D model to ensure camera and object pose consistency over multiple views. Figure 2 illustrates the annotation process. Following are the steps involved:

i. Rendering synthetic views of a 3D model: Instead of directly matching keypoints between a 3D model and 2D images, we instead render synthetic views of the 3D model and perform 2D keypoint matching. We use the physically based rendering engine, Pyrender [29], to render synthetic views. This allows us to utilize robust keypoint matching algorithms developed for RGB images. The virtual camera poses for rendering are randomly sampled around the object by varying the camera distance, and azimuth/elevation angles with respect to the object. We verify the quality of each rendered image by checking if there are sufficient keypoint matches against the real images. 150 images are rendered for each object model.

ii. Feature matching: We perform exhaustive feature matching across as well as within the real and synthetic images using neural network based feature matching technique SuperGlue [39].

iii. Camera pose estimation: Given the keypoint matches, we estimate the camera poses of both the real and virtual cameras in the same world coordinate frame using the SfM tool COLMAP [40, 41].

iv. Object pose estimation: Let $\{\hat{\xi}_i \mid i = 1, ..., 150\}$ be the ground truth poses of the virtual cameras in object frame (we keep track of the ground truth poses during the rendering step). Let $\{\xi_i \mid i = 1, ..., 150\}$ be the corresponding poses estimated by COLMAP in world frame. By aligning $\{\xi_i\}$ and $\{\hat{\xi}_i\}$ we can estimate the object pose. We use the Kabsch-Umeyama algorithm [46] under Random Sample Consensus (RANSAC) [5] scheme to perform a 7-DOF (pose + scale) alignment. Since COLMAP only uses 2D image information, its poses have arbitrary scale; hence we perform a 7-DOF alignment instead of 6-DOF to obtain metric scale. After applying the Kabsch-Umeyama algorithm we get 7-DOF transformation S in $Sim(3)$ Lie Group parameterized as:

$$S = \begin{bmatrix} sR_s & t_s \\ 0 & 1 \end{bmatrix} \tag{4}$$

The camera poses from COLMAP can then be transformed to metric scale pose:

$$_w\xi_{cam_i} = \begin{bmatrix} R_s R_i & sR_s t_i + t_s \\ 0 & 1 \end{bmatrix} \tag{5}$$

where R_i and t_i are the rotation and translation component of the camera poses from COLMAP.

Since the ground truth virtual camera poses $\{\hat{\xi}_i | i = 1, ..., 150\}$ are in object frame, the transformation in Eq. (5) will lead to camera poses in object frame i.e. $_w\xi_{obj} = \mathbb{I}$ where $\mathbb{I}$ is the 4×4 identity matrix.

4.3 Textureless Object Annotation

While the pipeline outlined in Sub-section 4.2 can accurately annotate texture-rich objects, it will fail for textureless objects since correct feature matches among the images cannot be established. To tackle this problem we develop another annotation system shown in Fig. 3 that can handle objects lacking good textures which consists of the following steps:

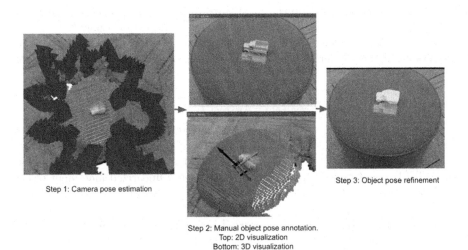

Fig. 3. Textureless object annotation. *Step 1*: Camera pose annotation (+ dense scene reconstruction). *Step 2*: Manual annotation of rough object pose where a transparent projection of the object model is superimposed over an RGB image for 2D visualization (top) and the 3D object is placed alongside the dense scene reconstruction for 3D visualization (bottom). *Step 3*: Object pose is refined such that the object projection overlaps with the ground truth mask (green). (Color figure online)

i. Camera pose estimation: Even when the object being scanned is textureless, our background has sufficient textures to allow successful camera pose estimation. We therefore utilize the RGB-D version of ORB-SLAM2 [32] to obtain the camera poses $\{_w\xi_{cam_i}\}$. Since it uses depth information alongside RGB, the poses are in metric scale.

ii. Manual annotation of rough object pose: We create an annotation interface as shown in Step 2 of Fig. 3 to estimate the rough object pose. To facilitate the annotation, we reconstruct the 3D scene using the RGB-D images and camera poses estimated in the previous step by employing Truncated Signed Distance Function (TSDF) fusion [56]. The object pose $_w\xi_{obj}$ is initialized to be a fixed distance in front of the first camera and the z-axis is aligned with the principle axis of the 3D scene found using Principal Component Analysis (PCA). An annotator can then update the 3 translation and 3 Euler angle (roll-pitch-yaw) components of the 6D object pose using keyboard to align the object model with the scene. In addition to the 3D scene, we also show the projection of the object model over an RGB image. The RGB image can be changed to verify the consistency of the object pose over multiple views.

iii. Object pose refinement: We find that obtaining accurate object pose through manual annotation is difficult, so we refine it further by aligning the projection of the 3D object model with ground truth object masks in different images. The ground truth object masks are obtained from Cascade Mask R-CNN [18] with a 152-layer ResNetXt backbone pretrained on ImageNet.

Let $_w\xi_{obj}$ be the rough object pose from manual annotation and $_w\xi_{cam_i}$ be the pose of the ith camera. The camera-centric object pose is represented as follows:

$$\xi = {}_{cam_i}\xi_{obj} = ({}_w\xi_{cam_i})^{-1} \times {}_w\xi_{obj} \qquad (6)$$

The transformation $\xi \in SE(3)$ is used to differentiably render [36] the object model onto the image of camera i to obtain the rendered object mask by applying the projection model of Eq. (3). Since direct optimization in the manifold space $SE(3)$ is not possible, we instead optimize the linearized increment of the manifold around ξ. This is a common technique in SLAM and Visual Odometry [11,32].

Let $\delta\xi \in \mathfrak{se}(3)$ represent the linearized increment of ξ belonging to the Lie algebra $\mathfrak{se}(3)$ corresponding to Lie Group $SE(3)$ [47]. The updated object pose is given by:

$$\xi' = \xi \times exp(\delta\xi) \qquad (7)$$

Here, exp represents the exponential map that transforms $\mathfrak{se}(3)$ to $SE(3)$. The object pose w.r.t. world frame can also be updated by right multiplication of the initial pose with $exp(\delta\xi)$.

We can optimize $\delta\xi$ in order to increase the overlap between the rendered mask M at ξ' and ground truth mask $\hat{M}$ using least-squares minimization of the mask loss:

$$\mathcal{L}_{mask} = mean(\|M \ominus \hat{M}\|_2) \qquad (8)$$

where $\ominus$ represents element-wise subtraction.

The optimization is performed using stochastic gradient descent for each camera for 30 iterations in PyTorch [35] library. Since $\delta\xi \in \mathfrak{se}(3)$ cannot represent large changes in pose, we update the pose $\xi \leftarrow \xi'$ every 30 iterations and relinearize $\delta\xi$ around the new ξ.

5   Dataset Statistics

We collected in total 998 objects. It typically takes about 20 min to scan the 3D model of an object and record a video, but about 2 h to register the scanned 3D model to all the video frames. Table 2 shows the category distribution of objects in our dataset along with the method used to annotate the object (texture-rich vs textureless). Each category in our dataset contains 39–115 objects, with average 67 objects per category. A majority of the objects (89%) were annotated using texture-rich pipeline which requires no user input. Table 3 shows the distribution of images over the categories. We have on average 56K images for each category.

Table 2. Annotation statistics.

Category	Bottle	Bowl	Cleanser	Cup	Eating utensils	Box	Plate	Toy animal	Toy car	Toy fruit	Toy aerocraft	Toy boat	Toy food	Toy figure	Misc	Total
Texture-rich annotation	60	61	51	39	27	83	45	69	115	12	61	39	82	95	51	890
Textureless annotation	0	11	0	12	14	0	6	32	0	33	0	0	0	0	0	108
Total	60	72	51	54	41	83	51	101	115	45	61	39	82	95	51	998

Table 3. Image distribution over the categories. Number of images in each category has been rounded to nearest 1000.

Bottle	Bowl	Cleanser	Cup	Eating utensils	Box	Plate	Toy animal	Toy car	Toy fruit	Toy aerocraft	Toy boat	Toy food	Toy figure	Misc	Total
54K	61K	44K	45K	33K	68K	45K	82K	104K	38K	51K	32K	69K	78K	43K	849K

6   Evaluation

To verify the usefulness of our dataset, we train and evaluate state-of-the-art multi-view 3D reconstruction baselines exclusively on our dataset. From each object, we randomly sample 100 different 3-view image tuples as the multi-view inputs. To ensure fair evaluation and avoid overfitting we split our dataset into training, testing and validation sets in approximately 70%-20%-10% ratio. The train-test-validation split is performed such that the distribution in each object category is also 70%-20%-10%. Only the data in training set is used to fit the baseline models while validation set is used to decide when to save the model parameters during training (known as checkpointing). All the evaluation results presented here are on the test set entirely held out during the training process.

6.1   Experiments

We evaluate our datasets with several recent learning-based 3D reconstruction baseline methods, including Multi-view Pixel2Mesh (MVP2M) [50], Pixel2Mesh++ (P2M++) [50], Multi-view extension of Mesh R-CNN [15] (MV M-RCNN) provided by [43], MeshMVS [43], DVR [33], IDR [55] and COLMAP [40,41]. We use the 'Sphere-Init' version of Mesh R-CNN and 'Back-projected depth' version of MeshMVS.

MVP2M pools multi-view image features and uses it to deform an initial ellipsoid to the desired shape. Pixel2Mesh++ deforms the mesh predicted by MVP2M by taking the weighted sum of deformation hypothesis sampled near the MVP2M mesh vertices. MV M-RCNN improves on MVP2M with a deeper backbone, better training recipe and higher resolution initial shape.

MeshMVS first predicts depth images using Multi-view Stereo and uses the depths to obtain a coarse shape which is deformed using similar techniques as MVP2M and MV MR-CNN. To train the depth prediction network of Mesh-MVS, we use depths rendered from the 3D object models since the recorded depth can be inaccurate or altogether missing at close distances. We also evaluate the baseline MeshMVS (RGB-D) which uses ground truth depths instead of predicted depths to obtain the coarse shape, essentially performing shape completion instead of prediction.

We also include per-scene optimized baselines DVR, IDR and COLMAP which do not require training generalizable priors with 3D supervision. DVR and IDR perform NeRF [30] like optimization to learn 3D models from images using implicit neural representation. COLMAP performs Structure-from-Motion (SfM) to first generate sparse point cloud which are further densified using Patch Match Stereo algorithm [41]. These methods require larger number of images to produce satisfactory results, hence we use 64 input images. Since the time required to reconstruct a scene is large for these methods, we evaluate these methods only on 30 scenes from the test set - 2 from each category.

All of the baselines require the object in the images to be segmented out of the background. We do this by rendering the 2D image masks of 3D object models using the annotated camera/object pose. Also, we transform the images to the size and intrinsics (Eq. (2)) required by the baselines before training/testing.

Metrics: We follow recent works [15, 43, 50] and choose F1-score (harmonic mean of precision and recall) at a thresholds $\tau = 0.3$ as our evaluation metric. Precision in this context is defined as the fraction of points in predicted model within τ distance from the ground truth points while recall is the fraction of point in ground truth model within τ distance from the predicted points.

We also report Chamfer Distance between a predicted model P and ground truth model Q which measures the mean distance between the closest pairs of points $\Lambda_{P,Q} = \{(p, arg\ min_q \|p - q\|) : p \in P, q \in Q\}$ in the two models:

$$\mathcal{L}_{\text{chamfer}}(P, Q) = |P|^{-1} \sum_{(p,q) \in \Lambda_{P,Q}} \|p - q\|^2 + |Q|^{-1} \sum_{(q,p) \in \Lambda_{Q,P}} \|q - p\|^2 \qquad (9)$$

We uniformly sample 10k points from predicted and ground truth meshes to evaluate these metrics. Following [12,15], we rescale the 3D models so that the longest edge of the ground truth mesh bounding box has length 10.

Results: The quantitative comparison results of different learning-based 3D reconstruction baselines on our dataset are presented in Table 4. Note that both training and testing set contain objects from all categories, but test F1-score on individual categories as well as over all categories are reported here. Figure 4 visualizes the shapes generated by different methods for qualitative evaluation.

We can see that overall Pixel2Mesh++ performs the best (barring MeshMVS RGB-D). This is contrary to the results on ShapeNet reported in [43] where MeshMVS performs the best. This can be attributed to the high depth prediction error of MeshMVS (average depth error is ∼6% of the total depth range). When predicted depth is replaced with ground truth depth, we indeed see a significant improvement in the performance of MeshMVS indicating that depth prediction is the main bottleneck in its performance.

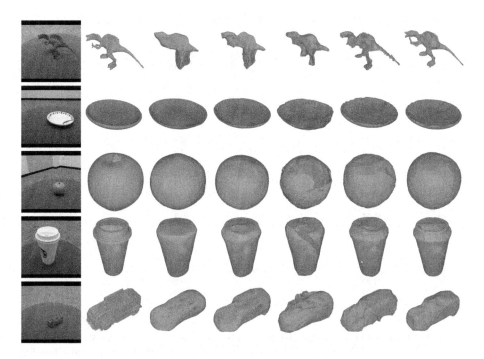

Fig. 4. Qualitative Evaluation. Left to right, shown are an input image, ground truth mesh, results from MVP2M, P2M++, MV M-RCNN, MeshMVS, and MeshMVS (RGB-D) respectively.

Table 5 shows the quantitative comparison between different unsupervised, per-scene optimized baselines. Here, IDR outperforms the other two baselines which is in line with the results presented in [55] on the DTU dataset. COLMAP performs worse than the rest because the textures on most of the objects are insufficient for dense reconstruction using Patch Match stereo leading to sparse and noisy results (Fig. 5).

Single Category Training: We compare the difference in the performance when each category is trained

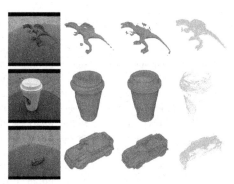

Fig. 5. Qualitative evaluation. Left to right: Input image, results from DVR, IDR, COLMAP.

and evaluated separately. In this case, there will be a different set of model parameters for each category. For these experiments we sample 200 different 3-view images as inputs from each scene. Table 6 shows the results for MV M-RCNN baseline when each category is trained separately versus when all are

Table 4. Quantitative comparison of state-of-the-art learning-based multi-view 3D reconstruction methods on our dataset. We report F1-score and Chamfer Distance on each semantic category as well as over all categories. The baseline MeshMVS (RGB-D) is not considered for highlighting the best performance since it uses ground truth depth as additional input.

Category	F1@0.3 ↑					Chamfer ↓				
	MVP2M	P2M++	MV M-RCNN	MeshMVS	MeshMVS (RGB-D)	MVP2M	P2M++	MV M-RCNN	MeshMVS	MeshMVS (RGB-D)
Bottle	74.86	**81.72**	67.12	55.35	94.11	0.23	**0.19**	1.78	0.53	0.06
Bowl	74.49	**80.60**	70.94	59.69	91.88	0.31	**0.23**	1.41	0.46	0.09
Box	61.32	**72.24**	67.90	59.28	91.04	0.39	**0.29**	0.84	0.48	0.10
Cleanser	68.69	**80.90**	72.37	64.01	95.97	0.30	**0.19**	0.96	0.39	0.04
Cup	65.31	**73.67**	66.00	52.41	87.40	0.39	**0.30**	1.59	0.64	0.12
Eating utensils	74.34	**88.40**	81.67	72.74	96.08	0.24	**0.12**	0.84	0.26	0.04
Plate	76.13	**81.65**	66.69	72.03	82.70	0.34	**0.26**	3.42	0.27	0.16
Toy boat	55.77	**65.57**	57.95	59.58	88.19	0.46	**0.37**	6.54	5.22	5.79
Toy aerocraft	52.85	**65.31**	56.91	64.94	91.13	0.73	0.55	2.91	**0.34**	0.08
Toy animals	49.46	**68.12**	64.07	59.89	93.53	0.81	0.51	0.94	**0.42**	0.06
Toy food	60.92	**71.24**	61.08	49.12	90.16	0.35	**0.25**	2.78	0.59	0.10
Toy fruit	56.78	**72.85**	59.84	41.28	88.86	0.55	**0.37**	3.77	0.87	0.11
Miscellaneous	56.54	**69.40**	66.34	61.57	91.40	0.63	**0.46**	0.96	0.47	0.11
Toy car	59.32	**71.33**	63.90	57.65	88.28	0.37	**0.25**	1.47	0.47	0.10
Toy figure	50.42	**68.32**	57.23	58.63	91.39	0.70	**0.46**	5.12	0.52	0.08
All	61.25	**73.30**	64.77	58.79	90.85	0.47	**0.33**	2.24	0.65	0.29

Table 5. Quantitative comparison of state-of-the-art NeRF-based 3D reconstruction methods along with COLMAP on our dataset. We report F1-score and Chamfer Distance on each semantic category as well as over all categories.

Category	F1@0.3 ↑			Chamfer ↓		
	DVR	IDR	COLMAP	DVR	IDR	COLMAP
Bottle	**92.95**	91.90	25.80	0.11	**0.09**	1.36
Bowl	69.20	**83.50**	14.72	**0.60**	0.62	1.81
Box	75.97	**78.95**	34.64	0.70	**0.22**	1.66
Cleanser	86.61	**98.32**	45.54	0.09	**0.02**	1.38
Cup	70.77	**78.69**	14.86	**0.64**	0.68	3.23
Eating utensils	87.93	**95.12**	41.34	0.08	**0.04**	1.10
Plate	62.46	75.01	**76.98**	0.50	0.45	**0.14**
Toy boat	86.71	**99.87**	45.66	0.08	**0.01**	0.37
Toy aerocraft	78.48	**99.07**	86.37	0.24	**0.02**	0.09
Toy animals	85.26	**90.61**	53.31	0.19	**0.11**	0.67
Toy food	86.06	**89.59**	34.74	0.12	**0.08**	0.96
Toy fruit	63.27	**90.25**	0.55	0.75	**0.09**	40.56
Miscellaneous	89.21	**89.31**	45.96	0.10	**0.09**	0.66
Toy car	76.25	**94.26**	27.24	0.24	**0.06**	1.32
Toy figure	82.25	**97.60**	49.39	0.16	**0.03**	0.32
All	79.56	**89.54**	39.81	0.30	**0.17**	3.71

trained together. We see that the performance is generally better when using all categories, showing that 3D reconstruction models can learn to generalize over multiple categories in our dataset.

Table 6. Single Vs All Category Training evaluation on MV M-RCNN baseline.

Category	F1@0.3 ↑		Chamfer ↓	
	All	Single	All	Single
Bottle	**67.12**	64.02	**1.78**	3.33
Bowl	**70.94**	53.41	**1.41**	27.37
Box	**67.90**	65.81	**0.84**	1.85
Cleanser	72.37	**73.00**	**0.96**	1.21
Cup	**66.00**	61.95	**1.59**	1.61
Eating utensils	**81.67**	77.06	0.84	**0.80**
Plate	**66.69**	62.15	**3.42**	50.72
Toy boat	**57.95**	55.39	**6.54**	10.21
Toy aerocraft	**56.91**	43.51	**2.91**	5.16
Toy animals	**64.07**	62.32	**0.94**	1.16
Toy food	61.08	**62.02**	**2.78**	4.92
Toy fruit	**59.84**	20.54	**3.77**	67.82
Miscellaneous	**66.34**	44.29	**0.96**	3.71
Toy car	63.90	**65.18**	1.47	**1.26**
Toy figure	**57.23**	50.81	**5.12**	9.0
Mean	**64.77**	58.15	**2.24**	10.57

7 Discussion

The results presented in Tables 4 and 6 as well as the qualitative evaluation of Fig. 4 show that the problem of generalizable multi-view 3D reconstruction is far from solved. While works like Pixel2Mesh++, Mesh R-CNN and MeshMVS have offered promising avenues for advancement of the state-of-the-art, more research is still needed in this direction. Table 5 and Fig. 5 shows the limitations of traditional 3D reconstruction methods like COLMAP. While more recent NeRF-based methods like DVR and IDR generates high quality reconstruction, their running time is at the order of 10 h in general and requires a larger number of input images (64 in our case). We hope that our dataset can serve as a challenging benchmark for these problems; aiding and inspiring future work in 3D shape generation.

8 Conclusion

We present a large scale dataset of 3D models and their real world multi-view images. Two methods were developed for annotation of the dataset which can provide high accuracy camera and object poses. Experiments show that our dataset can be used for training and evaluating multi-view 3D reconstruction methods, something that has been lacking in existing real world datasets.

References

1. Ahmadyan, A., Zhang, L., Ablavatski, A., Wei, J., Grundmann, M.: Objectron: A large scale dataset of object-centric videos in the wild with pose annotations. In: Proceedings of the IEEE/CVF Conference on Computer Vision and Pattern Recognition, pp. 7822–7831 (2021)
2. Bogo, F., Romero, J., Loper, M., Black, M.J.: Faust: Dataset and evaluation for 3d mesh registration. In: Proceedings of the IEEE conference on computer vision and pattern recognition, pp. 3794–3801 (2014)
3. Cadena, C., et al.: Past, present, and future of simultaneous localization and mapping: toward the robust-perception age. IEEE Trans. Rob. **32**(6), 1309–1332 (2016)
4. Calli, B., Walsman, A., Singh, A., Srinivasa, S., Abbeel, P., Dollar, A.M.: Benchmarking in manipulation research: Using the Yale-CMU-Berkeley object and model set. IEEE Robot. Autom. Mag. **22**(3), 36–52 (2015)
5. Cantzler, H.: Random sample consensus (RANSAC). Action and Behaviour, Division of Informatics, University of Edinburgh, Institute for Perception (1981)
6. Chang, A.X., et al.: ShapeNet: an information-rich 3d model repository. arXiv preprint arXiv:1512.03012 (2015)
7. Choi, S., Zhou, Q.Y., Miller, S., Koltun, V.: A large dataset of object scans. arXiv preprint arXiv:1602.02481 (2016)
8. Choy, C.B., Xu, D., Gwak, J.Y., Chen, K., Savarese, S.: 3D-R2N2: a unified approach for single and multi-view 3d object reconstruction. In: Leibe, B., Matas, J., Sebe, N., Welling, M. (eds.) ECCV 2016. LNCS, vol. 9912, pp. 628–644. Springer, Cham (2016). https://doi.org/10.1007/978-3-319-46484-8_38
9. Dai, A., Chang, A.X., Savva, M., Halber, M., Funkhouser, T., Nießner, M.: ScanNet: Richly-annotated 3d reconstructions of indoor scenes. In: Proceedings of the IEEE Conference on Computer Vision and Pattern Recognition, pp. 5828–5839 (2017)
10. Deng, J., Dong, W., Socher, R., Li, L.J., Li, K., Fei-Fei, L.: ImageNet: a large-scale hierarchical image database. In: 2009 IEEE Conference on Computer Vision and Pattern Recognition, pp. 248–255. IEEE (2009)
11. Engel, J., Schöps, T., Cremers, D.: LSD-SLAM: large-scale direct monocular SLAM. In: Fleet, D., Pajdla, T., Schiele, B., Tuytelaars, T. (eds.) ECCV 2014. LNCS, vol. 8690, pp. 834–849. Springer, Cham (2014). https://doi.org/10.1007/978-3-319-10605-2_54
12. Fouhey, D.F., Gupta, A., Hebert, M.: Data-driven 3d primitives for single image understanding. In: Proceedings of the IEEE International Conference on Computer Vision, pp. 3392–3399 (2013)
13. Fu, Q., Xu, Q., Ong, Y.S., Tao, W.: Geo-Neus: geometry-consistent neural implicit surfaces learning for multi-view reconstruction. arXiv preprint arXiv:2205.15848 (2022)
14. Gao, X.S., Hou, X.R., Tang, J., Cheng, H.F.: Complete solution classification for the perspective-three-point problem. IEEE Trans. Pattern Anal. Mach. Intell. **25**(8), 930–943 (2003)
15. Gkioxari, G., Malik, J., Johnson, J.: Mesh R-CNN. In: Proceedings of the IEEE/CVF International Conference on Computer Vision, pp. 9785–9795 (2019)
16. Groueix, T., Fisher, M., Kim, V.G., Russell, B.C., Aubry, M.: A papier-mâché approach to learning 3d surface generation. In: Proceedings of the IEEE Conference on Computer Vision and Pattern Recognition, pp. 216–224 (2018)

17. Gwak, J., Choy, C.B., Chandraker, M., Garg, A., Savarese, S.: Weakly supervised 3d reconstruction with adversarial constraint. In: 2017 International Conference on 3D Vision (3DV), pp. 263–272. IEEE (2017)
18. He, K., Gkioxari, G., Dollár, P., Girshick, R.: Mask R-CNN. In: Proceedings of the IEEE International Conference on Computer Vision, pp. 2961–2969 (2017)
19. Hodan, T., Haluza, P., Obdržálek, Š., Matas, J., Lourakis, M., Zabulis, X.: T-less: an RGB-D dataset for 6d pose estimation of texture-less objects. In: 2017 IEEE Winter Conference on Applications of Computer Vision (WACV), pp. 880–888. IEEE (2017)
20. Jensen, R., Dahl, A., Vogiatzis, G., Tola, E., Aanæs, H.: Large scale multi-view stereopsis evaluation. In: 2014 IEEE Conference on Computer Vision and Pattern Recognition, pp. 406–413. IEEE (2014)
21. Kar, A., Häne, C., Malik, J.: Learning a multi-view stereo machine. Adv. Neural. Inf. Process. Syst. **30**, 1–11 (2017)
22. Knapitsch, A., Park, J., Zhou, Q.Y., Koltun, V.: Tanks and temples: benchmarking large-scale scene reconstruction. ACM Trans. Graph. (ToG) **36**(4), 1–13 (2017)
23. Kuznetsova, A., et al.: The open images dataset v4. Int. J. Comput. Vision **128**(7), 1956–1981 (2020)
24. Lai, K., Bo, L., Ren, X., Fox, D.: A large-scale hierarchical multi-view RGB-D object dataset. In: 2011 IEEE International Conference on Robotics and Automation, pp. 1817–1824 (2011). https://doi.org/10.1109/ICRA.2011.5980382
25. Lei, J., Sridhar, S., Guerrero, P., Sung, M., Mitra, N., Guibas, L.J.: Pix2Surf: learning parametric 3D surface models of objects from images. In: Vedaldi, A., Bischof, H., Brox, T., Frahm, J.-M. (eds.) ECCV 2020. LNCS, vol. 12363, pp. 121–138. Springer, Cham (2020). https://doi.org/10.1007/978-3-030-58523-5_8
26. Lepetit, V., Moreno-Noguer, F., Fua, P.: EPNP: an accurate O(n) solution to the PNP problem. Int. J. Comput. Vision **81**(2), 155–166 (2009)
27. Lim, J.J., Pirsiavash, H., Torralba, A.: Parsing IKEA objects: fine pose estimation. In: 2013 IEEE International Conference on Computer Vision, pp. 2992–2999 (2013). https://doi.org/10.1109/ICCV.2013.372
28. Lin, T.-Y., et al.: Microsoft COCO: common objects in context. In: Fleet, D., Pajdla, T., Schiele, B., Tuytelaars, T. (eds.) ECCV 2014. LNCS, vol. 8693, pp. 740–755. Springer, Cham (2014). https://doi.org/10.1007/978-3-319-10602-1_48
29. Matl, M.: Pyrender (2019). https://github.com/mmatl/pyrender
30. Mildenhall, B., Srinivasan, P.P., Tancik, M., Barron, J.T., Ramamoorthi, R., Ng, R.: NeRF: representing scenes as neural radiance fields for view synthesis. In: Vedaldi, A., Bischof, H., Brox, T., Frahm, J.-M. (eds.) ECCV 2020. LNCS, vol. 12346, pp. 405–421. Springer, Cham (2020). https://doi.org/10.1007/978-3-030-58452-8_24
31. Moré, J.J.: The Levenberg-Marquardt algorithm: implementation and theory. In: Watson, G.A. (ed.) Numerical Analysis. LNM, vol. 630, pp. 105–116. Springer, Heidelberg (1978). https://doi.org/10.1007/BFb0067700
32. Mur-Artal, R., Montiel, J.M.M., Tardos, J.D.: ORB-SLAM: a versatile and accurate monocular slam system. IEEE Trans. Rob. **31**(5), 1147–1163 (2015)
33. Niemeyer, M., Mescheder, L., Oechsle, M., Geiger, A.: Differentiable volumetric rendering: learning implicit 3d representations without 3d supervision. In: Proceedings of the IEEE/CVF Conference on Computer Vision and Pattern Recognition, pp. 3504–3515 (2020)
34. Pan, J., Han, X., Chen, W., Tang, J., Jia, K.: Deep mesh reconstruction from single RGB images via topology modification networks. In: Proceedings of the IEEE International Conference on Computer Vision, pp. 9964–9973 (2019)

35. Paszke, A., et al.: Pytorch: an imperative style, high-performance deep learning library. In: Advances in Neural Information Processing Systems, vol. 32, pp. 8024–8035. Curran Associates, Inc. (2019)

36. Ravi, N., et al.: Accelerating 3d deep learning with pytorch3d. arXiv:2007.08501 (2020)

37. Reizenstein, J., Shapovalov, R., Henzler, P., Sbordone, L., Labatut, P., Novotny, D.: Common objects in 3d: Large-scale learning and evaluation of real-life 3d category reconstruction. In: International Conference on Computer Vision (2021)

38. Runz, M., et al.: Frodo: from detections to 3d objects. In: Proceedings of the IEEE/CVF Conference on Computer Vision and Pattern Recognition. pp. 14720–14729 (2020)

39. Sarlin, P.E., DeTone, D., Malisiewicz, T., Rabinovich, A.: Superglue: learning feature matching with graph neural networks. In: Proceedings of the IEEE/CVF Conference on Computer Vision and Pattern Recognition, pp. 4938–4947 (2020)

40. Schönberger, J.L., Frahm, J.M.: Structure-from-motion revisited. In: Conference on Computer Vision and Pattern Recognition (CVPR) (2016)

41. Schönberger, J.L., Zheng, E., Frahm, J.-M., Pollefeys, M.: Pixelwise view selection for unstructured multi-view stereo. In: Leibe, B., Matas, J., Sebe, N., Welling, M. (eds.) ECCV 2016. LNCS, vol. 9907, pp. 501–518. Springer, Cham (2016). https://doi.org/10.1007/978-3-319-46487-9_31

42. Shilane, P., Min, P., Kazhdan, M., Funkhouser, T.: The Princeton shape benchmark. In: Proceedings Shape Modeling Applications, 2004, pp. 167–178. IEEE (2004)

43. Shrestha, R., Fan, Z., Su, Q., Dai, Z., Zhu, S., Tan, P.: MeshMVS: multi-view stereo guided mesh reconstruction. In: 2021 International Conference on 3D Vision (3DV), pp. 1290–1300. IEEE (2021)

44. Sun, X., et al.: Pix3d: Dataset and methods for single-image 3d shape modeling. In: Proceedings of the IEEE Conference on Computer Vision and Pattern Recognition, pp. 2974–2983 (2018)

45. Tang, J., Han, X., Pan, J., Jia, K., Tong, X.: A skeleton-bridged deep learning approach for generating meshes of complex topologies from single RGB images. In: Proceedings of the IEEE Conference on Computer Vision and Pattern Recognition, pp. 4541–4550 (2019)

46. Umeyama, S.: Least-squares estimation of transformation parameters between two point patterns. IEEE Trans. Pattern Anal. Mach. Intell. **13**(4), 376–380 (1991). https://doi.org/10.1109/34.88573

47. Varadarajan, V.S.: Lie Groups, Lie Algebras, and their Representations. Graduate Text in Mathematics. GTM, vol. 102. Springer Science & Business Media, New York (2013). https://doi.org/10.1007/978-1-4612-1126-6

48. Wang, N., Zhang, Y., Li, Z., Fu, Y., Liu, W., Jiang, Y.-G.: Pixel2mesh: generating 3d mesh models from single RGB images. In: Ferrari, V., Hebert, M., Sminchisescu, C., Weiss, Y. (eds.) ECCV 2018. LNCS, vol. 11215, pp. 55–71. Springer, Cham (2018). https://doi.org/10.1007/978-3-030-01252-6_4

49. Wang, P., Liu, L., Liu, Y., Theobalt, C., Komura, T., Wang, W.: Neus: learning neural implicit surfaces by volume rendering for multi-view reconstruction. Adv. Neural. Inf. Process. Syst. **34**, 27171–27183 (2021)

50. Wen, C., Zhang, Y., Li, Z., Fu, Y.: Pixel2mesh++: multi-view 3d mesh generation via deformation. In: Proceedings of the IEEE/CVF International Conference on Computer Vision, pp. 1042–1051 (2019)

51. Xiang, Y., et al.: ObjectNet3D: a large scale database for 3d object recognition. In: Leibe, B., Matas, J., Sebe, N., Welling, M. (eds.) ECCV 2016. LNCS, vol. 9912, pp. 160–176. Springer, Cham (2016). https://doi.org/10.1007/978-3-319-46484-8_10

52. Xiang, Y., Mottaghi, R., Savarese, S.: Beyond pascal: a benchmark for 3d object detection in the wild. In: IEEE Winter Conference on Applications Of Computer Vision, pp. 75–82. IEEE (2014)

53. Yao, Y., et al.: BlendedMVS: a large-scale dataset for generalized multi-view stereo networks. In: Computer Vision and Pattern Recognition (CVPR) (2020)

54. Yao, Y., Schertler, N., Rosales, E., Rhodin, H., Sigal, L., Sheffer, A.: Front2back: single view 3d shape reconstruction via front to back prediction. In: Proceedings of the IEEE/CVF Conference on Computer Vision and Pattern Recognition, pp. 531–540 (2020)

55. Yariv, L., et al.: Multiview neural surface reconstruction by disentangling geometry and appearance. Adv. Neural. Inf. Process. Syst. **33**, 2492–2502 (2020)

56. Zhou, Q.Y., Koltun, V.: Dense scene reconstruction with points of interest. ACM Trans. Graph. (ToG) **32**(4), 1–8 (2013)

REALY: Rethinking the Evaluation of 3D Face Reconstruction

Zenghao Chai[1], Haoxian Zhang[2], Jing Ren[2], Di Kang[2],
Zhengzhuo Xu[1], Xuefei Zhe[2], Chun Yuan[1,3], and Linchao Bao[2]

[1] Shenzhen International Graduate School, Tsinghua University, Beijing, China
yuanc@sz.tsinghua.edu.cn
[2] Tencent AI Lab, Bellevue, China
linchaobao@gmail.com
[3] Peng Cheng National Laboratory, Shenzhen, China

Abstract. The evaluation of 3D face reconstruction results typically relies on a rigid shape alignment between the estimated 3D model and the ground-truth scan. We observe that aligning two shapes with different reference points can largely affect the evaluation results. This poses difficulties for precisely diagnosing and improving a 3D face reconstruction method. In this paper, we propose a novel evaluation approach with a new benchmark REALY, consists of 100 globally aligned face scans with accurate facial keypoints, high-quality region masks, and topology-consistent meshes. Our approach performs region-wise shape alignment and leads to more accurate, bidirectional correspondences during computing the shape errors. The fine-grained, region-wise evaluation results provide us detailed understandings about the performance of state-of-the-art 3D face reconstruction methods. For example, our experiments on single-image based reconstruction methods reveal that DECA performs the best on nose regions, while GANFit performs better on cheek regions. Besides, a new and high-quality 3DMM basis, HIFI3D^{++}, is further derived using the same procedure as we construct REALY to align and retopologize several 3D face datasets. We will release REALY, HIFI3D^{++}, and our new evaluation pipeline at https://realy3dface.com.

Keywords: 3D Face Reconstruction · Evaluation · Benchmark · 3DMM

1 Introduction

3D face reconstruction is a hotspot with broad applications in real world including face alignment [29,73], face recognition [8,13,64], and face animation [10,12]

Z. Chai and H. Zhang—Equal Contributions.

Supplementary Information The online version contains supplementary material available at https://doi.org/10.1007/978-3-031-20074-8_5.

Fig. 1. REALY: a <u>Re</u>gion-<u>a</u>ware benchmark based on the <u>LY</u>HM [18] dataset. Our benchmark contains 100 high-quality face shapes and *each* individual has **(a)** a rescaled and globally aligned scan, **(b)** 5 synthesized *multi-view* images with various GT camera parameters and illuminations, **(c)** a retopologized full-head mesh in HIFI3D [4] topology with consistent and semantically meaningful 68 keypoints, **(d)** 4 consistent region masks defined on both the retopologized mesh and the original scan, and **(e)** HIFI3D^{++} 3DMM: the first three PCs with the mean shape show the ethnic diversity.

among many others. How to estimate high fidelity 3D facial mesh [19,34,57] from monocular RGB(-D) images or image collections is a challenging problem in the fields of computer vision, computer graphics and machine learning.

Various methods have been proposed to tackle this problem, among which DNNs, especially CNNs [51,57,59] and GCNs [25,36], have made great progress due to their great expressiveness. However, developing new reconstruction methods and evaluating different methods or 3DMM basis are severely constrained by available datasets. Existing open-source 3D face datasets [2,46,68,70] have some unneglectable flaws. For example, the face scans are in different scales and random poses, and the provided keypoints are not accurate or discriminative enough, which makes it extremely hard to align the input shapes to the predicted face for evaluation. Moreover, due to the lack of ground-truth annotations in the original face scans, standard evaluation pipeline relies on nearest-neighboring correspondences to measure the similarity between the scan and the estimated face shape, which completely ignores substantive characteristics and discards shape geometry of human faces.

To fill this gap, we propose a new benchmark named REALY for evaluating 3D face reconstruction methods. REALY contains 3D face scans of 100 individuals from the LYHM [18] dataset, where the face scans are consistently rescaled, globally aligned, and wrapped into topology-consistent meshes. More importantly, since we have predefined facial keypoints and masks of the retopologized mesh template, the keypoints and masks can be transferred to original face scans. In this case, we get the high-quality facial keypoints and masks of the original raw face scans, which enable us to perform more accurate alignments and fine-grained, region-wise evaluations for estimated 3D face shapes. See Fig. 1 for an illustration. Our benchmark contains individuals from different ethnic, age, and gender groups (see Fig. 2 for some examples). Utilizing the retopologizing procedure built for REALY, we further present a high-quality and powerful 3DMM basis named HIFI3D^{++} by aligning and retopologizing several 3D face datasets. We conduct extensive experiments to evaluate state-of-the-art 3D face reconstruction methods and 3DMMs, which reveal several interesting observations and potential future research directions.

Fig. 2. Examples from REALY. *Top*: aligned high-resolution scans with textures. *Middle*: retopologized meshes in HIFI3D topology with semantically consistent keypoints (red points). *Bottom*: high quality face region masks of each scan.

Contributions. To summarize, our main contributions are:

- A new 3D face benchmark REALY that contains prealigned scans with accurate facial keypoints and region masks, retopologized meshes, and rendered high-fidelity multi-view images with camera parameters.
- A thorough investigation of the flaws in the standard evaluation pipeline for measuring face reconstruction quality.
- A novel, informative evaluation approach for 3D face reconstruction, with an elaborated region-wise, bidirectional alignment pipeline.
- Extensive experiments for benchmarking state-of-the-art 3D face reconstruction methods and 3DMMs.
- A new full-head 3DMM basis HIFI3D^{++} built from several 3D face datasets with high-quality, consistent mesh topology.

2   Related Work

Face reconstruction has drawn great attention in the past decades in both computer vision and computer graphics communities [33,37,54,63,65,72,73]. Below we review the topics that are most closely related to our work, and a full in-depth review can be found in [9,21,76].

3D Face Database. High quality 3D scan datasets greatly promote the development in the field of 3D face reconstruction. Massive face databases [32,40,73] have made it possible to train models for face reconstruction in a self-supervised manner. However, the 3D face scans in the existing datasets [2,18,46,70] are in different scales and random poses, and only a small set of inaccurate keypoints are provided for alignment. Another type of databases [11,68,70] contains retopologized meshes that are registered from high fidelity scans where all the meshes share the same topology. This type of databases is essential to construct 3D Morphable Models (3DMMs) [6,8,45,68], statistical models of facial shape and texture, which can be used for face regression and editing.

Single-View 3D Face Reconstruction. 3D face reconstruction from a single-view image has received glaring attention over the past decades, though estimating 3D information from a single 2D image is challenging and severely ill-posed. With the help of 3D morphable face models [6,11,21,35,48,55], the reconstruction problem is simplified into a tractable parametric regression. A straightforward solution to estimate 3DMM coefficients is based on analysis-by-synthesis [7,30,58,67], where the optimization objective usually consists of facial landmark alignment, photo consistency and statistical regularizers. These optimization-based approaches are computationally expensive and sensitive to initialization. Recently, many deep learning based models [28,51,57,59] are proposed to predict the 3DMM coefficients in a supervised or self-supervised way. This type of methods is robust for face reconstruction but has limited expressive power. To address this issue, GANFit [26,27] proposes to parameterize the texture maps using the latent code of a Texture GAN for face regression. Some nonlinear 3DMMs [60–62] are proposed for stronger expressiveness of face geometry. Some other work [17,22,31,63,75] utilize additional geometry and appearance representation (such as displacement and normal maps) to recover high-frequency details. Moreover, a recent surge of end-to-end approaches try to reconstruct 3D face shape directly from a depth map or UV position map [23,41,43,53,66,71]. However, these non-3DMM methods are prone to produce unrealistic and malformed faces compared to 3DMM-based methods.

Evaluation of Face Reconstruction. Existing evaluation protocols usually utilize the off-the-shelf datasets [2,11,46,70] to estimate the similarity between the reconstructed shape and the raw scan. Specifically, the reconstructed shape and the input scan are aligned using some predefined keypoints [17,24,38,75] or ICP [5,19,26–28,52]. Then Root Mean Square Error (RMSE) [16,19,42,59] or Normalized Mean Square Error (NMSE) [34,39,60,75] is calculated between the corresponding points on the input scan and the reconstructed shape. The correspondences are usually established in two ways, namely finding the nearest neighbor with smallest point-to-point distance [17,75] or point-to-plane distance [19,39,41]. Some benchmarks [24,42,52] propose to use predefined keypoints or disk-shaped region masks to measure shape similarity. Such measurement contains semantic prior but does not faithfully represent the overall face shape.

3   Background

3.1   Notation & Preliminaries

We use *triangle* mesh $S = \{V, F\}$ to represent face models with vertex positions V and triangle face list F. A *region-of-interest* of the mesh S is denoted as $\mathcal{R}_S$, which can be represented as an indicator function or a list of face IDs. We denote the *keypoints* on the mesh S as $\mathcal{K}_S$, which is a list of manually selected or automatically detected vertices that are semantically meaningful on S.

For a specific face shape, we consider three associated meshes: (1) S_H: the *ground-truth* mesh with *high* resolution, which is constructed from multi-view images; (2) S_L: the *ground-truth* retopologized mesh with *low* resolution, which is obtained by wrapping the HIFI3D [4] mesh topology to the shape S_H; (3) S_P: the *predicted* face mesh constructed from existing techniques. Note that different

Table 1. Overview of 3DMMs.

	BFM [45]	FWH [11]	FLAME [35]	LSFM [8]	LYHM [18]	FS [68]	HIFI3D [4]	HIFI3D^A [4]	*Ours*
# scans	200	140	3800	8402	1212	938	200	200	1957
n_v	53215	11510	5023	53215	11510	26317	20481	20481	20481
n_f	105840	22800	9976	105840	22800	52261	40832	40832	40832
# basis	199	50	300	158	100	300	200	500	526

HIFI3D^A stands for the "augmented" version of HIFI3D [4], which employs data augmentation techniques to construct 3DMM from 200 scans.

reconstruction methods may choose different mesh topologies (i.e., different size of V_P and F_P). For simplicity of notation, we denote the *regions* and *keypoints* defined on shape $S_H/S_L/S_P$ as $\mathcal{R}_H/\mathcal{R}_L/\mathcal{R}_P$ and $\mathcal{K}_H/\mathcal{K}_L/\mathcal{K}_P$ respectively.

A *map* between the shape S_i and S_j is denoted as $T_{i \rightarrow j}$, where the subscript represents the map *direction*. For example, $T_{p \rightarrow h}$ represents a map from the predicted mesh S_P to the high-resolution GT mesh S_H. We consider two different types of map, the vertex-to-vertex map $T_{i \rightarrow j}^{\mathrm{vtx}}$ and the vertex-to-point (also called vertex-to-plane) map $T_{i \rightarrow j}^{\mathrm{pts}}$. Specifically, $T_{i \rightarrow j}^{\mathrm{vtx}}$ maps each vertex in shape S_i to a *vertex* on S_j, and $T_{i \rightarrow j}^{\mathrm{pts}}$ maps each vertex on shape S_i to a *point* in a face of shape S_j. We will use the superscript to disambiguate the two maps when necessary.

Normalized Mean Square Error (NMSE) computes the distance between two surfaces S_i and S_j based on a given map $T_{i \rightarrow j}$ and is denoted as $e(T_{i \rightarrow j})$:

$$e(T_{i \rightarrow j}) = \frac{1}{n_v} \sum_{v \in S_i} \left\| v - T_{i \rightarrow j}(v) \right\|_F^2 \tag{1}$$

where n_v is the number of vertices in shape S_i, and $T_{i \rightarrow j}(v)$ gives the *coordinates* of the mapped position (of a vertex/point on shape S_j) for vertex $v \in S_i$.

Iterative Closest Point (ICP) can be applied to align two shapes via solving a rigid transformation and a nearest neighbor map iteratively to minimize NMSE:

$$\min_{\mathbf{R}, \mathbf{t}, T_{i \rightarrow j}} \sum_{v \in S_i} \left\| \mathbf{R}v + \mathbf{t} - T_{i \rightarrow j}(v) \right\|_F^2, \tag{2}$$

where the 3D rotation matrix $\mathbf{R}$ and the 3D translation vector $\mathbf{t}$ are computed to align S_i to S_j. For simplicity, we denote $[\mathbf{R}, \mathbf{t}, T_{i \rightarrow j}, S_i^*] = \mathbf{ICP}(S_i \rightarrow S_j)$, where S_i^* is obtained by transforming S_i via $(\mathbf{R}, \mathbf{t})$. For the purpose of efficiency, some previous works [17,24,38] only consider a small set of predefined corresponding keypoints to solve for $\mathbf{R}$ and $\mathbf{t}$ instead of using every vertex $v \in S_i$.

3.2 3DMM and Face Reconstruction

Formulation. The goal is to reconstruct a 3D face shape S_P from a single RGB(-D) image or an image collection. To reduce the search space of plausible faces, 3DMM is commonly used for face representation: $S = \bar{S} + \Phi \alpha$, where $\bar{S}$ is the *mean* shape, and Φ is the *principle components* (PCs) trained on some 3D face scans with neutral expression. Then the face reconstruction problem is reduced to a regression problem of solving for the facial parameter α. Existing methods either use deep networks to predict the α [17,19,22,28,29,57] or optimize various energy terms (e.g., most commonly used keypoint loss and photometric loss [3,7, 26,27,58,67]) with different regularization terms (e.g., not deviate too far from mean face [4,26,27,44,58]).

3DMM. The facial basis Φ determines the expressiveness power of the corresponding 3DMM and affect the reconstruction quality. Publicly available 3DMMs include BFM [6,45], LSFM [8], FLAME [35], LYHM [18], FaceScape (FS) [68], FaceWareHouse (FWH) [11], and HIFI3D/HIFI3D^A [4] (see Table 1).

Standard Evaluation Pipeline. Some datasets [2,24,46,52,75] also provide ground-truth scans, i.e., S_H with keypoints $\mathcal{K}_H$, that are associated with the input images, which allow us to evaluate the quality of the reconstructed shape S_P. Standard evaluation process consists of three steps: (1) first rescale and align S_P with S_H based on some sparse keypoints or applying ICP, (2) find the map $T_{p \to h}$ [16,20,41,47,50] or $T_{h \to p}$ [25,49,52,69] between the aligned shapes by nearest neighbor searching, (3) compute the NMSE of the nn-map $e(T_{p \to h})$ or $e(T_{h \to p})$.

4 Motivation

Multiple methods have been proposed to tackle the face reconstruction problem. However, to the best of our knowledge, there does not exist an effective evaluation protocol to fairly and reliably compare reconstructed faces from different methods. We observe the following issues in existing protocols:

(1) Global alignment is extremely sensitive to the provided keypoints and local changes. The NMSE metric based on global alignment often fails to reflect the true shape difference. Take the inset figure as an example: we have the ground-truth high-res mesh S_H colored in white, and the ground-truth low-res mesh S_L colored in yellow. We then modify the nose region of S_L while keeping the

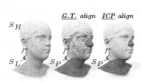

rest part unchanged, which leads to a toy predicted mesh S_P colored in blue. Perceptually, we expect S_P to be aligned with S_H in the same way as S_L (as shown in the middle) to compute the shape differences. However, ICP computes the alignment in a global way and as shown on the right, S_P is rotated backwards w.r.t. S_H, having the complete facial region of S_P behind S_H, which leads to exaggerated errors. In this case, considering region-based alignment can help to avoid global mismatch (see Fig. 4).

(2) Another limitation is that it is hard to establish accurate and meaningful correspondences based on the global *rigid* alignment from a single direction (i.e., from S_P to S_H only). For example, the inset figure shows two aligned lips and we are supposed to measure the NMSE on the nn-map from S_P to S_H.

For the red vertex $x \in S_P$, its nearest neighbor in S_H is the blue vertex y_1. In this case, considering the map in the other direction, i.e., from S_H to S_P, can help to establish the correct correspondence from y_2 to x.

These observations inspire us to consider *region-based* and *bidirectional* alignment for establishing semantically more meaningful correspondences between the predicted mesh S_P to the ground-truth mesh S_H. However, to make this happen, meshes S_H with ground-truth region masks $\mathcal{R}_H$ are requested, which are not available in any of the open datasets [2,18,46,56,68,75]. To fill the gap, we propose a new benchmark REALY, which provides ground-truth high-res mesh S_H and retopologized mesh S_L in HIFI3D topology, with accurate ground-truth keypoints and region masks. To justify the usefulness of our benchmark, we show two applications: evaluating and comparing (1) the reconstruction quality of faces obtained from 9 different methods in different choices of topology, (2) the expressiveness power of 8 different 3DMM basis for face regression.

Paper Structure. Section 5 discusses the details of REALY benchmark and our 3DMM. Section 6 illustrates our novel region-aware bidirectional evaluation pipeline. In Sect. 7 we extensively justify the usefulness of REALY and the advantages of our evaluation pipeline over the standard one on face reconstruction task, and demonstrate that HIFI3D^{++} is more expressive than existing 3DMMs.

5   REALY: A New 3D Face Benchmark

Overview. Our benchmark REALY contains 100 individuals, and each individual is modelled by a ground-truth high-resolution mesh S_H (the aligned 3D scan from LYHM [18]) and a retopologized low-resolution mesh S_L using HIFI3D [4] topology in neutral expression (see Fig. 2 for some examples). The meshes (S_H, S_L) of all individuals are consistently *scaled* and *aligned*. We also provide 68 keypoints and 4 region masks, which are semantically meaningful, for *both* S_H and S_L of *each* individual. For each individual, five high-quality and realistic multi-view images (including one frontal image) are rendered with well designed lighting condition and ground-truth camera parameters.

We explain the detailed construction procedure of REALY as follows.

HIFI3D Topology. We choose this topology for our benchmark for the following reasons: (1) LYHM has overdense samplings at the boundary of the eyes and mouth. (2) LSFM does not have edge loops to define the contours of the eyes and mouth. (3) FLAME has unnatural triangulation which cannot model some realistic muscle movements such as raising the eyebrows. As a comparison, HIFI3D has better triangulation and balanced samplings to make realistic and nuanced expressions. Besides, HIFI3D also has eyeballs, interior structure of the mouth, and the shoulder region, which all benefit downstream applications such as talking head. See supplementary for visualized comparisons.

Construction Pipeline. We start by collecting 1235 scans from LYHM and preparing a template shape S_{temp} in HIFI3D topology (see Fig. 1(c)) with predefined 68 keypoints $\mathcal{K}_{\text{temp}}$ and 4 region masks $\mathcal{R}_{\text{temp}}$ (including nose, mouth, forehead and cheek region). Firstly, we re-scale and rigidly align the input scans to the template shape S_{temp}, leading to our ground-truth high-resolution meshes S_H (i.e., aligned scans). We then follow [24,52] to define an evaluation region which is a disk centered on the nose tip. Secondly, we "wrap" (i.e., perform non-rigid registration) S_{temp} to each S_H to get the retopologized S_L such that S_L have the same topology as S_{temp} but reflect the shape of S_H. Note that we have keypoints $\mathcal{K}_L = \mathcal{K}_{\text{temp}}$ and regions $\mathcal{R}_L = \mathcal{R}_{\text{temp}}$ since S_L and S_{temp} share the same HIFI3D topology. We then transfer $\mathcal{K}_L$ and $\mathcal{R}_L$ from S_L to S_H for each individual. We also set up a rendering pipeline for synthesizing *multi-view* images for the textured high-resolution mesh S_H. Such a controlled environment enables REALY to focus on reflecting the reconstruction ability of different methods. Finally, we filter out samples with wrapping error larger than 0.2mm and ask an expert artist with 3 year modeling experience to select 100 individuals among all the processed scans with the highest model quality, across different genders, ethnicity, and ages, to obtain our REALY benchmark.

Challenges & Solutions. We observe two major challenges during the above construction procedure: (1) the raw scans are in different scales and poses with inaccurate sparse keypoints [74], which makes it difficult to align them consistently. To tackle this problem, we iterate through the following steps until convergence: first, render a frontal face image of S_H with texture using the initial/estimated transformation to align S_H to S_{temp} (note that the frontal pose needs to be determined from the alignment transformation as the frontal facing pose is unknown for a given scan); second, detect a set of 2D facial keypoints on the rendered image of S_H using state-of-the-art landmark detector; third, project the 2D keypoints into 3D using the rendering camera pose; fourth, update the alignment transformation from S_H to S_{temp} using the correspondences between the projected 3D keypoints on S_H and the known 3D keypoints on S_{temp}.

(2) Another challenge is, after we get the retopologized S_L, how to accurately transfer the region mask from the low-resolution mesh S_L (inherited from S_{temp}) to the high-resolution mesh S_H. One naive solution would be using nearest neighbor mapping from S_L to S_H to transfer the region mask. However, since the resolution of S_H can be 50× larger than that of S_L, this naive solution will introduce disconnected and noisy region mask. To avoid such flaws, we use the vertex-to-point mapping from both directions to find candidate regions on S_H. As much more correspondences can be established during the mapping from S_H to S_L, higher-quality, smoother region masks can be obtained. Finally, we filter out noisy regions (e.g., nostril, eyeballs) and return the largest connected region.

HIFI3D^{++}. With the above procedure, we can further construct a 3DMM basis by retopologizing more 3D face models. Specifically, based on the 200 individuals from HIFI3D [4], we additionally process and retopologize 3D face models of 846 individuals from FaceScape dataset [68] into HIFI3D topology. Together with the aforementioned processed models of 1235 individuals from LYHM [18], we collect and then select 1957 most representative meshes consisting of individuals from various ethnic groups. We then apply PCA [6] to obtain our new basis with 526 PCs (with 99.9% cumulative explained variance), which we name as HIFI3D^{++}. Table 1 shows the comparison of HIFI3D^{++} to other 3DMMs. Note that previous 3DMMs are more or less ethnics-biased. For example, BFM [45] is constructed mostly from Europeans, FLAME [35] is constructed from scans of the US and European, while HIFI3D [4] and FS [68] is constructed from scans of Asians. The LSFM and FLAME contains 50 : 1 and 12 : 1 of Caucasian and Asian respectively. In contrast, HIFI3D^{++} is constructed from high-quality models across more balanced ethnic groups that ensures 1 : 1 between Caucasian and Asian (plus a few subjects from other ethnicities). We examine the expressive powers and reconstruction qualities of different 3DMMs in Sect. 7.3.

Algorithm 1. $S_P^* = rICP(S_P \rightarrow S_H @ \mathcal{R}_H)$

Goal Rigidly align S_P to the *region R_H* of S_H.

Input: High-res mesh S_H with region R_H and keypoints $\mathcal{K}_H$; a predicted mesh S_P with keypoints $\mathcal{K}_P$; weights $w_\mathcal{K}$ for keypoints alignment; maximum iteration $\mathbb{K}$.

1: $S_P^{(0)} = gICP(S_P \rightarrow S_H)$
2: **for** $0 \leq k \leq \mathbb{K}$ **do**
3:    Find nn-map T from region $\mathcal{R}_H$ to $S_P^{(k)}$.
4:    Solve $[\mathbf{R}, \mathbf{t}] = \arg\min \sum_{v \in \mathcal{R}_H} \left\| \mathbf{R}T(v) + \mathbf{t} - v \right\|_F^2 + w_\mathcal{K} \left\| \mathbf{R}\mathcal{K}_P + \mathbf{t} - \mathcal{K}_H \right\|_F^2$.
5:    Obtain $S_P^{(k+1)}$ by transforming $S_P^{(k)}$ via $(\mathbf{R}, \mathbf{t})$.
6: **end for**
7: Set $S_P^* \leftarrow S_P^{(\mathbb{K})}$.

Algorithm 2. $[S_P^*, \mathcal{R}_H^*] = bICP(S_P \leftrightarrow S_H @ \mathcal{R}_H)$

Goal Rigidly align S_P and non-rigidly deform $\mathcal{R}_H$ for better alignment in region $\mathcal{R}_H$

1: $S_P^* = rICP(S_P \rightarrow S_H @ \mathcal{R}_H)$ % *call Algo. 1*
2: Find nn-map T from region $\mathcal{R}_H$ to S_P^*
3: $\mathcal{R}_H^* = nICP\left(\mathcal{R}_H \,|\, V_{\mathcal{R}_H} \rightarrow T(V_{\mathcal{R}_H})\right) + w_\mathcal{K}\ nICP\left(\mathcal{R}_H \,|\, \mathcal{K}_H \rightarrow \mathcal{K}_P\right)$ % *where $nICP(S \,|\, X \rightarrow Y)$ applies non-rigid ICP to deform S such that the points X on S are expected to be mapped to new positions Y*

---

6   A Novel Evaluation Pipeline

To evaluate the quality of a reconstructed or predicted face S_P, the standard pipeline first globally aligns S_P with the ground-truth high-resolution mesh S_H to find the nearest-neighbor map $T_{p \rightarrow h}$ (or $T_{h \rightarrow p}$). The similarity or reconstruction error is then measured by the NMSE error $e(T_{p \rightarrow h})$ (or $e(T_{h \rightarrow p})$). We propose a new evaluation pipeline based on a region-aware and bidirectional alignment.

We focus on how to accurately establish correspondences between S_P and a particular region $\mathcal{R}_H$ in the ground-truth shape S_H (denoted as $S_H @ \mathcal{R}_H$ for short), which consists of two main steps: (1) *rICP* (region-aware ICP): we first get the rigidly transformed shape S_P^* from S_P by aligning S_P to $\mathcal{R}_H$ such that the corresponding *region* on S_P is well aligned to $\mathcal{R}_H$ without taking the rest part of the face into consideration (see Algorithm 1). (2) **bICP** (non-rigid and bidirectional ICP): with the above established correspondences between S_P^* and $\mathcal{R}_H$ as initialization, we further refine the correspondences by applying non-rigid ICP (**nICP**) [1] to deform $\mathcal{R}_H$ to fit S_P^* (see Algorithm 2). This step yields a deformed shape $\mathcal{R}_H^*$ from $\mathcal{R}_H$, as well as the correspondences between $\mathcal{R}_H$ and S_P^* induced from $\mathcal{R}_H^*$ (using vertex-to-surface projection). Our region-wise alignment and the two step coarse-to-fine registration effectively guarantee that **nICP** can converge to a reasonable deformed shape $\mathcal{R}_H^*$ (see supplementary for details). The resulting correspondences are used for computing errors between $\mathcal{R}_H$ and S_P^*. Note that the second alignment step can be regarded as upsampling S_P^* such that it has a similar resolution to the dense ground-truth scan $S_H@\mathcal{R}_H$, which makes the evaluation of reconstructed meshes in different resolutions easier.

We observe that the correspondences established between the rigidly transformed shape S_P^* and deformed region $\mathcal{R}_H^*$ are more accurate than the correspondences detected between the original shapes S_P and S_H for evaluating the similarity between the two shapes in region $\mathcal{R}_H$. Figure 3 shows such an example. We visualize the corresponding points on S_H of the mouth keypoints on S_P in blue/green/yellow established by **gICP**/**rICP**/**bICP** respectively, where the red points are the ground-truth mouth keypoints on S_H.

We can see that **bICP** gives more accurate correspondences since it focus on the mouth region and considers correspondences from both directions. As a result, y_3 obtained by **bICP** is closer to the ground-truth y, while y_1 obtained by **gICP** is far from y. We validate the above analysis with detailed experiments in Sect. 7.1. We use the above established correspondences to measure the NMSE error of the region-wise aligned S_P^* compared to ground-truth S_H on four predefined regions including nose, mouth, forehead, and cheek, respectively (see Fig. 1d). The NMSE error is then transformed back to

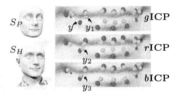

Fig. 3. Correspondence established by different ICPs and the GT correspondences (red). (Color figure online)

the physical scale of the raw scan in millimeters (note that each ground-truth S_H in our benchmark is rigidly transformed from raw scan, see Sect. 5). Evaluation on each region individually provides us fine-grained understandings of the qualities of the reconstructed meshes. We present extensive experiments for benchmarking state-of-the-art single-image 3D face reconstruction methods in Sect. 7.2.

7 Experiment

In this section we first demonstrate the effectiveness of our **bICP** which can establish more accurate correspondences than standard ICP for reliably evaluating 3D face reconstructions. We then compare different face reconstruction

Table 2. The distance $e(\cdot)$ between S_P (aligned by ***r*ICP**/***g*ICP**, or with G.T. alignment) and S_L of the four examples in Fig. 4.

$\mathcal{R}^{\text{rm}}$ / e(mm/10)	*r*ICP (ours) @nose	@mouth	@forehead	@cheek	all	*g*ICP $e(T_{p\to l}^{\text{vtx}})$	G.T. $e(T_{p\to l}^{\text{vtx}})$
nose	**8.376**	0.331	1.200	1.484	11.392	40.490	11.972
mouth	0.550	**4.372**	1.164	3.053	9.139	20.889	5.195
forehead	0.636	0.165	**7.107**	0.630	8.537	12.695	6.463
cheek	1.417	0.397	0.547	**3.631**	5.992	18.754	3.943

methods and 3DMMs using our evaluation protocol to investigate fine-grained shape differences based on regions in a systematically way.

7.1 Ablation Study: *b*ICPv.s. *g*ICP

To demonstrate the advantages of our region-based and bidirectional evaluation protocol over the standard one, we design a controlled experiment illustrated in Fig. 4 and Tables 2 and 3. Specifically, we carefully construct four predicted shapes S_P by modifying the same ground-truth mesh S_L such that the ground-truth correspondences between S_P and S_L are known for reference.

Table 3. Error of the nn-map obtained via different ICPs (Fig. 4).

$\mathcal{R}^{\text{rm}}$ / e(mm)	*g*ICP	*r*ICP	*b*ICP
nose	2.882	0.706	**0.670**
mouth	1.699	0.459	**0.407**
forehead	0.707	0.581	**0.520**
cheek	1.219	0.107	**0.105**

As illustrated in Fig. 4, we replace the nose/mouth/forehead/cheek region of shape S_L with the corresponding region from four different reference shapes $S_i (i = 1, 2, 3, 4)$ respectively. We then visualize the shape differences computed using ***b*ICP** (w.r.t. the four specified regions) and ***g*ICP** (w.r.t. the complete face) in Fig. 4 where large (small) errors are colored in red (blue).

We compare our evaluation pipeline to the standard one in two-fold: (1) we report the alignment error, the distance between the aligned S_P and the input S_L using ground-truth correspondences in Table 2, where the alignment is computed using our region-wise ***r*ICP** and the global-wise ***g*ICP**. (2) we report the accuracy of correspondences established via ***g*ICP**, ***r*ICP** (our intermediate step), and ***b*ICP** in Table 3 compared to the ground-truth correspondences.

We can see that gICP is extremely sensitive to local changes. For example, replacing the nose only can lead to errors in the complete face (first row in Fig. 4) and replacing the mouth can lead to errors even in forehead (second row) according to gICP. As a comparison, our bICP can correctly localizes the shape differences in the modified regions and lead to more accurate alignment than gICP as shown in Table 2. This suggests that region-based alignment can better quantify shape differences especially in the case of

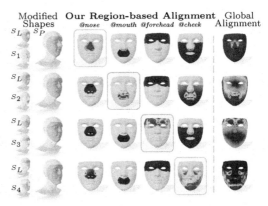

Fig. 4. We visualize the shape difference between S_P and S_L using our bICP (shown on separate regions) and gICP, where S_P is constructed by replacing S_L's nose/mouth/forehead/cheek region with the corresponding region from $S_1/S_2/S_3/S_4$. (Color figure online)

local or subtle changes. Moreover, Table 3 shows that both our rICP and bICP help to find more accurate correspondences to evaluate shape differences.

7.2 Evaluating Face Reconstruction Methods

We compare recent state-of-the-art face reconstruction methods on our REALY benchmark using our new evaluation protocol including: (1) linear-3DMM based methods: ExpNet [14,15,59], RingNet [52], MGCNet [54], Deep3D [19], 3DDFA-v2 [29], GANFit [26,27], DECA-coarse [22], and (2) non(linear)-3DMM methods: PRNet [23], Nonlinear 3DMM (N-3DMM) [60–62].

We report the statistics (mean and std.) of errors over 100 shapes in REALY using our bICP (in each separate region and complete face) and using standard gICP (in complete face) in Table 4. gICP suggests that DECA and Deep3D are the best among the tested methods for face reconstruction. However, our bICP suggests that DECA models the nose region in a much better and more accurate way than others, but it obtains less satisfactory result in the mouth region. Figure 5 shows some qualitative results, where the best reconstructed face selected using bICP (gICP) is highlighted in orange (blue&purple) box. We also conduct user study to ask people to vote for the best (labeled ⋆) and second best (labeled †) face. We can see that the faces selected by bICP are indeed visually more similar (validated by our user study) to the G.T. shapes than those selected by gICP.

Moreover, another advantage of our bICP evaluation protocol is its region-aware nature, which allows us to compare different methods in some particular region. Figure 6 shows such an example, where we select the best matched region from different methods according to our region-aware bICP and merge them

Input [15]   [52]   [54]   [23]   [19]   [29]   [26]   [61]   [22]   G.T.

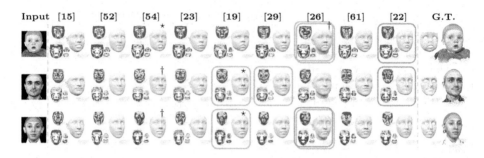

Fig. 5. Comparing different face reconstruction methods. We visualize the reconstruction error of each face using the standard evaluation pipeline (top left) and our novel evaluation pipeline (bottom left, shown in four regions), where large (small) errors are colored in red (blue). Note only the cropped region shown in G.T. is counted for evaluation. The best reconstructed face selected by our measurement (orange boxes) is visually closer to the ground-truth meshes than the ones selected using the standard measurements (blue & purple boxes). See more examples in our supplementary.

Table 4. Comparing different face reconstruction methods on REALY. We report the statistics of errors measured using our new pipeline (*b*ICP) and the standard one (*g*ICP from both directions). The best (second best) method w.r.t. average error is highlighted in red (blue).

methods / e (mm)	*b*ICP (ours)								*g*ICP			
	@$\mathcal{R}_N$ (nose)		@$\mathcal{R}_M$ (mouth)		@$\mathcal{R}_F$ (forehead)		@$\mathcal{R}_C$ (cheek)		all	$e(T_{p \to h}^{\text{pts}})$		$e(T_{h \to p}^{\text{pts}})$	
	avg.	std.	avg.	std.	avg.	std.	avg.	std.	avg.	avg.	std.	avg.	std.
ExpNet [15]	2.509	0.486	1.912	0.450	3.084	1.005	1.717	0.590	2.306	2.650	0.549	2.297	0.616
RingNet [52]	1.934	0.458	2.074	0.616	2.995	0.908	2.028	0.720	2.258	2.016	0.489	2.762	1.016
MGCNet [54]	1.771	0.380	**1.417**	0.409	**2.268**	0.503	1.639	0.650	**1.774**	2.388	0.865	2.094	0.750
PRNet [23]	1.923	0.518	1.838	0.637	2.429	0.588	1.863	0.698	2.013	3.036	0.933	2.302	0.747
Deep3D [19]	**1.719**	0.354	**1.368**	0.439	**2.015**	0.449	1.528	0.501	**1.657**	2.142	0.651	**1.908**	0.553
3DDFA-v2 [29]	1.903	0.517	1.597	0.478	2.477	0.647	1.757	0.642	1.926	2.788	0.951	2.279	0.765
GANFit [26]	1.928	0.490	1.812	0.544	2.402	0.545	**1.329**	0.504	1.868	**1.899**	0.730	**1.999**	0.748
N-3DMM [61]	2.936	0.810	2.375	0.599	4.582	1.448	1.918	0.801	2.953	3.681	1.566	3.252	1.198
DECA-c [22]	**1.697**	0.355	2.516	0.839	2.349	0.576	**1.479**	0.535	2.010	**1.698**	0.397	2.183	0.798

into a new face. Perceptually, the merged face is clearly better than the face reconstructed using DECA (selected by *g*ICP).

7.3   Evaluating Different 3DMMs

We use our new evaluation approach to compare different 3DMMs on REALY including: LYHM [18], BFM [45], FLAME [35], LSFM [8], FaceScape basis (FS) [68], HIFI3D and HIFI3D^A [4]. In this test, we use different basis and run standard RGB(-D) fitting algorithm [4] using photo loss (with/without depth loss), ID loss, landmark loss and regularization loss to regress the 3DMM coefficients from the given 2D images provided by REALY. For RGB fitting, we use

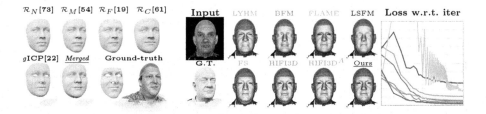

Fig. 6. We use our region-aware metric to find the best matched nose $\mathcal{R}_N$, mouth $\mathcal{R}_M$, cheek $\mathcal{R}_C$, and forehead $\mathcal{R}_F$ from existing methods, and merge them into a new face. Our merged face is more similar to the G.T. shape than DECA, the best reconstructed face voted by gICP.

Fig. 7. Comparing the fitting errors of different 3DMMs. We visualize an example of the RGB-D fitting errors during the optimization iterations using different 3DMMs and the corresponding reconstructed faces. We observe that HIFI3D^A and HIFI3D^{++} give the most realistic reconstructed faces (especially in the mouth region) and show superior converging rate with smallest converged loss among the tested 3DMMs. As a comparison, FS and LSFM show instability during the fitting process and lead to erroneous reconstruction results.

Table 5. Comparing different 3DMM basis on REALY. The best (second best) methods w.r.t. average error are highlighted in red (blue).

3DMMs / e (mm)	RGB Fitting									RGB-D Fitting								
	@$\mathcal{R}_N$		@$\mathcal{R}_M$		@$\mathcal{R}_F$		@$\mathcal{R}_C$		all	@$\mathcal{R}_N$		@$\mathcal{R}_M$		@$\mathcal{R}_F$		@$\mathcal{R}_C$		all
	avg.	std.	avg.	std.	avg.	std.	avg.	std.	avg.	avg.	std.	avg.	std.	avg.	std.	avg.	std.	avg.
BFM [45]	2.925	0.704	2.175	0.550	3.359	0.660	1.742	0.410	2.550	1.700	0.277	1.170	0.355	2.308	0.501	0.587	0.100	1.441
FLAME [35]	**2.700**	0.543	2.616	0.476	3.891	0.786	2.737	0.687	2.986	1.687	0.232	1.397	0.354	2.178	0.609	0.495	0.125	1.439
LSFM [8]	**2.455**	0.666	2.446	0.768	4.062	0.807	3.756	1.292	3.180	1.727	0.320	1.906	0.638	2.370	0.612	0.869	0.218	1.718
FS [68]	2.852	0.776	2.524	0.827	2.430	0.613	1.739	0.450	2.386	2.181	0.494	2.468	0.866	2.057	0.597	1.003	0.208	1.927
HIFI3D [4]	2.974	0.752	**1.285**	0.364	2.519	0.490	2.070	0.533	2.212	**1.653**	0.258	0.909	0.332	1.343	0.366	0.468	0.121	1.093
HIFI3D^A [4]	3.076	0.709	**1.201**	0.399	2.527	0.561	1.866	0.566	**2.167**	1.746	0.271	**0.607**	0.338	**1.235**	0.363	**0.302**	0.084	**0.972**
LYHM* [18]	2.723	0.578	1.988	0.556	3.752	0.716	**1.475**	0.439	2.485	2.144	0.331	1.654	0.520	3.174	0.676	0.673	0.155	1.911
Ours*	2.898	0.732	1.288	0.408	**2.216**	0.612	**1.599**	0.537	**2.000**	**1.542**	0.258	**0.621**	0.341	**1.085**	0.359	**0.265**	0.080	**0.878**

*Some of the test shapes in REALY are used to construct LYHM and our 3DMM.

a frontal face image of each individual as input. For RGB-D fitting, a frontal rendered depth image in addition to the RGB image is used. Figure 7 shows the fitting errors over iterations using different 3DMMs. The qualitative and quantitative comparisons are presented in Fig. 8 and Table 5, respectively. Note that both LYHM and our 3DMM basis in Table 5 use some test shapes in REALY to construct the 3DMM. They are listed in the table only for reference.

As shown in Table 5, HIFI3D^A, HIFI3D, and FS achieve similar performance in RGB fitting, while HIFI3D^A and HIFI3D perform much better than the other 3DMMs in RGB-D fitting, indicating that HIFI3D^A and HIFI3D are more expressive and can better fit the geometry especially in RGB-D fitting with extra depth information. To directly justify the expressive power of our new 3DMM basis HIFI3D^{++}, we compare HIFI3D^{++} to HIFI3D/HIFI3D^A over 3 shapes that are unused by all three 3DMMs. We fit the 3D ground-truth scans using

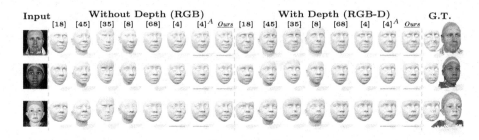

Fig. 8. Comparing different 3DMMs. From *Left to right*: LYHM [18], BFM [45], FLAME [35], LSFM [8], FS [68], HIFI3D [4], HIFI3D^A [4], and HIFI3D^{++}. We highlight the best (second best) reconstructed face via red (blue) underline. Only the cropped region shown in G.T. is counted for evaluation. See more examples in supplementary.

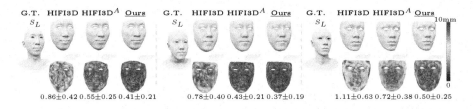

Fig. 9. Comparing our 3DMM to HIFI3D and HIFI3D^A. *Top*: Fitted faces S_P, *Bottom*: Fitting errors, where large (small) errors are colored in red (blue). (Color figure online)

the 3DMMs. Figure 9 shows the error heatmaps. The average error with our new basis decreases over 20% compared to HIFI3D^A.

Finally, an important observation from Tables 4–5 is that, while top performing single image reconstruction methods achieve results of $1.657 \sim 2.953$, the best RGB-D fitting records 0.878, which is far better than them. It implies that there is still much room for improvements in single image reconstruction methods.

8   Conclusions

In this work, we introduce a new benchmark REALY for 3D face reconstruction that provides accurate and consistent facial keypoints, region masks on the scans, and consistently retopologized meshes. During the construction procedure of the benchmark, we also derive a new powerful 3DMM basis HIFI3D^{++}. The benchmark allows us to design a novel region-aware and bidirectional evaluation pipeline to measure shape similarity, which is justified to be more reliable than the standard evaluation pipeline based on global alignment. Furthermore, we compare and analyse existing single-image face reconstruction methods and state-of-the-art 3DMM basis using our new evaluation approach on REALY, which is the first to obtain fine-grained region-wise analyses in the 3D face community. Moreover, it would be interesting to research how our benchmark can be used for supervised learning of face reconstruction.

Acknowledgment. This work was supported by SZSTC Grant No. JCYJ20190 809172201639 and WDZC20200820200655001, Shenzhen Key Laboratory ZDSY S20210623092001004.

References

1. Amberg, B., Romdhani, S., Vetter, T.: Optimal step nonrigid ICP algorithms for surface registration. In: CVPR (2007)
2. Bagdanov, A.D., Bimbo, A.D., Masi, I.: The Florence 2d/3d hybrid face dataset. In: J-HGBU@MM (2011)
3. Bai, Z., Cui, Z., Liu, X., Tan, P.: Riggable 3d face reconstruction via in-network optimization. In: CVPR (2021)
4. Bao, L., et al.: High-fidelity 3d digital human head creation from RGB-D selfies. TOG (2021)
5. Besl, P.J., McKay, N.D.: A method for registration of 3d shapes. TPAMI (1992)
6. Blanz, V., Vetter, T.: A morphable model for the synthesis of 3d faces. In: SIGGRAPH (1999)
7. Blanz, V., Vetter, T.: Face recognition based on fitting a 3d morphable model. TPAMI (2003)
8. Booth, J., Roussos, A., Zafeiriou, S., Ponniah, A., Dunaway, D.: A 3d morphable model learnt from 10,000 faces. In: CVPR (2016)
9. Brunton, A., Salazar, A., Bolkart, T., Wuhrer, S.: Review of statistical shape spaces for 3d data with comparative analysis for human faces. In: CVIU (2014)
10. Cao, C., Weng, Y., Lin, S., Zhou, K.: 3d shape regression for real-time facial animation. TOG **32**, 1 (2013)
11. Cao, C., Weng, Y., Zhou, S., Tong, Y., Zhou, K.: Facewarehouse: a 3d facial expression database for visual computing. TVCG **20**, 413–425 (2014)
12. Cao, C., Wu, H., Weng, Y., Shao, T., Zhou, K.: Real-time facial animation with image-based dynamic avatars. TOG **35**, 1–13 (2016)
13. Cao, K., Rong, Y., Li, C., Tang, X., Loy, C.C.: Pose-robust face recognition via deep residual equivariant mapping. In: CVPR (2018)
14. Chang, F., Tran, A.T., Hassner, T., Masi, I., Nevatia, R., Medioni, G.G.: Faceposenet: making a case for landmark-free face alignment. In: ICCV Workshops (2017)
15. Chang, F., Tran, A.T., Hassner, T., Masi, I., Nevatia, R., Medioni, G.G.: ExpNet: landmark-free, deep, 3d facial expressions. In: FG (2018)
16. Chaudhuri, B., Vesdapunt, N., Shapiro, L., Wang, B.: Personalized face modeling for improved face reconstruction and motion retargeting. In: Vedaldi, A., Bischof, H., Brox, T., Frahm, J.-M. (eds.) ECCV 2020. LNCS, vol. 12350, pp. 142–160. Springer, Cham (2020). https://doi.org/10.1007/978-3-030-58558-7_9
17. Chen, Y., Wu, F., Wang, Z., Song, Y., Ling, Y., Bao, L.: Self-supervised learning of detailed 3d face reconstruction. TIP **29**, 8696–8705 (2020)
18. Dai, H., Pears, N.E., Smith, W.A.P., Duncan, C.: Statistical modeling of craniofacial shape and texture. IJCV **128**, 547–571 (2020)

19. Deng, Y., Yang, J., Xu, S., Chen, D., Jia, Y., Tong, X.: Accurate 3d face reconstruction with weakly-supervised learning: From single image to image set. In: CVPR Workshops (2019)
20. Dib, A., Thebault, C., Ahn, J., Gosselin, P., Theobalt, C., Chevallier, L.: Towards high fidelity monocular face reconstruction with rich reflectance using self-supervised learning and ray tracing. In: ICCV (2021)
21. Egger, B., et al.: 3d morphable face models - past, present, and future. TOG. **39**, 1–38 (2020)
22. Feng, Y., Feng, H., Black, M.J., Bolkart, T.: Learning an animatable detailed 3d face model from in-the-wild images. In: SIGGRAPH (2021)
23. Feng, Y., Wu, F., Shao, X., Wang, Y., Zhou, X.: Joint 3D face reconstruction and dense alignment with position map regression network. In: Ferrari, V., Hebert, M., Sminchisescu, C., Weiss, Y. (eds.) Computer Vision – ECCV 2018. LNCS, vol. 11218, pp. 557–574. Springer, Cham (2018). https://doi.org/10.1007/978-3-030-01264-9_33
24. Feng, Z., et al.: Evaluation of dense 3d reconstruction from 2d face images in the wild. In: FG (2018)
25. Gao, Z., Zhang, J., Guo, Y., Ma, C., Zhai, G., Yang, X.: Semi-supervised 3d face representation learning from unconstrained photo collections. In: CVPR Workshops (2020)
26. Gecer, B., Ploumpis, S., Kotsia, I., Zafeiriou, S.: GANFIT: generative adversarial network fitting for high fidelity 3d face reconstruction. In: CVPR (2019)
27. Gecer, B., Ploumpis, S., Kotsia, I., Zafeiriou, S.: Fast-GANFIT: generative adversarial network for high fidelity 3d face reconstruction. TPAMI (2021)
28. Genova, K., Cole, F., Maschinot, A., Sarna, A., Vlasic, D., Freeman, W.T.: Unsupervised training for 3d morphable model regression. In: CVPR (2018)
29. Guo, J., Zhu, X., Yang, Y., Yang, F., Lei, Z., Li, S.Z.: Towards Fast, Accurate and Stable 3D Dense Face Alignment. In: Vedaldi, A., Bischof, H., Brox, T., Frahm, J.-M. (eds.) ECCV 2020. LNCS, vol. 12364, pp. 152–168. Springer, Cham (2020). https://doi.org/10.1007/978-3-030-58529-7_10
30. Hu, L., et al.: Avatar digitization from a single image for real-time rendering. TOG **36**, 1–4 (2017)
31. Jiang, D., et al.: Reconstructing recognizable 3d face shapes based on 3d morphable models. CoRR, abs/2104.03515 (2021)
32. Karras, T., Laine, S., Aila, T.: A style-based generator architecture for generative adversarial networks. In: CVPR (2019)
33. Lattas, A., et al.: Avatarme: Realistically renderable 3d facial reconstruction "in-the-wild". In: CVPR (2020)
34. Lee, G., Lee, S.: Uncertainty-aware mesh decoder for high fidelity 3d face reconstruction. In: CVPR (2020)
35. Li, T., Bolkart, T., Black, M.J., Li, H., Romero, J.: Learning a model of facial shape and expression from 4d scans. TOG (2017)
36. Lin, J., Yuan, Y., Shao, T., Zhou, K.: Towards high-fidelity 3d face reconstruction from in-the-wild images using graph convolutional networks. In: CVPR (2020)
37. Lin, J., Yuan, Y., Zou, Z.: Meingame: create a game character face from a single portrait. In: AAAI (2021)
38. Liu, F., Zhu, R., Zeng, D., Zhao, Q., Liu, X.: Disentangling features in 3d face shapes for joint face reconstruction and recognition. In: CVPR (2018)
39. Liu, P., Han, X., Lyu, M.R., King, I., Xu, J.: Learning 3d face reconstruction with a pose guidance network. In: ACCV (2020)

40. Liu, Z., Luo, P., Wang, X., Tang, X.: Deep learning face attributes in the wild. In: ICCV (2015)
41. Luo, H., et al.: Normalized avatar synthesis using styleGAN and perceptual refinement. In: CVPR (2021)
42. Lyu, J., Li, X., Zhu, X., Cheng, C.: Pixel-face: A large-scale, high-resolution benchmark for 3d face reconstruction. arXiv preprint arXiv:2008.12444 (2020)
43. Ma, S., et al.: Pixel codec avatars. In: CVPR (2021)
44. Pan, X., Dai, B., Liu, Z., Chen, C.L., Luo, P.: Do 2d GANs know 3d shape? Unsupervised 3d shape reconstruction from 2d image GANs. In: ICLR (2021)
45. Paysan, P., Knothe, R., Amberg, B., Romdhani, S., Vetter, T.: A 3d face model for pose and illumination invariant face recognition. In: AVSS (2009)
46. Phillips, P.J., et al.: Overview of the face recognition grand challenge. In: CVPR (2005)
47. Piao, J., Sun, K., Wang, Q., Lin, K., Li, H.: Inverting generative adversarial renderer for face reconstruction. In: CVPR (2021)
48. Ploumpis, S., Wang, H., Pears, N.E., Smith, W.A.P., Zafeiriou, S.: Combining 3d morphable models: a large scale face-and-head model. In: CVPR (2019)
49. R, M.B., Tewari, A., Seidel, H., Elgharib, M., Theobalt, C.: Learning complete 3d morphable face models from images and videos. In: CVPR (2021)
50. Ramon, E., et al.: H3D-Net: few-shot high-fidelity 3d head reconstruction. In: ICCV (2021)
51. Richardson, E., Sela, M., Kimmel, R.: 3d face reconstruction by learning from synthetic data. In: 3DV (2016)
52. Sanyal, S., Bolkart, T., Feng, H., Black, M.J.: Learning to regress 3d face shape and expression from an image without 3d supervision. In: CVPR (2019)
53. Sela, M., Richardson, E., Kimmel, R.: Unrestricted facial geometry reconstruction using image-to-image translation. In: ICCV (2017)
54. Shang, J., et al.: Self-supervised monocular 3d face reconstruction by occlusion-aware multi-view geometry consistency. In: Vedaldi, A., Bischof, H., Brox, T., Frahm, J.-M. (eds.) ECCV 2020. LNCS, vol. 12360, pp. 53–70. Springer, Cham (2020). https://doi.org/10.1007/978-3-030-58555-6_4
55. Smith, W.A.P., Seck, A., Dee, H., Tiddeman, B., Tenenbaum, J.B., Egger, B.: A morphable face albedo model. In: CVPR (2020)
56. Stratou, G., Ghosh, A., Debevec, P.E., Morency, L.P.: Effect of illumination on automatic expression recognition: a novel 3d relightable facial database. In: FG (2011)
57. Tewari, A., et al.: MoFA: Model-based deep convolutional face autoencoder for unsupervised monocular reconstruction. In: ICCV (2017)
58. Thies, J., Zollhöfer, M., Stamminger, M., Theobalt, C., Nießner, M.: Face2face: Real-time face capture and reenactment of RGB videos. In: CVPR (2016)
59. Tran, A.T., Hassner, T., Masi, I., Medioni, G.G.: Regressing robust and discriminative 3d morphable models with a very deep neural network. In: CVPR (2017)
60. Tran, L., Liu, F., Liu, X.: Towards high-fidelity nonlinear 3d face morphable model. In: CVPR (2019)
61. Tran, L., Liu, X.: Nonlinear 3d face morphable model. In: CVPR (2018)
62. Tran, L., Liu, X.: On learning 3d face morphable model from in-the-wild images. TPAMI **43**, 157–171 (2021)
63. Wen, Y., Liu, W., Raj, B., Singh, R.: Self-supervised 3d face reconstruction via conditional estimation. In: ICCV (2021)
64. Wright, J., Yang, A.Y., Ganesh, A., Sastry, S.S., Ma, Y.: Robust face recognition via sparse representation. TPAMI (2009)

65. Wu, F., et al.: MVF-Net: multi-view 3d face morphable model regression. In: Proceedings of the IEEE/CVF Conference on Computer Vision and Pattern Recognition, pp. 959–968 (2019)

66. Wu, S., Rupprecht, C., Vedaldi, A.: Unsupervised learning of probably symmetric deformable 3d objects from images in the wild. In: CVPR (2020)

67. Yamaguchi, S., et al.: High-fidelity facial reflectance and geometry inference from an unconstrained image. TOG. **37**, 1–4 (2018)

68. Yang, H., et al.: Facescape: a large-scale high quality 3d face dataset and detailed riggable 3d face prediction. In: CVPR (2020)

69. Yenamandra, T., et al.: i3DMM: deep implicit 3d morphable model of human heads. In: CVPR (2021)

70. Yin, L., Wei, X., Sun, Y., Wang, J., Rosato, M.J.: A 3d facial expression database for facial behavior research. In: FG (2006)

71. Zeng, X., Peng, X., Qiao, Y.: DF2Net: a dense-fine-finer network for detailed 3d face reconstruction. In: ICCV (2019)

72. Zhang, Z., et al.: Learning to aggregate and personalize 3d face from in-the-wild photo collection. In: CVPR (2021)

73. Zhu, X., Liu, X., Lei, Z., Li, S.Z.: Face alignment in full pose range: a 3d total solution. TPAMI. **41**, 18–92 (2019)

74. Zhu, X., Ramanan, D.: Face detection, pose estimation, and landmark localization in the wild. In: CVPR (2012)

75. Zhu, X., et al.: Beyond 3DMM space: towards fine-grained 3d face reconstruction. In: Vedaldi, A., Bischof, H., Brox, T., Frahm, J.-M. (eds.) ECCV 2020. LNCS, vol. 12353, pp. 343–358. Springer, Cham (2020). https://doi.org/10.1007/978-3-030-58598-3_21

76. Zollhöfer, M., et al.: State of the art on monocular 3d face reconstruction, tracking, and applications. In: CGF (2018)

Capturing, Reconstructing, and Simulating: The UrbanScene3D Dataset

Liqiang Lin⓪, Yilin Liu⓪, Yue Hu, Xingguang Yan, Ke Xie,
and Hui Huang$^{(\boxtimes)}$⓪

Shenzhen University, Shenzhen, China
huihuang@szu.edu.cn

Abstract. We present *UrbanScene3D*, a large-scale data platform for research of urban scene perception and reconstruction. UrbanScene3D contains over 128k high-resolution images covering 16 scenes including large-scale real urban regions and synthetic cities with 136 km^2 area in total. The dataset also contains high-precision LiDAR scans and hundreds of image sets with different observation patterns, which provide a comprehensive benchmark to design and evaluate aerial path planning and 3D reconstruction algorithms. In addition, the dataset, which is built on Unreal Engine and Airsim simulator together with the manually annotated unique instance label for each building in the dataset, enables the generation of all kinds of data, e.g., 2D depth maps, 2D/3D bounding boxes, and 3D point cloud/mesh segmentations, etc. The simulator with physical engine and lighting system not only produce variety of data but also enable users to simulate cars or drones in the proposed urban environment for future research. The dataset with aerial path planning and 3D reconstruction benchmark is available at: https://vcc.tech/UrbanScene3D.

Keywords: UAV · Urban scene dataset · Aerial path planning · 3D acquisition · 3D reconstruction · City simulation

1 Introduction

With the development of digital photography and 3D scanning technologies, we have witnessed the explosive growth of data in recent years. Rich data sources and interaction methods bring rapid research progress in computer vision, computer graphics and robotics. For indoor scenes, with the help of sufficient data and real-time interactions [1,28,30,40], many fundamental problems, such as 2D/3D object detection and segmentation [16,33], depth estimation [24,43], 3D reconstruction [7–9,14,41] and autonomous navigation [6,15,50], have been better solved in a data-driven manner. However, things are different for outdoor

Supplementary Information The online version contains supplementary material available at https://doi.org/10.1007/978-3-031-20074-8_6.

S. Avidan et al. (Eds.): ECCV 2022, LNCS 13668, pp. 93–109, 2022.
https://doi.org/10.1007/978-3-031-20074-8_6

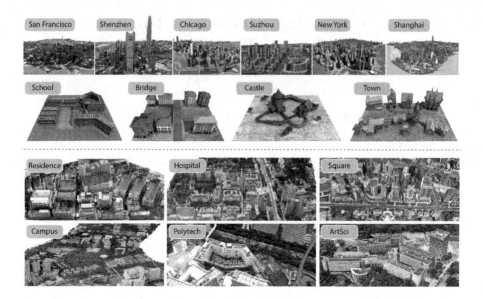

Fig. 1. A glance of synthetic (top) and real (bottom) scenes in UrbanScene3D.

study. The lack of effective devices and the extensive scales dramatically increase the difficulty of outdoor data capturing [48]. Also, due to the varied weather and light conditions, the outdoor scenes change fast and thus pose additional challenges to structure the data and design robust acquisition algorithms.

The current outdoor datasets are usually built by onboard equipment [10, 13,38], e.g., RGB cameras and/or LiDAR. Nonetheless, it is challenging to use these sensors to thoroughly capture the whole environment due to the limited field of views and routing choices. Other urban datasets [37,48] constructed by 3D modelers are usually clean and complete, but the models inside generally lack geometric and textural details. The gap between the proposed datasets and real-world scenarios remains large.

To tackle these problems, we present a large-scale urban scene dataset, *Urban-Scene3D*, which consists of both man-made and real-world reconstruction scenes in different scales, together with a convenient simulator built on Unreal Engine and AirSim. The man-made scene models have compact structures, which are carefully constructed/designed by professional artists; see the top of Fig. 1. Probably more important, UrbanScene3D also offers dense, detailed scene models reconstructed by aerial images through multi-view stereo (MVS) techniques; check out the bottom of Fig. 1, where the scene models are with realistic textures and meticulous geometric structures.

In particular, to investigate how to better acquire and reconstruct outdoor scenes, we select a set of scene representatives and capture them with a drone flying along a set of aerial paths. These flights are calculated by different planning algorithms for 3D urban scene reconstruction. Thus, for each representative environment, we are able to provide a variety of reconstructed meshes with the corresponding scene observations (aerial acquisition paths and the captured image sets). Besides, with the help of a high-precision laser scanner applied in the real world and the synthetic ground-truth models, we have constructed a benchmark that provides the point-level accuracy and completeness analysis of each reconstructed mesh. This enables a robust evaluation of both path planning strategies and MVS algorithms. In addition, the physical engine of AirSim enables users to simulate the robots (cars/drones) and test a variety of autonomous tasks in the proposed environments. The involvement of both synthetic and real scenes effectively extends the generalization ability of resulting algorithms.

In summary, our main contributions include: i) a large-scale urban scene dataset (Sect. 3) that facilitates research in various areas; ii) a comprehensive benchmark (Sect. 5) for investigating the impact of different factors in aerial path planning (Sect. 4) for 3D urban reconstruction; iii) an easy-to-use simulation platform (Sect. 6) for autonomous driving, robotics, and embodied AI research.

2   Related Work

Outdoor Datasets. The fast development of autonomous driving involves enormous outdoor datasets [2,10,13,38,39]. They often offer stereo sequences, 3D LiDAR point clouds, camera calibration, and 3D object tracklet labels for outdoor scenes, thus promoting many applications and research. Although these ground-based sensors can capture small-scale scenes [19], they usually have very restricted views and routing choices, which cause significant challenges to cover large-scale urban areas. Meanwhile, the unmanned aerial vehicles (UAVs) or drones, have much better visibility and more freedom to maneuver, making them suitable for a complete coverage of wide regions. However, most existing UAV based datasets are not designed for capturing the entire scene. Instead, they only provide partial observations for perception tasks, such as semantic segmentation [25], object detection [12,26,49], action recognition [5], gesture recognition [31,32], or tracking [3,29]. On the contrary, we carefully plan the drone path to obtain a complete capture, from which the entire 3D scene can be reconstructed with MVS methods.

Synthetic CAD Datasets. Different from real-world datasets, building synthetic datasets with CAD models [4,21] can offer a complete structured environment at a much lower cost, but lack geometric and textural details. To bridge the gap, HoliCity [48] aligns the real-world panoramas with the CAD models to provide real texture. However, the discrepancy is still significant since the geometry is too coarse and the panoramas only covers a portion of the entire scene. Instead, our UrbanScene3D contains both real-world and synthetic CAD scenes, facilitating research for both high-quality urban reconstruction and holistic scene understanding. Similar to Mueller et al. [29], we also provide a simulator that stimulates the research of online real-time capturing and understanding of 3D urban scenes.

Aerial Path Planning for Urban Scene Capture. To capture urban scenes with drones, aerial path planning plays a vital role; see a recent survey [47]. Manual control and Zig-Zag patterns are inefficient, difficult to achieve decent coverage,

Table 1. Statistics of UrbanScene3D with 10 synthetic and 6 real scenes. Area: the covered area of the scene model; Size: the size of the scene model; Texture: the number of texture images contained in the scene model; Texture: the size of texture; Object: the number of objects in the scene model.

Scene	Area(m^2)	Size(Mb)	Texture(#)	Texture(Mb)	Object(#)
New York	7.4×10^6	86	762	122	744
Chicago	2.4×10^7	146	2277	227	1629
San Francisco	5.5×10^7	225	2865	322	2801
Shenzhen	3.0×10^6	50	199	73	1126
Suzhou	7.0×10^6	191	395	24	168
Shanghai	3.7×10^7	308	2285	220	6850
School	1.7×10^4	25	47	488	3
Bridge	1.3×10^4	28	237	44	8
Castle	7.0×10^3	9	47	184	6
Town	4.4×10^3	112	73	348	17
Campus	1.3×10^6	1859	122	3676	178
Residence	1.0×10^5	356	52	1760	34
Square	1.1×10^6	3665	799	980	156
Hospital	5.0×10^5	6266	94	744	114
Polytech	1.5×10^4	3523	50	221	3
ArtSci	1.6×10^4	25395	118	556	3

and challenging to fulfill practical factors, such as safety restriction and battery capacity. To deal with these problems, existing methods [17,20,34,36,37,44,46] optimize the drone path according to certain goals and constraints with a coarse proxy model or a top view image as input. Specifically, Smith et al. [37] designs an optimization objective for better multi-view stereo results, ensuring the completeness and accuracy of the reconstruction. Further, Zhang el al. [44] propose a continuous path planner to adequately shorten the path length and reduce sharp turns. To be able to do offsite planning, Zhou et al. [46] utilize a satellite image to estimate a 2.5D proxy for view selection. For online planning, the researchers learn to construct 2.5D height maps [23] or estimate 3D bounding boxes of buildings [22] on-the-fly for drone navigation and exploration. Due to the lack of valid data, these methods usually rely on a handcraft heuristic function to optimize the capturing views or the flight trajectories. However, the quality of the final reconstruction is constrained by the high-order relation among observations, which is difficult to model by heuristics and optimization designs. Our data and benchmark will efficaciously facilitate future research on this topic.

3   The UrbanScene3D Dataset

The goal of UrbanScene3D is to provide a general data platform for 3D vision, graphics and robotics research in urban scene environments with different scales. UrbanScene3D provides 10 synthetic and 6 real-world scenes with CAD and

Table 2. More path planning statistics of 4 synthetic and 2 real representative scenes selected from UrbanScene3D. Tri: the number of triangles of the scene model; Proxy: the number of different levels of proxies provided; Overlap: the overlap rate used to sample the proxies; Planner: the number of different planners used to generate aerial paths; Path: the total number of generated flight paths of the scene; Image: the total number of captured images of the scene.

Scene	Tri(#)	Proxy(#)	Overlap(%)	Planner(#)	Path(#)	Image(#)
School	250,282	4	70 & 90	4	25	14,897
Bridge	394,022	4	70 & 90	4	25	13,228
Castle	109,513	4	70 & 90	4	25	7,414
Town	1,197,751	4	70 & 90	4	25	8,948
Polytech	2,613,608	3	90	4	13	19,635
ArtSci	4,524,028	3	90	4	13	12,261

reconstructed mesh models and the corresponding aerial images; see Fig. 1 and Table 1 for more details. The synthetic CAD scenes consist of various compact primitive structures including buildings, bridges, streets, and vegetation, all of which are built by professional artists. For real scenes, we use a drone to capture images for MVS. We program the drone to follow an aerial path generated with oblique photography, a commonly used industrial solution conducted by *DJI-Terra*[1] for 3D city acquisition. Based on these images, we reconstruct the scenes with *ContextCapture*[2], a commercial MVS solution. Specially, the selected representative scenes for our benchmark include additional huge volume of capture data using various path planners under different settings; see Table 2.

For oblique photography planner, we use a professional *DJI M300RTK*[3] drone loaded with five HD *PSDK 102S* aerial cameras. For the other planners, we use a single-camera *DJI PHANTOM 4 RTK*[4] drone.

Table 3 summarizes the difference between UrbanScene3D and the existing outdoor datasets. We further highlight the features of UrbanScene3D as follows.

Up in the Air. Most outdoor datasets are ground based and the capture usually do not cover the entire scene. The capture is incomplete even for aerial dataset like UAVDet [12], since its goal is object detection. Similar to BlendedMVS [42], we provide aerial captures that are suitable for MVS. Specifically for the representative scenes, we adopt multiple optimized aerial paths for the capture, which lead to greater quality urban scenes. Our approach not only provides a high-quality dataset for local perception research but also enables the research of global understanding for real 3D urban scenes.

---

[1] https://www.dji.com/dji-terra.
[2] https://www.bentley.com/en/products/brands/contextcapture.
[3] https://www.dji.com/matrice-300.
[4] https://www.dji.com/phantom-4-rtk.

Table 3. Comparing UrbanScene3D with existing 3D outdoor datasets. Area stands for the maximum area across all scenes in the dataset. Path stands for the number of flights/rides for capturing. Note that for BlendedMVS, we only show the estimated statistics of the urban scenes.

Datasets	Scene	Type	Area(km^2)	Path(#)	Image(#)	Diversity	Simulator	Semantics
KITTI [13]	Driving	LiDAR	/	1	93 k	5 scans	/	/
Cityscape [10]	Driving	Stereo	/	/	25 k	50 cities	/	2D
HoliCity [48]	Urban	CAD	20	/	6.3 k	1 city	/	3D
BlendedMVS [42]	Mixed	MVS	0.02	29	17 k	29 scenes	/	/
SYNTHIA [35]	Driving	CAD	/	/	50 k	1 city	Car	3D
Mueller2016 [29]	Mixed	CAD	/	/	/	/	Drone	3D
Smith2018 [37]	Urban	CAD	0.03	/	/	5 scenes	/	/
UrbanScene3D	Urban	CAD&MVS	55	130	128 k	16 cities/scenes	Car&drone	3D

Extensive Scale. Many existing datasets do not offer the complete capture of large-scale scenes; see Table 3. While Holicity offers a 20 km^2 scene of London, our dataset includes three large-scale city scenes that cover above 24 km^2 area. Meanwhile, we offer multiple real-world complete scenes, which include two extensive scenes that cover above 1 km^2 area, whose scale is unseen in previous datasets like BlendedMVS [42]. More diverse urban scenes and the corresponding aerial images with shot poses are also available. Additionally, our drone flight path length can be up to 17 km, which benefits the research for SLAM or SfM.

Path Planning Research. For current path planning methods, factors such as the proxy accuracy and overlap rate play an vital role. Our path planning benchmark specifically include different settings for these factors. We show their influence on the final reconstruction quality and acquisition efficiency; see Sect. 5. In contrast, existing benchmark [37] for path planning does not consider these factors and only includes synthetic scenes. Besides, our benchmark includes hundreds of flight paths, which will boost the future research for path planning techniques.

Multiple Captures. The different weather and lighting conditions in outdoor environment pose huge challenges for perception and reconstruction in general. Our benchmark offers multiple drone flights for each scene over different times, this greatly increases the variety of data, which can benefit learning based methods to in turn solve this problem. For example, the abundance (10k+) of the real scene images in the benchmark under different lighting conditions allows the future research for NeRFs [27] that can decouple geometry, material and light.

Simulation Environment. The sim-to-real gap is a critical problem for the robotics and embodied AI research. Our simulator can directly import our real-world scenes and simulate the drones inside them, hence this gap would be greatly shortened. In contrast, most existing simulator for autonomous driving or UAVs operate only for virtual scenes. Further, our simulator can show the coverage of the scene in real-time, which is useful for research on UAV exploration.

4   Scene Acquisition with Aerial Path Planning

UrbanScene3D offers a wide variety of potential applications, from instance segmentation, multi-view stereo, to depth estimation and novel view synthesis. See Sect. 6 for further details. In this section, we extend the UrbanScene3D dataset to a benchmark to evaluate the quality and efficiency of different path planning algorithms, as well as the impact of input proxies in Sect. 5.

UrbanScene3D contains all the data needed for testing path planning algorithms and analyzing the reconstructed results, including proxies, ground-truth models/point clouds, paths, images, and reconstructed results; see Table 2.

The majority of path planners usually rely on a pre-computed coarse model (also called *proxy* [37]) of the environment. The proxy can be obtained by various methods, including a quick reconstruction after a simplified oblique photography pass [34,37], satellite image [46], map providers or even through a real-time reconstruction [22]. The quality of the proxy, including the accuracy of the topology and the face normal, can affect the final quality of the reconstruction.

In Sect. 4.1, we briefly introduce the 4 path planners we used to generate different trajectories. To evaluate the influence of the proxy in the path planning, we then introduce different proxies we used in the dataset in Sect. 4.2.

4.1   Aerial Path Planning Methods

In order to offer more paths and images, we use four different path planners, including oblique photography and the methods proposed by Smith et al. [37], Zhou et al. [46], and Zhang et al. [44], to generate the paths on the different proxies mentioned in Sect. 4.2 with different overlap rates for different scenes, resulting in 100 different paths for synthetic scenes and 26 paths for real scenes. Figure 2 shows an illustration of the paths generated with the four different planners on the synthetic scene School and the real scene Polytech.

Oblique Photography. Given the image overlap and ground sample distance (GSD), Oblique photography generate an S-shaped trajectory at a fixed height (calculated by the GSD) and compute the required capture location. The S-shaped trajectory is usually computed by *Complete Coverage Path Planning* (CCPP) algorithm, which could guarantee the complete coverage of an area even with an irregular shape [45]. Also, the number of turns is minimized, which could significantly increase the capturing efficiency.

Planner Proposed by Smith et al. [37]. Unlike Oblique photography, Smith et al. [37] directly optimize viewpoints according to a heuristic function, *reconstructability*, which consider both the potential error of triangulation and feature matching in the *Multi-view Stereo* (MVS) process. In each iteration, Smith et al. [37] first compute the so-called *reconstructability* of each point respect to the current viewpoint set. Then they try to maximize this measurement by adjusting the position and orientation of each viewpoint.

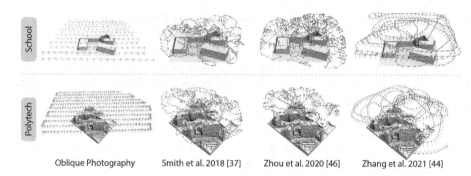

Fig. 2. The comparison of the paths generated with different aerail planning methods on the synthetic scene School and the real scene Polytech.

Planner Proposed by Zhou et al. [46]. Similar to Smith et al. [37], Zhou et al. [46] also consider the reconstructability of each point during the planning. However, they only use this measurement to reduce useless viewpoints. They first generate a large viewpoint set, which suppose to be *complete* but highly *redundant*. In each iteration, they define the *view redundancy* on the computed reconstructability and delete the most redundant viewpoint accordingly.

Planner Proposed by Zhang et al. [44]. Compared with Oblique photography, Smith et al. [37] and Zhou et al. [46] generate trajectories with higher capturing quality. However, the heuristic function which is defined on the viewpoints brings many sharp turns in the final trajectories. The drastic speed change significantly decreases the capturing efficiency. Thus, Zhang et al. [44] involves path smoothness in the heuristic function and utilize *Rapidly-exploring random* (RRT) tree to search for an efficient and high-quality trajectory.

4.2 Geometric Proxies

The proxies are essential for aerial path planning methods. Detailed proxy usually leads to much better reconstruction results. Previous works either use a rough scene proxy [37,44] or a 2.5D model extracted from satellite images [46] to plan the path. UrbanScene3D provides proxies in different levels of details, which could be used to analyze the relations between proxies, paths, and the corresponding qualities of the reconstructed models; see Fig. 3.

The box proxy (*box*) is the roughest level of proxy with incorrect topology. It is built by replacing the building set in the scene with its bounding box. For the real scene, the box proxy is deprecated due to the safety issue. Similar to *box* proxy, *coarse* proxy is also built by finding the bounding box of each building in the scene. However, the *coarse* proxy has more accurate topology, which might lead more accurate path planning result. The intermediate proxy (*inter*) is reconstructed by downsampled images which are captured by oblique photography. The ground-truth meshes (*fine*) for the synthetic scenes can also be

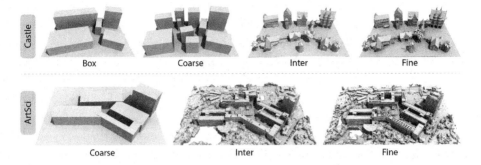

Fig. 3. The proxies of scene School in different levels of details. Box: the roughest proxy; Coarse: the coarse level of proxy; Inter: the intermediate level of proxy; Fine: the finest level of proxy.

used as proxies, which is supposed to provide the largest geometric information during the path planning process. The *fine* proxy for the real scenes are reconstructed with non subsampled images captured by oblique photography. Since there are no ground-truth meshes for real scenes, we use reconstructed models by high-density images as their corresponding fine proxies.

5   Scene Reconstruction Benchmarks

In this section, we evaluate the paths generated with different path planning methods for both energy cost, aerotriangulation accuracy, and reconstruction quality, providing the point-level accuracy and completeness analysis of the reconstructed mesh. The statistics of energy consumption of UAV capturing is given in Sect. 5.2. In Sect. 5.3, we analyze the aerotriangulation results of different planners. And finally, we evaluate the reconstruction results in Sect. 5.4. The Sect. 5.5 give a overall comparison of all the four planners.

Other information, e.g., the evaluation of different overlaps, the cost of model reconstruction, and the reconstruction evaluation on the other scenes are included in the supplementary material.

5.1   High-Precision LiDAR Scan

The synthetic scenes come with ground-truth meshes for evaluation. For the real scenes, we scan the entire building with high-precision LiDAR scanners loaded with GPS localization devices. The point clouds are then registered with each other, resulting in a high-precision LiDAR scan of the whole building.

The LiDAR scanner is Trimble X7 with self-calibration and self-registration techniques. The ranging noise is 0.5 mm, the ranging accuracy is 2 mm, the angular accuracy is 21″, and the accuracy of 3D points is 1.5 mm at 10 m and 2.4 mm at 20 m. Each scan, including self-calibration, takes 2 min and 34 s. For real scene Polytech, the overall error of registration is 6 mm; for real scene ArtSci, the overall error of registration is 3 mm.

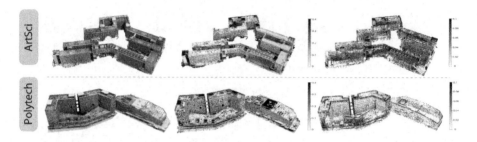

Fig. 4. The visualization of scanned point clouds and reconstruction error maps for real scene ArtSci and Polytech.

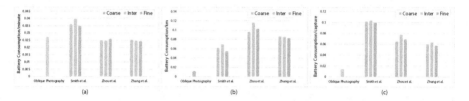

Fig. 5. Battery consumption of different methods with different proxies on the real scene ArtSci. (a): battery consumption per minute (%/minute) ↓; (b): battery consumption per Km (10^{-3}%/km) ↓; (c): battery consumption between two captures (10^{-2}%) ↓.

Figure 4 shows the scanned point clouds, the accuracy maps, and the completeness maps for both the real scene ArtSci and Polytech.

5.2   UAV Capturing Cost

Along with the length of the flight path, the efficiency of the path, such as the total turning angles, affects the overall energy consumption. The drone consumes more energy when it accelerates and decelerates near the turns.

Figure 5 shows the battery consumption statistics of the flight paths planned with different methods on the real scene ArtSci. As we can see in this figure, the capturing cost, or the efficiency of the flight path, is mainly affected by the path pattern. Since oblique photography has the simplest path (Fig. 2), it has nearly the lowest battery cost. Generally, the method proposed by Zhang et al. [44] has a lower battery consumption than the other two methods, since they explicitly optimize the path efficiency in their cost function.

5.3   Aerotriangulation Error

Before reconstructing the scenes, a process named aerotriangulation, which is a triangulation with aerial images is first performed on the captured images to determine the pose of the cameras and to obtain a sparse point cloud of the environment.

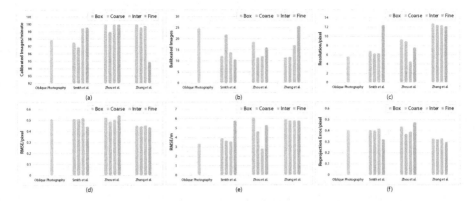

Fig. 6. Aerotriangulation error of different methods with different proxies on the synthetic scenes Town. (a): calibrated images per minute ($\#/m$) ↑; (b): the rate of successfully calibrated images (%) ↑; (c): average resolution per pixel ($1e^{-3}m/pixel$) ↓; (d): root mean square error in pixel ($1e^{-3}$pixel) ↓; (e): root mean square error in meter ($1e^{-3}$ m) ↓; (f): reprojection error (pixel) ↓.

Figure 6 shows the statistics of the aerotriangulation error on different proxies with the overlap as 90% tested on the scene Town. As indicated in Fig. 6, the aerotriangulation results of the method proposed by Smith et al. [37] and the method proposed by Zhou et al. [46] are quite sensitive to the different levels of proxies. For the method proposed by Zhang et al. [44], the RMS-pixel (root mean square error in pixel), RMS-meter (root mean square error in meter), and the reprojection error decrease as the proxy go finer. However, compared to Zhou et al. [46], some images captured with this method are not calibrated well. The aerotriangulation results of Zhou et al. [46] and Zhang et al. [44] have lower RMSE in meter than Smith et al. [37]. The images captured by oblique photography are also well-calibrated and have a low aerotriangulation error as the images are overlapped with each other strictly.

5.4   Reconstruction Accuracy and Completeness

We evaluate the reconstruction results of the four planners with different proxies and the results of reconstruction accuracy and completeness are shown in Fig. 7. The evaluation is performed on scene School with 90% overlap.

The value of 90% or 95% accuracy x means that for all the closest points of the vertices of the reconstruction model on the ground-truth model, 90% or 95% of them have a distance less than x. The value of 0.02 m, 0.075 m, or 0.075 m completeness x% means that for all the closest points of the vertices of the ground-truth model on the reconstruction model, x% of them have a distance less than 0.02 m, 0.05 m, or 0.075 m. A smaller 90% and 95% accuracy value mean higher accuracy and a larger 0.02 m, 0.05 m, or 0.075 m completeness value means higher completeness.

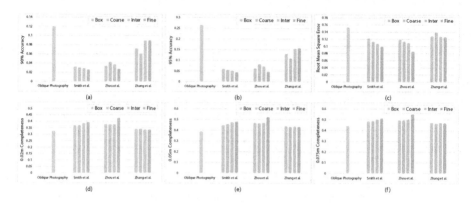

Fig. 7. Reconstruction error of different methods with different proxies on the synthetic scene School. (a): 90% accuracy (m) ↓; (b): 95% Accuracy (m) ↓; (c): root mean square error (m) ↓; (d): 0.02 m completeness (%) ↑; (e): 0.05 m completeness (%) ↑; (f): 0.075 m completeness (%) ↑.

As shown in Fig. 7, both the accuracy and the completeness of reconstructed results of the methods proposed by Smith et al. [37] and Zhou et al. [46] increase as the proxy goes finer. The accuracy and completeness of the results by Zhang et al. [44] are not quite consistent with the proxy.

The visualization of the reconstructed results and reconstruction error is shown in Fig. 8. The values for accuracy and completeness are clamped to $0 \sim 0.04$ and $0 \sim 0.1$. As one could expect, the complex geometry and high occlusion induce lower accuracy and completeness of reconstruction.

In general, the method proposed by Smith et al. [37] and Zhou et al. [46] get higher accuracy and completeness compared to oblique photography and Zhang et al. [44]. However, the paths produced by the method proposed by Zhang et al. [44] have higher quality and consume less energy.

5.5   Comparison of Different Planners

The path generated with oblique photography simply follows a Zig-Zag pattern thus the target scene is completely covered and the captured images are well calculated. As the baseline planner, oblique photography has the lowest energy cost among all the four planners but results in a roughest reconstruction. The reconstruction error mainly comes from the occlusion between different buildings and other objects since it can not dive into the space between them. Both the method propose by Smith et al. [37] and Zhou et al. [46] get a much higher quality reconstruction than oblique photography. In general, the method proposed by Zhou et al. [46] cost less energy compared to the Smith et al. [37]. For the method proposed by Zhang et al. [44], although they get a higher reconstruction error than Smith et al. [37] and Zhou et al. [46], the battery consumption is reduced due to the continuity of the generated paths.

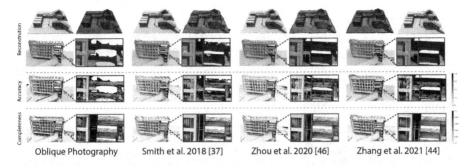

Oblique Photography   Smith et al. 2018 [37]   Zhou et al. 2020 [46]   Zhang et al. 2021 [44]

Fig. 8. Visual comparisons of the resulting 3D reconstruction and the corresponding reconstruction error produced by different methods. A higher value means lower accuracy and less completeness for the second and the third rows.

6   Simulator and Applications

Although there are 3D instance segmentation datasets, e.g., S3DIS [1], Scan-Net [11] and SceneNN [18], they are all collected from indoor scenes and still not enough for deep learning based methods. Please note that there is basically no decent dataset for learning 3D building instance segmentation in spacious outdoor scenes, especially for complicated urban regions.

In this context, our released UrbanScene3D provides rich, large-scale urban scene building annotation data for 3D instance segmentation research. To segment and label 3D architectures, we manually extract all single building models from the entire scene model. Every building is then assigned a unique label, forming an instance segmentation map; see the top right of Fig. 9 for an example. The 3D textured models with instance segmentation labels in UrbanScene3D allow users to obtain all kinds of data they would like to have: instance segmentation map, depth map in arbitrary resolution, 3D point cloud/mesh in both visible and invisible places, etc. UrbanScene3D also offers 4K captured aerial videos in some specific real scenes aimed for 3D reconstruction; see the top left of Fig. 9. Together with high-precision laser scans as ground-truth, these data can be effectively used to train and evaluate various SLAM algorithms.

Moreover, with UrbanScene3D, users can also simulate the robots (cars or drones) to test a variety of autonomous tasks in the proposed city environments. The gravity, inertia and collision can be handled by the physical engine of Airsim. Thus, users can easily generate highly realistic data for many tasks, such as depth estimation, autonomous navigation, and novel view synthesis. Meanwhile, both the lighting condition and the weather of each urban scene can be manipulated by users too. That is, users are able to simulate a rainy night campus or a foggy morning campus; see e.g., the bottom of Fig. 9. Such data endowed with large diversity would reduce the discrepancy between the simulated and real-world environments, and hence increase the generalization of proposed algorithms.

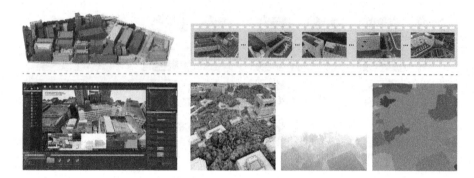

Fig. 9. UrbanScene3D also provides the building instance ID for each environment (top left) , 4K aerial videos that are aimed at the real scene acquisition (top right), and a simulator built on Unreal Engine and AirSim (bottom).

7   Conclusion and Future Work

We present a large-scale dataset, *UrbanScene3D*, which offers rich data annotations and a wide variety of observations of six representative environments. The corresponding reconstruction results and the ground-truth models/scans can be used to evaluate path planning and MVS algorithms. Besides, the proposed simulator allows users to further explore and capture urban scenes in various data patterns with different lighting/weather conditions. The release of UrbanScene3D would largely benefit the community.

In the future, we plan to do high-level geometric descriptions in the dataset, such as 3D structural points, cross-sectional profiles, wire-frames, or plane segments, etc., to support further research in both computer vision and computer graphics. UrbanScene3D will constantly grow to make more contributions to the data-driven study.

Acknowledgements. This work was supported in parts by NSFC (62161146005, U21B2023, U2001206), GD Talent Program (2019JC05X328), DEGP Innovation Team (2022KCXTD025), Shenzhen Science and Technology Program (KQTD202108110900 44003, RCJC20200714114435012, JCYJ20210324120213036), and Guangdong Laboratory of Artificial Intelligence and Digital Economy (SZ).

References

1. Armeni, I., Sax, A., Zamir, A.R., Savarese, S.: Joint 2D–3D-semantic data for indoor scene understanding. arXiv preprint arXiv:1702.01105 (2017)
2. Behley, J., et al.: SemanticKITTI: a dataset for semantic scene understanding of lidar sequences. In: Proceedings of International Conference on Computer Vision, pp. 9297–9307 (2019)
3. Bergmann, P., Meinhardt, T., Leal-Taixe, L.: Tracking without bells and whistles. In: Proceedings of IEEE International Conference on Pattern Recognition, pp. 941–951 (2019)

4. Brunel, A., Bourki, A., Strauss, O., Demonceaux, C.: FLYBO: a unified benchmark environment for autonomous flying robots. In: International Conference on 3D Vision, pp. 1420–1431 (2021)

5. Chaquet, J.M., Carmona, E.J., Fernández-Caballero, A.: A survey of video datasets for human action and activity recognition. In: Computer Vision and Image Understanding, pp. 633–659 (2013)

6. Chen, K., et al.: A behavioral approach to visual navigation with graph localization networks. In: Proceedings of Robotics: Science and Systems, pp. 1–10 (2019)

7. Chen, Z., Tagliasacchi, A., Zhang, H.: BSP-Net: generating compact meshes via binary space partitioning. In: Proceedings of IEEE Conference on Computer Vision & Pattern Recognition, pp. 45–54 (2020)

8. Chen, Z., Zhang, H.: Learning implicit fields for generative shape modeling. In: Proceedings of IEEE Conference on Computer Vision & Pattern Recognition, pp. 5939–5948 (2019)

9. Choy, C.B., Xu, D., Gwak, J.Y., Chen, K., Savarese, S.: 3D-R2N2: a unified approach for single and multi-view 3d object reconstruction. In: Leibe, B., Matas, J., Sebe, N., Welling, M. (eds.) ECCV 2016. LNCS, vol. 9912, pp. 628–644. Springer, Cham (2016). https://doi.org/10.1007/978-3-319-46484-8_38

10. Cordts, M., et al.: The cityscapes dataset for semantic urban scene understanding. In: Proceedings of IEEE Conference on Computer Vision & Pattern Recognition, pp. 3213–3223 (2016)

11. Dai, A., Chang, A.X., Savva, M., Halber, M., Funkhouser, T., Nießner, M.: ScanNet: richly-annotated 3D reconstructions of indoor scenes. In: Proceedings of IEEE Conference on Computer Vision & Pattern Recognition, pp. 2432–2443 (2017)

12. Du, D., et al.: The unmanned aerial vehicle benchmark: Object detection and tracking. In: Proceedings of European Conference on Computer Vision Workshops, pp. 370–386 (2018)

13. Geiger, A., Lenz, P., Urtasun, R.: Are we ready for autonomous driving? The KITTI vision benchmark suite. In: Proceedings of IEEE Conference on Computer Vision & Pattern Recognition, pp. 3354–3361 (2012)

14. Groueix, T., Fisher, M., Kim, V.G., Russell, B.C., Aubry, M.: AtlasNet: a Papier-Mâché approach to learning 3D surface generation. In: Proceedings of IEEE Conference on Computer Vision & Pattern Recognition, pp. 216–224 (2018)

15. Gupta, S., Davidson, J., Levine, S., Sukthankar, R., Malik, J.: Cognitive mapping and planning for visual navigation. In: Proceedings of IEEE Conference on Computer Vision & Pattern Recognition, pp. 2616–2625 (2017)

16. He, K., Gkioxari, G., Dollár, P., Girshick, R.B.: Mask R-CNN. In: Proceedings of International Conference on Computer Vision, pp. 2980–2988 (2017)

17. Hepp, B., Nießner, M., Hilliges, O.: Plan3D: Viewpoint and trajectory optimization for aerial multi-view stereo reconstruction. ACM Trans. Graph. **38**, 4:1–4:17 (2018)

18. Hua, B.S., Pham, Q.H., Nguyen, D.T., Tran, M.K., Yu, L.F., Yeung, S.K.: SceneNN: a scene meshes dataset with aNNotations. In: International Conference on 3D Vision, pp. 92–101 (2016)

19. Knapitsch, A., Park, J., Zhou, Q.Y., Koltun, V.: Tanks and temples: benchmarking large-scale scene reconstruction. ACM Trans. Graph. (Proc. SIGGRAPH). **36**, 78:1–78:13 (2017)

20. Koch, T., Körner, M., Fraundorfer, F.: Automatic and semantically-aware 3D UAV flight planning for image-based 3D reconstruction. Remote Sens. **11**, 1550 (2019)

21. Liu, J., Ji, S.: A novel recurrent encoder-decoder structure for large-scale multi-view stereo reconstruction from an open aerial dataset. In: Proceedings IEEE Conference on Computer Vision & Pattern Recognition, pp. 6050–6059 (2020)

22. Liu, Y., Cui, R., Xie, K., Gong, M., Huang, H.: Aerial path planning for online real-time exploration and offline high-quality reconstruction of large-scale urban scenes. ACM Trans. Graph. (Proc. SIGGRAPH Asia). 226:1–226:16 (2021)
23. Liu, Y., Xie, K., Huang, H.: VGF-Net: Visual-geometric fusion learning for simultaneous drone navigation and height mapping. Graph. Models. **116**, 101108:1–101108:9 (2021)
24. Luo, X., Huang, J., Szeliski, R., Matzen, K., Kopf, J.: Consistent video depth estimation. ACM Trans. Graph. (Proc. SIGGRAPH). **39**, 71:1–71:13 (2020)
25. Lyu, Y., Vosselman, G., Xia, G.S., Yilmaz, A., Yang, M.Y.: UAVid: a semantic segmentation dataset for UAV imagery. ISPRS J. Photogram. Remote Sens. **165**, 108–119 (2020)
26. Mandal, M., Kumar, L.K., Vipparthi, S.K.: MOR-UAV: a benchmark dataset and baselines for moving object recognition in UAV videos. In: Proceedings of ACM Conference on Multimedia, pp. 2626–2635 (2020)
27. Mildenhall, B., Srinivasan, P.P., Tancik, M., Barron, J.T., Ramamoorthi, R., Ng, R.: NeRF: representing scenes as neural radiance fields for view synthesis. In: Vedaldi, A., Bischof, H., Brox, T., Frahm, J.-M. (eds.) ECCV 2020. LNCS, vol. 12346, pp. 405–421. Springer, Cham (2020). https://doi.org/10.1007/978-3-030-58452-8_24
28. Mo, K., et al.: PartNet: a large-scale benchmark for fine-grained and hierarchical part-level 3D object understanding. In: Proceedings of IEEE Conf. on Computer Vision & Pattern Recognition, pp. 909–918 (2019)
29. Mueller, M., Smith, N., Ghanem, B.: A benchmark and simulator for UAV tracking. In: Leibe, B., Matas, J., Sebe, N., Welling, M. (eds.) ECCV 2016. LNCS, vol. 9905, pp. 445–461. Springer, Cham (2016). https://doi.org/10.1007/978-3-319-46448-0_27
30. Silberman, N., Hoiem, D., Kohli, P., Fergus, R.: Indoor segmentation and support inference from RGBD images. In: Fitzgibbon, A., Lazebnik, S., Perona, P., Sato, Y., Schmid, C. (eds.) ECCV 2012. LNCS, vol. 7576, pp. 746–760. Springer, Heidelberg (2012). https://doi.org/10.1007/978-3-642-33715-4_54
31. Perera, A.G., Law, Y.W., Chahl, J.: UAV-GESTURE: a dataset for UAV control and gesture recognition. In: Leal-Taixé, L., Roth, S. (eds.) ECCV 2018. LNCS, vol. 11130, pp. 117–128. Springer, Cham (2019). https://doi.org/10.1007/978-3-030-11012-3_9
32. Pisharady, P.K., Saerbeck, M.: Recent methods and databases in vision-based hand gesture recognition: a review. In: Computer Vision and Image Understanding, pp. 152–165 (2015)
33. Qi, C.R., Yi, L., Su, H., Guibas, L.J.: PointNet++: deep hierarchical feature learning on point sets in a metric space. In: Proceedings of Conference on Neural Information Processing Systems, pp. 5099–5108 (2017)
34. Roberts, M., et al.: Submodular trajectory optimization for aerial 3D scanning. In: Proceedings of International Conference on Computer Vision, pp. 5324–5333 (2017)
35. Ros, G., Sellart, L., Materzynska, J., Vazquez, D., Lopez, A.M.: The Synthia dataset: a large collection of synthetic images for semantic segmentation of urban scenes. In: Proceedings of IEEE Conference on Computer Vision & Pattern Recognition, pp. 3234–3243 (2016)
36. Schmid, K., Hirschmüller, H., Dömel, A., Grixa, I., Suppa, M., Hirzinger, G.: View planning for multi-view stereo 3D reconstruction using an autonomous multicopter. J. Intell. Robot. Syst. **65**, 309–323 (2012)

37. Smith, N., Moehrle, N., Goesele, M., Heidrich, W.: Aerial path planning for urban scene reconstruction: a continuous optimization method and benchmark. ACM Trans. Graph. (Proc. SIGGRAPH Asia). **36**, 183:1–183:15 (2018)

38. Song, X., et al.: ApolloCar3D: a large 3D car instance understanding benchmark for autonomous driving. In: Proceedings of IEEE Conference on Computer Vision & Pattern Recognition, pp. 5447–5457 (2019)

39. Sun, P., et al.: Scalability in perception for autonomous driving: Waymo open dataset. In: Proceedings of IEEE Conference on Computer Vision & Pattern Recognition, pp. 2446–2454 (2020)

40. Xia, F., R. Zamir, A., He, Z.Y., Sax, A., Malik, J., Savarese, S.: Gibson ENV: real-world perception for embodied agents. In: Proceedings of IEEE Conference on Computer Vision & Pattern Recognition, pp. 9068–9079 (2018)

41. Xu, Q., Wang, W., Ceylan, D., Mech, R., Neumann, U.: DISN: deep implicit surface network for high-quality single-view 3D reconstruction. Proc. Conf. on Neural Information Processing Systems pp. 490–500 (2019)

42. Yao, Y., et al.: BlendedMVS: a large-scale dataset for generalized multi-view stereo networks. In: Proceedings of IEEE Conference on Computer Vision & Pattern Recognition, pp. 1790–1799 (2020)

43. Yin, W., et al.: Learning to recover 3D scene shape from a single image. In: Proceedings of IEEE Conference on Computer Vision & Pattern Recognition, pp. 204–213 (2021)

44. Zhang, H., Yao, Y., Xie, K., Fu, C.W., Zhang, H., Huang, H.: Continuous aerial path planning for 3D urban scene reconstruction. ACM Trans. Graph. (Proc. SIGGRAPH Asia). **40**, 225:1–225:15 (2021)

45. Zhang, X., Zhao, P., Hu, Q., Ai, M., Hu, D., Li, J.: A UAV-based panoramic oblique photogrammetry (POP) approach using spherical projection. J. Photogramm. Remote Sens. **159**, 198–219 (2020)

46. Zhou, X., Xie, K., Huang, K., Liu, Y., Zhou, Y., Gong, M., Huang, H.: Offsite aerial path planning for efficient urban scene reconstruction. ACM Trans. Graph. (Proc. SIGGRAPH Asia). **39**, 192:1–192:16 (2020)

47. Zhou, X., Yi, Z., Liu, Y., Huang, K., Huang, H.: Survey on path and view planning for UAVs. Virtual Real. Intell. Hardw. **2**, 56–69 (2020)

48. Zhou, Y., Huang, J., Dai, X., Luo, L., Chen, Z., Ma, Y.: HoliCity: a city-scale data platform for learning holistic 3D structures. arXiv preprint arXiv:2008.03286 (2020)

49. Zhu, P., et al.: Visdrone-vid2019: the vision meets drone object detection in video challenge results. In: Proceedings of International Conference on Computer Vision Workshops, pp. 1–9 (2019)

50. Zhu, Y., et al.: Target-driven visual navigation in indoor scenes using deep reinforcement learning. In: Proceedings of IEEE International Conference on Robotics & Automation, pp. 3357–3364 (2017)

3D CoMPaT: Composition of Materials on Parts of 3D Things

Yuchen Li[1], Ujjwal Upadhyay[1], Habib Slim[1], Ahmed Abdelreheem[1],
Arpit Prajapati[2], Suhail Pothigara[2], Peter Wonka[1],
and Mohamed Elhoseiny[1]([✉])

[1] KAUST, Thuwal, Saudi Arabia
{yuchen.li,ujjwal.upadhyay,habib.slim,ahmed.abdelreheem,peter.wonka,
mohamed.elhoseiny}@kaust.edu.sa
[2] Poly9 Inc., San Francisco, California, USA
{arpit,suhail}@polynine.com

Abstract. We present 3D CoMPaT, a richly annotated large-scale
dataset of more than 7.19 million rendered compositions of Materials on
Parts of 7262 unique 3D Models; 990 compositions per model on average. 3D CoMPaT covers 43 shape categories, 235 unique part names, and
167 unique material classes that can be applied to parts of 3D objects.
Each object with the applied part-material compositions is rendered from
four equally spaced views as well as four randomized views, leading to a
total of 58 million renderings (7.19 million compositions ×8 views). This
dataset primarily focuses on stylizing 3D shapes at part-level with compatible materials. We introduce a new task, called Grounded CoMPaT
Recognition (GCR), to collectively recognize and ground compositions
of materials on parts of 3D objects. We present two variations of this
task and adapt state-of-art 2D/3D deep learning methods to solve the
problem as baselines for future research. We hope our work will help ease
future research on compositional 3D Vision. The dataset and code are
publicly available at https://www.3dcompat-dataset.org/.

1 Introduction

Various datasets have been proposed to facilitate 3D visual understanding including ShapeNet [4], ModelNet [33], and PartNet [26]. Recently, 3D-FUTURE [12]
was proposed, which contains 9,992 industrial 3D CAD shapes of furniture with
textures developed by professional designers. Despite these significant efforts to
create 3D datasets, current 3D object datasets (e.g., [4,26,33]) and 3D Scene
datasets (e.g., [8]) lack part-level material information. The availability of material
information has multiple benefits. First, material information provides additional
semantic information about an object. Second, material information enables more
realistic renderings making the models more suitable for synthetic to real transfer. Third, the same geometric 3D shape can be rendered with different material
assignments leading to more variability during training (see Fig. 1).

Y. Li , U. Upadhyay and H. Slim—Co-first authors.

S. Avidan et al. (Eds.): ECCV 2022, LNCS 13668, pp. 110–127, 2022.
https://doi.org/10.1007/978-3-031-20074-8_7

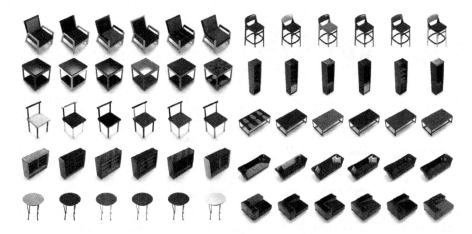

Fig. 1. Stylized models in the 3D CoMPaT dataset. We show several compositions of 8 selected models in the dataset, stylized with different materials.

We introduce a richly annotated large-scale dataset, dubbed as *3D CoMPaT*, Compositions of Materials on Parts of 3D Things. The dataset contains more than 7.19 million rendered model styles from 8 views, covers 43 shape categories, 235 unique and distinguishable part names, and 167 unique and distinguishable materials from 10 material classes that can be applied to parts of 3D objects. Each object with the applied part-material compositions is rendered from four equally spaced views, leading to 58 million (7.19 million compositions ×8 views) images in total. Examples of some rendered compositions and views can be seen in Fig. 1 and 2 respectively.

We start with 7262 unique shapes with a total of 37198 segmented parts (i.e., 5.12 segmented parts per shape on average), and we annotate the list of compatible/applicable materials for each part. Then, we sample a model by enumerating randomly over the compatible materials for each part with a limit of 1000 compositions per shape, leading to 7.19 million compositions of 3D objects.

Connection and Differences to Existing Datasets. The proposed dataset is different from the currently available datasets in the literature in the following ways. First, the dataset contains a diverse set of high-quality materials beyond mere texture maps. Second, for each part found in every 3D model, the dataset defines a set of materials that may be applied to this part in that model, allowing us to generate multiple material combinations for a single model (we call each combination a *style*). The models in 3D-FUTURE [12] and ShapeNet [4] do not have multiple styles, and also, in the ShapeNet dataset, only a small portion of 3D shapes are stylized. The following four key aspects can characterize our 3D CoMPaT dataset in contrast to existing datasets.

–*(a) human-generated vs. 3D scanned geometry.* For example, ScanNet [8] and Matterport3D [3] datasets are scanned 3D geometry. Conversely, ShapeNet [4] and our 3D CoMPaT dataset are human-generated.

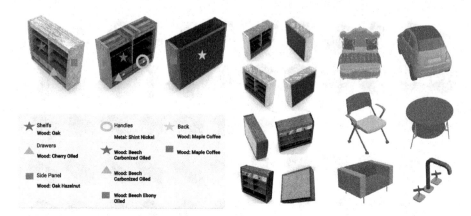

Fig. 2. 3D CoMPaT Dataset. **Left:** Examples of a stylized cabinet. The cabinet has five parts, shelves, drawers, handles, back and side panel, indicated as highlighted. The box below contains the material names for the indicated parts in different stylized cabinets. **Middle:** Each 3D object is rendered in four canonical and four randomized views. **Right:** Part segmentation masks for randomly selected shapes from our dataset.

–*(b) part segmentation information.* For some datasets, none or only a subset of the shapes have segmented part information, which is an important aspect of datasets like PartNet [26] and is also a characteristic of our dataset.

–*(c) texture coordinates, textures, and materials.* Since stylizing the composition of 3D model parts is at the heart of our work, our models have texture coordinates and material compatibility information to enable high-quality rendering of hundreds of compositions of materials on each shape. This is the most important distinguishing characteristic of our 3D CoMPaT dataset compared to existing datasets. There was some earlier effort to augment a subset of ShapeNet with material information [24]. This dataset has fewer shapes (3080 vs 7262), parts, and materials compared to our work.

–*(d) automatically generated vs. human-generated information.* 3D CoMPaT part names are consistent and come from a list of allowable part names per model category. All models are manually segmented at a part level rather than being segmented with deep learning models like OpenRooms [23]. Furthermore, in 3D CoMPaT all texture coordinates are developed and verified by humans (refer to Sec. 3 for more details).

We validate our dataset with experiments covering main 3D recognition tasks, including 3D object classification, 3D part recognition, and material tagging.

Grounded CoMPaT Recognition (GCR) Task. Finally, we introduce a novel task, dubbed as CoMPaT recognition. It aims at recognizing and grounding the shape category collectively with the part-material pairs associated with the shape, e.g., recognizing that the example in Fig. 2 is a "Cabinet", with a handle made of "shiny nickel (metal)" and a back made of "maple coffee wood".

Contributions

- We propose a new dataset of 7.19 million stylized models to study composition of Materials on Parts of 3D Things. Our dataset contains (a) a diverse set of 167 materials for 3D shapes. (b) The material assignment is done at part-level. (c) Segmentation masks in 2D and 3D are provided, alongside (d) human-verified texture coordinates. We hope this dataset may also facilitate future research on retrieving objects in 3D scenes (e.g., localizing a specific "chair" or "table" from Fig. 2).
- We validate our dataset by a set of experiments involving 2D/3D shape classification, part recognition (detection and segmentation), and material tagging.
- We also propose Grounded CoMPaT Recognition, a novel task of collectively recognizing and grounding compositions of materials on parts of 3D objects. We introduce two variants of this task, and adapt 2D/3D state-of-the-art methods as baselines for this problem.

2   Related Work

Datasets of 3D Shapes and Scenes. ModelNet [33] is a large-scale 3D CAD model dataset covering 40 categories. ShapeNet [4] is a richly-annotated, large-scale repository of shapes with semantic categories and organizes them under the WordNet taxonomy. PartNet [26] assigned rich fine-grained segmentation labels on the part level. Recently, 3D-FUTURE [12] was proposed, which contains 9,992 unique industrial 3D CAD shapes of furniture with high-resolution informative textures developed by professional designers. In contrast to 3D-FUTURE, Part-Net, and ShapeNet, where only a small portion of 3D shapes can be assigned materials, our dataset contains 7262 models, all of which can be stylized with different textures. PhotoShape [27] is a dataset similar to ours. More specifically, it uses a technique to automatically apply materials to existing models, mainly from ShapeNet [4]. Some rendered models are not that realistic. The texture coordinates are generated automatically, while ours are human-generated and human-verified. PhotoShape only has a single shape category, i.e., chair, and has only five material classes (leather, fabric, wood, metal, plastic). In comparison, our dataset has 43 shape categories and thirteen material classes (wood, metal, fabric, marble, ceramic, glass, leather, paint, paper, plastic, rubber, granite, wax). OpenRooms [23] is a large dataset containing indoor scenes. The authors automatically segment CAD models of the scenes into parts based on a segmentation model trained on the PartNet dataset. Hence, OpenRooms parts are restricted by the part classes present in PartNet. This also may introduce some segmentation errors in part localization and naming since learned predictions are not as accurate as human annotations. In contrast, our models are manually annotated and verified. Furthermore, our dataset contains models of objects and not indoor scenes, which gives users more flexibility. The major difference between OpenRooms and 3D CoMPaT is that OpenRooms uses scanned geometry captured by sensors while our dataset is manually constructed. We also note that Lin et al. [24] introduced 3080 stylized models for three categories with five material classes and part information. However, the scale of our dataset is much larger.

Texture Generation. TM-Net [13] is a novel deep generative model that generates meshes with detailed textures and synthesizes plausible textures for a given shape. Their work is inspired by SDM-NET [14]. Their method produces texture maps for each part, which means it works in a part-aware fashion. Each part is represented as a deformed box. They encode geometry and texture separately and learn the texture probability distribution conditioned on the geometry. This allows their method to be a generic framework for different application scenarios.

High-Level 3D Vision. Encouraging progress in 3D scene understanding, ScanNet [8] introduced a large-scale dataset of 1513 real-world scenes. More recently and at the intersection of 3D vision and natural language, ScanRefer [5] and Referit3D [2] datasets were recently introduced on top of ScanNet to study 3D object identification based on free-form natural language descriptions. The detailed composition of the shape category and part-material pairs provided in 3D CoMPaT can serve as a rich semantic description of shapes, and hence may facilitate more fine-grained visual grounding of language referring to 3D objects and scenes.

3   3D CoMPaT: Data Collection, Benchmark, and Validation

The 3D CoMPaT dataset collection pipeline comprises three main processes: 3D CAD models collection, materials collection, material assignment, and rendering.

3.1   3D CAD Models Collection

3D CoMPaT is based on a collection of 3D CAD models managed by Poly9 Inc.. The initial data has high-quality 3D models, but the part names, segmentation information, class information, and material information is often missing or faulty. Repetitions of the same CAD model may be present, and some CAD models contain a set of similar parts. The team for building 3D CoMPaT consisted of professional CAD modelers, researchers, and crowd-sourced workers from AMT. The process for creating 3D CoMPaT consists of frequent review meetings between researchers and professional modelers discussing issues with part names, shape categories, materials, and shape segmentation continuing for over one year. Based on these reviews, the professional modelers would adapt their processes, such as labeling instructions, or the allowable list of part names. While professional modelers did all the labeling and modeling work, researchers focused on automatic and manual quality control. While ultimately most of the class names, part names, and material assignments had to be changed during our effort, we only selected shapes that already had high geometric quality and texture coordinates so that little effort was needed to fix problems in the geometry. Due to our multi-stage verification process, each 3D shape was manually inspected more than once. Models that failed a stage of the quality control pipeline were sent back to the team of professional modelers.

– **(A) Shape and Part Category Labeling:** Each 3D CAD model is assigned a shape category label (e.g., chair, desk, table). All models are consistenly segmented into parts and every part in every model is assigned a part name (e.g., "seat, back, or legs"). Each part in each 3D CAD model is also assigned a list of compatible material types, e.g., for one particular chair a modeler could assign that the legs of the chair can be made of either metal or wood. Designing a consistent list of allowable part names for each shape category is a considerable effort. We sourced information from online retailers, other datasets such as Part-Net [26], names used in 3D CAD models, crowdsourcing services and our own experience. In particular, we started with a smaller subset of shapes and some initial labeling of part names to verify these annotations using Amazon Mechanical Turk (AMT). Even though our goal to fix the list of allowable part names early in the process, we had to adapt the list over time in the review meetings as new shapes were being processed.

– **(B) Duplicates and Near-duplicates Removal:** Some 3D CAD models are repeated more than once or contain multiple instances of the same model (e.g., a 3D CAD model representing a set of vases with different sizes). we implemented an automatic procedure to detect duplicates and near-duplicates to remove them from the dataset.

– **(C) Part Segmentation:** Every CAD model should be part-segmented; i.e., every CAD model consists of a set of separated part meshes. We manually check the segmentation of each shape in a 3D viewer and correct them if they are not consistent with the defined part categories.

Fig. 3. Examples of materials found in the dataset. We show examples of wood, metal, and fabric materials in the first, second, and third rows respectively.

Fig. 4. Left: Examples of texture coordinate checks. Right: Blender rendering environment. The environment contains three light sources (a directional light source and three area lights) and a plane at the bottom. The 3D CAD model is normalized, centered on the origin, and placed on the plane.

– **(D) Texture Coordinates Quality Check.** For a proper material assignment, the quality of texture coordinates was verified qualitatively. We followed two strategies. First, we overlay different materials over each part and check how it renders in different settings (we used an increasing level of light bounces to see how textures look). Second, we applied checkered textures to visually inspect the texture coordinates; as illustrated in Fig. 4 (left). For the evaluation of the 3D geometry, we checked that the models are watertight and that they have outward-pointing normals.

Crowdsourcing the Verification of Shape and Category labels. To verify annotated class names of a given 3D model, we asked five MTurk participants to choose from the following four options: (1) "yes, I would name the model the same," "(2) yes, but I would have given the model a different name," (3) "no, this is a wrong name (please specify a name)" or (4) "no, the model cannot be given a specific name.". We used a similar interface to verify the part class names; the part-annotation and model-annotation verification interface used in our AMT experiments is shown in the supplementary material [22].

3.2 Materials Collection

For materials, we use the free and open-source Nvidia vMaterials library. The Nvidia vMaterials library has over 2150 real-world materials and continues to grow. These materials are defined by the Nvidia MDL specification, allowing PBR materials with higher visual quality than basic materials based on diffuse textures. Materials from this library have the infinite tiling feature, allowing textures to be spread across large areas without a clear repeating pattern. The library provides class labels for every material organized in a hierarchical tree (e.g., an antique oxidized aluminum is a rusted aluminum metal). Table 1 presents the count of distinct subtypes for each material class (10). In total, the number of materials in our dataset is 167.

We manually inspected these materials, ignoring materials that may not be realistic when applied to specific parts. For example, a fabric material that has a mesh-like appearance is not suitable to be used for chair cushions (see Fig. 3).

Table 1. 3D CoMPaT material classes and number of materials per class.

Wood	Metal	Fabric	Marble	Ceramic	Glass
40	32	35	14	8	6
Leather	Plastic	Rubber	Granite	Wax	**Total**
13	10	5	3	1	**167**

3.3 Part-Material Assignment

One of the novel aspects of 3D CoMPaT is the presence of material compatibility information for parts present in each 3D model. Human workers conduct the process of material assignment. This process was realized at the instance level, i.e., the shape and parts of each 3D model were considered to compose them with appropriate materials. For example, the legs of one particular table could be assigned either metal or wood and the legs of another table could be assigned wood or plastic. The assignment space for this process is $7262 \times 5.12 \times 10$ (where 10 is the number of material categories). We only assign material classes. For example, all 32 metals can be assigned to a shape part in the material sampling stage if a metal is a possible assignment. We also control compatibility to some extent through grouping information. For example, all table legs have to be assigned the same material. However, we do not explicitly control complex material combinations, as this is hard to integrate into the currently used 3D modeler. This has advantages and disadvantages. An advantage of the current solution is that we allow a greater variety of models which can be a good source of data augmentation. As a disadvantage, several sampled stylized models may not be aesthetically beautiful. Overall, we believe that the consistency of the material assignments is better controlled at sampling process that assigns materials. For example, the sampler could select the same material for chair back and legs significantly more often than different materials. We believe that is more efficient and compatible with our current approach while an explicit control of material combinations suffers from an exponential explosion of possible combinations that need to be controlled. To analyze this issue further will require a significant effort in synthetic to real transfer which we leave to future work.

3.4 Rendering Composition of Materials on Parts of the Collected CAD Models

Once material assignments for each part are available, this information is used to sample materials from the assigned categories. For example, if a tabletop is made of wood, we can sample one of the 40 wood types, like teak, oak, hazelnut, etc. In what follows, we refer to the combination of these materials assigned to parts of a given CAD model as a *composition*. The application of one such composition to the CAD model is called a *style* of the model.

For each 3D CAD model, we randomly select a material for each part from the list of its compatible materials. We sample at most 1000 styles per 3D model.
– **(A) Rendering.** We use Blender [1] to render each CAD model into RGB images from 8 different views, with the camera placed far enough for the entire object to be visible. For the lighting setup, we use three light sources; see Fig. 4 (right). We render each stylized model in 4 standard views (front and back with default model orientation and front left and back right with the model rotated with 30°C around the z (up) axis). Further, we also render each model from 4 random views. The camera for random views is parameterized with elevation angle θ_{cam} (in degree) $\in [0, 90]$, while keeping the x, y same. The model is rotated parameterized with random rotation angle θ_{model} (in degree) $\in [0, 360]$.
– **(B) Segmentation and Depth Maps.** The rendered images in the 3D CoMPaT dataset will be accompanied by corresponding segmentation maps and depth maps. These maps will be rendered with the same four fixed views and four random views.

– **(C) Stylized 3D models.** We plan to release the stylized 3D models, which will enable their use in many 3D computer vision applications, including retrieval, reconstruction, and 3D generation.

3.5 Dataset Statistics

3D CoMPaT contains 7262 unique 3D shapes covering 43 shape categories. The top 6 classes are (table, tray, bowl, chair, desk, cabinet). The dataset contains 37198 part instances covering 235 part classes, and 167 different materials from 10 material classes. The top 5 material classes are (metal, wood, fabric, paint, marble); please see the supplementary for more details about shape classes, the number of object instances per shape class, part, and material classes [22]. In Table 2, we show how our proposed dataset has more variety in the number of materials and the number of materials assignments (styles) than the currently available datasets.

Table 2. Comparison of 3D CoMPaT with other datasets in the literature. To our knowledge, our dataset is the first one to have many different materials applied to different parts in the same 3D model. ✓*: only a subset of shapes are textured and the remaining shapes are with unidentified textures. ?: unknown. HVT stands for Human Verified Textures.

Benchmarks	Shapes no.	Categories	Material classes	Materials	Shape source	Stylized models	HVT	Parts per lpe
3D-Future [12]	9992	34	14(+1)	?	industry	102972	×	10.3
3D Front [11]	13151	50	23	?	3D-Future	13151	×	6.5
PhotoShape [27]	5830	1	5	363	ShapeNet, industry	11000	×	1–3
ShapeNetCore [4]	51300	55	×	✓*	online, crowdsource	×	×	×
ShapeNetSem [4]	~12000	270	×	✓*	online	×	×	×
ShapeNetPart [35]	31963	16	×	✓*	online	×	×	2.92
ModelNet [33]	151128	660	×	×	online	×	×	×
ObjectScans [6]	1,900	44	×	×	Scans	×	×	×
PartNet [26]	26671	24	×	×	ShapeNet	×	×	21.5
Lin et.al., [24]	3080+115	3	5	×	online, ShapeNet	3080+115 ?	×	5.16
3D CoMPaT	**7262**	**43**	**10**	**167**	**industry**	**7.19 million**	✓	**5.12**

Figure 5a and Fig. 5b show the frequency with which different shape classes and parts occur in the dataset. We observe that the dataset has an uneven distribution as some parts, model classes, and materials are more frequent than others. Figure 5c shows the distribution of subsets of parts in different model classes. The size of the bubble represents the occurrences of a part in a certain model class, which we further categorized as very frequent, frequent, or less frequent. It can be inferred from Fig. 5c that some parts are centered around a single "model class"; for example, the "top" is mostly centered around the "table" class, indicating the very frequent tabletop part in the dataset. Some parts have high variability across different models. From Fig. 5c, we can see that "leg" is a part that frequently occurs in "table" models but also in several other models like "chair", "cabinet", and "desk".

Table 3 shows the statistics of 3D CoMPaT in different aspects including parts, model classes, material and styles. The scale of material compositions on model parts is a key difference of 3D CoMPaT when compared to existing datasets, enabling styling of all existing model classes with different part-material combina-

Table 3. Dataset statistics.

Total number of models	7262
Total number of model classes	43
Total number of parts	37198
Total number of parts classes	235
Minimum number of parts per model	1
Maximum number of parts per model	17
Average number of parts per model	5.12
Average compositions per model	990
Total number of materials	167
Total number of stylized models	7.19 million

tions that are compatible. As we pointed out earlier, some materials cannot be applied to some parts (e.g., wood in exchange for glass).

3.6   Dataset Split and Non-compositional Validation Experiments

We create training, validation, and test splits for the renderings. All renderings and stylized versions of a 3D shape have to be assigned together to either training, validation, or test. Therefore, the splits are defined on shapes to prevent data leak. The training set has 5597 shapes, the test set 924 shapes and the validation set 477 shapes. Despite compositional recognition being the focus of our work, a variety of standard tasks can benefit from our proposed dataset, including 3D object classification, 3D semantic segmentation, shape classification, image shape retrieval, shape reconstruction from single/multiple images. We conducted experiments on some of these tasks to validate the properties of our proposed 3D CoMPaT dataset.

3D Shape and Part Classification. Our dataset has an uneven distribution, so some models and parts have more examples and hence help in better generalization. Some parts and models resemble their more frequently occurring counterparts (e.g. jar and container), making classification challenging. Note that there is some intersection between model class and part names, namely basket, bowl, candle holder, glass, shelf, table, tray, vase. This is because some models are parts of other larger models (e.g. shelf as part of shelf structure or cabinet). The presence of various materials to style the 3D object gives our dataset an edge over other existing datasets. We conduct shape classification experiments for the 3D models and the 3D parts. Results are reported in Table 4, where we benchmark Point Cloud Transformer (PCT) [16], DGCNN [32] , and Pointnet++ [29] on shape classification and Pointnet++ and PCT on part classification; see results in Table 4.

2D and 3D Material Segmentation. We benchmark BPNet [19], a 2D and 3D joint UNet, for our 2D and 3D Material Segmentation in Table 4.

Table 4. 3D CoMPaT non-compositional validation experiments.

Architecture	Task	Test performance
Pointnet++ [29]	3D shape classification	57.95% Accuracy
DGCNN [32]		68.32% Accuracy
PCT [15]		69.09% Accuracy
Pointnet++ [29]	3D part classification	24.18% Accuracy
PCT [15]		37.37% Accuracy
BPNet 2D [19]	2D material segmentation	35.75% mIOU
BPNet 3D [19]	3D material segmentation	17.03% mIOU
ResNet50 [18]	2D material tagging	0.53 F1, 0.67 AP
ResNet50 [18]	2D shape classification	76.82% Accuracy

2D Material Tagging/ Shape Classification. We use a ResNet50 [18] backbone for encoding the rendered images, to train a multi-label classifier over the 167 materials in the rendered images. The F1 score and average precision were 0.53 and 0.67 respectively. We also report a 2D shape classification performance of 76.82% using ResNet50, on 50 canonical compositions; see Table 4.

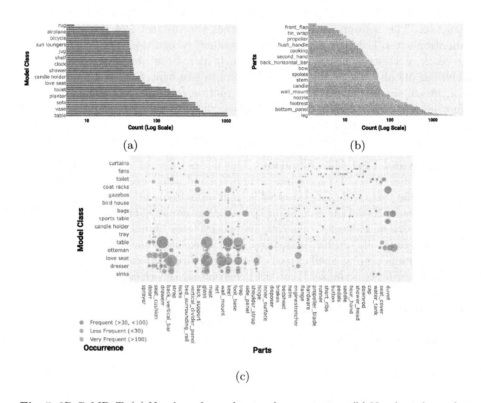

(a)   (b)

(c)

Fig. 5. 3D CoMPaT. (a) Number of samples per shape category. (b) Number of samples per part class. (c) Frequency of occurrence of part and model pair. Note that both visualizations do not cover all shape and part labels because of space constraints; more details are provided in the supplementary [22].

Sim2Real 3D Shape Recognition. We trained a PointMLP [25] model on ModelNet40 and 3D CoMPaT (with only one sampled composition/shape) and evaluated on the hardest variant of ScanObjectNN [31] (*without finetuning*). Table 5 shows 3D shape classification results for 9 classes. Results show that pretraining on 3DCoMPaT shapes leads to better generalization to real-world data than pretraining on ModelNet40.

Table 5. Sim2Real transfer: Accuracy results for PointMLP [25] trained on ModelNet40 and 3DCoMPaT (1 random composition), on ScanObjectNN's hardest variant.

Dataset	Acc. (%)
ModelNet40	24.33
3DCoMPaT	**29.21**

4 2D/3D Grounded CoMPaT Recognition (GCR) Task, Baselines, and Results

The goal of compositional modeling on 3D CoMPaT is to recognize the entire composition of materials on parts of a given 3D model. More specifically, we aim at correctly predicting the object category, part categories and the associated material for every part in the 3D model. Figure 6 visualizes some ground truth and prediction examples for this task. This task is challenging because 96.31% of the compositional frames at test time are unseen. We define a 3D CoMPaT compositional frame as a shape category and a set of part-material categorical pairs. Two compositional frames are different if they differ in a single part or material assignment. In standard recognition settings the model only has to select the correct shape class and examples of all shape classes have been seen before. By contrast, several proposed metrics require the correct recognition of compositional frames. The number of compositional frames is much higher than the number of shape classes and for most compositional frames in the test set there are no examples in the training set. This can be related to zero-shot recognition, which aims at recognizing unseen categories that are defined by unseen compositions of visual attributes (e.g., [9,10,17,21]). This is also connected to existing yet different compositional 2D computer vision tasks, including situation recognition [28,34], which aims at identifying an activity like "surfing" in an image, the engaged entities with their roles (e.g., "agent: woman", "tool: surfboard", and "place: ocean"), and bounding-box groundings of entities.

Metrics. Inspired by the metrics proposed in [28,34] for compositional situation recognition of activities in images, we define the compositional metrics of the 2D/3D **G**rounded **C**oMPaT **R**ecognition (**GCR**) task as follows:

(a) **Shape Accuracy**: accuracy of the predicted shape category. (b) **Value:** accuracy of predicting both part category and the material of a given part correctly. (c) **Value-all:** accuracy of predicting all the (part, material) pairs of a shape correctly. We similarly define grounding metrics to check segmentation masks. A grounding is correct if the IoU of a predicted part and ground truth part is more than 0.5; it can be IoU on segmentation masks. (d) **Grounded-value**: accuracy of predicting both part category and the material of a given

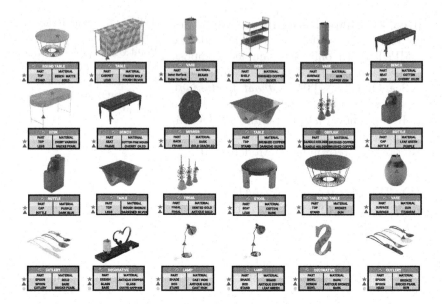

Fig. 6. Example realized materials over parts of certain model classes. Below each image is a table where the first row is the model class, the left column is part names, and the right column is material name for those parts. On the left outlined in gold are ground truth. The output from our material recognition, part recognition, and model recognition model is on the right. Incorrect part names and material names are highlighted in red, whereas correct ones are green. (Color figure online)

part as well as correctly grounding it. **(e) Grounded-value-all**: accuracy of predicting all the (part, material) pairs of a given shape correctly and grounding all of them correctly. All these metrics are calculated for each shape and then averaged across them to avoid bias toward shapes with more parts.

Given the shape dependence of metrics, we define three settings: **(a) Ground Truth Shape**: the ground truth shape is assumed to be correct. **(b) Top-1 Shape**: Shape category is predicted correctly. **(C) Top-5 Shape**: Shape category is in the top-5 predictions. For (b) and (c), part-material pairs and their groundings are considered incorrect if shape is not in top-1 or top-5 predictions, respectively. We investigate two variants of the GCR task:

– **(A) Joint 2D/3D GCR-SEG Setting and Baseline:** 2D/3D GCR-SEG aims at solving the GCR Task in 2D or 3D, where grounding of parts is measured at the pixel precision for 2D and mesh triangle precision for 3D. Hence, we adopted a segmentation approach to solve it, specifically the joint 2D/3D BPNet segmentation model [19]; see Fig. 7. We adapted [19] to jointly predict shape, part, and material recognition in the Grounded CoMPat recognition task. As shown in Fig. 7, our adapted network consists of two branches: according to their functional domains, we denote the left one as the 2D UNet branch and the right as the 3D MinkowskiUNet branch. A Bidirectional Projection Module (BPM) bidirectionally fuses the multi-view 2D and 3D features between two branches.

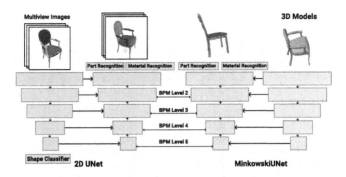

Fig. 7. 2D/3D GCR-SEG: Modified 2D/3D BPNet segmentation [19] architecture with 2D UNet [30] on the left and 3D MinkowskiUNet [7] on the right with same number of pyramid levels.

Features from the encoder of the U-Net are fed to a fully connected layer for shape classification. Images and voxels can be aggregated in a coarse-to-fine manner. BPNet can collect low-level and advanced complementary information; see more details in the supplementary [22].

– **(B) 3D GCR-SEG Setting and Baseline:** Similar to (A), but in 3D only, where part label and material labels are predicted at the point precision for grounding. [20]. We built on PointGroup [20], a point cloud based method for 3D segmentation; see PointGroup adaptation details in the supplementary [22].

Results. Table 6 shows the results for 2D GCR-SEG using BPNet, 3D GCR-SEG using our joint 2D/3D BPNet-based baseline. We report the "Standard" compositional metrics described earlier in this section, on ten compositions. To demonstrate how perfect prediction of either material or part influence the performance, we also report results where we use ground truth materials as the predicted material labels ("GT Material"), and ground truth parts as predicted parts ("GT Part"). It is not surprising that compared to "Standard", some metrics improve under "GT Material" and "GT Part" evaluation, especially for the value and value-all metrics that depend on the predicted part and the material labels. Note that all these baselines are composed of one model that jointly predicts shape and part material pairs in 2D or 3D. These models have a shape recognition performance ranging between 15.64% and 38.29% top-1 accuracy., and between 62.32% and 85.2% top-5 accuracy.; see Table 6. This limits the compositional performance, especially as we showed earlier in Table 4 that separate 2D and 3D Shape classifiers can reach 76.8% and 69.1% Top-1 Acc respectively. Hence, we also evaluated our BPNet-based 3D GCR-SEG approach where shape classes are predicted with a separate 3D PCT [15] classifier, leading to improved compositional performance. We observe similar behavior with PointGroup-based 3D GCR-SEG solution; see supplementary for materials for details [22]. The results suggest that designing a single model capable of performing well on GCR metrics is a challenge, and we hope that our 3D CoMPaT dataset and GCR baselines help ease future research.

Table 6. 2D/3D grounded CoMPaT recognition (GCR) results.

Exp.	Top-1 predicted shape					Top-5 predicted shape					Ground Truth Shape			
	Shape Acc.	Value	Value-all	Value-grnd	Value-all grnd	Shape Acc.	Value	Value-all	Value-grnd	Value-all grnd	Value	Value-all	Value-grnd	Value-all grnd
2D GCR-SEG (BPNet)														
Standard	36.91	6.81	3.54	3.29	0.07	39.07	7.29	3.74	3.48	0.07	65.07	27.72	36.15	2.89
GT Material	36.91	7.10	3.54	4.30	0.60	39.07	7.59	3.74	4.51	0.60	69.54	27.72	40.46	4.80
GT Part	36.91	7.52	5.77	4.94	1.20	39.07	8.07	6.28	5.37	1.49	86.54	71.73	71.83	44.80
2D GCR-SEG (BPNet) + Separate 2D Shape Classifier														
Standard	67.86	40.39	16.57	23.23	1.78	77.60	49.28	20.67	27.50	1.89	65.07	27.72	36.15	2.89
GT Material	67.86	42.98	16.57	26.40	3.46	77.60	52.33	20.67	31.18	3.64	69.54	27.72	40.46	4.80
GT Part	67.86	55.12	46.58	46.02	30.08	77.60	66.89	57.36	55.81	37.30	86.54	71.73	71.83	44.80
3D GCR-SEG (BPNet)														
Standard	36.91	5.39	2.02	0.65	0.03	39.07	5.68	2.07	0.70	0.03	41.35	11.48	4.62	0.03
GT Material	36.91	6.10	2.02	1.34	0.15	39.07	6.43	2.07	1.40	0.15	46.39	11.48	7.80	0.27
GT Part	36.91	6.30	4.13	2.05	0.82	39.07	6.72	4.40	2.29	0.92	77.40	66.47	46.73	39.03
3D GCR-SEG (BPNet) + Separate 3D Shape Classifier														
Standard	67.53	29.83	8.12	3.25	0.46	87.23	38.34	11.07	4.30	0.47	44.59	12.52	4.92	0.47
GT Material	67.53	33.72	8.12	6.07	0.63	87.23	43.15	11.07	7.38	0.66	50.71	12.52	8.23	0.66
GT Part	67.53	50.08	42.42	27.86	22.65	87.23	63.53	54.06	36.44	29.31	77.27	65.30	44.83	36.57

5   Conclusion

We introduce 3D CoMPaT, a large-scale dataset of Compositions of Materials on Parts of 3D Things. It contains 7.19 million styled models stemming from 7262 CAD models from 43 object categories. The unique aspect of 3D CoMPaT is that it contains 3D shapes, part segmentation information, texture coordinates, and material compatibility information, so that multiple high-quality PBR materials can be assigned to the same shape part. We also propose a new task, dubbed as 2D/3D Grounded CoMPaT Recognition (GCR), that the dataset enables and introduce baseline methods to solve them.

Acknowledgments. The authors wish to thank Poly9 Inc. participants for all the hard work, without whom this work would not be possible. This research is supported by King Abdullah University of Science and Technology (KAUST).

References

1. Blender foundation, blender.org - home of the blender project - free and open 3d creation software (2021)
2. Achlioptas, P., Abdelreheem, A., Xia, F., Elhoseiny, M., Guibas, L.: ReferIt3D: neural listeners for fine-grained 3D object identification in real-world scenes. In: Vedaldi, A., Bischof, H., Brox, T., Frahm, J.-M. (eds.) ECCV 2020. LNCS, vol. 12346, pp. 422–440. Springer, Cham (2020). https://doi.org/10.1007/978-3-030-58452-8_25
3. Chang, A., et al.: Matterport3d: learning from rgb-d data in indoor environments. In: International Conference on 3D Vision (3DV) (2017)
4. Chang, A.X., et al.: Shapenet: an information-rich 3d model repository. Technical Report. arXiv:1512.03012 [cs.GR], Stanford University – Princeton University – Toyota Technological Institute at Chicago (2015)
5. Chen, D.Z., Chang, A.X., Nießner, M.: Scanrefer: 3D object localization in rgb-d scans using natural language. arXiv preprint arXiv:1912.08830 (2019)
6. Choi, S., Zhou, Q.Y., Miller, S., Koltun, V.: A large dataset of object scans (2016)
7. Choy, C., Gwak, J., Savarese, S.: 4D spatio-temporal convnets: minkowski convolutional neural networks. In: Proceedings of the IEEE/CVF Conference on Computer Vision and Pattern Recognition, pp. 3075–3084 (2019)
8. Dai, A., Chang, A.X., Savva, M., Halber, M., Funkhouser, T., Nießner, M.: Scannet: richly-annotated 3D reconstructions of indoor scenes. In: Proceedings of Computer Vision and Pattern Recognition (CVPR). IEEE (2017)
9. Elhoseiny, M., Saleh, B., Elgammal, A.: Write a classifier: zero-shot learning using purely textual descriptions. In: Proceedings of the IEEE International Conference on Computer Vision, pp. 2584–2591 (2013)
10. Farhadi, A., Endres, I., Hoiem, D., Forsyth, D.: Describing objects by their attributes. In: CVPR 2009, pp. 1778–1785. IEEE (2009)
11. Fu, H., et al.: 3D-front: 3D furnished rooms with layouts and semantics (2021)
12. Fu, H., et al.: 3D-future: 3D furniture shape with texture. arXiv preprint arXiv:2009.09633 (2020)
13. Gao, L., Wu, T., Yuan, Y., Lin, M., Lai, Y., Zhang, H.: TM-NET: deep generative networks for textured meshes. CoRR abs/2010.06217 (2020), https://arxiv.org/abs/2010.06217

14. Gao, L., et al.: SDM-NET: deep generative network for structured deformable mesh. CoRR abs/1908.04520 (2019). http://arxiv.org/abs/1908.04520

15. Guo, M.H., Cai, J.X., Liu, Z.N., Mu, T.J., Martin, R.R., Hu, S.M.: Pct: point cloud transformer (2021)

16. Guo, M.H., et al.: Pct: point cloud transformer. Comput. Visual Media **7**(2), 187–199 (2021). https://doi.org/10.1007/s41095-021-0229-5

17. Guo, Y., Ding, G., Han, J., Gao, Y.: Synthesizing samples for zero-shot learning. In: IJCAI (2017)

18. He, K., Zhang, X., Ren, S., Sun, J.: Deep residual learning for image recognition (2015)

19. Hu, W., Zhao, H., Jiang, L., Jia, J., Wong, T.T.: Bidirectional projection network for cross dimension scene understanding. In: Proceedings of the IEEE/CVF Conference on Computer Vision and Pattern Recognition, pp. 14373–14382 (2021)

20. Jiang, L., Zhao, H., Shi, S., Liu, S., Fu, C.W., Jia, J.: Pointgroup: dual-set point grouping for 3D instance segmentation. In: Proceedings of the IEEE/CVF Conference on Computer Vision and Pattern Recognition, pp. 4867–4876 (2020)

21. Lampert, C.H., Nickisch, H., Harmeling, S.: Learning to detect unseen object classes by between-class attribute transfer. In: CVPR, pp. 951–958. IEEE (2009)

22. Li, Y., et al.: Supplementary material for 3D CoMPaT: composition of materials on parts of 3D things (2022). https://3dcompat-dataset.org/pdf/supplementary.pdf, version 1.0

23. Li, Z., et al.: Openrooms: an end-to-end open framework for photorealistic indoor scene datasets (2021)

24. Lin, H., et al.: Learning material-aware local descriptors for 3D shapes. In: 2018 International Conference on 3D Vision (3DV) (2018). https://doi.org/10.1109/3dv.2018.00027

25. Ma, X., Qin, C., You, H., Ran, H., Fu, Y.: Rethinking network design and local geometry in point cloud: a simple residual mlp framework. arXiv preprint arXiv:2202.07123 (2022)

26. Mo, K., et al.: PartNet: a large-scale benchmark for fine-grained and hierarchical part-level 3D object understanding. In: The IEEE Conference on Computer Vision and Pattern Recognition (CVPR) (June 2019)

27. Park, K., Rematas, K., Farhadi, A., Seitz, S.M.: Photoshape: photorealistic materials for large-scale shape collections. ACM Trans. Graph. **37**(6) (2018)

28. Pratt, S., Yatskar, M., Weihs, L., Farhadi, A., Kembhavi, A.: Grounded situation recognition. In: Vedaldi, A., Bischof, H., Brox, T., Frahm, J.-M. (eds.) ECCV 2020. LNCS, vol. 12349, pp. 314–332. Springer, Cham (2020). https://doi.org/10.1007/978-3-030-58548-8_19

29. Qi, C.R., Yi, L., Su, H., Guibas, L.J.: Pointnet++: deep hierarchical feature learning on point sets in a metric space. Adv. Neural Inf. Process. Syst., 5099–5108 (2017)

30. Ronneberger, O., Fischer, P., Brox, T.: U-Net: convolutional networks for biomedical image segmentation. In: Navab, N., Hornegger, J., Wells, W.M., Frangi, A.F. (eds.) MICCAI 2015. LNCS, vol. 9351, pp. 234–241. Springer, Cham (2015). https://doi.org/10.1007/978-3-319-24574-4_28

31. Uy, M.A., Pham, Q.H., Hua, B.S., Nguyen, D.T., Yeung, S.K.: Revisiting point cloud classification: a new benchmark dataset and classification model on real-world data. In: International Conference on Computer Vision (ICCV) (2019)

32. Wang, Y., Sun, Y., Liu, Z., Sarma, S.E., Bronstein, M.M., Solomon, J.M.: Dynamic graph cnn for learning on point clouds. ACM Trans. Graph. (TOG) **38**, 1–12 (2019)

33. Wu, Z., et al.: 3D shapenets: a deep representation for volumetric shapes. In: Proceedings of the IEEE Conference on Computer Vision and Pattern Recognition, pp. 1912–1920 (2015)
34. Yatskar, M., Zettlemoyer, L., Farhadi, A.: Situation recognition: visual semantic role labeling for image understanding. In: Proceedings of the IEEE Conference on Computer Vision and Pattern Recognition, pp. 5534–5542 (2016)
35. Yi, L., et al.: A scalable active framework for region annotation in 3d shape collections. ACM Trans. Graph. (ToG) **35**(6), 1–12 (2016)

PartImageNet: A Large, High-Quality Dataset of Parts

Ju He[1(✉)], Shuo Yang[2], Shaokang Yang[3], Adam Kortylewski[1,4,5],
Xiaoding Yuan[1], Jie-Neng Chen[1], Shuai Liu[3], Cheng Yang[3], Qihang Yu[1],
and Alan Yuille[1]

[1] Johns Hopkins University, Baltimore, USA
jhe47@jh.edu
[2] University of Technology Sydney, Ultimo, Australia
[3] ByteDance Inc., Beijing, China
[4] Max Planck Instutite for Informatics, Saarbrücken, Germany
[5] University of Freiburg, Freiburg im Breisgau, Germany

Abstract. It is natural to represent objects in terms of their parts.
This has the potential to improve the performance of algorithms for
object recognition and segmentation but can also help for downstream
tasks like activity recognition. Research on part-based models, however,
is hindered by the lack of datasets with per-pixel part annotations. This
is partly due to the difficulty and high cost of annotating object parts
so it has rarely been done except for humans (where there exists a big
literature on part-based models). To help address this problem, we propose PartImageNet, a large, high-quality dataset with part segmentation
annotations. It consists of 158 classes from ImageNet with approximately
24, 000 images. PartImageNet is unique because it offers part-level annotations on a general set of classes including non-rigid, articulated objects,
while having an order of magnitude larger size compared to existing part
datasets (excluding datasets of humans). It can be utilized for many
vision tasks including Object Segmentation, Semantic Part Segmentation, Few-shot Learning and Part Discovery. We conduct comprehensive
experiments which study these tasks and set up a set of baselines.

1 Introduction

When humans observe objects we can effortlessly parse them into their component parts. Studies in cognitive psychology show that humans learn rich hierarchical representations of objects [20] and can decompose objects into parts
taking into account their spatial relationships [1]. Partly inspired by these findings, computer vision researchers have studied how to model parts and to represent objects in terms of parts. The big literature on these topics includes
deformable templates [45], pictorial structures [11], constellation models [10, 38]

Supplementary Information The online version contains supplementary material
available at https://doi.org/10.1007/978-3-031-20074-8_8.

Fig. 1. Example figures of annotated images in PartImageNet. We offer high-quality precise and dense part segmentation annotation on a wide range of general species including both non-rigid and rigid objects. In total there are around 24,000 images of 158 classes from ImageNet annotated.

and grammar-based models [15,50]. In particular, there have been work [37,40] on segmenting object parts and studying whether this helps improve the segmentation of objects, and later studies of the use of these part segmentation for downstream tasks, e.g., describing pedestrians and facilitating person retrieval [32]. Most recently, part representations have been proposed to improve panoptic segmentation [14]. It has also been argued that object-part models will play an important role in few-shot learning [18,39,43] and hence help to alleviate the the computer vision communities dependence on annotated large-scale datasets. In short, object-part models are promising for improving computer vision on many different tasks (Fig. 1).

But in the big data era, research on part-based models and their applications is hindered due to the shortage of datasets with per-pixel part annotations. Current datasets are almost always restricted to humans or to a small number of object categories, e.g., PASCAL-Part [5]. There is a need to extend this datasets to include many more object categories, as suggested by [14]. Existing part datasets almost always focus on humans or a few rigid classes such as cars. This is partly caused by the difficulty of per-pixel part annotations compared to other types of annotation like bounding boxes. It requires much more effort to ensure accuracy and quality consistency, especially for non-rigid objects. The few works [17,32,43] that attempt to use parts as a mid-level representation, often learnt without supervision, also suffer from this lack of annotated datasets which makes it hard to evaluate whether they have actually captured meaningful object parts.

This motivates us to introduce PartImageNet - a large, high-quality dataset with part annotation on a general set of object classes. Concretely speaking, we manually select 158 classes from ImageNet [9] and group them into 11 supercategory following the WordNet hierarchy of ImageNet. Part labels are designed according to the super-category while can be elaborated to fine-grained classes in a hierarchical way. A carefully designed pipeline is taken to ensure the high quality of our PartImageNet annotations. As far as we know, this is the only dataset after PASCAL-Part [5] that offers part-level annotations on more general classes instead of just humans and rigid objects. Compared to PASCAL-Part [5], we annotate much more images (24k v.s. 10k) on much more classes (158 v.s. 20). Extensive experiments on PartImageNet are conducted to show that parts could help general object segmentation and few-shot learning and set up a set of baselines of different downstream tasks on this benchmark. We believe that with this dataset, the research on part-based models and their applications will be facilitated a lot. In summary, we make the following contributions in this work:

1. We briefly review the history of part-based models and introduce their potential applications in downstream tasks.
2. We introduce PartImageNet - a large, high-quality dataset with part annotations on a general set of classes. From our perspective, part-level annotation, especially on non-rigid objects, is very rare and valuable.
3. We set up a set of baselines on PartImageNet in different vision tasks with state-of-the-art methods which shows the broad usage of the dataset.
4. We conduct experiments to show that introducing parts annotations is beneficial to the object segmentation and few-shot learning which points out to a promising future direction.

2   Related Work

2.1   Part-based Models

Modeling objects in terms of parts is a long-standing problem in computer vision and there is rich history of research on this topic. Starting from Pictorial Structures in the early 1970's [13], plenty of different models [10,11,15,38,45,50] have been proposed to explicitly model parts and their spatial relations to the whole object. There have been a variety of technical approaches but a common theme is that object-part models provide rich representations of objects and help interpretablity. In recent years, partly due to the availability of big data, research on part-based models also includes part segmentation and unsupervised part exploitation.

Supervised Part Segmentation. Annotated human parts datasets have long existed and there has been much work [6,40] on human part detection and semantic segmentation of human parts. Sun et al. [32] proposed to exploit part-level features for pedestrian image description and thus facilitate person retrieval. There has also been some work [37,40] on semantic segmentation of parts of a limited class of other objects.

Unsupervised Part Exploitation on General Tasks. Due to the lack of annotated data on a more general set of classes, research on parts for non-human object classes is often unsupervised. Thewlis et al. [33] proposed to enforce the equivariance of landmark locations under artificial transformations of images to generate semantic meaningful parts of objects. Lorenz et al. [25] improved part discovery by simultaneously exploiting the invariance and equivariance constraints between synthetically transformed images and disentangling the shape and appearance of objects. Recently, parts have shown to be beneficial to unsupervised, or few-shot, object learning since the modeling of parts helps alleviates the scarcity of training data provided the parts can be shared between different classes. He et al. [18] exploited the fact that the feature vectors in the CNN can be viewed approximately as part detectors and their geometry relations could be estimated by clustering. Additionally, it has been shown that few-shot segmentation benefits from the modeling of parts. Liu et al. [24] decomposes the holistic class representation into a set of part-aware prototypes, capable of capturing diverse and fine-grained object features, which benefits semantic segmentation.

However, the part modeling of these methods mainly relies on unsupervised clustering combined with attention mechanisms. Without strong supervision, the results produced by these methods are not very satisfactory, because they only generate meaningful part segmentation in a few simple scenarios. It remains unclear if these approaches can really lead to the learning of semantically meaningful parts without evaluation. Thus it is important to introduce dataset with part annotation to analyze the actual effectiveness of such part modeling and promote the further research on this promising direction.

2.2   Part Datasets

2D Part Datasets. There exists multiple ways to annotate object parts in images. Among them, bounding boxes and keypoints are relatively easy to annotate while per-pixel segmentation is much harder due to the extreme fine-grained difficulty and high cost. The type of objects (i.e. rigid v.s. non-rigid) also plays an important role in deciding the difficulty of annotation. Wang et al. [36] provides dense bounding box annotation for parts on 6 vehicle categories. PASCAL3D+ [41], CarFusion [27] and Apollocar3D [31] offer keypoint annotation on a few rigid object categories especially on cars. ADE20K [49] contains part segmentation annotation on many rigid object categories. As for non-rigid objects, CUB-200–2011 [35] provides keypoint location for birds parts. LIP [21], MHP [48], CIHP [16] include instance-aware, part-level annotations for human.

As far as we are concerned, PASCAL-Part [5] is the only existing dataset that offers part-level annotation on a more general set of categories in a per-pixel segmentation format. However, it contains relatively small number of images and only a small set of classes. We introduce a much larger, high-quality dataset of parts to support more research on part-based models.

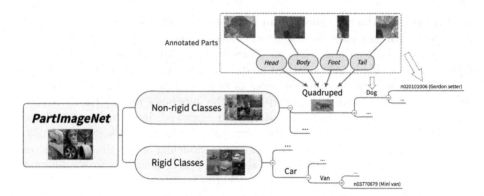

Fig. 2. Overview of the PartImageNet dataset. Accurate part segmentation masks on both non-rigid and rigid objects are offered. The part labels are defined on the super-category (e.g. Quadruped) level but can be easily transferred to mid-level or class-level part labels according to the need (e.g. Quadruped Head → Dog Head → Gordon setter Head) following the WordNet hierarchy as shown by the red dotted arrow. (Color figure online)

3D Part Dataset. 3D Part datasets also play a crucial role in the advances of 3D shape understanding tasks. Yi et al. [44] first takes an active learning approach to annotate the 3D models selected from 16 categories in ShapeNet [2]. PartNet [26] further provides hierarchical part annotations on 3D models covering 24 object categories, most of which are indoor furniture. Recently, CGPart [23] proposes to use computer graphics model to efficiently generate a large-scale vehicle dataset which offers part annotation. Although these datasets have shown their effectiveness in helping data-driven models, they still suffer from the problem of a lacking annotation of non-rigid object categories. The different domains also limit their usage in the image part-level parsing.

3   PartImageNet Dataset

In this section, we present the details of how we collect and annotate the data, followed by statistics and analyze on the quality of the PartImageNet dataset. The overview of the PartImageNet is shown in Fig. 2.

3.1   Data Collection

Data Source. As suggested by the name, we collect images from the ILSVRC-12 dataset [9]. There are in total 158 object classes selected to be annotated in our dataset. All the images conform to licensing for research purposes.

Object Categories. Analogous to tieredImageNet [28], which is also a subset of ILSVRC-12 [9], we group classes into super-categories corresponding to higher-level nodes in the ImageNet hierarchy. There are 11 super-categories in total.

To make the dataset more challenging and more valuable, we pick up fewer rigid objects such as vehicle but choose more animals to annotate. Thus for super-categories like Quadruped, they contain around 40 classes while for super-categories such as vehicle, boat, they only have less than 10 classes. In total, there exists 118 classes out of 158 which are non-rigid objects.

Filtering Unsuitable Images. As our PartImageNet dataset focuses on part segmentation, we eliminate those images which have no proper parts to annotate due to possible occlusion or improper viewpoints. Besides, to simplify the annotation process and avoid ambiguity during annotation, we discard all the images that contain more than one desired object with qualified parts to be annotated. (i.e. all annotated parts in an image are guaranteed to belong to one object).

3.2   Annotation

Instead of annotating bounding boxes or keypoints which is much easier, we aim at annotating high-quality part segmentation mask at pixel-level. The part labels for classes are determined by the corresponding super-categories (i.e. classes under the super-category share the same part labels). It is difficult to ensure that all the classes under the same semantic category have the same detailed parts so we only annotate those that are most important. Take horns for example, some mammals have horns while others do not, to simplify the definition and the annotation process, we do not create a horn label for mammals. Instead, only head label exists and for mammals with horns, the horns are also counted as part of the head during annotation. The detailed part labels for different categories are shown in Table 1. Notice that though the part labels are defined at the super-category level, they can easily be transferred to mid-level or class-level part labels according to the need following the WordNet hierarchy of the ImageNet as shown in Fig. 2.

Annotation Pipeline. Due to the extreme difficulty of annotating part segmentation mask at pixel level, a good annotation pipeline is of great importance to ensure the high quality and maintain the consistency of the annotation. Motivated by existing works on datasets such as ImageNet [9], COCO [22], Objects365 [29], we divide our annotation pipeline into three steps. First as we sample our images from ImageNet, we already have the class and super-category label information for the images, thus we split the annotation task into 11 (equals to the number of super-categories) sub-tasks to alleviate the workload of annotators. The second step is to choose whether to keep the image for the PartImageNet or not following the requirements in Sect. 3.1. In the last step, the annotators are going to annotate the segmentation mask of specific parts for the corresponding super-category. The specific part labels to be annotated are automatically generated according to the super-category label, thus the annotators do not need to pick the right parts among all possible parts of other super-categories which significantly improves the overall accuracy and efficiency.

Annotation Team. We divide our annotation team into three groups: annotators, inspectors, examiners. All the images are first annotated by annotators, then a subset of annotated images will be randomly chosen to be checked by the inspectors. In the end, the examiners can check as many images as they want and see if the quality meets the requirement. Any failures in the above steps will result in re-annotation of the job.

Annotator. The annotators' job is to annotate all the images following the pipeline introduced in Sect. 3.2. Before starting the official annotation, all annotators are going to take courses from the inspectors and go for a test annotation round. During the whole annotation process, the annotators can contact the inspectors at any time if they have questions regarding the current task.

Inspector. The duty of the inspectors is to ensure the quality of the annotation made by the annotators. The inspectors will first have a meeting with the annotators before annotation to teach them the annotation rules. Then they will review all the annotated images during the test annotation round and provide feedback to the annotators. For the official annotation, a random subset of annotated images will also be reviewed by them. If there is an obvious error or the annotation fails to meet the quality requirement, the task will be rejected and re-annotated. If the rejection ratio of an annotator is too high, then all his annotated tasks will be discarded and assigned to other annotators.

Examiner. Examiners design the annotation rules and discuss with the inspectors to make the quality requirement. They are also responsible for answering all the ambiguity questions. After all annotations are done, they review most of the annotated images to ensure the quality and unqualified ones will be rejected and re-annotated.

3.3 Annotation Quality and Consistency

Part segmentation annotation is very hard due to the variance of objects pose, orientation, occlusion. Besides, another important problem that does not exist in other annotation tasks is the ambiguity of how to define the separation of different parts (i.e. how do we define the boundary between head and body). It is impossible to make clear annotation rules that can keep all annotators consistent on the boundary annotation and handle so many different variations. Thus, to make the annotation of parts as accurate and consistent as we can, we make the following efforts:

Maximize Possible Information. The annotators are asked to annotate all visible and distinguishable parts no matter how small they are in order to keep as much information as we can. We believe that such kind of small parts also need to be studied and should be handled during the algorithm design stage instead of the annotation stage.

Accurate Boundary Segmentation. To keep the annotations accurate so they do not contain too many background pixels. We set strict annotation rules to guide the annotators to create tight segmentation masks in most situations (the requirements are relaxed under fuzzy situations). The occluders are also required to be masked out of the annotation.

Consistent Annotation Task Assignment. As our part labels are set according to the super-categories of the images. To keep the consistency among images of the same super-category, we divide the annotators into sub-groups where each sub-group is responsible for annotating one super-category and can communicate freely within the group. In this way, we alleviate the inconsistency of boundary separation especially among the same super-category.

3.4   Statistics

Category and Class Mapping. As introduced in Sect. 3.1, our PartImageNet focuses more on the challenging animals categories instead of rigid object categories. Thus we pick far more classes in animals than cars, boats, planes etc. The detailed number of classes per category is shown in Table 1. In summary, we annotated 158 classes and 118 of them are non-rigid objects. By contrast, PASCAL-Part [5] annotated 20 classes and 12 of them are non-rigid objects.

Total Annotated Images. Based on our proposed annotation pipeline, around 24,000 images are annotated in the PartImageNet dataset. We randomly sampled 85%, 5% and 10% images per class into training, validation and testing set. The detailed numbers of images and annotated parts in each set is shown in Table 2.

Table 1. Number of classes and annotated parts for each category in PartImageNet. The number in the brackets after the category name indicates the total number of classes under the category.

Category	Annotated parts
Quadruped (46)	Head, Body, Foot, Tail
Biped (17)	Head, Body, Hand, Foot, Tail
Fish (10)	Head, Body, Fin, Tail
Bird (14)	Head, Body, Wing, Foot, Tail
Snake (15)	Head, Body
Reptile (20)	Head, Body, Foot, Tail
Car (23)	Body, Tire, Side Mirror
Bicycle (6)	Head, Body, Seat, Tire
Boat (4)	Body, Sail
Aeroplane (2)	Head, Body, Wing, Engine, Tail
Bottle (5)	Body, Mouth

Table 2. The annotation split of the PartImageNet dataset.

	Images	Parts
Train	20481	95059
Validation	1206	5626
Test	2408	11275
All	24095	111960

Table 3. The annotation density of the PartImageNet dataset.

Number of parts	Proportion (%)
1–2	22.00
3–6	57.65
7–9	18.61
10+	1.74

Annotation Density. Though we directly offer more high-level part annotation compared to PASCAL-Part [5], PartImageNet still has a high density of part annotations with 111960 part instances in total. We compute the proportion of number of annotations per image as shown in Table 3. Most images contain around 3–6 annotations which is quite dense and considered our overall dataset size, it should provide enough training examples for most algorithms.

Class Distribution. To dive into the details of the PartImageNet, we provide the overall class distribution in Fig. 3. Though the original number of images per class in ImageNet [9] is roughly the same. After our annotation process, some classes will have more images be ruled out due to multiple objects in one image or occlusion (e.g. bottle). Thus PartImageNet naturally has a few tail classes that contain few images. However, compared to the PASCAL-Part [5]

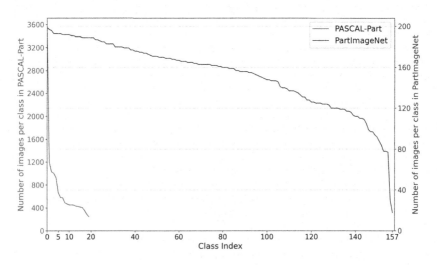

Fig. 3. Number of images per class in PartImageNet and PASCAL-Part [5]. Class index is sorted according to the number of images in the class. Our PartImageNet exhibits a more balanced distribution with a few tail classes that contain few images. By contrast, PASCAL-Part exhibits a more sharpen drop tendency.

dataset, PartImageNet exhibits a much more balanced distribution. The number of images of the most majority class in PASCAL-Part is roughly 9 times more than that of the middle class, while that ratio in PartImageNet is only 1.25.

4   Experiments

In this section, we conduct extensive experiments on our proposed PartImageNet for different tasks including semantic part segmentation, object segmentation and few-shot learning. We broadly evaluate classic methods along with some of the state-of-the-art models to set up a set of baselines on this benchmark. While all these methods do not take part annotations into account, we further show that by exploiting annotated parts, the performance on object segmentation and few-shot learning could get a non-trivial improvement.

4.1   Semantic Part Segmentation

We conduct experiments on semantic part segmentation PartImageNet using Semantic FPN [19], Deeplabv3+ [4] and SegFormer [42]. Semantic FPN [19] and Deeplabv3+ [4] are classic convolution-based semantic segmentation methods. SegFormer [42] is one of the state-of-the-art transformer-based semantic segmentation frameworks. We use Resnet-50 as backbone for Semantic FPN [19] and Deeplabv3 [3]. MiT-b2 (Mix Transformer encoders) is adopted for Segformer [42].

Table 4 summaries the results for semantic part segmentation and Fig. 4 shows the qualitatively visualizations. As can be observed, methods with strong supervision can generally produce satisfactory results on the semantic part segmentation especially when the background and the shape are relatively easy. However, they still suffer from three main challenges: 1) inaccurate boundary between semantic parts, 2) wrong label assignments on similar semantic parts, 3) ignoring small semantic parts (e.g. See row3 - row5 of Fig. 4). Besides, we also notice that the recent progress in methods for general object segmentation does not seem to bring expected improvement in the context of semantic part segmentation (e.g. SegFormer only bring limited improvement based on Deeplabv3+). This reveals the difficulty of part segmentation and indicates that special architecture or module design is needed for effectively solving the challenge.

Table 4. Experimental results of Part Segmentation on PartImageNet. Performance are evaluated in terms of mIoU and scores on validation and testing set are reported.

Model	Backbone	Crop size	Val mIoU	Test mIoU
Semantic FPN [19]	ResNet-50	512×512	60.36	58.69
Deeplab v3+ [4]	ResNet-50	512×512	64.20	64.83
SegFormer [42]	MiT-B2	512×512	65.27	65.17

Ground Truth	Semantic FPN	Deeplabv3+	SegFormer

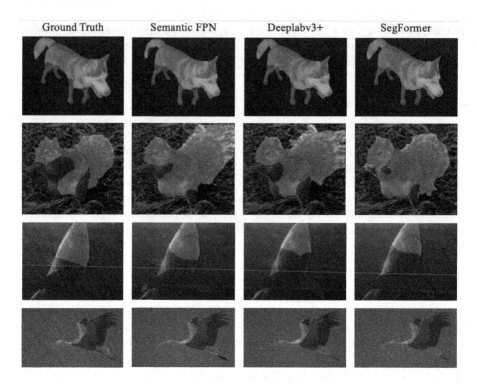

Fig. 4. Example figures of semantic part segmentation results. The quality of the results highly depend on the background, shape of the objects, occlusion situation and the class itself. More visualizations are shown in supplementary materials.

4.2 Object Segmentation

While we offer part-level segmentation masks, they could easily be integrated to offer a full object segmentation mask and thus serves as a benchmark for Salient Object Segmentation. As this role, PartImageNet is a relatively easy one compared to popular MS-COCO [22] and CityScapes [8] since it is a salient holistic segmentation of a single object. However, it is unique as it offers the opportunity to conduct research on the relation between parts and whole objects as shown below. Besides, it also has the advantage that it could be evaluated at a hierarchy level (i.e. super-category & fine-grained class).

Baseline. We still adopt Semantic FPN [19], Deeplabv3+ [4] and SegFormer [42] for object segmentation. The experimental setup and training pipeline are in line with those in semantic part segmentation.

Table 5 summarizes the results of Object Segmentation on PartImageNet. Here the mIoU on the fine-grained classes is reported as it is more challenging than segmenting the super-category object labels. As can be observed, existing methods already achieve quite good results on the benchmark as expected. We are more interested in whether parts can help the general object segmentation.

Table 5. Experimental results of Object Segmentation on PartImageNet. Performance are evaluated in terms of mIoU and scores on validation and testing set are reported.

Model	Backbone	Crop size	Val mIoU	Test mIoU
Semantic FPN [19]	ResNet-50	512×512	63.09	60.50
Deeplab v3+ [4]	ResNet-50	512×512	74.04	71.79
SegFormer [42]	MiT-B2	512×512	81.22	78.56

Can Parts Help Object Segmentation? Motivated by the intuition that it would be a natural way for models to first learn to group similar pixels together at the early stage followed by gradually forming a whole object mask, we design experiments to validate whether object segmentation can be improved by introducing part annotations as deep supervision. We take Deeplabv3+ [4] here for concrete analysis and ablation study.

Table 6 summaries the experimental results of adding part annotations as deep supervision in Deeplabv3+ [4] at different stages of the backbone. We observe that adding part annotations at early stage such as stage 2 does not have an obvious effect on the results probably because the features are still too local without the ability to capture semantic meanings. While starting from stage 3, the deep supervision gradually increases the performance of object segmentation. When adding it at the stage 4, the model achieves largest improvement by 1.63% and 1.05% mIoU on the validation and testing set respectively.

Table 7 further conducts ablation study on the type of deep supervision when adding at the 4th stage. We first show that by adding object masks as deep supervision, the performance decreases a little which reveals that by simply introducing object segmentation mask as deep supervision, the performance can not be improved. Then we show that when adding part annotations, it should be supervised with binary cross entropy loss (i.e. only the current part class is considered) in the sense that we should encourage pixels that belong to the same part to be similar while avoiding penalizing wrong classification of the part classes. The reasons for that are two-folded: firstly semantic part segmentation is a harder task compared to object segmentation, we should not do the full part of it at the early stage of the network, secondly some pixels of different parts are very similar at the pixel level which makes them hard to be distinguished when semantic meanings have not be well-learned at the shallow stage.

Table 6. Experimental results of exploiting part segmentation as deep supervision at different stages of the backbone. DS stands for Deep Supervision. mIoU on validation and testing sets are reported.

DS stage	Val mIoU	Test mIoU
None	74.04	71.79
Stage 2	74.21	71.75
Stage 3	74.47	72.26
Stage 4	**75.67**	**72.84**

Table 7. Exploiting different kinds of part segmentation as deep supervision at Stage 4. CE stands for training with Cross Entropy loss and BCE stands for training with Binary Cross Entropy loss.

DS type	Val mIoU	Test mIoU
None	74.04	71.79
Object	72.45	71.02
Part CE	73.88	71.61
Part BCE	**75.67**	**72.84**

4.3 Few-shot Learning

We could also organize our PartImageNet in an another way by splitting non-overlapping classes into training, validation and testing set, thus it naturally becomes a few-shot learning and transfer learning benchmark. The new split especially designed for Few-shot Learning contains 109 classes in training set, 19 classes in validation set and 30 classes in testing set. Unlike tieredImageNet [28], we do not try to avoid semantic overlap between training and testing sets. The details of the split will be presented in the supplementary materials. By converting PartImageNet into a few-shot benchmark, it offers the community a chance to validate and research on the effects of parts in this domain.

Baseline. We follow the conventional setting in few-shot classification to resize images to 84 * 84 pixels and adopt Conv4 and ResNet-12 as backbones with respect to different methods. We conduct experiments on PartImageNet using MAML [12], Prototypical Networks [30], RFS [34], Meta-Baseline [7], COMPAS [18] and DeepEMD [47]. Among them, MAML [12] and Prototypical Networks [30] are classic few-shot classification methods, RFS [34] and Meta-Baseline [7] are representative works for large-training-corpus methods and meta-training methods respectively while COMPAS [18] and DeepEMD [47] are recent works based on exploitation of parts or key regions to facilitate few-shot learning.

Table 8 summaries the results of selected methods on PartImageNet and miniImageNet. As can be observed, recent methods can obtain similar performances on PartImageNet as miniImageNet which shows that PartImageNet itself can serves as a good benchmark for evaluating few-shot algorithms. Besides, we also observe that though PartImageNet theoretically contains more classes with part structures, models [18,47] that claim to exploit part information do not show obvious advantages compared to others when training without directly using the part annotations.

Table 8. Experimental results of Few-shot Learning on PartImageNet and miniImageNet. Average classification accuracies(%) with 95% confidence intervals are reported.

Model	Backbone	PartImageNet 5-way		miniImageNet 5-way	
		1-shot	5-shot	1-shot	5-shot
MAML [12]	Conv4	46.9 ± 1.4	58.1 ± 0.7	48.7 ± 1.8	63.1 ± 0.9
Prototypical Networks [30]	Conv4	50.0 ± 0.6	65.4 ± 0.5	49.4 ± 0.8	68.2 ± 0.7
RFS [34]	ResNet-12	66.8 ± 0.9	81.7 ± 0.6	64.8 ± 0.6	82.1 ± 0.4
Meta-Baseline [7]	ResNet-12	68.0 ± 0.3	82.7 ± 0.2	63.2 ± 0.2	79.3 ± 0.2
COMPAS [18]	ResNet-12	67.1 ± 0.5	82.3 ± 0.2	65.7 ± 0.5	82.0 ± 0.3
DeepEMD [43]	ResNet-12	67.3 ± 0.6	82.7 ± 0.4	65.9 ± 0.8	82.4 ± 0.5

Can Parts Help Few-shot Learning? Based on the initial results, we are interested in whether parts can actually help few-shot learning. We take two representative methods-COMPAS [18] and DeepEMD [47] here to validate it.

COMPAS [18] originally constructs a part dictionary D of important regions by using K-Means on the feature representations of the backbone and further builds a map dictionary S of the spatial activation distribution of these regions. To exploit the part annotation on COMPAS, we first convert the part segmentation annotations into bounding boxes followed by using pre-trained backbone to extract feature representations of these parts. Then we apply K-Means on the feature representations to obtain a better initialization of the part dictionary D. Similarly, we directly calculate the spatial distribution of these bounding boxes to offer a better initialization of the map dictionary S.

For DeepEMD [47], it originally tries to get a dense representations of images and then compute the Earth Mover's Distance to generate the optimal matching flows between the representation sets of images. The optimal matching cost is further used as the distance metric to measure the similarity of two images. In the updated version DeepEMD V2 [46], the authors find that instead of generating dense representations of images, it is better to randomly sample a set of regions in the images and only compute the EMD between these regions. Thus it is natural to replace these randomly generated regions with annotated part regions and their concatenated regions to see if the results get better.

Table 9 summaries the results of COMPAS and DeepEMD w/ and w/o using part annotations on PartImageNet meta-testing set. Both methods achieve nontrivial improvement with explicit exploitation of annotated parts. Concretely speaking, COMPAS gets a 0.9% and 0.6% performance gain and DeepEMD achieves a 1.2% and 0.9% performance gain on 1-shot and 5-shot scenarios respectively. This reveals the great potential of introducing parts into few-shot learning. Potential research direction lies at how to integrate part detector into current few-shot learning pipeline. We leave such interesting works to the future.

Table 9. Experimental results of COMPAS and DeepEMD w & w/o using part annotations. Average classification accuracies(%) with 95% confidence intervals are reported.

Model	Backbone	PartImageNet 5-way	
		1-shot	5-shot
COMPAS [18]	ResNet-12	67.1 ± 0.5	82.3 ± 0.2
COMPAS w/ Part annotations	ResNet-12	$\mathbf{68.0 \pm 0.5}$	$\mathbf{82.9 \pm 0.3}$
DeepEMD [47]	ResNet-12	67.3 ± 0.6	82.7 ± 0.4
DeepEMD w/ Part annotations	ResNet-12	$\mathbf{68.5 \pm 0.7}$	$\mathbf{83.6 \pm 0.3}$

5   Conclusion

Parts provide a good intermediate representation of objects that have many advantages. Once obtained, they can be exploited to increase the accuracy of recognition, localization and benefit many downstream tasks such as pose estimation. In this work, we introduce PartImageNet-a large, high-quality dataset with part annotation on a general set of classes. A set of new baselines are further set of different vision tasks including semantic part segmentation, object segmentation and few-shot learning. We further show that introducing parts is beneficial to object segmentation and few-shot learning. We also reveal that existing works have certain limitations which hinder them to produce satisfactory semantic part segmentation results under complex backgrounds and variations. We hope that with the propose of our PartImageNet, we could attract more attention to the research of part-based models to address these difficulties and make parts great again.

Acknowledgements. The authors gratefully acknowledge supports from NSF BCS-1827427 and ONR N00014-21-1-2812. AK acknowledges support via his Emmy Noether Research Group funded by the German Science Foundation (DFG) under Grant No. 468670075.

References

1. Biederman, I.: Recognition-by-components: a theory of human image understanding. Psychol. Rev. **94**(2), 115 (1987)
2. Chang, A.X., et al.: Shapenet: an information-rich 3D model repository. arXiv preprint arXiv:1512.03012 (2015)
3. Chen, L.C., Papandreou, G., Schroff, F., Adam, H.: Rethinking atrous convolution for semantic image segmentation. arXiv preprint arXiv:1706.05587 (2017)
4. Chen, L.C., Zhu, Y., Papandreou, G., Schroff, F., Adam, H.: Encoder-decoder with atrous separable convolution for semantic image segmentation. In: Proceedings of the European Conference on Computer Vision (ECCV), pp. 801–818 (2018)

5. Chen, X., Mottaghi, R., Liu, X., Fidler, S., Urtasun, R., Yuille, A.: Detect what you can: Detecting and representing objects using holistic models and body parts. In: Proceedings of the IEEE Conference on Computer Vision and Pattern Recognition, pp. 1971–1978 (2014)
6. Chen, X., Yuille, A.L.: Articulated pose estimation by a graphical model with image dependent pairwise relations. Adv. Neural Inf. Process. Syst. **27** (2014)
7. Chen, Y., Liu, Z., Xu, H., Darrell, T., Wang, X.: Meta-baseline: exploring simple meta-learning for few-shot learning. In: Proceedings of the IEEE/CVF International Conference on Computer Vision, pp. 9062–9071 (2021)
8. Cordts, M., et al.: The cityscapes dataset for semantic urban scene understanding. In: Proceedings of the IEEE Conference on Computer Vision and Pattern Recognition, pp. 3213–3223 (2016)
9. Deng, J., Dong, W., Socher, R., Li, L.J., Li, K., Fei-Fei, L.: Imagenet: a large-scale hierarchical image database. In: 2009 IEEE Conference on Computer Vision and Pattern Recognition, pp. 248–255. Ieee (2009)
10. Fei-Fei, L., Fergus, R., Perona, P.: One-shot learning of object categories. IEEE Trans. Pattern Anal. Mach. Intell. **28**(4), 594–611 (2006)
11. Felzenszwalb, P.F., Huttenlocher, D.P.: Pictorial structures for object recognition. Int. J. Comput. Vision **61**(1), 55–79 (2005)
12. Finn, C., Abbeel, P., Levine, S.: Model-agnostic meta-learning for fast adaptation of deep networks. In: International Conference on Machine Learning, pp. 1126–1135. PMLR (2017)
13. Fischler, M.A., Elschlager, R.A.: The representation and matching of pictorial structures. IEEE Trans. Comput. **100**(1), 67–92 (1973)
14. de Geus, D., Meletis, P., Lu, C., Wen, X., Dubbelman, G.: Part-aware panoptic segmentation. In: Proceedings of the IEEE/CVF Conference on Computer Vision and Pattern Recognition, pp. 5485–5494 (2021)
15. Girshick, R., Felzenszwalb, P., McAllester, D.: Object detection with grammar models. Adv. Neural Inf. Process. Syst. **24**, 442–450 (2011)
16. Gong, K., Liang, X., Li, Y., Chen, Y., Yang, M., Lin, L.: Instance-level human parsing via part grouping network. In: Proceedings of the European Conference on Computer Vision (ECCV), pp. 770–785 (2018)
17. He, J., et al.: Transfg: a transformer architecture for fine-grained recognition. arXiv preprint arXiv:2103.07976 (2021)
18. He, J., Kortylewski, A., Yuille, A.: Compas: representation learning with compositional part sharing for few-shot classification. arXiv preprint arXiv:2101.11878 (2021)
19. Kirillov, A., Girshick, R., He, K., Dollár, P.: Panoptic feature pyramid networks. In: Proceedings of the IEEE/CVF Conference on Computer Vision and Pattern Recognition, pp. 6399–6408 (2019)
20. Lake, B.M., Salakhutdinov, R., Tenenbaum, J.B.: Human-level concept learning through probabilistic program induction. Science **350**(6266), 1332–1338 (2015). https://doi.org/10.1126/science.aab3050, https://www.science.org/doi/abs/10.1126/science.aab3050
21. Liang, X., Gong, K., Shen, X., Lin, L.: Look into person: joint body parsing & pose estimation network and a new benchmark. IEEE Trans. Pattern Anal. Mach. Intell. **41**(4), 871–885 (2018)
22. Lin, T.-Y., Maire, M., Belongie, S., Hays, J., Perona, P., Ramanan, D., Dollár, P., Zitnick, C.L.: Microsoft COCO: common objects in context. In: Fleet, D., Pajdla, T., Schiele, B., Tuytelaars, T. (eds.) ECCV 2014. LNCS, vol. 8693, pp. 740–755. Springer, Cham (2014). https://doi.org/10.1007/978-3-319-10602-1_48

23. Liu, Q., et al.: Cgpart: a part segmentation dataset based on 3D computer graphics models. arXiv preprint arXiv:2103.14098 (2021)

24. Liu, Y., Zhang, X., Zhang, S., He, X.: Part-aware prototype network for few-shot semantic segmentation. In: Vedaldi, A., Bischof, H., Brox, T., Frahm, J.-M. (eds.) ECCV 2020. LNCS, vol. 12354, pp. 142–158. Springer, Cham (2020). https://doi.org/10.1007/978-3-030-58545-7_9

25. Lorenz, D., Bereska, L., Milbich, T., Ommer, B.: Unsupervised part-based disentangling of object shape and appearance. In: Proceedings of the IEEE/CVF Conference on Computer Vision and Pattern Recognition (CVPR) (2019)

26. Mo, K., et al.: Partnet: a large-scale benchmark for fine-grained and hierarchical part-level 3D object understanding. In: Proceedings of the IEEE/CVF Conference on Computer Vision and Pattern Recognition, pp. 909–918 (2019)

27. Reddy, N.D., Vo, M., Narasimhan, S.G.: Carfusion: combining point tracking and part detection for dynamic 3D reconstruction of vehicles. In: Proceedings of the IEEE Conference on Computer Vision and Pattern Recognition, pp. 1906–1915 (2018)

28. Ren, M., et al.: Meta-learning for semi-supervised few-shot classification. arXiv preprint arXiv:1803.00676 (2018)

29. Shao, S., et al.: Objects365: a large-scale, high-quality dataset for object detection. In: Proceedings of the IEEE/CVF International Conference on Computer Vision, pp. 8430–8439 (2019)

30. Snell, J., Swersky, K., Zemel, R.S.: Prototypical networks for few-shot learning. arXiv preprint arXiv:1703.05175 (2017)

31. Song, X., et al.: Apollocar3d: a large 3D car instance understanding benchmark for autonomous driving. In: Proceedings of the IEEE/CVF Conference on Computer Vision and Pattern Recognition, pp. 5452–5462 (2019)

32. Sun, Y., Zheng, L., Yang, Y., Tian, Q., Wang, S.: Beyond part models: person retrieval with refined part pooling (and a strong convolutional baseline). In: Proceedings of the European Conference on Computer Vision (ECCV), pp. 480–496 (2018)

33. Thewlis, J., Bilen, H., Vedaldi, A.: Unsupervised learning of object landmarks by factorized spatial embeddings. In: Proceedings of the IEEE International Conference on Computer Vision, pp. 5916–5925 (2017)

34. Tian, Y., Wang, Y., Krishnan, D., Tenenbaum, J.B., Isola, P.: Rethinking few-shot image classification: a good embedding is all you need? In: Vedaldi, A., Bischof, H., Brox, T., Frahm, J.-M. (eds.) ECCV 2020. LNCS, vol. 12359, pp. 266–282. Springer, Cham (2020). https://doi.org/10.1007/978-3-030-58568-6_16

35. Wah, C., Branson, S., Welinder, P., Perona, P., Belongie, S.: The Caltech-UCSD Birds-200-2011 Dataset. Technical Report CNS-TR-2011-001, California Institute of Technology (2011)

36. Wang, J., Zhang, Z., Xie, C., Premachandran, V., Yuille, A.: Unsupervised learning of object semantic parts from internal states of cnns by population encoding. arXiv preprint arXiv:1511.06855 (2015)

37. Wang, P., Shen, X., Lin, Z., Cohen, S., Price, B., Yuille, A.L.: Joint object and part segmentation using deep learned potentials. In: Proceedings of the IEEE International Conference on Computer Vision, pp. 1573–1581 (2015)

38. Weber, M., Welling, M., Perona, P.: Unsupervised learning of models for recognition. In: Vernon, D. (ed.) ECCV 2000. LNCS, vol. 1842, pp. 18–32. Springer, Heidelberg (2000). https://doi.org/10.1007/3-540-45054-8_2

39. Wu, J., Zhang, T., Zhang, Y., Wu, F.: Task-aware part mining network for few-shot learning. In: Proceedings of the IEEE/CVF International Conference on Computer Vision, pp. 8433–8442 (2021)

40. Xia, F., Wang, P., Chen, X., Yuille, A.L.: Joint multi-person pose estimation and semantic part segmentation. In: Proceedings of the IEEE Conference on Computer Vision and Pattern Recognition, pp. 6769–6778 (2017)

41. Xiang, Y., Mottaghi, R., Savarese, S.: Beyond pascal: a benchmark for 3D object detection in the wild. In: IEEE Winter Conference on Applications of Computer Vision, pp. 75–82. IEEE (2014)

42. Xie, E., Wang, W., Yu, Z., Anandkumar, A., Alvarez, J.M., Luo, P.: Segformer: simple and efficient design for semantic segmentation with transformers. arXiv preprint arXiv:2105.15203 (2021)

43. Xu, W., Wang, H., Tu, Z., et al.: Attentional constellation nets for few-shot learning. In: International Conference on Learning Representations (2020)

44. Yi, L., et al.: A scalable active framework for region annotation in 3D shape collections. ACM Trans. Graph. (ToG) **35**(6), 1–12 (2016)

45. Yuille, A.L., Hallinan, P.W., Cohen, D.S.: Feature extraction from faces using deformable templates. Int. J. Comput. Vision **8**(2), 99–111 (1992)

46. Zhang, C., Cai, Y., Lin, G., Shen, C.: Deepemd: differentiable earth mover's distance for few-shot learning (2020)

47. Zhang, C., Cai, Y., Lin, G., Shen, C.: Deepemd: few-shot image classification with differentiable earth mover's distance and structured classifiers. In: Proceedings of the IEEE/CVF Conference on Computer Vision and Pattern Recognition, pp. 12203–12213 (2020)

48. Zhao, J., Li, J., Cheng, Y., Sim, T., Yan, S., Feng, J.: Understanding humans in crowded scenes: Deep nested adversarial learning and a new benchmark for multi-human parsing. In: Proceedings of the 26th ACM international conference on Multimedia, pp. 792–800 (2018)

49. Zhou, B., Zhao, H., Puig, X., Fidler, S., Barriuso, A., Torralba, A.: Scene parsing through ade20k dataset. In: Proceedings of the IEEE Conference on Computer Vision and Pattern Recognition, pp. 633–641 (2017)

50. Zhu, S.C., Mumford, D.: A Stochastic Grammar of Images. Now Publishers Inc. (2007)

A-OKVQA: A Benchmark for Visual Question Answering Using World Knowledge

Dustin Schwenk[1], Apoorv Khandelwal[1], Christopher Clark[1], Kenneth Marino[2], and Roozbeh Mottaghi[1(✉)]

[1] PRIOR @ Allen Institute for AI, Seattle, USA
roozbehm@allenai.org
[2] Carnegie Mellon University, Pittsburgh, USA
http://a-okvqa.allenai.org

Abstract. The Visual Question Answering (VQA) task aspires to provide a meaningful testbed for the development of AI models that can jointly reason over visual and natural language inputs. Despite a proliferation of VQA datasets, this goal is hindered by a set of common limitations. These include a reliance on relatively simplistic questions that are repetitive in both concepts and linguistic structure, little world knowledge needed outside of the paired image, and limited reasoning required to arrive at the correct answer. We introduce A-OKVQA, a crowdsourced dataset composed of a diverse set of about 25K questions requiring a broad base of commonsense and world knowledge to answer. In contrast to existing knowledge-based VQA datasets, the questions generally cannot be answered by simply querying a knowledge base, and instead require some form of commonsense reasoning about the scene depicted in the image. We demonstrate the potential of this new dataset through a detailed analysis of its contents and baseline performance measurements over a variety of state-of-the-art vision–language models.

1 Introduction

The original conception of the Visual Question Answering (VQA) problem was as a Visual Turing Test [10]: can a computer answer questions about an image well enough to fool us into thinking it's human? To truly solve this Turing Test, the computer would need to mimic several human capacities including: visual recognition in the wild, language understanding, basic reasoning abilities, and a background knowledge about the world. In the years after VQA was formulated, many of these aspects have been studied. Early datasets mostly studied the perception and language understanding problem on natural image

---

Supplementary Information The online version contains supplementary material available at https://doi.org/10.1007/978-3-031-20074-8_9.

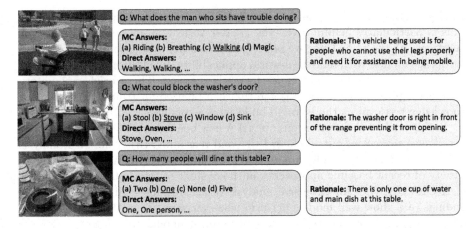

Fig. 1. A-OKVQA dataset includes questions that require reasoning via a variety of knowledge types such as commonsense, world knowledge and visual knowledge. We provide Multiple-Choice (MC) as well as Direct Answer evaluation settings. There are 3 rationales (one shown) associated to each question in the train set providing the explanation/knowledge for answering the question.

datasets [2,11,29]. Other datasets studied complex chains of reasoning about procedurally generated images [20]. More recent datasets include questions requiring factual [31,46,47] or commonsense knowledge [52] to answer.

But, VQA has largely been a victim of its own success. With the advent of large-scale pre-training of vision–language models [4,7,27,28,37,49,53] and other breakthroughs in multi-modal architectures, much of the low-hanging fruit in the field has been plucked and many of the benchmarks have seen saturated performance. Even performance on newer knowledge-based datasets has been improved by such models [53]. So how can we continue developing yet more challenging datasets? A good start is to ask which human capabilities are not yet expressed by current models.

We propose the following options. First, continuing the direction of past work in knowledge-requiring VQA, we further expand the areas of knowledge required. Our dataset requires diverse forms of outside knowledge including explicit fact-based knowledge that is likely to be contained in knowledge bases, commonsense knowledge about human social behavior, intuitive understanding of physics, and visual knowledge. Second, we increase the complexity of reasoning needed to answer questions. Our questions require models to recognize the image, understand the question, recall relevant knowledge, and use reasoning to arrive at an answer. For instance, in the first question shown in Fig. 1, the model should reason that people use that type of cart to avoid walking, and therefore the old man likely has trouble with this activity. In general, our dataset requires additional types of world knowledge compared to our previous work OK-VQA [31]. Hence, we call it Augmented OK-VQA (A-OKVQA).

A-OKVQA is composed of about 25K questions paired with both multiple choice (MC) answer options and ten free-form answers to allow for direct answer (DA) evaluation. The MC component of the dataset bypasses many difficulties inherent in (DA) evaluation and allows for a simple, clean accuracy score. This is particularly helpful given the greater variety in answers in A-OKVQA questions. At the same time, we believe direct answer evaluation is important to encourage models with more real-world applicability. In addition to the questions and answers, we provide *rationales* for each question. These brief explanatory statements provide extra information that can be used for training reasoning or knowledge retrieval methods, or to build more explainable VQA models.

In this work, our contributions are: (i) A new benchmark VQA dataset requiring diverse sources of outside knowledge and reasoning; (ii) A detailed analysis of the dataset that highlights its diversity and difficulty; (iii) An evaluation of a variety of recent baseline approaches in the context of the challenging questions in A-OKVQA; (iv) An extensive analysis of the results leading to interesting findings (e.g., how well models perform when answers are in the tail of the distribution, and the complementarity of the studied models).

2   Related Work

Visual Question Answering. Visual Question Answering (VQA) has been a common and popular form of vision–language reasoning. Many datasets for this task have been proposed [2,8,22,29,39,45,51,55] but most of these do not require much outside knowledge or reasoning, often focusing on recognition tasks such as classification, attribute detection, and counting.

Knowledge-Based VQA Datasets. Several previous works have studied the problem of knowledge-based VQA. The earliest explicitly knowledge-based VQA datasets were KB-VQA [46] and FVQA [47]. While these benchmarks did specifically require knowledge for questions, the knowledge required for these benchmarks is completely "closed". FVQA [47] is annotated by selecting a triplet from a fixed knowledge graph. KVQA [40] is based on images in Wikipedia articles. Because of the source of the images, these questions tend to mostly test recognizing specific named entities (e.g., Barrack Obama) and then retrieving Wikipedia knowledge about that entity rather than commonsense knowledge.

Most similar to our work is OK-VQA [31]. This dataset was an improvement over prior work in terms of scale, and the quality of questions and images. It also has the property that the required knowledge was not "closed" or explicitly drawn from a particular source, and could be called "open"-domain knowledge. While this is an improvement over the previous works, it still suffers from problems which we address in this work. The knowledge required, while "open" is still biased towards simple lookup knowledge (e.g., what is the capital of this country?) and most questions do not require much reasoning. In contrast, our dataset is explicitly drawn to rely on more common-sense knowledge and to require more reasoning to solve. In addition, our dataset includes "rationale" annotations, which allow knowledge-based VQA systems to more densely annotate their knowledge acquisition and reasoning capabilities. S3VQA [18] analyzes OK-VQA and creates a new dataset which includes questions that require detecting an object in the image, replacing the question with the word for that object and then querying the web to find the answer. Like OK-VQA, its questions have the shortcoming of generally requiring a single structured knowledge-retrieval, rather than commonsense knowledge and reasoning.

Another related line of work is Visual Commonsense Reasoning (VCR) [52]. VCR is also a VQA dataset, but is collected from movie scenes and is quite focused on humans and their intentions (e.g. "why is [PERSON2] doing this"), whereas our dataset considers questions and knowledge about a variety of objects. Additionally, the Ads Dataset [17] is a dataset requiring knowledge about the topic and sentiments of the ads. Other datasets have considered knowledge-based question answering for a sitcom [9] and by using web queries [5].

Explanation/Reasoning VQA. Visual reasoning on its own has been studied in several VQA datasets. In CLEVR [20], the image and question are automatically generated from templates and explicitly require models to go through multiple steps of reasoning to correctly answer. This dataset and similar datasets which rely on simulated images suffer from lack of visual realism and lack of richness in the images and questions and are thus prone to be overfit to with methods achieving nearly 100% accuracy [50]. Our dataset requires reasoning on real images and free-form language. Other works [23,33] have collected or extracted justifications on the VQAv2 [11] dataset. However, VQAv2 mostly focuses on questions about object attributes, counting and activities, which do not require reasoning on outside knowledge.

3   A-OKVQA Collection

Image Source. The most important attribute of an image source for this knowledge-based VQA task is that it contains an abundance of visually rich and interesting images. Images containing a small number of objects are typically quite challenging to write interesting questions requiring outside knowledge to answer. We used images from the 2017 partitioning of the COCO dataset [24] in the creation of A-OKVQA, because it (1) has many images cluttered with multiple objects and entity types, and (2) is an established dataset with many associated models already in existence. To ensure suitable images for annotation, we do some additional filtering to remove uninteresting images: for the training and validation sets, we define images with more than three objects as "interesting" and select those for question writing. For the test set, which lacks object annotations, we train a ResNet-50 classifier to distinguish such "interesting" images, achieving an accuracy of **78%** on our validation set. After multiple rounds of filtering (described below), we obtain 23.7K unique images.

Question Collection & Filtering. The questions in A-OKVQA were written and refined over several rounds of annotation by 437 crowd-workers on the Amazon Mechanical Turk platform and refined through several manual and automated filtering steps to increase overall quality. As a first quality assurance measure, workers completed a qualification task to demonstrate their ability to write questions that met our criteria, namely that questions: (1) require looking at the image to answer, (2) need some commonsense or specialized knowledge, (3) involve some thinking beyond merely recognizing an object, and (4) not be too similar to previous questions.

To help ensure the last point, we clustered images by CLIP [36] visual features and batched similar images together such that the same worker wrote questions sequentially for related images (e.g., a worker might write questions for several images showing baseball games in one task) to cut down on repetitive questions. As an added measure to encourage question diversity, we maintained a database of questions written and required users to check a new question against these by displaying the five previous questions most similar in terms of their RoBERTa [26] embeddings. We used a simple VQA model (Pythia [43] pre-trained on VQAv2) to automatically find and remove questions we considered trivial (which the model answered correctly). Questions were then screened by three other workers and only included if the majority agreed that it met our criteria for inclusion. In all, 37,687 questions, or **60%** of post-qualification questions were excluded from the dataset by this process.

Answers. We asked workers to provide the correct answer along with three distractors for the questions they wrote. After all questions and multiple-choice options were gathered, we collected nine additional free-form answers per question from a separate pool of workers.

Rationales. After questions and answers were collected and validated, we performed a separate task to collect three rationales per question. Workers were given a question and its multiple choice options and asked to explain why a particular answer was correct (in one to two simple sentences, including any necessary facts or prior world knowledge not shown by the images).

4   Dataset Statistics

The A-OKVQA dataset contains **24,903** (Question + Answer + Rationale) triplets in 17.1K (train)/1.1K (val)/6.7K (test) splits. These preserve the train/val/test splits in COCO 2017. The average lengths of and numbers of unique words in the questions, answers, and rationales are shown in Table 1.

In Fig. 2a we show the distribution of answer options in our dataset. What we see is a fairly typical long-tail distribution of labels, as is seen in many open-labeled image tasks [54]. A few answers occur quite often in the dataset, but most fall into the long tail of the distribution.

We are also interested in the amount of answer set overlap between the training set and the validation/testing sets. We find that 87.6% of val set and 82.7% of test set questions have correct answers that appear as options in the train set. While this demonstrates a reasonable similarity between our splits, there remains a significant portions the test set that requires an answer not seen during training. Thus, models must be able to generate answers that are out-of-distribution or based on some knowledge outside of the dataset.

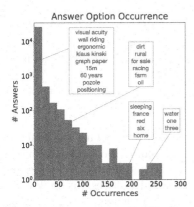

(a) Answer occurrence distribution of A-OKVQA.

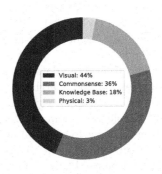

(b) Knowledge type distribution for a random subset of the dataset.

Fig. 2. Dataset statistics.

Table 1. Comparison of knowledge-based VQA datasets. Data based on reported numbers and available annotations. Thus, some statistics may exclude test sets. Answer statistics for A-OKVQA is based on the direct answer set. Rationales are not available (or not in sentence form) in all datasets. Q: question, I: image, A: answer, R: rationale, DA: Direct Answer, MC: Multiple Choice.

	Q	I	Rationale	Knowledge type	Ans type	Avg. length (Q/A/R)	Unique words (Q/A/R)
KB-VQA [46]	2,402	700	✗	Fixed KB	DA	6.8/2.0/—	530/1,296/—
FVQA [47]	5,826	2,190	✓	Fixed KB	DA	9.5/1.2/—	3,010/1,287/—
OK-VQA [31]	14,055	14,031	✗	Factoid	DA	8.1/1.3/—	5,703/11,125/—
S3VQA [18]	7,515	7,515	✗	Factoid	DA	12.7/2.8/—	7,515/8,301/—
VCR [52]	290k	99,904	✓	People actions	MC	8.7/7.7/16.8	11,254/18,861/28,751
A-OKVQA	24,903	23,692	✓	Common/world	DA/MC	8.8/1.3/11.0	7,248/17,683/20,629

Comparison with Other Datasets. In Table 1, we show dataset properties and statistics for A-OKVQA compared to related datasets. We have 2–10x more questions than the more knowledge-focused natural image datasets, such as OK-VQA, while VCR (focused on images of people in movies) has 10x more than ours. This is unsurprising because we intentionally filter out similar questions, making our questions more diverse (see Table 2). However, these are also difficult to collect at scale. Unlike these other datasets, ours has both multiple choice and direct answer annotations. Our dataset also has rationales, unlike OK-VQA, S3VQA and KB-VQA. Rationales in FVQA are in the form of knowledge tuples, rather than full sentences. VCR has the most similar rationales to our own. Since our rationales are more knowledge-based and have more possible variations per question, we collect three, unlike both FVQA and VCR which collect just one. Our questions are longer on average than in all datasets besides S3VQA and FVQA. Ours also contain the most unique words besides S3VQA (which has a similar number) and VCR (which has many more questions).

Knowledge Types. The most significant factor differentiating our dataset is the kind of knowledge required. Datasets such as FVQA have fixed knowledge bases that are used to write the questions, and so the knowledge required can be found in e.g. ConceptNet [25] directly. OK-VQA and S3VQA focus on more factoid knowledge (e.g., years of invention or countries of origin). Researchers have found that these datasets take the form of finding an entity in the image and/or question and searching and retrieving knowledge about that particular entity [18]. VCR requires images to have people in them and overwhelmingly depicts people interacting in television shows and movies. Thus, the required knowledge is very focused on commonsense about human behavior and intentions. In our dataset, we require broader areas of knowledge, including the factoid knowledge likely to be contained in knowledge bases (as in FVQA, KBVQA, OKVQA and S3VQA) and commonsense knowledge (similar to VCR, but broader in scope).

To analyze the knowledge required in A-OKVQA more quantitatively, we annotated a randomly sampled subset of 1,000 questions in the test set. In this experiment, we asked the annotators to label the knowledge type required to answer each question: (1) **Commonsense** knowledge about human social behavior (e.g. that many donuts being made in a cart implies they are for sale rather than for personal consumption), (2) **Visual knowledge** (e.g. muted color pallets are associated with the 1950s)s), (3) **Knowledge bases** (e.g. hot dogs were invented in Austria), and (4) **Physical knowledge** about the world that humans learn from their everyday experiences (e.g., shaded areas have a lower temperature than other areas). The distribution is shown in Fig. 2b. Most of our questions cluster around commonsense and visual knowledge. It should be noted that sometimes there is no clear distinction between these two categories, and a question can belong to either category.

Question Diversity. To compare the diversity of A-OKVQA to other datasets, we use the average pairwise cosine distance between questions for every dataset. We embed our questions with a sentence transformer[1]. We see from Table 2 that our dataset has the most diversity on this metric. In particular, we see a large difference compared to VCR which has many similar questions such as "What is going to happen next?" and questions relating to what specific people in the scene are doing and why. We also compare the diversity of rationales to VCR and VQAv2 (using rationales from VQA-X [33] rationales), and we find that our rationales are much more diverse than in these datasets. Qualitatively, we also find that our dataset tends to have much more varied questions because it is taken from the more visually diverse COCO dataset (a quality shared by OK-VQA and VQAv2 which do almost as well on this metric) and requires more diverse kinds of knowledge.

Finally, we use the same mean pairwise distance to look in particular at how different our questions are from OK-VQA which is the most similar prior work to ours. To do this we compare the minimum pairwise distance between every

---

[1] Specifically multi-qa-MiniLM-L6-cos-v1 [14] to avoid overlap with RoBERTa.

Table 2. Question and Rationale Diversity. Mean pairwise cosine distances in a sentence transformer space. ✗ indicates lack of rationale. Rationales for VQAv2 come from the VQA-X. dataset [33].

Dataset	Mean Q distance	Mean rationale distance
FVQA [47]	0.6199	✗
VCR [52]	0.7095	0.8017
KB-VQA [46]	0.7192	✗
S3VQA [18]	0.8050	✗
VQAv2 [11]	0.8405	0.8228
OK-VQA [31]	0.8428	✗
A-OKVQA	0.8564	0.8779

question in the OK-VQA training set to every question in the OK-VQA test set and our test set. We find that the average minimum distance from OK-VQA train to test is **0.256** compared to **0.311** between OK-VQA train and our test set[2]. This shows that there is in fact a significant difference between our question set and OK-VQA in this feature space.

5   Experiments

Next, we benchmark the A-OKVQA dataset and compare the performance of different models. We consider three classes of methods: (1) **large-scale pre-trained models** such as CLIP [36] and GPT-3 [4], (2) **models that generate and use rationales,** and (3) **specialized models** that are designed for knowledge-based VQA (KRISP [30]) or tested for VQA (e.g., ViLBERT [27]).

5.1   Evaluation

In the *multiple choice (MC)* setting, a model chooses its answer from one of four options and we compute accuracy as the evaluation metric. In the *direct answer (DA)* setting, a model can generate any text as its answer and we use the standard VQA evaluation from [2].

5.2   Large-scale Pre-trained Models

We compare three types of large-scale pre-trained models (discriminative, contrastive, and generative) in Table 3. We also test these models in different input settings (where questions, images, or both are provided).

---

[2] To make this comparison even, we chose a random subset of our test set to be the same size as OK-VQA test set so that the minimum is over the same number of possible choices in both cases.

We compute BERT [7,15] and CLIP ViT-B/32 text encoder representations for questions. We also compute ResNet-50 [12] and CLIP ViT-B/32 features for images. These are provided as inputs to the appropriate discriminative and contrastive models. We provide questions as tokens and CLIP RN50 × 4 image representations as inputs to the generative models. We generate a vocabulary from a subset of training set answers and choices to use across all appropriate models. We describe this vocabulary further in Appx. B.

Discriminative Models. We train a multi-label linear classifier (i.e. MLP with one hidden layer and sigmoid activation function) on top of BERT (row d), ResNet (row i), and CLIP (rows $e/j/m$) representations to score answers from the vocabulary. When questions and images are both provided, we first concatenate their representations. For the DA setting, we predict the top scoring vocabulary answer. For the MC setting, we instead predict the nearest neighbor[3] choice to the top scoring vocabulary answer.

Contrastive Models. We also evaluate models which match input questions and/or images with answers using their CLIP encodings. First, we evaluate the zero-shot setting (rows $f/k/n$). If both questions and images are provided as inputs, we first add their representations. We select the answer whose encoding has the greatest cosine similarity to our input representation. We select from vocabulary answers in DA and the given choices in MC.

We also train a single-layer MLP on top of our input representations (rows $g/l/o$). If both questions and images are provided, we first concatenate their representations. Our MLP produces a 512-d embedding and we train this with a CLIP-style contrastive loss between embeddings and their corresponding answers. We describe this loss further in Appx. B. We repeat the evaluation from the zero-shot setting, using these learned embeddings.

Generative Models. We also evaluate models (GPT-3 [4] and ClipCap [32]) that generate answers directly as text. For both models, we predict the generated text for DA and the generated text's nearest neighbor choice for MC.

We prompt GPT-3[4] (row h) with 10 random questions and answers from the training set, followed by a new question, and let GPT-3 generate an answer to that question, in a manner similar to [48]. We provide GPT-3 with the prompt template "Question: ... Answer: [...]", expecting it to complete the answer for each evaluation question.

ClipCap [32] (row p) is an image captioning method that passes CLIP image features through a trained network to GPT-2 (as input tokens). We adapt this model by adding question tokens (and answer choices if applicable) to the prompt of GPT-2, generate answers instead of captions, and fine-tune on our data. We provide additional details, diagrams, and variations in Appx. B.

---

[3] Cosine similarity between mean GloVe [16,34] word embeddings.

[4] We use the second largest available GPT-3 model, Curie, as in [48].

Table 3. Large-scale pre-trained models. We also compare with no input heuristics (rows *a-c*). *Random* is a uniform sampling from choices (for MC) or answers in the training set (for DA). *Random (weighted)* uses weighted sampling proportional to correct answer frequencies. *Most Common* selects the most frequent answer in train.

Method	Multiple Choice		Direct Answer	
	Val.	Test	Val.	Test
(a) Random	26.70	25.36	0.03	0.06
(b) Random (weighted)	29.49	**30.87**	0.15	0.10
(c) Most Common	**30.70**	30.33	**1.75**	**1.26**
Question				
(d) BERT [7] (classifier)	32.93	33.54	9.52	8.41
(e) CLIP [36] (classifier)	32.74	33.54	**13.10**	10.24
(f) CLIP [36] (zero-shot)	30.42	30.58	0.44	0.57
(g) CLIP [36] (contrastive)	**37.40**	**38.58**	5.56	3.83
(h) GPT-3 [4]	35.07	35.21	12.98	**11.49**
Image				
(i) ResNet [12] (classifier)	28.19	28.81	2.68	2.30
(j) CLIP [36] (classifier)	33.21	32.56	**5.15**	**4.38**
(k) CLIP [36] (zero-shot)	**56.28**	**53.94**	2.24	2.29
(l) CLIP [36] (contrastive)	52.56	50.09	2.33	2.45
Question & Image				
(m) CLIP (classifier)	40.84	38.30	18.95	14.27
(n) CLIP (zero-shot)	48.19	45.72	1.08	0.71
(o) CLIP (contrastive)	53.77	51.01	10.36	7.10
(p) ClipCap [32]	**56.93**	**51.43**	**30.89**	**25.90**

Results. Table 3 shows the results of our evaluation of these models. Rows *a-c* show the biases in our dataset, but that the direct answer setting is appropriately challenging. Question-only baselines (rows *d-h*) show poor performance in both MC and DA settings. However, it is interesting that GPT-3 performs similarly to the fine-tuned CLIP models (whichever is better per setting). The zero-shot CLIP model (row *f*) is least effective, indicating that training is necessary to repurpose CLIP text encodings for language-only tasks. Unsurprisingly, CLIP image features are very strong for zero-shot multiple choice matching (row *k*). However, they are not as strong as for the fine-tuned classifier (row *j*) in DA. ClipCap (row *p*) outperforms all other baselines in DA, because we use powerful image features and also fine-tune a strong language model for our task.

5.3 Rationale Generation

We are interested in whether we can improve GPT-3 prompting results by providing additional image- and question- specific context and report results for the following methods in Table 4. So, we fine-tune ClipCap (given images and questions, but not choices) as above, but for the task of generating rationales instead of answers. Our model scores **10.2** (val) / **9.58** (test) on SacreBLEU [35] and **0.271** (val) / **0.256** (test) on METEOR [3]. We can then prompt GPT-3 (as above) but also provide these generated rationales as "Context: ...". This model is denoted by 'ClipCap → Ratl. → GPT'. We provide additional details, diagrams, and examples of generated rationales in Appx. C. We repeat this experiment using captions (generated from only images) from the original ClipCap model: 'ClipCap → Cap. → GPT'.

Results. We show results from these experiments in Table 4. Interestingly, prompting GPT-3 with ground-truth rationales (row d) is competitive with the best model in Sec. 5.2 (Table 3, row p) in MC and significantly outperforms the question-only GPT-3 method (Table 3, row h). When we prompt GPT-3 with ground-truth rationales (row d), we see higher performance than when we pro-

Table 4. Models using generated and GT rationales as described in Sect. 5.3. We are unable to evaluate the GT Caption → GPT setting on the test set, as captions are not available in the COCO [6] test set.

Method	Multiple Choice		Direct Answer	
	Val.	Test	Val.	Test
(a) ClipCap → Cap. → GPT	42.51	43.61	16.59	15.79
(b) ClipCap → Ratl. → GPT	**44.00**	**43.84**	**18.11**	**15.81**
Oracles				
(c) GT Caption → GPT	45.40	—	16.39	—
(d) GT Rationale → GPT	**56.74**	56.75	**24.02**	20.75

Table 5. Specialized models results. Baselines trained for VQA or knowledge-based VQA, and fine-tuned on A-OKVQA. The bottom two rows are not comparable with the others since they use ground-truth rationales at test time.

Method	Multiple-Choice		Direct Answer	
	Val.	Test	Val.	Test
(a) Pythia [19]	49.0	40.1	25.2	21.9
(b) ViLBERT [27] - OK-VQA	32.8	34.1	9.1	9.2
(c) ViLBERT [27] - VQA	47.7	42.1	17.7	12.0
(d) ViLBERT [27]	49.1	41.5	30.6	25.9
(e) LXMERT [44]	51.4	41.6	30.7	25.9
(f) KRISP [30]	51.9	42.2	33.7	27.1
(g) GPV-2 [21]	**60.3**	**53.7**	**48.6**	**40.7**
Oracles				
(h) GPV-2 [21] + Masked Ans	65.1	58.3	52.7	43.9
(i) GPV-2 [21] + GT Ratl	73.4	67.2	58.9	51.7

vide ground-truth captions (row c). This affirms that rationales contain useful information (i.e. specific to our questions and answers) in addition to captions. However, the additional performance of prompting GPT-3 using generated rationales (row b) over generated captions (row a) is not as significant. This indicates potential room for improvement in our approach for generating rationales.

5.4 Specialized Models

In this section, we evaluate some recent high-performing, open-source models trained on knowledge-based VQA or the traditional VQA. The models we consider are Pythia [19], ViLBERT [27], LXMERT [44], KRISP [30], and GPV-2 [21]. As the first four models are part of MMF [42], it is easier to compare them fairly. KRISP is a high-performing model on OK-VQA [31]. It provides a suitable baseline as it was designed to perform well on knowledge-based VQA. GPV-2 performs multiple vision and vision–language tasks and has learned a large number of concepts, so it can be a strong baseline for A-OKVQA. All of these models are fine-tuned on A-OKVQA. We adapt them to MC using the nearest choice method described above. See Appx. D for the details of each model.

Results. Unsurprisingly, these models, which are specialized for DA and some of which are specialized for knowledge-based VQA perform very well on the DA evaluation and quite well on MC. Of the models trained only on A-OKVQA KRISP does the best, likely because it is trained to directly use outside knowledge graphs. GPV-2, however, performs best of all, beating all other models (that do not use ground-truth rationales) in all settings, possibly because of the large number of concepts it has learned.

Transfer Results. We train ViLBERT on VQAv2 and OK-VQA datasets (denoted by 'ViLBERT-VQA' and 'ViLBERT-OK-VQA' in Table 5) to evaluate whether the knowledge from those datasets is sufficient for A-OKVQA. The low performance shows that significant differences exist between these datasets and A-OKVQA.

Ground-Truth Rationales. To evaluate how well the model performs if it is provided with high-quality rationales, we use ground-truth rationales at test. We show these results with GPV-2 (our best model). Ground-truth rationales are appended to questions as additional input text ('GPV-2 + GT Ratl.'). For this experiment, we used only one of the rationales. Comparing rows g and i of Table 5 shows rationales are helpful. To evaluate how much of this improvement can be attributed to rationales and not the fact that sometimes rationales contain the answer, we replaced answers in the rationales with [answer] token. The performance drops (row i vs row h), however, it is still higher than the case that we do not use rationales (row h vs row g).

6 Analysis of Models

Next, we analyze the predictions that our baseline models make to see if we can learn more about A-OKVQA: what kinds of questions do different types of approaches do better/worse on? For these experiments, we choose some of the best performing models on Direct Answer: VilBERT [27], LXMERT [44], KRISP [30], ClipCap [32] and GPV-2 [21]. We also use the ClipCap → Rationale → GPT model from Table 4, which will be referred to as 'GR-GPT' for Generated Rationales GPT.

Answer Frequency. First, we look at how answer frequency affects performance in Table 6. We first count the number of times any answer appears in the direct answers in the training set. We then divide these into bins and look at the direct DA test accuracy of our baselines for each of these frequency bins. We find that GPV-2, and to a lesser extent ClipCap and GR-GPT perform better on questions whose answers do not appear often in the training set (1–5 and 6–10 columns of Table 6). GPV-2 in particular (which is fine-tuned on several vision and language tasks) is able to predict these tail answers much better than other methods, especially the discriminative methods such as LXMERT.

Table 6. Results across different answer frequencies. The questions are categorized based on the frequency of the GT answer in the training set. Columns show accuracy for answers that appear 1–5 times, 6–10 times, etc. If multiple direct choices, we default to most common one.

Model	1–5	6–10	11–20	21–50	51–100	101–200	201+
VilBERT [27]	0.00	0.00	3.68	10.97	19.95	26.53	35.91
LXMERT [44]	0.00	0.00	4.29	13.73	20.18	26.69	34.31
KRISP [30]	0.00	0.61	6.34	13.99	21.78	28.55	35.22
ClipCap [32]	4.71	4.24	9.10	17.90	25.93	29.44	33.99
GR-GPT	8.18	9.29	9.41	17.39	18.31	21.98	24.65
GPV-2 [21]	**10.16**	**12.12**	**22.60**	**31.04**	**38.40**	**41.60**	**44.69**

Prediction Overlap/Difference. Finally, we look at some statistics on a question by question level in the A-OKVQA test set. Specifically we look at the overlap in which methods answered which questions correctly[5].

First, we find that only **5.85%** of questions in test were answered correctly by all models and **30.96%** of questions had no model predict a correct answer for. Considering the worst performing model of these gets **15.81%** DA accuracy and

---

[5] For ease of analysis we count a binary yes/no of whether a model answered correctly if it answered any possible answer in the direct answer set.

the best gets **40.7%**, it implies that there is actually a large variation between these models beyond some just being generally better than others and thus getting "hard" questions right and keeping performance on "easy" questions.

In Table 7, we show the difference between the questions each model gets right on A-OKVQA test. Each row shows the percentage of that method's correctly answered questions that were not correctly answered by the comparison model in each column. If we look at the row for the lowest performing model (GR-GPT) for the column for the best performing model (GPV-2), we still see that **29.2%** of GR-GPT's correctly answered questions are answered wrongly by GPV-2!

Finally, to further illustrate the point that different models have very different mistake patterns, we take the prediction of all of these models except for GPV-2 for each question and take the majority vote between these. This majority vote combination gets an accuracy of **29.5** compared to the best of these models which gets **27.1**. This does not work when GPV-2 is added (this majority model gets **35.60** which is lower than GPV-2's **40.7**). We can also look at the Oracle combination accuracy. That is, from our six models, choose the answer with the highest ground-truth value and take that as the oracle combination answer. This DA accuracy is **56.87** versus the single best performance of **40.7**, again showing that even worse performing models get many questions right that the best model gets wrong.

Table 7. Pairwise difference between correctly answered questions. For row i and column j of this table the value is percentage of questions answered correctly by model i that j did not answer correctly.

Model	VilBERT	LXMERT	KRISP	ClipCap	GR-GPT	GPV-2
VilBERT [27]	0.00	29.00	27.19	43.72	59.72	26.33
LXMERT [44]	28.07	0.00	26.57	44.39	59.73	27.44
KRISP [30]	30.44	30.76	0.00	44.18	60.29	27.43
ClipCap [32]	48.72	49.98	46.76	0.00	55.94	26.64
GR-GPT	50.27	50.91	48.67	40.30	0.00	29.20
GPV-2 [21]	51.09	52.46	49.57	46.56	61.94	0.00

Qualitative Analysis. We extracted questions that all of the discussed models fail at. Figure 3 shows an example from each knowledge type. This shows what type of reasoning is missing in top performing models.

Collectively, these analyses reveal several interesting findings. First, aside from being generally difficult, the A-OKVQA dataset shows a surprising lack of overlap in the specific questions different models answer correctly. Second, we see that different methods handle rare answers very differently. Thirdly, different methods perform differently based on the type of knowledge required to answer questions. Together, these features suggests that A-OKVQA contains a

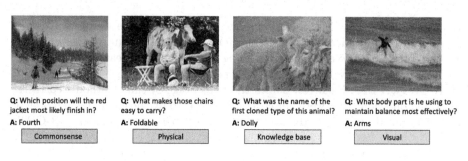

Q: Which position will the red jacket most likely finish in?
A: Fourth

Commonsense

Q: What makes those chairs easy to carry?
A: Foldable

Physical

Q: What was the name of the first cloned type of this animal?
A: Dolly

Knowledge base

Q: What body part is he using to maintain balance most effectively?
A: Arms

Visual

Fig. 3. Example questions that all discussed models fail at.

wide variety of challenging questions which are able to reveal and contrast the strengths and weaknesses of VQA methods.

7   Conclusion

Vision–language models have become progressively more powerful, however, evaluation of the reasoning capabilities of these models have not received adequate attention. To take a step in this direction, we propose a new knowledge-based VQA benchmark called A-OKVQA, which primarily includes questions that require reasoning using commonsense and world knowledge. We provide *rationales* for each question so models can learn the line of reasoning that leads to the answer. We evaluate a large set of recent, high performance baselines. While they show impressive performance on the proposed task, it is evident that they lack the reasoning capability and/or the knowledge required to answer the questions, and there is a large room for improvement.

References

1. Anderson, P., et al.: Bottom-up and top-down attention for image captioning and visual question answering. In: CVPR (2018)
2. Antol, S., et al.: VQA: visual question answering. In: ICCV (2015)
3. Banerjee, S., Lavie, A.: METEOR: An automatic metric for MT evaluation with improved correlation with human judgments. In: ACL Workshop on Intrinsic and Extrinsic Evaluation Measures for Machine Translation and/or Summarization (2005)
4. Brown, T.B., et al.: Language models are few-shot learners. In: NeurIPS (2020)
5. Chang, Y., Narang, M.B., Suzuki, H., Cao, G., Gao, J., Bisk, Y.: WebQA: multihop and multimodal QA. arXiv (2021)
6. Chen, X., et al.: Microsoft COCO captions: data collection and evaluation server. arXiv (2015)
7. Devlin, J., Chang, M.W., Lee, K., Toutanova, K.: BERT: pre-training of deep bidirectional transformers for language understanding. In: NAACL (2019)
8. Gao, H., Mao, J., Zhou, J., Huang, Z., Wang, L., Xu, W.: Are you talking to a machine? dataset and methods for multilingual image question. In: NeurIPS (2015)

9. García, N., Otani, M., Chu, C., Nakashima, Y.: KnowIT VQA: answering knowledge-based questions about videos. In: AAAI (2020)
10. Geman, D., Geman, S., Hallonquist, N., Younes, L.: Visual turing test for computer vision systems. Proc. Natl. Acad. Sci. **112**, 3618–3623 (2015)
11. Goyal, Y., Khot, T., Summers-Stay, D., Batra, D., Parikh, D.: Making the V in VQA matter: elevating the role of image understanding in visual question answering. In: CVPR (2017)
12. He, K., Zhang, X., Ren, S., Sun, J.: Deep residual learning for image recognition. In: CVPR (2016)
13. Hudson, D.A., Manning, C.D.: GQA: a new dataset for real-world visual reasoning and compositional question answering. In: CVPR (2019)
14. HuggingFace: https://huggingface.co/sentence-transformers/multi-qa-MiniLM-L6-cos-v1
15. HuggingFace: https://huggingface.co/sentence-transformers/nli-bert-base
16. HuggingFace: https://huggingface.co/sentence-transformers/average_word_ embeddings_glove.6B.300d
17. Hussain, Z., et al.: Automatic understanding of image and video advertisements. In: CVPR (2017)
18. Jain, A., Kothyari, M., Kumar, V., Jyothi, P., Ramakrishnan, G., Chakrabarti, S.: Select, substitute, search: a new benchmark for knowledge-augmented visual question answering. In: SIGIR (2021)
19. Jiang, Y., Natarajan, V., Chen, X., Rohrbach, M., Batra, D., Parikh, D.: Pythia v0.1: the winning entry to the VQA challenge 2018. arXiv (2018)
20. Johnson, J., Hariharan, B., van der Maaten, L., Fei-Fei, L., Zitnick, C.L., Girshick, R.: CLEVR: a diagnostic dataset for compositional language and elementary visual reasoning. In: CVPR (2017)
21. Kamath, A., Clark, C., Gupta, T., Kolve, E., Hoiem, D., Kembhavi, A.: Webly supervised concept expansion for general purpose vision models. arXiv (2022)
22. Krishna, R., et al.: Visual Genome: connecting language and vision using crowd-sourced dense image annotations. IJCV **123**, 32–73 (2017)
23. Li, Q., Fu, J., Yu, D., Mei, T., Luo, J.: Tell-and-answer: towards explainable visual question answering using attributes and captions. In: EMNLP (2018)
24. Lin, T.-Y., Maire, M., Belongie, S., Hays, J., Perona, P., Ramanan, D., Dollár, P., Zitnick, C.L.: Microsoft COCO: common objects in context. In: Fleet, D., Pajdla, T., Schiele, B., Tuytelaars, T. (eds.) ECCV 2014. LNCS, vol. 8693, pp. 740–755. Springer, Cham (2014). https://doi.org/10.1007/978-3-319-10602-1_48
25. Liu, H., Singh, P.: ConceptNet-a practical commonsense reasoning tool-kit. BT Technol. J. **22**, 211–226 (2004)
26. Liu, Y., et al.: RoBERTa: a robustly optimized bert pretraining approach. arXiv (2019)
27. Lu, J., Batra, D., Parikh, D., Lee, S.: ViLBERT: pretraining task-agnostic visiolinguistic representations for vision-and-language tasks. In: NeurIPS (2019)
28. Lu, J., Goswami, V., Rohrbach, M., Parikh, D., Lee, S.: 12-in-1: Multi-task vision and language representation learning. In: CVPR (2020)
29. Malinowski, M., Fritz, M.: A multi-world approach to question answering about real-world scenes based on uncertain input. In: NeurIPS (2014)
30. Marino, K., Chen, X., Parikh, D., Gupta, A.K., Rohrbach, M.: KRISP: integrating implicit and symbolic knowledge for open-domain knowledge-based VQA. In: CVPR (2021)
31. Marino, K., Rastegari, M., Farhadi, A., Mottaghi, R.: OK-VQA: a visual question answering benchmark requiring external knowledge. In: CVPR (2019)

32. Mokady, R., Hertz, A., Bermano, A.H.: ClipCap: CLIP prefix for image captioning. arXiv (2021)
33. Park, D.H., et al.: Multimodal explanations: justifying decisions and pointing to the evidence. In: CVPR (2018)
34. Pennington, J., Socher, R., Manning, C.D.: GloVe: global vectors for word representation. In: EMNLP (2014)
35. Post, M.: A call for clarity in reporting BLEU scores. In: Conference on Machine Translation (2018)
36. Radford, A., et al.: Learning transferable visual models from natural language supervision. In: ICML (2021)
37. Radford, A., Wu, J., Child, R., Luan, D., Amodei, D., Sutskever, I.: Language models are unsupervised multitask learners. OpenAI blog (2019)
38. Raffel, C., et al.: Exploring the limits of transfer learning with a unified text-to-text transformer. JMLR **21**, 1–67 (2020)
39. Ren, M., Kiros, J., Zemel, R.S.: Exploring models and data for image question answering. In: NeurIPS (2015)
40. Shah, S., Mishra, A., Yadati, N., Talukdar, P.P.: KVQA: knowledge-aware visual question answering. In: AAAI (2019)
41. Sharma, P., Ding, N., Goodman, S., Soricut, R.: Conceptual captions: a cleaned, hypernymed, image alt-text dataset for automatic image captioning. In: ACL (2018)
42. Singh, A., et al.: MMF: a multimodal framework for vision and language research (2020). https://github.com/facebookresearch/mmf
43. Singh, A., et al.: Towards VQA models that can read. In: CVPR (2019)
44. Tan, H.H., Bansal, M.: LXMERT: learning cross-modality encoder representations from transformers. In: EMNLP (2019)
45. Tapaswi, M., Zhu, Y., Stiefelhagen, R., Torralba, A., Urtasun, R., Fidler, S.: MovieQA: understanding stories in movies through question-answering. In: CVPR (2016)
46. Wang, P., Wu, Q., Shen, C., Dick, A.R., van den Hengel, A.: Explicit knowledge-based reasoning for visual question answering. In: IJCAI (2017)
47. Wang, P., Wu, Q., Shen, C., van den Hengel, A., Dick, A.R.: FVQA: fact-based visual question answering. TPAMI **40**, 2413–2427 (2017)
48. West, P., et al.: Symbolic knowledge distillation: from general language models to commonsense models. arXiv preprint arXiv:2110.07178 (2021)
49. Yang, Z., et al.: An empirical study of GPT-3 for few-shot knowledge-based VQA. arXiv (2021)
50. Yi, K., Wu, J., Gan, C., Torralba, A., Kohli, P., Tenenbaum, J.B.: Neural-symbolic VQA: disentangling reasoning from vision and language understanding. In: NeurIPS (2018)
51. Yu, L., Park, E., Berg, A.C., Berg, T.L.: Visual madlibs: fill in the blank description generation and question answering. In: ICCV (2015)
52. Zellers, R., Bisk, Y., Farhadi, A., Choi, Y.: From recognition to cognition: visual commonsense reasoning. In: CVPR (2019)
53. Zhang, P., et al.: VinVL: revisiting visual representations in vision-language models. In: CVPR (2021)
54. Zhu, X., Anguelov, D., Ramanan, D.: Capturing long-tail distributions of object subcategories. In: CVPR (2014)
55. Zhu, Y., Groth, O., Bernstein, M.S., Fei-Fei, L.: Visual7W: grounded question answering in images. In: CVPR (2016)

OOD-CV: A Benchmark for Robustness to Out-of-Distribution Shifts of Individual Nuisances in Natural Images

Bingchen Zhao[1], Shaozuo Yu[2], Wufei Ma[3], Mingxin Yu[4], Shenxiao Mei[3], Angtian Wang[3], Ju He[3], Alan Yuille[3], and Adam Kortylewski[3,5,6(✉)]

[1] University of Edinburgh, Edinburgh, Scotland
[2] The Chinese University of Hong Kong, Hong Kong, China
[3] Johns Hopkins University, Baltimore, USA
[4] Peking University, Beijing, China
[5] Max Planck Instutite for Informatics, Saarbrücken, Germany
akortyle@mpi-inf.mpg.de
[6] University of Freiburg, Freiburg im Breisgau, Germany

Abstract. Enhancing the robustness of vision algorithms in real-world scenarios is challenging. One reason is that existing robustness benchmarks are limited, as they either rely on synthetic data or ignore the effects of individual nuisance factors. We introduce OOD-CV , a benchmark dataset that includes out-of-distribution examples of 10 object categories in terms of pose, shape, texture, context and the weather conditions, and enables benchmarking models for image classification, object detection, and 3D pose estimation. In addition to this novel dataset, we contribute extensive experiments using popular baseline methods, which reveal that: 1) Some nuisance factors have a much stronger negative effect on the performance compared to others, also depending on the vision task. 2) Current approaches to enhance robustness have only marginal effects, and can even reduce robustness. 3) We do not observe significant differences between convolutional and transformer architectures. We believe our dataset provides a rich testbed to study robustness and will help push forward research in this area.

1 Introduction

Deep learning sparked a tremendous increase in the performance of computer vision systems over the past decade, under the implicit assumption that the training and test data are drawn independently and identically distributed (IID) from the same distribution. However, Deep Neural Networks (DNNs) are still far from reaching human-level performance at visual recognition tasks in real-world environments. The most important limitation of DNNs is that they fail to give

---

Supplementary Information The online version contains supplementary material available at https://doi.org/10.1007/978-3-031-20074-8_10.

S. Avidan et al. (Eds.): ECCV 2022, LNCS 13668, pp. 163–180, 2022.
https://doi.org/10.1007/978-3-031-20074-8_10

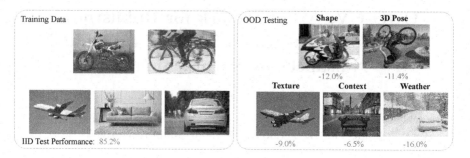

Fig. 1. Computer vision models are not robust to real-world distribution shifts at test time. For example, ResNet50 achieves 85.2% accuracy on our benchmark, when tested on images that are similarly distributed as the training data (IID). However, its performance deteriorates significantly when individual nuisance factors in the test images break the IID assumption. Our benchmark makes it possible, for the first time, to study the robustness of image classification, object detection and 3D pose estimation to OOD shifts in individual nuisances.

reliable predictions in unseen or adverse viewing conditions, which would not fool a human observer, such as when objects have an unusual pose, texture, shape, or when objects occur in an unusual context or in challenging weather conditions (Fig. 1). The lack of robustness of DNNs in such out-of-distribution (OOD) scenarios is generally acknowledged as one of the core open problems of deep learning, for example by the Turing award winners Yoshua Bengio, Geoffrey Hinton, and Yann LeCun [4]. However, the problem largely remains unsolved.

One reason for the limited progress in OOD generalization of DNNs is the lack of benchmark datasets that are specifically designed to measure OOD robustness. Historically, datasets have been pivotal for advancement of the computer vision field, e.g. in image classification [10], segmentation [13,31], pose estimation [44,50,51], and part detection [7]. However, benchmarks for OOD robustness have important limitations, which limit their usefulness for real-world scenarios. Limitations of OOD benchmarks can be categorized into three types: Some works measure robustness by training models on one dataset and testing them on another dataset without fine-tuning [1,20,23,54]. However, cross-dataset performance is only a very coarse measure of robustness, which ignores the effects of OOD changes to individual nuisance factors such as the object texture, shape or context. Other approaches artificially generate corruptions of individual nuisance factors, such as weather [35], synthetic noise [20] or partial occlusion [46]. However, some nuisance factors are difficult to simulate, such as changes in the object shape or 3D pose. Moreover, artificial corruptions only have limited generalization ability to real-world scenarios. The third type of approach obtains detailed annotation of nuisance variables by recording objects in fully controlled environments, such as in a laboratory [6] or using synthetic data [26]. But such controlled recording can only be done for limited amount of objects and it remains unclear if the conclusions made transfer to real-world scenarios.

In this work, we introduce OOD-CV, a dataset for benchmarking OOD robustness on real images with annotations of individual nuisance variables and labels for several vision tasks. Specifically, the training and IID testing set in OOD-CV consists of 10 rigid object categories from the PASCAL VOC 2012 [14] and ImageNet [10] datasets, and the respective labels for image classification, object detection, as well as the 3D pose annotation from the PASCAL3D+ dataset [50]. Our main contribution is the collection and annotation of a comprehensive out-of-distribution test set consisting of images that vary w.r.t. the training data in PASCAL3D+ in terms individual nuisance variables, i.e. images of objects with an unseen shape, texture, 3D pose, context or weather (Fig. 1). Importantly, we carefully select the data such that each of our OOD data samples only varies w.r.t. one nuisance variable, while the other variables are similar as observed in the training data. We annotate data with class labels, object bounding boxes and 3D object poses, resulting in a total dataset collection and annotation effort more than 650 h. Our ROBIN dataset, for the first time, enables studying the influence of individual nuisances on the OOD performance of vision models. In addition to the dataset, we contribute an extensive experimental evaluation of popular baseline methods for each vision task and make several interesting observations, most importantly: 1) Some nuisance factors have a much stronger negative effect on the model performance compared to others. Moreover, the negative effect of a nuisance depends on the downstream vision task, because different tasks rely on different visual cues. 2) Current approaches to enhance robustness using strong data augmentation have only marginal effects in real-world OOD scenarios, and sometimes even reduce the OOD performance. Instead, some results suggest that architectures with 3D object representations have an enhanced robustness to OOD shifts in the object shape and 3D pose. 3) We do not observe any significant differences between convolutional and transformer architectures in terms of OOD robustness. We believe our dataset provides a rich testbed to benchmark and discuss novel approaches to OOD robustness in real-world scenarios and we expect the benchmark to play a pivotal role in driving the future of research on robust computer vision.

2   Related Works

Robustness Benchmark on Synthetic Images. There has been a lot of recent work on utilizing synthetic images to test the robustness of neural networks [20,29,35]. For example, ImageNet-C [20] evaluates the performance of neural networks on images with synthetic noises such as JPEG compression, motion-blur and Gaussian noise by perturbing the standard ImageNet [10] test set with these noises. [35] extends this idea of perturbing images with synthetic noises to the task of object detection by adding these noises on COCO [31] and Pascal-VOC [13] test sets. Besides perturbation from image processing pipelines, there are also work [16] benchmarks the shape and texture bias of DNNs using images with artificially overwritten textures. Using style-transfer [15] as augmentation [16] or using a linear combination between strongly augmented images and the original images [22] have been shown as effective ways of improving the robustness against these synthetic image noises or texture changes. However, these benchmarks are limited in a way that synthetic image perturbations are not able to mimic real-world 3-dimensional nuisances such as novel shape or novel pose of objects. Our experiments in Sect. 4 also show that style-transfer [15] and strong augmentation [22] does not help with shape and pose changes. In addition, these benchmarks are limited to single tasks, for example, ImageNet-C [20] only evaluates the robustness on image classification, COCO-C [35] only evaluates on the tasks of object detection. DomainBed [17] also benchmarks algorithm on OOD domain generalization on the task of classification. In our work, we evaluate the robustness on real world images, while also evaluate the robustness across different tasks including image classification, object detection, and pose estimation.

Robustness Benchmark on Real World Images. Distribution shift in real-world images are more than just synthetic noises, many recent works [20,23,39] focus on collecting real-world images to benchmark robustness of DNN performances. ImageNet-V2 [39] created a new test set for ImageNet [10] by downloading images from Flickr, and found this new test set causes the model performance to degrade, showing that the distribution shift in the real images has an important influence on DNN models. By leveraging an adversarial filtration technique that filtered out all images that a fixed ResNet-50 [18] model can correctly classifies, ImageNet-A [23] collected a new test set and shows that these adversarially filtered images can transfer across other architectures and cause the performance to drop by a large margin. Although ImageNet-A [23] shows the importance of evaluating the robustness on real-world images, but cannot isolate the nuisance factor. Most recently, ImageNet-R [19] collected four OOD testing benchmarks by collecting images with distribution shifts in texture, geo-location, camera parameters, and blur respectively, and shows that not one single technique can improve the model performance across all the nuisance factors. There are also benchmarks to test how well a model can learn invariant features from unbalanced datasets [43]. And benchmarks composed of many real world shifts [25]. We introduce a robustness benchmark that is complementary to prior datasets, by disentangling individual OOD nuisance factors that correspond to semantic aspects of an image, such as the object texture and shape, the context object, and the weather conditions. Due to rich annotation of our data, our benchmark also enables studying OOD robustness for various vision tasks.

Techniques for Improving Robustness. To close the gap between the performance of vision models on datasets and the performance in the real-world, many techniques has been proposed [37]. These techniques for improving robustness can be roughly categorized into two types: data augmentation and architectural changes. Adversarial training by adding the worst case perturbation to images at training-time [49], using stronger data augmentation [8,47], image mixtures [12,22,55], and image stylizations [16] during training, or augmenting in the feature space [19] are all possible methods for data augmentation. These data augmentation methods have been proven to be effective for synthetic perturbed images [16,22]. Architectural changes are another way to improve the robustness by adding additional inductive biases into the model. [53] proposed to perform de-noise to the feature representation for a better adversarial robustness. Analysis-by-synthesis appoaches [28,45] can handle scenarios like occlusion by leveraging a generative object model and through top-down feedback [52]. Transformers are a newly emerged architecture for computer vision [11,32,42], and there are works showing that transformers may have a better robustness than CNNs [5,34], although our experiments suggest that this is not the case. Object-centric representations [33,48] have also been show to improve robustness. Self-supervised learned representations also show improvement on OOD examples [9,21,56,58] Our benchmark enables the comprehensive evaluation of such techniques to improve the robustness of vision models on realistic data, w.r.t. individual nuisances and vision tasks. We find that current approaches to enhance robustness have only marginal effects, and can even reduce robustness, thus highlighting the need for an enhanced effort in this research direction.

Fig. 2. Examples from our dataset with OOD variations of individual nuisance factors including the object shape, pose, texture, context and weather conditions.

3   Dataset Collection

In this section, we introduce the design of the OOD-CV benchmark and discuss the data collection process to obtain the OOD images and annotations.

3.1   What Are Important Nuisance Factors?

The goal of the OOD-CV benchmark is to measure the robustness of vision models to realistic OOD shifts w.r.t. important individual nuisance factors. To achieve this, we define an ontology of nuisance factors that are relevant in real-world scenarios following related work on robust vision [2,27,36,38,41] and taking inspiration from the fact that images are 3D scenes with a hierarchical compositional structure, where each component can vary independently of the other components. In particular, we identify five important nuisance factors that vary strongly in real-world scenarios: the object shape, its 3D pose, and texture appearance, as well as the surrounding context and the weather conditions. These nuisance factors can be annotated by a human observer with reasonable effort, while capturing a large amount of the variability in real-world images. Notably, each nuisance can vary independently from the other nuisance factors, which will enable us to benchmark the OOD effect of each nuisance individually.

3.2   Collecting Images

OOD data can only be defined w.r.t. some reference distribution of training data. For our dataset, the reference training data is based on the PASCAL3D+ [50] dataset which is composed of images from Pascal-VOC [13] and ImageNet [10] datasets, and contains annotations of the object class, bounding box and 3D pose. Our goal is to collect images where only one nuisance factor is OOD w.r.t. training data, while other factors are similar as in training data.

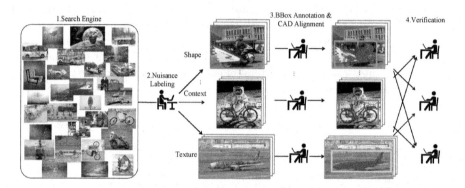

Fig. 3. The data is collected from internet using a predefined set of search keywords, we then manually filter out all images that do not have OOD nuisances or have multiple nuisances. After collecting and splitting the data into different collections with different nuisance, we label images with object bounding boxes and align a CAD model to estimate the 3D pose of the object. The CAD models are overlaid on the images in blue. After each image annotation has been verified by at least two other annotators, we include it in our final dataset. (Color figure online)

To collect data with OOD nuisance factors, we search the internet using a curated set of search keywords that are combinations of the object class from the PASCAL3D+ dataset and attribute words that may retrieve images with OOD attributes, e.g. "car+hotdog" or "motorbike+batman", a comprehensive list of our search keywords used can be found in the supplementary material. Note that we only use 10 object categories from PASCAL3D+, as we could not find sufficient OOD test samples for all nuisances for the categories "bottle" and "television". We manually filtered images with multiple nuisances and put an effort in retaining images that significantly vary in terms of one nuisance only. Following this approach, we collect 2632 images with OOD nuisances in terms of shape, texture, context and weather. Examples images are shown in Fig. 2.

To create OOD dataset splits regarding 3D pose and shape we leverage the shape and pose annotations from PASCAL3D+. These allow us to split the dataset such that 3D pose and shape of training and testing set do not overlap. We augment these OOD splits in pose and shape with additional data that we collect from internet. Statistics of our dataset are shown in the supplementary. On average we have 52 images per nuisance and object class which is comparable to other datasets, e.g. ImageNet-C with an average of 50 images.

Overall, the OOD-CV benchmark is an image collection with a total of 13297 images composed from PASCAL3D+ and internet where 10665 images are from PASCAL3D+ and 2632 images are collected and annotated by us. To ensure that test data is really OOD, three annotators went through all training data from PASCAL3D+ and filtered out images from training set that were too similar to OOD test data. To enable us to benchmark OOD robustness, the nuisance factors and vision tasks were annotated as discussed in the next section.

3.3   Data Annotation

A schematic illustration of the annotation process is shown in Fig. 3. After collecting the images from internet, we first classify the images according to OOD nuisance factor following the ontology discussed in Sect. 3.1. Subsequently, we annotate the images to enable benchmarking of a variety of vision tasks. In particular, we annotate the object class, 2D bounding box and 3D object pose. Note that we include the 3D pose, despite the large additional annotation effort compared to class labels and 2D bounding boxes, because we believe that extracting 3D information from images is an important computer vision task.

The annotation of the bounding boxes follows the coco format [31]. We used a web-based annotation tool[1] that enables the data annotation with multiple annotators in parallel. The 3D pose annotation mainly follows the pipeline of PASCAL3D+ [50] and we use a slightly modified annotation tool from the one used in the PASCAL3D+ toolkit[2]. Specifically, to annotate the 3D pose each annotator selects a CAD model from the ones provided in PASCAL3D+, which best resembles the object in the input image. Subsequently, the annotator labels several keypoints to align the 6D pose of the CAD model to the object in input image. After we have obtained annotations for the images, we count the distribution of number of images in each category and for categories with less images than average, we continue to collect additional images from internet for the minority categories. Following this annotation process, we collected labels for all 2632 images covering all nuisance factors. Finally, the annotations produced by every annotator are verified by at least two other annotators to ensure the annotation is correct. We have a total of 5 annotators, and it took about 15 min per image, resulting in more than 650 h of annotation effort.

Dataset Splits. To benchmark the IID performance, we split the 10665 images that we retained from the PASCAL3D+ dataset into 8532 training images and 2133 test images. The OOD dataset splits for the nuisances "texture", "context", and "weather" can be directly used from our collected data. As the Pascal3D+ data is highly variable in terms of 3D pose and shape, we create OOD splits w.r.t. the nuisances "pose" and "shape" by biasing the training data using the pose and shape annotations, such that the training and test set have no overlap in terms of shape and pose variations. These initial OOD splits are further enhanced using

---

[1] https://github.com/jsbroks/coco-annotator.
[2] https://cvgl.stanford.edu/projects/pascal3d.html.

the data we collected from the internet. The dataset and a detailed documentation of the dataset splits is available online[3].

4 Experiments

We test the robustness of vision models w.r.t. out-of-distribution shifts of individual nuisance factors in Sect. 4.1 and evaluate popular methods for enhancing the model robustness of vision models using data augmentation techniques (Sect. 4.2) and changes to the model architecture (Sect. 4.3). Finally, we study the effect when multiple nuisance factors are subject to OOD shifts in Sect. 4.4 and give a comprehensive discussion of our results in Sect. 5.

Experimental Setup. Our OOD-CV dataset enables benchmark vision models for three popular vision tasks: image classification, object detection, and 3D pose estimation. We study robustness of popular methods for each task w.r.t. OOD shifts in five nuisance factors: object shape, 3D pose, object texture, background context and weather conditions. We use the standard evaluation process of mAP@50 and Acc@$\frac{\pi}{6}$ for object detection and 3D pose estimation respectively. For image classification, we crop the objects in the images based on their bounding boxes to create object-centric images, and use the commonly used Top-1 Accuracy to evaluate the performance of classifiers. In all our experiments, we control variables such as the number of model parameters, model architecture, and training schedules to be comparable and only modify those variables we wish to study. The models for image classification are pre-trained on ImageNet [10] and fine-tuned on our benchmark. As datasets for a large-scale pre-training are not available for 3D pose estimation, we randomly initialize the pose estimation models and directly train them on the OOD-CV training split. Detailed training settings for vision models and data splits can be found in our supplementary.

Table 1. Robustness to individual nuisances of popular vision models for different vision tasks. We report the performance on i.i.d. test data and OOD shifts in the object shape, 3D pose, texture, context and weather. Note that image classification models are most affected by OOD shifts in the weather, while detection and pose estimation models mostly affected by OOD shifts in context and shape, suggesting that vision models for different tasks rely on different visual cues.

Task		i.i.d	Shape	Pose	Texture	Context	Weather
Image Classification	ResNet50	85.2% ± 2.1%	73.2% ± 1.9%	73.8% ± 2.0%	76.2% ± 2.6%	78.7% ± 2.8%	69.2% ± 1.9%
	MbNetv3-L	81.5% ± 1.7%	68.2% ± 2.0%	71.4% ± 1.6%	72.1% ± 2.4%	75.9% ± 2.9%	66.5% ± 2.5%
Object Detection	Faster-RCNN	72.6% ± 1.7%	61.6% ± 2.4%	62.4% ± 1.7%	56.3% ± 1.1%	35.6% ± 1.8%	50.7% ± 1.6%
	RetinaNet	74.7% ± 1.6%	64.1% ± 2.0%	65.8% ± 1.9%	61.5% ± 2.0%	40.3% ± 2.2%	54.2% ± 2.0%
3D Pose Estimation	Res50-Specific	62.4% ± 2.4%	43.5% ± 2.5%	45.2% ± 2.8%	51.4% ± 1.8%	50.8% ± 1.9%	49.5% ± 2.1%
	NeMo	66.7% ± 2.3%	51.7% ± 2.3%	56.9% ± 2.7%	52.6% ± 2.0%	51.3% ± 1.5%	49.8% ± 2.0%

---

[3] http://ood-cv.org/, Also see the supplementary material.

4.1   Robustness to Individual Nuisances

The OOD-CV benchmarks enables, for the first time, to study the influence of OOD shifts in individual nuisance factors on tasks of classification, detection and pose estimation. We first study the robustness of one representative methods for each task. In Table 1, we report the test performance on a test set with i.i.d. data, as well as the performance under OOD shifts to all five nuisance factors that are annotated in the OOD-CV benchmark. We observe that for image classification, the performance of the classic ResNet50 architecture [18] drops significantly for every OOD shift in the data. The largest drop is observed under OOD shifts in the weather conditions (−16.0%), while the performance drop for OOD context is only −6.5%. The results suggests that the model does not rely very much on contextual cues but rather focuses more on the overall gist of the image, which is largely affected by changing weather conditions. Moreover, the classification model is more affected by OOD shifts in geometric cues such as the shape and the 3D pose, compared to the object texture. On the contrary, for object detection the performance of a Faster-RCNN [40] model drops the most under OOD context (−37% mAP@50), showing that detection models rely strongly on contextual cues. While the performance of the detection model also decreases significantly across all OOD shifts, the appearance-based shifts like texture, context and weather have a stronger influence compared to OOD shifts in the shape and pose of the object. For the task of 3D pose estimation, we study a ResNet50-Specific [57] model, which is a common pose estimation baseline that treats pose estimation as a classification problem (discretizing the pose space and then classifying an image into one of the pose bins). We observe that the performance for 3D pose estimation drops significantly, across all nuisance variables and most prominently for OOD shifts in the shape and pose.

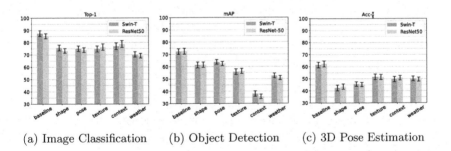

(a) Image Classification   (b) Object Detection   (c) 3D Pose Estimation

Fig. 4. Performance of CNN and Transformer on our benchmark. Transformers have a higher in-domain performance, but CNNs and transformers degrades mostly the same on OOD testing examples.

In summary, our experimental results show that **OOD nuisances have different effect on vision models for different visual tasks**. This suggests OOD robustness should not be simply treated as a domain transfer problem between datasets, but instead it is important to study the effects of individual nuisance factors. Moreover, OOD robustness might require different approaches for each vision tasks, as we observe clear differences in the effect of OOD shifts in individual nuisance factors between vision tasks.

4.2   Data Augmentation for Enhancing Robustness

Data augmentation techniques have been widely adopted as an effective means of improving the robustness of vision models. Among such data augmentation methods, stylizing images with artistic textures [16], mixing up the original image with a strongly augmented image (AugMix [22]), and adversarial training [49] are the most effective methods. We test these data augmentation methods on OOD-CV to find out if and how they affect the OOD robustness. The experimental results are summarized in Table 2. Overall, AugMix [22] improves the OOD robustness the most for image classification and pose estimation. While AugMix is not directly applicable to object detection, we observe that strong data augmentation style transfer [15] leads to a better improvement compared to

Table 2. Effect of data augmentation techniques on OOD robustness for three vision tasks. We report the performance of one baseline model for each task, as well as the same model trained with different augmentation techniques: Stylizing , AugMix [22] and Adversarial Training [49]. We evaluate all models on i.i.d. test data and OOD shifts in the object shape, 3D pose, texture, context and weather. Strong data augmentation only improves robustness to appearance-based nuisances but even decreases the performance to geometry-based nuisances like shape and 3D pose.

top-1	i.i.d	Shape	Pose	Texture	Context	Weather
ResNet-50	85.2%	73.2%	73.8%	76.2%	78.7%	69.2%
Style Transfer	86.4%	72.8%	72.6%	78.9%	78.8%	73.6%
AugMix	87.6%	73.0%	73.3%	82.1%	82.6%	75.2%
Adv. Training	83.7%	72.1%	71.6%	77.9%	79.9%	72.6%

(a) Top-1 accuracy results on image classification

mAP-50	i.i.d	Shape	Pose	Texture	Context	Weather
Faster-RCNN	72.6%	61.6%	62.4%	56.3%	35.6%	50.7%
Style Transfer	73.1%	59.8%	61.3%	58.4%	39.4%	53.5%
Adv. Training	71.3%	60.4%	60.1%	57.4%	36.9%	52.8%

(b) mAP@50 results on object detection

Acc-$\frac{\pi}{6}$	i.i.d	Shape	Pose	Texture	Context	Weather
Res50-Spec.	62.4%	43.5%	45.2%	51.4%	50.8%	49.5%
Style Transfer	63.1%	41.8%	44.7%	55.8%	54.3%	53.8%
AugMix	64.8%	44.1%	44.8%	56.7%	54.7%	55.6%
Adv. Training	61.1%	41.7%	43.5%	52.4%	51.7%	50.9%

(c) Acc-$\frac{\pi}{6}$ results on pose estimation

Table 3. OOD robustness of models with different capacities. While the performance degradation of MobileNetv3-Large (MbNetv3-L) are about the same as those of ResNet-50, training with data augmentation technique has smaller effect on MbNetv3-L due to the limited capacity.

	i.i.d	Shape	Pose	Texture	Context	Weather
ResNet50	85.2%	73.2%	73.8%	76.2%	78.7%	69.2%
+AugMix [22]	87.6%	73.0%	73.3%	82.1%	82.6%	75.2%
MbNetv3-L [24]	81.5%	68.2%	71.4%	72.1%	75.9%	66.5%
+AugMix [22]	83.1%	67.8%	71.6%	74.3%	76.8%	69.7%

adversarial training. Importantly, these data augmentation methods improve the OOD robustness mostly w.r.t. appearance-based nuisances like texture, context, and weather. However, in all our experiments *data augmentation slightly reduces the performance* under OOD shape and 3D pose. We suspect that this happens because data augmentation techniques mostly change appearance-based properties of the image and do not change the geometric properties of the object (i.e. shape and 3D pose). Similar trends are observed across all three of the tasks we tested, image classification, object detection, and pose estimation. These results suggest that two categories of nuisances exists, namely *appearance-based* nuisances like novel texture, context, and weather, and *geometric-based* nuisances like novel shape and pose. We observe that **data augmentation only improves robustness of appearance-based nuisances but can even decrease the performance w.r.t. geometry-based nuisances.**

4.3 Effect of Model Architecture on Robustness

In this section, we investigate four popular architectural changes that have proven to be useful in real world applications. Paricularly, we evaluate *CNNs vs Transformers*, the *model capacity*, *one stage vs two stage* detectors, and models with *integrated 3D priors*. Note that when we change the model architecture we keep other parameters such as number of parameters and capacity the same.

CNNs vs Transformers. Transformers have emerged as a promising alternative to convolutional neural networks (CNNs) as an architecture for computer vision tasks recently [11,32]. While CNNs have been extensively studied for robustness, the robustness of vision transformers are still under-explored. Some works [5,34] have shown that transformer architecture maybe more robust to adversarial examples, but it remains if this result holds for OOD robustness. In the following, we compare the performance of CNNs and transformers on the tasks of image classification, object detection and 3D pose estimation on the OOD-CV benchmark. Specifically, we replace the backbone the vision models for each task from ResNet-50 to Swin-T [32]. Our experimental results are presented in Fig. 4. Each experiment is performed five times and we report mean

Table 4. Comparison between one-stage method and two-stage object detection methods. One-stage methods are more robust compared to two-stage methods.

	i.i.d	Shape	Pose	Texture	Context	Weather
RetinaNet [30]	74.7%	64.1%	65.8%	61.5%	40.3%	54.2%
+Style Transfer [16]	75.8%	62.7%	64.2%	63.7%	44.7%	55.8%
Faster-RCNN [40]	72.6%	61.6%	62.4%	56.3%	35.6%	50.7%
+Style Transfer [16]	73.1%	59.8%	61.3%	58.4%	39.4%	53.5%

Table 5. Robustness of 3D pose estimation methods. We compare "Res50-Specific", which treats pose estimation as classification problem, and "NeMo", which represents the 3D object geometry explicitly. We observe OOD shifts in shape and pose leads to more performance degradation. NeMo has a significantly enhanced performance to OOD shifts in object shape and pose.

	i.i.d	Shape	Pose	Texture	Context	Weather
Res50-Specific	62.4%	43.5%	45.2%	51.4%	50.8%	49.5%
+AugMix [22]	64.8%	44.1%	44.8%	56.7%	54.7%	55.6%
NeMo [45]	66.7%	51.7%	56.9%	52.6%	51.3%	49.8%
+AugMix [22]	67.9%	53.1%	58.6%	57.8%	55.1%	56.7%

performance and standard deviation. It can be observed that CNNs and vision transformers have a comparable performance across all tasks as the difference between their performances are within the margin of error. Particularly, we do not observe any enhanced robustness as OOD shifts in individual nuisance factors lead to a similar decrease in performance in both the transformer and the CNN architecture. While we observe a slight performance gain on i.i.d. data in image classification (as reported in many other works), our results suggest that **Transformers do not have any enhanced OOD robustness compared to CNNs**. Note our findings here contrast with previous work on this topic [3], we argue that this is because our benchmark enables the study for individual nuisance factors on real world images, and the control over different individual nuisances give us opportunity to observe more errors in current vision models.

Model Capacity. For deployment in real applications, smaller models are preferred because they can yield better efficiency than regular models. In the following, we compare image classification performance of MobileNetV3 [24] in Table,3. Compared to ResNet-50, MobileNetv3 suffers a similar performance degradation under OOD shifts in the data. However, data augmentations does not improve the robustness of MobileNetV3 [24] as much as for ResNet-50, *e.g.*, performance on context nuisances improved by 3.9% for ResNet-50, but the improvement is only 0.9% for MobileNetV3. This suggests that **OOD robustness is more difficult to achieve for efficient models with a limaited capacity.**

One Stage vs Two Stage for Detection. It is a common belief in object detection community that two-stage detectors are more accurate, while one-stage detectors are more efficient. For object detection task, two popular types of architecture exist, namely one-stage and two stage models. We tested two representative models from these architecture types, RetinaNet [30], a one-stage detector, and Faster-RCNN [40], which is a two-stage detector. From our results in Table,4, we observe that RetinaNet achieves a higher performance compared to Faster-RCNN on the OOD-CV benchmark. However, when accounting for improved i.i.d performance, the OOD performance degradation are similar between two models. These initial result suggests that **two-stage methods achieve a higher score than one-stage methods, but are not necessarily more robustness**.

Models with Explicit 3D Object Geomtery. Recently, Wang et al. [45] introduced NeMo, a neural network architecture for 3D pose estimation that explicitly models 3D geometery, and they demonstrated promising results on enhancing robustness to partial occlusion and unseen 3D poses. In Table,5, we compare NeMo [45] model and a general Res50-Specific model on task of pose estimation on OOD-CV benchmark. NeMo [45] shows a stronger robustness against geometric-based nuisances (shape and pose), while robustness on appearance-based nuisances is comparable. This result suggests that, **neural networks with an explicit 3D object representation have a largely enhanced robustness to OOD shifts in geometry-based nuisances**. These results seem complementary to our experiments in the previous section, which demonstrate that strong data augmentation can help to improve the robustness of vision models to appearance-based nuisances, but not to geometry-based nuisances.

We further investigate, if robustness against all nuisance types can be improved by combining data augmentation with architectures that explicitly represent the 3D object geometry. Specifically, we train NeMo [45] with strong augmentations like AugMix [22] and our results in Table,5 show that this indeed largely enhances the robustness to OOD shifts in appearance-based nuisances, while retaining (and slightly improving) the robustness to geometry-based nuisances. Result suggests that enhancements of robustness to geometry-based nuisances can be developed independently to those for appearance-based nuisances.

4.4 OOD Shifts in Multiple Nuisances

In our experiments, we observed that geometry-based nuisances have different effects compared to appearance-based nuisances. In the following, we test the effect when OOD shifts happen in both of these nuisance types. Specifically, we introduce new dataset splits, which combine appearance-based nuisances, including texture, context, or weather, with the geometry-based nuisances shape and pose. From Table 6, we observe **OOD shifts in multiple nuisances amplify each other**. For example, for image classification, an OOD shift in only the 3D pose reduces the performance by 11.4% from 85.2% to 73.8%, and an OOD shift in the context reduces the performance by 6.6%. However, when pose and context are combined the performance reduces by 24.5%. We observe a similar amplification behaviour across all three tasks, suggesting that it is a general effect that is likely more difficult to address compared to single OOD shifts.

Table 6. Robustness to OOD shifts in multiple nuisances. When combined, OOD shifts in appearance-based nuisances and geometric-based nuisances amplifies each other, leads to further decrease compared to effects in individual nuisances.

	i.i.d	Texture	Context	Weather
Classification	85.2%	76.2%	78.7%	69.2%
+shape	73.2%	62.8%	63.6%	51.2%
+pose	73.8%	61.9%	60.7%	49.8%
Detection	72.6%	56.3%	35.6%	50.7%
+shape	61.6%	41.2%	24.3%	30.7%
+pose	62.4%	45.6%	26.1%	29.8%
Pose estimation	62.4%	51.4%	50.8%	49.5%
+shape	43.5%	33.1%	31.0%	29.8%
+pose	45.2%	30.2%	29.7%	28.1%

5   Conclusion

We have shown that proposed OOD-CV benchmark enables a thorough diagnosis of robustness of vision models to realistic OOD shifts in individual nuisance factors. Overall, we observe that OOD shifts poses a great challenge to current state-of-the-art vision models and requires significant attention from the research community to be resolved. Notably, we found that nuisance factors have a different effect on different vision tasks, suggesting that we might need different solutions for enhancing the OOD robustness for different vision tasks. In our experiments, it can also be clearly observed that the nuisances can be roughly separated into two categories, *appearance-based nuisances* like texture, context, or weather, and another one is *geometry-based nuisances* such as shape or pose. We showed that strong data augmentation enhances the robustness against appearance-based nuisances, but has very little effect on geometric-based nuisances. On the other hand, neural network architectures with an explicit 3D object representation achieve an enhanced robustness against geometric-based nuisances. While we observe that OOD robustness is largely an unsolved and severe problem for computer vision models, our results also suggest a way forward to address OOD robustness in the future. Particularly, that approaches to enhance the robustness may need to be specifically designed for each vision tasks, as different vision tasks focus on different visual cues. Moreover, we observed a promising way forward to a largely enhanced OOD robustness is to develop neural network architectures that represent the 3D object geometry explicitly and are trained with strong data augmentation to address OOD shifts in both geometry-based and appearance-based nuisances combined.

Acknowledgements. AK acknowledges support via his Emmy Noether Research Group funded by the German Science Foundation (DFG) under Grant No. 468670075. BZ acknowledges compute support from LunarAI. AY acknowledges grants ONR N00014-20-1-2206 and ONR N00014-21-1-2812.

References

1. Robust Vision Challenge 2020. http://www.robustvision.net/
2. Alcorn, M.A., et al.: Strike (with) a pose: neural networks are easily fooled by strange poses of familiar objects. In: Proceedings of the IEEE Conference on Computer Vision and Pattern Recognition, pp. 4845–4854 (2019)
3. Bai, Y., Mei, J., Yuille, A.L., Xie, C.: Are Transformers more robust than CNNs? Adv. Neural Inf. Process. Syst. **34**, 26831–26843 (2021)
4. Bengio, Y., Lecun, Y., Hinton, G.: Deep learning for AI. Commun. ACM **64**(7), 58–65 (2021)
5. Bhojanapalli, S., Chakrabarti, A., Glasner, D., Li, D., Unterthiner, T., Veit, A.: Understanding robustness of transformers for image classification. In: International Conference on Computer Vision (2021)
6. Borji, A., Izadi, S., Itti, L.: ilab-20m: a large-scale controlled object dataset to investigate deep learning. In: IEEE Conference on Computer Vision Pattern Recognition (2016)
7. Chen, X., Mottaghi, R., Liu, X., Fidler, S., Urtasun, R., Yuille, A.: Detect what you can: Detecting and representing objects using holistic models and body parts. In: IEEE Conference Computer Vision Pattern Recognition (2014)
8. Cubuk, E. D., Zoph, B., Mane, D., Vasudevan, V., Le, Q.V.: Autoaugment: learning augmentation policies from data. In: IEEE Conference on Computer Vision Pattern Recognition (2018)
9. Cui, Q., et al. Discriminability-transferability trade-off: an information-theoretic perspective. In: European Conference on Computer Vision (2022)
10. Deng, J., Dong, W., Socher, R., Li, L.J., Li, K., Fei-Fei, L.: Imagenet: a large-scale hierarchical image database. In: IEEE Conference Computer Vision Pattern Recognition (2009)
11. Dosovitskiy, A., et al.: An image is worth 16×16 words: transformers for image recognition at scale. In: International Conference Learning Representation (2020)
12. Erichson, N.B., Lim, S.H., Utrera, F., Xu, W., Cao, Z., Mahoney, M.W.: Noisymix: boosting robustness by combining data augmentations, stability training, and noise injections. arXiv preprint arXiv:2202.01263, 2022
13. Everingham, M., Eslami, S.M., Van Gool, L., Williams, C.K., Winn, J., Zisserman, A.: The pascal visual object classes challenge: a retrospective. Int. J. Comput. Vision **111**(1), 98–136 (2015)
14. Everingham, M., Van Gool, L., Williams, C.K.I., Winn, J., Zisserman, A.: The PASCAL Visual Object Classes Challenge 2012 (VOC2012) Results. http://www.pascal-network.org/challenges/VOC/voc2012/workshop/index.html
15. Gatys, L.A., Ecker, A.S., Bethge, M.: Image style transfer using convolutional neural networks. In: IEEE Conference on Computer Vision Pattern Recognition (2016)
16. Geirhos, R., Rubisch, P., Michaelis, C., Bethge, M., Wichmann, F.A., Brendel, W.: Imagenet-trained CNNs are biased towards texture; increasing shape bias improves accuracy and robustness. In: International Conference on Learning Representation (2019)

17. Gulrajani,I., Lopez-Paz, D.: In search of lost domain generalization. In: International Conference Learning Representation (2021)
18. He, K., Zhang, X., Ren, S., Sun, J.: Deep residual learning for image recognition. In: IEEE Conference Computer Vision Pattern Recognition (2015)
19. Hendrycks, D., et al. The many faces of robustness: a critical analysis of out-of-distribution generalization. In: International Conference on Computer Vision (2021)
20. Hendrycks, D., Dietterich, T.: Benchmarking neural network robustness to common corruptions and perturbations. In: International Conference on Learning Representation (2019)
21. Hendrycks, D., Mazeika, M., Kadavath, S., Song, D.: Using self-supervised learning can improve model robustness and uncertainty. Adv. Neural Inf. Process. Syst. **32** (2019)
22. Hendrycks, D., Mu, N., Cubuk, E.D., Zoph, B., Gilmer, J., Lakshminarayanan, B.: Augmix: a simple data processing method to improve robustness and uncertainty. In: International Conference on Learning Representation (2020)
23. Hendrycks, D., Zhao, K., Basart, S., Steinhardt, J., Song, D.: Natural adversarial examples. In: IEEE Conference on Computer Vision Pattern Recognition (2021)
24. Howard, A., et al. Searching for mobilenetv3. In: International Conference on Computer Vision (2019)
25. Koh, P.W., et al. Wilds: a benchmark of in-the-wild distribution shifts. In: International Conference on Machine Learning (2021)
26. Kortylewski, A., Egger, B., Schneider, A., Gerig, T., Morel-Forster, A., Vetter, T.: Empirically analyzing the effect of dataset biases on deep face recognition systems. In: Proceedings of the IEEE Conference on Computer Vision and Pattern Recognition Workshops (2018)
27. Kortylewski, A., Egger, B., Schneider, A., Gerig, T., Morel-Forster, A., Vetter, T.: Analyzing and reducing the damage of dataset bias to face recognition with synthetic data. In: Proceedings of the IEEE Conference on Computer Vision and Pattern Recognition Workshops (2019)
28. Kortylewski, A., Liu, Q., Wang, A., Sun, Y., Yuille, A.: Compositional convolutional neural networks: a robust and interpretable model for object recognition under occlusion. Int. J. Comput. Vision **129**(3), 736–760 (2021)
29. Kurakin, A., Goodfellow, I., Bengio, S.: Adversarial machine learning at scale. In: International Conference Learning Representation (2017)
30. Lin, T.Y., Goyal, P., Girshick, R., He, K., Dollár, P.: Focal loss for dense object detection. In: International Conference on Computer Vision (2017)
31. Lin, T.-Y., et al.: Microsoft COCO: common objects in context. In: Fleet, D., Pajdla, T., Schiele, B., Tuytelaars, T. (eds.) ECCV 2014. LNCS, vol. 8693, pp. 740–755. Springer, Cham (2014). https://doi.org/10.1007/978-3-319-10602-1_48
32. Liu, Z., et al. Swin transformer: hierarchical vision transformer using shifted windows. In: International Conference on Computer Vision (2021)
33. Francesco, L., et al.: Object-centric learning with slot attention. Adv. Neural Inform. Process. Syst. **33**, 11525–11538 (2020)
34. Mahmood, K., Mahmood, R., Van Dijk, M.: On the robustness of vision transformers to adversarial examples. In: International Conference on Computer Vision (2021)
35. Michaelis, C., et al. Benchmarking robustness in object detection: autonomous driving when winter is coming. Adv. Neural Inf. Process. Syst. (2019)
36. Michaelis, C., et al. Benchmarking robustness in object detection: autonomous driving when winter is coming. arXiv preprint arXiv:1907.07484 (2019)

37. Mohseni, S., Wang, H., Zhiding, Y., Xiao, C., Wang, Z., Yadawa, J.: Practical machine learning safety: a survey and primer. ArXiv (2021)
38. Qiu, W., Yuille, A.: UnrealCV: connecting computer vision to unreal engine. In: Hua, G., Jégou, H. (eds.) ECCV 2016. LNCS, vol. 9915, pp. 909–916. Springer, Cham (2016). https://doi.org/10.1007/978-3-319-49409-8_75
39. Recht, B., Roelofs, R., Schmidt, L., Shankar, V.: Do imagenet classifiers generalize to imagenet? In: International Conference Machine Learning (2019)
40. Ren, S., He, K., Girshick, R., Sun, J.: Faster r-cnn: towards real-time object detection with region proposal networks. Adv. Neural Inf. Processing Syst. **28** (2015)
41. Rosenfeld, A., Zemel, R., Tsotsos, J.K.: The elephant in the room. arXiv preprint arXiv:1808.03305 (2018)
42. Shao, J., Wen, X., Zhao, B., Xue, X.: Temporal context aggregation for video retrieval with contrastive learning. In: IEEE Winter Conference on Applications of Computer Vision (2021)
43. Tang, K., Tao, M., Qi, J., Liu, Z., Zhang, H.: Invariant feature learning for generalized long-tailed classification. In: Europe Confernce on Computer Vision (2022)
44. Tremblay, J., To, T., Birchfield, S.: Falling things: a synthetic dataset for 3D object detection and pose estimation. In: Proceedings of the IEEE Conference on Computer Vision and Pattern Recognition Workshops (2018)
45. Wang, A., Kortylewski, A., Yuille, A.: Nemo: neural mesh models of contrastive features for robust 3D pose estimation. In: International Conference on Learning Representation (2021)
46. Wang, A., Sun, Y., Kortylewski, A., Yuille, A.L.: Robust object detection under occlusion with context-aware compositional nets. In: IEEE Conference on Computer Vision Pattern Recognition (2020)
47. Wang, H., Xiao, C., Kossaifi, J., Zhiding, Y., Anandkumar, A., Wang, Z.: Augmax: adversarial composition of random augmentations for robust training. In: NeurIPS (2021)
48. Wen, X., Zhao, B., Zheng, A., Zhang, X., Qi, X.: Self-supervised visual representation learning with semantic grouping (2022). arxiv: 2205.15288
49. Wong, E., Rice, L., Kolter, J.Z.: Represent, fast is better than free: revisiting adversarial training. In: International Conference on Learning (2020)
50. Xiang, Y., Mottaghi, R., Savarese, S.: Beyond pascal: a benchmark for 3D object detection in the wild. In: IEEE Winter Conference on Applications of Computer Vision (2014)
51. Xiang, Y., Schmidt, T., Narayanan, V., Fox, D.: Posecnn: a convolutional neural network for 6D object pose estimation in cluttered scenes. In Robotics: Science and Systems (RSS) (2018)
52. Xiao, M., Kortylewski, A., Wu, R., Qiao, S., Shen, W., Yuille, A.: TDMPNet: prototype network with recurrent top-down modulation for robust object classification under partial occlusion. In: Bartoli, A., Fusiello, A. (eds.) ECCV 2020. LNCS, vol. 12536, pp. 447–463. Springer, Cham (2020). https://doi.org/10.1007/978-3-030-66096-3_31
53. Xie, C., Wu, Y., van der Maaten, L., Yuille, A.L., He, K.: Feature denoising for improving adversarial robustness. In IEEE Conference on Computer Vision Pattern Recognition (2019)
54. Ye, N., et al.: Ood-bench: benchmarking and understanding out-of-distribution generalization datasets and algorithms. arXiv preprint arXiv:2106.03721 (2021)
55. Yun, S., Han, D., Oh, S.J., Chun, S., Choe, J., Yoo, Y.: Cutmix: regularization strategy to train strong classifiers with localizable features. In: International Conference on Computer Vision (2019)

56. Zhao, B., Wen, X.: Distilling visual priors from self-supervised learning. In: Bartoli, A., Fusiello, A. (eds.) ECCV 2020. LNCS, vol. 12536, pp. 422–429. Springer, Cham (2020). https://doi.org/10.1007/978-3-030-66096-3_29
57. Zhou, X., Karpur, A., Luo, L., Huang, Q.: Starmap for category-agnostic keypoint and viewpoint estimation. In: European Conference on Computer Vision (2018)
58. Zhu, R., Zhao, B., Liu, J., Sun, Z., Chen, C.W.: Improving contrastive learning by visualizing feature transformation. In: International Conference Computer Vision (2021)

Facial Depth and Normal Estimation Using Single Dual-Pixel Camera

Minjun Kang[1], Jaesung Choe[1], Hyowon Ha[4], Hae-Gon Jeon[2],
Sunghoon Im[3], In So Kweon[1], and Kuk-Jin Yoon[1(✉)]

[1] KAIST, Daejeon, South Korea
kmmj2005@kaist.ac.kr
[2] GIST, Gwangju, South Korea
[3] DGIST, Daegu, South Korea
[4] Meta Reality Labs, Menlo Park, USA
https://github.com/MinJunKang/DualPixelFace

Abstract. Recently, Dual-Pixel (DP) sensors have been adopted in many imaging devices. However, despite their various advantages, DP sensors are used just for faster auto-focus and aesthetic image captures, and research on their usage for 3D facial understanding has been limited due to the lack of datasets and algorithmic designs that exploit parallax in DP images. It is also because the baseline of sub-aperture images is extremely narrow, and parallax exists in the defocus blur region. In this paper, we introduce a DP-oriented Depth/Normal estimation network that reconstructs the 3D facial geometry. In addition, to train the network, we collect DP facial data with more than 135K images for 101 persons captured with our multi-camera structured light systems. It contains ground-truth 3D facial models including depth map and surface normal in metric scale. Our dataset allows the proposed network to be generalized for 3D facial depth/normal estimation. The proposed network consists of two novel modules: Adaptive Sampling Module (ASM) and Adaptive Normal Module (ANM), which are specialized in handling the defocus blur in DP images. Finally, we demonstrate that the proposed method achieves state-of-the-art performances over recent DP-based depth/normal estimation methods.

Keywords: Dual-Pixel · Depth/Normal estimation

1 Introduction

A huge number of facial images are posted every day on social media. In 2020, for example, about 70% of photos were taken using cameras on smartphones and 24 billion selfies were uploaded to Google Photos App [19,20]. Accordingly, acquiring facial geometry from images has emerged as an interesting research topic, since 3D facial geometry can be used for various applications [69] such as

---

Supplementary Information The online version contains supplementary material available at https://doi.org/10.1007/978-3-031-20074-8_11.

face recognition [25,37,40], performance-based animation, real-time facial reenactment [5,68], facial biometrics [65], face-based interfaces, visual speech recognition, face-based search in visual assets, creating personalized avatars [35,43] or 3D printing of faces for entertainment or medicine, facial puppetry, face replacement [5,68], speech-driven animation, virtual make-up, and face image editing [63], etc. 3D facial geometry can be obtained by either using multiple cameras [4,15] or active sensing devices [30,32]. However, these methods often suffer from uncontrolled lighting conditions or hardware synchronization.

Recently, **Dual-Pixel (DP)** sensors get noticed due to their various advantages and are applied to the many portable imaging devices such as iPhone13 ProMax and Samsung Galaxy 22. DP sensors are perfectly synchronized with the same exposure, white balance, and geometric rectification. Such strengths derive from their hardware configuration that captures two images in a single camera at once. Based on these properties, currently, these novel sensors are mainly specialized in the fast auto-focus operation and more aesthetic image captures. However, thanks to their characteristics, DP sensors have great potential for other tasks. For example, a few previous studies [16,45,46,57,61,67] envision the new possibility of DP images for scene depth estimation. Usually, these studies regard DP images as extremely narrow-baseline stereo images having defocus-blur to infer high-quality depth maps. Here, it is worthy to note that although the DP sensors are being actively used to take face pictures, there has been a limited study [60] that recovers facial geometry using a Dual-Pixel camera. We found that previous methods have difficulty in facial geometry estimation, which is due to the lack of a facial DP dataset with precise 3D geometry and an appropriate algorithm for generalized estimation.

To address the issue, we present a DP-oriented 3D facial dataset and a depth/normal estimation network toward high-quality facial geometry reconstruction with DP cameras. We represent the 3D facial geometry not only with the depth map but also with the normal map for various applications such as face relighting. Our dataset involves 135,744 face data for 101 persons consisting of DP images and their corresponding depth maps and surface normal maps, which are captured by our structured light camera system. Based on these data, we train our depth/normal estimation network, called stereoDPNet, to infer 3D facial information from DP images. In particular, our stereoDPNet is fully oriented from the properties of dual-pixel images that have an extremely small range of disparity with defocus-blur. Our network design carefully treats these distinctive properties through our Adaptive Sampling Module (ASM) and Adaptive Normal Module (ANM). Finally, the contributions are as follows:

- DP-oriented 3D facial dataset with more than 135K DP images and their corresponding high-quality 3D models.
- Novel depth/normal estimation network for facial 3D reconstruction from a DP image with better generalization.

2   Related Work

Defocus-Disparity in Dual-Pixel. Dual-Pixel images can be considered as a pair of stereo images since the DP camera captures two sub-aperture images

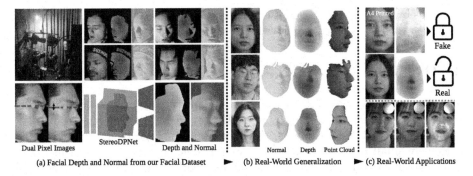

(a) Facial Depth and Normal from our Facial Dataset   ▶   (b) Real-World Generalization   ▶   (c) Real-World Applications

Fig. 1. Using our Dual-Pixel Facial datasets, our network aims at generalized estimation of unmet facial geometry, which can be used for various applications, such as face spoofing or relighting.

with small parallax. However, since the DP camera is equipped with a micro-lens array in front of a camera sensor, the pixel disparity in DP images is extremely narrow ($-$4px$\sim$+4px) [67] compared to conventional stereo images. For this reason, Zhang et al. [67] contend that a single pair of DP images is not suitable for cost volume-based disparity regression due to the narrow baseline ($<\sim$1 mm). Other works [16] also adopt simple 2D U-Net architectures for affine-transformed depth regression. Meanwhile, the disparity of DP images is induced by different left/right point spread functions (PSFs) instead of view parallax of stereo, called defocus-disparity [46]. Based on this observation, Punnappurath et al. [46] propose an optimization-based disparity regression using a parametrized PSF. The pioneering works [16,46,57] allow us to formulate depth-disparity conversion.

Geometry Dataset for Dual-Pixel. Owing to the growing research interest in DP photography, several real/synthetic DP datasets [3,16,45,46] have been released. Garg et al. [16] propose a real-world DP dataset that includes scene-scale images captured by an array of smartphones. Despite of their success, the estimated depth is up to scale because their training data contains a relative-scaled 3D geometry computed by a multiview stereo algorithm (COLMAP [51]).

Face Dataset. Facial datasets have typically been created whenever new types of commercial imaging devices are introduced. Since it is only available to reconstruct faces from monocular images with a limited assumption [59], many 3D face regression methods [14,21,49] rely on a given face morphable model [7,56] and modify the shape with facial keypoints [14,52] and landmarks [6,13]. Recently, several face regression models [6,58] utilize multi-view images as input. However, it is challenging to estimate facial geometry from DP images since blurry features are hardly captured from homogeneous regions of the face. This property brings difficulty in finding correspondence between left/right DP images. We observe that the previous DP-oriented methods [16,46] have difficulty estimating the 3D geometry of human faces as well. Many of the applications with facial images require both a high-quality depth and a surface normal for pleasing aesthetic effects [68]. Therefore, we satisfy the increasing industrial and academic

demands by providing high-quality and absolute scale facial depth/normal maps
that are captured with cameras with DP sensors.

3   Overview

This paper covers dual-pixel based facial understanding: from data acquisition
(Sect. 4) to general estimation by stereoDPNet (Sect. 5). Different from natural images from typical cameras, dual-pixel sensors capture images having an
extremely small range of disparity as well as defocus-blur, as shown in Fig. 4.
Through our carefully designed dataset and network, we design a well-generalized
methodology that even can infer facial geometry from unmet DP facial images.

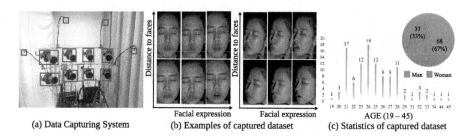

(a) Data Capturing System   (b) Examples of captured dataset   (c) Statistics of captured dataset

Fig. 2. Examples of our facial dataset. (a) The proposed hardware setup:
(2×4 multi-camera array (blue), 6 LEDs (red), a projector (green), and a LED con-
troller (magenta). (b) DP images with various facial expressions (horizontal axis) and
distances from the hardware to faces (vertical axis). There are two additional images
taken in different heading directions (center/rightward). (c) Our dataset has 68 men
and 33 women and age distribution of them ranges from 19 to 45. (Color figure online)

4   Dual-Pixel Facial Dataset

In this section, we explain the construction of DP-oriented facial dataset. Since
defocus-disparity in DP images is highly sensitive to image resolution, our
dataset should contain both high resolution and high quality ground truth
depth. By considering these requirements, we first explain the data configuration
(Sect. 4.1), details of capturing system (Sect. 4.2), and describe a ground-truth
depth/normal acquisition process (Sect. 4.3).

4.1   Dataset Configuration

Given an array of multiple DP cameras, we capture various human faces with
different expressions and light conditions. The dataset consists of 135,744 photos,
which are a combination of 101 people, eight cameras, seven different lighting
condition, four facial heading directions (left, right, center and upward), three
facial expressions (normal, open mouth and frown), and two fixed distances of
subjects from the camera array, as illustrated in Fig. 2. The distances between the

camera array and subjects range from 80 *cm* to 110 *cm*. Since the focus distance is about 97 *cm*, our captured images contain both front focused and back focused cases. Our dataset includes 44,352 female photos as well as 91,392 male photos, ages range from 19 to 45. The detailed statistics are provided in Fig. 2-(c). In main experiments, we use 76 people (76%) as a train set and the others (24%) as a test/validation set without any overlap with the train set.

4.2 Hardware Setup

For facial data acquisition, we set up the DP-oriented camera-projector system. The system consists of eight synchronized Canon 5D Mark IV cameras on a 2×4 grid, with one commercial projector (1920 × 1080 pixels) and six LED lights, as shown in Fig. 2 which enables capturing high-quality ground truths by using both structured light and photometric stereo. These cameras are available to capture DP images [2,3,45]. Each camera is equipped with a Canon 135 mm L lens. The 17° field of view (FOV), which the lens affords, can cover an approximately 16.7 cm × 25 cm area at about one-meter distance, which is suitable for capturing human faces. We take our dataset with a camera aperture of F5.6, exposure time 1/30", and ISO 1600. The shape of the camera rig mimics a spherical dome with a one-meter radius. All of the cameras are located on the rig looking at the same point near the sphere's center. The projector is positioned at the center of the camera array. The LED lights are installed at various positions so that face images can be taken under varying lighting conditions.

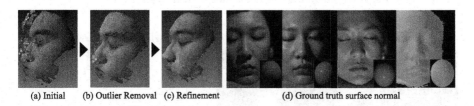

(a) Initial   (b) Outlier Removal   (c) Refinement   (d) Ground truth surface normal

Fig. 3. Ground-truth depth and surface normal acquisition. (a) Initial depth from the structured light. (b) Depth after removing outliers. (c) Depth via fusion of the initial depth and the surface normal obtained from the photometric stereo in (c).

4.3 Ground Truth Data Acquisition

Structured light systems are designed for high-quality 3D geometry acquisition under controlled environments by projecting pre-defined patterns on surfaces of objects [12,23,50] and by analyzing the projected patterns to measure 3D shapes of the objects. It is extensively used for ground-truth depth maps in stereo matching benchmarks [1,27,54] and shape from shading [24]. In this work, we tailor the structured light-based facial 3D reconstruction method [22] with our well-synchronized multi-camera system. Thanks to our capturing system and structured light-based reconstruction method, we obtain dense, high-quality facial 3D corresponding to high-resolution DP images in Fig. 1(a). Moreover, we calibrate point light directions by using a chrome ball and applying a photometric stereo in [44] to obtain accurate surface normal maps of subjects' faces in Fig. 3(d). We utilize the RANSAC algorithm in obtaining both surface normal and albedo for robust estimation by excluding severe specular reflection. By using the surface normals, initial depth is refined by conforming the initial facial depth and the surface normal [44], as illustrated in Fig. 3(a), (b), and (c).

To the end, we find an exact conversion between a defocus-disparity and a metric depth by using the relationship of signed defocus-blur $\bar{b}(x, y)$ and disparity d (Eq. 1) introduced in [16] with the paraxial and thin-lens approximations.

$$
\begin{aligned}
d(x, y) &= \alpha \bar{b}(x, y) \\
&\approx \alpha \frac{Lf}{1 - f/g} \left(\frac{1}{g} - \frac{1}{Z(x, y)} \right) \\
&\triangleq A(L, f, g) + \frac{B(L, f, g)}{Z(x, y)},
\end{aligned}
\tag{1}
$$

where $(x, y, Z(x, y))$ indicates 3D coordinates in camera space, α is a proportional term, and L is the diameter of the camera aperture. f represents the focal length of the lens and g is the focus distance of the camera. By using this relationship, we obtain a ground-truth defocus-disparity from the ground-truth depth in Fig. 4. This conversion is used to back-project our defocus-disparity to metric 3D space, and will be utilized to support absolute metric information for our depth and surface normal estimation network in Sect. 5.

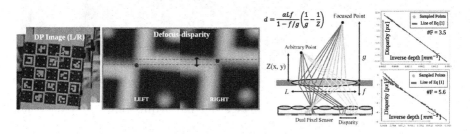

Fig. 4. Dual-Pixel Geometry. Disparity in DP images exists in blurry regions, called defocus-disparity (left). The ground-truth depth obtained by a plane homography and a defocus-disparity from the matching pairs are used to robustly find parameters of Eq. 1. This relationship is used to back-project our prediction to metric-scale depth (right).

5   Facial Depth and Normal Estimation

Based on our dataset, we design StereoDPNet for the general estimation of facial depth and normal. In real applications, dual-pixel images can be captured with various camera parameters, such as focus distance or focal length. The proposed network should cope with various hardware setups as well.

In this point of view, stereo matching methods [9,31,62,66] show strength in generalization toward unmet environments and robust to camera configuration thanks to its corresponding search. Since a pair of DP images can also be regarded as stereo images having a short disparity range, we build our StereoDPNet based on the stereo-based depth/normal method [34] for our dual-pixel based depth/normal estimation.

Nonetheless, the stereo matching methods often require all-in-focus and well-textured images for pixel-wise correspondence search, which is not always guaranteed for DP images due to its defocus-blur and homogeneous/textureless faces. Thus, we propose our two novel modules, Adaptive Sampling Module (ASM) and Adaptive Normal Module (ANM), to further fit the properties of dual-pixel images. As in Fig. 5, our StereoDPNet consists of four parts: feature extraction layer, ASM, cost aggregation layer, and ANM.

5.1 Overall Architecture

Given DP images with left I^L and right I^R, stereoDPNet is trained to infer a disparity map $\hat{d}$ and a surface normal map $\hat{n}$. To do so, first, the feature extraction layer infers DP image features F^L and F^R, respectively. Our feature extractor captures multi-scale information with a large receptive field by adopting Atrous Spatial Pyramid Pooling [11] and Feature Pyramid Network [39] to encode various sizes of defocus blur in the DP images. Second, using F^L and F^R, the proposed ASM captures an amount of spatially varying blur in dynamic ranges, and then adaptively samples the features. Then, the sampled features G^L and G^R are stacked into a cost volume $\mathcal{V}$. Third, the cost volume is aggregated through three stacked hourglass modules to infer the aggregated cost volume C_A. Lastly, this aggregated volume C_A is used to regress a disparity map following the baseline and infer a surface normal map by ANM. The details of ASM and ANM are described in Sect. 5.2 and Sect. 5.3.

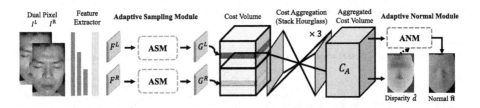

Fig. 5. Architecture of StereoDPNet. Given DP images, our network is trained to infer facial depth/normal maps. Our two key modules, Adaptive Sampling Module and Adaptive Normal Module, overcome the extremely narrow baseline in DP images by capturing disparities in blurry regions. Note that we use the pre-defined relationship between disparity and depth in Sect. 4.3 to convert disparity to metric depth.

5.2   Adaptive Sampling Module

In contrast to the widely used stereo images such as KITTI Stereo Bench-mark [17,18], dual-pixel images inherently have a small disparity range and defocus-blur. To cope with this issue, we design ASM inspired by defocus blur matching method [10] and depth from narrow-baseline light-field image [29]. As illustrated in Fig. 6-(a), our ASM dynamically samples blurry texture features for narrow-baseline stereo matching. To this end, the input features (F^L, F^R) pass through a *dynamic feature sampling layer* and a *self-3D attention layer* to obtain the locally dominant features G^L, G^R.

According to Jeon *et al.* [29], the sub-pixel shift from different sampling strategies to construct cost volume for matching provides varying results depend-ing on the local scene configurations. In particular, phase-shift interpolation ensures a denser sampling field at sub-pixel precision and reduces the burden from blurriness compared to other interpolation methods [29]. To take advan-tage of various conventional sampling methods, we incorporate them into ASM. The dynamic sampling layer in ASM is designed with a combination of nearest-neighbor, bilinear, and phase-shift interpolation, which can have various recep-tive fields to find varying blur sizes and can obtain subpixel-level shifted features. To this end, the shifted features from the three different sampling strategies are concatenated into one channel as a volumetric feature $\mathcal{V}$.

To extract useful features from given volumetric feature $\mathcal{V}$, we design a self-3D attention layer. Our self-3D attention layer adaptively selects sampling strategies to include prominent texture information in an extracted feature map. The layer consists of several 3D convolutional layers and the Sigmoid function. This obtains a soft mask as attention map $\mathcal{W}$ and selects features along the channel where $\mathcal{V}$ is concatenated. The soft mask $\mathcal{W}$ is multiplied with the feature $\mathcal{V}$ to sample useful features and the final feature volume $\mathcal{V}_S$ is produced through a softmax layer. Finally, the sampled features with the sub-pixel shift, G^L and G^R, are obtained by averaging the volume $\mathcal{V}_S$. The matching cost volume, constructed from the selected feature maps (G^L, G^R), contains rich texture information with relative blur and performs effective matching in homogeneous regions as well [10].

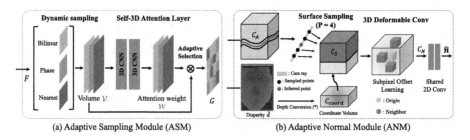

(a) Adaptive Sampling Module (ASM)   (b) Adaptive Normal Module (ANM)

Fig. 6. Proposed Modules of StereoDPNet. (a) Adaptive Sampling Module (ASM) consists of a dynamic sampling and a self-3D attention layer. (b) Adaptive Normal Module (ANM) consists of a surface sampling and a 3D deformable convolu-tional layer for surface normal regression.

5.3 Adaptive Normal Module

As illustrated in Fig. 6-(b), ANM aims to produce a surface normal map complementary to an estimated defocus-disparity map and to model 3D surface of human faces. The ANM consists of *surface sampling module* to capture surface by sampling the aggregated cost volume C_A and *deformable 3D convolutional layer* to consider dynamic ranges of neighbors to compute normal vectors.

According to [34], an accurately aggregated cost volume contains an implicit function representation of underlying surfaces for depth estimation. Since the surface normal mainly depends on the shape of the local surface, it is redundant to use all voxel embeddings in C_A for facial normal estimation. We thus sample the P candidates of hypothesis planes among M planes from the aggregated volume C_A using the estimated disparity map (Eq. 2). Since the surface normal is defined with the metric scale depth, we convert disparity to a depth map using Eq. 1 in Sect. 4.3 and provide this volumetric information with our network denoted as coordinate volume C_{coord}. The details of surface sampling process is explained in the supplementary material.

Since a human face has a variety of curved local surfaces, we need to consider dynamic ranges of neighbors to extract a local surface from the sampled hypothesis planes C_S in the previous stage. To do this, we follow the assumption of local plane in [41,42,47] and forms a local plane by a small set of neighbor points. Since these local patches have arbitrary shapes and sizes composed with its sampled neighboring points, we use 3D deformable convolutions [64] to consider the neighboring points within the dynamic ranges. The learnable offsets of the deformable convolution in 3D space allow us to adaptively sample neighbors and to find the best local plane. The final feature volume C_N is predicted after passing two 3D deformable convolution layers to extract surface normal information from the sampled volume C_S.

5.4 Depth and Normal Estimation

The aggregated volume C_A passes through a classifier to produce a final matching cost $\mathcal{A}$, and the softmax function $\sigma(\cdot)$ is applied to regress the defocus-disparity $\hat{d}$. Accordingly, we compute the disparity as follows:

$$\hat{d}_{u,v} = \sum_{m=1}^{M} d^m \cdot \sigma\left(\mathcal{A}_{u,v}^m\right), \tag{2}$$

where $\hat{d}_{u,v}$ is the defocus-disparity and $\mathcal{A}_{u,v}$ is the final matching cost at a pixel (u, v). M and d^m are the range of defocus-disparity, and predefined discrete disparity labels, respectively, whose details are described in Sect. 5.5. Following [9], we minimize a disparity loss $\mathcal{L}_{\text{disp}}$ using a smooth L_1 loss as follows:

$$\mathcal{L}_{\text{disp}} = \frac{1}{H \cdot W} \sum_{u=1}^{W} \sum_{v=1}^{H} \mathcal{M}_{u,v} \cdot \text{smooth}_{L_1}\left(d_{u,v} - \hat{d}_{u,v}\right), \tag{3}$$

where $d_{u,v}$ is a ground-truth defocus-disparity at a pixel (u, v) converted from the ground-truth metric scale depth and $\mathcal{M}_{u,v}$ is the facial mask in Sect. 4.3.

For the surface normal estimation, shared 2D convolutions are applied to the feature volume C_N to regress a surface normal. The final convolutional layers follow the same structure of the baseline architecture in [34]. Finally, we train ANM by minimizing a cosine similarity normal loss $\mathcal{L}_{\text{normal}}$ as:

$$\mathcal{L}_{\text{normal}} = \frac{1}{H \cdot W} \sum_{u=1}^{W} \sum_{v=1}^{H} \mathcal{M}_{u,v} \cdot (1 - \mathbf{n}_{u,v} \cdot \hat{\mathbf{n}}_{u,v}), \qquad (4)$$

where $\mathbf{n}_{u,v}$ and $\hat{\mathbf{n}}_{u,v}$ are a ground-truth, and a predicted normal at a pixel (u, v).

$$\mathcal{L}_{\text{total}} = \mathcal{L}_{\text{disp}} + \mathcal{L}_{\text{normal}} \qquad (5)$$

Our StereoDPNet is fully supervised by our ground-truth depth/normal maps. The network is trained by minimizing the combination of Eq. 3 and Eq. 4.

5.5   Implementation Details

The depth in our facial dataset ranges from 80 cm to 110 cm as described in Sect. 4.1 and the focus distance is about 97 cm. Therefore, our valid disparity range on original images is from –12 to 32 pixels. We note that the resolution of input images used is 1680×1120, which is downsampled four-fold due to GPU memory limitations. We thus set the minimum and maximum disparity of Eq. 2 to –4 and 12 pixels. We also set the number of levels in the cost volume M to 8, which represents a 0.5 pixel accuracy at least. We train our network with a batch size of four, and use Adam optimizer [33] starting from the initial learning rate 10^{-4} with a constant decay of 0.5 at every 35 epochs.

Table 1. Depth Benchmark Results. We show that our proposed method outperforms the existing stereo matching methods (PSMNet [9], StereoNet [31]), DP-oriented state-of-the-art methods (DPNet [16], MDD [46]), monocular depth estimation (BTS [36]), and depth/normal network for stereo matching (NNet [34]). Note that since MDD adopts another a defocus-disparity geometry different from [16], it is not measured by the absolute metrics. ST, DP, M, and DN denotes "Stereo Matching", "DP-oriented method", "Monocular", and "Depth and Normal", respectively.

Method	Task	Absolute error metric [mm] ↓					Affine error metric [px] ↓			Accuracy metric ↑	
		AbsRel	AbsDiff	SqRel	RMSE	RMSElog	WMAE	WRMSE	$1-\rho$	$\delta<1.01$	$\delta<1.01^2$
PSMNet [9]	ST	0.006	5.314	0.054	6.770	0.008	0.093	0.126	0.054	0.818	0.983
StereoNet [31]	ST	0.005	4.306	0.038	5.811	0.006	0.112	0.150	0.087	0.903	0.991
DPNet [16]	DP	0.008	7.175	0.092	8.833	0.010	0.110	0.148	0.086	0.688	0.959
MDD [46]	DP	–	–	–	–	–	1.830	2.348	0.575	–	–
BTS [36]	M	0.007	6.575	0.081	8.102	0.009	0.111	0.150	0.077	0.731	0.964
NNet [34]	DN	0.004	3.608	0.027	4.858	0.005	0.073	0.102	0.048	0.934	0.995
Ours	**DN**	**0.003**	**2.864**	**0.019**	**3.899**	**0.004**	**0.064**	**0.091**	**0.034**	**0.966**	**0.995**

Table 2. Ablation Study of ANM. NNet [34] is a baseline model of our overall architecture. We compare the performance of depth and surface normal estimation by adding each component. SS denotes "Surface Sampling" and D3D denotes "Deformable 3D convolution" of ANM respectively.

Method	ANM		Absolute [mm] ↓		Affine [px] ↓			Accuracy ↑		Normal [deg] ↓	
	SS	D3D	AbsDiff	RMSE	WMAE	WRMSE	$1-\rho$	$\delta<1.01$	$\delta<1.01^2$	MAE	RMSE
ASM Only			4.895	6.223	0.095	0.127	0.056	0.850	0.992	–	–
NNet [34]			3.608	4.858	0.073	0.102	0.048	0.934	0.995	9.634	11.877
ASM + NNet			3.271	4.434	0.064	0.090	**0.033**	0.947	**0.997**	9.072	11.045
ASM + NNet	✓		3.214	4.519	**0.062**	**0.089**	0.037	0.943	0.990	8.894	10.837
StereoDPNet	✓	✓	**2.864**	**3.899**	0.064	0.091	0.034	**0.966**	0.995	**7.479**	**9.386**

Table 3. Ablation Study of ASM. We test various sampling strategies in ASM and determine the final structure of ASM. Here, we only use ASM to strictly compare the inference of each sampling strategies. Bi denotes bilinear sampling.

Method	Absolute error metric [mm] ↓			Accuracy metric ↑	
	AbsDiff	SqRel	RMSE	$\delta<1.01$	$\delta<1.01^2$
Bilinear (Bi)	7.956	0.116	9.842	0.615	0.928
Phase	8.287	0.132	10.487	0.606	0.916
Phase + Bi	6.030	0.067	7.522	0.754	0.980
Nearest + Bi	5.841	0.062	7.287	0.772	0.984
Nearest + Phase	5.831	0.062	7.247	0.773	0.985
ASM	**4.895**	**0.045**	**6.223**	**0.850**	**0.992**

6 Experiments

To evaluate the effectiveness and the robustness of our work, we carry out various experiments on our dataset as well as DP images captured under real-world environments. For a fair comparison, all the methods are trained on identical training sets of our dataset from scratch. We then evaluate the quality of estimated depth/normal maps on the same test split of our facial dataset. Note that we use the facial mask for training and the test, given by the data acquisition process in Sect. 4.1. For the real-world samples, we use a facial mask from a pretrained face segmentation network[1].

6.1 Comparison Results

Evaluation Metrics. In our dataset benchmark, we convert our predicted disparity to depth (Sect. 4.3). Thus, we use both evaluation metrics in a public benchmark suite[2]: AbsRel, AbsDiff, SqRel, RMSE, RMSElog, and inlier pixel

---

[1] https://github.com/zllrunning/face-parsing.PyTorch.

[2] http://www.cvlibs.net/datasets/kitti/.

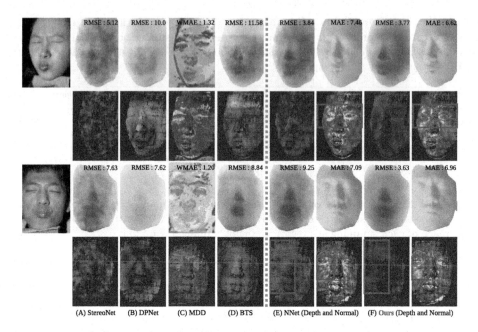

Fig. 7. Qualitative results on test set. We report AbsRel map of depths and MAE map of normals as the error map of predictions. The error map from MDD is the WMAE map because it predicts relative scale depth maps. We note that the range of error map is 0.0∼1.0 (AbsRel [mm]) and 0.0∼15.0 (MAE [degree]).

Fig. 8. Real-world results. We capture faces in unmet real-world and compare our method with the others in Table 1. StereoDPNet clearly captures surface and boundary depth of the face. Please refer to the supplementary material for more examples.

ratios ($\delta < 1.01^i$ where $i \in \{1, 2, 3\}$)[3] and affine invariant metrics [16] for the evaluation of predicted disparity/depth. To measure the quality of a surface normal map, we utilize a Mean Angular Error (MAE) and a Root Mean Square Angular Error (RMSAE) in degree unit following the DiLiGenT benchmark [53].

---

[3] All equations of the metrics are described in Supplementary material.

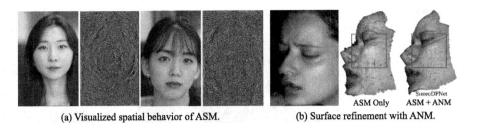

(a) Visualized spatial behavior of ASM.   (b) Surface refinement with ANM.

Fig. 9. (a) Spatial behavior of ASM (bilinear, nearest, and phase). (b) We compare 3D point cloud of the method of only ASM and with our full method of ASM and ANM. The result demonstrates that ANM refines surface of the facial 3D. (Color figure online)

Depth Benchmark. We compare our method with recent DP-based depth estimation approaches [16,46] as well as widely used stereo matching networks [9, 31], a depth/normal network for stereo matching, NNet [34] and a state-of-the-art monocular depth estimation network, BTS [36], whose results are reported in Table 1 and in Fig. 7. Since there is no published code for [16], we implement DPNet [16] to predict disparity instead of inverse depth following them, and check that the performance is similar on their dataset.

Due to the small range of the defocus-disparity from DP images (-4px to 12px), the cost volume with the discrete hypotheses leads to unstable training [67]. As a result, typical stereo matching based depth estimations, PSM-Net [9], StereoNet [31] do not work well. The methods in Table 1 except ours fail to handle defocus blur or struggle to find correspondances in human faces. For example, both DPNet and BTS suffer from blurry predictions, and MDD [46] is sensitive to the textureless regions in human faces. Although NNet [34] show relatively promising results, our method still outperforms them. Moreover, real-world results in Fig. 8 demonstrates that our network is specialized in finding defocus-disparity from facial DP images and robust to blur which produces robust results from the unmet facial scene.

Surface Normal Benchmark. To the best of our knowledge, this is the first attempt to estimate both the surface normal and the defocus-disparity from single DP images. Since the basic structure of ANM is derived from the recent depth and normal network [34] for multi-view stereo, we show the performance improvement of our ANM, compared to the baseline method [34] by adding each component in Table 2. We find that joint learning of disparity and surface normal leads to geometrically consistent and high-quality depth and surface normal shown in Fig. 9, which has been demonstrated in previous works [26,48].

6.2   Ablation Study

Analysis of ASM and ANM. First, we compare various subpixel sampling strategies in ASM as an ablation study. In Table 3, including whole attention maps from three different interpolations as proposed in ASM, shows the best

Fig. 10. Depth from single DP images in the wild. We show depth estimation results of StereoDPNet on outdoor photos, which are directly captured by us (left side) and in a public real-world DP dataset [2] for deblurring (right side).

(a) Depth and normal from public dataset [2]   (b) Depth and normal from our captured examples

Fig. 11. Depth and normal results in the wild. (a) public DP dataset [2], and (b) our captured natural DP images.

performance over any combination of two interpolations. We also provide spatial attention of W in ASM following the illustration scheme for selective matching costs in [28]. It shows that different sampling schemes are adaptively chosen. Second, we show that our surface normal estimation greatly improves the prediction of the disparity in Table 2. ANM captures local surface and refines the surface via cost volume and leads to major performance improvement as shown in Fig. 9. We attribute this outstanding performance to our sub-modules (ASM and ANM), which overcome the extremely narrow baselines in DP images.

Real World Experiment. To verify the generalizability of our method, we newly capture outdoor DP images using the Canon DSLR camera. We capture faces with various camera parameters (focus distance from 1.0 m to 1.5 m and F-number from 2.0 to 7.1) to demonstrate our method's robustness. Some of the results are shown in Fig. 8. Surprisingly, our StereoDPNet trained solely on our facial dataset also works well with general scenes (Fig. 10, Fig. 11), which

Table 4. Comparisons on the public dataset [46]. We provide quantitative comparison result of the methods in Table 1 on the public dataset [46].

Metrics	Method					
	PSMNet [9]	StereoNet [31]	DPNet [16]	MDD [46]	NNet [34]	**Ours**
WMAE (↓)	0.102	0.111	0.132	0.107	0.103	**0.085**
WRMSE (↓)	0.154	0.214	0.192	0.168	0.143	**0.133**
$1-\rho$ (↓)	0.351	0.261	0.420	**0.187**	0.345	0.276

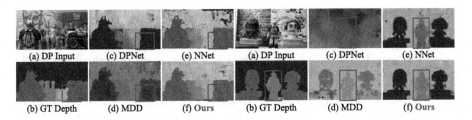

(a) DP Input   (c) DPNet   (e) NNet   (a) DP Input   (c) DPNet   (e) NNet

(b) GT Depth   (d) MDD   (f) Ours   (b) GT Depth   (d) MDD   (f) Ours

Fig. 12. Generalization on the public dataset [46]. We show qualitative results of depth from the methods in Table 1 on the public dataset [46].

demonstrates that our method is generalized well. Some of the scenes in Fig. 10 are from public DP dataset [2] (focus distance from 1.46 m to 1.59 m).

Generalization on the Public Dataset [46]. We conduct an additional experiment on another real-world DP dataset [46] to validate the generalization of our network. Although our method is generalized well in real-world scenarios in Fig. 10 and in Fig. 11, we augment our network by using an additional synthetic DP dataset in [3]. This is because there is no currently available large real-world DP dataset captured with DSLR for training except ours. For a fair comparison, we don't apply any post-processing (i.e. bilateral or guided filter) to the predictions. As illustrated in Fig. 12 and Table 4, our network shows promising results on the non-facial dataset [46] as well.

7   Conclusion

We present a high-quality facial DP dataset incorporating 135,744 face images for 101 subjects with corresponding depth maps in metric scale and surface normal maps. Moreover, we introduce DP-oriented StereoDPNet for both depth and surface normal estimation. StereoDPNet successfully shows impressive results in the wild by effectively handling the narrow baseline problem in DP.

Potential Societal Impact. We have already received consent from participants to use our facial dataset for only academic purposes. Thus, our dataset will be available to the computer vision community to promote relevant research.

Limitation. Although we show that our method is generalized to real-world DP scenes with various focus distances, our dataset is captured with fixed focus distance which is a clear limitation. Moreover, our ground truth acquisition of surface normal doesn't fully consider the complex specular reflection of the face which still remains as a challenging issue [35,55]. We also recognize that our dataset has an inherent bias in skin tone. However, these limitations can be resolved by capturing more dataset with various camera parameters and considering advanced non-Lambertian shape from shading methods [8,35,38]. We will refine the dataset sustainably and try to resolve these limitations.

Acknowledgements. This work is in part supported by the Ministry of Trade, Industry and Energy (MOTIE) and Korea Institute for Advancement of Technology (KIAT) through the International Cooperative R&D program in part (P0019797), 'Project for Science and Technology Opens the Future of the Region' program through the INNOPOLIS FOUNDATION funded by Ministry of Science and ICT (Project Number: 2022-DD-UP-0312), and also supported by the Samsung Electronics Co., Ltd (Project Number: G01210570).

References

1. Aanæs, H., Jensen, R.R., Vogiatzis, G., Tola, E., Dahl, A.B.: Large-scale data for multiple-view stereopsis. In: Proceedings of the IEEE/CVF International Conference on Computer Vision (ICCV), pp. 1–16 (2016)
2. Abuolaim, A., Brown, M.S.: Defocus deblurring using dual-pixel data. In: Vedaldi, A., Bischof, H., Brox, T., Frahm, J.-M. (eds.) ECCV 2020. LNCS, vol. 12355, pp. 111–126. Springer, Cham (2020). https://doi.org/10.1007/978-3-030-58607-2_7
3. Abuolaim, A., Delbracio, M., Kelly, D., Brown, M.S., Milanfar, P.: Learning to reduce defocus blur by realistically modeling dual-pixel data. In: Proceedings of the IEEE/CVF International Conference on Computer Vision (ICCV), pp. 2289–2298 (2021)
4. Apple: Apple iphone 11 pro (2019). https://www.apple.com/iphone-11-pro/, Accessed 20 Sept 2019
5. ARCore: Augmented faces. https://developers.google.com/ar/develop/java/augmented-faces (2019), accessed: 2019–12-18
6. Bai, Z., Cui, Z., Rahim, J.A., Liu, X., Tan, P.: Deep facial non-rigid multi-view stereo. In: Proceedings of the IEEE/CVF Conference on Computer Vision and Pattern Recognition (CVPR), pp. 5850–5860 (2020)
7. Blanz, V., Vetter, T.: A morphable model for the synthesis of 3D faces. In: Proceedings of the 26th Annual Conference on Computer Graphics and Interactive Techniques, pp. 187–194 (1999)
8. Boss, M., Jampani, V., Kim, K., Lensch, H., Kautz, J.: Two-shot spatially-varying brdf and shape estimation. In: Proceedings of the IEEE/CVF Conference on Computer Vision and Pattern Recognition, pp. 3982–3991 (2020)
9. Chang, J.R., Chen, Y.S.: Pyramid stereo matching network. In: Proceedings of the IEEE/CVF Conference on Computer Vision and Pattern Recognition (CVPR) (2018)
10. Chen, C.H., Zhou, H., Ahonen, T.: Blur-aware disparity estimation from defocus stereo images. In: Proceedings of the IEEE/CVF International Conference on Computer Vision (ICCV), pp. 855–863 (2015)

11. Chen, L.C., Zhu, Y., Papandreou, G., Schroff, F., Adam, H.: Encoder-decoder with atrous separable convolution for semantic image segmentation. In: Proceedings of the European conference on computer vision (ECCV) (2018)
12. Chen, W., Mirdehghan, P., Fidler, S., Kutulakos, K.N.: Auto-tuning structured light by optical stochastic gradient descent. In: Proceedings of the IEEE/CVF Conference on Computer Vision and Pattern Recognition (CVPR) (2020)
13. Deng, Y., Yang, J., Xu, S., Chen, D., Jia, Y., Tong, X.: Accurate 3D face reconstruction with weakly-supervised learning: From single image to image set. In: Proceedings of the IEEE/CVF Conference on Computer Vision and Pattern Recognition (CVPR) Workshops (2019)
14. Feng, Y., Wu, F., Shao, X., Wang, Y., Zhou, X.: Joint 3D face reconstruction and dense alignment with position map regression network. In: Proceedings of the European conference on computer vision (ECCV) (2018)
15. Galaxy: Samsung galaxy s10 (2019). https://www.samsung.com/us/mobile/galaxy-s10/, Accessed 08 Mar 2019
16. Garg, R., Wadhwa, N., Ansari, S., Barron, J.T.: Learning single camera depth estimation using dual-pixels. In: Proceedings of the IEEE/CVF International Conference on Computer Vision (ICCV) (2019)
17. Geiger, A., Lenz, P., Stiller, C., Urtasun, R.: Vision meets robotics: The kitti dataset. Int. J. Rob. Res. **32**(11), 1231–1237 (2013)
18. Geiger, A., Lenz, P., Urtasun, R.: Are we ready for autonomous driving? the kitti vision benchmark suite. In: 2012 IEEE Conference on Computer Vision and Pattern Recognition, pp. 3354–3361. IEEE (2012)
19. Google: Google photos: One year, 200 million users, and a whole lot of selfies (2016). https://blog.google/products/photos/google-photos-one-year-200-million/, Accessed 27 May 2016
20. Google: More controls and transparency for your selfies (2020). https://blog.google/outreach-initiatives/digital-wellbeing/more-controls-selfie-filters/, Accessed 01 Oct 2020
21. Guo, J., Zhu, X., Yang, Y., Yang, F., Lei, Z., Li, S.Z.: Towards fast, accurate and stable 3D dense face alignment. In: Vedaldi, A., Bischof, H., Brox, T., Frahm, J.-M. (eds.) ECCV 2020. LNCS, vol. 12364, pp. 152–168. Springer, Cham (2020). https://doi.org/10.1007/978-3-030-58529-7_10
22. Ha, H., Oh, T.H., Kweon, I.S.: A multi-view structured-light system for highly accurate 3D modeling. In: International Conference on 3D Vision (3DV) (2015)
23. Ha, H., Park, J., Kweon, I.S.: Dense depth and albedo from a single-shot structured light. In: International Conference on 3D Vision (3DV), pp. 127–134 (2015)
24. Han, Y., Lee, J.Y., So Kweon, I.: High quality shape from a single rgb-d image under uncalibrated natural illumination. In: Proceedings of the IEEE/CVF International Conference on Computer Vision (ICCV) (2013)
25. Hu, P., Ramanan, D.: Finding tiny faces. In: Proceedings of the IEEE Conference on Computer Vision and Pattern Recognition, pp. 951–959 (2017)
26. Im, S., Ha, H., Choe, G., Jeon, H.G., Joo, K., Kweon, I.S.: High quality structure from small motion for rolling shutter cameras. In: Proceedings of the IEEE/CVF International Conference on Computer Vision (ICCV) (2015)
27. Jensen, R., Dahl, A., Vogiatzis, G., Tola, E., Aanæs, H.: Large scale multi-view stereopsis evaluation. In: Proceedings of the IEEE/CVF Conference on Computer Vision and Pattern Recognition (CVPR) (2014)
28. Jeon, H.G., Park, J., Choe, G., Park, J., Bok, Y., Tai, Y.W., Kweon, I.S.: Depth from a light field image with learning-based matching costs. IEEE Trans. Pattern Anal. Mach. Intell. **41**(2), 297–310 (2018)

29. Jeon, H.G., Pet al.: Accurate depth map estimation from a lenslet light field camera. In: Proceedings of the IEEE/CVF Conference on Computer Vision and Pattern Recognition (CVPR) (2015)
30. Keselman, L., Iselin Woodfill, J., Grunnet-Jepsen, A., Bhowmik, A.: Intel realsense stereoscopic depth cameras. In: Proceedings of the IEEE/CVF Conference on Computer Vision and Pattern Recognition (CVPR) Workshops (2017)
31. Khamis, S., Fanello, S., Rhemann, C., Kowdle, A., Valentin, J., Izadi, S.: Stereonet: guided hierarchical refinement for real-time edge-aware depth prediction. In: Proceedings of the European Conference on Computer Vision (ECCV), pp. 573–590 (2018)
32. Kinect2: Kinect for windows sdk 2.0 (2014). https://developer.microsoft.com/en-us/windows/kinect/, Accessed 21 Oct 2014
33. Kingma, D.P., Ba, J.: Adam: a method for stochastic optimization. arXiv preprint arXiv:1412.6980 (2014)
34. Kusupati, U., Cheng, S., Chen, R., Su, H.: Normal assisted stereo depth estimation. In: Proceedings of the IEEE/CVF Conference on Computer Vision and Pattern Recognition (CVPR) (2020)
35. Lattas, A., et al.: Avatarme: Realistically renderable 3D facial reconstruction " in-the-wild". In: Proceedings of the IEEE/CVF Conference on Computer Vision and Pattern Recognition, pp. 760–769 (2020)
36. Lee, J.H., Han, M.K., Ko, D.W., Suh, I.H.: From big to small: multi-scale local planar guidance for monocular depth estimation. arXiv preprint arXiv:1907.10326 (2019)
37. Liang, J., Tu, H., Liu, F., Zhao, Q., Jain, A.K.: 3D face reconstruction from mugshots: application to arbitrary view face recognition. Neurocomputing **410**, 12–27 (2020)
38. Lichy, D., Wu, J., Sengupta, S., Jacobs, D.W.: Shape and material capture at home. In: Proceedings of the IEEE/CVF Conference on Computer Vision and Pattern Recognition, pp. 6123–6133 (2021)
39. Lin, T.Y., Dollár, P., Girshick, R., He, K., Hariharan, B., Belongie, S.: Feature pyramid networks for object detection. In: Proceedings of the IEEE/CVF Conference on Computer Vision and Pattern Recognition (CVPR) (2017)
40. Liu, F., Zhao, Q., Liu, X., Zeng, D.: Joint face alignment and 3D face reconstruction with application to face recognition. IEEE Trans. Pattern Anal. Mach. Intell. **42**(3), 664–678 (2018)
41. Long, X., et al.: Adaptive surface normal constraint for depth estimation. In: Proceedings of the IEEE/CVF International Conference on Computer Vision (ICCV) (2021)
42. Long, X., Liu, L., Theobalt, C., Wang, W.: Occlusion-aware depth estimation with adaptive normal constraints. In: Vedaldi, A., Bischof, H., Brox, T., Frahm, J.-M. (eds.) ECCV 2020. LNCS, vol. 12354, pp. 640–657. Springer, Cham (2020). https://doi.org/10.1007/978-3-030-58545-7_37
43. Luo, H., et al.: Normalized avatar synthesis using stylegan and perceptual refinement. In: Proceedings of the IEEE/CVF Conference on Computer Vision and Pattern Recognition, pp. 11662–11672 (2021)
44. Nehab, D., Rusinkiewicz, S., Davis, J., Ramamoorthi, R.: Efficiently combining positions and normals for precise 3D geometry. ACM Trans. Graph. (ToG) **24**(3), 536–543 (2005)

45. Pan, L., Chowdhury, S., Hartley, R., Liu, M., Zhang, H., Li, H.: Dual pixel exploration: simultaneous depth estimation and image restoration. In: Proceedings of the IEEE/CVF Conference on Computer Vision and Pattern Recognition (CVPR), pp. 4340–4349 (2021)
46. Punnappurath, A., Abuolaim, A., Afifi, M., Brown, M.S.: Modeling defocus-disparity in dual-pixel sensors. In: 2020 IEEE International Conference on Computational Photography (ICCP) (2020)
47. Qi, X., Liao, R., Liu, Z., Urtasun, R., Jia, J.: Geonet: geometric neural network for joint depth and surface normal estimation. In: Proceedings of the IEEE/CVF Conference on Computer Vision and Pattern Recognition (CVPR), pp. 283–291 (2018)
48. Qiu, J., et al.: Deeplidar: deep surface normal guided depth prediction for outdoor scene from sparse lidar data and single color image. In: Proceedings of the IEEE/CVF Conference on Computer Vision and Pattern Recognition (CVPR) (2019)
49. Richardson, E., Sela, M., Or-El, R., Kimmel, R.: Learning detailed face reconstruction from a single image. In: Proceedings of the IEEE/CVF Conference on Computer Vision and Pattern Recognition (CVPR), pp. 1259–1268 (2017)
50. Scharstein, D., Szeliski, R.: High-accuracy stereo depth maps using structured light. In: Proceedings of the IEEE/CVF Conference on Computer Vision and Pattern Recognition (CVPR), vol. 1 (2003)
51. Schönberger, J.L., Zheng, E., Frahm, J.-M., Pollefeys, M.: Pixelwise view selection for unstructured multi-view stereo. In: Leibe, B., Matas, J., Sebe, N., Welling, M. (eds.) ECCV 2016. LNCS, vol. 9907, pp. 501–518. Springer, Cham (2016). https://doi.org/10.1007/978-3-319-46487-9_31
52. Shang, J., et al.: Self-supervised monocular 3D face reconstruction by occlusion-aware multi-view geometry consistency. In: Vedaldi, A., Bischof, H., Brox, T., Frahm, J.-M. (eds.) ECCV 2020. LNCS, vol. 12360, pp. 53–70. Springer, Cham (2020). https://doi.org/10.1007/978-3-030-58555-6_4
53. Shi, B., Wu, Z., Mo, Z., Duan, D., Yeung, S.K., Tan, P.: A benchmark dataset and evaluation for non-lambertian and uncalibrated photometric stereo. In: Proceedings of the IEEE/CVF Conference on Computer Vision and Pattern Recognition (CVPR) (2016)
54. Silberman, N., Fergus, R.: Indoor scene segmentation using a structured light sensor. In: Proceedings of the IEEE/CVF International Conference on Computer Vision (ICCV) - Workshop on 3D Representation and Recognition (2011)
55. Song, G., Zheng, J., Cai, J., Cham, T.J.: Recovering facial reflectance and geometry from multi-view images. Image Vision Comput. **96**, 103897 (2020)
56. Tran, L., Liu, X.: Nonlinear 3D face morphable model. In: Proceedings of the IEEE/CVF Conference on Computer Vision and Pattern Recognition (CVPR), pp. 7346–7355 (2018)
57. Wadhwa, N.: Synthetic depth-of-field with a single-camera mobile phone. ACM Trans. Graph. (ToG) **37**(4), 1–13 (2018)
58. Wu, F., et al.: Mvf-net: Multi-view 3D face morphable model regression. In: Proceedings of the IEEE/CVF Conference on Computer Vision and Pattern Recognition (CVPR), pp. 959–968 (2019)
59. Wu, S., Rupprecht, C., Vedaldi, A.: Unsupervised learning of probably symmetric deformable 3D objects from images in the wild. In: Proceedings of the IEEE/CVF Conference on Computer Vision and Pattern Recognition (CVPR) (2020)
60. Wu, X., Zhou, J., Liu, J., Ni, F., Fan, H.: Single-shot face anti-spoofing for dual pixel camera. IEEE Trans. Inf. Forensics Secur. **16**, 1440–1451 (2020)

61. Xin, S., et al.: Defocus map estimation and deblurring from a single dual-pixel image. Proceedings of the IEEE/CVF International Conference on Computer Vision (ICCV) (2021)
62. Xu, H., Zhang, J.: Aanet: adaptive aggregation network for efficient stereo matching. In: Proceedings of the IEEE/CVF Conference on Computer Vision and Pattern Recognition (CVPR), pp. 1959–1968 (2020)
63. Yang, F., Wang, J., Shechtman, E., Bourdev, L., Metaxas, D.: Expression flow for 3D-aware face component transfer. In: ACM SIGGRAPH 2011 papers, pp. 1–10 (2011)
64. Ying, X., Wang, L., Wang, Y., Sheng, W., An, W., Guo, Y.: Deformable 3D convolution for video super-resolution. IEEE Signal Process. Lett. **27**, 1500–1504 (2020)
65. Yu, Z., Qin, Y., Li, X., Zhao, C., Lei, Z., Zhao, G.: Deep learning for face anti-spoofing: a survey. arXiv preprint arXiv:2106.14948 (2021)
66. Zhang, F., Prisacariu, V., Yang, R., Torr, P.H.: Ga-net: guided aggregation net for end-to-end stereo matching. In: Proceedings of the IEEE/CVF Conference on Computer Vision and Pattern Recognition (CVPR), pp. 185–194 (2019)
67. Zhang, Y., Wadhwa, N., Orts-Escolano, S., Häne, C., Fanello, S., Garg, R.: Du^{2}Net: learning depth estimation from dual-cameras and dual-pixels. In: Vedaldi, A., Bischof, H., Brox, T., Frahm, J.-M. (eds.) ECCV 2020. LNCS, vol. 12346, pp. 582–598. Springer, Cham (2020). https://doi.org/10.1007/978-3-030-58452-8_34
68. Zhou, H., Hadap, S., Sunkavalli, K., Jacobs, D.W.: Deep single-image portrait relighting. In: Proceedings of the IEEE/CVF International Conference on Computer Vision (ICCV) (2019)
69. Zollhöfer, M., et al.: State of the art on monocular 3D face reconstruction, tracking, and applications. In: Computer Graphics Forum, vol. 37, pp. 523–550. Wiley Online Library (2018)

The Anatomy of Video Editing: A Dataset and Benchmark Suite for AI-Assisted Video Editing

Dawit Mureja Argaw[1,2(✉)], Fabian Caba Heilbron[1], Joon-Young Lee[1], Markus Woodson[1], and In So Kweon[2]

[1] Adobe Research, San Jose, USA
dawitmureja@kaist.ac.kr
[2] KAIST, Daejeon, South Korea

Abstract. Machine learning is transforming the video editing industry. Recent advances in computer vision have leveled-up video editing tasks such as intelligent reframing, rotoscoping, color grading, or applying digital makeups. However, most of the solutions have focused on video manipulation and VFX. This work introduces the Anatomy of Video Editing, a dataset, and benchmark, to foster research in AI-assisted video editing. Our benchmark suite focuses on video editing tasks, beyond visual effects, such as automatic footage organization and assisted video assembling. To enable research on these fronts, we annotate more than 1.5M tags, with relevant concepts to cinematography, from 196176 shots sampled from movie scenes. We establish competitive baseline methods and detailed analyses for each of the tasks. We hope our work sparks innovative research towards underexplored areas of AI-assisted video editing. Code is available at: https://github.com/dawitmureja/AVE.git.

1 Introduction

What does the future of video editing look like? Arguably AI-based technologies will have a strong influence on this creative industry. In fact, the computer vision community has already delivered technologies such as automatic rotoscoping [30] as a teaser of the opportunities to transform video editing. Most research development has centered around enabling AI-based VFX (visual effects) [10,16,23,26,30,33,38]; however, editing video involves more than that. Despite their importance towards AI-assisted video editing, topics such as understanding cinematography concepts for automatic organization and assisting editors to assembly edits remain underexplored in the computer vision community.

Research progress toward AI-assisted video editing has been hindered by the lack of formally defined tasks relevant to the editing process. This observation sparked recent works to study film properties or learn cutting patterns

---

Supplementary Information The online version contains supplementary material available at https://doi.org/10.1007/978-3-031-20074-8_12.

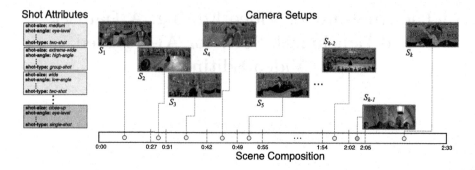

Fig. 1. Anatomy of Video Editing (AVE) dataset and benchmark suite. Our dataset decomposes movie scenes into sequence of shots by identifying the cuts in the scene. Each shot composing the scene has cinematographic attributes and camera setup labels.

from movie data [14,31,44]. MovieNet [14] touches on cinematography style by providing annotations for two attributes: view scale and camera movement. While automatically tagging these concepts already provides value to the automatic organization, the cinematographic vocabulary comprises a much larger set. Learning to Cut [31] recommends the best moments to cut a pair of shots by looking at motion. This task is indeed an important editing task, but there are still other decisions such as establishing the order of shots and the most suitable composition to assist video assembling. The progress is exciting, but the existing tasks cover a limited span of video editing.

To enable research development on AI-assisted video editing, we introduce the Anatomy of Video Editing (AVE), a dataset and benchmark suite. Movies require extensive hours of assistant editors to organize and tag footage and they depict the most creative and artistic forms of video editing. These properties motivate us to build the AVE dataset upon 5591 movie scenes. We recover the temporal composition of each scene by annotating the shot transitions and the camera setups. In total, we annotate 196176 shots among eight cinematography properties, yielding more than 1.5M labels. Figure 1 illustrates one annotated movie scene from our dataset.

Our benchmark suite facilitates research in two areas to advance AI-assisted video editing. We define two tasks related to automatically organizing footage and introduce three tasks that aim to learn editors' patterns in video assembling. Equally crucial to defining the right tasks is establishing solid baselines, metrics, and initial analyses. Our baselines include modern video understanding methods, providing a competitive start. Nevertheless, our analyses discuss opportunities to develop new models to improve upon our baselines on the proposed tasks.

Contributions. To summarize, our contributions are two-fold:

(1) We introduce the AVE dataset, which includes the composition of 5591 movie scenes with more than 1.5M cinematography labels for 196176 shots (Sect. 3).
(2) We establish a benchmark suite that includes five different tasks for AI-assisted video editing (Sect. 4). Along with each task definition, we imple-

ment competitive baselines and provide extensive experimental analyses (Sect. 5).

2   Related Works

Movie Datasets. Several movie-based datasets have been presented by previous works [2,14,22,41,44,50] for various video understanding tasks. Zhu *et al.* [50] proposed the MovieBook dataset for aligning stories from books and movies. Tapaswi *et al.* [41] introduced the MovieQA dataset. Bain *et al.* [2] proposed Condensed Movies, which contains 33K short movie clips and high-level text descriptions for text-to-video retrieval task. Liu *et al.* [22] proposed MUSES, which contains 31477 clips collected from several drama episodes and annotated with 25 action categories for temporal event localization task. Wu *et al.* [44] explored the long-term video understanding problem on movie clips dataset by formulating high-level prediction tasks. Recently, Huang *et al.* [14] proposed the MovieNet, which contains 1100 full movies and 60K trailers with diverse annotations to learn various tasks such as genre prediction, scene segmentation, and character recognition. While previous works primarily focus on high-level video content understanding tasks at a clip level, our work goes one step further and studies the sequence of shots in movie scenes by proposing a large-scale dataset with shot-level attributes and scene-level composition annotations.

Shot Assembly in Video Editing. Here we focus on previous works that studied cinematography patterns in film editing. For an in-depth discussion on video editing, in general, we invite the reader to [49]. Given a script and different takes of a scene, Leake *et al.* [20] attempted to generate a scene by selecting a relevant clip for each line of dialogue in a given script. Wu *et al.* [45,46] used shot relation attributes to formulate film editing pattern syntax and provided an interactive editing platform. Minh *et al.* [12] decomposed a video scene into an ordered sequence of relevant shots to remove abrupt discontinuities for improved human action recognition. Other works [3,31,32,35] studied cutting patterns in movie scenes. Although some previous works [20,45,46] attempted to study the film editing process, they are limited to a particular type of scene, *e.g.* dialogue, or cannot generalize to new editing patterns beyond a predefined set. Our work aims at learning general editing patterns from a large set of publicly-available movie scenes using a data-driven approach.

3   Anatomy of Video Editing: Dataset

Here we describe the collection of the Anatomy of Video Editing (AVE) dataset, a large-scale shot attribute set that contains approximately 196, 176 shots dissected from 5, 591 publicly available movie scenes [2,31][1].

---

[1] We crawled the movie scenes from the MovieClips YouTube Channel.

3.1   Shot Attributes

Following the standard definition of shot properties in cinematography [7,28], we label eight attributes, which we define below, for each shot in AVE.

Shot size is defined as how much of the setting or subject is displayed within a given shot. Shot size has *five* categories: 1) Extreme wide (EW) shots barely show the subject and the shot's main focus is the subject's surrounding; 2) Wide (W) shots, also known as long shot, show the entire subject and their relation to the surrounding environment; 3) Medium (M) shots depict the subject approximately from the waist up emphasizing both the subject and their surrounding; 4) Close-up (CU) shots are taken at a close range intended to show greater detail to the viewer; 5) Extreme close-up (ECU) shots frame a subject very closely where the outer portions of the subject are often cut off by the frame's edges.

Shot angle is the location where the camera is placed to take a shot. Shot angle has *five* categories: 1) Aerial (A) shot is captured from an elevated vantage point; 2) Overhead (O) shot is when the camera is placed directly above the subject; 3) Eye level (EL) shot is a shot where the camera is positioned directly at the subject's eye level; 4) High angle (HA) shot is when the camera points down on the subject from above; 5) Low angle (LA) shot is when the camera is positioned below the eye level and looks up at the subject.

Shot type refers to the composition of a shot in terms of the number of featured subjects and their physical relationship to each other and the camera. Shot type has *six* categories: 1) Over-the-shoulder (OTS) shot shows the main subject from behind the shoulder of another subject; 2) Single (S) shot captures one subject; 3) Two (2) shot has two subjects featured in the frame; 4) Three (3) shot has three characters in the frame 5) Insert (I) shot is any shot whose purpose is to draw the viewer's attention to a specific detail within a scene; 6) Group (G) shot features a group of subjects in the shot.

Shot motion is defined as the movement of the camera when taking a shot. Shot motion has *five* categories: 1) Pan/Truck (P/T) shot is when the camera is moving horizontally while its base remains in a fixed position; 2) Tilt/Pedestal (T/P) shot is when the camera moves vertically up or down with its base fixated to a certain point; 3) Locked (L) shot is taken without shifting the position of the camera; 4) Zoom/Dolly (Z/D) shot is when the camera moves forward and backward adding depth to a scene; 5) Handheld (H) shot is taken with the camera being supported only by the operator's hands and shoulder.

Shot location refers to the environment where the shot is taken. Shot location has *two* categories: 1) Exterior (Ext) shot is taken outdoors; 2) Interior (Int) shot is taken indoors.

Shot subject is the main subject featured or conveyed in the shot. Shot subject has *seven* categories: 1) Animal, 2) Location, 3) Object, 4) Human, 5) Limb, 6) Face and 7) Text.

Num. of people is the number of humans displayed in the shot and it has *six* categories: 1) None (0), 2) One (1), 3) Two (2), 4) Three (3), 5) Four (4) and 6) Five (5) if the shot has five or more people.

Sound source refers to the source of sound in the shot. Sound source has *four* categories: 1) On screen (OnS) - the source is a subject within the shot;

Table 1. Comparison with related datasets.

	Num. of shots	Num. of videos	Num. of shot attributes	Scene composition	Camera setup
Lie 2014 [4]	327	327	1	✗	✗
Context 2011 [48]	3,206	4	1	✗	✗
Cinema 2013 [5]	3,000	12	1	✗	✗
Taxon 2009 [43]	5054	7	1	✗	✗
MovieSD 2020 [35]	46,857	7,858	2	✗	✗
AVE	196,176	5,591	8	✓	✓

Table 2. Statistics of AVE.

	Train	Val	Test	Total
Num. of scenes	3914	559	1,118	5,591
Num. of shots	151,053	15,040	30,083	196,176
Avg. duration of shots (sec.)	3.83	3.71	3.78	3.81
Avg. number of shots per scene	34.71	35.42	35.69	35.09
Avg. number of camera setups	5.71	6.11	5.69	5.74

2) Off screen (OfS) - the sound comes from a subject not shown in the shot; 3) External narration (EN) - the source is a narration outside the shot; 4) External music (EM) - the only sound in the shot is music.

3.2 Scene Composition and Camera Setups

In addition to the attributes of the individual shots, we also provide annotation for the shot sequence composition, where we label the start and end time of each shot within a scene. We also group the shots that belong to the same camera setup and annotate the total number of takes used in the edited scene. These annotations will enable our studies on shot pattern selection and sequencing.

3.3 Annotation Procedure

We recruited a task force of 15 professional video editors. To reduce the amount of manual effort, we pre-segmented each video (scene) into shots using a pre-trained shot-boundary detector [39]. Then, the annotation process consisted of two steps. First, we asked the annotators to verify the automatic shot boundaries are correct and to group the shots in a scene by camera setup. Second, we asked the task force to label each shot with the attributes listed in Sect. 3.1.

3.4 Dataset Statistics

The Anatomy of Video Editing (AVE) dataset consists of 196,176 holistically annotated shots, collected from 5,591 movie scenes that cover a wide range of

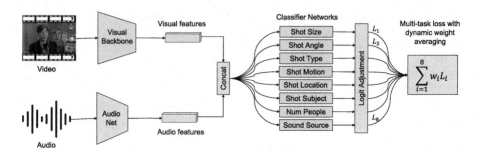

Fig. 2. Overview of shot attributes classification framework. Given a shot clip, we first extract audio-visual features using a common backbone network. The extracted features are then feed into eight classifiers to predict the attributes of the shot.

genres. In Table 1, we compare AVE with related datasets. Our dataset is considerably larger in size with significantly more comprehensive, and relevant to video editing, annotations. Previous works primarily focus on individual shot properties to analyze certain cinematic techniques, but AVE goes beyond shot level attributes by offering the temporal sequencing of shots and the composition of scenes. Table 2 presents detailed statistics for our train-val-test splits.

4   Anatomy of Video Editing: Benchmark Suite

In this section, we introduce five tasks for AI-assisted Video editing. The first two tasks focus on benchmarking the ability to automatically organize and tag footage according to cinematography properties. The last three tasks center around predicting editing patterns used in movie scenes.

Notation. Let $\mathcal{M}$ represent a movie scene which is defined as a sequence of k shots, i.e. $\mathcal{M} = \{\mathcal{S}_1, \mathcal{S}_2, \ldots, \mathcal{S}_k\}$, where $\mathcal{S}$ denotes a shot clip. Each shot $\mathcal{S}$ is composed of visual (v) and audio (a) representations, i.e. $\mathcal{S} = \langle v, a \rangle$. The audio-visual features encoded from each shot clips are denoted as $\{u_1, u_2, \ldots, u_k\}$.

4.1   Shot Attributes Classification

Given a shot $\mathcal{S}$, shot attributes classification aims to predict the attributes of $\mathcal{S}$: shot size, shot angle, shot type, shot motion, shot location, shot subject,number of people and sound source as discussed in Sect. 3.1. This task would be useful for an editor to automatically classify and organize shots by their attributes during the editing process. It can also be coupled with other tasks such as video content understanding [2,14,22,44] to establish a user query system, where shots can be retrieved by their content and attributes.

As each attribute has its own classes independent of others, shot attributes classification can be defined in a *multi-task* setting, where multiple classifiers are jointly optimized together in an end-to-end manner. We design a general framework for shot attributes classification by cascading an audio-visual encoder network with eight classifier networks as shown in Fig. 2. We use `ResNet-101` [11] and `R-3D` [42] as visual backbone networks to extract features from image and video inputs, respectively. To incorporate features from the audio input, we design a network called `AudioNet`, which is a feed-forward network with 3 convolutional and 2 linear layers. The features extracted from different input representations are then cascaded to obtain a cross-modal feature via concatenation. This cross-modal feature is then fed into each classifier network which outputs the predicted class for the respective shot attribute. Each classifier is a simple network with 2 linear layers and ReLU activation units.

Shot attributes inherently exhibit a long tail label distribution. For instance, *medium* is the most common `shot size` in movie scenes while *extreme close-up* is hardly used. This imbalance makes naive training to be biased toward the dominant label [15,27,40]. To address this problem, we implement the idea of logit adjustment [27] on each classifier output according to the label frequencies in the respective shot attribute. The training loss for our network is defined as an aggregate of the cross entropy losses from the different classifiers. To better explore the cross-task correlation during training, we use dynamic weight averaging technique [21] to scale the loss of each task (attribute) during training.

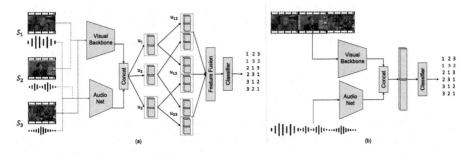

Fig. 3. Shot ordering baselines. (a) Late feature fusion, where we first extract features from each shot in the sequence and then combine the features at later stage (b) Early input fusion, where the input shot clips are first concatenated before extracting feature.

4.2 Camera Setup Clustering

Movie scenes in general contain highly frequent shot cuts as they are professionally edited by connecting several shots captured using a multi-camera system. This phenomenon can also be observed in the proposed dataset (see Table 2) which contains approximately 35 shots and 6 camera setups per scene. Given a list of shots $\{S_1, S_2, \ldots, S_k\}$ in any order, shot clustering is defined as grouping shots that belong to the same camera setup. This task could be useful during

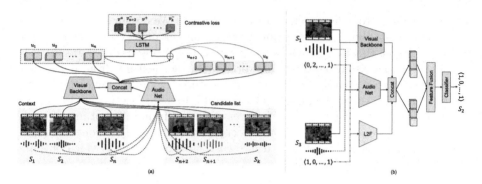

Fig. 4. (a) Overview of next shot selection. We use a contrastive approach to learn positive (matching) and negative (non-matching) shot sequence patterns. (b) Missing shot attributes prediction. We predict the attributes of an intermediate shot given its left and right neighboring shots.

the editing process in order to catalog different shots of a scene or various takes of a particular shot into the respective camera setup they belong to.

We formulate this task as a high-dimensional feature clustering problem. We extract features from the given shot set and evaluate the performance of several state-of-the-art clustering algorithms. We use both traditional, *i.e.* SIFT [25], and learning-based, *i.e.* ResNet-101 [11], CLIP [34] and R-3D [42], feature extraction methods. To establish baselines for shot clustering task, we experiment with standard clustering algorithms such as K-Means [24], Hierarchical Agglomerative Clustering (HAC) [29], OPTICS [1], but also novel methods such as FINCH [36].

4.3   Shot Sequence Ordering

Shots are fundamental units in the filmmaking process. Film editors create scenes by assembling shots in a coherent pattern that best depicts the story of the scene. As previous studies [3,20,45,46] have indicated, several factors go into the selection and sequencing of shots, which can be highly subjective at times. In this task, we aim to learn general shot ordering patterns in movie scenes following a data-driven approach, where we break down a movie scene into shots, randomly shuffle the shots, and target to reconstruct the movie scene by reordering the shuffled shots. Given a sequence of *contiguous* but randomly shuffled shots, *i.e.* $\text{rand}\{\mathcal{S}_1, \mathcal{S}_2, \ldots, \mathcal{S}_k\}$, shot ordering can be formulated as a classification task. If a given scene has k shots, there are $k!$ (factorial of k) possible ways of ordering them, *i.e.* $k!$ classes. We set $k = 3$ at a time for convenience and define shot order prediction as a 6-way classification problem.

We experiment with two types of baselines for shot order prediction as shown in Fig. 3. First, we follow previous video representation learning works [47,48] and perform late feature fusion, where we extract features from the input shot clips and then perform a hierarchical fusion of features. The combined features are then passed to a classifier network to predict the order (see Fig. 3a). As a second baseline, we perform early fusion at an input level where we concatenated the shot clips and then extract features from the resulting input (see Fig. 3b).

Compared to existing works on video clips order prediction [9,19,47,48], shot ordering is a more challenging problem for two main reasons. First, previous works mostly deal with ordering different segments of a video with a single camera setup. This makes it convenient to exploit semantic and geometric correspondences across clips to analyze their temporal coherence. In contrast, the neighboring clips in a given shot sequence are often from different camera setups and there is much less content overlap across inputs making it very challenging to learn ordering patterns from only the visual stream. Second, in previous works [9,19,47,48] problem formulation, there is always a unique solution for ordering the input clips given that the interval between the clips is not too large. In comparison, due to the subjective (and artistic) nature of the task, there could be multiple ways of ordering shot clips in a movie scene [3,20,45,46].

4.4   Next Shot Selection

During film editing, the process of assembling shots occurs in a sequential manner. Given a partial sequence of shots as a context, this task aims to anticipate the next shot from the list of available shots. Let $\{\mathcal{S}_1, \mathcal{S}_2, \ldots, \mathcal{S}_n\}$ denote the sequence of n shots provided as a history and $\mathbf{rand}\{\mathcal{S}_{n+1}, \mathcal{S}_{n+2} \ldots, \mathcal{S}_k\}$ represent the list of $k - n$ possible candidates to follow $\mathcal{S}_n$. Next shot selection is then defined as a multiple choice problem where a model makes the decision based on the affinity of each candidate shot to the previous sequence.

We formulate this task following a contrastive learning approach. First, we extract features from each shot in the given context and candidate list using an `audio-visual encoder` network (see Fig. 4). It is important to learn the shot sequence pattern from the given context in order to anticipate the next shot candidate. Thus, we feed the extracted feature sequence $\{u_1, u_2, \ldots, u_n\}$ into an `LSTM` [13] module, $i.e.$ $v^a = \mathrm{LSTM}\{u_1, u_2, \ldots, u_n\}$. The output of the LSTM module is defined as an $anchor$ feature v^a which represents an embedding for the context sequence. To generate a positive (matching) feature v^+ during training, we cascade the context and the correct next shot $\mathcal{S}_{n+1}$ and input the resulting sequence into the `LSTM` module, $i.e.$ $v^+ = \mathrm{LSTM}\{u_1, u_2, \ldots, u_n, u_{n+1}\}$. The intuition here is to learn that $\{\mathcal{S}_1, \mathcal{S}_2, \ldots, \mathcal{S}_n\}$ and $\{\mathcal{S}_1, \mathcal{S}_2, \ldots, \mathcal{S}_n, \mathcal{S}_{n+1}\}$ are feasible shot sequence patterns that appear in actual movie scenes. In contrast, the negative (non-matching) features are created by cascading any shot **except** $\mathcal{S}_{n+1}$ to the context, $i.e.$ $\{v_i^-\}_{i=1} = \mathrm{LSTM}\{u_1, u_2, \ldots, u_n, u_i\}$, where $i \neq n + 1$. We experiment with two types of negative samples generation: i) `in-sequence`, where $k - n - 1$ negatives are sampled per each input using all incorrect choices in the respective candidate list and ii) `in-batch`, where all other shot sequences in the batch are additionally used, $i.e.$ $bk - n - 1$ negative samples per each input for a batch size of b. We use the supervised NT-Xent loss [6,18] to train our network. During inference, we compute the affinity score, the cosine similarity, between the anchor feature v^a and the feature $v^c = \mathrm{LSTM}\{u_1, u_2, \ldots, u_n, u_c\}$,

Table 3. Quantitative analysis on shot attributes classification.

Attribute	Multi-task training								Single-task training			
	Video				Video + Audio				Video + Audio			
	Naïve		Logit adj.		Naïve		Logit adj.		Naïve		Logit adj.	
	Val	Test	Val	Test	Val	Test	Val	Test	Val	Test	Val	Test
Shot size	35.7	35.5	67.8	66.9	36.2	36.4	66.8	65.0	38.7	39.1	70.9	67.6
Shot angle	25.8	25.8	62.2	53.2	27.6	27.7	58.6	49.5	29.1	28.9	63.0	49.8
Shot type	59.5	60.8	63.9	64.9	59.8	61.0	63.7	65.3	60.1	62.3	64.9	66.7
Shot motion	32.1	31.7	42.8	42.7	32.3	31.8	44.6	43.2	32.3	31.2	47.4	43.7
Shot location	82.9	81.9	84.4	83.3	83.0	80.9	83.7	83.7	83.4	82.8	83.9	84.0
Shot subject	40.0	39.8	50.8	47.4	40.0	39.7	50.2	46.7	42.2	40.7	54.2	48.0
Num. of people	55.0	55.1	61.3	61.2	55.1	55.3	60.9	61.4	56.1	57.1	61.5	63.5
Sound source	25.0	25.0	34.4	32.6	25.0	25.0	41.0	38.9	25.0	25.0	38.1	35.3
Average	44.5	44.4	**58.4**	**56.5**	44.9	44.7	**58.7**	**56.7**	45.9	45.9	**60.5**	**57.3**

where c is an index for a shot in the candidate list. The shot with the highest score is then selected as the next shot.

4.5 Missing Shot Attributes Prediction

With the goal of learning editing patterns in movie scenes, here, we define another task that aims to predict the attributes of a missing shot in a given incomplete shot sequence. This is different from the task in Sect. 4.4 as it targets to predict the likely attributes of the shot that best completes the given sequence irrespective of the shot availability. Let $\{S_1, S_2, \ldots, S_k\}$ denote a given incomplete sequence without S_i, where $1 < i < k$. Then, missing shot attribute prediction is formulated as a classification problem, where we predict the attributes of S_i using the input sequence of shots and their attributes as a context. In this work, we consider a simple setup with $k = 3$, i.e. $\{S_1, S_3\}$ is given as an input and we predict the attributes of S_2. A more generalized formulation with longer sequences and missing shot(s) at arbitrary time steps is left for future work.

Figure 4b depicts the framework for missing shot attribute prediction. We first extract features from S_1 and S_3 using a pretrained backbone network. The attributes of S_1 and S_2 are also added as an input. For this purpose, we designed a simple 1-layered linear network called `label-2-feature` (L2F) which transforms an attribute vector of size 8 into a feature embedding. The extracted features are then concatenated and fed into multiple classifier networks which predict the different attributes of the missing shot S_2. Like the task in Sect. 4.1, logit adjustment is applied to the output of the classifiers during training to prevent the network from being biased to the dominant labels. The training is done in a multi-task setting using dynamic weight averaging [21] to scale the cross entropy losses from the different classifiers.

5   Experimental Results and Discussion

Dataset. We follow a `train-val-test` scene split of 70-10-20 in all experiments (see Table 2). As the scenes in the proposed dataset are non-overlapping, the train, validation, and test splits are disjoint sets. For the shot attributes classification task, we use all the shots in the respective scene split for training and evaluation. For shot ordering and missing shot attributes prediction tasks, we generate train, validation, and test sets by sampling 3 consecutive shots from a scene at a time. For the next shot selection task, on the other hand, we sample 9 consecutive shots at a time. The first 4 shots in the sequence are used as a context. The remaining 5 shots are used to make a candidate list.

Evaluation Metrics. For shot attributes classification and missing shot attributes prediction tasks, we report the `average per-class accuracy` to take the long tail distribution problem into account. For shot ordering and next shot selection tasks, we simply evaluate the `overall accuracy`. For shot clustering task, we evaluate the quality of the generated clusters with respect to ground truth clusters on 3 different metrics: Purity score (`PS`), Normalized mutual information (`NMI`) and Rand index (`RI`) [37].

Implementation Details. We use `ResNet-101` [11] and `R-3D` [42] as visual backbone networks to extract features from image and video inputs, respectively. In all experiments, the backbone network is initialized with pretrained weights (`ResNet-101` - pretrained on ImageNet [8] and `R-3D` - pretrained on Kinetics-400 [17]) and fine-tuned during training. We uniformly sample 16 frames from a shot clip as an input to `R-3D`, while we use the central frame of a shot for `ResNet-101`. Refer to the supplementary for task-level implementation details.

5.1   Experimental Results

Shot Attributes Classification. In Table 3, we present the performance of our network trained in two different settings: i. `multi-task`, where all eight classifiers are jointly trained together in an end-to-end manner, and ii. `single-task`, where one classifier is optimized at a time. As can be inferred from Table 3, individually training each classifier generally results in a better accuracy compared to training all classifiers together. It can also be noticed from Table 3 that taking the long tail distribution problem into account during training consistently leads to a significantly better result in comparison with Naïve training. For example, in a single-task setting, applying logit adjustment (Logit adj.) during training results in a 31.8% and 24.8% average accuracy improvement on validation and test sets, respectively. For attributes with imbalanced label distributions such as **shot size** and **shot angle**, we have observed that Naïvely trained network performs very well for the dominant classes but extremely poorly for low-frequency classes. On the other hand, a network trained with logit adjustment gives a relatively balanced per-class accuracy, and hence better overall performance.

We use different types of input representations for shot attributes classification. Table 3 compares their performance. Using video features as an input gives a competitive performance for most shot attributes except for **sound source**,

Table 4. Quantitative analysis on camera setup clustering.

Method	Parameter-based						Parameter-free					
	K-Means [24]			HAC [29]			OPTICS [1]			FINCH [36]		
	RI	NMI	PS	RI	NMI	PS	RI	NMI	PS	RI	NMI	PS
SIFT [25]	0.863	0.779	0.837	0.865	0.785	0.840	0.786	0.685	0.790	0.795	0.692	0.777
ResNet-101 [11]	**0.947**	**0.913**	**0.937**	**0.946**	**0.914**	**0.939**	0.784	0.718	0.801	0.887	0.834	0.887
CLIP [34]	0.907	0.858	0.894	0.912	0.867	0.899	0.836	0.769	0.865	0.845	0.780	0.851
ResNet-101 (Ours)	0.921	0.873	0.908	0.922	0.876	0.909	**0.868**	**0.802**	**0.889**	**0.889**	**0.838**	**0.895**
R-3D [42]	0.906	0.846	0.891	0.910	0.856	0.897	0.693	0.601	0.723	0.814	0.728	0.813
R-3D (Ours)	0.902	0.840	0.882	0.903	0.844	0.884	0.850	0.775	0.871	0.872	0.805	0.866

where adding audio features results in a 19.3% performance boost on both validation and test sets. Our baselines achieve a relatively low accuracy when predicting
shot motion and sound source. The lack of explicit modeling of motion could
be one contributing factor to the low performance on shot motion [35]. The
low accuracy sound source classification is most likely due to the fine-grained
nature of the task. For instance, it could be very ambiguous to differentiate
between on-screen, off-screen and external-narration classes. Incorporating motion information in the form of optical flow along with other input modalities and exploring the correlation of audio and visual features with a carefully
designed attention mechanism are interesting research directions.

Camera Setup Clustering. We perform scene-level shot clustering, where we
group the shots of a given scene into different camera setups. The averaged results
for all scenes in the dataset are summarized in Table 4. We use image-based and
video-based feature extraction methods to establish baselines. We also compare
the visual backbone of our framework trained on shot attribute prediction task in
Sect. 3.1. For clustering, we experiment with four standard clustering algorithms.
K-Means [24] and HAC [29] require the number of clusters as an input parameter,
i.e. parameter-based, while OPTICS [1] and FINCH [36] generate clusters without
relying on the number of clusters as an input, *i.e. parameter-free*.

Table 4 shows that image-based feature extraction methods generally perform
better than video-based backbones. It is also worth noting that, for parameter-
based clustering, ResNet-101 [11] pretrained on ImageNet [8] achieves the highest clustering accuracy on all metrics. However, for parameter-free clustering, ResNet-101 pretrained on the proposed dataset consistently outperforms
ResNet-101 (pretrained on ImageNet). The same notion can also be observed
for R-3D [42] which is pretrained on Kinetics-400 [17]. These results highlight
that shot attributes classification could be used as a pretext task for better
shot clustering as the ground truth for the number of clusters is not generally
available.

Table 5. Quantitative analysis on shot sequence ordering.

Method	Frame			Video			Audio + Video		
	Val	Test	Survey	Val	Test	Survey	Val	Test	Survey
Random	16.6	16.6	16.6	16.6	16.6	16.6	16.6	16.6	16.6
Baseline-I	21.0	21.5	20.0	21.7	22.4	23.3	23.1	24.4	26.7
Baseline-II	25.0	25.7	26.7	26.5	27.4	33.3	**29.3**	**30.7**	33.3
Human	-	-	32.0	-	-	39.9	-	-	**55.6**
Cinematography patterns									
Baseline-I (insert)	26.2	25.8	-	27.9	27.5	-	30.1	29.8	-
Baseline-II (insert)	39.6	37.3	-	41.5	38.4	-	42.2	39.5	-
Baseline-I (intensify)	29.6	30.1	-	30.7	31.4	-	32.2	33.1	-
Baseline-II (intensify)	34.1	35.8	-	38.1	40.5	-	44.2	48.0	-

Shot Sequence Ordering. The results for the shot order prediction task are presented in Table 5. We evaluate two baselines for shot order prediction: i. `Baseline-I`, where we first extract features from each shot in the sequence and then perform hierarchical feature fusion in the later stage as shown in Fig. 3a, and ii. `Baseline-II`, where we first concatenate the shots in the given input and then extract features from the resulting sequence (see Fig. 3b). We evaluate the two baselines for different input representations. As shot ordering is a 6-way classification problem, random order prediction has an accuracy of 16.6%. As can be seen from Table 5, the best performance for both baselines is achieved when using `audio + video` compared to using only `video` or a single `frame` as an input. This is intuitive as audio-visual features provide a richer context for the network to find correspondence between the shots when predicting order.

Table 5 also shows that early fusion of inputs leads to significantly better results compared to late feature fusion. For example, when using `audio + video`, `Baseline-II` outperforms `Baseline-I` by a margin of 26.8% and 25.8% on validation and test sets, respectively. This is mainly because early fusion enables the model to implicitly learn the correlation between shots at different levels of abstraction since all inputs are processed simultaneously. Instead, late feature fusion only learns limited correspondences as each shot is encoded independently.

The results in Table 5 are low mainly because predicting the order of shots is a very challenging problem. As discussed in Sect. 4.3, the shots in the input sequence are often from different camera setups, and hence, it is very difficult to exploit semantic and geometric correspondences which are crucial to learning order. To further analyze the performance of our models in comparison with humans, we conducted a survey. We sampled 30 triplets from the test set and asked more than 160 people to predict the order of the randomly shuffled shots, where each shot is represented using a single `frame`, `video` and `video + audio`. To prevent people from exploiting very noticeable transitions between shots, we embedded blank frames between the shot clips.

As can be concluded from Table 5, despite the better accuracy compared to our baselines, the task of ordering shots is also difficult for humans particularly when the shots are represented using a `frame` or `video`. The significant performance surge for humans in `audio + video` setting is most likely because

Table 6. Quantitative analysis on next shot selection.

Method	Frame		Video		Audio + Video	
	Val	Test	Val	Test	Val	Test
`Random`	20.0	20.0	20.0	20.0	20.0	20.0
`Cosine Sim.`	14.3	13.4	13.3	13.4	-	-
`Ours (in-sequence)`	34.1	34.0	37.9	37.5	39.0	38.7
`Ours (in-batch)`	38.4	38.2	41.3	41.0	**41.6**	**41.4**

humans can comprehend the content of the audio. For instance, if there is a dialogue between subjects in the given shots, humans can easily establish the order of the shots based on the speech of the subjects. An exciting future work would be to further exploit the content of the audio in the form of speech or other relevant representations in order to imitate human comprehension.

Although a broadly formulated shot ordering problem could be challenging, we analyze the performance of our baselines for shot sequences that contain commonly used cinematography patterns [3,20,45,46]. First, we evaluate the `insert` pattern, where one of the shots in the sequence is an `insert` shot. In this case, the number of possibilities for ordering decreases to 2 since the `insert` shot should always be in the middle. It is worth noting that a model doesn't have this pre-existing knowledge. As can be seen from Table 5, the performance of both baselines significantly increases for validation and test samples that contain an `insert` shot. The same phenomenon can also be observed for `intensify` pattern, where an editor uses a sequence of shots moving gradually closer, *i.e.* decreasing `shot size`, to build up emotion[2]. These results highlight that our baselines have implicitly learned common cinematography patterns during training.

Next Shot Selection. Table 6 shows the results for next shot selection task. We experiment with a shot sequence length of 9 for quantitative evaluation, where the first 4 shots are used as context and the remaining 5 are randomly shuffled and fed into the network as a candidate list for the next shot. In this setup, the random chance of accurately selecting the next shot is 20%. To further demonstrate the previously mentioned concept that the neighboring shots in a movie scene are usually from different camera setups, we use a Naïve `cosine similarity` between the end shot in the given context, *i.e.* S_4, and each shot in the candidate list as a baseline for next shot selection task. Here, we extract features from the shots using pretrained backbone networks and evaluate the cosine similarity between the extracted features. As can be seen from Table 6, Naïve `cosine similarity` performs even worse than random chance. In comparison, our proposed baselines (Sect. 4.4) perform significantly better. Our approach achieves an accuracy of 41.6% and 41.4% on validation and test sets, respec-

---

[2] We consider 3 `intensify` patterns: `extreme-wide - wide - medium`, `wide - medium - close-up`, `medium - close-up - extreme-close-up`.

Table 7. Quantitative analysis on missing shot attributes prediction.

Method	Shot size		Shot angle		Shot type		Shot motion	
	Val	Test	Val	Test	Val	Test	Val	Test
Dominant label	20.0	20.0	20.0	20.0	16.7	16.7	20.0	20.0
Frame	40.9	32.4	22.6	30.5	26.6	26.1	25.0	25.8
Frame + Attributes	**47.8**	**44.6**	28.5	34.1	32.0	34.5	31.0	31.8
Video	34.3	32.8	29.0	34.7	31.3	33.2	30.1	30.7
Video + Attributes	38.3	35.3	30.4	37.2	32.7	35.0	31.9	32.1
Video + Audio	36.4	35.3	31.5	35.8	31.9	33.4	30.5	30.9
Video + Audio + Attributes	39.2	37.2	**33.7**	**39.0**	**32.9**	**35.4**	**32.3**	**33.2**

tively. We also observe that using a larger number of negatives (in-batch) during training improves performance.

Missing Shot Attributes Prediction. This task targets to predict the attributes of an intermediate shot given its left and right neighboring shots. In Table 7, we present the results on four shot attributes, *i.e.* shot size, shot angle, shot type and shot motion, for a model trained in a multi-task setting. To confirm that the proposed model indeed uses the input shots as a context and does not simply converge to always predicting the dominant labels, we evaluated the accuracy of predicting the dominant label every time for each shot attribute. As can be inferred from the table, the proposed model outperforms the Naïve dominant label prediction baseline by a large margin. It can also be noticed that incorporating the attributes of the input shots along with other representations consistently improves model accuracy across all attributes.

As can be inferred from Table 7, the multi-task training setup does not always lead to a balanced performance for the missing shot attributes prediction task. For instance, when using frame as an input, the performance gap between shot size and other attributes is notably large in comparison with using other input representations. This is mainly because the model overfitted to the shot size attribute for this particular input setup.

6   Conclusion

We introduced the Anatomy of Video Editing (AVE) dataset and benchmark. We gathered more than 1.5M manually labeled tags, with relevant concepts to cinematography, from 196176 shots sampled from movie scenes. We also annotated the shot transitions and camera setup in movie scenes, which allowed us to recover the scene composition. We also define five tasks to help attain research progress in automatic footage organization and assisted video assembling. We hope that our work will inspire new computer vision technologies and spur research in machine listening, speech and language understanding, and graphics. Moreover, we believe our dataset will foster the design of new relevant tasks for AI-assisted editing. For instance, our sound-source annotations can facilitate the study of music selection for video. The scene composition labels can enable tasks related to recommending pace and rhythm for cutting.

References

1. Ankerst, M., Breunig, M.M., Kriegel, H.P., Sander, J.: Optics: ordering points to identify the clustering structure. ACM SIGMOD Rec. **28**(2), 49–60 (1999)
2. Bain, M., Nagrani, A., Brown, A., Zisserman, A.: Condensed movies: story based retrieval with contextual embeddings (2020)
3. Baxter, M.: Comparing cutting patterns-a working paper. Present Webpage Question **3** (2013)
4. Bhattacharya, S., Mehran, R., Sukthankar, R., Shah, M.: Classification of cinematographic shots using lie algebra and its application to complex event recognition. IEEE Trans. Multimedia **16**(3), 686–696 (2014)
5. Canini, L., Benini, S., Leonardi, R.: Classifying cinematographic shot types. Multimedia Tools Appl. **62**(1), 51–73 (2013)
6. Chen, T., Kornblith, S., Norouzi, M., Hinton, G.: A simple framework for contrastive learning of visual representations. In: International Conference on Machine Learning, pp. 1597–1607. PMLR (2020)
7. Dancyger, K.: The Technique of Film and Video Editing: History, Theory, and Practice. Routledge, London (2018)
8. Deng, J., Dong, W., Socher, R., Li, L.J., Li, K., Fei-Fei, L.: Imagenet: a large-scale hierarchical image database. In: 2009 IEEE Conference on Computer Vision and Pattern Recognition, pp. 248–255. IEEE (2009)
9. El-Nouby, A., Zhai, S., Taylor, G.W., Susskind, J.M.: Skip-clip: self-supervised spatiotemporal representation learning by future clip order ranking. arXiv preprint arXiv:1910.12770 (2019)
10. Gao, C., Saraf, A., Huang, J.-B., Kopf, J.: Flow-edge guided video completion. In: Vedaldi, A., Bischof, H., Brox, T., Frahm, J.-M. (eds.) ECCV 2020. LNCS, vol. 12357, pp. 713–729. Springer, Cham (2020). https://doi.org/10.1007/978-3-030-58610-2_42
11. He, K., Zhang, X., Ren, S., Sun, J.: Deep residual learning for image recognition. In: Proceedings of the IEEE Conference on Computer Vision and Pattern Recognition, pp. 770–778 (2016)
12. Hoai, M., Zisserman, A.: Thread-safe: towards recognizing human actions across shot boundaries. In: Cremers, D., Reid, I., Saito, H., Yang, M.-H. (eds.) ACCV 2014. LNCS, vol. 9006, pp. 222–237. Springer, Cham (2015). https://doi.org/10.1007/978-3-319-16817-3_15
13. Hochreiter, S., Schmidhuber, J.: Long short-term memory. Neural Comput. **9**(8), 1735–1780 (1997)
14. Huang, Q., Xiong, Yu., Rao, A., Wang, J., Lin, D.: MovieNet: a holistic dataset for movie understanding. In: Vedaldi, A., Bischof, H., Brox, T., Frahm, J.-M. (eds.) ECCV 2020. LNCS, vol. 12349, pp. 709–727. Springer, Cham (2020). https://doi.org/10.1007/978-3-030-58548-8_41
15. Kang, B., et al.: Decoupling representation and classifier for long-tailed recognition. arXiv preprint arXiv:1910.09217 (2019)
16. Kasten, Y., Ofri, D., Wang, O., Dekel, T.: Layered neural atlases for consistent video editing. ACM Trans. Graph. (TOG) **40**(6), 1–12 (2021)
17. Kay, W., et al.: The kinetics human action video dataset. arXiv preprint arXiv:1705.06950 (2017)

18. Khosla, P., et al.: Supervised contrastive learning. In: Larochelle, H., Ranzato, M., Hadsell, R., Balcan, M.F., Lin, H. (eds.) Advances in Neural Information Processing Systems, vol. 33, pp. 18661–18673. Curran Associates, Inc. (2020). https://proceedings.neurips.cc/paper/2020/file/d89a66c7c80a29b1bdbab0f2a1a94af8-Paper.pdf
19. Kim, D., Cho, D., Kweon, I.S.: Self-supervised video representation learning with space-time cubic puzzles. In: Proceedings of the AAAI Conference on Artificial Intelligence, vol. 33, pp. 8545–8552 (2019)
20. Leake, M., Davis, A., Truong, A., Agrawala, M.: Computational video editing for dialogue-driven scenes. ACM Trans. Graph. 36(4), 130-1 (2017)
21. Liu, S., Johns, E., Davison, A.J.: End-to-end multi-task learning with attention. In: Proceedings of the IEEE/CVF Conference on Computer Vision and Pattern Recognition, pp. 1871–1880 (2019)
22. Liu, X., Hu, Y., Bai, S., Ding, F., Bai, X., Torr, P.H.: Multi-shot temporal event localization: a benchmark. In: Proceedings of the IEEE/CVF Conference on Computer Vision and Pattern Recognition, pp. 12596–12606 (2021)
23. Liu, Y.L., Lai, W.S., Yang, M.H., Chuang, Y.Y., Huang, J.B.: Learning to see through obstructions with layered decomposition. IEEE Trans. Pattern Anal. Mach. Intell. (2021)
24. Lloyd, S.: Least squares quantization in PCM. IEEE Trans. Inf. Theory 28(2), 129–137 (1982)
25. Lowe, D.G.: Distinctive image features from scale-invariant keypoints. Int. J. Comput. Vision 60(2), 91–110 (2004)
26. Lu, E., Cole, F., Dekel, T., Zisserman, A., Freeman, W.T., Rubinstein, M.: Omnimatte: associating objects and their effects in video. In: Proceedings of the IEEE/CVF Conference on Computer Vision and Pattern Recognition, pp. 4507–4515 (2021)
27. Menon, A.K., Jayasumana, S., Rawat, A.S., Jain, H., Veit, A., Kumar, S.: Long-tail learning via logit adjustment. arXiv preprint arXiv:2007.07314 (2020)
28. Metz, C.: Film Language: A Semiotics of the Cinema. University of Chicago Press, Chicago (1991)
29. Müllner, D.: Modern hierarchical, agglomerative clustering algorithms. arXiv preprint arXiv:1109.2378 (2011)
30. Oh, S.W., Lee, J.Y., Xu, N., Kim, S.J.: Video object segmentation using space-time memory networks. In: Proceedings of the IEEE/CVF International Conference on Computer Vision, pp. 9226–9235 (2019)
31. Pardo, A., Caba, F., Alcázar, J.L., Thabet, A.K., Ghanem, B.: Learning to cut by watching movies. In: Proceedings of the IEEE/CVF International Conference on Computer Vision, pp. 6858–6868 (2021)
32. Pardo, A., Heilbron, F.C., Alcázar, J.L., Thabet, A., Ghanem, B.: Moviecuts: a new dataset and benchmark for cut type recognition. arXiv preprint arXiv:2109.05569 (2021)
33. Patwardhan, K.A., Sapiro, G., Bertalmío, M.: Video inpainting under constrained camera motion. IEEE Trans. Image Process. 16(2), 545–553 (2007)
34. Radford, A., et al.: Learning transferable visual models from natural language supervision. In: International Conference on Machine Learning, pp. 8748–8763. PMLR (2021)
35. Rao, A., et al.: A unified framework for shot type classification based on subject centric lens. In: Vedaldi, A., Bischof, H., Brox, T., Frahm, J.-M. (eds.) ECCV 2020. LNCS, vol. 12356, pp. 17–34. Springer, Cham (2020). https://doi.org/10.1007/978-3-030-58621-8_2

36. Sarfraz, S., Sharma, V., Stiefelhagen, R.: Efficient parameter-free clustering using first neighbor relations. In: Proceedings of the IEEE/CVF Conference on Computer Vision and Pattern Recognition, pp. 8934–8943 (2019)
37. Schütze, H., Manning, C.D., Raghavan, P.: Introduction to Information Retrieval, vol. 39. Cambridge University Press, Cambridge (2008)
38. Smith, J.R., Joshi, D., Huet, B., Hsu, W., Cota, J.: Harnessing AI for augmenting creativity: application to movie trailer creation. In: Proceedings of the 25th ACM International Conference on Multimedia, pp. 1799–1808 (2017)
39. Souček, T., Lokoč, J.: Transnet V2: an effective deep network architecture for fast shot transition detection. arXiv preprint arXiv:2008.04838 (2020)
40. Tan, J., et al.: Equalization loss for long-tailed object recognition. In: Proceedings of the IEEE/CVF Conference on Computer Vision and Pattern Recognition, pp. 11662–11671 (2020)
41. Tapaswi, M., Zhu, Y., Stiefelhagen, R., Torralba, A., Urtasun, R., Fidler, S.: Movieqa: understanding stories in movies through question-answering. In: Proceedings of the IEEE Conference on Computer Vision and Pattern Recognition, pp. 4631–4640 (2016)
42. Tran, D., Wang, H., Torresani, L., Ray, J., LeCun, Y., Paluri, M.: A closer look at spatiotemporal convolutions for action recognition. In: Proceedings of the IEEE Conference on Computer Vision and Pattern Recognition, pp. 6450–6459 (2018)
43. Wang, H.L., Cheong, L.F.: Taxonomy of directing semantics for film shot classification. IEEE Trans. Circuits Syst. Video Technol. 19(10), 1529–1542 (2009)
44. Wu, C.Y., Krahenbuhl, P.: Towards long-form video understanding. In: Proceedings of the IEEE/CVF Conference on Computer Vision and Pattern Recognition, pp. 1884–1894 (2021)
45. Wu, H.Y., Christie, M.: Analysing cinematography with embedded constrained patterns. In: WICED-Eurographics Workshop on Intelligent Cinematography and Editing (2016)
46. Wu, H.Y., Palù, F., Ranon, R., Christie, M.: Thinking like a director: film editing patterns for virtual cinematographic storytelling. ACM Trans. Multimedia Comput. Commun. Appl. (TOMM) 14(4), 1–22 (2018)
47. Xiao, J., et al.: Explore video clip order with self-supervised and curriculum learning for video applications. IEEE Trans. Multimedia 23, 3454–3466 (2021). https://doi.org/10.1109/TMM.2020.3025661
48. Xu, M., et al.: Using context saliency for movie shot classification. In: 2011 18th IEEE International Conference on Image Processing, pp. 3653–3656. IEEE (2011)
49. Zhang, X., Li, Y., Han, Y., Wen, J.: AI video editing: a survey (2022)
50. Zhu, Y., et al.: Aligning books and movies: Towards story-like visual explanations by watching movies and reading books. In: Proceedings of the IEEE International Conference on Computer Vision, pp. 19–27 (2015)

StyleBabel: Artistic Style Tagging and Captioning

Dan Ruta[1(✉)], Andrew Gilbert[1], Pranav Aggarwal[2], Naveen Marri[2], Ajinkya Kale[2], Jo Briggs[3], Chris Speed[4], Hailin Jin[2], Baldo Faieta[2], Alex Filipkowski[2], Zhe Lin[2], and John Collomosse[1,2]

[1] University of Surrey, Guildford, UK
dan.sebastian.ruta@gmail.com
[2] Adobe Research, San Jose, USA
[3] University of Northumbria, Newcastle upon Tyne, UK
[4] University of Edinburgh, Edinburgh, UK

Abstract. We present StyleBabel, a unique open access dataset of natural language captions and free-form tags describing the artistic style of over 135K digital artworks, collected via a novel participatory method from experts studying at specialist art and design schools. StyleBabel was collected via an iterative method, inspired by 'Grounded Theory': a qualitative approach that enables annotation while co-evolving a shared language for fine-grained artistic style attribute description. We demonstrate several downstream tasks for StyleBabel, adapting the recent ALADIN architecture for fine-grained style similarity, to train cross-modal embeddings for: 1) free-form tag generation; 2) natural language description of artistic style; 3) fine-grained text search of style. To do so, we extend ALADIN with recent advances in Visual Transformer (ViT) and cross-modal representation learning, achieving a state of the art accuracy in fine-grained style retrieval.

Keywords: Datasets and evaluation · Image and video retrieval · Vision + language · Vision applications and systems

1 Introduction

Artistic style is the distinctive appearance of an artwork; i.e. how an artist has depicted their subject matter [14]. Describing the artistic style of digital artwork is an open challenge for computer vision, which has focused on stylization, classification, and search in the style domain. However, automated style description has potential applications in summarization, analytics, and accessibility. For the first time, this paper shows that a set of descriptive tags, or even complete caption sentences, may be automatically generated to describe the fine-grained artistic style of an image – distinct from its content [10,28,55], or the emotions it evokes [2]. Our core contribution enabling this is **StyleBabel**, a novel dataset of fine-grained [32,51,54] annotations describing the artistic style of ∼135K digital artworks[1], collected from expert participants via a novel

---

[1] The dataset is released for open access (CC-BY 4.0).

Supplementary Information The online version contains supplementary material available at https://doi.org/10.1007/978-3-031-20074-8_13.

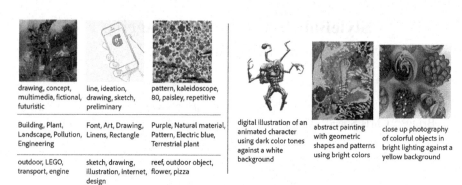

drawing, concept, multimedia, fictional, futuristic	line, ideation, drawing, sketch, preliminary	pattern, kaleidoscope, 80, paisley, repetitive	digital illustration of an animated character using dark color tones against a white background	abstract painting with geometric shapes and patterns using bright colors	close up photography of colorful objects in bright lighting against a yellow background
Building, Plant, Landscape, Pollution, Engineering	Font, Art, Drawing, Linens, Rectangle	Purple, Natural material, Pattern, Electric blue, Terrestrial plant			
outdoor, LEGO, transport, engine	sketch, drawing, illustration, internet, design	reef, outdoor object, flower, pizza			

Fig. 1. Results *generated* from models trained on StyleBabel to describe style using free-form tags (left) and captions (right). The top row of tags contains tags generated by our models trained with StyleBabel. The middle row contains tags from a commercial image tagging Google product, and the bottom from a similar commercial product from Microsoft. We show the importance of the style domain-specific information within StyleBabel, for generating relevant style captions.

participatory method that forms a further contribution of this paper. Specifically, our novel contributions are (Fig. 1):

1. StyleBabel Dataset. We present a new dataset of over ∼135K {image, tags, natural language (NL) caption} pairs for digital artwork images annotated by a combination of crowd-sourcing and 48 domain experts drawn from design and art schools. StyleBabel is the first dataset containing all three data types for every data sample. Furthermore, the images contained have vastly greater style variation than existing datasets [16,42] which predominantly focus on small subsets of fine art, sometimes further limited to only European or Asian [3,27,53]. Not only is StyleBabel's domain more diverse, but our annotations also differ. StyleBabel focuses on the visual appearance of images (which can include stroke/colouring type, lighting, shading, patterns, shapes, composition, medium, layout, theme etc.), we avoid external, high level information such as artists, time periods, surrounding meaning, emotions evoked, provenance facts, context or content. This enables new avenues for research not possible before, some of which we explore in this paper.

We do not seek to align our work to a formal ontology or definition of style (something heavily debated even by academics [14,35]). Instead, we explicitly build, evolve, and rely on the emergent structure of style information from the collective, harmonized experience of expert collaborators from art and design universities during our data collection process. In previous work [17], the working definition of style has been the similarity of gram matrices at specific layers in CNN backbones such as VGG [45]. During our data pre-processing/initialization, ahead of style annotation, we similarly use a working definition as similarity in the ALADIN [41] style model's embedding space, previously shown to accurately represent a variety of artistic styles in a metric space.

During annotation, images are grouped into ∼6K moodboards (grids of style-consistent images). Each moodboard is annotated by a group of experts, both with tags and free-form captions, to yield a description of visual style. The vocabulary used for both annotation forms is unconstrained. The moodboard annotations are cross-validated as part of the collection process and refined further via the crowd to obtain individual, image-level fine-grained annotations.

2. Grounded Annotation Methodology. We present a new data annotation methodology inspired by *Grounded Theory* (GT) [6,44], a qualitative research method used in the humanities and social sciences. In GT, participant groups engage in an unconstrained data clustering exercise while simultaneously evolving a shared vocabulary for describing those clusters. Working with these disciplines, we adapted this process to evolve a shared vocabulary for annotation while annotating groups ('moodboards') of images with similar artistic styles. The moodboards are obtained by clustering artworks within the ALADIN fine-grained embedding for style similarity [41]. Our iterative methodology comprises individual and participatory group stages and a validation stage.

3. Artistic Retrieval and Description. We incorporate a Visual Transformer [46] into a fine-grained visual style representation architecture [41], (ALADIN-ViT). ALADIN-ViT provides state of the art performance at fine-grained style similarity search. We train models for several cross-modal tasks using ALADIN-ViT and StyleBabel annotations. Using CLIP [36], we train with StyleBabel to generate free-form tags describing the artistic style, generalizing to unseen styles. We show that we may apply these tags for text based style search. We similarly demonstrate the synthesis of descriptive natural language captions for digital art.

2   Related Work

Representation learning for visual style has focused primarily on neural style transfer (NST) and style classification.

Style Transfer. Classical approaches learned patch-based representation of style by analogy from paired data. Gatys et al. [17] enabled NST by extracting disentangled representations separating content and style from unpaired data, using a Grammian computed across layers of a pre-trained VGG-19 [45] model. Similarly, feed-forward networks used the Grammian to train fast encoder-decoder models for NST specialized to pre-trained styles [23,47]. Extensions to multi-scale [50] and video [40] NSTS were later presented. To relax the constraint to pre-trained styles, feature based NST was proposed using Adaptive Instance Normalization (AdaIN) [18,21]. This approach was further generalized by the whitening and coloring transform (WCT), which matched feature covariances [29]. Recently unsupervised style transfer was enabled via MUNIT [22] and swapping autoencoder [34]. The latent style codes of encoder-decoder networks for NST were recently adapted for style-based visual representation learning, using weak supervision to learn a metric embedding for fine-grained similarity using the ALADIN model [41].

Style analytics via classification has been explored for digital artwork [52], smaller fine-art collections [24,57], product designs [4], and to identify both painters [7] and genres [43]. Style-based visual search has also been proposed for coarse-grained style using triplet [9] and constrastive training for fine-grained style via ALADIN [41].

Style Datasets. No prior dataset of fine-grained artistic style description exists. However, several annotated datasets of artwork have been produced. **Behance Artistic Media – BAM** [52] comprises 2M diverse digital artworks from the Behance.net platform, with 7 coarse-grained style and 4 emotion tags and no descriptions. **Omniart** (432K images) and Wikiart (81K) are datasets of fine art with associated metadata but no descriptions or tags. The **SemArt** dataset [16] focuses on very high level contextual semantic information, rarely containing style (visual appearance) information, and narrowly focuses solely on 8th-19th century European fine art. The **BAM-FG** (BAM Fine-grained) dataset comprises 2.62M images grouped into 310K style-consistent groupings but no descriptive text or labels. Our work also uses `Behance.net`, to provide expert style tags and natural language descriptions over 135K images. The **AVA** dataset [5] studies aesthetics information in *photographic* images only, and the follow-up **AVA-captions** dataset [19] adds captions for these, sourced from noisy internet comments sections. Recently, ArtEmis [2] released non-expert annotations capturing the emotions felt by viewers of fine art in WikiArt. Our proposed StyleBabel dataset is aligned to this contemporary work in that it also seeks to ascribe text to visual art. However, our focus is also on digital, not just fine artwork. We also differ in that our annotation is led by expert students in specialized art and design schools, not exclusively by non-expert crowd-workers. Notably, our annotations focus on the style alone, deliberately *avoiding* the description of the subject matter or the emotions that matter evokes. **ArtEmis** instead describes *exclusively the emotions evoked* by both the style and content of the artwork, both of which feature in the descriptions. To recap, StyleBabel is unique in providing tags and textual descriptions of the artistic style, doing so at a large scale and for a wider variety of styles than existing datasets, with labels sourced from a large, diverse group of experts across multiple areas of art.

Image captioning and visual question answering methods [49] initially learned LSTM language models, leveraging semantic image embeddings e.g. via ResNet/ImageNet. Later image captioning work [10,28,55,56] made use of object detection; regions of interest (ROI). Their relationships yielded improved semantics captioning models, though often due to the bias of co-present context that hinted at the image narrative. This is incompatible with our domain of artistic style, where this localization bias is not something we can use. Recently, there has been an influx of research combining the visual and text domains [36–38]. Established methods [13,25], have primarily functioned by generating captions from templates. Though this approach benefits from generating grammatically correct captions, its inflexibility has led to diminished interest in its application, despite recent implementation by OpenAI's CLIP [36]. Here, captioning capabilities generate tags and insert them into templates, using two encoders – for text and image modalities. This model then performs cross-modal training via contrastive loss. More recently, Attention-on-attention [20] can generate state-of-the-art quality captions from an image embedding by filtering out irrelevant attention results. VirTex [11] recently demonstrates that caption annotations are more efficient for representation learning of images, with better or comparable representation quality on ImageNet despite much less training data.

Grounded Theory (GT) [44] is a qualitative method used in the humanities and social sciences to codify data – i.e. to identify and name apparent or emergent patterns across different data sources and types. Through interpretation, participants collaboratively agree on an initial set of summative 'open' codes that are then iteratively combined into larger groups, until eventually, participants arrive, by consensus, at the common themes in the data [6]. We adopt this approach to collecting expert annotation to describe the artistic style of clusters of digital artwork. Free-form textual input from various participants can vary in writing style, creating a very noisy dataset. GT mitigates this by guiding participants to align their responses to a consistent format.

3   StyleBabel Dataset

StyleBabel is a new dataset for cross-modal representation learning. It comprises 135k digital artwork images from the public creative portfolio website `Behance.net` (in turn, available via the BAM dataset). Each image is annotated with a set of keyword tags and natural language descriptions *'captions'* describing its *fine-grained artistic style* – the distinctive appearance of the image – in the English language. We focus mainly on attributes that we can visually depict, rather than more high level and abstract concepts such as emotions [2]. StyleBabel enables the training of models for style retrieval and generates a textual description of fine-grained style within an image: automated natural language style description and tagging (e.g. style2text). We train state of the art proof of concept models for these tasks using our dataset in Sect. 5.

3.1   Study Context

We determined via early initial trials with crowd annotation platforms (AMT) that the quality, coarseness, and diversity of data generated by non-experts is inadequate for style description tasks. We collaborated with graduate schools specializing in digital art and design to address this. Together with academic experts at these schools, we designed a novel multi-staged participatory method to enable novel style vocabulary gathering, tagging, and caption generation, recruiting 48 expert staff and student participants. We particularly sought (but did not make a prerequisite) participants familiar with Behance. The final cohort comprised a representative balance of gender and ethnic background of both graduate and undergraduate cohorts - anecdotally, the gender split was equal. Expertise was at that of a final year undergraduate student, with more senior faculty members participating in the discussions. Their program's specialisms were primarily communication design (graphics, illustration), industrial design, fashion, and animation.

We executed the group exercise online using a *collaborative whiteboard* interactive platform[2], that provides capabilities for multiple users to move and annotate components freely in real time. We built 1300 unique pages of moodboards (Fig. 2) to allow participants to move sticky notes with related tags naturally in a collaborative process. The process simulated in-person group collaboration, enabling the formation of tag clusters and aligning to processes of GT codification. The combined use of Miro and Zoom supported real-time spatial organization of information and associated discussion. Workers were paid significantly higher than the national minimum, with a total dataset cost of approximately $160k, which we freely contribute as CC-BY 4.0.

3.2   StyleBabel Grounded Annotation

StyleBabel *does not* aim to develop an ontology to categorize style, with agreement on a diverse ontology eluding art practitioners [14]. Yet, consistency of language is essential for learning of effective representations. Therefore we propose an annotation

---

[2] https://miro.com/.

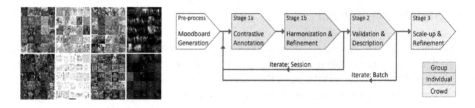

Fig. 2. The StyleBabel Grounded Annotation process. Moodboards (examples, left) are annotated via an iterative process (right) that encourages groups of participants to evolve and converge to a shared language for describing style. See Subsect. 3.2 for stage descriptions.

methodology that enables annotations at scale (multiple participants) and encourages co-evolution of a harmonized natural language to describe the style.

Our annotation process instead is inspired by Grounded Theory (GT) [6,44]; a qualitative method often used for data analysis in the humanities and social sciences. A systematic research process to 'codify' empirical data, identify themes from the data, and associate data with those themes. This process is distinct from fitting (or 'annotating') data to pre-existing categories. GT is an iterative process in which participants co-evolve a language to describe the data as they work on clustering and labeling it with that shared language. Concretely, GT often begins with a discussion around a subset of the data during which clusters are formed. Data is moved freely between clusters during the debate, from which a shared understanding and, ultimately, a shared terminology evolves for describing those clusters. With further data, this language identifies and names patterns apparent or emergent in the data.

Grounded Annotation Process. We propose a multi-stage process for compiling the StyleBabel dataset comprised of initial individual and subsequent group sessions and a final individual stage. Each batch of these sessions was estimated to take around 10 h, run over a week, and run four sets over four weeks.

Experts annotate images in small clusters (referred to as image 'moodboards'). Moodboards are obtained by automatically clustering artworks within a fine-grained style embedding [41]. Our annotation process thus pre-determines the clusters for expert annotation. Still, it encourages expert groups to evolve a harmonized language during the iterative annotation process (as in GT) to improve data consistency. We refer to this process as 'grounded annotation'.

Pre-processing - *Moodboard generation (Automated)*

We downloaded an initial dataset of 150 million digital artwork (static image assets) from Behance.net. We encode all images into a metric search embedding [41], that we then clustered into 6.5K clusters, with L_2 distance to identify the 25 nearest image neighbors to each cluster center. The images from each cluster were arranged in a 5×5 grid for presentation as a moodboard. Thus, we start the annotation process using 6,500 moodboards (162.5K images) of 6,500 different fine-grained styles.[3]. The extremely

---

[3] We redacted a minimal number of adult-themed images due to ethical considerations.

Changed (Re-moved or added tags in Stage 1b)	line, both have the same white backgrounds with very little tonal variations/ just block colours, no difference in tones, bright white background, b+w, constructed by lines, no colour, hand drawing linear, pen and ink	b+w black and white, pen and ink, fantasy, intricate, white space, central position, linear, illustration
Final tags after Stage 1b cleaning	ink work, sketches, black and white, white clean, monotonal, drawing, illustration, linear, pen and ink	bright, graphic, drawing, background, pen and ink, simple, space, central	black and white, fantasy, intricate, white composition, linear, illustration

Fig. 3. Before and after harmonization (Stage 1b), showing the benefits of the GT approach. Two moodboards receive linguistically different tag sets in Stage 1a (individual) but are conformed to the shared vocabulary evolved by the participant group in Stage 1b (group). The moodboard styles and the tag sets differ but draw upon a shared vocabulary (underscored tags) despite the board not being shown in the same session to workers. Tags removed are in red, and additions are in green. (Color figure online)

high data density from this internet-scale data corpus ensures that the small clusters formed are very stylistically consistent. Figure 2 (left) shows examples of moodboards.

Stage 1a - *Contrastive Annotation (Individual)*

Participants were individually presented with a pair of 5×5 moodboards and asked to generate a list of textual tags ('*style attributes*') that occur in one moodboard, but not another, and a list of style attributes which are shared by both. The moodboards were sampled such that they were close neighbors within the ALADIN style embedding. In the annotation, comparative language (e.g. 'X is brighter than Y') was not permitted to encourage standalone descriptions (e.g. 'bright' was allowed).

This paired approach encouraged the suggestion of fine-grained style attributes, supporting participants to suggest characteristics that may otherwise not have been considered when looking at individual styles. Multiple participants annotated each moodboard in this way to produce a rich initial set of attributes.

Stage 1b - *Harmonization and Refinement (Group)*

A collaborative workspace was synthesized within Miro, in which 5 moodboards and their associated style tags from Stage 1a are displayed (as 'sticky notes' below each moodboard).

After an initial briefing and group discussion, each group considered moodboards collectively, one moodboard at a time. All participants were asked to add new tags to the pre-populated list of tags that we had already gathered from Stage 1a (the individual task), modify the language used, or remove any tags they agreed were not appropriate. Each moodboard was considered 'finished' when no more changes to the tags list

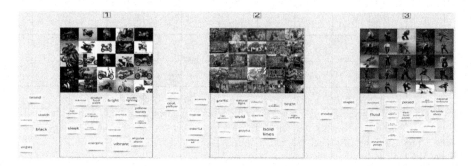

Fig. 4. Virtual environment for collaborative Stage 1b. Style attributes (as 'sticky notes') are added, modified and removed from each moodboard to harmonize and filter language.

could be readily determined (generally within 1 min). Workers spent at most 2h 15m per session, including all breaks. At least one facilitator was always present throughout to ensure high engagement. Figure 4 displays an example of moodboards presented during this part of the study via the Miro platform. Figure 3 provides an illustrative example of language harmonization. Two Stage 1a moodboards with initially very different language but similar style resulted in similar attributes post-Stage 1b.

Stage 2 - *Validation and Description (Individual)*
The participants completed the final stage individually. Each participant was presented with a random collection of 5 moodboards and a set of tags generated during the previous sessions for just one of these moodboards. Participants engaged in ESP-like game [1] to identify which moodboard the tags had been generated to describe, to verify accuracy. Further, we then asked them to create natural language captions, using as many presented tags as possible. We stressed to include as many tags as possible as by now, they had all been thoroughly cleaned and refined.

Stage 3 - *Scale-up and Refinement (Individual)*
Following these sessions with our subject experts, we ran a different task with non-experts (workers on Amazon Mechanical Turk (AMT)). We asked at an *image level* (rather than at the 5×5 cluster/moodboard level as previously) to discard any tags they considered not appropriate. Though the moodboards presented to these non-expert participants are style-coherent, there was still variation in the images, meaning that certain tags apply to most but not all of the images depicted. This step helped us to refine the final tags to individual images further. Unlike novel vocabulary generation, this verification step can be readily performed by non-experts, as detecting invalid tags is a much easier task than novel tag generation. We collected 3 responses per image and performed majority consensus to determine the final tags to use at the per-image level.

We additionally performed a large-scale crowd annotation exercise to individualize cluster-level captions to individual images. Trained workers were presented with individual images, its tags, and the moodboard caption and were asked to compose (potentially many) natural language captions using the tags and caption, ensuring the full set of tags were incorporated across those sentences. A constant set of workers were trained with feedback, for several months, together with a Quality Control (QC)

Fig. 5. Visualizing the top 250 tags captured within the StyleBabel annotation over 135K images.

Table 1. Excerpt of StyleBabel dataset. Four images and the corresponding tags and captions collected via our Grounded Annotation.

Image				
Tags	dim, concept, action, fantasy, powerful, digital, photography, animated, prototype, masculine, detailed, professional, lighting	abstract, moody, portrait, oil, painting, drawing, artistic, melancholic, pleasing	cold, digital, book, bright, colors, drawing, child, stroke, busy, clear, illustration, festive, blue	experimental, analog, line, development, black, drawing, sketch, figure, commercial, white, scamp, stroke, product, pencil, rough, thin, isometric
Caption	Fantasy themed digital illustration featuring an animated male character, dim highlighting and a hazy, dark and cluttered background. The illustration highlights the powerful masculine character with sharp objects around.	Portrait oil painting of a female character featuring abstract shapes and psychedelic patterns against a dark background. The artistic artwork is melancholic and using thin repetitive strokes and shades.	Digital bright fantasy anthropomorphism cartoon illustration created with soft diffused blended hues, brush strokes, lines, and geometric forms in neutral and cool tones.	Analog experimental sketches with thin pencil strokes and lines. The isometric drawing expresses commercial product development.

process to ensure high quality annotation. The QC process included grammatical correctness checking, and rejection of any description of content or emotion the descriptive captions.

Language Processing. Aside from the crowd data filtering, we cleaned the tags emerging from Stage 1b through several steps, including removing duplicates, filtering out invalid data or tags with more than 3 words, singularization, lemmatization, and manual spell checking for every tag. The spell checking step was carried out in 3 passes. The accuracy of the validation step in Stage 2 was found to be 90%.

The final StyleBabel dataset contains 135k images with an average of 12.8 tags per image, over 6k style groups (of the 6,500 initially sampled, with 6k completed by workers in the available time). The tags dictionary contains 3,151 unique tags, and the captions contain 5,475 unique words. Prepositions, determiners, and conjunctions were filtered out. Cardinals (e.g. *80s*) are kept. 9 cardinals, 2098 nouns, 500 verbs, 55 adverbs, and 482 adjectives are captured. Figure 5 visualizes a word cloud from the 250 most common style attributes in StyleBabel, and Table 1 shows the richness of the tags and captions.

4   Visual Embedding (ALADIN-ViT)

ALADIN is a two branch encoder-decoder network that seeks to disentangle image content and style. It works by pooling Adaptive Instance Normalization (AdaIN) statistics across multiple layers in the style encoder to produce an embedding for fine-grained style similarity using a VGG-19 convolutional backbone for the style encoder. In our later experiments, we require to use a Visual Transformer [12] (ViT) model for the vision domain. To achieve this, we adapt ALADIN to use ViT as the style encoder backbone; we refer to this as ALADIN-ViT (Fig. 6). We retrain ALADIN-ViT on BAM-FG following the same training method [41], i.e. using both the reconstruction loss and the weakly supervised contrastive loss and using the implicit style grouping in BAM-FG. Having swapped the style encoder for a transformer, it is no longer possible to sample AdaIN statistics from feature maps in the encoder. However, we retain the use of the style code as pairs of values to be split and used in the decoder stage, again keeping the size of the style code at double the number of feature maps in the decoder.

We achieve the state of the art fine grained style retrieval accuracy on the BAM-FG test partition (Table 2) at **64.48** Top-1, beating not only ALADIN (58.98) but also their fused variant (62.18), which incorporates ResNet embeddings into a concatenated embedding. We, in part, attribute the gains in accuracy to the larger receptive input size (in the pixel space) of earlier layers in the Transformer model, compared to early layers in CNNs. Given that style is a global attribute of an image, this greatly benefits our domain as more weights are trained on more global information.

5   StyleBabel Experimental Setup

Data Partitions. We define train/validation/test partitions within StyleBabel for our experiments as follows. Splits were separated on a moodboard basis, to avoid overlap. The training split has 133k images in 5,974 groups with 3,167 unique tags at an average of 13.05 tags per image. The validation and test splits contain 1k unique images for each validation and test, with 1,256/1,570/10.86 and 1,263/1,636/10.96 unique tags/groups/average tags per image. Captions have an average of 2.4 sentences, with an average of 19.3 words, from 6119 unique words. 1000 samples were extracted for each of the test/validation splits.

Implementation. The models were trained with a maximum batch size of 11k on a 12GB GTX Titan, with a learning rate of 0.003, Adam optimizer, and weight decay of $1e-6$. Logit accumulation [41] was employed to reach the maximum batch size possible in the GPU VRAM capacity. We trained all models to convergence. The learning rate was decayed using cosine annealing, as per SimCLR [8]. For the VirTex captioning experiments, a batch size of 105 was used, on a V100, with a learning rate of $2e-4$.

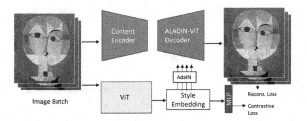

Fig. 6. ViT-ALADIN architecture used for StyleBabel experiments; as per ALADIN [41] but swapping the style encoder for ViT [12] (change in green) and retrained end-to-end on BAM-FG. (Color figure online)

Table 2. Fine grained style retrieval on the BAM-FG dataset [41] of proposed method ALADIN-ViT, compared to previous methods.

Data	Model	IR-1
BAM-FG-C_5	ALADIN	58.98
BAM-FG-C_5	ResNet	45.22
BAM-FG-C_5	ALADIN (Fused)	62.18
BAM-FG-C_5	ViT	57.91
BAM-FG-C_5	ALADIN-ViT	**64.48**

6   Experiments and Discussion

We illustrate the potential of our StyleBabel dataset for three cross-modal learning tasks:

1. Style Auto-tagging: (style2text) Using StyleBabel tags, we train a CLIP [36] model to learn a cross-modal embedding between image and text embeddings. We generate several tags for unseen StyleBabel images and explore the generated tags' accuracy and the model's ability to generalize.

2. Style Description: (style2text) We similarly make use of the natural language captions collected in StyleBabel, and showcase the generation of natural language captions describing the style of images.

3. Text Based Style Retrieval: (text2style) We explore the efficacy of our tag generation for text based style search.

6.1   Style Auto-tagging (style2text)

Recent literature in image captioning has transitioned to making use of object detectors in their model pipelines. This makes sense in semantics, as such features are most often localized to a subset of the image. Style, however, is typically a global attribute of an image, and object detectors are not compatible. Style is more abstract and seldom localized to any specific region of an image. We use the CLIP [36] training methodology to

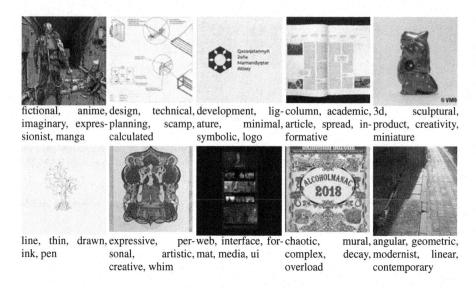

fictional,   anime, design,   technical, development,   lig- column, academic, 3d,   sculptural,
imaginary,   expres- planning, scamp,   ature,   minimal, article, spread, in- product, creativity,
sionist, manga   calculated   symbolic, logo formative   miniature

line, thin,   drawn, expressive,   per- web, interface, for- chaotic,   mural, angular, geometric,
ink, pen   sonal,   artistic, mat, media, ui   complex,   decay, modernist, linear,
                      creative, whim   overload   contemporary

Fig. 7. Style2Text tag generation experiment, using CLIP trained with ALADIN-ViT encoder.

learn a joint embedding space between the publicly available CLIP text encoder and our new vision transformer (ALADIN-ViT). CLIP is traditionally formed of two transformers, the first for text encoding and the second for image encoding. Two MLP heads are trained together through contrastive loss to learn a joint text/image embedding, adding invariance to the modality. We freeze both pre-trained transformers and train the two MLP layers (ReLU separated fully connected layers) to project their embeddings to the shared space. We follow CLIP, using contrastive loss, with the same training set-up.

When using the model for inference, we pass the entire dictionary of available tags through the text encoder and multi-modal MLP head to generate text embeddings. Next, we infer the image embedding using the image encoder and multi-modal MLP head, and calculate similarity logits/scores between the image and each of the text embeddings. We evaluate accuracy via WordNet similarity [15] using the *nltk*[4] library to first compute synsets for the N ground truth tags for an image. Next, we sort the tags in the dictionary by the logit scores following the embedding inference similarity. We select the top N "retrieved" tags, and for each, and calculate the WordNet similarity to each ground truth tag. The similarity ranges from 0 to 1, where 1 represents identical tags. We save the top value (the similarity score for the closest/most relevant ground truth tag) and repeat it for each test image. These values are averaged to form our *WordNet score*. We use this instead of precision/recall, as multiple tags in the dataset can represent very similar (but not identical) concepts. A soft score better encapsulates perceived accuracy of the tags.

We experiment with training CLIP on variants of StyleBabel, presenting results in Table 3. In particular, we quantify the difference in quality between collecting annotation via non-expert crowd annotation (StyleBabel-mturk) and gathering expert anno-

---

[4] https://www.nltk.org/.

Table 3. Ablation experiments for tag generation under the CLIP training setting. We show the benefit of annotating StyleBabel via the proposed GT annotation versus non-expert crowd-sourcing (StyleBabel-mturk). We further demonstrate the benefits of tag annotations individualised to the image-level (FG), compared to cluster-level (coarse).

Data	Model	WordNet score
CLIP Webscale	CLIP [36] baseline	0.168
StyleBabel-mturk	ALADIN-ViT	0.164
StyleBabel (coarse)	CLIP [36]	0.187
StyleBabel (coarse)	ALADIN-ViT	0.225
StyleBabel (FG)	CLIP	0.215
StyleBabel (FG)	ALADIN-ViT	**0.352**

tations using our GA process (StyleBabel/ALADIN-ViT). We also show the value of the final stage, where we refine tags to the image-level (FG) rather than moodboard-level (coarse). We train the MLP heads atop the CLIP image encoder embeddings (the 'CLIP' model) and atop embeddings from our ALADIN-ViT model (the 'ALADIN-ViT' model). The former is not based on the ALADIN-ViT style embedding and under-performs by 40%. The best performing model is the proposed ALADIN-ViT trained via StyleBabel data collected using GA on FG labels, with a WordNet score of **0.352**, double the CLIP [36] baseline. Figure 7 shows some examples of tags generated for various images, using the ALADIN-ViT based model trained under the CLIP method with StyleBabel (FG).

MS-COCO	a woman with a painting of a face on it	a close up of a remote with a remote	a kite that is hanging in the air	a room with a lot of windows and a clock	a person riding a surf-board in the water
StyleBabel CL+IL	digital illustration of a fictional character using dark color tones against a black background	product photography of business cards with text and logo in soft light-ing against a white background	digital illustration featuring characters and typog-raphy using bright colors	illustration architectural photog-raphy of a modern in-terior design in bright lighting using a neu-tral color palette	abstract painting using brush strokes and shading effects	watercolor paint and shading effects

Fig. 8. Examples of natural language captions generated for various art styles; Generated captions are compared from VirTex models trained on MS-COCO and Stylebabel CL+IL, showing the benefit of the style information present in the dataset.

We run a user study on AMT to verify the correctness of the tags generated, present-ing 1000 randomly selected test split images alongside the top tags generated for each. For each image/tags pair, 3 workers are asked to indicate tags that don't fit the image. We score tags as correct if all 3 workers agree they belong. The absolute accuracy of this study is 89.86%, indicating high tag generation accuracy.

Finally, we explore the model's generalization to new styles by evaluating the average WordNet score of images from the test split. In Fig. 9, we group the data samples into 10 *bins* of distances from their respective style cluster centroid, in the style embedding space. As before, we compute the WordNet score of tags generated using our model and compare it to the baseline CLIP model. Though the quality of the CLIP model is constant as samples get further from the training data, the quality of our model is significantly higher for the majority of the data split. At worst, our model performs similar to CLIP and slightly worse for the 5 most extreme samples in the test split. But for the majority of the test data, our model considerably outperforms CLIP.

Table 4. (top) VirTex caption generation metrics on 1k holdout StyleBabel test data, at cluster-level (CL), and image-level (IL). We also run CL+IL, where we fine-tune a CL model with IL data labels. (middle) Results with a baseline LSTM model trained over either ResNet or ALADIN image embeddings (bottom) Additional experiments showing performance of a VirTex model trained on an existing dataset (Artemis), and also evaluated on the StyleBabel (SB) test set.

Data	Model	Bleu-1	Bleu-2	Bleu-3	Bleu-4	METEOR	Rouge-L	CIDEr
MS-COCO baseline	VirTex	0.162	0.053	0.016	0.005	0.037	0.145	0.022
StyleBabel (CL)	VirTex	0.127	0.049	0.022	0.010	0.054	0.135	0.076
StyleBabel (IL)	VirTex	0.331	0.187	0.113	0.071	0.129	0.288	0.350
StyleBabel (CL+IL)	VirTex	**0.335**	**0.189**	**0.118**	**0.078**	**0.131**	**0.288**	**0.372**
StyleBabel (CL+IL)	ResNet LSTM	0.087	0.021	0.008	0.002	0.033	0.080	0.017
StyleBabel (CL+IL)	ALADIN-ViT LSTM	0.094	0.030	0.013	0.006	0.042	0.089	0.034
Artemis	VirTex+AoANet	0.185	0.083	0.041	0.023	0.081	0.182	0.146
Artemis (SB)	VirTex+AoANet	0.120	0.031	0.013	0.005	0.034	0.108	0.029

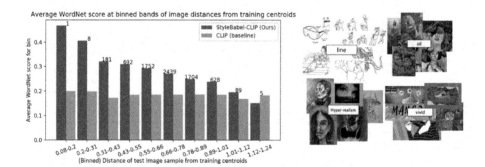

Fig. 9. (left) Generalization experiment for tag generation using baseline CLIP [36] and our Style-Babel trained model using ALADIN-ViT. The test set was sorted by distance in the style embedding space to closest training cluster. Their WordNet scores were binned into 10 quantized distance bands. The numbers atop the bars indicate the number of samples in the corresponding bin. (right) Top 5 style retrieval using textual tags. Using tags generated by ALADIN-ViT/CLIP over the StyleBabel test partition, we perform a keyword based search for artistic style.

6.2 Style Description (style2text)

We explore the feasibility of using the StyleBabel dataset for generating natural language captions. We conduct our experiments using a fusion of the VirTex [11] backbone for the visual representation learning of image/caption pairs, and Attention on Attention (AoA) [20] for the caption decoding. VirTex encodes images without using scene graphs, therefore avoiding issues related to style not being localized in an image. VirTex replaces the Faster-RCNN [39] component in AoA to generate feature maps. We use the pre-trained VirTex on COCO [31], and fine-tune the entire setup, end-to-end on final StyleBabel captions. As per standard practice, during data pre-processing, we remove words with only a single occurrence in the dataset. Removing 45.07% of unique words from the total vocabulary, or 0.22% of all the words in the dataset. We test the caption generation on the StyleBabel test data across Bleu [33], METEOR [26], Rouge [30], and CIDEr [48], as shown in Table 4. See the supplementary material for further analysis.

We would like to stress that these metrics are not comparable with values from these metrics on standard literature, as we are solving a new task. In literature, these metrics are used for semantic, localized features in images, whereas our task is to generate captions for global, style features of an image. We include an MS-COCO baseline, to show comparative accuracy versus a dataset with no style information. Figure 8 displays captions generated using this method.

6.3 Text Based Style Retrieval (text2style)

We explore the potential of the ALADIN-ViT+CLIP model trained in Subsect. 6.1 to perform image retrieval, using textual tag queries. By first indexing the score assigned to each tag in the dictionary at the image level, we can then use a tag query to retrieve images based on the sorted scores for that tag. We use nearest-neighbour search using the image embeddings, reversing the tags generation experiment. Figure 9 shows some example image retrievals using text queries.

To measure the quality of the results, we run all text tags as queries. For each, we compute the WordNet similarity of the query text tag to the kth top tag associated with the image, following a tag retrieval using a given image. We vary k and collect the average scores at values of 1, 5, 10, and 25. The scores at these values are 0.72, 0.467, 0.392, and 0.332, respectively.

7   Conclusion

We proposed StyleBabel, a novel unique dataset of digital artworks and associated text describing their fine-grained artistic style. Our annotation approach was inspired by Grounded Theory (GT) [44], to support the 'emergence' of themes from the corpus of digital artwork – as opposed to fitting images to pre-existing categories [6]. These sessions generated discussion while simultaneously evolving and arriving through consensus at a shared vocabulary for describing image clusters of similar style.

We extended ALADIN [41] to incorporate a visual transformer [12] (ALADIN-ViT) encoder, obtaining state of the art style similarity discrimination, leveraging StyleBabel for the automated description of artwork images using keyword tags and captions. We also showed text-based image retrieval of images based on the generated style tags. Further work could explore use of tags as priors in generating captions, and exploring more downstream tasks using StyleBabel.

Acknowledgement. We would like to thank Thomas Gittings, Tu Bui, Alex Black, and Dipu Manandhar for their time, patience, and hard work, assisting with invigilating and managing the group annotation stages during data collection and annotation.

References

1. von Ahn, L., Dabbish, L.A.: ESP: labeling images with a computer game, pp. 91–98 (2005)
2. Achlioptas, P., Ovsjanikov, M., Haydarov, K., Elhoseiny, M., Guibas, L.: Artemis: affective language for visual art. In: Proceedings of CVPR (2021)
3. Bai, Z., Nakashima, Y., Garcia, N.: Explain me the painting: multi-topic knowledgeable art description generation. CoRR, arXiv:2109.05743 (2021)
4. Bell, S., Bala, K.: Learning visual similarity for product design with convolutional neural networks. In: Proceedings of ACM SIGGRAPH (2015)
5. Bianco, S., Celona, L., Napoletano, P., Schettini, R.: Predicting image aesthetics with deep learning. In: Blanc-Talon, J., Distante, C., Philips, W., Popescu, D., Scheunders, P. (eds.) ACIVS 2016. LNCS, vol. 10016, pp. 117–125. Springer, Cham (2016). https://doi.org/10.1007/978-3-319-48680-2_11
6. Kathy, C.: Constructing Grounded Theory: A Practical Guide through Qualitative Analysis. Sage, London (2006)
7. Cetinic, E., Grgic, S.: Automated painter recognition based on image feature extraction. In: Proceedings of ELMAR (2013)
8. Chen, T., Kornblith, S., Norouzi, M., Hinton, G.: A simple framework for contrastive learning of visual representations. arXiv preprint arXiv:2002.05709 (2020)
9. Collomosse, J., Bui, T., Wilber, M., Fang, C., Jin, H.: Sketching with style: visual search with sketches and aesthetic context. In: Proceedings of ICCV (2017)
10. Cornia, M., Stefanini, M., Baraldi, L., Cucchiara, R.: Meshed-memory transformer for image captioning. arXiv preprint arXiv:1912.08226 (2020)
11. Desai, K., Johnson, J.: Virtex: learning visual representations from textual annotations. CoRR, arXiv:2006.06666 (2020)
12. Dosovitskiy, A., et al.: An image is worth 16x16 words: transformers for image recognition at scale. arXiv preprint arXiv:2010.11929 (2020)
13. Farhadi, A., et al.: Every picture tells a story: generating sentences from images. In: Daniilidis, K., Maragos, P., Paragios, N. (eds.) ECCV 2010. LNCS, vol. 6314, pp. 15–29. Springer, Heidelberg (2010). https://doi.org/10.1007/978-3-642-15561-1_2
14. Eric, F.: Art History and its Methods: A Critical Anthology. Phaidon, London (1995)
15. Fellbaum, C.: WordNet: An Electronic Lexical Database. Bradford Books (1998)
16. Garcia, N., Vogiatzis, G.: How to read paintings: semantic art understanding with multimodal retrieval. CoRR, arXiv:1810.09617 (2018)
17. Gatys, L.A., Ecker, A.S., Bethge, M.: A neural algorithm of artistic style. arXiv preprint arXiv:1508.06576 (2015)
18. Ghiasi, G., Lee, H., Kudlur, M., Dumoulin, V., Shlens, J.: Exploring the structure of a real-time, arbitrary neural artistic stylization network. arXiv preprint arXiv:1705.06830 (2017)
19. Ghosal, K., Rana, A., Smolic, A.: Aesthetic image captioning from weakly-labelled photographs. CoRR, arXiv:1908.11310 (2019)

20. Huang, L., Wang, W., Chen, J., Wei, X.: Attention on attention for image captioning. CoRR, arXiv:1908.06954 (2019)
21. Huang, X., Belongie, S.: Arbitrary style transfer in real-time with adaptive instance normalization. In: Proceedings of ICCV (2017)
22. Huang, X., Liu, M.-Y., Belongie, S., Kautz, J.: Multimodal unsupervised image-to-image translation. In: Ferrari, V., Hebert, M., Sminchisescu, C., Weiss, Y. (eds.) ECCV 2018. LNCS, vol. 11207, pp. 179–196. Springer, Cham (2018). https://doi.org/10.1007/978-3-030-01219-9_11
23. Johnson, J., Alahi, A., Fei-Fei, L.: Perceptual losses for real-time style transfer and super-resolution. In: Leibe, B., Matas, J., Sebe, N., Welling, M. (eds.) ECCV 2016. LNCS, vol. 9906, pp. 694–711. Springer, Cham (2016). https://doi.org/10.1007/978-3-319-46475-6_43
24. Karayev, S., et al.: Recognizing image style. In: Proceedings of BMVC (2014)
25. Kulkarni, G., et al.: Babytalk: understanding and generating simple image descriptions. IEEE Trans. Pattern Anal. Mach. Intell. **35**(12), 2891–2903 (2013)
26. Lavie, A., Agarwal, A.: Meteor: an automatic metric for MT evaluation with high levels of correlation with human judgments, pp. 228–231 (2007)
27. Xu, L., Meroño-Peñuela, A., Huang, Z., Harmelen, F.V.: An ontology model for narrative image annotation in the field of cultural heritage. In: WHiSe@ISWC (2017)
28. Li, X., et al.: Oscar: object-semantics aligned pre-training for vision-language tasks. arXiv preprint arXiv:2004.06165 (2020)
29. Li, Y., Fang, C., Yang, J., Wang, Z., Lu, X., Yang, M.: Universal style transfer via feature transforms. In: Proceedings of NIPS (2017)
30. Lin, C.-Y.: Rouge: a package for automatic evaluation of summaries, p. 10 (2004)
31. Lin, T.-Y., et al.: Microsoft COCO: common objects in context. CoRR, arXiv:1405.0312 (2014)
32. Pang, K., Yang, Y., Hospedales, T.M., Xiang, T., Song, Y.: Solving mixed-modal jigsaw puzzle for fine-grained sketch-based image retrieval. In: 2020 IEEE/CVF Conference on Computer Vision and Pattern Recognition (CVPR), Los Alamitos, CA, USA, pp. 10344–10352. IEEE Computer Society (2020)
33. Papineni, K., Roukos, S., Ward, T., Zhu, W.-J.: Bleu: a method for automatic evaluation of machine translation. In: Proceedings of the 40th Annual Meeting on Association for Computational Linguistics, USA, ACL 2002, pp. 311–318. Association for Computational Linguistics (2002)
34. Park, T., et al.: Swapping autoencoder for deep image manipulation. In: Proceedings of ECCV (2020)
35. Pinotti, A.: Formalism and the History of Style, pp. 75–90. Brill, Leiden (2012)
36. Radford, A., et al.: Learning transferable visual models from natural language supervision. arXiv preprint arXiv:2103.00020 (2021)
37. Ramesh, A., et al.: Zero-shot text-to-image generatio. arXiv preprint arXiv:2102.12092 (2021)
38. Ramesh, A., et al.: Zero-shot text-to-image generation. arXiv preprint arXiv:2102.12092 (2021)
39. Ren, S., He, K., Girshick, R., Sun, J.: Faster R-CNN: towards real-time object detection with region proposal networks. CoRR, arXiv:1506.01497 (2015)
40. Ruder, M., Dosovitskiy, A., Brox, T.: Artistic style transfer for videos. In: Proceedings of GCPR (2016)
41. Ruta, D., et al.: Aladin: all layer adaptive instance normalization for fine-grained style similarity. arXiv preprint arXiv:2103.09776 (2021)
42. Saleh, B., Elgammal, A.: Large-scale classification of fine-art paintings: learning the right metric on the right feature (2015)

43. Shamir, L., Macura, T., Orlov, N., Eckley, D.: Impressionism, expressionism, surrealism: automated recognition of painters and schools of art. IEEE Trans. Appl. Percept. (2010)

44. Simondsen, J., Roberton, T.: Routledge International Handbook of Participatory Design. Routledge, London (2013)

45. Simonyan, K., Zisserman, A.: Very deep convolutional networks for large-scale image recognition. arXiv preprint arXiv:1409.1556 (2014)

46. Srinivas, A., Lin, T.-Y., Parmar, N., Shlens, J., Abbeel, P., Vaswani, A.: Bottleneck transformers for visual recognition. arXiv preprint arXiv:2101.11605 (2021)

47. Ulyanov, D., Lebedev, V., Vedaldi, A., Lempitsky, V.: Texture networks: feed-forward synthesis of textures and stylized images. In: Proceedings of ICML (2016)

48. Vedantam, R., Lawrence Zitnick, C., Parikh, D.: Cider: consensus-based image description evaluation. CoRR, arXiv:1411.5726 (2014)

49. Vinyals, O., Toshev, A., Bengio, S., Erhan, D.: Show and tell: a neural image caption generator. arXiv preprint arXiv:1411.4555 (2015)

50. Wang, X., Oxholm, G., Zhang, D., Wang, Y.-F.: Multimodal transfer: a hierarchical deep convolutional neural network for fast artistic style transfer. In: Proceedings of CVPR (2017)

51. Wei, X.-S., Luo, J.-H., Wu, J., Zhou, Z.-H.: Selective convolutional descriptor aggregation for fine-grained image retrieval. arXiv preprint arXiv:1604.04994 (2017)

52. Wilber, M.J., Fang, C., Jin, H., Hertzmann, A., Collomosse, J., Belongie, S.: Bam! the behance artistic media dataset for recognition beyond photography. arXiv preprint arXiv:1704.08614 (2017)

53. Xu, L., Wang, X.: Semantic description of cultural digital images: using a hierarchical model and controlled vocabulary. D Lib Mag. 21(5/6) (2015)

54. Yao, B., Khosla, A., Fei-Fei, L.: Combining randomization and discrimination for fine-grained image categorization. In: CVPR 2011, pp. 1577–1584 (2011)

55. Zhang, P., et al.: Vinvl: revisiting visual representations in vision-language models. arXiv preprint arXiv:2101.00529 (2021)

56. Zhou, L., Palangi, H., Zhang, L., Hu, H., Corso, J.J., Gao, J.: Unified vision-language pretraining for image captioning and VQA. arXiv preprint arXiv:1909.11059 (2019)

57. Zujovic, J., Gandy, L., Friedman, S., Pardo, B., Pappas, T.N.: Classifying paintings by artistic genre: an analysis of features and classifiers. In: Proceedings of IEEE Workshop on Multimedia Signal Processing (MMSP) (2009)

PANDORA: A Panoramic Detection Dataset for Object with Orientation

Hang Xu[1,2], Qiang Zhao[2(✉)], Yike Ma[2], Xiaodong Li[3], Peng Yuan[3], Bailan Feng[3], Chenggang Yan[1,4], and Feng Dai[2(✉)]

[1] Hangzhou Dianzi University, Hangzhou, China
{hxu,cgyan}@hdu.edu.cn
[2] Institute of Computing Technology, Chinese Academy of Sciences, Beijing, China
{zhaoqiang,ykma,fdai}@ict.ac.cn
[3] Huawei Noah's Ark Lab, Beijing, China
{lixiaodong33,yuanpeng126,fengbailan}@huawei.com
[4] State Key Laboratory of Media Convergence Production Technology and Systems, Beijing, China

Abstract. Panoramic images have become increasingly popular as omnidirectional panoramic technology has advanced. Many datasets and works resort to object detection to better understand the content of the panoramic image. These datasets and detectors use a Bounding Field of View (BFoV) as a bounding box in panoramic images. However, we observe that the object instances in panoramic images often appear with arbitrary orientations. It indicates that BFoV as a bounding box is inappropriate, limiting the performance of detectors. This paper proposes a new bounding box representation, Rotated Bounding Field of View (RBFoV), for the panoramic image object detection task. Then, based on the RBFoV, we present a PANoramic Detection dataset for Object with oRientAtion (PANDORA). Finally, based on PANDORA, we evaluate the current state-of-the-art panoramic image object detection methods and design an anchor-free object detector called R-CenterNet for panoramic images. Compared with these baselines, our R-CenterNet shows its advantages in terms of detection performance. Our PANDORA dataset and source code are available at https://github.com/tdsuper/SphericalObjectDetection.

Keywords: PANDORA · Panoramic · Object detection · RBFoV

1 Introduction

In the past few years, with the numerous development of panoramic cameras with omnidirectional vision, the applications of panoramic images are also becoming

H. Xu and Q. Zhao—This work was done when Hang Xu and Qiang Zhao were at ICT.

Supplementary Information The online version contains supplementary material available at https://doi.org/10.1007/978-3-031-20074-8_14.

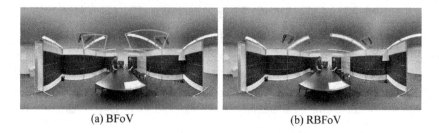

(a) BFoV   (b) RBFoV

Fig. 1. Visualization of two annotation methods (i.e., BFoV and RBFoV). (a) is a failure case of the BFoV annotation, which brings high overlap compared to (b). In our PANDORA dataset, we use the RBFoV as the bounding box.

more and more extensive, such as virtual reality [9], robotics [8], street view [2, 38,39], etc. As these panoramic data increase, the demand for panoramic object detection tasks increases [20,27,34]. Object detection has achieved an excellent performance in planar images, even comparable to human vision [12,25,32,40]. This is mainly attributed to the publication of large-scale planar image object detection datasets such as Pascal VOC [5], COCO [13], etc. However, object detection in panoramic images is still challenging for the following two reasons, as listed below:

Appropriate Annotations are Lacking. Object detection necessitates the location of objects and the computation of metrics, i.e., bounding box (BB) and intersection-over-union (IoU). Previous works either introduced bias in the BB [11,26] or could not calculate the IoU accurately [1]. Recent works [33,35] use the Bounding Field of View (BFoV) [24] as BB and precisely compute IoU by spherical geometry, making the BFoV the dominant representation of the bounding box in panoramic object detection. Objects without many orientations can be adequately annotated with this method. However, the object instances in panoramic images often appear with arbitrary orientations, depending on the observer's perspective. In an actually common condition as shown in Fig. 1, the overlap between two BFoVs is so large that state-of-the-art (SOTA) object detectors cannot differentiate them. In Sect. 6.1, we provide the quantifications regarding the overlap issue and show that using RBFoV we proposed enhances the detector's performance.

Labeling Objects are Complex. First, since the panoramic image has a 360° view, there are many objects of different sizes and categories in a panoramic image. Second, panoramic image is typically represented by equirectangular projection (ERP) [4]. The ERP is generated by polar transformation and thus suffers from distortion in the polar regions and discontinuity on the boundary [36]. Especially, the distortion in the polar regions is severe, which causes the annotator to be unable to identify these objects in the polar regions well. For these reasons, the development of panoramic object detection is greatly limited, resulting in the poor performance of the existing methods.

To address the above challenges, we propose a new bounding box representation, Rotated Bounding Field of View (RBFoV), for the panoramic image object detection task. Then, based on the RBFoV, we develop a new annotation tool to annotate objects at the polar regions and the boundary in panoramic images easily, and we present a PANoramic Detection dataset for Object with oRientAtion (PANDORA) in this work. To our best knowledge, PANDORA is the first dataset to use the RBFoV as the bounding box. It can be used to develop and evaluate object detectors in panoramic images. Finally, based on PANDORA, we evaluate the current SOTA methods and design an anchor-free object detector called R-CenterNet. Compared with these baselines, our R-CenterNet shows its advantages in terms of detection performance.

2   Related Work

2.1   Existing Bounding Boxes

The existing bounding box definitions are mainly divided into three representations, i.e., planar rectangle, circle and spherical rectangle. The works in [29,31] and [26] use the planar rectangle as the bounding box. This bounding box representation does not consider the distortions of panoramic images. Thus it is biased representations and has large errors. The work in [11] exploit the circular as the bouding box in the panoramic object detection. However, circular may exceed panoramic's upper or lower boundaries when the objects are near the pole. The works in [1,33] and [35] utilizes the Bounding Field of View (BFoV) as the bounding box. This bounding box is called a spherical rectangle, which is an unbiased representation. The BFoV is currently the most dominant bounding box representation in panoramic object detection.

2.2   Panoramic Object Detection Dataset

Till now, existing panoramic image object detection datasets can be roughly divided into two subsets, i.e., synthetic dataset and natural scenes dataset. Because of the difficulty of panoramic image annotation, early methods [1,23,33] for panoramic object detection used synthetic datasets. However, the synthetic dataset cannot adequately reflect the problem complexity in the natural scene. The natural scenes dataset popular benchmarks mainly include OSV [31], ERA [29] and 360-indoor [3]. These datasets are manually annotated on panoramic images of natural scenes. Therefore, they can better validate the performance of the panoramic object detection model compared to the synthetic datasets above. However, the bounding box they use is not the suitable in panoramic object detection task.

As a result, we present a PANoramic Detection dataset for Object with oRientAtion (PANDORA) in this work. Table 1 lists the existed panoramic object detection dataset for comparison.

Table 1. Existing panoramic object detection dataset comparison. The BBoX is the planar rectangle.

Dataset	Domain	Annotation	#Category	#Boxes
OSV [31]	Street scenes	BBoX	5	5,636
FlyingCars [1]	Synthesis cars	BFoV	1	6,000
ERA [29]	Dynamic activities	BFoV	10	7,199
360-Indoor [3]	Indoor scenes	BFoV	37	89,148
PANDORA	Indoor scenes	**RBFoV**	**47**	**94,353**

2.3 Panoramic Image Object Detection

Multi-projection YOLO [29] handles projection distortions by making multiple stereographic sub-projections. Then each sub-projection is separately processed by the YOLO detector. Multi-kernel [26] introduces multi-kernel layers for improving accuracy for distorted object detection and adds position information into the model for learning spatial information. Sphere-SSD [1] is the spherical single shot multi-box detector with the RMSProp optimizer to panoramic images. SpherePHD [11] utilizes a spherical polyhedron to represent Omni-directional views, which minimizes the variance of the spatial resolving power on the sphere surface. Reprojection R-CNN [33] is a two-stage panoramic object detector. The first stage generates coarse proposals, and the second stage refines the proposals to yield precise BFoVs. Sph-CenterNet [35] is an anchor-free object detection algorithm for spherical images. It adds the geometry for spherical images.

3 RBFoV

3.1 RBFoV Representation

The bounding box and IoU are a fundamental part of the object detector, where the positive and negative sample definition, NMS [16] and mAP [6] are all defined on those two elements. Therefore, it is important to establish a reasonable bounding box representation and an accurate and efficient IoU calculation method for the panoramic image object detection task.

We use the RBFoV as the bouding box. The RBFoV is defined by $(\theta, \phi, \alpha, \beta, \gamma)$, where θ and ϕ are the longitude and latitude coordinates of the object center, and α, β denote the up-down and left-right field-of-view angles of the object's occupation, γ represents the angle (clockwise is positive, counterclockwise is negative) of the rotation of the tangent plane of the RBFoV along the axis $\vec{OM}$ (The M is the tangent point (θ, ϕ)), as shown in Fig. 2(a,b). The range of values of γ is $[-90, 90]$.

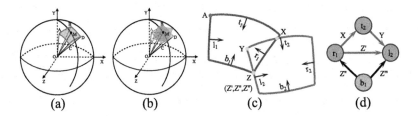

Fig. 2. (a) The RBFoV can be represented by either a spherical rectangle (red) or a tangent plane (blue) with M as the tangent point. (b) The angle γ (i.e., $\angle AMA'$) in the RBFoV is obtained by rotating the tangent plane along the axis $\vec{OM}$. (c) The intersection area of two RBFoVs is determined from the normal vectors $[\vec{t}_i, \vec{b}_i, \vec{l}_i, \vec{r}_i]$ of the planes that the neighboring sides of each RBFoV lie on. (d) We create the directed graph and use the DFS algorithm [19] to remove duplicated points. (Color figure online)

3.2 IoU Calculation Between Two RBFoVs

The shape of a RBFoV $(\theta, \phi, \alpha, \beta, \gamma)$ can be regarded as a spherical rectangle. The work in [35] gives the formula of the area for a spherical rectangle:

$$Area(B) = 4\arccos(-\sin\frac{\alpha}{2}\sin\frac{\beta}{2}) - 2\pi. \tag{1}$$

In order to compute the intersection area between two RBFoVs, we need to obtain the normal vectors $[\vec{t}, \vec{b}, \vec{l}, \vec{r}]$ of the planes that the neighboring sides of each RBFoV lie on. The normal vector derivation is given in the supplementary material. Next, the intersection points are obtained by normal vectors. The intersection points may contain the vertices of RBFoVs and the intersection points of boundaries. Vertices can be easily calculated by cross multiplication of two normal vector of RBFoV boundary planes, e.g. Vertex A is obtained by $\vec{t}_1 \times \vec{l}_1$ shown in Fig. 2(c). The intersection points of boundaries can be computed by cross multiplication of two normal vectors, one is from the first RBFoV and another from the second, e.g., as shown in Fig. 2(c), Point X is computed by $\vec{r}_1 \times \vec{t}_2$. In addition, some points that are duplicate or outside the intersection region must be removed. We first conduct dot product of points and normal vectors, and all result values not less than 0 are the inner points. Then we remove duplicated points, such as Point Z shown in Fig. 2(c), by creating the directed graph and using DFS algorithm [19] to find real intersection points in red Fig. 2(d). Finally, normal vectors of boundaries for real intersection points are conducted by dot product to calculate spherical angles of the intersection region. Based on spherical angles, we can find the area of the intersection region using the following formula [28]:

$$A(B_1 \cap B_2) = \sum_{i=1}^{n} \omega_i - (n-2)\pi, \tag{2}$$

where n is the number of intersection points, ω is the spherical angle of the intersection region.

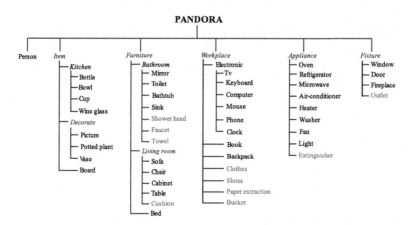

Fig. 3. Categories in our PANDORA dataset. The italic font denotes the super-categories, and the black font denotes the 37 categories in the existing 360-indoor [3] dataset, and the red font denotes the 10 categories added to our PANDORA dataset. There are 47 categories in our PANDORA dataset. (Color figure online)

4   PANDORA Dataset

In this section, based on the RBFoV, we present a PANoramic Detection dataset for Object with oRientAtion (PANDORA).

4.1   Image Collection

We aim to cover diverse indoor scenarios in our PANDORA dataset. We selected some popular indoor scenes. Based on these scenes, we collected 3, 000 panoramic images, of which most are from the 360cities and Flickr. Specifically, we consider three main aspects when selecting images, namely, **1)** images of the real world, **2)** many instances per image, and **3)** many different indoor scenes, which make the dataset approach real-world applications. All images are with 1, 920 × 960 resolution.

4.2   Category Selection

Forty-seven categories are chosen and annotated in our PANDORA dataset. The first 37 categories are in the existing dataset [3], we keep them all. Others are added mainly from the values in real applications. For example, we select *extinguishers* considering that measures for conflagration prevention are of significant importance indoor. We also add some categories which are common in the indoor scenes, such as *shoes, clothes, cushion*, etc. Next, similar to 360-indoor, we classify the object categories into five super-categories, except *person*. Each super-category represents a kind of scene. Figure 3 shows the 48 categories selected for annotation and the super categories in the PANDORA.

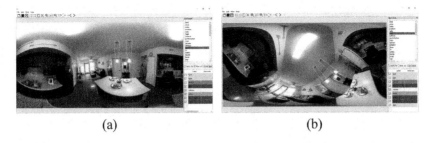

(a)   (b)

Fig. 4. The annotation tool of object detection for panoramic images. For objects with orientation, the annotator can rotate the annotation box to better bounding the object, as shown in (a). For objects of the poles, the annotator can rotate the image to find the appropriate annotation view, as shown in (b).

4.3   Image Annotation

In existing panoramic image annotation tools, such as the tool in [3], annotators are asked first to choose a viewpoint and use the buttons to adjust the bounding box size. Compared with LabelImg [14], which is inefficient. According to the particularity of panoramic images, we find that the planar rectangle in the panoramic image can be converted to the spherical rectangle. Based on this, we designed an annotation tool similar to LabelImg, as shown in Fig. 4 For objects in the polar regions and on the boundary, annotators can rotate the panoramic image to find the appropriate annotation view, as shown in Fig. 4(b).

4.4   Dataset Statistics

Next, we analyze the properties of the PANDORA dataset. Our PANDORA contains 3,000 images, including 94,353 bounding box from 47 categories. We split the dataset into trainning and testing set with 0.7 and 0.3. Firstly, we show the distribution of the top 10 categories and the number of per image instances in Fig. 5(a) and Fig. 5(b). In addition, aspect ratio (AR) is an essential factor for object detection models, such as Faster RCNN [22], SSD [15] and YOLOv2 [21]. We count the AR for all the instances in our PANDORA dataset to provide a reference for better model design. Figure 5(c) illustrates the distribution of aspect ratio for instances in our PANDORA dataset. We can see that instances varies greatly in aspect ratio. Moreover, there are a large number of instances with a large aspect ratio in our dataset. Finally, we analyze the distribution of latitude coordinates of object center in PANDORA in Fig. 5(d). The majority of objects appear between latitudes of $0°$ to $\pm 50°$. It is common because objects appear more often at the image center than at the polar regions in indoor scenes. There is less distortion of the object in the panoramic image center, but the distortion becomes more pronounced when the object is near the polar regions. The PANDORA dataset provides data of many objects at the polar regions that can assist the model in recognizing the high latitudes region.

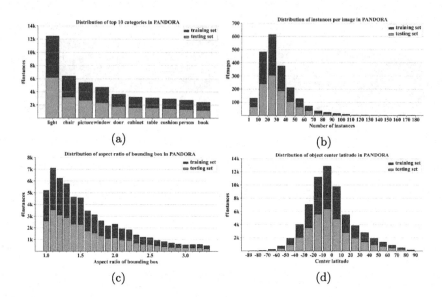

Fig. 5. Statistics of instances in PANDORA. (a) Number of annotated instances per category in the top 10 categories for PANDORA. (b) Number of annotated instances per image for PANDORA. (c) The aspect ratio of bounding box. (d) Distribution of latitude coordinates of object center in PANDORA.

5   R-CenterNet

We propose an anchor-free object detection method based on Sph-CenterNet [35], called R-CenterNet, to evaluate our PANDORA dataset better. In addition, we propose a panoramic rotation data augmentation technique that can increase the diversity of training data.

5.1   Network Architecture and Loss Definition

We use the anchor-free detection Sph-CenterNet [35] as the baseline. First, we need to clarify that the network has not changed the output of the original regression branch. To predict the RBFoV, we add a branch to regress the rotation angle γ of the RBFoV, as illustrated in Fig. 6. We use direct and indirect two forms for the regression of γ.

First, for direct regression, the model directly predicts the angle $\hat{\gamma}$ to match the ground truth γ:

$$L_{direct} = \frac{1}{N} \sum_{i=1}^{N} |\gamma_i - \hat{\gamma}_i|, \tag{3}$$

where γ_i and $\hat{\gamma}_i$ are the target and predicted rotation angles for object i; and N is the number of positive samples.

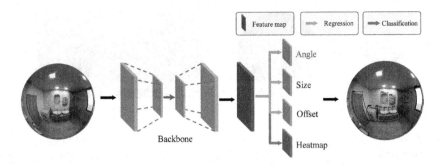

Fig. 6. Overall framework of our R-CenterNet. The network takes panoramic images as input, and predicts heatmaps, offsets, sizes and angles.

Second, for indirect regression, the R-CenterNet predicts two vectors ($\sin \hat{\gamma}$ and $\cos \hat{\gamma}$) to match the two targets from the ground truth ($\sin \gamma$ and $\cos \gamma$):

$$L_{indirect} = \frac{1}{N} \sum_{i=1}^{N} |\sin \gamma_i - \sin \hat{\gamma}_i| + |\cos \gamma_i - \cos \hat{\gamma}_i| . \tag{4}$$

We will carry out the normalization processing to make $\sin \hat{\gamma}^2 + \cos \hat{\gamma}^2 = 1$:

$$\sin \hat{\gamma} = \frac{\sin \hat{\gamma}}{\sqrt{\sin^2 \hat{\gamma} + \cos^2 \hat{\gamma}}}, \quad \cos \hat{\gamma} = \frac{\cos \hat{\gamma}}{\sqrt{\sin^2 \hat{\gamma} + \cos^2 \hat{\gamma}}}. \tag{5}$$

Thus, the overall training objective of our model is

$$L_{det} = L_{cls} + \lambda_{size} L_{size} + \lambda_{off} L_{off} + \lambda_{ang}(L_{direct} + L_{indirect}), \tag{6}$$

where L_{cls}, L_{size} and L_{off} are the losses of center point recognition, scale regression, and offset regression, which are the same as Sph-CenterNet; and λ_{size}, λ_{off} and λ_{ang} are constant factors, set to 0.1 in our experiments.

5.2   Implementation Details

Generating Ground-Truth Heatmaps. When assigning ground-truth information to heatmaps in the Sph-CenterNet, cells around the center point of a bounding box showed an independent Gaussian density, which draws a circle in the sphere regardless of the actual shape and orientation of the object in panoramic images. We propose a new method of assigning ground-truth that can change the shape of the Gaussian according to the shape and orientation of the objects, as illustrated in Fig. 7.

First, for each point (u, v) within the RBFoV, the corresponding coordinates in tangent plane $\Pi[\theta, \phi]$ could be calculated via the gnomonic projection [18,37]:

$$x(u, v) = \frac{\cos u \, \sin(v - \phi)}{\sin \theta \, \sin u + \cos \theta \, \cos u \, \cos(v - \phi)},$$

$$y(u, v) = \frac{\cos \theta \, \sin v - \sin \theta \, \cos u \, \cos(v - \phi)}{\sin \theta \, \sin u + \cos \theta \, \cos u \, \cos(v - \phi)}. \tag{7}$$

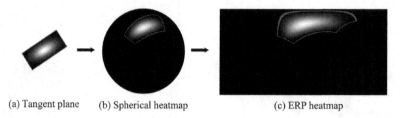

(a) Tangent plane   (b) Spherical heatmap   (c) ERP heatmap

Fig. 7. (a) We convert the tangent plane Π of the RBFoV into a 2-D Gaussian distribution. (b) The tangent plane Π projects back onto the spherical heatmap. (c) We project the spherical heatmap to the ERP heatmap.

The $\Pi[\theta, \phi]$ is an oriented rectangle $B(\theta, \phi, w, h, \gamma)$, where $w = 2\tan(0.5\alpha)$ and $h = 2\tan(0.5\beta)$. As illustrated in Fig. 7(a), we convert the Π into a 2-D Gaussian distribution $\mathcal{N}(\mu, \sigma^2)$ by the following formula [30]:

$$\sigma = \mathbf{R\Lambda R}^\top = \begin{pmatrix} \cos\gamma & -\sin\gamma \\ \sin\gamma & \cos\gamma \end{pmatrix} \begin{pmatrix} \frac{w}{2} & 0 \\ 0 & \frac{h}{2} \end{pmatrix} \begin{pmatrix} \cos\gamma & \sin\gamma \\ -\sin\gamma & \cos\gamma \end{pmatrix} \tag{8}$$

$$\mu = (\theta, \phi)$$

where $\mathbf{R}$ represents the rotation matrix, and $\mathbf{\Lambda}$ represents the diagonal matrix of eigenvalues.

Then, as illustrated in Fig. 7(b), the inverse gnomonic projection is used to prject the $\Pi[\theta, \phi]$ back onto the spherical heatmap by the following formula [18]:

$$u(x, y) = \sin^{-1}(\cos\nu\sin\theta + \frac{y\sin\nu\cos\theta}{\rho}),$$

$$v(x, y) = \phi + \tan^{-1}\left(\frac{x\sin\nu}{\rho\cos\theta\cos\nu - y\sin\theta\sin\nu}\right). \tag{9}$$

where $\rho = \sqrt{x^2 + y^2}$ and $\nu = \tan^{-1}\rho$.

Last, we project the spherical heatmap to the ERP heatmap, As illustrated in Fig. 7(c). The ERP heatmap is the ground-truth Y_{xyc}. If two Gaussians of the same class overlap, we take the element-wise maximum.

5.3   Panoramic Rotation Data Augmentation

For a panoramic image, we propose to rotate the panoramic image by η angle along n-axis in 3-D space to augment training data, where η and n are arbitrary values. To achieve this goal, we first represent each pixel under UV space as (u, v) where $u \in [-\pi, \pi], v \in [-\pi/2, \pi/2]$. The coordinate (u, v) can be easily computed as the column and row of an equirectangular image. We project the pixels to 3-D space and multiply their x, y, z by the rotation matrix $\mathcal{T}(n, \eta)$, where n is the axis and η is the angle of rotation along the axis. The equation

$n = (0,0,0), \eta = 0$ $n = (1,1,1), \eta = 30$

$n = (0,1,1), \eta = 30$ $n = (1,1,1), \eta = 60$

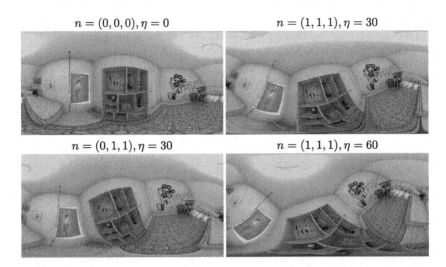

Fig. 8. Visualization of the proposed *Panoramic Rotation Data Augmentation*. We rotate the panoramic image by η angle along n-axis. The green bounding box is RBFoV. This augmentation strategy improves our quantitative results under experiment settings (Table 4).

of rotated x', y', z' are shown in Eq. 10.

$$\begin{pmatrix} x' \\ y' \\ z' \end{pmatrix} = \mathcal{T}(n,\eta) \cdot \left(x \ y \ z \right)^\top = \mathcal{T}(n,\eta) \cdot \begin{pmatrix} \cos(v) \cdot \sin(u) \\ \sin(v) \\ \cos(v) \cdot \cos(u) \end{pmatrix} \quad (10)$$

We can then project the rotated points back to the sphere by Eq. 11 for further equirectangular projection. $atan2$ in the equation is 2-argument arctangent.

$$\begin{aligned} u' &= atan2(x', z'), \\ v' &= atan2(y', \sqrt{(x')^2 + (z')^2}). \end{aligned} \quad (11)$$

After that, we need to obtain the parameters in the RBFoV after the panoramic image rotation. As we rotate the panoramic image by η angle along n-axis, the $b(\theta, \phi, \alpha, \beta, \gamma)$ become $b'(\theta', \phi', \alpha, \beta, \gamma')$. The θ' and ϕ' can be obtained from Eq. 10–11. The vertex A^* is obtained from the bounding box $(\theta', \phi', \alpha, \beta, 0)$, which can be found by rotating vertice A^* by γ' angle along the axis $\vec{OM}$ (M is the tangent point (θ', ϕ')) to obtain vertice A'.

$$\gamma' = \arccos(\vec{MA'}, \vec{MA^*}) \quad (12)$$

Figure 8 is the visualization we proposed Panoramic Rotation Data Augmentation.

Table 2. Quantify the study of BFoV and RBFoV as bounding boxes in panoramic images. Ground truths for BFoV experiments are generated by calculating the minimum bounding BFoVs over original annotated RBFoVs.

Method	Bounding box	$\mathbb{A}$	$\mathbb{B}$	$\mathbb{C}$	AP_{50}
Sph-CenterNet	BFoV	0.23	0.19	0.27	20.3
	RBFoV	0.11	0.07	0.18	**21.4** (+1.1)

6   Experiment

6.1   Quantify BFoV and RBFoV

Figure 1 is a visual example, which clearly shows how BFoVs lead to the significant overlap in bounding boxes where there should be none. To further explore the effect of the BFoV and RBFoV on the detector's performance, we design three metrics as follows:

$$\mathbb{A} = \frac{affected\ instances}{total\ instances}, \quad \mathbb{B} = \frac{overlap\ misses}{total\ misses}, \quad \mathbb{C} = \frac{overlap\ misses}{overlap\ cases}. \tag{13}$$

When IoU ≥ 0.3, we consider this an *affected instance* or *overlap case*. We consider it an *overlap miss* when the affected instance is incorrectly recognized or location (i.e., the IoU of predicted RBFoV and ground truth RBFoV ≥ 0.5). In addition to presenting Fig. 1, $\mathbb{A}$ is to quantify how common two nearby objects overlapped with BFoVs and RBFoVs representations in our dataset. $\mathbb{B}$ quantifies the percentage of all missed detections due to this overlap, which gives an idea of how different box impacts total performance. $\mathbb{C}$ quantities the percentage of times this overlap is not detected when it should have been, which gives an idea of how bad SOTA detection methods are at addressing this inappropriate bounding box.

We use Sph-CenterNet [35] as baseline. To input a image, aim of Sph-CenterNet is to predict the BFoV for each object. To predict the RBFoV, we add a branch to regress the rotation angle of the RBFoV and use direct and indirect regression loss for angle γ. As shown in Table 2, we provide the quantifications regarding the overlap issue and show that using RBFoV reduces these error percentages. The results in Table 2 verify our analysis: compared with BFoV, RBFoV is more reasonable as the bounding box for panoramic image object detection.

6.2   Evaluations

Dataset Splits. The train set and test set of PANDORA contain 2,100 and 900 images, respectively. Considering the limitation of the computation source, we resize all the images in PANDORA into 1024×512 for training and testing.

Metric. We use standard mAP [6] as the evaluation metric for object detection in panoramic images. Please note that as original evaluation metrics used in the baseline methods are biased, we use our IoU method for evaluation.

Table 3. Numerical results (AP) of baseline models evaluated with RBFoV ground-truths on PANDORA test-dev. We add a branch to the output of these methods for predicting the angle of the RBFoV and use L1 loss.

Bounding box	Methods	Backbone	AP	AP_{50}	AP_{75}
RBFoV	Multi-Kernel [26]	ResNet-101	3.8	13.7	1.0
	Sphere-SSD [1]	ResNet-101	3.2	12	0.6
	Reprojection R-CNN [33]	ResNet-101	4.3	16.6	0.7
	Sph-CenterNet [35]	ResNet-101	5.5	19.9	1.1
	Our R-CenterNet	ResNet-101	**7.3**	**22.7**	**2.6**

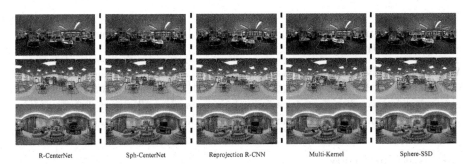

R-CenterNet   Sph-CenterNet   Reprojection R-CNN   Multi-Kernel   Sphere-SSD

Fig. 9. Visualization results of different methods on the PANDORA dataset.

Training Details. Our approach is implemented in PyTorch [17], and training is done on 8 GeForce RTX 2080Ti GPUs with a batch size of 32. We utilize Adam [10] to optimize the overall parameters objective for 160 epochs with the initial learning rate of 1.25×10^{-4}, and at 90 and 120 epochs, the learning rate is divided by 10.

Evaluation Tasks. We take Multi-Kernel [26], Sphere-SSD [1], Reprojection R-CNN [33] and Sph-CenterNet [35] as our baseline methods. To make it fair, we keep all the experiments' settings and hyper parameters the same as depicted in corresponding papers. All the methods take the ERP image as input, and the backbone networks are all the same ResNet-101 [7] architecture. The SphereNet Kerner [1] instead of the regular kernel in the CNN and the IoU use all we proposed except Multi-Kernel. Since its output bounding boxes are planar rectangles for Multi-Kernel, we still use the original planar IoU calculation method in its first stage. After these planar rectangles are predicted, we convert them to spherical rectangles. We add a branch to the output of these methods for predicting the angle of the RBFoV and use L1 loss.

Quantitative Results. The results of prediction are shown in Table 3. It is obvious that the two-stage approach Multi-Kernel and Reprojection R-CNN achieve better performance than the one-stage Sphere-SSD. Multi-Kernel uses a planar IoU calculation method in the first stage, resulting in a lower performance than Reprojection R-CNN. Since we change the generating ground-truth

Table 4. Ablation study demonstrates the effectiveness of each component. The PRDA is Panoramic Rotation Data Augmentation. The DR and IDR are direct and indirect regression for angle γ, respectively.

Method	Our heatmap	PRDA	IDR	DR	AP_{50}
Sph-CenterNet [35]				✓	19.9
	✓			✓	**20.5** (+0.6)
		✓		✓	**21.6** (+1.7)
			✓	✓	**21.4** (+1.5)
	✓	✓	✓	✓	**22.7** (+2.8)

heatmaps, and use *Panoramic Rotation Data Augmentation*, our R-CenterNet effect is better than Sph-CenterNet.

Visual Detection Results. As illustrated in Fig. 9, we give the results of the visualization of different methods on the PANDORA dataset. As shown, the R-CenterNet has good performance in both dense and small object detection. The visualization results are consistent with the data results in Table 3.

6.3   Ablation Study

Ablation experiments are presented in Table 4. We choose Sph-CenterNet [35] as the baseline for ablation study. For fairness, all experimental data and parameter settings are strictly consistent. We use AP_{50} as a measure of performance. It also can be evidenced in Table 4 that the detection results have been improved to varying degrees after adding each of the components we propose, and the total AP_{50} increased by 2.8%.

7   Conclusion

In this paper, we propose a new bounding box representation, RBFoV, for the panoramic image object detection task. Then, based on the RBFoV, we present a PANoramic Detection dataset for Object with oRientAtion (PANDORA). To our best knowledge, PANDORA is the first dataset to use the RBFoV as the bounding box. Finally, based on PANDORA, we evaluate the current SOTA methods and design an anchor-free object detector called R-CenterNet for panoramic images. Compared with these baselines, our R-CenterNet shows its advantages in terms of detection performance. By releasing PANDORA, We believe it will promote the development of object detection algorithms in panoramic images.

Acknowledgements. This work is supported by the National Key Research and Development Program of China (2020YFB1406604) and the National Natural Science Foundation of China (62072438, U1936110, 61931008, U21B2024).

References

1. Coors, B., Condurache, A.P., Geiger, A.: Spherenet: learning spherical representations for detection and classification in omnidirectional images. In: ECCV (2018)
2. Anguelov, D., et al.: Google street view: capturing the world at street level. Computer **43**(6), 32–38 (2010)
3. Chou, S.H., Sun, C., Chang, W.Y., Hsu, W.T., Sun, M., Fu, J.: 360-indoor: towards learning real-world objects in 360deg indoor equirectangular images. In: WACV (2020)
4. Cormack, R.: Flattening the earth: two thousand years of map projections by John P. Snyder; two by two: twenty-two pairs of maps from the newberry library illustrating five hundred years of western cartographic history by James Akerman; Robert Karrow; David Buisseret. ISIS **85**(3), 488–489 (1994)
5. Everingham, M., Gool, L.V., Williams, C.K.I., Winn, J., Zisserman, A.: The pascal visual object classes (VOC) challenge. IJCV **88**(2), 303–338 (2010)
6. Everingham, M., Eslami, S.M., Van Gool, L., Williams, C.K., Winn, J., Zisserman, A.: The pascal visual object classes challenge: a retrospective. IJCV **111**(1), 98–136 (2015)
7. He, K., Zhang, X., Ren, S., Sun, J.: Deep residual learning for image recognition. In: CVPR (2016)
8. Hu, H.N., Lin, Y.C., Liu, M.Y., Cheng, H.T., Chang, Y.J., Sun, M.: Deep 360 pilot: learning a deep agent for piloting through 360 sports videos. In: CVPR (2017)
9. Huang, J., Chen, Z., Research, A., Ceylan, U.D., Hailin, U.: 6-DOF VR videos with a single 360-camera. In: VR (2017)
10. Kingma, D., Ba, J.: Adam: a method for stochastic optimization. Comput. Sci. (2014)
11. Lee, Y., Jeong, J., Yun, J., Cho, W., Yoon, K.J.: SpherePHD: applying CNNs on a spherical PolyHeDron representation of 360 images (2019)
12. Lin, T.Y., Dollar, P., Girshick, R., He, K., Hariharan, B., Belongie, S.: Feature pyramid networks for object detection. In: CVPR (2017)
13. Lin, T.-Y., et al.: Microsoft COCO: common objects in context. In: Fleet, D., Pajdla, T., Schiele, B., Tuytelaars, T. (eds.) ECCV 2014. LNCS, vol. 8693, pp. 740–755. Springer, Cham (2014). https://doi.org/10.1007/978-3-319-10602-1_48
14. Lin, T.: Labelimg (2015)
15. Liu, W., et al.: SSD: single shot MultiBox detector. In: Leibe, B., Matas, J., Sebe, N., Welling, M. (eds.) ECCV 2016. LNCS, vol. 9905, pp. 21–37. Springer, Cham (2016). https://doi.org/10.1007/978-3-319-46448-0_2
16. Neubeck, A., Gool, L.: Efficient non-maximum suppression. In: ICPR (2006)
17. Paszke, A., et al.: Automatic differentiation in pytorch (2017)
18. Pearson, F.: Map Projections: Theory and Applications. CRC Press, Boca Raton (1990)
19. Putri, S.E., Tulus, T., Napitupulu, N.: Implementation and analysis of depth-first search (DFS) algorithm for finding the longest path. In: InteriOR (2011)
20. Ran, L., Zhang, Y., Zhang, Q., Tao, Y.: Convolutional neural network-based robot navigation using uncalibrated spherical images. Sensors **17**(6), 1341 (2017)
21. Redmon, J., Farhadi, A.: Yolo9000: better, faster, stronger. In: CVPR (2017)
22. Ren, S., He, K., Girshick, R., Sun, J.: Faster R-CNN: towards real-time object detection with region proposal networks. In: NIPS (2015)
23. Su, Y.C., Grauman, K.: Learning spherical convolution for fast features from 360 imagery. In: CVPR (2017)

24. Su, Y., Jayaraman, D., Grauman, K.: Pano2vid: automatic cinematography for watching 360° videos. In: ACCV (2016)
25. Tian, Z., Shen, C., Chen, H., He, T.: FCOS: fully convolutional one-stage object detection. In: ICCV (2020)
26. Wang, K.H., Lai, S.H.: Object detection in curved space for 360-degree camera. In: ICASSP (2019)
27. Lai, W.-S., Huang, Y., Joshi, N., Buehler, C., Yang, M.-H.: Semantic-driven generation of hyperlapse from 360[formula: see text] video. TVCG **24**(9), 2610–2621 (2017)
28. Wikipedia contributors: Spherical trigonometry (2021). https://en.wikipedia.org/w/index.php?title=Spherical_trigonometry&oldid=1016967508
29. Yang, W., Qian, Y., Cricri, F., Fan, L., Kamarainen, J.K.: Object detection in equirectangular panorama (2018)
30. Yang, X., Yan, J., Qi, M., Wang, W., Xiaopeng, Z., Qi, T.: Rethinking rotated object detection with gaussian wasserstein distance loss. In: International Conference on Machine Learning (2021)
31. Yu, D., Ji, S.: Grid based spherical CNN for object detection from panoramic images. Sensors **19**(11), 2622 (2019)
32. Zhang, S., Chi, C., Yao, Y., Lei, Z., Li, S.Z.: Bridging the gap between anchor-based and anchor-free detection via adaptive training sample selection. In: CVPR (2020)
33. Zhao, P., You, A., Zhang, Y., Liu, J., Tong, Y.: Spherical criteria for fast and accurate 360° object detection. In: AAAI, vol. 34, pp. 12959–12966 (2020)
34. Zhao, Q., Zhu, C., Dai, F., Ma, Y., Zhang, Y.: Distortion-aware CNNs for spherical images. In: Twenty-Seventh International Joint Conference on Artificial Intelligence IJCAI 2018 (2018)
35. Zhao, Q., et al.: Unbiased IOU for spherical image object detection. In: AAAI (2022)
36. Zhao, Q., Feng, W., Wan, L., Zhang, J.: Sphorb: a fast and robust binary feature on the sphere. Int. J. Comput. Vision **113**(2), 143–159 (2015)
37. Zhao, Q., Wan, L., Feng, W., Zhang, J., Wong, T.T.: Cube2video: navigate between cubic panoramas in real-time. IEEE Trans. Multimedia **15**(8), 1745–1754 (2013)
38. Zheng, J., et al.: Gait recognition in the wild with multi-hop temporal switch. In: ACM MM (2022)
39. Zheng, J., Liu, X., Liu, W., He, L., Yan, C., Mei, T.: Gait recognition in the wild with dense 3D representations and a benchmark. In: CVPR, pp. 20228–20237 (2022)
40. Zhou, X., Wang, D., Krhenbühl, P.: Objects as points. arXiv (2019)

FS-COCO: Towards Understanding of Freehand Sketches of Common Objects in Context

Pinaki Nath Chowdhury[1,2]([✉]), Aneeshan Sain[1,2], Ayan Kumar Bhunia[1], Tao Xiang[1,2], Yulia Gryaditskaya[1,3], and Yi-Zhe Song[1,2]

[1] SketchX, CVSSP, University of Surrey, Guildford, UK
p.chowdhury@surrey.ac.uk
[2] iFlyTek-Surrey Joint Research Centre on Artificial Intelligence, Guildford, UK
[3] Surrey Institute for People Centred AI, CVSSP,
University of Surrey, Guildford, UK

Abstract. We advance sketch research to scenes with the first dataset of freehand scene sketches, FS-COCO. With practical applications in mind, we collect sketches that convey scene content well but can be sketched within a few minutes by a person with any sketching skills. Our dataset comprises $10,000$ freehand scene vector sketches with per point space-time information by 100 non-expert individuals, offering both object- and scene-level abstraction. Each sketch is augmented with its text description. Using our dataset, we study for the first time the problem of fine-grained image retrieval from freehand scene sketches and sketch captions. We draw insights on: (i) Scene salience encoded in sketches using the strokes temporal order; (ii) Performance comparison of image retrieval from a scene sketch and an image caption; (iii) Complementarity of information in sketches and image captions, as well as the potential benefit of combining the two modalities. In addition, we extend a popular vector sketch LSTM-based encoder to handle sketches with larger complexity than was supported by previous work. Namely, we propose a hierarchical sketch decoder, which we leverage at a sketch-specific "pretext" task. Our dataset enables for the first time research on freehand scene sketch understanding and its practical applications. We release the dataset under CC BY-NC 4.0 license: FS-COCO dataset (https://github.com/pinakinathc/fscoco).

1 Introduction

As research on sketching thrives [5,16,21,41], the focus shifts from an analysis of quick single-object sketches [6–8,40] to an analysis of scene sketches [12,17,29,61], and professional [19] or specialised [53] sketches. In the age of data-driven computing, conducting research on sketching requires representative datasets. For instance, the inception of object-level sketch datasets [16,20,21,41,45,58] enabled

---

Supplementary Information The online version contains supplementary material available at https://doi.org/10.1007/978-3-031-20074-8_15.

Fig. 1. Comparison of our sketches to the scene sketches from `SketchyCOCO`, the latter are obtained by combining together sketches of individual objects. Our freehand scene sketches contain abstraction at the object and scene level and better capture the content of reference scenes. This figure demonstrates a large domain gap between freehand scene sketches and available scene sketches, motivating the need for new datasets. Our sketches contain stroke temporal order information, which we visualize using the "Parula" color scheme: strokes in "blue" are drawn first, strokes in "yellow" are drawn last. (Color figure online)

and propelled research in diverse applications [4, 5, 13]. Recently, increasingly more attempts are conducted towards not only collecting the data but also understanding how humans sketch [5, 20, 22, 54, 57]. We extend these efforts to scene sketches by introducing FS-COCO (Freehand Sketches of Common Objects in COntext), the first dataset of 10, 000 unique freehand scene sketches, drawn by 100 non-expert participants. We envision this dataset to permit a multitude of novel tasks and to contribute to the fundamental understanding of visual abstraction and expressivity in scene sketching. With our work, we make the first stab in this direction: We study fine-grained image retrieval from freehand scene sketches and the task of scene sketch captioning.

Thus far, research on scene sketches leveraged semi-synthetic [17, 29, 61] datasets that are obtained by combining together sketches and clip-arts of individual objects. Such datasets lack the holistic scene-level abstraction that characterises real scene sketches. Figure 1 shows a visual comparison between the existing semi-synthetic [17] scene sketch dataset and ours FS-COCO. It shows interactions between scene elements in our sketches and diversity of objects depictions. Moreover, our sketches contain more object categories than previous datasets: Our sketches contain more than 92 categories from the COCO-stuff [9], while sketches in SketchyScene [61] and SketchyCOCO [17] contain 45 and 17 object categories, respectively.

Our dataset collection setup is practical applications-driven, such as the retrieval of a video frame given a quick sketch from memory. This is an important task because, while the text-based retrieval achieved impressive results in recent years, it might be easier to communicate via sketching fine-grained details. However, this will only be practical if users can provide a quick sketch and are not expected to be good sketchers. Therefore, we collect *easy to recognize but quick to create* freehand scene sketches from recollection (similar to object sketches collected previously [16, 41]). As reference images, we select photos from the MS-COCO [28], a benchmark dataset for scene understanding that ensures diversity of scenes and is complemented with rich annotations in a form of semantic segmentation and image captions.

Equipped with our FS-COCO dataset, we for the first time study the problem of a fine-grained image retrieval from freehand scene sketches. First, we show the presence of a domain gap between freehand sketches and semi-synthetic ones [17,61], which are easier to collect, on the example of fine-grained sketch-based image retrieval. Then, in our work we aim at understanding how scene-sketch-based retrieval compares to text-based retrieval, and what information sketch captures. To obtain a thorough understanding, we collect for each sketch its text description. The text description makes the subject who created the sketch, eliminating the noise due to sketch interpretation. By comparing sketch text descriptions with image text descriptions from the MS-COCO [28] dataset, we draw conclusions on the complementary nature of the two modalities: sketches and image text descriptions.

Our dataset of freehand scene sketches enables analysis towards insights into how humans sketch scenes, not possible with earlier datasets [17]. We continue the recent trend on understanding and leveraging strokes order [5,19,20,54] and observe the same trends of coarse-to-fine sketching in scene sketches: We study stroke order as a factor of its salience for retrieval. Finally, we study sketch-captioning as an example of a sketch understanding task.

Collecting human sketches is costly, and despite our dataset being relatively large-scale, it is hard to reach the scale of the existing datasets of photos [33,43,47]. To tackle this known problem of sketch data, recent work [4,34] to improve the performance of the encoder-decoder-based architectures on the downstream tasks proposed to pre-train the encoder relying on some auxiliary task. In our work, we build on [4] and consider the auxiliary task of raster sketch to vector sketch generation. Since our sketches are more complex than those of single objects considered before, we propose a dedicated hierarchical RNN decoder. We demonstrate the efficiency of the pre-training strategy and our proposed hierarchical decoder on fine-grained retrieval and sketch-captioning.

In summary, our contributions are: (1) We propose the first dataset of freehand scene sketches and their captions; (2) We study for the first time fine-grained freehand-scene-sketch-based image retrieval (3) and the relations between sketches, images and their captions. (4) Finally, to address the challenges of scaling sketch datasets and complexity of scene sketches, we introduce a novel hierarchical sketch decoder that exploit temporal stroke order available for our sketches. We leverage this decoder at the pre-training stage for fine-grained retrieval and sketch captioning.

2   Related Work

Single-Object Sketch Datasets. Most freehand sketch datasets contain sketches of individual objects, annotated at the category level [16,21] or part level [18], paired to photos [41,45,58] or 3D shapes [38]. Category-level and part-level annotations enable tasks such as sketch recognition [42,59] and sketch generation [5,18]. *Paired* datasets allow to study practical tasks such as sketch-based image retrieval [58] and sketch-based image generation [52].

However, collecting fine-grained paired datasets is time-consuming since one needs to ensure accurate, fine-grained matching while keeping the sketching task

Table 1. Properties of scene sketch datasets.

Dataset	Abstraction		# pho-tos	Stroke temporal order	Cap-tions	Free-hand
	Object	Scene				
SketchyScene [61]	✓	✗	7,264	✗	✗	✗
SketchyCOCO [17]	✗	✓	14,081	✗	✗	✗
FS-COCO	✓	✓	10,000	✓	✓	✓

natural for the subjects [24]. Hence, such paired datasets typically contain a few thousand sketches per category, *e.g.*, QMUL-Chair-V2 [58] consists of 1432 sketch-photo pairs on a single 'chair' category, Sketchy [41] has an average of 600 sketches per category, albeit over 125 categories.

Our dataset contains *10,000 scene sketches*, each paired with a 'reference' photo and text description. It contains scene sketches rather than sketches of individual objects and excels the existing fine-grained datasets of single-object sketches in the amount of paired instances.

Scene Sketch Datasets. Probably the first dataset of 8,694 freehand scene sketches was collected within the multi-model dataset [2]. It contains sketches of 205 scenes, but the examples are not paired between modalities. Scene sketch datasets with the pairing between modalities [17,61] have started to appear, however they are *'semi-synthetic'*. Thus, the SketchyScene [61] dataset contains 7, 264 sketch-image pairs. It is obtained by providing participants with a reference image and clip-art like object sketches to drag-and-drop for scene composition. The augmentation is performed by replacing object sketches with other sketch instances belonging to the same object category. SketchyCOCO [17] was generated automatically relying on the segmentation maps of photos from COCO-Stuff [9] and leveraging freehand sketches of single objects from [16,21,41].

Leveraging the semi-synthetic datasets, previous work studied scene sketch semantic segmentation [61], scene-level fine-grained sketch based image retrieval [29], and image generation [17]. Nevertheless, sketches in the existing datasets are not representative of freehand human sketches as shown in Fig. 1, and therefore the existing results can be only considered preliminary. Unlike existing semi-synthetic datasets, our dataset of freehand scene sketches captures abstraction at the object level and holistic scene level, and contains stroke temporal information. We provide a comparative statistics with previous datasets in Table 1, discussed in Sect. 4.1. We demonstrate the benefit and importance of the newly proposed data on two problems: image retrieval and sketch captioning.

3   Dataset Collection

Targeting practical applications, such as sketch-based image retrieval, we aimed to collect representative freehand scene sketches with object- and scene-levels of abstraction. Therefore, we define the following requirements towards collected sketches: (1) created by non-professionals, (2) fast to create, (3) recognizable, (4) paired with images, and (5) supplemented with sketch-captions.

Data Preparation. We randomly select 10*k* photos from MS-COCO [28], a standard benchmark dataset for scene understanding [10, 11, 39]. Each photo in this dataset is accompanied by image captions [28] and semantic segmentation [9]. Our selected subset of photos includes 72 *"things"* instances (well-defined foreground objects) and 78 *"stuff"* instances (background instances with potentially no specific or distinctive spatial extent or shape: e.g., "trees", "fence"), according to the classification introduced in [9]. We present detailed statistics in Sect. 4.1.

Task. We built a custom web application[1] to engage 100 participants, each annotating a distinct subset of 100 photos. Our objective is to collect easy-to-recognize freehand scene sketches drawn from memory, alike single-object sketches collected previously [16, 41]. To imitate real world scenario of sketching from memory, following the practice of single object dataset collection, we showed a reference scene photo to a subject for a limited duration of 60 seconds, determined through a series of pilot studies. To ensure recognizable but not overly detailed drawings, we also put time limits on the duration of the sketching. We determined the optimal time limits through a series of pilot studies with 10 participants, which showed that 3 min were sufficient for participants to comfortably sketch recognizable scene sketches. We allow repeated sketching attempts, with the subject making an average of 1.7 attempts. Each attempt repeats the entire process of observing an image and drawing on a blank canvas. Upon satisfaction with their sketch, we ask the same subject to describe their sketch in text. The instructions to write a sketch caption are similar to that of Lin *et al.* [28] and are provided in supplemental materials. To reduce fatigue that can compromise data quality, we encourage participants to take frequent breaks and complete the task over multiple days. Thus, each participant spent 12–13 h to annotate 100 photos over an average period of 2 days.

Quality Check. We check the quality of sketches. We hired as a *human judge* one appointed person (1) with experience in data collection and (2) non-expert in sketching. The human judge instructed to "mark sketches of scenes that are *too difficult to understand or recognize.*" The tagged photos were sent back to their assigned annotator. This process guarantees the resulting scene sketches are recognizable by a human, and therefore, should be understood by a machine.

Participants. We recruited 100 non-artist participants from the age group 22–44, with an average age of 27.03, including 72 males and 28 females.

4   Dataset Composition

Our dataset consists of 10, 000 (a) unique freehand scene sketches, (b) textual descriptions of the sketches (sketch captions), (c) reference photos from the MS-COCO [28] dataset. Each photo in [28] contains 5 associated text descriptions (image captions) by different subjects [28]. Figures 1 and 3 show samples from our dataset, and supplemental materials visualize more sketches from our dataset.

---

[1] https://github.com/pinakinathc/SketchX-SST.

Table 2. Comparison of scene sketch datasets based on the distribution of categories in sketch-image pairs. 'FG' denotes subsets of datasets that are recommended for use in Fine-Grained tasks, such as fine-grained retrieval. e_l/e_c denotes estimates based on semantic segmentation labels in images and based on the occurrence of a word in a sketch caption, respectively. See Sect. 4 for details.

Dataset	# photos	#categories	# categories per sketch				# sketches per category			
			Mean	Std	Min	Max	Mean	Std	Min	Max
SketchyScene [61]	7,264	45	7.88	1.96	4	20	1079.76	1447.47	31	5723
SketchyCOCO [17]	14,081	17	3.33	0.9	2	7	1932.41	3493.01	33	9761
SketchyScene FG	2,724	45	7.71	1.88	4	20	394.51	540.30	3	2154
SketchyCOCO FG	1,225	17	3.28	0.89	2	6	164.71	297.79	5	824
FS-COCO (e_c)	10,000	92	1.37	0.57	1	5	99.42	172.88	1	866
FS-COCO (e_l)	10,000	150	7.17	3.27	1	25	413.18	973.59	1	6789

4.1 Comparison to Existing Datasets

Table 2 provides comparison with previous dataset and statistics on distribution of object categories in our sketches, which we discuss in more detail below.

Categories. First, we obtain a joint set of labels from the labels in [17,61] and [9]. To compute statistics on the categories present in [17,61], we use the semantic segmentation labels available in these datasets. For our dataset, we compute two estimates of the category distribution across our data: (1) e_l, based on semantic segmentation labels in images and (2) e_c, based on the occurrence of a word in a sketch caption. As can be seen from Fig. 3, the participants do not exhaustively describe in the caption all the objects present in sketches. Our dataset contains $e_c/e_l = 92/150$ categories, which is more than double the number of categories in previous scene sketch datasets (Table 2). On average, each category is present in $e_c/e_l = 99.42/413.18$ sketches. Among the most common category in all three datasets are 'cloud', 'tree' and 'grass' common to outdoor scenes. In our dataset 'person' is also among one of the most frequent categories along with common animals such as 'horse', 'giraffe', 'dog', 'cow' and 'sheep'. Our dataset, according to lower/upper estimates, contains $33/71$ indoor categories and $59/79$ outdoor categories. We provide detailed statistics in supplemental materials.

Sketch Complexity. Existing datasets of freehand sketches [16,41] contain sketches of single objects. The complexity of scene sketches is unavoidably higher than the one of single-object sketches. Sketches in our dataset have a median stroke count of 64. For comparison, a median strokes count in the popular Tu-Berlin [16] and Sketchy [41] datasets is 13 and 14, respectively.

5 Towards Scene Sketch Understanding

5.1 Semi-synthetic Versus Freehand Sketches

To study the domain gap between existing 'semi-synthetic' and our freehand scene sketches, we evaluate the state-of-the-art methods for Fine Grained Sketch

Table 3. Evaluation of a domain gap between 'semi-synthetic' sketches [17,61] and freehand sketches FS-COCO. The details on the compared methods are in Sect. 5.1. Top-1/Top-10 accuracy (R@1/R@10) is the percentage of test sketches for which the ground-truth image is among the first 1/10 ranked retrieval results.

Methods	Trained On																	
	SketchyScene (S-Scene) [61]						SketchyCOCO (S-COCO) [17]						FS-COCO (Ours)					
	Evaluate on						Evaluate on						Evaluate on					
	S-Scene		S-COCO		FS-COCO		S-Scene		S-COCO		FS-COCO		S-Scene		S-COCO		FS-COCO	
	R@1	R@10	R@1	R@10	R@1	R@10	R@1	R@10	R@1	R@10	R@1	R@10	R@1	R@10	R@1	R@10	R@1	R@10
Siam.-VGG16 [58]	22.8	43.5	1.1	4.1	1.8	6.6	0.3	2.1	37.6	80.6	<0.1	0.4	5.8	24.5	2.4	11.6	23.3	52.6
HOLEF [46]	22.6	44.2	1.2	3.9	1.7	5.9	0.4	2.3	38.3	82.5	0.1	0.4	6.0	24.7	2.2	11.9	22.8	53.1
CLIP zero-shot [39]	1.26	9.70	–	–	–	–	–	–	1.85	9.41	–	–	–	–	–	–	1.17	6.07
CLIP*	8.6	24.8	1.7	6.6	2.5	8.2	1.3	5.1	15.3	43.9	0.6	3.1	1.6	11.9	2.6	12.5	5.5	26.5

Based Image Retrieval (FG-SBIR) on the three datasets: SketchyCOCO [17], SketchyScene [61] and FS-COCO (ours) (Table 3).

Methods and Training Details. Siam.-VGG16 adapts the pioneering method of Yu et al. [58] by replacing the Sketch-a-Net [59] feature extractor with VGG16 [44] trained using triplet loss [50,55], as we observed that this increases retrieval performance. *HOLEF* [46] extends *Siam.-VGG16* by using spatial attention to better capture fine-scale details and introducing a novel trainable distance function in the context of triplet loss.

We also explore CLIP [39], a recent method that has shown an impressive ability to generalize across multiple photo datasets [28,37]. *CLIP (zero-shot)* uses the pre-trained photo encoder, trained on 400 million text-photo pairs that do not include photos from the MS-COCO dataset. In our experiments, we use the publicly available ViT-B/32 version[2] of CLIP, which uses the visual transformer backbone as a feature extractor. Finally, *CLIP** means CLIP fine-tuned on the target data. Since we found training CLIP to be very unstable, we train only the layer normalization [3] modules and add a fully connected layer to map the sketch and photo representations to a shared 512 dimensional feature space. We train *CLIP** using triplet loss [50,55] with a margin value set to 0.2 with a batch size 256 and a low learning rate of 0.000001.

Train and Test Splits. We train *Siam.-VGG16* and *HOLEF*, and fine-tune *CLIP** on the sketches from one of three datasets: SketchyCOCO [17], SketchyScene [61] and FS-COCO. For our FS-COCO dataset 70% of each user sketches are used for training and the remaining 30% for testing. This results in a training/tasting sets of 7,000 and 3,000 sketch-image pairs. For [17,61] we use subsets of sketch-image pairs, since both datasets contain noisy data, which leads to performance degradation when used for the fine-grained tasks such as fine-grained retrieval. For SketchyCOCO [17], following Liu *et al.* [29], we sort the sketches based on the number of the foreground objects and select the top 1,225 scene sketch-photo pairs. We then randomly split those into training and

---

[2] https://github.com/openai/CLIP.

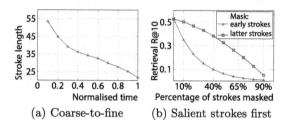

(a) Coarse-to-fine   (b) Salient strokes first

Fig. 2. Sketching strategies in our freehand scene sketches: Sect. 5.2. (a) Humans follow a coarse-to-fine sketching strategy, drawing longer strokes first. (b) Humans draw strokes more salient for the retrieval task early on. We plot the Top-10 (R@10) retrieval accuracy when certain strokes during testing are masked out. Top-10 accuracy calculates the percentage of test sketches for which the ground-truth image is among the first 10 ranked retrieval results.

test sets of $1,015$ and 210 pairs, respectively. For SketchyScene [61] we follow their approach used to evaluate image retrieval, and manually select sketch-photo pairs that have same categories present in images and sketches. We obtain training and test sets of $2,472$ and 252 pairs, respectively. The statistics on object categories in these subsets are given in Table 2 ('FG'). Note that in each experiment, the image gallery size is equal to the test set size. Therefore, in the case of our dataset, the retrieval is performed among the largest number of images.

Evaluation. Table 3 shows that training on 'semi-synthetic' sketch datasets like SketchyCOCO [17] and SketchyScene [61] does not generalize to freehand scene sketches from our dataset: training on FS-COCO/SketchyCOCO/SketchyScene and testing on our data results in $R@1$ of $23.3/ < 0.1/1.8$. Training with the sketches from [61] rather than from [17] results in better performance on our sketches, probably due to the larger variety of categories in [61] (46 categories) than in [17] (17 categories). Table 3 also shows a large domain gap between all three datasets.

As the image gallery is larger when tested on our sketches than for other datasets, the performance on our sketches in Table 3 is lower, even when trained on our sketches. For a fairer comparison, we create 10 additional test sets consisting of 210 sketch-image pairs (the size of the SketchyCOCO dataset's image gallery) by randomly selecting them from the initial set of 3000 sketches. For Siam-VGG16, the average retrieval accuracy and its standard deviation over ten splits are: Top-1 is $50.39\% \pm 2.15\%$ and Top-10 is $89.38\% \pm 2.0\%$. For $CLIP^*$, the average retrieval accuracy and its standard deviation over ten splits are: Top-1 is $42.53\% \pm 3.16\%$ and Top-10 is $87.93\% \pm 2.14\%$. These high performance numbers show the high quality of the sketches in our dataset.

5.2   What Does a Freehand Sketch Capture?

Sketching Strategy. We observe that humans follow a coarse-to-fine sketching strategy in scene sketches: in Fig. 2(a) we show that the average stroke length decreases with time. Similarly, coarse-to-fine sketching strategies has previously been observed in single object sketch datasets [16,20,41,54]. We also verify the hypothesis that humans draw salient and recognizable regions early [5,16,41]. We first train the classical SBIR method [58] on sketch-image pairs from our dataset: 70% of each user's sketches are used for training and 30% for testing. During the evaluation, we follow two strategies: (i) We gradually mask out a certain percentage of strokes drawn early, which is indicated by the red line in Fig. 2(b). (ii) We then gradually mask out strokes drawn towards the end, which is indicated by the blue line in Fig. 2(b). We observe that masking strokes towards the end has a smaller impact on the retrieval accuracy than masking early strokes. Thus we quantify that humans draw longer (Fig. 2a) and more salient for retrieval (Fig. 2b) strokes early on.

Sketch Captions vs. Image Captions. To gain insights into what information sketch captures, we compare sketch and image captions (Fig. 3 and 4). The vocabulary of our sketch captions matches 81.50% vocabulary of image captions. Specifically, comparing sketch and image captions for each instance reveals that on average 66.5% words in sketch captions are common with image captions, while 60.8% of words overlap among the 5 available captions of each image. This indicates that sketches preserve a large fraction of information in the image. However, the sketch captions in our dataset are on average shorter (6.55 words) than image captions (10.46). We explore this difference in more detail by visualizing the word clouds for sketch and image captions. From Fig. 4 we observe that, unlike image captions, sketch descriptions do not use "color" information. Also, we compute the percentage of nouns, verbs, and adjectives in sketch and image captions. Figure 4(c) shows that our sketch captions are likely to focus more on objects (i.e., nouns like "horse") and their actions (i.e., verbs like "standing") instead of focusing on attributes (i.e., adjectives like "a brown horse").

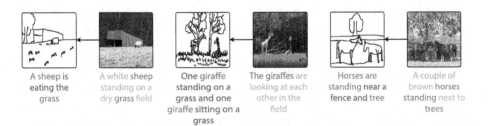

A sheep is eating the grass | A white sheep standing on a dry grass field

One giraffe standing on a grass and one giraffe sitting on a grass | The giraffes are looking at each other in the field

Horses are standing near a fence and tree | A couple of brown horses standing next to trees

Fig. 3. A qualitative comparison of image and sketch captions. The overlapping words are marked in blue, the words present only in image-captions are marked in red, while the words present only in sketch-captions are marked in green. (Color figure online)

Freehand Sketches vs. Image Captions. To understand the potential of quick freehand scene sketches in image retrieval, we compare freehand scene sketch with textual description as queries for fine-grained image retrieval (Table 4).

| | (a) Image captions | | (b) Sketch captions | | (c) Statistics |

Fig. 4. (a, b) Word clouds show frequently occurring words in image and sketch captions, respectively. The large the word, the more frequent it is. It shows that color information such as *"white"*, *"green"* is present in image captions but is missing from sketch captions. (c) Percentage of nouns, verbs, and adjectives in image and sketch captions, and their overlapping words. (Color figure online)

Methods. For text-based image retrieval, we evaluate two baselines: (1) *CNN-RNN* the simple and classic approach where text is encoded with an LSTM and images are encoded with a CNN encoder (VGG-16 in our implementation) [25, 49], and (2) CLIP [39] which is one of state-of-the-art methods alongside [26] in text-based image retrieval. For purity of experiments we evaluate here CLIP, as its training data did not include MS-COCO dataset from which the reference images in our dataset are coming from. *CLIP zero-shot* uses off-the-shelf ViT-B/32 weights. *CLIP** is fine-tuned on our sketch-captions by fine-tuning only layer normalization modules [3] with batch size 256 and learning rate $1e-7$.

Training Details. CNN-RNN and CLIP* are trained with triplet loss [50,55], with a margin value is set to 0.2. We use the same split to train/test sets as in Sect. 5.1. For retrieval from image captions, we randomly select one of 5 available caption versions.

Evaluation. Table 4 shows that image captions result in better retrieval performance compared to sketch captions, which we attribute to the color information in image captions. However, we observe that *CLIP**-based retrieval from image captions is slightly inferior to *Siam.-VGG16*-based retrieval from sketches. Note that *CLIP** is pre-trained on 400 million text-photo pairs, while *Siam.-VGG16* was trained on a much smaller set of 7000 sketch-photo pairs. Therefore, with even larger sketch datasets the retrieval accuracy from sketches will further increase. There is an intuitive explanation for this since scene sketches intrinsically encode fine-grained visual cues that are difficult to convey in text.

Table 4. Text-based versus sketch-based image retrieval.

| Methods | Retrieval accuracy | | | | | |
| | Image captions | | Sketch captions | | Sketches | |
	R@1	R@10	R@1	R@10	R@1	R@10
Siam.-VGG16 [58]	–	–	–	–	**23.3**	**52.6**
CNN-RNN [45]	11.1	31.1	7.2	23.6	–	–
CLIP zero-shot [39]	21.0	50.9	11.5	35.3	1.17	6.07
CLIP*	<u>22.1</u>	<u>52.3</u>	14.8	36.6	5.5	26.5

Predicted Captions

- ○ Two zebras standing on field
- ○ Zebras standing on grassland.

- ○ A giraffe is standing on the grass.
- ○ A giraffe is standing in the bushes.

- ○ Horses standing near tree.
- ○ Horses standing on the field.

- ○ A plane is taking off.
- ○ A plane is flying in the sky.

Fig. 5. Qualitative results showing predicted captions from LNFMM (H-Decoder) for scene sketches from our dataset.

Text and Sketch Synergy. While we have shown that scene sketches have strong ability in expressing fine-grained visual cues, image captions convey additional information such as "color". Therefore, we are exploring whether the two query modalities combined can improve fine-grained image retrieval. Following [30], we use two simple approaches to combine sketch and text: (-concat) we concatenate sketch and text features and (-add) we add sketch and text features. The combined features are then passed through a fully connected layer. Comparing the results in Table 5 and Table 4 shows that combining image captions and scene sketches improves fine-grained image retrieval. This confirms that the scene sketch complements the information conveyed by the text.

Table 5. Fine-grained image retrieval from the combined input of scene sketches and textual image descriptions.

Methods	R@1	R@10	Methods	R@1	R@10
CNN-RNN [45] -add	**25.3**	**55.0**	CLIP* -add	23.9	53.5
CNN-RNN [45] -concat	24.3	53.9	CLIP* -concat	23.3	52.6

Table 6. Sketch captioning (Sect. 5.3): our dataset enables captioning of scene sketches. We provide the results of the popular captioning methods developed for photos. For the evaluation, we use the standard metrics: BELU (B4) [35], METEOR (M) [14], ROUGE (R) [27], CIDEr (C) [48], SPICE (S) [1].

Methods	B4	M	R	C	S
Xu *et al.* [56]	13.7	17.1	44.9	69.4	14.5
AG-CVAE [51]	16.0	18.9	49.1	80.5	15.8
LNFMM [31]	16.7	21.0	52.9	90.1	16.0
LNFMM with pre-training (H-Decoder)	**17.3**	**21.1**	**53.2**	**95.3**	**17.2**

5.3 Sketch Captioning

While scene sketches are a pre-historic form of human communication, scene sketch understanding is nascent. Existing literature has solidified captioning as a hallmark task for scene understanding. The lack of paired scene-sketch and text datasets is the biggest bottleneck. Our dataset allows us to study this problem for the first time. We evaluate several popular and SOTA methods in Table 6: Xu *et al.* [56] is one of the first popular works to use the attention mechanism with an LSTM for image captioning. AG-CVAE [50] is a SOTA image captioning model that uses a variational auto-encoder along with an additive gaussian prior. Finally, LNFMM [31] is a recent SOTA approach using normalizing flows [15] to capture the complex joint distribution of photos and text. We show qualitative results in Fig. 5 using the LNFMM model with the pre-training strategy we introduce in Sect. 6.

6 Efficient "Pretext" Task

Our dataset is large (10,000 scene sketches!) for a sketch dataset. However, scaling it up to millions of sketch instances paired with other modalities (photos/text) to match the size of the photo datasets [47] might be intractable in the short term. Therefore, when working with freehand sketches, it is important to find ways to go around the limited dataset size. One traditional approach to address this problem is to solve an auxiliary or "pretext" task [32,36,60]. Such tasks exploit self-supervised learning, allowing to pre-train the encoder for the 'source' domain leveraging unpaired/unlabeled data. In the context of sketching, solving jigsaw puzzles [34] and converting raster to vector sketch [4] "pretext" tasks were considered. We extend the state-of-the-art sketch-vectorization [4] "pretext" task to support the complexity of scene sketches, exploiting the availability of time-space information in our dataset. We pre-train a raster sketch encoder with the newly proposed decoder that reconstructs a sketch in a vector format as a sequence of stroke points. Previous work [4] leverages a single layer Recurrent Neural Network (RNN) for sketch decoding. However, it can only reliably model up to around 200 stroke points [21], while our scene sketches can contain more than 3000 stroke points, which makes modeling scene sketches challenging. We observe that, on average, scene sketches consist of only 74.3 strokes, with each stroke containing around 41.1 stroke points. Modeling such number of strokes or stroke points *individually* is possible using a standard LSTM network [23]. Therefore, we propose a novel 2-layered hierarchical LSTM decoder (Fig. 6).

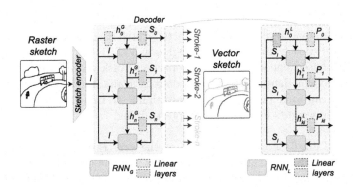

Fig. 6. The proposed hierarchical decoder used for pre-training a sketch encoder.

6.1   Proposed Hierarchical Decoder (H-Decoder)

We denote a raster sketch encoder that our proposed decoder pre-trains as $E(\cdot)$. Let the output feature map of $E(\cdot)$ be $F \in \mathbb{R}^{h' \times w' \times c}$, where h', w' and c denotes height, width, and number of channels, respectively. We apply a global max pooling to F, with consequent flattening, to obtain a latent vector representation of the raster sketch, $l_R \in \mathbb{R}^{512}$.

Naively decoding l_R using a single layer RNN is intractable [21]. We propose a two-level decoder consisting of two LSTMs, referred to as global and local. The global LSTM (RNN_G) predicts a sequence of feature vectors, each representing a stroke. The second local LSTM (RNN_L) predicts a sequence of points for any stroke, given its predicted feature vector.

We initialize the hidden state of the global RNN_G using a linear embedding as follows: $h_0^G = W_h^G l_R + b_h^G$. The hidden state h_i^G of decoder RNN_G is updated as follows: $h_i^G = RNN_G(h_{i-1}^G; [l_R, S_{i-1}])$, where $[\cdot]$ stands for a concatenation operation and $S_{i-1} \in \mathbb{R}^{512}$ is the last predicted stroke representation computed as: $S_i = W_y^G h_i^G + b_y^G$.

Given each stroke representation S_i, the initial hidden state of local RNN_L is obtained as: $h_0^L = W_h^L S_i + b_h^L$. Next, h_j^L is updated as: $h_j^L = RNN_L(h_{j-1}^L; [S_i, P_{t-1}])$, where P_{t-1} is the last predicted point of the i-th stroke. A linear layer is used to predict a point: $P_t = W_y^L h_j^L + b_j^L$, where $P_t = (x_t, y_t, q_t^1, q_t^2, q_t^3)$ is of size $\mathbb{R}^{2+3}$ whose first two logits represent absolute coordinate (x, y), and the later three denote the pen's state (q_t^1, q_t^2, q_t^3) [21].

We supervise the prediction of the absolute coordinate and pen state using the mean-squared error and categorical cross-entropy loss, as in [4].

6.2 Evaluation and Discussion

We use our proposed H-Decoder for pre-training a raster sketch encoder for fine-grained image retrieval (Table 7) and sketch captioning (Table 6).

Training Details. We start pre-training VGG-16 based *Siam.VGG16* (Table 7) and *LNFMM* (Table 6) encoders on QuickDraw [21], a large dataset of freehand object sketches, by coupling a VGG16 raster sketch encoder with our H-Decoder. For *CLIP** we start from the model weights in ViT-B/32. We then train *CLIP** and VGG-16-based encoders with our "pretext" task on *all* sketches from our dataset. We exploit here that the test data is available but does not have the paired data – captions, photos. After pre-training, training for downstream tasks starts with the weights learned during pre-training.

Evaluation. Table 6 shows the benefit of the pre-training with the proposed decoder. With this pre-training strategy the performance of LNFMM [31] on sketches approaches the performance on images (CIDEr score of 98.4[3]), increasing, *e.g.*, the CIDEr score from 90.1 to 95.3.

This pre-training also slightly improves the performance of sketch-based retrieval (Table 7). Next, we compare pre-training with the proposed H-Decoder and a more naive approach. We simplify scene sketches with the Ramer-Douglas Peucker (RDP) algorithm (Fig. 7): On average, the simplified sketches contain 165 stroke points, while the original sketches contain 2437 stroke points. Then, we pre-train with a single layer RNN, as proposed in [4]. In this case *Siam.VGG16* achieves *R@10* of 52.1, which is lower than the performance without pre-training (Table 7). This further demonstrates the importance of the proposed hierarchical decoder to scene sketches.

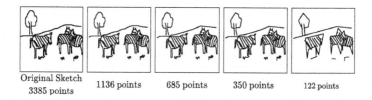

Original Sketch
3385 points   1136 points   685 points   350 points   122 points

Fig. 7. Simplifying scene sketch with the RDP algorithm looses salient information. RNNs can reliably model around 200 points. The training of a single-layer RNN exploits the simplification level of the most right image.

---

[3] The performance of image captioning goes up to 170.5 when 100 generated captions are evaluated against the ground-truth instead of 1.

Table 7. The role of pre-training with H-Decode in retrieval.

	Baseline		H-Decoder	
Method	R@1	R@10	R@1	R@10
Siam.-VGG16	23.3	52.6	**24.1**	**54.3**
CLIP*	5.5	26.5	5.7	27.1

7 Conclusion

We introduce the first dataset of freehand scene sketches with fine-grained paired text information. With the dataset, we took the first step towards freehand scene sketch understanding, studying tasks such as fine-grained image retrieval from scene sketches and scene sketches captioning. We show that relying on off-the-shelf methods and our data promising image retrieval and sketch captioning accuracy can be obtained. We hope that future work will leverage our findings to design dedicated methods exploiting the complementary information in sketches and image captions. In the supplemental materials, we provide a thorough comparison of modern encoders and state-of-the-art methods, and show how meta-learning can be used for few-shot sketch adaptation to an unseen user style. Finally, we proposed a new RNN-based decoder that exploits time-space information embedded in our sketches for a 'pre-text' task, demonstrating substantial improvement on sketch-captioning. We hope that our dataset will promote research on image generation from freehand scene sketches, sketch captioning, and novel sketch encoding approaches that are well suited for the complexity of freehand scene sketches.

References

1. Anderson, P., Fernando, B., Johnson, M., Gould, S.: SPICE: semantic propositional image caption evaluation. In: Leibe, B., Matas, J., Sebe, N., Welling, M. (eds.) ECCV 2016. LNCS, vol. 9909, pp. 382–398. Springer, Cham (2016). https://doi.org/10.1007/978-3-319-46454-1_24
2. Aytar, Y., Castrejon, L., Vondrick, C., Pirsiavash, H., Torralba, A.: Cross-modal scene networks. IEEE-TPAMI **40**(10), 2303–2314 (2018)
3. Ba, J., Kiros, J.R., Hinton, G.E.: Layer normalization. In: NIPS Deep Learning Symposium (2016)
4. Bhunia, A.K., Chowdhury, P.N., Yang, Y., Hospedales, T.M., Xiang, T., Song, Y.Z.: Vectorization and rasterization: self-supervised learning for sketch and handwriting. In: CVPR (2021)
5. Bhunia, A.K., et al.: Pixelor: a competitive sketching AI agent. So you think you can beat me? In: SIGGRAPH Asia (2020)
6. Bhunia, A.K., et al.: Doodle it yourself: class incremental learning by drawing a few sketches. In: CVPR (2022)
7. Bhunia, A.K., et al.: Sketching without worrying: Noise-tolerant sketch-based image retrieval. In: CVPR (2022)

8. Bhunia, A.K., et al.: Adaptive fine-grained sketch-based image retrieval. In: ECCV (2022)
9. Caesar, H., Uijlings, J., Ferrari, V.: Coco-stuff: thing and stuff classes in context. In: CVPR (2018)
10. Chen, J., Guo, H., Yi, K., Li, B., Elhoseiny, M.: VisualGPT: data-efficient adaptation of pretrained language models for image captioning. arXiv preprint arXiv:2102.10407 (2021)
11. Chen, L.C., Papandreou, G., Kokkinos, I., Murphy, K., Yuille, A.L.: DeepLab: semantic image segmentation with deep convolutional nets, atrous convolution, and fully connected CRFs. arXiv preprint arXiv:1606.00915 (2016)
12. Chowdhury, P.N., Bhunia, A.K., Gajjala, V.R., Sain, A., Xiang, T., Song, Y.Z.: Partially does it: towards scene-level FG-SBIR with partial input. In: CVPR (2022)
13. Das, A., Yang, Y., Hospedales, T., Xiang, T., Song, Y.-Z.: BézierSketch: a generative model for scalable vector sketches. In: Vedaldi, A., Bischof, H., Brox, T., Frahm, J.-M. (eds.) ECCV 2020. LNCS, vol. 12371, pp. 632–647. Springer, Cham (2020). https://doi.org/10.1007/978-3-030-58574-7_38
14. Denkowski, M.J., Lavie, A.: Meteor universal: language specific translation evaluation for any target language. In: WMT@ACL (2014)
15. Dinh, L., Krueger, D., Bengio, Y.: Nice: non-linear independent components estimation. In: ICLR, Workshop Track Proc (2015)
16. Eitz, M., Hays, J., Alexa, M.: How do humans sketch objects? ACM Trans. Graph. (2012)
17. Gao, C., Liu, Q., Wang, L., Liu, J., Zou, C.: Sketchycoco: image generation from freehand scene sketches. In: CVPR (2020)
18. Ge, S., Goswami, V., Zitnick, C.L., Parikh, D.: Creative sketch generation. In: ICLR (2021)
19. Gryaditskaya, Y., Hähnlein, F., Liu, C., Sheffer, A., Bousseau, A.: Lifting freehand concept sketches into 3D. In: SIGGRAPH Asia (2020)
20. Gryaditskaya, Y., Sypesteyn, M., Hoftijzer, J.W., Pont, S., Durand, F., Bousseau, A.: Opensketch: a richly-annotated dataset of product design sketches. ACM Trans. Graph. (2019)
21. Ha, D., Eck, D.: A neural representation of sketch drawings. In: ICLR (2018)
22. Hertzmann, A.: Why do line drawings work? Perception (2020)
23. Hochreiter, S., Schmidhuber, J.: Long short-term memory. Neural Comput. (1997)
24. Holinaty, J., Jacobson, A., Chevalier, F.: Supporting reference imagery for digital drawing. In: ICCV Workshop (2021)
25. Karpathy, A., Fei-Fei, L.: Deep visual-semantic alignments for generating image descriptions. IEEE-TPAMI (2017)
26. Li, X., et al.: OSCAR: object-semantics aligned pre-training for vision-language tasks. In: Vedaldi, A., Bischof, H., Brox, T., Frahm, J.-M. (eds.) ECCV 2020. LNCS, vol. 12375, pp. 121–137. Springer, Cham (2020). https://doi.org/10.1007/978-3-030-58577-8_8
27. Lin, C.Y.: Rouge: a package for automatic evaluation of summaries. In: Text Summarization Branches Out (2004)
28. Lin, T.-Y., et al.: Microsoft COCO: common objects in context. In: Fleet, D., Pajdla, T., Schiele, B., Tuytelaars, T. (eds.) ECCV 2014. LNCS, vol. 8693, pp. 740–755. Springer, Cham (2014). https://doi.org/10.1007/978-3-319-10602-1_48
29. Liu, F., et al.: SceneSketcher: fine-grained image retrieval with scene sketches. In: Vedaldi, A., Bischof, H., Brox, T., Frahm, J.-M. (eds.) ECCV 2020. LNCS, vol. 12364, pp. 718–734. Springer, Cham (2020). https://doi.org/10.1007/978-3-030-58529-7_42

30. Liu, K., Li, Y., Xu, N., Nataranjan, P.: Learn to combine modalities in multimodal deep learning. arXiv preprint arXiv:1805.11730 (2018)
31. Mahajan, S., Gurevych, I., Roth, S.: Latent normalizing flows for many-to-many cross-domain mappings. In: ICLR (2020)
32. Noroozi, M., Favaro, P.: Unsupervised learning of visual representations by solving jigsaw puzzles. In: Leibe, B., Matas, J., Sebe, N., Welling, M. (eds.) ECCV 2016. LNCS, vol. 9910, pp. 69–84. Springer, Cham (2016). https://doi.org/10.1007/978-3-319-46466-4_5
33. Ordonez, V., Kulkarni, G., Berg, T.: Im2text: describing images using 1 million captioned photographs. In: NIPS (2011)
34. Pang, K., Yang, Y., Hospedales, T.M., Xiang, T., Song, Y.Z.: Solving mixed-modal jigsaw puzzle for fine-grained sketch-based image retrieval. In: CVPR (2020)
35. Papineni, K., Roukos, S., Ward, T., Zhu, W.J.: Bleu: a method for automatic evaluation of machine translation. In: ACL (2002)
36. Pathak, D., Krahenbuhl, P., Donahue, J., Darrell, T., Efros, A.A.: Context encoders: feature learning by inpainting. In: CVPR (2016)
37. Plummer, B.A., Wang, L., Cervantes, C.M., Caicedo, J.C., Hockenmaier, J., Lazebnik, S.: Flickr30k entities: collecting region-to-phrase correspondences for richer image-to-sentence models. In: ICCV (2015)
38. Qi, A., et al.: Toward fine-grained sketch-based 3D shape retrieval. IEEE-TIP **30**, 8595–8606 (2021)
39. Radford, A., et al.: Learning transferable visual models from natural language supervision. arXiv preprint arXiv:2103.00020 (2021)
40. Sain, A., Bhunia, A.K., Potlapalli, V., Chowdhury, P.N., Xiang, T., Song, Y.Z.: Sketch3T: test-time training for zero-shot SBIR. In: CVPR (2022)
41. Sangkloy, P., Burnell, N., Ham, C., Hays, J.: The sketchy database: learning to retrieve badly drawn bunnies. ACM Trans. Graph. (2016)
42. Schneider, R.G., Tuytelaars, T.: Sketch classification and classfication-driven analysis using fisher vectors. In: SIGGRAPH Asia (2014)
43. Sharma, P., Ding, N., Goodman, S., Soricut, R.: Conceptual captions: a cleaned, hypernymed, image alt-text dataset for automatic image captioning. In: ACL (2018)
44. Simonyan, K., Zisserman, A.: Very deep convolutional networks for large-scale image recognition. In: ICLR (2015)
45. Song, J., Song, Y.Z., Xiang, T., Hospedales, T.M.: Fine-grained image retrieval: the text/sketch input dilemma. In: BMVC (2017)
46. Song, J., Yu, Q., Song, Y.Z., Xiang, T., Hospedales, T.M.: Deep spatial-semantic attention for fine-grained sketch-based image retrieval. In: ICCV (2017)
47. Srinivasan, K., Raman, K., Chen, J., Bendersky, M., Najork, M.: Wit: Wikipedia-based image text dataset for multimodal multilingual machine learning. arXiv preprint arXiv:2103.01913 (2021)
48. Vedantam, R., Zitnick, C.L., Parikh, D.: Cider: consensus-based image description evaluation. In: CVPR (2015)
49. Vinyals, O., Toshev, A., Bengio, S., Erhan, D.: Show and tell: a neural image caption generator. In: CVPR (2015)
50. Wang, J., et al.: Learning fine-grained image similarity with deep ranking. In: CVPR (2014)
51. Wang, L., Schwing, A.G., Lazebnik, S.: Diverse and accurate image description using a variational auto-encoder with an additive gaussian encoding space. In: NeurIPS (2017)

52. Wang, S.Y., Bau, D., Zhu, J.Y.: Sketch your own GAN. In: ICCV (2021)
53. Wang, T.Y., Ceylan, D., Popovic, J., Mitra, N.J.: Learning a shared shape space for multimodal garment design. In: SIGGRAPH Asia (2018)
54. Wang, Z., Qiu, S., Feng, N., Rushmeier, H., McMillan, L., Dorsey, J.: Tracing versus freehand for evaluating computer-generated drawings. ACM Trans. Graph. **40**(4), 1–12 (2021)
55. Wen, Y., Zhang, K., Li, Z., Qiao, Yu.: A discriminative feature learning approach for deep face recognition. In: Leibe, B., Matas, J., Sebe, N., Welling, M. (eds.) ECCV 2016. LNCS, vol. 9911, pp. 499–515. Springer, Cham (2016). https://doi.org/10.1007/978-3-319-46478-7_31
56. Xu, K., et al.: Show, attend and tell: Neural image caption generation with visual attention. In: ICML (2015)
57. Yan, C., Vanderhaeghe, D., Gingold, Y.: A benchmark for rough sketch cleanup. ACM Trans. Graph. **39**(6), 1–14 (2020)
58. Yu, Q., Liu, F., Song, Y.Z., Xiang, T., Hospedales, T.M., Loy, C.C.: Sketch me that shoe. In: CVPR (2016)
59. Yu, Q., Yang, Y., Song, Y.Z., Xiang, T., Hospedales, T.: Sketch-a-net that beats humans. In: BMVC (2015)
60. Zhang, R., Isola, P., Efros, A.A.: Colorful image colorization. In: Leibe, B., Matas, J., Sebe, N., Welling, M. (eds.) ECCV 2016. LNCS, vol. 9907, pp. 649–666. Springer, Cham (2016). https://doi.org/10.1007/978-3-319-46487-9_40
61. Zou, C., et al.: Sketchyscene: Rickly-annotated scene sketches. In: ECCV (2018)

Exploring Fine-Grained Audiovisual Categorization with the SSW60 Dataset

Grant Van Horn[1]([✉]), Rui Qian[1], Kimberly Wilber[2], Hartwig Adam[2], Oisin Mac Aodha[3], and Serge Belongie[4]

[1] Cornell University, Ithaca, USA
gvanhorn@cornell.edu
[2] Google, Menlo Park, USA
[3] University of Edinburgh, Edinburgh, UK
[4] University of Copenhagen, Copenhagen, Denmark

Abstract. We present a new benchmark dataset, Sapsucker Woods 60 (SSW60), for advancing research on audiovisual fine-grained categorization. While our community has made great strides in fine-grained visual categorization on images, the counterparts in audio and video fine-grained categorization are relatively unexplored. To encourage advancements in this space, we have carefully constructed the SSW60 dataset to enable researchers to experiment with classifying the same set of categories in three different modalities: images, audio, and video. The dataset covers 60 species of birds and is comprised of images from existing datasets, and brand new, expert curated audio and video datasets. We thoroughly benchmark audiovisual classification performance and modality fusion experiments through the use of state-of-the-art transformer methods. Our findings show that performance of audiovisual fusion methods is better than using exclusively image or audio based methods for the task of video classification. We also present interesting modality transfer experiments, enabled by the unique construction of SSW60 to encompass three different modalities. We hope the SSW60 dataset and accompanying baselines spur research in this fascinating area.

Keywords: Multi-modal learning · Fine-grained · Audio · Video

1 Introduction

Image-based fine-grained visual categorization (FGVC) of natural world categories has seen impressive performance gains over the last decade of research. This progression has been fueled by both larger datasets and improved techniques for classification. For example, consider the domain of bird species classification. The popular CUB200 [81] dataset (covering 200 classes of birds, each with 30 train and 30 test images) has seen top-1 accuracy improve from 10.3% [81]

The first two authors contributed equally. https://github.com/visipedia/ssw60.

Supplementary Information The online version contains supplementary material available at https://doi.org/10.1007/978-3-031-20074-8_16.

Fig. 1. Why audiovisual? Left: American Crow and Common Raven are visually confusing but aurally distinguishable, as illustrated by the spectrograms. Right: Yellow Warbler and Chestnut-sided Warbler are aurally confusing but visually distinguishable. Individually, audio and visual modalities have both advantages and disadvantages. We present the Sapsucker Woods 60 dataset (SSW60), a new dataset to facilitate work in fine-grained audiovisual categorization.

to over 91.7% [29]. This dataset motivated the construction of the larger and better curated NABirds [77] dataset (covering 400 species of birds, each with 60 train and 60 test images), which subsequently gave rise to the larger iNaturalist competition datasets [1]. The latest dataset in this series has 1,486 species of birds, most with 300 training examples, and the winners of the 2021 iNaturalist competition [1] achieved 94% top-1 accuracy on these species (using geographic location information). The release of the CUB200 dataset was a catalyst for FGVC research, motivating the construction of improved datasets as well as providing the means to benchmark progress. But what about the challenge of fine-grained categorization (FGC) in modalities besides images?

Audio and video modalities receive less attention than images for the task of fine-grained categorization. What opportunities and challenges do these modalities present (see Fig. 1)? More importantly, which existing datasets allow us to study cross-modality performance and where do they fall short? Large-scale audiovisual datasets such as AudioSet [25] and VGGSound [13], provide a class hierarchy more akin to coarse grained categories as perceived by humans than fine-grained categories as typically used in the context of FGC (with classes such as "Chirp, tweet" and "Hoot" for bird vocalizations in AudioSet).

There are a few existing bird video datasets [23,66,90], each focused primarily on benchmarking the performance of video frame classification, as opposed to cross-modality or audiovisual analysis. The YouTube-Birds dataset [90] almost checks all the boxes, except upon close inspection we find multiple inconveniences, e.g. it consists of a collection of YouTube links, of which at least 7% are broken at the time of writing, it contains labelling errors (typical for fine-grained datasets curated by non-experts), and the videos are not trimmed to the content of interest and are thus long and unwieldy. Both VB100 [23] and IBC127 [66] sampled their videos from higher quality data sources, but they each lack the full complement of unpaired audio and image modalities that we require for exploring audiovisual categorization. Finally, none of the prior art show the utility of audiovisual fusion methods for FGC.

In this paper, we aim to fill this dataset gap and open up new avenues of research in FGC. Our new dataset, SSW60, spans 60 species of birds that all occur in a specific geographic location: Sapsucker Woods in Ithaca, New York, (unlike the random collection of species present in the existing video datasets [23,66,90]). SSW60 contains a new collection of expert curated ten-second video clips for each species, totaling 5,400 video clips. SSW60 also contains an "unpaired" expert curated set of ten-second audio recordings for the same set of species, totaling 3,861 audio recordings. Finally, we also collate image data for the same species from the existing expert curated NABirds dataset [77] and the citizen science collected iNat2021 dataset [78].

With this new dataset in hand, we perform a thorough investigation of audiovisual classification performance. Our baseline methods utilize state-of-the-art backbones trained on visual and audio modalities. We experiment with several different fusion methods to combine information from both modalities and make audiovisual informed classifications. These experiments reveal that audiovisual methods outperform their respective single modality counterparts, advancing the state of the art for fine-grained bird species classification. As SSW60 contains images and unpaired audio examples, we conduct additional experiments to investigate the utility of pretraining on these individual modalities prior to working with video. We identify several insights from these experiments, including the unexpected negative impact of pretraining on high quality images, and the high utility of pretraining on unpaired audio samples.

In summary, we make the following contributions: 1) A new fine-grained dataset that contains expert curated video and audio data for a shared set of object categories. 2) A detailed analysis of cross-modality learning in the context of fine-grained object categories, as well as benchmark results for fine-grained audiovisual categorization.

2   Related Work

2.1   Image, Audio, and Video Datasets

Fine-Grained Image Datasets. The most commonly used classification datasets in computer vision predominantly deal with coarse-grained object reasoning, e.g. [19,28,40,48,65,89]. In contrast, fine-grained datasets contain subordinate categories that can be much more challenging for non-expert human annotators to discriminate. There are many fine-grained datasets spanning a wide range of visual concepts including airplanes [53,80], automobiles [24,42,49,86], dogs [39,50,60], fashion [34], plants [44,57,58], food [10,33], and the natural world [78,79], to name a few.

Datasets featuring images of different species of birds have been particularly popular in the vision community [9,41,77,81]. As a taxonomic group they present an interesting set of challenges that make them well suited for benchmarking advances in vision. For example, their appearance can differ based on life stage or sex, their shape can vary significantly, and some species can be very challenging for even expert humans to tell apart. Inspired by this, we propose a new multi-modal bird dataset that contains data from three different modalities: images, audio, and video.

Fine-Grained Video Datasets. The most commonly used video action recognition datasets also tend to focus on coarse-grained concepts [11,17,36,37,43, 71], with some emphasizing temporal reasoning [27,54,68]. Fewer fine-grained datasets exist, but those that do cover concepts such as sports [47,62,69] and cars [4,90]. Most relevant to this work are the small number of existing video datasets containing birds [23,66,90], see Table 1 for an overview. IBC127 [66] contains 8,014 videos across 127 bird categories. In the paper, experiments are performed for bird (127 classes) and action (4 classes) classification from video. VB100 [23] contains 1,416 videos from 100 bird species and evaluates on the task of species classification from video. While a small number of audio files are also available, no experiments are actually performed using this data. Finally, YouTube-Birds [90] contains 18,350 videos spanning the same 200 classes represented in the CUB200 image dataset [81]. The exact same set of videos are also used in [31]. Experiments are performed on the task of bird classification from video, and they show that their approach gives a minor performance improvement compared to simple baselines [82] which do not use any temporal information. The YouTube-Birds data is provided as a list of YouTube video URLs, and at the time of writing only 17,031 videos are still publicly available.

While these existing fine-grained datasets are very related to our work, they stop short of performing any cross-modal experiments, and do not show the benefit of audiovisual fusion methods for fine-grained categorization. Further, the distribution of data in these datasets is highly skewed and the included species were obviously dictated by data availability from web scraping. The SSW60 dataset provides a nearly uniform data distribution for a set geo-spatially co-located species. See the supplementary material for additional details.

Fine-Grained Audio Datasets. There are numerous examples of human speech focused [22,63], coarse-grained audio classification [21,25,61,67], and binary sound event [52,72] datasets. However, in contrast to images, there are fewer established datasets for fine-grained audio classification. One task that is highly representative of a fine-grained audio challenge is that of species identification. As a result, there exists a number of audio datasets focused on species identification. Examples include bird [15,16,31,51,55] and bat [64,88] species classification. Like their image counterparts, these datasets can be challenging to collect and accurately annotate [7]. These annotation issues can also be compounded by factors such as background noise and low quality recordings. The audio recordings in the SSW60 dataset have been manually vetted by domain experts to ensure that the labels are reliable.

Audiovisual Datasets. In addition to visual content, video data can also contain rich and descriptive audio information. For some fine-grained concepts, this information can be highly complementary to the visual cues, see Fig. 1. Inspired by these types of relationships, the vision community has developed several benchmarks to facilitate the exploration of multi-modal reasoning. Several different approaches have been used to construct these types of datasets.

The most basic approach is to query video media websites with keywords of interest, with the assumption that relevant sound events will also be present. This is the approach taken by the Flickr-SoundNet dataset [6], which contains 2M video clips with audio downloaded from Flickr, and was queried using tags from YFCC100M [73]. An alternative approach is to use automatic filtering, e.g. by making use of image or audio classification models. VGG-Sound [13] consists of 200k, ten-second video clips from 300 different audio classes. The

Table 1. Overview of existing bird datasets. °Only 17,031 videos are currently available online. *Contains the same images as [81]. †Contains the same videos as [90]. ‡Only spectrogram images are available, no audio files are included.

Dataset	Classes	Images	Videos	Audio
CUB200 [81]	200	11,788	-	-
NABirds [77]	555	48,562	-	-
VB100 [23]	100	-	1,416	502
IBC127 [66]	127	-	8,014	-
YouTube-Birds [90]	200	11,788*	18,350°	-
PKU FG-XMedia [31]	200	11,788*	18,350†	12,000‡
Ours	60	31,221	5,400	3,861

object that emits each sound is visible in the video clip, however, each clip is only labeled with one class even though multiple audio-visual events can be present. ACAV100M [45] contains 100M ten-second clips and was constructed using an automatic curation pipeline that maximized the mutual information between the audio and visual channels. The final dataset construction approach is to manually annotate some or all of the data. Kinetics-Sounds [5] features 19k, ten-second, audio-visual clips covering 34 human orientated action classes. The videos are a subset of the Kinetics dataset [37], which were manually filtered to ensure the presence of the actions of interest. More detailed annotations include localizing sound events in time or space. AVE (Audio-Visual Event) [75] is a subset of the AudioSet dataset [25], and contains 4,143 ten-second videos covering 28 event categories with manually labeled temporal event boundaries. Each video contains at least one two-second long audio-visual event. The LLP dataset [74] contains 11,849 YouTube video clips with 25 event categories labeled. The goal of the dataset is audio-visual parsing, i.e. deciding whether an event is audible, visible, or both. Manual temporal event annotations are provided for a subset of the videos. Finally, [12] adds image bounding boxes to audible sound sources for 5k videos in VGG-Sound [13]. In addition, the community has been working on audiovisual datasets for violence detection [83], as well as VQA [46,87]

None of the above datasets explore the problem of fine-grained audiovisual reasoning. In this work, we make use of high quality image and audio classifiers in order to select video clips that are highly likely to contain the discriminative audiovisual events for a set of 60 bird species.

2.2 Multi-modal Learning

Audiovisual Fusion. There is large and growing literature on multi-modal fusion for audiovisual understanding. Early methods adopted straightforward early or score fusion strategies, e.g. [14]. Subsequent research applied modality-specific networks with learning-driven information combinations in mid or late stage fusion strategies. Representative methods include activation summations [38], lateral connections [84], attention based re-weighting [20], among others. A comprehensive review can be found in [8]. The recent success of adopting

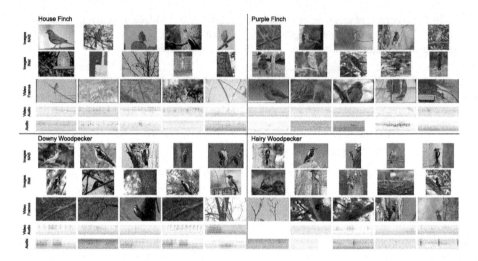

Fig. 2. Visual and audio examples (frames and spectrograms) for example bird species from the SSW60 dataset. Clockwise from top left: House Finch, Purple Finch, Hairy Woodpecker, and Downy Woodpecker. For each species, the five rows show modality samples from: (1) "Images NAB" - from NABirds [77]; (2) "Images iNat" - from iNaturalist2021 [78]; (3) "Video Frames" - center frames; (4) "Video Audio" - spectrogram that covers the three seconds of audio near the center frame; and (5) "Audio" - spectrogram generated from three seconds near the center of the file.

transformer architectures in the vision [18] and audio [26] communities empowered more advanced audiovisual fusion methods. A representative state-of-the-art work [56] carefully studied audiovisual fusion with transformers and we adopt this as our primary baseline.

Cross-Modal Analysis. [35] defined and measured the impact of several different domain shift factors in the context of training object detectors on video frames and images. These factors included the accuracy of the training bounding boxes, appearance diversity, image quality, and object size. They showed that these factors, in combination, are almost completely responsible for the performance difference as compared to training and testing on the same domain. Their conclusion was that if one wants to achieve the best performance they should train and test on the same domain. In this work, we analyse domain differences arising from depictions of the same concept (i.e. fine-grained bird categories) across different modalities.

3   SSW60 Dataset

In this section we describe the SSW60 dataset and the steps taken to construct it. The dataset is built around 60 species of birds that have a high propensity to be seen or heard on a live "feeder-cam" (i.e. , a static camera monitoring a bird feeder) that is continuously recording in Ithaca, New York. These species, therefore, represent a realistic fine-grained challenge experienced by humans (unlike, e.g. , CUB200 where the categories of birds come from all over the world). A model that can recognize these species and interpret their behaviors will be particularly relevant in assisting biologists with analyzing large collections of video footage from these cameras. We plan for future versions of this dataset to directly incorporate video from the live cams. For each of the 60 species we sampled data from three different modalities: videos (containing paired frames and audio), audio recordings, and images. Here videos are unique as they contain both visual and audio modalities, while the additional unpaired audio recordings and image datasets only consist of one modality respectively. See Fig. 2 for examples from the various modalities and Table 2 for per-modality statistics.

Video. The videos in SSW60 come from recordings archived at the Macaulay Library at the Cornell Lab of Ornithology [2]. These videos are contributed by professional and enthusiast videographers from the around the world, and can range in duration from a few seconds to multiple minutes. The camera view points are not fixed and can move in order to track the bird as it moves through the environment. Each video is associated with a particular "target species" that is known to be present in the video. For each video we isolated a ten-second clip where the task of species classification is particularly relevant. To accomplish this, we applied the following procedure: 1) For each of the 60 species of birds, we sampled all of their respective videos in the Macaulay Library. 2) We then used an image based bird detector and classifier (trained on the 30M+ images from the Macaulay Library) to identify the sections of video where the target species was present. This gave us candidate video sections to extract ten-second clips. 3) To further refine the candidate clips, we ran the Merlin Sound ID model [3], a high performing acoustic bird classification model, across the audio tracks of the candidate clips to determine if the target species was vocalizing. 4) For each video, we keep the clip with the highest likelihood of the target species vocalizing. 5) Finally, for each species, we select 90 video clips for the dataset, where each clip comes from a unique video.

We found that most videos in the Macaulay Library do not have complete metadata indicating the exact recording time and date. We therefore split the video files into train and test sets by splitting on the videographers. All of the videos from a particular videographer are either in the train split or the test split. We found that this tactic was necessary to prevent multiple, highly similar videos uploaded by the same videographer winding up in both the train and test sets (a problem found in existing datasets [23,66]). All videos are converted to a frame rate of 25FPS. This modality is referred to as "Video Frames" in the experiment section when considering only the frames of the videos, and is referred to as "Video Audio" when considering only the audio channel.

Note that some of the ten-second clips in SSW60 do not have the target species vocalizing; we do not treat this as a problem but view it as a challenge and inherent property of "in-the-wild" video. The process of a human uploading a video (as opposed to an audio recording) to the Macaulay Library, means that the videos in SSW60 will be biased towards visually relevant information

Table 2. Summary of the train/test split sizes for each modality in SSW60, along with information about the number of examples per class.

	Source	Total	Min	Max	Median
Images NAB	[77]	5050, 5171	30, 31	221, 214	60, 60
Images iNat	[78]	18000, 3000	300, 50	300, 50	300, 50
Audio	ours	2597, 1264	28, 12	52, 30	45, 21
Video	ours	3462, 1938	38, 22	68, 52	59, 31

for classification, as opposed to aurally relevant information. Using an acoustic classifier to find those sections of video with both visual and aurally relevant information helps mitigate this, but does not completely remove the visual bias.

Audio. All 60 bird species in SSW60 have unpaired audio recordings from the Macaulay Library. These recordings are unpaired in the sense that they do not have any associated visual data, i.e. no videos or images. Each audio recording is annotated with a particular "target species" that is known to be vocalizing in the file. However, it is not specified at what moment in time the target species is vocalizing, and recordings can be multiple minutes long. We sampled audio recordings for each of our 60 species and had an expert ornithologist provide temporal onset and offset annotations for the target species. We then trimmed the audio files to ten-second clips that contain the target species' vocalization. The result is an expert curated audio dataset for each of the 60 species in SSW60. The audio files are stored in WAV format at a sampling rate of 22.05kHz.

Audio is split between train and test sets by ensuring that audio files from the same recording session are placed in the same split. This prevents models from exploiting common background noise that might be heard across multiple recordings from the same location and time. This modality is referred to as "Audio" in the experiment section.

Images. Finally, we also preform experiments with images from two existing datasets: NABirds [77] and iNat2021 [78]. The 60 species in SSW60 conveniently overlap with the species in these existing datasets, and we incorporate all images available into SSW60 while maintaining the original train/test splits. For the NABirds dataset, we merged the respective "visual categories" that comprise each species. The images in NABirds are of particularly high quality, representing a best case scenario for visual classification (i.e. someone using high quality camera equipment to carefully compose a photograph for the goal of visual identification). The images in iNat2021 are more mixed in terms of quality and therefore represent a more difficult visual classification task. See Fig. 2 for sample images from both datasets. These modalities are referred to as "Images NAB" and "Images iNat" in the experiment section.

4   Methods

We are interested in exploring fine-grained categorization in two areas: **cross-modal analysis** and **audiovisual fusion**.

For **cross-modal analysis**, we assume a fixed backbone architecture that can be utilized for processing data from multiple modalities. For the audio modality, we convert the waveforms to spectrogram images. For videos, we adopt TSN [82] style methods using 2D image backbones to encode features and perform fusion on top of them. Our experimental procedure is straightforward: we train the backbone model using a particular training modality (see Sect. 3 for the options) and then evaluate the performance on an evaluation modality directly. As we have the same species in each modality, the trained backbone can be used directly on the evaluation modality. However, there is a domain transfer problem to consider (i.e. moving from images to video frames), so we also evaluate the trained backbone by first fine-tuning the weights using the training split of the evaluation modality, and then evaluate on that evaluation modality. We use top-1 accuracy as the evaluation criteria for all experiments. Unlike existing bird video datasets [23,66,90], our evaluation splits are uniform for each species, which makes top-1 accuracy across examples an unbiased assessment of performance. All backbone models are trained using softmax cross-entropy.

In addition to cross-modality analysis, we study fine-grained **audiovisual fusion** using the paired "Video Frames" and "Video Audio" data in SSW60. We adopt a transformer-based backbone and experiment with mid-fusion through the state-of-the-art multimodal bottleneck fusion approach of [56], as well as late and score-fusion. Thanks to the image and audio recordings provided in SSW60, we are able to study the effect of different pretraining dataset choices (e.g. ImageNet, Images iNat, and Images NAB) on audiovisual fusion.

4.1 Implementation Details

Image Modality. We adopt the standard ImageNet [65] training paradigm. During training, we randomly crop and resize a square portion of the image to 224×224 pixels, followed by a random flip augmentation; during evaluation, the shorter edge of the image is resized to 256 pixels first, and then a center crop of 224×224 is extracted for classification. We perform evaluation using a CNN-based ResNet50 [30] and transformer-based ViT-B [18] for experiments on the image modality, as they are the most popular choices in the image recognition community. Both are initialized with ImageNet pretrained weights.

Audio Modality. For audio processing, we convert the audio waveforms into spectrogram images. Concretely, the raw audio signal is resampled to a rate of 16kHz. We then apply the short-time Fourier transform algorithm using a window size of 512 and a stride length of 128. The frequency values are then transformed using the "mel-scale" with 128 bins. Finally we convert the magnitude values to decibel units and normalize to generate the final spectrogram image. This image is duplicated three times to create the RGB input for the network. For a 10-second long audio clip, the shape of the generated spectrogram image is approximately 128×1250, where 128 is the number of mel-scaled frequency bands and 1250 is the temporal span. During training, we utilize two augmentations to avoid overfitting: time cropping and frequency masking [59].

For time cropping, we randomly sample a window of length 400 time bins (spanning all 128 frequency bands) from the original spectrogram image (400 time bins corresponds to approximately 3 s of audio). For frequency masking, we randomly mask out 15 consecutive frequency bands. During evaluation, we densely sample five windows of length 400 time bins (spanning all 128 frequency bins) from the original spectrogram images using a stride of 150. We average the logits across the 5 windows to use as the final prediction. Earlier work [32] used VGG-style [70] backbones which we also compare to for completeness.

Video Frame Modality. We adopt the segment sampling strategy of TSN [82] where we first divide the video clip into eight uniform segments. During training we randomly sample one frame from each segment, while for evaluation we select the center frame of each segment. Each of the eight selected frames is passed through the 2D ResNet50 or ViT-B backbone for feature extraction using images of size 224×224 pixels. We then average the eight feature vectors to generate the final feature representation for the video clip. This global feature is then passed through a fully connected layer to produce a vector of logits. We initially conducted experiments with video-specific 3D convolution networks with dense frame sampling using S3D [85]. However we found that S3D (pretrained on Kinetics-400 [37]) performed worse than our TSN-style baselines (pretrained on ImageNet) for SSW60. Furthermore, using a 2D network like ResNet50 or ViT-B as the backbone provides the flexibility for easily studying feature transfer between video frames and images. We leave experimentation with more sophisticated video backbones for future work.

Audiovisual Fusion. We briefly recap the transformer architecture and then describe how we conduct audiovisual fusion experiments. Given an input image or audio spectrogram, it is first divided into non-overlapping patches. Each patch is projected to a token using a linear layer and a special learnable classification token is added. More details can be find in the original ViT paper [18]. After tokenization, the tokens are passed through a stack of transformer layers. We denote the input of the l-th layer as $\mathbf{z}^l$, which results in $\mathbf{z}^{l+1} = trans\_layer_l(\mathbf{z}^l)$. The computation inside $trans\_layer_l$ can be written as

$$\mathbf{y}^l = \mathrm{MSA}(\mathrm{LN}(\mathbf{z}^l)) + \mathbf{z}^l, \tag{1}$$

$$\mathbf{z}^{l+1} = \mathrm{MLP}(\mathrm{LN}(\mathbf{y}^l)) + \mathbf{y}^l, \tag{2}$$

where LN denotes layer normalization, MSA denotes multi-head self-attention. In our audiovisual fusion, we use two identical $L = 12$ layer transformers to take the visual and audio input separately. The forward process for the visual modality is thus $\mathbf{z}_v^{l+1} = v\_trans\_layer_l(\mathbf{z}_v^l)$, and $\mathbf{z}_a^{l+1} = a\_trans\_layer_l(\mathbf{z}_a^l)$ for the audio modality.

For mid-fusion, we use the state-of-the-art multimodal bottleneck transformer [56]. Here a set of learnable tokens $\mathbf{z}_b$ are used as the fusion bottleneck

$$[\mathbf{z}_v^{l+1}||\hat{\mathbf{z}}_b] = v\_trans\_layer_l([\mathbf{z}_v^l||\mathbf{z}_b]), \tag{3}$$

$$[\mathbf{z}_a^{l+1}||\mathbf{z}_b] = a\_trans\_layer_l([\mathbf{z}_a^l||\hat{\mathbf{z}}_b]). \tag{4}$$

$[.||.]$ denotes the concatenation of tokens. In each layer, $\mathbf{z}_b$ first interacts with the visual tokens $\mathbf{z}_v^l$ and gets updated to $\hat{\mathbf{z}}_b$. Then $\hat{\mathbf{z}}_b$ interacts with the audio tokens $\mathbf{z}_a^l$ to finish the audio visual fusion. Following [56], we conduct this fusion in the last four layers of the transformer.

For late fusion, we concatenate the class tokens of both modalities after the last transformer block, written as $[\mathbf{z}_v^{L+1}[0]||\mathbf{z}_a^{L+1}[0]]$ and apply a linear classifier on top of it. For score fusion, we take the predictions from both modalities and use a weighted sum of the combined final predictions. In practice, we use a weight of 0.5 for both the visual and audio modalities.

5 Experiments

We first perform cross-modal experiments on the video and audio modalities separately, and then explore multi-modal fusion for audiovisual categorization.

Visual Modality Categorization. Here we benchmark the performance achieved on the Video Frames of SSW60. Table 3 (Left) shows the top-1 accuracy on the Video Frame test set when using a ResNet50 backbone trained on either the Images iNat, Images NAB, or the Video Frames training datasets. We split the results depending on whether we fine-tune (FT) the trained backbone on the Video Frames training dataset. Training directly on the Video Frames dataset achieves a top-1 accuracy of 54.92%. Interestingly, we see that evaluating the Images iNat model directly on the Video Frames achieves an even higher top-1 accuracy of 60.47%. This is further improved to 71.88% when fine-tuning on the Video Frames train split. We compare these numbers to those achieved by a model trained on the Images NAB dataset: 24.05% and 56.55%, top-1 accuracy respectively. The Images iNat dataset has more training samples than Images NAB, however, the images in the NABirds dataset are aesthetically higher quality (see Sect. 3). These results seem to indicate that performance on "in-the-wild" videos benefits more from "lower quality" training images.

Audio Modality Categorization. We next benchmark the new unpaired audio dataset component of SSW60. Table 4 contains the results of these experiments. We trained and evaluated VGG16 and 19 [70], ResNet18 and 50 [30], and the transformer-based ViT-B [18] architectures. As expected, we see a progression of top-1 accuracy as we move from older architectures (52.1% for VGG16)

Table 3. Top-1 accuracy on SSW60 Video-Frames using a ResNet50 backbone (left) and SSW60 Video-Audio using a ResNet18 backbone (right) when training on different datasets (columns). Results are presented with and without finetuning (FT) on the respective video modality.

Cross-Modal - Video Frames				Cross-Modal - Video Audio		
FT	Images iNat	Images NAB	Video Frames	FT	Unpair Audio	Video Audio
	60.47	24.05	54.92		24.41	10.37
✓	71.88	56.55	-	✓	15.33	-

Table 4. Comparison of audio backbones trained and tested on the unpaired audio modality in SSW60. All models are initialized from ImageNet pretrained weights. '↑384' indicates that a model is fine-tuned on ImageNet with a higher resolution [76] and 'AS' is further fine-trained on AudioSet [26] before use.

Backbone	VGG16	VGG19	ResNet18	ResNet50	ViT-B	ViT-B↑384	ViT-B↑384 AS
Top 1 Acc	52.1%	56.1%	59.01%	63.7%	66.8%	65.9%	67.4%

to the latest architectures (66.8% for ViT-B). We attempted to push accuracy further by using a ViT-B model pretrained on a higher resolution image input (224 vs 384), but we actually see performance decrease to 65.9%. However, if we take this higher resolution model and add an additional pretraining step of training on AudioSet [25] then we achieve a top-1 accuracy of 67.4%.

We now benchmark the Video Audio component of SSW60. For these experiments we chose a ResNet18 backbone for convenience, but expect a more powerful backbone to be slightly more performant (see Table 4 and Table 5 (Direct Eval)). The obvious result is the low performance achieved when training exclusively with the Video Audio data, achieving a top-1 accuracy of just 10.37%. Directly using a model trained on the unpaired audio achieves 24.41%, a significant improvement. Interestingly, fine-tuning the unpaired audio model on the Video Audio training samples leads to a decrease in performance, down to 15.33%. This points to a recurring theme: video is biased to visual features (simply by the nature through which it was collected), and while it contains an audio channel, the ability to use the audio channel for classification appears to be difficult. We show in the next section however that it is possible to improve overall classification accuracy by incorporating audio.

Table 5. Audiovisual fine-grained categorization results on SSW60 videos using ViT models. We split results into two different scenarios: evaluation on the modalities individually ("Direct Eval" and "No Fusion") and on both modalities together ("Fusion"). All numbers reflect top-1 accuracy. "Direct Eval" means we can conduct direct evaluation for modalities pretrained on datasets with the same 60 species. "No Fusion" means we take a pretrained network and fine-tune it on the respective modality from the SSW60 training videos. For the Mid and Late fusion algorithms in "Fusion", we initialize the model with pretrained weights from individual models trained on the "Pretrain" datasets. For Score fusion, we take the best individual model for each modality (considering both "Direct Eval" and "No Fusion" variants) and fuse their scores by a weighted sum.

Pretrain		Direct Eval		No Fusion		Fusion		
Visual	Audio	Vid Frames	Vid Audio	Vid Frames	Vid Audio	Mid	Late	Score
ImageNet	ImageNet	-	-	59.0%	14.3%	54.3%	**59.8%**	58.9%
ImageNet	Unpair Audio	-	28.3%	59.0%	30.4%	62.0%	62.5%	**63.5%**
Images NAB	Unpair Audio	60.0%	28.3%	64.4%	30.4%	67.5%	**68.4%**	68.2%
Images iNat	Unpair Audio	78.0%	28.3%	76.2%	30.4%	73.5%	78.3%	**80.6%**

Audiovisual Fine-Grained Categorization. In contrast to the rich literature of audiovisual fusion on coarse-grained video datasets, audiovisual fine-grained categorization (FGC) remains under-explored due to a lack of appropriate datasets. SSW60 fills this gap and allows us to conduct a comprehensive analysis that explores the impacts of various pretraining and fusion methods on audiovisual FGC. We follow the paradigm employed by Nagragni et al. [56] and use two uni-modal models to process the audio and visual modalities separately. We adopt the ViT-B [18] backbone for both modalities (see Sect. 4.1). We are interested in two research questions: 1) What is the effect of different fusion methods? and 2) What is the effect of different pretraining datasets? For fusion methods, we use the state-of-the-art MBT [56] as the mid-fusion algorithm, and compare to late and score fusion techniques. For pretraining datasets, we utilize ImageNet, Images NAB, and Images iNat for the visual modality, and ImageNet and unpaired audio recordings for the audio modality. By construction, once a backbone has been trained on Images NAB, Images iNat, or the unpaired audio, we are able to directly evaluate on the corresponding modality of the SSW60 video dataset, since all datasets share the same 60 species. Our results are summarized in Table 5. We also provide per-class analysis between uni-modal and audiovisual fusion performance in Fig. 3. Our best result on SSW60 (80.6% top-1 accuracy) comes from fusing the scores of a visual model pretrained on Images iNat (and **not** fine-tuned on the SSW60 video frames), and an audio model pretrained on the unpaired audio and further fine-tuned on the audio channels of the SSW60 videos.

We highlight three conclusions from our audiovisual fusion investigations. **First, the best result from audiovisual fusion is always better than training on each modality separately.** For each row in Table 5, the highest top-1 accuracy is always in the Fusion column, meaning that combining information from both modalities is always better than using a single modality. This finding aligns well with our motivation of audiovisual fusion in Fig. 1. **Second, there is no "best" fusion method.** In the four different pretraining configurations, we find that late fusion works best half the time, and score fusion works best in the other half. It is interesting that the state-of-the-art mid-fusion method does not work as well as the simpler methods. We leave this as an open question for the community to explore more advanced mid-fusion methods for audiovisual FGC. **Third, pretraining on external datasets can be *very* beneficial.** We observe a $\sim 20\%$ increase in top-1 performance when fine-tuning the ImageNet backbones on Images iNat and the unpaired audio (Fusion column, row 1 vs row 4 in Table 5).

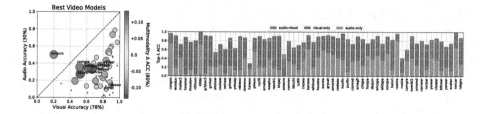

Fig. 3. Per-species audio and visual modality performance along with the resulting audiovisual performance after score fusion. These results correspond to the bottom right fusion model in Table 5. The size and color of the dots on the scatter plot indicate the resulting top-1 accuracy change (from the best uni-modal model) when fusing the predictions for audiovisual classification. Large blue dots correspond to better audiovisual accuracy. Large red dots correspond to worse audiovisual accuracy. Species with the largest positive and negative audiovisual changes have been labeled. The bars for each species in the bar plot are ordered by the modality performance. Purple bars on top reveal those species with improved audiovisual accuracy. 27 species improved, 27 species remained the same, and 6 species decreased after fusion. (Color figure online)

6   Conclusion

We present SSW60, a new dataset for advancing fine-grained audiovisual categorization. This expert curated dataset provides researchers with the tools to explore categorization across three different modalities, enabling a comprehensive exploration of cross-modal and audiovisual fusion. Similar to how the CUB200 dataset paved the way for the larger, and better curated, NABirds and iNaturalist datasets, we envision SSW60 as a vital first step towards studying audiovisual fine-grained categorization. The availability of live "feeder-cam" video featuring the bird species in SSW60 also provides an interesting avenue for studying the deployment of trained models for real-time audiovisual categorization - an important problem for biodiversity monitoring. At its current size, SSW60 can also be used as an evaluation dataset for self-supervised audiovisual models. We envision SSW60 broadly benefiting the vision community by providing ample directions for future work on FGC and video analysis more generally.

Limitations. The size of the SSW60 dataset is a potential limitation for training models from scratch, which is why we used ImageNet pretrained models. ImageNet does contain ∼60 classes of birds, but all models started from an ImageNet pretrained backbone. The video and audio annotations in SSW60 are "weak" in the sense that they apply to the entire ten-second clip, as opposed to temporally localized annotations.

Acknowledgment. Serge Belongie is supported in part by the Pioneer Centre for AI, DNRF grant number P1. These investigations would not be possible without the help of the passionate birding community contributing their knowledge and data to the Macaulay Library; thank you!

References

1. iNaturalist 2021 Challenge. http://www.kaggle.com/c/inaturalist-2021. Accessed 7 Mar 2022
2. Macaulay Library. http://www.macaulaylibrary.org. Accessed 7 Mar 2022
3. Merlin Sound ID. http://merlin.allaboutbirds.org/sound-id. Accessed 7 Mar 2022
4. Alsahafi, Y., Lemmond, D., Ventura, J., Boult, T.: Carvideos: a novel dataset for fine-grained car classification in videos. In: International Conference on Information Technology-New Generations (2019)
5. Arandjelovic, R., Zisserman, A.: Look, listen and learn. In: ICCV (2017)
6. Aytar, Y., Vondrick, C., Torralba, A.: Soundnet: learning sound representations from unlabeled video. In: NeurIPS (2016)
7. Baker, E., Vincent, S.: A deafening silence: a lack of data and reproducibility in published bioacoustics research? Biodivers. Data J. (2019)
8. Bayoudh, K., Knani, R., Hamdaoui, F., Mtibaa, A.: A survey on deep multimodal learning for computer vision: advances, trends, applications, and datasets. Vis. Comput. **38**(8), 2939–2970 (2021)
9. Berg, T., Liu, J., Lee, S.W., Alexander, M.L., Jacobs, D.W., Belhumeur, P.N.: Birdsnap: large-scale fine-grained visual categorization of birds. In: CVPR (2014)
10. Bossard, L., Guillaumin, M., Van Gool, L.: Food-101 – mining discriminative components with random forests. In: Fleet, D., Pajdla, T., Schiele, B., Tuytelaars, T. (eds.) ECCV 2014. LNCS, vol. 8694, pp. 446–461. Springer, Cham (2014). https://doi.org/10.1007/978-3-319-10599-4_29
11. Carreira, J., Zisserman, A.: Quo vadis, action recognition? A new model and the kinetics dataset. In: CVPR (2017)
12. Chen, H., Xie, W., Afouras, T., Nagrani, A., Vedaldi, A., Zisserman, A.: Localizing visual sounds the hard way. In: CVPR (2021)
13. Chen, H., Xie, W., Vedaldi, A., Zisserman, A.: Vggsound: a large-scale audio-visual dataset. In: International Conference on Acoustics, Speech and Signal Processing (ICASSP) (2020)
14. Chen, T., Rao, R.R.: Audio-visual integration in multimodal communication. Proc. IEEE **86**(5), 837–852 (1998)
15. Chronister, L., Rhinehart, T., Place, A., Kitzes, J.: An annotated set of audio recordings of Eastern North American birds containing frequency, time, and species information. Ecology (2021)
16. Cramer, J., Lostanlen, V., Farnsworth, A., Salamon, J., Bello, J.P.: Chirping up the right tree: incorporating biological taxonomies into deep bioacoustic classifiers. In: International Conference on Acoustics, Speech and Signal Processing (ICASSP) (2020)
17. Damen, D., et al.: Scaling egocentric vision: the epic-kitchens dataset. In: ECCV (2018)
18. Dosovitskiy, A., et al.: An image is worth 16x16 words: transformers for image recognition at scale. In: ICLR (2021)
19. Everingham, M., Van Gool, L., Williams, C.K., Winn, J., Zisserman, A.: The pascal visual object classes (VOC) challenge. In: IJCV (2010)
20. Fayek, H.M., Kumar, A.: Large scale audiovisual learning of sounds with weakly labeled data. arXiv:2006.01595 (2020)
21. Fonseca, E., Favory, X., Pons, J., Font, F., Serra, X.: FSD50K: an open dataset of human-labeled sound events. arXiv:2010.00475 (2020)

22. Garofolo, J.S.: Timit acoustic phonetic continuous speech corpus. Linguistic Data Consortium (1993)
23. Ge, Z., et al.: Exploiting temporal information for DCNN-based fine-grained object classification. In: International Conference on Digital Image Computing: Techniques and Applications (2016)
24. Gebru, T., Krause, J., Wang, Y., Chen, D., Deng, J., Fei-Fei, L.: Fine-grained car detection for visual census estimation. In: AAAI (2017)
25. Gemmeke, J.F., et al.: Audio set: an ontology and human-labeled dataset for audio events. In: International Conference on Acoustics, Speech and Signal Processing (ICASSP) (2017)
26. Gong, Y., Chung, Y.A., Glass, J.: AST: audio spectrogram transformer. In: Interspeech (2021)
27. Goyal, R., et al.: The "something something" video database for learning and evaluating visual common sense. In: ICCV (2017)
28. Gupta, A., Dollar, P., Girshick, R.: LVIS: a dataset for large vocabulary instance segmentation. In: CVPR (2019)
29. He, J., et al.: TransFG: a transformer architecture for fine-grained recognition. arXiv:2103.07976 (2021)
30. He, K., Zhang, X., Ren, S., Sun, J.: Deep residual learning for image recognition. In: CVPR, pp. 770–778 (2016)
31. He, X., Peng, Y., Xie, L.: A new benchmark and approach for fine-grained cross-media retrieval. In: International Conference on Multimedia (2019)
32. Hershey, S., et al.: CNN architectures for large-scale audio classification. In: ICASSP (2017)
33. Hou, S., Feng, Y., Wang, Z.: VegFru: a domain-specific dataset for fine-grained visual categorization. In: ICCV (2017)
34. Jia, M., et al.: Fashionpedia: ontology, segmentation, and an attribute localization dataset. In: Vedaldi, A., Bischof, H., Brox, T., Frahm, J.-M. (eds.) ECCV 2020. LNCS, vol. 12346, pp. 316–332. Springer, Cham (2020). https://doi.org/10.1007/978-3-030-58452-8_19
35. Kalogeiton, V., Ferrari, V., Schmid, C.: Analysing domain shift factors between videos and images for object detection. PAMI 38(11), 2327–2334 (2016)
36. Karpathy, A., Toderici, G., Shetty, S., Leung, T., Sukthankar, R., Fei-Fei, L.: Large-scale video classification with convolutional neural networks. In: CVPR (2014)
37. Kay, W., et al.: The kinetics human action video dataset. arXiv:1705.06950 (2017)
38. Kazakos, E., Nagrani, A., Zisserman, A., Damen, D.: Epic-fusion: audio-visual temporal binding for egocentric action recognition. In: ICCV (2019)
39. Khosla, A., Jayadevaprakash, N., Yao, B., Fei-Fei, L.: Novel dataset for fine-grained image categorization. In: First Workshop on Fine-Grained Visual Categorization (2011)
40. Krasin, I., et al.: Openimages: a public dataset for large-scale multi-label and multi-class image classification (2017). http://storage.googleapis.com/openimages/web/index.html
41. Krause, J., et al.: The unreasonable effectiveness of noisy data for fine-grained recognition. In: Leibe, B., Matas, J., Sebe, N., Welling, M. (eds.) ECCV 2016. LNCS, vol. 9907, pp. 301–320. Springer, Cham (2016). https://doi.org/10.1007/978-3-319-46487-9_19
42. Krause, J., Stark, M., Deng, J., Fei-Fei, L.: 3D object representations for fine-grained categorization. In: ICCV Workshops (2013)
43. Kuehne, H., Jhuang, H., Garrote, E., Poggio, T., Serre, T.: HMDB: a large video database for human motion recognition. In: ICCV (2011)

44. Kumar, N., et al.: Leafsnap: a computer vision system for automatic plant species identification. In: Fitzgibbon, A., Lazebnik, S., Perona, P., Sato, Y., Schmid, C. (eds.) ECCV 2012. LNCS, vol. 7573, pp. 502–516. Springer, Heidelberg (2012). https://doi.org/10.1007/978-3-642-33709-3_36

45. Lee, S., et al.: ACAV100M: automatic curation of large-scale datasets for audio-visual video representation learning. In: ICCV (2021)

46. Li, G., Wei, Y., Tian, Y., Xu, C., Wen, J.R., Hu, D.: Learning to answer questions in dynamic audio-visual scenarios. In: Proceedings of the IEEE/CVF Conference on Computer Vision and Pattern Recognition, pp. 19108–19118 (2022)

47. Li, Y., Li, Y., Vasconcelos, N.: RESOUND: towards action recognition without representation bias. In: Ferrari, V., Hebert, M., Sminchisescu, C., Weiss, Y. (eds.) ECCV 2018. LNCS, vol. 11210, pp. 520–535. Springer, Cham (2018). https://doi.org/10.1007/978-3-030-01231-1_32

48. Lin, T.-Y., et al.: Microsoft COCO: common objects in context. In: Fleet, D., Pajdla, T., Schiele, B., Tuytelaars, T. (eds.) ECCV 2014. LNCS, vol. 8693, pp. 740–755. Springer, Cham (2014). https://doi.org/10.1007/978-3-319-10602-1_48

49. Lin, Y.-L., Morariu, V.I., Hsu, W., Davis, L.S.: Jointly optimizing 3D model fitting and fine-grained classification. In: Fleet, D., Pajdla, T., Schiele, B., Tuytelaars, T. (eds.) ECCV 2014. LNCS, vol. 8692, pp. 466–480. Springer, Cham (2014). https://doi.org/10.1007/978-3-319-10593-2_31

50. Liu, J., Kanazawa, A., Jacobs, D., Belhumeur, P.: Dog breed classification using part localization. In: Fitzgibbon, A., Lazebnik, S., Perona, P., Sato, Y., Schmid, C. (eds.) ECCV 2012. LNCS, vol. 7572, pp. 172–185. Springer, Heidelberg (2012). https://doi.org/10.1007/978-3-642-33718-5_13

51. Lostanlen, V., Salamon, J., Farnsworth, A., Kelling, S., Bello, J.P.: Birdvox-full-night: a dataset and benchmark for avian flight call detection. In: International Conference on Acoustics, Speech and Signal Processing (ICASSP) (2018)

52. Mac Aodha, O., et al.: Bat detective-deep learning tools for bat acoustic signal detection. PLoS Comput. Biol. **14**(3), e1005995 (2018)

53. Maji, S., Rahtu, E., Kannala, J., Blaschko, M., Vedaldi, A.: Fine-grained visual classification of aircraft. arXiv:1306.5151 (2013)

54. Monfort, M., et al.: Moments in time dataset: one million videos for event understanding. PAMI **42**(2), 502–508 (2019)

55. Morfi, V., Bas, Y., Pamuła, H., Glotin, H., Stowell, D.: NIPS4Bplus: a richly annotated birdsong audio dataset. PeerJ Comput. Sci. **5**, e223 (2019)

56. Nagrani, A., Yang, S., Arnab, A., Jansen, A., Schmid, C., Sun, C.: Attention bottlenecks for multimodal fusion. In: NeurIPS (2021)

57. Nilsback, M.E., Zisserman, A.: A visual vocabulary for flower classification. In: CVPR (2006)

58. Nilsback, M.E., Zisserman, A.: Automated flower classification over a large number of classes. In: Indian Conference on Computer Vision, Graphics & Image Processing (2008)

59. Park, D.S., et al.: SpecAugment: a simple data augmentation method for automatic speech recognition. In: Interspeech (2019)

60. Parkhi, O.M., Vedaldi, A., Zisserman, A., Jawahar, C.V.: Cats and dogs. In: CVPR (2012)

61. Piczak, K.J.: ESC: dataset for environmental sound classification. In: International Conference on Multimedia (2015)

62. Piergiovanni, A., Ryoo, M.S.: Fine-grained activity recognition in baseball videos. In: CVPR Workshops (2018)

63. Robinson, T., Fransen, J., Pye, D., Foote, J., Renals, S.: WSJCAMO: a British English speech corpus for large vocabulary continuous speech recognition. In: International Conference on Acoustics, Speech, and Signal Processing (1995)
64. Roemer, C., Julien, J.F., Bas, Y.: An automatic classifier of bat sonotypes around the world. Methods Ecol. Evol. **12**(12), 2432–2444 (2021)
65. Russakovsky, O., et al.: Imagenet large scale visual recognition challenge. In: IJCV (2015)
66. Saito, T., Kanezaki, A., Harada, T.: IBC127: video dataset for fine-grained bird classification. In: International Conference on Multimedia and Expo (2016)
67. Salamon, J., Jacoby, C., Bello, J.P.: A dataset and taxonomy for urban sound research. In: International Conference on Multimedia (2014)
68. Sevilla-Lara, L., Zha, S., Yan, Z., Goswami, V., Feiszli, M., Torresani, L.: Only time can tell: discovering temporal data for temporal modeling. In: WACV (2021)
69. Shao, D., Zhao, Y., Dai, B., Lin, D.: FineGym: a hierarchical video dataset for fine-grained action understanding. In: CVPR (2020)
70. Simonyan, K., Zisserman, A.: Very deep convolutional networks for large-scale image recognition. In: ICLR (2015)
71. Soomro, K., Zamir, A.R., Shah, M.: UCF101: a dataset of 101 human actions classes from videos in the wild. arXiv:1212.0402 (2012)
72. Stowell, D., Wood, M.D., Pamuła, H., Stylianou, Y., Glotin, H.: Automatic acoustic detection of birds through deep learning: the first bird audio detection challenge. Methods Ecol. Evol. **10**(3), 368–380 (2019)
73. Thomee, B., et al.: YFCC100M: the new data in multimedia research. Commun. ACM **59**(2), 64–73 (2016)
74. Tian, Y., Li, D., Xu, C.: Unified multisensory perception: weakly-supervised audio-visual video parsing. In: Vedaldi, A., Bischof, H., Brox, T., Frahm, J.-M. (eds.) ECCV 2020. LNCS, vol. 12348, pp. 436–454. Springer, Cham (2020). https://doi.org/10.1007/978-3-030-58580-8_26
75. Tian, Y., Shi, J., Li, B., Duan, Z., Xu, C.: Audio-visual event localization in unconstrained videos. In: Ferrari, V., Hebert, M., Sminchisescu, C., Weiss, Y. (eds.) ECCV 2018. LNCS, vol. 11206, pp. 252–268. Springer, Cham (2018). https://doi.org/10.1007/978-3-030-01216-8_16
76. Touvron, H., Cord, M., Douze, M., Massa, F., Sablayrolles, A., Jégou, H.: Training data-efficient image transformers & distillation through attention. In: ICML (2021)
77. Van Horn, G., et al.: Building a bird recognition app and large scale dataset with citizen scientists: the fine print in fine-grained dataset collection. In: CVPR (2015)
78. Van Horn, G., Cole, E., Beery, S., Wilber, K., Belongie, S., Mac Aodha, O.: Benchmarking representation learning for natural world image collections. In: CVPR (2021)
79. Van Horn, G., et al.: The inaturalist species classification and detection dataset. In: CVPR (2018)
80. Vedaldi, A., et al.: Understanding objects in detail with fine-grained attributes. In: CVPR (2014)
81. Wah, C., Branson, S., Welinder, P., Perona, P., Belongie, S.: The caltech-UCSD birds-200-2011 dataset. Technical report, CNS-TR-2011-001 (2011)
82. Wang, L., et al.: Temporal segment networks for action recognition in videos. PAMI **41**(11), 2740–2755 (2018)
83. Wu, P., et al.: Not only look, but also listen: learning multimodal violence detection under weak supervision. In: Vedaldi, A., Bischof, H., Brox, T., Frahm, J.-M. (eds.) ECCV 2020. LNCS, vol. 12375, pp. 322–339. Springer, Cham (2020). https://doi.org/10.1007/978-3-030-58577-8_20

84. Xiao, F., Lee, Y.J., Grauman, K., Malik, J., Feichtenhofer, C.: Audiovisual slowfast networks for video recognition. arXiv:2001.08740 (2020)
85. Xie, S., Sun, C., Huang, J., Tu, Z., Murphy, K.: Rethinking spatiotemporal feature learning: speed-accuracy trade-offs in video classification. In: Ferrari, V., Hebert, M., Sminchisescu, C., Weiss, Y. (eds.) ECCV 2018. LNCS, vol. 11219, pp. 318–335. Springer, Cham (2018). https://doi.org/10.1007/978-3-030-01267-0_19
86. Yang, L., Luo, P., Change Loy, C., Tang, X.: A large-scale car dataset for fine-grained categorization and verification. In: CVPR (2015)
87. Yun, H., Yu, Y., Yang, W., Lee, K., Kim, G.: Pano-AVQA: grounded audio-visual question answering on 360deg videos. In: Proceedings of the IEEE/CVF International Conference on Computer Vision, pp. 2031–2041 (2021)
88. Zamora-Gutierrez, V., et al.: Acoustic identification of Mexican bats based on taxonomic and ecological constraints on call design. Methods Ecol. Evol. **7**(9), 1082–1091 (2016)
89. Zhou, B., Lapedriza, A., Khosla, A., Oliva, A., Torralba, A.: Places: a 10 million image database for scene recognition. PAMI **40**(6), 1452–1464 (2017)
90. Zhu, C., et al.: Fine-grained video categorization with redundancy reduction attention. In: Ferrari, V., Hebert, M., Sminchisescu, C., Weiss, Y. (eds.) ECCV 2018. LNCS, vol. 11209, pp. 139–155. Springer, Cham (2018). https://doi.org/10.1007/978-3-030-01228-1_9

The Caltech Fish Counting Dataset: A Benchmark for Multiple-Object Tracking and Counting

Justin Kay[1,5]([✉]), Peter Kulits[1], Suzanne Stathatos[1], Siqi Deng[2], Erik Young[3], Sara Beery[1], Grant Van Horn[4], and Pietro Perona[1,2]

[1] California Institute of Technology, Pasadena, USA
[2] AWS AI Labs, Shanghai, China
[3] Trout Unlimited, Arlington, USA
[4] Cornell University, Ithaca, USA
[5] Ai.Fish, Stavanger, Norway
justin@ai.fish

Abstract. We present the Caltech Fish Counting Dataset (CFC), a large-scale dataset for detecting, tracking, and counting fish in sonar videos. We identify sonar videos as a rich source of data for advancing low signal-to-noise computer vision applications and tackling domain generalization in multiple-object tracking (MOT) and counting. In comparison to existing MOT and counting datasets, which are largely restricted to videos of people and vehicles in cities, CFC is sourced from a natural-world domain where targets are not easily resolvable and appearance features cannot be easily leveraged for target re-identification. With over half a million annotations in over 1,500 videos sourced from seven different sonar cameras, CFC allows researchers to train MOT and counting algorithms and evaluate generalization performance at unseen test locations. We perform extensive baseline experiments and identify key challenges and opportunities for advancing the state of the art in generalization in MOT and counting.

Keywords: Detection · Tracking · Counting · Video dataset

1 Introduction

Diverse and high-quality datasets collected from the natural world have enabled progress on fundamental computer vision tasks such as fine-grained visual categorization [9–11,66,81,101,106–108] and individual re-identification [50,68,85]. This progress has had valuable impact in the same natural-world domains, and automated visual systems are now used in the field every day by ecologists, citizen scientists, and conservationists to improve the accuracy and efficiency of biodiversity monitoring efforts around the globe [1,12,41,65,105,106]. However, the range of computer vision tasks that these systems can perform is still limited, with most current algorithms and their supporting datasets focusing largely on

Supplementary Information The online version contains supplementary material available at https://doi.org/10.1007/978-3-031-20074-8_17.

visual classification in relatively high-quality imagery. Methods developed for existing datasets can fail to transfer to tasks where video analysis or non-RGB imagery is involved.

We present the Caltech Fish Counting Dataset (CFC), a large video dataset containing over half a million annotations for detecting, tracking, and counting migrating fish in sonar video. In addition to providing a challenging benchmark in a novel application domain, the dataset allows for detailed study in three areas that have received limited attention from the computer vision community and lack supporting benchmarks:

1. Multiple-object Tracking (MOT) in Natural Environments with Animal Targets. Most existing MOT datasets focus on human [34,67,77] and vehicle [44,100,112,119] tracking in cities. Animal targets provide a rich source of variability for developing trackers that are not biased toward urban domains, in addition to having numerous beneficial applications in conservation [105], neuroscience [75], and animal husbandry [42]. Furthermore, many state-of-the-art methods make extensive use of visual re-identification for performing association [87,115,125]. In contrast, CFC provides a benchmark sourced from low signal-to-noise recording equipment in challenging natural-world environments where tracking targets are difficult to resolve from background clutter and each other, making frame-to-frame visual association less effective.

The dataset is large, well-annotated, and challenging. It consists of 1,567 video sequences sourced from seven different sonar cameras on three rivers located in the U.S. states of Alaska and Washington. The videos are single-channel (i.e. grayscale), vary in resolution from 288×624 to $1,086 \times 2,125$, have frame rates between 6.7 and 13.3 frames per second, and are an average of 336 frames (38 s) in duration. Tracking annotations were collected through a paid annotation service for 8,254 fish across 527k frames, totaling 516k bounding boxes in 16.7 h of video.

2. Video-Based Counting. Existing video counting benchmarks focus on crowd counting in urban environments [25,26,40,40,113,114] and emphasize density estimation over trajectory-based counting. Methods developed for these datasets have limitations in applications where information about individuals, such as size or direction of motion, is required, since crowd density is largely treated as a regional feature [94]. The community is in need of a benchmark which can support both tracking and counting concurrently. CFC provides both a challenging MOT benchmark and an evaluation protocol for video-based counting that is motivated by a real-world metric. Ground-truth detections, trajectories, and counts are provided for every video sequence.

3. Generalization of Tracking and Counting Methods to New Domains. While generalization in computer vision has been extensively studied in object recognition [10,30,63,130], it is still relatively understudied within MOT and counting. CFC presents significant generalization challenges that are highlighted by the dataset design, providing a strong benchmark for the study of generalization and efficient adaptation in the context of MOT and counting. We enable this study by constraining training data to a single camera location, while sourcing test data from a variety of different out-of-sample rivers and cameras.

Finally, CFC is the first annotated video dataset sourced from the domain of fish counting in sonar, an application area with significant impacts in

Table 1. Comparison of video tracking and counting datasets. CFC is the first dataset that supports all three tasks of interest: detection, tracking, and counting, with more tracking annotations than existing animal-centric tracking datasets. (* indicates annotations are points, not bounding boxes)

Dataset	Vids	Frames	Annos	Animals	Detect	Track	Count
3D-ZeF [86]	8	28,800	86,400	✓ (100%)	✓	✓	
BIRDSAI [19]	48	62,400	154,000	✓ (78%)	✓	✓	
GMOT-40 [7]	40	9,643	256,341	✓ (38%)		✓	
MOT16 [77]	14	11,235	292,733		✓	✓	
MOT20 [34]	8	13,410	1.65 M		✓	✓	
UA-DETRAC [112]	100	140,000	1.21 M		✓	✓	
TAO [33]	2,907	4.44 M	332,401	✓ (∼10%)	✓	✓	
AnimalDrone [132]	162	53,644	4.05 M*	✓ (100%)			✓
DroneCrowd [114]	112	33,600	4.86 M*			✓	✓
Crossing-line [128]	5	3,100	5,900*			✓	✓
FDST [40]	100	15,000	394,081*				✓
Iowa DOT [80]	200	90,000	0				✓
Mall [27]	1	2,000	62,315*				✓
UCSD [25]	1	2,000	49,885*				✓
WorldExpo [120]	1,132	3,980	199,923*				✓
CFC	1,567	527,215	515,933	✓ (100%)	✓	✓	✓

conservation ecology. Salmon are keystone species that support at least 137 other animal species and provide food and nutrients to a wide range of ecosystems during their seasonal migration [43]. Sonar imaging provides a non-invasive way to monitor *escapement*—the number of salmon returning home each season to spawn—helping inform sustainable fisheries management. Automation using computer vision could enable current sonar-based monitoring programs to scale from a few locations to entire watersheds. We hope that our dataset will encourage computer vision researchers to work on this high-impact challenge.

Our contributions are: (1) a large and challenging dataset for tracking and counting in video that enables the study of generalizing algorithms to new locations; (2) an evaluation protocol that mimics the procedure used by field technicians when manually counting fish in sonar video; (3) a baseline method that utilizes a novel input structure to improve generalization performance at unseen test locations. The dataset and evaluation code are available here.

2 Related Work

Multiple-object Tracking (MOT). Several popular benchmarks have supported recent progress in MOT, particularly in the domains of pedestrian and vehicle tracking [34,44,67,77,100,112,119]. Large-scale benchmarks for tracking animals in the wild are less common. TAO [33] and GMOT-20 [7] focus on tracking all foreground objects with limited class information, and include some animal tracking sequences. The BIRDSAI [19] dataset focuses on human and animal tracking in the wild, and—similar to ours—contains non-RGB (in their case, thermal infrared) sequences, though it is sourced from moving aerial cameras rather than in-situ monitoring devices. With over half a million MOT annotations, the CFC dataset is larger than existing benchmarks for animal tracking in the wild, with a unique additional focus on video-based counting and generalization challenges. See Tab. 1 for a comparison with prior work.

Recent advancements in object detection [54,133] have helped popularize the *tracking-by-detection* paradigm in MOT, which divides the tracking problem into two steps: (1) an object detector predicts object locations (e.g. bounding boxes) in each frame, and (2) a tracker associates detections over time into object trajectories. While there has been significant progress in recent years (see recent surveys [29,71]), there are two notable shortcomings. First, the tracking-by-detection paradigm implicitly assumes that detection is possible and accurate in each frame. This is not universally valid, and our dataset can stimulate research in algorithms that do not rely on this assumption due to the difficulty in resolving fish locations frame-to-frame. Second, much recent progress can be attributed to the development of complex visual-feature representations for target re-identification. These techniques are often domain-specific according to the benchmark dataset. For example, [129] use a generative model to create synthetic pedestrian data consisting of various combinations of person appearance and structure information to achieve state-of-the-art performance, a technique that has been adopted by other top-performing MOT methods [52]. Our dataset introduces a challenging MOT benchmark in which individuals are visually indistinct, offering little opportunity to make use of visual features for individual re-identification, which can motivate the development of tracking methods that are not dependent upon complex appearance matching.

Counting in Video. Datasets for object counting are predominantly image-based [4,8,22,45,53,55,57,60,82,88,96,109,111,116,120,121,126]. Video-based counting datasets are more limited. Most are focused on estimating the number of people [25,26,40,40,113,114] or animals [132] in crowded scenes, combining the challenges of crowd-density estimation and camera motion compensation. While a limited number of video counting datasets incorporate trajectory information [114,128], existing benchmarks primarily model object locations as points and do not contain bounding box labels. CFC supports the study of all three tasks (detection, tracking, and counting), while containing over five times the number of annotated video frames as existing video counting benchmarks (see Tab. 1).

Methods for video-based counting can be roughly divided into *regression-based* methods, *density-based* methods, and *detection-based* methods. Regression-based methods attempt to predict counts directly by mapping image features to counting numbers [59,78], while density-based methods predict per-pixel crowd density in each frame and then analyze densities over time to obtain counts [4,83,122,126,128]. These methods are typically designed for counting large numbers of densely clustered objects where individual object detection is challenging. In contrast, detection-based methods utilize object detection in each frame to localize objects of interest and count them over time. These approaches typically employ a tracking-by-detection pipeline followed by counting based on either *region-of-interest* (ROI) [24,73] or *line-of-interest* (LOI) [62,72,128]. ROI-based methods attempt to estimate the number of objects passing through a subregion of the frame, such as a traffic lane or onramp in the case of vehicle counting [24]. LOI-based methods instead draw a virtual line through the field of view, counting objects when their trajectories intersect this line. In this work we use LOI-based counting, as it matches the approach currently used by fishery managers for counting fish in sonar [61].

Animal-Centric Datasets. Existing computer vision datasets in animal ecology primarily target the tasks of species classification [9,11,81,101,106–108], detection [2,6,9,10,20,31,35,57,84,89,93,98,101–103,118,127], and individual identification [50,68,85]. These datasets consist predominantly of RGB imagery where visual features are key signals for recognition; in contrast, our dataset consists of single-channel sonar video, in which the animals of interest are difficult to distinguish from background, debris, and each other.

For this reason CFC shares some characteristics with video datasets for studying animal behavior, including mice [3,5,17,46,47,51,99], rats [32], flies [37,38], bees [16,21,74,91], and fish [23,86,131]. As in our dataset, the visual similarities between individuals in these datasets mean that tracking must rely heavily on prediction of motion or behavior rather than using visual features for association. Our work, however, entails additional challenges not typically present in laboratory tracking and behavior study, such as complex background, difficult frame-by-frame detection, and unknown numbers of individuals in a scene.

Generalization in Computer Vision. *Domain generalization* is a type of domain shift—i.e. a difference in training and test data distributions—in which training and test data come from distinct, but related, domains. For example, in our dataset the domain generalization challenge comes from training and test data sourced from distinct sonar camera deployments on different rivers. Crucially, as opposed to *domain adaptation*, in which data from the test domain is available during model training, in domain generalization data from the test domain is considered inaccessible [15,79,104]. Within computer vision this has been most extensively studied for the task of object recognition [30,48,117,130], with a number of supporting datasets [10,39,63,92]. While there has been some study of domain generalization in other computer vision tasks such as semantic segmentation [28,49,123] and action recognition [64,97,110], it has been relatively understudied in the context of MOT and counting. Some MOT and counting datasets do represent domain generalization challenges in their test sets—for example, in MOT20 [34] one of the three test locations is from a new location, and in UA-DETRAC [112] (MOT) and WorldExpo [120] (crowd counting) all test data is from different locations than training data. Our dataset makes it possible to evaluate generalization for both MOT and video-based counting concurrently, while providing more out-of-distribution test videos than existing options.

Imaging Sonar. Only a very limited amount of annotated sonar imaging data has been released. [76] collected 524 sonar video clips with video-level species

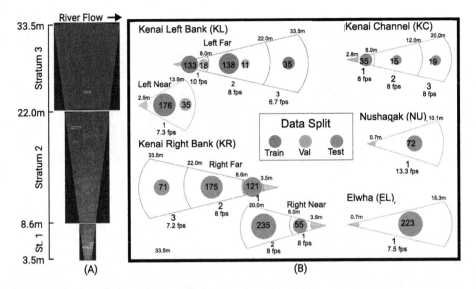

Fig. 1. Illustration of camera strata and data split. (**A**) Three example frames, one from each range window ("stratum") of the far-range camera at the KR location. Sonar cameras typically cycle between multiple strata periodically. White bounding boxes are ground-truth fish locations. (**B**) All cameras in the dataset. There are seven cameras total distributed among the five locations in the dataset, each with between one and three strata. Data split is indicated by the colored circles, and the number of training, validation, and testing sequences are indicated for each camera/stratum.

labels, [95] collected a small dataset of 143 sonar images to test image-level classification of fish and dolphin species, and [69] collected dot annotations for counting fish in 537 sonar images. Our work is the first to release detection and tracking annotations for fish in sonar, and it is several orders of magnitude larger than existing sonar datasets.

3   Dataset

Here we describe how we collected, annotated, and split CFC , and give an overview of common challenges.

Data Collection. The dataset was curated from 2,056 h of sonar video obtained from the Alaska Department of Fish and Game, the U.S. National Marine Fisheries Service, the U.S. National Park Service, and the Lower Elwha Klallam Tribe. It contains video from five distinct locations which we use to study out-of-sample performance: three locations on the Kenai River in Alaska, which we refer to as **KL** (**K**enai **L**eft Bank), **KR** (**K**enai **R**ight Bank), and **KC** (**K**enai **C**hannel); one location, **NU**, on the **Nu**shagak River in Alaska; and one location, **EL**, on the **El**wha River in Washington (sonar configurations shown in Fig. 1).

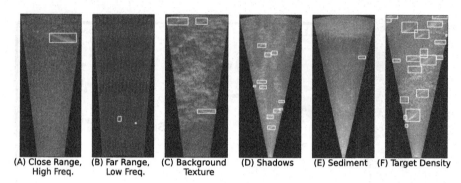

(A) Close Range,   (B) Far Range,   (C) Background   (D) Shadows   (E) Sediment   (F) Target Density
High Freq.   Low Freq.   Texture

Fig. 2. Example frames and common challenges in sonar video. Ground-truth fish locations are boxed in white. **(A)** Close range, high operating frequency: ideal conditions, fish is large, visible, and well-defined. Some speckle noise is still present. **(B)** Far range, low operating frequency: The fish are small and very coarsely defined due to scattering of sound waves at long range. **(C)** Background texture: The riverbed is very visible, occluding fish. **(D)** Shadows: Fish cast acoustic shadows which may occlude one another. **(E)** Sediment: Dirt, debris, and glacial silt occlude fish. **(F)** Target density: Dense crowds of fish, intersecting trajectories and occlusion.

The data had already been analyzed by experts ("manually marked") to obtain fish counts. Most of the video contained no fish. Since our focus is on detection, tracking, and counting, we used the manual markings to extract shorter 200–300 frame video clips known to contain fish. If any of these clips overlapped, we merged them into one longer clip. In total we extracted 1,233 clips from the Kenai River, containing 4,300 fish; 262 clips from the Elwha River, containing 884 fish; and 72 clips from the Nushagak River, containing 3,070 fish.

Annotation. We hired a third-party annotation service to collect multiple-object tracking annotations for all fish in the extracted clips. Annotators were provided with the raw video clips and instructed to box all visible fish tightly using the vatic.js GUI [18]. For any stationary fish, they were required to annotate every fifth frame, and we interpolated between those annotations in the intermediate frames; for all other tracks, all bounding boxes in all frames were annotated manually. The annotation service had their own internal quality-management procedures whereby multiple annotators inspected each clip before it was finalized. In total, 515,933 bounding boxes for 8,254 fish tracks were collected in 527,215 frames from seven different cameras.

Data Split. We designed a dataset splitting protocol that allows us to study generalization to new locations, a known challenge for current computer vision methods [10,63]. Our test data comes from deployment locations never seen during training or validation. We chose KL as our training and validation location due to its sufficient size for model training. Data from this location spans 16 d in total. We selected one of these days at random to hold out as a validation set, and the other 15 d serve as our training set. This gives us 162,680 training images containing 1,762 tracks and 132,220 bounding boxes, and 30,518 validation images containing 207 tracks and 18,565 bounding boxes.

The other locations (KR, KC, NU, and EL) serve as test sets for evaluating generalization performance under different conditions. These locations cover a range of generalization scenarios that may be faced in the real world: KR includes a new camera deployment on the same body of water; KC includes a new deployment in a nearby, but separate, body of water; NU and EL include deployments on new rivers in different geographic regions with different species distributions. The data split is illustrated in Fig. 1. In total the dataset contains 334,017 test images with 6,285 tracks and 365,148 bounding boxes. For all experiments we report results on all test locations individually.

Challenges. We have identified a number of challenges inherent to detecting and tracking fish using sonar, which we have illustrated in Fig. 2. Some of these challenges are constant across all data in this domain (e.g. speckle noise and shadows), while some vary across locations due to hardware settings or environmental factors, presenting generalization challenges (e.g. presence of sediment, riverbed shape and texture, and hardware operating frequency). More details on the causes of these challenges can be found in the supplemental material.

4 Metrics

4.1 Counting Protocol

We follow the counting procedure used by field technicians when counting fish in sonar video [61]. A vertical line-of-interest (LOI) is drawn in the middle of the frame, and a fish is considered to have moved left or right if its trajectory start and end positions are on different sides of the LOI. Note that not every fish in a clip will cross the LOI. Some fish are stationary throughout the entire clip, while others enter and exit on the same side of the frame without crossing the LOI. These fish are excluded from the count totals, which matches the protocol used by the field technicians.

4.2 Counting Metric

In the target application, fish-counting error is measured as the sum of upstream and downstream counting errors, and error is normalized separately at each river to account for variations in fish abundance. We classify direction of movement as "left" or "right" rather than "upstream" or "downstream" to make our system agnostic to the orientation of the camera. Based on this we define the absolute counting error for the ith video clip, E_i, as the sum of the absolute left and right (i.e. upstream and downstream) counting errors:

$$E_i = |z_{left_i} - \hat{z}_{left_i}| + |z_{right_i} - \hat{z}_{right_i}| \tag{1}$$

where z_i and $\hat{z}_i$ are the predicted and ground-truth counts for clip i, respectively. Overall counting error is reported as normalized Mean Absolute Error (nMAE):

$$nMAE = \frac{\frac{1}{N}\sum_{i=1}^{N} E_i}{\frac{1}{N}\sum_{i=1}^{N} \hat{z}_i} = \frac{\sum_{i=1}^{N} E_i}{\sum_{i=1}^{N} \hat{z}_i} \tag{2}$$

where N is the number of video clips at a given location and $\hat{z}_i = \hat{z}_{left_i} + \hat{z}_{right_i}$ is the ground-truth count for clip i.

We choose a metric that is normalized *per location*, giving *equal weight to each fish* at a given location regardless of variance in fish density across clips at that location. We do this because video clips in CFC are arbitrarily generated and are much shorter in duration than videos in the target application, thus *per-clip* normalization—i.e. giving equal weight to each *clip*—would not be appropriate. We consider this the main metric for the dataset, since it is the most important in the target application. Achieving at most 10% counting error on a river would make an algorithm on par with human experts and feasible for augmenting counting in the field [61].

4.3 Detection and Tracking Metrics

In addition to counting, CFC has been annotated to measure detection and tracking performance as well. For our detection metric we choose the PascalVOC [36] evaluation of mean Average Precision with IoU ≥ 0.5 (AP50). For tracking, we report the CLEAR [13], IDF1 [90], and HOTA [70] metrics.

The CLEAR MOT metrics [13] are computed *per-frame* by matching detections from predicted tracks with ground-truth detections. This matching allows the number of true positive (TP), false positive (FP), and false negative (FN) detections to be computed using an IoU threshold between predicted and ground-truth boxes. Recall (CLR_Re) and precision (CLR_Pr) are defined as normal according to the number of TPs, FPs, and FNs, and Multiple Object Tracking Accuracy ($MOTA$) is defined as:

$$MOTA = \frac{TP - FP - IDSW}{TP + FN} \tag{3}$$

where $IDSW$ is the sum of all "ID switches", i.e. the number of times a predicted track changes its matched ground-truth track and vice versa. In practice, $IDSW \ll TP$ and MOTA becomes predominantly a measure of detection quality in the tracks. Since this scoring occurs per-frame, MOTA does not capture long-term tracking performance.

In contrast, IDF1 [90] first computes a *global* (per-video-clip) *track* matching, i.e. a bipartite matching between all ground-truth and predicted tracks. From this matching, ID true positives ($IDTP$), false positives ($IDFP$), and false negatives ($IDFN$) are computed, and the IDF1 score is defined as the harmonic mean of ID Precision (IDP) and ID Recall (IDR):

$$IDF1 = 2 \cdot \frac{IDP \times IDR}{IDP + IDR}, \quad IDP = \frac{IDTP}{IDTP + IDFP}, \quad IDR = \frac{IDTP}{IDTP + IDFN} \tag{4}$$

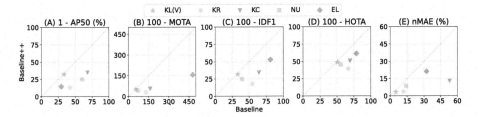

Fig. 3. Baseline (Sec. 5.1) and Baseline++ (Sec. 5.3) results on CFC . All results are displayed in terms of error, i.e. the lower-left of each plot represents the best performance. Baseline++ improves performance on all tasks across all locations and reduces generalization gaps between the validation location and testing locations. Generalization challenges remain, most notably at KC and EL.

Since this matching is restricted to be static for the length of the clip, IDF1 is a measure of long-term tracking performance.

HOTA [70] is designed to measure both short-term and long-term tracking performance. It is the geometric mean of a detection score ($DetA$) and an association score ($AssA$), each defined as the Jaccard index of detection/association TPs, FPs, and FNs. Thus it can be easily decomposed into detection/association precision and recall ($DetRe$ and $DetPr$, and $AssRe$ and $AssPr$, respectively). In this formulation, AssRe is inversely correlated with the number of track splits, while AssPr is inversely correlated with the number of track merges.

5   Experiments

We evaluate state-of-the-art methods on CFC to provide a baseline for future work and give insight into the generalization challenges of object detection, multiple-object tracking, and counting. In Sec. 5.1 we propose a tracking-by-detection approach to fish counting which allows us to evaluate each of these tasks, and study its performance. In Sec. 5.2 we perform ablation studies and investigate the upper bounds of this approach and its generalization capabilities. In Sec. 5.3 we introduce an improved baseline method to address these challenges, establish the state of the art on CFC , and discuss remaining challenges.

5.1   Baseline

Our baseline method uses the YOLOv5 [56] object detector and SORT [14] tracker. Trajectories are then analyzed as described in Sec. 4.1 to predict counts.

We chose YOLOv5 after an initial architecture search. These experiments as well as training settings are included in the supplemental material. We chose SORT because it has shown to be a popular and robust tracker across a range of applications, recently achieving state-of-the-art performance on several MOT datasets with minor modifications [124]. It performs tracking using a motion model based on the Kalman filter [58] without using appearance information

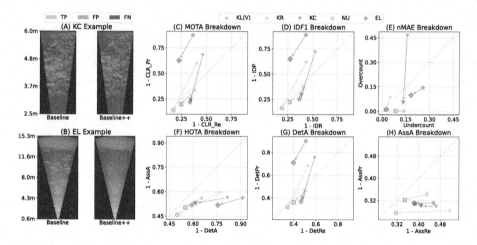

Fig. 4. Baseline and Baseline++ error analysis and comparison. (A)–(B) Example frames at the KC and EL locations. Note the large reduction in FP and FN detections between the two methods. **(C)–(H)** Breakdowns of MOTA, IDF1, HOTA, and nMAE into component submetrics. Arrows point from Baseline results to Baseline++ results; Baseline++ markers are larger and have a black edge. All results are displayed in terms of error. This breakdown shows that the low tracking scores of our baseline method at out-of-distribution locations are predominantly due to FP detections (i.e. low detection precision) that cause low CLR_Pr (C), low IDP (D), and low DetPr leading to low DetA (F)–(G). The proposed Baseline++ method succesfully targets a large portion of these FPs, improving all tracking metrics and submetrics. **(E)** nMAE decomposed into undercounting and overcounting errors, normalized by ground-truth counts. Baseline++ significantly reduces both types of errors.

for association. We verified our hypothesis that appearance features are not a strong signal for association in CFC by training a visual re-identification model that performed poorly on our validation set. More details of this experiment are provided in the supplemental material. See Figs. 3 and 4 for our performance on the various locations with this baseline method. A tabular version of these results is included in the supplemental material.

Analysis. Our baseline method performs on par with human experts at the location where it is trained, with a validation counting error of less than 5%. Counting generalization performance is best at KR, which matches intuition given that this data is sourced from a nearby location to the training set (KL). However, generalization performance at the other locations is quite poor. We examine the two most challenging locations, KC (53% nMAE) and EL (32.3% nMAE), in Fig. 4. At KC, false positive (FP) and false negative (FN) detections are caused by the presence of complex background information (Fig. 4A), while at EL the errors are overwhelmingly FPs caused by sediment and other noise resulting from the camera's very large range window (Fig. 4B).

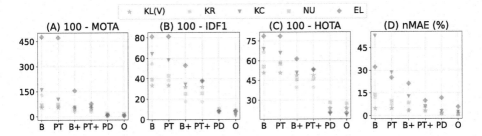

Fig. 5. Baseline and upper bound tracking and counting performance. Baseline methods are compared to methods that use various amounts of ground-truth data. X axis key: **B**aseline, **P**erfect **T**racker, **B**aseline++, **P**erfect **T**racker++, **P**erfect **D**etector, **O**racle. Note the performance difference between Baseline and Perfect Detector: there is a large performance boost when using ground-truth detections. Using a tracker that can perfectly generalize to different locations improves performance as well, but not as much as the Perfect Detector.

We can see the direct impact of these detection errors on our tracking and counting metrics in Fig. 4C–H. At both locations, we see that abundant FPs cause very low CLR Precision (Fig. 4C), ID Precision (Fig. 4D), and Detection Precision (Fig. 4G), negatively impacting MOTA, IDF1, and HOTA, respectively. Interestingly, while FPs cause overcounting errors at KC, the majority of counting errors at EL are actually due to undercounting (Fig. 4E). From manual inspection we diagnosed that this is often caused by TP tracks merging with hallucinated detections, causing the loss of a track before it has the chance to cross the counting line. These challenges demonstrate why counting, in addition to detection and tracking, is an important metric for researchers to consider.

Our baseline results indicate that (1) there are indeed generalization challenges in this domain, (2) they appear to be largely caused by location-specific environmental changes, and (3) these challenges affect all three tasks of interest: detection, tracking, and counting. Further, the low counting error on the validation set indicates that our overall tracking-by-detection approach is feasible at in-distribution locations and that the key challenges are in generalization. To verify this, in the next section we perform ablation studies and examine the upper-bound generalization capabilities of the proposed tracking-by-detection baseline, and use these results to motivate an improved baseline in Sec. 5.3.

5.2 Ablation Study and Generalization Upper Bounds

To evaluate generalization potential, we perform a set of "reversed" ablation studies and compare our baseline results with three different upper bounds that utilize different types of ground-truth information (Fig. 5):

1. Perfect Tracker Generalization. We use the detections from our baseline detector, but we fit the tracker hyperparameters directly to each test set based on counting performance. This results in five different trackers, one for each test set, with the best possible tracker parameter settings at each location.

This gives an upper bound for the counting performance of a multiple-object tracker which can perfectly generalize to new locations.

2. Perfect Detector. This model takes *ground-truth* detections as input. The tracker hyperparameters are fit to counting performance on the validation set as in our baseline. This gives an upper bound for the counting performance of our tracker when given perfect detections.

3. Oracle. This model combines the first two upper bounds. It takes ground-truth detections as input and fits the tracker hyperparameters to each test set. This gives us the overall upper bound on counting performance for our baseline approach given perfect detections and perfect tracker generalization.

Analysis. The most apparent result is the very strong performance at all locations given a Perfect Detector. In most cases, with perfect detections our tracker achieves near-Oracle performance and generalizes well without modification. Only one location (EL) shows significant further improvements in counting error in the Oracle method compared to the Perfect Detector method. Meanwhile, Perfect Tracker Generalization does improve performance in most cases, but not as much as the Perfect Detector. This indicates that the proposed motion-based tracking approach is indeed feasible but is dependent upon a strong detector with strong generalization capabilities. Therefore the most effective improvement to overall system-generalization performance appears to be improving the generalization capabilities of the detector, which we address in the next section.

5.3 Baseline++

Given the results from our upper bound analysis, we implemented an improved baseline method, "Baseline++," with the primary goal of improving object-detection generalization performance. We noticed that the background (1) varies significantly across locations and (2) occludes fish (see Fig. 2 for frame examples). Thus, we appended two additional channels to our image input: (1) a background-subtracted version of each frame, where the background for each clip is obtained by averaging all frames, and (2) the difference between each background-subtracted frame and its preceding frame, to capture motion information. Example frames illustrating these transformations are included in the supplemental material. We trained a new detector and tracker with this input in the same way as the baseline model. Results are shown in Figs. 3, 4, and 5.

Analysis. In Fig. 3, we see that our Baseline++ method leads to modest improvements on our validation set (+1.6 AP50, –1.7% nMAE), but *significant* improvements in generalization performance (e.g. –40.2% nMAE at KC). In Fig. 4, we dissect these improvements by looking at: (A)–(B) two example frames from KC and EL, and (C)–(H) breakdowns of tracking and counting metrics across all locations. We see the efficacy of simple background subtraction as a generalization mechanism, helping significantly reduce the number of FPs and FNs in the example KC and EL frames as well as at all test locations. We also see evidence of some outstanding issues: one FN remains in the KC example due to a small, stationary fish that appears to have been removed by the background-subtraction routine, and one FP remains in the EL example due to noise near the transducer. IDR now lags behind IDP at all locations except for EL, indicating that most remaining tracking problems are track splits causing undercounting errors. These trends are also indicated in the HOTA decompositions (Fig. 4F–H), which show that DetRe now lags behind DetPr at all locations except EL, and while AssRe has improved (i.e. track splits have been reduced), it is still lower than AssPr.

6   Conclusions

We present the Caltech Fish Counting Dataset , a natural-world sonar video dataset that allows us to study object detection, multiple-object tracking, and counting under challenging real-world domain shifts. Due to the visual qualities of the source domain of river-based sonar, the dataset poses challenges to existing methods developed primarily for urban environments and provides a benchmark for video-based counting in the wild, a task that lacks supporting benchmarks.

Our experiments show that there is still significant room for improvement in the generalization performance of tracking and counting algorithms. There are also opportunities to improve tracker generalization and making trackers more robust to noisy detections. Robust algorithms that work across the range of generalization challenges in CFC will certainly be impactful in other domains, and we hope that our dataset will provide a useful testing ground for the computer vision community to push forward progress on these tasks. High-performing methods would enable sonar-based fish counting to scale globally and have real-world impact in managing some of the world's most sensitive and valuable ecosystems.

In the future, the dataset will be expanded to include additional input formats, locations, and species. One additional path forward for the community is to explore the impact of utilizing unlabeled data for unsupervised domain adaptation or self-supervised pretraining on unseen locations, which we plan to make possible by releasing additional unlabeled data from all test locations.

Acknowledgment. We are grateful to AWS for a gift to Trout Unlimited (TU) that supported data annotations, computational and storage costs, and to the Resnick Sustainability Institute at Caltech for funding to SB and PP. An NSF Fellowship supported SB. JK, SD, and EY volunteered their time. GVH was supported by the Macaulay Library at Cornell University. For collecting the dataset, and for feedback, encouragement, and moral support, we are grateful to: George Pess and Oleksandr Stefankiv (Northwest Fisheries Science Center); James Miller, Carl Pfisterer, Dawn Wilburn, Brandon Key, Suzanne Maxwell, Gregory Buck, April Faulkner, and Jordan Head (Alaska Department of Fish and Game); Dave Kajtaniak and Michael Sparkman (California Department of Fish and Wildlife); Dean Finnerty (TU's Wild Steelhead Project); and Keith Denton, Mike McHenry, and the Lower Elwha Klallam Tribe.

References

1. Ahumada, J.A., et al.: Wildlife insights: a platform to maximize the potential of camera trap and other passive sensor wildlife data for the planet. Environ. Conserv. **47**(1), 1–6 (2020)
2. Anton, V., Hartley, S., Geldenhuis, A., Wittmer, H.U.: Monitoring the mammalian fauna of urban areas using remote cameras and citizen science. J. Urban Ecol. **4**(1), juy002 (2018)
3. Arac, A., Zhao, P., Dobkin, B.H., Carmichael, S.T., Golshani, P.: DeepBehavior: a deep learning toolbox for automated analysis of animal and human behavior imaging data. Front. Syst. Neurosci. **13**, 20 (2019)
4. Arteta, C., Lempitsky, V., Zisserman, A.: Counting in the wild. In: Leibe, B., Matas, J., Sebe, N., Welling, M. (eds.) ECCV 2016. LNCS, vol. 9911, pp. 483–498. Springer, Cham (2016). https://doi.org/10.1007/978-3-319-46478-7_30
5. Austin, C.P., et al.: The knockout mouse project. Nat. Genet. **36**(9), 921 (2004)
6. Australian Institute of Marine Science (AIMS) and University of Western Australia (UWA) and Curtin University: Ozfish dataset - machine learning dataset for baited remote underwater video stations (2019)
7. Bai, H., Cheng, W., Chu, P., Liu, J., Zhang, K., Ling, H.: Gmot-40: a benchmark for generic multiple object tracking. In: Proceedings of the IEEE/CVF Conference on Computer Vision and Pattern Recognition, pp. 6719–6728 (2021)
8. Beery, S., Agarwal, A., Cole, E., Birodkar, V.: The iWildCam 2021 competition dataset. arXiv preprint arXiv:2105.03494 (2021)
9. Beery, S., Van Horn, G., Mac Aodha, O., Perona, P.: The iWildCam 2018 challenge dataset. arXiv preprint arXiv:1904.05986 (2019)
10. Beery, S., Van Horn, G., Perona, P.: Recognition in terra incognita. In: Proceedings of the European Conference on Computer Vision (ECCV), pp. 456–473 (2018)
11. Berg, T., Liu, J., Woo Lee, S., Alexander, M.L., Jacobs, D.W., Belhumeur, P.N.: Birdsnap: large-scale fine-grained visual categorization of birds. In: Proceedings of the IEEE Conference on Computer Vision and Pattern Recognition, pp. 2011–2018 (2014)
12. Berger-Wolf, T.Y., et al.: Wildbook: crowdsourcing, computer vision, and data science for conservation. arXiv preprint arXiv:1710.08880 (2017)
13. Bernardin, K., Stiefelhagen, R.: Evaluating multiple object tracking performance: the clear mot metrics. EURASIP J. Image Video Process. **2008**, 1–10 (2008)
14. Bewley, A., Ge, Z., Ott, L., Ramos, F., Upcroft, B.: Simple online and realtime tracking. In: 2016 IEEE International Conference on Image Processing (ICIP), pp. 3464–3468. IEEE (2016)
15. Blanchard, G., Lee, G., Scott, C.: Generalizing from several related classification tasks to a new unlabeled sample. In: Advances in Neural Information Processing Systems, vol. 24 (2011)
16. Boenisch, F., Rosemann, B., Wild, B., Dormagen, D., Wario, F., Landgraf, T.: Tracking all members of a honey bee colony over their lifetime using learned models of correspondence. Front. Robot. AI **5**, 35 (2018)
17. Bogue, M.A., et al.: Mouse phenome database: a data repository and analysis suite for curated primary mouse phenotype data. Nucleic Acids Res. **48**(D1), D716–D723 (2020)
18. Bolkensteyn, D.: dbolkensteyn/vatic.js, May 2020. https://github.com/dbolkensteyn/vatic.js. Original-date: 2016–11-23T12:39:07Z

19. Bondi, E., et al.: BIRDSAI: a dataset for detection and tracking in aerial thermal infrared videos. In: WACV (2020)
20. Boom, B., et al.: A research tool for long-term and continuous analysis of fish assemblage in coral-reefs using underwater camera footage. Ecol. Inf. **23**, 83–97 (2014)
21. Bozek, K., Hebert, L., Mikheyev, A.S., Stephens, G.J.: Towards dense object tracking in a 2d honeybee hive. In: Proceedings of the IEEE Conference on Computer Vision and Pattern Recognition, pp. 4185–4193 (2018)
22. Brandt, M., et al.: An unexpectedly large count of trees in the west African Sahara and Sahel (2020). https://doi.org/10.3334/ORNLDAAC/1832
23. Bruslund Haurum, J., Karpova, A., Pedersen, M., Hein Bengtson, S., Moeslund, T.B.: Re-identification of zebrafish using metric learning. In: Proceedings of the IEEE/CVF Winter Conference on Applications of Computer Vision Workshops, pp. 1–11 (2020)
24. Bui, N., Yi, H., Cho, J.: A vehicle counts by class framework using distinguished regions tracking at multiple intersections. In: Proceedings of the IEEE/CVF Conference on Computer Vision and Pattern Recognition Workshops, pp. 578–579 (2020)
25. Chan, A.B., Liang, Z.S.J., Vasconcelos, N.: Privacy preserving crowd monitoring: Counting people without people models or tracking. In: 2008 IEEE Conference on Computer Vision and Pattern Recognition, pp. 1–7. IEEE (2008)
26. Change Loy, C., Gong, S., Xiang, T.: From semi-supervised to transfer counting of crowds. In: Proceedings of the IEEE International Conference on Computer Vision, pp. 2256–2263 (2013)
27. Chen, K., Loy, C.C., Gong, S., Xiang, T.: Feature mining for Localised crowd counting. In: Bmvc. vol. 1, p. 3 (2012)
28. Chen, Y., Li, W., Gool, L.V.: Road: reality oriented adaptation for semantic segmentation of urban scenes. In: 2018 IEEE/CVF Conference on Computer Vision and Pattern Recognition, pp. 7892–7901 (2018)
29. Ciaparrone, G., Sánchez, F.L., Tabik, S., Troiano, L., Tagliaferri, R., Herrera, F.: Deep learning in video multi-object tracking: a survey. Neurocomputing **381**, 61–88 (2020)
30. Csurka, G.: Domain adaptation for visual applications: a comprehensive survey. arXiv preprint arXiv:1702.05374 (2017)
31. Cutter, G., Stierhoff, K., Zeng, J.: Automated detection of rockfish in unconstrained underwater videos using Haar cascades and a new image dataset: labeled fishes in the wild. In: 2015 IEEE Winter Applications and Computer Vision Workshops, pp. 57–62. IEEE (2015)
32. van Dam, E.A., van der Harst, J.E., ter Braak, C.J., Tegelenbosch, R.A., Spruijt, B.M., Noldus, L.P.: An automated system for the recognition of various specific rat behaviours. J. Neurosci. Methods **218**(2), 214–224 (2013)
33. Dave, A., Khurana, T., Tokmakov, P., Schmid, C., Ramanan, D.: TAO: a large-scale benchmark for tracking any object. In: Vedaldi, A., Bischof, H., Brox, T., Frahm, J.-M. (eds.) ECCV 2020. LNCS, vol. 12350, pp. 436–454. Springer, Cham (2020). https://doi.org/10.1007/978-3-030-58558-7_26
34. Dendorfer, P., et al.: Mot20: a benchmark for multi object tracking in crowded scenes. arXiv preprint arXiv:2003.09003 (2020)
35. Ditria, E.M., Connolly, R.M., Jinks, E.L., Lopez-Marcano, S.: Annotated video footage for automated identification and counting of fish in unconstrained seagrass habitats. Front. Mar. Sci. **8**, 160 (2021)

36. Everingham, M., Van Gool, L., Williams, C.K., Winn, J., Zisserman, A.: The pascal visual object classes (VOC) challenge. Int. J. Comput. Vision **88**(2), 303–338 (2010)
37. Eyjolfsdottir, E., Branson, K., Yue, Y., Perona, P.: Learning recurrent representations for hierarchical behavior modeling. arXiv preprint arXiv:1611.00094 (2016)
38. Eyjolfsdottir, E., et al.: Detecting social actions of fruit flies. In: Fleet, D., Pajdla, T., Schiele, B., Tuytelaars, T. (eds.) ECCV 2014. LNCS, vol. 8690, pp. 772–787. Springer, Cham (2014). https://doi.org/10.1007/978-3-319-10605-2_50
39. Fang, C., Xu, Y., Rockmore, D.N.: Unbiased metric learning: on the utilization of multiple datasets and web images for softening bias. In: Proceedings of the IEEE International Conference on Computer Vision, pp. 1657–1664 (2013)
40. Fang, Y., Zhan, B., Cai, W., Gao, S., Hu, B.: Locality-constrained spatial transformer network for video crowd counting. In: 2019 IEEE International Conference on Multimedia and Expo (ICME), pp. 814–819. IEEE (2019)
41. Fennell, M., Beirne, C., Burton, A.C.: Use of object detection in camera trap image identification: assessing a method to rapidly and accurately classify human and animal detections for research and application in recreation ecology. bioRxiv (2022). https://doi.org/10.1101/2022.01.14.476404, https://www.biorxiv.org/content/early/2022/01/21/2022.01.14.476404
42. Fernandes, A.F.A., Dórea, J.R.R., Rosa, G.J.D.M.: Image analysis and computer vision applications in animal sciences: an overview. Front. Vet. Sci. **7**, 551269 (2020)
43. Rahr, G.: Why protect salmon. https://www.wildsalmoncenter.org/why-protect-salmon/
44. Geiger, A., Lenz, P., Urtasun, R.: Are we ready for autonomous driving? the Kitti vision benchmark suite. In: 2012 IEEE Conference on Computer Vision and Pattern Recognition, pp. 3354–3361. IEEE (2012)
45. van Gemert, J.C., Verschoor, C.R., Mettes, P., Epema, K., Koh, L.P., Wich, S.: Nature conservation drones for automatic localization and counting of animals. In: Agapito, L., Bronstein, M.M., Rother, C. (eds.) ECCV 2014. LNCS, vol. 8925, pp. 255–270. Springer, Cham (2015). https://doi.org/10.1007/978-3-319-16178-5_17
46. Geuther, B.Q., et al.: Robust mouse tracking in complex environments using neural networks. Commun. Biol. **2**(1), 1–11 (2019)
47. Geuther, B.Q., Peer, A., He, H., Sabnis, G., Philip, V.M., Kumar, V.: Action detection using a neural network elucidates the genetics of mouse grooming behavior. Elife **10**, e63207 (2021)
48. Gulrajani, I., Lopez-Paz, D.: In search of lost domain generalization. arXiv preprint arXiv:2007.01434 (2020)
49. Hoffman, J., Wang, D., Yu, F., Darrell, T.: FCNs in the wild: pixel-level adversarial and constraint-based adaptation (2016)
50. Holmberg, J., Norman, B., Arzoumanian, Z.: Estimating population size, structure, and residency time for whale sharks Rhincodon Typus through collaborative photo-identification. Endangered Species Res. **7**(1), 39–53 (2009)
51. Hong, W., Kennedy, A., Burgos-Artizzu, X.P., Zelikowsky, M., Navonne, S.G., Perona, P., Anderson, D.J.: Automated measurement of mouse social behaviors using depth sensing, video tracking, and machine learning. Proc. Natl. Acad. Sci. **112**(38), E5351–E5360 (2015)
52. Hornakova, A., Henschel, R., Rosenhahn, B., Swoboda, P.: Lifted disjoint paths with application in multiple object tracking. In: International Conference on Machine Learning, pp. 4364–4375. PMLR (2020)

53. Hsieh, M.R., Lin, Y.L., Hsu, W.H.: Drone-based object counting by spatially regularized regional proposal network. In: Proceedings of the IEEE International Conference on Computer Vision, pp. 4145–4153 (2017)
54. Huang, J., et al.: Speed/accuracy trade-offs for modern convolutional object detectors. In: Proceedings of the IEEE Conference on Computer Vision and Pattern Recognition, pp. 7310–7311 (2017)
55. Idrees, H., et al.: Composition loss for counting, density map estimation and localization in dense crowds. In: Proceedings of the European Conference on Computer Vision (ECCV), pp. 532–546 (2018)
56. Jocher, G., et al.: Ultralytics/yolov5: v6.1 - TensorRT, TensorFlow Edge TPU and OpenVINO Export and Inference, February 2022. https://doi.org/10.5281/zenodo.6222936
57. Jones, F.M., et al.: Time-lapse imagery and volunteer classifications from the zooniverse penguin watch project. Sci. Data 5(1), 1–13 (2018)
58. Kalman, R.E.: A new approach to linear filtering and prediction problems. J. Basic Eng. 82(1), 35–45 (1960). https://doi.org/10.1115/1.3662552, https://asmedigitalcollection.asme.org/fluidsengineering/article/82/1/35/397706/A-New-Approach-to-Linear-Filtering-and-Prediction
59. Kamenetsky, D., Sherrah, J.: Aerial car detection and urban understanding. In: 2015 International Conference on Digital Image Computing: Techniques and Applications (DICTA), pp. 1–8. IEEE (2015)
60. Kellenberger, B., Marcos, D., Tuia, D.: Detecting mammals in UAV images: best practices to address a substantially imbalanced dataset with deep learning. Remote Sens. Environ. 216, 139–153 (2018)
61. Key, B., Miller, J., Huang, J.: Operational plan: Kenai river chinook salmon sonar assessment at river mile 13(7), 2020–2022 (2020)
62. Kocamaz, M.K., Gong, J., Pires, B.R.: Vision-based counting of pedestrians and cyclists. In: 2016 IEEE Winter Conference on Applications of Computer Vision (WACV), pp. 1–8. IEEE (2016)
63. Koh, P.W., et al.: Wilds: a benchmark of in-the-wild distribution shifts. In: International Conference on Machine Learning, pp. 5637–5664. PMLR (2021)
64. Kuehne, H., Jhuang, H., Garrote, E., Poggio, T., Serre, T.: HMDB: a large video database for human motion recognition. In: 2011 International Conference on Computer Vision, pp. 2556–2563. IEEE (2011)
65. Kulits, P., Wall, J., Bedetti, A., Henley, M., Beery, S.: ElephantBook: a semi-automated human-in-the-loop system for elephant re-identification. In: ACM SIG-CAS Conference on Computing and Sustainable Societies, pp. 88–98 (2021)
66. Kumar, N., et al.: Leafsnap: a computer vision system for automatic plant species identification. In: Fitzgibbon, A., Lazebnik, S., Perona, P., Sato, Y., Schmid, C. (eds.) ECCV 2012. LNCS, vol. 7573, pp. 502–516. Springer, Heidelberg (2012). https://doi.org/10.1007/978-3-642-33709-3_36
67. Leal-Taixé, L., Milan, A., Reid, I., Roth, S., Schindler, K.: Motchallenge 2015: towards a benchmark for multi-target tracking. arXiv preprint arXiv:1504.01942 (2015)
68. Li, S., Li, J., Lin, W., Tang, H.: Amur tiger re-identification in the wild. arXiv e-prints pp. arXiv-1906 (2019)
69. Liu, L., Lu, H., Cao, Z., Xiao, Y.: Counting fish in sonar images. In: 2018 25th IEEE International Conference on Image Processing (ICIP), pp. 3189–3193, October 2018. https://doi.org/10.1109/ICIP.2018.8451154. iSSN: 2381-8549
70. Luiten, J., et al.: Hota: a higher order metric for evaluating multi-object tracking. Int. J. Comput. Vision 129(2), 548–578 (2021)

71. Luo, W., Xing, J., Milan, A., Zhang, X., Liu, W., Kim, T.K.: Multiple object tracking: a literature review. Artif. Intell. **293**, igence, x (2021)
72. Ma, Z., Chan, A.B.: Crossing the line: Crowd counting by integer programming with local features. In: Proceedings of the IEEE Conference on Computer Vision and Pattern Recognition, pp. 2539–2546 (2013)
73. Mandal, V., Adu-Gyamfi, Y.: Object detection and tracking algorithms for vehicle counting: a comparative analysis. J. Big Data Anal. Transp. **2**(3), 251–261 (2020)
74. Marstaller, J., Tausch, F., Stock, S.: Deepbees-building and scaling convolutional neuronal nets for fast and large-scale visual monitoring of bee hives. In: Proceedings of the IEEE International Conference on Computer Vision Workshops (2019)
75. Mathis, M.W., Mathis, A.: Deep learning tools for the measurement of animal behavior in neuroscience. Curr. Opin. Neurobiol. **60**, 1–11 (2020)
76. McCann, E., Li, L., Pangle, K., Johnson, N., Eickholt, J.: An underwater observation dataset for fish classification and fishery assessment. Sci. Data **5**(1), 1–8 (2018)
77. Milan, A., Leal-Taixé, L., Reid, I., Roth, S., Schindler, K.: Mot16: A benchmark for multi-object tracking. arXiv preprint arXiv:1603.00831 (2016)
78. Moranduzzo, T., Melgani, F.: Automatic car counting method for unmanned aerial vehicle images. IEEE Trans. Geosci. Remote Sens. **52**(3), 1635–1647 (2013)
79. Muandet, K., Balduzzi, D., Schölkopf, B.: Domain generalization via invariant feature representation. In: International Conference on Machine Learning, pp. 10–18. PMLR (2013)
80. Naphade, M., et al.: The 5th AI city challenge. In: Proceedings of the IEEE/CVF Conference on Computer Vision and Pattern Recognition, pp. 4263–4273 (2021)
81. Nilsback, M.E., Zisserman, A.: A visual vocabulary for flower classification. In: 2006 IEEE Computer Society Conference on Computer Vision and Pattern Recognition (CVPR 2006), vol. 2, pp. 1447–1454. IEEE (2006)
82. Norouzzadeh, M.S., et al.: Automatically identifying, counting, and describing wild animals in camera-trap images with deep learning. Proc. Natl. Acad. Sci. **115**(25), E5716–E5725 (2018)
83. Oñoro-Rubio, D., López-Sastre, R.J.: Towards perspective-free object counting with deep learning. In: Leibe, B., Matas, J., Sebe, N., Welling, M. (eds.) ECCV 2016. LNCS, vol. 9911, pp. 615–629. Springer, Cham (2016). https://doi.org/10.1007/978-3-319-46478-7_38
84. Pardo, L.E., et al.: Snapshot safari: a large-scale collaborative to monitor Africa's remarkable biodiversity. S. J. Sci. **117**(1–2), 1–4 (2021)
85. Parham, J.R., Crall, J., Stewart, C., Berger-Wolf, T., Rubenstein, D.: Animal population censusing at scale with citizen science and photographic identification. In: 2017 AAAI Spring Symposium Series (2017)
86. Pedersen, M., Haurum, J.B., Bengtson, S.H., Moeslund, T.B.: 3d-zef: a 3d zebrafish tracking benchmark dataset. In: Proceedings of the IEEE/CVF Conference on Computer Vision and Pattern Recognition, pp. 2426–2436 (2020)
87. Revaud, J., Weinzaepfel, P., Harchaoui, Z., Schmid, C.: Deepmatching: Hierarchical deformable dense matching. Int. J. Comput. Vision **120**(3), 300–323 (2016)
88. Rey, N., Volpi, M., Joost, S., Tuia, D.: Detecting animals in African savanna with UAVs and the crowds. Remote Sens. Environ. **200**, 341–351 (2017)
89. Richards, B.L., Drazen, J.C., Virginia Moriwake, V.: Hawai'i deep-7 bottomfish training and validation image dataset: Noaa pacific islands fisheries science center botcam stereo-video (2014)

90. Ristani, E., Solera, F., Zou, R., Cucchiara, R., Tomasi, C.: Performance measures and a data set for multi-target, multi-camera tracking. In: Hua, G., Jégou, H. (eds.) ECCV 2016. LNCS, vol. 9914, pp. 17–35. Springer, Cham (2016). https://doi.org/10.1007/978-3-319-48881-3_2

91. Rodriguez, I.F., Megret, R., Acuna, E., Agosto-Rivera, J.L., Giray, T.: Recognition of pollen-bearing bees from video using convolutional neural network. In: 2018 IEEE Winter Conference on Applications of Computer Vision (WACV), pp. 314–322. IEEE (2018)

92. Saenko, K., Kulis, B., Fritz, M., Darrell, T.: Adapting visual category models to new domains. In: Daniilidis, K., Maragos, P., Paragios, N. (eds.) ECCV 2010. LNCS, vol. 6314, pp. 213–226. Springer, Heidelberg (2010). https://doi.org/10.1007/978-3-642-15561-1_16

93. Saleh, A., Laradji, I.H., Konovalov, D.A., Bradley, M., Vazquez, D., Sheaves, M.: A realistic fish-habitat dataset to evaluate algorithms for underwater visual analysis. Sci. Rep. **10**(1), 1–10 (2020)

94. Sam, D.B., Peri, S.V., Sundararaman, M.N., Kamath, A., Radhakrishnan, V.B.: Locate, size and count: accurately resolving people in dense crowds via detection. IEEE Trans. Pattern Anal. Mach. Intell. **43**(8), 2739–2751 (2020)

95. Schneider, S., Zhuang, A.: Counting fish and dolphins in sonar images using deep learning. arXiv preprint arXiv:2007.12808 (2020)

96. Shao, W., Kawakami, R., Yoshihashi, R., You, S., Kawase, H., Naemura, T.: Cattle detection and counting in UAV images based on convolutional neural networks. Int. J. Remote Sens. **41**(1), 31–52 (2020)

97. Soomro, K., Zamir, A.R., Shah, M.: Ucf101: a dataset of 101 human actions classes from videos in the wild. arXiv preprint arXiv:1212.0402 (2012)

98. Stierhoff, K., Cutter, G.: Rockfish (sebastes spp.) training and validation image dataset: Noaa southwest fisheries science center remotely operated vehicle (ROV) digital still images (2013)

99. Sun, J.J., et al.: The multi-agent behavior dataset: mouse dyadic social interactions. arXiv preprint arXiv:2104.02710 (2021)

100. Sun, P., et al.: Scalability in perception for autonomous driving: Waymo open dataset. In: Proceedings of the IEEE/CVF Conference on Computer Vision and Pattern Recognition, pp. 2446–2454 (2020)

101. Swanson, A., Kosmala, M., Lintott, C., Simpson, R., Smith, A., Packer, C.: Snapshot Serengeti, high-frequency annotated camera trap images of 40 mammalian species in an African savanna. Sci. Data **2**(1), 1–14 (2015)

102. Tabak, M.A., et al.: Machine learning to classify animal species in camera trap images: applications in ecology. Methods Ecol. Evol. **10**(4), 585–590 (2019)

103. The Nature conservancy: channel islands camera traps 1.0 (2021)

104. Torralba, A., Efros, A.A.: Unbiased look at dataset bias. In: CVPR 2011, pp. 1521–1528. IEEE (2011)

105. Tuia, D., et al.: Perspectives in machine learning for wildlife conservation. Nat. Commun. **13**(1), 1–15 (2022)

106. Van Horn, G., et al.: Building a bird recognition app and large scale dataset with citizen scientists: the fine print in fine-grained dataset collection. In: Proceedings of the IEEE Conference on Computer Vision and Pattern Recognition, pp. 595–604 (2015)

107. Van Horn, G., et al.: The INaturalist species classification and detection dataset. In: Proceedings of the IEEE Conference on Computer Vision and Pattern Recognition, pp. 8769–8778 (2018)

108. Wah, C., Branson, S., Welinder, P., Perona, P., Belongie, S.: The Caltech-UCSD birds-200-2011 dataset (2011)
109. Wang, Q., Gao, J., Lin, W., Li, X.: NWPU-Crowd: a large-scale benchmark for crowd counting and localization. IEEE Trans. Pattern Anal. Mach. Intell. **43**(6), 2141–2149 (2020)
110. Weinland, D., Ronfard, R., Boyer, E.: Free viewpoint action recognition using motion history volumes. Comput. Vis. Image Underst. **104**(2–3), 249–257 (2006)
111. Weinstein, B.G., et al.: A remote sensing derived data set of 100 million individual tree crowns for the national ecological observatory network. Elife **10**, e62922 (2021)
112. Wen, L., et al.: UA-DETRAC: a new benchmark and protocol for multi-object detection and tracking. Comput. Vis. Image Underst. **193**, 102907 (2020)
113. Wen, L., et al.: Detection, tracking, and counting meets drones in crowds: a benchmark. In: Proceedings of the IEEE/CVF Conference on Computer Vision and Pattern Recognition, pp. 7812–7821 (2021)
114. Wen, L., et al.: Detection, tracking, and counting meets drones in crowds: a benchmark. In: CVPR (2021)
115. Wojke, N., Bewley, A., Paulus, D.: Simple online and realtime tracking with a deep association metric. In: 2017 IEEE International Conference on Image Processing (ICIP), pp. 3645–3649. IEEE (2017)
116. Wu, Z., Fuller, N., Theriault, D., Betke, M.: A thermal infrared video benchmark for visual analysis. In: Proceedings of the IEEE Conference on Computer Vision and Pattern Recognition Workshops, pp. 201–208 (2014)
117. Ye, N., et al.: OoD-Bench: quantifying and understanding two dimensions of out-of-distribution generalization. In: Proceedings of the IEEE/CVF Conference on Computer Vision and Pattern Recognition, pp. 7947–7958 (2022)
118. Yousif, H., Kays, R., He, Z.: Dynamic programming selection of object proposals for sequence-level animal species classification in the wild. IEEE Trans. Circuits Syst. Video Technol. (2019)
119. Yu, F., et al.: Bdd100k: a diverse driving video database with scalable annotation tooling, vol. 2, no. 5, p. 6 (2018). arXiv preprint arXiv:1805.04687
120. Zhang, C., Kang, K., Li, H., Wang, X., Xie, R., Yang, X.: Data-driven crowd understanding: a baseline for a large-scale crowd dataset. IEEE Trans. Multimedia **18**(6), 1048–1061 (2016)
121. Zhang, C., Li, H., Wang, X., Yang, X.: Cross-scene crowd counting via deep convolutional neural networks. In: Proceedings of the IEEE Conference on Computer Vision and Pattern Recognition, pp. 833–841 (2015)
122. Zhang, S., Wu, G., Costeira, J.P., Moura, J.M.: FCN-rLSTM: deep spatio-temporal neural networks for vehicle counting in city cameras. In: Proceedings of the IEEE International Conference on Computer Vision, pp. 3667–3676 (2017)
123. Zhang, Y., David, P., Gong, B.: Curriculum domain adaptation for semantic segmentation of urban scenes. In: 2017 IEEE International Conference on Computer Vision (ICCV), pp. 2039–2049 (2017)
124. Zhang, Y., et al.: Bytetrack: multi-object tracking by associating every detection box. arXiv preprint arXiv:2110.06864 (2021)
125. Zhang, Y., Wang, C., Wang, X., Zeng, W., Liu, W.: Fairmot: on the fairness of detection and re-identification in multiple object tracking. arXiv preprint arXiv:2004.01888 (2020)
126. Zhang, Y., Zhou, D., Chen, S., Gao, S., Ma, Y.: Single-image crowd counting via multi-column convolutional neural network. In: Proceedings of the IEEE Conference on Computer Vision and Pattern Recognition, pp. 589–597 (2016)

127. Zhang, Z., He, Z., Cao, G., Cao, W.: Animal detection from highly cluttered natural scenes using spatiotemporal object region proposals and patch verification. IEEE Trans. Multimedia **18**(10), 2079–2092 (2016)

128. Zhao, Z., Li, H., Zhao, R., Wang, X.: Crossing-line crowd counting with two-phase deep neural networks. In: Leibe, B., Matas, J., Sebe, N., Welling, M. (eds.) ECCV 2016. LNCS, vol. 9912, pp. 712–726. Springer, Cham (2016). https://doi.org/10.1007/978-3-319-46484-8_43

129. Zheng, Z., Yang, X., Yu, Z., Zheng, L., Yang, Y., Kautz, J.: Joint discriminative and generative learning for person re-identification. In: Proceedings of the IEEE/CVF Conference on Computer Vision and Pattern Recognition, pp. 2138–2147 (2019)

130. Zhou, K., Liu, Z., Qiao, Y., Xiang, T., Loy, C.C.: Domain generalization in vision: a survey (2021)

131. Zhou, Y., Yu, H., Wu, J., Cui, Z., Zhang, F.: Fish behavior analysis based on computer vision: a survey. In: Mao, R., Wang, H., Xie, X., Lu, Z. (eds.) ICPCSEE 2019. CCIS, vol. 1059, pp. 130–141. Springer, Singapore (2019). https://doi.org/10.1007/978-981-15-0121-0_10

132. Zhu, P., Peng, T., Du, D., Yu, H., Zhang, L., Hu, Q.: Graph regularized flow attention network for video animal counting from drones. IEEE Trans. Image Process. (2021)

133. Zou, Z., Shi, Z., Guo, Y., Ye, J.: Object detection in 20 years: a survey. arxiv preprint arXiv:1905.05055 (2019)

A Dataset for Interactive Vision-Language Navigation with Unknown Command Feasibility

Andrea Burns[1]([✉]), Deniz Arsan[2], Sanjna Agrawal[1], Ranjitha Kumar[2],
Kate Saenko[1,3], and Bryan A. Plummer[1]

[1] Boston University, Boston, MA 02215, USA
{aburns4,sanjna,saenko,bplum}@bu.edu
[2] University of Illinois Urbana-Champaign, Champaign, IL 61820, USA
{darsan2,ranjitha}@illinois.edu
[3] MIT-IBM Watson AI Lab, Cambridge, MA 02142, USA

Abstract. Vision-language navigation (VLN), in which an agent follows language instruction in a visual environment, has been studied under the premise that the input command is fully feasible in the environment. Yet in practice, a request may not be possible due to language ambiguity or environment changes. To study VLN with unknown command feasibility, we introduce a new dataset Mobile app Tasks with Iterative Feedback (MoTIF), where the goal is to complete a natural language command in a mobile app. Mobile apps provide a scalable domain to study real downstream uses of VLN methods. Moreover, mobile app commands provide instruction for interactive navigation, as they result in action sequences with state changes via clicking, typing, or swiping. MoTIF is the first to include feasibility annotations, containing both binary feasibility labels and fine-grained labels for why tasks are unsatisfiable. We further collect follow-up questions for ambiguous queries to enable research on task uncertainty resolution. Equipped with our dataset, we propose the new problem of feasibility prediction, in which a natural language instruction and multimodal app environment are used to predict command feasibility. MoTIF provides a more realistic app dataset as it contains many diverse environments, high-level goals, and longer action sequences than prior work. We evaluate interactive VLN methods using MoTIF, quantify the generalization ability of current approaches to new app environments, and measure the effect of task feasibility on navigation performance.

Keywords: Vision-language navigation · Task feasibility · Mobile apps

1 Introduction

Vision-language navigation (VLN) has made notable progress toward natural language instruction following [5,17,31,32,38,39,44]. While navigation datasets

---

Supplementary Information The online version contains supplementary material available at https://doi.org/10.1007/978-3-031-20074-8_18.

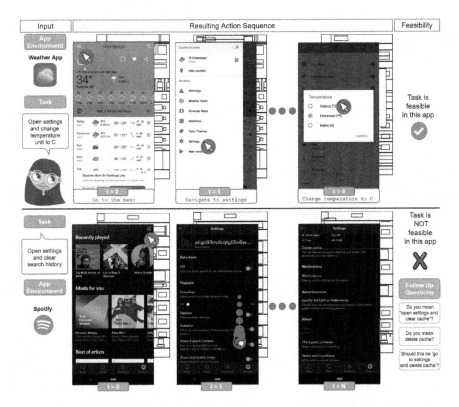

Fig. 1. MoTIF natural language commands which may not be possible. At each time step, action coordinates (*i.e.*, where clicking, typing, or scrolling occurs), the app screen, and view hierarchy (*i.e.*, the app backend, illustrated behind it) are captured

exist for home environments [3,8,19,38] and digital environments like mobile apps and websites [25,26,33,37], none capture the possibility that the language request may not be feasible in the given environment. When high-level natural language goals are requested, they may not be feasible for various reasons: the request may be ambiguous or state dependent, refer to functionality that is no longer available, or is reasonable in a similar environment but not satisfiable in the current. Task feasibility has been studied to determine question relevance for text-only [12] and visual question answering [14,30,36], but it has not been explored in interactive multimodal environments.

To study interactive task feasibility, we propose Mobile app Tasks with Iterative Feedback (MoTIF)[1], the largest dataset designed to support interactive methods for completing natural language tasks in mobile apps. As illustrated in Fig. 1, a sample includes the natural language command (*i.e.*, task), app view hierarchy, app screen image, and action coordinates for each time step. MoTIF contains both feasible and infeasible requests, unlike any VLN dataset to date. In addition to these binary feasibility labels for each task, we collect subclass annotations for why tasks are infeasible and natural language follow-up questions.

---

[1] https://github.com/aburns4/MoTIF.

Our dataset provides a domain with practical downstream applications to study vision-language navigation, as well as data for investigating app design [9,10,27], human-computer interfaces [21–23], and document understanding [4,20,43].

We propose a baseline model for task feasibility prediction and confirm app exploration is necessary, with visual inputs key to accuracy. Surprisingly, prior representation learning approaches specific to the mobile app domain (*e.g.*, app icon features) do not result in the best performance. We then evaluate methods for automating MoTIF's commands and find MoTIF's diverse test set are challenging for prior work. Performance trends between seen and unseen app environments point to the need for more in-app exploration during training and qualitative failures in the best baseline model demonstrate the importance of visual understanding for MoTIF.

We summarize our contributions below:

- A new vision-language navigation dataset, Mobile app Tasks with Iterative Feedback (MoTIF). MoTIF has free form natural language commands for interactive goals in mobile apps, a subset of which are infeasible. It contains natural language tasks for the most app environments to date. MoTIF also captures multiple interactions including clicking, swiping and typing actions.
- A new vision-language task: interactive task feasibility classification, along with subclass annotations on why tasks are infeasible and follow-up questions for research toward resolving task uncertainty via dialogue.
- Benchmarks for feasibility classification and task automation with MoTIF. A thorough feature exploration is performed to evaluate the role of vision and language in task feasibility. We compare several methods on mobile app task automation, analyze generalization, and examine the effects of feasibility.

2   Related Work

We now discuss the key differences between MoTIF and existing datasets; we provide a side-by-side comparison in Table 1.

Task Feasibility. Vision-language research has recently begun to study task feasibility. Gurari *et al.* introduced VizWiz [14], a visual question answering dataset for images taken by people that are blind, resulting in questions which may not be answerable. To the best of our knowledge, VizWiz is the only vision-language dataset with annotations for task feasibility, but it only addresses question answering over static images. Additionally, images that cannot be used to answer visual questions are easily classified, as they often contain blurred or random scenes (*e.g.*, the floor). Gardner *et al.* [12] explored question-answer plausibility prediction, but the questions used were generated from a bot, which could result in extraneous questions also easy to classify as implausible. Both are significantly different from the nuanced tasks of MoTIF with human generated queries, for which exploration is necessary to determine feasibility. MoTIF's infeasible tasks are always relevant to the Android app category, making it more challenging to discern feasibility compared to the distinct visual failures present in VizWiz.

Table 1. Comparison of MoTIF to existing datasets. We consider the number of natural language commands, command granularity, existence of feasibility annotations, the number of environments and whether the visual state is included in annotations

Dataset	Language annotations			Dataset environment	
	# Human annotations	Task granularity	Feasibility	# Environments	Visual state
(a) House					
R2R [3]	21,567	Low	✗	90	✓
IQA [13]	✗	High	✗	30	✓
ALFRED [38]	25,743	High & Low	✗	120	✓
(b) Webpage					
MiniWoB [37]	✗	High	✗	100	✗
PhraseNode [33]	50,000	Low	✗	1,800	✗
(c) Mobile App					
RicoSCA [25]	✗	Low	✗	9,700	✗
PIXELHELP [25]	187	Low	✗	4	✗
MoTIF (Ours)	6,100	High & Low	✓	125	✓

Vision-Language Navigation There are datasets that strictly navigate to locations like Room-to-Room [3] and Room-Across-Room [19], as well as inter-active datasets where agents perform actions in the environment to complete a goal like ALFRED [38]. MoTIF is most similar to interactive VLN, as the natural language instructions are intended to complete a goal for the user, which requires clicking, typing, or swiping actions in the environment. However, an advantage of MoTIF is that it is a real, non-simulated domain to study interactive navigation, unlike all VLN prior work which uses simulated data [13,34,38,45].

Digital Task Automation. Prior work has not studied web task automation in a multimodal setting, ignoring the rendered website image [33,37]. The existing datasets MiniWoB [37] and PhraseNode [33] also lack realism, as MiniWoB consists of handcrafted HTML and PhraseNode only captures single action commands on the home screen of websites. Unlike these datasets which limit interaction to a single screen, MoTIF contains action sequences with many different states (as shown in Fig. 1), with a median of eight visited screens.

RicoSCA and PIXELHELP were introduced for mobile app task automation by Li *et al.* [25]. RicoSCA makes use of the mobile app dataset Rico [9], which captures random exploration in Android apps. Li *et al.* synthetically generate random commands with templates like *"click on* **x**" and stitch multiple together to any prescribed length. These generated step-by-step instructions do not reflect downstream use, where users ask for a high-level goal. For MoTIF, we instead collect free form high-level goals, and then post-process our data to automatically generate the low level subgoal instructions. PIXELHELP is a small mobile app dataset, but most commands are device specific. *I.e.*, the tasks refer to the phone itself, such as *"in the top control menu click the battery saver,"* and are not in-app tasks like those in Fig. 1. PIXELHELP also only contains clicking, while MoTIF has clicking, typing and swiping actions.

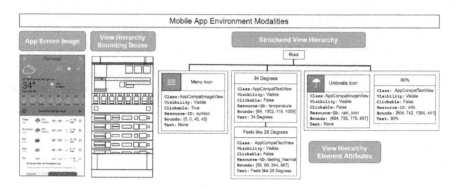

Fig. 2. We illustrate captured app modalities: the rendered screen and view hierarchy, which contains element metadata such as the Android class, resource ID, and text

3 MoTIF Dataset

For a mobile app task dataset, we need natural language tasks for apps and their resulting action sequence. Figure 1 illustrates MoTIF tasks like *"open settings and change temperature unit to C."* For each command, we collect expert demonstrations of attempts to complete the request. At each time step we capture the app screen, the app backend view hierarchy, what type of action is taken, and where the action occurred. We show the modalities captured at each time step in greater detail in Fig. 2. The Android app backend, *i.e.*, view hierarchy, is a tree-like structure akin to the Document Object Model (DOM) used for HTML. It organizes each screen element hierarchically, and contains additional metadata like the Android class of an element (*e.g.*, a text view or image view), its resource identifier, the text it contains, whether it is clickable, and other attributes.

3.1 Data Collection

We provide a general framework for others to collect natural language data with unknown feasibility; Fig. 3 illustrates the collection pipeline. We select 125 apps for MoTIF over 15 app categories (the complete app list can be found in the Supplementary). Ten apps with (1) at least 50k downloads and (2) a rating higher than or equal to 4/5 were chosen for each category. Next, a first set of annotators writes commands. A list of (app, task) pairs are then provided to a second set of annotators in an interactive session, where they attempt the task, specify if it is not feasible, and can ask a clarifying question if not. The Supplementary includes annotator demographics, payment, and collection interface details.

Natural Language Commands. To collect natural language tasks, we instruct workers to write commands as if they are asking the app to perform the task for them. Annotators can explore the app before deciding on their list of tasks. We ask them to write functional or navigational tasks, and not commands requiring text comprehension like summarizing an article. We neither structure the written tasks nor prescribe a specific number of tasks to be written for each app.

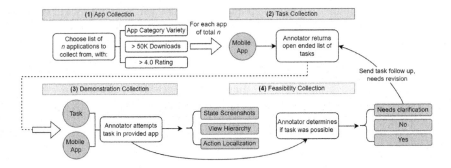

Fig. 3. The data collection pipeline (see Sect. 3.1). Colored boxes (app, task, demonstration, and feasibility collection) are stages of curating the dataset (Color figure online)

Task-Application Pairing. When collecting natural language tasks, annotators can first explore the app. Once we have tasks for every app, we introduce additional feasibility uncertainty for the demonstration stage by collecting demos for both the original (app, task) list, as well as tasks paired with apps they were not originally written for. We create these additional (app, task) pairs by clustering tasks within each Android category (for example, clustering all tasks for Music and Audio Android apps) and selecting representatives from each cluster. These representative tasks are then collected for all apps of that category, which we coin "*category-clustered*." Specifically, we cluster the mean FastText embedding [7] of the language commands using K-Means [28].

Clusters are visualized with T-SNE [29] (see Supplementary). If a particular app's tasks are isolated from other clusters, we retain "*app-specific*" pairings, *i.e.*, the (app, task) pairs for tasks specifically written for the given app. This resulted in 40 apps having only app-specific tasks. If two apps' tasks are closely clustered, we group them; 17 apps' tasks were gathered this way. Figure 1 (bottom) shows a category-clustered task which was deemed infeasible by annotators. The command "*open settings and clear search history*" was paired with the music app Spotify even though it was not written for it. This is a sensible request given that Spotify is a music streaming app. Yet, no search history is found under settings, only the option to "delete cache," and follow-up questions are asked.

Task Demonstration and Feasibility Annotations. Once the language commands are paired with apps, we instruct new annotators to demonstrate the task in the given app. We provide a website interface connected to physical Android phones for crowd workers to interact with, as well as anonymized login credentials so that no personally identifiable information is collected. They are instructed to record their demonstration after they have logged in (we consider logging in to be a separate task). After attempting to complete the task, they are brought to a post-survey where they provide details on whether or not the task was successfully completed. We therefore have demonstrations of actions taken both

Table 2. Task feasibility and follow-up question breakdown. Annotators can state the action: can't be completed (impossible), is under-specified (unclear), may be possible, but are unsure how or other tasks need to be completed first (premature)

#	Feasible	Infeasible			Total
		Impossible	Unclear	Premature	
Task demonstrations	3,337	911	159	300	4,707
Follow-up questions	93	253	136	164	646

in successful and unsuccessful episodes, which may provide interesting insight toward how to reason about whether a task is or is not feasible, and why.

3.2 Dataset Analysis

Natural Language Commands. We collected over 6.1k natural language tasks across 125 Android apps. The vocabulary size was 3,763 after removing non-alphanumeric characters. The average number of tasks submitted per app is 56, with average length being 5.6 words. The minimum task length is one, consisting of single action tasks like 'refresh' or 'login,' with the longest at 44 words. Word cloud visualizations, additional examples and statistics are in the Supplementary.

Feasibility Annotations. We collect at least five expert demonstrations per (app, task) pair for two purposes: to reach a majority feasibility label and to capture different attempts of the same task, as some tasks can be completed in multiple ways. See the Supplementary for an annotator agreement histogram.

Of the resulting tasks, 29.2% are deemed infeasible by at least five crowd workers. However, the tasks considered infeasible do not always correlate to mismatched (app, task) pairs, *i.e.*, some *app-specific* tasks are deemed infeasible during demonstration. This confirms the need to study commands with unknown feasibility, as someone familiar with an app can still pose requests that are either not possible, ambiguous, or state dependent. Of the infeasible tasks, 16.8% are from app-specific pairs. *E.g.*, the request *"click shuttle and station"* originally written for the NASA app was labeled infeasible because the app has changing interactive features. Thus app changes and dynamic features also motivate studying infeasible requests, as a task that was once feasible may not always be.

Table 2 provides statistics on the number of task demonstrations and follow-up questions per feasibility category. There are three options for annotators to choose from: (1) the action cannot be completed in the app, (2) the action is unclear or under-specified, or (3) the task seems to be possible, but they cannot figure out how or other tasks need to be completed first. These map to Table 2's impossible, unclear, and premature columns. If a crowd worker cannot complete the task, they are prompted to ask a follow-up question. We instruct them to write the question(s) such that if they had the answer, they may now be able to complete the original action or perform an alternative task for the user.

4   Task Feasibility Experiments

We first perform experiments with MoTIF for task feasibility. Given a natural language command and the app states visited during its demonstration, the purpose of task feasibility prediction is to classify if the command can be completed. To determine feasibility, we expect a model to learn the most relevant state for the requested task and if the functionality needed to complete it is present. Our results provide an initial upper bound on performance, as the input action sequences can be considered the ground truth exploration needed to determine feasibility, as opposed to a learned agent's exploration. MoTIF has 4.7k demonstrations and we reserve 10% for testing. Note that our test set only includes (app, task) pairs for which all annotators agreed on their feasibility annotation.

4.1   Models

We propose a Multi-Layer Perceptron (MLP) baseline with two hidden layers that outputs a binary feasibility prediction. Each MLP is trained for 50 epochs with cross entropy using Stochastic Gradient Descent with a learning rate of 1e-2. The natural language command is always input to the classifier, and we ablate which app environment features are additional input. In addition to the feature ablations, we ablate how the demonstration sequence is aggregated (averaging or concatenating over time steps or using the last hidden state of an LSTM [16]).

Features. We encode the task command and view hierarchy elements per step with mean pooled features. Specifically, we try both FastText [6] and CLIP [35] (trained with a Transformer backbone for its image and text encoders [11,41]). As seen in Fig. 2, the view hierarchy captures all rendered app elements and their attributes: the element's text (ET), resource-identifier (ID) and class labels (CLS) which provide content and type information. We use the best combination of these attributes in Table 3 and have more ablations in the Supplementary. We also include Screen2Vec [24] in our view hierarchy representations. Screen2Vec is a semantic embedding of the view hierarchy, representing the view hierarchy with a GUI, text, and layout embedder. The GUI and text encoders make use of BERT features while the layout features are learned with an autoencoder. Thus, it tries to encode both textual and structural features, but no visual information.

For visual features, we extract ResNet152 [15] features for ten crops of each app image and CLIP features of each whole app image. We also include icon features by cropping all icon images per screen (*e.g.*, the menu and umbrella icons shown in Fig. 2). We embed each icon image using the embedding layer of a CNN trained for the downstream task of icon classification by Liu *et al.* [27].

Metrics. We report the average F1 score over ten runs with different random initialization. "Infeasible" is defined as the positive class, as we care more about correctly classifying tasks that are infeasible, than misclassifying feasible tasks.

Table 3. Task feasibility F1 score using our MLP. We ablate input features and action sequence aggregation. The random baseline predicts a feasibility label given the train distribution. On the right is a confusion matrix for the predictions of our best classifier

C_{feas} Input Features	Demo Aggregation		
	Avg	Cat	LSTM
Random		20.1	
(a) View Hierarchy			
FastText [6] (ET, ID)	16.7	43.6	34.1
CLIP [35] (ET, ID)	28.0	50.9	36.2
Screen2Vec [24]	25.9	33.7	36.0
(b) App Screen Image			
ResNet [15]	31.3	41.9	35.9
Icons [27]	0.4	40.0	15.2
CLIP [35]	44.7	58.2	42.8
(c) Best Combination			
CLIP [35] (Screen, ET, ID)	44.8	61.1	40.9

(c) Best Combination

Ground Truth

	Feasible	Infeasible
Prediction — Feasible	76.4%	8.6%
Prediction — Infeasible	4.0%	11.0%

4.2 Results

Our best task feasibility classifier (Table 3(c) left) achieves an F1 score of 61.1 when CLIP embeds the task, view hierarchy, and app screen image. This is still fairly low, and feature ablations demonstrate room to improve both the language and visual representations. While CLIP has shown significant performance gains in other vision-language tasks, it is somewhat surprising that domain-specific embeddings (*e.g.*, Screen2Vec, Icons) are not as competitive. The combination of view hierarchy and app screen features does not largely outperform the app screen image CLIP results (and does worse with LSTM aggregation), suggesting a need for better vision-language encodings which can pull features together from different modalities such as the view hierarchy.

We include the confusion matrix on the right of Table 3 for our best model. In downstream use, the classifier would result in 5% of tasks being missed out on; *i.e.*, 5% of tasks were incorrectly classified as infeasible. This reduces the utility of assistive applications, where we'd like all possible commands to correctly be completed. However, the 44% of infeasible tasks that were incorrectly classified as feasible can have more negative consequences. In application, this means a vision-language model would attempt to complete an unsatisfiable request, resulting in unknown behavior. We need downstream models to behave in reliable ways, especially for users that cannot verify the task was reasonably completed.

Table 3(a) left compares methods of encoding the view hierarchy. Using CLIP for view hierarchy elements results in notably better performance than FastText, albeit less significant when input demos are aggregated with an LSTM. Our final view hierarchy embedding is Screen2Vec which performs worse than CLIP and on par with FastText, despite being trained on mobile app data. Screen2Vec may not capture enough low level view hierarchy information to predict feasibility, and methods trained on huge data, even if from another domain, are more powerful.

In Table 3(b) left we ablate over the visual representations of the app screen. While icon representations are trained on images from the same domain as MoTIF, they are significantly less effective than ResNet and CLIP. The F1 score nearly drops to zero when the average icon feature is used, illustrating that the average icon does not carry useful information for feasibility classification. Icon features may be too low-level or require improved aggregation methods.

Comparing demonstration aggregation methods (averaging, concatenating, or LSTM), there is a trend that concatenating time steps is the best method, suggesting a sequential representation of the action sequence is needed. However, when the best representations for the view hierarchy and app screen are combined in Table 3(c), averaging manages to outperform the LSTM performance.

In future work we hope to learn hierarchical representations in order to encode global information such as that of Screen2Vec as well as local information from icon embeddings. Taking advantage of the tree structure from the view hierarchy via Transformers or Graph Neural Networks may help learn structured app features. Additionally, all current approaches do not take into account any notion of app "affordance," *i.e.*, which app elements are most actionable.

5   Task Automation Experiments

In app task automation, we are given an app environment (with all of its modalities) and a language command. The goal is to interact with the app and output a sequence of app actions that complete the task, akin to interactive VLN. At each time step there are two predictions: an action (clicking, typing, or swiping) and a localization (grounding visually on the app screen or classifying over the app elements). We benchmark several methods and analyze performance below.

5.1   Models

We adapt three models for the mobile app domain with as few changes as possible. The VLN approaches described below (Seq2Seq and MOCA) take both the high-level goal and low level instructions as input while Seq2Act only supports low level instruction. In the supplementary we include input language ablations to consider what performance with real downstream use would look like.

Seq2Seq is a VLN model for the ALFRED, a dataset of actionable commands for tasks in household environments. It originally predicts an action and binary mask at each time step. The mask isolates the household object on which the action is performed. The features at each time step include the attended language instruction, the current step's visual features, the last predicted action, and the hidden state of a BiLSTM which takes the former as input. The previous step's BiLSTM hidden state attends to the language input. These features are passed to a fully connected layer with Softmax for action prediction and a deconvolutional network for mask prediction. We replace the mask prediction network for three fully connected layers that predict a point in the app screen and minimize the mean squared error. Action prediction is trained via cross entropy.

MOCA [39], also proposed for ALFRED, decouples the action and grounding predictions of each step in a VLN sequence. One model stream is for the action prediction policy, and another for interaction grounding. Both streams first use a BiLSTM language encoder, which take the high-level goal or low level instruction as input, respectively. The encoded tokens are attended to using ResNet visual features via dynamic attention filters. Then, two LSTM decoders are used: one for the action policy stream and another for the interaction grounding.

At test time MOCA makes use of an off-the-shelf object segmentation model to perform grounding given the predicted object class. To adapt the object class prediction to mobile apps, we instead perform app element type prediction (prediction is over twelve classes, including button, checkbox, edit text, image view, and more). As no such segmentation model exists for mobile apps yet, we also predict bounding box localization directly using the LSTM decoder output, but use the app element type prediction to narrow grounding options at evaluation.

Seq2Act. [25] models mobile app task automation in two stages: action phrase extraction and action grounding. Both stages are modeled with Transformers. The first model predicts a span (*i.e.*, substring) of the original input command that corresponds to the action type, action location, and action input. It has an encoder-decoder architecture: the encoder embeds the instruction's text tokens and the decoder computes a query vector for the action type, location, and input phrases given the previously decoded spans. A text span is selected for each decoder query (action type, action location, action input) via cosine similarity.

The action grounding model takes each extracted phrase as input to predict an action type and location (which app element it is performed on). Actions are predicted given the encoder embedding of the predicted action type span via a Multi-Layer Perception (MLP). To localize the action, a Transformer is trained to embed app elements using the view hierarchy attributes as shown in Fig. 2. A Softmax is applied to the similarities of the predicted app location span embeddings and the latent app element representations. The max scoring app element becomes the grounding prediction for that time step.

Datasets. We evaluate task automation on two MoTIF test splits: an app seen and an app unseen split to study generalization to new environments; generalization of tasks across apps is provided in the Supplementary. We jointly train VLN models on MoTIF and RicoSCA for additional data (see the Supplementary for additional experiments trained solely on MoTIF). Seq2Act was originally trained on RicoSCA and we adapt its training data split to be able to evaluate seen versus unseen apps at test time.

Features. Visual features for Seq2Seq and MOCA are from the last convolutional layer of a ResNet18, as done for the original models; these features are needed for meaningful localization on the mobile app screen. We also include CLIP features of the screen at each time step. Note that VLN methods require a test-time environment; we build an offline version of each Android app to approximate a complete state-action space graph. Details on the creation of these graphs can be found in

Table 4. Mobile app task accuracy on MoTIF. We evaluate the Seq2Seq and MOCA navigation models and the Transformer grounding model Seq2Act

Model	App seen			App unseen		
	Action	Ground	Action + Ground	Action	Ground	Action + Ground
(a) Seq2Seq [38]						
Complete Sequence	68.5	22.5	22.5	54.3	18.0	17.7
Partial Sequence	89.5	40.4	40.1	81.7	31.3	30.6
(b) MOCA [39]						
Complete Sequence	51.1	21.3	20.7	44.8	17.0	15.1
Partial Sequence	78.5	40.0	38.6	72.2	32.7	30.0
(c) Seq2Act [25]						
Complete Sequence	<u>98.8</u>	<u>27.6</u>	<u>27.6</u>	<u>94.9</u>	<u>23.5</u>	<u>23.5</u>
Partial Sequence	<u>99.7</u>	<u>64.4</u>	<u>64.3</u>	<u>98.9</u>	<u>62.2</u>	<u>61.7</u>

the Supplementary. Seq2Act does not use off-the-shelf features as input; all text and app element embeddings are learned from scratch.

Metrics. We report complete and partial sequence accuracy per [25]: the complete score for an action sequence is 1 if the predicted and ground truth sequences have the same length and the same predictions at each step, else 0. The partial sequence score is the fraction of predicted steps that match the ground-truth. These are reported for action prediction (Action), action grounding (Ground), or both jointly. Seq2Seq localization is correct if the predicted point falls within the bounding box of the ground truth app element. MOCA localization is correct if the predicted bounding box and ground truth have an IoU greater than 0.5.

5.2 Results

Despite MOCA being a more recent model for interactive vision-language navigation, it generally does not outperform Seq2Seq. The app element type prediction MOCA uses may be responsible for the similar or lower accuracy, as the original intention of object class prediction was to narrow down grounding interaction to very few options. *E.g.*, in the home environments of ALFRED, which MOCA evaluated on, the object class predicted may be apple. If there is only a single apple in the scene, the object segmentation model would be highly effective for grounding. The mobile app domain differs in that there are many app elements per time step of the same type, *e.g.*, there are many app icons or app buttons, and this prediction may not significantly reduce the grounding prediction space.

The Seq2Seq and MOCA models perform worse than Seq2Act. While additional model ablations may improve performance, it is clear that action localization on the continuous app screen is more challenging. Seq2Act achieves the highest performance for all metrics. Seq2Act was originally evaluated with PIXEL-HELP [25] and achieved 70.6% complete Action + Ground accuracy on it, much higher than the accuracy reported on MoTIF. This may be due to PIXELHELP containing click-only tasks for four test environments, which does not reflect the

Fig. 4. Seq2Act text matching. Green and red boxes are valid and invalid predictions, respectively; black are additional valid ground truth. The left shows valid text matching, identifying "notifications" in the app Pinterest. The right shows Seq2Act incorrectly matching "my" in the input task to the app element "My favorite" in the Opera news app (Color figure online)

model's performance on a greater variety of apps or tasks. MoTIF's step-by-step instructions also contain location descriptions for app elements which don't contain text, differing from the Seq2Act training data distribution.

Qualitatively inspecting misclassifications, we find one culprit to be Seq2Act overly relying on matching input task text to view hierarchy text. In Fig. 4, we show Seq2Act's text matching tendency, which can result in failure. For example, Seq2Act predicts the app element with the word "my" in it for the input command *"go to my profile."* These results, in addition to the high visual performance from the feasibility classifier, verifies the need for visual input to correct model bias to match input task text directly to the view hierarchy.

Performance is unsurprisingly worse for unseen app environments. We suspect that current model formulations do not learn enough about app elements outside of the ground truth action sequences during training. None of the benchmark models include exploration, and as a result, may be biased to the small subset of elements seen in expert demonstration. In future work, using pre-trained generic app features or incorporating exploration into the training process through reinforcement learning approaches may alleviate this.

6   Discussion

We find our best task feasibility prediction results to be low at a 61.1 F1 score, given that the input demonstrations serve as the oracle exploration needed to determine feasibility. In addition to improving vision-language feasibility reasoning, a necessary next step is to instead use learned explorations during training. Our ablations demonstrate that visual inputs are useful for feasibility prediction, and research toward better mobile app features that actually use the rendered screen could increase performance. Building hierarchical visual and textual features may provide stronger context clues for determining command feasibility in the app environment. We also hope to perform experiments classifying why tasks are not feasible and automating question generation in response, making use of MoTIF's subclass annotations for infeasible tasks and follow up questions.

By evaluating action and grounding performance independently, we found that models for completing mobile app tasks can have more difficulty grounding and consistently perform more poorly in new app environments. Better representations of app elements are needed; specifically, incorporating pretraining tasks for improved app features or allowing for exploration outside of ground truth action sequences may be necessary to diversify test time predictions.

Limitations. The MoTIF dataset is not on the scale of pretraining datasets used in other VL tasks (*e.g.*, Alt-Text [18], JFT-300M [40]), as it is very expensive and time costly to collect natural language commands and feasibility labels. MoTIF is nonetheless useful to the research community as it can be used to evaluate how existing methods would solve language-based digital tasks in realistic settings.

Societal Impact. Methods for automating language commands and predicting command feasibility can be used to assist people who are not able to interact with apps, either situationally (*e.g.*, while driving) or physically (*e.g.*, users who are low-vision or blind). Improving mobile app task automation could better balance the capabilities of current assistive technologies, which typically lack agency or flexibility [42]. *E.g.*, screen readers are primarily used for web browsing and information consumption (lacking agency), while interactive virtual assistants (*e.g.*, Siri, Alexa) have limited, structured commands (lacking flexibility).

MoTIF's collection was designed to ensure no personally identifiable information is captured. But, in downstream use of app task automation, user privacy is of concern. People who use assistive tools (*e.g.*, people who are blind) already expose sensitive information to other humans to receive help [1,2]. To mitigate potential harm, deployment of our research can be limited to apps which do not require log in information; these are less likely to include name, address, or payment data. MoTIF does not have tasks which require payment, and we can deny payment related tasks to prevent fraud and other undesired outcomes.

7   Conclusion

We introduced Mobile app Tasks with Iterative Feedback (MoTIF), a new VLN dataset that contains natural language commands for tasks in mobile apps which may not be feasible. MoTIF is the first dataset to capture task uncertainty for interactive visual environments and contains greater linguistic and visual diversity than prior work, allowing for more research toward robust vision-language methods. We introduced the task of feasibility prediction and evaluate prior methods for automating mobile app tasks. Results verify that MoTIF poses new vision-language challenges, and that the vision-language community can make use of more realistic data to evaluate and improve upon current methods.

Acknowledgements. This work is funded in part by Boston University, the Google Ph.D. Fellowship program, the MIT-IBM Watson AI Lab, the Google Faculty Research Award and NSF Grant IIS-1750563.

References

1. Ahmed, T., Hoyle, R., Connelly, K., Crandall, D., Kapadia, A.: Privacy concerns and behaviors of people with visual impairments. In: Proceedings of the 33rd Annual ACM Conference on Human Factors in Computing Systems, CHI 2015, pp. 3523–3532. Association for Computing Machinery, New York (2015). https://doi.org/10.1145/2702123.2702334
2. Akter, T., Dosono, B., Ahmed, T., Kapadia, A., Semaan, B.C.: "I am uncomfortable sharing what I can't see": privacy concerns of the visually impaired with camera based assistive applications. In: USENIX Security Symposium (2020)
3. Anderson, P., et al.: Vision-and-language navigation: Interpreting visually-grounded navigation instructions in real environments. In: Proceedings of the IEEE Conference on Computer Vision and Pattern Recognition (CVPR) (2018)
4. Appalaraju, S., Jasani, B., Kota, B.U., Xie, Y., Manmatha, R.: Docformer: end-to-end transformer for document understanding. In: 2021 IEEE/CVF International Conference on Computer Vision (ICCV) (2021)
5. Blukis, V., Paxton, C., Fox, D., Garg, A., Artzi, Y.: A persistent spatial semantic representation for high-level natural language instruction execution (2021)
6. Bojanowski, P., Grave, E., Joulin, A., Mikolov, T.: Enriching word vectors with subword information. Trans. Assoc. Comput. Linguist. **5**, 135–146 (2017)
7. Conneau, A., Lample, G., Ranzato, M., Denoyer, L., Jégou, H.: Word translation without parallel data. In: International Conference on Learning Representations (ICLR) (2018)
8. Das, A., Datta, S., Gkioxari, G., Lee, S., Parikh, D., Batra, D.: Embodied question answering. In: Proceedings of the IEEE Conference on Computer Vision and Pattern Recognition (CVPR) (2018)
9. Deka, B., et al.: Rico: a mobile app dataset for building data-driven design applications. In: 30th Annual Symposium on User Interface Software and Technology (UIST) (2017)
10. Deka, B., Huang, Z., Kumar, R.: Erica: Interaction mining mobile apps. In: 29th Annual Symposium on User Interface Software and Technology (UIST) (2016)
11. Dosovitskiy, A., et al.: An image is worth 16 x 16 words: transformers for image recognition at scale (2021)
12. Gardner, R., Varma, M., Zhu, C., Krishna, R.: Determining question-answer plausibility in crowdsourced datasets using multi-task learning. In: W-NUT@EMNLP (2020)
13. Gordon, D., Kembhavi, A., Rastegari, M., Redmon, J., Fox, D., Farhadi, A.: IQA: visual question answering in interactive environments. In: 2018 IEEE/CVF Conference on Computer Vision and Pattern Recognition (CVPR), pp. 4089–4098 (2018). https://doi.org/10.1109/CVPR.2018.00430
14. Gurari, D., et al.: Vizwiz grand challenge: answering visual questions from blind people. In: Conference on Computer Vision and Pattern Recognition (CVPR) (2018)
15. He, K., Zhang, X., Ren, S., Sun, J.: Deep residual learning for image recognition. In: 2016 IEEE Conference on Computer Vision and Pattern Recognition (CVPR), pp. 770–778 (2016). https://doi.org/10.1109/CVPR.2016.90

16. Hochreiter, S., Schmidhuber, J.: Long short-term memory. Neural Comput. **9**(8), 1735–1780 (1997). https://doi.org/10.1162/neco.1997.9.8.1735
17. Irshad, M.Z., Ma, C.Y., Kira, Z.: Hierarchical cross-modal agent for robotics vision-and-language navigation. In: Proceedings of the IEEE International Conference on Robotics and Automation (ICRA) (2021). https://arxiv.org/abs/2104.10674
18. Jia, C., et al.: Scaling up visual and vision-language representation learning with noisy text supervision (2021)
19. Ku, A., Anderson, P., Patel, R., Ie, E., Baldridge, J.: Room-across-room: Multilingual vision-and-language navigation with dense spatiotemporal grounding. In: Proceedings of the 2020 Conference on Empirical Methods in Natural Language Processing (EMNLP), pp. 4392–4412. Association for Computational Linguistics, November 2020. https://doi.org/10.18653/v1/2020.emnlp-main.356, https://aclanthology.org/2020.emnlp-main.356
20. Li, P., et al.: Selfdoc: self-supervised document representation learning. In: 2021 IEEE/CVF Conference on Computer Vision and Pattern Recognition (CVPR) (2021)
21. Li, T.J.J., Azaria, A., Myers, B.A.: Sugilite: creating multimodal smartphone automation by demonstration. In: Proceedings of the 2017 CHI Conference on Human Factors in Computing Systems, CHI 2017, pp. 6038–6049. Association for Computing Machinery, New York (2017)
22. Li, T.J.J., Chen, J., Xia, H., Mitchell, T.M., Myers, B.A.: Multi-modal repairs of conversational breakdowns in task-oriented dialogs, pp. 1094–1107. Association for Computing Machinery, New York (2020)
23. Li, T.J.-J., Mitchell, T.M., Myers, B.A.: Demonstration + natural language: multimodal interfaces for GUI-based interactive task learning agents. In: Li, Y., Hilliges, O. (eds.) Artificial Intelligence for Human Computer Interaction: A Modern Approach. HIS, pp. 495–537. Springer, Cham (2021). https://doi.org/10.1007/978-3-030-82681-9_15
24. Li, T.J.J., Popowski, L., Mitchell, T.M., Myers, B.A.: Screen2vec: semantic embedding of GUI screens and GUI components. In: Proceedings of the SIGCHI Conference on Human Factors in Computing Systems, CHI 2021 (2021)
25. Li, Y., He, J., Zhou, X., Zhang, Y., Baldridge, J.: Mapping natural language instructions to mobile UI action sequences. In: Proceedings of the 58th Annual Meeting of the Association for Computational Linguistics, pp. 8198–8210. Association for Computational Linguistics, July 2020. https://doi.org/10.18653/v1/2020.acl-main.729, https://www.aclweb.org/anthology/2020.acl-main.729
26. Li, Y., Li, G., Zhou, X., Dehghani, M., Gritsenko, A.A.: VUT: versatile UI transformer for multi-modal multi-task user interface modeling. CoRR abs/2112.05692 (2021). https://arxiv.org/abs/2112.05692
27. Liu, T.F., Craft, M., Situ, J., Yumer, E., Mech, R., Kumar, R.: Learning design semantics for mobile apps. In: 31st Annual Symposium on User Interface Software and Technology (UIST) (2018)
28. Lloyd, S.: Least squares quantization in PCM. In: IEEE Transactions on Information Theory (1982)
29. van der Maaten, L., Hinton, G.: Visualizing data using t-SNE. J. Mach. Learn. Res. **9**, 2579–2605 (2008). http://www.jmlr.org/papers/v9/vandermaaten08a.html
30. Massiceti, D., Dokania, P.K., Siddharth, N., Torr, P.H.S.: Visual dialogue without vision or dialogue. CoRR abs/1812.06417 (2018). http://arxiv.org/abs/1812.06417
31. Min, S.Y., Chaplot, D.S., Ravikumar, P., Bisk, Y., Salakhutdinov, R.: Film: following instructions in language with modular methods (2021)

32. Nguyen, K., Daumé III, H.: Help, anna! visual navigation with natural multimodal assistance via retrospective curiosity-encouraging imitation learning. In: Proceedings of the Conference on Empirical Methods in Natural Language Processing (EMNLP), November 2019
33. Pasupat, P., Jiang, T.S., Liu, E.Z., Guu, K., Liang, P.: Mapping natural language commands to web elements. In: Empirical Methods in Natural Language Processing (EMNLP) (2018)
34. Puig, X., et al.: Virtualhome: simulating household activities via programs. In: 2018 IEEE/CVF Conference on Computer Vision and Pattern Recognition (CVPR), pp. 8494–8502. IEEE Computer Society, Los Alamitos, CA, USA, June 2018. https://doi.org/10.1109/CVPR.2018.00886, https://doi.ieeecomputersociety.org/10.1109/CVPR.2018.00886
35. Radford, A., et al.: Learning transferable visual models from natural language supervision. CoRR abs/2103.00020 (2021). https://arxiv.org/abs/2103.00020
36. Ray, A., Christie, G., Bansal, M., Batra, D., Parikh, D.: Question relevance in VQQ: identifying non-visual and false-premise questions (2016)
37. Shi, T., Karpathy, A., Fan, L., Hernandez, J., Liang, P.: World of bits: An open-domain platform for web-based agents. In: 34th International Conference on Machine Learning (ICML) (2015)
38. Shridhar, M., et al.: ALFRED: a benchmark for interpreting grounded instructions for everyday tasks. In: The IEEE Conference on Computer Vision and Pattern Recognition (CVPR) (2020). https://arxiv.org/abs/1912.01734
39. Singh, K.P., Bhambri, S., Kim, B., Mottaghi, R., Choi, J.: Factorizing perception and policy for interactive instruction following. In: Proceedings of the IEEE/CVF International Conference on Computer Vision (ICCV) (2021)
40. Sun, C., Shrivastava, A., Singh, S., Gupta, A.: Revisiting unreasonable effectiveness of data in deep learning era. CoRR abs/1707.02968 (2017). http://arxiv.org/abs/1707.02968
41. Vaswani, A., et al.: Attention is all you need. In: Conference on Neural Information Processing Systems (NeurIPS) (2017)
42. Vtyurina, A., Fourney, A., Morris, M.R., Findlater, L., White, R.W.: Bridging screen readers and voice assistants for enhanced eyes-free web search. In: International ACM SIGACCESS Conference on Computers and Accessibility (ASSETS) (2019)
43. Yamaguchi, K.: Canvasvae: learning to generate vector graphic documents. In: Proceedings of the IEEE/CVF International Conference on Computer Vision (ICCV) (2021)
44. Zhu, F., Zhu, Y., Chang, X., Liang, X.: Vision-language navigation with self-supervised auxiliary reasoning tasks. In: 2020 IEEE/CVF Conference on Computer Vision and Pattern Recognition (CVPR), pp. 10009–10019 (2020). https://doi.org/10.1109/CVPR42600.2020.01003
45. Zhu, Y., et al.: Visual semantic planning using deep successor representations. In: 2017 IEEE International Conference on Computer Vision (ICCV) (2017)

BRACE: The Breakdancing Competition Dataset for Dance Motion Synthesis

Davide Moltisanti[1]([✉])(iD), Jinyi Wu[2](iD), Bo Dai[3](iD), and Chen Change Loy[2](iD)

[1] University of Edinburgh, Edinburgh, Scotland
davide.moltisanti@ed.ac.uk
[2] S-Lab, Nanyang Technological University, Singapore, Singapore
jinyi002@e.ntu.edu.sg, ccloy@ntu.edu.sg
[3] Shanghai AI Laboratory, Shanghai, China
daibo@pjlab.org.cn

Abstract. Generative models for audio-conditioned dance motion synthesis map music features to dance movements. Models are trained to associate motion patterns to audio patterns, usually without an explicit knowledge of the human body. This approach relies on a few assumptions: strong music-dance correlation, controlled motion data and relatively simple poses and movements. These characteristics are found in all existing datasets for dance motion synthesis, and indeed recent methods can achieve good results. We introduce a new dataset aiming to challenge these common assumptions, compiling a set of dynamic dance sequences displaying complex human poses. We focus on breakdancing which features acrobatic moves and tangled postures. We source our data from the Red Bull BC One competition videos. Estimating human keypoints from these videos is difficult due to the complexity of the dance, as well as the multiple moving cameras recording setup. We adopt a hybrid labelling pipeline leveraging deep estimation models as well as manual annotations to obtain good quality keypoint sequences at a reduced cost. Our efforts produced the BRACE dataset, which contains over 3 h and 30 min of densely annotated poses. We test state-of-the-art methods on BRACE, showing their limitations when evaluated on complex sequences. Our dataset can readily foster advance in dance motion synthesis. With intricate poses and swift movements, models are forced to go beyond learning a mapping between modalities and reason more effectively about body structure and movements.

1 Introduction

Audio-conditioned generative models [11,14,22,27] for dance motion synthesis learn a mapping between music features and the aligned dance movements. Models typically tackle this task treating the skeleton sequence as an additional

---

D. Moltisanti and B. Dai—Work done while at Nanyang Technological University.
D. Moltisanti and J. Wu—Equal contribution.

Supplementary Information The online version contains supplementary material available at https://doi.org/10.1007/978-3-031-20074-8_19.

S. Avidan et al. (Eds.): ECCV 2022, LNCS 13668, pp. 329–344, 2022.
https://doi.org/10.1007/978-3-031-20074-8_19

Fig. 1. Challenges and characteristics of BRACE's video source. Acrobatic moves make our dataset unique compared to previous dance datasets. Complex poses are difficult to estimate automatically. Occlusion, multiple cameras setup with frequent shot changes and aerial views, dynamic lighting with strong flashes and motion blur add to the difficulty of extracting keypoints for the dancer.

modality to be "remembered" when "hearing" a particular music beat or melody. Models are trained to capture correspondences between a sequence of music features and a sequence of keypoints, often without explicitly modelling the body's structure and movements. This is a reasonable approach when the following conditions are met: i) there is a strong correlation between music and dance movement, i.e. a choreography can be observed; ii) poses and movements are relatively simple or not too diverse and iii) motion data is controlled, i.e. all the captured movement is related to the dance, without keypoint shifts induced by camera movements. Current datasets [2,7,11–14,22,27] satisfy these constraints, where videos are captured either in a controlled environment [2,14,22,27], with a static camera [7,11,12] or are even synthesised [13].

We propose a new dataset aiming to challenge such assumptions. Our goal is to gather data that: i) contains diverse and complex human poses and movements; ii) exhibits a weaker correlation between music and movement; iii) is captured in a real-world setting, i.e. multiple moving cameras record dancers from a variety of viewpoints. We look after these characteristics to push generative models to go beyond learning a mapping between modalities. With weak music-dance correlation, less controlled motion and difficult movements and poses, models are forced to effectively reason about body structure and movement. The properties we are seeking are amply available in videos of breakdancing, which is an athletic form of dance with swift movements and tangled poses. Music is typically a looping sequence providing a rhythmic beat rather than a base for a choreography, and as such it is weakly correlated with the dance.

We use videos from the Red Bull BC One contests featuring the best dancers in the world. Thanks to recent progress in deep pose estimation models, keypoints are typically entirely estimated, and good results can be achieved when poses are relatively simple. However, the dynamic nature of breakdancing and the recording setting in our video source introduce several challenges to keypoint estimation. Due to the complex posture assumed by the dancers, pose estimation models are pushed to their limits. Motion blur induced by fast and acrobatic moves, occlusion and dynamic lighting further complicate the task, as we show in Fig. 1. Under these circumstances, it is not possible to solely rely

Table 1. Comparing recent datasets for dance motion synthesis. A: automatic (estimated with a model). M: manually annotated. C: obtained from MoCap. *not available.

Name	Year	Sequences	Size	Dancers	Styles	Annotations	Source	FPS	Movement	Pose
Groove net [2]	2017	4	0 h 23 m	1	1	3D joints (C)	Hired dancer	NA*	NA*	NA*
Dance with melody [22]	2018	61	1 h 34 m	NA	4	3D joints (C), basic dance movements	Hired dancers	25	1.918	0.193
Dancing 2 music [12]	2019	361K	71 h	NA	3	2D keypoints (A)	YouTube	15	0.704	0.071
Music 2 dance [27]	2020	2	0 h 58 m	2	2	3D joints (C)	Hired dancers	60	1.583	0.205
AIST++ [14]	2021	1.4K	5 h 11 m	30	10	2D/3D keypoints and SMPL body models (A)	Hired dancers	60	1.450	0.135
Dance revolution [11]	2021	790	12 h	NA	3	2D keypoints (A)	YouTube	15	0.804	0.137
Phantom dance [13]	2021	300	12 h	1	4	3D quaternion	Synthesised	60	1.962	0.251
Learning to dance [7]	2021	298	0h24 m	NA	3	2D keypoints (A)	YouTube	24	1.161	0.111
BRACE (Ours)	2022	465	3h 32m	64	1	2D keypoints (A/M), movement categories, dancer IDs, shot bounds	YouTube	25–30	2.388	0.235

on pose estimation models to obtain good quality keypoints. At the same time, manually annotating poses in videos is very expensive and time consuming. To overcome these issues we design a hybrid annotation pipeline using both automatic and manual annotations, striking a good balance between keypoint quality and labelling burden. Our efforts produced the BRACE dataset, a collection of dynamic dance sequences annotated with high quality 2D keypoints. As reported in Table 2, our dataset amounts to over 3 h and 30 min of footage. We also provide fine-grained labels annotating the key elements of breakdancing. We test recent state-of-the-art methods on BRACE, showing the limitations of current approaches when evaluated on more dynamic and complex data.

To summarise, our contributions are: i) a new high quality dataset featuring complex poses and dynamic movements; ii) a hybrid automatic-manual annotation pipeline designed to efficiently annotate human keypoints under challenging conditions; iii) a study of recent work on our new dataset, showing the challenges posed by its unique characteristics. BRACE is publicly available online[1].

2   Related Work

2.1   Dance Datasets

Table 1 reports recent datasets for music conditioned dance motion generation. Earlier efforts [2, 22] collect a small amount of highly curated data, with motion

---

[1] https://github.com/dmoltisanti/brace/.

capture setups recording hired dancers. AIST++ [14] offers 2D/3D keypoints and SMPL models extracted for a subset of AIST [23]. Synthetic datasets have also been proposed [13], where digital artists produce video animations of dance videos. As pose estimation models grow increasingly reliable, sourcing videos from YouTube and extracting keypoints has become a common option [7,11,12]. We partially follow this approach, sourcing videos from YouTube and using a hybrid approach combining automatic and manual annotations.

A common characteristic of current datasets is their relative simplicity of pose and motion. Dancer in datasets such as Dancing 2 Music [12], Dance Revolution [11] and Learning to Dance [7] are mostly in an upright position and do not perform particularly dynamic moves. AIST++ [14] includes breakdancing, however these amount to only 30 min of footage (10% of the whole dataset). Furthermore, based on our observations breakdancing sequences in AIST++ mostly feature simple moves and upright poses. We next quantify the differences amongst these datasets and BRACE measuring movement and pose diversity.

Measuring Movement and Pose Diversity. We need to normalise all keypoints in a consistent way for a fair comparison. We also wish to marginalise apparent movements that could be induced by a camera change, zoom or panning. We extract the tightest box/cuboid enclosing all keypoints and normalise each keypoint with respect to the tightest box/cuboid. For example in 2D, given the tightest box $B = (x_b, y_b, w, h)$ and a keypoint $P = (x_p, y_p)$, the normalised keypoint is $\bar{P} = ((x_p - x_b)/w, (y_p - y_b)/h)$. To measure movements we take into account the FPS of the videos, since a small FPS may produce an unrealistic large displacement and vice-versa. For a given node p its movement is thus calculated as $v_i = d(p_i, p_{i+1})/dt$, where $d(p_i, p_{i+1})$ is the Euclidean distance between frames i and $i+1$ and $dt = 1/fps$. We measure such frame-wise distance for each node independently and take the average on all sequences in a given dataset. This is what we report under "Movement" in Table 1. To measure pose diversity we calculate the standard deviation of each node. We calculate the *std* of each node in a sequence and take the average across all sequences in a dataset and across all nodes. This gives us a 2D or 3D vector depending on the dimension of the keypoints. We report the average of this vector under "Pose" in Table 1. To further reduce camera movement bias, we calculate metrics within shot boundaries. As the table shows, our dataset offers by far the most dynamic sequences thanks to the very nature of breakdancing. While Phantom Dance exhibits a slightly larger pose diversity, it should be noted that this is a synthesised dataset.

2.2   Dance Motion Synthesis

Sequence-to-Sequence Approaches. [11,14,22,27] are a common choice for audio-conditioned dance motion generation. Huang *et al.* [11] design an Encoder-Decoder (ED) architecture, where the Encoder is a transformer that encodes music features in a latent space. The decoder is an RNN that produces the dance movement as a sequence of keypoints. Li *et al.* [14] also adopt a sequence-to-sequence framework, using a group of transformers. When motion data is controlled a sequence mapping can successfully produce good dance motion by

Table 2. The BRACE dataset at a glance. Each dancer performs multiple sequences in a video. Sequences are annotated into segments according to their dance element.

Frames	334,538	Sequences	465
Manually annotated frames	26,676 (8%)	**Segments**	1,352
Duration	3 h 32 m	**Avg. segments per sequence**	2.91
Dancers	64	**Avg. sequence duration**	27.48 s
Videos	81	**Avg. segment duration**	9.45 s

implicitly learning movements from the data. However, when data is less controlled, i.e. data captures motion induced by camera movements (e.g. zooming, panning, camera change), we expect models to produce similar artefacts since they learn to replicate the training sequences. While normalisation techniques can mitigate this issue, ultimately it becomes harder for a model to learn motion when this is captured "in the wild". When poses and motion are more diverse and complex the mapping task also becomes intrinsically harder. We test [11,14] on BRACE, where these challenges are widely present, to study the limitations of sequence-to-sequence approaches.

Other Approaches. [12] extracts music and dance units from the data. Music units are extracted with an audio beat detection algorithm. Dance units are found detecting abrupt changes in motion magnitude and angle. Dance sequences are decomposed into such units. An auto-encoder models these atomic moves, and a GAN composes multiple units to form a dance sequence. The motion unit decomposition of this method is likely to be challenged when dance sequences exhibit swift movements and acrobatic poses as in BRACE, as we show in Sect. 4. In [13] an ED generates key poses, while another ED generates motion curves between these key poses. The authors propose a Kinematic Chain Network where features are embedded with MLPs that are chained following the body structure, using a tree topology. In [25] a latent space is constructed sampling from a Gaussian process. The latent space encodes an abstract motion signal, and a GCN is then trained to map such signal to a skeleton sequence. [25] does not condition motion generation on music, which is done in [7] through a GCN-based generative model trained in an adversarial fashion.

3   The BRACE Dataset

We choose the Red Bull BC One breakdancing competition as our data source, which features the best dancers in the world competing one against each other. The competition follows the knockout tournament format, where two dancers compete in a 1-vs-1 battle taking turns to perform a number of sequences. Video recordings of the shows are available on YouTube[2] (we use videos from years 2011/13/14/17/18/20). Figure 1 illustrates the videos characteristics and the difficulties involved in extracting human poses. Videos were shot using multiple cameras and feature wide panning, long zooming, aerial views and abrupt

---

[2] https://www.youtube.com/channel/UC9oEzPGZiTE692KucAsTY1g.

shot changes, all of which makes automatic pose extraction not trivial. Lighting is also a challenge, since strong flashes and dimly lit scenes are common in the videos. Furthermore, the very nature of breakdancing makes keypoint extraction intrinsically difficult. Complex poses and motion blur induced by quick movements stretch the capabilities of pose estimation models. We design a pipeline to address such challenges to extract 2D keypoints from the videos, adopting a hybrid annotation paradigm. Our objective is to obtain dense and good quality poses while minimising manual annotations cost. Our pipeline is flexible and can be adopted for other pose estimation datasets.

It should be noted that we are not affiliated with Red Bull and that all video-audio copyright belongs to Red Bull. We release our processed keypoint sequences and our temporal labels, providing a link to the original YouTube videos. We also release audio features extracted with Librosa [17].

3.1 Data Acquisition

Figure 2 shows our approach to obtain human keypoints for the active dancer. We first employ state-of-the-art human pose estimators to extract automatic poses. We then process keypoints to select the active dancer and temporally annotate dance sequences. As discussed earlier, we cannot solely rely on automatic pose estimation. We thus find bad keypoints corresponding to difficult poses and manually label them. We later detect automatic pose outliers and also manually label these. Finally, we merge automatic and manual annotations interpolating the keypoint sequences with Bézier curves. Table 2 summarises our dataset.

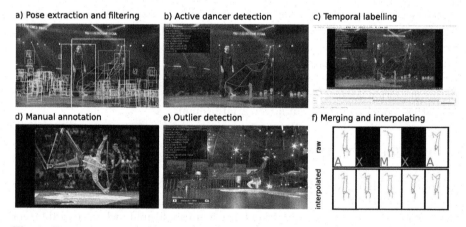

Fig. 2. Data acquisition pipeline. We start extracting automatic poses with a model ensemble, which produces a large number of annotations (a). We then filter poses and detect the active dancer throughout the video (b) before annotating dance segments (c). Subsequently, we select bad poses and manually label them (d). Automatic pose outliers are then detected (e) and manually labelled. Finally, manual and automatic pose are merged and interpolated to produce our dance keypoint sequences (f, where "A", "X" and "M" indicate automatic, missing and manual poses respectively). (Color figure online)

Automatic Pose Estimation. We employ a model ensemble to extract human poses from video frames. We favour this option over a single model to boost the chance of getting good keypoints for difficult poses. We choose a top-down approach to first detect humans in frames and then estimate their pose, using MMDetection [18] and MMPose [19]. We use the top 3 human detectors ranked on the COCO dataset [15]: HTC [6] with backbones ResNet 50/100 [9] and Cascade R-CNN [3] with backbone ResNet 50. Accordingly, we utilise the top 3 pose estimators ranked on COCO: HRNet [21] and a cascaded HRNet+DarkPose [26] with two different configurations (32 and 64 channels for the bottleneck block). All models were pre-trained on COCO. We obtain poses for each detector/estimator combination, gathering a total of 9 sets of poses for each frame.

Filtering Multiple Pose Estimations. We start rejecting poses with low confidence scores. We keep the 4 largest boxes produced by each model at a given frame, which removes most poses captured for people in the audience. Finally we apply a standard object-detection NMS. Figure 2 (a) shows all poses detected with the model ensemble before filtering. Notice the abundant number of detections. Figure 2 (b) illustrates the automatically selected pose for the active dancer.

Active Dancer Detection. We automatically find the active dancer by building people tracks. These are obtained by linking boxes across frames if their IOU is above a certain threshold (0.4). For robustness we look for overlapping boxes in a window of 10 frames, i.e. given a box at frame t, if there is no overlapping box at frame $t + 1$ we search for a box in frames $[t + 2, t + 10]$, choosing the temporally closest overlapping box. This simple method based entirely on boxes is good enough for our purpose. We measure the movement of each tracked person by calculating the change in pixel area of the tracked box across frames. We select the box corresponding to the track exhibiting the highest movement as our active dancer, and use the corresponding keypoints as the pose candidate.

Temporal Labelling. We generate a new copy of each video overlaying the keypoints of the detected active dancer. We then label the start/end of each dance element, annotating the type of movement (toprock, footwork and powermove, presented in Sect. 3.3) as well as the dancer ID. We also annotate segments where the active dancer estimation was incorrect, i.e. frames where the pose candidate corresponded to the idle dancer or another person in the video. We use these labels to later retrieve keypoints for the correct person automatically.

Manual Pose Annotation. The quality of keypoint estimation degrades when the dancer's pose is extreme or when frames are too blurry. We manually label such difficult poses. To automatically find which frames need manual annotation we aggregate a labelling score. This is obtained multiplying the candidate's box confidence score and the average keypoint confidence score (a low labelling score indicates the pose is likely bad). We treat frames with a low labelling score as missing frames we need to manually annotate. We then apply a labelling discount to reduce annotation time and cost. Thanks to our Bézier interpolation, we can allow for a certain number of missing frames in a given window, while still recovering a good keypoint sequence. We allow for a maximum of 2 consecutive and a total of 5 missing frames in a window of 10 frames. The selected frames are then labelled by our locally sourced annotators. With our discount method we annotated only 57.17% of frames initially marked for labelling.

Outlier Detection. Some bad automatic poses may not be selected for manual annotations due to a noisy high confidence score. We find such poses with an outlier detection method. Once we have manually annotated frames for a video, we merge automatic and manual poses. We then employ a sliding window median filter to detect noisy outliers. Figure 2 (e) shows an outlier found with this algorithm. Green segments indicate the head, thus the person is incorrectly detected in an upright position. We search for outliers within the labelled segments and shot boundaries (detected with [5]). All outliers are manually labelled.

Merging and Interpolating Poses. At this point we have a mix of manual and automatic annotations, with missing poses for a few frames due to our labelling discount. In order to obtain smooth dance sequences we interpolate the keypoint series using Bézier curves. We slide an overlapping window throughout a sequence of keypoints and fit a Bézier curve to each node trajectory separately. Curves are fitted using a least-square algorithm. Sequences are interpolated within dance segments and shot boundaries. The interpolated sequences constitute our final keypoints data. More details can be found in the supplementary material.

Table 3. Quality control measures for BRACE. Incorrect pose shows the percentage of the whole dataset where we spotted wrong keypoints. GT/Raw - Interpolated MAE refers to the Mean Absolute Error calculated for a fully manually annotated sequence.

Incorrect pose		GT - Interpolated MAE		GT - Raw MAE
Automatic	Manual	All frames	Rejected frames	Rejected frames
0.63%	0.12%	27px	35px	60px

3.2   Quality Control

We carefully reviewed all the final interpolated sequences to spot incorrect poses. This is to validate the automatic selection of bad poses as well as the manual annotations themselves. We generated and watched videos overlaying the keypoints, marking all frames with a bad pose. An odd-looking frame in the interpolated sequence is introduced when automatic or manual keypoints are incorrect. Table 3 reports how many of these we spotted. In total 0.63% and 0.12% of the total frames were found incorrect for automatic and manual keypoints. These very low error percentages reflect the reliability of our data acquisition pipeline. Wrong automatic keypoints were outliers that were not detected. This typically happens when many consecutive poses are noisy, i.e. a bad pose is no longer an outlier in a window of frames according to the rolling window median filter. This can be fixed by tuning the outlier detector parameters. Manual incorrect annotations were found over frames with severe occlusion or where annotators labelled the idle dancer. This issue can be alleviated by showing annotators a few neighbouring frames in addition to the frame to be labelled.

We also implemented another quality control measure. We manually labelled a sequence of 1,472 frames (1 min). The sequence contains toprocks, footworks and powermoves. The Mean Absolute Error (MAE, averaged across frames and joints) between the GT and the interpolated sequence is 27px (frame area: 1920 × 1080), as reported in Table 3. The low MAE is indicative of BRACE's quality. 355 frames (24%) of the raw keypoints were rejected (bad pose). 7% of these frames were manually annotated for the interpolated sequence. Looking only at the rejected frames (i.e. those with a difficult pose), the GT-raw MAE is 60px whereas the GT-interpolated MAE is 35px. This further highlights the efficiency of our pipeline to obtain good poses labelling fewer frames (7 vs 24%).

3.3 Dance Elements

A breakdancing sequence can be decomposed into three main elements: toprock, footwork and powermove. We label sequences into such constituent parts, and here we describe them briefly. A toprock features a dancer in the upright position performing a variety of free-style steps. A footwork involves a dancer supporting themselves on the floor using their hands while performing moves with their legs and feet. Powermoves are the most dynamic movements where performers engage in complex moves such as acrobatic aerial flips and head/back spins. Figure 3 illustrates a few frames for each dance element. Note the complexity of the dancer poses, especially for powermove and footwork. Next, we analyse how such movements are combined temporally.

Fig. 3. The primary elements of breakdancing: toprock, footwork and powermove.

Cypher Format. We investigate here whether the alternating battle format brings any patterns in the dance. In Fig. 4 we plot each sequence according to their order in the competition. For each sequence we illustrate the segments anno-tated with the corresponding dance element (bottom of the figure). We observe that the vast majority of dancers begins their competition (1st sequence) with toprock movements, which is a common practice in breakdancing. Some dancers though do not follow such convention and start off with powermoves. We also notice that the most common pattern in a sequence is (toprock, powermove, foot-work), which is interestingly more evident in the 1st sequence. Figure 4 (top) also

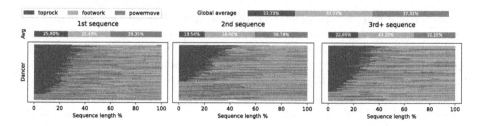

Fig. 4. Analysing dance elements patterns emerging from the battle-format. We split sequences according to their order in the battle. Bottom: each line shows a sequence from a single dancer, with coloured segments corresponding to the three different movements we labelled. Segments are normalised according to the sequence length. We report the average percentage of frames labelled with each movement, both according to the sequence order (top) and globally (top right). (Color figure online)

illustrates how often each movement was performed in a sequence (calculated as average percentage of the total length). We again see that the highest concentration of toprock appears in the 1st sequence. The percentage of footwork grows according to the order of the sequence. Interestingly, powermove percentage is virtually unchanged in the first two sequences but drops by 7% in the last sequence, which suggests that dancers become more tired towards the end of the competition, given that powermoves are very strenuous. Finally, Fig. 4 (top right) reports global movement percentages. Footwork and powermove are the dominant movements, confirming the dynamism of BRACE. We will look at global movement percentages again when testing our dataset.

We believe the alternating battle format is an interesting novel aspect of BRACE. Indeed, by considering a sequence not just as a stand-alone progression of movements but as part of a longer and more complex scenario one could devise more creative models simulating dance competitions. While here we focus on breakdancing competitions, other styles too are often performed following such battle format (e.g. modern styles such as Hip-Hop, Krump and Street Jazz).

3.4 Audio Correlation

Although breakdancing has a weaker audio correlation, dancers still closely follow the music and its rhythm. Quoting from Red Bull BC One website[3], dancers use especially toprock movements to *"showcase their rhythmic style and their ability to play with the music"*. As another example, dancers also follow the music to perform a freeze. Quoting again from (See footnote 3): *"a freeze is when a dancer holds a solid shape with their body for a few seconds. This is usually done to hit a prominent sound in the music"*. While the *melody* of the music might be less correlated with the dance, the *rhythm* is the foundation of the movements. Models are pushed to their limits, however the fundamental premise of the audio-

---

[3] https://www.redbull.com/us-en/understand-the-basic-elements-of-breaking.

conditioned generative task remains solid, i.e. there is sufficient correlation in the data for a model to learn to generate sequences based on the music.

Finally, we note that audio files contain live commentary of the performances. Theoretically, these could provide cues models could exploit. We watched 8 random full videos from all years (23 min of footage, 11% of the dataset) and labelled segments with commentary. We found that 17% of the labelled sequences contained a vocal comment of the performance. Based on these numbers, we conclude commentary is present but not likely to influence generative models.

4 Testing Generative Models on BRACE

Testing models that were designed with specific assumptions on data where such constraints are more loose might not appear fair. Our intention is to test a new benchmark to encourage novel approaches to tackle more challenging data, rather than cast a bad light onto existing work. Here we evaluate Dance revolution [11], AIST++ [14] and Dancing 2 Music [12], reviewed in Sect. 2.2.

4.1 Evaluation Metrics

We follow AIST++ [14] and report the commonly used Fréchet Inception Distance [10] (FID) calculated directly in the nodes pose space. More precisely, we first normalise keypoints as explained in Sect. 2.1. To calculate the FID, we stack all keypoints and estimate their mean and covariance. We report two dance-music correlation metrics introduced in [14]: Beat Alignment Score and Beat Dynamic-Time-Warping (DTW) Cost. These metrics measure the alignment and similarity between music and kinematics beats. Music beats were obtained using the Essentia library [24]. Kinematics beats were obtained by finding peaks in the averaged second-order derivatives of keypoint movements.

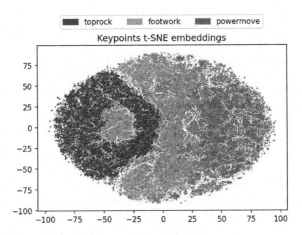

Fig. 5. t-SNE embeddings of all keypoints in BRACE. A good separation of the three main dance elements emerges from static poses.

We also analyse the ability of the models to generate a sensible breakdancing sequence by looking at the distribution of the three dance elements. As we saw in Fig. 3, our sequences are mostly composed of footwork and powermove movements, both around 37% of all frames, with toprock movements amounting to around 23% of the data. We check if the generated sequences reflect this distribution. We conduct this study by looking at frame poses. We first inspect whether static poses have a clear enough separation for our study to be sensible. We do this by plotting t-SNE embeddings [16] of all keypoints in BRACE. As depicted in Fig. 5, we observe a good separation of the three dance elements from static poses. This motivates us to train a classifier to recognise poses from single frames and use its predictions to estimate the distribution of dance elements in the generated sequences. Specifically, we train a spatial GCN model [20], which attained 73.1% top-1 accuracy on the test set.

4.2   Results

We divide our dataset in a 70/30 training/test split and ensure all models reach training convergence before testing. Table 4 reports results obtained on the selected models. The "GT Reference" baseline reports evaluation metrics calculated on the ground truth test set, i.e., on real dance sequences as opposed to generated ones. Since this is a new dataset, this helps us understand the results of the evaluated models. We observe that all baselines struggle to achieve optimal performance. In fact, pose FID and beat alignment score are far from the reference baseline, which indicates that the generated sequences are not very realistic. However, models are able to generate poses resembling breakdancing postures. This is indicated by the classifier predictions of toprock, footwork and powermove. Nevertheless, except for AIST++, all models generate more toprock and fewer powermove poses, which are respectively the easiest and hardest breakdancing postures. This demonstrates the challenges BRACE poses to existing state-of-the-art models when evaluated on complex scenes. Dancing 2 Music achieves the worst FID and beat alignment score. As noted in Sect. 2.2, this method splits sequences automatically into atomic dance units, and the model is trained to compose such units to form a dance sequence. Motion decomposition is done by measuring the displacement of each joint between neighbouring frames. Breakdancing moves with their large displacements stress this approach, which explains the poor performance of the method.

Interestingly, we notice that models attain a better beat DTW cost compared to the GT Reference baseline, but their beat alignment score is worse. Breakdancing songs feature fast-tempo music with regular beats. While dancer follow the tempo and flow of the music, naturally they do not perform a movement for every beat, hence the higher beat DTW cost of the reference baseline. This suggests models learn to "blindly" follow the music beat, i.e. they generate sequences full of strong movements which however do not necessarily mimic a real breakdancing, which typically displays a good mix of slow and fast moves.

Qualitative evaluation is as important as quantitative analysis for dance motion synthesis. We visually inspect the generated sequences and notice that

Table 4. Testing recent generative models on BRACE. Note that toprock, footwork and powermove averages for the GT reference baseline were predicted with the GCN classifier. Actual statistical average in the test set were (toprock = 25.52, footwork = 39.72, powermove = 34.76). ↓ lower is better, ↑ higher is better.

Baseline	Pose FID ↓	Beat alignment score ↑	Beat DTW cost ↓	Toprock avg	Footwork avg	Powermove avg
GT reference	0.0032	0.451	36.50	7.84	48.45	43.71
Dance revolution [11]	0.5158	0.264	11.88	10.59	51.60	37.72
AIST++ [14]	0.5743	0.136	12.92	6.39	40.73	52.89
Dancing 2 music [12]	0.5884	0.129	11.60	16.04	50.09	33.87

while motion appears plausible, ultimately sequences look disconnected, showing repeating movements. Although the pose classifier shows that models are able to generate toprock, footwork and powermove, we observe that the way these are mixed is not very realistic and diverse. This is most likely due to the weaker correlation of music and motion in breakdancing. The generated sequences also display motion induced by camera panning and zooming, which was expected since the tested methods assume the input motion data is controlled. We show these findings in the supplementary material video[4].

Lastly, we evaluate the impact of two hyper-parameters when training Dance Revolution [11], namely the number of layers (2–4) for the encoder and the sliding window size of the local self-attention (15, 25, 50, 100, 200). In Table 4 we report results obtained with the best parameters, i.e. 3 layers and window size 15 (all results in supplementary material). The number of layers did not affect performance much. The attention size instead played an important role, with performance degrading as the window enlarged. This parameter controls the receptive field of the encoder, i.e. the temporal neighbourhood each element in the input sequence can attend to. Performance deterioration with larger windows is linked to the fact that our sequences contain motion with very quick and large displacement, which are hard to model well with a large receptive field.

Table 5. Evaluating BRACE for pose estimation. We compare the performance of HRNet [21] pre-trained on COCO [15] before and after fine-tuning.

Model	BRACE AP	BRACE AR	Ext. powermoves AP	Ext. powermoves AR
COCO-pretrained	0.158	0.202	0.462	0.513
BRACE-finetuned	0.357	0.445	0.598	0.642

5   Pose Estimation on BRACE

We show here that BRACE can also be useful for 2D keypoint estimation since it contains well-labelled skeletons with motion blur and extreme poses. We use

---

[4] https://youtu.be/-5N6uBDfMoM.

the 26K manually annotated skeletons and split them into 80/20 train/test sets. We use HRNet [21] pretrained on COCO [15] as base model and compare performance before and after finetuning on BRACE. Table 5 reports a large improvement after fine-tuning. While this was expected, it proves manual annotations are consistent and models can learn from the data. The poor performance of COCO-pretrained also corroborates that our pipeline successfully detected bad automatic key-points: frames are then manually labelled but have complex postures, so performance before finetuning is low. Besides showing improvements on the test split of BRACE, the BRACE-finetuned model also outperforms COCO-pretrained when tested on an external powermove video[5]. This video is a compilation of powermoves shot with a very different setting compared to BRACE. We randomly sample 200 frames from the video and manually annotate these frames. Although camera movements and angles as well as lighting in the external video are very different from those in our dataset, the BRACE-finetuned model shows a substantial improvement. This proves that BRACE is useful to help the model learn pose estimation in extreme postures.

6 Conclusion

We presented BRACE, a new dataset for audio-conditioned dance motion synthesis. BRACE was collected to challenge the main assumptions taken by motion synthesis models, i.e. relative simple poses and movement captured with controlled data. We designed an efficient pipeline to annotate poses in videos, striking a good balance between labelling cost and keypoint quality. Our pipeline is flexible and can be adopted for any pose estimation task involving complex movements and dynamic recording settings. We further enrich our dataset with temporal segments labelling the constituent elements of breakdancing. BRACE, while restricted to a specific dance genre, readily pushes models to go beyond a modality mapping approach, to reason more efficiently about motion and poses and to deal with less constrained scenarios.

Future Research. Because audio cues are not as strong as in other datasets, future models will have to creatively find other ways to generate good results on BRACE. For example, the movement labels could be exploited. This could be achieved by injecting the movement category in a model through positional encoding, i.e. by modelling the relative position of a movement in the sequence together with its type. Knowing that a given dance segment is a specific movement, models could generate more varied sequences by enforcing a given distribution or order of the movement categories. This is just one of the possible ideas one could develop with our fine-grained labels. Another interesting direction for further research is the generation of dance sequences in a finer granularity and more controlled manner. Current methods lack the ability to adjust generated sequences according to human intervention or conditioning. If we could decompose sequences into shorter actions, e.g. by effectively clustering poses and

---

[5] https://www.youtube.com/watch?v=q5Xr0F4a0iU.

movements, we could then introduce user input as another modality to generate dance movements that follow a designated pattern. For example, a user might specify a target combination of toprocks, footworks and powermoves. Such work would be extremely helpful for animation and gaming industries. Since breakdancing is one of the most granular dance genre, we believe BRACE constitutes a good dataset to experiment such methods on.

Longevity of BRACE. While it is common practice to utilise YouTube videos to compile research datasets (e.g. Kinetics [4], AVA [8], YouTube8M [1]), this comes with a risk. Because videos can disappear from YouTube and since researchers in most cases cannot publish their own copy of the videos, YouTube-based datasets are sometimes difficult to compare results on, and missing videos intrinsically diminish the usefulness of a dataset. We are aware of this issue, however for dance motion synthesis, the main scope of our work, this problem is not as severe. We release our keypoint sequences together with Librosa [17] audio features, thus even if all the corresponding YouTube videos were removed, our dataset would still be entirely usable and future generative models can be compared accordingly. We note this is common practice in other skeleton-based datasets for dance synthesis [7,11,12] and we follow this approach accordingly.

Acknowledgement. This study is supported under the RIE2020 Industry Alignment Fund - Industry Collaboration Projects (IAF-ICP) Funding Initiative, as well as cash and in-kind contribution from the industry partner(s). The project is also supported by Singapore MOE AcRF Tier 1 (RG16/21).

References

1. Abu-El-Haija, S., et al.: YouTube-8M: a large-scale video classification benchmark. arXiv preprint arXiv:1609.08675 (2016)
2. Alemi, O., Françoise, J., Pasquier, P.: Groovenet: real-time music-driven dance movement generation using artificial neural networks. Networks 8(17), 26 (2017)
3. Cai, Z., Vasconcelos, N.: Cascade R-CNN: high quality object detection and instance segmentation. Trans. Pattern Anal. Mach. Intell. **43**(5), 1483–1498 (2019)
4. Carreira, J., Zisserman, A.: Quo vadis, action recognition? A new model and the kinetics dataset. In: Conference on Computer Vision and Pattern Recognition (2017)
5. Castellano, B.: Pyscenedetect. https://pyscenedetect.readthedocs.io
6. Chen, K., et al.: Hybrid task cascade for instance segmentation. In: Conference on Computer Vision and Pattern Recognition (2019)
7. Ferreira, J.P., et al.: Learning to dance: a graph convolutional adversarial network to generate realistic dance motions from audio. Comput. Graph. **94**, 11–21 (2021)
8. Gu, C., et al.: Ava: a video dataset of spatio-temporally localized atomic visual actions. In: Conference on Computer Vision and Pattern Recognition (2018)
9. He, K., Zhang, X., Ren, S., Sun, J.: Deep residual learning for image recognition. In: Conference on computer vision and pattern recognition (2016)
10. Heusel, M., Ramsauer, H., Unterthiner, T., Nessler, B., Hochreiter, S.: GANs trained by a two time-scale update rule converge to a local nash equilibrium. In: Advances in Neural Information Processing Systems (2017)

11. Huang, R., Hu, H., Wu, W., Sawada, K., Zhang, M., Jiang, D.: Dance revolution: long-term dance generation with music via curriculum learning. In: International Conference on Learning Representations (2021)
12. Lee, H.Y., et al.: Dancing to music. In: Neural Information Processing Systems (2019)
13. Li, B., Zhao, Y., Sheng, L.: DanceNet3D: music based dance generation with parametric motion transformer. arXiv preprint arXiv:2103.10206 (2021)
14. Li, R., Yang, S., Ross, D.A., Kanazawa, A.: AI choreographer: music conditioned 3d dance generation with AIST++. In: International Conference on Computer Vision (2021)
15. Lin, T.Y., et al.: Microsoft COCO: common objects in context. In: European Conference on Computer Vision (2014)
16. Van der Maaten, L., Hinton, G.: Visualizing data using t-sne. J. Mach. Learn. Res. **9**, 2579–2605 (2008)
17. McFee, B., et al.: librosa: audio and music signal analysis in python. In: Python in science conference (2015)
18. MMDetection Contributors: OpenMMLab Detection Toolbox and Benchmark, August 2018. https://github.com/open-mmlab/mmdetection
19. MMPose Contributors: OpenMMLab Pose Estimation Toolbox and Benchmark, August 2020. https://github.com/open-mmlab/mmpose
20. Shi, L., Zhang, Y., Cheng, J., Lu, H.: Two-stream adaptive graph convolutional networks for skeleton-based action recognition. In: Conference on Computer Vision and Pattern Recognition (2019)
21. Sun, K., Xiao, B., Liu, D., Wang, J.: Deep high-resolution representation learning for human pose estimation. In: Conference on Computer Vision and Pattern Recognition (2019)
22. Tang, T., Jia, J., Mao, H.: Dance with melody: an lstm-autoencoder approach to music-oriented dance synthesis. In: ACM International Conference on Multimedia (2018)
23. Tsuchida, S., Fukayama, S., Hamasaki, M., Goto, M.: AIST dance video database: multi-genre, multi-dancer, and multi-camera database for dance information processing. In: International Society for Music Information Retrieval Conference (2019)
24. Universitat Pompeu Fabra, B.: Essentia. https://essentia.upf.edu
25. Yan, S., Li, Z., Xiong, Y., Yan, H., Lin, D.: Convolutional sequence generation for skeleton-based action synthesis. In: International Conference on Computer Vision (2019)
26. Zhang, F., Zhu, X., Dai, H., Ye, M., Zhu, C.: Distribution-aware coordinate representation for human pose estimation. In: Conference on Computer Vision and Pattern Recognition (2020)
27. Zhuang, W., Wang, C., Chai, J., Wang, Y., Shao, M., Xia, S.: Music2dance: dancenet for music-driven dance generation. Commun. Appl. ACM Trans. Multimedia Comput. **18**(2), 1–21 (2022)

Dress Code: High-Resolution Multi-category Virtual Try-On

Davide Morelli[1] , Matteo Fincato[1] , Marcella Cornia[1(✉)] ,
Federico Landi[1] , Fabio Cesari[2] , and Rita Cucchiara[1]

[1] University of Modena and Reggio Emilia, Modena, Italy
{davide.morelli,matteo.fincato,marcella.cornia,federico.landi,
rita.cucchiara}@unimore.it
[2] YOOX NET-A-PORTER, Bologna, Italy
fabio.cesari@ynap.com

Abstract. Image-based virtual try-on strives to transfer the appearance of a clothing item onto the image of a target person. Prior work focuses mainly on upper-body clothes (*e.g.* t-shirts, shirts, and tops) and neglects full-body or lower-body items. This shortcoming arises from a main factor: current publicly available datasets for image-based virtual try-on do not account for this variety, thus limiting progress in the field. To address this deficiency, we introduce Dress Code, which contains images of multi-category clothes. Dress Code is more than 3× larger than publicly available datasets for image-based virtual try-on and features high-resolution paired images (1024 × 768) with front-view, full-body reference models. To generate HD try-on images with high visual quality and rich in details, we propose to learn fine-grained discriminating features. Specifically, we leverage a semantic-aware discriminator that makes predictions at pixel-level instead of image- or patch-level. Extensive experimental evaluation demonstrates that the proposed approach surpasses the baselines and state-of-the-art competitors in terms of visual quality and quantitative results. The Dress Code dataset is publicly available at https://github.com/aimagelab/dress-code.

Keywords: Dress code dataset · Virtual try-on · Image synthesis

1 Introduction

Clothes, fashion, and style play a fundamental role in our daily life and allow people to communicate and express themselves freely and directly. With the advent of e-commerce, the variety and availability of online garments have become increasingly overwhelming for the customer. Consequently, user-oriented applications such as virtual try-on, in both 2D [4,12,13,42] and 3D [29,36,46,48]

F. Landi—Now at Huawei Technologies, Amsterdam Research Center, the Netherlands.

Supplementary Information The online version contains supplementary material available at https://doi.org/10.1007/978-3-031-20074-8_20.

S. Avidan et al. (Eds.): ECCV 2022, LNCS 13668, pp. 345–362, 2022.
https://doi.org/10.1007/978-3-031-20074-8_20

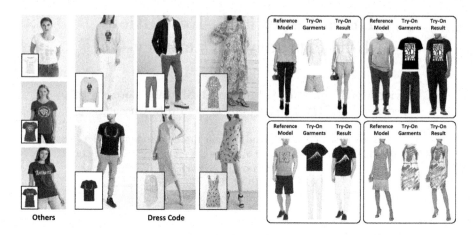

Fig. 1. Differently from existing publicly available datasets for virtual try-on, Dress Code features different garments, also belonging to lower-body and full-body categories, and high-resolution images.

settings, are increasingly important for online shopping, helping fashion companies to tailor the e-commerce experience and maximize customer satisfaction. Image-based virtual try-on aims at synthesizing an image of a reference person wearing a given try-on garment. In this task, while virtually changing clothing, the person's intrinsic information such as body shape and pose should not be modified. Also, the try-on garment is expected to properly fit the person's body while maintaining its original texture. All these elements make virtual try-on a very active and challenging research topic.

Due to the strategic role that virtual try-on plays in e-commerce, many rich and potentially valuable datasets are proprietary and not publicly available to the research community [23,24,30,43]. Public datasets, instead, either do not contain paired images of models and garments or feature a very limited number of images [13]. Moreover, the overall image resolution is low (mostly 256 × 192). Unfortunately, these drawbacks slow down progress in the field. In this paper, we present *Dress Code*: a new dataset of high-resolution images (1024 × 768) containing more than 50k image pairs of try-on garments and corresponding catalog images where each item is worn by a model. This makes Dress Code more than 3× larger than VITON [13], the most common benchmark for virtual try-on. Differently from existing publicly available datasets, which contain only upper-body clothes, Dress Code features upper-body, lower-body, and full-body clothes, as well as full-body images of human models (Fig. 1, *left*).

Current off-the-shelf architectures for virtual try-on are not optimized to work with clothes belonging to different macro-categories (*i.e.* upper-body, lower-body, and full-body clothes). In fact, this would require learning the correspondences between a particular garment class and the portion of the body involved in the try-on phase. For instance, trousers should match the legs pose, while a dress should match the pose of the entire body, from shoulders to hips and eventually knees. In this paper, we design an image-based virtual try-on architecture that can anchor the given garment to the right portion of the body. As a consequence, it is possible to perform a "complete" try-on over a given person by selecting different garments (Fig. 1, *right*). In order to produce high-quality results rich in visual details, we introduce a parser-based discriminator [26,31,38]. This component can increase the realism and visual quality of the results by learning an internal representation of the semantics of generated images, which is usually neglected by standard discriminator architectures [17,41]. This component works at pixel-level and predicts not only real/generated labels but also the semantic classes for each image pixel. We validate the effectiveness of the proposed approach by testing its performance on both our newly collected dataset and on the most widely used dataset for the task (*i.e.* VITON [13]).

The contributions of this paper are summarized as follows: (1) We introduce Dress Code, a novel dataset for the virtual try-on task. To the best of our knowledge, it is the first publicly available dataset featuring lower-body and full-body clothes. As a plus, all images have high resolution (1024 × 768). (2) To address the challenges of generating high-quality images, we leverage a Pixel-level Semantic-Aware Discriminator (PSAD) that enhances the realism of try-on images. (3) With the aim of presenting a comprehensive benchmark on our newly collected dataset, we train and test up to nine state-of-the-art virtual try-on approaches and three different baselines. (4) Extensive experiments demonstrate that the proposed approach outperforms the competitors and other state-of-the-art architectures both quantitatively and qualitatively, also considering different image resolutions and a multi-garment setting.

2   Related Work

The first popular image-based virtual try-on model [13] builds upon a coarse-to-fine network. First, it predicts a coarse image of the reference person wearing the try-on garment, then it refines the texture and shape of the previously obtained result. Wang *et al.* [40] overcame the lack of shape-context precision (*i.e.* bad alignment between clothes and body shape) and proposed a geometric transformation module to learn the parameters of a thin-plate spline transformation to warp the input garment. Following this work, many different solutions were proposed to enhance the geometric transformation of the try-on garment. For instance, Liu *et al.* [27] integrated a multi-scale patch adversarial loss to increase the realism in the warping phase. Minar *et al.* [28] and Yang *et al.* [42] proposed different regularization techniques to stabilize the warping process during training. Instead, other works [8,24] focused on the design of additional projections of the input garment to preserve details and textures of input clothing items.

Another line of work focuses on the improvement of the generation phase of final try-on images [4,7,9,14,18,19]. Among them, Issenuth *et al.* [18] introduced a teacher-student approach: the teacher learns to generate the try-on results using image pairs (sampled from a paired dataset) and then teaches the student how to deal with unpaired data. This paradigm was further improved in [10] with

Fig. 2. Sample image pairs from the Dress Code dataset with pose keypoints, dense poses, and segmentation masks of human bodies.

a student-tutor-teacher architecture where the network is trained in a parser-free way, exploiting both the tutor guidance and the teacher supervision. On a different line, Ge *et al.* [9] presented a self-supervised trainable network to reframe the virtual try-on task as clothes warping, skin synthesis, and image composition using a cycle-consistent framework.

A third direction of research estimates the person semantic layout to improve the visual quality of generated images [12,20,42,45]. In this context, Jandial *et al.* [20] proposed to generate a conditional segmentation mask to handle occlusions and complex body poses effectively. Very recently, Chen *et al.* [3] introduced a new scenario where the try-on results are synthesized in sequential poses with spatio-temporal smoothness. Using a recurrent approach, Cui *et al.* [5] designed a person generation framework for pose transfer, virtual try-on, and other fashion-related tasks. While almost all these methods generate low-resolution results, a limited subset of works focuses on the generation of higher-resolution images instead. Unfortunately, these works employ non-public datasets to train and test the proposed architectures [24,43].

3   Dress Code Dataset

Publicly available datasets for virtual try-on are often limited by one or more factors such as lack of variety, small size, low-resolution images, privacy concerns, or from the fact of being proprietary. We identify four main desiderata that the ideal dataset for virtual try-on should possess: (1) it should be publicly available for research purposes; (2) it should have corresponding images of clothes and reference human models wearing them (*i.e.* the dataset should consist of paired images); (3) it should contain high-resolution images and (4) clothes belonging to different macro-categories (tops and t-shirts belong to the upper-body category,

Table 1. Comparison between dress code and the most widely used datasets for virtual try-on and other related tasks.

Dataset	Public	Multi-category	# Images	# Garments	Resolution
O-VITON [30]	✗	✓	52,000	–	512 × 256
TryOnGAN [23]	✗	✓	105,000	–	512 × 512
Revery AI [24]	✗	✓	642,000	321,000	512 × 512
Zalando [43]	✗	✓	1,520,000	1,140,000	1024 × 768
VITON-HD [4]	✓	✗	27,358	13,679	1024 × 768
FashionOn [16]	✓	✗	32,685	10,895	288 × 192
DeepFashion [27]	✓	✗	33,849	11,283	288 × 192
MVP [6]	✓	✗	49,211	13,524	256 × 192
FashionTryOn [47]	✓	✗	86,142	28,714	256 × 192
LookBook [44]	✓	✓	84,748	9,732	256 × 192
VITON [13]	✓	✗	32,506	16,253	256 × 192
Dress code	✓	✓	107,584	53,792	1024 × 768

while skirts and trousers are examples of lower-body clothes and dresses are full-body garments). In addition to this, a dataset for virtual try-on with a large number of images is more preferable than other datasets with the same overall characteristics but smaller size. By looking at Table 1, we can see that Dress Code complies with all of the above desiderata, while featuring more than three times the number of images of VITON [13]. To the best of our knowledge, this is the first publicly available virtual try-on dataset comprising multiple macro-categories and high-resolution image pairs. Additionally, it is the biggest available dataset for this task at present, as it includes more than 100k images evenly split between garments and human reference models.

Image Collection and Annotation. All images are collected from different fashion catalogs of YOOX NET-A-PORTER containing both casual clothes and luxury garments. To create a coarse version of the dataset, we select images of different garment categories for a total of about 250k fashion items, each containing 2–5 images of different views of the same product. Since our goal is to create a dataset for virtual try-on and not all fashion items were released with the image pair required to perform the task, we select only those products where the front-view image of the garment and the corresponding full figure of the model are available. We exploit an automatic selection procedure: we only store the clothing items for which at least one image with the entire body of the model is present, using a human pose estimator to verify the presence of the neck and feet joints. In this way, all products without valid image pairs are automatically discarded. After this automatic stage, we manually validate all images and remove the remaining invalid image pairs, including those pairs for which the garment of interest is mostly occluded by other overlapping clothes. Finally, we group the annotated products into three categories: upper-body clothes (composed of tops, t-shirts, shirts, sweatshirts, and sweaters), lower-body clothes (composed of skirts, trousers, shorts, and leggings), and dresses. Overall, the dataset is composed of 53,795 image pairs: 15,366 pairs for upper-body clothes, 8,951 pairs for lower-body clothes, and 29,478 pairs for dresses.

Existing datasets for virtual try-on show the face and physiognomy of the human models. While this feature is not essential for virtual try-on, it also causes potential privacy issues. To preserve the models' identity, we partially anonymize all images by cutting them at the level of the nose. In this way, information about the physiognomy of the human models is not available. To further enrich our dataset, we compute the joint coordinates, the dense pose, and the segmentation mask for the human parsing of each model. In particular, we use OpenPose [2] to extract 18 keypoints for each human body, DensePose [11] to compute the dense pose of each reference model, and SCHP [25] to generate a segmentation mask representing the human parsing of model body parts and clothing items. Sample human model and garment pairs from our dataset with the corresponding additional information are shown in Fig. 2.

Comparison with Other Datasets. Table 1 reports the main characteristics of the Dress Code dataset in comparison with existing datasets for virtual try-on and fashion-related tasks. Although some proprietary and non-publicly available datasets have also been used [23,24,43], almost all virtual try-on literature [10,40,42] employs the VITON dataset [13] to train the proposed models and perform experiments. We believe that the use of Dress Code could greatly increase the performance and applicability of virtual try-on solutions. In fact, when comparing Dress Code with the VITON dataset, it can be seen that our dataset jointly features a larger number of image pairs (*i.e.* 53,792 vs 16,253 of the VITON dataset), a wider variety of clothing items (*i.e.* VITON only contains t-shirts and upper-body clothes), a greater variance in model images (*i.e.* Dress Code images can contain challenging backgrounds, accessories like bags, scarfs, and belts, and both male and female models), and a greater image resolution (*i.e.* 1024×768 vs 256×192 of VITON images).

4   Virtual Try-On with Pixel-Level Semantics

Architectures for virtual try-on address the task of generating a new image of the reference person wearing the input try-on garment. Given the generative nature of this task, virtual try-on methods are usually trained using adversarial losses that typically work at image- or patch-level and do not consider the semantics of generated images. Differently from previous works, we introduce a Pixel-level Semantic Aware Discriminator (PSAD) that can build an internal representation of each semantic class and increase the realism of generated images. In this section, we first describe the baseline generative architecture and then detail PSAD which improves the visual quality and overall performance.

4.1   Baseline Architecture

To tackle the virtual try-on task, we begin by building a baseline generative architecture that performs three main operations: (1) garment warping, (2) human parsing estimation, and finally (3) try-on. First, the warping module employs geometric transformations to create a warped version of the input try-on garment. Then, the human parsing estimation module predicts a semantic map for the reference person. Last, the try-on module generates the image of the reference person wearing the selected garment. Our baseline model is shown in Fig. 3 and detailed in the following.

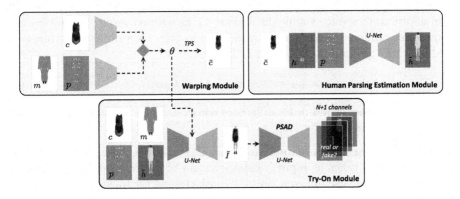

Fig. 3. Overview of the proposed architecture.

Network Inputs and Notation. Here, we define the different inputs for our network and related notation. We denote with c an image depicting a clothing item alone. This image contains information about the shape, texture, and color of the try-on garment. Details about the reference human model come in different forms: p, m, and h are three images containing respectively the pose of that person (p), the background and appearance of the portions of the body and outfit that are not involved in the try-on phase such as hands, feet, and part of the face (m), and the semantic labels of each of these regions (h). Our architecture can employ two different representations for the body pose: keypoints or dense pose [11]. In this section, as well as in Fig. 3, we consider the case of pose keypoints. However, it is possible to switch and use dense pose representation by accounting for the different number of channels. Finally, we denote with I the image depicting the person described by (p, m, h) wearing the garment c.

Warping Module. The warping module transforms the input try-on garment c into a warped image of the same item that matches the body pose and shape expressed respectively by p and m. As warping function we use a thin-plate spline (TPS) geometric transformation [33], which is commonly used in virtual try-on models [8,40,42]. Inside this module, we aim to learn the correspondence between the inputs (c, p, m) and the set θ of parameters to be used in the TPS transformation. Specifically, we follow the warping module proposed in [40] and compute a correlation map between the encoded representations of the try-on garment c and the pose and cloth-agnostic person representation (p and m), obtained using two separate convolutional networks. Then, we predict the spatial transformation parameters θ corresponding to the (x, y)-coordinate offsets of TPS anchor points. These parameters are used in the TPS function to generate the warped version $\tilde{c}$ of the input try-on garment:

$$\tilde{c} = \text{TPS}_\theta(c). \tag{1}$$

To train this network, we minimize the L_1 distance between the warped result $\tilde{c}$ and the cropped version of the garment $\hat{c}$ obtained from the ground-truth image I. In addition, to reduce visible distortions in the warped result, we employ the second-order difference constraint introduced in [42]. Overall, the loss function used to train this module is defined as follows:

$$\mathcal{L}_{warp} = \|\tilde{c} - \hat{c}\|_1 + \lambda_{const}\mathcal{L}_{const}, \tag{2}$$

where $\mathcal{L}_{const}$ is the second-order difference constraint and λ_{const} is used to weigh the constraint loss function [42].

Human Parsing Estimation Module. This module, based on the U-Net architecture [34], takes as input a concatenation of the warped try-on clothing item $\tilde{c}$ (Eq. 1), the pose image p, and the masked semantic image h, and predicts the complete semantic map $\tilde{h}$ containing the human parsing for the reference person:

$$\tilde{h} = \text{U-Net}_\mu(c, h, p), \tag{3}$$

where μ denotes the set of learnable weights in the network. Every pixel of $\tilde{h}$ contains a probability distribution over 18 semantic classes, which include *left/right arm, left/right leg, background, dress, shirt, skirt, neck*, and so on. We optimize the set of weights μ of this module using a pixel-wise cross-entropy loss between the generated semantic map $\tilde{h}$ and the ground-truth $\hat{h}$.

Try-On Module. This module produces the image $\tilde{I}$ depicting the reference person described by the triple $(p, m, \tilde{h})$ wearing the input try-on clothing item c. To this end, we employ a U-Net model [34] which takes as input c, p, m, and the one-hot semantic image obtained by taking the pixel-wise argmax of $\tilde{h}$. During training, instead, we employ the ground-truth human parsing $\hat{h}$. This artifice helps to stabilize training and brings better results.

At this stage, we take advantage of the previously learned geometric transformation TPS_θ to facilitate the generation of $\tilde{I}$. Specifically, we employ a modified version of the U-Net model featuring a two-branch encoder that generates two different representations for the try-on garment c and the reference person, and a decoder that combines these two representations to generate the final image $\tilde{I}$. The input of the first branch is the original try-on garment c, while the input of the second branch is a concatenation of the reference model and corresponding additional information. In the first branch, we apply the previously learned transformation TPS_θ. Thus, the skip connections, which are typical of the U-Net design, no longer perform an identity mapping, but compute:

$$E_i(c) = \text{TPS}_\theta(E_i(c)), \tag{4}$$

where $E_i(c)$ are the features extracted from the ith layer of the U-Net encoder.

During training, we exploit a combination of three different loss functions: an L_1 loss between the generated image $\tilde{I}$ and the ground-truth image I, a perceptual loss $\mathcal{L}_{vgg}$, also know as VGG loss [21], to compute the difference between the feature maps of $\tilde{I}$ and I extracted with a VGG-19 [39], and the adversarial loss $\mathcal{L}_{adv}$:

$$\mathcal{L}_{try\text{-}on} = \left\| \tilde{I} - I \right\|_1 + \mathcal{L}_{vgg} + \lambda_{adv}\mathcal{L}_{adv}, \tag{5}$$

where λ_{adv} is used to weigh the adversarial loss. For a formulation of $\mathcal{L}_{adv}$ using our proposed Pixel-level Parsing-Aware Discriminator (PSAD), we refer the reader to the next subsection (Eq. 6).

4.2   Pixel-Level Semantic-Aware Discriminator

Virtual try-on models are usually enriched with adversarial training strategies to increase the realism of generated images. However, most of the existing discriminator architectures work at image- or patch-level, thus neglecting the semantics of generated images. To address this issue, we draw inspiration from semantic image synthesis literature [26,31,38] and train our discriminator to predict the semantic class of each pixel using generated and ground-truth images as fake and real examples respectively. In this way, the discriminator can learn an internal representation of each semantic class (*e.g.* tops, skirts, body) and force the generator to improve the quality of synthesized images.

The discriminator is built upon the U-Net model [34], which is used as an encoder-decoder segmentation network. For each pixel of the input image, the discriminator predicts its semantic class and an additional label (real or generated). Overall, we have $N + 1$ classes (*i.e.* N classes corresponding to the ground-truth semantic classes plus one class for fake pixels) and thus we train the discriminator with a $(N + 1)$-class pixel-wise cross-entropy loss. In this way, the discriminator prediction shifts from a patch-level classification, typical of standard patch-based discriminators [17,41], to a per-pixel class-level prediction.

Due to the unbalanced nature of the semantic classes, we weigh the loss class-wise using the inverse pixel frequency of each class. Formally, the loss function used to train this Pixel-level Parsing-Aware Discriminator (PSAD) can be defined as follows:

$$\mathcal{L}_{adv} = -\mathbb{E}_{(I,\hat{h})} \left[\sum_{k=1}^{N} w_k \sum_{i,j}^{H \times W} \hat{h}_{i,j,k} \log D(I)_{i,j,k} \right]$$

$$-\mathbb{E}_{(p,m,c,\hat{h})} \left[\sum_{i,j}^{H \times W} \log D(G(p,m,c,\hat{h}))_{i,j,k=N+1} \right], \tag{6}$$

where I is the real image, $\hat{h}$ is the ground-truth human parsing, p is the model pose, m and c are respectively the person representation and the try-on garment given as input to the generator, and w_k is the class inverse pixel frequency.

5 Experiments

5.1 Experimental Setup

Datasets. First, we perform experiments on our newly proposed dataset, Dress Code, using 48,392 image pairs as training set and the remaining as test set (*i.e.* 5,400 pairs, 1,800 for each category). During evaluation, image pairs of the test set are rearranged to form unpaired pairs of clothes and front-view models. On Dress Code, we use three different image resolutions: 256×192 (*i.e.* the one typical used by virtual try-on models), 512×384, and 1024×768. Following our experiments on Dress Code, we evaluate our model on the standard VITON dataset [13], composed of 16,253 image pairs. We employ this dataset to evaluate our solution in comparison with other state-of-the-art architectures on a widely-employed benchmark. In VITON, all images have a resolution of 256×192 and are divided into training and test set with 14,221 and 2,032 image pairs respectively.

Table 2. Try-on results on the dress dode test set. Top-1 results are highlighted in bold, underlined denotes second-best.

Model	Upper-body			Lower-body			Dresses			All			
	SSIM ↑	FID ↓	KID ↓	SSIM ↑	FID ↓	KID ↓	SSIM ↑	FID ↓	KID ↓	SSIM ↑	FID ↓	KID ↓	IS ↑
CP-VTON [40]	0.812	46.99	3.236	0.782	54.66	3.656	0.816	34.95	1.759	0.803	35.16	2.245	2.817
CP-VTON+ [28]	0.863	28.93	1.856	0.819	41.37	2.506	0.826	32.27	1.630	0.836	25.19	1.586	3.002
CIT [32]	0.860	26.41	1.496	0.834	31.77	1.753	0.810	35.58	1.734	0.835	21.99	1.313	3.022
CP-VTON† [40]	0.898	23.03	1.338	0.887	26.96	1.409	0.838	33.04	1.668	0.874	18.99	1.117	**3.058**
CIT† [32]	0.912	17.66	0.895	0.896	23.15	1.005	0.855	23.87	0.969	0.888	13.97	0.761	3.014
VITON-GT [8]	0.922	18.90	0.994	0.916	21.88	0.949	0.864	29.45	1.402	0.899	13.80	0.711	3.042
WUTON [18]	0.924	17.74	0.893	0.918	22.57	1.008	0.866	28.93	1.304	0.902	13.28	0.771	3.005
ACGPN [42]	0.889	19.03	1.028	0.874	24.46	1.208	0.845	22.42	0.944	0.868	13.79	0.818	2.924
PF-AFN [10]	0.918	19.03	1.237	0.907	23.43	1.018	0.869	21.94	0.723	0.902	14.36	0.756	3.023
Dense Pose													
Ours (Patch)	<u>0.930</u>	18.21	0.929	<u>0.922</u>	21.95	0.992	<u>0.875</u>	21.84	0.768	<u>0.908</u>	12.82	0.692	3.042
Ours (PSAD)	0.928	<u>17.18</u>	<u>0.793</u>	0.921	<u>20.49</u>	<u>0.896</u>	0.872	**19.63**	**0.635**	0.906	<u>11.47</u>	<u>0.619</u>	2.987
Pose Keypoints													
Ours (NoDisc)	0.926	18.84	0.943	0.915	22.48	0.943	0.873	23.71	0.937	0.907	13.51	0.704	3.041
Ours (Binary)	0.925	18.39	0.872	0.914	22.52	0.98	0.871	22.35	0.816	0.906	12.89	0.645	3.017
Ours (Patch)	**0.931**	18.40	0.841	**0.923**	21.46	0.955	**0.876**	21.94	0.814	**0.909**	12.53	0.666	<u>3.043</u>
Ours (PSAD)	0.928	**17.04**	**0.762**	0.921	**20.04**	**0.795**	0.872	<u>20.98</u>	<u>0.672</u>	0.906	**11.40**	**0.570**	3.036

Evaluation Metrics. Following recent literature, we employ evaluation metrics that either compare the generated images with the corresponding ground-truths, *i.e.* Structural Similarity (SSIM), or measure the realism and the visual quality of the generation, *i.e.* Frechét Inception Distance (FID) [15], Kernel Inception Distance (KID) [1], and Inception Score (IS) [35].

Training. We train the three components of our model separately. Specifically, we first train the warping module and then the human parsing estimation module for 100k and 50k iterations respectively. Finally, we train the try-on module for other 150k iterations. We set the weight of the second-order difference constraint λ_{const} to 0.01 and the weight of the adversarial loss λ_{adv} to 0.1. All experiments are performed using Adam [22] as optimizer and a learning rate equal to 10^{-4}. More details on the architecture and training stage are reported in the supplementary material.

5.2 Experiments on Dress Code

Baselines and Competitors. In this set of experiments, we compare with CP-VTON [40], CP-VTON+ [28], CIT [32], VITON-GT [8], WUTON [18], ACGPN [42], and PF-AFN [10], that we re-train from scratch on our dataset using source codes provided by the authors, when available, or our re-implementations. In addition to these methods, we implement an improved version of [40] (*i.e.* CP-VTON†) and of [32] (*i.e.* CIT†) in which we use, as an additional input to the model, the person representation m. To validate the effectiveness of the Pixel-level Semantic Aware Discriminator (PSAD), we also test a model trained with a patch-based discriminator [17] (Patch), a model trained by removing in our discriminator the N semantic channels and only keeping the real/fake one [37] (Binary), and a baseline trained without the adversarial loss (NoDisc).

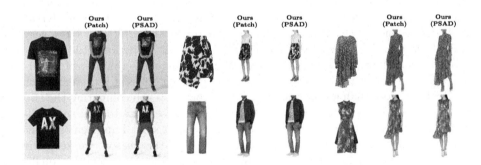

Fig. 4. Qualitative comparison between patch and PSAD.

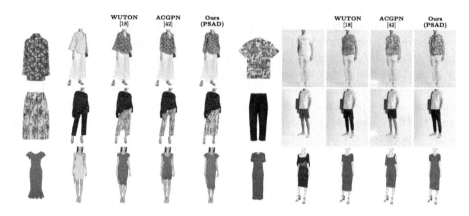

Fig. 5. Sample try-on results on the Dress Code test set.

Low-Resolution Results and Ablative Analysis. In this experiment, we compare our complete model (PSAD) with state-of-the-art architectures for virtual try-on and with the Patch, Binary, and NoDisc baselines. For these comparisons, we consider the standard resolution for virtual try-on (256×192). In Table 2, we report numerical results on the Dress Code test set. As it can be seen, our model obtains better results than competitors on all clothing categories in terms of almost all considered evaluation metrics. Quantitative results also confirm the effectiveness of PSAD in comparison with a pixel-level discriminator without semantics and with a standard patch-based discriminator, especially in terms of the realism of the generated images (*i.e.* FID and KID). PSAD is second to the Patch model only in terms of SSIM, and by a very limited margin. All discriminator-based configurations outperform the NoDisc baseline, thus showing the importance of incorporating a discriminator in a virtual try-on architecture. We also test the effect of using different representations for the body pose (human keypoints and dense pose). When comparing the two versions of our model, we find out that using dense pose helps to deal with full-body clothes (*i.e.* dresses), but does not bring a consistent improvement over the use of human keypoints in our architecture. For this reason, we keep the latter model version for all the next experiments. In Fig. 4, we report a qualitative comparison between the results obtained with our Patch model and the PSAD version. In Fig. 5, we compare our results with those obtained by state-of-the-art competitors. Overall, our model with PSAD can better preserve the characteristics of the original clothes such as colors, textures, and shapes, and reduce artifacts and distortions, increasing the realism and visual quality of the generated images.

High-Resolution Results. For this experiment, we train and test our models and competitors using higher-resolution images (512×384 and 1024×768). We compare with CP-VTON [40] and its improved version (CP-VTON†). Quantitative results for this setting are reported in Table 3 and refer to the entire test

Table 3. High-resolution results on the dress code test set.

Model	512 × 384				1024 × 768			
	SSIM ↑	FID ↓	KID ↓	IS ↑	SSIM ↑	FID ↓	KID ↓	IS ↑
CP-VTON [40]	0.831	29.24	1.671	3.096	0.853	36.68	2.379	3.155
CP-VTON† [40]	0.896	10.08	0.425	3.277	0.912	9.96	0.338	3.300
Ours (Patch)	**0.923**	9.44	**0.246**	3.310	**0.922**	9.99	0.370	3.344
Ours (PSAD)	0.916	**7.27**	0.394	**3.320**	0.919	**7.70**	**0.236**	**3.357**

Table 4. Multi-garment try-on results on the Dress Code test set.

Model	Resolution	FID ↓	KID ↓	IS ↑
CP-VTON† [40]	256 × 192	30.29	1.935	**2.912**
VITON-GT [8]	256 × 192	21.06	1.176	2.762
WUTON [18]	256 × 192	20.13	1.084	2.753
Ours (Patch)	256 × 192	19.86	1.006	2.784
Ours (PSAD)	256 × 192	**17.52**	**0.749**	2.832
CP-VTON† [40]	512 × 384	22.96	1.327	**3.273**
Ours (Patch)	512 × 384	21.90	1.155	3.073
Ours (PSAD)	512 × 384	**16.90**	**0.690**	3.160
CP-VTON† [40]	1024 × 768	23.30	1.393	3.261
Ours (Patch)	1024 × 768	20.26	0.841	**3.498**
Ours (PSAD)	1024 × 768	**17.19**	**0.681**	3.340

set of the Dress Code dataset. As it can be seen, our method outperforms the competitors. When generating images with resolution 1024×768, PSAD achieves the best results in terms of FID, KID, and IS with respect to the competitors and the Patch baseline (Fig. 6).

Multi-garment Try-On Results. As an additional experiment on the Dress Code dataset, we propose a novel setting in which the try-on is performed twice: first with an upper-body garment, and then with a lower-body item. This fully-unpaired setting aims to push further the difficulty of image-based virtual try-on, as it doubles the number of operations required to generate the resulting image. We remind that this experiment would have not been possible on the standard VITON dataset [13], as it contains only upper-body clothes. In Table 4, we report numerical results at varying image resolution. We can observe that PSAD outperforms the competitors and baselines on almost all the metrics for all the different image resolutions, with the only exception of the IS metric. Notably, the improvement of PSAD with respect to the Patch baseline ranges from 2.34 to 5.00 and from 0.16 to 0.46 in terms of FID and KID respectively.

Table 5. User study results. Our model is always preferred more than 50% of the time.

	CP-VTON	VITON-GT	WUTON	ACGPN	PF-AFN	Ours (Patch)
Realism	10.1/**89.9**	46.4/**53.6**	42.0/**58.0**	35.9/**64.1**	29.4/**70.6**	34.8/**65.2**
Coherency	11.5/**88.5**	32.1/**67.9**	41.6/**58.4**	23.1/**76.9**	25.0/**75.0**	36.9/**63.1**

Fig. 6. High-resolution results on the Dress Code test set in both single- and multi-garment try-on settings.

User Study. While quantitative metrics used in the previous experiments can capture fine-grained variations in the generated images, the overall realism and visual quality of the results can be effectively assessed by human evaluation. To further evaluate the quality of generated images, we conduct a user study measuring both the realism of our results and their coherence with the input try-on garment and reference person. In the first test (Realism test), we show two generated images, one generated by our model and the other by a competitor, and ask to select the more realistic one. In the second test (Coherency test), in addition to the two generated images, we include the images of the try-on garment and the reference person used as input to the try-on network. In this case, we ask the user to select the image that is more coherent with the given inputs. All images are randomly selected from the Dress Code test set. Overall, this study involves a total of 30 participants, including researchers and non-expert people, and we collect more than 3,000 different evaluations (*i.e.* 1,500 for each test). Results are shown in Table 5. For each test, we report the percentage of votes obtained by the competitor/by our model. We also include a comparison with the Patch baseline. Our complete model is always selected more than 50% of the time against all considered competitors, thus further demonstrating the effectiveness of our solution.

5.3 Experiments on VITON

To conclude, we train the try-on networks on the widely used VITON dataset [13]. For this experiment, we compare our PSAD and Patch models with other state-of-the-art architectures. In particular, we report results from CP-VTON [40] and CP-VTON+ [28] using source codes and pre-trained models

Table 6. Try-on results on the VITON test set [13]. Note that all models are trained exclusively on VITON.

Model	Resolution	SSIM ↑	FID ↓	KID ↓	IS ↑
CP-VTON [40]	256 × 192	0.798	19.06	0.906	2.601
CP-VTON+ [28]	256 × 192	0.828	16.31	0.784	2.821
SieveNet [20]	256 × 192	0.766	14.65	–	2.820
ACGPN [42]	256 × 192	0.845	–	–	2.829
DCTON [9]	256 × 192	0.830	14.82	–	**2.850**
Ours (Patch)	256 × 192	**0.893**	14.76	0.495	2.733
Ours (PSAD)	256 × 192	0.885	**13.71**	**0.412**	2.840

Fig. 7. Sample generated results on the VITON test set.

provided by the authors. For SieveNet [20], ACGPN [42], and DCTON [9], we use the results reported in the papers. Table 6 shows the quantitative results on the test set, while in Fig. 7 we report four examples of the generated try-on results. Also in this setting, PSAD contributes to increasing the realism and visual quality of synthesized images.

6 Conclusion

In this paper, we presented Dress Code: a new dataset for image-based virtual try-on. Dress Code, while being more than 3× larger than the most common dataset for virtual try-on, is the first publicly available dataset for this task featuring clothes of multiple macro-categories and high-resolution images. We also presented a comprehensive benchmark with up to nine state-of-the-art virtual try-on approaches and different baselines, and introduced a Pixel-level Semantic-Aware Discriminator (PSAD) that improves the generation of high-quality images and the realism of the results.

Acknowledgments. We thank CINECA, the Italian Supercomputing Center, for providing computational resources. This work has been supported by the PRIN project

"CREATIVE: CRoss-modal understanding and generATIon of Visual and tExtual content" (CUP B87G22000460001), co-funded by the Italian Ministry of University and Research.

References

1. Bińkowski, M., Sutherland, D.J., Arbel, M., Gretton, A.: Demystifying MMD GANs. In: ICLR (2018)
2. Cao, Z., Simon, T., Wei, S.E., Sheikh, Y.: Realtime multi-person 2d pose estimation using part affinity fields. In: CVPR (2017)
3. Chen, C.Y., Lo, L., Huang, P.J., Shuai, H.H., Cheng, W.H.: FashionMirror: co-attention feature-remapping virtual try-on with sequential template poses. In: ICCV (2021)
4. Choi, S., Park, S., Lee, M., Choo, J.: VITON-HD: high-resolution virtual try-on via misalignment-aware normalization. In: ICCV (2021)
5. Cui, A., McKee, D., Lazebnik, S.: Dressing in order: recurrent person image generation for pose transfer. In: ICCV, Virtual Try-On and Outfit Editing (2021)
6. Dong, H., et al.: Towards multi-pose guided virtual try-on network. In: ICCV (2019)
7. Fenocchi, E., Morelli, D., Cornia, M., Baraldi, L., Cesari, F., Cucchiara, R.: Dual-branch collaborative transformer for virtual try-on. In: CVPR Workshops (2022)
8. Fincato, M., Landi, F., Cornia, M., Fabio, C., Cucchiara, R.: VITON-GT: an image-based virtual try-on model with geometric transformations. In: ICPR (2020)
9. Ge, C., Song, Y., Ge, Y., Yang, H., Liu, W., Luo, P.: Disentangled cycle consistency for highly-realistic virtual try-on. In: CVPR (2021)
10. Ge, Y., Song, Y., Zhang, R., Ge, C., Liu, W., Luo, P.: Parser-free virtual try-on via distilling appearance flows. In: CVPR (2021)
11. Güler, R.A., Neverova, N., Kokkinos, I.: DensePose: dense human pose estimation in the wild. In: CVPR (2018)
12. Han, X., Hu, X., Huang, W., Scott, M.R.: ClothFlow: a flow-based model for clothed person generation. In: ICCV (2019)
13. Han, X., Wu, Z., Wu, Z., Yu, R., Davis, L.S.: VITON: an image-based virtual try-on network. In: CVPR (2018)
14. He, S., Song, Y.Z., Xiang, T.: Style-based global appearance flow for virtual try-on. In: CVPR (2022)
15. Heusel, M., Ramsauer, H., Unterthiner, T., Nessler, B., Klambauer, G., Hochreiter, S.: GANs trained by a two time-scale update rule converge to a Nash equilibrium. In: NeurIPS (2017)
16. Hsieh, C.W., Chen, C.Y., Chou, C.L., Shuai, H.H., Liu, J., Cheng, W.H.: FashionOn: semantic-guided image-based virtual try-on with detailed human and clothing information. In: ACM Multimedia (2019)
17. Isola, P., Zhu, J.Y., Zhou, T., Efros, A.A.: Image-To-Image translation with conditional adversarial networks. In: CVPR (2017)
18. Issenhuth, T., Mary, J., Calauzènes, C.: Do not mask what you do not need to mask: a parser-free virtual try-on. In: ECCV (2020)
19. Jae Lee, H., Lee, R., Kang, M., Cho, M., Park, G.: LA-VITON: a network for looking-attractive virtual try-on. In: ICCV Workshops (2019)
20. Jandial, S., Chopra, A., Ayush, K., Hemani, M., Krishnamurthy, B., Halwai, A.: SieveNet: a unified framework for robust image-based virtual try-on. In: WACV (2020)

21. Johnson, J., Alahi, A., Fei-Fei, L.: Perceptual losses for real-time style transfer and super-resolution. In: ECCV (2016)
22. Kingma, D.P., Ba, J.: Adam: a method for stochastic optimization. In: ICLR (2015)
23. Lewis, K.M., Varadharajan, S., Kemelmacher-Shlizerman, I.: TryOnGAN: body-aware try-on via layered interpolation. ACM Trans. Graphic. 40(4), 1–10 (2021)
24. Li, K., Chong, M.J., Zhang, J., Liu, J.: Toward accurate and realistic outfits visualization with attention to details. In: CVPR (2021)
25. Li, P., Xu, Y., Wei, Y., Yang, Y.: Self-correction for human parsing. IEEE Trans. PAMI 44(6), 3260–3271 (2022)
26. Liu, X., Yin, G., Shao, J., Wang, X., Li, H.: Learning to predict layout-to-image conditional convolutions for semantic image synthesis. In: NeurIPS (2019)
27. Liu, Z., Luo, P., Qiu, S., Wang, X., Tang, X.: DeepFashion: powering robust clothes recognition and retrieval with rich annotations. In: CVPR (2016)
28. Minar, M.R., Tuan, T.T., Ahn, H., Rosin, P., Lai, Y.K.: CP-VTON+: clothing shape and texture preserving image-based virtual try-on. In: CVPR Workshops (2020)
29. Mir, A., Alldieck, T., Pons-Moll, G.: Learning to transfer texture from clothing images to 3d humans. In: CVPR (2020)
30. Neuberger, A., Borenstein, E., Hilleli, B., Oks, E., Alpert, S.: Image based virtual try-on network from unpaired data. In: CVPR (2020)
31. Park, T., Liu, M.Y., Wang, T.C., Zhu, J.Y.: Semantic image synthesis with spatially-adaptive normalization. In: CVPR (2019)
32. Ren, B., et a;.: Cloth interactive transformer for virtual try-on. arXiv preprint arXiv:2104.05519 (2021)
33. Rocco, I., Arandjelovic, R., Sivic, J.: Convolutional neural network architecture for geometric matching. In: CVPR (2017)
34. Ronneberger, O., Fischer, P., Brox, T.: U-net: convolutional networks for biomedical image segmentation. In: MICCAI (2015)
35. Salimans, T., Goodfellow, I., Zaremba, W., Cheung, V., Radford, A., Chen, X.: Improved techniques for training GANs. In: NeurIPS (2016)
36. Santesteban, I., Thuerey, N., Otaduy, M.A., Casas, D.: Self-supervised collision handling via generative 3d garment models for virtual try-on. In: CVPR (2021)
37. Schonfeld, E., Schiele, B., Khoreva, A.: A u-net based discriminator for generative adversarial network. In: CVPR (2020)
38. Schönfeld, E., Sushko, V., Zhang, D., Gall, J., Schiele, B., Khoreva, A.: You only need adversarial supervision for semantic image synthesis. In: ICLR (2021)
39. Simonyan, K., Zisserman, A.: Very deep convolutional networks for large-scale image recognition. In: ICLR (2015)
40. Wang, B., Zheng, H., Liang, X., Chen, Y., Lin, L., Yang, M.: Toward characteristic-preserving image-based virtual try-on network. In: ECCV (2018)
41. Wang, T.C., Liu, M.Y., Zhu, J.Y., Tao, A., Kautz, J., Catanzaro, B.: High-resolution image synthesis and semantic manipulation with conditional GANs. In: CVPR (2018)
42. Yang, H., Zhang, R., Guo, X., Liu, W., Zuo, W., Luo, P.: Towards photo-realistic virtual try-on by adaptively generating-preserving image content. In: CVPR (2020)
43. Yildirim, G., Jetchev, N., Vollgraf, R., Bergmann, U.: Generating high-resolution fashion model images wearing custom outfits. In: ICCV Workshops (2019)
44. Yoo, D., Kim, N., Park, S., Paek, A.S., Kweon, I.S.: Pixel-level domain transfer. In: ECCV (2016)
45. Yu, R., Wang, X., Xie, X.: VTNFP: an image-based virtual try-on network with body and clothing feature preservation. In: ICCV (2019)

46. Zhao, F., et al.: M3D-VTON: a monocular-to-3d virtual try-on network. In: ICCV (2021)
47. Zheng, N., Song, X., Chen, Z., Hu, L., Cao, D., Nie, L.: Virtually trying on new clothing with arbitrary poses. In: ACM Multimedia (2019)
48. Zhu, H., et al.: DeepFashion3D: a dataset and benchmark for 3d garment reconstruction from single images. In: ECCV (2020)

A Data-Centric Approach for Improving Ambiguous Labels with Combined Semi-supervised Classification and Clustering

Lars Schmarje[1]([✉])(iD), Monty Santarossa[1](iD), Simon-Martin Schröder[1](iD),
Claudius Zelenka[1](iD), Rainer Kiko[2](iD), Jenny Stracke[3](iD), Nina Volkmann[4](iD),
and Reinhard Koch[1](iD)

[1] MIP, Computer Science, Kiel University, Kiel, Germany
{las,msa,sms,czw,rk}@informatik.uni-kiel.de
[2] LOV, Sorbonne Université, Paris, France
rainer.kiko@obs-vlfr.fr
[3] ITW, University of Bonn, Bonn, Germany
jenny.stracke@itw.uni-bonn.de
[4] WING & ITTN, University of Veterinary Medicine Hannover, Hanover, Germany
nina.volkmann@tiho-hannover.de

Abstract. Consistently high data quality is essential for the development of novel loss functions and architectures in the field of deep learning. The existence of such data and labels is usually presumed, while acquiring high-quality datasets is still a major issue in many cases. Subjective annotations by annotators often lead to ambiguous labels in real-world datasets. We propose a data-centric approach to relabel such ambiguous labels instead of implementing the handling of this issue in a neural network. A hard classification is by definition not enough to capture the real-world ambiguity of the data. Therefore, we propose our method "Data-Centric Classification & Clustering (DC3)" which combines semi-supervised classification and clustering. It automatically estimates the ambiguity of an image and performs a classification or clustering depending on that ambiguity. DC3 is general in nature so that it can be used in addition to many Semi-Supervised Learning (SSL) algorithms. On average, our approach yields a 7.6% better F1-Score for classifications and a 7.9% lower inner distance of clusters across multiple evaluated SSL algorithms and datasets. Most importantly, we give a proof-of-concept that the classifications and clusterings from DC3 are beneficial as proposals for the manual refinement of such ambiguous labels. Overall, a combination of SSL with our method DC3 can lead to better handling of ambiguous labels during the annotation process. (Source code is available at https://github.com/Emprime/dc3).

Keywords: Data-centric · Clustering · Ambiguous labels

Supplementary Information The online version contains supplementary material available at https://doi.org/10.1007/978-3-031-20074-8_21.

S. Avidan et al. (Eds.): ECCV 2022, LNCS 13668, pp. 363–380, 2022.
https://doi.org/10.1007/978-3-031-20074-8_21

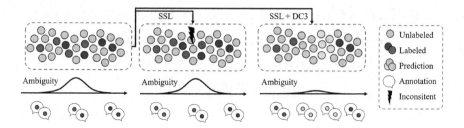

Fig. 1. Benefit of data-centric classification and clustering (DC3) over Semi-Supervised Learning (SSL) - Real-world datasets often suffer from intra- or interobserver variability (IIV) during the annotation and thus no clear separation of classes is given as in common benchmark datasets. Images with a high variability between the annotations therefore have a ambiguous label. These ambiguous labels can perturb SSL approaches (see lightning bolt) and result in inconsistent predictions. Our method DC3 can be used in combination with SSL to identify ambiguous images automatically and cluster them, while classifying the rest as usual. Therefore, we avoid label ambiguity during training and generate cluster proposals which can be used to create more consistent labels.

1 Introduction

In recent years, deep learning has been successfully applied to many computer vision problems [11,15,20,39,41,48]. The availability of large high-quality datasets was a main reason for this success, as this enabled machine learning to incorporate a wide variety of real world patterns [29]. Many novel loss functions and architectures have been proposed including options to handle imperfect data [50,58]. This model-centric view mostly tries to deal with issues like label bias [34], label noise [25] or ambiguous labels [17] instead of improving the dataset during the annotation process. Following recent data-centric literature [4,42,44], we therefore investigate in this paper an approach to improve the dataset during the annotation process.

Specifically, we study the impact of ambiguous labels due to *intra- or interobserver variability* (IIV). Such variability may arise from variability / inconsistency of annotations over time or between annotators. This issue is common when annotating data [5,14,16,19,23–25,36,38,42–46]. The literature names different possible reasons for this variability such as low resolution [38], bad quality [21,46], subjective interpretations of classes [24,36] or mistakes [25,32].

We assume that this variability can be modeled for each image with an unknown soft probability distribution $l \in [0,1]^k$ for a classification problem with k classes. Many previous methods use a hard label instead of a soft label for training and therefore can not model this issue by definition. We call a label and its corresponding image *certain* if all annotators would agree on the classification ($l \in \{0,1\}$) and *ambiguous* if they would disagree ($l \in (0,1)$). In other words, ambiguous images are likely to have different annotations due to IIV while certain images do not. It is problematic that the unknown distribution l can only be estimated with expensive operations such as the acquisition of multiple annotations. Real-world example images with certain and ambiguous labels are given in Fig. 3 and detailed definitions are given in Subsect. 2.1.

The goal of this paper is to introduce a method which provides predictions which are beneficial for improving ambiguous labels via relabeling in a downstream task. The quality of ambiguous labels and thus the performance of trained models [4,60] can easily be improved with more annotations. However, more annotations are associated with a higher cost in the form of human working hours. Semi-Supervised Learning (SSL) can reduce these costs because it has shown great potential in reducing the amount of required labeled data to 10% or even 1% while maintaining classification performance [8,11,26,48,61]. SSL can even boost performance further [39,59] on already large labeled datasets like ImageNet [29].

Therefore, we propose Data-Centric Classification & Clustering (DC3) which can be used in combination with many SSL algorithms to perform a combined semi-supervised classification and clustering. It simultaneously distinguishes between ambiguous and certain images, classifies the certain images and clusters visually similar ambiguous images. A graphical summary is provided in Fig. 1. We will show that this approach leads to better classifications and more compact clusters across multiple semi-supervised algorithms and non-curated datasets. Furthermore, we give a proof-of-concept that these improvements lead to a greater consistency of labels based on proposals from DC3.

The key contributions of this paper are: (1) DC3 allows an SSL algorithm to predict on average a 7.6% better F1-Score for classifications and a 7.9% lower inner distance of clustering across multiple algorithms and non-curated datasets. The hyperparameters of DC3 are fixed across all algorithms and datasets which illustrates the general applicability of our method. (2) We give a proof-of-concept that these improved predictions can be used to create labels on average 2.4-fold faster and 6.74% more consistent, in comparison to the non-extended algorithms and a consensus process. This leads to higher quality data for further evaluation or model training. (3) DC3 can be used in combination with many SSL algorithms without a noticeable trade-off in terms of run-time or memory consumption, which should enable many further applications.

1.1 Related Work

Our method is mainly related to Data-Centric Machine Learning, Semi-Supervised Learning and Classification & Clustering.

Data-Centric Machine Learning aims at improving the data quality rather then improving the model alone [35,44]. The data issues like imperfect, ambiguous or erroneous labels [1,4,13,14,23,51,60] are often handled in a model-centric approach by detecting errors or making the models more robust [2,9,25,49]. We want to use the predictions of our model to improve the annotation process and therefore prevent or minimize the quality issues before they need to be handled in particular.

Semi-Supervised Learning [10] is mainly developed on curated benchmark datasets [12,28,29] where the issue of IIV is not considered. In contrast to other SSL research [8,11,18,48,61], we are not evaluating on these curated benchmarks but work with new real-world datasets for two reasons. Firstly, curated datasets do not suffer so much from IIV because they were already cleaned. Recent research indicates that even these datasets suffer from errors in the labels which negatively impact the performance [4,38]. Secondly, if we want to evaluate the IIV issue, we need an approximation of the variability of the label for each image e.g. in the form of multiple annotations per image. However, this information is not provided for current state-of-the-art benchmarks except for datasets like [4,38].

Classification and Clustering was investigated in detail [6,7,37,40,53]. However, classical low dimensional approaches are difficult to extend to real-world images [6,37,40]. and many deep-learning methods use the clustering only as a proxy task before the actual classification [22,42,54] or iterate between classifications and clusters [7,53]. The work by Smieja et al. is a rare example where classification and clustering results are generated in parallel in each training step [47]. However, we want to automatically decide which data should be classified or clustered due to their underlying ambiguity.

2 Method

Our method Data-Centric Classification & Clustering (DC3) is not an individual method but an extension for SSL algorithms such as [3,30,31,48,52]. Any image classification model can be combined with DC3 as long as it is compatible with the definition of an arbitrary SSL algorithm below.

2.1 Definitions

We assume that every image $x \in X$ has an unknown soft probability distribution $l \in [0,1]^k$ for a classification problem with k classes. This assumption is based on two main reasons. Firstly, inconsistent annotations exist due to subjective opinions from the annotators, e.g. the grading of an illness [24]. A hard label $l \in \{0,1\}^k$ could not model such a difference over the complete annotator population. Secondly, if we consider biological processes, images of intermediate transition stages between two classes, such as the degeneration of a living underwater organism to dead biomass exist [42].

An image and its corresponding label l are *ambiguous* if $i,j \in \{1,..,k\}$ exist with $i \neq j, l_i > 0$ and $l_j > 0$. Otherwise the image and its label are *certain*. The ambiguity of a label is $1 - max_{i \in \{1,..,k\}} l_i$. An image might be ambiguous because it is actually an intermediate or uncertain combination of different classes as stated above. For this reason, ambiguous images are not just wrongly assigned images.

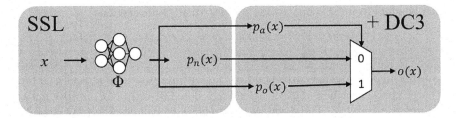

Fig. 2. Our method DC3 and an extended arbitrary SSL method – The SSL algorithm passes an image x through the network Φ and outputs a classification $p_n(x)$. We add two additional outputs: an overclustering $p_o(x)$ and a ambiguity estimation $p_a(x)$. The ambiguity estimation $p_a(x)$ is used to determine if the classification or the overclustering output is used for our method DC3. Only some labels are available for the classification output and therefore most images have to be trained completely self-supervised on all outputs.

An SSL algorithm uses a labeled dataset X_l and an unlabeled dataset X_u for the training of a neural network Φ with $X = X_l \cup X_u$. For all images $x \in X_l$ a hard label l is available while no label information is available for $x \in X_u$. The output $p_n(x) := \Phi(x)$ is a probability distribution over the k classes.

2.2   DC3

Our method DC3 extends an arbitrary SSL algorithm. The SSL algorithm passes an image x through the network Φ and predicts a classification $p_n(x) \in [0,1]^k$. DC3 calculates two additional outputs without a noticeable impact on training time or memory consumption: a clustering assignment $p_o(x) \in [0,1]^{k'}$ with $k' > k$ and an ambiguity estimation $p_a(x) \in [0,1]$. The cluster assignment partitions visually similar images in more clusters than classes exist (overclustering with $k' > k$). The ambiguity estimation is used to determine if a classification ($p_n(x)$) or an (over)clustering ($p_o(x)$) should be used as the final output. The image is predicted as certain and the classification is used if $p_a(x) < 0.5$. Otherwise, the image is estimated as ambiguous and the clustering is used as output (Fig. 2).

A key difference to previous literature [7,22,42] is that we do not create an additional or only a clustering of all samples. We create SSL classifications for certain images while ambiguous images are clustered without prescribed knowledge. Moreover, it is not feasible to determine ambiguous images before this classification/clustering and thus we have no ground-truth for this decision as well. These conditions led us to formulate three goals for our development: 1. The underlying SSL training must be possible and not negatively impacted while computing an additional overclustering. 2. A degeneration to one or random cluster assignments has to be avoided as no ground-truth is available for the clustering. 3. A balance between certain and ambiguous images is needed as the same argument (no-ground truth) applies to the ambiguity estimation $p_a(x)$ For this purpose, the network is trained by minimizing the following loss function which benefits from SSL but avoids the described degenerations.

$$L(x) = L_{SSL}(x) \cdot [1 - p_a(x)] + \lambda_{CE^{-1}} L_{CE^{-1}}(x) \cdot [1 - p_a(x)]$$
$$+ \lambda_a L_A(x) + \lambda_s L_S(x) \cdot p_a(x) \tag{1}$$

The first three loss terms correspond to the outputs $p_n(x), p_o(x)$ and $p_a(x)$ and the three goals described above, respectively. The last term (L_S) is optional and stabilizes the training. The λ values are weights to balance the impact of each term. The first loss L_{SSL} is the loss calculated by the original SSL algorithm and is only scaled with $[1 - p_a(x)]$ to prevent the original SSL training on images the network predicts as ambiguous.

The second loss $L_{CE^{-1}}$ incentives visually homogeneous clusters of the images by pushing images from different classes into different clusters. This loss is needed to prevent a degeneration of the clustering. A similar loss was used in [42] but could only be trained on labeled data, with pretrained networks and several inefficient stabilizing methods like repeating every sample 3–5 times per batch. We generalized the formula for two input images x, x' of the same mini-batch which should not be of the same class:

$$CE^{-1}(p_o(x), p_o(x')) = - \sum_{c=1}^{k} p_o(x)_c \cdot ln(1 - p_o(x')_c). \tag{2}$$

For the selection of x, x', we use either the ground-truth label l of x if it is available or the Pseudo-Label based on the network prediction $p_n(x)$. The loss is also scaled with $[1 - p_a(x)]$ because it uses an estimate of the class for an image which could be wrong / ill-suited for ambiguous images.

The third loss L_A allows the ambiguity estimation. As stated above, the underlying distribution l is unknown and thus we do not know during training if x is ambiguous or certain. However, we can expect to know or be given a prior probability $p_A \in [0, 1]$ of the expected percentage of ambiguous images in the total dataset. We set p_A to a fixed value which balances certain and ambiguous images and the details are given in Subsect. 3.3. Based on this probability, we can estimate a Pseudo-Label of the ambiguity of each image in a batch during training. The loss L_A is the binary cross-entropy between the Pseudo-Label $h(x)$ and $p_a(x)$. The usage of hot-encoded Pseudo-Labels forces the network to make more confident predictions. The formulation is given below with i as the index of the image x inside the given batch, when all images inside the batch are sorted in ascending order based on p_a.

$$L_A(x) = CE(h(x), p_a(x))$$
$$= -(1 - h(x)) \cdot ln(p_a(x = 0))$$
$$- h(x) \cdot ln(p_a(x = 1)) \text{ with} \tag{3}$$
$$h(x) = \begin{cases} 1 & i \leq \text{batch size} \cdot p_A \\ 0 & \text{else} \end{cases}$$

The fourth term L_S is the cross-entropy (CE) between $p_o(x)$ and $p_o(x')$ for two differently augmented versions x, x' of the same image. This loss is scaled with $p_a(x)$ and incentives that augmented versions of the same ambiguous image are in the same output cluster. We use CE because it indirectly minimizes also the entropy of $p_o(x)$ which leads to sharper predictions. Many SSL algorithms already use a differently augmented version x' of x as secondary input [3,22, 30,48,52] which allows an easy computation. Otherwise, the fourth term is not calculated and treated as zero.

It is important to note that only the proposed combination of the individual parts leads to a successful training of all desired outputs. We show in Subsect. 4 that the combined clustering and classification (CC) based on $p_a(x)$ and the loss L_{CE-1} are the two essential parts to DC3.

3   Experiments

3.1   Datasets

That our method can be applied to many SSL algorithms across different real-world ambiguous datasets without major changes is a major advantage. While many datasets [5,14,16,23–25,36,38,42,46] suffer from annotation variability, we do not know the unknown underlying distribution l to evaluate the ambiguity or any related metrics. We can approximate l with the average over multiple annotations from humans. An annotation is the hard coded guess $a = (a_1, ..., a_k) \in \{0,1\}^k$ of a class for an image from a human with exactly one $i' \in \{1, ..., k\} : a'_i = 1$ and for all $j \in \{1, ..., k\} \setminus \{i'\} : a_j = 0$. We assume that the approximation $\hat{l}$ as the average of n annotations is identical to the unknown distribution l for $n \longrightarrow \infty$. This leaves the issue that we need multiple annotations per image for a dataset with ambiguous labels which are often not available. However, all datasets summarized in Table 1 have multiple annotations and thus allow the approximation of $\hat{l}$. Nine visual examples for all datasets are given in Fig. 3 and the datasets are shortly introduced below.

The *Plankton* dataset was introduced in [42]. The dataset contains 10 plankton classes and has multiple labels per image due to the help of citizen scientists. In contrast to [42], we include ambiguous images in the training and validation set and do not enforce a class balance which results in a slightly different data split as shown in Fig. 3. Moreover, we processed the data by recentering the images and removing artifacts like scale bars.

The *Turkey* dataset was used in [56,57]. The dataset contains cropped images of potential injuries of the birds which were separately annotated by three experts as not injured or injured.

The *Mice Bone* dataset is based on raw data which was published in [46]. The raw data are 3D scans from collagen fibers in mice bones. The three proposed classes are similar as well as dissimilar collagen fiber orientations and not relevant regions due to noise or background. We used the given segmentations to cut image regions from the original 2D image slices which mainly consist of one class. We generated ambiguous GT labels on 10% of the generated images by averaging over three classifications from an expert.

Table 1. Overview of the used datasets – # is an abbreviation for number. The class imbalance is given as the percentage of the smallest and largest class with regard to the complete dataset. $\hat{p}_A$ is the expected prior ambiguity probability of the dataset. n is the average of annotations per image.

Name	# Classes	Input size [px]	# Images			Class imbalance [%]		$\hat{p}_A$ [%]	n
			Train	Val	Unlabeled	Smallest	Largest		
Plankton [42]	10	96×96	1964	2456	7860	4.16	30.37	44	24
Turkey [55]	2	96×96	1299	1542	5199	9.66	90.33	22	3
Mice Bone [46]	3	224×224	277	169	278	10.81	63.98	65	3
CIFAR-10H [38]	10	32×32	1600	2000	6400	9.88	10.16	32	51

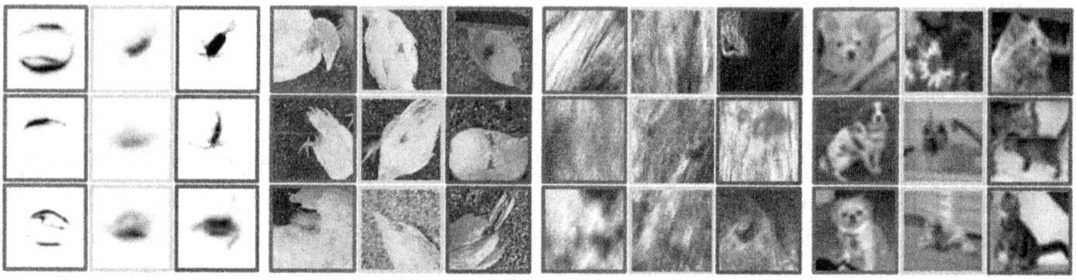

(a) Plankton [42]   (b) Turkey [56]   (c) Mice Bone [46]   (d) CIFAR-10H [38]

Fig. 3. Example images for the ambiguous real-world datasets – All datasets have certain images (red & blue) and ambiguous images between these classes (grey). The classes are Bubble & Copepod, Not Injured & Injured, Similar & Dissimilar Orientations and Dog & Cat respectively. (Color figure online)

The *CIFAR-10H* [38] dataset provides multiple annotations for the test set of CIFAR-10 [28]. This dataset is interesting because it illustrates that even the hard labels from benchmark datasets like CIFAR-10 are based on soft labels due to IIV.

As stated above the approximation of $\hat{l}$ is only possible with multiple annotations per image. For the *STL-10* dataset [12], only one annotation/label per image is given. We still include some results of this dataset to illustrate the performance on previous benchmarks.

For all datasets, we split our images X into a labeled X_l and an unlabeled X_u training set. We keep additional images as a validation subset. On X_l, we use for each image a random hard label sampled from the corresponding $\hat{l}$. This simulates the noisy approximation of the true ground truth label l. On X_u, we can only use the image information and not any label information. The validation data is used to compare the trained networks and to detect issues like overfitting.

3.2 Metrics

We want to measure the quality of classification and clusters over the certain and ambiguous data respectively which we assume are better proposals in the annotation or evaluation process. Based on this reasoning, we decided to use the weighted F1-Score on certain data and the mean inner distance on ambiguous data, The ambiguity is determined by the network output p_a. We define the metrics in detail below and give in Subsect. 3.5 a proof-of-concept for the higher consistency of labels based on proposals selected by the defined metrics. Common metrics like accuracy are not used as the class imbalance of several of our datasets would lead to misleading results.

During training we do not enforce a balance between ambiguous and certain predictions to keep the required prior knowledge minimal. This can lead to uninformative metrics and therefore we call a training *degenerated* if no more than 10% of the validation data are either predicted as ambiguous or certain. We use the *weighted F1-Score* on certain images, based on the number of images per class to avoid instability due to classes with no or very few certain (predicted) images. For the ambiguous images, we use the mean inner euclidean distance (d) to the centroid on the soft/ambiguous Ground-Truth (GT) labels. The metric d is based on the soft GT and thus also minimal for classifications of the majority class which allows an evaluation also on classified data. The equation for a set of clusters of images X is given in Eq. 4 with sets $C \in X$ as clusters and the corresponding approximated soft label distribution $\hat{l}_x$ for each image $x \in C$. The centroid per cluster is given as μ_C.

$$d(X) := \frac{1}{|X|} \sum_{C \in X} \frac{1}{|C|} \sum_{x \in C} ||\hat{l}_x - \mu_C||_2 \text{ with}$$

$$\mu_C := \frac{1}{|C|} \sum_{x \in C} \hat{l}_x \tag{4}$$

We use the vanilla (unchanged) SSL algorithms as baseline experiments. For these experiments and some ablation experiments, we have no ambiguity prediction $p_a(x)$. In these cases, we assume all images to be certain and use $p_n(x)$ as output. We often noticed that the classification improved while the clustering degenerated and the other way round. Therefore, we determine the best performance considering the difference ($d-$F1) between distance and F1-Score (smaller is better). It is important to note that this balancing is arbitrary, but we give a proof of concept that the proposals calculated by these metrics lead to more consistent annotations which justifies their definition. In general, we have 3 runs per setup but we exclude results that degenerate as described above. We report the best of these runs based on the ($d-$F1)-score over all non-degenerated runs. All scores are calculated on the validation data which is in general about 20% of all the data (see details in Table 1).

3.3   Implementation Details

All methods use the same code base and share major hyperparameters which is crucial for valid comparisons [27]. We use the prior ambiguity $p_A = 0.6$ and loss weights $\lambda_{CE^{-1}} = 10$, $\lambda_f = 0.1$ and $\lambda_s = 0.1$ across all experiments. It is important to note that we do not use the actual prior probability of ambiguous images

$\hat{p}_A$ as given in Table 1 because the probability is unknown or would require multiple annotations per image. We use a constant approximation across all datasets and show in Sect. 4 that this approximation is comparable or even better than $\hat{p}_A$. This parameter is essential for balancing the certain and ambiguous images. The batch size was 64 for all datasets except for the mice bone dataset with a batch size of 8. The additional losses L_A and L_S are only applied on the unlabeled data while $L_{CE^{-1}}$ is also calculated on the labeled data. These hyperparameters were determined heuristically on the Plankton dataset with Mean-Teacher and show strong results across different methods and datasets as shown in Subsect. 3.4. Most likely these parameters are not optimal for an individual combination of a method and a dataset but they show the general applicability across methods and datasets. We want to show that DC3 can be applied successfully to other datasets without hyperparameter optimization and thus did not investigate all combinations in detail. Nevertheless, we refer to the supplementary for more detailed insights about individual hyperparameters and the complete pseudo code for the loss calculation.

3.4   Evaluation

The comparison between different SSL algorithms and their extension with DC3 is given in Table 2. The best results were selected as described in Subsect. 3.2. The complete results and additional plots are given in the supplementary. We see that DC3 improves the classification and clustering performance across the majority of classes and methods by 5 to 10%. $(d-F1)$ is improved by up to 40% for 16 out of 19 method-dataset-combinations. On average, we achieve a 7.6% higher F1-Score for certain classifications and a 7.9% lower inner distance for clusterings of ambiguous images if we look at all non excluded method-dataset-combinations. Even on STL-10 (without the possibility to evaluate ambiguous labels) DC3 creates up to 9% better classifications. Overall, we see the most benefit on the Mice Bone and Turkey dataset which we attribute to the worse

Table 2. Performance across different methods and datasets – The vanilla algorithm is highlighted in light grey. Better results in comparison to the vanilla algorithm are marked bold. The definition of the metrics are given in Subsect. 3.2. CE stands for supervised Cross-Entropy training. All values are given in %. Reasons for exclusion: H - Hardware Restrictions

Methods	Plankton			Turkey			Mice Bone			CIFAR-10H			STL-10
	F1 ↑	d ↓	(d−F1) ↓	F1 ↑	d ↓	(d−F1) ↓	F1 ↑	d ↓	(d−F1) ↓	F1 ↑	d ↓	(d−F1) ↓	F1 ↑
CE	86.71	30.45	−56.26	83.84	42.98	−40.86	69.55	54.75	−14.80	67.71	55.80	−11.91	80.48
CE + DC3	78.24	**23.41**	−54.84	**85.79**	**27.64**	**−58.14**	**93.88**	**36.58**	**57.30**	**78.27**	**54.52**	**−23.75**	**88.45**
Mean-Teacher [52]	88..72	25.84	−62.88	81.82	45.12	−36.70	66.41	48.83	−17.58	73.53	46.93	−26.59	80.67
Mean-Teacher [52] + DC3	**91.30**	**24.84**	**−66.46**	**86.45**	**33.92**	**−52.53**	**89.4**	**35.11**	**−54.73**	**85.13**	**52.44**	**−32.69**	**89.28**
Pi-Model [30]	87.57	28.43	−59.14	82.11	39.46	−42.65	68.15	54.11	−14.04	71.53	49.13	−22.40	82.56
Pi-Model [30] + DC3	79.79	**19.08**	−60.71	**87.43**	**23.33**	**−64.10**	**88.01**	**30.99**	**−57.02**	**83.05**	**43.40**	**−39.65**	**89.54**
Pseudo-Label [31]	87.62	27.42	−60.20	82.37	44.88	−37.49	66.60	57.03	−9.57	69.70	53.30	−16.40	82.48
Pseudo-Label [31] + DC3	**89.31**	31.76	−57.55	**83.44**	**35.04**	**−48.41**	**86.58**	**37.52**	**−49.06**	**83.74**	**51.32**	**−32.42**	**88.87**
FixMatch [48]	85.81	30.29	−55.52	82.14	43.33	−38.81	H	H	H	78.09	41.99	−36.10	89.35
FixMatch [48] + DC3	**87.20**	31.28	**−55.92**	**83.56**	**28.17**	**−55.39**	H	H	H	**83.09**	49.49	**−33.60**	**91.45**

Table 3. Consistency comparison of generated labels from proposals – The first column describes the annotator selection and the used proposals. The Cohen's kappa coefficient κ measures the agreement of between the used repetitions and Time gives annotation time in minutes. Results which are within one percent or minute of the best result per dataset and annotator selection are marked bold.

	Plankton		Turkey		Mice Bone		CIFAR-10H	
	κ [%] ↑	Time [min] ↓	κ [%] ↑	Time [min] ↓	κ [%] ↑	Time [min] ↓	κ [%] ↑	Tim [min] ↓
A1	73.00 ± 1.51	51.09 ± 2.36	88.08 ± 3.43	14.56 ± 0.84	71,35 ± 2.56	13,94 ± 2.25	92.70 ± 1.69	40.58 ± 1.93
A1 + SSL	85.00 ± 2.52	12.69 ± 3.37	85.63 ± 3.66	10.70 ± 0.44	72.00 ± 2.87	6.59 ± 1.65	94.85 ± 0.91	14.33 ± 1.48
A1 + DC3	90.29 ± 1.41	11.32 ± 1.43	91.95 ± 1.22	11.57 ± 0.64	81.36 ± 2.17	6.74 ± 1.05	94.70 ± 0.52	14.65 ± 0.60
A2	85.25 ± 1.79	61.99 ± 10.98	81.54 ± 0.89	18.11 ± 4.30	68.63 ± 6.66	11.06 ± 3.60	98.81 ± 0.14	33.08 ± 5.36
A2 + SSL	94.88 ± 0.52	9.23 ± 0.76	81.10 ± 3.39	9.48 ± 0.83	59.63 ± 6.20	12.07 ± 4.77	98.00 ± 0.27	12.66 ± 0.69
A2 + DC3	94.04 ± 0.67	10.32 ± 0.07	81.83 ± 1.98	9.91 ± 0.39	72.19 ± 3.23	9.13 ± 2.98	98.29 ± 0.19	14.27 ± 0.69
A3	84.74 ± 1.02	21.54 ± 1.54	78.27 ± 1.08	19.35 ± 1.16	56.27 ± 4.03	10.15 ± 2.12	93.22 ± 1.01	21.96 ± 1.10
A3 + SSL	88.59 ± 0.84	9.02 ± 0.20	88.44 ± 1.74	13.24 ± 0.32	72.32 ± 0.61	8.02 ± 1.23	92.37 ± 1.78	9.79 ± 0.52
A3 + DC3	88.57 ± 0.62	7.76 ± 0.27	91.94 ± 1.04	14.05 ± 0.51	72.77 ± 2.74	9.56 ± 1.71	94.81 ± 0.96	9.50 ± 0.74

initial approximation of $\hat{l}$. The different vanilla algorithms achieve quite similar results for each dataset. Only FixMatch achieves a more than 5% better F1-Score on the curated STL-10 and CIFAR-10H dataset. In general, we see that DC3 can be beneficially applied to a variety of datasets and methods and predicts better classifications and more compact clusters.

Additional results about the impact of ambiguous data, the unlabeled data ratio and the interpretabiliy can be found in the supplementary.

3.5 Proof-of-Concept Improved Data Quality

We show above that DC3 can lead to better classifications and clusters than SSL alone. In accordance with previous literature [42, 44], we give a proof-of-concept in Table 3 that the annotation process can be improved with cluster-based proposals. As an SSL algorithm we used Mean-Teacher and for the datasets Plankton, Turkey and CIFAR-10H we used a random subsample of 10% for the evaluation. We conducted experiments with a pool of 6 annotators which consisted of domain experts and inexperienced hired workers which were paid a fixed wage per hour. We assigned 3 annotators from the pool per dataset. This means that annotator named e.g. A1 might be a different person between datasets in Table 3. We compare the annotations over time from each annotator. We investigated three different proposals for the annotation. The baseline is not using any proposals, the second is using the SSL predictions (classification) and the third is using the DC3 predictions (classification + clusters). For each cluster, a rough description was given as guidance during the annotation. After a training phase for the inexperienced annotators, we averaged across three repetitions for every annotator, proposal and dataset combination.

Table 4. Ablation results averaged over different methods – The vanilla algorithms/baselines are highlighted in light grey. Each lower row extends this baseline individually with CE^{-1} [42], Clustering & Classification (CC) or both (DC3). CC can be interpreted as DC3 without CE^{-1}. The prior ambiguity estimate p_A is given in brackets if applicable. Results that improve over the baseline are marked in bold. The metrics are defined in Subsect. 3.2. The column 'Ambiguous' gives the percentage of predicted ambiguous data and the last column gives the number of non-degenerated runs over which we averaged

	F1		d		$(d{-}F1)$		Ambiguous		# Runs
	best	mean ± std	best	mean ± std	best	mean ± std	best	mean ± std	
CIFAR-10H									
Baseline	0.7809	0.7153 ± 0.0359	0.4199	0.5027 ± 0.0469	-0.3611	-0.2126 ± 0.0827	-	-	15
+ CE^{-1}	0.7383	**0.7191 ± 0.0164**	0.4692	**0.4929 ± 0.0243**	-0.2691	-0.2262 ± 0.0404	-	-	12
+ CC ($p_A = 0.6$)	**0.8565**	**0.7471 ± 0.1246**	0.8657	0.8768 ± 0.0129	0.0092	0.1297 ± 0.1374	0.6145	0.5923 ± 0.0322	12
+ DC3 ($p_A = 0.32$)	0.6656	0.6970 ± 0.0469	0.2155	0.3684 ± 0.1227	-0.4501	-0.3286 ± 0.0836	0.2910	0.3115 ± 0.0140	12
+ DC3 ($p_A = 0.6$)	**0.8305**	**0.7457 ± 0.1097**	0.4340	**0.4741 ± 0.0584**	-0.3965	**-0.2716 ± 0.0928**	0.6125	0.5860 ± 0.0290	15
Plankton									
Baseline	0.8872	0.8652 ± 0.0212	0.2584	0.2915 ± 0.0240	-0.6287	-0.5737 ± 0.0444	-	-	15
+ CE^{-1}	**0.8896**	**0.8803 ± 0.0060**	0.2540	0.2690 ± 0.0098	-0.6356	-0.6113 ± 0.0154	-	-	12
+ CC ($p_A = 0.6$)	**0.8919**	**0.9128 ± 0.0427**	0.4085	0.7702 ± 0.1630	-0.4833	-0.1426 ± 0.1375	0.6242	0.5927 ± 0.0127	12
+ DC3 ($p_A = 0.44$)	0.8625	**0.9049 ± 0.0340**	0.2192	0.3269 ± 0.0526	-0.6433	-0.5780 ± 0.0305	0.4365	0.4451 ± 0.0204	11
+ DC3 ($p_A = 0.6$)	**0.9130**	**0.8768 ± 0.0640**	0.2484	0.3004 ± 0.0750	-0.6646	-0.5764 ± 0.0416	0.6164	0.5893 ± 0.0202	14
Turkey									
Baseline	0.8211	0.8213 ± 0.0069	0.3946	0.4428 ± 0.0209	-0.4265	-0.3786 ± 0.0230	-	-	15
+ CE^{-1}	0.7998	0.7998 ± 0.0000	**0.3338**	**0.3338 ± 0.0000**	-0.4660	-0.4660 ± 0.0000	-	-	12
+ CC ($p_A = 0.6$)	**0.8527**	**0.8264 ± 0.0469**	0.3400	0.3435 ± 0.0408	-0.5127	-0.4829 ± 0.0128	0.5837	0.5646 ± 0.0427	12
+ DC3 ($p_A = 0.22$)	0.7998	0.7998 ± 0.0000	**0.1675**	**0.2252 ± 0.0646**	-0.6322	-0.5746 ± 0.0646	0.5000	0.3674 ± 0.2054	4
+ DC3 ($p_A = 0.6$)	**0.8743**	**0.8432 ± 0.0350**	**0.2333**	**0.3270 ± 0.0692**	-0.6410	-0.5162 ± 0.0643	0.8093	0.6387 ± 0.2354	12

We see a general trend that the consistency improves and the annotation time decreases when proposals are used instead of None. Using DC3 proposals instead of SSL proposals, either leads to a similar or better consistency while the annotation time is often increased by one or two minutes. For this improvement, we credit the cleaner and more fine-grained outputs of the network. The additional verifications of the clusters could lead to the slightly increased annotation time. The individual benefits vary between the datasets and annotators. For example, the gains on the curated CIFAR-10H dataset are lower than on the uncurated Mice Bone dataset. On average across all annotators and datasets, we achieve an improved consistency of 6.74%, a relative speed-up of 2.4 and a maximum speed-up of 4.5 with DC3 proposals in comparison to the baseline.

4   Discussion

Ablation Study. We pooled the runs between all methods to evaluate the impact of the individual components of our method DC3 and show the results in Table 4. The method FixMatch and the Mice Bone dataset are excluded from this ablation due to the up to 12 times higher required GPU hours and degenerated runs as before. Across the datasets, we see the best $(d{-}F1)$-scores are achieved by DC3. The impact of the components varies between the datasets. We see that CE^{-1} positively impacts the clustering results which confirms the benefit of using CE^{-1} for overclustering [42]. CC often reaches a better F1-Score than the baseline and even surpasses DC3 sometimes. However, the inner distance (d) may increase as well. We conclude that CC and CE^{-1} on their own can lead to improvements but only the combination of both parts results in a stable algorithm across datasets and methods. Additionally, we see that the number of not degenerated runs is highest with the combination of CE^{-1} and CC. If we use an realistic amount of ambiguity $\hat{p}_A$ in each dataset as p_A, we see that in general the F1-Score decreases and d-score improves. We attribute this difference to the lower prior ambiguity p_A because DC3 tries to predict more certain than ambiguous images. This leads to a lower inner distance but also includes more difficult images in the classification of the certain data. We believe this parameter is essential for balancing the improvements in the F1- and d-score for a specified usecase. We chose a p_A of 0.6 because we wanted to weight certain and ambiguous images almost equally but ensure very certain /fewer classifications.

Qualitative Analysis with t-SNE. We investigated some t-SNE [33] visualizations in Fig. 4. Comparing the predicted (DC3) classes and ambiguity with the ground truth (GT), we see more wrong classifications on ambiguous images. DC3 outputs higher ambiguity than expected due to the higher value of p_A, but the predicted ambiguous clusters are often located nearby of ambiguous regions in the GT. Additionally, the clusters in (c) partition the feature space in smaller regions which can be more easily verified by humans as shown in Subsect. 3.5. Overall, we see a better representation of the ambiguous feature space.

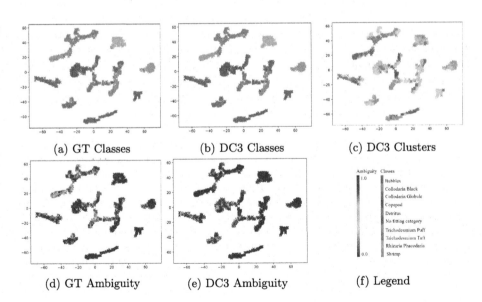

(a) GT Classes	(b) DC3 Classes	(c) DC3 Clusters
(d) GT Ambiguity	(e) DC3 Ambiguity	(f) Legend

Fig. 4. t-SNE plots for Plankton dataset with Mean-Teacher – The same color was used 2–3 times for different clusters to ensure distinct colors. (Color figure online)

Limitations. We showed that DC3 generalizes to different SSL algorithms and datasets without hyperparameter changes. However, the datasets only consist of up to several thousand images. Due to the required multiple annotations per image for the evaluation it is difficult to obtain datasets with millions of images. We focused on improving the classification and clustering and gave a proof-of-concept for the increased consistency of relabeled data. Due to the required human labor during the relabeling step, we could not investigate the consistency across more datasets and algorithms or investigate the usage of the improved data. We proposed to improve the annotation process based on human-validated network predictions. This could introduce a not-desired bias into the data. This might lead to a negative impact for humans or a group of humans for certain use-cases but we believe a small bias can be accepted in most applications because it is human controlled and systematically.

5   Conclusion

In real-world datasets, we often encounter ambiguous labels, due to intra- or interobserver variability, but also as intermediate classes might exist. We propose our method DC3 which is an extension to many SSL algorithms and allows to classify images with certain labels and cluster ambiguous ones. DC3 also automatically determines which image should be treated as certain or ambiguous only based on a given prior probability p_A. On average, we achieve an increased F1-Score of 7.6% and a lower inner distance of clusters of 7.9% over all method-dataset-combinations. We give a proof-of-concept that these improved predictions can be used beneficially as proposals to create more consistent annotations. On average, we achieve an improved consistency of 6.74% and a relative speed-up of 2.4 when using DC3 proposals instead of no proposals. Therefore, SSL algorithms with DC3 are better suited to handle real-world datasets including ambiguous labeled images either by an improved classification / clustering or as a proposal during the annotation process with more insight.

Acknowledgements. We acknowledge funding of LS by the ARTEMIS project (grant no. 01EC1908E) funded by the Federal Ministry of Education and Research (BMBF), Germany. SMS was funded by BMBF projects CUSCO (grant no. 03F0813D) and MOSAiC (grant no. 03F0917B). RKi was supported via a "Make Our Planet Great Again" grant of the French National Research Agency within the "Programme d'Investissements d'Avenir"; reference "ANR-19-MPGA-0012". Funding for Plank-tonID project were granted to RKi and RKo (CP1733) by the Cluster of Excellence 80 "Future Ocean" within the Excellence Initiative by the Deutsche Forschungsgemein-schaft on behalf of the German federal and state governments. Turkey data set was collected in the project "RedAlert - detection of pecking injuries in turkeys using neu-ral networks" which was supported by the "Animal Welfare Innovation Award" of the "Initiative Tierwohl".

References

1. Addison, P.F.E.E., et al.: A new wave of marine evidence-based management: emerging challenges and solutions to transform monitoring, evaluating, and reporting. ICES J. Mar. Sci. **75**(3), 941–952 (2018). https://doi.org/10.1093/icesjms/fsx216
2. Algan, G., Ulusoy, I.: Image classification with deep learning in the presence of noisy labels: a survey. Knowl.-Based Syst. (2020). https://doi.org/10.1016/j.knosys.2021.106771
3. Berthelot, D., Carlini, N., Goodfellow, I., Papernot, N., Oliver, A., Raffel, C.A.: Mixmatch: a holistic approach to semi-supervised learning. In: Advances in Neural Information Processing Systems, pp. 5050–5060 (2019)
4. Beyer, L., Hénaff, O.J., Kolesnikov, A., Zhai, X., van den Oord, A.: Are we done with ImageNet? arXiv preprint arXiv:2006.07159 (2020)
5. Brünger, J., Dippel, S., Koch, R., Veit, C.: 'Tailception': using neural networks for assessing tail lesions on pictures of pig carcasses. Animal **13**(5), 1030–1036 (2019). https://doi.org/10.1017/S1751731118003038
6. Cai, W., Chen, S., Zhang, D.: A simultaneous learning framework for clustering and classification. Pattern Recogn. **42**(7), 1248–1259 (2009). https://doi.org/10.1016/j.patcog.2008.11.029
7. Caron, M., Bojanowski, P., Joulin, A., Douze, M.: Deep clustering for unsupervised learning of visual features. In: Proceedings of the European Conference on Computer Vision (ECCV), pp. 132–149 (2018)
8. Caron, M., Goyal, P., Misra, I., Bojanowski, P., Mairal, J., Joulin, A.: Unsupervised Learning of Visual Features by Contrasting Cluster Assignments. In: Proceedings of Advances in Neural Information Processing Systems (NeurIPS) (2020)
9. Cevikalp, H., Benligiray, B., Gerek, O.N.: Semi-supervised robust deep neural networks for multi-label image classification. Pattern Recogn. **100**, 107164 (2020). https://doi.org/10.1016/j.patcog.2019.107164
10. Chapelle, O., Scholkopf, B., Zien, A., Schölkopf, B., Zien, A.: Semi-supervised learning. IEEE Trans. Neural Netw. **20**(3), 542 (2006)
11. Chen, T., Kornblith, S., Swersky, K., Norouzi, M., Hinton, G.: Big self-supervised models are strong semi-supervised learners. In: Advances in Neural Information Processing Systems 33 Pre-Proceedings (NeurIPS 2020) (2020)
12. Coates, A., Ng, A., Lee, H.: An analysis of single-layer networks in unsupervised feature learning. In: Proceedings of the Fourteenth International Conference on Artificial Intelligence and Statistics, pp. 215–223 (2011)
13. Crawford, K., Paglen, T.: Excavating AI: the politics of images in machine learning training sets. AI Soc. 1–12. https://doi.org/10.1007/s00146-021-01162-8
14. Culverhouse, P., Williams, R., Reguera, B., Herry, V., González-Gil, S.: Do experts make mistakes? A comparison of human and machine identification of dinoflagellates. Mar. Ecol. Prog. Ser. **247**, 17–25 (2003). https://doi.org/10.3354/meps247017
15. Damm, T., et al.: Artificial intelligence-driven hip fracture prediction based on pelvic radiographs exceeds performance of DXA: the "study of osteoporotic fractures" (SOF). J. Bone Miner. Res. **37**, 193–193 (2021)
16. De Fauw, J., et al.: Clinically applicable deep learning for diagnosis and referral in retinal disease. Nat. Med. **24**(9), 1342–1350 (2018)
17. Gao, B.B., Xing, C., Xie, C.W., Wu, J., Geng, X.: Deep label distribution learning with label ambiguity. IEEE Trans. Image Process. **26**(6), 2825–2838 (2017)

18. Grill, J.B., et al.: Bootstrap your own latent: a new approach to self-supervised learning. In: Advances in Neural Information Processing Systems 33 Pre-proceedings (NeurIPS 2020) (2020)
19. Grossmann, V., Schmarje, L., Koch, R.: Beyond hard labels: investigating data label distributions. arXiv preprint arXiv:2207.06224 (2022)
20. He, K., et al.: Mask R-CNN. In: Proceedings of the IEEE International Conference on Computer Vision, pp. 2961–2969 (2017)
21. Jenckel, M., Parkala, S.S., Bukhari, S.S., Dengel, A.: Impact of training LSTM-RNN with fuzzy ground truth. In: ICPRAM (2018)
22. Ji, X., Henriques, J.F., Vedaldi, A.: Invariant information clustering for unsupervised image classification and segmentation. In: Proceedings of the IEEE International Conference on Computer Vision, pp. 9865–9874. No. Iic (2019)
23. Jungo, A., et al.: On the effect of inter-observer variability for a reliable estimation of uncertainty of medical image segmentation. In: Frangi, A.F., Schnabel, J.A., Davatzikos, C., Alberola-López, C., Fichtinger, G. (eds.) MICCAI 2018. LNCS, vol. 11070, pp. 682–690. Springer, Cham (2018). https://doi.org/10.1007/978-3-030-00928-1_77
24. Karimi, D., Nir, G., Fazli, L., Black, P.C., Goldenberg, L., Salcudean, S.E.: Deep learning-based Gleason grading of prostate cancer from histopathology images-role of multiscale decision aggregation and data augmentation. IEEE J. Biomed. Health Inf. $24(5)$, 1413–1426 (2020). https://doi.org/10.1109/JBHI.2019.2944643
25. Karimi, D., Dou, H., Warfield, S.K., Gholipour, A.: Deep learning with noisy labels: exploring techniques and remedies in medical image analysis. Med. Image Anal. 65, 101759 (2020)
26. Kim, B., Choo, J., Kwon, Y.D., Joe, S., Min, S., Gwon, Y.: SelfMatch: combining contrastive self-supervision and consistency for semi-supervised learning (NeurIPS) (2021)
27. Kolesnikov, A., Zhai, X., Beyer, L.: Revisiting self-supervised visual representation learning. In: Proceedings of the IEEE conference on Computer Vision and Pattern Recognition, pp. 1920–1929 (2019)
28. Krizhevsky, A., Hinton, G., Others: Learning multiple layers of features from tiny images. Technical Report (2009)
29. Krizhevsky, A., Sutskever, I., Hinton, G.E.: ImageNet classification with deep convolutional neural networks. In: Advances in Neural Information Processing Systems, vol. 60, pp. 1097–1105. Association for Computing Machinery (2012). https://doi.org/10.1145/3065386
30. Laine, S., Aila, T.: Temporal ensembling for semi-supervised learning. In: International Conference on Learning Representations (2017)
31. Lee, D.H.: Pseudo-label: the simple and efficient semi-supervised learning method for deep neural networks. In: Workshop on Challenges in Representation Learning, ICML, vol. 3, p. 2 (2013)
32. Li, J., Socher, R., Hoi, S.C.H.: DivideMix: learning with noisy labels as semi-supervised learning. In: International Conference on Learning Representations, pp. 1–14 (2020)
33. der Maaten, L., Hinton, G.: Visualizing data using t-SNE. J. Mach. Learn. Res. $9(11)$, 2579–2605 (2008)
34. Menon, A.K., et al.: Disentangling sampling and labeling bias for learning in large-output spaces. In: International Conference on Machine Learning (2021)
35. Motamedi, M., Sakharnykh, N., Kaldewey, T.: A data-centric approach for training deep neural networks with less data. In: NeurIPS 2021 Data-centric AI Workshop (2021)

36. Ooms, E.A., et al.: Mammography: interobserver variability in breast density assessment. Breast **16**(6), 568–576 (2007). https://doi.org/10.1016/j.breast.2007.04.007

37. Peikari, M., Salama, S., Nofech-mozes, S., Martel, A.L.: A cluster-then-label semi-supervised learning approach for pathology image classification. Sci. Rep. 1–13 (2018). https://doi.org/10.1038/s41598-018-24876-0

38. Peterson, J., Battleday, R., Griffiths, T., Russakovsky, O.: Human uncertainty makes classification more robust. In: Proceedings of the IEEE International Conference on Computer Vision 2019-October, pp. 9616–9625 (2019). https://doi.org/10.1109/ICCV.2019.00971

39. Pham, H., Dai, Z., Xie, Q., Luong, M.T., Le, Q.V.: Meta Pseudo Labels (2020)

40. Qian, Q., Chen, S., Cai, W.: Simultaneous clustering and classification over cluster structure representation. Pattern Recogn. **45**(6), 2227–2236 (2012). https://doi.org/10.1016/j.patcog.2011.11.027

41. Santarossa, M., et al.: MedRegNet: unsupervised multimodal retinal-image registration with GANs and ranking loss. In: Medical Imaging 2022: Image Processing, vol. 12032, pp. 321–333. SPIE (2022)

42. Schmarje, L., Brünger, J., Santarossa, M., Schröder, S.M., Kiko, R., Koch, R.: Fuzzy Overclustering: semi-supervised classification of fuzzy labels with overclustering and inverse cross-entropy. Sensors **21**(19), 6661 (2021). https://doi.org/10.3390/s21196661

43. Schmarje, L., et al.: Is one annotation enough? A data-centric image classification benchmark for noisy and ambiguous label estimation. arXiv preprint arXiv:2207.06214 (2022)

44. Schmarje, L., Koch, R.: Life is not black and white - combining semi-supervised learning with fuzzy labels. In: Proceedings of the Conference "Lernen, Wissen, Daten, Analysen" (2021)

45. Schmarje, L., Liao, Y.H., Koch, R.: A data-centric image classification benchmark. In: NeurIPS 2021 Data-centric AI workshop (2021)

46. Schmarje, L., Zelenka, C., Geisen, U., Glüer, C.-C., Koch, R.: 2D and 3D segmentation of uncertain local collagen fiber orientations in SHG microscopy. In: Fink, G.A., Frintrop, S., Jiang, X. (eds.) DAGM GCPR 2019. LNCS, vol. 11824, pp. 374–386. Springer, Cham (2019). https://doi.org/10.1007/978-3-030-33676-9_26

47. Śmieja, M., Struski, Ł., Figueiredo, M.A.T.: A classification-based approach to semi-supervised clustering with pairwise constraints (2020)

48. Sohn, K., et al.: FixMatch: simplifying semi-supervised learning with consistency and confidence. In: Advances in Neural Information Processing Systems 33 Pre-proceedings (NeurIPS 2020) (2020)

49. Song, H., Kim, M., Park, D., Lee, J.G., Shin, Y., Lee, J.G.: Learning from noisy labels with deep neural networks: a survey. In: IEEE Transactions on Neural Networks and Learning Systems, pp. 1–19 (2022). https://doi.org/10.1109/TNNLS.2022.3152527

50. Tajbakhsh, N., Jeyaseelan, L., Li, Q., Chiang, J.N., Wu, Z., Ding, X.: Embracing imperfect datasets: a review of deep learning solutions for medical image segmentation. Med. Image Anal. **63**, 101693 (2020). https://doi.org/10.1016/j.media.2020.101693

51. Tarling, P., Cantor, M., Clapés, A., Escalera, S.: Deep learning with self-supervision and uncertainty regularization to count fish in underwater images, pp. 1–22 (2021)

52. Tarvainen, A., Valpola, H.: Mean teachers are better role models: weight-averaged consistency targets improve semi-supervised deep learning results. In: ICLR (2017)

53. Tian, Y., Henaff, O.J., van den Oord, A.: Divide and contrast: self-supervised Learning from uncurated data (2021)
54. Van Gansbeke, W., Vandenhende, S., Georgoulis, S., Proesmans, M., Van Gool, L.: Scan: learning to classify images without labels. In: Proceedings of the European Conference on Computer Vision, pp. 268–285 (2020)
55. Volkmann, N., et al.: So much trouble in the herd: detection of first signs of cannibalism in turkeys. In: Recent Advances in Animal Welfare Science VII Virtual UFAW Animal Welfare Conference, p. 82 (2020)
56. Volkmann, N., et al.: Learn to train: improving training data for a neural network to detect pecking injuries in turkeys. Animals **2021**(11), 1–13 (2021). https://doi.org/10.3390/ani11092655
57. Volkmann, N., et al.: Keypoint detection for injury identification during turkey husbandry using neural networks. Sensors **22**(14), 5188 (2022). https://doi.org/10.3390/s22145188
58. Wei, Y., Feng, J., Liang, X., Cheng, M.M.: Object region mining with adversarial erasing : a simple classification to object region mining with adversarial. In: CVPR (March), pp. 1568–1576 (2017)
59. Xie, Q., et al.: Self-training with noisy student improves ImageNet classification. In: IEEE/CVF Conference on Computer Vision and Pattern Recognition (CVPR), pp. 10684–10695. IEEE (2020). https://doi.org/10.1109/CVPR42600.2020.01070
60. Yun, S., Oh, S.J., Heo, B., Han, D., Choe, J., Chun, S.: Re-labeling ImageNet: from single to multi-labels, from global to localized labels. In: Proceedings of the IEEE/CVF Conference on Computer Vision and Pattern Recognition (CVPR), pp. 2340–2350 (2021)
61. Zbontar, J., Jing, L., Misra, I., LeCun, Y., Deny, S.: Barlow twins: self-supervised learning via redundancy reduction (2021)

ClearPose: Large-scale Transparent Object Dataset and Benchmark

Xiaotong Chen[(✉)], Huijie Zhang, Zeren Yu, Anthony Opipari,
and Odest Chadwicke Jenkins

University of Michigan, Ann Arbor, MI 48109, USA
{cxt,huijiezh,yuzeren,topipari,ocj}@umich.edu

Abstract. Transparent objects are ubiquitous in household settings and pose distinct challenges for visual sensing and perception systems. The optical properties of transparent objects leave conventional 3D sensors alone unreliable for object depth and pose estimation. These challenges are highlighted by the shortage of large-scale RGB-Depth datasets focusing on transparent objects in real-world settings. In this work, we contribute a large-scale real-world RGB-Depth transparent object dataset named *ClearPose* to serve as a benchmark dataset for segmentation, scene-level depth completion and object-centric pose estimation tasks. The ClearPose dataset contains over 350K labeled real-world RGB-Depth frames and 5M instance annotations covering 63 household objects. The dataset includes object categories commonly used in daily life under various lighting and occluding conditions as well as challenging test scenarios such as cases of occlusion by opaque or translucent objects, non-planar orientations, presence of liquids, etc. We benchmark several state-of-the-art depth completion and object pose estimation deep neural networks on ClearPose. The dataset and benchmarking source code is available at https://github.com/opipari/ClearPose.

Keywords: Transparent objects · Depth completion · Pose estimation · Dataset and benchmark

1 Introduction

Transparent and translucent objects are prevalent in daily life and household settings. When compared with opaque and Lambertian objects, they present additional challenges to visual perception systems. The first challenge is that transparent objects do not exhibit consistent RGB color features across varying scenes. Since the visual appearance of these objects depends on a given scene's background, lighting, and organization, their visual features can drastically differ

---

Supplementary Information The online version contains supplementary material available at https://doi.org/10.1007/978-3-031-20074-8_22.

S. Avidan et al. (Eds.): ECCV 2022, LNCS 13668, pp. 381–396, 2022.
https://doi.org/10.1007/978-3-031-20074-8_22

between scenes thereby confounding feature-based perception systems. The second challenge is the inaccurate depth measurements among RGB-Depth (RGB-D) cameras on transparent or translucent materials due to the lack of reliable reflections. This challenge is especially meaningful for state-of-the-art pose estimation approaches that require accurate depth measurements as input. To overcome these challenges, computational perception algorithms have been proposed for a variety of visual tasks, including image segmentation, depth completion, and object pose estimation. In this paper, our aim is to complement recent work in transparent object perception by providing a large-scale, real-world RGB-D transparent object dataset. Furthermore, we use the new large-scale dataset to perform benchmark analysis of state-of-the-art perception algorithms on transparent object depth completion and pose estimation tasks.

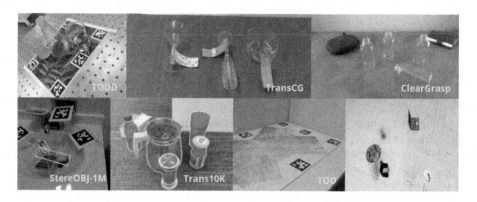

Fig. 1. Sample images from existing transparent datasets. TOD and StereOBJ-1M are collected using stereo RGB cameras, and other datasets used RGB-D cameras (except for Omniverse which is completely synthetic). (Color figure online)

Table 1. Comparison between existing transparent object datasets and ClearPose. *Trans10K is a transparent segmentation dataset and has no object-centric pose labels. *StereObj1M is not publicly available at the time of submission so the #frame and #pose annotation are estimated based on the published ratio of transparent objects in the entire object set [12]

Dataset	Modality	#obj	#Frame	#Pose annotation
TOD [13]	RGB-D	15	48K(real)	∼0.1M
ClearGrasp [15]	RGB-D	10	50K(syn)+286(real)	∼0.2M
TODD [22]	RGB-D	6	15K(real)	∼0.1M
Omniverse [26]	RGB-D	9	60K(syn)	∼0.2M
TransCG [7]	RGB-D	51	58K(real)	∼0.2M
Trans10K* [20]	RGB	10K	15K(real)	Seg only
ProLIT [25]	Light-Field	5	75K(syn)+300(real)	∼0.1M
StereObj1M* [12]	Stereo	7	∼150K(real)	∼0.6M
ClearPose (ours)	RGB-D	63	**350K(real)**	**∼5M**

There are several existing datasets focusing on transparent object perception with commodity RGB stereo or RGB-D sensors, as summarized in Fig. 1. While these datasets target transparent object perception, most are relatively small-scale (no more than 50K real-world frames), include few cluttered scenes (typically with less than 3 objects per image), do not offer diverse categories of commonplace household objects, and record limited lighting changes. These limitations motivate the introduction of **ClearPose**, a large-scale real-world transparent object dataset labeled with ground truth pose, depth, instance-level segmentation masks, surface normals, etc. that (1) has a comparable size with ordinary opaque object pose estimation datasets like YCB-Video [19]; (2) contains challenging heavy clutter scenes including multiple layers of occlusion between transparent objects; (3) contains a variety of commonplace household object categories (bottle, cup, wine, container, bowl, plate, spoon, knife, fork, and some chemical lab supplies); (4) covers diverse lighting conditions and multiple adversarial testing scenes. Further details of ClearPose in relation to existing datasets are included in Table 1 with sample images from ClearPose shown in Fig. 2.

Fig. 2. Sample images from ClearPose dataset. On the left, we show RGB images taken for different object subsets under various lighting conditions and backgrounds. On the right, we show examples of different types of testing scenes, such as covered by a translucent box (top-left), novel background with opaque distractor objects (top-right), non-planar cases (middle-left), filled with liquid (middle-right), and heavy clutters of transparent objects (bottom). (Color figure online)

The labeling of such a large-scale dataset requires both efficiency and accuracy. To achieve these qualities in ClearPose, we take advantage of a recently published pipeline named ProgressLabeller [5]. The ProgressLabeller pipeline combines visual SLAM and an interactive graphical interface with multi-view sil-houette matching-based object alignment to enable efficient and accurate label-ing of the transparent object poses from RGB-D videos, which realizes rapid data annotation and exempts from the broken depth problem by transparent objects. Given the unique scale and relevance of ClearPose, we envision it will serve beneficial as a benchmark dataset on transparent perception tasks. In this current paper, we include benchmark analysis for a set of state-of-the-art visual perception algorithms on ClearPose. We target our benchmark analysis on the tasks of depth completion and RGB-D pose estimation.

2   Related Works

2.1   Transparent Dataset and Annotation

As mentioned in Table 1, there are several existing datasets and associated anno-tation pipelines that focus on transparent objects. With the exception of works such as Trans10k [20], TransCut [23] and TOM-Net [3] that are focused on 2D image segmentation or matting, most recent transparent perception datasets are collected in an object-centric 3D setting using RGB-D, stereo or light-field sensor modalities.

Similar to the case of opaque objects, datasets created in simulation, sup-porting photo-realistic rendering with ray-tracing, are more readily created and can produce very realistic examples of transparent object appearance. Exam-ples of such simulated datasets include those [15] rendered by Blender, [25] by Unreal Engine and [26] by Nvidia Omniverse platform. While simulated datasets are appealing for their ease of creation, they often lack realistic feature artifacts (e.g. sensor noise, object wear marks, true lighting etc.) which can impact down-stream perception systems that rely on the synthetic dataset (i.e. the syn-to-real gap).

Among existing real-world datasets, TOD [13] and StereObj1M [12] use RGB stereo cameras together with AprilTags. First, camera pose transforms are solved from AprilTag detection, and then several 2D keypoints on the objects are man-ually annotated in keyframes that are farthest to each other in the sequence. The corresponding 3D keypoint positions are solved by multi-view triangulation from those labeled 2D keypoints, and finally, the object 6D poses are solved from 3D keypoints as an Orthogonal Procrustes problem and propagated to all frames. In TOD, the authors also introduced a method to record ground truth depth images: they record the positions of transparent objects in the scene, and put their opaque counterparts that share the same shape at the same pose in separate collects. This pipeline was also used for real-world data collection in ClearGrasp [15], however, it's extremely inefficient to replace transparent objects and their counterparts repetitively. Moreover, it is unclear how or whether this approach could be applied to data collection in complex scenes with cluttered objects as is typical in household settings. In Xu et al. [22], transparent objects are placed in several fixed locations relative to AprilTag arrays, with pose dis-tribution diversity achieved by attaching a camera to a robot end-effector. This method still restricts the relative position between objects and is inefficient for complex scenes. In Fang et al. [7], all objects are attached to a large visual IR marker so that an optical tracking algorithm can estimate the objects' 6D poses. In this way, the collection can support dynamic scenes. On the other hand, all the object instances in collected data are accompanied by visually obscuring external labels which may not exist in natural environments.

Overall, datasets except for StereObj1M are still not large-scale and require external efforts on hardware, such as deploying robotic arms, calibration between multiple sensors, fiducial or optical markers. Instead of using markers or complex robotic apparatuses, we take advantage of an existing labeling system, Progress-Labeller [5], that is based on visual SLAM to produce accurate camera poses efficiently on recorded RGB-D videos. There are two assumptions in our labeling pipeline, both of which can be easily met: our pipeline assumes static scenes during video capturing and that scene backgrounds have adequate RGB features for visual SLAM processing.

2.2 Transparent Depth Completion and Object Pose Estimation

Zhang et al. [24] presented early work on the problem of depth completion from inaccurate depth using deep neural networks. Zhang et al. introduced an approach to estimate surface normal and boundaries from RGB images that then solved for the completed depth using optimization. ClearGrasp [15] adapted the method to work for transparent objects and demonstrated robotic grasping experiments on transparent objects from completed depth. Tang et al. [16] integrated the ClearGrasp network structure with adversarial learning to improve depth completion accuracy. Zhu et al. [26] proposed a framework that learns local implicit depth functions from the inspiration of neural radiance fields and performs self-refinement to complete the depth of transparent objects. Xu et al. [22] proposed to first complete the point cloud by projecting the original depth using a 3D encoder-decoder U-Net and then re-project the completed point cloud back to depth, and finally complete this depth using another encoder-decoder network given the ground truth mask. Fang et al. [7] also used a U-Net architecture to perform depth completion and demonstrated robotic grasping capabilities with their approach.

KeyPose [13] was proposed for keypoint-based transparent object pose estimation on stereo images. It outperformed DenseFusion [18], even with ground truth depth, and achieved high accuracy on the TOD dataset. Chang et al. [2] proposed a 3D bounding box representation and reported results comparable to KeyPose in multi-view pose estimation. StereObj1M [12] benchmarked KeyPose and another RGB-based object pose estimator, PVNet [14], on more challenging objects and scenes, where both methods achieved lower accuracy with respect to the ADD-S AUC metric (introduced in [19]) with both monocular and stereo input. Xu et al. [21] proposed a two-stage pose estimation framework that performs image segmentation, surface normal estimation, and plane approximation in the first stage. The second stage then combines output from the first stage

with color and depth RoI features for input to an RGB-D pose estimator originally designed for opaque objects [17] to regress 6D object poses. This method
also outperformed DenseFusion and [17] fed with ClearGrasp output depth by a
large margin. In this paper, we evaluate how well state-of-the-art RGB-D methods [9] designed for opaque object pose estimation can perform on transparent
objects compared with [21].

3   Dataset

3.1   Dataset Objects and Statistics

As shown in Fig. 3, there are 63 objects included in the ClearPose dataset. There
are 49 household objects, including 14 water cups, 9 wine cups (with a thin stem
compared with water cups), 5 bottles (with an opening smaller than the cross-
section of the cylindrical body), 6 bowls, 5 containers (with 4 corners while bowls
are classified with round shapes), and several other objects like pitcher, mug,
spoon, etc. Moreover, the dataset contains 14 chemical supply objects, including
a syringe, a glass stick, 2 reagent bottles, 3 pans, 2 graduated cylinders, a funnel,
a flask, a beaker, and 2 droppers.

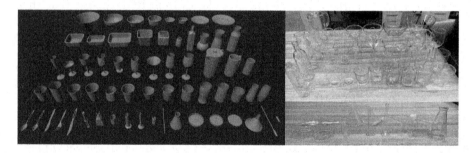

Fig. 3. Objects included in the ClearPose dataset. On the left, we show the rendered
CAD models for each object. From top to bottom there are bowls and plates (1st row),
containers and bottles (2nd row), wine cups, two mugs and a pitcher (3rd row), water
cups (4th row), and spoons, a fork, knives as well as chemical supplies (bottom row).
On the right, we show real images of household objects on the top right, and chemical
supplies on the bottom right.

All the images are collected using a RealSense L515 RGB-depth camera, with
a raw resolution of 1280 × 720. After object pose annotation, the central part of
each image is cropped and reshaped to 640 × 480 for reduced storage space and
faster CNN training and inference. For the training set, we separate all 63 objects
into 5 separate subsets and collected 4–5 scenes with different backgrounds for
each subset. Each scene is scanned by the hand-held camera moving around the
tabletop scene at 3 different heights with 3 different lighting conditions (bright
room light, dim room light, dim room light with sidelight from a photography

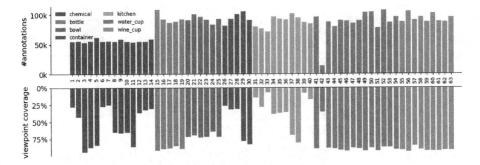

Fig. 4. Distribution of instance annotations and viewpoint orientation coverage statistics for every object in the ClearPose dataset. The 'kitchen' category includes fork, spoon, knife, mug, plate and pitcher objects.

lighting board). For the testing set, as the appearance of transparent objects depends on their context within a scene, we consider 6 different test cases and collect corresponding scenes as follows: (1) different backgrounds: novel backgrounds that never appeared in the training scenes with each object subset. (2) heavy occlusions: cluttered scenes each with about 25 objects that form multiple layers of occlusion when viewed from the table's side. (3) translucent/transparent covers: scenes with all transparent objects placed inside a translucent box. (4) together with opaque objects: transparent objects placed together with opaque YCB and HOPE objects, which did not appear in the training set. (5) filled with liquid: scenes with transparent objects filled with different colored liquid. (6) non-planar configuration: scenes with objects placed onto different surfaces with multiple heights. Sample RGB images from both training and test sets are included in Fig. 2.

We calculate several statistics about the ClearPose dataset. In total there are 354,481 RGB-D frames captured in 51 scenes, with 5,052,429 object instance annotations with 6 DoF poses, segmentation masks, surface normals, and ground truth depth images. The distribution of object instance annotation and camera viewpoint coverage are shown in Fig. 4 colored by object category, where we see our dataset has roughly even viewpoint coverage for most objects. Viewpoint coverage is calculated by projecting collected object orientations onto a unit sphere and counting the covered region percentage over the sphere's surface. For symmetrical objects, regions with the same object appearance are considered together. Some objects like plates, forks, large bowls can only be placed in certain orientations, so they have reduced viewpoint coverage. The 2nd water_cup was broken during the data collection process so it has fewer instance annotations.

3.2 Pose Annotation

We use the ProgressLabeller [5] to annotate the 6D poses of transparent objects and render object-wise segmentation masks, ground truth depths, surface

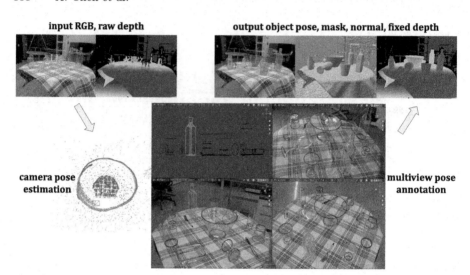

Fig. 5. Transparent object pose annotation pipeline using ProgressLabeller. On top-left we show one sample of aligned RGB-D images from continuous streams captured by the camera. The frames are fed into visual SLAM to estimate camera trajectory, then the objects' poses are annotated in a multi-view silhouette alignment interface shown at the bottom-right. Finally, the object poses, surface normals, and fixed depths are calculated and rendered as output. (Color figure online)

normals, etc. from the labeled poses. As shown in Fig. 5, the first step of the ProgressLabeller pipeline is to run ORB-SLAM3 [1] on collected RGB-D video frames to produce camera pose estimates. During data collection, we notice ORB-SLAM3 sometimes couldn't estimate camera pose well in case of extreme transparent object clutter, where background RGB features are heavily distorted. In these cases, the camera view needs to capture some background area or other landmark objects that can provide stable features. The next step is to import the reconstructed scene (cameras and point cloud) into the Blender workspace, select several camera views from different orientations, and import the object 3D CAD model into the workspace. Then, the object silhouettes/boundaries can be directly compared and matched with original RGB images from multiple views simultaneously when the user drags the object across the scene to tune its position and orientation. Figure 5 shows an example case of a matched transparent bottle. Optionally, the user can select to first locate the object onto the 2D fitting plane of the support table, etc., as shown on top-left of Fig. 5. After labeling all objects' poses in the 3D workspace, their poses in every camera frame are calculated by dividing them with estimated camera poses. The output ground truth depth images (fixed depth) are generated by overlaying rendered object CAD model depth to the original depth images. Then the surface normals are calculated from the depth images. It takes around 30 min to finish labeling one scene using this pipeline, including visual SLAM for camera pose estimation, object pose manual alignment, and output image rendering.

4   Benchmark Experiments

In this section, we provide benchmark results of recent research on depth-related transparent object perception using deep neural networks, including scene level depth completion, and both instance-level and category-level RGB-D pose estimation. As mentioned in Sect. 3.1, we test the generalization capability of such systems on 6 aspects of appearance novelty with transparent objects: new background, heavy occlusion, translucent cover, opaque distractor objects, filled with liquid, and non-planar placement. Specifically, around 200K images are selected for training, and for each of 6 test cases, 2K images from corresponding scenes are randomly sampled to compose the testing set for evaluation.

4.1   Depth Completion

We selected two recent depth completion works that are publicly available, ImplicitDepth [26] and TransCG [7] as baseline methods for the depth completion task on transparent object scenes. (ClearGrasp [15] was shown to be less accurate than both works, and Transparenet [22] was released around the date of this submission.) ImplicitDepth is a two-stage method that learns local implicit depth functions in the first stage through ray-voxel pairs similar to neural rendering and refines the depth in the second stage. TransCG is built on DFNet [11] which was initially developed for image completion. We trained both networks following their original papers' training iterations and hyper-parameters. Specifically, ImplicitDepth was trained on a 16G RTX3080 GPU with a 0.001 learning rate and iterated around 2M frames for each of the two stages. TransCG was trained on an 8G RTX3070 GPU with a fixed 0.001 learning rate and iterated around 900K frames in total. Both works use Adam as the optimizer. Then we evaluated the two works on 6 test sets mentioned in Sect. 3.1 with metrics defined in [6]. The results are shown in Table 2. TransCG surpassed Implicit-Depth in most tests with fewer training iterations, which implies that methods using DFNet can outperform designs using voxel-based PointNet for transparent depth completion. Across different tests, both methods perform poorly in Translucent Cover scenes and achieved the best performance in New Background scenes. Other scene variations such as Filled Liquid, Opaque Distractor, and Non Planar do not substantially impact the methods' accuracy. Figure 6 shows examples of qualitative results from both methods compared with the ground truth.

4.2   Instance-Level Object Pose Estimation

There is one recent work of Xu et al. [21] focusing on transparent object pose estimation using raw RGB and depth images. This work doesn't have source code publicly available, so we re-implemented the proposed method following the original paper for inclusion in our benchmark analysis. This method is implemented as a two-stage pipeline, for which we trained Mask R-CNN [8] for instance-level segmentation and DeepLabv3 [4] for surface normal estimation, and with an XYZ 3D coordinate map of the supporting plane feature in the first stage. The

Table 2. Depth completion benchmark results of ImplicitDepth and TransCG on 6 different test scenarios of the ClearPose dataset.

Testset	Metric	RMSE↓	REL↓	MAE↓	$\delta_{1.05}$ ↑	$\delta_{1.10}$ ↑	$\delta_{1.25}$ ↑
New background	ImplicitDepth	0.07	0.05	0.04	67.00	87.03	97.50
	TransCG	0.03	0.03	0.02	86.50	97.02	99.74
Heavy occlusion	ImplicitDepth	0.11	0.09	0.08	41.43	66.52	91.96
	TransCG	0.06	0.04	0.04	72.03	90.61	98.73
Translucent cover	ImplicitDepth	0.16	0.16	0.13	22.85	41.17	73.11
	TransCG	0.16	0.15	0.14	23.44	39.75	67.56
Opaque distractor	ImplicitDepth	0.14	0.13	0.10	34.41	55.59	83.23
	TransCG	0.08	0.06	0.06	52.43	75.52	97.53
Filled liquid	ImplicitDepth	0.14	0.13	0.11	32.84	53.44	84.84
	TransCG	0.04	0.04	0.03	77.65	93.81	99.50
Non planar	ImplicitDepth	0.18	0.16	0.15	20.34	38.57	74.02
	TransCG	0.09	0.07	0.07	55.31	76.47	94.88

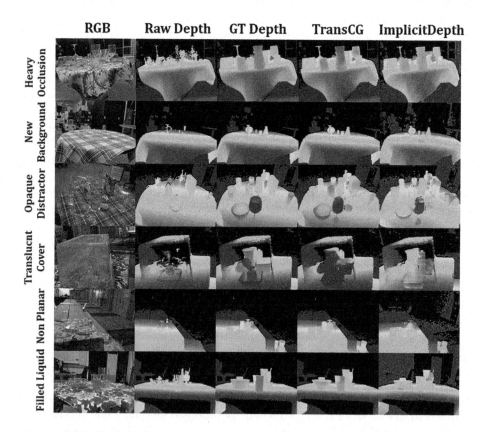

Fig. 6. Qualitative depth completion results. From left to right, there are RGB image, raw depth, ground truth depth rendered using object CAD models, completed depth by TransCG and ImplicitDepth.

second stage replicates most of the architecture and loss functions described in [17] to ultimately regress dense pixel-wise 3D translation, 3D rotation delta from a set of fixed rotation anchors, and confidence scores. In practice, we trained the networks on an RTX2080-SUPER GPU. Mask R-CNN has trained 5 epochs with SGD optimizer, batch size of 5, and learning rate of 0.005. DeepLabv3 was trained 2 epochs with Adam optimizer, batch size of 4 and learning rate of 0.0001, and second stage network was trained around 180K iterations with Adam optimizer, batch size of 4, and learning rate of 0.0005. We compare this method [21] with a state-of-the-art RGB-D pose estimator that was originally designed for opaque objects, FFB6D [9]. The FFB6D estimator follows a two-stream RGB and point cloud encoder-decoder architecture with fusion between blocks. FFB6D is trained on a 16G RTX3080 GPU for 5 epochs with batch size 6. All the hyper-parameters follow the default value from the original implementation. For our analysis of FFB6D pose estimation performance, we run experiments with different depth options in training and testing: with raw, ground truth, and completed depth from TransCG, as detailed in Table 3.

Table 3. Pose estimation accuracy comparison on different test sets of the ClearPose dataset. FFB6D$_{r/r}$ refers to train and test FFB6D model both on raw depth. Similarly, FFB6D$_{g/c}$, FFB6D$_{g/g}$ refer to train on ground truth, test on completed depth from TransCG, and train and test both on ground truth, respectively. The values are averaged across all objects in the dataset.

Testset	Metric	Xu et al	FFB6D$_{r/r}$	FFB6D$_{g/c}$	FFB6D$_{g/g}$
New background	Accuracy	50.958	44.264	49.517	59.694
	ADD(-S)	45.233	43.452	47.691	58.224
Heavy occlusion	Accuracy	24.193	14.723	15.160	26.331
	ADD(-S)	22.953	17.869	17.862	31.875
Translucent cover	Accuracy	14.353	5.5617	4.5345	13.433
	ADD(-S)	14.311	7.5983	5.8054	17.620
Opaque distractor	Accuracy	42.630	0.4618	1.3331	2.3525
	ADD(-S)	39.036	0.7628	1.5516	3.0685
Filled liquid	Accuracy	34.500	7.6908	9.0584	16.228
	ADD(-S)	32.251	11.153	10.828	18.583
Non planar	Accuracy	21.024	7.4924	7.5843	15.567
	ADD(-S)	18.411	7.8021	6.7339	16.986

For evaluation, we use two metrics based on Average-point-Distance (ADD and ADD-S) from [19]. ADD is calculated as the average Euclidean distance of corresponding point pairs from two object point clouds separately at the ground truth pose and predicted pose. ADD-S is calculated as the minimum distance of every point from the predicted point cloud to the ground truth point cloud. In Table 3, 'Accuracy' is calculated as the percentage of all pose estimates on the test set with ADD error less than 10cm. 'ADD(-S)' is calculated as Accuracy-Under-Curve area integrated from 0–10cm error, which is then scaled from 1 to 100 as the percentage.

As shown in Table 3, from the comparison between different training and testing combination within FFB6D, the upper bound performance appears when the network are both trained and tested on ground truth depth. When both the training and testing data come to raw, the metric drops a lot. Obviously, inaccurate depth would be the difficulty for transparent object pose estimation. It should be mentioned that training on ground truth depth, testing on completed depth (from TransCG) almost display the same accuracy. Although TransCG is good at depth completion, the disparity between ground truth and depth completion would make the network in vain. Generally, the easiest test case is New Background, and the accuracy drops a lot in the other 5 scenarios. When we compare the accuracy of Xu et al. with variants of FFB6D, we find they are comparable in New Background, Heavy Occlusion, Translucent Cover, and Non Planar scenes, while Xu et al. is much better in Opaque Distractor and

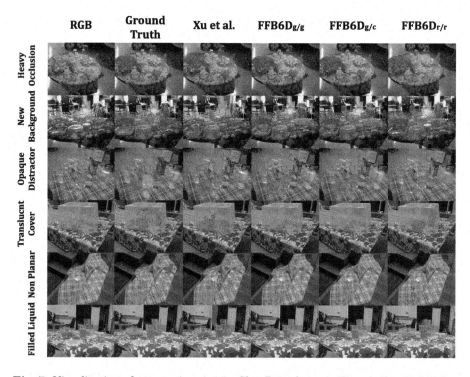

Fig. 7. Visualization of pose estimation in ClearPose dataset. From left to right, they are raw image, ground truth object poses, pose estimation results of method from Xu et al., FFB6D$_{g/g}$, FFB6D$_{g/c}$, FFB6D$_{r/r}$. From top to bottom, results are shown in different test scenes in Table 3. Objects are projected to color masks based on their pose estimates, with their 6DoF poses marked as the red-green-blue coordinate frame.

Filled Liquid scenes. One possible reason is that there are some unseen colors mixing in the transparent objects, adding remarkable noise to object keypoint regression during the FFB6D inference process, which is not used by Xu et al. Overall, the pose estimation accuracy of current methods is still much worse than that on opaque objects with RGB features (with ADD-S around 90 on public datasets [10]). Some qualitative examples of pose estimates are shown in Fig. 7.

5   Discussions

There are some common classes of objects with transparency/translucency not included in our dataset, for example, those with colored transparent/translucent materials, with markers or labels, together with opaque parts, etc. Instead, our focus in the ClearPose dataset is to investigate pure transparency that exhibits relatively few features for perception. On the other hand, we anticipate the open-source ProgressLabeller [5] will facilitate more large-scale customized transparent datasets in the future.

As for benchmarking perception models, we didn't include a complete list of recent state-of-the-art approaches due to resource constraints (i.e. compute and time limitations). Based on our current dataset and benchmark results, there are several possible extensions: (1) Comparison of RGB-only pose estimators with RGB-D methods that are free of transparent object broken depth issues. (2) Category-level pose estimation for transparent objects, for which the ClearPose dataset has categories of bowls, bottles, wine_cups, etc. that are with similar 3D shape and topology. (3) Neural rendering on transparent objects considering environment contexts, such as varied lighting and occlusions. (4) Transparent object grasping and manipulation experiment in practical scenes, including the 6 test scenarios mentioned in the benchmark.

Besides, an especially interesting problem emerging from our heavy cluttered, and translucent covered test scenes is the multi-layer appearance of transparent

Fig. 8. Examples of multi-layer transparent object appearance. In the left image, the annotated bounding boxes show large overlap between object pairs, where the objects behind are still perceivable in some cases with less light distortion. In the right image, objects behind the translucent surface are still detectable as well.

objects. As shown in Fig. 8, because of transparency/translucency, some image pixels could belong to more than one object. New detection and segmentation annotation rules, such as bounding box non-maximum suppression threshold, or segmentation mask format over the image, could be proposed and explored based on our dataset as future work.

6 Conclusions

In this paper, we described the contribution of **ClearPose**, a new large-scale RGB-D transparent object dataset with annotated poses, masks, and associated labels created using a recently proposed pipeline. We performed a set of benchmarking experiments on depth completion and object pose estimation tasks using state-of-the-art methods over 6 different generalization test cases that are common in practical scenarios. Results from our experiments demonstrate that there is still much room for improvement in some cases, such as heavy clutter, transparent objects filled with liquid, or being covered by other translucent surfaces. The dataset and benchmark code implementations will be made public with the intention to support further research progress in transparent RGB-D visual perception.

Acknowledgement. We thank greatly the support from Dr. Peter Gaskell and Weishu Wu at the University of Michigan, who provided devices and objects for dataset collection.

References

1. Campos, C., Elvira, R., Rodríguez, J.J.G., Montiel, J.M., Tardós, J.D.: Orb-slam3: an accurate open-source library for visual, visual-inertial, and multimap slam. IEEE Trans. Robot. **37**(6), 1874–1890 (2021)
2. Chang, J., et al.: GhostPose:*: multi-view pose estimation of transparent objects for robot hand grasping. In: 2021 IEEE/RSJ International Conference on Intelligent Robots and Systems (IROS), pp. 5749–5755. IEEE (2021)
3. Chen, G., Han, K., Wong, K.Y.K.: Tom-net: learning transparent object matting from a single image. In: Proceedings of the IEEE Conference on Computer Vision and Pattern Recognition, pp. 9233–9241 (2018)
4. Chen, L.C., Papandreou, G., Schroff, F., Adam, H.: Rethinking atrous convolution for semantic image segmentation. arXiv preprint arXiv:1706.05587 (2017)
5. Chen, X., Zhang, H., Yu, Z., Lewis, S., Jenkins, O.C.: ProgressLabeller: visual data stream annotation for training object-centric 3d perception. arXiv preprint arXiv:2203.00283 (2022)
6. Eigen, D., Puhrsch, C., Fergus, R.: Depth map prediction from a single image using a multi-scale deep network. In: Advances in neural Information Processing Systems, vol. 27 (2014)
7. Fang, H., Fang, H.S., Xu, S., Lu, C.: TransCG: a large-scale real-world dataset for transparent object depth completion and grasping. arXiv preprint arXiv:2202.08471 (2022)

8. He, K., Gkioxari, G., Dollár, P., Girshick, R.: Mask R-CNN. In: Proceedings of the IEEE International Conference on Computer Vision, pp. 2961–2969 (2017)

9. He, Y., Huang, H., Fan, H., Chen, Q., Sun, J.: Ffb6d: a full flow bidirectional fusion network for 6d pose estimation. In: Proceedings of the IEEE/CVF Conference on Computer Vision and Pattern Recognition, pp. 3003–3013 (2021)

10. Hodaň, T., et al.: BOP challenge 2020 on 6d object localization. In: Bartoli, A., Fusiello, A. (eds.) ECCV 2020. LNCS, vol. 12536, pp. 577–594. Springer, Cham (2020). https://doi.org/10.1007/978-3-030-66096-3_39

11. Hong, X., Xiong, P., Ji, R., Fan, H.: Deep fusion network for image completion. In: Proceedings of the 27th ACM International Conference on Multimedia, pp. 2033–2042 (2019)

12. Liu, X., Iwase, S., Kitani, K.M.: Stereobj-1 m: large-scale stereo image dataset for 6d object pose estimation. In: Proceedings of the IEEE/CVF International Conference on Computer Vision, pp. 10870–10879 (2021)

13. Liu, X., Jonschkowski, R., Angelova, A., Konolige, K.: KeyPose: multi-view 3d labeling and keypoint estimation for transparent objects. In: Proceedings of the IEEE/CVF Conference on Computer Vision and Pattern Recognition, pp. 11602–11610 (2020)

14. Peng, S., Liu, Y., Huang, Q., Zhou, X., Bao, H.: PVNet: pixel-wise voting network for 6dof pose estimation. In: Proceedings of the IEEE/CVF Conference on Computer Vision and Pattern Recognition, pp. 4561–4570 (2019)

15. Sajjan, S., et al.: Clear grasp: 3d shape estimation of transparent objects for manipulation. In: 2020 IEEE International Conference on Robotics and Automation (ICRA), pp. 3634–3642. IEEE (2020)

16. Tang, Y., Chen, J., Yang, Z., Lin, Z., Li, Q., Liu, W.: DepthGrasp: depth completion of transparent objects using self-attentive adversarial network with spectral residual for grasping. In: 2021 IEEE/RSJ International Conference on Intelligent Robots and Systems (IROS), pp. 5710–5716. IEEE (2021)

17. Tian, M., Pan, L., Ang, M.H., Lee, G.H.: Robust 6d object pose estimation by learning rgb-d features. In: 2020 IEEE International Conference on Robotics and Automation (ICRA), pp. 6218–6224. IEEE (2020)

18. Wang, C., et al.: DenseFusion: 6d object pose estimation by iterative dense fusion. In: Proceedings of the IEEE/CVF Conference on Computer Vision and Pattern Recognition, pp. 3343–3352 (2019)

19. Xiang, Y., Schmidt, T., Narayanan, V., Fox, D.: PoseCNN: a convolutional neural network for 6d object pose estimation in cluttered scenes. Robot. Sci. Syst. (2018)

20. Xie, E., Wang, W., Wang, W., Ding, M., Shen, C., Luo, P.: Segmenting transparent objects in the wild. In: Vedaldi, A., Bischof, H., Brox, T., Frahm, J.-M. (eds.) ECCV 2020. LNCS, vol. 12358, pp. 696–711. Springer, Cham (2020). https://doi.org/10.1007/978-3-030-58601-0_41

21. Xu, C., Chen, J., Yao, M., Zhou, J., Zhang, L., Liu, Y.: 6dof pose estimation of transparent object from a single RGB-D image. Sensors 20(23), 6790 (2020)

22. Xu, H., Wang, Y.R., Eppel, S., Aspuru-Guzik, A., Shkurti, F., Garg, A.: Seeing glass: joint point cloud and depth completion for transparent objects. arXiv preprint arXiv:2110.00087 (2021)

23. Xu, Y., Nagahara, H., Shimada, A., Taniguchi, R.i.: Transcut: transparent object segmentation from a light-field image. In: Proceedings of the IEEE International Conference on Computer Vision, pp. 3442–3450 (2015)

24. Zhang, Y., Funkhouser, T.: Deep depth completion of a single RGB-d image. In: Proceedings of the IEEE Conference on Computer Vision and Pattern Recognition, pp. 175–185 (2018)

25. Zhou, Z., Chen, X., Jenkins, O.C.: Lit: light-field inference of transparency for refractive object localization. IEEE Robot. Autom. Lett. **5**(3), 4548–4555 (2020)
26. Zhu, L., et al.: RGB-d local implicit function for depth completion of transparent objects. In: Proceedings of the IEEE/CVF Conference on Computer Vision and Pattern Recognition, pp. 4649–4658 (2021)

When Deep Classifiers Agree: Analyzing Correlations Between Learning Order and Image Statistics

Iuliia Pliushch[1]([✉]), Martin Mundt[2], Nicolas Lupp[1], and Visvanathan Ramesh[1]

[1] Goethe University Frankfurt, Frankfurt, Germany
{pliushch,vramesh}@em.uni-frankfurt.de
[2] TU Darmstadt and hessian.AI, Darmstadt, Germany
martin.mundt@tu-darmstadt.de

Abstract. Although a plethora of architectural variants for deep classification has been introduced over time, recent works have found empirical evidence towards similarities in their training process. It haswrapfig been hypothesized that neural networks converge not only to similar representations, but also exhibit a notion of empirical agreement on which data instances are learned first. Following in the latter works' footsteps, we define a metric to quantify the relationship between such classification agreement over time, and posit that the agreement phenomenon can be mapped to core statistics of the investigated dataset. We empirically corroborate this hypothesis across the CIFAR10, Pascal, ImageNet and KTH-TIPS2 datasets. Our findings indicate that agreement seems to be independent of specific architectures, training hyper-parameters or labels, albeit follows an ordering according to image statistics.

Keywords: Neural network learning dynamics · Deep classifier agreement · Data instance ordering · Image dataset statistics

1 Introduction

Can we make the learning process of a neural network more transparent? Is there any order in which a network is learning dataset instances? Various prior works posit that certain data instances are easier to learn than others. Arpit *et al.* [3] argue that neural networks prioritize simple patterns first during the learning process by analyzing the nature of the decision boundary. Mangalam and Prabhu [35] extend the results, showing that neural networks first learn instances, classified correctly by shallow models like Random Forests and Support Vector Machines. Geirhos *et al.* [14] and Shah *et al.* [41] specify which patterns are simple for neural networks to learn, namely that they exhibit a *simplicity bias* during training by relying on simple-but-noisy features like color and

---

Supplementary Information The online version contains supplementary material available at https://doi.org/10.1007/978-3-031-20074-8_23.

S. Avidan et al. (Eds.): ECCV 2022, LNCS 13668, pp. 397–413, 2022.
https://doi.org/10.1007/978-3-031-20074-8_23

texture, instead of shape. Recently, Hacohen *et al.* [15] have shown that there is agreement over learned examples throughout the entire learning process of a neural network, which is independent of initialization and batch-sampling and occurs also when changing different hyperparameter settings, like learning rate, optimizer, weight-decay and architecture. If certain examples are easier for a neural network to learn than others, it can be hypothesized that the difficulty of an example depends on dataset and image statistics to a larger degree than the learner itself. Hence, different neural networks would learn the same (easy) examples at the same time, despite common epoch-wise random shuffling of the data during the training process and strong regularization through noise of mini-batch stochastic gradient descent. In this spirit, we extend the analysis to a stricter agreement metric and not only replicate the presence of agreement, but also correlate it to chosen image statistics, in an attempt to clarify the reason why certain image examples are more difficult to learn than others. Our contributions are:

- We design a strict instance-based agreement metric to quantify how learning progresses and data instances are classified correctly across neural networks.
- With our metric, we replicate insights on classifier agreement from Hacohen *et al.* [15] in terms of consistent neural network agreement across batch-sizes and architectures, as well as investigate the role of labels through a label randomization study.
- We select promising image statistics to correlate with neural network data instance agreement. We empirically corroborate correlations for metrics such as entropy, segment count, number of relevant frequency coefficients and summed edge strengths on popular image classification datasets: CIFAR10, Pascal, KTH-TIPS2b and ImageNet.

The analysis we conduct might help to better understand the tools - neural networks - we use for training. Further, as the next step, these insights could drive us towards the design of a *learning curriculum* [4,16,27,29], in which the dataset instances could be sampled according to a high correlation between observed agreement and the inspected metrics. We posit that this could lead to training speed ups and performance improvements. Our code is available at: https:// github.com/ccc-frankfurt/intrinsic_ordering_nn_training.

2   Problem Statement and Motivation

Let us first recall the general procedure of neural network training and the rationale behind it. Assume that we have a training set $X = (x_n, y_n)_{n=1}^{N}$, where x_n are our (i.i.d.) dataset instances, y_n the corresponding labels and the number of dataset instances N. We also assume access to a similarly designed non-overlapping test set. We want to optimize a defined loss to measure and minimize the discrepancy between our network prediction and the ground truth. For that, we ideally want to integrate the loss L of our neural network - function f_θ with parameters θ, over the dataset distribution:

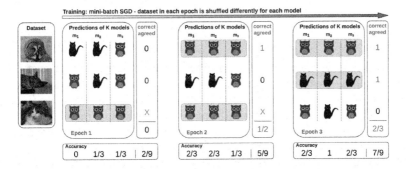

Fig. 1. Agreement visualization: For each image the classification results are compared across networks and, in addition to *average accuracy over networks*, *true positive agreement* calculated, which is the ratio of images that all networks classify correctly per epoch to those that at least one network classifies correctly.

$$\int L(f_\theta(x), y) dP(x, y) \tag{1}$$

In practice, we only have a limited amount of samples from the dataset distribution. Hence we compute an *approximation*. Typically a noisy gradient estimate (see appendix) is leveraged for such empirical optimization, by presenting our data in mini-batches over several epochs t and shuffling the dataset after every epoch, i.e. when the network has seen all the data (at least) once. Of course, when the networks have fully converged and learnt a sufficiently large amount of data, the dataset instances they have learnt trivially overlap. It is however not self-evident that different approximators would learn the data in a similar way or in other words that despite shuffling and mini-batch updating, neural networks would learn data in the same order. We first provide a definition for such agreement and then consider when networks necessarily start to agree on the dataset instances during learning. Hacohen *et al.* [15] define one form of *agreement* as "the largest fraction of classifiers that predict the same label" for the same data instance, as well as *true positive agreement* as an "average accuracy of a single example over multiple models". In order to take the next step and try to quantify the difficulty of the images for training, we step back from agreement as an average and define *(true positive)* agreement of an instance per epoch as an *exact match*, such that all K networks classify the same instance correctly in epoch t, where K is the number of networks we have trained. *True positive agreement per epoch* can then be computed as the sum of instances classified correctly by *all* classifiers in that epoch, normalized by the sum of instances classified correctly by *any* classifier in that epoch. Formally, true positive agreement TPa per epoch t is defined as:

$$TPa^{(t)}(x,y) = \frac{\sum_{n \in N} \prod_{k \in K} \mathbb{1}_{f_k^{(t)}(x_n)=y_n}}{\sum_{n \in N} \max_{k \in K} \mathbb{1}_{f_k^{(t)}(x_n)=y_n}} \qquad (2)$$

During training, we now monitor the true positive agreement in every epoch for each training instance. Suppose that we train K networks, as in Fig. 1. In the first epoch, some models classify some dataset instances correctly (indicator function, $\mathbb{1}_{f_k^t(x_n)=y_n}$ being the condition for a prediction match), but for no instance it is the case that all models classify it correctly. In the second epoch - one dataset instance is classified correctly by all models. As during training more models classify instances correctly, if they learn the same instances first, then as soon as all models agree, it will be reflected in the agreement scores. Perfect agreement of 100% can be reached if all models learn the same instances. So, agreement - fraction of correctly classified instances over all models compared to learned at all by at least one model - can be higher than average model accuracy per epoch, which is the fraction of correctly classified instances from the whole train set, averaged over the trained models. False positive agreement (all models misclassify an instance in the same way), as in the case of the partly white cat in the first two epochs (blue shaded box in Fig. 1), is left out of the true positive agreement. However, it could analyzed in future work.

To assess, how trivial it is that neural networks agree *before* convergence we consider the minimum possible agreement - the *lower bound*. When do the models necessarily start to agree to learn the same instances? Let us assume that we train 2 networks and every one is 50% correct at some epoch t. Then every network can learn the fraction of data that the other one did not. The same applies if we train 3 networks and the accuracy is 2/3 per network, because if we split the data into 3 portions, every network can learn 2 portions of the data such that there is not one portion common to all 3 networks. The same occurs for K networks with accuracy being $\frac{K-1}{K}$. In all these cases the sum of errors err_k^e all networks make is $K * \frac{1}{K} = 1$ or 100%. As the accuracy rises higher than that and the error gets lower, the networks will necessarily start to learn the fractions of data others are learning. Hence, the lower bound is 0% when the sum of errors the networks make is bigger or equal to 100%. The lower bound fraction, reported in the remainder of the paper in percent, can be defined as:

$$LBa^t(x,y) = 1 - \min(\sum_{k \in K} \underbrace{1 - acc_k^e}_{err_k^e}, 1). \qquad (3)$$

In particular, the difference between agreement and lower bound shows us the portion of agreement which could not have been predicted on the basis of the lower bound alone.

Lastly, since one of the datasets we test our hypotheses on is *multilabel*, in this scenario we extend the definition of agreement and lower bound such that agreement and accuracy are calculated on the basis of *exact match*, meaning that for all present and absent labels in an image, the prediction should exactly match: the presence and absence of a label should be predicted correctly for all labels. This is a criterion which is non-forgiving: if one of the two labels has been predicted correctly, the exact match still classifies this image as wrongly predicted. On the other hand, it is a strong criterion to test agreement on, since what we are after is a *full* and not *partial* agreement. It is also a much stronger criterion than investigated in Hacohen *et al.* [15]. Notably, our TP-agreement is thus also different from an *observed agreement*, i.e. the sum over instances given estimators classify correctly (true positives) and incorrectly (true negatives) divided by the total number of instances [18]. Our choice to separate out true positive agreement is intended to avoid potential confusion, as the number of true positives and negatives is not equal during training and can complicate the assessment of reliability across estimators. The alternative Cohen's kappa, for example, suffers from the prevalence problem: it is non-representatively low in case of uneven frequencies of events. An alternative PABAK measure counter-acting the prevalence bias [6] is a linear function of observed agreement, which takes both true positives and negatives into account. We provide a deeper discussion on alternatives in the appendix, in context of the preliminary results shown in the upcoming section.

3 Agreement for Different Batch-Sizes and Architectures, as Well as for Random Labels

To reiterate, the general procedure is to train several (in our case 5) networks on the same dataset and track examples, classified correctly per epoch per network. Upon training several networks for the same amount of epochs, *agreement per epoch* is defined as the sum of images *every* network classified correctly, normalized by the sum of images *any* network classified correctly. We have seen on the example of the *lower bound* that a quite high accuracy is necessary for the networks to unavoidably learn the same instances and that this relation depends on the number of networks trained: the more networks, the higher accuracy each of those has to obtain to start learning the same data portion. Hence, it is not self-evident that agreement does occur during neural network training.

If networks agree on what to learn, which factors does this agreement depend on? To provide an intuition for above paragraphs, as well as to replicate prior insights obtained by Hacohen *et al.* [15], we first test for the overall presence of agreement. Then, we extend our experiments to different batch-sizes and architectures. Presence of agreement in all these diverse conditions supports the hypothesis that agreement is not dependent on the *model*, but on the (sampled) dataset population itself in terms of the nature of the true unknown underlying distribution and the intrinsic characteristic of the difficulty of classification [7]. To further investigate whether the *joint* dataset and label distribution leads to agreement, or whether it is independent of labels, we test the presence of agreement in case of random labels.

As hypothesized, mirroring prior hypothesis of Hacohen *et al.* [15], but using our strict agreement criterion, we found visually clear agreement during training of CIFAR10 [28] on DenseNet121 [22], presented in Fig. 2a. Particularly in

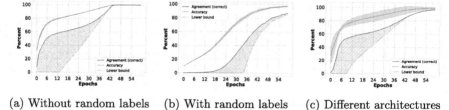

(a) Without random labels   (b) With random labels   (c) Different architectures

Fig. 2. Ablation study on **CIFAR10**: training DenseNet121 with and without randomization, as well as with different architectures: LeNet5, VGG16, ResNet50, DenseNet121. The **blue area** demonstrates the difference between agreement and lower bound. The **red area** is the epoch-wise standard deviation from average accuracy across trained networks. (Color figure online)

the first epochs, as the accuracy grows, the area between agreement and the lower bound, shaded in blue, is the most prominent. It shows that throughout training we observe growing agreement on the learned instances, i.e. certain data instances are labelled correctly in earlier stages than others, which is most remarkable in the training epochs before networks converge and the accuracy plateaus.

Agreement persists also when training different architectures. We have chosen 4 diverse architectures, ranging from simple ones like LeNet5 [30] and VGG16 [43] to the more complex ones like ResNet50 [19] and DenseNet121 [22]. Training CIFAR10 on them for the same amount of epochs, we could observe visually prominent agreement as well, see Fig. 2c (training details and additional plots in the appendix). The agreement is similar to that for the same architecture. The differences in learning speed are reflected in the standard deviation across different model accuracies, shaded in red. Note that accuracy deviation has been almost negligible when the same architectures have been trained.

We have also replicated the presence of agreement for different batch-sizes in the appendix. A comparison shows that agreement curves are similar for simpler architectures and smaller batch-sizes, as well as more complex architectures and larger batch-sizes, suggesting that model capacity and enhanced randomness when training with smaller batch sizes slow down the learning and agreement.

Above experiments suggest that batch-size or architecture type are not the underlying causes for agreement during training. Next, we test whether it is the structure of the data itself, or the relationship between the training data and its human assigned labels that account for it. To test this hypothesis, we assess agreement under label randomization. State-of-the-art convolutional networks can fit random labels with ease [49]. Maennel *et al.* [34] argue further that during training with random labels an alignment between the principal components of data and network parameters takes place. Hence, if the dataset structure is responsible for agreement, it should be visible also in case of random labels. Figure 2b supports this hypothesis. We observe that the accuracy grows at a slower pace and that agreement grows more slowly than during training with ground truth labels. This may reflect the fact that it takes longer for the network to start learning the dataset structure without label guidance. Nonetheless, there is still sufficient agreement once accuracy starts to rise. Interestingly, here we disagree with [15], who did not find agreement with randomized labels.

To conclude, we have observed a clear gap between theoretical lower-bound and observed agreement, independence on semantic labels and architecture, even coherence in between them. This supports the existence of a fundamental core mechanism linked to more elemental dataset properties. To further support and strengthen our early results, we show in the appendix that observed trends of true positive agreement clearly surpassing the lower-bound persist even when comparing it to the *expected random agreement*. The latter is computed as the product of accuracies for a given epoch. It is based on the assumption that networks classify instances independently of each other, which does not seem to be the case, partly because, as we show, the dataset structure plays an important role. In addition, we also compute the standard deviation on agreement for Pascal in the appendix, showing that it is negligibly small.

4 Dataset Metrics

In the face of the insight that dataset properties are the probable cause of agreement, we proceed by choosing several diverse datasets, as well as dataset metrics to establish a correlation between them and training agreement. We have chosen the following datasets to validate our agreement hypothesis: a tiny-sized CIFAR10 [28] for ablation experiments, a diverse dataset with objects differing in illumination, size and scale - Pascal Visual Object Classes (VOC) 2007 and 2012 [10,11], a large-scale ILSVRC-2012 (ImageNet) [9,40], as well as a texture dataset KTH-TIPS2b [8]. CIFAR10, Pascal and ImageNet have been gathered by means of search engines and then manual clean-up. In case of ImageNet, classes to search for were obtained from the hierarchical structure of WordNet and the manual clean-up proceeded by means of the crowdsourcing platform Amazon Mechanical Turk. On the example of the person category, Yang *et al.* [48] elaborate that a dataset gathered in such a manner is as strong as the semantic label assumptions and distinctions on which it is based, the quality of the images obtained using search engines (e.g. lack of image diversity), as well as the quality of the clean-up (annotation) procedure. In distinction to the above three datasets, though KTH-TIPS2b is a quite small dataset, it has been carefully designed, controlling for several illumination and rotation conditions, and varying scales.

Prior Work: What surrogate image statistics may be used to study the agreement between classifiers on the order of learning? Let us look at some prior works in this direction. First, some dataset properties make learning difficult in general, namely the diverse nature of the data itself: the difficulty of assigning image categories due to possible image variation, e.g. rotation, lighting, occlusion, deformation [38]. Second, learning algorithms also show preferences for particular kinds of data. Russakovsky *et al.* [39] analyze the impact onto ImageNet classification and localization performance of several dataset properties on the image and instance level, like object size, whether the object is human- or man-made, whether it is textured or deformable. Their insights are consistent with the intuition that object classification algorithms rely more on texture and color as cues than shape. They further argue that object classification accuracy is higher for natural than man-made objects. Hoiem *et al.* [21] analyze the impact of object characteristics on errors in several non-neural network object detectors, coming to the conclusion that the latter are sensitive to object size and confusion with semantically similar objects.

In an attempt to mimic the decisions of a human learner, several image features have been related to image memorability and object importance. Isola *et al.* [25] investigate memorability of an image as a stable property across viewers and its relation to basic image and object statistics, like mean hue and number of objects in the image. Spain and Perona [45], on the other hand, establish the connection between image object features and the importance of this object in the image, which is the probability that a human observer will name it upon seeing the image. Berg *et al.* [5] extends this analysis to encompass semantic features like object categories and scene context.

Knowing which image cues the learning process is sensitive to gives room for improving it. Alexe *et al.* [2] design an objectness measure generic over classes from image features (multi-scale saliency, color contrast, edge density and superpixels straddling) which can be used as a location prior for object detection. Extending the latter work, Lee and Grauman [31] use this objectness measure, as well as an additional familiarity metric (whether it belongs to a familiar category) to design a learing procedure which first considers easy objects. Liu *et al.* [33] fit a linear regression model with several image features, like color, gradient and texture, to estimate the difficulty of segmenting an image. In [46] an active learner is designed, which partly on the basis of edge density and color histogram metrics, proposes which instances to annotate and estimates the annotation cost for the multi-label learning task. Notably the question of whether the networks learn the same examples first is different from the question whether they learn the same representations [32,47], but if the former is correct, then the latter is more probable.

Our Choice: Several works have correlated basic image statistics to various human-related concepts, like memorability [25], importance [45] or image difficulty [24], or directly attempted to find out the influence of such metrics onto object classification [2,39]. Inspired by these approaches, we have chosen 4 image statistics to correlate agreement to: segment count [12], (sum of) edge strengths [26], (mean) image intensity entropy [13,44] and percentage of coefficients needed to reconstruct the image based on the DCT coefficient matrix [1]. First 3 metrics are shown in Fig. 3 (DCT coefficients matrix in the appendix).

The choice of the first two is inspired by [24], who correlate several image properties, including segment count and (sum of) edge strengths, to the *image difficulty score*, defined as a normalized response time needed for human annotations to detect the objects in the image. Their hypothesis is that segments divide the image into homogeneous textural regions, such that the more regions - the

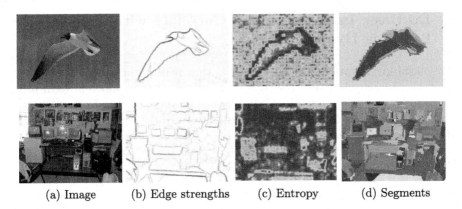

(a) Image   (b) Edge strengths   (c) Entropy   (d) Segments

Fig. 3. Visualization of selected metrics on Pascal examples. For intuition, we have chosen an "easy" and a "difficult" image according to Ionescu *et al.* [24]. Implementation details can be found in the appendix.

more cluttered an image might be (and the more difficult an object to find). The same line of reasoning goes for the sum of edge strengths: the more edges, the more time might be needed to get a grasp of the image. If the way humans search for objects in the image corresponds to some degree to the way a neural networks learns to predict their presence, segment count and the (sum of) edge strengths might be predictive for the agreement during training. Mean image entropy and DCT coefficients have been chosen for a similar line of reasoning. Both entropy and DCT coefficients, similar to edge strengths and segment count, provide a measure of variability: how uniform the variation in image pixels is in the case of entropy and how many (vertical and horizontal) frequencies are needed to describe an image in the case of DCT coefficients. Recently, [36] have analyzed how certain dataset features relate to classification, stating, for instance, that for MNIST and ImageNet the decision boundary is small for low frequency and high for high frequency components. In other words, the classifier develops a strong invariance along high frequencies. Hence, frequency-related information might influence agreement.

In addition, for Pascal, which contains further annotations, we considered the *number of object instances* (since it is a *multilabel* dataset such that several label instances may be present in the same image) and *the bounding box area* (ratio of the area taken by objects divided by the image size), as well as the *image difficulty scores* described above, computed by [24]. KTH-TIPS2b, is constructed in such a way that for each texture type, there are 4 texture samples, each of which varies in *illumination, scale* and *rotation*, which we also considered. Finally, for the CIFAR10 test set, Peterson *et al.* [37] have computed soft labels, reflecting human uncertainty that the given target class is in the image, to test whether networks trained on soft labels are more robust to adversarial attacks and generalize better than those trained on hard one-hot labels. *Soft label entropy* shows weak negative correlation with test agreement (see Fig. 5 of the appendix).

5   Do Basic Image Statistics Correlate with Training Learning Dynamics?

Our initial investigation of Sect. 3 suggests that neither the labels, nor the precisely chosen neural architecture or optimization hyper-parameters seem to be the primary source for agreement, eliminating all factors of Eq. 1 other than the data distribution itself. As such, we investigate the question *"do image statistics provide a sufficient description in correlation for agreement?"* on four datasets: Pascal [11], CIFAR10 [28], KTH-TIPS2b [8], and ImageNet [9].

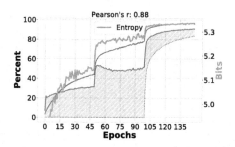

Fig. 4. Pascal DenseNet: Agreement visualization on *train set*. In addition to accuracy (**red**), agreement (**blue** curve) and its difference to lower-bound (shaded **blue** area) (left y-axis), dataset metric values are shown in **purple** (right y-axis). *Pearson's correlation coefficient* between agreement (**blue** curve) and metric values (in **purple**) quantitatively supports the visible correlation. (Color figure online)

To make the full upcoming results easier to follow, we first start by visualizing and discussing one example metric, namely entropy on Pascal in Fig. 4. In a given epoch, the agreement (blue) and accuracy (red) curves can be compared to the average entropy of the agreed upon instances (in purple). Again, the shaded blue area accentuates the difference between lower bound and agreement. Since we have chosen a step-wise learning rate scheduler for training, in order to reach roughly 50% exact match accuracy on the test set, the step-wise learning is reflected in the accuracy and agreement curve. As a new addition to our previously shown figures, we now notably also observe a strong positive correlation with the dataset entropy metric. This correlation between network agreement and the entropy of the correspondingly agreed upon instances is further quantified through a high Pearson correlation coefficient of 0.88.

We continue our analysis in this form for all other mentioned metrics and dataset combinations in Fig. 6 and Fig. 7. To better evaluate the shown correlations, we have visualized the distribution (in the form of a histogram) of the values for each dataset metric on the train sets in the appendix. Since the metrics fluctuate a lot in the first epochs due to predictions being primarily random, we omit plotting them for the first 5 epochs. For reference, we provide the agreement, accuracy and lower-bound curves in the style of our previous figures in

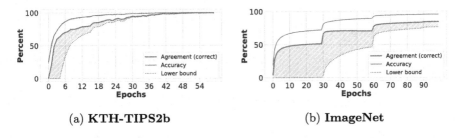

(a) **KTH-TIPS2b**   (b) **ImageNet**

Fig. 5. On DenseNet: Agreement, accuracy and lower bound as in Fig. 4

Fig. 5. To clarify potential correlations, these curves are then followed by visualizations and quantitative Pearson's r values of only agreement to the set of chosen image metrics in Fig. 6 and Fig. 7.

For the **Pascal** dataset, shown in Fig. 6a, the correlations between agreement and average dataset metrics are apparent (apart from sum of edge strengths). The correlations suggest that as the models learn, they in progression first learn dataset instances with lower entropy, segment count, number of significant DCT coefficients and number of object instances, meaning that less labels are present in the same image. The distribution for the number of instances (in the appendix) shows that the number of labels in most images is only 1 (equivalent to the single label classification), less for 2 and 3. This is reflected in the correlation, which goes up from 1.1 to 1.4. There is also a correlation between image difficulty (how much time humans need to find the objects in the image) and agreement, which is consistent with the other metrics, namely that easy examples are learnt first. This result is further supported by the bounding box size, where we see an inverse correlation, such that large objects are learnt first, in agreement with insights presented in the dataset metrics section. However, note that particularly for segment count, frequency coefficients and "image difficulty" the dataset metric curve first goes down, before it reverses its direction for the remainder of epochs. What we observe is that when accuracy is low and the model is trying to find an optimal trajectory to learn, there are more random fluctuations, due to the stochasticity of the learning process. In the appendix we show the correlations for Pascal ResNet with the same training setup. There, the trend of metric values first going down in first epochs (until the agreement approximatively reaches 20%) and then up is even more pronounced for some metrics.

Correlations are also present on **KTH-TIPS2b**, visualized in Fig. 6b. However, for this texture dataset, the tendency observed in Pascal is reversed, such that entropy, summed edge strengths, segment count and frequency percentage are inversely correlated with the dataset metric. In addition to these metrics, the way in which the dataset has been designed allows to extract additional ones, namely several illuminations, rotations and scales. The corresponding correlations are visualized in Fig. 6c. For illumination and rotation, instead of building an average over the metric values per epoch, we calculate for each illumination kind and rotation direction the fraction of values agreed upon, normalized by all

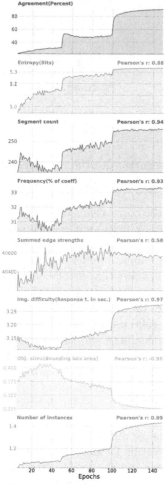

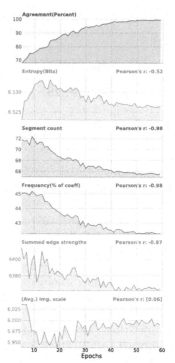

(b) **KTH-TIPS2b DenseNet:** Agreement and metric values in analogy to fig. 6a

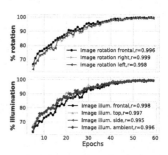

(a) **Pascal DenseNet:** Correlation between agreement (in blue) to per epoch averaged dataset metric values for correctly agreed upon training instances, on a shared x-axis (in analogy to the purple curve in fig. 4). Pearson correlation coefficient between agreement and the metric is provided. It is in rectangular brackets if the 2-tailed p-value is $>= 0.001$, see appendix for details.

(c) **KTH-TIPS2b DenseNet:** For illumination and rotation types, the percentage learned per category per epoch has been visualized separately for immediate comparison.

Fig. 6. Visualization of correlations between agreement and dataset metrics on *train sets* for **Pascal** and **KTH-TIPS2b**.

metric values of that type. For frontal illumination, for example, we count the instances that models agree on and divide by the number of instances of that type in the train set. We observe that texture patterns *illuminated* from the front are agreed on slower than other illumination types, while texture patterns *captured* from the front are agreed on quicker than other rotation directions. Correlation for texture scale seems absent.

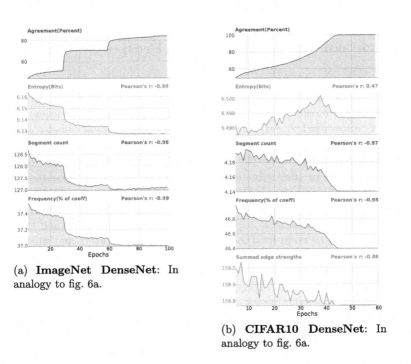

(a) **ImageNet DenseNet**: In analogy to fig. 6a.

(b) **CIFAR10 DenseNet**: In analogy to fig. 6a.

Fig. 7. Visualization of correlations between agreement and dataset metrics on *train sets* for **ImageNet** and **CIFAR10**.

We have seen that correlations on Pascal and KTH-TIPS2b diverge. In Fig. 7a we also see that on **ImageNet** correlations, albeit on a small scale, are present and they seem to be congruent with those on KTH-TIPS2b rather than Pascal. Namely, first images with higher segment count, entropy and number of relevant frequency coefficients are learned. Pascal and ImageNet are datasets of objects, while KTH-TIPS2b of texture. Why the difference? If we follow recent hypotheses on neural networks exhibiting simplicity bias and primarily using texture to discriminate [14,41], then correlation directions on KTH-TIPS2b and ImageNet would be the same (which our results indicate). On both Pascal and ImageNet random-crop is used to get train images of the same size, which has been argued by [20] to enhance texture bias. The way objects are presented in Pascal and ImageNet differs however, for ImageNet objects are centered and not much background is present, which is not the case for Pascal, making latter classification more challenging, but also effects of random-crop eventually different.

On **CIFAR10**, the direction of correlations is more consistent with KTH-TIPS2b and ImageNet (see Fig. 7b). The correlations are marginal, however, given that metric value range is very small. The presence of agreement with little correlation can also be an indication that there are some other metrics which explain it, though it may be some humanly non-interpretable noise patterns [23].

6   Discussion on Limitations and Prospects

Although agreement is present for *every* dataset, the previous sections have exposed a dataset dependency with respect to how precisely correlations between agreement and dataset metrics manifest. This means that the order, in which dataset instances are learned, is to a large degree independent of network parameters, but instead dependent on the general dataset statistics. This seems congruent with the ideas that a classifier compactly encodes the data in the first layers [42], as well as that agreement results from the principal component bias [17] in that learning order is influenced by the principal components of the data at earlier stages. Hence, in order to better understand the learning process of neural networks (and make a leap from correlation to causation, see appendix), agreement should be computed for carefully designed datasets and suitable metrics, for which the generative process and dataset statistics are well known.

Another research direction is to assess generalization and analyze the agreement on unknown *test sets*. Though these are often assumed to follow the same distribution as their training counterparts, it is practically not always the case. Supposedly, if the subset statistics are sufficiently similar, then agreement and metrics correlations should similarly manifest, as we exemplify in the appendix.

Last but not least, as mentioned in the introduction, the insights on agreement could help us design a more efficient *learning curriculum*, for which an appropriate pacing function [16] should be chosen with care.

7   Conclusions and Outlook

In this paper we have defined a new notion of agreement, characterising the learning process of neural networks in a more detailed way. We have demonstrated agreement on the train (and test set) for CIFAR10, Pascal, ImageNet and KTH-TIPS dataset. We have further correlated agreement on these datasets to several image statistics, in an attempt to explain why neural networks prefer to learn dataset instances in the way they do. Our results have shown several positive and negative correlations to dataset metrics, though different for each dataset. For future research is left the opportunity to test the results on further datasets, to test the correlation for further metrics, as well as to design curricula for training neural networks based on these insights.

Acknowledgements. This work was supported by the German Federal Ministry of Education and Research (BMBF) funded project 01IS19062 "AISEL" and the European Union's Horizon 2020 project No. 769066 "RESIST".

References

1. Ahmed, N., Natarajan, T., Rao, K.R.: Discrete cosine transform. IEEE Trans. Comput. **C-24**(1), 90–93 (1974)
2. Alexe, B., Deselaers, T., Ferrari, V.: Measuring the objectness of image windows. IEEE Trans. Pattern Anal. Mach. Intell. (TPAMI) **34**(11), 2189–2202 (2012)
3. Arpit, D., et al.: A closer look at memorization in deep networks. In: International Conference on Machine Learning (ICML) (2017)
4. Bengio, Y., Louradour, J., Collobert, R., Weston, J.: Curriculum learning. In: International Conference on Machine Learning (ICML) (2009)
5. Berg, A.C., et al.: Understanding and predicting importance in images. In: IEEE Conference on Computer Vision and Pattern Recognition (CVPR) (2012)
6. Byrt, T., Bishop, J., Carlin, J.B.: Bias, prevalence and kappa. J. Clin. Epidemiol. **46**(5), 423–429 (1993)
7. Caelen, O.: A Bayesian interpretation of the confusion matrix. Ann. Math. Artif. Intell. **81**(3–4), 429–450 (2017)
8. Caputo, B., Hayman, E., Mallikarjuna, P.: Class-specific material categorisation. In: International Conference on Computer Vision (ICCV) (2005)
9. Deng, J., Dong, W., Socher, R., Li, L.J., Li, K., Fei-Fei, L.: ImageNet: a large-scale hierarchical image database. In: IEEE Conference on Computer Vision and Pattern Recognition (CVPR) (2009)
10. Everingham, M., Eslami, S.M., Van Gool, L., Williams, C.K., Winn, J., Zisserman, A.: The pascal visual object classes challenge: a retrospective. Int. J. Comput. Vision **111**(1), 98–136 (2015)
11. Everingham, M., Van-Gool, L., Williams, C.K.I., Winn, J., Zisserman, A.: The pascal visual object classes (VOC) challenge. Int. J. Comput. Vision **88**(2), 303–338 (2010)
12. Felzenszwalb, P.F., Huttenlocher, D.P.: Efficient Graph-Based Image Segmentation. Int. J. Comput. Vision **59**, 167–181 (2004)
13. Frieden, B.R.: Restoring with maximum likelihood and maximum entropy. J. Optical Soc. America (JOSA) **62**(4), 511–518 (1972)
14. Geirhos, R., Michaelis, C., Wichmann, F.A., Rubisch, P., Bethge, M., Brendel, W.: Imagenet-trained CNNs are biased towards texture; increasing shape bias improves accuracy and robustness. International Conference on Learning Representations (ICLR) (2019)
15. Hacohen, G., Choshen, L., Weinshall, D.: Let's agree to agree: neural networks share classification order on real datasets. In: International Conference on Learning Representations (ICLR) (2020)
16. Hacohen, G., Weinshall, D.: On the power of curriculum learning in training deep networks. In: International Conference on Machine Learning (ICML) (2019)
17. Hacohen, G., Weinshall, D.: Principal components bias in over-parameterizyed linear models, and its manifestation in deep neural networks. J. Mach. Learn. Res. **23**, 1–46 (2022)
18. Hallgren, K.A.: Computing Inter-Rater Reliability for Observational Data: An Overview and Tutorial. Tutor Quant Methods Psychol. **8**(1), 23–34 (2012)

19. He, K., Zhang, X., Ren, S., Sun, J.: Deep residual learning for image recognition. In: IEEE Conference on Computer Vision and Pattern Recognition (CVPR), pp. 770–778 (2016)
20. Hermann, K.L., Chen, T., Kornblith, S.: The origins and prevalence of texture bias in convolutional neural networks. In: Neural Information Processing Systems (NeurIPS) 34 (2020)
21. Hoiem, D., Chodpathumwan, Y., Dai, Q.: Diagnosing error in object detectors. In: Fitzgibbon, A., Lazebnik, S., Perona, P., Sato, Y., Schmid, C. (eds.) ECCV 2012. LNCS, vol. 7574, pp. 340–353. Springer, Heidelberg (2012). https://doi.org/10.1007/978-3-642-33712-3_25
22. Huang, G., Liu, Z., Van Der Maaten, L., Weinberger, K.Q.: Densely connected convolutional networks. In: IEEE Conference on Computer Vision and Pattern Recognition (CVPR), pp. 2261–2269 (2017)
23. Ilyas, A., Santurkar, S., Tsipras, D., Engstrom, L., Tran, B., Madry, A.: Adversarial examples are not bugs, they are features. In: Neural Information Processing Systems (NeurIPS) (2019)
24. Ionescu, R.T., Alexe, B., Leordeanu, M., Popescu, M., Papadopoulos, D.P., Ferrari, V.: How hard can it be? estimating the difficulty of visual search in an image. In: IEEE Conference on Computer Vision and Pattern Recognition (CVPR), pp. 2157–2166 (2016)
25. Isola, P., Xiao, J., Parikh, D., Torralba, A., Oliva, A.: What makes a photograph memorable? IEEE Trans. Pattern Anal. Mach. Intell. (TPAMI) 36(7), 1469–1482 (2014)
26. Isola, P., Zoran, D., Krishnan, D., Adelson, E.H.: Crisp boundary detection using pointwise mutual information. In: Fleet, D., Pajdla, T., Schiele, B., Tuytelaars, T. (eds.) ECCV 2014. LNCS, vol. 8691, pp. 799–814. Springer, Cham (2014). https://doi.org/10.1007/978-3-319-10578-9_52
27. Jiang, L., Meng, D., Zhao, Q., Shan, S., Hauptmann, A.G.: Self-paced curriculum learning. In: Proceedings of the National Conference on Artificial Intelligence, vol. 4, pp. 2694–2700 (2015)
28. Krizhevsky, A.: Learning Multiple Layers of Features from Tiny Images. Technical report Toronto (2009)
29. Kumar, M., Packer, B., Koller, D., Kumar, P., Packer, B., Koller, D.: Self-paced learning for latent variable models. In: Neural Information Processing Systems (NeurIPS) (2010)
30. LeCun, Y., Bottou, L., Bengio, Y., Haffner, P.: Gradient-based learning applied to document recognition. Proc. IEEE 86(11), 2278–2323 (1998)
31. Lee, Y.J., Grauman, K.: Learning the easy things first: Self-paced visual category discovery. In: IEEE Conference on Computer Vision and Pattern Recognition (CVPR), pp. 1721–1728 (2011)
32. Li, Y., Yosinski, J., Clune, J., Lipson, H., Hopcroft, J.: Convergent Learning: do different neural networks learn the same representations? In: International Conference on Learning Representations (ICLR) (2016)
33. Liu, D., Xiong, Y., Pulli, K., Shapiro, L.: Estimating image segmentation difficulty. In: Perner, P. (ed.) MLDM 2011. LNCS (LNAI), vol. 6871, pp. 484–495. Springer, Heidelberg (2011). https://doi.org/10.1007/978-3-642-23199-5_36
34. Maennel, H., et al.: What do neural networks learn when trained with random labels? In: Neural Information Processing Systems (NeurIPS) (2020)
35. Mangalam, K., Prabhu, V.: Do deep neural networks learn shallow learnable examples first? In: International Conference on Machine Learning (ICML), Deep Phenomena Workshop (2019)

36. Ortiz-Jiménez, G., Modas, A., Moosavi-Dezfooli, S.M., Frossard, P.: Hold me tight! Influence of discriminative features on deep network boundaries, Neural Information Processing Systems (NeurIPS) (2020)
37. Peterson, J.C., Battleday, R.M., Griffiths, T.L., Russakovsky, O.: Human uncertainty makes classification more robust. In: International Conference on Computer Vision (ICCV) (2019)
38. Pinto, N., Cox, D.D., DiCarlo, J.J.: Why is real-world visual object recognition hard? PLoS Comput. Biol. **4**(1), 0151–0156 (2008)
39. Russakovsky, O., Deng, J., Huang, Z., Berg, A.C., Fei-Fei, L.: Detecting avocados to Zucchinis: what have we done, and where are we going? In: International Conference on Computer Vision (ICCV) (2013)
40. Russakovsky, O., Deng, J., Su, H., Krause, J., Satheesh, S., Ma, S., Huang, Z., Karpathy, A., Khosla, A., Bernstein, M., Berg, A.C., Fei-Fei, L.: ImageNet large scale visual recognition challenge. Int. J. Comput. Vision **115**(3), 211–252 (2015)
41. Shah, H., Tamuly, K., Raghunathan, A., Jain, P., Netrapalli, P.: The pitfalls of simplicity bias in neural networks. In: Neural Information Processing Systems (NeurIPS) (2020)
42. Shwartz-Ziv, R., Tishby, N.: Opening the Black Box of Deep Neural Networks via Information. Why & when Deep Learning works: looking inside Deep Learning ICRI-CI (2017)
43. Simonyan, K., Zisserman, A.: Very deep convolutional networks for large-scale image recognition. In: International Conference on Learning Representations (ICLR) (2015)
44. Skilling, J., Bryan, R.: Maximum entropy image reconstruction: general algorithm. Mon. Not. R. Astron. Soc. **211**, 111–124 (1984)
45. Spain, M., Perona, P.: Some objects are more equal than others: measuring and predicting importance. In: Forsyth, D., Torr, P., Zisserman, A. (eds.) ECCV 2008. LNCS, vol. 5302, pp. 523–536. Springer, Heidelberg (2008). https://doi.org/10.1007/978-3-540-88682-2_40
46. Vijayanarasimhan, S., Grauman, K.: What's it going to cost you? Predicting effort vs. informativeness for multi-label image annotations. In: IEEE Conference on Computer Vision and Pattern Recognition (CVPR) (2009)
47. Wang, L., Hu, L., Gu, J., Wu, Y., Hu, Z., He, K., Hopcroft, J.: Towards understanding learning representations: to what extent do different neural networks learn the same representation. In: Neural Information Processing Systems (NeurIPS) (2018)
48. Yang, K., Qinami, K., Fei-Fei, L., Deng, J., Russakovsky, O.: Towards fairer datasets: Filtering and balancing the distribution of the people subtree in the ImageNet hierarchy. In: Conference on Fairness, Accountability, and Transparency (FAT), pp. 547–558 (2020)
49. Zhang, C., Bengio, S., Hardt, M., Recht, B., Vinyals, O.: Understanding deep learning requires rethinking generalization. In: International Conference on Learning Representations (ICLR) (2017)

AnimeCeleb: Large-Scale Animation CelebHeads Dataset for Head Reenactment

Kangyeol Kim[1,4], Sunghyun Park[1], Jaeseong Lee[1], Sunghyo Chung[2], Junsoo Lee[3], and Jaegul Choo[1,4(✉)]

[1] KAIST, Daejeon, South Korea
{kangyeolk,psh01087,wintermad1245,jchoo}@kaist.ac.kr
[2] Korea University, Seoul, South Korea
s94021@korea.ac.kr
[3] Naver Webtoon, Seongnam-si, South Korea
junsoolee93@webtoonscorp.com
[4] Letsur Inc., Seongnam-si, South Korea

Abstract. We present a novel Animation CelebHeads dataset (Anime-Celeb) to address an animation head reenactment. Different from previous animation head datasets, we utilize a 3D animation models as the controllable image samplers, which can provide a large amount of head images with their corresponding detailed pose annotations. To facilitate a data creation process, we build a semi-automatic pipeline leveraging an open 3D computer graphics software with a developed annotation system. After training with the AnimeCeleb, recent head reenactment models produce high-quality animation head reenactment results, which are not achievable with existing datasets. Furthermore, motivated by metaverse application, we propose a novel pose mapping method and architecture to tackle a cross-domain head reenactment task. During inference, a user can easily transfer one's motion to an arbitrary animation head. Experiments demonstrate an usefulness of the AnimeCeleb to train animation head reenactment models, and the superiority of our cross-domain head reenactment model compared to state-of-the-art methods. Our dataset and code are available at *this url*.

Keywords: Animation dataset · Head reenactment · Cross-domain

1 Introduction

Recent head reenactment methods [4,15,17] show impressive results on controlling a human head motion after trained with large-scale human talking head

---

K. Kim, S. Park and J. Lee—Equal contributions

Supplementary Information The online version contains supplementary material available at https://doi.org/10.1007/978-3-031-20074-8_24.

S. Avidan et al. (Eds.): ECCV 2022, LNCS 13668, pp. 414–430, 2022.
https://doi.org/10.1007/978-3-031-20074-8_24

Fig. 1. (Better viewed in color) Examples of our AnimeCeleb. Including a canonical head (*Neutral*), the AnimeCeleb contains expression-changed (*+Expression*) and head-rotated (*+Rotation*) images with varying shaders. (Color figure online)

video datasets [5,14]. The common approaches [15,17,20,21] for this task is to learn diverse motion changes between two contiguous frames, which require a large amount of head videos to train a high-performing neural network model. Due to the dependency of human video datasets, such approaches show weak generalization capacity on the animation domain, because animation characters have distinct appearances (*e.g.*, explicit lines and large eyes) compared to the human head ones. Our key contribution is to construct a large-scale animation head dataset, AnimeCeleb, for head reenactment, which deems as a data-centric solution to produce high-quality reenactment results on the animation domain.

Obviously, a standard approach to build an animation dataset would be to collect the images from comic books and cartoon films. Instead, we propose a principled manner to construct animation dataset, where 3D animation models serve as valuable image samplers. This leads to three following benefits. First, we can ceaselessly simulate the specified pose[1] of a 3D animation model, enabling to generate an *unlimited* number of multi-pose images of the same identity. Second, the simulated poses are easily obtainable as detailed pose vectors, where each dimension represents an individual semantic of an expression or a head angle. Lastly, a 3D vector graphics environment gives freedom to render the *arbitrary* resolution images with various shaders (See Fig. 1 horizontal axis). These strengths bring multiple use cases including the animation head reenactment and intuitive pose editing.

Technically, our data creation process involves 3D animation model collection, semantic annotation and image rendering. In this process, we first collect the 3D animation models spanning a wide range of animation characters. The collected 3D models contain a set of morphs that can deform appearances of the 3D models in face and body part. To identify suitable morphs relevant

---

[1] Throughout this paper, we mean by the 'pose' the information about head rotation, translation, and facial expression.

to the head reenactment task, we develop an annotation system to filter the expression-irrelevant morphs. We employ Blender[2] that can execute codes for a head detection and a pose manipulation to enable an automatic image rendering.

A great interest of an animation domain is to transfer a user's motion to the animation character, which is potentially applicable in a metaverse and a virtual avatar system. In this paper, we focus on transferring a user's pose to the animation character, and refer to this problem as a *cross-domain head reenactment task*. A plausible solution to the task is building a shared pose representation space across the domains (*i.e.*, human and animation). We use 3D morphable model (3DMM) parameters as the shared pose representation, which is widely used in recent numerous head reenactment studies [7,8,15,18,22]. 3DMM is a parametric face modeling method that provides powerful tools for describing human heads with semantic parameters. Since the AnimeCeleb pose vector is not compatible with 3DMM, we newly propose a *pose-mapping* method to transform an AnimeCeleb pose vector to 3DMM parameters. To be specific, we compute a set of distinct 3DMM parameters to describe the semantics that the AnimeCeleb includes, and combine it to obtain 3DMM parameters corresponding to a AnimeCeleb pose vector. Owing to the pose mapping, we can guarantee that both the AnimeCeleb and VoxCeleb [14], a human head video dataset, share the pose representations. Furthermore, we propose a new architecture called an animation motion model (*AniMo*), in which datasets from different domains are used to learn how to manipulate a head image according to the motion residing in the shared representations. In this manner, our model is capable of transferring a human head motion represented as 3DMM parameters to an animation head.[3]

In summary, our contributions to animation research are as follows:

– We propose a *novel data creation pipeline* and present a *public large-scale animation head dataset* AnimeCeleb, which contains groups of high-quality images and their corresponding pose vectors.
– We newly propose a *pose-mapping* method and a cross-domain head reenactment model *AniMo*, which jointly lead to a seamless motion transfer from a **human head** to an **animations head**.
– We demonstrate the effectiveness of AnimeCeleb in training head reenactment baselines, and experimental results show the superiority of *AniMo* on cross-domain head reenactment compared to state-of-the-art methods.

2   Animation CelebHeads Dataset

We first describe each step of the data creation of the AnimeCeleb in Sect. 2.1. Next, AnimeCeleb properties and statistics are given in Sect. 2.2. In Sect. 2.3, we show the animation head reenactment results on the AnimeCeleb and other animation datasets.

---

[2] https://www.blender.org/.
[3] Related work regarding to the AnimeCeleb and the proposed algorithm is provided in supplementary material.

2.1   Data Creation Process

Figure 2 depicts the overall process of the data creation pipeline. In the following, we provide details of each step from (A) to (D).

Data Collection (A). We collected 3D animation models from two different web sites: DevianArt[4] and Niconi solid[5]. Since all 3D animation models are copyrighted by their creators, we carefully confirmed the scope of rights and obtained permission from reachable authors. Finally, we acquired 3613 usable 3D animation models in total. We will release all 3D animation model *artists' list* along with the AnimeCeleb to acknowledge the credits of the artists.

The collected 3D animation models contain two essential components. The first component is the **morphs** that can alter appearances of a 3D animation model on face or body parts. We are able to change an individual morph's continuous value ranging from $[0, 1]$, and obtain a transformed appearance of a 3D animation model; for example, an animation head with open mouth in 0.3 proportion can be generated. The second one is the **bones** that can control head angles (*i.e.*, yaw, pitch and roll axes). In specific, the head angles are controlled by applying a rotation matrix to the neck bone.

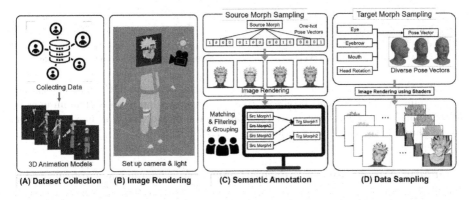

Fig. 2. Dataset Creation Pipeline Overview. 3D animation models are collected from two different websites (A). Then, a head part of the collected model are rendered after applying a morph with maximum intensity (B); these are then used for semantic annotation (C). In a data sampling step, sampled target morphs are used to compose pose vectors that serve as conditions to produce multi-pose images with diverse facial expressions and head rotations.

Image Rendering (B). To achieve an automatic sampling using 3D animation models, we develop a 2D head image creation pipeline built on Blender: an open source 3D computer graphics software that supports the visualization, manipulation and rendering of 3D animation models. To successfully render the

---

[4] https://www.deviantart.com/.
[5] https://3d.nicovideo.jp/.

animation head images in Blender, we need to consider three aspects: (1) camera position, (2) light condition, and (3) image resolution.

We set the camera position based on a neck bone position with the aim of capturing the head part. In respect to the light condition, we use a directional light point along the negative y-axis: frontal direction of an animation character (See Fig. 2(B)). Before rendering, we set the resolution of the images as 256 × 256, which is a standard resolution used in previous head reenactment methods [15,17]. Nonetheless, since the AnimeCeleb images are rendered from a 3D vector graphics model, we can create a higher image resolution (*e.g.*, 1024 × 1024). To demonstrate its extensive usage, we present various generated samples under different conditions in the supplementary material. Note that the rendered images contain an alpha channel as a transparent background, which can separate the foreground animation character and the background.

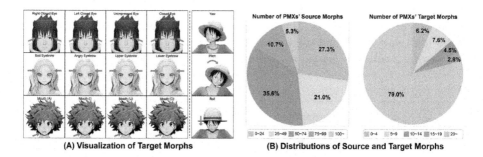

(A) Visualization of Target Morphs   (B) Distributions of Source and Target Morphs

Fig. 3. (A) Visualizing target morphs' examples and head rotation. (B) The percentage of the number of source and target morphs on 3D animation models. The number of source morphs are widely distributed ranging from 0 to over 100, and most animation models have dense usable annotations (*i.e.*, target morphs).

Semantic Annotation (C). Each 3D animation model has a significantly different number of morphs ranging from zero to even over 100. However, a morph naming convention is different according to a creator, which makes it difficult to apply a standardized criterion before annotating an accurate semantic of an individual morph. A goal of the semantic annotation is to *identify* expression-related morphs and *annotate* the morphs according to the unified naming convention. Importantly, this allows to sample a properly functioning expression-related source morph from a 3D animation model during rendering. For example, when a morph あ attached to a specific 3D animation model is identified as indicating a semantic of pronouncing the syllable 'ah' with a mouth, then it can be annotated as the target morph (*i.e.*, Mouth (A)). After annotation, that source morph あ of the 3D model is used, when the target morph Mouth (A) is determined to control the mouth shape.

To achieve the semantic annotation, we first define 23 *target* morphs, these are deemed as meaningful semantics to represent the facial expressions. We select the target morphs out of candidates collaborated with animation experts who work with cartoon makers. Figure 3(A) shows the examples of the target morphs

Table 1. Comparison between the AnimeCeleb and public animation head datasets.

Dataset	Num. of images	Identity labels	Face Align.	Unified style	Image source	Attribute Anno.
Kaggle Anime Face [1]	63K	✗	✗	✗	Media	–
Danbooru 2019 [3]	302K	✓	✗	✗	Media	–
iCartoonFace [23]	0.39M	✓	✗	✗	Media	3D Head Pose, Bounding Box Gender
AnimeCeleb (Ours)	2.4M	✓	✓	✓	3D Models	3D Head Pose, Expression, Foreground Mask Artistic Style

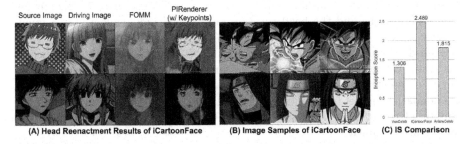

(A) Head Reenactment Results of iCartoonFace   (B) Image Samples of iCartoonFace   (C) IS Comparison

Fig. 4. (A) Head reenactment results trained with the iCartoonFace that bear an identity leakage problem. (B) An intra-variation within the same identity of the iCartoonFace is extremely large. (C) Average inception score comparison on three datasets; the average scores using 1000 identities indicate that iCartoonFace contains relatively inconsistent styles within the identity than those of the VoxCeleb and the AnimeCeleb.

that include meaningful semantics for three parts: eyes, eyebrows, and a mouth. Conversely to the target morphs, we denote the original morphs as *source* morphs in the remainder of this section. Next, we attempt to match the source morphs to the target morphs. Fortunately, a group of the source morphs with the identical name tends to portray the same semantics. Therefore, we take a two-stage approach: a group annotation and an individual inspection. The former collectively match a group of the source morphs under the same name to a target morph; the latter is responsible for inspecting the matched source morphs one-by-one to confirm whether it works correctly. During the group annotation, we count the number of source morphs that 3D models have, and remove the source morphs under 50. The individual inspection reduces the erroneous annotations that occur at the group annotation.

For this, we first render the head images after applying the entire source morphs independently and a neutral image without applying any morph using a 3D animation model (Fig. 2(C) upper part). Afterwards, we match a group of source morphs to one of the target morphs (*i.e.*, group annotation) and correct the results in a single morph-level via comparing a neutral and a morph-applied image for each source morph (*i.e.*, individual inspection). The entire procedure is conducted on the newly developed annotation system (Fig. 2(C) lower part). We provide the details of the defined target morphs and annotation system in the supplementary material.

Data Sampling (D). Throughout the data sampling, randomly selected target morphs for each part (*i.e.,* eyes, eyebrows and a mouth) are applied to a 3D animation model. The magnitudes of the morphs are determined by sampling from a uniform distribution, $\mathcal{U}(0, 1)$, independently. In respect to the head rotation, a 3D rotation matrix is computed taking yaw, pitch and roll values sampled between -20° and 20°. We render a transformed head after applying the morphs and the rotation, and also acquire a paired pose vector $\mathbf{p} \in \mathbb{R}^{20}$. A detailed description of the pose sampling process is provided in supplementary material.

A real-time rendering engine that Blender provides is used to produce the manipulated images and paired pose vectors. During rendering, we utilize 4 different types of shaders as shown in Fig. 2 to provide diverse textured 2D images. Since the morphs and the head rotation are applied independently, two image groups: a group of frontalized images with expression (*frontalized-expression*) and head rotated images with expression (*rotated-expression*) are included in the AnimeCeleb. The number of images sampled from the 3D model are determined differently depending on the number of annotated target morphs that a 3D animation model has. When a 3D animation model contains more than five annotated target morphs, we generate 100 images; if not (*e.g.,* zero), just 20 images are obtained.

2.2   Dataset Description

AnimeCeleb Properties. Figure 3(A) shows the examples of multiple target morphs for each part and head rotation results. The target morphs consist of 9 eye-related morphs, 9 eyebrow-related morphs and 5 mouth-related morphs. Note that the pre-defined target morphs include the semantics related to both eyes or eyebrows, which fill two values (*e.g.,* left and right eye) of a 17-dimensional pose vector (*expression* part). In total, 3613 different 3D models are used to generate the AnimeCeleb. As can be seen in Fig. 3(B) left, the number of source morphs of collected raw 3D animation models are widely distributed, averaging 49 morphs. After the semantic annotation, most animation models have more than 20 target morphs as shown in Fig. 3(B) right; this indicates the source morphs are densely matched to the target morphs.

Comparison with Other Datasets. As shown in Table 1, the AnimeCeleb has three advantages compared to the public existing animation head datasets [1, 3,23]. The advantages mainly stem from exploiting the power of 3D software and 3D animation models. First, detailed annotations such as facial expressions and head rotations can be easily gained because we are able to manipulate the head using our morph annotation (Table 1 Attribute Anno.). Second, the AnimeCeleb provides a massive amount of animation images that have unified styles (Table 1 Num. of Images, Unified Style). We believe that these properties help to develop high-performing neural networks in broad applications. Lastly, the AnimeCeleb contains four different unified styles in consideration of different cartoon textures. A similar approach [13] has been proposed using 3D animation models to construct an animation face dataset, and achieve a promising results on head reenactment. The contribution of AnimeCeleb is the first publicly available dataset that contains animation faces with pose annotations as well as the data sampling pipeline.

2.3 Animation Head Reenactment

Overview. The head reenactment aims to transfer a pose from a driving image to a source image. A common training scheme of the head reenactment model is to extract a pose from a driving image, and feed it with a source image to a decoder to reconstruct the driving image. Therefore, training a high-performing head reenactment model requires a large-scale video dataset, containing a set of the same identity images that can serve as a source and driving image pair. In a human domain, the VoxCeleb [14], a large-scale talking head dataset, plays this role. We believe that the AnimeCeleb is analogous to the VoxCeleb in an animation domain, which bears a potential to train a high-performing animation head reenactment model.

Prior head reenactment approaches are categorized into two groups whether a pre-computed pose annotation is utilized during training or not. The FOMM does not use the pose annotation, and learn relative motion between two images to convey the pose to a source image. In contrast, numerous studies [15,20,21] take advantage of the pose annotations such as keypoints and 3DMM parameters obtained from off-the-shelf pose extractors. Among them, we train two represen-

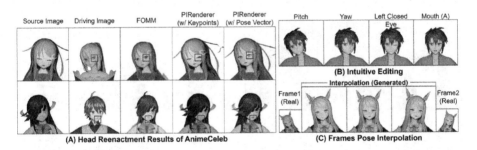

Fig. 5. (A) Qualitative results of the FOMM and PIRenderer trained with the AnimeCeleb. (B) Intuitive editing of an animation head image with different pose vectors. (C) Filling in-between frames using linearly interpolated pose vectors.

Table 2. Quantitative results of animation head reenactment. Obviously, for the AnimeCeleb dataset, the PIRenderer trained with pose vector outperforms the PIRenderer with keypoints and the FOMM.

Model	Same-Identity		Cross-identity
	FID$\downarrow$	SSIM$\uparrow$	FID$\downarrow$
FOMM	23.45	0.824	29.94
PIRenderer(w/ keypoints)	27.84	0.770	21.48
PIRenderer(w/ pose vector)	**20.27**	**0.826**	**16.52**

tative head reenactment baselines [15, 17] from each category with the Anime-Celeb: the FOMM [17] and the PIRenderer [15], which uses 3DMM parameters to describe a head pose.

Experiment Setup. When training the PIRenderer, we replace 3DMM with the pose vectors of the AnimeCeleb. For the dataset comparison, we additionally train the baselines [15, 17] using the iCartoonFace [23]. Although there exist other animation head datasets [1, 3], we select the iCartoonFace as a comparison dataset, acknowledging the size of it and accurate identity labels. Furthermore, with the aim of pose annotation comparison, we train the PIRenderer leveraging the keypoints for both datasets. We utilize an off-the-shelf animation keypoint detector[6] that gives 28 keypoints of an animation head image. All implementations are conducted following the hyperparameters denoted the papers with 3319 train set and 294 test dataset created with the first shader style.

We evaluate the trained models on (1) Self-identity task where the same character provides the source and driving image, and (2) Cross-identity task where two frames of different character sampled from the AnimeCeleb serve as the source and driving image. For evaluation, Frechet Inception Distance (FID) [11] and Structural Similarity (SSIM) [19] are adopted to measure the generated images quality. Note that the AnimeCeleb is applicable to other existing head reenactment models [9, 20, 21] that need image keypoints, yet we implement two representative baselines here.

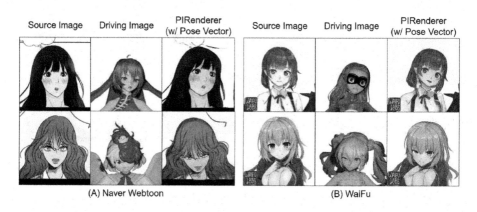

Fig. 6. Head reenactment results on other animation datasets.

Experimental Results with the iCartoonFace. Figure 4(A) shows the cross-identity head reenactment outputs of two models trained with the iCartoonFace. Despite the attempts to train the FOMM and PIRenderer with the iCartoonFace, we have found that the trained models show poor performance, producing blurry outputs. We assume that excessive variation within a single

---

[6] https://github.com/hysts/anime-face-detector.

identity is the main cause of the results. In fact, considering that the iCartoon-Face consists of the images collected from different appearance scenes, most images have own properties as seen in Fig. 4(B). For quantitative analysis, we measure the Inception Score (IS) [16] by averaging 1,000 image sets of the same identity. As seen in Fig. 4(C), we confirm that the iCartoonFace records higher IS score, compared to the VoxCeleb and the AnimeCeleb. This indicates that the iCartoonFace contains unacceptable appearance complexity, hence learning from such images goes beyond the capacity of existing head reenactment models.

Advantage of Pose Annotation. As seen in Fig. 5(A), the FOMM trained with the AnimeCeleb produces plausible outputs, yet still has undesirable deformation. Different from it, the trained PIRenderers successfully preserve the source head structure while imitating a given driving image with both pose annotations (*i.e.*, keypoints and pose vector). Especially, the PIRenderer(w/ pose vector) accurately conveys a driving pose to the source image as shown in Fig. 5(A) red boxes. It is because the AnimeCeleb pose vectors hold more direct guidance (*e.g.*, 80% mouth openness) than the keypoints. This results can be quantitatively confirmed in Table 2, where the PIRenderer(w/ pose vector) outperforms other baselines on both same-identity and cross-identity head reenactment tasks. Besides, the PIRenderer(w/ pose vector) is able to intuitively edit head poses based on given pose vectors (Fig. 5(B)) and generate the in-between frames by interpolating the pose vectors of two different frames (Fig. 5(C)).

Other Animation Results. We demonstrate the generalization capacity of the trained model on other animation datasets. In an experiment, we evaluate the PIRenderer(w/ pose vector) on different collected head datasets including Waifu Labs[7] and Naver Webtoons[8]. As seen in Fig. 6, the model successfully transfer a given driving image pose to an animation head. We provide the details of the collected animation head datasets and additional results on other examples in supplementary material.

3   Cross-domain Head Reenactment

Overview. Although we show a promising animation head reenactment result in Sect. 2.3, controlling characters' head pose as a human user wants (*i.e.*, cross-domain head reenactment) is another important application that bears a potential to be used in a virtual YouTuber system and a cartoon production. In this section, we address the cross-domain head reenactment using the proposed pose mapping method and the *AniMo*.

In a standard head reenactment training scheme, two frames are sampled from a video: a source image s and driving image d, and reconstruct d. Different from previous methods [15,17], we leverage two videos from different domains, respectively. Since a direct supervision across domains is not available during training, the source and driving image pair from animation domain: $s^{(a)}$, $d^{(a)}$ and human domain: $s^{(r)}$, $d^{(r)}$ are utilized to reconstruct the driving images, $d^{(a)}$

---

[7] https://waifulabs.com/.
[8] https://comic.naver.com/.

and $d^{(r)}$, respectively. In the following, we illustrate the details of a driving pose representation (Sect. 3.1). Then, we describe a training pipeline and its objective functions (Sect. 3.2).

Difference from PIRenderer. Our architecture design is inspired by PIRenderer [15], yet two novel components, a pose-mapping method and separate domain-specific networks, are proposed to improve cross-domain head reenactment performance. The pose-mapping method enables to align blendshape and 3DMM, which gives the capability to handle a pose from human domain (*i.e.*, cross domain). Also, the domain-specific networks help to preserve a given source image's textures for each domain, and improve the quality of image. Note that our pose-mapping method can help PIRenderer to improve the performance on cross-domain head reenactment task.

3.1 Driving Pose Representations

Human Pose Representation. Our approach employs the 3DMM parameters to describe a pose of a driving human head image. With the 3DMM, a 3D human face shape $\mathbf{S}$ can be represented as $\mathbf{S} = \bar{\mathbf{S}} + \alpha\mathbf{B}_{id} + \beta\mathbf{B}_{exp}$, where $\bar{\mathbf{S}}$ is the average face shape, $\mathbf{B}_{id}$ and $\mathbf{B}_{exp}$ denote the principal components of identity and expression based on 200 scans of human faces [2], respectively. Also, $\alpha \in \mathbb{R}^{80}$ and $\beta \in \mathbb{R}^{64}$ indicate the coefficients that control the relative magnitude between the facial shape and expression basis. The head rotation and translation are defined as $\mathbf{R} \in SO(3)$ and $\mathbf{t} \in \mathbb{R}^3$. We use a pre-trained 3D face reconstruction model [6] to extract the 3DMM parameters from the human head images. Discarding α for excluding an identity-related information, we only exploit a subset space of the 3DMM parameters $\mathcal{M}$ to represent a human head pose, where $\mathbf{m} \in \mathcal{M}$ comprises of expression coefficients, head rotation and translation: $\mathbf{m} \equiv \{\beta, \mathbf{R}, \mathbf{t}\} \in \mathbb{R}^{70}$.

Pose Mapping. The AnimeCeleb pose vector $\mathbf{p} \in \mathbb{R}^{20}$ consists of independent coefficients $\mathbf{b} \in \mathcal{B}$ and head angles $\mathbf{h} \in \mathcal{H}$, where $\mathcal{B}$ denotes a 17-dimensional space of concatenated expression coefficient and $\mathcal{H}$ indicates a 3D head angle space. In this step, we aim at discovering a mapping relationship from the AnimeCeleb pose vector to the 3DMM parameters. To this end, we propose a pose mapping function: $\mathcal{T} : \mathcal{B} \times \mathcal{H} \rightarrow \mathcal{M}$, which is responsible to find its corresponding 3DMM parameters, given a pose vector. We construct a direct mapping relationship between the coefficients $\mathbf{b}$ and the 3DMM expression parameters β using facial landmarks as a proxy space and expressing the each coefficient's semantics via manually manipulating the landmark positions. In the following, we elaborate the details step-by-step with Fig. 7(A).

(T.0) Before the landmark manipulation, we first obtain an initial landmark position, which corresponds to a neutral 3DMM coefficient. To be specific, the initial landmark position is obtained from a rendered mesh with setting the entire 3DMM coefficients as $\mathbf{0}$ expressed as $\{\alpha_0, \beta_0, \mathbf{R}_0, \mathbf{t}_0\}$, meaning that the average face shape $\bar{\mathbf{S}}$ at center location offers the initial landmark position. (T.1) Next, the initial landmarks are manipulated according to each semantic; for example, *left closed eye* landmarks can be achieved by minimizing the distances between the upper and the lower eyelid keypoints at the left eye. (T.2 and T.3) Then, the manipulated landmarks l^k with k-th semantic are used to update the initial β by minimizing the ℓ_2 distance between l^k and the landmarks extracted from the rendered mesh using β. Also, we employ a ℓ_2 regularization during updating β. Completing this process for each landmark, we can gain the fitted 3DMM expression parameters for each semantic: $\Phi = \{\beta^k\}_{k=1}^{17} \in \mathbb{R}^{17 \times 64}$. Finally, the pose mapping function can be written as: $\mathbf{m}_i = \mathcal{T}(\mathbf{b}_i, \mathbf{h}_i) = (\mathbf{b}_i \cdot \Phi) \oplus \Pi(\mathbf{h}_i) \oplus \mathbf{0} \in \mathcal{M}$, where Π denotes a mapping to convert a degree into radian measurement and $\oplus, i$ indicate a concatenation operation and a data index, respectively. In addition, $\mathbf{0} \in \mathbb{R}^3$ is concatenated to represent translation parameters.

3.2   Training Pipeline

Figure 7 depicts an overview of our framework, which consists of three networks described below.

Motion Network. Given a driving pose $\mathbf{m}$, our motion network F generates a latent pose code $\mathbf{z} \in \mathcal{Z}$, where $\mathcal{Z}$ denotes a latent pose space. Formally, this can be written as: $\mathbf{z}^{(a)} = F(\mathbf{m}^{(a)}), \mathbf{z}^{(r)} = F(\mathbf{m}^{(r)})$, where $\mathbf{m}^{(a)} = \mathcal{T}(\mathbf{b}, \mathbf{h})$ is a transformed driving pose corresponding to the driving image $d^{(a)}$ in an animation domain and $\mathbf{m}^{(r)}$ denotes a subset of 3DMM paramters obtained from the driving image $d^{(r)}$ in a human domain, respectively. Thanks to the pose mapping method, the motion network F can be designed as *domain-agnostic* manner. The learned latent pose code $\mathbf{z}$ is transformed to estimate the affine parameters for adaptive instance normalization (AdaIN) [12] operations. The pose information parameterized as the affine parameters plays a role in predicting an optical flow in the warping network W and injecting a fine-detailed pose in the editing network G.

Warping & Editing Network. For sake of simplicity, we omit the domain notation unless needed, such as $\mathbf{z} = \{\mathbf{z}^{(a)}, \mathbf{z}^{(r)}\}$, $d = \{d^{(a)}, d^{(r)}\}$, and $s = \{s^{(a)}, s^{(r)}\}$ in the descriptions of warping and editing network. Inspired by the PIRenderer [15], we employ *domain-specific* warping networks and an editing network for each domain. A warping network W takes a source image s and latent pose code $\mathbf{z}$ to predict the optical flow $\mathbf{u}$ that approximates the coordinate offsets to reposition a source head alike a driving head.

Next, the source image is fed into an encoder part of a editing network G and the optical flow $\mathbf{u}$ is applied to the intermediate multi-scale feature maps. This leads to spatial deformation of the feature maps according to the driving pose. During decoding in G, the AdaIN operation is used to inject the pose information. After training, the warping network mainly focuses on causing a large pose, including the head rotation, whereas the editing network serves to portrait an detailed expression-related pose. We train our framework with a reconstruction loss and a style loss following the PIRenderer [15]. The architecture, implementation details and objective functions are elaborated in the supplementary material.

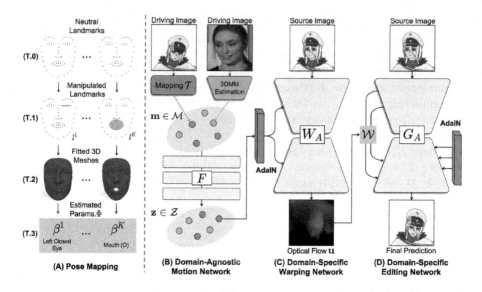

Fig. 7. Overview of (A) pose mapping method and (B)-(D) *AniMo*.

3.3   Experiments

Experiment Setup. Different from Sect. 2.3, we use both cartoon texture shader style AnimeCeleb and the VoxCeleb [14] as a training dataset. The Vox-Celeb contains 22,496 talking-head videos collected from online videos, and we use downloadable 18,503 videos for the train set and 504 videos for test set.

We evaluate the trained models on self-identity, and cross-domain head reen-actment where the images of the AnimeCeleb and the VoxCeleb alternatively serve as a source and a driving image respectively. Similar to Sect. 2.3, FID and SSIM are used to assess the quality of generated images. In addition, we introduce a Head Angle Error (HAE) that measures the ℓ_1 distances between the driving image's head angles and those of the generated image with the aim of evalu-ating head rotating ability. To be specific, we take advantage of a pre-trained head angle regressor, based on ResNet-18 [10] architecture and trained with the AnimeCeleb train set using ℓ_1 distance objective function between a predicted angle and the ground-truth **h**. In experiments, we use randomly sampled 1,000 pairs of source and driving images to compute evaluation metrics.

Comparison with State of the Art. We compare the *AniMo* with state-of-the-art models [4,15,17] quantitatively and qualitatively. Since we leverage two datasets during training, comparable baselines are trained on either the VoxCeleb following their original implementations or both the VoxCeleb and AnimeCeleb. During evaluation, we make an inference of manipulated animation or human head by optionally leveraging the decoder of each domain. We describe the details of the baselines and settings in the supplementary material.

Table 3 shows quantitative comparisons between the *AniMo* and the baselines on the self-identity and the cross-domain head reenactment. When evaluating

Table 3. Quantitative comparison with baselines on self-identity and cross-domain head reenactment tasks. The expression A → B denotes that transferring a A's motion to B's a source image.

Train Dataset	Methods	Self-identity (AnimeCeleb)		Self-identity (VoxCeleb)		Cross-domain (Vox.→Anime.)		Cross-domain (Anime.→-Vox.)
		FID↓	SSIM↑	FID↓	SSIM↑	FID↓	HAE↓	FID↓
Single Dataset	FOMM	47.91	0.648	**16.10**	**0.803**	122.83	0.177	94.23
(VoxCeleb)	PIRenderer	134.91	0.532	19.67	0.604	95.75	0.176	96.42
	LPD	–	–	–	–	166.54	0.171	–
Joint Datasets	FOMM	45.01	**0.748**	19.60	0.748	144.88	0.196	126.49
(AnimeCeleb,	PIRenderer+$\mathcal{T}$	16.07	0.735	18.98	0.611	69.80	0.195	61.67
VoxCeleb)	**Ours**	**16.05**	0.738	19.34	0.606	**18.78**	**0.128**	**41.04**

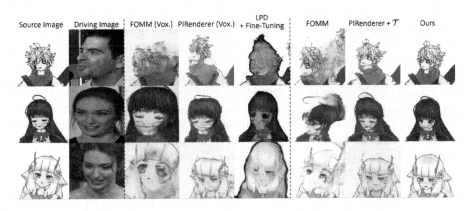

Fig. 8. Qualitative comparison between our model and the baselines.

the self-identity head reenactment within the AnimeCeleb, it is obvious that the models trained on both the AnimeCeleb and the VoxCeleb surpass those trained on the VoxCeleb. On the contrary, quantitative results on self-identity head reenactment within the VoxCeleb demonstrate that joint datasets may be harmful to the reconstruction task. Unlike these results, our model outperforms all baselines on cross-domain head reenactment tasks in terms of an image quality and an imitating head pose, indicating the superiority of our model in transferring a pose across the domains.

Figure 8 shows qualitative comparisons between the *AniMo* and the baselines on the cross-domain head reenactment. The FOMM, which relies on the unsupervised landmarks, does not work well, because the model attempts to align the appearance of the source image as the driving image's head structure, and this leads to the identity leakage problem as well as introducing blurring artifacts. In contrast, the PIRenderer and latent pose descriptor (LPD) [4], where the pose is injected by the AdaIN operations, successfully retain a head structure of the source image, yet produce rather blurry outputs. As seen in the PIRenderer+$\mathcal{T}$, the blurry artifacts can be improved by incorporating the AnimeCeleb as an additional training dataset with the pose mapping $\mathcal{T}$. Meanwhile, our model clearly outperforms the baselines, preserving more vivid textures of the source image and accurately reflecting the pose of the driving image with the aid of the domain-specific networks. We conclude that the shared pose space introduced by the pose mapping and the domain-specific design help the model to transfer the pose across domains. We include more results in the supplementary material.

4   Conclusions

In this paper, we present the AnimeCeleb, a large-scale animation head dataset, which is a valuable and practical resource for developing animation head reenactment model. Departing from existing animation datasets, we utilize 3D animation models to construct our animation head dataset by simulating facial expressions and head rotation, resulting in neatly-organized animation head dataset with rich annotations. For this purpose, we built a semi-automatic data creation pipeline based on Blender and a semantics annotation tool. We believe that the AnimeCeleb would boost and contribute to animation-related research. On the other hand, we propose the pose mapping and architecture to address cross-domain head reenactment to admit transferring a given human head motion to an animation head. Conducted experiments demonstrate the effectiveness of the *AniMo* on cross-domain head reenactment and intuitive image editing. In the future work, we plan to extend the AnimeCeleb and develop more advanced cross-domain head reenactment model.

Acknowledgements. This work was supported by the Institute of Information & communications Technology Planning & Evaluation (IITP) grant funded by the Korean government (MSIT) (No. 2019-0-00075, Artificial Intelligence Graduate School Program (KAIST), No. 2021-0-01778, Development of human image synthesis and discrimination technology below the perceptual threshold), and the Air Force Research Laboratory, under agreement number FA2386-22-1-4024. The U.S. Government is authorized to reproduce and distribute reprints for Governmental purposes notwithstanding any copyright notation thereon. Finally, we thank all researchers at NAVER WEBTOON Corp.

References

1. Kaggle animation face. https://www.kaggle.com/splcher/animefacedataset
2. Blanz, V., Vetter, T.: A morphable model for the synthesis of 3d faces. In: Proceedings of the 26th Annual Conference on Computer Graphics and Interactive Techniques, pp. 187–194 (1999)
3. Branwen, G., Anonymous, Community, D.: Danbooru 2019: A large-scale anime character illustration dataset. https://www.gwern.net/Crops, May 2020. https://www.gwern.net/Crops, accessed: DATE
4. Burkov, E., Pasechnik, I., Grigorev, A., Lempitsky, V.: Neural head reenactment with latent pose descriptors. In: Proceedings of the IEEE Conference on Computer Vision and Pattern Recognition (CVPR), pp. 13786–13795 (2020)

5. Chung, J.S., Nagrani, A., Zisserman, A.: Voxceleb2: deep speaker recognition. arXiv preprint arXiv:1806.05622 (2018)
6. Deng, Y., Yang, J., Xu, S., Chen, D., Jia, Y., Tong, X.: Accurate 3d face reconstruction with weakly-supervised learning: from single image to image set. In: Proceedings of the IEEE Conference on Computer Vision and Pattern Recognition Workshop (CVPRW) (2019)
7. Gafni, G., Thies, J., Zollhofer, M., Nießner, M.: Dynamic neural radiance fields for monocular 4d facial avatar reconstruction. In: Proceedings of the IEEE Conference on Computer Vision and Pattern Recognition (CVPR), pp. 8649–8658 (2021)
8. Guo, Y., Chen, K., Liang, S., Liu, Y.J., Bao, H., Zhang, J.: Ad-nerf: audio driven neural radiance fields for talking head synthesis. In: Proceedings of the IEEE International Conference on Computer Vision (ICCV), pp. 5784–5794 (2021)
9. Ha, S., Kersner, M., Kim, B., Seo, S., Kim, D.: Marionette: few-shot face reenactment preserving identity of unseen targets. In: Proceedings of the AAAI Conference on Artificial Intelligence (AAAI), vol. 34, pp. 10893–10900 (2020)
10. He, K., Zhang, X., Ren, S., Sun, J.: Deep residual learning for image recognition. In: Proceedings of the IEEE Conference on Computer Vision and Pattern Recognition (CVPR), pp. 770–778 (2016)
11. Heusel, M., Ramsauer, H., Unterthiner, T., Nessler, B., Hochreiter, S.: GANs trained by a two time-scale update rule converge to a local nash equilibrium. In: Proceedings of the Advances in Neural Information Processing Systems (NeurIPS) (2017)
12. Huang, X., Belongie, S.: Arbitrary style transfer in real-time with adaptive instance normalization. In: Proceedings of the IEEE International Conference on Computer Vision, pp. 1501–1510 (2017)
13. Khungurn, P.: Talking head anime from a single image 2: More expressive (2021). https://pkhungurn.github.io/talking-head-anime-2/. Accessed: YYYY-MM-DD
14. Nagrani, A., Chung, J.S., Zisserman, A.: Voxceleb: a large-scale speaker identification dataset. arXiv preprint arXiv:1706.08612 (2017)
15. Ren, Y., Li, G., Chen, Y., Li, T.H., Liu, S.: Pirenderer: controllable portrait image generation via semantic neural rendering. In: Proceedings of the IEEE International Conference on Computer Vision (ICCV), pp. 13759–13768 (2021)
16. Salimans, T., Goodfellow, I., Zaremba, W., Cheung, V., Radford, A., Chen, X.: Improved techniques for training gans. In: Advances in neural information processing systems 29 (2016)
17. Siarohin, A., Lathuilière, S., Tulyakov, S., Ricci, E., Sebe, N.: First order motion model for image animation. In: Proceedings of the Advances in Neural Information Processing Systems (NeurIPS) 32, pp. 7137–7147 (2019)
18. Wang, C., Chai, M., He, M., Chen, D., Liao, J.: Cross-domain and disentangled face manipulation with 3d guidance. arXiv preprint arXiv:2104.11228 (2021)
19. Wang, Z., Bovik, A.C., Sheikh, H.R., Simoncelli, E.P.: Image quality assessment: from error visibility to structural similarity. IEEE Trans. Image Process. **13**(4), 600–612 (2004)
20. Zakharov, E., Ivakhnenko, A., Shysheya, A., Lempitsky, V.: Fast bi-layer neural synthesis of one-shot realistic head avatars. In: Vedaldi, A., Bischof, H., Brox, T., Frahm, J.-M. (eds.) ECCV 2020. LNCS, vol. 12357, pp. 524–540. Springer, Cham (2020). https://doi.org/10.1007/978-3-030-58610-2_31
21. Zakharov, E., Shysheya, A., Burkov, E., Lempitsky, V.: Few-shot adversarial learning of realistic neural talking head models. In: Proceedings of the IEEE Conference on Computer Vision and Pattern Recognition (CVPR), pp. 9459–9468 (2019)

22. Zhang, C., et al.: Facial: synthesizing dynamic talking face with implicit attribute learning. In: Proceedings of the IEEE International Conference on Computer Vision (ICCV), pp. 3867–3876 (2021)
23. Zheng, Y., Zhao, Y., Ren, M., Yan, H., Lu, X., Liu, J., Li, J.: Cartoon face recognition: a benchmark dataset. In: Proceedings of the 28th ACM International Conference on Multimedia, pp. 2264–2272 (2020)

MUGEN: A Playground for Video-Audio-Text Multimodal Understanding and GENeration

Thomas Hayes[1], Songyang Zhang[2]([✉]), Xi Yin[1], Guan Pang[1], Sasha Sheng[1], Harry Yang[1], Songwei Ge[3], Qiyuan Hu[1], and Devi Parikh[1]

[1] Meta AI, New York, USA
{thayes427,yinxi,gpang,sash,harryyang,isabellehu,dparikh}@fb.com
[2] University of Rochester, Rochester, USA
szhang83@ur.rochester.edu
[3] University of Maryland, College Park, USA
songweig@umd.com
https://mugen-org.github.io/

Abstract. Multimodal video-audio-text understanding and generation can benefit from datasets that are narrow but rich. The narrowness allows bite-sized challenges that the research community can make progress on. The richness ensures we are making progress along the core challenges. To this end, we present a large-scale video-audio-text dataset MUGEN, collected using the open-sourced platform game CoinRun. We made substantial modifications to make the game richer by introducing audio and enabling new interactions. We trained RL agents with different objectives to navigate the game and interact with 13 objects and characters. This allows us to automatically extract a large collection of diverse videos and associated audio. We sample 375K video clips (3.2 s each) and collect text descriptions from human annotators. Each video has additional annotations that are extracted automatically from the game engine, such as accurate semantic maps for each frame and templated textual descriptions. Altogether, MUGEN can help progress research in many tasks in multimodal understanding and generation. We benchmark representative approaches on tasks involving video-audio-text retrieval and generation. Our dataset and code are released at: https://mugen-org.github.io/.

Keywords: Video · Audio · Language · Multimodal · Retrieval · Generation

---

T. Hayes and S. Zhang—equal contribution, ordered alphabetically.

Supplementary Information The online version contains supplementary material available at https://doi.org/10.1007/978-3-031-20074-8_25.

1   Introduction

Research in multimodal understanding and generation brings together the sub-fields of vision and language in AI. Significant progress has been made on image-text understanding and generation tasks, such as CLIP [54] for image-text retrieval and DALL-E [55] for text-to-image generation. This progress has been made possible with large-scale image-text datasets [6,53,61,64,73] that are collected from the web. However, progress in the video-text domain lags due to challenges in data collection and modeling of spatiotemporal information.

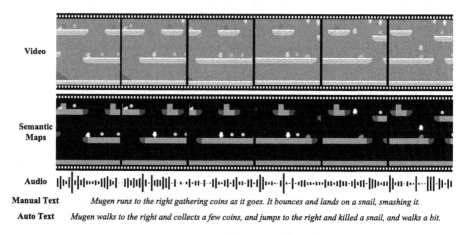

Fig. 1. An example from our dataset. For each 3.2 s video clip, we have rich annotations including accurate semantic maps, synchronized audio, manual text collected from human annotators, and auto-text generated based on certain rules.

Many existing video-text datasets [40,50,68,79] are collected in the wild and are proposed for understanding tasks such as video-text retrieval [50], video question answering [40], and generation tasks like video captioning [68]. Yet the performance on these tasks is still far behind their image counterparts [10,42,76] due to the challenges in understanding the complex dynamics in these in-the-wild videos. Moreover, such video-text pairs are too challenging for text-to-video generation, where more constrained datasets are used instead, e.g., bouncing MNIST [33], KTH [51] and UCF-101 [48]. However, these are limited in actions and interactions between entities which are crucial to modeling real-world videos.

In this paper, we introduce MUGEN, a large-scale controllable video-audio-text dataset with rich annotations for multimodal understanding and generation. MUGEN is collected in a closed world based on the open-sourced platform game CoinRun [11]. We have made substantial modifications to the game engine to make the videos more diverse (and delightful) by introducing audio, adjusting camera zoom and stabilization, and enabling new interactions between characters. We name the protagonist "Mugen", and collected videos about Mugen's interactions with the other characters and objects.

To collect videos, we train reinforcement learning (RL) agents to navigate the world and record gameplay. To increase video diversity and reduce bias towards the actions of any single agent, we trained 14 RL agents with different objectives. We record 233K videos of gameplay where the game environment is procedurally generated, so there are no video duplicates. We then sample 375K 3.2 s video clips from this video set to collect text descriptions from human annotators (which we call "manual text"). For each video clip, there are additional annotations that come for free: 1) audio is generated from a set of background music and foreground sound effects; 2) accurate semantic maps are generated for each frame using the game assets; 3) automatic text descriptions ("auto-text") are generated based on Mugen's actions and language templates. This results in 375K video-audio-text samples in the MUGEN dataset. One example is shown in Fig. 1.

Table 1. Comparison between MUGEN and other video-text datasets. Sent., Sem. and Cust. represent sentence, semantic and customizable. M, A, W and ASR represent descriptions that are manually annotated, alt-text collected from the web, and translated from speech. R and G represent sound recorded with the video and generated based on the video.

Dataset	Video Content	Sent. Source	Number of			Properties		
			Sent.	Videos	Clips	Sem.	Audio	Cust.
BMNIST [33]	Digit	A	–	–	–	✗	✗	✓
KTH [51]	Human action	A	2K	–	2K	✗	✗	✗
TVR [41]	TV show	M	11K	–	22K	✗	R	✗
YouCook2 [79]	Cooking	M	14K	2K	14K	✗	R	✗
MSVD [7]	Open	M	70K	–	2K	✗	R	✗
A2D [67]	Human action	M	7K	–	4K	✓	R	✗
Charades [62]	Daily life	M	16K	–	10K	✗	R	✗
FLINTSTONES [25]	Cartoon	M	25K	–	25K	✓	R	✗
MSRVTT [68]	Human activity	M	200K	7180	10K	✗	R	✗
WebVid-10M [5]	Open	W	10.7M	–	10.7M	✗	R	✗
HowTo100M [50]	Instructional	ASR	136K	1.2M	136M	✗	R	✗
HD-VILA-100M [69]	Open	ASR	100M	3.3M	100M	✗	R	✗
MUGEN (ours)	Platform game	M+A	379K	233K	375K	✓	G	✓

Table 1 shows a comparison between MUGEN and other multimodal datasets. There are several advantages of MUGEN. First, the videos in MUGEN are collected in a closed world with a limited set of visually simple objects and scenes (i.e., simpler than in-the-wild datasets) but with diverse motions and interactions between entities that capture some of the core challenges in video understanding and generation (i.e., richer than other closed world datasets). Not only does the narrowness allow for bite-sized challenges to make progress on, it also alleviates the need for web-scale data and correspondingly massive compute resources in studying multimodal understanding and generation. Second, there are rich annotations for each video including accurate semantic maps, synchronized audio, and auto-text and manual text descriptions that can enable a wide variety of tasks in multimodal research. Third, the game engine setup allows us to render videos at different resolutions on the fly, which is more flexible and storage efficient. Fourth, the game engine is modifiable, and once released, will allow the research community to collect more data to study a diverse set of problems.

MUGEN enables study of many multimodal video-audio-text tasks. In this paper, we focus on several tasks including retrieval and generation between all pairs of modalities. For the research community to make progress, it is vital to have consistent evaluation protocols. While many automatic metrics have been proposed for evaluation of generative models, human judgement is still the gold standard. Prior works have compared to ground-truth for text [12] or audio generation [9], but video generation evaluation is usually conducted by comparing to baselines because ground-truth is too challenging. This makes it difficult to compare methods and calibrate progress over time. Given that MUGEN is a closed world dataset with simplified visual elements, it is possible to compare to ground-truth videos for evaluation. In this paper, we conduct a comprehensive human evaluation for various cross-modal generation baselines. We evaluate both the generation quality as well as faithfulness to input modality. We hope this evaluation protocol will be adopted by the community. We will make our evaluation interfaces publicly available.

We summarize the contributions of this paper as follows:

- We propose MUGEN, a large-scale dataset of 375K video-audio-text samples with additional annotations of semantic maps and auto-text to facilitate research in multimodal understanding and generation.
- We benchmark the performance of video-audio-text retrieval and generation between every pair of modalities in a unified framework. To our knowledge, this is the first work that benchmarks all these tasks on one dataset.
- We formulate a standard protocol for human evaluation of quality and faithfulness for four generation tasks.
- We will release the dataset and the game platform so the community can generate more data for a variety of tasks to push the field forward.

2   Related Work

Multimodal Datasets. Existing multimodal datasets belong to two categories based on the visual content: open world (in-the-wild environments) and closed world (constrained environments). Open world datasets such as MSCOCO [45], ConceptualCaptions [6], and WIT [64] are widely used for image-text research. CLEVR [30] is a closed world dataset collected by arranging different 3D shapes on a clean background, which enables systematic progress in visual reasoning by reducing the complexity and bias from the real world.

Most video-text datasets are open world. MSRVTT [68], ANetCap [37], MSVD [7], and DiDeMo [3] contain videos of sports and human actions collected from the web. YouCook2 [79] and HowTo100M [50] contain instructional videos collected from YouTube. TVR [41], TVQA [40], and LSMDC [57] are collected from TV series and movies. Ego4D [24] is collected by people wearing an egocentric camera recording everyday activities around the world. Videos in these datasets contain complex backgrounds and diverse events, which makes them very challenging. Datasets from constrained environments, *e.g.* Bouncing MNIST (BMNIST) [33] and KTH [51], have been proposed. These datasets don't capture some of the core challenges in videos such as multiple entities interacting with each other in meaningful ways. FLINTSTONES [25] is created from an animated series, but the scenes are too diverse for the size of the dataset. In contrast, MUGEN simplifies the visual complexities of the scenes and objects, but captures complex motion and interactions between multiple entities.

The text in existing datasets are either collected from humans [25,68,79] or extracted from speech [50]. Besides human descriptions, MUGEN also allows generating templated auto-text descriptions for videos of arbitrary lengths.

Most open world video-text datasets are associated with audio recorded from human speech and/or events. AudioSet [22] and VGGSound [8] are collected with video-audio pairs for audio event recognition. However, the video and audio are often not well-aligned. (E.g., the speech may describe things not related to or aligned with the video and background noise is common.) In contrast, the video and audio in MUGEN are synchronized based on Mugen's actions, making it feasible to study less explored tasks like audio generation from video or text.

Multimodal Understanding and Generation. Multimodal research typically involves four modalities: image, video, audio and text. Image-text tasks are widely studied, such as VQA [4], image captioning [1,31,72], image-text retrieval [32], visual storytelling [27], text-to-image generation [56], etc. Earlier methods aimed to design effective models for specific tasks [23,43,52,71]. Later work [10,42,78] focused on large-scale pre-training to learn cross-modal representations that can be transferred to various downstream tasks. More recently, CLIP [54], CogView [14], and DALL-E [55] leverage even larger-scale training to improve model generalization and zero-shot learning. FLAVA [63] and Florence [74] were proposed as foundation models for both vision and language.

Many video-text tasks have been proposed, such as video QA [40], video-text retrieval [68], video grounding [19], video captioning [68], text-to-video generation [25], etc. Similar to image-text research, early approaches focused on a single task [17,20,38,77]. Some recent work proposed novel architectures to learn task-agnostic video-text embeddings, such as MIL-NCE [49] and Clip-BERT [39]. Compared to video-text retrieval and video captioning, text-to-video generation is relatively understudied, largely due to a lack of feasible datasets. Early methods [44,46,51] were evaluated on simple datasets like BMNIST [33] and KTH [51]. Mazaheri and Shah [48] annotated 10 action classes from UCF-101 [48]. However, the limited motion in these datasets restricts the diversity of the collected text descriptions, making them sub-optimal for studying text-to-video generation.

There are also efforts on audio, such as audio-text retrieval [36], audio captioning [35], audio-to-video generation [47], video-to-audio generation [28], etc.

We explore video-audio-text retrieval and generation between all pairs of modalities on MUGEN, and conduct extensive evaluations including human evaluation.

3   MUGEN Dataset

Environment. In-the-wild video understanding and generation poses several challenges, including understanding motion of objects, interactions among objects, physics, camera vs. object and scene motion, 3D depth of scenes, diverse object appearances and semantics, lighting conditions, etc. Our goal was to develop a dataset that is rich along some of these dimensions, but narrower along others, to enable focused advances in some of the core challenges of multimodal video research. Specifically, we desired a closed world dataset where physics are simplified, the camera angle is fixed, the number of objects is limited, and lighting is consistent. Yet, we sought diverse motions and interactions between entities (dataset statistics are shown in Fig. 2). For these purposes, we chose an open source video game which (1) enables training RL agents to collect video data at scale and (2) gives access to the game engine that provides additional high quality annotations for free, such as precise frame-level semantic maps and automatic text descriptions. Amongst open source games, we chose OpenAI's CoinRun [11] because of its ease of modification.

OpenAI's CoinRun is a platform game developed for quantifying generalization of RL agents [11,15,29]. The game has a single main character (who we call Mugen) with the objective to collect coins without being killed by monsters. Each level has a number of coins and monsters, and the level ends when Mugen collects all coins, Mugen is killed by a monster, or the level times out after 21 seconds. The environment is procedurally generated, with each level having a unique configuration of platforms, coins, and monsters.

We made a number of modifications to increase the diversity of game events and enhance richness, such as adding audio, slowing game physics, adjusting camera zoom and stabilization, and enabling new interactions between characters. Altogether, our updated version of CoinRun features Mugen, 10 monsters, coin and gem objects, and 2 world themes, space and snow. Mugen can take 16 different actions (see Fig. 2c for the most frequent actions). Monsters differ in their action vocabulary; some walk, others hop, and one flies. A full list of modifications, before and after videos highlighting these changes, and images of these characters, objects, and themes can be found in the appendix.

Audio. The audio consists of two layers, sound effects and background music. We chose 8 sound effects corresponding to Mugen's core actions: walk, jump, collect coin, kill monster, power-up, climb ladder, bump head, die. Each sound effect is triggered by these actions, and one sound effect plays at a time. Background music features 2 themes for the space and snow game themes. Background music is layered with the sound effect audio to produce the full audio track.

Video Collection. We train RL agents to navigate the environment and collect gameplay videos. We use an IMPALA-CNN architecture [16] and train agents

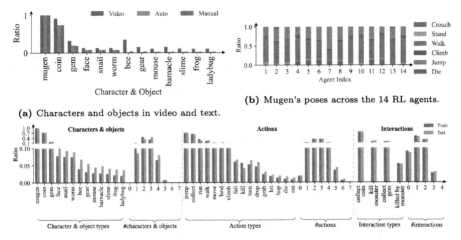

(a) Characters and objects in video and text.

(b) Mugen's poses across the 14 RL agents.

(c) Characters, objects, actions and interactions in three splits and their occurrence per video.

Fig. 2. Distribution of characters, objects, actions and interactions.

with Proximal Policy Optimization [59]. Inputs to the agent include the current game frame and the agent's velocity. The agent's performance in the game is immaterial to us; we care about maximizing the diversity of video data. To this end, we trained 14 agents with modified reward functions to achieve different behaviors. For example, decreasing the reward discount factor makes the agent more myopic and risk-tolerant, so the agent dies frequently. Figure 2b shows the distribution of Mugen's poses for each agent where the variation in time spent in different poses indicates differing actions. To further increase diversity, we ensured that the seed for map procedural generation is always unique. We have verified there are no duplicate videos in MUGEN.

To efficiently handle large-scale game video data and enable easy data customization (e.g., swapping characters or objects, changing background), we do not save the rendered videos. Instead, we save all metadata such as world layout and character movements in a json format, from which we can render RGB frames and pixel-accurate segmentation maps at any resolution up to 1400×1400 on-the-fly, resulting in more efficient data storage.[1]

We recorded 233K videos of gameplay ranging from 3.2 s to 21 s (level timeout) at 30 frames per second. Each video corresponds to a whole level of gameplay. We will release the game engine so others can customize the data environment or agents for their own purposes.

Manual Text. We split the 233K videos into 3.2 s (96 frames) clips and ask annotators to describe in 1–2 sentences what happens in the short video. After filtering low quality annotations, MUGEN consists of $378, 902$ text descriptions

---

[1] Storage is $>100\times$ smaller than 1024×1024 videos stored with lossless encoding.

for $375, 368$ video clips.[2] Refer to the appendix for the annotation interface and details on annotation quality control.

Auto-Text. In addition to collecting human annotation, we also developed a template-based algorithm to automatically generate textual descriptions for videos based on game engine metadata. See the appendix for details.

Note that both video and auto-text can be generated automatically. We can generate arbitrary amounts of video-text data with arbitrary lengths. This makes it feasible to study more tasks where manual annotations are expensive to acquire, such as text-conditioned long video generation [21], video grounding [75], and dense video captioning [37]. Auto-text is also highly structured in nature. This simplifies the text and improves model explainability since each action and interaction in the video has a unique description in the text.

Dataset Statistics. In total, MUGEN consists of 375K 3.2 s video clips paired with 379K manual text descriptions, as well as 233K longer (3.2 s to 21 s) videos. Each video clip or long video also comes with semantic maps, auto-text, and audio. There are 11 characters, 2 objects, 16 different actions for Mugen, and 4 classes of interactions with other objects and characters: collect coin, collect gem (power up), kill monster, killed by monster.

We first analyze the occurrences of characters and objects in video, manual text, and auto-text in Fig. 2a.[3] We observe that not all characters and objects appearing in the video are mentioned in the text. This is because annotators are more likely to describe characters that interact with Mugen than those in the background. Given the unbalanced distribution of characters and objects, when splitting our dataset, we sample fewer videos featuring only Mugen or Mugen's interaction with coins for the validation and test sets. Both validation and test sets contain only one manual text per video. This results in $349, 666, 12, 851,$ $12, 851$ video clips in training, validation, and test sets, respectively.

The distributions of characters and objects, actions, and interactions are shown in Fig. 2b. "Jump" and "collect" are the top 2 most frequent actions, consistent with "collect coin" being the most frequent class of interaction (this is CoinRun after all!). The rarest interaction type is Mugen being killed by a monster. We also show the distribution of the number of characters and objects, actions, and interactions in each video. Most videos contain 2–4 characters and objects, 2–4 actions, and 2–3 interactions. This is more diverse than other closed world datasets with one or two digits moving [33] or a single person moving in a scene [51]. We also show the location heatmap of each charchater/object and temporal heatmap of each action/interaction in the appendix.

As shown in Table 1, MUGEN is several orders of magnitude larger than existing closed world datasets such as BMNIST [33], KTH [51] and FLINT-STONES [25]. While it is smaller than some open world datasets including HowTo100M [50] and WebVid-2M [5], it is also visually less diverse, making it feasible to train effective models without having to work with web-scale

---

[2] A very small portion of the clips have more than one description.

[3] The occurrence of one character is counted at most once in each video/text.

data. Moreover, our dataset provides audio aligned with video, accurate frame-level semantic maps, and automatically generated text descriptions which enable studying a variety of tasks. Finally, this dataset is customizable with the released game engine, so the community can generate more data of different distributions.

4 Video-Audio-Text Retrieval and Generation

While MUGEN can enable many tasks, we focus on retrieval and generation between every pair of modalities. We first present the cross-modal retrieval framework and then a unified pipeline for cross-modal generation.

4.1 Video-Audio-Text Retrieval

Cross-modal retrieval, which retrieves samples from one modality given a query from another, is a fundamental task with many real-world applications. For example, text-to-video retrieval is widely used for video search.

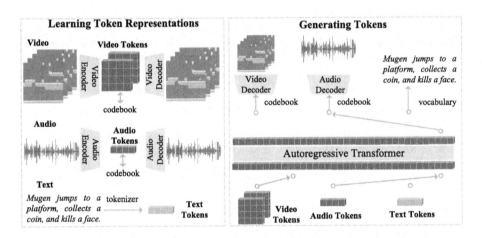

Fig. 3. A unified framework for generation between every pairs of modalities. The right part shows an example of video-to-audio generation.

We use an encoder F_x to map input x of each modality to a feature vector $\mathbf{f}_x = F_x(x)$. It is projected into a joint embedding space $\mathbf{e}_x = \mathbf{f}_x \cdot \mathbf{W}_x$, where $\mathbf{W}_x$ are the learnable parameters. Given inputs p and q from two modalities P and Q, the similarity can be computed by a scaled cosine function, $s(p,q) = cos(\mathbf{e}_p, \mathbf{e}_q) \cdot e^{\tau_{PQ}}$, where τ_{PQ} is a learnable temperature parameter. The matching loss L_{PQ} is computed as:

$$L_{PQ} = -\frac{1}{2N} \sum_{i=1}^{N} (\log(\frac{e^{s(p_i,q_i)}}{\sum_{j=1}^{N} e^{s(p_i,q_j)}}) + \log(\frac{e^{s(p_i,q_i)}}{\sum_{k=1}^{N} e^{s(p_k,q_i)}})), \qquad (1)$$

where N is the number of samples in a batch, p_i and q_i represent the ith sample from P and Q modalities within the batch.

We train three models with L_{VA}, L_{VT} and L_{AT} separately for video(V)-audio(A), video-text(T), and audio-text retrieval. For comparison, we also sum three losses to learn a joint model.

During inference, to retrieve samples from modality P given a query from modality Q, we rank the samples based on the similarities $s(p, q)$. To retrieve modality P based on queries from two modalities Q and R, we sum the similarity from two modalities, $s(p, q) + s(p, r)$. $s(p, q)$ and $s(p, r)$ can either come from two models independently trained by L_{PQ} and L_{PR} or the joint model.

4.2 Video-Audio-Text Generation

Cross-modal generation has gained increasing interest in recent years. Amongst video-audio-text cross-modal generation tasks, video-to-text generation (video captioning) is most studied, while other tasks (video-to-audio, text-to-video, etc.) are relatively under-explored.

Table 2. Performance comparison on video(V)-audio(A)-text(T) retrieval. For retrieval in modality P, $Q + R$ denotes the ensemble of two models independently trained by L_{PQ} and L_{PR}; $Q + R*$ denotes the joint model. Recalls are shown in percentage (%).

Query	Video retrieval			Query	Audio retrieval			Query	Text retrieval		
Type	R1	R5	R10	Type	R1	R5	R10	Type	R1	R5	R10
A	58.59	88.83	94.41	V	61.14	88.99	94.59	V	10.61	25.72	34.70
T	8.54	22.50	31.71	T	2.40	8.35	13.38	A	2.95	9.36	14.80
A+T	**81.50**	**96.10**	**98.26**	V+T	**69.59**	**92.48**	**96.42**	V+A	**11.68**	**27.13**	**36.60**
A+T*	62.54	87.33	92.62	V+T*	41.83	73.04	82.68	V+A*	10.95	26.24	35.33

Inspired by the success of using a VQ-VAE [65] and transformer for image [55] and video [70] generation, we adopt a similar and unified framework for cross-modal generation, as shown in Fig. 3. For each modality, we first learn a discrete codebook to encode the data. Then an decoder-only transformer is used to learn token generation from one modality to another.

Learning Token Representations. For video representation, we train a 3D VQ-VAE to learn a codebook following the training losses in [70]. The encoder is used to encode videos as inputs for the transformer during training, and the decoder is used for video generation during inference. Similarly, we train a 1D VQ-VAE to learn audio compression following the training losses in [13]. For text representation, we learn a tokenizer from manual text in the training set.

Generating Tokens. We use a decoder-only transformer to do auto-regressive token generation. During training, the input to the transformer is a sequence of tokens concatenated from modality P and Q. Video tokens are flattened from 3D latent codes into 1D. Text tokens are truncated or padded to have the same length. Causal attention is used where each token can only attend to prior tokens. The transformer learns to predict the token ids at every location. The loss functions for the two modalities are summed, similar to DALL-E [55]. During inference, given the tokens from P, we auto-regressively generate all tokens for Q. For audio or video, we use the predicted tokens to look up the codebook embeddings and feed them into VQ-VAE's decoder to reconstruct the video or audio. For text, the vocabulary is used to reconstruct the sentences.

5 Experiments

5.1 Video-Audio-Text Retrieval

The retrieval task is to find the true match from the test set in one modality, given queries of either one of the other modalities or both modalities. For retrieval based on queries from two modalities, we compare the ensemble of two separately trained models and the joint model. We report recall at rank 1, 5 and 10. For all experiments, if not specified, the video dimension is $256 \times 256 \times 32$, where the 32 frames are evenly sampled from the 96 frames to save computation.

Implementation Details. Pre-trained models are used as initialization including ResNet-18 [26] pre-trained on VGGSound [8] for the audio encoder, S3D [66] pre-trained on Kinetics 400 [34] for the video encoder, and DistilBERT [58] for the text encoder. The parameters in the text encoder are fixed[4] and the other two encoders are learnable. The temperature τ_{PQ} is initialized as 0.07 and the maximum is 100, the learning rate is 0.001, and batch size is 16. All models are trained for 400K steps and checkpoints are selected based on the validation set.

Results. The results are shown in Table 2. We have the following observations: 1) across all single modality retrieval tasks, video-to-audio and audio-to-video retrieval perform the best and text-to-audio and audio-to-text perform the worst. This is because video and audio are synchronized, while audio and text are only sparsely aligned on Mugen's actions and interactions; different text descriptions can map to similar audio samples. 2) retrieval based on two modalities with an ensemble of models $(P+Q)$ consistently outperforms single modality retrieval. This is because the other modality can provide complementary information. For example, text contains information of Mugen's moving direction that is available in video but not audio. 3) the performance of the joint model $(P + Q^*)$ typically falls between the separately trained models, which indicates that it is challenging to learn a joint embedding space for all modalities.

5.2 Video-Audio-Text Generation

We evaluate cross-modal generation for all pairs of modalities. We use V, A, T to denote video, audio, text, and P2Q to represent the task (e.g., T2V for

---

[4] Our initial experiments show unstable training with learnable text encoder.

text-to-video generation). We focus on quantitative evaluations of the quality of the output and faithfulness to the input.

Implementation Details. The 3D VQ-VAE is similar to [70] except that we use a kernel size of 3, which significantly sped up training compared to the original kernel size of 4. We use a down-sample ratio of $32 \times 32 \times 4$ for video compression and a vocabulary of size 2048. The 3D VQ-VAE is trained for 600K steps with a learning rate of 0.003 and a batch size of 8. The 1D VQ-VAE for audio features non-causal, dilated 1D convolutions where the dilation is grown

Table 3. Performance comparison on all generation tasks. D.S. denotes the down-sampled training set. F(V/A)D denotes FVD for video quality and FAD for audio quality. R.Sim. denotes the Relative Similarity to evaluate the faithfulness to the input. "B4", "M.", "R." and "C." denote BLEU4, METEOR, ROUGE and CIDEr. "Q." and "F." stand for quality and faithfulness. Video frame lengths map to different frame rates (8/16/32 represent 2.5/5/10 frames per second). Audio token lengths map to different compression ratios (68/137/275/551 represent 1024/512/256/128 compression ratios in VQ-VAE). All metrics except F(V/A)D are shown in percentage (%). All metrics are better when higher except F(V/A)D, which is the lower the better.

Out Mod.	In Mod.	Train Data	Out Len.	In Len.	Text Type	Auto F(V/A)D	R.Sim.	B4	M.	R.	C.	Human Q.	F.
Text	Video	Full	–	8	M	–	83.5	7.4	20.2	27.9	18.2	–	–
				16			101.5	**7.8**	20.8	28.7	**20.2**	–	–
				32			**108.0**	**7.8**	**21.3**	**29.1**	19.9	**31.3**	**42.6**
	Audio	Full	–	68	M	–	101.0	6.0	19.3	26.5	14.1	–	–
				137			103.9	6.3	19.3	26.6	14.4		
				275			106.7	6.5	19.3	26.8	14.7		
				551			**107.5**	**6.7**	**19.4**	**27.1**	**15.5**		
Video	Text	Full	8	–	M	$112.7_{\pm0.2}$	39.5	5.1	15.2	21.7	11.1	–	–
			16		M	$72.7_{\pm2.0}$	63.9	7.3	18.5	26.5	15.3	–	–
			32		M	$61.0_{\pm0.6}$	64.9	8.1	19.9	28.1	**19.2**	**17.0**	**31.6**
			32		A	$140.7_{\pm3.1}$	14.3	6.4	17.8	25.3	14.9	9.2	11.7
			32		M+A	$61.4_{\pm1.0}$	**66.5**	**8.2**	**20.0**	**28.2**	19.1	–	–
		D.S.	8	–	M	$112.7_{\pm1.1}$	42.0	5.0	15.3	21.9	11.0	–	–
			16		M	$72.2_{\pm1.7}$	69.5	7.3	18.6	26.7	15.8	–	–
			32		M	$62.0_{\pm0.7}$	70.6	7.9	20.0	28.2	19.0	**18.8**	**35.7**
			32		A	$151.7_{\pm3.4}$	20.5	6.2	17.7	24.9	14.2	12.1	13.1
			32		M+A	$61.0_{\pm1.4}$	**72.2**	**8.2**	**20.2**	**28.4**	**19.7**	–	–
	Audio	Full	32	68	–	$64.0_{\pm0.9}$	79.9	–	–	–	–	–	–
				137		$66.4_{\pm0.4}$	91.4					–	–
				275		$63.4_{\pm0.4}$	93.1					**17.6**	**37.1**
				551		$64.5_{\pm1.0}$	**93.6**					–	–
Audio	Video	Full	68	32	–	$523.8_{\pm1.0}$	86.5	–	–	–	–	–	–
			137			$128.5_{\pm0.4}$	95.4					–	–
			275			$52.3_{\pm0.5}$	**96.7**					15.2	31.1
			551			**$50.0_{\pm0.8}$**	92.7					–	–
	Text	Full	68	–	M	$574.0_{\pm2.8}$	**91.3**	7.0	18.5	26.5	15.3	–	–
			137			$171.1_{\pm2.2}$	88.8	6.9	18.5	26.5	15.0		
			275			**$93.7_{\pm1.6}$**	86.9	**7.1**	18.5	**26.9**	**16.2**		
			551			$109.4_{\pm2.3}$	78.7	6.9	18.1	26.1	15.9		

by a factor of 3. The vocabulary size is 1024. Audio sample rate is 22 kHz. The 1D VQ-VAE is trained for 1M steps with a learning rate of 0.0003 and a batch size of 4. We use Byte-Pair Encoding (BPE) [18,60] for text tokenization and train a tokenizer from the manual text annotations in the training set. All P2Q generation models are trained with the same transformer architecture and optimization hyper-parameters. For the transformer, we use 12 layers with a hidden dimension of 768 and 8 attention heads. All models are trained for 600K steps with a learning rate of 0.0003 and batch size of 4. Model checkpoints are selected based on the performance on the validation set.

Inference. During inference, we perform token sampling from the estimated distribution with filtering. For video or audio generation, we use top-k = 100 and top-p = 0.9 for filtering. For text generation, we use top-k = 1, which is the same as beam search [2] with size 1 in the common captioning setup.

Automatic Evaluation. For text generation, we use metrics that are widely used in captioning evaluation including BLEU4, METEOR, ROUGE, and CIDEr. For video quality, we follow prior practices and use I3D pre-trained on Kinetics 400 to calculate FVD. For audio quality, we use the pre-trained audio encoder on VGGSound to calculate FAD. To automatically evaluate faithfulness to input, we propose a new metric Relative Similarity (R.Sim.) that leverages the retrieval models. Specifically, we calculate the average similarity between the input and output divided by the average similarity between the input and the ground truth. For T2V and T2A generation, we use the V2T and A2T models applied on the generated video/audio to calculate the captioning metrics.

Human Evaluation. We establish a human evaluation protocol to calibrate towards the Ground Truth (GT). We randomly selected 512 samples from the test set and manually inspected the descriptions to ensure the samples were diverse and not too simple (e.g., to avoid multiple samples where Mugen simply jumps onto a platform). For each task, we evaluate both quality and faithfulness. We use "quality"[5] to measure the single modality quality and "faithfulness" to measure the alignment between the input and output modality. As it is not straightforward for humans to judge the alignment between audio and text, we do not evaluate T2A and A2T but focus on the other cross-modal generation tasks. For quality, we ask human judges to select the higher quality sample (video, audio, or text) between the generation and GT. For faithfulness, human judges are asked to select the media which better aligns with the input[6]. Each comparison is evaluated by 5 judges and the majority vote is taken. We report the percentage of samples that are chosen over the GT as the final metric. The upper bound for these evaluations is around 50% when a human judge cannot tell the difference between the generation and the GT.

We took several steps to mitigate bias and improve replicability in human evaluation. We shuffle sample order, shuffle the presentation order of models,

---

[5] Even within "quality", there are different kinds of deficiencies and more fine-grained evaluation could be part of future work.

[6] We will release the annotation UIs for others to follow this protocol.

anonymize model generations, and recruit diverse raters with Amazon Mechanical Turk. We also remove confounding factors. For instance, for video comparison, we render the GT video using the same theme (snow or space), frame rate, and resolution as the generated video. For generated text, several post-processing steps are used: capitalize the first letter of the first word in each sentence, use "Mugen" to replace "mugen", and remove duplicated spaces.

Text Generation from Video or Audio. As shown in Table 3, we vary the video frame rate and audio compression ratio (a higher compression ratio results in fewer tokens) for comparison. For V2T generation, higher frame rate leads to stronger performance. Human evaluation shows high faithfulness with 42.6% of samples chosen over GT, and relatively lower quality with 31.25% of samples considered more realistic than GT. For A2T generation, a smaller compression ratio (more tokens) is better. A2T performs worse than V2T as video-text are more densely aligned than audio-text.

Video Generation from Audio or Text. For T2V generation, we experiment with training using manual text and auto-text. As mentioned earlier, we balanced the characters in the validation and test sets. Correspondingly, to study the effects of data balancing, we also generate a smaller training set with 233K samples by down-sampling videos with Mugen or Mugen and coins only. As shown in Table 3, for T2V generation, we have the following observations: 1) Larger frame rate leads to better performance in all automatic metrics. 2) Auto-text performs worse than manual text and cannot noticeably improve performance when combined with manual text. This is because we evaluate on manual text for all comparisons. We hypothesize that auto-text may be useful when manual text is not available or is limited. 3) Models trained on the down-sampled training set consistently outperform those on the full set. Future work can explore other sampling strategies to fully utilize the training set. 4) Human evaluation results show better faithfulness compared to quality. The trends between automatic metrics and human evaluation results are similar.

For A2V generation, a smaller compression ratio (longer token sequence) leads to better quality and faithfulness in the automatic metrics. Human evaluation shows higher faithfulness compared to quality, similar to the T2V task.

Audio Generation from Video or Text. For audio generation, generating a longer audio sequence (less compression) leads to better quality in FAD for both T2A and V2A. But the R.Sim. may not follow the same trend. Human evaluation also shows higher faithfulness than quality, similar to other tasks.

When comparing the human evaluation results for all tasks, we see V2T is the easiest with the highest quality and faithfulness. V2T is also the most studied task in literature. For the other three tasks, faithfulness is considerably higher than quality. Improving video and audio reconstruction in VQ-VAE can potentially lead to higher quality. This also suggests that humans can reasonably ignore generation quality in faithfulness evaluation. We also compare the diversity of generated samples in Appendix C.

6 Conclusion

We introduce MUGEN – a closed world, large-scale multimodal dataset based on a significantly enhanced version of the platform game CoinRun [11]. MUGEN has videos, human-annotated text descriptions, automatically generated templated text descriptions, frame-level pixel-accurate semantic segmentation maps, as well as audio. The multiple modalities and rich annotations in MUGEN enable research progress in various tasks in multimodal understanding and generation without requiring web-scale data or massive compute. We explore retrieval and generation between every pair of modalities. To evaluate generative models, we establish a human evaluation protocol by calibrating towards the ground-truth samples, making it easier to compare performance and show progress. The MUGEN dataset, the modified game engine, our training code and models, and the human evaluation UIs can be found at: https://mugen-org.github.io/.

References

1. Agrawal, H., et al.: NoCaps: novel object captioning at scale. In: Proceedings of the IEEE/CVF International Conference on Computer Vision, pp. 8948–8957 (2019)
2. Anderson, P., Fernando, B., Johnson, M., Gould, S.: Guided open vocabulary image captioning with constrained beam search. arXiv preprint arXiv:1612.00576 (2016)
3. Anne Hendricks, L., Wang, O., Shechtman, E., Sivic, J., Darrell, T., Russell, B.: Localizing moments in video with natural language. In: Proceedings of the IEEE International Conference on Computer Vision, pp. 5803–5812 (2017)
4. Antol, S., et al.: VQA: visual question answering. In: Proceedings of the IEEE International Conference on Computer Vision, pp. 2425–2433 (2015)
5. Bain, M., Nagrani, A., Varol, G., Zisserman, A.: Frozen in time: a joint video and image encoder for end-to-end retrieval. In: IEEE International Conference on Computer Vision (2021)
6. Changpinyo, S., Sharma, P., Ding, N., Soricut, R.: Conceptual 12M: pushing web-scale image-text pre-training to recognize long-tail visual concepts. In: Proceedings of the IEEE/CVF Conference on Computer Vision and Pattern Recognition, pp. 3558–3568 (2021)
7. Chen, D., Dolan, W.B.: Collecting highly parallel data for paraphrase evaluation. In: Proceedings of the 49th Annual Meeting of the Association for Computational Linguistics: Human Language Technologies, pp. 190–200 (2011)
8. Chen, H., Xie, W., Vedaldi, A., Zisserman, A.: VGGSound: a large-scale audio-visual dataset. In: ICASSP 2020–2020 IEEE International Conference on Acoustics, Speech and Signal Processing (ICASSP), pp. 721–725. IEEE (2020)
9. Chen, L., Srivastava, S., Duan, Z., Xu, C.: Deep cross-modal audio-visual generation. In: 2017 Proceedings of the on Thematic Workshops of ACM Multimedia, pp. 349–357 (2017)
10. Chen, Y.-C., et al.: UNITER: UNiversal image-TExt representation learning. In: Vedaldi, A., Bischof, H., Brox, T., Frahm, J.-M. (eds.) ECCV 2020. LNCS, vol. 12375, pp. 104–120. Springer, Cham (2020). https://doi.org/10.1007/978-3-030-58577-8_7
11. Cobbe, K., Klimov, O., Hesse, C., Kim, T., Schulman, J.: Quantifying generalization in reinforcement learning. In: International Conference on Machine Learning, pp. 1282–1289. PMLR (2019)

12. Cui, Y., Yang, G., Veit, A., Huang, X., Belongie, S.: Learning to evaluate image captioning. In: Proceedings of the IEEE Conference on Computer Vision and Pattern Recognition, pp. 5804–5812 (2018)
13. Dhariwal, P., Jun, H., Payne, C., Kim, J.W., Radford, A., Sutskever, I.: Jukebox: a generative model for music. arXiv preprint arXiv:2005.00341 (2020)
14. Ding, M., et al.: CogView: mastering text-to-image generation via transformers. In: Advances in Neural Information Processing Systems, vol. 34 (2021)
15. Edwards, A., Sahni, H., Schroecker, Y., Isbell, C.: Imitating latent policies from observation. In: International Conference on Machine Learning, pp. 1755–1763. PMLR (2019)
16. Espeholt, L., et al.: IMPALA: scalable distributed deep-RL with importance weighted actor-learner architectures. In: International Conference on Machine Learning, pp. 1407–1416. PMLR (2018)
17. Gabeur, V., Sun, C., Alahari, K., Schmid, C.: Multi-modal transformer for video retrieval. In: Vedaldi, A., Bischof, H., Brox, T., Frahm, J.-M. (eds.) ECCV 2020. LNCS, vol. 12349, pp. 214–229. Springer, Cham (2020). https://doi.org/10.1007/978-3-030-58548-8_13
18. Gage, P.: A new algorithm for data compression. C Users J. **12**(2), 23–38 (1994)
19. Gao, J., Sun, C., Yang, Z., Nevatia, R.: TALL: temporal activity localization via language query. In: ICCV (2017)
20. Gao, L., Guo, Z., Zhang, H., Xu, X., Shen, H.T.: Video captioning with attention-based LSTM and semantic consistency. IEEE Trans. Multimed. **19**(9), 2045–2055 (2017)
21. Ge, S., et al.: Long video generation with time-agnostic VQGAN and time-sensitive transformer. arXiv preprint arXiv:2204.03638 (2022)
22. Gemmeke, J.F., et al.: AudioSet: an ontology and human-labeled dataset for audio events. In: 2017 IEEE International Conference on Acoustics, Speech and Signal Processing (ICASSP), pp. 776–780. IEEE (2017)
23. Goyal, Y., Khot, T., Summers-Stay, D., Batra, D., Parikh, D.: Making the V in VQA matter: elevating the role of image understanding in visual question answering. In: Proceedings of the IEEE Conference on Computer Vision and Pattern Recognition, pp. 6904–6913 (2017)
24. Grauman, K., et al.: Ego4D: around the world in 3,000 hours of egocentric video. arXiv preprint arXiv:2110.07058 (2021)
25. Gupta, T., Schwenk, D., Farhadi, A., Hoiem, D., Kembhavi, A.: Imagine this! Scripts to compositions to videos. In: Proceedings of the European Conference on Computer Vision (ECCV), pp. 598–613 (2018)
26. He, K., Zhang, X., Ren, S., Sun, J.: Deep residual learning for image recognition. In: Proceedings of the IEEE Conference on Computer Vision and Pattern Recognition, pp. 770–778 (2016)
27. Huang, T.H., et al.: Visual storytelling. In: NAACL (2016)
28. Iashin, V., Rahtu, E.: Taming visually guided sound generation. arXiv preprint arXiv:2110.08791 (2021)
29. Igl, M., et al.: Generalization in reinforcement learning with selective noise injection and information bottleneck. In: Advances in Neural Information Processing Systems, vol. 32 (2019)
30. Johnson, J., Hariharan, B., Van Der Maaten, L., Fei-Fei, L., Lawrence Zitnick, C., Girshick, R.: CLEVR: a diagnostic dataset for compositional language and elementary visual reasoning. In: Proceedings of the IEEE Conference on Computer Vision and Pattern Recognition, pp. 2901–2910 (2017)

31. Johnson, J., Karpathy, A., Fei-Fei, L.: DenseCap: fully convolutional localization networks for dense captioning. In: Proceedings of the IEEE Conference on Computer Vision and Pattern Recognition, pp. 4565–4574 (2016)

32. Johnson, J., et al.: Image retrieval using scene graphs. In: Proceedings of the IEEE Conference on Computer Vision and Pattern Recognition, pp. 3668–3678 (2015)

33. Kahou, S.E., Michalski, V., Memisevic, R., Pal, C., Vincent, P.: RATM: recurrent attentive tracking model. In: 2017 IEEE Conference on Computer Vision and Pattern Recognition Workshops (CVPRW), pp. 1613–1622. IEEE (2017)

34. Kay, W., et al.: The kinetics human action video dataset. arXiv preprint arXiv:1705.06950 (2017)

35. Kim, C.D., Kim, B., Lee, H., Kim, G.: AudioCaps: generating captions for audios in the wild. In: NAACL-HLT (2019)

36. Koepke, A.S., Oncescu, A.M., Henriques, J., Akata, Z., Albanie, S.: Audio retrieval with natural language queries: a benchmark study. IEEE Trans. Multimed. (2022)

37. Krishna, R., Hata, K., Ren, F., Fei-Fei, L., Niebles, J.C.: Dense-captioning events in videos. In: International Conference on Computer Vision (ICCV) (2017)

38. Le, T.M., Le, V., Venkatesh, S., Tran, T.: Hierarchical conditional relation networks for video question answering. In: Proceedings of the IEEE/CVF Conference on Computer Vision and Pattern Recognition, pp. 9972–9981 (2020)

39. Lei, J., et al.: Less is more: ClipBERT for video-and-language learning via sparse sampling. In: Proceedings of the IEEE/CVF Conference on Computer Vision and Pattern Recognition, pp. 7331–7341 (2021)

40. Lei, J., Yu, L., Bansal, M., Berg, T.L.: TVQA: localized, compositional video question answering. In: EMNLP (2018)

41. Lei, J., Yu, L., Berg, T.L., Bansal, M.: TVR: a large-scale dataset for video-subtitle moment retrieval. In: Vedaldi, A., Bischof, H., Brox, T., Frahm, J.-M. (eds.) ECCV 2020. LNCS, vol. 12366, pp. 447–463. Springer, Cham (2020). https://doi.org/10.1007/978-3-030-58589-1_27

42. Li, X., et al.: Oscar: object-semantics aligned pre-training for vision-language tasks. In: Vedaldi, A., Bischof, H., Brox, T., Frahm, J.-M. (eds.) ECCV 2020. LNCS, vol. 12375, pp. 121–137. Springer, Cham (2020). https://doi.org/10.1007/978-3-030-58577-8_8

43. Li, Y., et al.: StoryGAN: a sequential conditional GAN for story visualization. In: Proceedings of the IEEE/CVF Conference on Computer Vision and Pattern Recognition, pp. 6329–6338 (2019)

44. Li, Y., Min, M., Shen, D., Carlson, D., Carin, L.: Video generation from text. In: Proceedings of the AAAI Conference on Artificial Intelligence, vol. 32 (2018)

45. Lin, T.-Y., et al.: Microsoft COCO: common objects in context. In: Fleet, D., Pajdla, T., Schiele, B., Tuytelaars, T. (eds.) ECCV 2014. LNCS, vol. 8693, pp. 740–755. Springer, Cham (2014). https://doi.org/10.1007/978-3-319-10602-1_48

46. Liu, Y., Wang, X., Yuan, Y., Zhu, W.: Cross-modal dual learning for sentence-to-video generation. In: Proceedings of the 27th ACM International Conference on Multimedia, pp. 1239–1247 (2019)

47. Mama, R., Tyndel, M.S., Kadhim, H., Clifford, C., Thurairatnam, R.: NWT: towards natural audio-to-video generation with representation learning. arXiv preprint arXiv:2106.04283 (2021)

48. Mazaheri, A., Shah, M.: Video generation from text employing latent path construction for temporal modeling. arXiv preprint arXiv:2107.13766 (2021)

49. Miech, A., Alayrac, J.B., Smaira, L., Laptev, I., Sivic, J., Zisserman, A.: End-to-end learning of visual representations from uncurated instructional videos. In: CVPR (2020)

50. Miech, A., Zhukov, D., Alayrac, J.B., Tapaswi, M., Laptev, I., Sivic, J.: HowTO100M: learning a text-video embedding by watching hundred million narrated video clips. In: Proceedings of the IEEE/CVF International Conference on Computer Vision, pp. 2630–2640 (2019)

51. Mittal, G., Marwah, T., Balasubramanian, V.N.: Sync-DRAW: automatic video generation using deep recurrent attentive architectures. In: Proceedings of the 25th ACM International Conference on Multimedia, pp. 1096–1104 (2017)

52. Niu, Y., Tang, K., Zhang, H., Lu, Z., Hua, X.S., Wen, J.R.: Counterfactual VQA: a cause-effect look at language bias. In: Proceedings of the IEEE/CVF Conference on Computer Vision and Pattern Recognition, pp. 12700–12710 (2021)

53. Ordonez, V., Kulkarni, G., Berg, T.: Im2Text: describing images using 1 million captioned photographs. In: Advances in Neural Information Processing Systems, vol. 24 (2011)

54. Radford, A., et al.: Learning transferable visual models from natural language supervision. In: International Conference on Machine Learning, pp. 8748–8763. PMLR (2021)

55. Ramesh, A., et al.: Zero-shot text-to-image generation. In: International Conference on Machine Learning, pp. 8821–8831. PMLR (2021)

56. Reed, S., Akata, Z., Yan, X., Logeswaran, L., Schiele, B., Lee, H.: Generative adversarial text to image synthesis. In: International Conference on Machine Learning, pp. 1060–1069. PMLR (2016)

57. Rohrbach, A., Rohrbach, M., Tandon, N., Schiele, B.: A dataset for movie description. In: Proceedings of the IEEE conference on computer vision and pattern recognition. pp. 3202–3212 (2015)

58. Sanh, V., Debut, L., Chaumond, J., Wolf, T.: DistilBERT, a distilled version of BERT: smaller, faster, cheaper and lighter. arXiv preprint arXiv:1910.01108 (2019)

59. Schulman, J., Wolski, F., Dhariwal, P., Radford, A., Klimov, O.: Proximal policy optimization algorithms. arXiv preprint arXiv:1707.06347 (2017)

60. Sennrich, R., Haddow, B., Birch, A.: Neural machine translation of rare words with subword units. In: Proceedings of the 54th Annual Meeting of the Association for Computational Linguistics (Volume 1: Long Papers), pp. 1715–1725. Association for Computational Linguistics, Berlin, Germany (2016). https://doi.org/10.18653/v1/P16-1162, https://aclanthology.org/P16-1162

61. Sharma, P., Ding, N., Goodman, S., Soricut, R.: Conceptual captions: a cleaned, hypernymed, image alt-text dataset for automatic image captioning. In: Proceedings of the 56th Annual Meeting of the Association for Computational Linguistics (Volume 1: Long Papers), pp. 2556–2565 (2018)

62. Sigurdsson, G.A., Varol, G., Wang, X., Farhadi, A., Laptev, I., Gupta, A.: Hollywood in homes: crowdsourcing data collection for activity understanding. In: Leibe, B., Matas, J., Sebe, N., Welling, M. (eds.) ECCV 2016. LNCS, vol. 9905, pp. 510–526. Springer, Cham (2016). https://doi.org/10.1007/978-3-319-46448-0_31

63. Singh, A., et al.: FLAVA: a foundational language and vision alignment model. arXiv preprint arXiv:2112.04482 (2021)

64. Srinivasan, K., Raman, K., Chen, J., Bendersky, M., Najork, M.: WIT: Wikipedia-based image text dataset for multimodal multilingual machine learning. In: SIGIR (2021)

65. Van Den Oord, A., Vinyals, O., et al.: Neural discrete representation learning. In: Advances in Neural Information Processing Systems, vol. 30 (2017)

66. Xie, S., Sun, C., Huang, J., Tu, Z., Murphy, K.: Rethinking spatiotemporal feature learning: speed-accuracy trade-offs in video classification. In: Proceedings of the European Conference on Computer Vision (ECCV), pp. 305–321 (2018)

67. Xu, C., Hsieh, S.H., Xiong, C., Corso, J.J.: Can humans fly? Action understanding with multiple classes of actors. In: Proceedings of the IEEE Conference on Computer Vision and Pattern Recognition, pp. 2264–2273 (2015)

68. Xu, J., Mei, T., Yao, T., Rui, Y.: MSR-VTT: a large video description dataset for bridging video and language. In: Proceedings of the IEEE Conference on Computer Vision and Pattern Recognition, pp. 5288–5296 (2016)

69. Xue, H., et al.: Advancing high-resolution video-language representation with large-scale video transcriptions. In: International Conference on Computer Vision and Pattern Recognition (CVPR) (2022)

70. Yan, W., Zhang, Y., Abbeel, P., Srinivas, A.: VideoGPT: video generation using VQ-VAE and transformers (2021)

71. Yang, Z., Gong, B., Wang, L., Huang, W., Yu, D., Luo, J.: A fast and accurate one-stage approach to visual grounding. In: The IEEE International Conference on Computer Vision (ICCV) (2019)

72. You, Q., Jin, H., Wang, Z., Fang, C., Luo, J.: Image captioning with semantic attention. In: Proceedings of the IEEE Conference on Computer Vision and Pattern Recognition, pp. 4651–4659 (2016)

73. Young, P., Lai, A., Hodosh, M., Hockenmaier, J.: From image descriptions to visual denotations: new similarity metrics for semantic inference over event descriptions. Trans. Assoc. Comput. Linguist. **2**, 67–78 (2014)

74. Yuan, L., et al.: Florence: a new foundation model for computer vision. arXiv preprint arXiv:2111.11432 (2021)

75. Zeng, R., Xu, H., Huang, W., Chen, P., Tan, M., Gan, C.: Dense regression network for video grounding. In: Proceedings of the IEEE/CVF Conference on Computer Vision and Pattern Recognition, pp. 10287–10296 (2020)

76. Zhang, P., et al.: VinVL: revisiting visual representations in vision-language models. In: Proceedings of the IEEE/CVF Conference on Computer Vision and Pattern Recognition, pp. 5579–5588 (2021)

77. Zhang, S., Peng, H., Fu, J., Lu, Y., Luo, J.: Multi-scale 2D temporal adjacent networks for moment localization with natural language. TPAMI (2021)

78. Zhou, L., Palangi, H., Zhang, L., Hu, H., Corso, J., Gao, J.: Unified vision-language pre-training for image captioning and VQA. In: Proceedings of the AAAI Conference on Artificial Intelligence, vol. 34, pp. 13041–13049 (2020)

79. Zhou, L., Xu, C., Corso, J.J.: Towards automatic learning of procedures from web instructional videos. In: Thirty-Second AAAI Conference on Artificial Intelligence (2018)

A Dense Material Segmentation Dataset for Indoor and Outdoor Scene Parsing

Paul Upchurch$^{(\boxtimes)}$ and Ransen Niu

Apple Inc., One Apple Park Way, Cupertino, CA, USA
paulup@gmail.com

Abstract. A key algorithm for understanding the world is material segmentation, which assigns a label (metal, glass, etc.) to each pixel. We find that a model trained on existing data underperforms in some settings and propose to address this with a large-scale dataset of 3.2 million dense segments on 44,560 indoor and outdoor images, which is 23x more segments than existing data. Our data covers a more diverse set of scenes, objects, viewpoints and materials, and contains a more fair distribution of skin types. We show that a model trained on our data outperforms a state-of-the-art model across datasets and viewpoints. We propose a large-scale scene parsing benchmark and baseline of 0.729 per-pixel accuracy, 0.585 mean class accuracy and 0.420 mean IoU across 46 materials.

1 Introduction

A goal of computer vision is to develop the cognitive ability to plan manipulation of something and predict how it will respond to stimuli. This is informed by the properties of what something is made of. Those properties can be discovered by segmenting a photograph into recognized materials. Material recognition can be understood through the science of material perception starting with Adelson's [1] proposal to divide the world into *things* (countable objects) and *stuff* (materials). Adelson argued stuff is important because of its ubiquity in everyday life. Ritchie *et al.* [25] describe material perception in two parts. The first part is categorical recognition of what something is made of. The second part is recognizing material properties (*e.g.*, glossy, flexible, sound absorbent, sticky) which tells us how something will feel or how it will interact with other objects. While Schwartz *et al.* [30] proposed to recognize properties from local image patches we follow Bell *et al.* [3] who segmented images by recognizing material classes.

Deep learning-based material recognition builds on some key developments. Sharan *et al.* [31] showed that people can recognize 10 kinds of materials in the

---

P. Upchurch and R. Niu—Equal Contribution.

Supplementary Information The online version contains supplementary material available at https://doi.org/10.1007/978-3-031-20074-8_26.

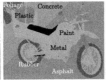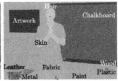

Fig. 1. Densely annotated materials. Our annotations are full-scene, highly detailed and enable prediction of 46 kinds of materials.

wild [32] with 85% accuracy. Bell *et al.* [2], following [27], built an efficient annotation tool to create a large-scale material database from crowds and Internet photos. Next, Bell *et al.* [3] introduced large-scale training data and a deep learning approach leading to material segmentation as a building-block for haptics, material assignment, robotic navigation, acoustic simulation and context-aware mixed reality [4,8,11,23,29,43]. Xiao *et al.* [37] introduced a multi-task scene parsing model which endows a photograph with a rich prediction of scene type, objects, object parts, materials and textures.

Despite widespread adoption of material segmentation, a lack of large-scale data means evaluation rests on the only large-scale segmentation dataset, OpenSurfaces [2]. We find there is room for improvement and propose the Dense Material Segmentation dataset (DMS) which has 3.2 million segments across 44k densely annotated images, and show empirically that our data leads to models which further close the gap between computer vision and human perception.

There are goals to consider for a material dataset. First, we need a general-purpose set of material labels. We want to mimic human perception so we choose distinguishable materials even if they are of the same type. For example, we separate clear from opaque plastic rather than have a single label for all plastics. We define fine-grained labels which have useful properties, physical or otherwise. For example, a painted whiteboard surface has utility not found in a *paint* label—it is appropriate for writing, cleaning and virtual content display. These functional properties come from how the material is applied rather than its physical structure. Ultimately we choose a set of 52 labels based on prior work and useful materials we found in photographs (details in Sect. 3.1).

Following [30], we also want indoor and outdoor scenes. Counter-intuitively, this could be unnecessary. Material is recognizable regardless of where it occurs in the world, and deep learning methods aim to create a model which generalizes to unseen cases. Thus, an indoor residential dataset [2] could be sufficient. We find this is not the case. In Sect. 4.1 we show that a model trained on [2] performs worse on outdoor scenes. This is a key finding which impacts all algorithms which use [2] for training. We also show that a model trained on our dataset is consistent across indoor and outdoor scenes.

We want our database to support many scene parsing tasks so we need broad coverage of objects and scene attributes (which include activities, *e.g.*, eating). In Sect. 3.2 we show that we achieve better coverage compared to [2].

We propose nine kinds of photographic types which distinguish different view-points and circumstances. Our motivation was to quantitatively evaluate cases where we had observed poor performance. This data can reveal new insights on how a model performs. We find that a state-of-the-art model underperforms in some settings whereas a model fit to our data performs well on all nine types.

Our final goal is to have diversity in skin types. Skin is associated with race and ethnicity so it is crucial to have fair representation across different types of skin. We compare our skin type data to OpenSurfaces [2] in Sect. 3.2 and show our data has practical benefits for training in Sect. 4.2.

The paper is organized as follows. In Sect. 2 we review datasets. In Sect. 3 we describe how we collected data to achieve our goals. In Sect. 4 we compare our dataset to state-of-the-art data and a state-of-the-art model, study the impact of skin types on training, propose a material segmentation benchmark, and demonstrate material segmentation on real world photos.

In summary, our contributions are:

– We introduce DMS, a large-scale densely-annotated material segmentation dataset and show it is diverse with extensive analysis (Sect. 3).
– We advance fairness toward skin types in material datasets (Sect. 3.2).
– We introduce photographic types which reveal new insights on prior work and show that a model fit to our data performs better across datasets and viewpoints compared to the state-of-the-art (Sect. 4.1).
– We propose a new large-scale indoor and outdoor material segmentation benchmark of 46 materials and present a baseline result (Sect. 4.3).

2   Related Work

Material Segmentation Datasets. The largest dataset is OpenSurfaces [2] which collected richly annotated polygons of residential indoor surfaces on 19k images, including 37 kinds of materials. The largest material recognition dataset is the Materials in Context Database [3] which is 3M point annotations of 23 kinds of materials across 437k images. This data enables material segmentation by CNN and a dense CRF tuned on OpenSurfaces segments. The Local Materials Database [30] collected segmentations, with the goal of studying materials using only local patches, of 16 kinds of materials across 5,845 images sourced from existing datasets. The Light-Field Material Dataset [35] is 1,200 4D indoor and outdoor images of 12 kinds of materials. The Multi-Illumination dataset [21] captured 1,016 indoor scenes under 25 lighting conditions and annotated the images with 35 kinds of materials. Table 1 lists the largest datasets.

Materials have appeared in purpose-built datasets. The Ground Terrain in Outdoor Scenes (GTOS) database [39] and GTOS-mobile [38] are 30k images of hundreds of instances of 40 kinds of ground materials and 81 videos of 31 kinds of ground materials, respectively. The Materials in Paintings dataset [34] is bounding box annotations and extracted segmentations on 19k paintings of 15 kinds

Table 1. Large-scale datasets. We propose a dataset with 23× more segments, more classes and 2.3× more images as the largest segment-annotated dataset.

Dataset	Annotation	Classes	Images	Scenes
OpenSurfaces [2]	137k segments	37	19,447	Indoor residential
Materials in context [3]	3M points	23	436,749	Home interior & exterior
Local materials [30]	9.4k segments	16	5,845	Indoor & outdoor
DMS (Ours)	3.2M segments	52	44,560	Indoor & outdoor

of materials depicted by artists, partly distinguished into 50 fine-grained categories. COCO-Stuff [6] is segmentations of 91 kinds of stuff on 164k COCO [18] images. While this is a source of material data, it is not a general-purpose material dataset because important surfaces (*e.g.*, objects labeled in COCO) are not assigned material labels. ClearGrasp [28] is a dataset of 50k synthetic and 286 real RGB-D images of glass objects built for robotic manipulation of transparent objects. The Glass Detection Dataset [20] is 3,916 indoor and outdoor images of segmented glass surfaces. The Mirror Segmentation Dataset [41] is 4,018 images with segmented mirror surfaces across indoor and outdoor scenes. Fashionpedia [15] is a database of segmented clothing images of which 10k are annotated with fashion attributes which include fine-grained clothing materials. Figaro [33] is 840 images of people with segmented hair distinguished into 7 kinds of hairstyles.

Categorical Material Names. Bell *et al.* [2] created a set of names by asking annotators to enter free-form labels which were merged into a list of material names. This approach is based on the appearance of surfaces as perceived by the annotators. Schwartz *et al.* [30] created a three-level hierarchy of material names where materials are organized by their physical properties. Some categories were added for materials which could not be placed in the hierarchy. In practice, both approaches resulted in a similar set of entry-level [22] names which also closely agree with prior studies of categorical materials in Internet images [14,32].

3   Data Collection

DMS is a set of dense polygon annotations of 52 material classes across 44,560 images, which are a subset of OpenImages [17]. We followed a four step process. First, a set of labels was defined. Next, a large set of images was studied by people and algorithms to select images for annotation. Next, the selected images were fully segmented and labeled by a human annotator. Finally, each segmented image was relabeled by multiple people and a final label map was created by fusing all labels. The last three steps were followed multiple times.

3.1   Material Labels

We choose to predefine a label set which is the approach of COCO-Stuff [6]. This encourages annotators to create consistent labels suitable for machine learning.

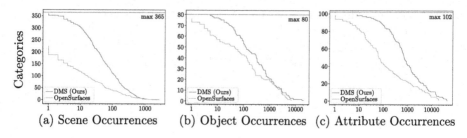

(a) Scene Occurrences   (b) Object Occurrences   (c) Attribute Occurrences

Fig. 2. Image diversity. We plot number of categories (y-axis) vs. occurrence in images (log-scale x-axis) of Places365 scene type (a), COCO objects (b), and SUN attributes (c). Our dataset (*blue*) is larger, more diverse and more balanced across categories (higher slope) compared to the largest segmentation dataset (*orange*).

We instructed annotators to assign *not on list* to recognized materials which do not fit in any category and *I cannot tell* to unknown and unrecognizable surfaces (*e.g.*, watermarks and under-/over-saturated pixels).

We defined a label set based on appearance, which is the approach of Open-Surfaces [2]. A label can represent a solid substance (*e.g.*, wood), a distinctive arrangement of substances (*e.g.*, brickwork), a liquid (*e.g.*, water) or a useful non-material (*e.g.*, sky). We used 35 labels from OpenSurfaces and *asphalt* from [30].

We added 2 fine-grained people and animal categories (*bone* and *animal skin*). We introduced 3 labels for workplaces (*ceiling tile*, *whiteboard* and *fiberglass wool*), 6 for indoor scenes (*artwork*, *clutter*, *non-water liquid*, *soap*, *pearl* and *gemstone*) and 4 for outdoors (*sand*, *snow*, *ice* and *tree wood*). *Artwork* identifies an imitative surface which is photographic or fine art—affording further analysis by Materials In Paintings [34]. *Clutter* is a region of visually indistinguishable manufactured stuff (typically a mixture of metal, plastic and paper) which occurs in trash piles. Lastly, we defined a label called *engineered stone* for artificial surfaces which imitate stone, which includes untextured and laminated solid surfaces. See Fig. 4 for an example of each label.

3.2   Image Selection

Bell *et al.* [3] found that a balanced set of material labels can achieve nearly the same performance as a 9× larger imbalanced set. Since we collect dense annotations we cannot directly balance classes. Instead, we searched 191k images for rare materials and assumed common materials would co-occur. Furthermore, we ran Detectron [12] to detect COCO [18] objects, and Places365 [45] to classify scenes and recognize SUN [24] attributes. EXIF information was used to infer country. These detections were used to select images of underrepresented scenes, objects and countries. Figure 2 compares the diversity of the 45k images in DMS to the 19k images in OpenSurfaces by a plot of the number of categories, y, which have at least x occurrences. Occurrences of scene type, object and SUN attribute are plotted. Note that the x-axis is logarithmic scale. We find our

Table 2. Skin types. We report estimated occurrences. Our dataset has 12× more occurrences of the smallest group and 4.8× more fair representation by ratio.

	OpenSurfaces	DMS (Ours)
Type I–II (light)	2,332	4,535
Type III–IV (medium)	3,889	9,776
Type V–VI (dark)	375	5,899
Ratio of largest to smallest group	10.37 : 1	2.16 : 1

dataset is more diverse having more classes present in greater amounts (more than can be explained by the 2.24× difference in image count).

We balance the distribution of skin appearance in DMS so that algorithms trained with our data perform well on all kinds of skin [5]. We use Fitzpatrick [10] skin type to categorize skin into 3 groups, inspired by an approach used by [40]. We ran the DLIB [16] face detector and labeled a subset of the faces. Our 157 manual annotations were used to calibrate a preexisting face attribute predictor (trained on a different dataset) which was then used to predict skin types for the rest of DMS. We found that the ratio of the largest group to the smallest was 9.4. Next, we selected images which would increase the most underrepresented skin type group and found this reduced the ratio to 2.2. We calibrated the same detector for OpenSurfaces faces and measured its ratio as 10.4. According to the findings of [5], we expect skin classifiers trained on OpenSurfaces would underperform on dark skin. Table 2 shows the distribution of skin types.

We used Places365 scene type detection to select outdoor images but we found this did not lead to outdoor materials. We took two steps to address this. First, we annotated our images with one of nine *photographic types* which distinguish outdoor from indoor from unreal images. Table 3 shows the annotated types. Next, we used these labels to select outdoor scenes and underrepresented viewpoints. This was effective—growing the dataset by 17% more than doubled 9 kinds of outdoor materials: *ice* (3×), *sand* (4.4×), *sky* (8×), *snow* (9.5×), *soil* (3×), *natural stone* (2.4×), *water* (2.5×), *tree wood* (2.3×) and *asphalt* (9.2×).

3.3   Segmentation and Instances

Images were given to annotators for polygon segmentation of the entire image. We instructed annotators to segment parts larger than a fingertip, ignore gaps smaller than a finger, and to follow material boundaries tightly while ignoring geometry and shadow boundaries. Following [2], annotators were instructed to segment glass and mirror surfaces rather than the covered or reflected surfaces. Unreal elements such as borders and watermarks were segmented separately. Images with objectionable content (*e.g.*, violence) were not annotated.

Annotators segmented resized images, with median longest edge of 1024 pixels, creating over 3.2 million segments (counting only those larger than 100 pixels) with a mean of 72 segments per image. The created segments are detailed—

Table 3. Photographic types. Our data contains indoor views (*top*), outdoor views (*middle*), and close-up and unusual views (*bottom*).

Photographic Type	Images	
An area with visible enclosure	16,013	
A collection of indoor things	6,064	
A tightly cropped indoor thing	2,634	
A ground-level view of reachable outdoor things	3,127	
A tightly cropped outdoor thing	1,196	
Distant unreachable outdoor things	971	
A real surface without context	847	
Not a real photo	805	
An obstructed or distorted view	204	

Table 4. Annotator agreement rates. High rates indicate consistent label assignment. Low rates indicate disagreement, confusion or unstructured error.

Hair	0.95	Glass	0.80	Wood	0.67	Non-clear plastic	0.60
Skin	0.93	Paper	0.76	Tree wood	0.66	Leather	0.53
Foliage	0.86	Carpet/rug	0.73	Tile	0.66	Cardboard	0.53
Sky	0.86	Nat. stone	0.72	Metal	0.65	Artwork	0.51
Food	0.84	Ceramic	0.70	Paint/plaster	0.62	Clear plastic	0.50
Fabric/cloth	0.82	Mirror	0.68	Rubber	0.61	Concrete	0.45

wires, jewelry, teeth, eyebrows, shoe soles, wheel rims, door hinges, clasps, buttons and latches are some of the small and thin materials segmented separately. See Fig. 1 and Fig. 3 for examples of detailed segmentations.

We defined a material instance as materials of the same type from the same manufacturing source. For example a wooden cabinet should be segmented separately from a wood floor but the planks making up a single-source floor would be one instance. DMS is the first large-scale densely segmented dataset to have detailed material instances.

3.4   Labeling

The annotator who segmented an image also assigned labels based on their judgment and our instruction. We found that surfaces coated with another material or colored by absorbing ink required clarification. Appearance-changing coatings were labeled *paint* while clear or appearance-enhancing coatings (*e.g.*, varnish, cosmetics, sheer hosiery) were labeled as the underlying material. Small amounts of ink (*e.g.*, printed text) are disregarded. Some surfaces imitate the appearance of other materials (*e.g.*, laminate). High-quality imitations were labeled as the imitated material and low-quality imitations as the real material.

Fig. 3. Fused labels. We show segmentation quality and variety of scenes, activities and materials (*left to right:* building exterior, workplace, road, swimming pool, shop, dining room). See Table 5 for color legend. Black pixels are unlabeled (no consensus).

Table 5. Material occurrence in images. We report the number of images in which a label occurs. The colors are used for visualizations.

	Paint/plaster	39,323		Sky	3,306		Chalkboard	668
	Fabric/cloth	31,489		Mirror	3,242		Asphalt	474
	Non-clear plas	30,506		Cardboard	3,150		Fire	412
	Metal	30,504		Food	2,908		Gemstone	369
	Glass	28,934		Concrete	2,853		Sponge	326
	Wood	24,248		Ceiling tile	2,524		Eng. stone	299
	Paper	20,763		Natural stone	2,076		Liquid	294
	Skin	18,524		Water	2,063		Pearl	282
	Hair	17,766		Tree wood	2,026		Cork	273
	Foliage	11,384		Wicker	1,895		Sand	272
	Tile	10,173		Soil/mud	1,855		Snow	191
	Carpet/rug	9,516		Pol. stone	1,831		Soap	154
	Ceramic	8,314		Brickwork	1,654		Clutter	128
	Rubber	7,811		Fur	1,567		Ice	96
	Leather	7,354		Whiteboard	1,171		Styrofoam	88
	Clear plastic	6,431		Wax	1,107		Fiberglass wool	33
	Artwork	4,344		Wallpaper	1,076			
	Bone/horn	3,751		Animal skin	1,007			

Our instructions were refined in each iteration and incorrect labels from early iterations were corrected. Some cases needed special instruction. We instructed annotators to label electronic displays as *glass* and vinyl projection screens as *not on list*. Uncovered artwork or photographs were to be labeled *artwork* while glass-covered art should be labeled *glass*. In ambiguous cases, we assume framed artwork has a glass cover. *Sky* includes day sky, night sky and aerial phenomenon (*e.g.*, clouds, stars, moon, and sun).

We collected more opinions by presenting a segmentation, after removing labels, to a different annotator who relabeled the segments. The relabeling annotator could fix bad segments by adjusting polygons or assign special labels to indicate a segment does not follow boundaries or is made of multiple material types. We collected 98,526 opinions across 44,560 images consisting of 8.2 million segment labels (counting only segments larger than 100 pixels).

We studied label agreement by counting occurrences of a segment label and matching pixel-wise dominant label by a different annotator. We found an agreement rate of 0.675. In cases of agreement, 8.9% were unrecognizable (*I cannot tell*) and 0.6% were *not on list*. Table 4 shows the agreement rate for classes larger than the median number of segments per class. Among the largest classes the most agreed-upon labels are *hair*, *skin*, *foliage*, *sky*, and *food*. We only analyze the largest classes since unstructured error (*e.g.*, misclicks) can overwhelm the statistics of small classes, which are up to 2,720 times smaller.

3.5 Label Fusion

Each annotator's segments are rendered to create a label map. Label maps were inspected for correctness and we fixed incorrect labels in 1,803 images. Next, we

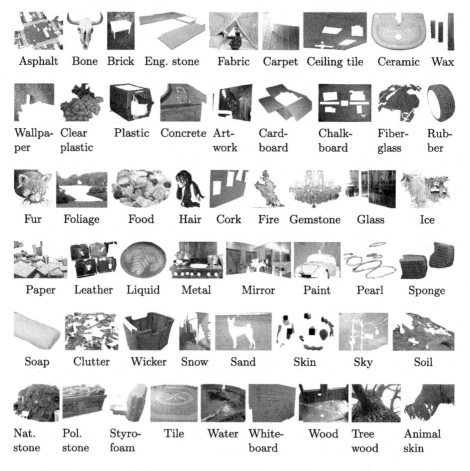

Fig. 4. Material labels. For each label we show a cut-out example.

create a single *fused label map* for each image. First, we combined label maps pixel-wise by taking the strict majority label. Next, we overlaid manual corrections and reassigned non-semantic labels (*e.g.*, I cannot tell) to *no label*. The fused maps have a mean labeled area fraction of 0.784. For comparison, we created fused label maps for OpenSurfaces and found its density is 0.210. DMS is 2.3× larger and 3.7× denser, which is 8.4× more labeled area. Compared to the 3M points in MINC [3], DMS has 3.2M fused segments which carry more information about shape, boundary and co-occurrences. While MINC annotations span 10× more images, point annotations cannot evaluate segmentation boundaries for scene parsing tasks. Example fused maps and class occurrences are shown in Fig. 3 and Table 5. The smallest class appears in 33 images whereas the largest class, *paint*, appears in 39,323 images, which is 88% of the images.

4   Experiments

First, we investigate the impact of our data on training deep learning models with a cross-dataset comparison (Sect. 4.1). Then, we compare the impact of skin type distributions on fairness of skin recognition (Sect. 4.2). Next, we establish a material segmentation benchmark for 46 kinds of materials (Sect. 4.3). Finally, we show predictions on real world images (Sect. 4.4).

Splits. We created train, validation and test splits for our data by assigning images according to material occurrence. The smallest classes are assigned a ratio of $1:1:1$, which increases to $2.5:1:1$ for the largest. An image assignment impacts the ratio of multiple classes so small classes are assigned first. There are 24,255 training images, 10,139 validation images and 10,166 test images.

4.1   Cross-Dataset Comparison

Does training with our data lead to a better model? This experiment compares a model fit to our data against two baselines fit to OpenSurfaces data—the strongest published model [37] and a model with the same architecture as ours. There are two sources of data. The first is OpenSurfaces data with the splits and 25 labels proposed by [37]. The second is comparable DMS training and validation data ([37] does not define a test split) created by translating our labels to match [37]. The evaluation set, which we call Avg-Val, is made of both parts—the validation sets of OpenSurfaces and DMS, called OS-Val and DMS-Val, respectively—weighted equally. For evaluation of our data we fit models to DMS training data and choose the model that performs best on DMS-Val. This model, which we call DMS-25, is a ResNet-50 architecture [13] with dilated convolutions [7,42] as the encoder, and Pyramid Pooling Module from PSP-Net [44] as the decoder. The first baseline (Table 6, row 2) is UPerNet [37], a multitask scene parsing model which uses cross-domain knowledge to boost material segmentation performance. The second baseline (Table 6, row 3), called OS-25, has the same architecture as DMS-25 but is fit to OpenSurfaces training data. Table 6 shows the results. We report per-pixel accuracy (Acc), mean class accuracy (mAcc), mean intersection-over-union (mIoU) and Δ, the absolute difference in a metric across DMS-Val and OS-Val. A low Δ indicates a model is more consistent across datasets. We find that fitting a model to DMS

Table 6. Training data evaluation. We compare segmentation of 25 materials with our training data (*row 1*) to OpenSurfaces data with two kinds of models (*rows 2 and 3*). Avg-Val is the equally-weighted validation sets of each dataset, DMS-Val and OS-Val. Δ is the difference in a metric across datasets. A convnet fit to our data achieves higher performance and is more consistent across datasets.

Training data	Model	Metric	Avg-Val ↑	Δ ↓	DMS-Val ↑	OS-Val ↑
DMS (Ours)	DMS-25	Acc	**0.777**	**0.047**	0.753	0.800
		mAcc	**0.689**	**0.006**	0.686	0.692
		mIoU	**0.500**	**0.014**	0.507	0.493
OpenSurfaces [2]	UPerNet [37]	Acc	0.682	0.310	0.527	0.837
		mAcc	0.486	0.274	0.349	0.623
		mIoU	0.379	0.298	0.230	0.528
OpenSurfaces [2]	OS-25	Acc	0.705	0.231	0.589	0.820
		mAcc	0.606	0.193	0.509	0.702
		mIoU	0.416	0.199	0.316	0.515

training data leads to higher performance and lower Δ on all metrics. We also report the metrics on each validation set and find that both baselines underperform on DMS-Val. We find that DMS-25 performs 0.01 lower on OS-Val mAcc compared to a model trained on OpenSurfaces data. This may be due to differences in annotation and image variety. We use our photographic type labels to investigate the larger performance gaps on DMS-Val.

Why do models trained with OpenSurfaces underperform on our validation images? In Table 7 we report per-pixel accuracy of DMS-25, UPerNet, and OS-25 across nine categories. We find that DMS-25 performs consistently across categories with the lowest performing category (unreal images) 0.071 below the highest performing category (images of enclosed areas). UPerNet shows lower performance across all categories with a drop of 0.426 from images of enclosed areas to images of distant outdoor things. And OS-25 shows similar performance with a drop of 0.407. We observe that both UPerNet and OS-25 have low performance on outdoor images and images without any context. This study shows that photographic types can improve our understanding of how material segmentation models perform in different settings. And, these results justify our decision to collect outdoor images and images of different photographic types.

4.2 Recognition of Different Skin Types

Models trained on face datasets composed of unbalanced skin types exhibit classification disparities [5]. Does this impact skin recognition? Without any corrections for skin type imbalance we find that DMS-25 has a 3% accuracy gap among different skin types on DMS-val (Type I–II: 0.933, Type III–IV: 0.924, Type V–VI: 0.903) while OS-25 has a larger gap of 13.3% (Type I–II: 0.627, Type III–IV: 0.571, Type V–VI: 0.494). This confirms that skin type imbalance

Table 7. Performance analysis with photographic types. A model fit to our data, DMS-25 (*Table 6, row 1*), performs well on all photographic types whereas two models fit to OpenSurfaces, UPerNet and OS-25 (*Table 6, rows 2–3*) have low performance outdoors (*middle*) and on surfaces without any context (*row 7*).

Photographic type	Per-Pixel accuracy		
	DMS-25 (Ours)	UPerNet [37]	OS-25
An area with visible enclosure	0.756	0.615	0.632
A collection of indoor things	0.752	0.546	0.622
A tightly cropped indoor thing	0.710	0.441	0.561
A view of reachable outdoor things	0.750	0.265	0.388
A tightly cropped outdoor thing	0.731	0.221	0.359
Distant unreachable outdoor things	0.736	0.189	0.225
A real surface without context	0.691	0.222	0.348
Not a real photo	0.685	0.528	0.551
An obstructed or distorted view	0.729	0.370	0.496

impacts skin recognition. Our contribution lies in providing more data for all skin types (Table 2), which makes it easier for practitioners to create fair models.

4.3 A Material Segmentation Benchmark

It is common practice to select large categories and combine smaller ones (our smallest occurs in only 12 training images) for a benchmark. Yet, we cannot know *a priori* how much training data is sufficient to learn a category. We choose to be guided by the validation data. We fit many models to all 52 categories then inspect the results to determine which categories can be reliably learned. We select ResNet50 [13] with dilated convolutions [7, 42] as the encoder, and Pyramid Pooling Module from PSPNet [44] as the decoder. We choose this architecture because it has been shown to be effective for scene parsing [44,47]. Our best model, which we call DMS-52, predicts 52 materials with per-pixel accuracy 0.735, mean class accuracy 0.535 and mIoU 0.392 on DMS-val.

We inspected a few strongest DMS-52 fitted models and found that 6 categories consistently stood out as underperforming—having 0 accuracy in some cases and, at best, not much higher than chance. Those categories are *non-water liquid, fiberglass, sponge, pearl, soap* and *styrofoam*, which occur in 129, 12, 149, 129, 58 and 33 training images, respectively. Guided by this discovery we select the other 46 material labels for a benchmark.

We train a model, called DMS-46, to predict the selected categories, with the same architecture as DMS-52. We use a batch size of 64 and stochastic gradient descent optimizer with 1e-3 base learning rate and 1e-4 weight decay. We use ImageNet pretraining [46,47] to initialize the encoder weights, and scale the learning rate for the encoder by 0.25. We update the learning rate with a

Table 8. Test set results. We report metrics for our model, DMS-46. 17 materials, in italics, are new—not predicted by prior general-purpose models [3,30,37].

Category	Acc	IoU	Category	Acc	IoU	Category	Acc	IoU
Sky	0.962	0.892	*Chalkboard*	0.712	0.548	*Artwork*	0.454	0.301
Fur	0.910	0.707	Paint/plaster	0.694	0.632	Mirror	0.452	0.278
Foliage	0.902	0.761	Wicker	0.674	0.460	*Sand*	0.444	0.340
Skin	0.886	0.640	Natural stone	0.665	0.436	*Ice*	0.440	0.362
Hair	0.881	0.673	Glass	0.653	0.483	*Tree wood*	0.428	0.261
Food	0.868	0.668	Asphalt	0.628	0.442	Pol. stone	0.379	0.236
Ceiling tile	0.867	0.611	Leather	0.615	0.373	*Clear plastic*	0.360	0.222
Water	0.866	0.712	*Snow*	0.610	0.465	Rubber	0.255	0.163
Carpet/rug	0.849	0.592	Concrete	0.603	0.304	*Clutter*	0.182	0.152
Whiteboard	0.838	0.506	Metal	0.575	0.303	*Fire*	0.176	0.147
Fabric/cloth	0.801	0.692	*Wax*	0.573	0.371	*Gemstone*	0.116	0.096
Wood	0.797	0.635	Cardboard	0.570	0.363	Eng. stone	0.088	0.071
Ceramic	0.757	0.427	Wallpaper	0.544	0.329	*Cork*	0.082	0.066
Brickwork	0.746	0.491	*Non-clear plastic*	0.519	0.321	*Bone/horn*	0.074	0.070
Paper	0.729	0.508	Soil/mud	0.511	0.332			
Tile	0.722	0.550	*Animal skin*	0.472	0.308			

cosine annealing schedule with warm restart [19] every 30 epochs for 60 epochs. Because the classes are imbalanced we use weighted symmetric cross entropy [36], computed across DMS training images, as the loss function, which gives more weight to classes with fewer ground truth pixels. We apply stochastic transformations for data augmentation (scale, horizontal and vertical flips, color jitter, Gaussian noise, Gaussian blur, rotation and crop), scale inputs into $[0, 1]$, and normalize with mean $= [0.485, 0.456, 0.406]$ and std $= [0.229, 0.224, 0.225]$ from ImageNet [9]. The training tensor has height and width of 512.

DMS-46 predicts 46 materials with per-pixel accuracy 0.731/0.729, mean class accuracy 0.598/0.585 and mIoU 0.435/0.420 on DMS-val/DMS-test respectively. We report the test set per-class accuracy and IoU in Table 8. We find that *sky, fur, foliage, skin* and *hair* have the highest recognition rates, similar to the findings of [3]. 17 materials do not appear in any prior large-scale material benchmarks. Among these new materials we report high recognition rates for *ceiling tile, whiteboard* and *chalkboard*. To our knowledge, DMS-46 is the first material segmentation model evaluated on large-scale dense segmentations and predicts more classes than any general-purpose model.

4.4   Real-World Examples

In Fig. 5 we demonstrate DMS-46 on indoor and outdoor photos from daily life. Our model recognizes and localizes *food* on *ceramic* plates, workplace materials (*whiteboard* and *ceiling tile*), ground cover materials (*soil, stone, foliage* and *snow*), unprocessed *tree wood*, and *fire* on a *wax* candle.

A Failure Case. The last image is a failure case where our model is confused by decorative tile artwork. We also see opportunities for further improving boundaries and localizing small surfaces.

Fig. 5. Real-world examples. Our model, DMS-46, predicts 46 kinds of indoor and outdoor materials. See Table 5 for color legend.

5 Discussion and Conclusion

Dense Annotation. Prior works [2,3,30] instruct annotators to locate and segment regions made of a given material. Our approach is different. We instruct annotators to segment and label the entire image. This approach collects different data because annotators address all surfaces—not just those which are readily recognized. We hypothesize this creates a more difficult dataset, and propose this approach is necessary for evaluation of scene parsing, which predicts all pixels.

Real vs. Synthetic. Synthetic data has achieved high levels of realism (*e.g.*, Hypersim [26]) and may be a valuable generator of training data. We opted to label real photos because models trained on synthetic data need a real evaluation dataset to confirm the domain gap from synthetic to real has been bridged.

Privacy. Material predictions can be personal. Knowing a limb is not made of skin reveals a prosthetic. The amount of body hair reveals one aspect of appearance. Precious materials in a home reveals socio-economic status. Clothing material indicates degree of nakedness. Care is needed if material segmentation is tied to identity. Limiting predicted materials to only those needed by an application or separating personal materials from identity are two ways, among many possible ways, to strengthen privacy and protect personal information.

6 Conclusion

We present the first large-scale densely-annotated material segmentation dataset which can train or evaluate indoor and outdoor scene parsing models.[1] We propose a benchmark on 46 kinds of materials. Our data can be a foundation for

---

[1] Our data is available at https://github.com/apple/ml-dms-dataset..

algorithms which utilize material type, make use of physical properties for simulations or functional properties for planning and human-computer interactions. We look forward to expanding the number of materials, finding new methods to reach even better full-scene material segmentation, and combining the point-wise annotations of MINC [3] with our data in future work.

Acknowledgements. We thank Allison Vanderby, Hillary Strickland, Laura Snarr, Mya Exum, Subhash Sudan, Sneha Deshpande, and Doris Guo for their help with acquiring data; Richard Gass, Daniel Kurz and Selim Ben Himane for their support.

References

1. Adelson, E.H.: On seeing stuff: the perception of materials by humans and machines. In: Human vision and electronic imaging VI, vol. 4299, pp. 1–12. SPIE (2001)
2. Bell, S., Upchurch, P., Snavely, N., Bala, K.: OpenSurfaces: a richly annotated catalog of surface appearance. ACM Trans. Graph. (TOG) **32**(4), 1–17 (2013)
3. Bell, S., Upchurch, P., Snavely, N., Bala, K.: Material recognition in the wild with the Materials in Context database. In: Proceedings of the IEEE Conference on Computer Vision and Pattern Recognition, pp. 3479–3487 (2015)
4. Brandao, M., Shiguematsu, Y.M., Hashimoto, K., Takanishi, A.: Material recognition CNNs and hierarchical planning for biped robot locomotion on slippery terrain. In: 2016 IEEE-RAS 16th International Conference on Humanoid Robots (Humanoids), pp. 81–88. IEEE (2016)
5. Buolamwini, J., Gebru, T.: Gender shades: intersectional accuracy disparities in commercial gender classification. In: Conference on Firness, Accountability and Transparency, pp. 77–91. PMLR (2018)
6. Caesar, H., Uijlings, J., Ferrari, V.: COCO-Stuff: Thing and stuff classes in context. In: Proceedings of the IEEE Conference on Computer Vision and Pattern Recognition, pp. 1209–1218 (2018)
7. Chen, L.C., Papandreou, G., Kokkinos, I., Murphy, K., Yuille, A.L.: DeepLab: semantic image segmentation with deep convolutional nets, atrous convolution, and fully connected CRFs. IEEE Trans. Pattern Anal. Mach. Intell. **40**(4), 834–848 (2017)
8. Chen, L., Tang, W., John, N.W., Wan, T.R., Zhang, J.J.: Context-aware mixed reality: a learning-based framework for semantic-level interaction. In: Computer Graphics Forum, vol. 39, pp. 484–496. Wiley Online Library (2020)
9. Deng, J., Dong, W., Socher, R., Li, L.J., Li, K., Fei-Fei, L.: ImageNet: a large-scale hierarchical image database. In: 2009 IEEE Conference on Computer Vision and Pattern Recognition, pp. 248–255. IEEE (2009)
10. Fitzpatrick, T.B.: The validity and practicality of sun-reactive skin types I through VI. Arch. Dermatol. **124**(6), 869–871 (1988)
11. Gao, Y., Hendricks, L.A., Kuchenbecker, K.J., Darrell, T.: Deep learning for tactile understanding from visual and haptic data. In: 2016 IEEE International Conference on Robotics and Automation (ICRA), pp. 536–543. IEEE (2016)
12. Girshick, R., Radosavovic, I., Gkioxari, G., Dollár, P., He, K.: Detectron (2018). https://github.com/facebookresearch/detectron

13. He, K., Zhang, X., Ren, S., Sun, J.: Deep residual learning for image recognition. In: Proceedings of the IEEE Conference on Computer Vision and Pattern Recognition, pp. 770–778 (2016)
14. Hu, D., Bo, L., Ren, X.: Toward robust material recognition for everyday objects. In: BMVC, vol. 2, p. 6. Citeseer (2011)
15. Jia, M.: Fashionpedia: ontology, segmentation, and an attribute localization dataset. In: Vedaldi, A., Bischof, H., Brox, T., Frahm, J.-M. (eds.) ECCV 2020. LNCS, vol. 12346, pp. 316–332. Springer, Cham (2020). https://doi.org/10.1007/978-3-030-58452-8_19
16. King, D.E.: Dlib-ml: a machine learning toolkit. J. Mach. Learn. Res. **10**, 1755–1758 (2009)
17. Krasin, I., et al.: OpenImages: a public dataset for large-scale multi-label and multi-class image classification (2017). https://storage.googleapis.com/openimages/web/index.html
18. Lin, T.-Y., et al.: Microsoft COCO: common objects in context. In: Fleet, D., Pajdla, T., Schiele, B., Tuytelaars, T. (eds.) ECCV 2014. LNCS, vol. 8693, pp. 740–755. Springer, Cham (2014). https://doi.org/10.1007/978-3-319-10602-1_48
19. Loshchilov, I., Hutter, F.: SGDR: stochastic gradient descent with warm restarts. In: International Conference on Learning Representations (2017)
20. Mei, H., et al.: Don't hit me! glass detection in real-world scenes. In: Proceedings of the IEEE/CVF Conference on Computer Vision and Pattern Recognition, pp. 3687–3696 (2020)
21. Murmann, L., Gharbi, M., Aittala, M., Durand, F.: A dataset of multi-illumination images in the wild. In: Proceedings of the IEEE/CVF International Conference on Computer Vision, pp. 4080–4089 (2019)
22. Ordonez, V., Deng, J., Choi, Y., Berg, A.C., Berg, T.L.: From large scale image categorization to entry-level categories. In: Proceedings of the IEEE International Conference on Computer Vision, pp. 2768–2775 (2013)
23. Park, K., Rematas, K., Farhadi, A., Seitz, S.M.: PhotoShape: photorealistic materials for large-scale shape collections. ACM Trans. Graph. **37**(6) (2018)
24. Patterson, G., Hays, J.: SUN attribute database: discovering, annotating, and recognizing scene attributes. In: 2012 IEEE Conference on Computer Vision and Pattern Recognition, pp. 2751–2758. IEEE (2012)
25. Ritchie, J.B., Paulun, V.C., Storrs, K.R., Fleming, R.W.: Material perception for philosophers. Philos Compass **16**(10), e12777 (2021)
26. Roberts, M., et al.: Hypersim: a photorealistic synthetic dataset for holistic indoor scene understanding. In: Proceedings of the IEEE/CVF International Conference on Computer Vision, pp. 10912–10922 (2021)
27. Russell, B.C., Torralba, A., Murphy, K.P., Freeman, W.T.: LabelMe: a database and web-based tool for image annotation. Int. J. Comput. Vis. **77**(1), 157–173 (2008)
28. Sajjan, S., et al.: ClearGrasp: 3D shape estimation of transparent objects for manipulation. In: 2020 IEEE International Conference on Robotics and Automation (ICRA), pp. 3634–3642. IEEE (2020)
29. Schissler, C., Loftin, C., Manocha, D.: Acoustic classification and optimization for multi-modal rendering of real-world scenes. IEEE Trans. Vis. Comput. Graph. **24**(3), 1246–1259 (2017)
30. Schwartz, G., Nishino, K.: Recognizing material properties from images. IEEE Trans. Pattern Anal. Mach. Intell. **42**(8), 1981–1995 (2019)
31. Sharan, L., Liu, C., Rosenholtz, R., Adelson, E.H.: Recognizing materials using perceptually inspired features. Int. J. Comput. Vis. **103**(3), 348–371 (2013)

32. Sharan, L., Rosenholtz, R., Adelson, E.H.: Accuracy and speed of material categorization in real-world images. J. Vis. **14**(9), 12–12 (2014)
33. Svanera, M., Muhammad, U.R., Leonardi, R., Benini, S.: Figaro, hair detection and segmentation in the wild. In: 2016 IEEE International Conference on Image Processing (ICIP), pp. 933–937. IEEE (2016)
34. Van Zuijlen, M.J., Lin, H., Bala, K., Pont, S.C., Wijntjes, M.W.: Materials in paintings (MIP): an interdisciplinary dataset for perception, art history, and computer vision. PLoS ONE **16**(8), e0255109 (2021)
35. Wang, T.-C., Zhu, J.-Y., Hiroaki, E., Chandraker, M., Efros, A.A., Ramamoorthi, R.: A 4D light-field dataset and CNN architectures for material recognition. In: Leibe, B., Matas, J., Sebe, N., Welling, M. (eds.) ECCV 2016. LNCS, vol. 9907, pp. 121–138. Springer, Cham (2016). https://doi.org/10.1007/978-3-319-46487-9_8
36. Wang, Y., Ma, X., Chen, Z., Luo, Y., Yi, J., Bailey, J.: Symmetric cross entropy for robust learning with noisy labels. In: Proceedings of the IEEE/CVF International Conference on Computer Vision, pp. 322–330 (2019)
37. Xiao, T., Liu, Y., Zhou, B., Jiang, Y., Sun, J.: Unified perceptual parsing for scene understanding. In: Proceedings of the European Conference on Computer Vision (ECCV), pp. 418–434 (2018)
38. Xue, J., Zhang, H., Dana, K.: Deep texture manifold for ground terrain recognition. In: Proceedings of the IEEE Conference on Computer Vision and Pattern Recognition, pp. 558–567 (2018)
39. Xue, J., Zhang, H., Dana, K., Nishino, K.: Differential angular imaging for material recognition. In: Proceedings of the IEEE Conference on Computer Vision and Pattern Recognition, pp. 764–773 (2017)
40. Yang, K., Qinami, K., Fei-Fei, L., Deng, J., Russakovsky, O.: Towards fairer datasets: filtering and balancing the distribution of the people subtree in the ImageNet hierarchy. In: Proceedings of the 2020 Conference on Fairness, Accountability, and Transparency, pp. 547–558 (2020)
41. Yang, X., Mei, H., Xu, K., Wei, X., Yin, B., Lau, R.W.: Where is my mirror? In: Proceedings of the IEEE/CVF International Conference on Computer Vision, pp. 8809–8818 (2019)
42. Yu, F., Koltun, V.: Multi-scale context aggregation by dilated convolutions. In: International Conference on Learning Representations (2016)
43. Zhao, C., Sun, L., Stolkin, R.: A fully end-to-end deep learning approach for real-time simultaneous 3D reconstruction and material recognition. In: 2017 18th International Conference on Advanced Robotics (ICAR), pp. 75–82. IEEE (2017)
44. Zhao, H., Shi, J., Qi, X., Wang, X., Jia, J.: Pyramid scene parsing network. In: Proceedings of the IEEE Conference on Computer Vision and Pattern Recognition, pp. 2881–2890 (2017)
45. Zhou, B., Lapedriza, A., Khosla, A., Oliva, A., Torralba, A.: Places: a 10 million image database for scene recognition. IEEE Trans. Pattern Anal. Mach. Intell. **40**(6), 1452–1464 (2017)
46. Zhou, B., Zhao, H., Puig, X., Fidler, S., Barriuso, A., Torralba, A.: Scene parsing through ade20k dataset. In: Proceedings of the IEEE Conference on Computer Vision and Pattern Recognition (2017)
47. Semantic understanding of scenes through the ADE20K dataset. Int. J. Comput. Vis. **127**(3), 302–321 (2019)

MimicME: A Large Scale Diverse 4D Database for Facial Expression Analysis

Athanasios Papaioannou[3(✉)], Baris Gecer[3], Shiyang Cheng[3],
Grigorios Chrysos[3], Jiankang Deng[3], Eftychia Fotiadou[3], Christos Kampouris[3],
Dimitrios Kollias[3], Stylianos Moschoglou[3], Kritaphat Songsri-In[3],
Stylianos Ploumpis[3], George Trigeorgis[3], Panagiotis Tzirakis[3],
Evangelos Ververas[3], Yuxiang Zhou[3], Allan Ponniah[4], Anastasios Roussos[1,2],
and Stefanos Zafeiriou[3]

[1] University of Exeter, Exeter, UK
[2] Institute of Computer Science, Foundation for Research and Technology Hellas,
Heraklion, Greece
troussos@ics.forth.gr
[3] Imperial College London, London, UK
apapaion@gmail.com, s.zafeiriou@imperial.ac.uk
[4] Department of Plastic Surgery, Royal. Free Hospital, London, UK

Abstract. Recently, Deep Neural Networks (DNNs) have been shown
to outperform traditional methods in many disciplines such as computer
vision, speech recognition and natural language processing. A prerequisite for the successful application of DNNs is the big number of data.
Even though various facial datasets exist for the case of 2D images, there
is a remarkable absence of datasets when we have to deal with 3D faces.
The available facial datasets are limited either in terms of expressions
or in the number of subjects. This lack of large datasets hinders the
exploitation of the great advances that DNNs can provide. In this paper,
we overcome these limitations by introducing MimicMe, a novel large-scale database of dynamic high-resolution 3D faces. MimicMe contains
recordings of 4, 700 subjects with a great diversity on age, gender and
ethnicity. The recordings are in the form of 4D videos of subjects displaying a multitude of facial behaviours, resulting to over 280, 000 3D meshes
in total. We have also manually annotated a big portion of these meshes
with 3D facial landmarks and they have been categorized in the corresponding expressions. We have also built very powerful blendshapes for
parameterising facial behaviour. MimicMe will be made publicly available upon publication and we envision that it will be extremely valuable
to researchers working in many problems of face modelling and analysis, including 3D/4D face and facial expression recognition[†]. We conduct
several experiments and demonstrate the usefulness of the database for
various applications. ([†]https://github.com/apapaion/mimicme)

A. Papaioannou, B. Gecer, S. Cheng, G. Chrysos, J. Deng, E. Fotiadou, C. Kampouris,
D. Kollias, S. Moschoglou, K. Songsri-In, S. Ploumpis, G. Trigeorgis, P. Tzirakis, E.
Ververas, Y. Zhou were with Imperial College London during this work.

S. Avidan et al. (Eds.): ECCV 2022, LNCS 13668, pp. 467–484, 2022.
https://doi.org/10.1007/978-3-031-20074-8_27

Fig. 1. Synthetic 3D faces with random identity, appearance and expression generated by the non-linear model that we built from the proposed MimicMe database. The collected large-scale 4D data (4,700 identities and over 280,000 high-resolution 3D meshes) alongside the proposed especially-designed processing framework yield models and results of unprecedented realism and quality.

1   Introduction

Arguably, 3D Morphable Models (3DMMs) have dominated the field of 3D statistical shape modelling the last 20 years since their introduction by the seminal work of Blanz and Vetter [5]. They have been used in a variety of applications and in different fields such as creative media, medical image analysis, biometrics, computer vision, human behavioral analysis, computer graphics, craniofacial surgery and large-scale facial phenotyping, see e.g. [2,18,19,30,38,39,44,58].

In essence, a face 3DMM is constructed by bringing all the facial 3D meshes of the training set into dense correspondence and then performing some form of dimensionality reduction, typically principal component analysis (PCA). When a set of 3D meshes is in dense correspondence, then vertices with the same index in different meshes represent the same part (e.g. a vertex with index i represents the nose tip in every mesh of the set). After the construction of a 3DMM, a new face shape is represented by a few parameters.

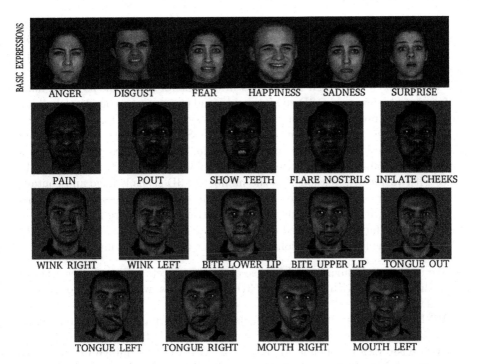

BASIC EXPRESSIONS

| ANGER | DISGUST | FEAR | HAPPINESS | SADNESS | SURPRISE |

| PAIN | POUT | SHOW TEETH | FLARE NOSTRILS | INFLATE CHEEKS |

| WINK RIGHT | WINK LEFT | BITE LOWER LIP | BITE UPPER LIP | TONGUE OUT |

| TONGUE LEFT | TONGUE RIGHT | MOUTH RIGHT | MOUTH LEFT |

Fig. 2. Expressions included in the dataset. In the first row, the basic expressions are shown. These snapshots are taken from the video that subjects were watching in order to mimic the corresponding facial expressions.

During the last years, the rise of Deep Neural Networks (DNNs), with Convolution Neural Networks (CNNs) as the catalyst, revolutionized computer vision. It was only natural that 3D shape modelling was among the fields that were significantly influenced by this trend. Two main lines of research have emerged. The first one has attempted to re-model the 3DMMs by introducing some form of nonlinearity replacing the PCA part of 3DMMs with autoencoders [10,13,26,41]. The other one has attempted to leverage the success of DNNs in 2D images by applying these models in 2D representations of the 3D images like UV maps [22,23,35].

A common ground for both approaches is the need for large datasets. Even though this is trivial for the case of 2D images and videos, where numerous databases have been proposed for various applications, such as 2D-based face identification, in-the-wild face analysis, age estimation, facial emotion recognition, etc., the relevant advances in the field of 3D modelling are still rather limited. This is due to the fact that 3D acquisition devices are usually expensive, can be found only in specialised products or are used for medical purposes (i.e. CT, MRI). The majority of previous 3DMMs have been built using either neutral faces, or a small sample size of people under various expressions. Thus, the community is still lacking a database that combines large numbers in subjects, expressions and 3D images per subject.

In this work, we overcome the aforementioned limitations by constructing a large scale dynamic facial expression database, hereby coined as MimicMe. Our dataset includes 4,700 subjects performing various facial expressions. It contains over 280,000 high resolution 3D facial scans. Due to the demographic richness of our dataset, we expect that MimicMe will become an invaluable asset for many different problems such as 3D/4D face and facial expression recognition, building high-quality expressive blendshapes, as well as synthesizing 3D faces for training deep learning systems. In addition, we revisit LSFM [9], a fully automated and robust Morphable Model construction pipeline, to incorporate the advances in landmarks' localization, and extend it to handle not only neutral faces but also faces with various expressions. As the number of 3D scans is huge and contains particularly large demographic variability (the capture process was performed in a museum with people from various countries), there were some flawed 3d registrations which we proposed to amend them by exploiting a StyleGan [29].

In summary, the contributions of this paper are the following:

- We introduce MimicMe, a database of 4,700 subjects collected over a period of three months with over 280,000 3D facial meshes, with various posed facial behaviours.
- We have a number of 55,000 3D facial landmarks manually corrected, which leads to a subspace of sparse representations for 3D facial expressions.
- We revisit LSFM pipeline for registration to take advantage of DNNs' for landmarks' localization and generalize for all facial poses.
- We propose a new method to correct distorted 3D scans by training a Style-Gan to perform texture completion.
- We build novel expression blendshapes learned from our database that are more powerful than the off-the-shelf blendshapes provided by other datasets.
- We show that our dataset can be used to generate high-quality faces by capitalizing on the recent developments on Generative Adversarial Networks (GANs). We build a novel non-linear model that can synthesize shape, expression, texture and normals.

2   Related Work

2.1   3D/4D Face Datasets

As the existence of a dataset of 3D faces is a crucial factor to build a 3D Morphable Model and an expression blendshape model, there have been attempts in the past to build as large and diverse datasets as possible. Even though there are datasets that used 3DMM fitting process to reconstruct 3D faces from images [27,57], a process called analysis-by-synthesis [19], these datasets are usually of limited quality. Thus, we focus on datasets that have been created using depth sensors, scanners or multi-view camera systems. These 4D face datasets can be categorized according to the kind of facial movements, namely, datasets that include a variety of expressions (e.g. happiness, sadness, disguise), and datasets that focus on speech.

One of the first 3D datasets with expressions is BU-3DFE database [53], which includes articulated facial expressions from 100 adults. The age of subjects ranges from 18 years to 70 years old and included the 6 prototypic expressions (happiness, disgust, fear, angry, surprise and sadness). Bosphorus database [42] includes similar numbers of 105 individuals with a rich set of 34 expressions per subject, but it does not contain 3D meshes, as the data are in the form of depth maps and texture images. BU-4DFE [52] was an extension of BU-3DFE to dynamic 3D space using the same 6 facial expressions from 101 adults. FaceWare-house [12] is one more database which has been used to build 3D blendshapes. To this end, it includes both neutral 3D faces and 3D facial expressions. The capture process was implemented with a Kinect (RGBD camera) and the dataset size is of 150 subjects, aged 7–80 from various ethnic backgrounds. Expressions include the neutral expression and 19 others such as mouth-opening, smile, kiss, etc. 4DFAB [14] has been proposed recently and is one of the largest 4D datasets. It consists of over 1,800,000 3D meshes. 4DFAB contains recordings of 180 subjects captured in four different sessions spanned over a five-year period. Subjects performed not only the 6 prototypic expressions, but also spontaneous expressions and 9 words utterances. More recently, Ranjan et al. [41] propose the framework of convolutional mesh autoencoders (COMA) and introduce for the needs of their method a dataset of 12 different subjects with 20, 466 meshes of extreme expressions was also provided.

One other trend of 4D databases is to acquire databases which focus on speech and word utterance. In this category belongs VOCASET [17] which contains a collection of audio-4D scan pairs captured for 12 subjects. For each subject, 40 sequences of a sentence spoken in English, each of length three to five seconds have been collected. 4D Cardiff Conversation Database (4D CCDb) [34] contains 4 subjects captured while discussing topics of their own interest. In total 34 conversations, have been captured at a frame rate of 60 fps leading to 3500–4000 frames per sequence. [47] captured 4D sequences of 2 native and 2 non-native English speakers reading out the 500 words contained in the publicly-available Lipreading Words (LRW) in-the-wild dataset [15]. S3DFM [54] is a publicly-available dataset that focuses on speech-driven 3D facial dynamics across 77 subjects. Each subject read out 10 times a word and the whole process was captured with a high frame rate 3D video sensor (500 fps).

Table 1 provides a summary of the most recent 3D and 4D datasets, with details such as the number of subjects, the year of acquisition and the quality of their meshes.

2.2   3DMM and Blendshape Models

The construction of a 3DMM, as introduced by the seminal work of Blanz and Vetter [5], consists of four main steps, namely data pre-processing, bringing the facial meshes into a common space by removing rotation, scale and translation, establishing group-wise dense correspondence between a training set of facial meshes, and finally performing some kind of statistical analysis, usually PCA, on the registered data to produce a low-dimensional model. Variations on steps

Table 1. 3D and 4D facial datasets.

Dataset	Year	Type	Unique Participants	No vertices	Expressions	Public Available	Coverage
BU-4DFE [52]	2008	4D	101	35,000	6	Yes	Face
BOSPHORUS [42]	2008	3D	105	-	34	Yes	Face
BP4D-Spontaneous [56]	2014	4D	41	30,000–50,000	27 AU	Yes	Face
FaceWarehouse [12]	2014	4D	150	11,000	20	Yes	Face
4D CCDb [34]	2015	4D	4	30,000	Speech	Yes	Face
LSFM [9]	2016	3D	10,000	60,000	Neutral only	No	Face
LYHM [18]	2017	3D	1,200	180,000	Neutral only	Yes	Head
4D-FAB [14]	2018	4D	180	75,000	6	No	Face
COMA [41]	2018	4D	12	5023	11	Yes	Face
S3DFM [54]	2019	4D	77	-	Speech	Yes	Face
VOCASET [17]	2019	4D	127	5023	Speech	Yes	Face
SIAT-3DFE [51]	2020	4D	12	500K-1M	16	Yes	Face
FaceScape [50]	2020	4D	938	29,587	20	Yes	Face
MimicME (proposed)	2022	4D	4,700	60,000	20	Yes	Face

of the aforementioned process led to different versions of 3DMMs. Lüthi [33] proposes to use Gaussian Process (GP) in order to construct 3DMMs, which was shown to exhibit better capacity in this respect. A different approach was suggested in [20] where a dictionary learning was used to form a 3D face shape model leading to better performance in terms of reconstruction and fitting accuracy than the PCA-based 3DMM. [31] introduced Gaussian mixture model in 3DMMs by assuming that the global population was a mixture of Gaussian sub-populations, each with its own mean and a shared covariance.

In a similar manner, blendshapes models (or expression models) are 3DMMs that consider the identity and expression as two distinguishable parts and create two different models for each of these parts. Depending on the way that these two parts are combined, the models in the literature can be classified to three categories: **additive**, **multiplicative**, and **nonlinear models** [19].

Additive models represent the expressions as the offset between a shape with expression and the neutral shape of a subject [3,4,45]. **Multiplicative models** combine identity and expression in a multiplicative manner, which in most of the cases is done by exploiting tensors. The main concept is to stack the 3D face data into a tensor and performing higher-order tensor decomposition (HOSVD) instead of PCA [6,7,11,48,49]. These models are characterized by their expressiveness and simplicity but require data with semantic correspondence, specified by expression labels. Finally, in **nonlinear models**, facial variations are modelled with nonlinear transformations, such as a physical simulation [28] or Gaussian mixture models to represent facial shape and texture [31]. Li et al. [32] introduce FLAME, a non-linear 3D expressive head model that combines explicit control over jaw articulation with expression blendshapes. They register the 3D meshes based on a non-rigid ICP method regularized by the face model. Many of the recent DNN methods belong to this category. Several recent deep learning approaches adopt autoencoder frameworks to build nonlinear 3DMMs by learning a relevant latent space, see e.g. [1,46].

2.3 Appearance Models

In most cases, 3DMMs include also a modelling of the facial appearance. As in the case of the shape model, the appearance model of a 3DMM is built by performing statistics on the appearance information of the training shapes, which is represented either in terms of per-vertex values or as a texture in the so-called UV-space [19]. The latter is more popular as it does not require the shape and appearance to have the same resolution and the texture in the UV-space is treated as a 2D image, meaning that standard techniques for image processing and analysis are easily applied.

Appearance models of the facial texture in UV-space are grouped into **linear** and **nonlinear**. **Linear models** include the original work by Blanz and Vetter [5], the work of [18] for head and the work of [8] for face, to name a few. **Nonlinear models** include most of the recent deep learning-based approaches, which learn a joint shape and texture model, see e.g. [22,23]. For the successful training of these models, the existence of a large scale dataset of UV maps plays a crucial role. However, the solutions of the existing literature are not satisfactory and this is a gap that we fill with the proposed database.

3 MimicMe Database

3.1 Data Acquisition

The proposed database (MimicMe) was collected during a special exhibition in the Science Museum, London, over a period of 3 months. A large number of museums' visitors (4,700) volunteered to be recorded by a 3dMD[1] face capture system while performing various expressions. To avoid a biased dataset due to people's difficulties to act naturally, especially for the case of specific expressions [19], each subject had to watch twice a video of actors performing the expressions shown in Fig. 2. During the fist playback, the subject familiarized herself with the expressions she had to perform and in the second playback, when the capture process was happening, she had to mimic the actors' expressions. In that way, 20 expressions had been recorded. The frame rate of capture was between 2 and 4 frames per second. We also kept demographics information for each subject such as ethnicity, gender and age as it can be seen in Table 2 and Fig. 3. For each subject, a sequence of 70–120 3D images was created. The 3D triangular surface composed of approximately 120,000 vertices joined into approximately 250,000 triangles, along with a high-resolution texture map. The total number of captured 3D images is roughly 280, 760, which is larger than all previous expression-controlled 3D face datasets.

---

[1] https://3dmd.com/.

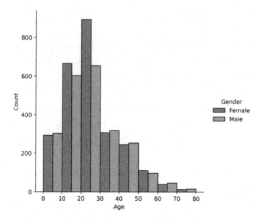

Table 2. Ethnicity distribution in MimicMe database.

Ethnicity	Number	Proportion
Caucasian	3,545	75.43%
Asian	612	13.02%
Black	112	2.38%
Mixed	326	6.94%
Other	105	2.23%

Fig. 3. Distribution of age and gender in MimicMe database.

3.2   Annotation and Registration Process

In order to be able to use the 3D data in a statistically meaningful way, we need to register them into a common template such that all the meshes share the same number of vertices joined into a common triangulation. In literature, the methods for performing 3D registration are classified into two categories based on the space where registration is done. The first category of methods exploits the advances of algorithms in 2D images and perform the dense registration in the 2D projections of the 3D meshes, namely their UV counterparts [16,40]. The second class of methods registers directly (i.e. in the 3D space) the mesh and the template [3,36].

As the former methods present some drawbacks like introducing non-linearities into the process and the need of rasterizing the UV image [8], we chose to register our 3D meshes using a method from the latter class of methods, namely performing the registration in the 3D space. There are plenty of methods and frameworks in this family like [8,25,59]. We opt for the framework used in building the LSFM [8], which is open source, publicly available and is based on Non-rigid Iterative Closest Point (NICP) for the 3D mesh registration. Since LSFM pipeline is used mainly on datasets with neutral faces, it is not suitable for datasets with faces with expressions. To address this problem, we need to adapt the template to handle each deformed face. We follow the updated approach of LSFM presented in [47] where the template used for registration is not the same for all the meshes to be registered but it is deformed driven by a set of landmarks of each mesh and the expression blendshape model built in [14] . More precisely, a face detection and alignment model [55] is applied to each mesh and its corresponding color image. Then, a set of 68 sparse 2D landmarks is predicted which are easily projected in their corresponding 3D landmarks by exploiting the correspondence between the color image and the depth map. The predicted 3D landmarks are used to align the mesh to the template. To reduce effects from the identity difference between the template and the mesh, we regis-

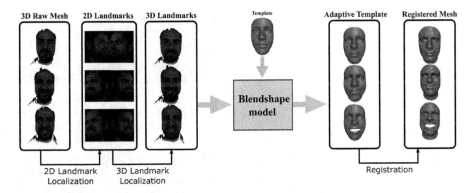

Fig. 4. Registration pipeline. The process starts by extracting 2D landmarks from the texture image, and then their corresponding position on the 3D mesh. By applying a regression between the 3D landmarks of the raw mesh and the neutral registered mesh, we create an adaptive template. Using this template and the 3D shape of the raw mesh, NICP can accurately register the raw mesh.

ter the neutral shape of each person, and we calculate the blendshape parameters c_b for a mesh through linear regression between the landmarks of the registered neutral shape and mesh's landmarks as follows:

$$||l_{\mathbf{x}_k} - \mathbf{A}(\mathbf{x}_n + \mathbf{U}_b \mathbf{c}_b)||_F^2 \tag{1}$$

where $l_{\mathbf{x}_k} \in \mathbb{R}^{3m}$ is a vector with the m landmarks, $\mathbf{A} \in \mathbb{R}^{3m \times K}$ is an indicator matrix, $\mathbf{x}_n \in \mathbb{R}^{3n}$ is the neutral registered shape, $\mathbf{U}_b \in \mathbb{R}^{3n \times s}$ is a matrix with the blendshapes and $\mathbf{c}_b \in \mathbb{R}^s$ is a vector with parameters for the blendshapes.

Finally, we perform dense registration with NICP between the adaptive template and the mesh. In addition, we compute the corresponding texture for each registered mesh. We use a rectangular UV map for representation of the extracted texture as shown in Fig. 6 in order to make the training of GAN simpler.

As compared to [47], our pipeline has several advantages that increase the accuracy of model building in such dynamic scenarios. The most crucial one is the automatic correction of the predicted landmarks. After predicting the 3D landmarks for each mesh, we manually selected one neutral and the apex meshes (meshes with maximum facial change) of each expression per person and corrected the 3D landmarks (Fig. 5) using a 3D landmarking tool[1]. In total, 55,000 meshes were manually annotated. A statistical shape model for the 3D landmarks was built using the manually corrected landmarks. This model was used to correct the rest of the automatic predicted 3D landmarks, adding one more step in our pipeline 4.

3.3 Texture Completion

During the collection of such large-scale dataset, it is inevitable to obtain scan failures for some portion of the data. Such failures are often due to misplacement

---

[1] https://github.com/menpo/landmarker.io.

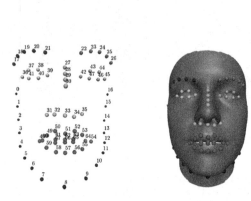

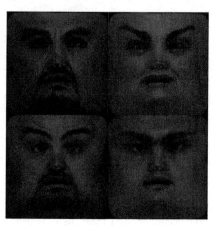

Fig. 5. Definition of the 68 3D facial landmarks (left) and an example of annotated template (right). Landmarks with the same color belong to the same semantic group (e.g. orange for the left eye).

Fig. 6. UV maps examples of registered meshes

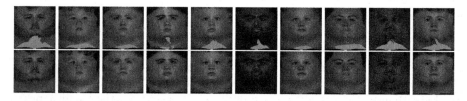

Fig. 7. Texture Completion by projecting visible part of the texture to a GAN that is trained with complete textures, as explained in [21].

of the subject with respect to the camera or self-occlusions, e.g. occlusions due to hair, clothes, accessories. We estimated that a non-negligible portion of our dataset is affected by such scanning failures and propose the following approach to inpaint missing parts of the texture maps.

We first gather a subset with samples where the subjects have been scanned properly and train a StyleGANv2 [29] from this subset dataset. Then, we project the remaining incomplete textures by using the method explained in [21], with a mask of visible texture, in order to hallucinate missing parts. Finally, we inpaint the texture by alpha blending between the original and hallucinated parts to achieve completed texture map. Some examples of this approach are shown in Fig. 7

3.4   Creating Expression Blendshapes

One of the ways that we have exploited our rich dynamic dataset was by using it to build a blendshape model following the standard process used in additive

Table 3. Recognition Rates (RR) [%] obtained from facial expression experiments using 7 expressions (AN-Anger, DI-Disgust, FE-Fear, HA-Happiness, SA-Sadness, SU-Surprise, PA-Pain)

Method	AN	DI	FE	HA	SA	SU	PA
FW	65.4	57.8	**44.4**	84.9	67.8	78.6	49.2
4DFAB	66.6	59.0	44.2	85.8	70.2	81.4	53.8
Ours	**69.4**	**61.7**	44.0	**86.1**	**70.6**	**81.6**	**62.9**

models, see e.g. [37]. In particular, we used the registered meshes from the previous step and the neutral shape of each sequence. For each of the sequences, we subtracted the neutral mesh of the sequence from each frame. After that, for each subject, we have a sequence of difference vectors, namely $\mathbf{d} \in \mathbb{R}^{3n}$ which were then stacked into a matrix $\mathbf{D} = [\mathbf{d}_1, \ldots, \mathbf{d}_k] \in \mathbb{R}^{3n \times k}$, where n is the number of vertices in our mesh. Finally, incremental PCA was applied to our difference matrix $\mathbf{D}$ to identify the deformation components. We keep 28 blendshapes which correspond to 99.9% of the total variance.

4   Experiments

4.1   Facial Expression Recognition

We performed the standard FER experiments on all the expressions, namely the 6 prototypic expressions anger, fear, disgust, surprise, happiness, sadness, and some proposed expressions like pain, flaring of nostrils, inflating of cheeks, pout, showing the teeth, winking each eye, biting the upper and lower lip and moving the mouth left and right. We selected 700 subjects of our dataset that haven't been used for the creation of our blendshape model for training and testing. In total, almost 7000 meshes were utilised. We created a 10-fold partition, every time one fold was used for testing, the others were used for training.

We selected the apex frames of each expression sequence, so for each subject we had 20 meshes. For each mesh, the difference from the neutral mesh of the sequence was calculated and then the weights were found by projecting the difference to each blendshape model. In this way, every mesh was represented by a set of 30 parameters. After this, a multi-class SVM was employed to classify expressions. Radial Basis Function (RBF) kernel was selected, whose parameters were chosen by an empirical grid search. We achieved a recognition rate of 66.1%, 63.9%, and 68.3%, for 4DFAB, FaceWarehouse and our blendshape model, respectively. Table 3 shows the recognition rate for some expressions.

4.2   Evaluation of the Expression Blendshape Model

We compare our blendshape model with FaceWarehouse (FW) [12] and 4DFAB [14] models in expression reconstruction. We randomly selected 2079 frames from 192 subjects that display various expressions, from which, we computed the facial deformation in the same way as described in [14] and reconstructed it using both blendshape models. We calculate the reconstruction error and plot the cumulative error curves for models with different number of expression components in Fig. 8. To provide a fair comparison with FW and 4DFAB, we report the performance of our model using the same number of components as the other models. It is clear that our blendshape model largely outperforms FW and 4DFAB models.

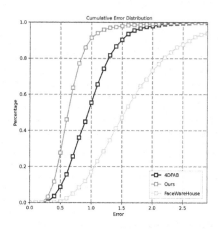

Fig. 8. Cumulative reconstruction errors achieved with different blendshapes over randomly selected expressions from our database.

Additionally, we plot some 3D expression transfer examples in Fig. 9. For visualization reasons, we removed the ears and neck from the faces. For each expression transfer, the facial deformation from the corresponding neutral face was calculated and the blendshape parameters were computed using the aforementioned blendshape models. We then cast the reconstructed expression on a mean face for visualisation. Note that we fixed the number of our expression components to be identical for every model. Our blendshape model can faithfully reconstruct expressive faces with correct expression meaning.

4.3   Non-linear 3D Expression Model

Generating realistic faces in 3D is of high importance for many computer graphics and computer vision applications. In recent studies [23,24,43], Generative Adversarial Networks (GANs) have been trained by large-scale *private* datasets to generate high-quality textures of faces. However, since these datasets are private, it is difficult to explore the potential of such direction.

In order to demonstrate that MimicMe dataset is useful for training more sophisticated 3D face models such as GANs, we train a joint GAN model [22] that can synthesize shape, expression, texture and normals. Figures 1 and 10

Ground Truth

FW

4DFAB

Ours

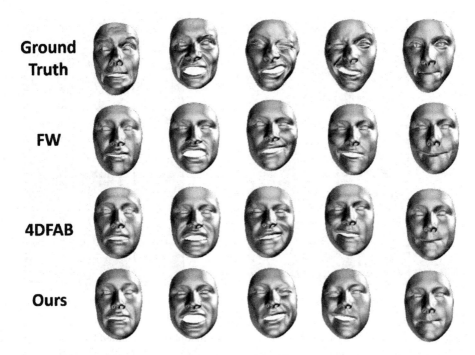

Fig. 9. Comparison of FaceWarehouse [12] blendshape model, 4DFAB [14] and our expression blendshape model. The face in which the blendshapes are applied is the mean face, namely we do not transfer details of face identity

shows some random generations from this generator. It is worth observing how the expression is reflected to both shape and texture and that the generator can synthesize wide range of expressions as well as identity.

Generally, the deformation caused by expressions is often split between shape and texture in the current capture systems. However, the modelling of expression is isolated from the modelling of shape and texture, placing a fundamental limit to the synthesis of semantically meaningful 3D faces. Therefore, our dataset becomes particularly useful for exploiting the correlation between expression, texture and shape by deep generative models.

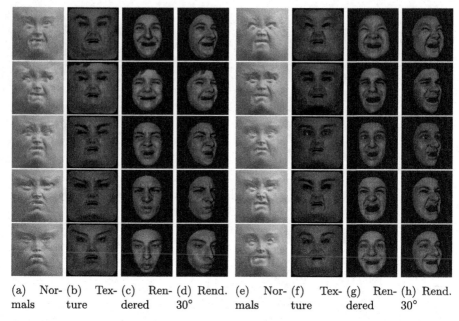

(a) Nor- (b) Tex- (c) Ren- (d) Rend. (e) Nor- (f) Tex- (g) Ren- (h) Rend.
mals   ture   dered   30°   mals   ture   dered   30°

Fig. 10. Random synthetic faces generated by our model that is trained by our dataset. Please note the correlation between expression, texture and shape as well as the identity and expression diversity. Such correlation can be only achieved using a dataset that consists of large number of different identities under various expression, such as MimicMe.

5   Conclusion

We have presented MimicMe, a large-scale detailed 3D facial dataset that can be used for biometric applications, facial expression analysis and generation of realistic faces in 3D for computer graphics. Compared to previous public large-scale 3D face datasets, MimicMe provides the largest diverse population, with high geometric quality. We demonstrate the usefulness of the database in a series of recognition experiments. Promising results are obtained with basic features and standard classifiers, thus we believe that even better results can be obtained using more recent deep methods. We built a powerful expression blendshape model from this database, which outperforms the state-of-the-art blendshape models and a Non-linear 3D Expression Model, which generated high-quality textures of synthetic faces. We make MimicMe database publicly available for research purposes, which we anticipate to have a significant impact on the research in this field.

Acknowledgements. S. Zafeiriou and part of research was funded by the EPSRC Fellowship DEFORM: Large Scale Shape Analysis of Deformable Models of Humans (EP/S010203/1).

References

1. Abrevaya, V.F., Wuhrer, S., Boyer, E.: Multilinear autoencoder for 3D face model learning. In: WACV 2018-IEEE Winter Conference on Applications of Computer Vision (2018)
2. Amberg, B., Knothe, R., Vetter, T.: Expression invariant 3D face recognition with a morphable model. In: 8th IEEE International Conference on Automatic Face & Gesture Recognition, 2008. FG 2008, pp. 1–6. IEEE (2008)
3. Amberg, B., Romdhani, S., Vetter, T.: Optimal step nonrigid ICP algorithms for surface registration. In: IEEE Conference on Computer Vision and Pattern Recognition, 2007, CVPR2007, pp. 1–8. IEEE (2007)
4. Blanz, V., Basso, C., Poggio, T., Vetter, T.: Reanimating faces in images and video. In: Computer Graphics Forum, vol. a22, pp. 641–650. Wiley Online Library (2003)
5. Blanz, V., Vetter, T.: A morphable model for the synthesis of 3D faces. In: Proceedings of the 26th Annual Conference on computer Graphics and Interactive Techniques, pp. 187–194. ACM Press/Addison-Wesley Publishing Co. (1999)
6. Bolkart, T., Wuhrer, S.: 3d faces in motion: fully automatic registration and statistical analysis. Comput. Vis. IDmage Underst. **131**, 100–115 (2015)
7. Bolkart, T., Wuhrer, S.: A robust multilinear model learning framework for 3d faces. In: Proceedings of the IEEE Conference on Computer Vision and Pattern Recognition, pp. 4911–4919 (2016)
8. Booth, J., Roussos, A., Ponniah, A., Dunaway, D., Zafeiriou, S.: Large scale 3D morphable models. Int. J. Comput. Vision **126**(2–4), 233–254 (2018)
9. Booth, J., Roussos, A., Zafeiriou, S., Ponniah, A., Dunaway, D.: A 3D morphable model learnt from 10,000 faces. In: Proceedings of the IEEE Conference on Computer Vision and Pattern Recognition, pp. 5543–5552 (2016)
10. Bouritsas, G., Bokhnyak, S., Ploumpis, S., Bronstein, M., Zafeiriou, S.: Neural 3D morphable models: spiral convolutional networks for 3D shape representation learning and generation. In: Proceedings of the IEEE International Conference on Computer Vision, pp. 7213–7222 (2019)
11. Brunton, A., Salazar, A., Bolkart, T., Wuhrer, S.: Review of statistical shape spaces for 3d data with comparative analysis for human faces. Comput. Vis. Image Underst. **128**, 1–17 (2014)
12. Cao, C., Weng, Y., Zhou, S., Tong, Y., Zhou, K.: Facewarehouse: a 3d facial expression database for visual computing. IEEE Trans. Visual Comput. Graphics **20**(3), 413–425 (2014)
13. Cheng, S., et al.: MeshGAN: non-linear 3D morphable models of faces. arXiv preprint arXiv:1903.10384 (2019)
14. Cheng, S., Kotsia, I., Pantic, M., Zafeiriou, S.: 4DFAB: a large scale 4d database for facial expression analysis and biometric applications. In: Proceedings of the IEEE Conference on Computer Vision and Pattern Recognition (CVPR), June 2018
15. Chung, J.S., Senior, A., Vinyals, O., Zisserman, A.: Lip reading sentences in the wild. In: 2017 IEEE Conference on Computer Vision and Pattern Recognition (CVPR), pp. 3444–3453. IEEE (2017)
16. Cosker, D., Krumhuber, E., Hilton, A.: A FACS valid 3D dynamic action unit database with applications to 3D dynamic morphable facial modeling. In: 2011 International Conference on Computer Vision, pp. 2296–2303 (2011). https://doi.org/10.1109/ICCV.2011.6126510
17. Cudeiro, D., Bolkart, T., Laidlaw, C., Ranjan, A., Black, M.J.: Capture, learning, and synthesis of 3d speaking styles. In: Proceedings of the IEEE Conference on Computer Vision and Pattern Recognition, pp. 10101–10111 (2019)

18. Dai, H., Pears, N., Smith, W., Duncan, C.: A 3D morphable model of craniofacial shape and texture variation. In: 2017 IEEE International Conference on Computer Vision (ICCV), pp. 3104–3112. IEEE (2017)
19. Egger, B.: 3d morphable face models-past, present, and future. ACM Trans. on Grap. **39**(5), 1–38 (2020)
20. Ferrari, C., Lisanti, G., Berretti, S., Del Bimbo, A.: Dictionary learning based 3D morphable model construction for face recognition with varying expression and pose. In: International Conference on 3D Vision (3DV), pp. 509–517. IEEE (2015)
21. Gecer, B., Deng, J., Zafeiriou, S.: OSTeC: one-shot texture completion. In: Proceedings of the IEEE/CVF Conference on Computer Vision and Pattern Recognition, pp. 7628–7638 (2021)
22. Gecer, B., Lattas, A., Ploumpis, S., Deng, J., Papaioannou, A., Moschoglou, S., Zafeiriou, S.: Synthesizing Coupled 3D Face Modalities by Trunk-Branch Generative Adversarial Networks. In: Vedaldi, A., Bischof, H., Brox, T., Frahm, J.-M. (eds.) ECCV 2020. LNCS, vol. 12374, pp. 415–433. Springer, Cham (2020). https://doi.org/10.1007/978-3-030-58526-6_25
23. Gecer, B., Ploumpis, S., Kotsia, I., Zafeiriou, S.: GanFit: GEnerative adversarial network fitting for high fidelity 3d face reconstruction. In: Proceedings of the IEEE Conference on Computer Vision and Pattern Recognition, pp. 1155–1164 (2019)
24. Gecer, B., Ploumpis, S., Kotsia, I., Zafeiriou, S.P.: Fast-GANFit: gnerative adversarial network for high fidelity 3D face reconstruction. IEEE Trans Pattern Anal. Mach. Intell. **44**, 4879–4893 (2021)
25. Gilani, S.Z., Mian, A., Shafait, F., Reid, I.: Dense 3d face correspondence. IEEE Trans. Pattern Anal. Mach. Intell. **40**(7), 1584–1598 (2017)
26. bibitemch27gong19 Gong, S., Chen, L., Bronstein, M., Zafeiriou, S.: SpiralNet++: a fast and highly efficient mesh convolution operator. In: Proceedings of the IEEE International Conference on Computer Vision Workshops, pp. 0–0 (2019)
27. Guo, Y., Cai, J., Jiang, B., Zheng, J., et al.: Cnn-based real-time dense face reconstruction with inverse-rendered photo-realistic face images. IEEE Trans. Pattern Anal. Mach. Intell. **41**(6), 1294–1307 (2018)
28. Ichim, A.E., Kadleček, P., Kavan, L., Pauly, M.: Phace: physics-based face modeling and animation. ACM Transactions on Graphics (TOG) **36**(4), 1–14 (2017)
29. Karras, T., Laine, S., Aittala, M., Hellsten, J., Lehtinen, J., Aila, T.: Analyzing and improving the image quality of stylegan. In: Proceedings of the IEEE/CVF Conference on Computer Vision and Pattern Recognition, pp. 8110–8119 (2020)
30. Knoops, P.G., et al.: A machine learning framework for automated diagnosis and computer-assisted planning in plastic and reconstructive surgery. Sci. Rep.D **9**(1), 1–12 (2019)
31. Koppen, P., et al.: Gaussian mixture 3d morphable face model. Pattern Recogn. **74**, 617–628 (2018)
32. Li, T., Bolkart, T., Black, M.J., Li, H., Romero, J.: Learning a model of facial shape and expression from 4d scans. ACM Trans. Graph. **36**(6), 194 (2017)
33. Lüthi, M., Gerig, T., Jud, C., Vetter, T.: Gaussian process morphable models. IEEE Trans. Pattern Anal. Mach. Intell. **40**, 1860–1873 (2017)
34. Marshall, A.D., Rosin, P.L., Vandeventer, J., Aubrey, A.: 4D Cardiff conversation database (4D CCDB): a 4D database of natural, dyadic conversations. Audit. Vis. Speech Process. {AVSP} **2015**, 157–162 (2015)
35. Moschoglou, S., Ploumpis, S., Nicolaou, M.A., Papaioannou, A., Zafeiriou, S.: 3dfacegan: Adversarial nets for 3d face representation, generation, and translation. Int. J. Comput. Vision **128**, 2534–2551 (2020)

36. Myronenko, A., Song, X.: Point set registration: coherent point drift. IEEE Trans. Pattern Anal. Mach. Intell. **32**(12), 2262–2275 (2010)
37. Neumann, T., Varanasi, K., Wenger, S., Wacker, M., Magnor, M., Theobalt, C.: Sparse localized deformation components. ACM Trans. Graph. **32**(6), 179 (2013)
38. O'Sullivan, E., et al.: The 3D skull 0–4 years: a validated, generative, statistical shape model. Bone Rep. **15** (2021)
39. O'Sullivan, E., et al.: Convolutional mesh autoencoders for the 3-dimensional identification of FGFR-related craniosynostosis. Sci. Rep. **12**(1), 1–8 (2022)
40. Patel, A., Smith, W.A.: 3D morphable face models revisited. In: IEEE Conference on Computer Vision and Pattern Recognition, 2009. CVPR 2009, pp. 1327–1334. IEEE (2009)
41. Ranjan, A., Bolkart, T., Sanyal, S., Black, M.J.: Generating 3d faces using convolutional mesh autoencoders. In: Ferrari, V., Hebert, M., Sminchisescu, C., Weiss, Y. (eds.) ECCV 2018. LNCS, vol. 11207, pp. 725–741. Springer, Cham (2018). https://doi.org/10.1007/978-3-030-01219-9_43
42. Savran, A., et al.: Bosphorus database for 3D face analysis. In: BIOID, pp. 47–56 (2008)
43. Slossberg, R., Shamai, G., Kimmel, R.: High quality facial surface and texture synthesis via generative adversarial networks. In: Leal-Taixé, L., Roth, S. (eds.) ECCV 2018. LNCS, vol. 11131, pp. 498–513. Springer, Cham (2019). https://doi.org/10.1007/978-3-030-11015-4_36
44. Staal, F.C., Ponniah, A.J., Angullia, F., Ruff, C., Koudstaal, M.J., Dunaway, D.: Describing crouzon and pfeiffer syndrome based on principal component analysis. J. Cranio-Maxillof. Surg. **43**(4), 528–536 (2015). https://doi.org/10.1016/j.jcms.2015.02.005, http://www.sciencedirect.com/science/article/pii/S101051821500027X
45. Thies, J., Zollhofer, M., Stamminger, M., Theobalt, C., Nießner, M.: Face2Face: real-time face capture and reenactment of RGB videos. In: Proceedings of the IEEE Conference on Computer Vision and Pattern Recognition, pp. 2387–2395 (2016)
46. Tran, L., Liu, X.: Nonlinear 3D face morphable model. In: Proceedings of the IEEE Conference on Computer Vision and Pattern Recognition, pp. 7346–7355 (2018)
47. Tzirakis, P., Papaioannou, A., Lattas, A., Tarasiou, M., Schuller, B., Zafeiriou, S.: Synthesising 3D facial motion from in-the-wild-speech. In: 2020 15th IEEE International Conference on Automatic Face and Gesture Recognition (FG 2020)(FG), pp. 627–634 (2020)
48. Vlasic, D., Brand, M., Pfister, H., Popović, J.: Face transfer with multilinear models. ACM Trans. Graph. **24**(3), 426–433 (2005)
49. Wang, M., Panagakis, Y., Snape, P., Zafeiriou, S.: Learning the multilinear structure of visual data. In: Proceedings of the IEEE Conference on Computer Vision and Pattern Recognition, pp. 4592–4600 (2017)
50. Yang, H., et al.: Facescape: a large-scale high quality 3D face dataset and detailed riggable 3D face prediction. In: Proceedings of the IEEE/CVF Conference on Computer Vision and Pattern Recognition, pp. 601–610 (2020)
51. Ye, Y., Song, Z., Guo, J., Qiao, Y.: Siat-3dfe: A high-resolution 3d facial expression dataset. IEEE Access **8**, 48205–48211 (2020)
52. Yin, L., Chen, X., Sun, Y., Worm, T., Reale, M.: A high-resolution 3D dynamic facial expression database. In: 2008 8th IEEE International Conference on Automatic Face Gesture Recognition, pp. 1–6 (2008). https://doi.org/10.1109/AFGR.2008.4813324

53. Yin, L., Wei, X., Sun, Y., Wang, J., Rosato, M.J.: A 3D facial expression database for facial behavior research. In: 7th International Conference on Automatic Face and Gesture Recognition (FGR 2006), pp. 211–216. IEEE (2006)

54. Zhang, J., Fisher, R.B.: 3d visual passcode: Speech-driven 3d facial dynamics for behaviometrics. Signal Process. **160**, 164–177 (2019)

55. Zhang, K., Zhang, Z., Li, Z., Qiao, Y.: Joint face detection and alignment using multitask cascaded convolutional networks. IEEE Signal Process. Lett. **23**(10), 1499–1503 (2016)

56. Zhang, X., Yin, L., Cohn, J.F., Canavan, S., Reale, M., Horowitz, A., Liu, P., Girard, J.M.: Bp4d-spontaneous: a high-resolution spontaneous 3d dynamic facial expression database. Image Vis. Comput. **32**(10), 692–706 (2014)

57. Zhu, X., Lei, Z., Liu, X., Shi, H., Li, S.Z.: Face alignment across large poses: a 3D solution. In: Proceedings of the IEEE Conference on Computer Vision and Pattern Recognition, pp. 146–155 (2016)

58. Zollhöfer, M., et al.: State of the art on monocular 3D face reconstruction, tracking, and applications. In: Computer Graphics Forum, vol. 37, pp. 523–550. Wiley Online Library (2018)

59. Zulqarnain Gilani, S., Shafait, F., Mian, A.: Shape-based automatic detection of a large number of 3D facial landmarks. In: Proceedings of the IEEE Conference on Computer Vision and Pattern Recognition, pp. 4639–4648 (2015)

Delving into Universal Lesion Segmentation: Method, Dataset, and Benchmark

Yu Qiu and Jing Xu[✉]

College of Artificial Intelligence, Nankai University, Tianjin 300350, China
yqiu@mail.nankai.edu.cn, xujing@nankai.edu.cn

Abstract. Most efforts on lesion segmentation from CT slices focus on one specific lesion type. However, universal and multi-category lesion segmentation is more important because the diagnoses of different body parts are usually correlated and carried out simultaneously. The existing universal lesion segmentation methods are weakly-supervised due to the lack of pixel-level annotation data. To bring this field into the fully-supervised era, we establish a large-scale universal lesion segmentation dataset, SegLesion. We also propose a baseline method for this task. Considering that it is easy to encode CT slices owing to the limited CT scenarios, we propose a Knowledge Embedding Module (KEM) to adapt the concept of dictionary learning for this task. Specifically, KEM first learns the knowledge encoding of CT slices and then embeds the learned knowledge encoding into the deep features of a CT slice to increase the distinguishability. With KEM incorporated, a Knowledge Embedding Network (KEN) is designed for universal lesion segmentation. To extensively compare KEN to previous segmentation methods, we build a large benchmark for SegLesion. KEN achieves state-of-the-art performance and can thus serve as a strong baseline for future research. The data and code have released at https://github.com/yuqiuyuqiu/KEN.

Keywords: Universal lesion segmentation · Lesion segmentation · Dictionary learning · Knowledge embedding

1 Introduction

When reading medical images such as computed tomography (CT), radiologists first need to search across the image to find lesions for further characterization and measurement [45]. To reduce radiologists' burden and improve accuracy, much effort has been paid to develop automatic lesion segmentation techniques [2,7,26,31,41,43,53,59]. Moreover, automatic lesion segmentation from CT slices also plays a crucial role in many computer-aided diagnosis (CAD) tasks such as pathology detection [34], tumor growth monitoring [20], and quantitative disease progression [28]. Recently, great progress has been brought to this field with the fast development of convolutional neural networks (CNNs), especially fully convolutional networks (FCNs) [38].

S. Avidan et al. (Eds.): ECCV 2022, LNCS 13668, pp. 485–503, 2022.
https://doi.org/10.1007/978-3-031-20074-8_28

It is widely accepted for semantic segmentation models [10,38,42,48,55] that the performance gains mainly benefit from large amounts of accurately labeled training data such as Cityscapes [12] and ADE20K [58] datasets. However, unlike natural images, medical images are difficult to obtain due to their high privacy and secrecy. What's worse, medical image annotation is not only time-consuming and expensive but also requires extensive clinical expertise, resulting in the lack of publicly available medical segmentation data [16,29,40]. Therefore, the biggest challenge of training an accurate lesion segmentation model is the lack of a large-scale dataset.

Besides the limited data scale, another problem is that the existing medical datasets only contain a particular lesion type such as the liver dataset [40], kidney tumor dataset [16], breast mass datasets [23,29], and lung nodules dataset [3]. Based on this, the existing lesion segmentation models usually focus on segmenting one specific lesion type from the corresponding body part [8,11,25]. However, in fact, many types of lesions are correlated with each other. For example, metastases can spread to new areas of the body through the lymph system or bloodstream. In practice, a patient should have radiological examinations on different body parts at the same time so that the radiologists are able to make a more accurate diagnosis by observing relevant clinical findings. Therefore, it is necessary to develop a universal and multi-category CAD framework, capable of segmenting multiple lesion types.

To address the above problems, we first establish a new large-scale multi-category radiological image dataset for lesion segmentation, namely **SegLesion**. SegLesion consists of 9623 lesions in 9456 CT slices with corresponding pixel-level annotations. These CT slices are collected from 4321 series of 3178 studies for 1356 unique patients. Different from existing datasets [3,16,23,29,40], SegLesion contains a variety of lesions, including lung nodules, liver lesions, enlarged lymph nodes, kidney lesions, bone lesions, and so on. SegLesion is based on the DeepLesion dataset [46] that only has bounding box annotations for universal lesion detection. With DeepLesion, many weakly-supervised lesion segmentation algorithms have been presented owing to the importance of lesion segmentation [2,7,41]. To bring universal lesion segmentation into the fully-supervised era, we establish SegLesion by carefully labeling the pixels of each lesion according to the bidimensional RECIST (Response Evaluation Criteria in Solid Tumours) diameters [13] (two short crossing lines on the lesion in Fig. 1) and the bounding boxes provided by DeepLesion.

Lesions of different types usually exhibit a wide variety of sizes, shapes, and appearances. For instance, as shown in Fig. 1, some lesions have a normal size, while other lesions only occupy a few pixels; and meanwhile, different shapes and appearances of lesions are also observed. As a result, it is suboptimal to directly apply the existing segmentation methods [5,9,10,14,32,36,38,42,48,51, 55–57,60] to universal lesion segmentation. To design a better universal lesion segmenter, we observe that the scenarios of CT slices are very limited (*i.e.*, just human organs) and thus easy to be encoded. Motivated by this, we consider adopting the concept of *dictionary learning* for this task. To this end, we

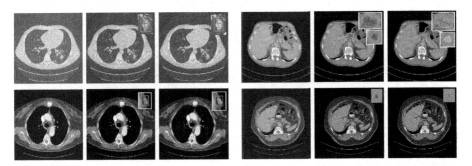

Fig. 1. Samples of CT slices without annotation, with RECIST-diameters and bounding-boxes, and with pixel-wise masks from left to right. Note that for visual clarity, we keep the bounding box in the right image.

propose a Knowledge Embedding Module (KEM). KEM first encodes the knowledge of CT scenarios by learning a *dictionary* as in dictionary learning. Then, the learned dictionary is embedded into the deep features of a CT slice to improve feature distinguishability. With KEM incorporated, we design an elegant network, *i.e.*, Knowledge Embedding Network (KEN). Despite the wide variety, KEN can accurately segment lesions through dataset-level knowledge encoding.

For extensively comparing our method with previous methods, we build a comprehensive benchmark, including well-known methods for both medical image segmentation and semantic image segmentation. We adopt four popular evaluation metrics in medical image segmentation for evaluation. Experimental results demonstrate that our method performs favorably against previous state-of-the-art methods and thus can be served as a strong baseline for future research on this topic. This comprehensive benchmark would also be useful for future research. We summarize our contributions as follows:

- We establish a large-scale multi-category lesion segmentation dataset, SegLesion, with high-quality annotations, for universal lesion segmentation.
- We propose a universal lesion segmentation method, KEN, by embedding the learned data knowledge of CT scenarios into the deep features of a CT slice to increase the distinguishability.
- We build a comprehensive segmentation benchmark for our new SegLesion dataset to promote future research on this topic.

2 Related Work

Lesion Segmentation Dataset. There have existed some lesion segmentation datasets for a specific lesion. For example, the 3D-IRCADb dataset [40] and the Liver Tumor Segmentation (LiTS) challenge organized in MICCAI 2017 [6] are two competitive and widely-used datasets for liver lesion segmentation. The 2019 Kidney Tumor Segmentation Challenge (KiTS19) [16] is for kidney tumor

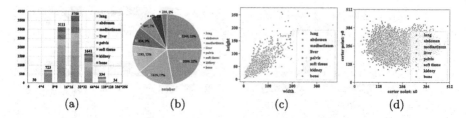

Fig. 2. Data statistics of the new SegLesion dataset. (a) Lesion size distribution; (b) Numbers of lesions of different types; (c) Lesions' height *vs.* width; (d) Coordinates of lesion center points.

segmentation by collecting arterial phase abdominal CT scans from 300 patients who underwent partial or radical nephrectomy. INbreast [29] and DDSM-CBIS [23] are two popular datasets for breast mass segmentation. There are also other datasets targeting on pelvic mass segmentation, thyroid nodule segmentation, axillary lymph node segmentation, and so on [3,4]. However, the scales of these datasets are limited, and each dataset only contains a specific lesion type, making it difficult to train a universal lesion segmentation framework.

Lesion Segmentation. Recently, CNNs, especially FCNs, have been widely applied for lesion segmentation, such as U-Net [36], UNet++ [60], and Attention U-Net [32]. For example, Cao *et al.* [8] proposed a dual-branch residual network for lung nodule segmentation. Christ *et al.* [11] designed a cascaded FCN for liver tumor segmentation. Besides, segmentation models designed for natural images [10,38,42,48,55] can also be used for medical image segmentation seamlessly. However, our SegLesion dataset is more challenging than existing datasets due to its lower contrast, more complicated distribution, and larger anatomical variability in size and shape, making previous segmentation methods unable to achieve satisfactory results. In this paper, we propose a dictionary-learning-based method according to the characteristics of medical images, which can serve as a strong baseline for future research on universal lesion segmentation.

3   SegLesion Dataset

3.1   Data Collection and Annotation

Yan *et al.* [46] introduced a large-scale medical image dataset, *i.e.*, DeepLesion, by releasing CT slices that have been collected for two decades in their institute. DeepLesion collects 32735 lesions in 32120 CT slices from 10594 studies of 4427 unique patients. Lesions of DeepLesion are annotated by bidimensional RECIST diameters (Response Evaluation Criteria in Solid Tumours) diameters [13] (two short crossing lines on the lesion in Fig. 1) that can tell us the location of each lesion. The authors automatically generated bounding boxes for these lesions by adding 5-pixel padding to each direction (left, top, right, and bottom) of the bounding box of RECIST diameters. The authors then selected 9816 lesions in

9624 CT slices and manually labeled them into eight types (*i.e.*, lung, abdomen, mediastinum, liver, pelvis, soft tissue, kidney, and bone) to form a universal and multi-category lesion detection dataset. With DeepLesion, many studies have emerged for lesion detection [46], weakly-supervised lesion segmentation [2,7,41], body part recognition [44], lesions relationship learning [47], and so on. Note that DeepLesion only provides bounding box annotations, so only weakly-supervised lesion segmentation can be explored on this dataset. Our goal of this paper is to bring universal lesion segmentation to the fully-supervised era.

To this end, we carefully label the selected 9816 lesions in 9624 CT slices with pixel-level masks. Unlike DeepLesion that automatically generates the bounding box for each lesion, we manually label the mask of each lesion using the online annotation tool of Polygon-RNN++[1] [1]. To ensure the accuracy and reliability, we conduct a triple-check annotation process, and the third annotator is an experienced doctor. In detail, the first annotator labels lesions with masks according to the RECIST diameters that have indicated the location of each lesion. After finishing this job, the first annotator checks the annotations carefully and re-annotates unsatisfactory ones (1st check). Then, the annotations are re-checked by the second annotator. If he has different opinions on some annotations, the first and second annotators will discuss and re-annotate these CT slices together (2nd check). At last, the annotations are further re-checked by the third annotator who is an experienced doctor. If he disagrees with some annotations, these three annotators will discuss and make re-annotations together (3rd check). Moreover, we abandon some CT slices with lesions whose boundaries are fuzzy for accurate recognition or whose masks are too small to label manually. Finally, SegLesion is composed of 9623 lesions in 9456 CT slices from 4321 series of 3178 studies of 1356 unique patients. We show eight examples with different annotation types in Fig. 1.

3.2 Data Statistics

All CT slices in SegLesion are in a resolution of 512×512. The distribution of the lesion sizes is shown in Fig. 2a, from which we can see that most lesions only occupy a small part of the whole image. In detail, about 71.3% of lesions have a size ranging from 64 pixels to 1024 pixels. The number of lesions whose sizes are over 4096 (64×64) pixels is 368, only accounting for 3.8% of all lesions in SegLesion. Among all lesions, the smallest one only has 8 pixels, and the largest one has 57161 pixels, occupying 21.8% of the entire image. We also plot a height *vs.* width figure for all lesions, as shown in Fig. 2c. It is easy to see that the lesions in SegLesion are very small in general. In Fig. 2d, we plot the locations of center points of lesions. We can observe that the lesions are randomly distributed on the CT slices without bias, indicating the universal property of SegLesion.

Following DeepLesion, we coarsely divide the 9456 CT slices of SegLesion into eight types, including lung (2346), abdomen (2099), mediastinum (1619), liver (1193), pelvis (834), soft tissue (647), kidney (479), and bone (239), as

---

[1] http://www.cs.toronto.edu/~amlan/demo/.

Table 1. Number of CT slices of different lesion types in each split. Note that data splitting is conducted at the patient level. ME: Mediastinum; ST: Soft tissue.

Splits	Lung	Abdomen	ME	Liver	Pelvis	ST	Kidney	Bone	Total
Training	1575	1435	1149	837	573	451	328	175	6523
Validation	354	333	242	167	139	114	84	35	1468
Test	417	331	228	189	122	82	67	29	1465
Total	2346	2099	1619	1193	834	647	479	239	9456

depicted in Fig. 2b. Mediastinum lesions are mainly lymph nodes in the chest. The abdomen type consists of miscellaneous lesions that are not in the liver or kidney. The soft tissue type refers to lesions in the muscle, skin, and fat. To facilitate and standardize the future use, SegLesion is randomly split into training, validation, and test sets *at the patient level*, accounting for about 70%, 15%, and 15% of lesions of each type, respectively. A summary of dataset splits and lesion types can be found in Table 1. Since SegLesion contains multi-category CT slices with a wide variety of sizes, shapes, and appearances, it is possible to use SegLesion to train universal lesion segmentation frameworks.

3.3   Potential Applications

The potential applications of SegLesion include:

- Lesion segmentation: This is a direct application of the SegLesion dataset. Unlike previous lesion segmentation for only one specific lesion type, SegLesion is the first public large-scale dataset for universal lesion segmentation. More future researches are expected to push this field to clinical applications.
- 3D lesion segmentation: By combining 2D masks with two-dimensional diameter measurements in DeepLesion [46], we can develop weakly-supervised 3D segmentation algorithms to analyze lesions in a 3D view.
- Lesion retrieval: With lesion masks, it is convenient to conduct region- and context-based lesion retrieval. This would benefit the clinical diagnosis by finding the most similar lesion cases given a query CT slice.
- Lesion growth analysis: Lesion masks in our SegLesion can provide better information than the bounding boxes in DeepLesion [46] for analyzing lesion changes based on their sizes, shapes, and appearances.

As discussed above, this paper explores universal lesion segmentation on the SegLesion dataset by proposing an effective baseline method and building a comprehensive segmentation benchmark.

3.4   Data Naming

We follow the similar naming pattern of DeepLesion [46], *i.e.*, the real patient IDs, accession numbers, and series numbers are replaced by self-defined indices of patient, study, and series (starting from 1) for anonymization. Therefore, each CT slice in SegLesion is named with the format "{patient index}_study index}_{series index}_{slice index}".

4   Methodology

4.1   Knowledge Embedding Module

Our technical motivation comes from the traditional concept of *sparse dictionary learning*, also called *sparse coding*. Sparse coding aims at representing the input data with a linear combination of basic elements. These basic elements are called *atoms* or *codewords*, which compose a *dictionary*. We observe that the scenarios of CT slices are very limited, *i.e.*, just medical imaging of human organs, unlike natural images that would have countless unforeseen new scenarios, so it is easy to encode CT scenarios. Instead of using traditional optimization algorithms for dictionary learning, this paper tries to adapt the idea of dictionary learning to deep learning. Specifically, we leverage CNNs to learn codewords for all CT training data. Then, we embed the learned knowledge, *i.e.*, codewords, into CT features to increase the distinguishability of abnormal and normal areas for easing subsequent pixel-wise classification, which is dubbed *knowledge embedding*.

In detail, we aim at learning K codewords $\mathbf{V}_k \in \mathbb{R}^C$ ($k \in \{1, 2, \cdots, K\}$), *i.e.*, $\mathbf{V} \in \mathbb{R}^{K \times C}$, which encodes the essential knowledge of *all CT slices*. We also learn a scale matrix $\mathbf{S} \in \mathbb{R}^{K \times C}$ for knowledge embedding. Hence, $\mathbf{V}$ and $\mathbf{S}$ are learnable encoding variables. Suppose $\mathbf{X} \in \mathbb{R}^{C \times H \times W}$ is the deep feature map extracted from a CT slice $\mathbf{I} \in \mathbb{R}^{H' \times W'}$ using a deep FCN. Here, C, H, and W are the number of channels, height, and width of the feature map, respectively. Similarly, H' and W' are height and width of the input CT slice, respectively. In this paper, we use the convolutional part of VGG16 [39] or ResNet50 [15] with a stride of 8 for feature extraction, so we have $H = H'/8$ and $W = W'/8$. Our specific idea is to first learn codewords $\mathbf{V}$ and scale $\mathbf{S}$ for all data and then embed the learned information into each pixel of the feature map $\mathbf{X}$ to get a new feature map $\mathcal{T}(\mathbf{X}) \in \mathbb{R}^{C \times H \times W}$, where $\mathcal{T}(\cdot)$ can be viewed as a transformation function for this process. Benefiting from the universal knowledge, the new feature map $\mathcal{T}(\mathbf{X})$ is expected to be easier for pixel-wise classification, and better segmentation results can thus be achieved.

With the above motivation and definitions, we continue by proposing KEM for our goal. As illustrated in Fig. 3, the feature map $\mathbf{X} \in \mathbb{R}^{C \times H \times W}$ is first reshaped to $\mathbb{R}^{N \times C}$ ($N = H \times W$) and then replicated to $\mathbb{R}^{N \times K \times C}$. We subtract $\mathbf{V}$ from $\mathbf{X}$ in the spirit of residual learning, which can be formulated as

$$\mathbf{D} = \mathbf{X} - \mathbf{V}, \quad \mathbf{D} \in \mathbb{R}^{N \times K \times C}, \tag{1}$$

where $\mathbf{V}$ is reshaped and replicated to the same size as $\mathbf{X}$ before subtraction. In this way, we obtain the residual values $\mathbf{D}$ between the feature of each point in $\mathbf{X}$ and each codeword in $\mathbf{V}$. Next, *local scale coefficients* are computed for aggregating $\mathbf{D}$ as

$$\mathbf{A}_{:,k,:} = \frac{\exp(\mathbf{S}_{k,:} \otimes \mathbf{D}^2_{:,k,:})}{\sum_{k' \in \{1,2,\cdots,K\}} \exp(\mathbf{S}_{k',:} \otimes \mathbf{D}^2_{:,k',:})}, \tag{2}$$
$$k \in \{1,2,\cdots,K\}, \qquad \mathbf{A} \in \mathbb{R}^{N \times K \times C},$$

in which $\otimes$ means element-wise multiplication, before which two matrices are replicated to the same size. Inspired by the *softmax* function, Eq. (2) ensures $\sum_{k \in \{1,2,\cdots,K\}} \mathbf{A}_{n,k,c} = 1$ for $\forall n \in \{1,2,\cdots,N\}$ and $\forall c \in \{1,2,\cdots,C\}$. In this way, the local scale coefficient matrix $\mathbf{A}$ is not only derived from the learnable variable $\mathbf{S}$ but also the residual values $\mathbf{D}$, containing both universal and input-related properties. Here, "local" means that the local weight $\mathbf{A}$ at each position is determined by $\mathbf{D}$ at the same position.

With $\mathbf{D}$ and $\mathbf{A}$ prepared, we can calculate the reweighted residual values as

$$\mathbf{D}' = \mathbf{D} \otimes \mathbf{A}, \quad \mathbf{D}' \in \mathbb{R}^{N \times K \times C}. \tag{3}$$

$\mathbf{D}'$ is aggregated along the dimension of K:

$$\mathbf{D}'' = \sum_{k \in \{1,2,\cdots,K\}} \mathbf{D}'_{:,k,:}, \tag{4}$$

after which $\mathbf{D}''$ is reshaped to $\mathbf{D}'' \in \mathbb{R}^{C \times H \times W}$, the same size as $\mathbf{X}$. Now, *global scale coefficients* are further computed for $\mathbf{D}''$ to enhance its intra-channel representation. This operation is called **Embedding Re-scaling (ER)**. ER first aggregates $\mathbf{D}'$ along the dimension of K to summarize the residual values in terms of different codewords, and then aggregates the result along the dimension of N to compute the global information of a CT slice, which can be expressed as

$$\mathbf{E} = \sum_{n \in \{1,2,\cdots,N\}} \sum_{k \in \{1,2,\cdots,K\}} \mathbf{D}'_{n,k,:}, \tag{5}$$

where we have $\mathbf{E} \in \mathbb{R}^C$ representing the overall encoder of the input CT slice $\mathbf{I}$. Next, $\mathbf{E}$ is transformed to an attention vector by

$$\mathbf{E}' = \sigma(\text{FC}(\mathbf{E})), \quad \mathbf{E}' \in \mathbb{R}^C, \tag{6}$$

in which $\text{FC}(\cdot)$ is a fully-connected layer and $\sigma(\cdot)$ is the standard *sigmoid* function. Then, $\mathbf{E}'$ is replicated to $\mathbf{E}' \in \mathbb{R}^{C \times H \times W}$. The output of KEM is easy to write as

$$\mathbf{Y} = \mathbf{D}'' \otimes \mathbf{E}' + \mathbf{D}'' + \mathbf{X}, \quad \mathbf{Y} \in \mathbb{R}^{C \times H \times W}. \tag{7}$$

This intra-channel representation enhancement is different from traditional channel attention [17] that only relies on the feature map (*i.e.*, self-attention), because $\mathbf{E}'$ is based on both the feature map and the learned universal data knowledge.

The proposed KEM can be viewed as an extension of traditional *dictionary learning*. Specifically, KEM defines learnable variables ($\mathbf{V}$ and $\mathbf{S}$) to encode the scenarios of CT slices, achieved by making the inherent dictionary differentiable.

$\mathbf{V} \in \mathbb{R}^{K \times C}$ can be viewed as K *codewords* of the dictionary. The learned dictionary is embedded into the feature map $\mathbf{X}$ in a pixel-wise manner to construct a new feature map $\mathbf{Y}$. The universal knowledge in the dictionary would increase the feature distinguishability, so it is easier to discriminate each pixel in $\mathbf{Y}$ to be normal or abnormal. The input $\mathbf{X}$ and output $\mathbf{Y}$ of KEM have the same size so that KEM is flexible to be plugged into any CNNs.

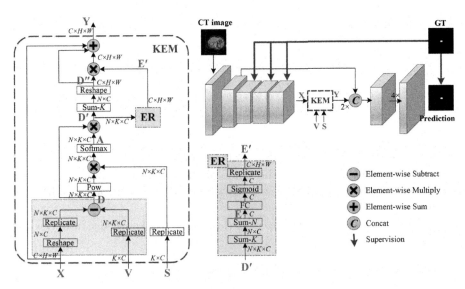

Fig. 3. Network architecture of the proposed KEN.

4.2 Knowledge Embedding Network

In this part, we elaborate on KEN by incorporating KEM. Let us take VGG16 [39] as an example, and the ResNet50 [15] version can be similarly defined. As shown in Fig. 3, we remove all fully-connected layers in VGG16 to obtain an FCN, so that we can obtain five convolutional feature maps, *i.e.*, $\mathbf{X}^{(i)}$ ($i \in 1, 2, \cdots, 5$), corresponding to five convolutional stages of VGG16. Besides the existing convolution layers, we add two more convolutions to deepen VGG16, *i.e.*,

$$\begin{aligned}
\mathbf{X}_1^{(6)} &= \text{ReLU}(\text{BN}(\text{Conv}^{3\times3}(\mathbf{X}^{(5)}))), \\
\mathbf{X}_2^{(6)} &= \text{ReLU}(\text{BN}(\text{Conv}^{1\times1}(\mathbf{X}_1^{(6)}))).
\end{aligned} \tag{8}$$

Here, $\text{Conv}^{3\times3}(\cdot)$ and $\text{Conv}^{1\times1}(\cdot)$ are a 3×3 convolution with 512 output channels and a 1×1 convolution with 1024 output channels, respectively. $\text{BN}(\cdot)$ and $\text{ReLU}(\cdot)$ are batch normalization [19] and ReLU [30] layers, respectively. Note that ResNet50 does not need these two more convolutions because ResNet50 is

Table 2. Effects of the main components of KEN. The symbol ✔ indicates that a design choice is used. The 0th column is the results of the standard FCN, and the 4th column is the results of our final model in this paper.

Components		0	1	2	3	4	5	6	7	8
$\mathbf{X}^{(6)}$			✔	✔	✔	✔	✔	✔	✔	✔
KEM			✔	✔	✔				✔	✔
Decoder				✔	✔	✔	✔			
Deep supervision					✔	✔	✔	✔	✔	✔
KEM w/o ER						✔				
KEM w/o $\mathbf{D}''$							✔			
Decoder w/ $\mathbf{X}^{(2)}$									✔	
Decoder w/ $\mathbf{X}^{(4)}$										✔
Metrics (%)	mIoU ↑	62.56	63.05	64.35	64.80	**65.78**	65.15	64.45	65.63	65.15
	SEN ↑	30.98	33.24	46.30	50.76	51.09	42.92	42.67	46.74	**52.11**
	SPE ↑	67.48	67.72	92.43	95.31	97.48	81.30	96.02	96.51	**97.94**
	DSC ↑	27.32	28.61	35.68	39.19	**41.01**	34.73	32.91	39.45	37.79

deep enough for lesion segmentation. Following previous segmentation methods [18,48,52,55–57,61], we change the stride of the last two downsampling layers from 2 to 1, leading to the smallest scale of 1/8. Dilated convolutions are used to keep the receptive field.

A KEM is put on top of $\mathbf{X}_2^{(6)}$ to embed the universal knowledge into it, which can be written as

$$
\dot{\mathbf{X}}^{(6)} = \mathrm{ReLU}(\mathrm{BN}(\mathrm{Conv}^{1 \times 1}(\mathbf{X}_2^{(6)}))),
$$
$$
\hat{\mathbf{X}}^{(6)} = \mathrm{ReLU}(\mathrm{BN}(\mathcal{T}(\dot{\mathbf{X}}^{(6)}))),
$$

$$(9)$$

where $\mathrm{Conv}^{1 \times 1}$ is a 1×1 convolution with 256 output channels. Then, we upsample $\hat{\mathbf{X}}^{(6)}$ from 1/8 scale to 1/4 scale and fuse it with $\mathbf{X}^{(3)}$ that is in 1/4 scale, like

$$
\hat{\mathbf{X}}^{(3)} = \mathrm{ReLU}(\mathrm{BN}(\mathrm{Conv}^{1 \times 1}(\mathbf{X}^{(3)}))),
$$
$$
\mathbf{X}^{\mathrm{concat}} = \mathrm{Concat}(\hat{\mathbf{X}}^{(3)}, \mathrm{Upsample}(\hat{\mathbf{X}}^{(6)}, 2)),
$$
$$
\mathbf{X}^{\mathrm{fuse}} = \mathrm{ReLU}(\mathrm{BN}(\mathrm{Conv}^{3 \times 3}(\mathbf{X}^{\mathrm{concat}}))),
$$

$$(10)$$

in which $\mathrm{Upsample}(\cdot, 2)$ upsamples a feature map by two times, $\mathrm{Conv}^{1 \times 1}$ is a 1×1 convolution with 64 output channels, and $\mathrm{Conv}^{3 \times 3}$ is a 3×3 convolution with 256 output channels. $\mathbf{X}^{\mathrm{fuse}}$ is used to predict the final lesion masks using a 1×1 convolution and upsampling by four times. During training, we also apply deep supervision [22] to $\mathbf{X}^{(4)}$, $\mathbf{X}^{(5)}$, and $\mathbf{X}^{(6)}$ for better optimization, as shown in Fig. 3.

5   Experiments

5.1   Experimental Setup

Implementation Details. The proposed method is implemented using the PyTorch framework [33]. We use ImageNet-pretrained VGG16 [39] or ResNet50 [15] as the backbone. We use $K = 24$ as the default setting. We initialize other convolution layers using the default setting of PyTorch. The Adam optimizer [21] is used for training. The learning rate policy is *poly*, in which the current learning rate equals the base one multiplying $(1 - curr\_iter/max\_iter)^{power}$, where the initial learning rate is set to 1e–4 and *power* is set to 0.9. The weight decay is 1e–4. We train our model for 50 epochs with a batch size of 16. In our experiments, we found that more than 50 epochs do not bring improvement for all models due to the large scale of our new SegLesion dataset. All experiments are conducted using a TITAN Xp GPU.

Table 3. Ablation studies for the hyper-parameter settings of KEN. "#Channels of decoder" means the numbers of channels for $\hat{\mathbf{X}}^{(3)}$ and $\hat{\mathbf{X}}^{(6)}$ in Eq. (10). The default settings are $K = 24$, $C = 512$, and #Channels $= (64, 256)$, respectively.

Configurations		Metrics (%)			
		mIoU ↑	SEN ↑	SPE ↑	DSC ↑
Default Configuration		65.78	51.09	97.48	**41.01**
K of KEM	16	65.47	51.31	97.81	39.61
	32	65.73	52.07	97.31	39.84
	48	65.63	46.50	96.97	38.40
C of KEM	128	65.90	48.78	98.54	39.36
	256	65.27	49.50	97.38	38.80
	1024	**66.31**	52.15	97.90	40.68
#Channels of decoder	(64, 128)	65.35	49.76	**98.63**	38.33
	(64, 512)	65.75	48.15	93.12	39.30
	(32, 128)	64.98	51.05	94.09	39.11
	(32, 256)	65.91	48.14	96.85	39.69
	(128, 256)	65.28	**52.83**	94.77	39.39

Table 4. Quantitative comparison between our KEN and 22 state-of-the-art segmentation methods.

Methods	Publication	Backbone	ImageNet	#Params	FLOPs	Speed	Metrics (%)			
							mIoU ↑	SEN ↑	SPE ↑	DSC ↑
U-Net	MICCAI'2015	-	No	33.72M	261.92G	27.86fps	61.62	39.92	82.72	27.76
FCN-8s	TPAMI'2017	VGG16	Yes	15.53M	105.97G	51.65fps	62.56	30.98	67.48	27.32
SegNet	TPAMI'2017	-	No	28.75M	160.44G	42.41fps	57.21	22.92	90.75	15.35
FRRN	CVPR'2017	-	No	17.30M	237.70G	17.41fps	62.74	37.80	81.19	28.41
PSPNet	CVPR'2017	ResNet50	Yes	64.03M	257.79G	26.52fps	64.67	31.59	72.72	27.93
DeepLabv3	CVPR'2017	ResNet50	Yes	38.71M	163.83G	20.59fps	66.06	42.11	86.34	36.36
DenseASPP	CVPR'2018	-	Yes	27.93M	122.28G	15.95fps	61.73	22.50	71.09	20.92
DFN	CVPR'2018	ResNet50	Yes	43.53M	81.88G	89.39fps	62.27	33.39	76.74	26.46
EncNet	CVPR'2018	ResNet50	Yes	51.25M	217.46G	23.21fps	64.45	33.73	68.28	29.19
DeepLabv3+	ECCV'2018	Xception	Yes	53.33M	82.87G	32.26fps	59.88	23.06	77.03	20.14
BiSeNet	ECCV'2018	ResNet18	Yes	12.50M	13.01G	335.50fps	60.52	20.14	68.51	17.15
UNet++	DLMIA'2018	-	No	35.77M	552.16G	10.56fps	62.52	34.10	74.34	26.61
Attention U-Net	arXiv'2018	-	No	34.06M	266.31G	24.25fps	61.69	35.47	81.11	25.95
OCNet	arXiv'2018	ResNet50	Yes	51.60M	220.69G	28.00fps	65.82	42.77	93.28	35.71
DUpsampling	CVPR'2019	ResNet50	Yes	28.46M	123.01G	31.26fps	65.99	34.82	66.69	30.28
DANet	CVPR'2019	ResNet50	Yes	64.87M	275.72G	24.53fps	65.18	32.94	64.93	28.21
CCNet	CVPR'2019	ResNet50	Yes	46.32M	197.92G	27.56fps	65.18	35.92	71.47	30.86
ANNNet	ICCV'2019	ResNet50	Yes	47.42M	203.07G	21.50fps	65.77	34.49	66.07	29.75
GFF	AAAI'2020	ResNet50	Yes	90.57M	374.03G	17.52fps	64.54	28.14	59.54	20.80
CPNet	CVPR'2020	ResNet50	Yes	48.59M	207.43G	22.58fps	64.59	30.24	62.90	27.55
OCRNet	ECCV'2020	ResNet50	Yes	37.94M	161.44G	28.07fps	65.70	37.31	82.61	32.89
DNL	ECCV'2020	ResNet50	Yes	46.51M	197.52G	26.07fps	64.36	35.38	69.83	30.13
KEN	-	VGG16	Yes	20.11M	148.99G	31.79fps	65.78	51.09	97.48	41.01
KEN	-	ResNet50	Yes	26.74M	139.36G	26.56fps	**66.64**	**58.48**	**97.82**	**42.06**

Evaluation Criteria. This paper adopts four popular segmentation metrics in medical image analysis, including mean intersection over union (mIoU), sensitivity (SEN), specificity (SPE), and dice similarity coefficient (DSC). The higher these metrics, the better the performance.

5.2   Ablation Studies

Here, we conduct ablation studies to evaluate the effect of various designs using the VGG16 backbone. We train the models on the SegLesion training set and evaluate on the validation set. We start with the standard FCN (the 0th column of Table 2), which is viewed as the baseline.

First, to prove the effect of $\mathbf{X}^{(6)}$, we add $\mathbf{X}^{(6)}$ to the baseline. The results are shown in the 1st column of Table 2. Note that we do not use $\mathbf{X}^{(6)}$ for ResNet50 owing to its enough depth. Second, we add KEM which is the key component of our model to the above 1th model to prove the effect of KEM and its designs. The results are put in the 2nd column of Table 2. Third, as shown in the 3rd column of Table 2, we prove the effect of the simple decoder of KEN, which fuses the features at 1/4 ($\mathbf{X}^{(3)}$) and 1/8 ($\mathbf{X}^{(6)}$) scales. Forth, we also show the effect of training with deep supervision in the 4th column of Table 2. The experimental results of above ablation studies indicate the significant improvement brought by each component of KEN, especially by KEM. Fifth, KEM uses ER to enhance

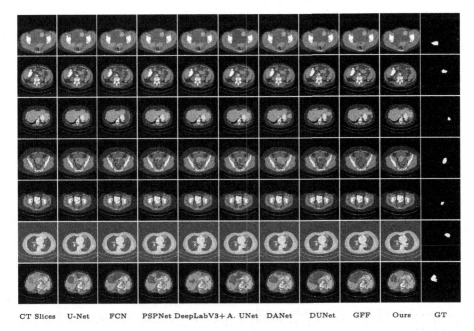

Fig. 4. Qualitative comparison between KEN and eight state-of-the-art competitors. GT: ground-truth lesion mask, A. UNet: Attention UNet. Red: true positive; Green: false negative; **Blue**: false positive. (Color figure online)

the intra-channel representation, as in Eq. (5)–Eq. (7). We provide the results of removing ER from KEM in the 5th column of Table 2. Sixth, another question would be what will happen if we only use ER for knowledge embedding, *i.e.*replacing $\mathbf{D}''$ in Eq. (7) with the input $\mathbf{X}$. The results of this study are given in the 6th column of Table 2. Finally, we try different decoders by replacing $\mathbf{X}^{(3)}$ with $\mathbf{X}^{(2)}$ (1/2 scale) or $\mathbf{X}^{(4)}$ (1/8 scale). The results of these two ablation studies are shown in 7th and 8th columns of Table 2, respectively. We can see that the default design of our model shows significant superiority over all above variants.

In Table 3, we evaluate the impact of the number of knowledge vectors K and the number of channels of the feature map C, which are the most important hyper-parameters of KEM. We also evaluate the impact of different numbers of channels of $\hat{\mathbf{X}}^{(3)}$ and $\hat{\mathbf{X}}^{(6)}$ in the decoder. We can see that KEN is robust to different parameter settings, and the default setting performs slightly better.

5.3   Performance Comparison

Quantitative Evaluation. On our SegLesion test set, we build a comprehensive benchmark for extensively comparing the proposed KEN with 22 state-of-the-art methods, including U-Net [36], FCN-8s [38], SegNet [5], FRRN [35], PSPNet [57], DeepLabv3 [9], DenseASPP [48], DFN [52], EncNet [56], DeepLabv3+ [10], BiSeNet [51], UNet++ [60], Attention U-Net [32], OCNet [55], DUpsampling

Table 5. Lesion segmentation accuracy of KEN for different lesion types on the SegLesion test set. This paper focuses on universal lesion segmentation, and this is table is just shown for clarification. ME: Mediastinum; ST: Soft tissue.

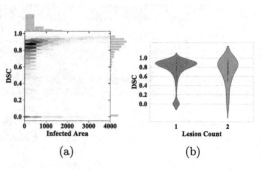

(a)   (b)

Lesion Types	Metrics (%)			
	mIoU↑	SEN ↑	SPE ↑	DSC ↑
All Types	65.78	51.09	97.48	41.01
Lung	73.91	66.26	98.01	53.60
Abdomen	61.72	37.01	97.03	30.33
ME	66.88	59.20	98.95	45.93
Liver	67.74	57.81	98.59	46.11
Pelvis	64.39	35.85	96.40	28.76
ST	58.52	30.64	91.26	24.67
Kidney	58.12	36.42	98.29	29.15
Bone	63.92	41.84	96.47	35.19

Fig. 5. Statistical analysis for KEN on the SegLesion test set. (a) The DSC score *vs.* the infected area; (b) The probability distribution of the DSC score *vs.* the lesion count in the corresponding CT slice.

[42], DANet [14], CCNet [18], ANNNet [61], GFF [24], CPNet [50], OCRNet [54], and DNL [49]. For a fair comparison, we use the code released by the authors. Besides the accuracy evaluation in terms of mIoU, SEN, SPC, and DSC, we also report the number of parameters, the number of FLOPs, and speed, where the default SegLesion resolution of 512 × 512 is adopted for testing.

The numeric comparison is summarized in Table 4. From this table, we can find that the proposed KEN significantly outperforms all competitors in terms of all metrics. The main reason may be that the SegLesion dataset exhibits a wide variety of sizes, shapes, and appearances, which are beyond the consideration of previous segmentation methods, resulting in the unsatisfactory performance of these methods for universal lesion segmentation. This also suggests that universal lesion segmentation is a new research field *worthy of study*. The ResNet50 version of KEN further boosts the performance compared to the VGG16 version. The number of parameters of KEN is also favorably small, implying that its improvement mainly comes from our idea of knowledge embedding learning. KEN is also one of the fastest methods because the proposed KEM is computationally flexible, and the computational load mainly comes from the backbone networks.

In Table 5, we provide the segmentation accuracy of KEN for different lesion types. KEN consistently achieves good performance for all lesion types. Specifically, KEN achieves the best performance for lung lesions and the worst performance for soft-tissue lesions. Note that previous lesion segmentation can only handle a single lesion type, which is the problem that our SegLesion resolves.

Note that this paper does not aim to solve/end a problem. Instead, our main contribution is to start a new task of universal lesion segmentation by proposing a large-scale dataset, a comprehensive benchmark, and a strong baseline method.

Although the performance of our baseline is not enough for clinical applications, we believe lots of studies will appear to push this field to clinical deployment.

Qualitative Evaluation. To explicitly show the effectiveness of the proposed KEN, we select some representative CT slices and display the qualitative comparison between KEN and eight state-of-the-art methods in Fig. 4. We can see that CT slices are with lower contrast compared with nature images, and different lesion types exhibit a wide variety of sizes, shapes, and appearances, making universal lesion segmentation very challenging. Generally, KEN can successfully segment the lesions with fine details, leading to better results.

Statistical Analysis. To further study the stability of the proposed KEN, we perform statistical analysis on our SegLesion dataset. Figure 5a shows the relationship between the most popular metric of DSC and the infected area. We can see that most CT images have DSC in the range of [0.6, 1.0]. Figure 5b displays the relationship between DSC and the lesion count in a CT slice. The medium DSC is above 0.8, regardless of lesion counts. These analyses demonstrate the effectiveness of the proposed KEN in universal lesion segmentation.

6   Conclusion

Universal lesion segmentation is of vital importance but has not been well explored due to the lack of labeled data. Currently, there only exist some weakly-supervised methods. To bring this field to the fully-supervised era, we establish a large-scale universal lesion segmentation dataset. Motivated by traditional dictionary learning, we propose a knowledge embedding approach, *i.e.*, KEN, for universal lesion segmentation. We also build a large benchmark to compare KEN to previous methods extensively. KEN consistently outperforms other competitors and can thus serve as a strong baseline for future research. The limitation of this paper would be that the proposed dataset is still not large enough like natural image datasets [27,37], although it is the largest dataset for universal lesion segmentation now. In the future, we will continue our work by extending this dataset as large as possible.

Acknowledgements. This work is supported by Science and Technology Planning Project of Tianjin, China (Grant No. 20YDTPJC01810), Tianjin Natural Science Foundation, China (Grant No. 21JCYBJC00110 and 19JCQNJC00300).

References

1. Acuna, D., Ling, H., Kar, A., Fidler, S.: Efficient interactive annotation of segmentation datasets with polygon-RNN++. In: Proceedings of the IEEE Conference on Computer Vision And Pattern Recognition (CVPR), pp. 859–868 (2018)
2. Agarwal, V., Tang, Y., Xiao, J., Summers, R.M.: Weakly-supervised lesion segmentation on CT scans using co-segmentation. In: Computer-Aided Diagnosis. vol. 11314, p. 113141J (2020)

3. Armato, S.G., et al.: The Lung Image Database Consortium (LIDC) and Image Database Resource Initiative (IDRI): A completed reference database of lung nodules on CT scans. Med. Phys. **38**(2), 915–931 (2011)
4. Armato, S.G., III.: Lung image database consortium: developing a resource for the medical imaging research community. Radiology **232**(3), 739–748 (2004)
5. Badrinarayanan, V., Kendall, A., Cipolla, R.: SegNet: a deep convolutional encoder-decoder architecture for image segmentation. IEEE Trans. Pattern Anal. Mach. Intell. (TPAMI) **39**(12), 2481–2495 (2017)
6. Bilic, P., et al.: The liver tumor segmentation benchmark (LiTS). arXiv preprint arXiv:1901.04056 (2019)
7. Cai, J., et al.: Accurate weakly-supervised deep lesion segmentation using large-scale clinical annotations: slice-propagated 3D mask generation from 2D RECIST. In: 4th International Conference on Medical Image Computing and Computer Assisted Intervention (MICCAI), pp. 396–404. Springer (2018)
8. Cao, H., et al.: Dual-branch residual network for lung nodule segmentation. Appl. Soft Comput. **86**, 105934 (2020)
9. Chen, L.C., Papandreou, G., Schroff, F., Adam, H.: Rethinking atrous convolution for semantic image segmentation. arXiv preprint arXiv:1706.05587 (2017)
10. Chen, Liang-Chieh., Zhu, Yukun, Papandreou, George, Schroff, Florian, Adam, Hartwig: Encoder-decoder with atrous separable convolution for semantic image segmentation. In: Ferrari, Vittorio, Hebert, Martial, Sminchisescu, Cristian, Weiss, Yair (eds.) ECCV 2018. LNCS, vol. 11211, pp. 833–851. Springer, Cham (2018). https://doi.org/10.1007/978-3-030-01234-2_49
11. Christ, P.F., et al.: Automatic liver and tumor segmentation of CT and MRI volumes using cascaded fully convolutional neural networks. arXiv preprint arXiv:1702.05970 (2017)
12. Cordts, M., et al.: The Cityscapes dataset for semantic urban scene understanding. In: IEEE Conference on Computer Vision and Pattern Recognition (CVPR), pp. 3213–3223 (2016)
13. Eisenhauer, E.A., et al.: New response evaluation criteria in solid tumours: Revised RECIST guideline (version 1.1). Eur. J. Cancer **45**(2), 228–247 (2009)
14. Fu, J., et al.: Dual attention network for scene segmentation. In: IEEE Conference on Computer Vision and Pattern Recognition (CVPR), pp. 3146–3154 (2019)
15. He, K., Zhang, X., Ren, S., Sun, J.: Deep residual learning for image recognition. In IEEE Conference on Computer Vision and Pattern Recognition (CVPR), pp. 770–778 (2016)
16. Heller, N., et al.: The KiTS19 challenge data: 300 kidney tumor cases with clinical context, CT semantic segmentations, and surgical outcomes. arXiv preprint arXiv:1904.00445 (2019)
17. Hu, J., Shen, L., Sun, G.: Squeeze-and-excitation networks. In: IEEE Conference on Computer Vision and Pattern Recognition (CVPR), pp. 7132–7141 (2018)D
18. Huang, Z., et al.: CCNet: criss-cross attention for semantic segmentation. In: IEEE Conference on Computer Vision and Pattern Recognition (CVPR), pp. 603–612 (2019)
19. Ioffe, S., Szegedy, C.: Batch normalization: accelerating deep network training by reducing internal covariate shift. In: International Conference on Machine Learning (ICML), pp. 448–456 (2015)
20. Katzmann, A., et al: Predicting lesion growth and patient survival in colorectal cancer patients using deep neural networks. In: International Conference on Microsoft Interface Definition Language (2018)

21. Kingma, D.P., Ba, J.: Adam: A method for stochastic optimization. In: International Conference on Learning Representations (ICLR) (2015)

22. Lee, C.Y., Xie, S., Gallagher, P., Zhang, Z., Tu, Z.: Deeply-supervised nets. In: International Conference on Artificial Intelligence and Statistics (AISTATS), pp. 562–570 (2015)

23. Lee, R.S., Gimenez, F., Hoogi, A., et al.: A curated mammography data set for use in computer-aided detection and diagnosis research. Sci. Data **4**, 170177 (2017)

24. Li, X., Zhao, H., Han, L., Tong, Y., Tan, S., Yang, K.: Gated fully fusion for semantic segmentation. In: AAAI Conference on Artificial Intelligence (AAAI), pp. 11418–11425 (2020)

25. Li, X., Chen, H., Qi, X., Dou, Q., Fu, C.W., Heng, P.A.: H-DenseUNet: hybrid densely connected UNet for liver and tumor segmentation from CT volumes. IEEE Trans. Med. Imaging (TMI) **37**(12), 2663–2674 (2018)

26. Lian, C., Ruan, S., Denœux, T., Li, H., Vera, P.: Joint tumor segmentation in PET-CT images using co-clustering and fusion based on belief functions. IEEE Trans. Image Process. (TIP) **28**(2), 755–766 (2019)

27. Lin, Tsung-Yi., Maire, Michael, Belongie, Serge, Hays, James, Perona, Pietro, Ramanan, Deva, Dollár, Piotr, Zitnick, C. Lawrence.: Microsoft COCO: common objects in context. In: Fleet, David, Pajdla, Tomas, Schiele, Bernt, Tuytelaars, Tinne (eds.) ECCV 2014. LNCS, vol. 8693, pp. 740–755. Springer, Cham (2014). https://doi.org/10.1007/978-3-319-10602-1_48

28. Lu, K., Bascom, R., Mahraj, R.P., Higgins, W.E.: Quantitative analysis of the central-chest lymph nodes based on 3D MDCT image data. In: Conference on Medical Imaging 2009: Computer-Aided Diagnosis. vol. 7260, p. 72600U (2009)

29. Moreira, I.C., Amaral, I., Domingues, I., Cardoso, A., Cardoso, M.J., Cardoso, J.S.: INbreast: toward a full-field digital mammographic database. Acad. Radiol. **19**(2), 236–248 (2012)

30. Nair, V., Hinton, G.E.: Rectified linear units improve restricted Boltzmann machines. In: International Conference on Machine Learning (ICML), pp. 807–814 (2010)

31. Nikan, S., et al.: PWD-3DNet: a deep learning-based fully-automated segmentation of multiple structures on temporal bone CT scans. IEEE Trans. Image Process. **30**, 739–753 (2020)

32. Oktay, O., et al.: Attention U-Net: Learning where to look for the pancreas. arXiv preprint arXiv:1804.03999 (2018)

33. Paszke, A., et al.: PyTorch: an imperative style, high-performance deep learning library. In: Annual Conference on Neural Information Processing System (NeurIPS), pp. 8026–8037 (2019)

34. Peng, Y., Yan, K., Sandfort, V., Summers, R.M., Lu, Z.: A self-attention based deep learning method for lesion attribute detection from CT reports. In: IEEE International Conference on Healthcare Informatics, pp. 1–5 (2019)

35. Pohlen, T., Hermans, A., Mathias, M., Leibe, B.: Full-resolution residual networks for semantic segmentation in street scenes. In: IEEE Conference on Computer Vision and Pattern Recognition (CVPR), pp. 4151–4160 (2017)

36. Ronneberger, Olaf, Fischer, Philipp, Brox, Thomas: U-Net: convolutional networks for biomedical image segmentation. In: Navab, Nassir, Hornegger, Joachim, Wells, William M.., Frangi, Alejandro F.. (eds.) MICCAI 2015. LNCS, vol. 9351, pp. 234–241. Springer, Cham (2015). https://doi.org/10.1007/978-3-319-24574-4_28

37. Russakovsky, O., Deng, J., Su, H., Krause, J., Satheesh, S., Ma, S., Huang, Z., Karpathy, A., Khosla, A., Bernstein, M., et al.: ImageNet large scale visual recognition challenge. Int. J. Comput. Vis. (IJCV) **115**(3), 211–252 (2015)

38. Shelhamer, E., Long, J., Darrell, T.: Fully convolutional networks for semantic segmentation. IEEE Trans. Pattern Anal. Mach. Intell. (TPAMI) **39**(4), 640–651 (2017)
39. Simonyan, K., Zisserman, A.: Very deep convolutional networks for large-scale image recognition. In: International Conference on Learning Representations (ICLR). pp. 1–14 (2015)
40. Soler, L., et al.: 3D image reconstruction for comparison of algorithm database: a patient-specific anatomical and medical image database. Tech. Rep, IRCAD, Strasbourg, France (2010)
41. Tang, Y., et al.: CT image enhancement using stacked generative adversarial networks and transfer learning for lesion segmentation improvement. In: International Workshop on Machine Learning in Medical Imaging, pp. 46–54 (2018)
42. Tian, Z., He, T., Shen, C., Yan, Y.: Decoders matter for semantic segmentation: data-dependent decoding enables flexible feature aggregation. In: IEEE Conference on Computer Vision and Pattern Recognition (CVPR), pp. 3126–3135 (2019)
43. Wang, Z., Wei, L., Wang, L., Gao, Y., Chen, W., Shen, D.: Hierarchical vertex regression-based segmentation of head and neck CT images for radiotherapy planning. IEEE Trans. Image Process. **27**(2), 923–937 (2018)
44. Yan, K., Lu, L., Summers, R.M.: Unsupervised body part regression via spatially self-ordering convolutional neural networks. In: IEEE International Symposium on Biomedical Imaging (ISBI), pp. 1022–1025 (2018)
45. Yam, X., et al.: MULAN: multitask universal lesion analysis network for joint lesion detection, tagging, and segmentation. In: Shen, D., et al. (eds.) MICCAI 2019. LNCS, vol. 11769, pp. 194–202. Springer, Cham (2019). https://doi.org/10.1007/978-3-030-32226-7_22
46. Yan, K., Wang, X., Lu, L., Summers, R.M.: DeepLesion: automated mining of large-scale lesion annotations and universal lesion detection with deep learning. J. Med. Imag. **5**(3), 036501 (2018)
47. Yan, K., et al.: Deep lesion graphs in the wild: Relationship learning and organization of significant radiology image findings in a diverse large-scale lesion database. In: IEEE Conference on Computer Vision and Pattern Recognition (CVPR), pp. 9261–9270 (2018)
48. Yang, M., Yu, K., Zhang, C., Li, Z., Yang, K.: DenseASPP for semantic segmentation in street scenes. In: IEEE Conference on Computer Vision and Pattern Recognition (CVPR), pp. 3684–3692 (2018)
49. Yin, Minghao, Yao, Zhuliang, Cao, Yue, Li, Xiu, Zhang, Zheng, Lin, Stephen, Hu, Han: Disentangled Non-local Neural Networks. In: Vedaldi, Andrea, Bischof, Horst, Brox, Thomas, Frahm, Jan-Michael. (eds.) ECCV 2020. LNCS, vol. 12360, pp. 191–207. Springer, Cham (2020). https://doi.org/10.1007/978-3-030-58555-6_12
50. Yu, C., Wang, J., Gao, C., Yu, G., Shen, C., Sang, N.: Context prior for scene segmentation. In: IEEE Conference on Computer Vision and Pattern Recognition (CVPR), pp. 12416–12425 (2020)
51. Yu, C., Wang, J., Peng, C., Gao, C., Yu, G., Sang, N.: BiSeNet: Bilateral segmentation network for real-time semantic segmentation. In: Eur. Conf. Comput. Vis. (ECCV). pp. 325–341 (2018)
52. Yu, C., Wang, J., Peng, C., Gao, C., Yu, G., Sang, N.: Learning a discriminative feature network for semantic segmentation. In: IEEE Conference on Computer Vision and Pattern Recognition (CVPR), pp. 1857–1866 (2018)
53. Yu, Q., Shi, Y., Sun, J., Gao, Y., Zhu, J., Dai, Y.: Crossbar-Net: A novel convolutional neural network for kidney tumor segmentation in CT images. IEEE Trans. Image Process. **28**(8), 4060–4074 (2019)

54. Yuan, Yuhui, Chen, Xilin, Wang, Jingdong: Object-contextual representations for semantic segmentation. In: Vedaldi, Andrea, Bischof, Horst, Brox, Thomas, Frahm, Jan-Michael. (eds.) ECCV 2020. LNCS, vol. 12351, pp. 173–190. Springer, Cham (2020). https://doi.org/10.1007/978-3-030-58539-6_11

55. Yuan, Y., Wang, J.: OCNet: object context network for scene parsing. arXiv preprint arXiv:1809.00916 (2018)

56. Zhang, H., et al.: Context encoding for semantic segmentation. In: IEEE Conference on Computer Vision and Pattern Recognition (CVPR), pp. 7151–7160 (2018)

57. Zhao, H., Shi, J., Qi, X., Wang, X., Jia, J.: Pyramid scene parsing network. In: IEEE Conference on Computer Vision and Pattern Recognition (CVPR). pp. 2881–2890 (2017)

58. Zhou, B., et al.: Semantic understanding of scenes through the ADE20K dataset. Int. J. Comput. Vis. (IJCV) **127**(3), 302–321 (2019)

59. Zhou, S., Nie, D., Adeli, E., Yin, J., Lian, J., Shen, D.: High-resolution encoder-decoder networks for low-contrast medical image segmentation. IEEE Trans. Image Process. **29**, 461–475 (2020)

60. Zhou, Zongwei, Rahman Siddiquee, Md Mahfuzur, Tajbakhsh, Nima, Liang, Jianming: UNet++: a nested u-net architecture for medical image segmentation. In: Stoyanov, D., et al. (eds.) DLMIA/ML-CDS -2018. LNCS, vol. 11045, pp. 3–11. Springer, Cham (2018). https://doi.org/10.1007/978-3-030-00889-5_1

61. Zhu, Z., Xu, M., Bai, S., Huang, T., Bai, X.: Asymmetric non-local neural networks for semantic segmentation. In: International Conference on Computer Vision Workshops (ICCV), pp. 593–602 (2019)

Large Scale Real-World Multi-person Tracking

Bing Shuai[⊠][iD], Alessandro Bergamo, Uta Büchler[iD], Andrew Berneshawi[iD],
Alyssa Boden[iD], and Joseph Tighe[iD]

AWS AI Labs, Seattle, USA
bshuai@amazon.com
https://github.com/amazon-research/tracking-dataset

Abstract. This paper presents a new large scale multi-person tracking dataset. Our dataset is over an order of magnitude larger than currently available high quality multi-object tracking datasets such as MOT17, HiEve, and MOT20 datasets. The lack of large scale training and test data for this task has limited the community's ability to understand the performance of their tracking systems on a wide range of scenarios and conditions such as variations in person density, actions being performed, weather, and time of day. Our dataset was specifically sourced to provide a wide variety of these conditions and our annotations include rich meta-data such that the performance of a tracker can be evaluated along these different dimensions. The lack of training data has also limited the ability to perform end-to-end training of tracking systems. As such, the highest performing tracking systems all rely on strong detectors trained on external image datasets. We hope that the release of this dataset will enable new lines of research that take advantage of large scale video based training data.

Keywords: Multi-object tracking · Dataset · MOT

1 Introduction

Large-scale datasets are the fuel that has driven the success of learning-based methods over the past decade. The introduction of large datasets, such as ImageNet [21], MSCOCO [34], LSUN [63] and Kinetics [11], has enabled the development of deep learning-based models which have rapidly advanced the field of computer vision. Unfortunately, no such large scale dataset has been collected for multi-object tracking to date. The multi-object tracking task [8,41,50,57,65,66] requires detection and ID assignment of all objects for each frame in a video. In practice many current datasets have people as the only objects (multi-person), which will also be our focus. The most popular datasets used today, MOT17 [39] and MOT20 [20], have just 14 and 8 videos respectively, greatly limiting the ability of researchers to develop data hungry models that require large tracking

---

Supplementary Information The online version contains supplementary material available at https://doi.org/10.1007/978-3-031-20074-8_29.

datasets as well as limiting the measure of generalizability of tracking methods given the small number of videos used for testing. In this work we present a new multi-person tracking dataset that is an order of magnitude larger than MOT17 [39] and MOT20 [20], while maintaining the high quality bar of annotation present in those datasets.

One reason for the lack of large scale multi-object tracking datasets is the significant cost to collecting such a dataset. The collection and annotation of these datasets is non-trivial as both the curation (sourcing) and labeling require significantly higher manual human labor than classification or detection based datasets. For person tracking, sourcing video is particularly challenging because though there is a large volume of video content available on the internet, it is mostly content that does not align with our target video domain or the content rights are restricted such that the videos cannot be easily included in an academic dataset. The Kinetics [11] dataset, for example, attempted to remove this challenge by only providing links to YouTube videos but over time those videos were removed, leaving researchers with incomplete train and test sets and making it difficult to reliably compare to other works.

In this work we collect videos from sources where we are given the rights to redistribute the content and participants have given explicit consent, such as the MEVA [17] dataset. Our dataset consists of 236 videos captured mostly from static-mounted cameras. Approximately 80% of these videos are carefully sourced from scratch from stock footage websites and 20% are collected from existing datasets such as PathTrack [37] or MEVA [17]. While building the dataset we place special importance on sourcing indoor and outdoor videos with different lightning conditions, diverse camera angles (from birds-eye view to low-angle view), varying weather conditions (sunny, raining, cloudy, night), various levels of occlusion and different crowd densities. Section 3 presents a detailed analysis of these factors.

In addition to sourcing, collecting high quality annotations is especially challenging for multi-object tracking datasets. This is largely due to the complexity of the task. Classification datasets [11,21] only require one or more labels to be tagged per entire image or video whereas detection datasets [24,34] increase the complexity by not only requiring a list of objects, but also the object's location specified by a bounding box. Multi-object tracking extends the idea of object detection even further by also requiring a unique object identifier for every labeled bounding box throughout a video recording. This annotation task is especially challenging in crowded scenes where even a human annotator could easily lose or confuse an object with another if they get partly or fully occluded.

In this work we adopt a two stage annotation pipeline that leverages AWS Sage-Maker GroundTruth (an iteration of Amazon MTurk). When annotating videos for tracking, many edge cases emerge and must be handled consistently to have a meaningful measure of an algorithm's quality. In our annotation process, we have thoroughly considered edge cases such as people with high occlusion or person reflections and defined strict protocols for dealing with each edge case. For example, we annotate reflections of people but tag such annotations specifically so they can be properly handled during training and evaluation. After carefully defining our annotation criteria, we use our trained workforce to annotate all videos from scratch. More details regarding our annotation protocol can be found in Sect. 4.

We demonstrate the benefit our large-scale dataset adds to the community by (1) comparing key statistics with existing MOT benchmarks (Sect. 5) and (2) training and evaluating state-of-the-art multi-object tracking models on our dataset (Sect. 6). The latter shows that our benchmark contains many challenging scenarios where current state-of-the-art models fail to perform well. We hope that the publication of our dataset will drive the tracking community towards developing more robust models that can generalize to a wide variety of smart home/city scenarios.

2   Related Work

Multi-object Tracking Datasets. MOT is an essential part of important applications such as autonomous driving [23,43,45], smart city [12,13,18,38] and activity recognition [5,58]. Especially the field of autonomous driving has grown significantly, which is also reflected in the number of large-scale benchmarks published for this scenario [9,14,16,22,27,31,52,62]. Some of these datasets have also been used to train and/or evaluate person tracking models [42,50]. The challenges such benchmarks entail are fast camera motions and quick position changes of pedestrians. However, the amount of occlusions and crowdness is rather limited and thus not sufficient enough to train robust tracking models that can operate in high-occlusion scenarios. In contrast, synthetic datasets that have been specifically created for pedestrian detection/tracking in urban scenarios [25,26] contain scenes with varying person densities and can therefore be very valuable for person tracking. The clear advantage is that they do not require any manual annotations. Although the quality of synthetic data improves steadily, the usage of such data is rather limited due to the apparent domain shift to real-world data.

Recently, a few real-world MOT datasets have been proposed. For instance, CroHD [53] dataset was introduced to track pedestrian's head in crowded scenes, GMOT-40 [4] was proposed for the purpose of general object tracking, and MVMHAT [61] and MMPTRACK [29] are adopted for multi-camera multi-person tracking. In general, their sizes are a magnitude smaller than our dataset. One of the biggest real-world MOT datasets is TAO [19], which provides a great variety of scenes. Since TAO is created for general object tracking, the number of challenging person tracking sequences is rather limited given that a large number of videos contain only a single person. Moreover, TAO provides full annotations for only a small fraction of videos, which makes it difficult to train on. In contrast, our dataset has been exhaustively annotated.

Finally, the MOT datasets that are most comparable to ours are HiEve [35], MOT17 [39] and MOT20 [20]. HiEve consists of 32 videos (13.5% of the size of our dataset) and provides annotations for different human-centric understanding tasks such as pedestrian tracking or pose estimation [15,36,51]. The main goal of HiEve is to provide a set of videos that are recorded during complex events

 Bird's eye view
Outdoor
Good light

 High-angle view
Indoor
Good light

 Mid-angle view
Outdoor
Poor light

 Low-angle view
Indoor
Good light

Fig. 1. The figure is best viewed in color. Frames in the video are exhaustively annotated with person boxes, each of which have a unique identifier (i.e. color-coded box). The videos in the dataset cover diverse tracking scenarios in terms of camera angles, weather/lighting condition and scenery types.

(e.g. earthquake escapes). Our dataset, on the other hand, has the objective of providing a wide variety of smart home/city scenarios during different seasons, varying lightning and weather conditions and diverse crowd densities without focusing solely on the complexity of events. The most popular MOT benchmark which has also a similar purpose as ours is MOT17 [39]. The benchmark consists of 14 videos that are recorded at 9 different scenes with different lightning and camera angles. MOT20 [39] extends the MOT17 benchmark by 8 additional videos, which was specifically created for tracking in crowds. Our dataset also contains very crowded scenes, but provides on top of that a wide variety of pedestrian densities indoor and outdoor.

Multi-object Tracking Methods. Many of the well-known MOT models follow the detection-by-tracking paradigm [8,32,47,50,55,57,59,60], in which object instances are firstly detected for every frame and then they are linked across frames to form object tracks. Recently, online trackers [42,50,56,65,67] have steadily gained ground by pushing the results on MOTChallenge [39] to new highs. Those trackers are usually deep neural networks that include key models for online tracking, which include a detection model [10,44,54,67], a motion model [7,8,33,50,57] and an optional person re-identification model [56,65]. Those models are usually jointly trained with tracking annotations, i.e. a bounding box with a unique identifier. Due to the scarcity of those annotations, self-supervised training techniques [49,50,65,66] were developed to leverage image-based object detection datasets for model pre-training. In this work, we train and evaluate three recent state-of-the-art online trackers on our dataset.

3   Video Sourcing

The creation of a dataset for training/evaluating person tracking algorithms needs to strike a balance between the need of (1) having videos that represent a large variety of real-world tracking applications; (2) having videos containing challenging scenarios for tracking algorithms (e.g. occlusions, small objects); and (3) ensuring that the data is collected in a responsible way such that it can be used in perpetuity. Following these guidelines, we source our dataset in two steps.

Data Source Selection. We select a pool of data sources based on the availability of video content suitable for tracking applications, as well as the presence of an appropriate license that allows the data to be used and remain available for academic research. We source videos from stock video services (Fillerstock [1], Pexels [2], Pixabay [3]) and from public academic datasets for human activity understanding (MEVA [17], Virat [40], PathTrack [37]) where proper licensing is available. The breakdown of the number of videos for each data source is provided in the supplementary material. Note that although MEVA and Virat come with incomplete person bounding boxes annotations, we re-annotate all videos included in our dataset to ensure consistency in annotations across all data sources. We first create an initial large candidate set of videos by automatically querying content from Fillerstock, Pexels, and Pixabay using a pre-defined set of search keywords such as "person walking in the shopping mall" (please refer to the supplementary material for the full list). The union of these videos and the videos from the public datasets form our candidate video set.

Manual Selection. Our initial candidate dataset includes 8000+ videos which are then manually inspected by a team of experts. The selection processes took into account the following criteria: (1) application aligned (fixed connected home or city level cameras), (2) moving crowds, (3) occlusion, (4) background variability, (5) static vs moving cameras, (6) camera position and (7) environment conditions (day/night, sunny/rain/snow/cloudy etc.). More details to the mentioned criteria are elaborated in the supplementary material. In total, we select 236 videos for manual annotation and inclusion in our dataset. The cumulative temporal duration of these videos is 139 min.

4   Annotation Pipeline

Annotating person boxes with identities is time-consuming and error-prone. To this end, we adopt AWS SageMaker GroundTruth (SMGT) service[1] (an advanced version of Amazon Mechanical Turk). This workflow works as follows. First, the annotator draws bounding boxes for all visible people in the starting frame. In the next frame, the SMGT service leverages a pre-trained model to predict the bounding box for each annotated person. The annotator first verify the quality of predicted bounding boxes and adjust the bounding boxes as needed. Then, the annotator draws bounding boxes for those persons that do not appear in earlier frames.

We employ professional annotators that have been specially trained for this task. We ask them to annotate every possible visible person in the video unless they are too small in size ($<20 \times 20$ pixels) to be accurately localized or they are

---

[1] https://docs.aws.amazon.com/sagemaker/latest/dg/sms-video-object-tracking.html.

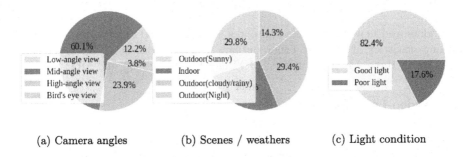

(a) Camera angles   (b) Scenes / weathers   (c) Light condition

Fig. 2. Video-level statistics of training videos in our dataset.

in a crowd. In the latter case, we ask the annotators to draw a bounding box with `crowd label` that includes all people in the crowd (e.g. Fig. 1(bottom left)). If a person enters the area labeled as crowd, with >95% of the person's bounding box covered by a crowd box, we label this occurrence as 'ignore' to ensure that the predicted tracks are not penalized on these cases. As shown in Fig. 1, we annotate with `amodal` bounding boxes, indicating that the full extent of the bounding box is annotated regardless of the visibility status of the underlying person. In addition, we also annotate the corresponding `visible` bounding boxes that only enclose the visible part of the person body. This inclusion of both annotation types give researchers the most flexibility when choosing how to train their models and evaluating these models on other datasets.

To ensure that the annotation is of high quality, we perform a second round of labeling where a separate group of annotators checks if (1) all people are annotated, (2) all bounding boxes are correctly localized and (3) the identity of a person track is consistent throughout the video. In case the annotators notice a mistake, they correct the error. Finally, the authors of this paper do a final verification pass on the data, sending back any videos that have errors for re-annotation. This rigorous process allows us to have high confidence of the quality of the provided annotations. We first annotate at 5 frames per second. Then, we linearly interpolate those annotations and let our trained annotators verify the correctness of those interpolations for every frame and person.

Given that not all annotated person boxes are equally interesting, and some might even be perceived as noise, we further annotate each person track with the following tags: 1) sitting/standing still person; 2) person in vehicle; 3) person on open-vehicle; 4) reflection; 5) severely occluded person; 6) person in background; 7) foreground person. These fine-grained track-level tags enable to train or evaluate models along different sets of person tracks based on the needs of various tracking applications. The definition and visual examples of those tags are provided in the supplementary materials.

5 Dataset

To understand how our dataset compares to current MOT datasets we analyze various statistics of our and other publicly available datasets. We specifically compare to three popular datasets: MOT17 [39], HiEve [35], and MOT20 [20].

5.1 Video-Level Statistics

Camera Angles. We categorize the angles of the cameras that are used to record the underlying videos into four buckets: (1) bird's-eye view, (2) high-angle view, (3) mid-angle view and (4) low-angle view. Visual examples are given in Fig. 1. As shown in Fig. 2a, our dataset contains 143 (60.1%) and 33 (23.9%) videos that are recorded by mid and low-angle-view cameras, respectively. On this front, the closest dataset to ours is MOT17 [39] that has 10 (71.4%) mid-angle-view and 4 (28.6%) high-angle-view videos. Out of 32 videos in HiEve dataset [35], only 2 (6.3%) videos are recorded with mid-angle-view cameras and the remaining 30 (93.7%) videos are with high-angle-view. For MOT20 dataset [20], all 8 videos are captured with high-angle-view cameras.

Scenes and Weather. We categorize the scene of a video into two buckets: (1) indoor (e.g. cafe house, mall, airport) and (2) outdoor (e.g. street, plaza, beach). For outdoor videos, we further annotate the weather condition. As shown in Fig. 2b, there are 63 (26.5%) indoor videos and the outdoor videos are evenly spread across three weather/light conditions (sunny, cloudy, night/dark). Furthermore as we show in Fig. 2c, there are 42 (17.6%) videos that have poor light condition, under which tracking people becomes increasingly challenging. Overall, our dataset provides a good diversity in terms of scene types and light conditions. In comparison, MOT17 [39] includes 2 indoor and 2 night videos.

People Density. We define the people density (d) of the scene to be the average number of people per frame, based on which we categorize each video into four buckets: low density ($d \leq 10$), medium density ($10 < d \leq 30$), high density ($30 < d \leq 60$) and extremely high density ($d > 60$). As shown in Fig. 3, our dataset has a similar distribution with MOT17 [39] and HiEve [35] dataset, although it has a significantly larger scale. Note that although there is a positive correlation between the tracking difficulty and the people density of the video when the camera angle and scene/light condition is similar, people density is not the only indicator of difficulty level of underlying videos. For example, tracking a person in a low-angle-view video with low density can be more challenging than that in a high-density bird's-eye video due to the high level of occlusion in the low-angle-view video.

In terms of the above factors, our dataset provides a set of videos that resembles a similar distribution with the current dataset MOT17 [39] but at an order of magnitude larger scale. Importantly our dataset is highly diverse which makes the training and evaluation of tracking models more representative to real-world person tracking challenges.

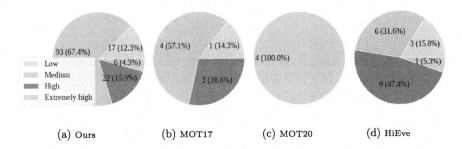

| | (a) Ours | (b) MOT17 | (c) MOT20 | (d) HiEve |

Fig. 3. Video-level people density distribution of training videos.

5.2 Track-Level Statistics

We further analyze the statistics of each track annotated in our dataset. We represent a person track as a temporally ordered set of bounding boxes $\mathcal{T} = [\text{bb}_{t_s}, \ldots, \text{bb}_t, \ldots, \text{bb}_{t_e}]$, in which t_s and t_e are the start and terminal timestamp of person track $\mathcal{T}$ respectively, $\text{bb}_t = (x_t, y_t, w_t, h_t)$ where (x_t, y_t) is the center point coordinates of person bounding box at time t and w_t, h_t its width and height. In total, 12,150 unique person tracks are annotated, out of which 7,096 tracks are from training videos, and the remaining 5,054 from test videos. Furthermore, 7,534 tracks are labeled with "foreground person" tag, based on which we derive the statistics of person tracks as follows.

Average Track Speed. We define the temporally normalized motion vector $\mathbf{m}_{(t_1 \rightarrow t_2)}$ for person track $\mathcal{T}$ between timestamp t_1 and t_2 ($t_2 > t_1$) as follows:

$$\mathbf{m}_{t_1 \rightarrow t_2} = \frac{1}{\zeta \cdot (t_2 - t_1)} (x_{t_2} - x_{t_1}, y_{t_2} - y_{t_1}) \tag{1}$$

in which ζ is the average length of the person bounding box at timestamp t_1 and t_2, that is $\zeta = 0.5 * (\sqrt{(w_{t_1} \cdot h_{t_1})} + \sqrt{(w_{t_2} \cdot h_{t_2})})$. Therefore, $\mathbf{m}_{(t_1 \rightarrow t_2)}$ indicates the direction of the person's motion between timestamp t_1 and t_2, and its $\mathbf{L}_2$ norm $||\mathbf{m}_{(t_1 \rightarrow t_2)}||_2$ reflects the speed of the corresponding person within a unit of time. Then, we derive the average speed $\mathbf{v}$ for a track with the following equation:

$$\mathbf{v}_{(\mathcal{T})} = \frac{1}{|\mathbf{T}| - 1} \sum_{i=2}^{|\mathbf{T}|} ||\mathbf{m}_{(\mathbf{T}[i-1] \rightarrow \mathbf{T}[i])}||_2 \tag{2}$$

where $\mathbf{T} = \{t_s, \ldots, t, \ldots, t_e\}$ is a sorted list of timestamps that the person appears. We bucketize each person track to have a static/slow, medium and fast speed if $\mathbf{v}_{(\mathcal{T})} < 0.2$, $0.2 \leq \mathbf{v}_{(\mathcal{T})} < 0.6$ and $\mathbf{v}_{(\mathcal{T})} \geq 0.6$. In Fig. 4a, we show the distribution of track speed of our dataset in comparison with MOT17 [39]. A few videos in MOT17 are recorded with moving camera, which leads to larger portion of higher-speed person tracks (e.g. a person standing still appears to be non-static in a video with moving background).

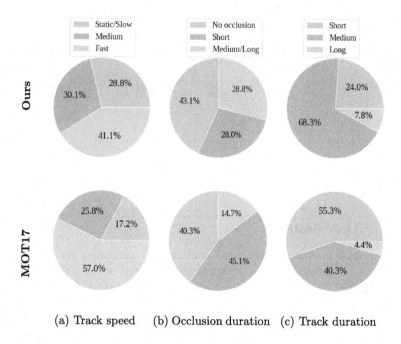

(a) Track speed   (b) Occlusion duration   (c) Track duration

Fig. 4. Key statistics of person tracks in training videos from our dataset and MOT17.

Occlusion Duration. A person becomes fully occluded if its appearance feature is not discernible at that particular time. In our case, this happens if the annotator is unable to locate their position without inferring from temporal context. Therefore, we define the occlusion duration of a person track to be the cumulative duration $(\mathbf{o}_{(\mathcal{T})})$ of the person being fully occluded. We further categorize each person track to have no, short and medium/long occlusion if $\mathbf{o}_{(\mathcal{T})} = 0$, $0 < \mathbf{o}_{(\mathcal{T})} < 2(s)$ and $\mathbf{o}_{(\mathcal{T})} \geq 2(s)$. As shown in Fig. 4b, our dataset includes a significantly higher portion of person tracks with medium/long occlusion in comparison to MOT17. In addition, there is a significant percentage (3.5%) of person tracks whose occlusion duration is longer than 10 s. A particular challenge in person/object tracking is to preserve the identity consistency before and after the object becomes fully occluded. In this respect, our dataset provides challenging and interesting cases.

Track Duration. The duration of a track $(\mathbf{l}_{(\mathcal{T})})$ is defined as the time range between the first and last appearance of the person in the video, that is $\mathbf{l}_{(\mathcal{T})} = t_e - t_s$. We classify each person track to be short, medium and long if $\mathbf{l}_{(\mathcal{T})} < 5(s)$, $5 \leq \mathbf{l}_{(\mathcal{T})} < 30(s)$ and $\mathbf{l}_{(\mathcal{T})} \geq 30(s)$ respectively. As shown in Fig. 4c, person tracks in our dataset tend to be longer in contrast to MOT17 [39]. Considering that tracking a person in a longer duration is both interesting and technically challenging, our dataset offers valuable testing cases along this aspect.

Table 1. Comparison of dataset statistics (of training set) between our and existing datasets. Annotated Frames refer to the frames that are manually annotated and those that are automatically interpolated and then manually verified.

Dataset	#Videos	Length (secs)	#Annotated frames	#Person tracks	Min Res.	Min. FPS
HiEve [35]	19	1,842	32,929	1,736	352 × 258	15
MOT17 [39]	7	215	5,316	546	640 × 480	14
MOT20 [20]	4	357	8,931	2,215	1173 × 880	25
Ours	138	4,736	118,685	7,096	720 × 480	15

In Table 1, we further compare our dataset with existing person tracking datasets. In comparison to MOT17 [39], the most popular dataset for multi-person tracking research, our dataset includes an order of magnitude larger number of unique person tracks and videos. Although MOT20 [20] includes more annotated person tracks, their scope is specifically for tracking people in crowds. Both the diversity of videos and the person tracks in our dataset are unparalleled w.r.t other dataset including HiEve [35], which makes it a more challenging and realistic evaluation benchmark for multi-person tracking.

5.3 Benchmarking

We randomly split the videos with 60% train and 40% test. To make sure that both subsets follow a similar distribution, we perform the split for each video source separately. Overall, there are 138 train and 98 test videos, and we treat it as the official split of this dataset. The statistics for both splits are listed in the supplementary materials.

We only evaluate on keyframes for bounding boxes with the "foreground person" and "standing/sitting still person" tag that aren't fully occluded. The key frames are identical with those used for manual annotation, so we are evaluating the results at 5FPS. With this evaluation protocol, we are discounting the influence from the detection failures but implicitly amplifying the effect from identity inconsistency. By doing this the missed detection on a fully occluded person are not penalized. We argue that it's more important to keep the identity prediction consistent before and after the person is fully occluded rather than inferring bounding boxes for a person that is not visible.

6   Experiments

We evaluate our dataset using three recent state-of-the-art online trackers, each including a person detection and person identity association model, which are jointly trained with tracking annotations. We briefly introduce the methods.

CenterTrack [66] is a single-stage online tracking model that performs joint detection and tracking and is built upon the CenterNet [67] framework. The model takes as input (1) the previous RGB frame, (2) the current RGB frame, and (3) a heatmap with the tracked object centers. The model predicts the object boxes for the current frame, conditioned on the tracking center points that are provided as input. In addition, the model outputs the estimated offset motion vectors, based on which an online solver is used to link the boxes across frames.

SiamMOT [50] is a two-stage tracking model which uses Faster R-CNN [44] for its person detection model. A Siamese-based tracker [28,30] is incorporated in the network as a motion model to associate the detection bounding boxes across frames. In this work, we use the best-performing motion model, EMM, as suggested in the original paper.

FairMOT [65] is a single-stage tracking model that uses CenterNet [67] as person detection model. In addition to CenterNet, this method adopts a parallel branch to extract a feature vector (embedding) for each person instance. Finally, the affinity between the person's location and its embedding, together with a motion model (Kalman filter) are used to link detected people across frames.

We choose the above three models as they cover both single-stage and two-stage detection models. Besides, they cover two mainstream linking techniques: CenterTrack [66] and SiamMOT [50] use learned motion models for bounding box linking, whereas FairMOT [65] leverages the similarity of person embeddings.

Implementation Details. All models use DLA-34 [64] as feature backbone, and they are pre-trained on the CrowdHuman dataset [48]. We use the official open-source implementations for all the algorithms provided by the original authors. We train and evaluate the model with `amodal` bounding boxes. Please refer to the supplementary materials for more details.

Evaluation Metrics. Following other literature, we report standard tracking metrics including MOTA and IDF1. In general, MOTA measures the overall performance of the end-to-end tracking system by accounting for both the detection and data association performance. IDF1, on the other hand, specifically indicates the performance of predicted identity consistency. For more details on these metrics we refer the reader to [6,46].

6.1   Model Evaluation

In Table 2, we show the results of three recent online trackers. In the default evaluation protocol [20,35,39], all valid person boxes on key frames are evaluated. Under such setting, all models achieve relatively low MOTA and IDF1 in comparison to the performance on MOT17 [39] and HiEve [35], which underscores the challenges of our dataset. As expected, the detection failure (False Positive (FP) and False Negative (FN)) heavily influences the MOTA metric. We observe that a significant number of detection failures results from missed detections when a person becomes fully occluded. As we elaborated in Sect. 5.3, we should not heavily penalize those missed detections as long as the predicted identity is consistent before and after the occlusion happens. To this end, we apply an occlusion filter process to exclude those boxes tagged as being fully occluded from evaluation. As shown in Table 2, FN is significantly decreased, which lifts MOTA by a large margin. Additionally, after applying the filter, a

Table 2. Result comparison on the test split of our dataset. Occlusion filter means that only bounding boxes without being tagged as occluded are used during evaluation.

Methods	Occlusion filter	IDF1 ($\uparrow$)	MOTA ($\uparrow$)	FP ($\downarrow$)	FN ($\downarrow$)	IDsw ($\downarrow$)
CenterTrack [66]	✗	43.04	52.31	24611	107037	10487
SiamMOT [50]	✗	49.84	59.56	13268	98069	9201
FairMOT [65]	✗	56.52	54.29	14568	116495	5179
CenterTrack [66]	✓	46.36	59.28	24340	71550	10319
SiamMOT [50]	✓	53.71	67.52	13217	62543	8942
FairMOT [65]	✓	61.05	61.79	14540	80034	5095

person track with occlusion is "reduced" in length, which in-turn benefits IDF1. Nonetheless, the improvement of IDF1 is less significant than that of MOTA.

As shown in Table 2, SiamMOT achieves significantly higher MOTA compared to CenterTrack and FairMOT. We conjecture that its underlying detector – Faster-RCNN [44] – works better than CenterNet [67] which underlies the other two tracking models. To validate it, we run inference of the two underlying detectors—FRCNN [44] and CenterNet [67] on the test set. FRCNN achieves 82.03% AP@0.5 and CenterNet achieves 78.51% AP@0.5.[2] Not surprisingly, Fair-MOT achieves a significantly better IDF1 than the other two motion-based tracking models, despite the fact that the detected boxes have more errors than that of SiamMOT. This result suggests that person re-identification is essential for tracking models to preserve the identity consistency of predicted tracks in the case of occlusion.

6.2   In-Depth Model Analysis

Small-Size Person Tracking. Being able to correctly track small scale objects is important for real-world application scenarios. We categorize a person track as *small* if the average areas of the associated bounding boxes is smaller than 0.5% relative to the video frame area. For example, any bounding box whose area is smaller than 50×90 for a standard 720p video is considered small in size. In our test set, 1,624 tracks are categorized as "small". As shown in Table 3a, there is a significant performance gap between tracking large-size and small-size persons on both MOTA and IDF1. This is expected as both detecting and re-identifying low-resolution objects remains a major challenge.

Static vs. Moving. In real-world scenarios, video sequences contain a mix of static and moving objects. For example, people might be sitting on chairs or benches (e.g. at a park or in a waiting room), as well as standing and not moving (e.g. waiting for the pedestrian green light). We find that the presence

---

[2] We encourage the researchers report detection AP@0.5 of their tracking models on our dataset.

Table 3. Result comparison of models on different subsets of person tracks.

Method	IDF1(↑)		MOTA(↑)	
	Small	Large	Small	Large
CenterTrack	34.3	52.7	34.5	70.1
SiamMOT	47.1	56.6	49.9	75.2
FairMOT	50.2	66.6	40.8	72.0

(a) Results for tracks associated to small-size vs large-size persons.

Method	IDF1(↑)		MOTA(↑)	
	Static	Moving	Static	Moving
CenterTrack	45.3	43.2	57.1	43.7
SiamMOT	52.6	52.6	67.2	57.9
FairMOT	59.3	60.2	60.0	53.7

(b) Results for static-to-slow vs medium-to-fast moving tracks.

Method	IDF1(↑)		MOTA(↑)	
	Long	Short	Long	Short
CenterTrack	32.5	51.2	37.6	59.6
SiamMOT	39.8	59.6	51.4	70.3
FairMOT	44.3	68.3	45.2	64.4

(c) Results for tracks with medium-to-long vs short-to-no occlusions.

Method	IDF1(↑)			MOTA(↑)		
	s	m	l	s	m	l
CenterTrack	42.9	47.4	41.4	-3.9	51.9	62.2
SiamMOT	51.3	54.4	50.7	16.4	62.1	73.0
FairMOT	52.3	61.7	58.9	13.2	58.2	64.6

(d) Results for tracks with short (s), medium (m) and long (l) duration.

of such objects can inflate the evaluation metrics given the fact that tracking static objects is perceptually easier than tracking moving ones. This is because static objects do not require sophisticated motion models and do not exhibit any change in appearance over time unless they are occluded. In Table 3b, we show the performance for static vs. moving objects. Overall, MOTA is significantly higher for static tracks than for moving tracks, which indicates that static/slow-moving people are easier to be detected in our dataset. However, IDF1 performance is similar for both set of tracks, which suggests that the person's motion velocity is not strongly correlated with of its level of tracking difficulty level in our dataset.

Tracks with Full Occlusion. Being able to track such scenarios is of great importance in real-world tracking applications, especially when the camera is close to the ground where person-to-person occlusion is common. Tracking through full occlusion and keeping its identity unchanged is challenging in particular in video sequences where a large number of people are present. To this end, we report results on tracks with short-to-no occlusion and with medium-to-long occlusion, which are defined in Sect. 5.2. As shown in Table 3c, both the MOTA and IDF1 are substantially lower for tracks with medium-to-long occlusion. In this case, people are more likely to be partially occluded, which leads to more detection failures that contributes to lower MOTA. The huge gap in terms of IDF1 for all models suggests that preserving the same identity before and after the person is occluded is challenging and we hope that future research can improve performance for online trackers to track through long occlusion.

Track Duration. In Table 3d, we show the break-down results for tracks with short, medium and long duration, as defined in Sect. 5.2. There are a few interesting observations: 1) the IDF1 for long-duration tracks is the lowest, despite the fact that its corresponding MOTA is the highest. We find that this happens because long-duration tracks usually appear in high-angle view cameras (e.g. MEVA [17], Virat [40]) in our dataset, therefore detecting person in those videos is easier, which positively correlates with a higher MOTA; 2) the MOTA for short-duration track is abysmal, although it has a decent IDF1. We notice that the presence of short tracks are correlated with various challenging occlusion scenarios, for example, short tracks are associated to people in large crowds or people walking behind various objects (trees, vehicles), where the people are first visible, then become partially-occluded and disappear quickly. The challenges presented in short, medium, and long tracks are diverse and depending on the application each could be important. Thus we hope that researchers will adopt the practice of reporting metrics on these three categories separately in the future to give further insight into their model performance.

In summary, our dataset provides interesting and challenging cases for real-world tracking that includes various duration tracks, tracks with medium-to-long occlusion and small-size person tracks, on which existing state-of-the-art online trackers struggle.

7   Conclusion and Discussion

In this paper, we introduced a large scale real-world multi-person tracking dataset. The dataset is meticulously curated by (1) sourcing a set of videos that are diverse in terms of people density, camera angles, weather and scenery types as well as lighting conditions and (2) exhaustively annotating all persons in every frame with rigorous annotation and verification protocol that accommodates robust edge case handling. We demonstrated the value of the dataset by comparing it against existing datasets including MOT17 [39], HiEve [35], and MOT20 [20]. Our dataset is a magnitude larger than the most popular MOT17 dataset in terms of unique person tracks, number of videos, and total video duration. We further performed in-depth analyses of existing state-of-the-art online trackers on our dataset and observed interesting cases where current online trackers fail to perform well. We hope that the publication of this dataset will spark a new wave of research towards developing more usable tracking models in real-world multi-person tracking.

Socially Responsible Usage of the Dataset. This dataset should primarily be used to improve person tracking algorithms, which can have a significant positive effect on many real-world video understanding problems including for example self-driving cars and human activity understanding. We ask the users of this dataset to use the data in a socially responsible manner, and request to not use the data to identify or generate biometric information of the people in the videos.

References

1. Fillerstock. http://fillerstock.com/
2. Pexels. http://www.pexels.com/
3. Pixabay. http://pixabay.com/

4. Bai, H., Cheng, W., Chu, P., Liu, J., Zhang, K., Ling, H.: GMOT-40: a benchmark for generic multiple object tracking. In: Proceedings of the IEEE/CVF Conference on Computer Vision and Pattern Recognition, pp. 6719–6728 (2021)
5. Beddiar, D.R., Nini, B., Sabokrou, M., Hadid, A.: Vision-based human activity recognition: a survey. Multimed. Tools Appl. **79**(41), 30509–30555 (2020). https://doi.org/10.1007/s11042-020-09004-3
6. Bernardin, K., Stiefelhagen, R.: Evaluating multiple object tracking performance: the CLEAR MOT metrics. EURASIP J. Image Video Process. **2008** (2008). https://doi.org/10.1155/2008/246309
7. Bertinetto, L., Valmadre, J., Henriques, J.F., Vedaldi, A., Torr, P.H.S.: Fully-convolutional siamese networks for object tracking. In: Hua, G., Jégou, H. (eds.) ECCV 2016. LNCS, vol. 9914, pp. 850–865. Springer, Cham (2016). https://doi.org/10.1007/978-3-319-48881-3_56
8. Bewley, A., Ge, Z., Ott, L., Ramos, F., Upcroft, B.: Simple online and realtime tracking. In: 2016 IEEE International Conference on Image Processing (ICIP), pp. 3464–3468. IEEE (2016)
9. Caesar, H., et al.: nuScenes: a multimodal dataset for autonomous driving. In: Proceedings of the IEEE/CVF Conference on Computer Vision and Pattern Recognition, pp. 11621–11631 (2020)
10. Carion, N., Massa, F., Synnaeve, G., Usunier, N., Kirillov, A., Zagoruyko, S.: End-to-end object detection with transformers. In: Vedaldi, A., Bischof, H., Brox, T., Frahm, J.-M. (eds.) ECCV 2020. LNCS, vol. 12346, pp. 213–229. Springer, Cham (2020). https://doi.org/10.1007/978-3-030-58452-8_13
11. Carreira, J., Noland, E., Hillier, C., Zisserman, A.: A short note on the Kinetics-700 human action dataset. arXiv preprint arXiv:1907.06987 (2019)
12. Chandrajit, M., Girisha, R., Vasudev, T.: Multiple objects tracking in surveillance video using color and hu moments. Sig. Image Process. Int. J. (SIPIJ) **7**(3), 16–27 (2016)
13. Chandrakar, R., Raja, R., Miri, R., Sinha, U., Kushwaha, A.K.S., Raja, H.: Enhanced the moving object detection and object tracking for traffic surveillance using RBF-FDLNN and CBF algorithm. Expert Syst. Appl. **191**, 116306 (2022)
14. Chang, M.F., et al.: Argoverse: 3D tracking and forecasting with rich maps. In: Proceedings of the IEEE/CVF Conference on Computer Vision and Pattern Recognition, pp. 8748–8757 (2019)
15. Chang, S., et al.: Towards accurate human pose estimation in videos of crowded scenes. In: Proceedings of the 28th ACM International Conference on Multimedia, pp. 4630–4634 (2020)
16. Cordts, M., et al.: The cityscapes dataset for semantic urban scene understanding. In: Proceedings of the IEEE Conference on Computer Vision and Pattern Recognition, pp. 3213–3223 (2016)
17. Corona, K., Osterdahl, K., Collins, R., Hoogs, A.: MEVA: a large-scale multiview, multimodal video dataset for activity detection. In: Proceedings of the IEEE/CVF Winter Conference on Applications of Computer Vision (WACV), pp. 1060–1068, January 2021
18. Datta, A., Shah, M., Lobo, N.D.V.: Person-on-person violence detection in video data. In: Object Recognition Supported by User Interaction for Service Robots, vol. 1, pp. 433–438. IEEE (2002)
19. Dave, A., Khurana, T., Tokmakov, P., Schmid, C., Ramanan, D.: TAO: a large-scale benchmark for tracking any object. In: Vedaldi, A., Bischof, H., Brox, T., Frahm, J.-M. (eds.) ECCV 2020. LNCS, vol. 12350, pp. 436–454. Springer, Cham (2020). https://doi.org/10.1007/978-3-030-58558-7_26

20. Dendorfer, P., et al.: MOT20: a benchmark for multi object tracking in crowded scenes. arXiv preprint arXiv:2003.09003 (2020)
21. Deng, J., Dong, W., Socher, R., Li, L.J., Li, K., Fei-Fei, L.: ImageNet: a large-scale hierarchical image database. In: CVPR 2009 (2009)
22. Dollár, P., Wojek, C., Schiele, B., Perona, P.: Pedestrian detection: a benchmark. In: 2009 IEEE Conference on Computer Vision and Pattern Recognition, pp. 304–311. IEEE (2009)
23. Ess, A., Schindler, K., Leibe, B., Van Gool, L.: Object detection and tracking for autonomous navigation in dynamic environments. Int. J. Robot. Res. **29**(14), 1707–1725 (2010)
24. Everingham, M., Van Gool, L., Williams, C.K.I., Winn, J., Zisserman, A.: The Pascal visual object classes (VOC) challenge. Int. J. Comput. Vis. **88**(2), 303–338 (2010). https://doi.org/10.1007/s11263-009-0275-4
25. Fabbri, M., et al.: MOTSynth: how can synthetic data help pedestrian detection and tracking? In: International Conference on Computer Vision (ICCV) (2021)
26. Fabbri, M., Lanzi, F., Calderara, S., Palazzi, A., Vezzani, R., Cucchiara, R.: Learning to detect and track visible and occluded body joints in a virtual world. In: Ferrari, V., Hebert, M., Sminchisescu, C., Weiss, Y. (eds.) ECCV 2018. LNCS, vol. 11208, pp. 450–466. Springer, Cham (2018). https://doi.org/10.1007/978-3-030-01225-0_27
27. Geiger, A., Lenz, P., Urtasun, R.: Are we ready for autonomous driving? The KITTI vision benchmark suite. In: Conference on Computer Vision and Pattern Recognition (CVPR) (2012)
28. Guo, D., Wang, J., Cui, Y., Wang, Z., Chen, S.: SiamCAR: siamese fully convolutional classification and regression for visual tracking. In: Proceedings of the IEEE/CVF Conference on Computer Vision and Pattern Recognition, pp. 6269–6277 (2020)
29. Han, X., et al.: MMPTRACK: large-scale densely annotated multi-camera multiple people tracking benchmark (2021)
30. Held, D., Thrun, S., Savarese, S.: Learning to track at 100 FPS with deep regression networks. In: Leibe, B., Matas, J., Sebe, N., Welling, M. (eds.) ECCV 2016. LNCS, vol. 9905, pp. 749–765. Springer, Cham (2016). https://doi.org/10.1007/978-3-319-46448-0_45
31. Houston, J., et al.: One thousand and one hours: self-driving motion prediction dataset. arXiv preprint arXiv:2006.14480 (2020)
32. Leal-Taixé, L., Canton-Ferrer, C., Schindler, K.: Learning by tracking: siamese CNN for robust target association. In: Proceedings of the IEEE Conference on Computer Vision and Pattern Recognition Workshops, pp. 33–40 (2016)
33. Li, B., Wu, W., Wang, Q., Zhang, F., Xing, J., Yan, J.: SiamRPN++: evolution of siamese visual tracking with very deep networks. In: Proceedings of the IEEE/CVF Conference on Computer Vision and Pattern Recognition, pp. 4282–4291 (2019)
34. Lin, T.-Y., et al.: Microsoft COCO: common objects in context. In: Fleet, D., Pajdla, T., Schiele, B., Tuytelaars, T. (eds.) ECCV 2014. LNCS, vol. 8693, pp. 740–755. Springer, Cham (2014). https://doi.org/10.1007/978-3-319-10602-1_48
35. Lin, W., et al.: Human in events: a large-scale benchmark for human-centric video analysis in complex events. arXiv preprint arXiv:2005.04490 (2020)
36. Liu, W., Bao, Q., Sun, Y., Mei, T.: Recent advances in monocular 2D and 3D human pose estimation: a deep learning perspective. arXiv preprint arXiv:2104.11536 (2021)

37. Manen, S., Gygli, M., Dai, D., Gool, L.V.: PathTrack: fast trajectory annotation with path supervision. In: 2017 IEEE International Conference on Computer Vision (ICCV), pp. 290–299 (2017)
38. Mathur, G., Somwanshi, D., Bundele, M.M.: Intelligent video surveillance based on object tracking. In: 2018 3rd International Conference and Workshops on Recent Advances and Innovations in Engineering (ICRAIE), pp. 1–6. IEEE (2018)
39. Milan, A., Leal-Taixé, L., Reid, I., Roth, S., Schindler, K.: MOT16: a benchmark for multi-object tracking. arXiv preprint arXiv:1603.00831 (2016)
40. Oh, S., et al.: A large-scale benchmark dataset for event recognition in surveillance video. In: CVPR 2011, pp. 3153–3160. IEEE (2011)
41. Pang, B., Li, Y., Zhang, Y., Li, M., Lu, C.: TubeTK: adopting tubes to track multi-object in a one-step training model. In: Proceedings of the IEEE/CVF Conference on Computer Vision and Pattern Recognition, pp. 6308–6318 (2020)
42. Pang, J., et al.: Quasi-dense similarity learning for multiple object tracking. In: Proceedings of the IEEE/CVF Conference on Computer Vision and Pattern Recognition, pp. 164–173 (2021)
43. Rangesh, A., Trivedi, M.M.: No blind spots: full-surround multi-object tracking for autonomous vehicles using cameras and lidars. IEEE Trans. Intell. Veh. **4**(4), 588–599 (2019)
44. Ren, S., He, K., Girshick, R., Sun, J.: Faster R-CNN: towards real-time object detection with region proposal networks. In: Advances in Neural Information Processing Systems, vol. 28 (2015)
45. Rezaei, M., Azarmi, M., Mir, F.M.P.: Traffic-Net: 3D traffic monitoring using a single camera. arXiv preprint arXiv:2109.09165 (2021)
46. Ristani, E., Solera, F., Zou, R., Cucchiara, R., Tomasi, C.: Performance measures and a data set for multi-target, multi-camera tracking. In: Hua, G., Jégou, H. (eds.) ECCV 2016. LNCS, vol. 9914, pp. 17–35. Springer, Cham (2016). https://doi.org/10.1007/978-3-319-48881-3_2
47. Ristani, E., Tomasi, C.: Features for multi-target multi-camera tracking and re-identification. In: Proceedings of the IEEE Conference on Computer Vision and Pattern Recognition, pp. 6036–6046 (2018)
48. Shao, S., et al.: CrowdHuman: a benchmark for detecting human in a crowd. arXiv preprint arXiv:1805.00123 (2018)
49. Shuai, B., Li, X., Kundu, K., Tighe, J.: Id-free person similarity learning. In: Proceedings of the IEEE/CVF Conference on Computer Vision and Pattern Recognition (2022)
50. Shuai, B., Berneshawi, A., Li, X., Modolo, D., Tighe, J.: SiamMOT: siamese multi-object tracking. In: Proceedings of the IEEE/CVF Conference on Computer Vision and Pattern Recognition, pp. 12372–12382 (2021)
51. Song, L., Yu, G., Yuan, J., Liu, Z.: Human pose estimation and its application to action recognition: a survey. J. Vis. Commun. Image Represent. **76**, 103055 (2021)
52. Sun, P., et al.: Scalability in perception for autonomous driving: Waymo open dataset. In: Proceedings of the IEEE/CVF Conference on Computer Vision and Pattern Recognition, pp. 2446–2454 (2020)
53. Sundararaman, R., De Almeida Braga, C., Marchand, E., Pettre, J.: Tracking pedestrian heads in dense crowd. In: Proceedings of the IEEE/CVF Conference on Computer Vision and Pattern Recognition, pp. 3865–3875 (2021)
54. Tian, Z., Shen, C., Chen, H., He, T.: FCOS: fully convolutional one-stage object detection. In: Proceedings of the IEEE/CVF International Conference on Computer Vision, pp. 9627–9636 (2019)

55. Wang, G., Wang, Y., Zhang, H., Gu, R., Hwang, J.N.: Exploit the connectivity: multi-object tracking with trackletnet. In: Proceedings of the 27th ACM International Conference on Multimedia, pp. 482–490 (2019)
56. Wang, Z., Zheng, L., Liu, Y., Li, Y., Wang, S.: Towards real-time multi-object tracking. In: Vedaldi, A., Bischof, H., Brox, T., Frahm, J.-M. (eds.) ECCV 2020. LNCS, vol. 12356, pp. 107–122. Springer, Cham (2020). https://doi.org/10.1007/978-3-030-58621-8_7
57. Wojke, N., Bewley, A., Paulus, D.: Simple online and realtime tracking with a deep association metric. In: 2017 IEEE International Conference on Image Processing (ICIP), pp. 3645–3649. IEEE (2017)
58. Wu, J., Osuntogun, A., Choudhury, T., Philipose, M., Rehg, J.M.: A scalable approach to activity recognition based on object use. In: 2007 IEEE 11th International Conference on Computer Vision, pp. 1–8. IEEE (2007)
59. Xu, J., Cao, Y., Zhang, Z., Hu, H.: Spatial-temporal relation networks for multi-object tracking. In: Proceedings of the IEEE/CVF International Conference on Computer Vision, pp. 3988–3998 (2019)
60. Xu, Y., Osep, A., Ban, Y., Horaud, R., Leal-Taixé, L., Alameda-Pineda, X.: How to train your deep multi-object tracker. In: Proceedings of the IEEE/CVF Conference on Computer Vision and Pattern Recognition, pp. 6787–6796 (2020)
61. Gan, Y., Han, R., Yin, L., Feng, W., Wang, S.: Self-supervised multi-view multi-human association and tracking. In: ACM MM (2021)
62. Yu, F., et al.: BDD100K: a diverse driving dataset for heterogeneous multitask learning. In: Proceedings of the IEEE/CVF Conference on Computer Vision and Pattern Recognition, pp. 2636–2645 (2020)
63. Yu, F., Seff, A., Zhang, Y., Song, S., Funkhouser, T., Xiao, J.: LSUN: construction of a large-scale image dataset using deep learning with humans in the loop. arXiv preprint arXiv:1506.03365 (2015)
64. Yu, F., Wang, D., Shelhamer, E., Darrell, T.: Deep layer aggregation. In: Proceedings of the IEEE Conference on Computer Vision and Pattern Recognition, pp. 2403–2412 (2018)
65. Zhang, Y., Wang, C., Wang, X., Zeng, W., Liu, W.: FairMOT: on the fairness of detection and re-identification in multiple object tracking. Int. J. Comput. Vis. **129**(11), 3069–3087 (2021). https://doi.org/10.1007/s11263-021-01513-4
66. Zhou, X., Koltun, V., Krähenbühl, P.: Tracking objects as points. In: Vedaldi, A., Bischof, H., Brox, T., Frahm, J.-M. (eds.) ECCV 2020. LNCS, vol. 12349, pp. 474–490. Springer, Cham (2020). https://doi.org/10.1007/978-3-030-58548-8_28
67. Zhou, X., Wang, D., Krähenbühl, P.: Objects as points. arXiv preprint arXiv:1904.07850 (2019)

D2-TPred: Discontinuous Dependency for Trajectory Prediction Under Traffic Lights

Yuzhen Zhang[1], Wentong Wang[2], Weizhi Guo[1], Pei Lv[1(✉)], Mingliang Xu[1], Wei Chen[3], and Dinesh Manocha[4]

[1] School of Computer and Artificial Intelligence, Zhengzhou University, Zhengzhou, China
zyzzhang@gs.zzu.edu.cn, {ielvpei,iexumingliang}@zzu.edu.cn
[2] Henan Institute of Advanced Technology, Zhengzhou University, Zhengzhou, China
wangwentong@gs.zzu.edu.cn
[3] State Key Lab of CAD&CG, Zhejiang University, Hangzhou, Zhejiang, China
chenwei@cad.zju.edu.cn
[4] Department of Computer Science, University of Maryland, College Park, MD, USA
dmanocha@umd.edu

Abstract. A profound understanding of inter-agent relationships and motion behaviors is important to achieve high-quality planning when navigating in complex scenarios, especially at urban traffic intersections. We present a trajectory prediction approach with respect to traffic lights, D2-TPred, which uses a spatial dynamic interaction graph (SDG) and a behavior dependency graph (BDG) to handle the problem of discontinuous dependency in the spatial-temporal space. Specifically, the SDG is used to capture spatial interactions by reconstructing sub-graphs for different agents with dynamic and changeable characteristics during each frame. The BDG is used to infer motion tendency by modeling the implicit dependency of the current state on priors behaviors, especially the discontinuous motions corresponding to acceleration, deceleration, or turning direction. Moreover, we present a new dataset for vehicle trajectory prediction under traffic lights called VTP-TL. Our experimental results show that our model achieves more than 20.45% and 20.78% improvement in terms of ADE and FDE, respectively, on VTP-TL as compared to other trajectory prediction algorithms. The dataset and code are available at: https://github.com/VTP-TL/D2-TPred.

Keywords: Spatial dynamic interaction graph · Behavior dependency graph · Discontinuous dependency · Traffic lights

1   Introduction

The interaction relationships and behavioral intentions of vehicles or agents are frequently used for autonomous driving [4,27,32]. A key problem is to predict the future trajectory of each vehicle or road agent, which is used to perform safe navigation or traffic forecasting [1,6,40,48]. Existing trajectory prediction methods are mainly designed to extract the spatial-temporal information

© The Author(s), under exclusive license to Springer Nature Switzerland AG 2022
S. Avidan et al. (Eds.): ECCV 2022, LNCS 13668, pp. 522–539, 2022.
https://doi.org/10.1007/978-3-031-20074-8_30

Fig. 1. Illustration of discontinuous dependency among vehicles at crossroad intersection near traffic lights. We highlight the local trajectories of four vehicles, $v_1 \ldots v_4$ using black directed curves. The orange boxes represent the influence area of the corresponding traffic lights, which are fixed regions and restrict the motion behavior of vehicles while they are passing. We show the position of three vehicles, v_1, v_2, v_3 at time t_1 and t_5, along with the corresponding green boxes which show the dynamic interaction area determined by the moving vehicles. The purple directed edges within each green box represent the interactions among vehicles. In this case, v_3 interacts with v_1 and v_2 at time t_1. However, v_3 is not affected by v_1 at time t_5, even though it is located in the same region. This indicates the discontinuity in the interaction between v_1 and v_3 during this time period. The vehicle v_4 located in the influence areas is not constrained by the red light because it is right-turning. (Color figure online)

from spatial interactions and behavior modeling. In terms of spatial interaction, most previous works determine the interaction among objects according to the predefined interaction areas, such as the entire scene [1,36,40,42,48], localized regions [2,6,12], and the area corresponding to visual attention [19]. However, these methods do not fully consider the varying interactions and dependency between neighbors that occur due to different behaviors, such as changing lanes or turning directions that can lead to new pairwise interactions. In terms of behavior dependency, these prediction algorithms obtain the relevant information of the current state from previous states based on LSTM-based methods [23,48] or graph-based approaches [29,38].

In this paper, we address the problem of trajectory prediction in areas close to traffic lights or intersections. Due to the constraints of traffic signs and traffic lights with red, green, and yellow states labeled by discrete indexes, the vehicles usually do not exhibit the first-order continuity in their movement behaviors with stopping, going straight, turning right, and turning left. Instead, their trajectory is governed by the discontinuous effects from the environment or other agents. For example, in the green boxes of Fig. 1, the interactions among vehicle v_1, v_2 and v_3 change from time t_1 to t_5. Even though these vehicles are within the same interaction regions determined by distance which shown using green boxes, the spatial and behavior interaction between the vehicles changes considerably and we need to model such changes. For vehicle v_4, the most important influence on its current state is the change in its behavior due to the right-turn, rather than the movement state in adjacent timestamp. We refer to these phenomena as *discontinuous dependency (D2)*, which makes accurate spatial-temporal feature extraction extremely challenging. Current trajectory prediction methods do not fully account for this property that the trajectories of traffic agents are usually not first-order continuous due to the frequent starting and stopping motions.

Main Results: In order to model the discontinuous dependency between traffic agents, we present a new trajectory prediction approach (D2-TPred). In our formulation, we construct a spatial dynamic interaction graph (SDG) for different traffic agents in one frame. Each traffic agent is regarded as a graph node and we compute appropriate edges to model its interactions with other changing neighboring agents determined by visual scope, distance, and lane index as well as discontinuous dependencies in terms of their relative positions. Moreover, a behavior dependency graph (BDG) is computed for each agent to model the discontinuities with respect to their behaviors at previous time instances, rather than only adjacent timestamp. Specifically, to avoid the key behavioral features such as acceleration, deceleration, or turning direction, may be filtered by forget gates or the error will be accumulated in sequential prediction by RNN network, the way of dependency information passing between adjacent frames is replaced by a GAT (graph attention network) [31], and the behavior dependency is modeled along the edges in the BDG. The SDG and BDG are used as part of a graph-based network for trajectory prediction.

We also present a new dataset for vehicle trajectory prediction, VTP-TL. Our dataset consists of traffic pattern at urban intersections with different traffic rules, such as crossroads, T-junctions intersections, and roundabouts, containing 2D coordinates of vehicle trajectory and more than 1000 annotated vehicles at each traffic intersection. The novel components of our work include:

1 We propose a novel trajectory prediction approach, D2-TPred, that accounts for various discontinuities in the vehicle trajectories and pairwise interactions near traffic lights and intersections.

2 We present two types of data structure to improve the performance of graph-based networks to model dynamic interactions and vehicle behaviors. SDG is used to model spatial interactions by reconstructing appropriate sub-graphs for dynamic agents with constantly changing neighbors in each frame. BDG is used to model the dynamically changing behaviors dependency of current state on previous behaviors. The usage of SDG and BDG improves the prediction accuracy by 22.45% and 29.39% in ADE and FDE.

3 We present a new dataset VTP-TL that corresponds to traffic video data near traffic lights and interactions. This includes 150 min of video clips at 30 fps corresponding to challenging urban scenarios. They are captured using drones at 70–120 m above the traffic intersections.

2   Related Work

A brief overview of prior work on graph neural networks, interaction models, and motion pattern dependency is given.

Graph Neural Networks: Graph Neural Network (GNN) [58] can model social or other interactions between agents. Prior trajectory prediction methods based on GNN can be divided into two categories. The first is based on undirected graphs, which utilize the graph structure to explicitly construct interactions and assign the same weight for each pair of nodes, e.g., STUGCN [55], Social-STGCNN [29]. The second is based on Graph attention networks (GAT) [31], which introduces an attention mechanism into the undirected graph to calculate asymmetric influence weights for interactive agents. The GAT-based approaches, such as Social-BiGAT [43], STGAT [23], EvolveGraph [24], and SGCN [38], can flexibly model asymmetric interactions to compute spatial-temporal features and improve the prediction accuracy. Meanwhile, EvolveGraph [24] and SGCN [38] introduce graph structure inference to generate dynamic and sparse interaction. Different from these methods, we directly construct one directed graph according to interactive objects determined by the visual scope, distance, and traffic rules, and use GATs to represent the asymmetric interactions among agents.

Social Interaction Models: Social interactions and related information are used by traffic agents to make reasonable decisions to avoid potential collisions. Social force-based methods [13,33,49] use different types of force to model acceleration and deceleration forces. Social pooling based approaches [1,2,12,40] try to integrate motion information of neighbors within a radius. GNN-based techniques [23,24,29,41–43,46] use graph structures to directly model the interactions among near and far agents. These methods assume that the underlying agents interact with all other agents in a predefined or nearby regions. They do not account for those neighbors need to be pruned, especially moving along the opposite lanes.

Motion Models: Motion models are used to infer the motion information as part of trajectory prediction. Early studies have focused on forecasting future trajectories based on a linear model, constant velocity model, or constant acceleration model [52]. However, these simple models can not handle complex traffic patterns. Furthermore, LSTM-based approaches [1,2,23,39] and graph structure-based approaches [29,38,54,55] are proposed to model the motion trajectories. Other techniques take into account driver behavior patterns [3,7]. Giuliari et al. [17] perform precise trajectory prediction using transformer networks. Here, the states of an agent in temporal sequence are regarded as nodes to construct directed graph, further achieve the direct influence between discontinuous timestamps, rather than only adjacent one.

3   D2-TPred

In this section, we present our novel learning-based trajectory prediction algorithm, which involves the influence of traffic lights on motion behaviors, and the architecture is shown in Fig. 2.

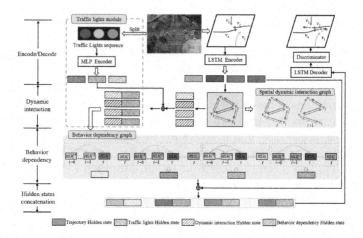

Fig. 2. Architecture of our proposed D2-TPred model. The spatial dynamic interaction graph is used to represent the dynamic interactions and we reconstruct the sub-graphs. The behavior dependency graph learns the movement features by estimating the effect of agent behavior. The discriminator is used to refine the predicted trajectories. The traffic light module is used to predict the trajectories at urban intersections.

3.1   Problem Formulation

Given spatial coordinate and traffic light state of N agents in each scenario, we aim to predict the most likely trajectories of these agents in the future. At any time t, the state of the ith agent Sq_i at time t can be denoted as $Sq_i^t = (Fid, Aid, x_i^t, y_i^t, Lid, pa_i^t, f_i^t, mb_i^t, lid_i^t, ls_i^t, lt_i^t)$, where $p_i^t = (x_i^t, y_i^t)$ represents the position coordinate and the other symbols represent the corresponding traffic light information described with more detail in Sect. 3.3. According to the inputs of all agents in the interval $[1 : t_{obs}]$, our method can predict their position at next moment $t_{pred} \in [t_{obs} + 1 : T]$. Different from the ground truth trajectory $Lq_i^{t_{pred}}$, $\hat{Lq}_i^{t_{pred}}$ notates the predicted trajectory.

3.2   Spatio-Temporal Dependency

Spatial Dynamic Interaction Graph. Unlike prior methods [23,29], we reconstruct the sub-graphs to model all the interactions in each frame. We illustrate our approach to model discontinuous dependency by highlighting one scenario with 7 vehicles and appropriate trajectories in Fig. 3. Similar to [19], the visual area of a subject is treated as frustum, where different visual ranges are set between road and intersection by considering the characteristics of human visual system. At time t_1, v_2, v_3, and v_7 are located in the visual area of neighborhood of v_1. However, the motion behavior of v_1 is not affected by v_7, which moves in the opposite lane. Hence, we construct sub-graph G_1 corresponding to the interactions among vehicles v_1, v_2, and v_3, and sub-graph G_3 for vehicles v_5 and v_6. Moreover, for vehicles v_4 and v_7 without nearby neighbors, we compute

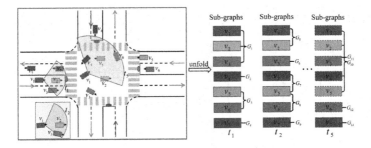

Fig. 3. The spatial dynamic interaction graph (SDG). The left part of the figure shows the scene from time t_1 to t_5, and the right part represents the reconstructed interaction sub-graphs at different time instances.

sub-graphs G_2 and G_4, respectively. Based on these sub-graphs, the intermediate states of these vehicles are updated. Since the interactions between the vehicles change dynamically, vehicle v_1 is not affected by vehicle v_3 at time t_2. Even though they are within the same interaction region determined by distance, the influence of vehicle v_3 on vehicle v_1 is not the same between adjacent frames. In this manner, we reconstruct the corresponding sub-graphs G_5, G_{13} to represent these varying interactions between the vehicles.

Considering the asymmetry of interactions among agents, we use a self-attention mechanism into these constructed directed graphs to model the spatial interactions. For agent i at time t, we first determine its interactive objects j according to the visual scope θ, distance d, and lane index Lid, and the corresponding matrix V, D, and L respectively.

$$
\begin{cases}
V[i,j] = 1, & if\ \theta(\vec{ij}) \in \theta, \\
D[i,j] = 1, & if\ \left\| p_j^t - p_i^t \right\|_2 \leq d, \\
L[i,j] = 1, & if\ Lid_i^t = Lid_j^t, \\
R = V \times D \times L
\end{cases}
\tag{1}
$$

where R filled with 0 and 1 represents adjacency matrix among agents, and we further construct sub-graph based on it. We then calculate the spatial state hs_i^t by integrating the hidden states h_j^t from interactive objects.

$$
e_i^t = \Phi(p_i^t, W_p), \quad h_i^t = LSTM(h_i^{t-1}, e_i^t, W_l), \tag{2}
$$

$$
hs_i^t = \sum_{j \in \mathcal{N}_i^t} (a_{ij}^t R_{ij}^t) h_j^t, \tag{3}
$$

where $\Phi(\cdot)$ is an embedding function, and e_i^t is the state vector of agent i at time t. Similar to method [14], a_{ij}^t represents the attention coefficient of agent j to i at timestamp t, W_p and W_l are embedding matrix and LSTM cell weight.

Behavior Dependency Graph. To avoid the key behavioral features may be filtered by forget gate of RNN network in process of information passing,

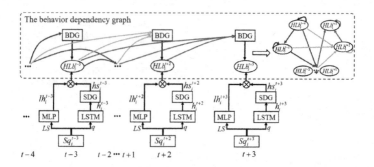

Fig. 4. The behavior dependency graph (BDG). The lower part refers to the encoding process of trajectories and traffic light signals. The upper part describes behavior dependency, where segments with the same color refer to a temporal dependency graph.

we model the discontinuous dependency from previous behaviors to the current state by using GATs, rather than only adjacent timestamps. Specifically, for a given vehicle, its states updated by SDG are regarded as nodes. We model discontinuous dependency in the temporal sequence as edges and construct a directed graph, where the behavior information is transferred along the directed edges. The detailed architecture of the BDG for a given agent is shown in Fig. 4.

Specifically, for agent i, we use directed segments with the same color to constitute an unfolded BDG, and different colors represent the behavior dependency graphs at different time instances. The BDG uses the state hs_i^t generated by the SDG. Its current state is updated and embed into the behavior dependency graph at the next time instance, where dependency weights among nodes are calculated by using a self-attention mechanism. As shown in the dashed box of Fig. 4, the motion state of agent i at current moment $t+2$ is governed by the previous behaviors at time $t+1$, t, $t-1$, $t-2$, $t-3$, and $t-4$, etc., whereas the next instance $t+3$ is governed by $t+2$, $t+1$, t, $t-1$, $t-2$, and $t-3$. In this way, the updated hidden state hb_i^t for agent i at time t is calculated as follows:

$$a_i^{tt'} = softmax(\frac{exp(LeakyReLU^*(\beta^T[Whs_i^t \| Whb_i^{t'}]))}{\sum_{t'}^t exp(LeakyReLU^*(\beta^T[Whs_i^t \| Whb_i^{t'}]))}),$$

$$hb_i^t = \sum_{t' \in (t-k) \; and \; t' \geq 0}^t a_i^{tt'}(hb_i^{t'}, hs_i^t), \qquad (4)$$

where k represents the experimental estimated time window whose quantitative results have the lowest prediction error by obtaining more effective behavior feature. β^T is the weight vector of a single-layer feedforward neural network. t' denotes a specific time instance in the previous frames from $t-k$ to t.

3.3 Trajectory Prediction Near Traffic Lights

In this section, we present two prediction schemes for the vehicle trajectory prediction. The first scheme considers the discontinuous constraints on vehicles' behaviors caused by the alternation of traffic light states, where the traffic lights are regarded as indicator signals with fixed position and alternating states. The second scheme is designed for scenarios without traffic lights, which is described in detail in the supplementary material https://github.com/VTP-TL/D2-TPred.

Given the observed sequence: $Sq_i^t = (Fid, Aid, x, y, Lid, pa, f, mb, lid, ls, lt)$, which is divided by the vehicle trajectory $q = (Fid, Aid, x, y, Lid, pa, f, mb)$ and the corresponding traffic light states sequence $LS = (Fid, lid, ls, lt)$. Fid, Aid, and Lid are the index of frame, vehicle, and lane where the vehicle located, respectively. lid_i^t is the traffic light index. pa_i^t describes whether vehicle v_i is within the influence area of corresponding traffic light. f_i^t indicates whether vehicle v_i is closest to the parking line in the influence area. mb_i^t represents the movement behavior of one agent, such as turning-left, turning-right, or going-straight. ls_i^t and lt_i^t respectively describe the state and duration of traffic light. We take into account that the vehicle trajectory is continuous and the traffic light states sequence is periodic and discontinuous. Therefore, the two different encoders, LSTM and MLP, are utilized to handle them and compute the corresponding hidden states h_i^t and $lh_i^t = MLP(LS_i^t, W_M)$, respectively. In SDG, we use GAT to integrate influencing features from nearby interacting agents and then compute the updated state hs_i^t of agent i. In terms of behavior dependency, we first concatenate the state hs_i^t (Eq. 4) and traffic lights state lh_i^t as input $\tilde{HL}_i^t$, and then use these results to construct BDG. Based on the BDG, we can model discontinuous constraints of traffic lights on the movement behaviors of vehicles, as shown in Fig. 4. In this stage, hidden state HLb_i^t is computed as a weighted sum of $HLb_i^{1:(t-1)}$, where the dependency weights are calculated by a self-attention mechanism. The resulting equations:

$$\tilde{HL}_i^t = integrate(hs_i^t, lh_i^t, W_l), \quad HLb_i^t = GAT(\tilde{HL}_i^t, HLb_i^{1:t}, W_{\tilde{\theta}}), \quad (5)$$

where $integrate(\cdot)$ is concatenation operation. W_l, and $W_{\tilde{\theta}}$ are the embedding weights. To augment behavior feature and avoid the feature loss filtered by forget gates in process of sequence, the intermediate state are generated by integrating the sate HLb_i^t and original state h_i^t. The predicted position is given by:

$$\hat{Lq}_i^{t_{pred}} = \sigma(D_{LSTM}([HLb_i^t, h_i^t], W_d)). \quad (6)$$

where D_{LSTM} and W_d are the decoder based LSTM and corresponding weight respectively. $\sigma(\cdot)$ represents a linear layer. Our method is also GAN-based model integrating a discriminator D_{cls} into the predicted approach, which utilizes LSTM and MLP to respectively encode the complete trajectory ($[Sq_i^{T_{obs}}$, $\hat{Lp}_i^{T_{pred}})]$ and traffic light sequence LS, and then concatenate them as the input into the *Discriminator* to output a real/fake probability $probL_i$ by a linear network.

$$probL_i = D_{cls}(LSTM([Sq_i^{t_{obs}}, \hat{Lq}_i^{t_{pred}}], W_l), MLP(LS_i, W_M)) \quad (7)$$

Table 1. VTP-TL vs other state-of-the-art traffic datasets. *Size* represents the number of annotated frames. E_V and B_V represent the egocentric vision and bird's view.

Datasets	Location	View	Night	Road type	Size	Traffic lights
CityScapes [10]	Europe	E_V	×	Urban	25K	×
Argoverse [9]	USA	E_V	√	Urban	22K	×
INTERACTION [45]	International	B_V	×	Urban	–	×
ApolloScape [50]	China	E_V	√	Urban + rural	144K	×
TRAF [6]	India	E_V	√	Urban + rural	72K	×
D2-city [57]	China	E_V	×	Urban	700K	×
inD [5]	Germany	B_V	×	Urban	–	×
Lyft Level5 [21]	USA	E_V	×	Urban	46K	×
nuScenes [20]	USA/Singapore	E_V	√	Urban	40K	×
Waymo [37]	USA	E_V	√	Urban	200K	√
Waterloo [44]	Canada	B_V	×	Urban	–	√
IDD [16]	India	E_V	×	Urban + rural	10K	×
METEOR [35]	India	E_V	√	Urban + rural	2027K	×
VTP-TL	China	B_V	√	**Urban**	**270K**	√

For each vehicle, we calculate displacement error by variety loss in [1]. The model predicts multiple trajectories K, and chooses the trajectory with the lowest distance error between them and ground-truth trajectory as the model output.

$$Loss_{variety} = \min_K \left\| Lq_i - \hat{Lq}_i^{K} \right\|_2. \tag{8}$$

Through considering the best trajectory, the loss encourages network to cover the space of outputs that conform to the past trajectory.

3.4 VTP-TL Dataset

Although plenty of datasets have been constructed to evaluate the performance of trajectory prediction (Table 1), they rarely contained the important attributes of traffic lights except for Waymo and Waterloo. More details and their differences are described in our supplementary materials. For our new traffic dataset, VTP-TL, we use drones to hover at 70 to 120 m above the traffic intersections in an urban setting, as statically as possible, to record vehicle trajectories passing through the area with a bird's-eye view in the daytime corresponding to non-rush hours, rush hours, and during the evening. The dataset contains more than 150 min video clips, over $270k$ annotated frames, and more than 4 million bounding boxes for traffic vehicles at three typical urban scenarios: crossroads, T-junctions, and roundabouts intersections. Specifically, according to these recorded videos including traffic lights when they are visible, we infer the invisible state in the videos since the pattern of traffic lights are fixed. Therefore, we manually mark the related attributes of traffic light signals as discrete index, such as the index, state, duration, and position coordinate, and high definition maps such as lanes,

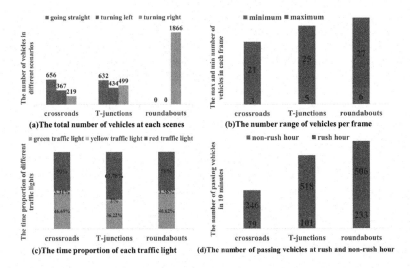

Fig. 5. We highlight the traffic light states and vehicles behaviors in various videos in VTP-TL. The detailed descriptions are given in the appendix.

crosswalks, and stop lines. Compared with Waymo, the traffic lights are annotated as independent objects, and modeled as agents with fixed position and changeable states in our prediction framework. The center of bounding box is regarded as the position coordinates of vehicle. Finally, we obtain a new dataset of vehicles trajectory prediction containing over 1288 vehicles driving straight, 801 vehicles turning left, and 2584 vehicles turning right. Our dataset is divided into training, validation, and testing sets at a ratio of 4:1:1, and down-sampled to 3 frames per second for experiments.

We also perform statistical analysis on the VTP-TL dataset, and the corresponding results are shown in Fig. 5. The number of vehicles with different motion behaviors at each urban intersection are shown in Fig. 5(a). Considering different traffic rules at various urban intersections, we also count the number range of passing vehicles per frame as Fig. 5(b). Meanwhile, to ensure the effective passing of vehicles, different cycle time for traffic lights is set at different intersections (shown in Fig. 5(c)). In Fig. 5(d), we count the number of vehicles in the daytime of the rush and non-rush hours in 10 min. These descriptions can fully represent a large number of vehicles' behaviors are constrained by traffic lights. The user identifiers and exact date of publication have been masked off to protect privacy. The dataset would only be available for research purposes. More details are given in the supplementary materials.

4   Experimental Evaluation

In our experiments, the dimension of the embedding layer and the hidden state are set as 16 and 32, respectively. We also set the fixed input dimension as 64 and use the attention layer of 64. During training, the Adam optimizer is applied with a learning rate of 0.01 and batch size of 64.

Table 2. Quantitative results of prediction performance on traffic datasets. The ADE/FDE are calculated for each dataset. The bold fonts correspond to the best results with the lowest error among predicted 20 possible trajectories for each agent, except INTER (INTERACTION) where the lowest error among predicted 6 possible trajectories. For Waymo, we implement those baseline methods according to their open source code, while the other experimental values of comparison methods are all described in open papers. - denotes methods have not been validated on those datasets.

Method	Apolloscape	Method	SDD	INTER	Method	Waymo
TPNet [15]	2.23/4.70	EvolveGraph [24]	13.9/22.9	-	SGAN [1]	6.01/11.40
CS-LSTM [12]	2.14/11.70	Goal-Gan [11]	12.2/22.1	-	Social-LSTM [2]	4.05/7.59
G-LSTMS [8]	1.12/2.05	SimAug [26]	10.27/19.71	-	STGAT [23]	1.68/3.70
SGAN [1]	3.98/6.75	LB-EBM [30]	8.87/**15.61**	-	SGCN [38]	1.02/2.26
TraPHic [6]	1.28/11.67	DESIRE [25]	19.3/34.1	0.32/0.88		
NLNI [56]	1.09/1.55	HEAT [28]	-	**0.19**/0.66		
AI-TP [53]	1.16/2.13	TNT [18]	-	0.21/0.67		
GRIP++ [47]	1.25/2.34	MultiPath [51]	-	0.30/0.99		
D2-TPred	**1.02/1.69**	D2-TPred	**8.24**/15.89	0.29/**0.62**	D2-TPred	**0.85/1.89**

Evaluation Datasets. We evaluate proposed model on four traffic datasets, Apolloscape [50], SDD [34], INTERACTION [45], and Waymo [37]. In addition, we also report the experiments on our new dataset VTP-TL.

Evaluation Metrics. We use the same evaluating metrics as [22,23,41]. *Average displacement error* (ADE) represents the average square error between the predicted trajectory and the ground truth trajectory for all agents at all frames. *Final displacement error* (FDE) represents the mean distance between the predicted path and ground truth trajectory for all agents at the final frame.

Comparable Methods. *Social-LSTM* [2] models spatial interaction by pooling mechanism. *CS-LSTM* [12], *TraPHic* [6] and *GRAPH-LSTM* [8] combine CNN with LSTM to perform trajectory prediction. *SGAN* [1], SGCN [38], and *Goal-Gan* [11] use GAN to model spatial interactions and physical attentions. *Social Attention* [42], AI-TP [53], *Trajectron++* [41], *GRIP++* [47], *NLNI* [56], *EvolveGraph* [24], and *STGAT* [23] integrate graph structure and attention mechanism to extract spatial-temporal interaction features. *TPNet* [15] and *DESIRE* [25], integrate scene contex into prediction framework. *NMMP* [22] models the directed interaction with the neural motion message passing strategy. SimAug [26] is trained only on 3D simulation data to predict future trajectories. LB-EBM [30] is a probabilistic model with cost function defined in the latent space to account for the movement history and social context for diverse human trajectories. *HEAT* [28], *TNT* [18], and *MultiPath* [51] are used on INTERACTION and reported in [18].

4.1 Quantitative Evaluation

We have performed the detailed quantitative evaluation. On traffic datasets Apolloscape, SDD, INTERACTION, Waymo, and VTP-TL, the quantitative

Table 3. Quantitative results on VTP-TL dataset. We compare with the baseline methods and compute the ADE and FDE metrics by using 8 time steps to predict 12 future frames. +TL represents that traffic light states is embedded into the trajectory prediction system. The bold fonts correspond to the best results, which are the lowest error among predicted 20 possible trajectories for each agent.

Metrics	Comparable models (in pixels)						
	Social Lstm	Social attention	SGAN	STGAT	Trajectron++	NMMP	D2-TPred
ADE	54.328	43.648	37.63	28.279	39.01	35.15	**20.685**
FDE	112.635	97.614	75.35	61.762	118.37	70.35	**47.296**
Metrics	Comparable models+TL (in pixels)						
	Social Lstm	Social attention	SGAN	STGAT	Trajectron++	NMMP	D2-TPred
ADE	45.04	34.460	31.56	21.245	35.456	32.33	**16.900**
FDE	78.52	75.825	65.67	43.620	114.365	66.35	**34.553**

results of prediction performance for D2-TPred and other trajector prediction methods are shown in Table 2 and Table 3.

Traffic Datasets Without Traffic Lights: Taking benefits from the SDG and BDG to extract spatio-temporal features, our method achieves competitive performance in the datasets shown in Table 2. Specifically, the performance of our method significantly outperforms comparative methods on Apolloscape. In SDD dataset with a large number of different scenarios, we observe the lowest error on ADE and the third-lowest error on FDE, as well as the lowest error on the FDE on INTER (INTERACTION). Moreover, we also achieve the best performance on Waymo Open Motion dataset by observing 8 frames to predict the next 12 frames. These demonstrate that our model can effectively capture the dynamic changeable interaction features and behavior dependency in complex traffic scenarios. More experimental results on other datasets such as ETH-UCY, Argoverse, nuScenes and inD are described in our supplementary materials.

VTP-TL Dataset with Traffic Lights: In this section, we describe D2-TPred+TL, which introduces traffic light states into D2-TPred approach. In Table 3, we evaluate our model against comparable methods, and all these methods against themselves with traffic lights. The experimental results show our method outperforms all other methods on the VTP-TL dataset in terms of ADE and FDE. Notably, compared with STGAT with the lowest prediction error, the ADE and FDE of D2-TPred+TL are reduced by 20.45% and 20.78%. This illustrates we can effectively model constraints of traffic lights on motion behaviors.

4.2 Ablation Studies

We present the ablation studies on VTP-TL with traffic light. This not only demonstrates the significance of each component but also highlights the benefits of modeling discontinuity due to traffic lights on vehicle movement behavior.

Table 4. The ablation results on VTP-TL dataset. **S** denotes spatial interaction achieved by GAT (S_G) or SDG (S_S). **B** denotes behavior dependency achieved by LSTM (B_L) or BDG (B_B). **TL** denotes traffic light encoder as LSTM (TL_L) or MLP (TL_M). **D** denotes the discriminator. The bold fonts correspond to the best results.

Setting	S		B		TL		D	Metrics
	GAT	SDG	LSTM	BDG	LSTM	MLP	D	ADE/FDE
$S_G + B_L + TL_M + D$	✓		✓			✓	✓	21.792/48.936
$S_G + B_B + TL_M + D$	✓			✓		✓	✓	19.635/41.804
$S_S + B_L + TL_M + D$		✓	✓			✓	✓	20.082/44.560
$S_S + B_B + TL_L + D$		✓		✓	✓		✓	17.896/37.629
$S_S + B_B + TL_M$		✓		✓		✓		18.626/39.598
$S_S + B_B + TL_M + D$		✓		✓		✓	✓	**16.900/34.553**

Evaluation of the SDG and BDG: To show the effectiveness of the SDG and BDG, we compare $S_G+B_B+TL_M+D$, $S_S+B_L+TL_M+D$ with $S_S+B_B+TL_M+D$ in Table 4. $S_S + B_B + TL_M + D$ can reduce ADE by 13.93% and 15.85%, and FDE by 17.34% and 22.46%, respectively. This directly illustrates that the SDG and BDG can effectively capture discontinuous dependency in spatial-temporal space to further improve the accuracy of prediction trajectories.

Evaluation of the Discriminator: We introduce a discriminator to refine the predicted trajectories. By comparing $S_S + B_B + TL_M$ with $S_S + B_B + TL_M + D$ in Table 4, the performances of the latter are increased by 9.26% and 12.74% in ADE and FDE, respectively. Moreover, the discriminator contributes to improving the accuracy of predicted trajectory.

Evaluation of Different Encoders: Due to the distinctive characteristics of traffic light states, we use the MLP and LSTM to encode them. By comparing $S_S+B_B+TL_L+D$ and $S_S+B_B+TL_M+D$ in Table 4, utilizing MLP to capture features of traffic light states can be further improved by 5.56% and 8.17% on ADE and FDE, respectively. This illustrates that a discontinuous sequence may not be suitable for being encoded by LSTM with strong context correlation.

Evaluation of the Function of Traffic Lights: For traffic lights, we compare the methods+TL with the corresponding baseline methods. The former directly uses the VTP-TL dataset, and the latter uses a dataset that consists of *Fid*, *Aid*, *x*, and *y* attributes split from the VTP-TL dataset. As shown in Table 3, it can further increase the performance by 8.02% to 24.87% and 3.38% to 30.29% in ADE and FDE, respectively. Therefore, we can clearly validate the necessity of traffic lights in trajectory prediction at urban intersections.

4.3   Qualitative Evaluation

In Fig. 6, the images of first two columns show the qualitative results derived from the Argoverse and Apolloscape. It can be seen our method without traffic lights also predicts acceptable future paths at urban intersections.

Argoverse   Apolloscape   VTP-TL

———— Ground Truth   ———— Observation   – – – Social-LSTM   – – – Social-Attention   – – – SGAN
– – – STGAT   – – – Trajectron++   – – – NMMP   – – – CS-LSTM   – – – GRAPH-LSTMS
······ TraPHic   ······ MATF-GAN   – – – GRIP++   – – – D2-TPred (Ours)

Fig. 6. The visualization results at urban intersections on traffic datasets and VTP-TL dataset. Note that the compared methods are not the same in different datasets. (Color figure online)

In the third column, we show the qualitative results on the VTP-TL dataset. For the first row, the current traffic light state is red on the vertical road. We only show five vehicles' trajectories, where vehicle v_1 drives straight, v_2 turns right under the red traffic light, v_3 goes straight under the green light, v_4 and v_5 are not in the influence area of traffic light signals. For v_1, the predicted trajectory of our method is closest to the ground truth. Although the trajectories of v_2, v_3, v_4, and v_5 are not affected by traffic light signals, our method also predicts acceptable trajectories. The next two images show the predicted trajectory at T-junctions and roundabout intersections, where the states of vehicles located in the former are changing from parking to driving under the traffic light states from red to green. This illustrates our model can flexibly respond to the dynamic changes of surrounding agents and traffic light states. Limited by the pages, more results and failure case are listed in supplementary materials.

5   Conclusions

We present *D2-TPred*, a new trajectory prediction approach by taking into traffic lights. The approach can not only model the dynamic interactions by reconstructing sub-graphs for all agents with constantly changing interaction objects (SDG), but also captures discontinuous behavior dependency by modeling the direct effects of behaviors at prior instances on the current state (BDG). Moreover, one new dataset VTP-TL for vehicles trajectory prediction with traffic lights is also released. Based on it, we describe two trajectory forecasting schemes and obtain competitive performance against other state-of-the-art.

Acknowledgments. This work was supported in part by the National Natural Science Foundation of China with Grant No. 61772474 and 62036010, Zhengzhou Major Science and Technology Project with Grant No. 2021KJZX0060-6. We thank all the reviewers for their valuable suggestions.

References

1. Agrim, G., Justin, J., Li, F.F., Silvio, S.: Social GAN: socially acceptable trajectories with generative adversarial networks. In: 2018 IEEE/CVF Conference on Computer Vision and Pattern Recognition (CVPR), pp. 2255–2264 (2018)
2. Alahi, A., Goel, K., Ramanathan, V., Robicquet, A., Fei-Fei, L., Savarese, S.: Social LSTM: human trajectory prediction in crowded spaces. In: 2016 IEEE Conference on Computer Vision and Pattern Recognition (CVPR), pp. 961–971 (2016). https://doi.org/10.1109/CVPR.2016.110
3. Angelos, M., Rohan, C., Dinesh, M.: B-GAP: behavior-guided action prediction for autonomous navigation. arXiv preprint arXiv:2011.03748 (2020)
4. Bai, H., Cai, S., Ye, N., Hsu, D., Lee, W.S.: Intention-aware online POMDP planning for autonomous driving in a crowd. In: 2015 IEEE International Conference on Robotics and Automation (ICRA), pp. 454–460 (2015)
5. Bock, J., Krajewski, R., Moers, T., Runde, S., Vater, L., Eckstein, L.: The inD dataset: a drone dataset of naturalistic road user trajectories at German intersections. In: 2020 IEEE Intelligent Vehicles Symposium (IV), pp. 1929–1934 (2019). https://doi.org/10.1109/IV47402.2020.9304839
6. Chandra, R., Bhattacharya, U., Bera, A., Manocha, D.: TraPHic: trajectory prediction in dense and heterogeneous traffic using weighted interactions. In: 2019 IEEE/CVF Conference on Computer Vision and Pattern Recognition (CVPR), pp. 8475–8484 (2019). https://doi.org/10.1109/CVPR.2019.00868
7. Chandra, R., Bhattacharya, U., Mittal, T., Bera, A., Manocha, D.: CMetric: a driving behavior measure using centrality functions. In: 2020 IEEE/RSJ International Conference on Intelligent Robots and Systems (IROS), pp. 2035–2042 (2020)
8. Chandra, R., et al.: Forecasting trajectory and behavior of road-agents using spectral clustering in graph-LSTMs. IEEE Robot. Autom. Lett. **5**(3), 4882–4890 (2020)
9. Chang, M.F., et al.: Argoverse: 3D tracking and forecasting with rich maps. In: Proceedings of the IEEE/CVF Conference on Computer Vision and Pattern Recognition, pp. 8748–8757 (2019)
10. Cordts, M., et al.: The cityscapes dataset for semantic urban scene understanding. In: 2016 IEEE Conference on Computer Vision and Pattern Recognition (CVPR), pp. 3213–3223 (2016)
11. Dendorfer, P., Oep, A., Laura, L.T.: Goal-GAN: multimodal trajectory prediction based on goal position estimation. In: Computer Vision - ACCV 2020 (2021)
12. Deo, N., Trivedi, M.M.: Convolutional social pooling for vehicle trajectory prediction. In: 2018 IEEE/CVF Conference on Computer Vision and Pattern Recognition Workshops (CVPRW), pp. 1468–1476 (2018)

13. Dirk, H., Peter, M.: Social force model for pedestrian dynamics. Phys. Rev. E **51**(5), 4282–4286 (1995)
14. Dzmitry, B., Kyunghyun, C., Yoshua, B.: Neural machine translation by jointly learning to align and translate. arXiv:1409.0473v7 (2014)
15. Fang, L., Jiang, Q., Shi, J., Zhou, B.: TPNet: trajectory proposal network for motion prediction. In: 2020 IEEE/CVF Conference on Computer Vision and Pattern Recognition (CVPR), pp. 6796–6805 (2020). https://doi.org/10.1109/CVPR42600.2020.00683
16. Girish, V., Anbumani, S., Anoop, N., Manmohan, C., Jawahar, C.V.: IDD: a dataset for exploring problems of autonomous navigation in unconstrained environments. In: 2019 IEEE Winter Conference on Applications of Computer Vision (WACV), pp. 1743–1751 (2021)
17. Giuliari, F., Hasan, I., Cristani, M., Galasso, F.: Transformer networks for trajectory forecasting. In: 2020 25th International Conference on Pattern Recognition (ICPR), pp. 10335–10342 (2020)
18. Hang, Z., Jiyang, G., Tian, L., Chen, S., Benjamin, S., Balakrishnan, V.: TNT: target-driven trajectory prediction. arXiv:2008.08294v2 (2020)
19. Hasan, I., et al.: Forecasting people trajectories and head poses by jointly reasoning on tracklets and vislets. IEEE Trans. Pattern Anal. Mach. Intell. **43**(4), 1267–1278 (2021)
20. Holger, C., Varun, K.R.B., Lang, A.H., Sourabh, V.: nuScenes: a multimodal dataset for autonomous driving. In: 2020 IEEE/CVF Conference on Computer Vision and Pattern Recognition (CVPR), pp. 11621–11631 (2020)
21. Houston, J., Zuidhof, G., Bergamini, L., Ye, Y., Ondruska, P.: One thousand and one hours: self-driving motion prediction dataset. In: Conference on Robot Learning (CoRL) (2020)
22. Hu, Y., Chen, S., Zhang, Y., Gu, X.: Collaborative motion prediction via neural motion message passing. In: 2020 IEEE/CVF Conference on Computer Vision and Pattern Recognition (CVPR), pp. 6318–6327 (2020)
23. Huang, Y., Bi, H., Li, Z., Mao, T., Wang, Z.: STGAT: modeling spatial-temporal interactions for human trajectory prediction. In: 2019 International Conference in Computer Vision, pp. 6272–6281 (2019)
24. Jiachen, L., Fan, Y., Tomizuka, M., Choi., C.: EvolveGraph: multi-agent trajectory prediction with dynamic relational reasoning. In: Proceedings of the Neural Information Processing Systems (NeurIPS), pp. 1–18 (2020)
25. Lee, N., Choi, W., Vernaza, P., Choy, C.B., Torr, P.H.S., Chandraker, M.: DESIRE: distant future prediction in dynamic scenes with interacting agents. In: 2017 IEEE Conference on Computer Vision and Pattern Recognition (CVPR), pp. 2165–2174 (2017). https://doi.org/10.1109/CVPR.2017.233
26. Liang, J., Jiang, L., Hauptmann, A.: SimAug: learning robust representations from 3D simulation for pedestrian trajectory prediction in unseen cameras **2**. arXiv preprint arXiv:2004.02022 (2020)
27. Luo, Y., Cai, P., Bera, A., Hsu, D., Lee, W.S., Manocha, D.: PORCA: modeling and planning for autonomous driving among many pedestrians. IEEE Robot. Autom. Lett. **3**(4), 3418–3425 (2018)
28. Mo, X., Huang, Z., Xing, Y., Lv, C.: Multi-agent trajectory prediction with heterogeneous edge-enhanced graph attention network. IEEE Trans. Intell. Transp. Syst. 1–14 (2022). https://doi.org/10.1109/TITS.2022.3146300

29. Mohamed, A., Qian, K., Elhoseiny, M., Claudel, C.: Social-STGCNN: a social spatio-temporal graph convolutional neural network for human trajectory prediction. In: 2020 IEEE Conference on Computer Vision and Pattern Recognition, pp. 14424–14432 (2020)
30. Pang, B., Zhao, T., Xie, X., Wu, Y.N.: Trajectory prediction with latent belief energy-based model. In: The IEEE/CVF Conference on Computer Vision and Pattern Recognition (CVPR), pp. 11814–11824, June 2021
31. Petar, V., Guillem, C., Arantxa, C., Adriana, R.: Graph attention networks. In: International Conference on Learning Representations (ICLR) (2018)
32. Pongsathorn, R., Takahiro, H., Masao, N.: Motion planning and control of autonomous driving intelligence system based on risk potential optimization framework. Int. J. Autom. Eng. **7**(1), 53–60 (2016)
33. Ramin, M., Alexis, O., Mubarak, S.: Abnormal crowd behavior detection using social force model. In: 2009 IEEE Conference on Computer Vision and Pattern Recognition, pp. 935–942 (2009)
34. Robicquet, A., Sadeghian, A., Alahi, A., Savarese, S.: Learning social etiquette: human trajectory understanding in crowded scenes. In: Leibe, B., Matas, J., Sebe, N., Welling, M. (eds.) ECCV 2016. LNCS, vol. 9912, pp. 549–565. Springer, Cham (2016). https://doi.org/10.1007/978-3-319-46484-8_33
35. Rohan, C., et al.: METEOR: a massive dense & heterogeneous behavior dataset for autonomous driving. arXiv preprint arXiv:2109.07648 (2021)
36. Sadeghian, A., Kosaraju, V., Sadeghian, A., Hirose, N., Rezatofighi, H., Savarese, S.: SoPhie: an attentive GAN for predicting paths compliant to social and physical constraints. In: 2019 IEEE/CVF Conference on Computer Vision and Pattern Recognition (CVPR), pp. 1349–1358 (2020)
37. Scott, E., et al.: Large scale interactive motion forecasting for autonomous driving: the waymo open motion dataset. arXiv preprint arXiv:2104.10133 (2021)
38. Shi, L., et al.: SGCN: sparse graph convolution network for pedestrian trajectory prediction. In: IEEE Conference on Computer Vision and Pattern Recognition (CVPR) (2021)
39. Song, X., et al.: Pedestrian trajectory prediction based on deep convolutional LSTM network. IEEE Trans. Intell. Transp. Syst. **22**(6), 3285–3302 (2021)
40. Song, Y., Bisagno, N., Hassan, S.Z., Conci, N.: AG-GAN: an attentive group-aware GAN for pedestrian trajectory prediction. In: 2020 25th International Conference on Pattern Recognition (ICPR), pp. 8703–8710 (2021)
41. Tim, S., Boris, I., Punarjay, C., Marco, P.: Trajectron++: multi-agent generative trajectory forecasting with heterogeneous data for control. In: IEEE Conference on Computer Vision and Pattern Recognition (CVPR), pp. 683–700 (2020)
42. Vemula, A., Muelling, K., Oh, J.: Social attention: modeling attention in human crowds, pp. 1–7 (2018)
43. Vineet, K., Amir, S., Roberto, M.M., Lan, R.: Social-BiGAT: multimodal trajectory forecasting using bicycle-GAN and graph attention networks. In: Advances in Neural Information Processing Systems (NeurIPS), pp. 137–146 (2019)
44. University of Waterloo: uwaterloo (2021). http://wiselab.uwaterloo.ca/waterloo-multi-agent-traffic-dataset/
45. Wei, Z., et al.: Interaction dataset: an international, adversarial and cooperative motion dataset in interactive driving scenarios with semantic maps. arXiv preprint arXiv:1910.03088 (2019)
46. Wu, Z., Pan, S., Chen, F., Long, G., Zhang, C., Yu, P.S.: A comprehensive survey on graph neural networks. IEEE Trans. Neural Netw. Learn. Syst. **32**(1), 4–24 (2019)

47. Xin, L., Xiaowen, Y., Chuah, M.C.: GRIP++: enhanced graph-based interaction-aware trajectory prediction for autonomous driving. arXiv preprint arXiv:1907.07792 (2020)
48. Xu, Y., Ren, D., Li, M., Chen, Y., Fan, M., Xia, H.: Tra2Tra: trajectory-to-trajectory prediction with a global social spatial-temporal attentive neural network. IEEE Robot. Autom. Lett. **6**(2), 1574–1581 (2021)
49. Yuexin, M., Dinesh, M., Wenping, W.: AutoRVO: local navigation with dynamic constraints in dense heterogeneous traffic. arXiv preprint arXiv:1804.02915 (2018)
50. Yuexin, M., Xinge, Z., Sibo, Z., Ruigang, Y., Wenping, W., Dinesh, M.: TrafficPredict: trajectory prediction for heterogeneous traffic-agents. In: Proceedings of the AAAI Conference on Artificial Intelligence, vol. 33, no. 01, pp. 6120–6127 (2019)
51. Yuning, C., Benjamin, S., Mayank, B., Dragomir, A.: MultiPath: multiple probabilistic anchor trajectory hypotheses for behavior prediction. arXiv:1910.05449 (2019)
52. Zernetsch, S., Kohnen, S., Goldhammer, M., Doll, K., Sick, B.: Trajectory prediction of cyclists using a physical model and an artificial neural network. In: 2016 IEEE Intelligent Vehicles Symposium (IV), pp. 833–838 (2016)
53. Zhang, K., Zhao, L., Dong, C., Wu, L., Zheng, L.: AI-TP: attention-based interaction-aware trajectory prediction for autonomous driving. IEEE Trans. Intell. Veh. 1 (2022). https://doi.org/10.1109/TIV.2022.3155236
54. Zhao, L., et al.: T-GCN: a temporal graph convolutional network for traffic prediction. IEEE Trans. Intell. Transp. Syst. **21**(9), 3848–3858 (2019)
55. Zhao, Z., Liu, C.: STUGCN: a social spatio-temporal unifying graph convolutional network for trajectory prediction. In: 2021 6th International Conference on Automation, Control and Robotics Engineering (CACRE), pp. 546–550 (2021)
56. Zheng, F., et al.: Unlimited neighborhood interaction for heterogeneous trajectory prediction. In: 2021 IEEE/CVF International Conference on Computer Vision (ICCV), pp. 13148–13157 (2021). https://doi.org/10.1109/ICCV48922.2021.01292
57. Zhengping, C., et al.: D^2-City: a large-scale dashcam video dataset of diverse traffic scenarios. arXiv preprint arXiv:1904.01975 (2019)
58. Zhou, J., et al.: Graph neural networks: a review of methods and applications. AI Open **1**, 57–81 (2020). https://doi.org/10.1016/j.aiopen.2021.01.001

The Missing Link: Finding Label Relations Across Datasets

Jasper Uijlings$^{(\boxtimes)}$, Thomas Mensink, and Vittorio Ferrari

Google Research, Zürich, Switzerland
jrru@google.com

Abstract. Computer vision is driven by the many datasets available for training or evaluating novel methods. However, each dataset has a different set of class labels, visual definition of classes, images following a specific distribution, annotation protocols, etc. In this paper we explore the automatic discovery of visual-semantic relations between labels across datasets. We aim to understand how instances of a certain class in a dataset relate to the instances of another class in another dataset. Are they in an *identity, parent/child, overlap* relation? Or is there no link between them at all? To find relations between labels across datasets, we propose methods based on language, on vision, and on their combination. We show that we can effectively discover label relations across datasets, as well as their type. We apply our method to four applications: understand label relations, identify missing aspects, increase label specificity, and predict transfer learning gains. We conclude that label relations cannot be established by looking at the names of classes alone, as they depend strongly on how each of the datasets was constructed.

1 Introduction

Progress in computer vision is fueled by the availability of many different datasets, covering a wide spectrum of appearance domains and annotated for various task types, like ImageNet for classification [6], Open Images for detection [15], and KITTI for semantic segmentation of driving scenes [8]. Each of these datasets has its own set of class labels, its own visual definition for each class, its own set of images following a specific distribution, its own annotation protocols, and was labeled by a different group of humans annotators. As a result, the visual-semantical meaning of a certain label in a particular dataset is unique [22,26]. A few examples: (1) a `sofa` in ADE20k refers to the same visual concept as a `couch` in COCO, even though their class label is different;

J. Uijlings and T. Mensink—Equal contribution.

Supplementary Information The online version contains supplementary material available at https://doi.org/10.1007/978-3-031-20074-8_31.

(2) ADE20k distinguishes `stool`, `armchair`, and `swivel chair` whereas COCO has a single concept `chair`. Moreover it is unclear if instances of `stool` would adhere to the annotation definition of the `chair` class in COCO; (3) ADE20k has the labels `floor` and `rug` whereas COCO distinguishes `floor-wood` and `rug-merged`. These are two ways of categorizing the visual world which are not fully compatible: a full-floor carpet is both a `floor` and a `rug-merged`, while a wooden floor is only a `floor` and a doormat is only a `rug-merged` (see also Fig. 1c).

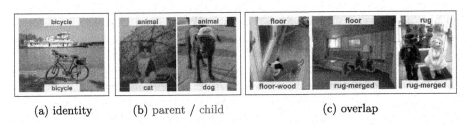

(a) identity   (b) parent / child   (c) overlap

Fig. 1. Examples of relations: (a) *identity*: both bicycle labels contain similar instances; (b) *parent/child*: the `animal` class contains instances which are either `cat` or `dog`; (c) `floor` and `rug-merged` *overlap* in the middle instance. But each label contains instances which are incompatible with the other label.

In this paper we want to automatically discover relations between labels across datasets. We aim to determine if the ADE20k `lake` and COCO `water-other` labels are related in their visual semantics. More specifically, are there visual instances which can be described by both labels? And what is the *type* of their relation? Do they represent the same visual concept? Are they in a parent/child relation? Or do they overlap like `floor` and `rug-merged`? Establishing such relations would enable combining datasets. This is useful for training on larger dataset with more visual concepts and more samples per concept, and also for evaluation purposes.

Joining datasets cannot be done by simply looking at the class label names; how labels across datasets are related really depends on the idiosyncrasies of each dataset involved. Indeed, Lambert et al. [16] recently proposed to unify multiple datasets into a single and consistent label space. This required a tremendous amount of manual work: matching all labels, visually verifying whether labels actually point to the same visual concepts, and re-annotating significant portions of each dataset into a single, mutually exclusive label space. Essentially [16] manually solved some of the kind of problems we want to address automatically. But also their result is prone to similar issues as described, their result depends on choices made for the definitions of labels, the annotation protocol, *etc.* Moreover as the number of datasets continues to grow, such heroic manual joining operation becomes infeasible and it will be necessary to do this automatically.

In this paper, we present methods for the automatic discovery of relations between labels across dataset. We distinguish different relation types

(Table 1): *identity* (e.g. ADE20k `bicycle` and COCO `bicycle`), *parent/child* (e.g. ADE20k `animal` and COCO `dog`), and *overlap* (e.g. ADE20k `floor` and COCO `rug-merged`). We introduce methods to establish these relations by leveraging language cues, visual cues, and a combination of both.

In short, this paper presents an exploration into the discovery of how labels across datasets relate to each other. Our contributions are as follows: (1) We introduce a variety of methods to discover the existence of relations between labels across datasets, as well as their type (Sect. 3). These methods include vision, language, and their combination. (2) We demonstrate that we can effectively and automatically discover label relations between three semantic segmentation datasets: COCO [5,13,17], ADE20k [33], and Berkeley Deep Drive (BDD) [31] (Sect. 4). To evaluate this quantitatively we leverage the MSeg annotations [16] to establish ground-truth label relations between these datasets. Additionally, we show that we can discover relations between different *types* of datasets by applying our method to ILSVRC12 image classification and COCO segmentation (supp. mat. Sect. A). (3) We demonstrate the usefulness of our method in four applications: *Understand label relations* (Sect. 5.1), in which we gain a deeper understanding of what types of relations exist and why they arise in practice; *Identify missing aspects* (Sect. 5.2), where we determine how datasets vary in covering appearance variability of a class; *Increase label specificity* (Sect. 5.3), where we can relabel instances of a class at a finer-grained level; *Predict transfer learning gains* (supp. mat. Sect. B), where our label relations can predict the gains brought by transfer learning.

2   Related Work

Dataset Creation and Evolution. In computer vision there is a long standing history to create datasets for training and benchmarking methods. There are too many to recall here, but interestingly many popular dataset have evolved over time, either by growing the number of images, like ImageNet [6], the number of classes, like PASCAL-VOC [7] from 4 classes in 2005 to 20 in 2007, or in the types of annotation, like COCO [17] to COCO-stuff [4] to COCO-panoptic [12]. Other datasets evolve by merging, for example the SUNRGB-D [34] dataset combined imagery from among others NYU-depth-v2 [25] and SUN3D [30], while the ADE20K [33] dataset contains imagery from SUN [29] and Places [34].

In this paper we use the COCO-panoptic dataset [5,12,17], ADE20K [33] and BDD [31]. Instead of considering these dataset individually, we explore how the visual concepts in these dataset *relate* to each other. The relations we find could be used when aiming to combine these datasets or when aiming to train more generic models across different datasets.

Learning over Diverse Image Domains. Any single dataset has issues by its design [22], bias [26], or evaluation robustness [32]. Therefore a recent trend is to train or evaluate algorithms over multiple datasets. For example in the Robust Vision Challenge [1] participants are asked to evaluate a single trained model over multiple datasets and the winner is based on the average performance. To facilitate this, collection of datasets have been introduced, for example, Visual Decathlon for image classification [24], Meta-Dataset for few-shot learning [27], and MSeg for semantic segmentation [16].

Training tactics to successfully use multiple datasets differ, from training a single model with different heads over all datasets jointly [14], to learn in stages, *i.e.*, first on ImageNet, then tune on COCO and finally fine-tune on PASCAL-VOC [19]; and from using manually merged labels [2,16], to post-hoc merging of labels for detection [35]. In contrast to these approaches, our aim is not to train a new model with better classifiers, but we aim to analyze more fundamentally how datasets relate to each other.

Table 1. Definition of types of label relations we distinguish. In this paper we aim to automatically identify all relations (Sect. 3) except the *part-of* relation.

Identity   Label a in one dataset indicates the same visual concept as label b in another dataset. For example `sofa` in ADE20k and `couch` in COCO represent the same visual concept.

Parent/child   A subcategory relationship. For example, `animal` in ADE20k is the parent of `cow` in COCO.

Overlap   Label a in one dataset and label b in another describe visual concepts which are not the same even though their sets of instances intersect. For example, the ADE20k `floor` and COCO `rug-merged` both describe a floor-covering carpet. Yet both concepts are broader in a mutually exclusive way: `floor` also includes a wooden floor which is not a `rug-merged`. Conversely, `rug-merged` also includes a rug which can be picked up which is not a `floor`.

Part-of   Label a in one dataset captures parts of instances of label b in another dataset. For example, `roof` in COCO describes part of an instance of `house` in ADE20k.

Zero-Shot and Open Set Segmentation. For both zero-shot and open set segmentation the goal is to obtain pixel-wise predictions for never-seen labels using zero training examples [3,9]. Both aim to learn classifiers which generalize the set of training classes to a fixed set of never seen labels [3] or open vocabulary queries [9]. This works by establishing (language) based relations between seen and unseen classes, for example based on large scale contrastive pre-training on images and textual queries [11,23]. In contrast to these methods, our aim is not to train generalizable classifiers, but to find the relations between visual concepts in both datasets, for which we can make use of the available annotations.

3   Method

In this paper we want to automatically discover relations between class labels across two given datasets A and B. We consider all possible pairs $\langle a, b \rangle$ of labels

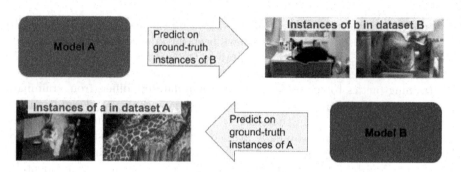

Fig. 2. Illustration of how to obtain label link scores between ADE20k `animal` and COCO `cat`, we estimate $S_{a \to b}(\texttt{animal}, \texttt{cat})$ using the model trained on ADE20K and $S_{b \to a}(\texttt{cat}, \texttt{animal})$ using the model trained on COCO.

a in A and b in B. For each pair we want to determine if they are *related*, i.e. where there are visual instances which are covered by both the definition of a and b, and we also want to determine the *type* of the relation (Table 1).

We distinguish *identity, parent/child, overlap,* and *part-of* (focusing mostly on the first three). Importantly, the existence of a relation between two labels and its type cannot be derived simply by considering their names. Instead, they are specific to the pair datasets from which they originate, because they depend on the design and construction of each dataset.

3.1   Discovering Relations Using Visual Information

We first discuss how we discover relations and their type using purely visual information, as illustrated in Fig. 2). We do this in the context of semantic segmentation, but our method would also work for object detection. To determine whether there exist a relation between label a in dataset A and b in dataset B, we use annotated *instances*[1] of these classes in their respective datasets.

We use a model p_A trained on dataset A to obtain predictions $p_A(a|i_b)$ for label a for an instance i_b with label b from dataset B. Next, we average these predictions:

$$S_{a \to b} = \frac{1}{n_b} \sum_{i_b \in B} p_A(a|i_b) \tag{1}$$

where n_b is the number of instances of label b in dataset B. Intuitively, this measures how likely it is that the instances of $i_{b=\texttt{cat}}$ from the COCO dataset (B) would be called $a = \texttt{animal}$ according to the model trained on ADE20k (dataset A). Similarly we obtain $S_{b \to a}$ by aggregating predictions of p_B over instances of dataset A. The final score is the average: $R_{a,b} = (S_{a \to b} + S_{b \to a})/2$. To determine whether there is a relation between label a and label b, we simply threshold $R_{a,b}$. This results in a set $\mathcal{R}$ of binary relations.

---

[1] An instance is either a single object (for thing classes, e.g. `cat`, `car`), or the union of all regions of a stuff class (e.g. `grass`, `water`), following the panoptic definition [13].

Experimentally we evaluate two different c $p_A(a|i_b)$:

- *Pixel Probabilities*: applying a segmentation model trained on dataset A directly on instances of dataset B. To convert to instance probabilities we average the pixel-wise probabilities over all pixels of the instance;
- *Visual Embeddings*: we extract instance visual features for both dataset A and dataset B by aggregating the pixel-wise visual features, using the same segmentation model (trained on dataset A) without the classification head. Then we use a 1-Nearest Neighbour classifier. This results in a binary prediction *i.e.* $p_A(a|i_b)$ is either 1 or 0. We do the analogue for $p_B(b|i_a)$.

Training Details. We train semantic segmentation models using an HRNetV2-W48 [28] backbone with a linear pixel-wise prediction head and a softmax-loss. This results in a strong model for semantic segmentation [16,19,28]. We unify the training setup to make the models compatible across datasets, using color normalization, horizontal flipping, random crop and resize to 713×713. We optimize using SGD with momentum, with lr $= 0.01$ decreased by a factor 10 after 2/3rd of the number of training steps (optimized per dataset).

While for semantic segmentation typically the `background` class is ignored during training and evaluation we find it useful to incorporate it explicitly. The `background` prediction can be interpreted as the model predicting *none of the classes from my label space*. Moreover, we find it beneficial to only aggregate over *easy* instances to factor out errors introduced by miss-classification of difficult instances. To do so we use instances which are classified correctly by the model trained on the same dataset. More specifically, we define instances to be easy for the pixel probability method if $p_B(b|i_b) > 0.5$. They are easy for the visual embedding method if $p_B(b|i_b) = 1$.

3.2   Relation Type Discovery

We estimate the *type* of relation (Table 1) in two different ways, one based on set theory and the other on the degree of asymmetry between $S_{a \rightarrow b}$ and $S_{b \rightarrow a}$.

Set Theory. To derive the relation types we make two assumptions: (1) There is only a relation between label a and label b if there are instances which can be categorized as both a and b, so $\langle a, b \rangle \in \mathcal{R}$; (2) Labels from the same dataset are mutually exclusive. Then we derive the types between a_k and b_l as follows:

- *identity*: a_k and b_l have an identity relation when neither a_k nor b_l has a relation with another label. More formally, $\langle a_k, b_l \rangle \in \mathcal{R}$, but $\nexists a_m, \langle a_m, b_l \rangle \in \mathcal{R}, a_m \neq a_k$ and $\nexists b_n, \langle a_k, b_n \rangle \in \mathcal{R}, b_n \neq b_l$.
- *parent/child*: A label a_k is a parent if it is related to at least two labels in B (including b_l), which are not related to any other label in A. More formally, for at least two labels b_l and b_n, $b_l \neq b_n$, it holds that $\langle a_k, b_l \rangle \in \mathcal{R}$ and $\langle a_k, b_n \rangle \in \mathcal{R}$. Yet, $\nexists a_m, [\langle a_m, b_l \rangle \in \mathcal{R} \lor \langle a_m, b_n \rangle \in \mathcal{R}], a_m \neq a_k$. Analogously, a_k is a child of b_l if their roles are reversed.

- *overlap*: both labels a_k and b_l are used in multiple relations. Formally, $\langle a_k, b_l \rangle \in \mathcal{R}$ and $\exists a_m, \langle a_m, b_l \rangle \in \mathcal{R}, a_m \neq a_k$ and $\exists b_n, \langle a_k, b_n \rangle \in \mathcal{R}, b_n \neq b_l$.

Score Asymmetry. We exploit the asymmetry between $S_{a \to b}$ and $S_{b \to a}$ to provide the type of the relation. Intuitively, for a *parent-child* relation, we expect that an `animal` classifier gives high scores on `cat` instances, while the `cat` classifier only gives high scores on *some* of the `animal` instances. Therefore, a large asymmetry between $S_{a \to b}$ and $S_{b \to a}$ suggests that the labels are in a *parent-child* relation. Given a pair of labels $(a, b) \in \mathcal{R}$ we derive the label as follows: 1) a is a *parent* of b, if $\frac{S_{a \to b}}{S_{b \to a}} > T$; else 2) a is a *child* of b, if $\frac{S_{b \to a}}{S_{a \to b}} > T$; otherwise 3) a and b are in an *identity* relation. Note this method cannot predict *overlap*.

3.3   Predicting Relation Types Using Language

We introduce two baseline methods which use language to discover relations.

WordNet. We use the WordNet [21] taxonomy and its graphical structure. Specifically, we map each class label to a WordNet noun-synset. Then, if a and b map to the same synset, they are in an *identity* relation. When the synset of a is an ancestor of the synset of b, then a is a *parent* of b. If two synsets share at least one descendant, they are in an *overlap* relation. For example, in WordNet `car` and `truck` overlap since they both have `minivan` as a descendent.

For each pair of labels (a, b) we estimate the `path similarity` between the two synsets, which is based on the proximity of their nearest common ancestor. Then we add 1 if a and b have a relation according to the taxonomy. This yields a dense matrix R, with pairs discovered as *identity* have a strength of 2, as *parent*, *child*, or *overlap* have a strength between 1 and 2, and the rest between 0 and 1.

Word2Vec. Our second baseline uses Word2Vec [20], based on the publicly available model trained on Wikipedia [10]. This maps each word to a 500-D embedding vector. The score between each paper of labels a, b is based on the cosine similarity between their embeddings. Since this is a symmetric similarity, we can only use the *set theory* method to determine relation types.

3.4   Discovering Relations by Combining Vision and Language

We combine our Visual Embeddings method with our WordNet method. We multiply the strength of the visual relation $R_{a,b}$ by a constant factor n if the synset of a and the synset of b are related according to the taxonomy (i.e. we discover *identity, parent, child,* or *overlap*).

To discover the relation type, we combine the visual *asymmetry* method and the WordNet predictions: If according to WordNet a and b are in an *identity* relation, we enlarge threshold T of the *asymmetry* method by a factor m. This makes it more likely that *identity* will be predicted. Similarly, when according to WordNet a and b are in a *parent/child* relation, we reduce T by a factor m.

3.5   Evaluation

To evaluate how well we are able to automatically discover relations between labels across datasets, we first establish ground-truth relations[2]. We leverage the MSeg dataset [16], who manually constructed a unified label space across a variety of different datasets, which we refer to as *MSeg labels* (Fig. 3). Based on this, we first map dataset A and dataset B to the MSeg label space, and then create direct relations between labels in A and B.

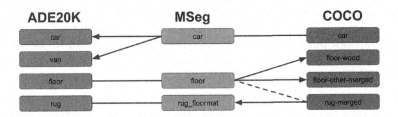

Fig. 3. To create relations between ADE20k and COCO, we first establish relations between each individual dataset and MSeg. Based on set theory (Sect. 3.1) we establish *identity* (—), *parent/child* (➔), and *overlap* (- -) relations. Afterwards, through MSeg we derive direct relations between ADE20k and COCO.

Establishing Relations to the MSeg Label Space. The MSeg dataset provides for all dataset which they cover a new ground-truth in the unified MSeg label space. This MSeg ground-truth covers a different set of labels than the original ground-truth for each dataset; for each dataset the authors merged some classes and re-annotated other classes to obtain a consistent labeling of each dataset according to the MSeg label space [16]. We compare the MSeg ground-truth with the original ground-truth to establish relations.

In particular, we count how many times an instance with a particular label in the original label space is relabeled to each MSeg label. For an instance to count being relabeled, more than 50% of its pixels need to have been relabeled. This makes the process robust against small manual corrections made during the MSeg relabeling effort. We manually inspect all label pairs with a positive count, and remove them when this is caused by a human error (low counts typically help identify these cases). For example, a few instances of COCO `tent` have been relabeled to the MSeg `kite`, while these labels are clearly unrelated. All remaining pairs are considered as related in our ground-truth.

To derive the type of relation, we apply the *set theory* method from Sect. 3.1, and then manually investigate all relations. We found that almost no human correction was needed at this stage. The only exception was that a few relations were changed to *part-of*, which the set theory method cannot automatically produce. For example, COCO `roof` is *part-of* the MSeg `building`.

---

[2] Available at: https://github.com/google-research/google-research/tree/master/missing_link.

Establishing Relations Between A and B. Through the MSeg labels, we can directly relate the original labels between datasets (Fig. 3). The type of relation depends on the type of the two individual relations with MSeg. When both relations are *identity*, the resulting relation is that as well. Two consecutive *child* relations or one *identity* and one *child* relation result in a *child* relation. For example, ADE20k `van` is a *child* of COCO `car`. The *parent* relation is analogous to *child*. If one relation is *part-of*, the resulting relation is *part-of* as well. For all other cases, we manually inspect visual examples to determine the relation type. Often this happens for *overlap* relations. But for example both COCO `person` and the ADE20k `person` have been sub-categorized by MSeg in `person`, `bicyclist`, `motorcyclist`, and `rider_other`. It requires manual inspection to verify that both `person` labels represent the same concept and hence have an *identity* relation. As before, after these steps we perform a final quality control by manually inspecting visual examples of label pairs.

Quantitative Evaluation. For two datasets, we compare our automatically predicted relations with the ground-truth we just established. We evaluate how good our methods are in predicting whether any relation is present, regardless of its type. To do so we order all possible label pairs according to their predicted strength, and calculate a Precision-Recall (PR) curve and its associated Area Under the Curve (AUC). We also measure how well our methods predicts relation types, where we also consider *no relation* predictions. We measure accuracy for each predicted type and average them to obtain an overall accuracy.

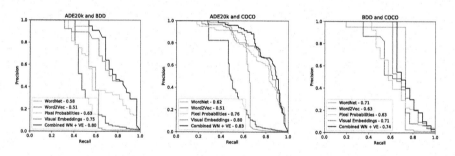

Fig. 4. Precision recall curves for different methods for (binary) label relation predictions. The visual methods perform (much) better than language-only methods and combining vision and language gives best performance.

4   Results

As our main experiment we apply and evaluate our method on all three possible pairs of the following semantic segmentation datsets: (1) ADE20k [33], a dataset of consumer photos, where we consider the 150 most frequent class labels as is common practice; (2) COCO Panoptic [5,13,17], which also contains consumer photos, with 133 classes; (3) Berkeley Deep Drive [31], a driving dataset containing 19 classes. For ease of exposition, we write the names of class labels for ADE20k in blue, for COCO in red, and for BDD in violet.

Additionally, in Sect. A of the supp. mat. we demonstrate that we can establish relations between labels of different types of datasets by applying our method to ILSVRC classification and COCO segmentation.

Relation Discovery. The Precision-Recall curves in Fig. 4 show that the language-based models are generally outperformed by the vision-based models. The model based on WordNet works better than Word2Vec, because Word2Vec gives high scores for labels which are semantically related but do not refer to the same object. For example, the Word2Vec cosine similarity between shower and toilet is 0.72 while these classes are really disjoint. The WordNet-based method has high accuracy for labels in an *identity* or *parent/child* relation according to the taxonomy, but a low recall for many other relations. Among the vision models, the Visual Embeddings method consistently outperforms the Pixel Probability method (Sect. 3.1). Finally, we obtain the best performance when combining WordNet with Visual Embeddings.

Relation Type Classification. Before we can determine relation types, we note that the *Set Theory* and *Score Asymmetry* methods have thresholds (Sect. 3.2). We establish these by optimizing accuracy with respect to the predictions made by the WordNet *taxonomy*. While the WordNet *taxonomy* method may not be fully accurate, as long as it is an unbiased estimate its optimal thresholds will also hold for the real ground-truth - which is indeed what we found.

The results in Table 2 generally align with our previous observations: WordNet is the best language-based model but the vision-based models work even better. Again, the Visual Embeddings method outperforms all others. From the two ways to determine the relation type, the one based on *Score Asymmetry* works best. Intuitively, it makes sense that this is a powerful mechanism: we expect an animal model to always yield high scores on cat instances, whereas a cat model will not give high scores to all animal instances. As before, the combination of WordNet and Visual Embeddings gives the best results.

In Fig. 5 we show the full confusion matrices for relations between ADE20k and COCO discovered by the WordNet *taxonomy*, Visual Embeddings with *Set Theory*, and Embeddings with *Asymmetry* methods. We can see that the WordNet taxonomy predicts both the identity and 'no relation' pretty well, but tends to over-predict 'no relation'. The Embeddings with *Set Theory* also over-predicts 'no relation', it is slightly worse in 'identity' but better in 'child' and 'overlap'. Embeddings with *Asymmetry* is significantly better in parent and child relations. However, it cannot predict 'overlap'.

5   Applications

We apply our method to four applications (Sect. 5.1, 5.2, 5.3, supp. mat Sect. B).

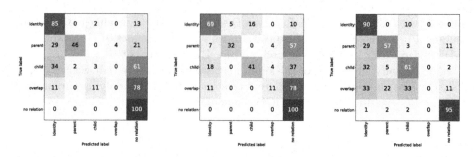

Fig. 5. Confusion matrices for relation types between ADE20K and COCO using WordNet-taxonomy (*left*), Embeddings with Set Theory (*middle*), and Embedding with Asymmetry (*right*).

Table 2. Accuracy (in percentage) of estimating relation types. Our vision-based models outperform language-only models for all pairs of datasets. and combining works best.

	Language		Vision				Vision+Language
	WordNet	Word2Vec	Pixel predictions		Visual embeddings		WordNet+Embeddings
	Taxonomy	*Set theory*	*Set theory*	*Asymmetry*	*Set theory*	*Asymmetry*	*taxonomy+asymmetry*
ADE20k, BDD	46	37	56	54	56	55	57
ADE20k, COCO	47	38	47	60	51	61	62
BDD, COCO	46	38	46	48	49	51	53
Average	46	38	50	54	52	56	57

5.1   Understand Label Relations

To gain insights into why and how labels relate, we visually inspect instances of labels with high-scoring relations, but whose labels do not exactly match. We do this for relations between ADE20k and COCO which we visualize in Fig. 6.

Identity. One of the highest scoring identity relations with non-matching labels is the ADE20k `sofa` and COCO `couch`. These are synonyms and indeed represent the same visual concept (see Fig. 6 *top left*). More interestingly, we also identify a relation between ADE20k `minibike` and COCO `motorcycle`. Semantically these are different concepts: usually a minibike denotes a tiny motorbike which is not higher than one's knees. But here both represent a full-sized motorcycle (Fig. 6 *top center*). Finally, another interesting, high-scoring identity relation we found is between `stove` and `oven` (Fig. 6 *second row*). In ADE20k the `stove` refers to the cooking panel on which you can put pots and pans, while including the oven underneath if it exists. In COCO, the `oven` refers to the closed heating compartment, including the stove if it exists. So even while `stove` and `oven` are synonyms and mostly represent the same visual concept, one could argue that the true relation is not identity but overlap, because there are instances which are `stove` but not `oven` (2nd row, left) and vice-versa (2nd row, right).

Parent/Child. One example of parent/child is between ADE20k `animal` and COCO `elephant` (Fig. 6 *top-right*). Others include `hill` and `mountain-merged`,

Fig. 6. Examples of instances of classes in ADE20k (in blue) and COCO (in red). The top rows shows examples for labels for which we find a relation. The second row shows how `stove` and `oven` categorize the visual world differently. The bottom shows different types of water which are difficult to distinguish, and different types of screens which are labeled inconsistently. (Color figure online)

`wall` and `wall-tile`. We also correctly identify that the ADE20k `tent` is a child of the COCO `tent`, since the latter also includes the ADE20k `awning`. Language alone would never be able to identify that `tent` and `tent` have a *child* relation.

Overlap. Here we look at several overlap relations found by our embeddings and logic method. It correctly identifies the overlap between `floor` and `rug-merged`. This overlap relation exists because both labels use a different reference frame of the world: `floor` emphasizes that the concept is *stuff* and not an *object*, while `rug-merged` emphasizes the function and type of material (*e.g.* fabric to walk on), see Fig. 1. We also predict an overlap relation between `water` and `water-other`, where the ground-truth relation is *child*. When visually inspecting examples, we found many examples where it was unclear what type of water the image depicts (Fig. 6 *bottom left*). Arguably, `water`, `river`, `sea`, `river`, and `water-other` all overlap, mostly caused by the visual ambiguity in images with these labels.

Inconsistencies. Finally, we found strong relations not only between `television receiver` and `tv`, but also between `crt screen`, `monitor`, `computer` and `tv`. Looking at instances, these labels often point to the same visual concepts (Fig. 6 *bottom right*). So strictly speaking, these labels visually overlap. However, this overlap is caused by labeling errors and inconsistencies in both datasets. In COCO, all displays (including computer monitors) are labeled as `tv`. Instead, in ADE20k computer monitors are alternatively labeled as `crt screen`, `monitor`, and `computer`. These concepts overlap even within ADE20k which makes the common assumption of mutually exclusive labels *within a dataset* invalid.

5.2   Identify Missing Aspects

We want to identify which appearance aspects of a class are common between two datasets, and which are covered by only one of them. Discovering this would enable combining examples from different datasets to cover the full range of visual appearances of a class. This could help train better recognition models.

For this experiment we focus on the COCO `car` and BDD `car` classes. We use the model trained on the COCO dataset and extract features for both COCO `car` and BDD `car` instances, which we aggregate per instance. We use these features to create a 2D visualisation using UMAP [18] in Fig. 7 and extract 6 different clusters for further analysis in Fig. 8.

Each of the shown clusters has some particular visual coherence, for example:

- Three clusters of cluttered streets differing in the shapes: the back of the car in the center, partial cars at the image border, and partial occluded cars.
- Two clusters with imagery captured at night, but with different instance shapes. Those clusters are mostly filled with images from the BDD dataset.
- A cluster with *parked cars next to sports*, filled with only COCO images.

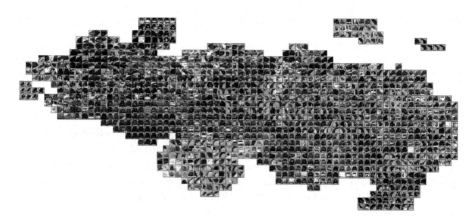

Fig. 7. Embedding of `car` instances (COCO with blue box, BDD with red). (Color figure online)

Fig. 8. Embedding with clusters of COCO `car` (orange dots) & BDD `car` (blue dots) instances (*left*) and example images sampled from each cluster (*right*). (Color figure online)

From this visual analysis we observe that there is a significant overlap in the kind of `car` segments: both datasets contain instances with a rear or side view, partially occluded instances, and instances at the edge of the image. However, we also find interesting differences in the imagery contained in the datasets: BDD is a driving dataset and hence the diversity in viewpoints of scenes is limited to the viewpoint from the dashboard. COCO, on the other hand, is a very diverse consumer dataset, where street imagery is present with much more viewpoints. That explains why we see cars near sport fields in COCO, but not in BDD.

Fig. 9. Confusion matrix (*left*) and example (*right*) evaluating re-annotation of ADE20k `animal` using the predictions of related child COCO classes.

5.3   Increase Label Specificity

In this experiment we illustrate how the discovered label relations could be used to annotate images with a finer level of annotation. Here we relabel the ADE20k `animal` instances into the related COCO classes: {`cow`, `dog`, ..., `zebra`} using the model trained on COCO, using the established label relation indicating that ADE20k `animal` is a parent class of these COCO classes.

For this experiment we use the model trained on COCO and use this model to predict fine-grained annotations on the instances belonging to the ADE20k `animal` class. In order to quantitatively evaluate these new annotations we make use of the MSeg annotations. These provide ground-truths for the ADE segments, which we use to evaluate the top-1 accuracy per class.

Figure 9 (*left*) shows the confusion matrix between MSeg ground-truths and COCO predictions on ADE instances. Figure 9 (*right*) shows examples of correctly and incorrectly classified segments. From the results we observe that for most labels the finer annotations are accurate and the errors are easily explainable.

6   Conclusion

In this paper we investigated the relations of labels across datasets. We introduced several methods to automatically discover relations and their types. Our experiments showed that our vision-based models outperformed our language-based models by a significant margin, demonstrating that relying on the semantics of the label names alone is insufficient for establishing such relationships.

We demonstrated the usefulness of establishing *visual-semantic* relationships on four applications. Among our findings, we discovered that the definition of labels across datasets can vary in subtle ways. Understanding these subtle relations is important when using multiple datasets, such as when training on a combination of datasets, when fine-tuning on a target dataset, or when merging two datasets. We hope that our work inspires more researchers to study how different datasets relate to each other and how to exploit these relations to address computer vision problems.

References

1. Robust vision challenge. http://www.robustvision.net/
2. Bevandić, P., Oršić, M., Grubišić, I., Šarić, J., Šegvić, S.: Multi-domain semantic segmentation with overlapping labels. In: Proceedings of the WACV (2022)
3. Bucher, M., Vu, T., Cord, M., Pérez, P.: Zero-shot semantic segmentation. In: NeurIPS (2019)
4. Caesar, H., Uijlings, J., Ferrari, V.: COCO-stuff dataset (2018). http://calvin.inf.ed.ac.uk/datasets/coco-stuff
5. Caesar, H., Uijlings, J., Ferrari, V.: COCO-stuff: thing and stuff classes in context. In: CVPR (2018)
6. Deng, J., Dong, W., Socher, R., Li, L.J., Li, K., Fei-fei, L.: ImageNet: a large-scale hierarchical image database. In: CVPR (2009)
7. Everingham, M., Eslami, S., van Gool, L., Williams, C., Winn, J., Zisserman, A.: The Pascal visual object classes challenge: a retrospective. IJCV **111**, 98–136 (2015). https://doi.org/10.1007/s11263-014-0733-5
8. Geiger, A., Lenz, P., Stiller, C., Urtasun, R.: Vision meets robotics: the KITTI dataset. Int. J. Robot. Res. **32**(11), 1231–1237 (2013)

9. Ghiasi, G., Gu, X., Cui, Y., Lin, T.: Open-vocabulary image segmentation. Technical report, ArXiV (2021)
10. Google: Wiki words 500 with normalization - a 500 dimensional wor2vec skip-gram model trained on English Wikipedia. https://tfhub.dev/google/Wiki-words-500-with-normalization/2
11. Jia, C., et al.: Scaling up visual and vision-language representation learning with noisy text supervision. In: ICML (2021)
12. Kirillov, A.: Panoptic challenge intro. COCO+Mapillary Joint Recognition Challenge Workshop. http://presentations.cocodataset.org/ECCV18/COCO18-Panoptic-Overview.pdf
13. Kirillov, A., He, K., Girshick, R., Rother, C., Dollár, P.: Panoptic segmentation. In: CVPR (2019)
14. Kokkinos, I.: UberNet: training a 'universal' CNN for low-, mid-, and high-level vision using diverse datasets and limited memory. In: CVPR (2017)
15. Kuznetsova, A., et al.: The open images dataset V4: unified image classification, object detection, and visual relationship detection at scale. IJCV **128**, 1956–1981 (2020). https://doi.org/10.1007/s11263-020-01316-z
16. Lambert, J., Liu, Z., Sener, O., Hays, J., Koltun, V.: MSeg: a composite dataset for multi-domain semantic segmentation. In: CVPR (2020)
17. Lin, T.-Y., et al.: Microsoft COCO: common objects in context. In: Fleet, D., Pajdla, T., Schiele, B., Tuytelaars, T. (eds.) ECCV 2014. LNCS, vol. 8693, pp. 740–755. Springer, Cham (2014). https://doi.org/10.1007/978-3-319-10602-1_48
18. McInnes, L., Healy, J., Saul, N., Grossberger, L.: UMAP: uniform manifold approximation and projection. J. Open Source Softw. **3**(29), 861 (2018)
19. Mensink, T., Uijlings, J., Kuznetsova, A., Gygli, M., Ferrari, V.: Factors of influence for transfer learning across diverse appearance domains and task types. IEEE Trans. PAMI (2021)
20. Mikolov, T., Chen, K., Corrado, G., Dean, J.: Efficient estimation of word representations in vector space. In: ICLR Workshop (2013)
21. Miller, G.: WordNet: a lexical database for English. Commun. ACM **38**(11), 39–41 (1995)
22. Ponce, J., et al.: Dataset issues in object recognition. In: Ponce, J., Hebert, M., Schmid, C., Zisserman, A. (eds.) Toward Category-Level Object Recognition. LNCS, vol. 4170, pp. 29–48. Springer, Heidelberg (2006). https://doi.org/10.1007/11957959_2
23. Radford, A., et al.: Learning transferable visual models from natural language supervision. In: ICML (2021)
24. Rebuffi, S.A., Bilen, H., Vedaldi, A.: Learning multiple visual domains with residual adapters. In: NeurIPS (2017)
25. Silberman, N., Hoiem, D., Kohli, P., Fergus, R.: Indoor segmentation and support inference from RGBD images. In: Fitzgibbon, A., Lazebnik, S., Perona, P., Sato, Y., Schmid, C. (eds.) ECCV 2012. LNCS, vol. 7576, pp. 746–760. Springer, Heidelberg (2012). https://doi.org/10.1007/978-3-642-33715-4_54
26. Torralba, A., Efros, A.: An unbiased look on dataset bias. In: CVPR (2011)
27. Triantafillou, E., et al.: Meta-dataset: a dataset of datasets for learning to learn from few examples. In: ICLR (2020)
28. Wang, J., et al.: Deep high-resolution representation learning for visual recognition. IEEE Trans. PAMI **43**(10), 3349–3364 (2020)
29. Xiao, J., Hays, J., Ehinger, K., Oliva, A., Torralba, A.: SUN database: large-scale scene recognition from Abbey to Zoo. In: CVPR (2010)

30. Xiao, J., Owens, A., Torralba, A.: SUN3D: a database of big spaces reconstructed using SfM and object labels. In: ICCV (2013)
31. Yu, F., et al.: BDD100K: a diverse driving dataset for heterogeneous multitask learning. In: CVPR (2020)
32. Zendel, O., Honauer, K., Murschitz, M., Humenberger, M., Fernandez Dominguez, G.: Analyzing computer vision data - the good, the bad and the ugly. In: CVPR (2017)
33. Zhou, B., Zhao, H., Puig, X., Fidler, S., Barriuso, A., Torralba, A.: Scene parsing through ADE20K dataset. In: CVPR (2017)
34. Zhou, B., Lapedriza, A., Xiao, J., Torralba, A., Oliva, A.: Learning deep features for scene recognition using places database. In: NeurIPS (2014)
35. Zhou, X., Koltun, V., Krähenbühl, P.: Simple multi-dataset detection. In: CVPR (2022)

Learning Omnidirectional Flow in 360° Video via Siamese Representation

Keshav Bhandari[1] , Bin Duan[2], Gaowen Liu[3], Hugo Latapie[3], Ziliang Zong[1], and Yan Yan[2(✉)]

[1] Texas State University, San Marcos, USA
[2] Illinois Institute of Technology, Chicago, USA
yyan34@iit.edu
[3] Cisco Research, San Jose, USA

Abstract. Optical flow estimation in omnidirectional videos faces two significant issues: the lack of benchmark datasets and the challenge of adapting perspective video-based methods to accommodate the omni-directional nature. This paper proposes the first perceptually natural-synthetic omnidirectional benchmark dataset with a 360° field of view, FLOW360, with 40 different videos and 4,000 video frames. We conduct comprehensive characteristic analysis and comparisons between our dataset and existing optical flow datasets, which manifest perceptual realism, uniqueness, and diversity. To accommodate the omnidirectional nature, we present a novel Siamese representation Learning framework for Omnidirectional Flow (SLOF). We train our network in a contrastive manner with a hybrid loss function that combines contrastive loss and optical flow loss. Extensive experiments verify the proposed framework's effectiveness and show up to 40% performance improvement over the state-of-the-art approaches. Our FLOW360 dataset and code are available at https://siamlof.github.io/.

Keywords: 360° optical flow dataset · Siamese flow estimation

1 Introduction

Optical flow estimation, as a fundamental problem in computer vision, has been studied over decades by early works [33,43] dated back to 80s. Before the era of modern deep learning, traditional optical flow estimation methods relied on hand-crafted features based optimizations [5,16,48], energy-based optimizations [13,32,55] and variational approaches [14,27,65]. Although deep learning-based approaches [34,38,40,58,60,69] have shown great advantages over these classical approaches, most of them are specially tailored for perspective videos. The availability of perspective optical flow datasets [6,15,28,29,47] heavily supports the advancement of these modern deep learning-based approaches. The

---

Supplementary Information The online version contains supplementary material available at https://doi.org/10.1007/978-3-031-20074-8_32.

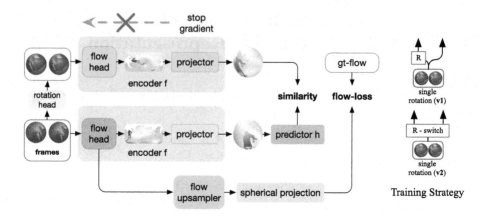

Fig. 1. Siamese Representation Learning for Omnidirectional Flow (SLOF).
Pairs of frame sequence (w/ and w/o random rotation) are passed as inputs to encoder
f (RAFT as a flow head backbone and a standard convolutional projector layer). A
predictor layer h is an MLP layer. The entire framework is trained by fusing the pre-
training and fine-tuning stage to combine the similarity and flow-loss in a single stage.
The model maximizes the similarity between latent representations of flow information from two streams and minimizes the flow loss. **Training Strategy (right):** Here
two different arrows ($left, right$) represent siamese streams or input pathways to our
model. **v1** and **v2** (either of the stream is subjected to rotational augmentation) are
similar strategies achieving overall better performance.

optical flow datasets are difficult to obtain and requires the generation of naturalistic synthetic dataset like Sintel [15]. As these datasets mark the foundation
for optical flow estimation research, the availability of reliable omnidirectional
datasets is equally important to advance the omnidirectional flow estimation
research. The need for the datasets brings up the first challenge: there is no
such reliable (perceptually natural and complex) 360° or omnidirectional video
dataset in the literature collected for omnidirectional optical flow estimation.
Another challenge of omnidirectional optical flow estimation is that current
perspective video-based deep networks fail to accommodate the nature of 360°
videos. These perspective optical flow estimation methods inevitably require fine-
tuning due to the presence of radial distortion [4] on 360° videos. This fine-tuning
task is effort-intensive and requires several transformation techniques to adapt
the distortion [22,57]. An intuitive solution is to fine-tune perspective-based
deep networks under omnidirectional supervised data. However, this brute-force
migration of perspective-based networks often requires enormous supervision
and still leads to significant performance degradation [9].

    We address the first challenge of reliable benchmark dataset shortage by
proposing a new dataset named FLOW360. To the best of our knowledge, this is
the first perceptually natural-synthetic 360° video dataset collected for omnidirectional flow estimation. Currently, existing omnidirectional datasets face two
significant issues i.e., lack of full 360° FOV (field of view) and lack of percep-

tual realism. Specifically, OmniFlow [51] dataset only has 180° FOV failing to address the omnidirectional nature, while the dataset proposed in OmniFlowNet [3] lacks perceptual realism in scene and motion. Meanwhile, perspective optical flow datasets such as [6,15,28] have facilitated researchers in investigating perspective optical flow estimation methods [21,34,38,60,69], where the availability of such omnidirectional videos dataset is essential to advance this particular field. It is worth noting that FLOW360 dataset can be used in various other areas such as continuous flow estimation in 3-frame settings with forward and backward consistency [37,42,45], depth [24,70] and normal map estimation [64].

The accommodation to the omnidirectional nature generally requires modification of convolution layers and further refinements on the target dataset due to the presence of radial distortions [9], which is caused by projecting 360° videos (spherical) to an equirectangular plane. Existing works design various convolution layers to address the distortion problem, such as spherical convolution [11,19,56,57], spectral convolution [18,23] and tangent convolution [22]. Although these methods can achieve better performance than classical CNNs, they require immense effort with layer-wise architecture design, which is impractical for high-demanding deployment in the real-world setting.

Instead of adding new convolution layers, we design a novel SLOF (Siamese representation Learning for Omnidirectional Flow) framework (Fig. 1), which leverages the rotation-invariant property of omnidirectional videos to address the radial distortion problem. The term rotation-invariant here implies that 360° videos are rotated in a random projection such that the reverse rotation of such projection is equal to the original projection. This rotation-invariant property ensures that omnidirectional videos can be projected to a planar representation with infinite projections by rotating the spherical videos on three different axis (X, Y, Z), namely "pitch", "roll" and "yaw" operations preserving overall information. Specifically, we design a siamese representation learning framework for learning omnidirectional flow from a pair of consecutive frames and their rotated counterparts, assuming that the representations of these two cases are similar enough to generate nearly identical optical flow in the spherical domain. Besides, we design and compare different combinations of rotational augmentation and derive guidelines for selecting the most effective augmentation scheme.

To summarize, we make three major contributions in this paper: (i) we introduce FLOW360, a new optical flow dataset for omnidirectional videos, to fill the dataset's need to advance the omnidirectional flow estimation field. (ii) We propose SLOF, a novel framework for optical flow estimation in omnidirectional videos, to mitigate the cumbersome framework adjustments for omnidirectional flow estimation. (iii) We demonstrate a new distortion-aware error measure for performance analysis that incorporates the relative error measure based on distortion. Finally, we compare our method with existing omnidirectional flow estimation techniques via kernel transformation [57] to address radial distortions. The FLOW360 dataset, the SLOF framework, and our experimental results provide a solid foundation for future exploration in this important field.

2   Related Work

Optical Flow Datasets. Perspective datasets such as [6,7,26,41,44,49] comprise synthetic image sequences along with synthetic and hand-crafted optical flow. However, these datasets fall short in terms of perceptual realism and complexities. Even though several optical flow datasets have been published recently in [28,29,46,47], they are primarily used in automotive driving scenarios. The other relevant dataset in the literature was Sintel [15], which provided a bridge to contemporary optical flow estimation and synthetic datasets that can be used in real-world situations.

All datasets, as mentioned earlier, are introduced for perspective videos thus cannot be used for omnidirectional flow estimation. So to address this problem, LiteFlowNet360 [9] on omnidirectional flow estimation was released to augment the Sintel dataset by introducing distortion artifacts for the domain adaptation task. Nevertheless, these augmented datasets are discontinuous around the edges and violate the 360° nature of omnidirectional videos. The closest datasets to ours are OmniFlow [51] and OmniFlowNet [3]. OmniFlow introduced a synthetic 180° FOV dataset, which is limited to indoor scenes and lacks full 360° FOV. Similarly, OmniFlowNet introduced a full 360° FOV dataset. However, both datasets lack complexities and evidence for perceptual realism. We show a detailed comparison of FLOW360, OmniFlow, and OmniFlowNet in Fig. 5. Compared to existing datasets in the literature, FLOW360 is the first perceptually natural benchmark 360° dataset and fills the void in current research.

Optical Flow Estimation. Advancements in optical flow estimation techniques largely rely on the success of data-driven deep learning frameworks. Flownet [21] marked one of the initial adoption of CNN- based deep learning frameworks for optical flow estimation. Several other works [2,34,38,39,50,61,62,67] followed the footsteps with improved results. Generally, these networks adopt an encoder-decoder framework to learn optical flow in a coarse-to-fine manner. The current framework RAFT [60] has shown improvements with correlation learning.

The methods mentioned above are insufficient on omnidirectional flow field estimation as they are designed and trained for perspective datasets. One of the initial work [52] on omnidirectional flow estimation was presented as flow estimation by back-projecting image points to the virtually curved retina, thus called back-projection flow. It showed an improvement over classical algorithms. Similarly, another classical approach [20] relied on spherical wavelet to compute optical flow on omnidirectional videos. However, these methods are limited to classical approaches as they are not relevant in existing deep learning-based approaches. One of the recent works, LiteFlowNet360 [9] tried to compute optical flow on omnidirectional videos using domain adaptation. This method utilized the kernel transformer technique (KTN [57]) to adapt convolution layers on Lite-FlowNet [34] and learn correct convolution mapping on spherical data. Similarly, OmniFlowNet [3] proposed a deep learning-based optical flow estimation technique for omnidirectional videos. The major drawback of these methods is the requirement to adapt convolution layers, which takes a substantial amount of time and makes portability a significant issue. For example, in LiteFlowNet360, each convolution layer in LiteFlowNet was transformed using KTN with additional training and adjustments. Similar to OmniFlowNet, every convolution layer in LiteFlowNet2 [35] was transformed using kernel mapping [25] based on different locations of the spherical image. These techniques incur computational overheads and limit the use of existing architectures. Such approaches demand explicit adaptation of convolution layers, which is hard to maintain when more up-to-date methods are published constantly. Contrary to these methods, we propose a Siamese Representation Learning for Omnidirectional Flow (SLOF) method to learn omnidirectional flow by exploiting existing architectures with designed representation learning objectives, significantly reducing the unnecessary effort of transforming or redesigning the convolution layer.

Siamese Representation Learning. Representation learning is a powerful approach in unsupervised learning. Siamese networks have shown great success in different vision-related tasks such as verification [12,12,59] and tracking [8]. A recent approach [17] in siamese representation learning showed impressive results in unsupervised visual representation learning via exploiting different augmentation views of the same data. They presented their work in pre-training and fine-tuning stages, where the former being the unsupervised representation learning. We use the representation learning scheme on omnidirectional data via rotational augmentations, maximizing the similarity for latent representations and minimizing the flow loss.

3   FLOW360 Dataset

FLOW360 is an optical flow dataset tailored for 360° videos using Blender [10]. This dataset contains naturalistic 360° videos, forward and backward optical flow, and dynamic depth information. The dataset comprises 40 different videos extracted from huge 3D-World 'The Room', 'Modern', 'Alien Planet', and 'City Rush'. Due to their size, this 3D-World cannot be rendered at once in a single video. We render several parts of this 3D-World, which provides enough qualitative variation in motion and visual perception like 3D-assets, textures, and illuminations. The nature of this large and diverse animated world provides relatively enough diversity to qualify for a standard benchmark dataset. The Fig. 3 shows some of the examples of motion and scene diversity of FLOW360. Similarly, samples from the dataset of different 3D-World are shown in Fig. 2. We build these 3D-World using publicly available 3D models [31,36,66] and 3D animated characters [1,54,63]. Meanwhile, we adopt Blender [10] for additional rigging and animation for the dataset.

FLOW360 contains 40 video clips extracted from different parts of huge 3D-World, 'The Room', 'Alien Planet', 'City Rush', and 'Modern'. The datasets also contain other information like depth maps and normal fields extracted from the 3D-World. The FLOW360 dataset has 4,000 video frames, 4,000 depth maps, and 3,960 flow fields. We divide the video frames into 2700/1300 train/test split. We render the video frames with the dimension of (512, 1024) to save the rendering time. However, FLOW360 can be rendered with higher resolution, as 3D models and Blender add-ons (provided in material) will also be public.

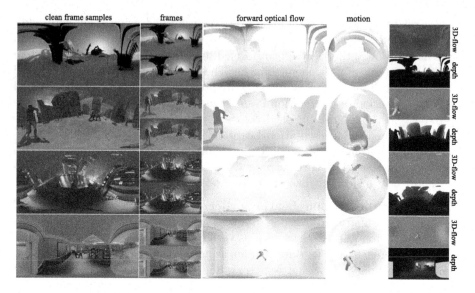

Fig. 2. The FLOW360 Dataset. Sample frames (first and second column, respectively) from some of the videos with corresponding forward optical flow and dynamic depth information. Motion in 3D Sphere (fourth column) is computed by transforming the motion vectors from Equirectangular plane (θ, ϕ) to unit sphere $f(x, y, z)$. Motion in the sphere is represented in RGBA color notation. RGB color representation (as suggested in Middlebury [6]) is encoded using (x, y) components, and the alpha color is encoded from z of a unit sphere. RGB encoding (fifth column) is an RGB color map of flow in 3D space. **Note:** flow fields are clipped for better visualization.

Diversity. We design FLOW360 datasets to include a diverse situation that resembles the real world scenario as much as possible. The statistical validity of the datasets in terms of perceptual realism of scene and motion is presented in Fig. 5. The datasets contain a wide range of motion complexity from smaller to larger displacement, occlusion, motion blur, and similar complexities on the scene using camera focus-defocus, shadow, reflections, and several distortion combinations. As these complexities are quite common in natural videos, the FLOW360 provides similar complexities. Similarly, the datasets cover diverse scenarios like environmental effects, textures, 3D assets, and diverse illuminations. The qualitative presentation of these diversities and complexities are presented in Fig. 3 and Fig. 4 respectively.

Fairness. The FLOW360 dataset contains custom-tailored animated 360 videos. We plan to release the dataset with the 3D models and our custom Blender add-ons to provide researchers a platform to create their custom optical flow datasets for all kinds of environments (perspective, 180° and 360° FOV). However, the release of 3D world scenes can raise questions regarding fairness. To mitigate this issue, we will perturb certain parts of 3D world scenes and not release any camera information related to the test set.

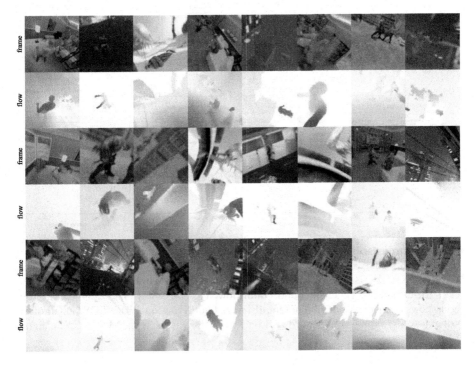

Fig. 3. Motion and Scene Diversity. Samples from FLOW360 Dataset with random projection (pitch, roll, yaw, fov) showing scene and motion diversity. The FLOW360 dataset has a vast scene consisting of several lighting scenarios, textures, diverse 3D assets, and motion complexity in different regions.

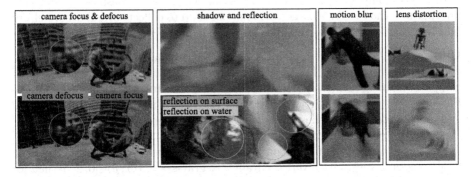

Fig. 4. Complexity of FLOW360 Dataset. Final frames in FLOW360 Dataset include complex characteristics like camera focus/defocus, motion blur, lens distortion, shadow, and reflections. Our dataset provides ambiance occlusion and environmental effects for a realistic visual appearance.

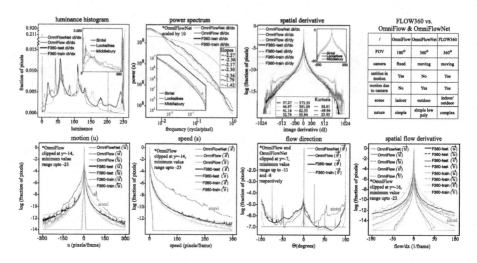

Fig. 5. Comparison of frames and flow statistics. Top row represents the frames statistics and comparison with Sintel, Lookalikes, Middlebury, OmniFlow [51] and OmniFlowNet [3]. Bottom row represents flow statistics and comparison with Sintel (red), OmniFlow (magenta) and OmniFlowNet (turquoise). The table on the top-right shows a brief comparision of OmniFlow & OmniFlowNet with FLOW360 dataset. **Note:** ($\rightarrow$, $\leftarrow$) represents forward and backward flow fields, respectively. (Color figure online)

Render Passes. We exploit several modern features from Blender-v2.92 like advanced ray-tracing as a render engine along with render passes like vector, normal, depth, mist, and so on to produce realistic 3D scenes. Additionally, we incorporate features like ambient occlusion, motion blur, camera focus/defocus, smooth shading, specular reflection, shadow, and camera distortion to introduce naturalistic complexity (shown in Fig. 4) in our dataset. Besides optical flow information, the FLOW360 3D-world may be used to collect several other helpful information like depth, normal maps, and semantic segmentation.

Dataset Statistics. We conduct a comprehensive analysis and compare our dataset with Sintel [15], Lookalikes (presented in the original Sintel paper to compare the image statistics with the simulated dataset), Middlebury [6], Omni-Flow [51] and OmniFlowNet [3]. The analysis shown in Fig. 5 shows the image and motion statistics in the top and bottom rows, respectively.

Based on analysis from Sintel, we present frame statistics with three different analysis: luminance histogram, power spectrum, and spatial derivative. For luminance statistics, we convert the frames to gray-scale, $I(x, y) \in [0, 255]$ then we compute histograms of gray-scale images across all pixels in the entire dataset. The luminance statistics show the FLOW360 has a similar distribution with the peak in the range between $[0-100]$ and decreasing luminosity beyond that range. Similarly, we estimate power spectra from the 2D FFT of the 512×512 in the center of each frame. We compute the average of these power spectra across all the datasets. We present power spectra analysis separately for the training and test set in this analysis. The power spectra analysis closely resembles the Sintel, Lookalikes, and Middlebury datasets. Based on [26,53], the real-world movies exhibit a characteristic of a power spectrum slope around -2, which is equivalent to a $1/f^2$ falloff. FLOW360 with the slope $(-2.30, -2.36)$ on test and training split shows such characteristics. We do not claim that FLOW360 is realistic, but it certainly exhibits perceptual similarity with natural movies. The spatial and temporal derivative analysis additionally supports this characteristic. The Kurtosis of frames spatial derivatives range from 32.74 to 57.27, peaked at zero. This characteristic shows that FLOW360 has a resemblance to natural scenes [26].

Regarding the flow field analysis we directly compare the distribution of motion $u(x, y)$, speed defined as $s(x, y) = \sqrt{u(x, y)^2 + v(x, y)^2}$, flow direction $\Theta(x, y) = \tan^{-1}(v(x, y)/u(x, y))$ and spatial flow derivative of u and v. The close resemblance of the flow field statistics between Sintel and FLOW360 suggests motion field resemblance with natural movies. Based on these comparisons, FLOW360 exhibits sufficient properties evident enough for its perceptual realism and complexities.

Comparison with OmniFlow and OmniFlowNet. OmniFlow [51] presents an omnidirectional flow dataset that is roughly similar to FLOW360. However, the major distinction between these datasets is the FOV. FLOW360 provides immersive 360° FOV, whereas OmniFlow provides only 180° FOV showing FLOW360 compared to OmniFlow is the true omnidirectional dataset. Similarly, OmniFlowNet [3] presents synthetic omnidirectional flow dataset with 360° FOV. However, this dataset contains low poly unnatural scenes, which can be explained by relatively larger kurtosis $(373.55, 391.09)$, characteristic of a power spectrum and luminance distribution (peaked at 255). The overall statistical analysis reveals FLOW360's better perceptual realism and diversity.

Applications. As we mentioned, the FLOW360 dataset contains frames and forward flow field and includes backward flow field, depth maps, and 3D-FLOW360 worlds, providing potential for applications like continuous flow-field estimation in 3 frames setting. Besides optical flow estimation, the FLOW360 dataset can be used in other applications such as depth and normal field estimation. Moreover, given 3D-FLOW360 animation data, the researcher can create as many optical flow datasets as needed.

4   SLOF

SLOF, as shown in Fig. 1, is inspired by the recent work on Siamese representation learning [17]. Since the method we rely on acts as a hub between several methods like contrastive learning, clustering, and siamese networks, it exhibits two special properties required for our case. First, this method has noncollapsing behavior. Here, the term collapsing refers to a situation where an optimizer finds possible minimum -1 similarity loss resulting degenerate solution (characterized by zero std of l_2-normalized output $z/||z||_2$ for each channel) while training without stop-gradient operations. Stop-gradient yields *std* value near $\frac{1}{\sqrt{d}}$ across each channel for all samples preventing such behaviour [17]. Second, it is useful when we have only positive discriminative cases. SLOF does not consider radial distortion mitigation via changing/transforming the convolution layers rather learns the equivariant properties of 360 videos via siamese representation. We claim that such transformation is trivial, based on the following fact. First, the omnidirectional videos are projected in angular domain, *w.r.t.* **polar**(θ), **azimuthal**(ϕ); $\theta\in(-\frac{\pi}{2},\frac{\pi}{2})$, $\phi\in(-\pi,\pi)$, so we can learn flow fields in these domains and convert these flow fields to spherical domain using planar to spherical transformations as shown in Eq. 1 and Eq. 2. Second, the intent of a convolution operator in optical flow architecture is relatively different from other applications like classification, detection, or segmentation network, where other tasks require convolution to learn relevant features (spatially consistent), the relevance of these features should stay consistent (strictly for better performance) throughout any spatial location of the images/videos. However, the convolution operation is dedicated to computing the pixel-wise displacement regardless of spatial inconsistency in the distorted region via equivariant representation learning [17]. Another important consideration of such a design is to make this method portable to any existing optical flow architecture. This eliminates the architecture re-adjustments tasks and make it powerful and portable.

Mapping Flow Field to Unit Sphere. Input to our model are equirectangular images projected in angular domain **polar**(θ), **azimuthal**(ϕ), where these angles are defined in radian as $\theta\in(-\frac{\pi}{2},\frac{\pi}{2})$, $\phi\in(-\pi,\pi)$, thus the predicted optical flow is in (θ,ϕ). These flow fields can be converted to unit sphere using planar to spherical co-ordinate transformation as shown below:

$$(x_s, y_s, z_s) = (\sin\theta\cos\phi, \sin\theta\sin\phi, \cos\theta). \tag{1}$$

We can compute sphere to catadioptric plane [30] projections to express the flow field in Cartesian co-ordinates as:

$$(x,y) = (\frac{x_s}{1-z_s}, \frac{y_s}{1-z_s}) = (\cot\frac{\theta}{2}\cos\phi, \cot\frac{\theta}{2}\sin\phi). \tag{2}$$

Design. Given a pair of input image sequence $X_1 = (x_1, x_2)$, the rotation head (R) computes augmented view of this sequence as $X_2 = (x_1', x_2')$ with rotation r using a random combination of "pitch", "yaw" and "roll" operations. These two augmented views are passed as an input to an encoder network f, defined as $f = P(R'(\Theta(E(R(X,r)))))$ where E is a flow prediction module, RAFT [60] in our case, Θ is a mapping of 2D flow to unit sphere, R' is a reverse rotation operation and P is a convolution based down-sampling head. A prediction head presented as h (an MLP head), transforms the output from the encoder f from one stream to match the other stream. The illustration of this process shown in Equation. 3 as maximization of cosine similarity two views from siamese stream:

$$D(p^{left}, z^{right}) = -\frac{p^{left}}{||p^{left}||_2} \cdot \frac{z^{right}}{||z^{right}||_2}. \tag{3}$$

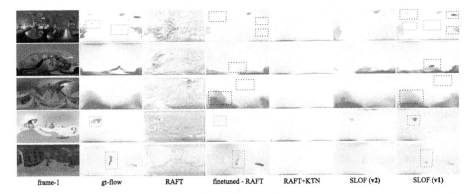

frame-1   gt-flow   RAFT   finetuned - RAFT   RAFT+KTN   SLOF (v2)   SLOF (v1)

Fig. 6. Qualitative results on FLOW360 test set. Qualitative results show our best model SLOF (**v1**) shows better results compared to fine-tuned RAFT trained with policy explained in [60]. The dotted (**black**) rectangle indicates the comparative improvements of our model over fine-tuned RAFT. RAFT+KTN method fails to predict flow-field correctly; instead, it only predicts shallow flow fields from camera motion. The weakness of our model can be seen on dotted (red) rectangle where smaller motion segments are missing. **Note:** Flows information is clipped for better visualization. (Color figure online)

Here, $p^{left} \triangleq h(f^{left}(X_1))$ and $z^{right} \triangleq f^{right}(X_2)$ denotes the output vectors to match from two different streams (f^{left}, f^{right}). This maximization problem can be viewed from another direction, with (p^{right}, z^{left}) as the second matching pair from siamese stream (f^{right}, f^{left}) respectively. Given two matching pairs, we can use following (Eq. 4) symmetrized similarity loss function L_{sim} (note that z^{left} and z^{right} are treated as a constant term using stop-grad operations to prevent a degenerate solution due to model collapse [17]). Similarly, the optical flow loss L_{flow} is computed as a sequence loss [60] over predicted flow field and ground truth. This loss (l_1 distance over predicted and ground truth flow f_{gt}) is computed and averaged over sequence of predictions iteratively generated for the same pair of input frames $\{f_1, f_2, ..., f_n\} = E(R(X, r))$ as shown in Eq. 4, where $\gamma = 0.8^{n-i-1}$ served as weights over sequence loss. Note that (n, i) denotes number of prediction(n) in sequence and prediction id(i) in predicted flow sequences. The design of the weighted schemes ensures different levels of confidence on predicted flows over time.

$$L_{sim} = \frac{1}{2}D(p^{left}, z^{right}) + \frac{1}{2}D(p^{right}, z^{left}), \ L_{flow} = \sum_{i=1}^{n} \gamma||R(f_{gt}, r) - f_i||. \ (4)$$

Given similarity loss(L_{sim}) and flow loss(L_{flow}) we implement a hybrid loss function $L = L_{sim} + L_{flow}$. The overall objective of this loss function is to maximize the similarity between latent representation of flow information while minimizing the loss between ground truth and predicted optical flow.

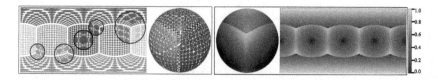

Fig. 7. Distortion density map. Illustrating different distortion intensity due to equirectangular projections. Left: upper (red) and lower (green) part of projections shows higher distortion in central part where as the equatorial region (cyan, pink, blue, gray) exhibit higher distortion rate away from the center of tangential plane. Right: shows the distortion density from $(0, 1)$. This distortion density map is used to evaluate the distortion aware EPE (EPE_d). **Note:** Each circle patch in left spherical projection have same area. (Color figure online)

5 Experiments

We evaluate SLOF on the FLOW360 test set. We use pre-trained RAFT on Sintel [15] and fine-tune on FLOW360 as a comparison baseline. The fine-tuning process is done using training protocols suggested in [60]. Moreover, to make a fair comparison with traditional methods, we transform RAFT (pre-trained) to adapt spherical convolution using KTN [57]. KTN transforms the convolution kernel to mitigate the radial distortions via estimating the spherical convolution function. Additionally, we run ablation studies on different training strategies and propose a distortion-aware evaluation. We will present details of the training procedure in the supplemental material.

Scope. The scope of our experiments are two folds: First, create a baseline for future researchers to explore novel methodologies. Second, address the validity of our method based on the fair comparison with a flow network designed for a spherical dataset. We formulate our baseline experiment on perspective optical flow network RAFT and modified version of RAFT with KTN [57] to compare the performance. The RAFT+KTN architecture simulates a domain adaptation similar to approaches like [3,9]. We choose KTN because of its success over alternative approaches like [18,19,23,56,68]. It is worth noting that the design of omnidirectional flow estimation can be extended to several techniques involving mitigation of radial distortions, making it practically impossible to cover all.

Augmentation Strategy. Given the nature of SLOF, we can train it using two different training strategies (**v1, v2**) as shown in Fig. 1(right). These strategies can be achieved by performing different rotational augmentation on the input sequences. The first strategy (**v1**) can be achieved by using set of inputs $(R(X_1, r_1), R(X_2, r_2))$ where $r_1 = (0, 0, 0)$, i.e., X_1 does not have any rotational augmentation, whereas $r_2 \neq (0, 0, 0)$ has rotation defined with random combinations of "pitch", "roll", and "yaw" operations. This setting is kept consistent throughout the training process. Alternatively, identical augmentation can be achieved by flipping this augmentation protocols. The second rotational scheme (**v2**) can be achieved by randomly switching rotation such that when r_1 is none, the r_2 is some random rotational augmentation and vice versa. This approach performs on par with **v1**.

$$\text{AE} = \arccos\left(\frac{u_e u_r + v_e v_r + 1}{\sqrt{u_r^2 + v_r^2 + 1}\sqrt{u_e^2 + v_e^2 + 1}}\right). \tag{5}$$

Table 1. Quantitative results on FLOW360 test set. $*$ denotes that we use EPE_d/AE_d as the metrics; otherwise, the normal EPE and AE. Compared to baseline, SLOF achieves lower end-point-error and angular error on both distortion aware (EPE_d and AE_d) and normal scheme. In terms of end-point-error (lower the better) our model (**v1**, **v2**) outperforms all the baseline. Similarly in terms of angular error (lower the better) our models (**v1**, **v2**) perform comparatively similar and outperform all the baseline. Though RAFT+KTN achieves comparable normal EPE, the distortion aware (Weighted) metrics (EPE_d and AE_d) are significantly larger. **Note:** metrics in range (all, less than (5, 10, 20) and greater than 20) is computed as an average, based on the speed ($\text{s}(x,y) = \sqrt{u(x,y)^2 + v(x,y)^2}$) only in the respective pixel regions.

Method	Version	Metric	Weighted $s \geq 0^*$	$s \geq 0$	$s < 5$	$s < 10$	$s < 20$	$s \geq 20$
Baselines	RAFT [60]	EPE	3.344	2.058	0.558	0.682	0.838	71.736
		AE	1.120	0.820	0.825	0.821	0.819	0.868
	Finetuned RAFT [60]	EPE	2.635	1.624	0.314	0.393	0.509	65.340
		AE	0.745	0.522	0.527	0.522	0.520	0.647
	RAFT + KTN [57]	EPE	3.899	2.222	0.598	0.742	0.924	76.426
		AE	2.020	0.912	0.912	0.910	0.911	1.0114
SLOF	Switch rotation (**v2**)	EPE	2.626	1.615	0.326	0.401	0.512	64.678
		AE	**0.691**	**0.485**	**0.489**	**0.484**	**0.482**	0.659
	Single rotation (**v1**)	EPE	**2.548**	**1.568**	**0.309**	**0.387**	**0.502**	62.476
		AE	0.708	0.497	0.501	0.497	0.495	**0.607**

Evaluation Strategy. We evaluate our method based on 2D-raw flow. Besides, using EPE (End Point Error in Eq. 6), i.e., Euclidean distance between the predicted flow and ground truth flow, as a single evaluation metric, we incorporate AE (Angular Error) as shown in Eq. 5 as the second measure. To explain the error in the omnidirectional setting, we introduce a distortion-aware measure called EPE_d as in Eq. 6. This metric penalizes the error in the distorted area based on the distortion density map.

$$\text{EPE} = \frac{1}{N}\sum_i^N \|f_{pred} - f_{gt}\|_2, \; \text{EPE}_d = \frac{1}{N}\sum_i^N \frac{\|f_{pred} - f_{gt}\|_2}{1 - d}. \tag{6}$$

As EPE_d, AE_d is calculated as $\frac{1}{N}\sum_i^N \frac{\text{AE}}{1-d}$ where, d represents the distortion density map illustrated in Fig. 7, $f_{pred} = (u_e, v_e)$ represents predicted flow, and $f_{gt} = (u_r, v_r)$ represents ground truth flow. Note that, to maintain lower metrics scale the distortion density is mapped between $[0.500, 1.000)$ from $(0.0, 1.0]$. Please refer to supplemental for additional details on distortion density map.

Results. Figure 6, Fig. 8 and Table 1 summarize our experimental results. The overall summary of qualitative results is presented in Fig. 6. SLOF performs better than baseline RAFT and kernel transformed RAFT+KTN methods. This result is evident enough to show that siamese representation learning can exploit the rotational properties of 360° videos to learn omnidirectional optical flow regardless of explicit architecture adjustments.

Our methods, SLOF (**v1**, **v2**) perform better than presented baselines. Among these methods **v1** has the best EPE score whereas, **v2** has better AE score. However, AE on both **v1** and **v2** are relatively similar, suggesting **v1** as our best method. This is clearly visible in qualitative results shown in Fig. 6.

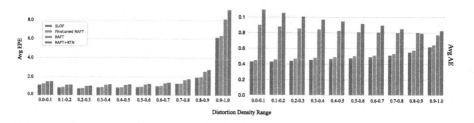

Fig. 8. Error distribution plot. Illustrating error (EPE and AE) in different distortion density ranges. SLOF relatively performs better in all distortion density ranges.

By investigating distortion-aware EPE, we can see that RAFT with KTN achieves significantly higher EPE regardless of comparable normal EPE with the other methods. This clearly explains why RAFT+KTN methods could not predict the motion around the distorted area; instead, it predicts shallow flow fields due to camera motion only. Moreover, comparing qualitative results in Fig. 6 and EPE measure in different distortion ranges in Fig. 8, we can see that our best method can predict smoother flow fields compared to baseline methods. These fields in the polar region are comparatively better and have better motion consistency in the edge region. However, our model might fail to predict relatively smaller motion regions in some cases, which leaves room for future improvements based on the proposed method. This concludes that RAFT+KTN requires additional re-engineering and domain adaptation, which is out of the scope of current work.

6   Conclusion

Omnidirectional flow estimation remains in its infancy because of the shortage of reliable benchmark datasets and tedious tasks dealing with inescapable radial distortions. This paper proposes the first perceptually natural-synthetic benchmark dataset, FLOW360, to close the gap, where comprehensive analysis shows excellent advantages over other datasets. Our dataset can be extended for other non-motion applications like segmentation and normal estimation task as well. Moreover, we introduce a siamese representation learning approach for omnidirectional flow (SLOF) instead of redesigning the convolution layer to adapt omnidirectional nature. Our method leverages the invariant rotation property of 360° videos to learn similar flow representation on various video augmentations. Meanwhile, we study the effect of different rotations on the final flow estimation, which provides a guideline for future work. Overall, the elimination of network redesigns aids researchers in exploiting existing architectures without significant modification leading faster deployment in real world setting.

Acknowledgements. This research was partially supported by NSF CNS-1908658, NeTS-2109982 and the gift donation from Cisco. This article solely reflects the opinions and conclusions of its authors and not the funding agents.

References

1. Adobe: Mixamo. www.mixamo.com/
2. Ahmadi, A., Patras, I.: Unsupervised convolutional neural networks for motion estimation. In: ICIP (2016)
3. Artizzu, C.O., Zhang, H., Allibert, G., Demonceaux, C.: OmniFlowNet: a perspective neural network adaptation for optical flow estimation in omnidirectional images. In: ICPR (2021)
4. Azevedo, R., Birkbeck, N., Simone, F., Janatra, I., Adsumilli, B., Frossard, P.: Visual distortions in 360-degree videos. TCSVT **2019**(8), 2524–2537 (2020)
5. Bailer, C., Taetz, B., Stricker, D.: Flow fields: dense correspondence fields for highly accurate large displacement optical flow estimation. In: ICCV (2015)
6. Baker, S., Roth, S., Scharstein, D., Black, M.J., Lewis, J., Szeliski, R.: A database and evaluation methodology for optical flow. In: ICCV (2007)
7. Barron, J.L., Fleet, D.J., Beauchemin, S.S.: Performance of optical flow techniques. IJCV **12**(1), 43–77 (1994)
8. Bertinetto, L., Valmadre, J., Henriques, J.F., Vedaldi, A., Torr, P.H.S.: Fully-convolutional Siamese networks for object tracking. In: Hua, G., Jégou, H. (eds.) ECCV 2016. LNCS, vol. 9914, pp. 850–865. Springer, Cham (2016). https://doi.org/10.1007/978-3-319-48881-3_56
9. Bhandari, K., Zong, Z., Yan, Y.: Revisiting optical flow estimation in 360 videos. In: ICPR (2021)
10. Blender: https://www.blender.org/
11. Boomsma, W., Frellsen, J.: Spherical convolutions and their application in molecular modelling. In: NeurIPS (2017)
12. Bromley, J., et al.: Signature verification using a "Siamese" time delay neural network. IJPRAI **7**(04), 669–688 (1993)
13. Brox, T., Bruhn, A., Papenberg, N., Weickert, J.: High accuracy optical flow estimation based on a theory for warping. In: Pajdla, T., Matas, J. (eds.) ECCV 2004. LNCS, vol. 3024, pp. 25–36. Springer, Heidelberg (2004). https://doi.org/10.1007/978-3-540-24673-2_3
14. Brox, T., Malik, J.: Large displacement optical flow: descriptor matching in variational motion estimation. TPAMI **33**(3), 500–513 (2010)

15. Butler, D.J., Wulff, J., Stanley, G.B., Black, M.J.: A naturalistic open source movie for optical flow evaluation. In: Fitzgibbon, A., Lazebnik, S., Perona, P., Sato, Y., Schmid, C. (eds.) ECCV 2012. LNCS, vol. 7577, pp. 611–625. Springer, Heidelberg (2012). https://doi.org/10.1007/978-3-642-33783-3_44

16. Chen, Q., Koltun, V.: Full flow: optical flow estimation by global optimization over regular grids. In: CVPR (2016)

17. Chen, X., He, K.: Exploring simple Siamese representation learning. In: CVPR (2021)

18. Cohen, T.S., Geiger, M., Koehler, J., Welling, M.: Spherical CNNs. arXiv (2018)

19. Coors, B., Condurache, A.P., Geiger, A.: SphereNet: learning spherical representations for detection and classification in omnidirectional images. In: Ferrari, V., Hebert, M., Sminchisescu, C., Weiss, Y. (eds.) ECCV 2018. LNCS, vol. 11213, pp. 525–541. Springer, Cham (2018). https://doi.org/10.1007/978-3-030-01240-3_32

20. Demonceaux, C., Kachi-Akkouche, D.: Optical flow estimation in omnidirectional images using wavelet approach. In: CVPRW (2003)

21. Dosovitskiy, A., et al.: FlowNet: learning optical flow with convolutional networks. In: ICCV (2015)

22. Eder, M., Shvets, M., Lim, J., Frahm, J.M.: Tangent images for mitigating spherical distortion. In: CVPR (2020)

23. Esteves, C., Allen-Blanchette, C., Makadia, A., Daniilidis, K.: Learning SO(3) equivariant representations with spherical CNNs. In: Ferrari, V., Hebert, M., Sminchisescu, C., Weiss, Y. (eds.) ECCV 2018. LNCS, vol. 11217, pp. 54–70. Springer, Cham (2018). https://doi.org/10.1007/978-3-030-01261-8_4

24. Feng, B.Y., Yao, W., Liu, Z., Varshney, A.: Deep depth estimation on 360° images with a double quaternion loss. In: 3DV (2020)

25. Fernandez-Labrador, C., Facil, J.M., Perez-Yus, A., Demonceaux, C., Civera, J., Guerrero, J.J.: Corners for layout: end-to-end layout recovery from 360 images. RA-L 5(2), 1255–1262 (2020)

26. Field, D.J.: Relations between the statistics of natural images and the response properties of cortical cells. Josa a 4(12), 2379–2394 (1987)

27. Garg, R., Roussos, A., Agapito, L.: A variational approach to video registration with subspace constraints. IJCV 104(3), 286–314 (2013)

28. Geiger, A., Lenz, P., Stiller, C., Urtasun, R.: Vision meets robotics: the kitti dataset. IJRR 32(11), 1231–1237 (2013)

29. Geiger, A., Lenz, P., Urtasun, R.: Are we ready for autonomous driving? The kitti vision benchmark suite. In: CVPR (2012)

30. Geyer, C., Daniilidis, K.: A unifying theory for central panoramic systems and practical implications. In: Vernon, D. (ed.) ECCV 2000. LNCS, vol. 1843, pp. 445–461. Springer, Heidelberg (2000). https://doi.org/10.1007/3-540-45053-X_29

31. Goralczyk, A.: Nishita sky demo (2020), creative Commons CC0 (Public Domain) - Blender Studio - cloud.blender.org

32. Horn, B.K., Schunck, B.G.: Determining optical flow. AI 17(1–3), 185–203 (1981)

33. Horn, B., Schunck, B.: Techniques and applications of image understanding (1981)

34. Hui, T.W., Tang, X., Loy, C.C.: LiteFlowNet: a lightweight convolutional neural network for optical flow estimation. In: CVPR (2018)

35. Hui, T.W., Tang, X., Loy, C.C.: A lightweight optical flow CNN -revisiting data fidelity and regularization. TPAMI 43(8), 2555–2569 (2021)

36. Hulle, S.V.: Bcon19 (2019), 2019 Blender Conference - cloud.blender.org

37. Hur, J., Roth, S.: MirrorFlow: exploiting symmetries in joint optical flow and occlusion estimation. In: ICCV (2017)

38. Ilg, E., Mayer, N., Saikia, T., Keuper, M., Dosovitskiy, A., Brox, T.: FlowNet 2.0: evolution of optical flow estimation with deep networks. In: CVPR (2017)
39. Yu, J.J., Harley, A.W., Derpanis, K.G.: Back to basics: unsupervised learning of optical flow via brightness constancy and motion smoothness. In: Hua, G., Jégou, H. (eds.) ECCV 2016. LNCS, vol. 9915, pp. 3–10. Springer, Cham (2016). https://doi.org/10.1007/978-3-319-49409-8_1
40. Jiang, S., Campbell, D., Lu, Y., Li, H., Hartley, R.: Learning to estimate hidden motions with global motion aggregation. arXiv (2021)
41. Liu, C., Freeman, W.T., Adelson, E.H., Weiss, Y.: Human-assisted motion annotation. In: CVPR (2008)
42. Liu, P., Lyu, M., King, I., Xu, J.: SelFlow: self-supervised learning of optical flow. In: CVPR (2019)
43. Lucas, B.D., Kanade, T.: An iterative image registration technique with an application to stereo vision. In: IJCAI, vol. 2 (1981)
44. McCane, B., Novins, K., Crannitch, D., Galvin, B.: On benchmarking optical flow. CVIU **84**(1) (2001)
45. Meister, S., Hur, J., Roth, S.: Unflow: unsupervised learning of optical flow with a bidirectional census loss. In: AAAI (2018)
46. Meister, S., Jähne, B., Kondermann, D.: Outdoor stereo camera system for the generation of real-world benchmark data sets. Opt. Eng. **51**(2), 021107 (2012)
47. Menze, M., Geiger, A.: Object scene flow for autonomous vehicles. In: CVPR (2015)
48. Menze, M., Heipke, C., Geiger, A.: Discrete optimization for optical flow. In: GCPR (2015)
49. Otte, M., Nagel, H.-H.: Optical flow estimation: advances and comparisons. In: Eklundh, J.-O. (ed.) ECCV 1994. LNCS, vol. 800, pp. 49–60. Springer, Heidelberg (1994). https://doi.org/10.1007/3-540-57956-7_5
50. Ranjan, A., Black, M.J.: Optical flow estimation using a spatial pyramid network. In: CVPR (2017)
51. Seidel, R., Apitzsch, A., Hirtz, G.: OmniFlow: human omnidirectional optical flow. In: CVPR (2021)
52. Shakernia, O., Vidal, R., Sastry, S.: Omnidirectional egomotion estimation from back-projection flow. In: CVPRW (2003)
53. Simoncelli, E.P., Olshausen, B.A.: Natural image statistics and neural representation. Annu. Rev. Neurosci. **24**(1), 1193–1216 (2001)
54. Sketchfab. https://sketchfab.com/
55. Steinbrücker, F., Pock, T., Cremers, D.: Large displacement optical flow computation without warping. In: ICCV (2009)
56. Su, Y.C., Grauman, K.: Learning spherical convolution for fast features from 360° imagery. In: NeurIPS (2017)
57. Su, Y.C., Grauman, K.: Kernel transformer networks for compact spherical convolution. In: CVPR (2019)
58. Sun, D., Yang, X., Liu, M.Y., Kautz, J.: Models matter, so does training: an empirical study of CNNs for optical flow estimation. TPAMI **42**(6), 1408–1423 (2019)
59. Taigman, Y., Yang, M., Ranzato, M., Wolf, L.: DeepFace: closing the gap to human-level performance in face verification. In: CVPR (2014)
60. Teed, Z., Deng, J.: RAFT: recurrent all-pairs field transforms for optical flow. In: Vedaldi, A., Bischof, H., Brox, T., Frahm, J.-M. (eds.) ECCV 2020. LNCS, vol. 12347, pp. 402–419. Springer, Cham (2020). https://doi.org/10.1007/978-3-030-58536-5_24

61. Teney, D., Hebert, M.: Learning to extract motion from videos in convolutional neural networks. In: ACCV (2016)
62. Tran, D., Bourdev, L., Fergus, R., Torresani, L., Paluri, M.: Deep end2end voxel2voxel prediction. In: CVPRW (2016)
63. Turbosquid: https://www.turbosquid.com
64. Wang, R., Geraghty, D., Matzen, K., Szeliski, R., Frahm, J.M.: VPLNet: deep single view normal estimation with vanishing points and lines. In: CVPR (2020)
65. Weinzaepfel, P., Revaud, J., Harchaoui, Z., Schmid, C.: DeepFlow: large displacement optical flow with deep matching. In: ICCV (2013)
66. Woliński, M.: City - 3d model, sketchfab.com
67. Wulff, J., Black, M.J.: Efficient sparse-to-dense optical flow estimation using a learned basis and layers. In: CVPR (2015)
68. Zhang, Z., Xu, Y., Yu, J., Gao, S.: Saliency detection in 360° videos. In: Ferrari, V., Hebert, M., Sminchisescu, C., Weiss, Y. (eds.) ECCV 2018. LNCS, vol. 11211, pp. 504–520. Springer, Cham (2018). https://doi.org/10.1007/978-3-030-01234-2_30
69. Zhao, S., Sheng, Y., Dong, Y., Chang, E.I., Xu, Y., et al.: MaskFlowNet: asymmetric feature matching with learnable occlusion mask. In: CVPR (2020)
70. Zioulis, N., Karakottas, A., Zarpalas, D., Daras, P.: OmniDepth: dense depth estimation for indoors spherical panoramas. In: Ferrari, V., Hebert, M., Sminchisescu, C., Weiss, Y. (eds.) ECCV 2018. LNCS, vol. 11210, pp. 453–471. Springer, Cham (2018). https://doi.org/10.1007/978-3-030-01231-1_28

VizWiz-FewShot: Locating Objects in Images Taken by People with Visual Impairments

Yu-Yun Tseng[✉], Alexander Bell, and Danna Gurari

University of Colorado Boulder, Boulder, USA
yuts1923@colorado.edu

Abstract. We introduce a few-shot localization dataset originating from photographers who authentically were trying to learn about the visual content in the images they took. It includes nearly 10,000 segmentations of 100 categories in over 4,500 images that were taken by people with visual impairments. Compared to existing few-shot object detection and instance segmentation datasets, our dataset is the first to locate holes in objects (e.g., found in 12.3% of our segmentations), it shows objects that occupy a much larger range of sizes relative to the images, and text is over five times more common in our objects (e.g., found in 22.4% of our segmentations). Analysis of three modern few-shot localization algorithms demonstrates that they generalize poorly to our new dataset. The algorithms commonly struggle to locate objects with holes, very small and very large objects, and objects lacking text. To encourage a larger community to work on these unsolved challenges, we publicly share our annotated few-shot dataset at https://vizwiz.org.

Keywords: Few-shot learning · Object detection · Instance segmentation

1 Introduction

Our paper is motivated by the belief that people who are blind or with low vision (BLV) would benefit from the ability to locate objects in images that they take, whether with a bounding box or fine-grained segmentation. For people with low vision, localization would enhance their use of magnification tools [4,30] by automatically enlarging the content of interest. For all BLV users, they

---

Y.-Y. Tseng and A. Bell—Equal contribution

Supplementary Information The online version contains supplementary material available at https://doi.org/10.1007/978-3-031-20074-8_33.

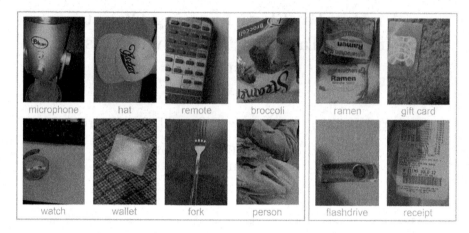

Fig. 1. Examples from our VizWiz-FewShot dataset showing instance segmentation annotations we collected for images taken by people with vision impairments. Annotated categories span those that are in common with prior work (left green box) and unique to our dataset (right blue box). These examples highlight novel aspects of our dataset, including that holes are permitted in our objects, objects vary considerably in how much of the image they occupy, and objects often feature text. (Annotation overlay colors were selected based on the order the instance segmentations appear in our dataset, and so not object categories.) (Color figure online)

could have stronger privacy guarantees with services[1] that describe their images if object localization algorithms were used in place of recognition algorithms. That is because services could use localizations to obfuscate all content except the detected regions needed to justify predictions[2] and so remove accidentally captured private information in the background of images, which is a common occurrence for people with vision impairments [16]. Finally, automatic localization would also support users to independently edit their images, which is a feature some BLV photographers have requested.

Observing that BLV photographers take pictures showing a large number of objects (e.g., 16,400 nouns were used to describe less than 40,000 images taken by BLV photographers [18]), we are interested in the problem of few-shot learning. Casting the problem as a few-shot learning problem means that developers can efficiently scale up the number of categories supported in order to locate the long-tail of categories. That is because few-shot learning methods learn to locate a novel object category by observing only K annotated examples, where K is typically 1, 5, or 10 examples.

---

[1] Visual assistance services include Microsoft's Seeing AI, Google's Lookout, and Tap-TapSee. The popularity of such services is exemplified by companies' reports about hundreds of thousands of users and tens of millions of requests [9,12,22].

[2] Recorded evidence can be needed by companies for legal reasons.

To support our aim, we introduce a few-shot localization dataset that consists of 100 segmented categories in over 4,500 images taken by people with vision impairments. The images were taken in authentic use cases where the photographers were soliciting human assistance to learn about their visual surroundings [3]. Examples of annotated images in our dataset are shown in Fig. 1.

We next analyze how our dataset compares to the four existing few-shot localization datasets [1,13,23,26,28] to reveal both how our dataset is similar to and different from prior work. We observe several unique aspects about our dataset. First, it is the only dataset that indicates when and where holes are located in objects. Holes are observed in 12.3% of our instance segmentations. Second, our dataset's objects exhibit a much larger range of sizes relative to the image sizes. Finally, our dataset's objects contain text much more frequently. Specifically, our analysis shows that 22.4% of objects in our dataset contain text versus 4.6% of the objects in the related instance segmentation dataset, COCO-20^i [26]. We suspect the latter two unique aspects of our dataset stem from how images were curated. While our images come from a real-world application where photographers were authentically trying to learn about their visual surroundings, existing datasets were contrived by scraping images from photo-sharing websites. Altogether, we believe that our new dataset fills important gaps of existing datasets in the vision community by capturing a greater diversity of challenges that can arise in real-world applications.

We also benchmark top-performing few-shot learning object detection and instance segmentation algorithms on our new dataset. We find that the algorithms perform poorly overall. Our fine-grained analysis reveals that the algorithms commonly fail for objects that contain holes, very small and very large objects, and objects that lack text.

In summary, our contributions include: (1) a new few-shot localization dataset based on images that were taken in a real-world application, (2) the first few-shot localization dataset with metadata showing where holes are located in objects, (3) fine-grained analysis revealing unique aspects of our dataset compared to existing few-shot localization datasets, and (4) analysis of top-performing few-shot localization algorithms that reveals open algorithmic challenges for the vision community. We expect this work will encourage the development of algorithms that can handle a greater diversity of challenges that arise in real-world applications. We expect these advancements will, in turn, benefit a larger audience by facilitating the improvement of algorithms for application domains, such as robotics and wearable lifelogging, that face similar challenges including holes in objects, varying object sizes, and presence of text.

2   Related Work

Few-Shot Learning Datasets for Image Localization. Several dataset challenges have been proposed for few-shot object detection and few-shot instance segmentation: PASCAL-5^i [1], COCO-20^i [26,28], ImageNet-LOC [8], and FSOD

Dataset [13]. A limitation of existing datasets is that images come from contrived settings rather than authentic use cases where people are seeking to learn about their images. Specifically, images were curated by scraping images from the Internet that were tagged with pre-defined categories of interest. To our knowledge, we are introducing the first few-shot dataset challenges based on images that originate from authentic use cases where people took pictures to learn about the content. Our dataset offers new categories that are applicable to real-world applications. In addition, our dataset provides metadata showing holes in objects, which is a unique feature that creates new challenges toward few-shot problems. Finally, it provides additional real-world challenges such as a larger range of object sizes and a higher prevalence of objects containing text.

Few-Shot Algorithms for Image Localization. Few-shot learning was introduced to the community in 2017 for object detection [10] and in 2018 for instance segmentation [26]. Since, a large number of algorithms have been proposed that largely are based on two types of approaches: meta-learning and fine-tuning. To assess how state-of-the-art methods perform on our new dataset, we benchmark the top-performing few-shot object detection and instance segmentation algorithms for which code is publicly-available. Overall, we observe poor performance from these algorithms [5,26,27,29]. From our fine-grained analysis, we find this dataset is challenging for algorithms due to the presence of holes in objects, very small objects, very large objects, and objects that lack text.

Datasets Originating from People With Vision Impairments. In recent years, a growing number of publicly-available datasets have been proposed to facilitate the development of algorithms that can work well on images taken by people with vision impairments [2,6,7,15–19,25,32]. For example, existing datasets support the development of algorithms for predicting answers to visual questions [17,19], recognizing objects in videos [25], and describing images with captions [18]. Complementing prior work, we introduce a dataset for localizing objects in images taken by BLV photographers, either using a bounding box or segmentation. We expect success with developing localization algorithms for images taken by BLV photographers to directly benefit BLV photographers and to, more generally, support a larger number of real-world applications that encounter similar visual characteristics found in our dataset, such as robotics and wearable lifelogging applications.

3   VizWiz-FewShot Dataset

We introduce a dataset that we call "VizWiz-FewShot". It consists of localization annotations for images taken by people with vision impairments who authentically were trying to learn about their visual surroundings.

3.1   Dataset Creation

Data Source. Our dataset extends the VizWiz-Captions dataset [18], which consists of images taken by people with vision impairments paired with five crowdsourced captions per image. The photographers took and shared these images in order to solicit assistance from remote humans in recognizing the contents in the images [3]. We leverage the data in both the train and validation splits, which offers a starting point of 31,181 captioned images.

Category Selection. We chose 100 categories to locate in the images. These categories both support backward compatibility with popular few-shot localization datasets and reflect important categories for people with vision impairments. To select the categories, we first quantified the frequency of all nouns that appeared in at least two of the five captions per image for our images. We then selected 72 non-ambiguous categories that overlap with four existing few-shot localization datasets: MS COCO [24], PASCAL VOC [11], FSS-1000 [23], and FSOD [13]. We also selected 28 non-ambiguous categories that are unique to our target population, by choosing categories that refer to physical objects. All 100 selected categories have at least 10 examples.

Data Filtering. We next filtered the images to only retain those that contained at least one of our 100 categories. First, we removed images which did not mention any of our categories within at least two of their respective captions. Then, the authors subsequently verified that each remaining image contained at least one object that fit the precise definition of at least one of our categories. For example, our automatic collection of images with the category "pen" retrieved some images of pencils without pens and so we removed those images. After filtering, we had total of 4,930 images.

Annotation Tasks. After iterative prototyping, we settled on a workflow similar to prior work [24], such that we first used an image classification task to flag which categories of interest are present in each image and then an instance segmentation task to locate every instance of each category. For both tasks, we utilized templates provided by Amazon Mechanical Turk (AMT).

For image classification, crowdworkers were shown an image and asked to select all categories that were present, if any. Since showing all 100 categories at the same time could overwhelm crowdworkers and ultimately lead to lower quality results, we instead showed a subset of categories at a time (i.e., ∼20).

For instance segmentation, crowdworkers were shown an image with the list of categories known to be present from the image classification task and asked to locate each instance of every category. Like prior work, our annotation tool supported users to create a series of clicks to generate polygons. Going beyond prior work, in addition to being able to draw 'positive' polygons to locate object boundaries, our tool also enabled users to create 'negative' polygons in order to capture when objects contained holes. We offered extensive instructions with our task to cover edge-case scenarios, including how to annotate the presence of holes and how to handle occlusions.

Annotation Collection. We implemented several quality control methods to support our collection of high-quality annotations. First, we only accepted workers who already had completed at least 500 AMT tasks with at least a 99% approval rating. For the more complex instance segmentation task, we also required workers to successfully pass a qualification test consisting of nine challenging annotation edge cases (described in the Supplementary Materials). We then collected redundant results from multiple unique workers for both tasks. For image classification, we collected three results per image and flagged a category as present if at least one worker indicated so. For instance segmentation, we collected two sets of annotations per image-category pair and then computed intersection over union (IoU) scores to determine how to establish a ground truth segmentation per image. When $IoU \geq 0.8$, we randomly chose one of the annotations as the ground truth. Otherwise, the authors reviewed the pair of annotations to choose one as the ground truth (or, in exceptional cases, discarded both annotations). Finally, we paid above minimum wage to better incentivize the workers.[3] Upon completion, we had a total of 9,861 segmented objects in 4,622 images.

3.2 Dataset Analysis

We now analyze the VizWiz-FewShot dataset and compare it to the other mainstream few-shot localization datasets.

VizWiz-FewShot-IS (Instance Segmentation). We first characterize our few-shot instance segmentation dataset and compare it to the only other few-shot instance segmentation dataset we are aware of: COCO-20[i] [24], which has a total of 80 categories. We compute for every instance segmentation the following metrics:

- **Mass center**: location of the center of mass pixel for each object relative to the image coordinates. Consequently, an object's x-coordinate and y-coordinate values can range from 0 to 1.
- **Boundary complexity**: ratio of the area of an instance to the length of its perimeter, also known as isoperimetric inequality. Values range from 0 to 1, with lower values representing more complex boundaries.
- **Image coverage**: percentage of pixels each instance segmentation occupies from the entire image.
- **Prevalence of text**: flag indicating if Microsoft Azure's optical character recognition (OCR) API returned text for an image, after masking out all content except for the instance segmentation.

---

[3] Average hourly wage was $8.00 and $9.61 for classification and IS respectively.

– **Prevalence of holes**: flag indicating if any holes are present paired with the percentage of pixels each hole occupies from the instance segmentation when any holes are present.

In what follows, we report the statistics summarizing the results for all instance segmentations for each dataset.[4]

Results for *boundary complexity*, object location (i.e., *mass center*), and *image coverage* are shown in Fig. 2(a). Amongst these metrics, the only major difference between the two datasets is *image coverage*. For example, objects in our dataset represent on average roughly six times more relative area in images than those in COCO-20^i. We exemplify this finding qualitatively by showing in Fig. 2(b) how annotations of two types of content, "sink" and "oven", dramatically differ in image coverage across the two datasets. We attribute the prevalence of larger relative object sizes in our dataset to the fact that photographers in an authentic use case where they are trying to learn about content take up-close pictures of the content. Another key distinction about our dataset is that we observe a considerably larger variability for the image coverage in our dataset. Qualitative results in Fig. 3 exemplify this range of relative area occupied by segmentations in our dataset. This finding highlights that a benefit of our dataset is that it encourages the design of algorithms that will be able to handle a larger range of relative object sizes in images.

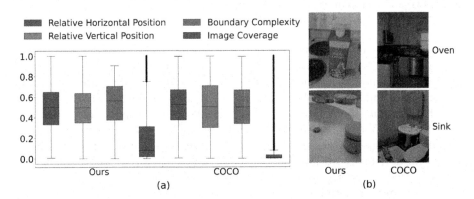

Fig. 2. Comparison of our dataset with the only existing few-shot instance segmentation dataset, COCO-20^i. (a) Summary statistics for all segmented objects in each dataset are shown in the box plot with respect to the location (i.e., relative x-coordinates and y-coordinates for mass center), boundary complexity, and image coverage. The box plot's central mark denotes the median score, box edges the 25th and 75th percentiles scores, whiskers the most extreme data points not considered outliers, and individually plotted points the outliers. (b) Annotations from both datasets exemplify our quantitative finding that an object with larger image coverage is an outlier in COCO-20^i while common in our dataset.

---

[4] For efficiency, we evaluated the presence of text for a random sample of images in COCO-20^i that is comparable to the number of images in our dataset: 8,000.

Fig. 3. Examples from our VizWiz-FewShot dataset illustrating its unique aspects, specifically the high variability of object size relative to images, high prevalence of text in objects, and inclusion of holes in segmentations.

When analyzing the *prevalence of text*, we find that 22.4% of instances in our dataset include text compared to only 4.6% in COCO-20^i. We show examples of objects in our dataset that contain text in Fig. 3, including of cups, menus, cereal boxes, and albums. We also show in Fig. 4 the frequency at which text is found in a sample of our categories. Categories that more commonly contain text include ramen, food menu, packet, and gift card. Categories that rarely contain text include dog, vase, house, and spoon. We hypothesize from our findings that algorithm developers working on COCO-20^i may have a bias to disregard text. We expect our dataset will inspire developers to consider how to take advantage of text recognition methods as potential predictive cues for locating objects with few-shot localization algorithms.

Finally, a unique feature of our dataset that is not supported in COCO-20^i is locating the *holes* in objects. We define a hole as any area in an object that does not belong to the object itself since our goal is to locate all pixels belonging to each category of interest. Thus, a hole may manifest as a property of an object itself (i.e. a ring), an object's orientation (i.e. a side view of an open armrest on a chair), or an occlusion on the object (i.e. a plate partially occluded by food). In total, 12.3% of the instances in our VizWiz-FewShot-IS contain holes. As shown in Fig. 5, some of the object categories with the highest proportion of instance segmentations that contain holes are chairs, sandals, bracelets, and bowls. For instance, 21.1% of the bowl instances have holes, likely because bowls

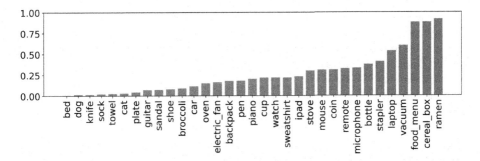

Fig. 4. Proportion of instances with text on a per-category basis for each third category in our dataset, sorted them by frequency of text.

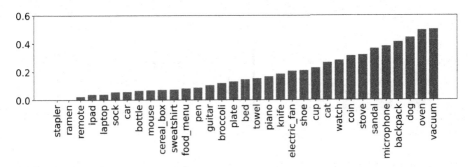

Fig. 5. Proportion of instances with holes on a per-category basis for each third category in our dataset, sorted by frequency of holes.

typically contain food in them. We attribute the high frequency of holes to two causes. First, is that the objects intrinsically contain them; e.g., chairs, stools, and sandals. The second reason is that large-appearing objects get occluded by foreground objects, such as occlusions on rugs, bowls, and plates. Corroborating this hypothesis, we find that the percentage of instances with holes increases with object size, suggesting that larger objects tend to have hole-type occlusions more frequently than smaller objects (results shown in the Supplementary Materials). We also observe that certain categories regularly have a larger percentage of hole pixels in them, such as bowls which typically are occluded by a large amount of food (results are shown in the Supplementary Materials). We anticipate the need to recognize holes will increase our dataset's difficulty for computer vision models since they will need to go beyond merely locating the outermost boundary of objects to also understanding which interior pixels should belong to the objects.

VizWiz-FewShot-OD (Object Detection). We next characterize our dataset in the object detection setting and how it compares to the three mainstream few-shot object detection datasets: COCO-20^i [28], PASCAL-5^i [1], and FSOD [13].[5] To support comparison, we convert each instance segmentation in our dataset into its bounding box representation. For every dataset, we compute for each object detection its relative position and image coverage.[6] Summary statistics for each dataset are shown in Fig. 6.

One key distinction of our dataset is the greater variability in the *relative positions* of its objects. This finding contrasts a common photographer's bias of beautifully capturing the contents of interest near the center of images. We suspect this greater diversity of object positions stems from the inability of BLV photographers to inspect the images to guarantee that they are centering the contents of interest in their images and their inability to verify that clutter gets excluded from the background of their images.

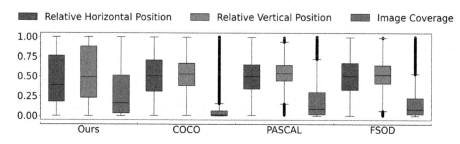

Fig. 6. Box plot showing how objects in our dataset compare to those in the three existing few-shot object detection datasets with respect to relative position and image coverage.

Another distinction in our dataset is its bias towards having objects positioned on the left side of images, as exemplified by the mean and median relative horizontal position being 0.45 and 0.39 respectively. One possible reason for this bias may be a commonality in how the photographers take images. Specifically, when a person is trying to learn about a particular object often the person holds the content of interest in the left hand while taking a picture of it with the right hand. This scenario assumes a tendency in society for people to be right-handed.

Finally, we observe that bounding boxes in our dataset tend to cover more of an image than two of the four existing datasets: COCO-20^i and FSOD. Image coverage of objects in our dataset is comparable to PASCAL, which we attribute to PASCAL's focus on iconic images with salient objects [24] and our dataset's inclusion of images of objects taken up-close for visual assistance.

---

[5] We use both the train and validation splits from each of the mainstream datasets for analysis. We randomly sample 10% of the annotations from COCO-20^i due to its large size, and we use all annotations from PASCAL-5^i and FSOD.

[6] We exclude from consideration the other three metrics used to analyze the instance segmentations because boundary complexity is no longer relevant, text prevalence could be incorrect due to the bounding box extending beyond an object's boundaries, and none of the other datasets located holes in objects.

4   Algorithm Benchmarking

We now present our results from benchmarking top-performing computer vision algorithms on our VizWiz-FewShot dataset.

To support use of our annotated data for few-shot localization tasks, we create a 4-fold cross-validation format and split our 100 object categories into four sets, where $i = 0, 1, 2, 3$ for the ith fold. This approach mimics the settings used for the few-shot datasets PASCAL-5^i [1] and COCO-20^i [26,28]. We refer to the resulting datasets for few-shot instance segmentation and few-shot object detection as VizWiz-FewShot-IS-25^i and VizWiz-FewShot-OD-25^i respectively.

We evaluate the trained models using mAP and mAP_{50}. mAP originates from the MS COCO object detection challenge [24] and is frequently used to evaluate algorithms for FSIS [14,26,27,31] and FSOD [20]. mAP refers to the mean of Average Precision (AP) for all categories and is an average across the IoU threshold of $0.5 : 0.05 : 0.95$ for ground truth and prediction regions. The only difference between FSOD and FSID is that that former is evaluated based on bounding boxes while the latter is evaluated based on mask areas. We also present results with respect to mAP_{50}, where only threshold 0.5 is used, since this approach facilitates the comparison with datasets such as Pascal VOC. Our evaluation is based on when $K = 1, 3, 5, 10$ shots are available.

4.1   Few-Shot Instance Segmentation Algorithms

We benchmarked the top-performing FSIS algorithm for which code is publicly-available and can be successfully deployed on modern GPUs[7]. Specifically, we evaluated the algorithm YOLACT [5], which was originally proposed outside of a few-shot setting, and then was subsequently shown to yield strong results on COCO-20^i when fine-tuned for FSIS [27]. When using the codebase as is on our new FSIS dataset, the performance on novel classes is consistently negligible (i.e., mAP around 0). We found this occurs because the default hyperparameters leads to training loss explosion. Consequently, we tested with different hyperparameters. Specifically, we (1) explored four learning rates in decreasing order from the original setting (i.e., 1e−3) to a value where saw convergence (i.e., 2e−5), (2) explored weights for the bounding box loss and mask loss in increasing order from 0 to 15 with an increment size of 1, (3) resized all images to match MS COCO's resolutions (i.e., 640×480), and (4) removed object instances of which the areas exceed that of MS COCO (i.e., instances are filtered based on the size range in MS COCO).

Overall Performance: Results are shown in Table 1. We report results with respect to each fold as well as the mean across all folds.

Overall, the model performs poorly on VizWiz-FewShot-IS-25^i. Moreover, the performance is much worse on our dataset than observed on the original

---

[7] We discuss the limitations of other FSIS algorithms for benchmarking on our dataset in the Supplementary Materials.

dataset for which it was proposed [27]; e.g., mAP_{50} score of 2.48 compared to 17.1 for 1-shot and 5.17 compared to 18.9 for 5-shot for VizWiz-FewShot-IS-25^i and COCO-20^i respectively. These findings motivate the benefit of our dataset in providing a challenging problem for the vision community.

Fine-Grained Analysis: To identify what make the dataset difficult, we next analyze the model's performances with respect to (1) image quality, (2) object size, and (3) presence of text. To do so, we distribute the test examples into subsets with respect to each of the following factors:

Table 1. Overall performance of the few-shot algorithms on our VizWiz-FewShot dataset presented in 4-fold validation style. The FSIS algorithm is benchmarked on VizWiz-FewShot-IS-25^i, and the FSOD algorithms are benchmarked on VizWiz-FewShot-OD-25^i.

	Shots	25^0		25^1		25^2		25^3		Mean	
		mAP	mAP_{50}	mAP	mAP_{50}	mAP	mAP_{50}	mAP	mAP_{50}	mAP	mAP_{50}
FSIS YOLACT	$k=1$	1.87	2.5	2.91	3.51	1.39	1.79	1.08	2.13	1.81	2.48
	$k=3$	2.31	2.81	4.48	5.24	2.35	2.78	3.59	4.52	3.18	3.84
	$k=5$	3.45	4.30	4.84	5.67	4.34	5.14	4.39	5.56	4.25	5.17
	$k=10$	5.97	7.69	7.71	9.02	6.18	7.18	5.82	7.38	6.42	7.82
FSOD DeFRCN	$k=1$	3.45	5.80	4.67	8.33	3.51	5.10	4.51	8.19	4.03	6.85
	$k=3$	6.80	11.65	7.81	13.85	7.26	11.74	7.88	14.05	7.43	12.82
	$k=5$	8.99	15.19	11.26	19.13	10.60	16.95	11.23	19.11	10.52	17.60
	$k=10$	11.24	21.34	13.36	25.68	11.94	22.07	13.91	24.76	12.61	23.46
FSOD YOLACT	$k=1$	2.05	2.61	2.84	3.66	1.61	1.97	1.91	2.26	2.10	2.63
	$k=3$	2.45	3.05	4.41	5.53	2.58	3.22	3.94	4.89	3.35	4.17
	$k=5$	3.46	4.44	4.87	5.88	4.82	5.68	4.72	5.81	4.47	5.45
	$k=10$	6.27	7.89	7.60	9.29	6.61	7.90	6.06	7.86	6.64	8.24

- **Image quality**: Leveraging metadata from prior work [18] which indicates how many from five crowdworkers indicated an image is insufficient quality to recognize the content, we classify an image as "high quality" when none indicate insufficient quality and "medium quality" when one or two crowdworkers flagged the image as insufficient quality. We exclude even lower quality images from our analysis since these are rare in our test set.
- **Object size**: The target object size is calculated based on the number of pixels in the instance segmentations. We divide the dataset into small, medium, and large sizes, such that the numbers of images in each set are evenly distributed. This resulted in the following thresholds: 350^2 and 900^2.
- **Presence of text**: We used the metadata collected for Sect. 3 that determined whether an object has text on it using OCR on background-masked instance images to flag whether text is present.
- **Presence of hole(s)**: We used additional metadata from Sect. 3, indicating if each instance segmentation contains a hole, to flag if a hole is present.

All fine-grained analysis results for YOLACT are shown in Table 2.

With respect to *image quality* and *object size*, our findings reinforce those of prior work. Specifically, like prior work [18], the algorithm typically performs better on images with higher quality. Like other prior work [21,33], algorithms typically perform worse for smaller objects. However, our findings extend those reported in [21,33] since we define object sizes differently; i.e., they use smaller thresholds of 32^2 and 96^2. To our knowledge, our work is the first to offer insights into performance on larger objects due to the novel presence of such larger instances in our dataset.

Table 2. Fine-grained analysis on the performance of FSIS and FSOD models on VizWiz-FewShot presented in mAP.

	Shots	Image quality		Object size			Presence of text		Presence of holes	
		Medium	High	Small	Medium	Large	Yes	No	Yes	No
FSIS YOLACT	$k = 1$	1.24	**2.11**	1.38	**2.19**	1.74	**1.83**	1.62	1.48	**1.99**
	$k = 3$	**3.31**	3.19	2.24	3.44	**3.80**	**3.26**	2.84	2.91	**3.21**
	$k = 5$	3.72	**4.29**	2.64	3.88	**5.19**	3.78	4.05	3.06	**4.22**
	$k = 10$	6.11	**6.50**	3.94	6.53	**7.30**	**6.16**	5.28	5.82	**6.29**
FSOD DeFRCN	$k = 1$	**2.46**	2.22	2.67	2.96	**3.57**	**4.97**	2.29	0.875	**3.99**
	$k = 3$	4.97	**5.26**	6.13	5.41	**6.81**	**7.93**	7.60	2.15	**7.60**
	$k = 5$	10.69	10.27	6.83	**16.95**	8.90	**13.48**	12.70	2.56	**9.78**
	$k = 10$	12.82	**13.62**	12.23	**18.18**	11.48	**17.45**	15.96	5.37	**12.49**
FSOD YOLACT	$k = 1$	1.36	**2.23**	1.49	**2.16**	1.93	**2.06**	1.72	1.71	**2.10**
	$k = 3$	3.42	3.36	2.51	3.42	**4.05**	**3.44**	3.05	3.30	**3.33**
	$k = 5$	3.99	**4.51**	3.02	3.80	**5.24**	3.78	**4.31**	3.40	**4.40**
	$k = 10$	6.19	**6.70**	4.43	6.36	**7.31**	**6.18**	5.60	6.09	**6.45**

With respect to the *presence of text*, overall the performance is slightly better for instances that contain text. Initially, we found this surprising. We expected the opposite trend since we suspected that the limited prevalence of text in prior datasets would have led algorithm designers to not consider the presence of text in their algorithm designs. We suspect part of the reason for our finding is that, if the text on the objects is clear enough to be visible, then the image is high quality. Additionally, the high frequency information from text regions in instance segmentations may be valuable predictive cues, despite the absence of the ability to recognize the text as text. Finally, the presence of text has a strong correlation with particular categories, which may influence our findings.

Finally, with respect to the *presence of holes*, the performance is consistently worse for objects that contain holes. The presence of holes raises the task complexity dramatically by requiring algorithms to go beyond locating object boundaries to also have a semantic understanding of all pixels within the object boundary. According to our analysis in Sect. 3 and the Supplementary Materials, objects with larger sizes tend to have more coverage by holes, including due to occlusion. Therefore, we suspect that the poor performance that we observed for larger sized objects could be correlated with the poor performance we observing with our analysis here on objects with holes.

4.2   Few-Shot Object Detection

We benchmarked two FSOD algorithms for which code is publicly-available. First, we chose Decoupled Faster R-CNN (*DeFRCN*) with its default hyperparameters [29], since it is the state-of-the-art FSOD model. It follows a two-stage fine-tuning paradigm. For our k-shot experiments, we randomly sample k images to use for fine-tuning the model. We also benchmark the YOLACT model used for FSIS by converting its segmentation results into bounding boxes.

Overall Performance: Overall results are shown in Table 1. These results resemble those observed for FSIS. Specifically, both algorithms perform poorly on our dataset and much worse on our dataset than reported for the original dataset on which they were evaluated. These results reinforce that our new dataset offers distinct challenges from existing datasets for FSOD algorithms.

Fine-Grained Analysis: We perform the same fine-grained analysis conducted for FSIS with the two benchmarked FSOD models, and results are also reported in Table 2. While we observe that the level of *image quality* does not correlate with algorithm performance, we do observe performance trends for the other three factors. Moreover, these trends match those discussed for FSIS. Specifically, both benchmarked models tend to perform the worst for small objects, perform better when text is present, and perform worse when holes are present.

Table 3. Generalization of models trained on MS COCO for few-shot object detection to matching categories in our VizWiz-Fewshot-OD dataset.

Model	Testing set	mAP				mAP$_{50}$			
		1	3	5	10	1	3	5	10
DeFRCN	MS COCO	6.63	12.32	14.20	16.69	12.50	21.69	24.87	29.15
	VizWiz	1.32	3.43	2.17	4.57	2.74	5.86	3.39	6.53

Cross-Dataset Analysis: Finally, we evaluated DeFRCN's generalization performance across datasets.[8] To do, so we randomly selected 20 of the 37 categories

---

[8] Of note, we also conducted cross-dataset experiments with YOLACT in the FSIS and FSOD settings however the cross-dataset performance was negligible. We attribute it to unsuccessful training with the chosen hyperparameters, both because the loss plateaued rather than converging with the new YOLACT hyperparameter values used in this paper and the loss exploded when using the original YOLACT values (i.e., the performance of YOLACT reported in the original paper could not be replicated when using the different set of training categories from MS COCO). In summary, the cross-dataset analysis results of YOLACT reinforce our initial findings that YOLACT performance is extremely sensitive to chosen hyperparameters and the training data, with custom tuning for each change.

found in both MS COCO and VizWiz-FewShot-OD-25^i as novel classes. Next, we trained DeFRCN on the remaining 60 MS COCO classes and then fine-tuned it with k-shot images randomly sampled from the 20 novel classes in MS COCO. The resulting model was evaluated on both the MS COCO test set as well as our VizWiz-FewShot-OD-25^i test set. Results are shown in Table 3. We observe significant gaps between scores on MS COCO and our dataset revealing that the algorithm generalizes poorly when encountering the domain shift between the two datasets. These findings reinforce that images in our dataset offers distinct algorithmic challenges from those observed in MS COCO.

5   Conclusions

We introduce the VizWiz-FewShot dataset to facilitate the community in designing few-shot learning models for object detection and instance segmentation that work well for the diverse set of challenges that emerge in real-world applications. Our benchmarking of top few-shot localization algorithms reveal that valuable directions for future work are to better support objects that contain holes, very small and very large objects, and objects that lack text.

Acknowledgments. This project was supported in part by a National Science Foundation SaTC award (#2148080) and gift funding from Microsoft AI4A. We thank Leah Findlater and Yang Wang for contributing to this research idea and the anonymous reviewers for their valuable feedback to improve this work.

References

1. Amirreza Shaban, Shray Bansal, Z.L.I.E., Boots, B.: One-shot learning for semantic segmentation. In: Proceedings of the British Machine Vision Conference (BMVC), pp. 167.1–167.13, September 2017
2. Bhattacharya, N., Li, Q., Gurari, D.: Why does a visual question have different answers? In: Proceedings of the IEEE/CVF International Conference on Computer Vision, pp. 4271–4280 (2019)
3. Bigham, J.P., et al.: VizWiz: nearly real-time answers to visual questions. In: Proceedings of the 23nd Annual ACM Symposium on User Interface Software and Technology, pp. 333–342 (2010)
4. American Federation for the Blind: Low vision optical devices. https://www.afb.org/node/16207/low-vision-optical-devices
5. Bolya, D., Zhou, C., Xiao, F., Lee, Y.J.: YOLACT: real-time instance segmentation. In: ICCV (2019)
6. Chen, C., Anjum, S., Gurari, D.: Grounding answers for visual questions asked by visually impaired people. In: Proceedings of the IEEE/CVF Conference on Computer Vision and Pattern Recognition, pp. 19098–19107 (2022)
7. Chiu, T.Y., Zhao, Y., Gurari, D.: Assessing image quality issues for real-world problems. In: Proceedings of the IEEE/CVF Conference on Computer Vision and Pattern Recognition, pp. 3646–3656 (2020)

8. Deng, J., Dong, W., Socher, R., Li, L.J., Li, K., Fei-Fei, L.: ImageNet: a large-scale hierarchical image database. In: 2009 IEEE Conference on Computer Vision and Pattern Recognition, pp. 248–255 (2009). https://doi.org/10.1109/CVPR.2009.5206848

9. Desmond, N.: Microsoft's Seeing AI founder Saqib Shaikh is speaking at Sight Tech Global. https://social.techcrunch.com/2020/08/20/microsofts-seeingai-founder-saqib-shaikh-is-speaking-at-sight-tech-global/

10. Dong, X., Zheng, L., Ma, F., Yang, Y., Meng, D.: Few-example object detection with model communication. IEEE Trans. Pattern Anal. Mach. Intell. **PP**, 1 (2018)

11. Everingham, M., Gool, L.V., Williams, C.K.I., Winn, J.M., Zisserman, A.: The pascal visual object classes (VOC) challenge. Int. J. Comput. Vis. (IJCV) **88**, 303–338 (2009)

12. Be My Eyes: Be My Eyes: Our story. https://www.bemyeyes.com/about

13. Fan, Q., Zhuo, W., Tang, C.K., Tai, Y.W.: Few-shot object detection with attention-RPN and multi-relation detector. In: Proceedings of the IEEE/CVF Conference on Computer Vision and Pattern Recognition (CVPR) (2020)

14. Fan, Z., et al.: FGN: fully guided network for few-shot instance segmentation. In: 2020 IEEE/CVF Conference on Computer Vision and Pattern Recognition (CVPR), pp. 9169–9178. Computer Vision Foundation/IEEE (2020)

15. Gurari, D., et al.: Predicting foreground object ambiguity and efficiently crowdsourcing the segmentation (s). Int. J. Comput. Vision **126**(7), 714–730 (2018)

16. Gurari, D., et al.: VizWiz-Priv: a dataset for recognizing the presence and purpose of private visual information in images taken by blind people. In: Proceedings of the IEEE/CVF Conference on Computer Vision and Pattern Recognition, pp. 939–948 (2019)

17. Gurari, D., et al.: VizWiz grand challenge: answering visual questions from blind people. In: Proceedings of the IEEE Conference on Computer Vision and Pattern Recognition, pp. 3608–3617 (2018)

18. Gurari, D., Zhao, Y., Zhang, M., Bhattacharya, N.: Captioning images taken by people who are blind. In: Vedaldi, A., Bischof, H., Brox, T., Frahm, J.-M. (eds.) ECCV 2020. LNCS, vol. 12362, pp. 417–434. Springer, Cham (2020). https://doi.org/10.1007/978-3-030-58520-4_25

19. Kim, J.-H., Lim, S., Park, J., Cho, H.: Korean localization of visual question answering for blind people. In: SK T-Brain - AI for Social Good Workshop at NeurIPS (2019)

20. Jiaxu, L., et al.: A comparative review of recent few-shot object detection algorithms (2021)

21. Kang, B., Liu, Z., Wang, X., Yu, F., Feng, J., Darrell, T.: Few-shot object detection via feature reweighting. In: 2019 IEEE/CVF International Conference on Computer Vision (ICCV), pp. 8419–8428, November 2019

22. Lee, S., Reddie, M., Tsai, C.H., Beck, J., Rosson, M.B., Carroll, J.M.: The emerging professional practice of remote sighted assistance for people with visual impairments. In: Proceedings of the 2020 CHI Conference on Human Factors in Computing Systems, pp. 1–12 (2020)

23. Li, X., Wei, T., Chen, Y.P., Tai, Y.W., Tang, C.K.: FSS-1000: a 1000-class dataset for few-shot segmentation. In: Proceedings of the IEEE/CVF Conference on Computer Vision and Pattern Recognition (CVPR) (2020)

24. Lin, T.-Y., et al.: Microsoft COCO: common objects in context. In: Fleet, D., Pajdla, T., Schiele, B., Tuytelaars, T. (eds.) ECCV 2014. LNCS, vol. 8693, pp. 740–755. Springer, Cham (2014). https://doi.org/10.1007/978-3-319-10602-1_48

25. Massiceti, D., et al.: Orbit: a real-world few-shot dataset for teachable object recognition. In: ICCV 2021, October 2021
26. Michaelis, C., Ustyuzhaninov, I., Bethge, M., Ecker, A.S.: One-shot instance segmentation. ArXiv (2018)
27. Nguyen, K., Todorovic, S.: FAPIS: a few-shot anchor-free part-based instance segmenter. In: 2021 IEEE/CVF Conference on Computer Vision and Pattern Recognition (CVPR), pp. 11094–11103 (2021)
28. Nguyen, K.D.M., Todorovic, S.: Feature weighting and boosting for few-shot segmentation. In: 2019 IEEE/CVF International Conference on Computer Vision (ICCV), pp. 622–631 (2019)
29. Qiao, L., Zhao, Y., Li, Z., Qiu, X., Wu, J., Zhang, C.: DeFRCN: decoupled faster R-CNN for few-shot object detection. ArXiv (2021)
30. Stangl, A.J., Kothari, E., Jain, S.D., Yeh, T., Grauman, K., Gurari, D.: BrowseWithMe: an online clothes shopping assistant for people with visual impairments. In: Proceedings of the 20th International ACM SIGACCESS Conference on Computers and Accessibility, pp. 107–118 (2018)
31. Yan, X., Chen, Z., Xu, A., Wang, X., Liang, X., Lin, L.: Meta R-CNN: towards general solver for instance-level low-shot learning. In: 2019 IEEE/CVF International Conference on Computer Vision (ICCV), October 2019
32. Zeng, X., Wang, Y., Chiu, T.Y., Bhattacharya, N., Gurari, D.: Vision skills needed to answer visual questions. Proc. ACM Hum.-Comput. Interact. 4(CSCW2), 1–31 (2020)
33. Zhao, Z.Q., Zheng, P., Xu, S.T., Wu, X.: Object detection with deep learning: a review. IEEE Trans. Neural Netw. Learn. Syst. PP, 1–21 (2019). https://doi.org/10.1109/TNNLS.2018.2876865

TRoVE: Transforming Road Scene Datasets into Photorealistic Virtual Environments

Shubham Dokania[1](✉), Anbumani Subramanian[1], Manmohan Chandraker[2], and C. V. Jawahar[1]

[1] IIIT Hyderabad, Hyderabad, Telangana, India
shubham.dokania@research.iiit.ac.in
[2] University of California San Diego, San Diego, CA, USA

Abstract. High-quality structured data with rich annotations are critical components in intelligent vehicle systems dealing with road scenes. However, data curation and annotation require intensive investments and yield low-diversity scenarios. The recently growing interest in synthetic data raises questions about the scope of improvement in such systems and the amount of manual work still required to produce high volumes and variations of simulated data. This work proposes a synthetic data generation pipeline that utilizes existing datasets, like nuScenes, to address the difficulties and domain-gaps present in simulated datasets. We show that using annotations and visual cues from existing datasets, we can facilitate automated multi-modal data generation, mimicking real scene properties with high-fidelity, along with mechanisms to diversify samples in a physically meaningful way. We demonstrate improvements in mIoU metrics by presenting qualitative and quantitative experiments with real and synthetic data for semantic segmentation on the Cityscapes and KITTI-STEP datasets. *All relevant code and data is released on github*[3] (https://github.com/shubham1810/trove_toolkit).

Keywords: Synthetic data · Road scenes · Self-driving · Semantic segmentation

1 Introduction

Computer vision applications, specifically autonomous driving systems, are constantly evolving owing to the rapid progress in the deep learning and machine vision community. At the core of such advancements lies the foundation created by high-quality, structured data, which augments the strengths of sophisticated architectures. While data acquisition and processing require expensive hardware setup and efforts to collect and process, there are several self-driving platforms

---

Supplementary Information The online version contains supplementary material available at https://doi.org/10.1007/978-3-031-20074-8_34.

Fig. 1. A sample of the scene generated with the proposed method. The first image shown is a real-world sample from nuScenes dataset. Using some existing annotation, we are able to generate extensions such as depth, instance segmentation, RGB images, semantic segmentation, and surface normals. These modalities represent a part of the capabilities of the proposed method.

which provide easier access to large volume of raw and processed data. However, data annotation still poses a huge challenge and is a resource extensive process. Even in the cases when it is feasible, the sheer number of possibilities in real-world diversity makes it unfathomable to observe all variations in object types, scenes, weathers, traffic densities, and sensor configurations. All these possibilities for variations create a near-insurmountable obstacle for dataset curation and annotations for self-driving and road scene scenarios. Use of synthetic data allows creation of such variations and extended diversity for a vast number of scenes, but requires expensive and expert manual efforts for simulations. In this work, we raise the question whether this abundant real-data can be used to automatically create synthetic datasets for training machine learning algorithms and be inclusive of large-variations while preserving real-world structural properties. Mimicking the physical properties of real-data in a synthetic pipeline helps towards minimizing domain gaps, while allowing to generate physically meaningful variations in scenes.

There have been several advancements in the preparation and utilization of synthetic datasets in recent times [18,19,22,40,42,49]. While synthetically generated data may not be a complete substitute for real-world data yet, some works [22,43,45] discuss the usefulness of augmenting real-world data with synthetic datasets for improved performance . There have been significant improvements in approaches for domain adaptation [12,23,43], transfer of synthetic-to-real scenes and improvement in photo-realism [28,38]. It becomes easier to add different environments, diversity in ambiance, lighting, weathers, and sensors using synthetic data. However, while the data synthesis through simulation is more straightforward than real-world dataset creation, it still requires a significant manual effort. Adding a new scene in such existing pipelines requires expertise to ensure a degree of photo-realism. Recent works highlight learning methods to generate novel trajectories and motion patterns [41,47,51]. Still, they may not necessarily delineate real-world behavior accurately, especially in complex scenes with varying crowd and traffic densities.

We propose an approach to model synthetic data based on real-world data distributions using available annotations and visual cues, mimicking real-world domain structure and enabling variations in a physically meaningful manner. Unlike most existing works, we show that using information from existing datasets for object placement and behavior can allow for fast construction of virtual environments while preserving the appeal of synthetic data generation systems for efficiency and diversity. We can use the same labels from a real scene to generate a diverse set of annotated data items from each scene (example shown in Figs. 1 and 3) with diverse environmental conditions.

Our approach utilizes the location information from existing real scenes and visual cues available either as annotations or extracted from driving video sequences using currently available approaches in computer vision. We generate high-fidelity environment maps using geographic data available online and supplement this data with extracted cues from existing datasets and scenes. Our physically-based method of scene generation allows us to match different aspects of the scenes such as object positions, orientations, appearances, and ambient factors to recreate virtual environments that mimic real-world. The proposed approach is not restricted to manual design or hand-crafted environments, so it can be extended to virtually any location and complexity configuration for which visual cues can be automatically generated or already available.

A prime example of such a method is to extend existing datasets by utilizing the available annotation from the vast set of high-quality datasets [10,21,24,44] and generate multiple variations for each scene to increase the data volume and annotation modalities available. To support our claims, we outline our approach in the forthcoming sections and use the nuScenes dataset [6] as a base for the core set of experiments. An overview of our approach is shown in Fig. 2. We use some parts of the already available annotations in nuScenes to generate new environments with traffic and pedestrian behavior similar to that available in the nuScenes dataset while varying the visual information to accommodate a diverse set of configurations. We show qualitative and quantitative analysis over segmentation tasks and compare validation metrics over popular datasets to outline the effectiveness of our data generation strategy for being physically consistent and adhering to real-world distributions. We highlight multiple modalities in our proposed dataset to enable various vision downstream tasks with different sensor configurations.

2   Related Work

Data acquisition and annotation for several downstream tasks can be challenging and resource-intensive. Especially for tasks like semantic segmentation, data preparation's cost and time estimate rise rapidly with data volume. There exist many real-world datasets in the community which targets specific problem statements such as vision tasks in indoor scenes [32], datasets with fine annotations for semantic segmentation and 3D object detection in outdoor scenes [2,15,16,48], and 3D LiDAR point cloud segmentation in urban environments [4,24,29]. However, considering the cost of expensive annotations, it is often the case that some datasets only focus on specific modalities. For example, the nuScenes dataset [6] consists of high-quality annotations for object detection, tracking, trajectory prediction, LiDAR segmentation, and panoptic LiDAR segmentation but does not contain fine semantic segmentation annotations due to the sheer volume of available images.

Simulator-Based Methods: Synthetic datasets have been shown to improve performances across a variety of tasks including, but not limited to, object detection [26,33], trajectory prediction [7,51], depth estimation [3,31], semantic and instance segmentation [5,49], human pose estimation [45], object 6DoF pose estimation [26], 3D reconstruction [9], tracking and optical flow [50]. CARLA [19] is a popular simulator that relies on manually designed environment maps and places 3D object assets for vehicles, pedestrians, and dynamic entities in the environment. CARLA simulates different traffic conditions, variations in lighting, and some weather changes, which are rendered in a photo-realistic manner to provide significant overlap with real-world scenarios. The base version of the CARLA simulator provides a limited number of 3D city environments; different scenarios are simulated, and annotations are generated, which can be either exported to train deep learning models or utilized via their API to evaluate autonomous driving benchmark tasks. LGSVL Simulator [39] is a recent addition to the available simulation engines that delivers high-fidelity data for autonomous driving scenarios. LGSVL is built with an integration of Apollo Auto [1], which provides various features for interfacing with autonomous driving runtimes. The 3D environment is generated to mimic several real-world locations and integrate multiple sensor types, including RGB, Radar, LiDAR, which can be configured to behave like real-world sensors such as the Velodyne VLP-16 LiDAR. A recent simulation suite built on CARLA is the SUMMIT engine for urban traffic scenarios [7]. SUMMIT simulates complex and unregulated behavior in dense traffic environments and utilizes real-world maps to replicate difficult areas like roundabouts, highways, and intersection junctions. SUMMIT uses a context-aware behavior model, Context-GAMMA, an extension of GAMMA [30], to formulate agents' motion in complex environments for dynamic crowd behavior.

Non-simulation Approaches: Several works in literature do not rely on simulation of the driving environment directly but provide structured fine annotations. A notable contribution to the community in this area is the Virtual KITTI dataset [22] which builds over the popular KITTI dataset [46] and extends the limited amount of annotated information by generating close-to-realistic images for digital-twins of sequences from the KITTI dataset. The Virtual KITTI dataset was recently extended in the Virtual KITTI 2 dataset [5], where the quality of images has been improved with a high definition render pipeline and the latest game engine (Unity 2018.4 LTS). The core approach in the Virtual KITTI dataset involves the acquisition of real-world data and measurements from the KITTI MOT benchmarks, then building a synthetic clone of the environments

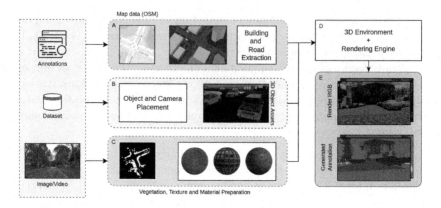

Fig. 2. An overview of the synthetic data generation pipeline. Given real-world input dataset with annotations for object locations, we follow the process depicted in the above figure. (A) Map data extraction from OSM for building and road extraction. (B) Retrieval of categorical information and 3D object placement in scene with sampled camera poses. (C) Extraction of background data such as vegetation mask in world coordinates and PBR texture preparation. (D) Fusion of artifacts in the 3D environment and initialization of rendering process. (E) Generated RGB data and corresponding annotations stored for further use.

semi-automatically. Then, the objects of interest are placed in the scene manually, and lighting is adjusted to match the real-scene visually. There also exist datasets like SYNTHIA [40], that do not rely on any visual or geometric cues from real-world datasets and build novel virtual worlds to facilitate synthetic data generation. SYNTHIA provides generated annotations over 13 classes for pixel-level semantic segmentation and frames rendered from multiple view-points in the virtual environment. SYNTHIA dataset consists of large-scale annotations of up to 200k images across four-season settings in the form of video sequences and a random split of data with 13.4k images generated from randomly sampled camera locations across the synthetic map. While the volume and impact of the SYNTHIA dataset is prominent, the data generation process involves exorbitant manual effort. Furthermore, the dynamic entities in the scenes are also programmed manually to capture Spatio-temporal information between different vehicles and pedestrians.

Learning-Based Methods: Some recent approaches focus on imitation training [27] for iterative generation of more training data, especially for scenes where the model performs poorly. The work presented in [35] deals explicitly with the problem of domain gap in synthetic data by employing self-supervised learning over scene graphs to learn the scene layout and compare generated images with unlabelled images in the target domain. A recurring limitation observed in most datasets tends to be a lack of proper replication of real-world structures in an automated way without learning data or scene-specific layouts. The simulators can construct high-quality environments with variations in multiple factors. They, however, do not replicate the behavior of traffic entities from across a variety of locations around the world, and learned behaviors can only reproduce such motion and trajectory, which is reflective of the training data. In our proposed method for generating synthetic datasets, we leverage visual cues and pre-existing annotations from public datasets and enable the construction of large-scale scenes in virtual environments while mapping driver and pedestrian behavior from actual data into a virtual space.

3   Our Approach

We describe the process for generating synthetic data automatically using either existing annotations from public datasets or visual cues from video sequences. We demonstrate the process with an example of the nuScenes dataset [6], but the same method can be applied to other datasets with available annotations [10,29,46]. The core components required to realize the data generation pipeline comprise of the geographic location and objects location/orientation in a given scene or video sequence. It is possible to construct a structured description of the scene and use it as configuration for the data generation process. To ensure diversity in object appearances, we use publicly available free 3D assets for different classes. The process of generating synthetic data using the proposed approach can be broken down into four major parts, which consist of (1) Building the world environment, (2) Placement of objects and camera in the scenes, (3) Applying textures and lighting information, and (4) Rendering and annotation processing. In the following subsections, we describe the steps in detail, referencing the overall process as shown in Fig. 2, and samples from intermediate stages shown in Fig. 4. All development of the 3D environment for our dataset is performed in Blender [13], an open-source 3D modeling and development software.

3.1   Building the Virtual Environment

Assuming the ego-vehicle to be the origin at each scene, we can estimate the geographic location using either GPS data (if available), or offset from scene geometry origin for which GPS information may be available.

Buildings: For generating the building placeholder, we refer to data from Open-StreetMaps (OSM) [34] through a blender add-on (blender-osm [36]). The meshes are generated without any texture initially. To extend variability in the scene, we choose buildings with an approximately rectangular layout and replace the mesh with a 3D building asset. The 3D assets used in this work were acquired from free-to-use resources on different forums such as [8,25]. To check whether a building (say b) qualifies for replacement, we take the points (x, y) from the base plane of b as $\{(x, y)|b_z = 0\}$ and compute the edge length as well as orientations for the building base polygon. Let the edges be denoted by $e_{1,2} = d((x_1, y_1), (x_2, y_2))$ and the orientations be $\theta_{1,2} = \arctan((y_2 - y_1)/(x_2 - x_1))$, where d represents the euclidean distance function. We then compute a histogram of orientations, weighted by the respective edge lengths and select the pairs with close to $\pi/2$ difference. The selected pair with the highest edge weight (lengths) are then chosen to estimate the orientation of the rectangular building base. If no such edges and orientations are found, we assume a complex building outline and mark the building for applying facade texture in a later stage. Optionally, we can also compute the area of the polygon by projecting the base plane on a raster grid and taking ratio of area with the enclosing convex polygon. However, to avoid additional computations, we do not employ this approach in the current pipeline.

Roads: The road meshes are extracted from OSM map data as well via blender-osm. The road meshes are connected together to form a joint mesh object for the entire road network in the current context. The road width is adjusted to approximately match the road width available from real-world annotations (for nuScenes, extracted from the LiDAR point cloud).

Fig. 3. Example of variations in synthetic data for the same scene configuration. (a) The real-dataset image depicting a scene from the nuScenes dataset. (b) Sample render with different buildings, vehicles, pedestrians and lighting (c) Rendered image from "b" after applying color transformation for the cityscapes dataset. (d) Render for the same scene from a different camera perspective. (e, f) Additional renders from the scene with variations in vehicles, buildings, lighting etc.

3.2   Object and Camera Placement

We utilize the annotations available in the real-world datasets for extracting bounding boxes and camera poses for each scene and lay out the process to replicate the same structure in the virtual environment.

3D Object Placement: To assign a 3D asset to each bounding box, we estimate a *quality-of-fit* metric based on the Intersection over Union (IoU) for 3D bounding boxes. For a given object bounding box (say o_i) and a set of N 3D assets with corresponding bounding boxes (say $\{o_j | j \in 1, ..., N\}$) centered at the origin, we scale the asset box such that the largest dimension of the asset box o_j matches that of the query box o_i, while preserving aspect ratios. We then compute the 3D IoU metric as follows:

$$IoU_{3D}(o_i, o_j) = IoU_{xy}(o_i, o_j) * min(z_{o_i}, z_{o_j}) \tag{1}$$

where, IoU_{xy} represents the 2D IoU metric for projection on the XY-plane, z_{o_i} is the length of the box along z-axis for object i. We are able to use a simplified implementation f the 3D IoU metric due to the known physical properties of both source and target object. We assign the asset with highest IoU_{3D} for a best match, or randomly sample from top-k to induce object diversity.

Camera Pose: We process the camera matrix and pose information from the source dataset and create virtual clones with similar configuration in the simulated environment. To extend the extent and visual coverage of generated images, we additionally sample camera poses from different vehicles in the scene (along with ego-vehicle), hence diversifying the view-points in a scene.

3.3   Textures, Lighting and Background

Texture and Lighting play a critical role towards achieving photo-realism in 3D virtual environment. Additionally, having dense background objects improves the content domain-gap and are a step forward towards realistic distribution of scene geometry.

Textures: We use high-quality 4K textures and PBR (Physically based rendering) materials from free-to-use forums [14]. High-resolution maps for color, displacement, roughness, normals, metallic, and emission are available, through which we create BSDF materials for building facades, roads, sidewalks, and ground/terrain.

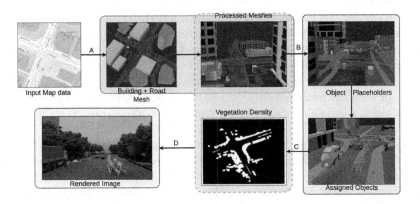

Fig. 4. Samples from different steps in the proposed approach. Step (A) corresponds to the Sect. 3.1 for Building and Road processing, (B) corresponds to object placeholder creation and placement, (C) shows vegetation texture density as image, and part of building/road texture in step (A) output. Finally, Stage (D) shows the rendered output for the given scene and the camera pose data.

Lighting: High-fidelity materials are important for photo-realism because the pixel-wise distribution of lighting, reflections and color impacts the level of visual perception. Lighting in virtual scenes is very important to accurately model scene dynamics from different view-points. We add different lighting environment models using High Dynamic Range Image (HDRI) to ensure a high range of illumination levels.

Background: We utilise LiDAR point cloud data from source and construct a 2D location density map for bushes and trees in the scene. To avoid unrealistic occurrences, we remove density data from road area by application of a binary mask. An example of the vegetation density in a scene is shown in Fig. 2(C). In the virtual scene, we apply a probability distribution over the ground plane using the vegetation density map and instantiate trees/bushes. We sample different types and number of trees from the available assets with variations in sizes and sample locations. A similar approach is used for generating traffic signs and poles along the sidewalks in the scene.

3.4   Data Processing and Training

Once the preparation of the virtual environment is completed with all objects and entities populated in the scene, we proceed towards rendering and dataset curation stages for synthetic data availability in experiments.

Rendering and Annotations: We use the Cycles rendering engine in Blender to render the 3D scene and generate multi-modal annotations for semantic and instance segmentation, optical flow, depth estimation, 2D and 3D object detection. We employ the library provided in BlenderProc [17] for annotation extraction. Annotations are generated for 20 classes (including void) namely; sky, car, bus, jeep, truck, van, human, building, road, barrier, ground, cycle rider, construction (vehicle), bushes, trees, motorcycle rider, traffic cone, traffic sign, sidewalk, and void. However, for fair comparison with common benchmarks, we further process the available data into 13 classes as follows: void, car, bus, truck, person, rider, road, sidewalk, building, traffic poles, vegetation, terrain, and sky.

Training Data: For training and evaluation purpose, we sample a set of 5000 images from our synthetic dataset which have been selected based on the class distribution in annotation maps such that each sample contains a minimum of 6–8 different classes. Additional attention towards imbalance due to background classes is necessary to improve class-wise distribution.

Color Processing: Since we render images in different lighting conditions, the visual pixel-distribution may vary compared to a dataset we wish to benchmark against. Towards this, we optionally add a color processing stage similar to what was proposed in [37]. We transform the source and target images to L*a*b* color space and adjust the mean and variance of the source domain to a scaled metric between the two domains. A visual example is presented in Fig. 3(b, c).

4   Experiments and Results

For a streamlined analysis and discussion about the experiments, we first outline details about the datasets used in our study and layout the experiment design. Then we analyse the results quantitatively and qualitatively to see how the proposed approach is useful to generate synthetic data that is useful for real-world model training and evaluation.

4.1   Datasets and Experiments

For our analysis, we use the Cityscapes [15] and KITTI-STEP [48] datasets. Both of these datasets have been selected for the fairly substantial amount of annotated data available in each.

Cityscapes: A widely used dataset for tasks related to visual odometry and perception for road scenes. The dataset provides 5000 finely annotated images for semantic and panoptic segmentation, and an additional 20000 images with coarse annotations with 30 class annotations. Collected over 50 cities in Europe, the dataset provides abundant diversity across scenes with different seasons, and some variations in weather. We use the full training set of the Cityscapes dataset (denoted as R) along with a random subset of 1000 images from the training set (denoted as P, partial) to show the impact of our synthetic dataset on evaluation of the validation set (denoted as V) from the real-world Cityscapes dataset. All images have been re-scaled to 512×256 without loss in aspect ratio for use in training semantic segmentation task. We only use the 5000 finely annotated (2975 for train and 500 for validation) for our experiments.

KITTI-STEP (Segmenting and Tracking Every Pixel) dataset, is an extension of the KITTI dataset with 21 training and 29 testing sequences from the raw KITTI dataset, based on the KITTI-MOTS [46] dataset and provides semantic as well as panoptic segmentation labels for each image in the sequence along with tracking IDs for non-background objects across frames in a scene. Since this dataset contains more samples compared to the KITTI semantic segmentation benchmark [2], we use the 5027 images in the train set and 2981 images in the validation set for our experiments. It is important to note that since the data is extracted from sequences, there is substantial overlap between many frames in the training set which will impact the results, as we shall see in the later analysis. We re-scale the images to a resolution of 620×188 without loss of aspect ratio for our experiments and perform semantic segmentation task. We follow the same notation where the full training data shall be denoted by R, partial data of 1000 images as P, and the validation set as V.

Training Details: We employ the Deeplab V2 architecture [11] with the resnet-50 backbone (pretrained with imagenet weights) without CRF. The architecture is kept consistent across all experiments to ensure fairness. For training, 5000 image samples from the generated synthetic dataset are considered, denoted as S. Each image is generated at a resolution of 1600×900, then appropriately downscaled and randomly cropped during training to adhere to aspect ratio in the image and match the real data for both training and validation, i.e., 512×256 for Cityscapes and 620×188 for KITTI-STEP. The color transformation scheme mentioned in Sect. 3.4 is optionally used and will be denoted as C wherever applicable in the results. For combined training of synthetic and real data, we use two methods; we can mix the real and synthetic images in the same batch while training the model (denoted by M) or train on synthetic data initially and then fine-tune with the real data (denoted by F). For an exhaustive comparison, we present results on all combinations of the settings and report the per-class IoU, mean IoU (mIoU), and global accuracy of each method. For training, we do not employ any additional augmentations apart from randomly cropping the synthetic image to adjust aspect ratio. The models are all trained for 30 epochs, with a batch size of 10 and initial learning rate $1e - 04$. The models are trained on a Nvidia RTX 2080Ti GPU using Pytorch-lightning [20]. The quantitative results from experiments on Cityscapes and KITTI-STEP are presented in Tables 1 and 2, respectively.

Table 1. Quantitative results for training on real and synthetic data and validation on Cityscapes dataset. We report class-wise IoU, mIoU and global accuracy for the 12 classes (excluding void)

Training method	Val. data	Sky	Car	Bus	Truck	Person	Rider	Road	Sidewalk	Building	Traffic Poles	Veget	Terrain	mIoU	Acc.
R	V	89.25	88.86	67.66	57.16	60.15	43.66	96.51	73.88	86.83	36.77	86.49	55.71	70.25	98.88
S	V	27.86	41.19	3.93	4.49	23.54	14.11	71.57	18.86	61.73	1.45	70.61	28.19	30.63	95.50
S + R [F]	V	89.03	88.86	68.27	51.16	60.53	43.21	96.67	74.88	86.89	**39.16**	86.51	57.62	70.23	98.89
S + R [M]	V	**90.06**	89.14	67.96	53.01	61.08	**44.73**	**96.84**	75.92	87.38	38.13	**87.04**	58.49	70.82	98.93
S + C	V	72.84	47.22	9.73	7.54	38.22	15.15	67.60	20.23	74.13	4.44	74.46	12.83	37.03	95.84
S + C + R [F]	V	88.95	88.83	69.07	57.38	60.33	43.99	96.66	74.83	86.97	38.20	86.49	57.07	70.73	98.89
S + C + R [M]	V	90.04	**89.51**	**72.09**	**65.48**	**61.28**	41.98	96.79	75.68	**87.46**	39.08	86.99	57.35	**71.98**	**98.94**
P	V	86.91	86.14	29.26	32.37	55.19	33.37	95.63	68.92	84.55	30.66	84.70	49.60	61.44	98.65
S + P [F]	V	88.00	86.71	46.71	35.02	55.22	28.40	96.03	70.62	84.99	32.80	85.03	53.16	63.56	98.70
S + P [M]	V	88.47	**87.25**	**58.44**	44.99	**57.92**	40.24	96.39	73.02	**85.86**	33.80	**85.78**	54.34	67.21	**98.80**
S + C + P [F]	V	87.19	86.71	49.94	36.39	55.05	26.36	95.61	68.59	85.13	33.20	85.10	48.05	63.11	98.69
S + C + P [M]	V	**89.05**	87.05	54.07	34.73	57.24	38.33	96.32	72.52	85.84	**34.01**	85.52	54.28	65.75	98.78

4.2 Result Analysis

In Table 1 and Table 2, we present the **mIoU** and IoU per class for the 12 classes (excluding void), along with the global accuracy for each of the different training methods. Furthermore, we present qualitative results on both Cityscapes and KITTI-STEP datasets for some of the methods in Fig. 5.

Cityscapes (Full Real): We notice that training with a mix of real and synthetic data results in a boost of $+1.73\%$ mIoU when the synthetic data has gone through color adjustment. It is interesting to note that while synthetic data in itself may not be enough for achieving high performance (mIoU 30.63%), whenever combined with real data, helps improve accuracy compared to real data only. This is clear in the qualitative results as well where the model trained with a mix of modified synthetic data and real data is able to generate better segmentation mask for the classes person, sky, traffic pole/sign. It is worth highlighting that for the example in first example (left-sub column) of Cityscapes dataset, the model trained on real data is not able to detect some instance of the person class, while the model trained on the mixture, even with partial, is able to detect the same for this particular sample. When considering autonomous driving scenarios and real-world use cases, this is a crucial detail to consider towards enhancing the performance of deep learning architectures through synthetic data.

Table 2. Quantitative results for training on real and synthetic data and validation on KITTI-STEM dataset. We report class-wise IoU, mIoU and global accuracy for the 12 classes (excluding void)

Training method	Val. data	Sky	Car	Bus	Truck	Person	Rider	Road	Sidewalk	Building	Traffic Poles	Veget	Terrain	mIoU	Acc.
R	V	91.31	86.66	0.14	18.52	**60.99**	27.93	**85.51**	59.32	81.54	44.20	89.57	72.06	59.81	98.39
S	V	26.44	27.29	28.85	1.95	29.94	14.34	41.21	18.96	26.73	2.53	68.75	44.81	27.64	92.96
S + R [F]	V	91.54	**87.34**	1.68	13.38	60.57	27.80	84.95	59.20	82.06	**45.49**	**90.22**	73.20	59.79	98.41
S + R [M]	V	91.61	**87.34**	**53.55**	**28.56**	60.39	30.44	85.14	58.31	81.84	42.83	90.12	**74.26**	**65.37**	**98.42**
S + C	V	80.18	71.03	34.60	15.97	45.35	19.29	48.00	21.96	63.61	12.80	83.06	57.79	46.14	95.92
S + C + R [F]	V	91.41	86.99	2.23	19.98	59.58	**33.22**	85.40	**59.43**	81.63	45.36	90.01	73.24	60.71	98.41
S + C + R [M]	V	**91.66**	85.20	45.98	25.32	59.85	29.05	84.60	57.75	**82.24**	42.99	90.03	72.55	63.93	98.38
P	V	90.41	84.54	0	6.16	56.09	17.61	84.39	56.23	80.23	39.54	89.62	72.30	56.44	98.28
S + P [F]	V	90.80	**85.87**	12.91	8.17	56.91	16.01	83.33	54.39	80.14	42.21	89.66	72.09	57.71	98.25
S + P [M]	V	90.64	85.31	31.85	16.13	59.17	**29.60**	**84.88**	**57.21**	80.90	**41.77**	**89.88**	**73.25**	61.72	**98.34**
S + C + P [F]	V	90.28	85.44	2.09	12.63	54.91	20.54	84.26	56.38	79.74	40.60	89.21	71.64	57.31	98.27
S + C + P [M]	V	**91.35**	85.54	**48.59**	**22.65**	59.25	26.97	84.50	55.65	**81.95**	39.00	89.82	71.80	**63.09**	98.33

Cityscapes (Partial Real): We also highlight that for Cityscapes dataset, the model trained with synthetic and partial data achieves a significant improvement (+5.77% mIoU) over the model trained with just partial data. This result emphasizes on the practical implications of synthetic data where scarcity of real-world annotated data availability may be a bottleneck. Qualitatively as well, the model (S + P [M]) is able to predict sharp segmentation masks for pedestrians crossing the road, compared to the large masks predicted by model (P), trained only on partial real data. The visual results are coherent with the per-class IoU metrics highlighted in Table 1. The road, sidewalk, and traffic sign/pole segmentation metric for partial data shows a gap in the performances with and without synthetic data, and the same is observable in example from column 2 (right) in the Cityscapes qualitative sample. The traffic poles are missing almost entirely in the prediction from (P) and the sidewalk structure shows significant noise. Whereas for the same sample, (S + P [M]) shows a higher degree of accuracy and even generates predictions for the poles which have low pixel density.

KITTI-STEP: To strengthen our claims, we bring attention to the results presented in Table 2 where training with synthetic data, assuming full training dataset, shows an improvement of +5.56% mIoU and with the partial real dataset available only, an improvement of +6.65% mIoU. The seemingly high difference

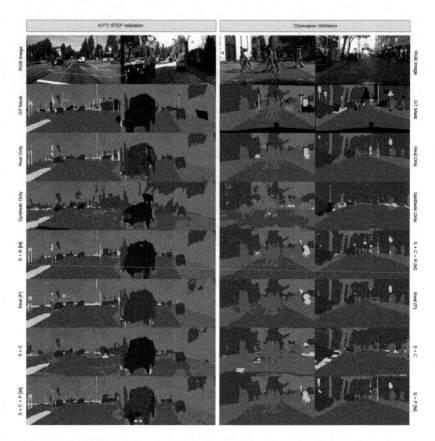

Fig. 5. Qualitative results for different training strategies using real and synthetic data across KITTI-STEP and Cityscapes datasets. The nomenclature is R: Real, S: Synthetic, P: Real (partial), [F]: Fine-tuned on real, [M]: Real mixed with synthetic, C: Color transformation

in the performance for these models can be attributed to the large performance gap in the "bus" and "truck" classes. The reason is that the number of annotated images with bus or truck appearing in the image is very low in the KITTI-STEP dataset. For qualitative confirmation of this case, we highlight column 2 (right) for KITTI-STEP dataset in Fig. 5. The models trained using only real data misclassify the pixels of the truck object as car, while the model trained with a combination of real and synthetic data accurately segments the object as truck in (S + R[M]). A similar case can be observed for the bus visible in column 1 where only the model trained with synthetic and real combined are able to correctly segment some portion of the bus object. It is important to note that while synthetic data is useful for enhancement of deep learning models, generating such datasets usually requires manual efforts and careful design. However, in this work, we showed a method to generate synthetic dataset fully automatically, hence avoiding the dependency on manual design.

4.3 Dataset Statistics

In the experiments presented, we use a sample of 5k images and semantic segmentation annotations, the 5k samples were selected after filtering out 2.8k samples with low variations in categorical labels per image. However, using the method described in this work, more data can be generated across different modalities including, but not limited to instance and panoptic segmentation, depth estimation, optical flow, surface normal estimation, 2D and 3D object detection, 6DoF object annotations, and 3D object reconstruction. We currently utilise 110 3D assets for different object categories and 40 PBR texture materials for roads, sidewalk, and building facades. In this work, we demonstrate the ability to generate synthetic data based on real-world annotations available in nuScenes dataset, however our approach can be extended to any public dataset to add more diversity in synthetic scenes. For each scene, we sample 20 images and corresponding annotations from different vehicles and camera poses. If OSM map data is available, it takes 25–30 s to generate a virtual scene otherwise 30–40 s considering an additional API call to OSM server to retrieve map data. Once a virtual scene is generated, it takes 65–85 s to render each image of size 1600×900 and the corresponding annotations using a RTX 2080Ti GPU. Essentially, we can generate annotated data in orders of 100,000 within a span of 1 week with 12 GPUs in parallel.

5   Conclusions

We propose a framework for automatic generation of synthetic data for visual perception using existing real-world data. Using a set of 5k synthetically generate images and corresponding semantic segmentation annotations, we show the efficiency of combining synthetic data with real data towards improvements in performance. Given the potential scale of data generation capabilities, various types of data selection strategies can be applied without losing precious annotations. Our approach avoids the pitfalls and limitations of bounded data volumes and variety unlike manually designed virtual environments. Making use of geographical data, our data generation process can be extended to different locations across the globe. Further work in this direction could explore additional modalities and improved photo-realism with more complex scenes generated from a diverse set of datasets and benchmarks on a multitude of tasks. We also highlight another future direction towards better automation by using only visual inputs from a user side.

Acknowledgements. This work is funded by iHub-data and mobility at IIIT Hyderabad.

References

1. Baidu Apollo team: Apollo: Open Source Autonomous Driving (2017). https:// github.com/apolloauto/apollo. Accessed 11 Feb 2022
2. Alhaija, H., Mustikovela, S., Mescheder, L., Geiger, A., Rother, C.: Augmented reality meets computer vision: efficient data generation for urban driving scenes. Int. J. Comput. Vis. (IJCV) **126**, 961–972 (2018)
3. Atapour-Abarghouei, A., Breckon, T.P.: Real-time monocular depth estimation using synthetic data with domain adaptation via image style transfer. In: Proceedings of the IEEE Conference on Computer Vision and Pattern Recognition, pp. 2800–2810 (2018)
4. Behley, J., et al.: Semantickitti: a dataset for semantic scene understanding of lidar sequences. In: Proceedings of the IEEE/CVF International Conference on Computer Vision, pp. 9297–9307 (2019)
5. Cabon, Y., Murray, N., Humenberger, M.: Virtual kitti 2. arXiv preprint arXiv:2001.10773 (2020)
6. Caesar, H., et al.: nuScenes: a multimodal dataset for autonomous driving. In: CVPR (2020)
7. Cai, P., Lee, Y., Luo, Y., Hsu, D.: SUMMIT: a simulator for urban driving in massive mixed traffic. In: 2020 IEEE International Conference on Robotics and Automation (ICRA), pp. 4023–4029 (2020). https://doi.org/10.1109/ICRA40945.2020.9197228
8. CGTrader: 3d model store. https://www.cgtrader.com/
9. Chang, A.X., et al.: ShapeNet: an information-rich 3d model repository. arXiv preprint arXiv:1512.03012 (2015)
10. Chang, M.F., et al.: Argoverse: 3d tracking and forecasting with rich maps. In: Proceedings of the IEEE/CVF Conference on Computer Vision and Pattern Recognition, pp. 8748–8757 (2019)
11. Chen, L.C., Papandreou, G., Kokkinos, I., Murphy, K., Yuille, A.L.: DeepLab: semantic image segmentation with deep convolutional nets, Atrous convolution, and fully connected CRFs. IEEE Trans. Pattern Anal. Mach. Intell. **40**(4), 834–848 (2017)
12. Chen, W., et al.: Contrastive syn-to-real generalization. In: International Conference on Learning Representations (2021). https://openreview.net/forum?id=F8whUO8HNbP
13. Blender Online Community: Blender - a 3D modelling and rendering package. Blender Foundation, Stichting Blender Foundation, Amsterdam (2018). http://www.blender.org
14. PolyHaven Community: 3d model and texture store. https://polyhaven.com/
15. Cordts, M., et al.: The cityscapes dataset for semantic urban scene understanding. In: Proceedings of the IEEE Conference on Computer Vision and Pattern Recognition (CVPR) (2016)
16. Cordts, M., et al.: The cityscapes dataset. In: CVPR Workshop on The Future of Datasets in Vision (2015)
17. Denninger, M., et al.: Blenderproc. arXiv preprint arXiv:1911.01911 (2019)
18. Devaranjan, J., Kar, A., Fidler, S.: Meta-Sim2: unsupervised learning of scene structure for synthetic data generation. In: Vedaldi, A., Bischof, H., Brox, T., Frahm, J.-M. (eds.) ECCV 2020. LNCS, vol. 12362, pp. 715–733. Springer, Cham (2020). https://doi.org/10.1007/978-3-030-58520-4_42

19. Dosovitskiy, A., Ros, G., Codevilla, F., Lopez, A., Koltun, V.: CARLA: an open urban driving simulator. In: Conference on Robot Learning, pp. 1–16. PMLR (2017)
20. Falcon, W., et al.: PyTorch lightning. GitHub **3**, 6 (2019). https://github.com/PyTorchLightning/pytorch-lightning
21. Gählert, N., Jourdan, N., Cordts, M., Franke, U., Denzler, J.: Cityscapes 3d: dataset and benchmark for 9 DoF vehicle detection. arXiv preprint arXiv:2006.07864 (2020)
22. Gaidon, A., Wang, Q., Cabon, Y., Vig, E.: Virtual worlds as proxy for multi-object tracking analysis. In: Proceedings of the IEEE Conference on Computer Vision and Pattern Recognition, pp. 4340–4349 (2016)
23. Hoyer, L., Dai, D., Van Gool, L.: DAFormer: improving network architectures and training strategies for domain-adaptive semantic segmentation. arXiv preprint arXiv:2111.14887 (2021)
24. Huang, X., et al.: The apolloscape dataset for autonomous driving. In: Proceedings of the IEEE Conference on Computer Vision and Pattern Recognition Workshops, pp. 954–960 (2018)
25. Trimble Inc: https://3dwarehouse.sketchup.com/
26. Josifovski, J., Kerzel, M., Pregizer, C., Posniak, L., Wermter, S.: Object detection and pose estimation based on convolutional neural networks trained with synthetic data. In: 2018 IEEE/RSJ International Conference on Intelligent Robots and Systems (IROS), pp. 6269–6276. IEEE (2018)
27. Kishore, A., Choe, T.E., Kwon, J., Park, M., Hao, P., Mittel, A.: Synthetic data generation using imitation training. In: Proceedings of the IEEE/CVF International Conference on Computer Vision, pp. 3078–3086 (2021)
28. Li, Z., et al.: OpenRooms: an end-to-end open framework for photorealistic indoor scene datasets. arXiv preprint arXiv:2007.12868 (2020)
29. Liao, Y., Xie, J., Geiger, A.: Kitti-360: a novel dataset and benchmarks for urban scene understanding in 2d and 3d. arXiv preprint arXiv:2109.13410 (2021)
30. Luo, Y., Cai, P., Hsu, D., Lee, W.S.: GAMMA: a general agent motion prediction model for autonomous driving. arXiv preprint arXiv:1906.01566 (2019)
31. Mayer, N.: What makes good synthetic training data for learning disparity and optical flow estimation? Int. J. Comput. Vision **126**(9), 942–960 (2018)
32. Silberman, N., Hoiem, D., Kohli, P., Fergus, R.: Indoor segmentation and support inference from RGBD images. In: Fitzgibbon, A., Lazebnik, S., Perona, P., Sato, Y., Schmid, C. (eds.) ECCV 2012. LNCS, vol. 7576, pp. 746–760. Springer, Heidelberg (2012). https://doi.org/10.1007/978-3-642-33715-4_54
33. Nowruzi, F.E., Kapoor, P., Kolhatkar, D., Hassanat, F.A., Laganiere, R., Rebut, J.: How much real data do we actually need: analyzing object detection performance using synthetic and real data. arXiv preprint arXiv:1907.07061 (2019)
34. OpenStreetMap contributors: planet dump retrieved from https://planet.osm.org (2017). https://www.openstreetmap.org
35. Prakash, A., et al.: Self-supervised real-to-sim scene generation. In: Proceedings of the IEEE/CVF International Conference on Computer Vision, pp. 16044–16054 (2021)
36. Prochitecture: Blender-OSM: OpenStreetMap and terrain for blender (2021). https://github.com/vvoovv/blender-osm
37. Reinhard, E., Adhikhmin, M., Gooch, B., Shirley, P.: Color transfer between images. IEEE Comput. Graphics Appl. **21**(5), 34–41 (2001)

38. Roberts, M., et al.: Hypersim: a photorealistic synthetic dataset for holistic indoor scene understanding. In: Proceedings of the IEEE/CVF International Conference on Computer Vision, pp. 10912–10922 (2021)

39. Rong, G., et al.: LGSVL simulator: a high fidelity simulator for autonomous driving. In: 2020 IEEE 23rd International Conference on Intelligent Transportation Systems (ITSC), pp. 1–6. IEEE (2020)

40. Ros, G., Sellart, L., Materzynska, J., Vazquez, D., Lopez, A.M.: The synthia dataset: a large collection of synthetic images for semantic segmentation of urban scenes. In: Proceedings of the IEEE Conference on Computer Vision and Pattern Recognition, pp. 3234–3243 (2016)

41. Ruiz, N., Schulter, S., Chandraker, M.: Learning to simulate. In: International Conference on Learning Representations (2019). https://openreview.net/forum?id=HJgkx2Aqt7

42. Shah, S., Dey, D., Lovett, C., Kapoor, A.: AirSim: high-fidelity visual and physical simulation for autonomous vehicles. In: Hutter, M., Siegwart, R. (eds.) Field and Service Robotics. SPAR, vol. 5, pp. 621–635. Springer, Cham (2018). https://doi.org/10.1007/978-3-319-67361-5_40

43. Tsai, Y.H., Hung, W.C., Schulter, S., Sohn, K., Yang, M.H., Chandraker, M.: Learning to adapt structured output space for semantic segmentation. In: Proceedings of the IEEE Conference on Computer Vision and Pattern Recognition, pp. 7472–7481 (2018)

44. Varma, G., Subramanian, A., Namboodiri, A., Chandraker, M., Jawahar, C.: IDD: a dataset for exploring problems of autonomous navigation in unconstrained environments. In: 2019 IEEE Winter Conference on Applications of Computer Vision (WACV), pp. 1743–1751 (2019). https://doi.org/10.1109/WACV.2019.00190

45. Varol, G., et al.: Learning from synthetic humans. In: Proceedings of the IEEE Conference on Computer Vision and Pattern Recognition, pp. 109–117 (2017)

46. Voigtlaender, P., et al.: MOTS: multi-object tracking and segmentation. In: Conference on Computer Vision and Pattern Recognition (CVPR) (2019)

47. Wang, J., et al.: AdvSim: generating safety-critical scenarios for self-driving vehicles. In: Proceedings of the IEEE/CVF Conference on Computer Vision and Pattern Recognition, pp. 9909–9918 (2021)

48. Weber, M., et al.: Step: segmenting and tracking every pixel. In: Neural Information Processing Systems (NeurIPS) Track on Datasets and Benchmarks (2021)

49. Wrenninge, M., Unger, J.: Synscapes: a photorealistic synthetic dataset for street scene parsing. arXiv preprint arXiv:1810.08705 (2018)

50. Wulff, J., Butler, D.J., Stanley, G.B., Black, M.J.: Lessons and insights from creating a synthetic optical flow benchmark. In: Fusiello, A., Murino, V., Cucchiara, R. (eds.) ECCV 2012. LNCS, vol. 7584, pp. 168–177. Springer, Heidelberg (2012). https://doi.org/10.1007/978-3-642-33868-7_17

51. Zheng, G., Liu, H., Xu, K., Li, Z.: Learning to simulate vehicle trajectories from demonstrations. In: 2020 IEEE 36th International Conference on Data Engineering (ICDE), pp. 1822–1825. IEEE (2020)

Trapped in Texture Bias? A Large Scale Comparison of Deep Instance Segmentation

Johannes Theodoridis[1,2]([✉]), Jessica Hofmann[1], Johannes Maucher[1], and Andreas Schilling[2]

[1] Institute for Applied AI - Hochschule der Medien, Stuttgart, Germany
{theodoridis,jh275,maucher}@hdm-stuttgart.de
[2] University of Tübingen, Tübingen, Germany
andreas.schilling@uni-tuebingen.de

Abstract. Do deep learning models for instance segmentation generalize to novel objects in a systematic way? For classification, such behavior has been questioned. In this study, we aim to understand if certain design decisions such as *framework*, *architecture* or *pre-training* contribute to the semantic understanding of instance segmentation. To answer this question, we consider a special case of robustness and compare pre-trained models on a challenging benchmark for object-centric, out-of-distribution texture. We do not introduce another method in this work. Instead, we take a step back and evaluate a broad range of existing literature. This includes Cascade and Mask R-CNN, Swin Transformer, BMask, YOLACT(++), DETR, BCNet, SOTR and SOLOv2. We find that YOLACT++, SOTR and SOLOv2 are significantly more robust to out-of-distribution texture than other frameworks. In addition, we show that deeper and dynamic architectures improve robustness whereas training schedules, data augmentation and pre-training have only a minor impact. In summary we evaluate 68 models on 61 versions of MS COCO for a total of 4148 evaluations.

Keywords: Robust vision · Instance segmentation · Deep learning · Object-centric · Out-of-distribution · Texture robustness

1 Introduction

In this study, we investigate a special case of robustness for deep learning based instance segmentation. More precisely, we want to learn how pre-trained models compare in the case of *out-of-distribution texture*, i.e. when learned objects contain textures that do not appear in the training data. In particular, we aim to understand if different *frameworks*, *architectures* and *pre-training schemes* contribute

Supplementary Information The online version contains supplementary material available at https://doi.org/10.1007/978-3-031-20074-8_35.

content image   style image   style transfer   stylized image   mask annotation   **Stylized**   **Stylized**   **Stylized**
(COCO)   (Painter by Numbers)   (AdaIN)   (Stylized COCO)   COCO   **COCO**   **Objects**   **Background**

Fig. 1. Left: Simplified creation process of the Stylized COCO dataset. Style images are randomly chosen from Kaggles Painter by Numbers dataset. Right: We use mask annotations to create counterfactual, object-centric versions of Stylized COCO. We include more examples of the creation process in the supplementary material

to model robustness in a systematic way. Despite their remarkable success in computer vision, deep neural networks still struggle in many challenging real-world scenarios [48,50,55,73]. One specific example are naturally adversarial objects [41]. Consider for instance a pedestrian with an unconventionally textured dress or a rare horse statue made out of bronze. The model might have seen many pedestrians or natural horses during training but still fails to detect these rare or unseen examples, often with high confidence. Generalizing to such instances is typically described as *out-of-distribution robustness* [29,41]. For classification, [29] suggest that improvements in this direction are more likely to come from computer vision architectures than from existing data augmentation or additional public datasets. Motivated by these findings, we take a step back and perform an extensive comparison of existing literature. Since instance segmentation methods are quite complex, our goal is to unveil the impact of different components and design decision. As a result, our systematic baseline enables more informed design decisions regarding segmentation robustness in the future.

The problem space we consider is inspired by work from [1] and [19] on texture bias in convolutional neural networks (CNNs). Both groups found that when compared to humans, CNNs for classification ignore object shape in favor of local texture cues. In fact, [5] have further shown that CNNs can robustly classify objects in texturized images where the global appearance of objects is fully mixed up. Since human vision is fairly robust to novel texture and sensitive to object shape, we hypothesize that segmentation models with a similar bias will generalize in more systematic ways as well. As a first step in this direction, we want to learn if existing methods may contain components and design decisions that promote such behavior. In consequence, we opted to evaluate an extensive range of pre-trained models on a challenging but easy to understand edge case.

As shown in Fig. 1 left, we utilize the AdaIN method [33] to create a stylized version of MS COCO [45]. The resulting dataset can be understood as a simulation of familiar objects with guaranteed novel texture, i.e. out-of-distribution texture. Crucially, it ensures that potentially confounding biases from the original data, such as class imbalance or specific view points, are preserved. The simulation is not perfect however. It introduces processing artifacts which we analyze in depth in our methods section. In addition, we control the strength of the style transfer and report results on the full range. This step is essential to distinguish between the effect of image corruption and actually novel object texture. In this sense, style transfer as a whole can be understood as a special type of image corruption. The statistical difference to classical corruption types, such as gaussian noise, is that the latter assumes the corruption to be independent from the signal. In style transfer, the *corruption* is by design not random and highly correlated with the shape and texture features of the content and style image respectively. Alternatives to our simulation approach are discussed in the related work part.

The complete benchmark setting is displayed in Fig. 1 right. As can be seen, we utilize the segmentation labels to create two additional object-centric versions of Stylized COCO. The motivation for this step is twofold. First, the masking ensures that object contour is recovered in cases where strong stylization results in a camouflage setting. Second and more importantly, it is more plausible to limit the texture simulation to actual object instances instead of the full image. In addition to this causal justification, we are interested to see if pre-trained models are able to exploit this *implicit encoding* of ground truth information which is trivial to spot for the human observer. The Stylized Background dataset can be seen as a control group that allows us to measure the importance of context information. In general, we expect all pre-trained models to degrade with increasing out-of-distribution texture. The approach we take is therefore a negative test, i.e. if some models degrade significantly less than others we consider them more robust.

2   Methods

In this section we describe the datasets, frameworks and models that are used in this study. The code to reproduce our results and the resulting detection and evaluation data can be found here: https://github.com/JohannesTheo/trapped-in-texture-bias.

2.1   An Object-Centric Version of Stylized COCO

Stylized COCO as shown in Fig. 1 left is an adaptation of Stylized-ImageNet by [19]. It was first used by [50][1] as data augmentation during training to improve the robustness of detection models against common corruption types, e.g. gaussian noise or motion blur. We instead use a stylized version of the val2017 subset to test pre-trained instance segmentation models directly on this data. By manual inspection of Stylized COCO, we found that strong stylization can sometimes lead to images where the object contour starts to vanish, up to the point where objects and their boundaries dissolve completely. This effect depends on the style image but affects objects of all scales alike. As shown in Fig. 2, we resolve this issue by using the ground truth mask annotations to limit the style transfer to the actual objects or the background. This not only ensures that object contours are preserved but also controls for global stylization as a confounding variable. By assuming an object-centric causal model, Stylized COCO allows us to ask interventional

---

[1] Stylized Datasets: https://github.com/bethgelab/stylize-datasets.

COCO instances Stylized COCO Stylized Objects Stylized Background

Fig. 2. Depending on the style image, object boundaries can vanish due to strong stylization. The Stylized Objects and Background versions of Stylized COCO resolve this issue

questions regarding the original COCO dataset, e.g. *"What happens if we change the texture of images?"*. By masking the style transfer to objects or background, we can also ask counterfactual questions such as *"Was it actually the object that caused the change in performance?"*, *"What if we change the background instead?"*. We will refer to the different dataset versions as Stylized COCO (●), Stylized Objects (▲) and Stylized Background (■).

A second problem that remains is that shape information within the object can also be lost due to strong stylization. We address this issue by controlling the strength of the AdaIN method. This can be done with an α parameter that acts as a mixing coefficient between the content and style image. More precisely, AdaIN employs a pre-trained VGG encoder f on both images, performs an interpolation step between the resulting feature maps and produces the final output with a learned decoder network g. In summary, a stylized image t is produced by

$$T(c, s, \alpha) = g((1 - \alpha)f(c) + \alpha \text{AdaIN}(f(c), f(s))) \tag{1}$$

where c and s are the content and style images respectively. We will refer to this method as blending in *feature space*. The top row of Fig. 3 shows two examples of the extreme points $\alpha = 0$ (no style) and $\alpha = 1$ (full style). Note that at $\alpha = 0$, the image colors are mostly preserved but the algorithm has already introduced artifacts in the form of subtle texture and shape changes. In response, we create a control group where we perform alpha blending between the pixel values of the original content image c and the stylized image t at a specific alpha value:

$$P(c, t_\alpha, \alpha) = (1 - \alpha) * c + \alpha * t_\alpha \tag{2}$$

We will refer to this method as blending in *pixel space*. In contrast to the feature space sequence, the control group should preserve textures and object shape over a longer range. The idea is to compare models on both sequences in order to attribute performance to either image corruption or actual out-of-distribution texture. In contrast to [19] who used a fixed style strength to modify ImageNet features ($\alpha = 1$), we produce the full alpha-range $\alpha \in (0.0, 0.1, 0.2, ..., 1.0)$ for both blending spaces. Note that every alpha value depicts a separate and complete copy of the accordingly styled COCO val2017 subset. The qualitative differences can be inspected in Fig. 3 bottom left (zoom in for better visibility).

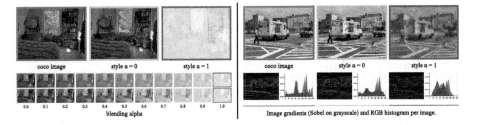

Fig. 3. Top row: Comparison of COCO and Stylized COCO at different alphas. The AdaIN method introduces subtle artifacts even at $\alpha = 0$ (no style). Bottom left: We control the style strength in feature space (yellow to pink) and pixel space (blue to pink). Every alpha depicts a complete version of the accordingly styled `val2017` subset. Bottom right: Comparison of image gradients and color histograms at different alphas. (Color figure online)

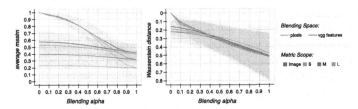

Fig. 4. Left: Average structural similarity between image gradients in relation to COCO (a score of 1 means that there is no difference between images). Right: Wasserstein distance between RGB histograms (reversed y-axis)

Quantitative measures have been calculated to validate our subjective impression of Stylized COCO. Figure 3 bottom right shows a comparison of image gradients and RGB histograms at the *extreme* points. Compared to the original image we can observe the subtle shape changes in the gradient map of $\alpha = 0$ and a significantly different color histogram at $\alpha = 1$. To describe this effect over the full alpha range, we compute the structural similarity index (SSIM) [70] between gradient images of corresponding image pairs. Between RGB histograms we compute the Wasserstein distance alike. We always compare against the original COCO data and report the mean distance averaged over the full dataset at a specific alpha. In addition to the image-to-image scores we also include an instance level comparison for the COCO scales S,M and L. Instances have been cropped based on bbox information. This step was added after we observed that small objects appear to be more affected by the AdaIN artifacts compared to medium and large instances. Figure 4 displays the results and confirms our assumption. Structural similarity depends on object size and is in fact, almost constant over the full feature space range for small objects. Furthermore, the control group preserves structural similarity over a longer range as intended. Color distance in contrast converges at around $\alpha = 0.3$. Based on these insights, we feel confident to better attribute potential performance dips to either image corruption or out-of-distribution texture and subsequently, determine the relative importance of each feature type.

2.2   Model Selection

To contribute a comprehensive overview on model robustness, we opted for a broad comparison of popular frameworks and architectures. The dimensions we consider to be impactful are *framework*, *architecture* and *pre-training*. The finally selected models can be found in Table 1.

Frameworks for instance segmentation can be categorized in different ways. A first distinction can be made between methods that solve the detection problem as a refinement process of box proposals (multi stage) and methods that predict bounding boxes directly (one stage). We include the popular multi-stage frameworks Mask R-CNN [25] and Cascade Mask R-CNN [6] that uses multiple refinement stages instead of one. Both frameworks formulate instance segmentation as a pixel-wise classification problem. Since this rather naive extension to Faster R-CNN [57] can ignore object boundaries and shapes, we include the boundary-preserving mask head alternative (Cascade-) BMask [13] for comparison. A remaining challenge to boundary detection are overlapping objects that occlude the ground truth contour of other instances. We therefore include the Bilayer Convolutional Network (BCNet) [38] as another mask head alternative. In BCNet, the occluded and occluding objects are detected separately and modeled explicitly in a layered representation. The mask head can then"consider the interaction between [the decoupled boundaries] during mask regression [38]." A second distinction between frameworks concerns the use of predefined anchor boxes. Anchor based methods predict relative transformations on these priors whereas anchor free methods predict absolute bounding boxes. We include YOLACT(++) [3,4] as a one-stage, anchor based framework. YOLACT is a real-time method that solves instance segmentation without explicit localization (feature pooling). Instead, it generates prototype masks over the entire image which are combined with per-instance mask coefficients to form the final output. The (++) version improves by adding a mask re-scoring branch [34] and deformable convolutions (v2) [14,76]. We include DETR [8] as a one-stage, anchor free framework that formulates object detection as a set prediction problem over image features. Note that it was not primarily designed for instance segmentation but offers a corresponding extension that we use in our study. Based on model availability we include BCNet in the FCOS [62] variant (F-BCNet). FCOS is a fully convolutional, one-stage, anchor-free alternative to Faster R-CNN that "solves object detection in a per-pixel prediction fashion, analogue to semantic segmentation [62]." Finally, we distinguish between top down frameworks where detection precedes segmentation and bottom up methods where bounding boxes are derived from mask predictions. We include the bottom-up methods SOLOv2 [69] and SOTR [23]. SOLO [68] divides the input into a fixed grid and predicts a semantic category and corresponding instance mask at each location. The final segmentation is obtained with non-maximum-suppression on the gathered grid results to resolve similar predictions of adjacent grid cells. SOLOv2 improves by introducing dynamic convolutions to the mask prediction branch, i.e. an additional input dependent branch that dynamically predicts the convolution kernel weights. A similar idea was used by [61]. SOTR uses a twin attention mechanism [35] to model global and semantic dependencies between encoded image patches. The final result is obtained by patch wise classification and a multi-level upsampling module with dynamic convolution kernels for mask predictions, similar to SOLOv2. For completeness, we also include YOLO(v3,4 and scaled v4) to our comparison since detection is a vital sub-task of top down frameworks [2,56,64].

Architectures used in instance segmentation can be divided into backbone, neck and functional heads. The latter output the final results and are framework specific. Backbones and necks however are typically chosen from a pool of established models which allows for a controlled comparison. The role of backbone networks is to extract meaningful feature representations from the input, i.e. to encode the input. The neck modules define which representations are available to the functional heads, i.e. define the information flow. We include the CNN backbones ResNet [27], ResNext [72] and RegNet [54], a network found with meta architecture search that outperforms EfficientNet [59]. Note that BCNet utilizes a Graph Convolutional Network (GCN) [39] within its mask heads to model long-range dependencies between pixels (to evade local occlusion). Furthermore, DETR and SOTR are hybrid frameworks that use transformer architectures to process the encoded backbone features. With Swin Transformer [47] we also include a convolution free backbone alternative based on the Vision Transformer approach (ViT) [15]. The most popular neck choice is the Feature Pyramid Network (FPN) [44]. It builds a hierarchical feature representation from intermediate layers to improve performance at different scales, e.g. small objects. For comparison we also include a ResNet conv4 neck (C4) as used in [57] and a ResNet conv5 neck with dilated convolution (DC5) as used by [14]. Finally we abbreviate FPN models that use deformable convolutions as DCN [14,76]. Similar to dynamic convolutions which predict kernel weights, DCNs learn to dynamically transform the sampling location of the otherwise fixed convolution filters.

Pre-training of backbone networks is commonly done as supervised learning on ImageNet (IN). Due to the recent success of self supervised learning (SSL) in classification, we are interested in how these representations perform in terms of object-centric robustness. In particular we are interested in the contrastive learning framework that seeks to learn "representations with enough invariance to be robust to inconsequential variations [60]". Based on availability we include the methods InstDis [71], MoCo [10,24], PIRL [51] and InfoMin [60]. Note that pre-trained backbones were only used as initialization for a supervised training on COCO. As a final comparison we include models that have been trained with

Table 1. Overview of frameworks, backbones and neck methods. (*) Swin Transformer use hierarchical representations similar to FPN necks in CNNs. RegNetY is similar to RegNetX but implements the Squeeze-and-Excitation operation [31]. Yolo consists of darknet (D), spatial pyramid pooling (SSP) [26] and a Path Aggregation Network (PAN) [46] in varying combinations with CSPNet (C) [65].

Backbone	Framework								
CNN	multi stage			one stage					
GCN	anchor based					anchor free			
Hybrid	top down (bbox→segm)								bottom up (segm→bbox)
ViT	Mask R-CNN	BMask	Cascade	YOLO(v3,4,s4)	YOLACT(++)	DETR	FCOS BCNet	SOTR	SOLOv2
R50	FPN, C4, DC5, DCN	FPN	FPN	-	FPN, DCN	FPN, DC5	-	-	FPN
R101	FPN, C4, DC5,	FPN	DCN	-	FPN, DCN	FPN	FPN	FPN, DCN	FPN
X101	FPN	-	-	-	-	-	-	-	-
X151	-	-	FPN, DCN	-	-	-	-	-	-
RegNetX	FPN	-	-	-	-	-	-	-	-
RegNetY	FPN	-	-	-	-	-	-	-	-
Swin-T	FPN*	-	FPN*	-	-	-	-	-	-
Swin-S	FPN*	-	FPN*	-	-	-	-	-	-
Swin-B	-	-	FPN*	-	-	-	-	-	-
D53	-	-	-	FPN	-	-	-	-	-
CD53	-	-	-	(C)PAN, SPP	-	-	-	-	-

random initialization and Large Scale Jittering (LSJ) [21] data augmentation as an alternative to pre-training.

From the overview in Table 1 we can now derive dimensions that allow for a fair evaluation of models. Specifically, we can fix the backbone and neck architecture (e.g. ResNet + FPN) for a controlled comparison between *frameworks*. Vice versa, we can investigate the impact of a specific backbone and neck combination within a fixed framework (e.g. Mask R-CNN). The complete list of models is displayed in Fig. 5. Note that we did not include the dimension of pre-training in the above overview for readability reasons. In our experiments however, we do compare training setups and learning schedules for a fixed model type (e.g. Mask R-CNN + ResNet + FPN).

3   Related Work

Robust vision can be approached from different perspectives. The classical view stems from signal processing and concerns image corruptions that are independent from the signal, e.g. salt and pepper noise [28,37,50,52]. A popular alternative is to compare model performance and failure cases against humans [17–20,58,63]. Since human vision is fairly robust, the hope is that vision models with a similar bias will generalize in more systematic ways as well. For instance, [18] and [63] show that transformer models perform closer to human behavior than CNNs. In support of the hypothesis, [49] find that transformer architectures are more robust against adversarial attacks. [48] on the other hand report that both model types are prone to small in-distribution changes in 3D perspective and lighting. The approach we take is inspired by these works but more direct. Instead of comparing to humans, it measures texture robustness in a challenging zero-shot setting. A third perspective originates from the long-tail distribution of real-world data. In such settings, robustness can be understood as the ability to adapt to uncommon or novel objects with efficient transfer learning [16,32], re-sampling [9,67] or regularization strategies [30,53,66]. Particular relevant are methods that handle object occlusion [11]. Since objects can be occluded in almost infinite ways, a common strategy is to represent object properties more explicitly, e.g. to decoupled shape and appearance for instance [13,16,38]. We expect these methods to be strong contenders in our comparison. As an alternative to our sensitivity benchmark, [36] analyze feature importance in latent representations and [7] use feature visualization to understand object detectors. Both leverage style transfer to simulate novel object appearances. The closest real-life alternative is the Natural Adversarial Objects (NAO) dataset [41]. It depicts a more realistic out-of-distribution setting but does not allow to control for pose and perspective, i.e. to observe the exact same objects with varying textures for instance. Other alternatives are the 3DB framework [42], a rendering engine that enables artifact free texture transfer on synthetic objects and SI-Score [74], a dataset for analyzing robustness to rotation, location and size. The key difference to work on reducing texture bias such as [19] and [43], is that these works do not control style strength, object contour and global stylization as potential confounders. As shown in Subsect. 2.1, this severely limits any analysis of the problem space. Our second contribution is the so far, most comprehensive selection of frameworks, architectures and pre-training schemes. This is crucial to allow for a fair comparison and rigorous analysis of model components which can not be easily derived from existing literature otherwise.

4   Results

In this section we present the zero-shot evaluation on Stylized COCO, Objects and Background. Each dataset version contains 20 copies of the accordingly styled COCO `val2017` subset. As a reference point, we *reproduce the evaluation* on the original `val2017` subset and report the absolute Average Precision (AP) for all models in Fig. 5. As can be seen, training schedule, data augmentation and architecture choice have the biggest impact within a framework. Overall, RegNets trained with LSJ and Swin Transformer models perform best. Note that SOTR and SOLO have worse APs but significantly better APm and APl compared to other frameworks (see supplementary material for all scores).

We now present the results of our sensitivity analysis. In total, we tested 68 pre-trained models[2] on 61 `val2017` replicas which sums up to 4148 subset evaluations. Since it is not expedient to report this amount of data in the form of tables, we communicate mainly with figures in the main paper. However, the exact numerical values will be released for inspection together with the code. To quantify out-of-distribution robustness, we calculate the relative zero-shot performance in comparison to the performance on uncorrupted data. For every dataset version, blending space and alpha step we calculate:

$$rP_\alpha = P_\alpha/P_{coco}; P \in \{AP, APs, APm, APl\} \tag{3}$$

---

[2] See supplementary material for the list of code projects and weight sources.

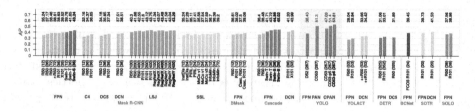

Fig. 5. Absolute performances on COCO `val2017`. Training schedules in epochs have been appended to model names. Note that Yolo is bounding box AP which is not comparable but included for model completeness. Methods that did not report scores for `val2017` have been validated on `test-dev2017` first (Color figure online)

Note that we focus on IoU type segmentation and the scale dependent APs, m, l metrics since COCO has an unbalanced distribution of 41% small, 34% medium and 24% large instances. We include more metrics, absolute scores and the corresponding figures for bounding box IoU in the supplementary material.

A large scale comparison of all models can be found in Fig. 6. Relative AP scores are displayed from left to right, datasets from top to bottom. The subfigures can be read as follows. From left to right ($\alpha : 0 \rightarrow 1$), how much of the original performance is lost with increasing out-of-distribution texture? Recall that at $\alpha = 0$, no out-of-distribution texture is used. For the feature space sequence (dark colors), this means that a loss in performance can be, at this point, attributed to image corruptions from the style transfer method. For the pixel space control sequence (light colors), this point depicts the original `val2017` score which is always 100% in our relative metric. For better visibility, we display an averaged model group per framework. This decision is not arbitrary however. Between all models, we calculated the average L2 distance over the full alpha range (see supplementary material for the resulting distance matrices). As a result of this analysis, we find models from the same framework to perform more similar to each other ($\mu_{L2} = 0.08 \pm 0.05$) than to models from other frameworks ($\mu_{L2} = 0.21 \pm 0.08$). Note that Swin Transformer is treated as a custom *framework* in this comparison even though it implements the (Cascade) Mask R-CNN strategies. In the following, we highlight a few key observations.

First subfigure (top left): The average framework AP on Stylized COCO starts from only $58 \pm 5\%$ due to the impact of image corruption. Revisit Fig. 3 to see how images look like at this point ($\alpha = 0$). After this initial loss, performance remains fairly constant up to $\alpha = 0.3$ from where it drops to $18 \pm 5\%$. Apparently, frameworks seem to maintain a consistent ranking over the full alpha range which we investigate in more detail in our controlled comparison.

First row (Stylized COCO): On small objects (rAPs), model performance is severely affected by image corruptions from the beginning: $19 \pm 6\% \rightarrow 4 \pm 2\%$. With increasing objects size, this effect seems to gradually vanish. On large

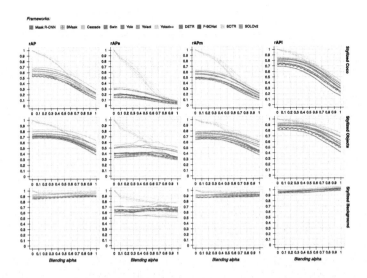

Fig. 6. General overview of model robustness against out-of-distribution texture (zoom in for better visibility). Yolo is displayed for completeness but not directly comparable.

objects (rAPl), the relative performance is then more affected by actual out-of-distribution texture than by corruption artifacts: $78 \pm 5\% \rightarrow 28 \pm 8\%$.

Second row (Stylized Objects): The average framework model is more robust to this type of data, e.g. rAP is now: $72\pm5\% \rightarrow 47\pm7\%$. In addition, models exhibit an extended range of robustness after the initial dip (now up to $\alpha = 0.5$). The apparent ranking of frameworks remains the same. Note the increasing variance towards the end of the blending sequence, e.g. rAPm: $70 \pm 5\% \rightarrow 48 \pm 9\%$, rAPl: $87 \pm 4\% \rightarrow 56 \pm 10\%$. We conclude that object contour is in fact an important property and that some models can exploit this feature more effectively than others. However, no model is able to exploit the implicit encoding of ground truth masks. Doing so would imply a high level of abstraction which we do not find to happen in existing models.

Third row (Stylized Background): In this dataset version, only background features are corrupted. This allows us to measure the importance of context information. As displayed in the second subfigure (rAPs), models do indeed rely on additional context information to segment small objects: $63 \pm 5\% \rightarrow 63 \pm 7\%$. With increasing object size, models depend less on background information. Interestingly, we observe a subtle performance gain on large objects with increasing stylization (rAPl): $96 \pm 2\% \rightarrow 101 \pm 2\%$. As before however, models do not exploit the implicit mask encoding in a more systematic way which is arguably even easier in this setting.

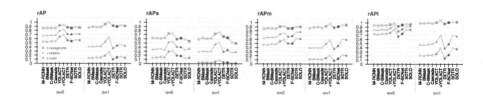

Fig. 7. A controlled comparison of framework robustness. Note that we compromise on ResNet-101 for SOTR and F-BCNet, see Table 1 for available backbones

A controlled comparison of frameworks, architectures and pre-training is presented in this subsection. Each comparison contributes to the main goal of our study which asks: *Do existing segmentation methods contain components or design decisions that promote systematic generalization regarding object-centric features?* Note that we focus on the extreme points $\alpha = 0$ and $\alpha = 1$.

Frameworks are compared first. For statistical fairness, we use the same backbone and neck method per framework (ResNet-50 + FPN). Figure 7 displays the results on the feature space sequence. As hypothesized earlier, we observe a consistent ranking between frameworks from $\alpha : 0 \to 1$ and across dataset versions. A noticeable difference is the amplified difference between frameworks and the increased distance between Stylized COCO and Stylized Objects at $\alpha = 1$. We conclude that robustness against semantic image corruption is correlated with robustness against out-of-distribution texture. However, some frameworks seem to exploit object contour more effectively than others. The most robust framework overall is YOLACT++. Its predecessor YOLACT is compatible on small objects. SOTR and SOLO(v2) perform best on medium and large objects. DETR appears as the least robust framework but we like to point out that it was not primarily designed for instance segmentation. Surprisingly, BMask and BCNet are not better than Cascade and Mask R-CNN.

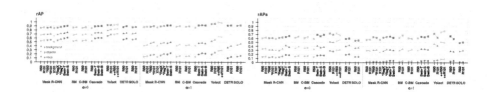

Fig. 8. Model robustness for different backbones. Scores for medium and large objects follow the trend of rAP and can be found in the supplementary material. Models marked with * are trained with LSJ

Backbones are compared next. In this analysis, we only use models with FPN neck and compare within the same framework. When available, we include model pairs with different data augmentation. The results are displayed in Fig. 8. As can be seen from the left subfigure (rAP), a clear trend is visible. When every other factor is controlled, deeper backbones improve robustness. Swin-T and S are comparable to ResNet-50 and 101 in model complexity but generally more robust than their CNN counterparts. For medium and large objects, a similar trend can be reported. For small objects, the behavior is less clear and surprisingly, often reversed.

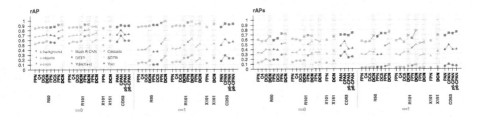

Fig. 9. Robustness by neck architecture. Deformable convolutions are highlighted for better visibility. Note that Yolo is only comparable to itself due to bounding box score

Neck methods are compared in Fig. 9. We only use models with a similar training schedule and group them by backbone and framework. Surprisingly, the popular FPN method is consistently the least robust option. In contrast, deformable convolutions (DCN) consistently improve robustness as highlighted for better visibility. For small objects, DC5 necks improve the robustness on Stylized Objects (triangle). Note that Yolo is only comparable against itself with the simple v4-csp model (CPAN) performing best.

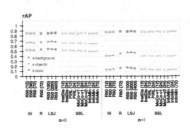

Fig. 10. Model robustness by pre-training and data augmentation. We distinguish between ImageNet (IN), random (R) and self supervised learning (SSL) initialization

Pre-training, training schedules and data augmentation have surprisingly, little to no impact on texture robustness. The result of this comparison is displayed Fig. 10. On the other hand we can report that supervised and unsupervised representations perform almost on par. We suspect that the supervised fine tuning on the segmentation task overshadows potential differences in the initial backbone representations. In comparison we find that random initialization with LSJ data augmentation is the most robust combination.

5   Discussion

As expected, we found deep learning models for instance segmentation to be vulnerable to image corruption and not particularly robust against novel object texture. Based on our in depth analysis, we now understand this problem space much better. In particular that the type of robustness depends heavily on object size. Small objects are predominantly affected by image corruption which confirms related findings from work on scale aware augmentation [12]. In consequence, we hypothesize that the difference between shape and texture simply collapses for (very) small objects in MS COCO. Furthermore, we find that segmentation models can exploit object contour independently from object texture (better performance on Stylized Objects). However, the question arises if this is not simply a byproduct of the limited area of effect in this dataset. To answer this question, we conduct an ablation study with salt and pepper noise which rejects this hypothesis. A second ablation with blurred object contour confirms the importance of this feature. The results can be found in the supplementary material. Note that more generally, the importance of contour for segmentation is acknowledged in the literature, e.g. by work on mask refinement [40,75]. It would be interesting to see how these methods adapt to unseen textures. For medium and large objects, we found models to be biased towards learned texture, i.e. out-of-distribution texture results in a significant performance loss after controlling for general image corruptions. In contrast to [19] who argue that this problem is induced by the ImageNet training data, we find no such correlation in terms of pre-training for instance segmentation. We conclude that either a similar bias is induced by the COCO dataset or that framework and architecture choice is simply more important as suggested by [29]. Our key findings support the latter hypothesis. In particular the results of YOLACT(++), SOTR and SOLOv2 unveil a new and promising starting point for more in depth research, e.g. on prototype masks and implicit localization. In the same spirit, [22] formulate *the binding problem* which is "the inability [of neural networks] to dynamically and flexibly combine (bind) information [... which] limits their ability to [...] accommodate different patterns of generalization". The consistently better results for dynamic architectures and components confirm this assumption.

6   Conclusion

In this study we contribute a comprehensive baseline on the texture robustness of deep learning based instance segmentation. As a result of our study, we find a noticeable texture bias in most existing methods. However, models do also exploit other features such as object contour. Based on this insight we feel optimistic that, with the right design decisions, vision models are not trapped in texture bias. The key finding of our study is that the frameworks YOLACT++, SOTR and SOLOv2 as well as deeper and dynamic architectures improve texture robustness. We hope that our rigorous analysis enables more in depth research and contributes to facilitate a systematic design approach to robust vision.

References

1. Baker, N., Lu, H., Erlikhman, G., Kellman, P.J.: Deep convolutional networks do not classify based on global object shape. PLoS Comput. Biol. **14**(12), e1006613 (2018)
2. Bochkovskiy, A., Wang, C.Y., Liao, H.Y.M.: YOLOv4: optimal speed and accuracy of object detection. CoRR abs/2004.10934 (2020)
3. Bolya, D., Zhou, C., Xiao, F., Lee, Y.J.: YOLACT: real-time instance segmentation. In: Proceedings of the IEEE/CVF International Conference on Computer Vision (ICCV) (Oct 2019)
4. Bolya, D., Zhou, C., Xiao, F., Lee, Y.J.: YOLACT++: better real-time instance segmentation. IEEE Trans. Pattern Anal. Mach. Intell. **44**, 1108–1121 (2020)
5. Brendel, W., Bethge, M.: Approximating CNNs with bag-of-local-features models works surprisingly well on ImageNet. In: International Conference on Learning Representations (2019)
6. Cai, Z., Vasconcelos, N.: Cascade R-CNN: delving into high quality object detection. In: Proceedings of the IEEE Conference on Computer Vision and Pattern Recognition (CVPR) (2018)
7. Cao, A., Johnson, J.: Inverting and understanding object detectors. CoRR abs/2106.13933 (2021)
8. Carion, N., Massa, F., Synnaeve, G., Usunier, N., Kirillov, A., Zagoruyko, S.: End-to-end object detection with transformers. In: Vedaldi, A., Bischof, H., Brox, T., Frahm, J.M. (eds.) Computer Vision – ECCV 2020, vol. 12346, pp. 213–229. Springer, Cham (2020). https://doi.org/10.1007/978-3-030-58452-8_13
9. Chang, N., Yu, Z., Wang, Y.X., Anandkumar, A., Fidler, S., Alvarez, J.M.: Image-level or object-level? A tale of two resampling strategies for long-tailed detection. In: Meila, M., Zhang, T. (eds.) Proceedings of the 38th International Conference on Machine Learning. Proceedings of Machine Learning Research, vol. 139, pp. 1463–1472. PMLR (2021)
10. Chen, X., Fan, H., Girshick, R.B., He, K.: Improved baselines with momentum contrastive learning. CoRR abs/2003.04297 (2020)
11. Chen, Y.T., Liu, X., Yang, M.H.: Multi-instance object segmentation with occlusion handling. In: Proceedings of the IEEE Conference on Computer Vision and Pattern Recognition (CVPR) (2015)
12. Chen, Y., et al.: Scale-aware automatic augmentation for object detection. In: Proceedings of the IEEE/CVF Conference on Computer Vision and Pattern Recognition (CVPR), pp. 9563–9572 (2021)
13. Cheng, T., Wang, X., Huang, L., Liu, W.: Boundary-preserving mask R-CNN. In: Vedaldi, A., Bischof, H., Brox, T., Frahm, J.M. (eds.) Computer Vision – ECCV 2020, vol. 12359, pp. 660–676. Springer, Cham (2020). https://doi.org/10.1007/978-3-030-58568-6_39
14. Dai, J., et al.: Deformable convolutional networks. In: Proceedings of the IEEE International Conference on Computer Vision (ICCV) (2017)
15. Dosovitskiy, A., et al.: An image is worth 16 × 16 words: transformers for image recognition at scale. In: International Conference on Learning Representations (2021)
16. Fan, Q., Ke, L., Pei, W., Tang, C.K., Tai, Y.W.: Commonality-parsing network across shape and appearance for partially supervised instance segmentation. In: Vedaldi, A., Bischof, H., Brox, T., Frahm, J.M. (eds.) Computer Vision – ECCV 2020, vol. 12353, pp. 379–396. Springer, Cham (2020). https://doi.org/10.1007/978-3-030-58598-3_23

17. Geirhos, R., Narayanappa, K., Mitzkus, B., Bethge, M., Wichmann, F.A., Brendel, W.: On the surprising similarities between supervised and self-supervised models (2020)
18. Geirhos, R., et al.: Partial success in closing the gap between human and machine vision. CoRR abs/2106.07411 (2021)
19. Geirhos, R., Rubisch, P., Michaelis, C., Bethge, M., Wichmann, F.A., Brendel, W.: ImageNet-trained CNNs are biased towards texture; increasing shape bias improves accuracy and robustness. In: International Conference on Learning Representations (2019)
20. Geirhos, R., Temme, C.R.M., Rauber, J., Schütt, H.H., Bethge, M., Wichmann, F.A.: Generalisation in humans and deep neural networks. In: Bengio, S., Wallach, H., Larochelle, H., Grauman, K., Cesa-Bianchi, N., Garnett, R. (eds.) Advances in Neural Information Processing Systems, vol. 31. Curran Associates, Inc. (2018)
21. Ghiasi, G., et al.: Simple copy-paste is a strong data augmentation method for instance segmentation. In: Proceedings of the IEEE/CVF Conference on Computer Vision and Pattern Recognition (CVPR). pp. 2918–2928 (2021)
22. Greff, K., van Steenkiste, S., Schmidhuber, J.: On the binding problem in artificial neural networks. CoRR abs/2012.05208 (2020)
23. Guo, R., Niu, D., Qu, L., Li, Z.: SOTR: segmenting objects with transformers. CoRR abs/2108.06747 (2021)
24. He, K., Fan, H., Wu, Y., Xie, S., Girshick, R.: Momentum contrast for unsupervised visual representation learning. In: IEEE/CVF Conference on Computer Vision and Pattern Recognition (CVPR) (2020)
25. He, K., Gkioxari, G., Dollar, P., Girshick, R.: Mask R-CNN. In: Proceedings of the IEEE International Conference on Computer Vision (ICCV) (Oct 2017)
26. He, K., Zhang, X., Ren, S., Sun, J.: Spatial pyramid pooling in deep convolutional networks for visual recognition. In: Fleet, D., Pajdla, T., Schiele, B., Tuytelaars, T. (eds.) Computer Vision – ECCV 2014, vol. 8691, pp. 346–361. Springer, Cham (2014). https://doi.org/10.1007/978-3-319-10578-9_23
27. He, K., Zhang, X., Ren, S., Sun, J.: Deep residual learning for image recognition. In: Proceedings of the IEEE Conference on Computer Vision and Pattern Recognition (CVPR) (2016)
28. Hendrycks, D., Dietterich, T.: Benchmarking neural network robustness to common corruptions and perturbations. In: International Conference on Learning Representations (2019)
29. Hendrycks, D., Zhao, K., Basart, S., Steinhardt, J., Song, D.: Natural adversarial examples. In: Proceedings of the IEEE/CVF Conference on Computer Vision and Pattern Recognition (CVPR), pp. 15262–15271 (2021)
30. Hsieh, T.I., Robb, E., Chen, H.T., Huang, J.B.: DropLoss for long-tail instance segmentation. In: Proceedings of the Workshop on Artificial Intelligence Safety 2021 (SafeAI 2021) Co-Located with the Thirty-Fifth AAAI Conference on Artificial Intelligence (AAAI 2021), Virtual, February 8, 2021 (2021)
31. Hu, J., Shen, L., Sun, G.: Squeeze-and-excitation networks. In: Proceedings of the IEEE Conference on Computer Vision and Pattern Recognition (CVPR) (2018)
32. Hu, R., Dollár, P., He, K., Darrell, T., Girshick, R.: Learning to segment every thing. In: Proceedings of the IEEE Conference on Computer Vision and Pattern Recognition (CVPR) (2018)
33. Huang, X., Belongie, S.: Arbitrary style transfer in real-time with adaptive instance normalization. In: Proceedings of the IEEE International Conference on Computer Vision (ICCV) (2017)

34. Huang, Z., Huang, L., Gong, Y., Huang, C., Wang, X.: Mask scoring R-CNN. In: Proceedings of the IEEE/CVF Conference on Computer Vision and Pattern Recognition (CVPR) (2019)

35. Huang, Z., Wang, X., Huang, L., Huang, C., Wei, Y., Liu, W.: CCNet: criss-cross attention for semantic segmentation. In: Proceedings of the IEEE/CVF International Conference on Computer Vision (ICCV) (2019)

36. Islam, M.A., et al.: Shape or texture: understanding discriminative features in {CNN}s. In: International Conference on Learning Representations (2021)

37. Kamann, C., Rother, C.: Benchmarking the robustness of semantic segmentation models with respect to common corruptions. Int. J. Comput. Vis. **129**(2), 462–483 (2021)

38. Ke, L., Tai, Y.W., Tang, C.K.: Deep occlusion-aware instance segmentation with overlapping BiLayers. In: Proceedings of the IEEE/CVF Conference on Computer Vision and Pattern Recognition (CVPR), pp. 4019–4028 (2021)

39. Kipf, T.N., Welling, M.: Semi-supervised classification with graph convolutional networks. In: International Conference on Learning Representations (ICLR) (2017)

40. Kirillov, A., Wu, Y., He, K., Girshick, R.: PointRend: image segmentation as rendering. In: IEEE/CVF Conference on Computer Vision and Pattern Recognition (CVPR) (2020)

41. Lau, F., Subramani, N., Harrison, S., Kim, A., Branson, E., Liu, R.: Natural adversarial objects. arXiv preprint arXiv:2111.04204 (2021)

42. Leclerc, G., et al.: 3DB: a framework for debugging computer vision models. CoRR abs/2106.03805 (2021)

43. Li, Y., et al.: Shape-texture debiased neural network training. In: International Conference on Learning Representations (2021)

44. Lin, T.Y., Dollar, P., Girshick, R., He, K., Hariharan, B., Belongie, S.: Feature pyramid networks for object detection. In: Proceedings of the IEEE Conference on Computer Vision and Pattern Recognition (CVPR) (2017)

45. Lin, T.Y., Maire, M., Belongie, S., Hays, J., Perona, P., Ramanan, D., Dollár, P., Zitnick, C.L.: Microsoft COCO: common objects in context. In: Fleet, D., Pajdla, T., Schiele, B., Tuytelaars, T. (eds.) Computer Vision – ECCV 2014, vol. 8693, pp. 740–755. Springer, Cham (2014). https://doi.org/10.1007/978-3-319-10602-1_48

46. Liu, S., Qi, L., Qin, H., Shi, J., Jia, J.: Path aggregation network for instance segmentation. In: Proceedings of the IEEE Conference on Computer Vision and Pattern Recognition (CVPR) (2018)

47. Liu, Z., et al.: Swin Transformer: hierarchical vision transformer using shifted windows. arXiv preprint arXiv:2103.14030 (2021)

48. Madan, S., Sasaki, T., Li, T.M., Boix, X., Pfister, H.: Small in-distribution changes in 3D perspective and lighting fool both CNNs and Transformers. CoRR abs/2106.16198 (2021)

49. Mahmood, K., Mahmood, R., van Dijk, M.: On the robustness of vision transformers to adversarial examples. In: Proceedings of the IEEE/CVF International Conference on Computer Vision (ICCV), pp. 7838–7847 (2021)

50. Michaelis, C., et al.: Benchmarking robustness in object detection: autonomous driving when winter is coming. In: Machine Learning for Autonomous Driving Workshop, NeurIPS 2019, vol. 190707484 (2019)

51. Misra, I., van der Maaten, L.: Self-supervised learning of pretext-invariant representations. In: IEEE/CVF Conference on Computer Vision and Pattern Recognition (CVPR) (2020)

52. Mummadi, C.K., Subramaniam, R., Hutmacher, R., Vitay, J., Fischer, V., Metzen, J.H.: Does enhanced shape bias improve neural network robustness to common corruptions? In: International Conference on Learning Representations (2021)
53. Pan, T.Y., et al.: On model calibration for long-tailed object detection and instance segmentation. In: Thirty-Fifth Conference on Neural Information Processing Systems (2021)
54. Radosavovic, I., Kosaraju, R.P., Girshick, R., He, K., Dollar, P.: Designing network design spaces. In: IEEE/CVF Conference on Computer Vision and Pattern Recognition (CVPR) (2020)
55. Recht, B., Roelofs, R., Schmidt, L., Shankar, V.: Do ImageNet classifiers generalize to ImageNet? In: Proceedings of Machine Learning Research, vol. 97, pp. 5389–5400. PMLR, Long Beach, California, USA (2019)
56. Redmon, J., Farhadi, A.: YOLOv3: An incremental improvement. CoRR abs/1804.02767 (2018)
57. Ren, S., He, K., Girshick, R., Sun, J.: Faster R-CNN: towards real-time object detection with region proposal networks. In: Cortes, C., Lawrence, N., Lee, D., Sugiyama, M., Garnett, R. (eds.) Advances in Neural Information Processing Systems, vol. 28. Curran Associates, Inc. (2015)
58. Shankar, V., Roelofs, R., Mania, H., Fang, A., Recht, B., Schmidt, L.: Evaluating machine accuracy on ImageNet. In: III, H.D., Singh, A. (eds.) Proceedings of the 37th International Conference on Machine Learning. Proceedings of Machine Learning Research, vol. 119, pp. 8634–8644. PMLR (Jul 2020)
59. Tan, M., Le, Q.: EfficientNet: rethinking model scaling for convolutional neural networks. In: Chaudhuri, K., Salakhutdinov, R. (eds.) Proceedings of the 36th International Conference on Machine Learning. Proceedings of Machine Learning Research, vol. 97, pp. 6105–6114. PMLR (2019)
60. Tian, Y., Sun, C., Poole, B., Krishnan, D., Schmid, C., Isola, P.: What makes for good views for contrastive learning? In: Larochelle, H., Ranzato, M., Hadsell, R., Balcan, M.F., Lin, H. (eds.) Advances in Neural Information Processing Systems, vol. 33, pp. 6827–6839. Curran Associates, Inc. (2020)
61. Tian, Z., Shen, C., Chen, H.: Conditional convolutions for instance segmentation. In: Vedaldi, A., Bischof, H., Brox, T., Frahm, J.M. (eds.) Computer Vision – ECCV 2020, vol. 12346, pp. 282–298. Springer, Cham (2020). https://doi.org/10.1007/978-3-030-58452-8_17
62. Tian, Z., Shen, C., Chen, H., He, T.: FCOS: Fully convolutional one-stage object detection. In: Proceedings of the IEEE/CVF International Conference on Computer Vision (ICCV) (2019)
63. Tuli, S., Dasgupta, I., Grant, E., Griffiths, T.L.: Are convolutional neural networks or transformers more like human vision? CoRR abs/2105.07197 (2021)
64. Wang, C.Y., Bochkovskiy, A., Liao, H.Y.M.: Scaled-YOLOv4: scaling cross stage partial network. In: Proceedings of the IEEE/CVF Conference on Computer Vision and Pattern Recognition (CVPR), pp. 13029–13038 (2021)
65. Wang, C.Y., Mark Liao, H.Y., Wu, Y.H., Chen, P.Y., Hsieh, J.W., Yeh, I.H.: CSPNet: a new backbone that can enhance learning capability of CNN. In: 2020 IEEE/CVF Conference on Computer Vision and Pattern Recognition Workshops (CVPRW), pp. 1571–1580. IEEE, Seattle, WA, USA (2020)
66. Wang, J., et al.: Seesaw loss for long-tailed instance segmentation. In: Proceedings of the IEEE/CVF Conference on Computer Vision and Pattern Recognition (CVPR), pp. 9695–9704 (2021)

67. Wang, T., et al.: The devil is in classification: a simple framework for long-tail instance segmentation. In: Vedaldi, A., Bischof, H., Brox, T., Frahm, J.M. (eds.) Computer Vision – ECCV 2020, vol. 12359, pp. 728–744. Springer, Cham (2020). https://doi.org/10.1007/978-3-030-58568-6_43

68. Wang, X., Kong, T., Shen, C., Jiang, Y., Li, L.: SOLO: segmenting objects by locations. In: Vedaldi, A., Bischof, H., Brox, T., Frahm, J.M. (eds.) Computer Vision – ECCV 2020, vol. 12363, pp. 649–665. Springer, Cham (2020). https://doi.org/10.1007/978-3-030-58523-5_38

69. Wang, X., Zhang, R., Kong, T., Li, L., Shen, C.: SOLOv2: dynamic and fast instance segmentation. In: Larochelle, H., Ranzato, M., Hadsell, R., Balcan, M.F., Lin, H. (eds.) Advances in Neural Information Processing Systems, vol. 33, pp. 17721–17732. Curran Associates, Inc. (2020)

70. Wang, Z., Bovik, A., Sheikh, H., Simoncelli, E.: Image quality assessment: from error visibility to structural similarity. IEEE Trans. Image Process. **13**(4), 600–612 (2004)

71. Wu, Z., Xiong, Y., Yu, S.X., Lin, D.: Unsupervised feature learning via non-parametric instance discrimination. In: Proceedings of the IEEE Conference on Computer Vision and Pattern Recognition (CVPR) (2018)

72. Xie, S., Girshick, R., Dollar, P., Tu, Z., He, K.: Aggregated residual transformations for deep neural networks. In: Proceedings of the IEEE Conference on Computer Vision and Pattern Recognition (CVPR) (2017)

73. Yuille, A., Liu, C.: Deep Nets: what have they ever done for vision? Technical Report 88, Center for Brains, Minds and Machines. CBMM, MIT CSAIL (2018)

74. Yung, J., et al.: SI-Score: an image dataset for fine-grained analysis of robustness to object location, rotation and size. CoRR abs/2104.04191 (2021)

75. Zhu, C., Zhang, X., Li, Y., Qiu, L., Han, K., Han, X.: SharpContour: a contour-based boundary refinement approach for efficient and accurate instance segmentation. In: Proceedings of the IEEE/CVF Conference on Computer Vision and Pattern Recognition (CVPR), pp. 4392–4401 (2022)

76. Zhu, X., Hu, H., Lin, S., Dai, J.: Deformable ConvNets V2: more deformable, better results. In: Proceedings of the IEEE/CVF Conference on Computer Vision and Pattern Recognition (CVPR) (2019)

Deformable Feature Aggregation for Dynamic Multi-modal 3D Object Detection

Zehui Chen[1], Zhenyu Li[2], Shiquan Zhang[3], Liangji Fang[3], Qinhong Jiang[3], and Feng Zhao[1(✉)]

[1] University of Science and Technology of China, Hefei, China
lovesnow@mail.ustc.edu.cn, fzhao956@ustc.edu.cn
[2] Harbin Institute of Technology, Harbin, China
zhenyuli17@hit.edu.cn
[3] SenseTime Research, Shanghai, China
{zhangshiquan,fangliangji,jiangqinhong}@senseauto.com

Abstract. Point clouds and RGB images are two general perceptional sources in autonomous driving. The former can provide accurate localization of objects, and the latter is denser and richer in semantic information. Recently, AutoAlign [6] presents a learnable paradigm in combining these two modalities for 3D object detection. However, it suffers from high computational cost introduced by the global-wise attention. To solve the problem, we propose Cross-Domain DeformCAFA module in this work. It attends to sparse learnable sampling points for cross-modal relational modeling, which enhances the tolerance to calibration error and greatly speeds up the feature aggregation across different modalities. To overcome the complex GT-AUG under multi-modal settings, we design a simple yet effective cross-modal augmentation strategy on convex combination of image patches given their depth information. Moreover, by carrying out a novel image-level dropout training scheme, our model is able to infer in a dynamic manner. To this end, we propose AutoAlignV2, a faster and stronger multi-modal 3D detection framework, built on top of AutoAlign. Extensive experiments on nuScenes benchmark demonstrate the effectiveness and efficiency of AutoAlignV2. Notably, our best model reaches 72.4 NDS on nuScenes test leaderboard, achieving new state-of-the-art results among all published multi-modal 3D object detectors. Code will be available at https://github.com/zehuichen123/AutoAlignV2.

Keywords: 3D object detection · Multi-modal learning · Sensor fusion · Camera sensor · LiDAR sensor

1 Introduction

3D object detection serves as a fundamental computer vision task in autonomous driving. Modern 3D object detectors [13,20,24,33] have demonstrated promising performance on competitive benchmarks including KITTI [10], Waymo [28],

S. Avidan et al. (Eds.): ECCV 2022, LNCS 13668, pp. 628–644, 2022.
https://doi.org/10.1007/978-3-031-20074-8_36

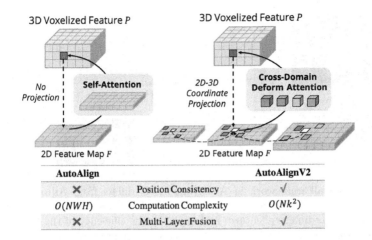

Fig. 1. The comparison between AutoAlignV2 and AutoAlign. AutoAlignV2 hints at the alignment module with general mapping relationship guaranteed by deterministic projection matrix, and simultaneously reserves the ability to automatically adjust the positions of feature aggregation. Due to the lightweight computational cost, AutoAlignV2 is able to aggregate multi-layer features for hierarchical imagery information.

and nuScenes [2] datasets. Despite the rapid progress in detection accuracy, the room for further improvement is still large. Recently, an upsurging stream in combining RGB images and LiDAR points for accurate detection has drawn many attentions [1,15,16,19,31,39]. Different from the point clouds which are beneficial for spatial localization, imagery data are more superior in providing semantic and textural information, *i.e.*, more suitable for classification. Therefore, it is believed that these two modalities are complementary to each other and can further promote the detection accuracy.

However, how to effectively combine these heterogeneous representations for 3D object detection has not been fully explored. In this work, we mainly attribute the current difficulties of training cross-modal detectors to two aspects. On one hand, the fusion strategy in combining imagery and spatial information remains sub-optimal. Due to the heterogeneous representations between RGB images and point clouds, features need to be carefully aligned before being aggregated together. This is often achieved by establishing deterministic correspondence between the point and the image pixel through LiDAR-camera projection matrix [27,31,39]. AutoAlign [6] proposes a learnable global-wise alignment module for automatic registration and achieves good performance. However, it has to be trained with the help of CSFI module to acquire the inner positional matching relationship between points and image pixels. Besides, the complexity of attention-style operation is quadratic to the image size, making it impractical to apply queries on high-resolution feature maps (*e.g.*, C_2, C_3). Such a limitation can lead to coarse and inaccurate image information and the loss of hierarchical representations brought by FPN (See Fig. 1). On the other hand, data augmen-

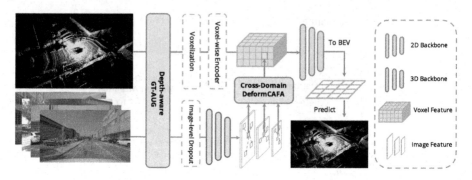

Fig. 2. The overall framework of AutoAlignV2. It differs from AutoAlign in three aspects: (i) the proposed Cross-Domain DeformCAFA module enhances the representations with better imagery features and improves the efficiency of the fusion process, (ii) the Depth-Aware GT-AUG algorithm greatly simplifies the synchronization issue among 2D-3D joint augmentations, and (iii) the adoption of image-level dropout training strategy enables our model to infer in a dynamic fusion manner.

tation, especially GT-AUG [33], is a crucial step for 3D detectors to achieve competitive results. In terms of multi-modal methods, an important problem is how to keep synchronization between images and point clouds when conducting cut and paste operations. MoCa [39] uses labor-intensive mask annotations in 2D domain for accurate image features. Box-level annotations are also applicable but delicate and complex points filtering is required [31].

In this work, we propose AutoAlignV2 to mitigate the aforementioned issues in a much simpler and more effective way. It hints at the alignment module with the general mapping relationship guaranteed by deterministic projection matrix and simultaneously reserves the ability to automatically adjust the positions of feature aggregation. As for the synchronization issue in 2D-3D joint augmentation, a novel depth-aware GT-AUG algorithm is introduced to cope with object occlusion in the image domain, getting rid of the complex point cloud filtering or the need for delicate mask annotations. We also present a new training scheme named image-level dropout strategy, which enables the model to infer results dynamically even without images. Through extensive experiments, we validate the effectiveness of AutoAlignV2 on two representative 3D detectors: Object DGCNN [32] and CenterPoint [36], and achieve new state-of-the-art performance on the competitive nuScenes benchmark.

2   Related Work

2.1   Object Detection with Point Cloud

Existing 3D object detectors can be broadly categorized as point-based and voxel-based approaches. Point-based methods directly predict the regression boxes from points [26,35]. For example, Point R-CNN [25] adopts a semantic network to segment the point clouds and then generates the proposals at each foreground point. 3DSSD [34] fully applies point-level predictions on the one-stage architecture, where an anchor-free head is designed after the PointNet-like feature extraction. Although the accurate 3D localization information is maintained, these algorithms often suffer from high computational cost [24]. Different from the point-wise detection, voxel-based approaches transform sets of unordered points into 2D feature map through voxelization, which can be directly applied with convolutional neural networks [8,22,41]. For instance, VoxelNet [41] is a widely-used paradigm where a VFE layer is proposed to extract unified features for each 3D voxel. Based on this, CenterPoint [36] presents a center-based label assignment strategy, achieving competitive performance in 3D object detection.

2.2 Multi-modal 3D Object Detection

Recently, there has been an increasing attention on multi-modal data for 3D object detection [17,21]. AVOD [12] and MV3D [5] are two pioneer works in this field, where 2D and 3D RoI are directly concatenated before box prediction. Qi et al. [23] utilized images to generate 2D proposals and then lifted them up to 3D space (frustum), which narrows the searching space in point clouds. 3D-CVF [37] and EPNet [11] explore the fusion strategy on feature maps across different modalities with a learned calibration matrix. Though easy-to-implement, they are likely to suffer from coarse feature aggregation. To mitigate this issue, various approaches [27,29,39] fetch pixel-wise image features with camera-LiDAR projection matrix given by 3D coordinates. As an example, MVX-Net [27] provides an easy-to-extend framework for cross-modal 3D object detection with joint optimization in 2D and 3D branches. AutoAlign [6] formulates the projection relationship as an attention map and automates the learning of such an alignment through the network. In this work, we explore a faster and more efficient alignment strategy to further boost the performance of point-wise feature aggregation.

3   AutoAlignV2

The aim of AutoAlignV2 is to effectively aggregate image features for further performance enhancement of 3D object detectors. We start with the basic architecture of AutoAlign: the paired images are input into a light-weight backbone, ResNet [30], followed by FPN [18] to get the feature maps. Then, relevant imagery information is aggregated through a learnable alignment map to enrich the 3D representations of non-empty voxels during the voxelization phase. Finally, the enhanced features will be fed into the subsequent 3D detection pipeline to generate the instance predictions.

Such a paradigm could aggregate heterogeneous features in a data-driven way. However, there are two main bottlenecks that still hinder the performance. The first one is inefficient feature aggregation. Although global-wise attention map automates the feature alignment between RGB images and LiDAR points, the computational cost is high: given the voxel number N and the size of image feature $W \times H$, the complexity is $O(NWH)$. Due to the large value of WH, AutoAlign discards other layers except C_5 to reduce the cost. The second one is complex data augmentation synchronization between image and points. GT-AUG is an essential step for high-performance 3D object detectors, but how to keep the semantic consistency between the points and the image during training remains a complicated problem.

In this section, we show that the aforementioned challenges can be effectively resolved through the proposed AutoAlignV2, which consists of two parts: Cross-Domain DeformCAFA module and Depth-Aware GT-AUG data augmentation strategy (see Fig. 2). We also present a novel image-level dropout training strategy, which enables our model to infer in a more dynamic manner.

3.1   Deformable Feature Aggregation

Revisiting to CAFA We first revisit the Cross-Attention Feature Alignment module proposed in AutoAlign. Instead of establishing deterministic correspondence with the camera-LiDAR projection matrix, it models the mapping relationship with a learnable alignment map, which enables the network to automate the alignment of non-homogenous features in a dynamic and data-driven manner. Specifically, given the feature map $F = \{f_1, f_2, ..., f_{hw}\}$ (f_i indicates the image feature of the ith spatial position) and voxel features $P = \{p_1, p_2, ..., p_J\}$ (p_j indicates each non-empty voxel feature) extracted from raw point clouds, each voxel feature p_j will query the whole image pixels and generate the attention weights based on the dot-product similarity between the voxel feature and the pixel feature. The final output of each voxel feature is the linear combination of values on all the pixel features according to the attention weights. Such a paradigm enables the model to aggregate semantically relevant spatial pixels to update p_j and demonstrates superior performance compared to bilinear interpolation of features. However, the huge computational cost limits the query candidate to C_5 only, losing the fine-grained information from high-resolution feature maps.

Cross-Domain DeformCAFA. The bottleneck of CAFA is that it takes all the pixels as possible spatial positions. Based on the attributes of 2D images, the most relative information is mainly located at *geometrically-nearby* locations. Therefore, it is unnecessary to consider all the positions but only several key-point regions. Inspired by this, we introduce a novel *Cross-Domain Deform-CAFA* operation (see Fig. 3), which greatly reduces the sampling candidates and dynamically decides the key-point regions on the image plane for each voxel query feature.

More formally, given the feature map $\mathbf{F} \in \mathbb{R}^{h \times w \times d}$ extracted from the image backbone (*e.g.*, ResNet, CSPNet) and non-empty voxel features $\mathbf{P} \in \mathbb{R}^{N \times c}$, we first compute the reference points $R_i = (r_x^x, r_y^i)$ in the image plane from each voxel feature center $V_i = (v_x^i, v_y^i, v_z^i)$ with the camera projection matrix $T_{cam-lidar}$,

$$R_i = \mathbf{RC} \cdot T_{cam-lidar} \cdot V_i, \tag{1}$$

where $\mathbf{RC}$ is the combination of the rectifying rotation matrix and calibration matrix of the camera. After obtaining the reference point R_i, we adopt bilinear interpolation to get the feature F_i in the image domain. The query feature Q_i is derived as the element-wise product of the image feature F_i and the corresponding voxel feature P_j (to be discussed later). The final deformable cross-attention feature aggregation is calculated by,

$$
\begin{aligned}
&\mathrm{DeformCAFA}(Q_i, R_i, \mathbf{F}) \\
&= \sum_{m=1}^{M} \mathbf{W}_m \left[\sum_{k=1}^{K} A_{mqk}(Q_i) \cdot \mathbf{W}'_m \mathbf{F}(R_i + \Delta R_{mqk}) \right],
\end{aligned} \tag{2}
$$

where $\mathbf{W}_m$ and $\mathbf{W}'_m$ are learnable weights, and A_{mqk} is a MLP to generate attention scores on the aggregated image features. Following the design of self-attention mechanism, we adopt M attention split heads. Here, K is the number of sampling positions ($K^2 \ll HW$, e.g., $K = 4$). With the help of dynamically generated sampling offset Δ_{mqk}, DeformCAFA is able to conduct cross-domain relational modeling much faster than vanilla operation. The complexity is reduced from $O(NWH)$ to $O(NK^2)$, enabling us to perform multi-layer feature aggregation, i.e., to fully utilize the hierarchical information provided by FPN layers. Another advantage of DeformCAFA is that it explicitly maintains the positional consistency with the camera projection matrix to obtain the reference points. Hence, even without adopting the CFSI module proposed in AutoAlign, our DeformCAFA can yield a semantically and positionally consistent alignment.

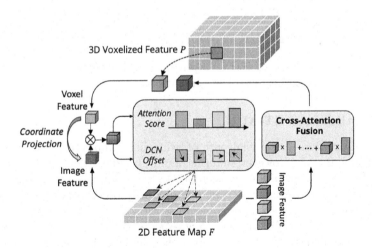

Fig. 3. Illustration of the Cross-Domain DeformCAFA module. It first combines coordinate-corresponding voxel and image features to generate cross-domain tokens, which are then used to guide the aggregated positions in 2D feature map through learnable convolutional offset. The final fused feature is obtained by the cross-attention fusion of aggregated image feature and original voxel feature.

Cross-Domain Token Generation. The sparse-style DeformCAFA greatly improves the efficiency compared to vanilla non-local operation. However, when directly applying voxel features as the token to generate attention weights and deformable offsets, the detection performance is barely comparable to or even worse than its bilinear-interpolation counterparts. After careful analysis, we find a cross-domain knowledge translation issue in the token generation process. Different from the original deformable operation, which is usually performed under the unimodal setting [3,43], cross-domain attention requires information from both modalities. However, the voxel features that only consist of spatial representations, can hardly perceive information in the image domain. Therefore, allowing interaction between different modalities is of great importance.

Motivated by [14], we hypothesize that the representation of each object can be explicitly disentangled into two components: the domain-specific and the instance-specific information. The former refers to the data related to the representation itself, including the built-in attributes of domain features, while the latter represents the identity information about the object, regardless of the domain it is encoded in. Concretely, given the corresponding paired image feature F_i and voxel feature P_j, we have,

$$F_i = D_i^{2D} \cdot M_{obj}^i, \; P_j = D_j^{3D} \cdot M_{obj}^j, \tag{3}$$

where D_i^{2D} and D_j^{3D} are domain-related features in the image and point domains, while M_{obj}^i and M_{obj}^j are the object-specific representations, respectively. Since F_i and P_j are the geometrically-paired features, M_{obj}^i and M_{obj}^j can be close in the instance-specific representation space (*i.e.*, $M_{obj} \approx M_{obj}^i \approx M_{obj}^j$). Based on this, we can implicitly interact features of different domain knowledges with,

$$Token = f(F_i \cdot P_j) = f(D_i^{2D} \cdot D_j^{3D} \cdot (M_{obj})^2), \tag{4}$$

where f is one fully connected (FC) layer to aggregate cross-domain information and improve the flexibility of token generation.

3.2   Depth-Aware GT-AUG

Data augmentation is a crucial part of achieving competitive results for most deep learning models. However, in terms of multi-modal 3D object detection, it is hard to keep synchronization between point clouds and images when combining them together in data augmentation, mainly due to object occlusions or changes in the viewpoints. To solve the problem, we design a simple yet effective cross-modal data augmentation named *Depth-Aware GT-AUG*. Different from the methods described in [31,39], our approach abandons the complex point cloud filtering process or the requirement of delicate mask annotation in the image domain. Instead, inspired by the MixUp proposed in [38], we incorporate the depth information from 3D object annotations to mix up the image regions.

Specifically, given the virtual objects P to paste, we follow the same 3D implementation in GT-AUG [33]. As for the image domain, we first sort them in

Fig. 4. Visualization of the augmented images with the proposed Depth-Aware GT-AUG. The samples are randomly selected from nuScenes dataset.

a far-to-near order. For each to-paste object, we crop the same region from the original image and combine them with a mix-up ratio of α on the target image. The detailed implementation is shown in Algorithm 1.

Algorithm 1: Depth-Aware GT-AUG

Input: Object Points Set $\mathbf{P^{3D}}$, Object Image Patches Set $\mathbf{P^{2D}}$, Object Depths Set $\mathbf{D}$, Points $\mathbf{P}$, Image $\mathbf{I}$.

1: ObjectInds $\leftarrow$ AscendingSort($\mathbf{D}$);
2: **for all** i such that $i \in$ ObjectInds **do**
3:     // point augmentation
4:     $\mathbf{P} \leftarrow \mathbf{P} + \mathbf{P_i^{3D}}$;
5:     // image augmentation
6:     $\mathbf{P_{origin}} = CROP(\mathbf{I}, \mathrm{Coord}(\mathbf{P_i^{2D}}))$;
7:     $\mathbf{P_{new}} = \alpha\mathbf{P_{origin}} + (1 - \alpha)\mathbf{P_i^{2D}}$;
8:     $\mathbf{I} \leftarrow PASTE(\mathbf{I}, \mathbf{P_{new}})$
9: **end for**

Output: $\mathbf{P}, \mathbf{I}$

Depth-Aware GT-AUG simply follows the augmentation strategy in the 3D domain, but at the same time, keeps the synchronization in the image plane through MixUp-based cut-and-paste. The key intuition is that the MixUp technique does not fully remove the corresponding information after pasting augmented patches on top of the original 2D image. On the contrary, it decays the compactness of such information with respect to the depth to guarantee the existence of the feature from the corresponding points. Concretely, if one object is occluded by other instances n times, the transparency of this object region will be decayed by a factor of $(1 - \alpha)^n$ according to its depth order.

3.3   Image-Level Dropout Training Strategy

Actually, image is usually an optional input and may not be supported in all 3D detection systems. Therefore, a more realistic and applicable solution to multi-modal detection should be in a dynamic fusion manner: when images are unavailable, the model detects objects based on raw point clouds; when images are available, the model conducts feature fusion and yields better prediction. To achieve this goal, we propose an image-level dropout training strategy by randomly dropping the aggregated image features at the image level and padding them with zeros during training, as shown in Fig. 5. Since the imagery information is intermittently missed, the model should gradually learn to utilize 2D features as one alternative input. Later, we will show that such a strategy not only speeds up the training speed greatly (with fewer images to process per batch) but also improves the final performance.

(a) Vanilla Image Fusion   (b) Image-Level Dropout Fusion

Fig. 5. Visualization of our proposed image-level dropout training strategy compared to the vanilla fusion method. We enable the model to acquire ad-hoc inference by randomly blinding several cameras during training. The images in while-black (b) denote the dropout RGB images where we pad them with zeros for fusion.

4   Experiments

4.1   Dataset and Experimental Setup

Dataset. The nuScenes dataset [2] is one of the most popular datasets for 3D object detection, consisting of 700 scenes for training, 150 scenes for validation, and 150 scenes for testing. For each scene, it includes 6 camera images to cover the whole viewpoint. In terms of the overlapping regions between images, we predefine the image fetching priority sequence to avoid the ambiguous problem.

Experimental Setup. We select Object DGCNN [32] and CenterPoint [36] as 3D base detectors for the nuScenes dataset. For the image branch, we adopt a light-weight backbone CSPNet [30], the same one used in YOLOX-Tiny [9], as the feature extractor, followed by PAFPN [18]. We also pretrain the image branch with 2D detection supervision on nuImages by adding an extra head [9]. The voxel size is set to (0.1 m, 0.1 m, 0.1 m) if not specified. To avoid the redundant computational cost, we adopt dynamic voxelization [40] to reduce the number of voxel features. As for the DeformCAFA module, the head number is set to 4 and the deformable point is set to 8. All the feature pyramid layers share the same weight for the feature aggregation operation. All runtimes are measure on a NVIDIA V100 GPU. The whole framework is optimized with hybrid optimizers in an end-to-end manner. The 3D branch is optimized with AdamW and the 2D branch is optimized with SGD. We use MMDetection3D [7] as our codebase and apply the default settings, if not specified.

4.2 Main Results

Results on 3D Object Detectors. We first implement AutoAlignV2 on two representative 3D detector baselines: CenterPoint (anchor/center-based) and Object DGCNN (transformer-based) on nuScenes validation subset. The final performance is reported in Table 1. Our AutoAlignV2 greatly boosts its vanilla 3D baselines by 3.7/4.5 on mAP and 2.4/2.4 on NDS score, respectively. This validates the effectiveness and generalization of the proposed method under different 3D detection frameworks.

Table 1. Comparison of detection results based on Object DGCNN and CenterPoint with and without AutoAlignV2 on nuScenes validation subset.

Method	AutoAlignV2	mAP	NDS
Object DGCNN [32]		60.73	67.14
Object DGCNN [32]	✓	**64.42**	**69.52**
CenterPoint [36]		62.56	68.84
CenterPoint [36]	✓	**67.05**	**71.23**

Comparison with State-of-the-Arts. In addition to offline results, we also report the detection performance on nuScenes test leaderboard compared to various detection approaches. The results are shown in Table 2. Our final model is based on CenterPoint with a voxel size of (0.075 m, 0.075 m, 0.2 m). It surpasses all the other counterparts including the recently developed MoCa [39] and PointAugmenting [31] by roughly 2.0 mAP, achieving new state-of-the-arts on this competitive benchmark. When observing the results in detail, we can find that the construction vehicle, motorcycle, and bicycle are separately improved by 13.1, 13.4, and 17.4 mAP. Such huge enhancements manifest the superiority of our proposed AutoAlignV2 to deal with hard-to-detect examples.

4.3 Ablation Studies

In this section, we provide extensive ablations to gain a deeper understanding of AutoAlignV2. For efficiency, 1/8 nuScenes training set is used.

Ablation Studies on AutoAlignV2. To understand how each component in AutoAlignV2 facilitates the detection performance, we test each module independently on the baseline detector: CenterPoint and report its performance in Table 3. The overall mAP score starts from 50.3. When we add the Cross-Domain DeformCAFA module together with the image branch, the mAP score is raised by 6.7%. Such a significant improvement validates the correctness of the incorporation of image features and the effectiveness of the proposed deformable feature alignment module. Then, we adopt the image-level dropout strategy to improve the training speed. The performance does not drop and is even slightly improved by another 0.1 mAP. When the depth-aware GT-AUG is added, the accuracy is further promoted by 1.4 mAP. Although the improvement is not remarkable, depth-aware GT-AUG greatly simplifies the synchronization process in the joint image-point augmentation.

Table 2. Comparison with previous methods on nuScenes test leaderboard. "C.V." and "Ped." are the abbreviations of construction vehicle and pedestrian, respectively. NDS score, mAP, and APs of each category are reported. The single class AP not reported in the paper is marked by "-". The best results are highlighted in bold.

Method	NDS	mAP	Car	Truck	Bus	Trailer	C.V	Ped.	Motor	Bicycle
3D-CVF [37]	49.8	42.2	79.7	37.9	55.0	36.3	-	71.3	37.2	-
PointPainting [29]	58.1	46.4	77.9	35.8	36.1	37.3	15.8	73.3	41.5	24.1
CVCNet [4]	66.6	58.2	82.6	49.5	59.4	51.1	16.2	83.0	61.8	38.8
AFDetV2 [42]	68.5	62.4	86.3	54.2	62.5	58.9	26.7	85.8	63.8	34.3
MVP [36]	70.5	66.4	86.8	58.5	67.4	57.3	26.1	89.1	70.0	49.3
MoCa [39]	70.9	66.6	86.7	58.6	67.2	60.3	32.6	87.1	67.8	52.0
AutoAlign [6]	70.9	65.8	85.9	55.3	67.7	55.6	29.6	86.4	71.5	51.5
PointAugmenting [31]	71.1	66.8	87.5	57.3	65.2	60.7	28.0	87.9	74.3	50.9
CenterPoint [36]	67.3	60.3	85.2	53.5	63.6	56.0	20.0	84.6	59.5	30.7
AutoAlignV2 (Ours)	**72.4**	**68.4**	87.0	59.0	69.3	59.3	33.1	87.6	72.9	52.1

Table 3. Effect of each component in our AutoAlignV2. Results are reported on nuScenes validation set with CenterPoint.

DeformCAFA	Image-level Dropout	Depth-aware GT-AUG	mAP	NDS
			50.28	58.71
✓			56.96	62.54
✓	✓		57.03	62.52
✓	✓	✓	**58.45**	**63.16**

Ablation Studies on Cross-Domain DeformCAFA

1) **Comparison with other fusion mechanisms.** In this experiment, we keep all settings the same except for the cross-modal feature fusion method for

Table 4. Comparison with different feature fusion strategies adopted in current multi-modal detectors. Methods with * indicate our own implementation.

Fusion Strategy	mAP	NDS
Baseline w/o Img	50.28	58.71
PointPainting* [27]	55.45	61.44
MoCa [39]	55.91	61.54
AutoAlign [6]	56.69	61.93
PointAugmenting* [31]	56.75	62.11
Cross-Domain DeformCAFA	**58.45**	**63.16**

a fair comparison. We consider the following strategies used in PointPainting [27], MoCa [39], AutoAlign [6], and PointAugmenting [31], and compare them with Cross-Domain DeformCAFA in Table 4. It can be found that AutoAlignV2 outperforms all the other fusion mechanisms by a large margin, verifying the effectiveness of our proposed approach. The enhancement mainly stems from two aspects: (i) multi-level features are fully utilized thanks to the optimization of computational complexity and (ii) superiority of relational modeling on cross-domain features across different modalities.

2) **Strategies on token generation.** To validate the necessity of the cross-domain token generation, we compare our method with various policies: generated from voxel features only, image features only, and their combinations including concatenation, addition, and multiplication. As given in Table 5, utilizing the voxel features as the query token cannot guarantee satisfying results, since 3D features can hardly perceive information in the interaction between cross-modal features. The result produced by the image features is also limited, possibly due to the lack of information from 3D points. The performance of simply concatenating or adding them together remains poor. We infer the reason that though both features contain the same identity information, it is still hard for the model to figure them out when blending with the domain-specific representation. Finally, we obtain the best performance with the multiplication version, which proves the assumption in Sect. 3.1.

Table 5. Ablations on different strategies in query token generation for Cross-Domain DeformCAFA module. "Operation" denotes the interact operation between the points and image features to generate tokens.

Points Feature	Images Feature	Operation	mAP	NDS
✓		-	57.10	61.77
	✓	-	57.77	62.08
✓	✓	Concat	58.01	62.32
✓	✓	Add	57.94	62.13
✓	✓	Multiply	**58.45**	**63.16**

Ablation Studies on Depth-Aware GT-AUG

1) **Comparison with other cross-modal GT-AUG.** We compare depth-aware GT-AUG together with other cross-modal data augmentation approaches proposed in MoCa [39] and PointAugmenting [31]. As shown in Table 6, the depth-aware GT-AUG slightly surpasses all the other strategies even without point filtering or 2D occlusion checking, which greatly overcomes the difficulty in cross-domain synchronization. Moreover, we can see from Fig. 4 that the depth-aware GT-AUG is able to produce smoother images for image fusion, which enhances the quality of 2D features during the cross-modal fusion process.

Table 6. Comparison with various cross-modal GT-AUG strategies. "2D Occlusion Check": abandoning the instance paste if it has certain overlap with the original instances in the images; "Points Filter": filtering the points to guarantee that points of one instance will not aggregate the image features from another occluded one.

Method	2D Occlusion Check	Points Filter	mAP	NDS
w/o Aug			40.12	45.39
MoCa [39]	✓		53.08	56.54
PointAugmenting [31]		✓	53.16	56.91
Depth-Aware GT-AUG			**53.48**	**57.16**

2) **GT-AUG Mix-up Ratio.** In Fig. 6, we investigate how the mix-up ratio α in the depth-aware GT-AUG affects the model performance. It can be seen that the detection result is not sensitive to the mix-up ratio ranging from 0.5 to 0.8, where the NDS only fluctuates within 0.1%. However, the score drops about 0.7 mAP with $\alpha = 1.0$, where the depth-aware GT-AUG degenerates to the original GT-AUG implementation in MoCa [39]. Since no occlusion checking or point filtering is performed, points may be fused with other imagery information, leading to the ambiguous learning issue.

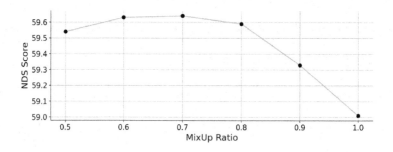

Fig. 6. Ablation study on the mix-up ratio α introduced in depth-aware GT-AUG.

Ablation Studies on Image-level Dropout Strategy. Considering that AutoAlignV2 can be dynamically trained with or without images, namely dynamic image fusion, we study such an attribute and how it contributes to the final performance. Concretely, we vary the number of images for training in our image-level dropout strategy and report the detection accuracy as well as the training time in Table 7. From the table, we can find that reducing the number of training images from 6 to 3 has little effect on the performance of the model but greatly reduces the training time by 1.5×. However, if continuously reducing this number to 1, the performance incurs an evident decline. We infer the reason that single image training is not enough for fully cross-modal fusion learning. Therefore, we adopt 3 images per scene in our experiments.

Table 7. Ablation studies on the number of images for fusion during the training process with our proposed image-level dropout strategy.

# Images	Training Time	mAP	NDS
0	7.6 h	50.28	58.71
1	8.5 h	57.93	62.84
3	9.7 h	58.45	**63.16**
6	14.1 h	**58.51**	63.11

4.4 Dynamic Inference and Runtime

Autonomous driving is a direct application of multi-modal 3D object detection. Therefore, the practicality and inclusiveness of the model are also vital. As mentioned in Sect. 3.1, AutoAlignV2 fits to different inference modes, no matter the images are available or not. We carefully measure the inference performance of AutoAlignV2 under different settings and report its runtime per frame in Table 8. Compared with the LiDAR-only detector: CenterPoint, our AutoAlignV2 takes only 123 ms for the extra 2D image branch, thanks to its light-weight backbone: CSPNet. We resize all the images to 640×1280 for efficient fusion. In addition to fully surrounding images for cross-modal fusion, our method is also qualified for the LiDAR-only scenarios without any extra computational cost compared to vanilla CenterPoint, but still maintains the detection accuracy.

Table 8. Inference time of AutoAlignV2 on nuScenes dataset. "# Images" means the number of images to load during inference.

Method	# Images	Inference Time	mAP	NDS
CenterPoint	-	85 ms	50.28	58.71
AutoAlignV2	6	208 ms	**58.45**	**63.16**
AutoAlignV2	3	181 ms	54.32	60.84
AutoAlignV2	0	87 ms	50.29	58.67

5 Conclusion

In this paper, we develop a dynamic and fast multi-modal 3D object detection framework, AutoAlignV2. It greatly speeds up the fusion process by utilizing multi-layer deformable cross-attention networks to extract and aggregate features from different modalities. We also design the depth-aware GT-AUG strategy to simplify the synchronization between 2D and 3D domains during the multi-modal data augmentation process. Interestingly, our AutoAlignV2 is much more flexible and can infer with and without images in an ad-hoc manner, which is more suitable for the real-world systems. We hope AutoAlignV2 can serve as a simple yet strong paradigm in multi-modal 3D object detection.

Acknowledgments. This work was supported by the USTC-NIO Joint Research Funds KD2111180313. We acknowledge the support of GPU cluster built by MCC Lab of Information Science and Technology Institution, USTC.

References

1. Bai, X., et al.: TransFusion: robust LiDAR-camera fusion for 3D object detection with transformers. In: Proceedings of the IEEE/CVF Conference on Computer Vision and Pattern Recognition, pp. 1090–1099 (2022)
2. Caesar, H., et al.: nuScenes: a multimodal dataset for autonomous driving. In: Proceedings of the IEEE/CVF conference on computer vision and pattern recognition, pp. 11621–11631 (2020)
3. Carion, N., Massa, F., Synnaeve, G., Usunier, N., Kirillov, A., Zagoruyko, S.: End-to-end object detection with transformers. In: Vedaldi, A., Bischof, H., Brox, T., Frahm, J.-M. (eds.) ECCV 2020. LNCS, vol. 12346, pp. 213–229. Springer, Cham (2020). https://doi.org/10.1007/978-3-030-58452-8_13
4. Chen, Q., Sun, L., Cheung, E., Yuille, A.L.: Every view counts: cross-view consistency in 3D object detection with hybrid-cylindrical-spherical voxelization. Adv. Neural Inf. Process. Syst., 21224–21235 (2020)
5. Chen, X., Ma, H., Wan, J., Li, B., Xia, T.: Multi-view 3D object detection network for autonomous driving. In: Proceedings of the IEEE Conference on Computer Vision and Pattern Recognition, pp. 1907–1915 (2017)
6. Chen, Z., et al.: AutoAlign: pixel-instance feature aggregation for multi-modal 3D object detection. IJCAI, pp. 1–7 (2022)
7. Contributors, M.: MMDetection3D: OpenMMLab next-generation platform for general 3D object detection. https://github.com/open-mmlab/mmdetection3D (2020)
8. Deng, J., Shi, S., Li, P., Zhou, W., Zhang, Y., Li, H.: Voxel R-CNN: towards high performance voxel-based 3D object detection. In: Proceedings of the AAAI Conference on Artificial Intelligence, vol. 35, pp. 1201–1209 (2021)
9. Ge, Z., Liu, S., Wang, F., Li, Z., Sun, J.: YOLOX: exceeding YOLO series in 2021. arXiv preprint arXiv:2107.08430, pp. 1–6 (2021)
10. Geiger, A., Lenz, P., Urtasun, R.: Are we ready for autonomous driving? The KITTI vision benchmark suite. In: Proceedings of the IEEE/CVF Conference on Computer Vision and Pattern Recognition, pp. 3354–3361. IEEE (2012)

11. Huang, T., Liu, Z., Chen, X., Bai, X.: EPNet: enhancing point features with image semantics for 3d object detection. In: Vedaldi, A., Bischof, H., Brox, T., Frahm, J.-M. (eds.) ECCV 2020. LNCS, vol. 12360, pp. 35–52. Springer, Cham (2020). https://doi.org/10.1007/978-3-030-58555-6_3

12. Ku, J., Mozifian, M., Lee, J., Harakeh, A., Waslander, S.L.: Joint 3D proposal generation and object detection from view aggregation. In: 2018 IEEE/RSJ International Conference on Intelligent Robots and Systems, pp. 1–8. IEEE (2018)

13. Lang, A.H., Vora, S., Caesar, H., Zhou, L., Yang, J., Beijbom, O.: PointPillars: fast encoders for object detection from point clouds. In: Proceedings of the IEEE/CVF Conference on Computer Vision and Pattern Recognition, pp. 12697–12705 (2019)

14. Li, Y., et al.: Fully convolutional networks for panoptic segmentation. In: Proceedings of the IEEE/CVF Conference on Computer Vision and Pattern Recognition, pp. 214–223 (2021)

15. Li, Y., et al.: DeepFusion: LiDAR-camera deep fusion for multi-modal 3D object detection. In: Proceedings of the IEEE/CVF Conference on Computer Vision and Pattern Recognition, pp. 17182–17191 (2022)

16. Li, Z., et al.: SimIPU: simple 2D image and 3D point cloud unsupervised pre-training for spatial-aware visual representations. In: Proceedings of the AAAI Conference on Artificial Intelligence. vol. 36, pp. 1500–1508 (2022)

17. Liang, M., Yang, B., Wang, S., Urtasun, R.: Deep continuous fusion for multi-sensor 3D object detection. In: Proceedings of the European Conference on Computer Vision, pp. 641–656 (2018)

18. Liu, S., Qi, L., Qin, H., Shi, J., Jia, J.: Path aggregation network for instance segmentation. In: Proceedings of the IEEE Conference on Computer Vision and Pattern Recognition, pp. 8759–8768 (2018)

19. Liu, Z., et al.: BEVFusion: multi-task multi-sensor fusion with unified bird's-eye view representation. arXiv preprint arXiv:2205.13542 (2022)

20. Mao, J., et al.: Voxel transformer for 3D object detection. In: Proceedings of the IEEE/CVF International Conference on Computer Vision, pp. 3164–3173 (2021)

21. Pang, S., Morris, D., Radha, H.: CLOCs: camera-LiDAR object candidates fusion for 3D object detection. In: 2020 IEEE/RSJ International Conference on Intelligent Robots and Systems, pp. 1–10. IEEE (2020)

22. Qi, C.R., Litany, O., He, K., Guibas, L.J.: Deep hough voting for 3D object detection in point clouds. In: Proceedings of the IEEE/CVF International Conference on Computer Vision, pp. 9277–9286 (2019)

23. Qi, C.R., Liu, W., Wu, C., Su, H., Guibas, L.J.: Frustum pointnets for 3D object detection from RGB-D data. In: Proceedings of the IEEE Conference on Computer Vision and Pattern Recognition, pp. 918–927 (2018)

24. Shi, S., et al.: PV-RCNN: point-voxel feature set abstraction for 3D object detection. In: Proceedings of the IEEE/CVF Conference on Computer Vision and Pattern Recognition, pp. 10529–10538 (2020)

25. Shi, S., Wang, X., Li, H.: Point RCNN: 3D object proposal generation and detection from point cloud. In: Proceedings of the IEEE/CVF Conference on Computer Vision and Pattern Recognition, pp. 770–779 (2019)

26. Shi, S., Wang, Z., Shi, J., Wang, X., Li, H.: From points to parts: 3D object detection from point cloud with part-aware and part-aggregation network. IEEE Transactions on Pattern Analysis and Machine Intelligence, pp. 1–14 (2020)

27. Sindagi, V.A., Zhou, Y., Tuzel, O.: MVX-Net: multimodal VoxelNet for 3D object detection. In: 2019 International Conference on Robotics and Automation (ICRA), pp. 7276–7282. IEEE (2019)

28. Sun, P., et al.: Scalability in perception for autonomous driving: waymo open dataset. In: Proceedings of the IEEE/CVF Conference on Computer Vision and Pattern Recognition, pp. 2446–2454 (2020)
29. Vora, S., Lang, A.H., Helou, B., Beijbom, O.: PointPainting: sequential fusion for 3D object detection. In: Proceedings of the IEEE/CVF Conference on Computer Vision and Pattern Recognition, pp. 4604–4612 (2020)
30. Wang, C.Y., et al.: CSPNet: a new backbone that can enhance learning capability of CNN. In: Proceedings of the IEEE/CVF Conference on Computer Vision and Pattern Recognition Workshops, pp. 390–391 (2020)
31. Wang, C., Ma, C., Zhu, M., Yang, X.: PointAugmenting: cross-modal augmentation for 3D object detection. In: Proceedings of the IEEE/CVF Conference on Computer Vision and Pattern Recognition, pp. 11794–11803 (2021)
32. Wang, Y., Solomon, J.M.: Object DGCNN: 3D object detection using dynamic graphs. In: Advances in Neural Information Processing Systems 34 (2021)
33. Yan, Y., Mao, Y., Li, B.: SECOND: sparsely embedded convolutional detection. Sensors **18**, 3337 (2018)
34. Yang, Z., Sun, Y., Liu, S., Jia, J.: 3DSSD: point-based 3D single stage object detector. In: Proceedings of the IEEE/CVF Conference on Computer Vision and Pattern Recognition, pp. 11040–11048 (2020)
35. Yang, Z., Sun, Y., Liu, S., Shen, X., Jia, J.: STD: sparse-to-dense 3D object detector for point cloud. In: Proceedings of the IEEE/CVF International Conference on Computer Vision, pp. 1951–1960 (2019)
36. Yin, T., Zhou, X., Krahenbuhl, P.: Center-based 3D object detection and tracking. In: Proceedings of the IEEE/CVF Conference on Computer Vision and Pattern Recognition, pp. 11784–11793 (2021)
37. Yoo, J.H., Kim, Y., Kim, J., Choi, J.W.: 3D-CVF: generating joint camera and LiDAR features using cross-view spatial feature fusion for 3D object detection. In: Vedaldi, A., Bischof, H., Brox, T., Frahm, J.-M. (eds.) ECCV 2020. LNCS, vol. 12372, pp. 720–736. Springer, Cham (2020). https://doi.org/10.1007/978-3-030-58583-9_43
38. Zhang, H., Cisse, M., Dauphin, Y.N., Lopez-Paz, D.: MixUp: beyond empirical risk minimization. arXiv preprint arXiv:1710.09412, pp. 1–12 (2017)
39. Zhang, W., Wang, Z., Loy, C.C., Zhang, W.: Improving data augmentation for multi-modality 3D object detection. arXiv preprint arXiv:2012.12741, pp. 1–10 (2021)
40. Zhou, Y., et al.: End-to-end multi-view fusion for 3D object detection in LiDAR point clouds. In: Conference on Robot Learning, pp. 923–932. PMLR (2020)
41. Zhou, Y., Tuzel, O.: VoxelNet: end-to-end learning for point cloud based 3D object detection. In: Proceedings of the IEEE Conference on Computer Vision and Pattern Recognition, pp. 4490–4499 (2018)
42. Zhu, B., Jiang, Z., Zhou, X., Li, Z., Yu, G.: Class-balanced grouping and sampling for point cloud 3D object detection. arXiv preprint arXiv:1908.09492, pp. 1–10 (2019)
43. Zhu, X., Su, W., Lu, L., Li, B., Wang, X., Dai, J.: Deformable DETR: deformable transformers for end-to-end object detection. In: International Conference on Learning Representations, pp. 1–12 (2020)

WeLSA: Learning to Predict 6D Pose from Weakly Labeled Data Using Shape Alignment

Shishir Reddy Vutukur[1,2]([✉]) [iD], Ivan Shugurov[1,2] [iD], Benjamin Busam[1] [iD], Andreas Hutter[2] [iD], and Slobodan Ilic[1,2] [iD]

[1] Technical University of Munich, Munich, Germany
shishirvutukur@gmail.com
[2] Siemens Technology, Munich, Germany

Abstract. Object pose estimation is a crucial task in computer vision and augmented reality. One of its key challenges is the difficulty of annotation of real training data and the lack of textured CAD models. Therefore, pipelines which do not require CAD models and which can be trained with few labeled images are desirable. We propose a weakly-supervised approach for object pose estimation from RGB-D data using training sets composed of very few labeled images with pose annotations along with weakly-labeled images with ground truth segmentation masks without pose labels. We achieve this by learning to annotate weakly-labeled training data through shape alignment while simultaneously training a pose prediction network. Point cloud alignment is performed using structure and rotation-invariant feature-based losses. We further learn an implicit shape representation, which allows the method to work without the known CAD model and also contributes to pose alignment and pose refinement during training on weakly labeled images. The experimental evaluation shows that our method achieves state-of-the-art results on LineMOD, Occlusion-LineMOD and TLess despite being trained using relative poses and on only a fraction of labeled data used by the other methods. We also achieve comparable results to state-of-the-art RGB-D based pose estimation approaches even when further reducing the amount of unlabeled training data. In addition, our method works even if relative camera poses are given instead of object pose annotations which are typically easier to obtain.

Keywords: Object pose estimation · Shape alignment · Weak supervision

1 Introduction

6D object pose estimation is a crucial task in computer vision and robotics with applications for robotic grasping [37], augmented reality [3], and autonomous

---

Supplementary Information The online version contains supplementary material available at https://doi.org/10.1007/978-3-031-20074-8_37.

driving [23]. 6D pose estimation comprises estimating rotation and translation of an object from the camera coordinate system to the object coordinate system.

With the rise of deep learning, we witnessed a rapid improvement of learning-based pose estimation from RGB images [18,27,30,32,33,36,38,40,40] as well as from RGBD data [5,8,9,34]. A common problem of deep learning-based methods is their dependence on access to a large number of images with ground truth labels. This is even more problematic for 6D pose estimation because pose labels cannot be manually annotated and, thus, require sophisticated labeling pipelines [17]. A possible solution would be to simulate synthetic scenes and train networks on rendered images. This, however, requires the availability of textured CAD models and significant time for simulation and rendering. As we can see from the results of the BOP Challenge [13], methods trained on synthetic data still lag behind their counterparts trained on real or mixed data. For RGBD-based methods [8,9,34], training on real data is also prevalent due to difficulty of realistic simulation of depth sensor noise [14]. To overcome these problems, we propose a novel training pipeline that uses a combination of a very small number of images with object pose or relative camera transformation labels and weakly-labeled images with only 2D segmentation masks. Besides, our training pipeline does not require access to CAD models.

Some approaches are proposed which do not require CAD model. For example, RLLG [4] proposes a training pipeline without CAD model by using labeled training RGB images to regress 2D-3D correspondences by implicitly reconstructing the model using multiview supervision. Similarly, we establish 3D-3D correspondences without CAD model by reconstructing the model implicitly by establishing correspondences in local reference frame of one of the training samples. RLLG [4] requires labeled data for the entire training data even though it doesn't require CAD model. To overcome the need of real training data and CAD model, Latent Fusion [26] proposes a generalized reconstruction pipeline from few labeled views of the unseen object which is then used to estimate pose for a given segmented image by iterative feature alignment. Even though it is a generalized network, the performance of Latent Fusion is not comparable to fully supervised approaches. Without requiring CAD model, our approach uses a combination of very few labeled data and weakly-labeled data and achieves accuracy on par with state-of-the-art supervised RGB-D approaches.

In this paper, we propose a novel deep learning architecture for pose estimation and a novel weakly supervised training pipeline. Since we don't use a CAD model, we use the reference frame of one of the labeled training sample as the canonical reference frame. During training, the network takes as input a point cloud of the object and outputs both implicit shape representation of the object and dense 3D-3D correspondences in the canonical reference frame defined by one of the labeled samples. Note that, since the CAD models are not available, the network is trained to learn the implicit shape representation of the object which is used for shape alignment and pose refinement. Thus, during training, the network learns to reconstruct the object. The predicted implicit shape is converted to the triangular mesh for ICP [1] refinement. During inference, we estimate pose using estimated 3D-3D correspondences and refine the pose using the shape reconstructed during training. The proposed training pipeline consists of three stages: 1) fully supervised training on fully labeled images; 2) fine-tuning on weakly labeled images; 3) auto-labeling weakly labeled images and then training on them in a fully supervised manner. The architecture and the training pipeline were evaluated on LineMOD, LineMOD-Occlusion and TLess datasets and showed very competitive results despite having been trained using a fraction of labeled training images compared to other approaches.

To this end, we contribute:

1. A novel RGB-D pose estimation architecture for 6D pose estimation from point clouds and color image, which fuses features from color, depth and normals and performs simultaneous object reconstruction and 6D pose estimation from very few images with pose labels. Two key components can be distinguished: We propose a feature decoder to improve pose estimation by associating pose invariant features in the shape alignment pipeline, and a shape network to learn the shape of the object which contributes to pose refinement and shape alignment.

2. A weakly supervised novel pose estimation pipeline that simultaneously learns a pose estimation network and auto-label weakly-labeled data with segmentation masks using labeled samples with relative pose labels leveraging shape alignment and feature alignment losses without the need of CAD model. The pipeline achieves accuracy on par with fully supervised RGB-D approaches.

3. Novel shape-based and feature-based rotation invariant losses, are proposed which are suitable for weakly supervised training. The training setup makes it suitable to handle symmetric objects as our approach is shape alignment based. Our approach works even if only the relative poses are available instead of absolute pose for few samples.

2   Related Work

Advances in deep learning enabled a rapid development of pose estimation methods from monocular RGB images. One line of work presented in [5,18,21,36,38] treat pose estimation as a regression problem by directly predicting rotation and translation of the object. [20,22,27,30,32,40] treat it as a correspondence estimation problem by regressing 2D-3D correspondences between image pixels and the 3D model of the object. The 6D pose is then estimated using PnP [19] and RANSAC. Alternatively, [16,28,33] estimate a predefined set of sparse keypoints instead of dense correspondences, which has proven to be more robust to occlusions. We have opted for a dense correspondence-based approach as dense 3D-3D correspondences are required for shape alignment. Despite that, our approach is robust to occlusions on par with keypoint based approaches.

Pose estimation from RGBD data, which was traditionally solved using geometric methods, such as Point Pair Features [6], has also attracted attention from the deep learning community. Most of the methods, such as [8,10,32,34], rely on a common idea of fusing the features estimated separately from RGB using a CNN and from Depth using a variant of Pointnet [29]. Similarly to pose estimation from RGB, some methods [8,10,32] are trained to predict 3D-3D correspondences, while [34] directly outputs rotation and translation.

There have been several attempts to lessen the dependence of pose estimation methods on hard-to-annotate pose labels. [31,35,39] propose to pre-train a model on synthetic images with full annotations and then use the network to label real images, which are then used for training. A CAD-free and 6D labels-free method that uses known bounding boxes, object size and multi-view constraints to train a direct pose regression was proposed in [21]. [41] proposes an approach to estimate domain invariant keypoints by training with labeled synthetic images and real data without pose labels. We propose a weakly-supervised approach using few labeled samples and weakly-labeled data to train a pose estimation pipeline and to label weakly-labeled data without requiring CAD model.

3   Method

3.1   Architecture

The proposed network takes a segmented point cloud and a segmented RGB image of the detected object and outputs 1) dense 3D-3D correspondences between the point cloud and the object model; 2) decoded rotation-invariant features; 3) implicit shape representation of the object. Figure 1 summarizes the architecture. Two separate encoders are used to map the input point cloud and the input image to their respective latent vector representations. Both vectors are stacked to form the vector z, which is used by the decoders. Vector z along with each 3D point in the point cloud are passed through two MLP decoders to predict point-wise 3D correspondences and point-wise feature values. The predicted correspondences are passed through an MLP shape network to predict their respective SDF values. The feature decoder and shape network are used only during the training of the network. We describe different components of our network in detail in the following section.

Encoders. The encoder E consists of two main components. A PointNet based encoder [24] is used to extract features from the point cloud, $X \in \mathbb{R}^{K \times 3}$. Each x of the K points is concatenated with its corresponding normal, n, and color, c, of the normal vector, N, and color vector, C, to use as input to point cloud encoder. The network extracts features from the input point cloud and its features, normals, and color, and outputs an intermediate latent vector.

A ResNet CNN [7] encoder extracts features from an RGB image, I. The CNN predicts another intermediate latent vector from a color image. The intermediate latent vectors from Pointnet and CNN are concatenated to pass through a fully connected layer to produce a global latent vector, z of length d.

The full encoder is mathematically defined as:

$$z = E(I, X, N, C) \tag{1}$$

Correspondence Decoder. Correspondence decoder is an MLP with 7 fully connected layers which takes the global latent vector z and a 3D point x and

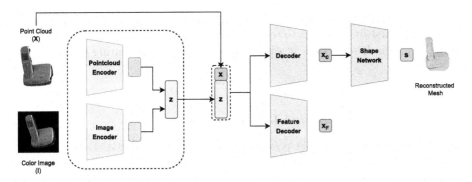

Fig. 1. Architecture: Our network takes in a segmented point cloud and segmented color image to predict 3D correspondences which are used to estimate 6D pose. A feature decoder and shape network are employed only during training to improve shape alignment. The encoder combines latent vectors from the point cloud encoder and image encoder to predict z. Each 3D point, x, in the point cloud, X, is concatenated with z to predict point-wise correspondences, x_C and pose invariant point-wise features, x_F using Correspondence decoder (Decoder) and Feature decoder respectively. The predicted correspondences are passed through the shape network to predict point-wise SDF value, s, which is used to improve shape alignment. The shape network learns implicit shape which is used to reconstruct shape used for pose refinement during training. (Color figure online)

predicts its corresponding 3D point $x_C \in \mathbb{R}^3$ in the canonical reference frame. We denote the decoder with D which is mathematically defined as:

$$x_C = D(z, x) \tag{2}$$

Feature Decoder. The feature decoder, F, has the same architecture as the correspondence decoder and has the same input. It takes a concatenated vector of z and x to predict a per-point pose invariant feature, x_F. The decoder serves an auxiliary role and is used only during training. The motivation behind the feature decoder is to incorporate pose-invariant features. This allows us to define loss functions even for unlabeled data. Since both decoders share the same input, losses formulated on features impact the correspondence prediction. By associating shape alignment with feature loss, we are able to avoid false matches where the structure is similar but features are different. This is illustrated in Fig. 4. In addition to explicit loss terms on shape alignment related feature losses, predicting pose invariant features for each point is an auxiliary task that improves the encoder performance.

$$x_F = F(z, x) \tag{3}$$

Shape Decoder. The shape decoder SN, similarly to DeepSDF [25], learns implicit shape representation in the canonical object pose space. It consists of an MLP with 7 fully connected layers which takes in a correspondence 3D point,

x_C, to predict its signed distance function value, s. The purpose of the decoder is twofold. First, it allows us to reconstruct the object during training and avoid using CAD models. Second, it allows for shape alignment during training.

$$s = SN(x_C) \tag{4}$$

3.2   Training Pipeline and Loss Functions

We aim to estimate the 6D pose of an object from an RGB-D image which involves estimating 3D rotation and 3D translation. We train a network to estimate dense 3D-3D correspondences, which are then used to estimate the 6D pose. To facilitate shape alignment and pose refinement, an implicit object shape is predicted. The model is trained in a weakly-supervised manner on a mix of weakly labeled data and a very small amount of fully labeled data. Fully-labeled images are provided with ground truth poses and segmentation masks. Only object masks are available for weakly-labeled images. We refer to the fully-labeled samples as fewshot samples as we use very few of them in our pipeline.

We employ a three-stage pipeline to train the network. In Stage 1, all parts of the network are trained in a fully supervised manner on the fewshot samples. The shape encoder, trained separately from the rest of the network, implicitly reconstructs the object shape. The pre-trained shape encoder is frozen after this stage. In Stage 2, we train the network along with the feature decoder using both fewshot data and weakly-labeled images using shape and feature deviation losses. We also use the frozen shape network to facilitate shape alignment for weakly-labeled samples. In Stage 3, we first estimate poses for weakly-labeled data using the trained network from Stage 2. The estimated poses are refined using ICP with the triangular mesh reconstructed from the shape network. The network is then trained in a fully supervised manner using the refined poses.

We use the following terminology in the rest of the paper. The camera reference frame is the local reference frame in which each image is observed which is specific to each image. The canonical reference frame is the reference frame to which we find the pose for all the samples. The reference frame of the first sample in the fewshot samples is treated as the canonical reference frame. We use relative pose between frames to generate pose for fewshot samples to the canonical reference frame which is the camera reference frame of the first sample. We estimate pose for all our samples treating the first sample in fewshot samples as the canonical reference frame.

Stage 1. In this stage, we train the network with fewshot samples for which we know the pose labels. It is depicted in Fig. 2. We use correspondence regression loss, L_C, to penalize L2 distance between ground-truth correspondences, X_G, and predicted correspondences. The ground-truth correspondences are obtained by transforming the input point cloud with ground truth rotation, R_G, and translation, T_G, to the canonical reference frame. Using relative pose between frames, we find the transformation to the first frame from every frame and use

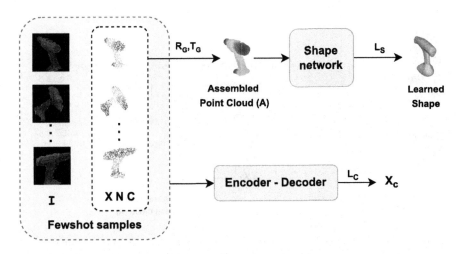

Fig. 2. Pipeline of Stage 1: Few shot samples comprises of RGB image, I, and point cloud, X, and its corresponding normals, N, and color, C. We use ground truth relative poses R_G, T_G to transform all the point clouds to the first image reference frame to get an assembled point cloud A. We train implicit shape network using A and loss, L_S. We also train the encoder-decoder using ground truth relative poses for fewshot samples using loss L_C.

it as a ground truth pose. We train the encoder-decoder network using loss function, L_C which is defined as follows:

$$X_G = X R_G + T_G \quad L_C = \|X_C - X_G\|_2 \tag{5}$$

We employ SDF loss, L_S, with the assembled point cloud, A and its normals, A_N to train the shape network. The assembled point cloud is obtained by combining the ground truth correspondences of the few shot point clouds. Since the assembled point cloud is supposed to lie on the object's surface, the SDF value should be zero for these points. To generate more samples to train the shape network and to learn shape better, we estimate point cloud normals and translate assembled point cloud along their per-point normals, A_N, by a scaling factor, P. For these samples, the SDF value should be equal to the scaling factor, P, and hence we formulate loss with the scaling factor as follows:

$$A' = A + P A_N$$
$$S = SN(A')$$
$$L_S = \|S - P\|_1$$

Stage 2. In this stage, the network is trained on both weakly-labeled and fewshot samples. It is depicted in Fig. 3. We freeze the shape network because it has already learned the signed distance function of the shape and is used to formulate shape deviation loss for weakly-labeled data. We present the loss functions used in this stage below.

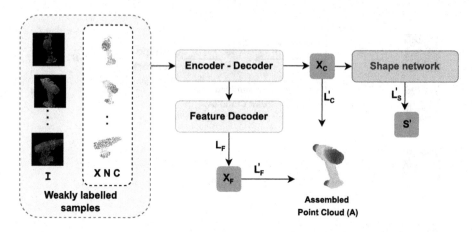

Fig. 3. Pipeline of Stage 2 : We train the encoder-decoder, feature decoder using a frozen shape network and assembled point cloud. Chamfer loss, L'_C, photometric loss, L'_F are formulated on correspondences, X_C and predicted features X_F. Correspondences are also passed through the frozen shape network to predict SDF, S' to formulate SDF loss, L'_S. (Color figure online)

We predict color as a feature using the feature decoder. We use color as pose-invariant feature to improve pose alignment. We employ a feature loss, L_F, between predicted feature, X_F, and color of the input point cloud, C. This loss is applied to all the samples.

$$L_F = \|X_F - C\|_2 \qquad (6)$$

We employ different loss functions for weakly-labeled samples as we do not know the pose for these samples. We employ a rigidity preserving loss, L'_R, between the input point cloud and predicted correspondences to predict the correspondences with the same structure as the input point cloud. We formulate a loss to preserve the inter-point euclidean distance between each pair of points between input point cloud, X, and predicted correspondences, X_C.

$$
\begin{aligned}
d^{ij} &= \|x^i - x^j\|_2 \\
d_C^{ij} &= \|x_C^i - x_C^j\|_2 \\
L'_R &= \sum_j \sum_i \|d^{ij} - d_C^{ij}\|_2
\end{aligned}
\qquad (7)
$$

We estimate rotation and translation between input point cloud, X, and predicted correspondences, X_C, using the differentiable Kabsch algorithm [15]. So, the loss formulated using the rotation and translation can be back propagated through the network. We transform input normals, N, and point cloud, X, to canonical reference frame using estimated rotation and translation as follows:

$$N_T = NR \quad X_T = XR + T \qquad (8)$$

We transform the input point cloud using R, T to constrain the shape alignment to rigid transform by parameterizing loss over R, T instead of predicted correspondences directly. If we formulate the chamfer shape loss with predicted correspondences, the degenerate solution is that all predicted correspondences can collapse to one point on the target shape. Although we have a structure preserving loss, L'_R, transforming input point cloud and formulating loss on R and T eliminates the sensitivity of network on weights assigned to structure preserving and shape aligning losses. Since we employ structure preserving loss even for noisy point clouds and parameterize shape based losses over rigid transformation, the entire point cloud undergoes a rigid transformation avoiding the need to include RANSAC for correspondence filtering.

To register weakly-labeled samples to the canonical reference frame, we employ chamfers distance, L'_C, to register the predicted correspondences with the assembled point cloud. We employ chamfers distance between assembled point cloud, A, its colors, A_C, its normals, A_N, and transformed input, X_T, predicted color, X_F, transformed normals, N_T.

Chamfer distance penalizes the structure deviation by penalizing the distance between the closest points on a target and source shape. We further combine features and correspondences by penalizing the feature deviation among the closest points in addition to structure deviation. We use color and normal features along with 3D points in chamfer distance to align the point clouds better. To propagate loss to the encoder through the features based on chamfer distance, we need to associate the feature loss to the pose. We achieve this by adding a feature decoder, which uses the same input as the correspondence decoder. Since we use same the latent space for both correspondence decoder and feature decoder, the pose alignment is impacted by losses formulated on correspondences as well as the features. Thus, we formulate feature loss on colors to propagate loss to improve the encoder to predict better correspondences and align the shapes better. The photometric consistency loss, L'_F, penalizes the color deviation between closest points on the transformed input cloud and the assembled point cloud.

We estimate rotation between the input point cloud and correspondences to rotate normals to the canonical reference frame. Losses formulated on rotated normals, N_T, propagates through rotation matrix to correspondences and to the network. The normal consistency loss, L'_N, penalizes normal deviation between closest points on the transformed input cloud and the assembled point cloud.

$$idx = \arg\min_{x \in A} ||x - x_T||_2$$
$$L'_C = ||A[idx] - x_T||_2$$
$$L'_F = ||A_C[idx] - x_F||_2 \tag{9}$$
$$L'_N = ||A_N[idx] - n_T||_2$$

By adding features into the pipeline and formulating loss function combining correspondences and features, the network automatically learns to predict the pose better as it impacts both the feature and correspondence decoder.

We employ another shape penalizing loss formulated using the frozen shape network. The predicted correspondences, X_C, from the weakly-labeled data are passed through the shape network to predict SDF values, S, for the correspondences. Since the correspondences are supposed to lie on the shape, the predicted SDF value should be 0 for the correspondences. Basically, the predicted SDF value measures how far the predicted correspondence is from the object surfaces. In the ideal case, when the correspondence is on the surface, SDF is 0. We formulate shape deviation SDF loss, L'_S, as follows:

$$L'_S = \|S\|_1 \tag{10}$$

The total loss, L_2, to train the stage 2 with coefficients β_1 and β_2 is as follows:

$$L_2 = \beta_1(L_C + L_F) + \beta_2(L'_R + L'_C + L'_F + L'_N + L'_S) \tag{11}$$

Stage 3. We train the network using the above losses until convergence in Stage 2. We observe that the predictions still need refinement to align perfectly with the shape. To further refine the pose predictions, we employ an ICP-based refinement pipeline to achieve exact alignment. We reconstruct the surface mesh of the object from the Shape network using the marching cubes algorithm. We project the mesh using the estimated pose from the predicted correspondences and then perform ICP with the input point cloud to find better alignment. After extracting the refined pose for all the weakly labeled samples, we employ correspondence loss, L_C, with the estimated refined poses as ground truth poses for weakly-labelled samples to improve the accuracy further. We train the third stage using estimated refined pose, R', T', for weakly-labelled data as follows:

$$X'_G = XR' + T' \quad L_3 = \|X_C - X'_G\|_2 \tag{12}$$

4   Results

We evaluate our approach on LineMOD [11], LineMOD-Occlusion [2] and TLess [12]. We employ ADD/ADD-S metric [11] for LineMOD, LineMOD-Occlusion and AR metric of BOP Challenge [13] for TLess. We demonstrate the effectiveness of our approach by comparing results we attained using a fraction of total data as labeled data in contrast to other approaches using full labeled data.

4.1   Training Data

We use ground truth masks to extract tight image patches containing the object and point clouds corresponding to the foregrounds of the object. For LineMOD, we sample 15% of data as training data similar to other approaches. Of the sampled training data, we consider ground truth training samples(1%) from the sampled data in a way that they cover the object from different viewpoints which are far apart from each other so that they cover the object to the maximal extent.

This is essential for our approach as we need an approximate point cloud of the object from the ground truth samples. The rest (14%) is treated as weakly-labeled data with only segmentation masks. If the absolute pose is given for the dataset, we use the first image in the fewshot samples as the canonical reference frame and convert the absolute poses of other fewshot samples to relative poses.

Table 1. Results on LineMOD dataset along with state of the art RGB and RGBD approaches. * denotes discrete symmetric objects. GT data and Total Data refer to the amount of ground truth data and total data used for training respectively. ICP refers to results with ICP refinement using the reconstructed model. CAD refers to training data synthetically generated using a CAD model.

Method/Object	Dpod		Dpodv2		PVN3D	G2L-Net	Ours					
RGB	✓	✓	✓	✓	✓	✓	✓	✓	✓	✓	✓	✓
Depth	✗	✗	✓	✓	✓	✓	✓	✓	✓	✓	✓	✓
GT Data	-	15%	-	15%	15%	5%	15%	1%	1%	1%	15%	15%
Total Data	-	15%	-	15%	15%	5%	15%	5%	15%	15%	15%	15%
ICP	✗	✗	✗	✗	✗	✗	✗	✗	✗	✓	✗	✓
CAD	✓	✓	✓	✓	✓	✓	✓	✗	✗	✗	✗	✗
Ape	37.2	53.2	62.14	80	97.3		96.8	94.2	97.2	98.2	99.1	99.3
Benchvice	66.7	95.3	88.39	99.7	99.7		9.1	94.9	97.9	99.9	99.5	99.5
Camera	24.2	90.3	92.51	99.2	99.6		98.2	94.1	97.9	99.3	98.8	98.8
Can	52.5	94.1	96.6	99.6	99.5		98	96.5	97.7	98.7	99.7	100
Cat	32.3	60.3	86.17	95.1	99.8		99.2	99.1	99.3	99.3	99.3	99.3
Driller	66.6	97.7	90.15	98.9	99.3		99.8	89.5	99.5	99.5	99.5	99.5
Duck	26.1	66	54.86	79.5	98.2		97.7	84.3	95.4	97.1	96.8	98.8
Egg box*	73.3	99.7	98.64	99.6	99.8		100	99.4	100	100	100	100
Glue*	74.9	93.8	95.4	99.8	100		100	99.9	99.8	99.8	99.9	99.9
Puncher	24.5	65.8	27	72.3	99.9		99	87.7	96.6	98.8	98.6	99
Iron	85	99.8	98.2	99.4	99.7		99.3	94.1	95.4	99.3	100	100
Lamp	57.2	88.1	91	96.3	99.8		99.5	90.2	99.1	99.1	99.1	99.1
Phone	29	74.2	74.3	96.8	99.5		98.9	98.5	99.9	99.9	99.9	99.9
Average	50	82.9	81.2	93.5	99.4	88.5	98.7	**94.03**	**98.1**	**99.1**	**99.2**	**99.4**

4.2 LineMOD Dataset

Most approaches use 15% of the total data as training data. Our training data consists of 1% samples with ground truth poses and 14% samples without known poses. We train DpodV2 [32] segmentation network with 15% ground truth data whereas the pose pipeline uses 1% ground truth data. During training, the pose accuracy of labels generated for weakly-labeled training samples after stage 2 is 90.6% without ICP and 99.2% with ICP. The ICP accuracy indicates the efficiency of our labeling pipeline and the gap in accuracy justifies the need for refinement in stage 3. From Table 1, we are able to achieve SOTA results using a fraction of ground truth pose data. We observe an improvement of 1.0% with ICP

Table 2. Results on LineMOD-Occlusion dataset along with state of the art RGB [33,38,40] and RGBD [8,9] approaches.

Method	PoseCNN	Dpod	Hybrid Pose	PVN3D	FFB6D	Ours
Average	24.9	47.3	47.5	63.2	66	**63.2**

refinement (99.1%) using the generated mesh from shape network. We achieve closer to benchmark accuracy when we use 15% ground truth data (99.2%).

4.3   LineMOD-Occlusion Dataset

On LineMOD-Occlusion, we achieve close to SOTA results even though we train on data obtained from the LineMOD instead of LineMOD-Occlusion and with only 1% labeled data. The results are presented in Table 2. Our method achieves the same accuracy as PVN3D [10] which shows that our network is capable of handling occluded objects on par with keypoint based approaches despite being a dense correspondence based approach.

4.4   TLess Dataset

We conducted experiments on TLess [12] to show the robustness of our method to occlusions and symmetries. We used 1.5% (20 samples) labeled training images to train the network compared to 100% ($\approx$ 1260) used by other approaches. During training, the AR score of labels generated for weakly-labeled training samples is 0.85 indicating that we are able to label most of the training samples correctly. The results on test set are presented in Table 3. We achieve a higher VSD score that measures shape alignment. This indicates that our shape matching is on par with other approaches despite using fewer labels. We observed a slightly low recall on MSSD, MSPD since there are some objects with minimal geometric differences leading to misalignments.

Table 3. Results on TLess along with supervised [27,32] approaches. GT data refer to the amount of ground truth training data. ICP refers to results with ICP refinement.

Method	Pix2Pose	DpodV2		Ours	
ICP	✓	✗	✓	✗	✓
GT data	100%	100%	100%	1.5%	1.5%
VSD	0.43	0.53	0.41	0.34	**0.46**
MSSD	0.54	0.55	0.51	0.28	0.36
MSPD	0.54	0.58	0.53	0.29	0.37
AR	0.51	0.56	0.49	0.30	0.4

5   Ablation Studies

5.1   Amount of Training Data

We achieve 94% accuracy with just 5% of training data with 1% labeled data as shown in Table 1. As expected, our accuracy increases with an increase in GT training data which is evident from the increase in training data from 1% to 15%. However, the increase in accuracy (1.1%) shows that our weakly-supervised approach is estimating very good poses for unlabelled samples during training even with very less labeled data. We observe that when we use only 5% of total data as training data with 1% ground truth data, we get better accuracy (94%) compared to G2L-Net with 5% ground truth training data(89%). To show that our architecture and training pipeline is on par with benchmark approaches, we evaluate our pipeline with full ground truth labels (15%) and observe that our accuracy(99.2%) is very close to the benchmark accuracy(99.4%).

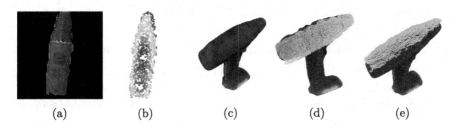

(a)	(b)	(c)	(d)	(e)

Fig. 4. Failure cases on Driller without Feature Decoder: a) Input Image, b) Input Point cloud, c) 3D Object Model d) Bad Correspondences without feature decoder , e) Correct Correspondences with feature decoder. (Color figure online)

5.2   Feature Decoder

In the LineMOD dataset, objects like driller which has a texture that is not constant, the performance increases by a significant margin when we use feature decoder. We especially added this module to solve some issues we encountered with the driller object. As shown in the Fig. 4, the pose is predicted wrongly in the fourth image. The failure cases happen when naive chamfer loss, L'_C, without feature decoder based losses (L'_F, L_F) are used. The failure cases occur as the structure is very similar to the object in both the third and fourth images. The distinguishing feature between correctly aligned fourth image and wrongly aligned third is the color of the point cloud as the structure is very similar in both the scenarios. If the failed sample is not present in the ground truth training data during training, the pose is predicted wrongly when the feature decoder is not present in the pipeline. The pose is predicted correctly in the presence of the feature decoder even if the specific sample is not present in the training set. We observe an increase in accuracy of weakly-labeled samples (8.9%) on driller when feature decoder is added as shown in Table 4.

Table 4. Ablation study on the contribution of different loss functions. We present the pose labeling accuracy of weakly-labeled training data on driller object after Stage 2 with combinations of chamfer loss, shape loss and feature decoder.

Losses	L_C'		L_S'	$L_C' + L_S'$	
Feature Decoder	✗	✓	✗	✗	✓
Average	89	96	87.5	90.5	99.4

5.3   Shape Network

The SDF loss, L_S', helps in aligning weakly-labeled samples to the shape. We observe a drop in pose accuracy by 1.5% when we remove SDF loss. The drop in accuracy is not significant as the chamfer loss serves a similar purpose. However, the approach works even when the shape loss L_S' is used without chamfers distance L_C' as shown in Table 4. Besides, the reconstructed shape used for pose refinement of the weakly-labeled samples improves the unrefined accuracy of the pipeline by a significant amount (6.6%) from stage 2 (91.5%) to stage 3 (98.1%).

5.4   Influence of Each Training Stage on the Final Performance

To show the significance of each stage, we evaluate the pose accuracy after each stage on the LineMOD dataset presented in Table 5. The accuracy (75.3%) is quite low after Stage 1 since it is only trained with around 10 fewshot samples. The accuracy after Stage 2 (91.5%) is higher since we incorporate different viewpoints ($\sim$ 160 samples) from weakly-labeled data, but it still needs improvement to achieve exact alignment. After Stage 3 (98.1%), the network achieves better accuracy as the estimated poses for weakly-labeled data are refined using reconstructed shape and thus network learns to predict more accurately.

Table 5. Accuracy on LineMOD after each stage of training

Training Stage	Stage 1	Stage 2	Stage 3
Average	75.3	91.5	98.1

6   Conclusion

We propose a novel weakly-supervised training pipeline for pose estimation, that does not require CAD models and requires a very small number of labeled images. The core idea is to develop a pipeline leveraging few fully labeled images to automatically label the rest of the images and then train on them. To achieve this, we propose novel rotation-invariant feature and shape -based losses used for weakly-supervised shape alignment. Absolute object poses can be replaced with relative camera transformations which are easier to obtain in practice without changes to the training pipeline. Experimental evaluation demonstrate the effectiveness of our pipeline despite using only a fraction of labeled training images.

Acknowledgements. This work was partially funded by the German BMWK under grant GEMIMEG-II-01MT20001A.

References

1. Arun, K.S., Huang, T.S., Blostein, S.D.: Least-squares fitting of two 3-D point sets. IEEE Trans. Pattern Anal. Mach. Intell. (1987)
2. Brachmann, E., Krull, A., Michel, F., Gumhold, S., Shotton, J., Rother, C.: Learning 6d object pose estimation using 3D object coordinates. In: ECCV (2014)
3. Busam, B.: High performance visual pose computation. Ph.D. Thesis, Technische Universität München (2021)
4. Cai, M., Reid, I.: Reconstruct locally, localize globally: a model free method for object pose estimation. In: 2020 IEEE/CVF Conference on Computer Vision and Pattern Recognition (CVPR) (2020)
5. Chen, W., Jia, X., Chang, H.J., Duan, J., Leonardis, A.: G2L-Net: global to local network for real-time 6d pose estimation with embedding vector features. In: IEEE/CVF Conference on Computer Vision and Pattern Recognition (CVPR) (2020)
6. Drost, B., Ulrich, M., Navab, N., Ilic, S.: Model globally, match locally: efficient and robust 3D object recognition. In: 2010 IEEE Computer Society Conference on Computer Vision and Pattern Recognition, pp. 998–1005. IEEE (2010)
7. He, K., Zhang, X., Ren, S., Sun, J.: Deep residual learning for image recognition. arXiv preprint arXiv:1512.03385 (2015)
8. He, Y., Huang, H., Fan, H., Chen, Q., Sun, J.: FFB6D: a full flow bidirectional fusion network for 6d pose estimation. In: Proceedings of the IEEE/CVF Conference on Computer Vision and Pattern Recognition, pp. 3003–3013 (2021)
9. He, Y., Sun, W., Huang, H., Liu, J., Fan, H., Sun, J.: PVN3D: a deep point-wise 3D keypoints voting network for 6dof pose estimation. In: CVPR (2020)
10. He, Y., Sun, W., Huang, H., Liu, J., Fan, H., Sun, J.: PVN3D: a deep point-wise 3D keypoints voting network for 6DoF pose estimation. In: Proceedings of the IEEE/CVF Conference on Computer Vision and Pattern Recognition (CVPR) (2020)
11. Hinterstoisser, S., et al.: Model based training, detection and pose estimation of texture-less 3D objects in heavily cluttered scenes (2012)
12. Hodaň, T., Haluza, P., Obdržálek, Š., Matas, J., Lourakis, M., Zabulis, X.: T-LESS: an RGB-D dataset for 6D pose estimation of texture-less objects. IEEE Winter Conference on Applications of Computer Vision (WACV) (2017)
13. Hodan, T., Melenovsky, A.: Bop: benchmark for 6d object pose estimation. https:// bop.felk.cvut.cz/home/ (2019)
14. Jung, H., Brasch, N., Leonardis, A., Navab, N., Busam, B.: Wild ToFu: improving range and quality of indirect time-of-flight depth with RGB fusion in challenging environments. In: 2021 International Conference on 3D Vision (3DV), pp. 239–248. IEEE (2021)
15. Kabsch, W.: A solution for the best rotation to relate two sets of vectors. Acta Crystallographica Section A (1976)
16. Kaskman, R., Shugurov, I., Zakharov, S., Ilic, S.: 6 DoF pose estimation of texture-less objects from multiple RGB frames. In: Bartoli, A., Fusiello, A. (eds.) ECCV 2020. LNCS, vol. 12536, pp. 612–630. Springer, Cham (2020). https://doi.org/10. 1007/978-3-030-66096-3_41

17. Kaskman, R., Zakharov, S., Shugurov, I., Ilic, S.: Homebreweddb: RGB-D dataset for 6d pose estimation of 3D objects. In: ICCV Workshops (2019)
18. Labbe, Y., Carpentier, J., Aubry, M., Sivic, J.: CosyPose: consistent multi-view multi-object 6D pose estimation. In: Proceedings of the European Conference on Computer Vision (ECCV) (2020)
19. Lepetit, V., Moreno-Noguer, F., Fua, P.: EPnP: an accurate o(n) solution to the PnP problem. Int. J. Comput. Vis. (2009). https://doi.org/10.1007/s11263-008-0152-6
20. Li, F., Shugurov, I., Busam, B., Li, M., Yang, S., Ilic, S.: PolarMesh: a star-convex 3D shape approximation for object pose estimation. IEEE Robot. Autom. Lett. **7**(2), 4416–4423 (2022)
21. Li, F., Shugurov, I., Busam, B., Yang, S., Ilic, S.: WS-OPE: weakly supervised 6-D object pose regression using relative multi-camera pose constraints. IEEE Robot. Autom. Lett. (2022)
22. Li, F., Yu, H., Shugurov, I., Busam, B., Yang, S., Ilic, S.: NeRF-Pose: a first-reconstruct-then-regress approach for weakly-supervised 6d object pose estimation. arXiv preprint arXiv:2203.04802 (2022)
23. Manhardt, F., Kehl, W., Gaidon, A.: ROI-10D: monocular lifting of 2D detection to 6D pose and metric shape. In: Proceedings of the IEEE/CVF Conference on Computer Vision and Pattern Recognition, pp. 2069–2078 (2019)
24. Mescheder, L., Oechsle, M., Niemeyer, M., Nowozin, S., Geiger, A.: Occupancy networks: Learning 3d reconstruction in function space. In: Proceedings IEEE Conference on Computer Vision and Pattern Recognition (CVPR) (2019)
25. Park, J.J., Florence, P., Straub, J., Newcombe, R., Lovegrove, S.: DeepSDF: learning continuous signed distance functions for shape representation. In: The IEEE Conference on Computer Vision and Pattern Recognition (CVPR) (2019)
26. Park, K., Mousavian, A., Xiang, Y., Fox, D.: LatentFusion: end-to-end differentiable reconstruction and rendering for unseen object pose estimation. In: Proceedings of the IEEE Conference on Computer Vision and Pattern Recognition (2020)
27. Park, K., Patten, T., Vincze, M.: Pix2Pose: pixel-wise coordinate regression of objects for 6D pose estimation. In: The IEEE International Conference on Computer Vision (ICCV) (2019)
28. Peng, S., Liu, Y., Huang, Q., Zhou, X., Bao, H.: PVNet: pixel-wise voting network for 6DoF pose estimation. In: CVPR (2019)
29. Qi, C.R., Su, H., Mo, K., Guibas, L.J.: PointNet: deep learning on point sets for 3D classification and segmentation. arXiv preprint arXiv:1612.00593 (2016)
30. Shugurov, I., Li, F., Busam, B., Ilic, S.: OSOP: a multi-stage one shot object pose estimation framework. In: Proceedings of the IEEE/CVF Conference on Computer Vision and Pattern Recognition (CVPR), pp. 6835–6844 (2022)
31. Shugurov, I., Pavlov, I., Zakharov, S., Ilic, S.: Multi-view object pose refinement with differentiable renderer. IEEE Robot. Autom. Lett. (2021)
32. Shugurov, I., Zakharov, S., Ilic, S.: DPODv2: dense correspondence-based 6 DoF pose estimation. IEEE Trans. Pattern Anal. Mach. Intell. (2021)
33. Song, C., Song, J., Huang, Q.: HybridPose: 6D object pose estimation under hybrid representations. In: Proceedings of the IEEE/CVF Conference on Computer Vision and Pattern Recognition (2020)
34. Wang, C., et al.: DenseFusion: 6D object pose estimation by iterative dense fusion (2019)

35. Wang, G., Manhardt, F., Shao, J., Ji, X., Navab, N., Tombari, F.: Self6D: self-supervised monocular 6D object pose estimation. In: The European Conference on Computer Vision (ECCV) (2020)
36. Wang, G., Manhardt, F., Tombari, F., Ji, X.: GDR-Net: geometry-guided direct regression network for monocular 6d object pose estimation. In: IEEE/CVF Conference on Computer Vision and Pattern Recognition (CVPR) (2021)
37. Wang, P., et al.: DemoGrasp: few-shot learning for robotic grasping with human demonstration. In: 2021 IEEE/RSJ International Conference on Intelligent Robots and Systems (IROS), pp. 5733–5740. IEEE (2021)
38. Xiang, Y., Schmidt, T., Narayanan, V., Fox, D.: PoseCNN: a convolutional neural network for 6D object pose estimation in cluttered scenes. In: Robotics: Science and Systems (RSS) (2018)
39. Zakharov, S., Kehl, W., Bhargava, A., Gaidon, A.: Autolabeling 3D objects with differentiable rendering of SDF shape priors. In: IEEE Computer Vision and Pattern Recognition (CVPR) (2020)
40. Zakharov, S., Shugurov, I., Ilic, S.: DPOD: 6D pose object detector and refiner. In: International Conference on Computer Vision (ICCV) (2019)
41. Zhang, S., Zhao, W., Guan, Z., Peng, X., Peng, J.: Keypoint-graph-driven learning framework for object pose estimation. In: 2021 IEEE/CVF Conference on Computer Vision and Pattern Recognition (CVPR) (2021)

Graph R-CNN: Towards Accurate 3D Object Detection with Semantic-Decorated Local Graph

Honghui Yang[1], Zili Liu[1,3], Xiaopei Wu[1], Wenxiao Wang[2(✉)], Wei Qian[3], Xiaofei He[1,3], and Deng Cai[1]

[1] State Key Lab of CAD&CG, Zhejiang University, Hangzhou, China
{yanghonghui,wuxiaopei,dcai}@zju.edu.cn
[2] School of Software Technology, Zhejiang University, Hangzhou, China
wenxiaowang@zju.edu.cn
[3] Fabu Inc., Hangzhou, China
{qianwei,hexiaofei}@fabu.ai

Abstract. Two-stage detectors have gained much popularity in 3D object detection. Most two-stage 3D detectors utilize grid points, voxel grids, or sampled keypoints for RoI feature extraction in the second stage. Such methods, however, are inefficient in handling unevenly distributed and sparse outdoor points. This paper solves this problem in three aspects. 1) Dynamic Point Aggregation. We propose the patch search to quickly search points in a local region for each 3D proposal. The dynamic farthest voxel sampling is then applied to evenly sample the points. Especially, the voxel size varies along the distance to accommodate the uneven distribution of points. 2) RoI-graph Pooling. We build local graphs on the sampled points to better model contextual information and mine point relations through iterative message passing. 3) Visual Features Augmentation. We introduce a simple yet effective fusion strategy to compensate for sparse LiDAR points with limited semantic cues. Based on these modules, we construct our Graph R-CNN as the second stage, which can be applied to existing one-stage detectors to consistently improve the detection performance. Extensive experiments show that Graph R-CNN outperforms the state-of-the-art 3D detection models by a large margin on both the KITTI and Waymo Open Dataset. And we rank first place on the KITTI BEV car detection leaderboard.

Keywords: 3D object detection · Point clouds · Multiple sensors

1 Introduction

In autonomous driving, 3D object detection is an essential task that has received substantial attention from industry [1,12,38] and academia [24,39,47]. Among the

---

Supplementary Information The online version contains supplementary material available at https://doi.org/10.1007/978-3-031-20074-8_38.

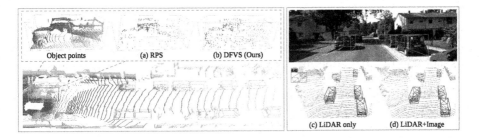

Fig. 1. Illustration of different sampling strategies: (a) random point sampling (RPS) in existing works and the proposed (b) dynamic farthest voxel sampling (DFVS). And the comparison of results using (c) LiDAR and (d) LiDAR and Image. We show the ground truth in pink bounding boxes and our detected objects in green bounding boxes. (Color figure online)

existing 3D detection methods, two-stage detectors [25,42] outperform most single-stage detectors [12,38] in accuracy due to the proposal refinement stage. Previous two-stage methods [7,14,17,24–26,40] have explored different RoI pooling methods to capture better proposal features for refinement. PointRCNN [25] and its subsequent works [14] sample keypoints from original point clouds near the 3D proposal and extract the features of the sampled points. Part-A^2 Net [26] divides each 3D proposal into regular voxel grids and applies sparse convolutions to capture the features of voxel grids. PV-RCNN [24] and its variants [7,17,35] sample grid points within each 3D proposal and use the set abstraction [22] to aggregate the features of grid points. The methods that utilize the sampled keypoints show more flexibility than others since they directly process raw points and avoid the predefined voxel grids [16,40] or grid points [6,31] as intermediaries for RoI feature extraction.

Nevertheless, existing methods relied on sampled points still have some problems: **1)** They ignore that points are unevenly distributed in different parts of an object, thus yield sub-optimal sampling strategy. As Fig. 1(a) shows, points for some parts are too sparse to preserve the structure information, which will hinder the prediction of the object's size. **2)** The point interrelation is not adequately utilized to model the contextual information of sparse points for object detection. **3)** Sparse LiDAR points in a single proposal provide limited semantic cues, which easily leads to a series of points that resemble a part of an object yielding high classification scores. Figure 1(c) shows that a wall corner is wrongly detected as a car. To surmount the above challenges, we introduce three modules:

1) Dynamic Point Aggregation (DPA). To efficiently and effectively group and sample context and object points for 3D proposals, we propose patch search (PS) and dynamic farthest voxel sampling (DFVS). We will start with PS to speed up grouping then move on to DFVS to solve the uneven distribution problem during sampling.

Previous methods [5,25,26] group points by searching all points to determine whether they belong to a proposal, which is time-consuming since the theoretical time complexity is $O(NM)$, where N and M are the number of points and proposals, respectively. Especially for the detection on Waymo Open Dataset [28], there are often about 180K points and 500 proposals per frame that need to be processed. In contrast, PS only searches the points falling in patches occupied by the proposal to group corresponding context and object points. Then, DFVS sample keypoints from the grouped points to well retain the objects' structure, as shown in Fig. 1(b). Specifically, instead of sampling points directly [14,23,25], DFVS splits each proposal into evenly distributed voxels and iteratively samples the most distant non-empty voxels (i.e., voxels involving at least one point). Further, to ensure the efficiency and accuracy of sampling, we resort to dynamic voxel size. That is, for nearby objects with many points, we use a large voxel size to reduce the sampling complexity. While for distant objects with sparse points, we use a relatively small voxel size to preserve the geometric details.

2) RoI-graph Pooling (RGP). To alleviate the missing detection, we utilize the graph neural network (GNN) to build connections among points to better model contextual information through iterative message passing. Compared with previous point-based methods [21,22], the GNN allows more complex features to be determined along the edges and avoids grouping and sampling the points repeatedly. Specifically, RGP constructs local graphs in each 3D proposal, which treats the sampled points as graph nodes. To compensate for the information loss caused by downsampling, we use PointNet [21] to encode neighbor points of each node into the initial features. Then, RGP iteratively aggregates messages from its neighbors on a k-NN graph to mine the relations among nodes. Finally, we propose multi-level attentive fusion (MLAF) to capture abundant spatial features from multi-level nodes with different receptive fields and fully exploit graph nodes to extract robust RoI features.

3) Visual Features Augmentation (VFA). Though LiDAR points provide accurate depth information, the lack of sufficient semantic features makes it difficult to distinguish objects with similar geometric structures. Thus, a simple yet effective fusion method is used to fuse geometric features from LiDAR and semantic features from images for suppressing the false positives, as shown in Fig. 1(d). We decorate local graphs with image features by bilinear interpolation since graph nodes serve as a natural bridge between the LiDAR and image. We train the two streams in an end-to-end manner and show the complex multi-modality cut-and-paste augmentation [30,45] is not necessary for our framework.

Based on the three modules, we present our Graph R-CNN that can replace the second stage of other two-stage detectors or supplement any one-stage detector for further improvement. Extensive experiments have been conducted on several detection benchmarks to verify the effectiveness of our approach. We consistently improve existing 3D detectors by a large margin and achieve new state-of-the-art results on both Waymo Open Dataset (WOD) [28] and KITTI [8].

Our contributions can be summarized as follows:

- We fully consider the uneven distribution of point clouds and propose dynamic point aggregation (DPA).
- We introduce RoI-graph Pooling (RGP) to capture the robust RoI features by iterative graph-based message passing.
- We demonstrate a simple yet effective fusion strategy (VFA) to fuse image features with point features during the refinement stage.

- We present an accurate and efficient 3D object detector (Graph R-CNN) that can be applied to existing 3D detectors. Extensive experiments are conducted to verify the effectiveness of our methods.

2   Related Works

3D Object Detection Using Point Cloud. Current 3D detectors can be mainly divided into two streams: one-stage and two-stage methods. One-stage detectors jointly predict an output class and location of objects at the projected volumetric grids or downsampled points. SECOND [38] rasterizes point cloud into 3D voxels and accelerates VoxelNet [50] by exploiting sparse 3D convolution. Point-Pillars [12] partitions points into pillars rather than voxels. 3DSSD [39] proposes a fusion farthest point sampling strategy by utilizing both feature and geometry distance for better classification performance.

Two-stage detectors first use a region proposal network (RPN) to generate coarse object proposals and then use a dedicated per-region head to classify and refine them. PointRCNN [25] generates RoIs based on foreground points from the scene and conducts canonical 3D box refinement after point cloud region pooling. PV-RCNN [24] incorporates the advantage from 3D voxel Convolutional Neural Network and Point-based set abstraction to learn discriminative point cloud features. Voxel R-CNN [7] proposes a voxel RoI pooling to extract RoI features directly from voxel features to refine proposals in the second stage. CenterPoint [42] detects centers of objects using a keypoint detector and refines these estimates using additional point features on the object.

3D Object Detection Using Multi-modality Fusion. Recently, much progress has been made to exploit the advantages of the camera and LiDAR sensors. MV3D [4] generates 3D proposals from the bird's eye view and fuses multi-view features via region-based representation. EPNet [11] proposes LI-Fusion module to fuse the deep features of point clouds and camera images in a point-wise paradigm. However, insufficient multi-modality augmentation makes these methods perform only marginally better or sometimes worse than approaches that only use point cloud. Recent works [30,45] overcome the constraint by extending the cut-and-paste augmentation [38] to multi-modality methods. But a complex process is needed to avoid collisions between objects in both point cloud and 2D imagery domain. PointPainting [29] augments LiDAR points with segmentation scores, which are suboptimal to cover color and textures in images.

3D Object Detection Using Graph Neural Networks. Graph Neural Networks [9] are introduced to model intrinsic relationships of graph-structured data. Since they are suitable for processing 3D point clouds, some works have adopted GNNs for 3D object detection. 3DVID [41] explores spatial relations among different grid regions by treating the non-empty pillar grids as graph nodes to enhance pillar features. Object DGCNN [33] uses DGCNN [34] to construct a graph between the queries for incorporating neighborhood information in object detection estimates. DOPS [19] creates a graph where the points are connected to those with similar center predictions for consolidating the per-point object predictions. Point-GNN [27] encodes point clouds in a fixed radius near-neighbors graph and predicts the category and shape of the object that each node in the graph belongs to. Our work differs from previous works by constructing local graphs during the refinement stage, which greatly saves computational and memory overhead since the k-nearest neighbor algorithm can be parallelly applied in each 3D proposal, and numerous background points can be avoided to build graphs.

3   Methods

In this section, we present the design of Graph R-CNN, as shown in Fig. 2. We first introduce dynamic point aggregation in Sect. 3.1. Next, we will demonstrate RoI-graph pooling in Sect. 3.2. Then, we will illustrate how to incorporate semantic features from the image into our framework in Sect. 3.3. Finally, we will show the definition of the loss function in Sect. 3.4.

3.1   Dynamic Point Aggregation

In this section, we present a differentiable dynamic point aggregation (DPA) to efficiently and effectively group and sample points and their features for each proposal. We first enlarge each proposal's size by σ to wrap enough object and context points. Then, DPA uses patch search (PS) to quickly group the points in each enlarged proposal and dynamic farthest voxel sampling (DFVS) to evenly sample the grouped points.

Patch Search. Unlike previous works [14,23,25] that need to search all points to determine whether they belong to an enlarged proposal, we divide the entire scene into patches and only search the points falling in patches occupied by the proposal, as shown in Fig. 3. PS consists of three major steps: 1) We turn the rotated box into an axis-aligned box to make it easier to find the occupied patches. 2) We build point2patch and patch2box index arrays, which store the point and patch indices as keys, and the corresponding patch and box indices as values, respectively. 3) We finally group the points for each proposal according to the point2patch and patch2box index arrays, as shown in Fig. 3(a). We note that all the steps can be conducted in parallel on GPUs. In this way, we reduce the theoretical time complexity from $O(NM)$ to $O(QK)$, where Q is the number of points that fall in all occupied patches, and K is the predefined maximum number of boxes per patch since the same patch may be occupied by multiple boxes. Notably, Q and K are much smaller than N and M, respectively.

Dynamic Farthest Voxel Sampling. Since the number of raw points in a box is usually far more than that of the sampled points (e.g., 70112 vs. 256, as Fig. 4(b) shows), it's nontrivial to ensure every part of an object is sampled. Therefore, we propose DFVS to balance sampling efficiency and accuracy. To be specific, DFVS partitions proposals into evenly distributed voxels and then iteratively sample the most distant non-empty voxels. Considering the number of points varies with the distance of the box, as Fig. 4(a) shows, the voxel size should be

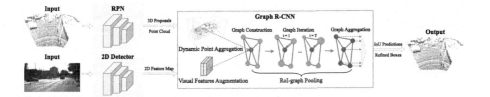

Fig. 2. The overall architecture. We take 3D proposals and points from the region proposal network (RPN) and 2D feature map from the 2D detector as inputs. We propose dynamic point aggregation to sample context and object points and visual features augmentation to decorate the points with 2D features. RoI-graph pooling serves sampled points as graph nodes to build local graphs for each 3D proposal. We iterate the graph for T times to mine the geometric features among the nodes. Finally, each node is fully utilized through graph aggregation to produce robust RoI features.

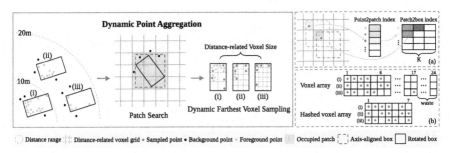

Fig. 3. Illustration of dynamic point aggregation, which includes (a) patch search and (b) dynamic farthest voxel sampling. In (a), we use different colors to represent different keys and values. In (b), we flatten the voxel grids of each proposal for better display.

changed dynamically according to the distance to ensure the sampling efficiency of nearby objects and accuracy of distant objects, as shown in Fig. 3. Formally, the voxel size V_i of the box b_i can be calculated by:

$$V_i = \lambda \cdot e^{-\frac{\sqrt{x_i^2 + y_i^2 + z_i^2}}{\delta}} \tag{1}$$

where (x_i, y_i, z_i) is the i-th box's center, and λ and δ determine the relationship between the voxel size and the distance from the box to the LiDAR sensor.

Assume we have grouped the points in the box b_i by patch search and obtained $\mathcal{P}_i = \{p_j^i = [x_j^i, y_j^i, z_j^i, r_j^i] \in \mathbb{R}^4 : j = 1, \cdots, N\}$, where (x_j^i, y_j^i, z_j^i) and r_j^i indicate j-th point's coordinate in the i-th box's canonical coordinate system and the reflectance intensity. We assign each point to evenly divided voxel grids, and the grid index of the point p_j^i is represented as $\{g_j^i = (\lfloor \frac{x_j^i}{V_i} \rfloor, \lfloor \frac{y_j^i}{V_i} \rfloor, \lfloor \frac{z_j^i}{V_i} \rfloor)\}$. Each non-empty voxel can be represented by a randomly selected point in the voxel. Next, farthest point sampling (FPS) [22] is applied to iteratively sample the most distant non-empty voxels.

A potential problem with DVFS lies in that, for the distant box, a small voxel size will divide the box into numerous voxels, of which the non-empty voxels only

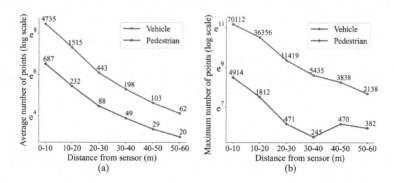

Fig. 4. The statistical plot of the (a) average and (b) maximum number of points in each ground truth on Waymo Open Dataset for vehicle and pedestrian.

occupy a small part. And to utilize the parallel computation of GPUs, voxel grids of other boxes need to be padded to the largest grid number, which will increase the memory overhead, as shown in Fig. 3(b). Since we only care about non-empty voxels, we use a hash table [18] to record the hashed grid indices of non-empty voxels and quadratic probing to resolve the collisions in the hash table.

3.2 RoI-Graph Pooling

In this section, we describe the process of RoI-graph pooling, as shown in Fig. 2, which treats sampled points as nodes to build local graphs in 3D proposals. It consists of graph construction, iteration, and aggregation.

Graph Construction. Given sampled points $\overline{\mathcal{P}} = \{p_j = [x_j, y_j, z_j, r_j] \in \mathbb{R}^4 : j = 1, \cdots, T\}$ for each proposal b (we drop the i subscript for ease of notation), we construct a local graph $\mathcal{G} = (\mathcal{V}, \mathcal{E})$, where node $v_j \in \mathcal{V}$ represents a sampled point $p_j \in \overline{\mathcal{P}}$, and edge $e_j^k \in \mathcal{E}$ indicates the connection between node v_j and v_k. To reduce the computational overhead, we define $\mathcal{G}$ as a k-nearest neighbor (k-NN) graph, which is built from the geometric distance among different nodes. Despite efficient, building graphs on down-sampled points inevitably loss fine-grained features. Thus, we use PointNet [21] to encode original neighbor points within a radiu r for each node. We note that neighbor query only induces a marginal computational overhead because it is only conducted for each proposal.

The same graph nodes may be wrapped by different proposals, which will result in the same pooling features and thus introduce ambiguity in the refinement stage [14,26]. Inspired by [23], we add the 3D proposal's local corners (i.e., the corners are transformed to the proposal's canonical coordinate system) for each node to make them have the ability to discriminate differences. In our experiments, we found that two diagonal corners are sufficient. Formally, the initial state s_j^0 of each node v_j at iteration step $t = 0$ can be represented by:

$$s_j^0 = [x_j, y_j, z_j, r_j, f_j, u_j, w_j],\qquad(2)$$

where $[\cdot, \cdot]$ is concatenation function, f_j is the features from PointNet, and u_j and w_j are two diagonal corners of the 3D proposal.

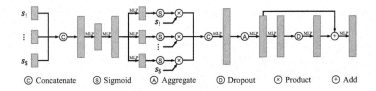

Fig. 5. Illustration of multi-level attentive fusion.

Graph Iteration. To mine the rich geometric relations among nodes, we iteratively pass the message on $\mathcal{G}$ and update the node's state at each iteration step. Concretely, at step t, a node v_j aggregates information from all the neighbor nodes $v_k \in \mathcal{N}_{v_j}$ in the k-NN graph. Following [2,33,41], we use EdgeConv [34] to update the state s_j^{t+1}:

$$s_j^{t+1} = \max_{v_k \in \mathcal{N}_{v_j}} \phi_\theta([s_k^t - s_j^t, s_j^t]),   (3)$$

where ϕ_θ is parameterized by a Multilayer Perceptron (MLP).

Graph Aggregation. To capture robust RoI features, we propose multi-level attentive fusion (MLAF) to fuse the nodes' features, as shown in Fig. 5. Specifically, we concatenate the nodes' features $[s_j^1, \cdots, s_j^T]$ from different iterations and feed them into several MLPs to learn the channel-wise weights. Then, we reweight $[s_j^1, \cdots, s_j^T]$ to enhance the features for final detection. After that, it's nontrivial to fully utilize every graph node for the proposal refinement. We explore several aggregation operations, e.g., the channel-wise Transformer [23], Set Transformer [13], attention sum, average pooling, and max pooling. Our final model uses max pooling as it provides the best empirical performance. Then, Dropout is used in later MLPs to reduce overfitting, and a shortcut connection is added to fuse more features without adding much cost.

3.3 Visual Features Augmentation

Cut-and-paste augmentation (CPA) [38] is widely used for 3D object detection to increase the training samples, which could speed up training convergence and improve the detection performance. Since our Graph R-CNN extracts RoI features directly from raw point clouds, we doubt whether CPA is required for our model. We carefully study its influence in Sect. 4.4 and find that our model does not depend on it. Thus, CPA is only used to pretrain the RPN and disabled when training the whole framework.

For the camera image, we extract high-level semantic features using a pretrained 2D detector. Then, we apply two 1×1 convolutional kernels to reduce the dimensionality of the output feature, as Fig. 2 shows. The benefit brought by it is twofold. Firstly, it can learn to select features that contribute greatly to the performance of the refinement. Secondly, it can ease the optimization to fuse low-dimensionality point features with high-dimensionality image features. Then, we project the graph node to the location in the camera image and collect the feature vector at that pixel in the camera image through bilinear interpolation. Lastly, the features will be appended to s_j^0 for each node v_j.

3.4 Loss Functions

Classification Loss. For class-agnostic confidence score prediction, we follow [24, 42] to use a score target I_i guided by the box's 3D IoU with the corresponding ground-truth bounding box:

$$I_i = \min\left(1, \max\left(0, 2 \times \text{IoU}_i - 0.5\right)\right), \tag{4}$$

where IoU_i is the IoU between the i-th proposal box and the ground truth. The training is supervised with a binary cross entropy loss:

$$\mathcal{L}_{cls} = \frac{1}{B} \sum_{i=1}^{B} -I_i \log\left(\hat{I}_i\right) - (1 - I_i) \log\left(1 - \hat{I}_i\right), \tag{5}$$

where $\hat{I}_i$ is the predicted confidence score, and B is the number of sampled region proposals at the training stage.

Regression Loss. For box prediction, we transform the 3D proposal $b_i = (x_i, y_i, z_i, l_i, w_i, h_i, \theta_i)$ and the corresponding 3D ground-truth bounding box $b_i^{gt} = (x_i^{gt}, y_i^{gt}, z_i^{gt}, l_i^{gt}, w_i^{gt}, h_i^{gt}, \theta_i^{gt})$ from the global reference frame to the canonical coordinate system of 3D proposal:

$$
\begin{aligned}
\tilde{b}_i &= (0, 0, 0, l_i, w_i, h_i, 0), \\
\tilde{b}_i^{gt} &= \left(x_i^{gt} - x_i, y_i^{gt} - y_i, z_i^{gt} - z_i, l_i^{gt}, w_i^{gt}, h_i^{gt}, \Delta\theta_i\right),
\end{aligned}
\tag{6}
$$

where $\Delta\theta_i = \theta_i^{gt} - \theta_i$. Then, the regression targets for center t_i^c, size t_i^s, and orientation t_i^o can be defined as:

$$
\begin{aligned}
t_i^c &= \left(x_i^{gt} - x_i, y_i^{gt} - y_i, z_i^{gt} - z_i\right), \\
t_i^s &= \left(l_i^{gt} - l_i, w_i^{gt} - w_i, h_i^{gt} - h_i\right), \\
t_i^o &= \Delta\theta_i - \lfloor \frac{\Delta\theta_i}{\pi} + 0.5 \rfloor \times \pi.
\end{aligned}
\tag{7}
$$

Having all the targets $t_i = (t_i^c, t_i^s, t_i^o)$, our regression loss is defined as:

$$\mathcal{L}_{reg} = \frac{1}{B_+} \sum_{i=1}^{B_+} \text{L1}\left(o_i - t_i\right), \tag{8}$$

where o_i is the output of the model's regression branch, and B_+ is the number of positive samples.

Total Loss. Finally, the overall loss is formulated as:

$$\mathcal{L} = \mathcal{L}_{cls} + \alpha\mathcal{L}_{reg}, \qquad (9)$$

where α is a hyperparameter to balance the loss, which is 1 by default.

4 Experiments

4.1 Datasets

Waymo Open Dataset is a large-scale autonomous driving dataset consisting of 798 scenes for training and 202 scenes for validation. The evaluation protocol consists of average precision (AP) and average precision weighted by heading (APH). It includes two difficulty levels: LEVEL_1 denotes objects containing more than 5 points, and LEVEL_2 denotes objects containing at least 1 point.

KITTI contains 7481 training samples and 7518 testing samples in autonomous driving scenes. We follow [4,7,24] to divide the training data into a *train* set with 3712 samples and a *val* set with 3769 samples. The performance on the *val* set and the test leaderboard are reported.

4.2 Implementation Settings

Implementation Details. The codebase of CenterPoint is used for WOD. Then, we replace the second stage of CenterPoint-Voxel with our method (i.e., Graph-Ce) and train the network separately. For the dynamic point aggregation, we sample 256 points for each proposal and set $\sigma = 0.4$. In dynamic farthest voxel sampling, we set hash size as 4099 and λ and δ as 0.18 and 50, respectively. In patch search, the K and patch size are set to 32 and 1.0, respectively. For the RoI-graph pooling, we set $r = 0.4$ and the embedding channels to $[16, 16]$ in PointNet. We update the graph with $T = 3$, and the output dimensions of the three iterations are $[32, 32, 64]$. The number k of nearest neighbors is set as 8. In MLAF, the embedding dimension is 256, and the dropout ratio is 0.1.

For KITTI, the codebase of OpenPCDet is used. We propose Graph-Pi, Graph-Vo, and Graph-Po that use the **pi**llar-based PointPillars, the **vo**xel-based SECOND, and the **po**int-based 3DSSD as their region proposal networks, respectively. We incorporate the image branch in Graph-Vo (i.e., Graph-VoI) to compare with previous multi-modality methods. For 2D detector, we use the CenterNet [48] with DLA-34 [44] backbone, which takes images with a resolution of 1280×384 as input. The dimension of the output features will be reduced to 32 by the feature reduction layer.

Training Details. For WOD, we use the same training schedules and assignment strategies as CenterPoint-Voxel. The second stage is trained for 6 epochs on 4 GTX 1080Ti GPUs with 8 batch size per GPU.

Table 1. Vehicle detection results on WOD validation sequences. CenterPoint-Voxel[†] is reproduced by us based on the officially released code. CenterPoint-Voxel[‡] is the first stage of CenterPoint-Voxel[†].

Difficulty	Methods	3D AP (IoU=0.7)				3D APH (IoU=0.7)				BEV AP (IoU=0.7)				BEV APH (IoU=0.7)			
		Overall	0–30 m	30–50 m	50 m-Inf	Overall	0–30 m	30–50 m	50 m-Inf	Overall	0–30 m	30–50 m	50 m-Inf	Overall	0–30 m	30–50 m	50 m-Inf
LEVEL 1	MVF [49]	62.93	86.30	60.02	36.02	-	-	-	-	80.40	93.59	79.21	63.09	-	-	-	-
	Pillar-od [32]	69.80	88.53	66.50	42.93	-	-	-	-	87.11	95.78	84.74	72.12	-	-	-	-
	PV-RCNN [24]	70.30	91.92	69.21	42.17	69.69	91.34	68.53	41.31	82.96	97.35	82.99	64.97	82.06	96.71	82.01	63.15
	VoTr-TSD [18]	74.95	92.28	73.36	51.09	74.25	91.73	72.56	50.01	-	-	-	-	-	-	-	-
	Voxel R-CNN [7]	75.59	92.49	74.09	53.15	-	-	-	-	88.19	**97.62**	87.34	77.70	-	-	-	-
	LiDAR R-CNN [14]	76.00	92.10	74.60	54.50	75.50	91.60	74.10	53.40	90.10	97.00	89.50	78.90	89.30	96.50	88.60	77.40
	Pyramid-PV [17]	76.30	92.67	74.91	54.54	75.68	92.20	74.21	53.45	-	-	-	-	-	-	-	-
	CenterPoint-Voxel[†] [42]	76.86	92.27	75.31	54.10	76.33	91.81	74.74	53.35	91.61	97.19	91.05	82.06	90.85	96.69	90.23	80.59
	CenterPoint-Voxel[‡] [42]	74.78	91.51	73.25	50.67	74.24	91.04	72.67	49.93	90.94	97.02	90.26	80.78	90.12	96.51	89.39	79.20
	Graph-Ce (Ours)	**80.77**	**93.59**	**79.68**	**60.41**	**80.28**	**93.20**	**79.16**	**59.62**	**92.69**	97.56	**92.15**	**84.31**	**92.01**	**97.15**	**91.43**	**82.94**
LEVEL 2	PV-RCNN [24]	65.36	91.58	65.13	36.46	64.79	91.00	64.49	35.70	77.45	94.64	80.39	55.39	76.60	94.03	79.40	53.82
	VoTr-TSD [18]	65.91	-	-	-	65.29	-	-	-	-	-	-	-	-	-	-	-
	Voxel R-CNN [7]	66.59	91.74	67.89	40.80	-	-	-	-	81.07	**96.99**	81.37	63.26	-	-	-	-
	Pyramid-PV [17]	67.23	-	-	-	66.68	-	-	-	-	-	-	-	-	-	-	-
	LiDAR R-CNN [14]	68.30	91.30	68.50	42.40	67.90	90.90	68.00	41.80	81.70	94.30	82.30	65.80	81.00	93.90	81.50	64.50
	CenterPoint-Voxel[†] [42]	69.09	91.41	69.43	42.40	68.59	90.96	68.89	41.78	85.43	96.35	86.44	70.06	84.66	95.86	85.63	68.66
	CenterPoint-Voxel[‡] [42]	66.66	90.63	66.90	39.50	66.17	90.16	66.36	38.90	84.87	96.21	85.69	69.08	84.04	95.69	84.81	67.58
	Graph-Ce (Ours)	**72.55**	**92.75**	**73.74**	**47.84**	**72.10**	**92.36**	**73.25**	**47.19**	**86.56**	96.79	**87.59**	**72.06**	**85.86**	**96.38**	**86.86**	**70.72**

Table 2. Vehicle, pedestrian, and cyclist results on WOD validation sequences.

Difficulty	Methods	Vehicle				Pedestrian				Cyclist			
		3D AP	3D APH	BEV AP	BEV APH	3D AP	3D APH	BEV AP	BEV APH	3D AP	3D APH	BEV AP	BEV APH
LEVEL 1	CenterPoint-Voxel[‡] [42]	74.78	74.24	90.94	90.12	75.95	69.75	82.01	75.05	72.27	71.12	75.95	74.70
	Graph-Ce (Ours)	80.77	80.28	92.69	92.01	82.35	76.64	86.75	80.51	75.28	74.21	77.42	76.30
LEVEL 2	CenterPoint-Voxel[‡] [42]	66.66	66.17	84.87	84.04	68.42	62.67	75.06	68.46	69.69	68.59	73.24	72.03
	Graph-Ce (Ours)	72.55	72.10	86.56	85.86	74.44	69.02	79.50	73.45	72.52	71.49	74.64	73.56

For KITTI, we use the same training configuration as PV-RCNN and train the whole model end-to-end for 80 epochs on 4 GTX 1080Ti GPUs with 4 batch size per GPU, and the pretrained RPN and 2D detector are frozen during training. For 2D detector, we pretrain CenterNet on WOD for 24 epochs and finetune it on KITTI for 12 epochs. We use Adam optimizer with one-cycle policy and set batch size to 2 and learning rate to 0.00025.

4.3 Comparison with State-of-the-Art Methods

Waymo Open Dataset. We compare Graph-Ce for the vehicle class at different distances on the full WOD validation with previous methods. Table 1 shows that Graph-Ce achieves the state-of-the-art results in both level 1 and level 2 among all the published papers with a single frame LiDAR input. In Table 2, we present our results for the vehicle, pedestrian, and cyclist classes. Compared with our baseline, i.e., CenterPoint-Voxel[‡], our method improves the 3D APH in level 2 for the vehicle, pedestrian, and cyclist by 5.93%, 6.35%, and 2.90%, respectively.

KITTI. We compare Graph-Pi, Graph-Vo, Graph-Po, and Graph-VoI with previous methods listed in Table 3. Graph-Pi achieves the fastest inference speed among all two-stage methods. Compared with methods using only LiDAR as input, Graph-Po ranks the 1st place in 3D AP and BEV AP with competitive inference speed. Graph-VoI outperforms all previous multi-modality methods by a large margin (+2.08% for 3D easy AP and +2.6% for 3D moderate AP).

Table 3. Performance comparison on the KITTI testing sever for 3D car detection. L and I represent the LiDAR point cloud and the camera image, respectively.

Methods	Modality	3D AP			BEV AP			FPS (Hz)
		Easy	Moderate	Hard	Easy	Moderate	Hard	
One-stage:								
Point-GNN [27]	L	88.33	79.47	72.29	93.11	89.17	83.90	1.7
3DSSD [39]	L	88.36	79.57	74.55	92.66	89.02	85.86	26.3
SA-SSD [10]	L	88.75	79.79	74.16	95.03	91.03	85.96	25.0
CIA-SSD [46]	L	89.59	80.28	72.87	93.74	89.84	82.39	**32.5**
SASA [3]	L	88.76	82.16	77.16	92.87	89.51	86.35	27.8
Two-stage:								
PV-RCNN [24]	L	90.25	81.43	76.82	94.98	90.65	86.14	12.5
Voxel R-CNN [7]	L	90.90	81.62	77.06	94.85	88.83	86.13	25.2
CT3D [23]	L	87.83	81.77	77.16	92.36	88.83	84.07	14.3
Pyramid-PV [17]	L	88.39	82.08	77.49	92.19	88.84	86.21	7.9
VoTr-TSD [18]	L	89.90	82.09	**79.14**	94.03	90.34	86.14	7.2
SPG [37]	L	90.50	82.13	78.90	94.33	88.70	85.98	6.4
PointPainting [29]	L+I	82.11	71.70	67.08	92.45	88.11	83.36	2.5
PI-RCNN [36]	L+I	84.37	74.82	70.03	91.44	85.81	81.00	10.0
MMF [15]	L+I	88.40	77.43	70.22	93.67	88.21	81.99	12.5
EPNet [11]	L+I	89.81	79.28	74.59	94.22	88.47	83.69	10.0
3D-CVF [43]	L+I	89.20	80.05	73.11	93.52	89.56	82.45	13.3
CLOCs_PVCas [20]	L+I	88.94	80.67	77.15	93.05	89.80	86.57	10.0
Graph-Pi (Ours)	L	90.94	82.42	77.00	95.06	91.52	86.42	**28.5**
Graph-Vo (Ours)	L	91.29	82.77	77.20	95.27	91.72	86.51	25.6
Graph-Po (Ours)	L	91.79	83.18	77.98	**95.79**	**92.12**	**87.11**	16.1
Graph-VoI (Ours)	L+I	**91.89**	**83.27**	77.78	95.69	90.10	86.85	13.3

Table 4. Performance of our model on the KITTI *val* set with AP calculated by 40 recall positions for car class. [†] indicates our reproduced results.

Methods	3D AP			BEV AP		
	Easy	Moderate	Hard	Easy	Moderate	Hard
Pointpillars[†] (**Pillar-based**) [12]	89.67	80.38	78.80	93.56	89.53	88.57
Graph-Pi (Ours)	93.16	85.87	83.29	96.18	91.84	89.46
SECOND[†] (**Voxel-based**) [38]	92.15	82.43	79.26	95.78	91.26	88.57
Graph-Vo (Ours)	93.33	86.12	83.29	96.35	92.16	91.54
Graph-VoI (Ours)	**95.67**	**86.87**	**84.09**	96.28	**92.68**	**92.11**
3DSSD[†] (**Point-based**) [39]	91.68	82.72	79.74	96.04	91.45	88.89
Graph-Po (Ours)	93.27	86.50	83.87	**96.64**	92.45	89.92

Table 4 shows our method could consistently improve PointPillars, SECOND, and 3DSSD by a large margin, demonstrating the efficacy of the method.

4.4 Ablation Study

Analysis of the Dynamic Point Aggregation. The third and fourth rows in Table 5 show that the dynamic point aggregation (DPA) contributes an improvement of 1.06% and 0.87% APH at level 2 for vehicle and pedestrian, respectively. Especially, Table 6 shows that DPA improves the baseline by 1.49% APH at 0–30m since the nearby objects suffer more from the uneven distribution problem.

Table 5. Ablation study of every module: RoI-graph pooling (RGP), multi-level attentive fusion (MLAF), dynamic point aggregation (DPA), PointNet (PN), and diagonal corners (DC). We show the 3D APH at level 2 on the WOD validation set.

w/ RGP	w/ MLAF	w/ DPA	w/ PN	w/ DC	Vehicle	Pedestrian
					66.17	62.67
✓					69.48	66.79
✓	✓				69.77	67.00
✓	✓	✓			70.83	67.87
✓	✓	✓	✓		71.04	67.96
✓	✓	✓	✓	✓	**72.10**	**69.02**

Table 6. Ablation study of the performance of DPA at different distances. We show the level 2 APH on the WOD validation set for vehicle class.

w/ DPA	Overall	0–30 m	30–50 m	50 m-Inf
	69.77	90.25	71.21	**45.40**
✓	**70.83**	**91.74**	**71.36**	**45.40**

Table 7. Ablation study of FPS and DFVS based on 3DSSD. We report the mAP on KITTI *val* set for car class and the runtime of sampling.

Methods	3D mAP	BEV mAP	Runtime (ms)
FPS	81.73	**88.57**	29.6
DFVS	**81.75**	88.55	**20.3**

Table 8. Ablation study of different sampling and searching strategies. [†] is tested by us based on the officially released code.

w/ PR[†]	w/ PS	w/ VS	w/ DVS	w/ DFVS	w/ FPS	APH	Runtime (ms)
✓						69.77	69.7
	✓					69.77	**1.9**
	✓	✓				70.39	2.2
	✓		✓			70.67	2.2
	✓			✓		**70.83**	2.8
	✓				✓	**70.83**	7.3

The first and second rows in Table 8 show that the patch search (PS) is 35× faster than the baseline, i.e., point cloud region pooling (PR) [25].

We also explore several sampling strategies in Table 8 to solve the uneven distribution problem, i.e., voxel sampling (VS), dynamic voxel sampling (DVS), dynamic farthest voxel sampling (DFVS), and farthest point sampling (FPS). We note that VS is a special case of DVS when δ is large, and FPS is a special case of DFVS when λ is small. Table 8 shows that DFVS achieves the best trade-off between accuracy and efficiency. Further, we explore the use of DFVS on point-based 3D object detectors as an alternative to FPS. Table 7 shows that DFVS achieves similar results with FPS but costs less runtime.

Table 9. Ablation study of the number of iterations to update the graph.

# iterations	Overall	0–30 m	30–50 m	50 m-Inf
T = 1	68.76	89.84	70.19	44.03
T = 2	69.07	89.95	70.60	44.49
T = 3	**69.48**	**89.97**	**71.02**	**45.18**

Table 10. Ablation study of different methods to aggregate nodes' features.

Methods	CT	ST	AS	AP	MP
Vehicle	71.67	71.82	71.86	71.85	**72.10**
Pedestrian	68.82	68.74	68.66	68.76	**69.02**

Table 11. Ablation study of image features and CPA. [†] and [‡] indicate CPA is used in RPN and refinement, respectively.

w/ CPA[†]	w/ CPA[‡]	w/ RGB	w/ Seg	w/ Feat	3D AP	BEV AP
					85.38	91.48
✓	✓				86.12	92.16
✓					86.11	92.23
✓		✓			86.20	92.35
✓			✓		86.38	92.59
✓				✓	**86.87**	**92.68**

Analysis of the RoI-Graph Pooling. The first and second rows in Table 5 show that the RoI-graph pooling (RGP) raises the APH at level 2 for vehicle and pedestrian by 3.31% and 4.12%, respectively. In Table 9, we study the effect of the number of iterations on the detection accuracy, where the number of neighbors is set to 8 by default to save GPU memory. This result suggests it is beneficial to iterate more times to mine geometric relations. Besides, we find accuracy gains for distant objects are greater than for nearby objects since the contextual information is better modeled to alleviate the missing detection of distant objects. For graph construction, we investigate the components used in the initial state of the graph node. The fourth and fifth rows in Table 5 show that using PointNet (PN) raises 0.21% APH for vehicle class since the downsampling introduces the loss of fine-grained details, and the fifth and sixth rows show that adding two diagonal corners (DC) for each node raises 1.06% APH for both vehicle and pedestrian. For graph aggregation, the second and third rows in Table 5 show that multi-level attentive fusion (MLAF) boosts the performance by 0.29% APH for vehicle class. Furthermore, we study influences of different aggregation methods in Table 10, i.e., channel-wise Transformer (CT), Set Transformer (ST), attention sum (AS), average pooling (AP), and max pooling (MP). Transformer does not achieve better results, probably because it has more parameters leading to overfitting.

Analysis of the Visual Features Augmentation. By comparing the fourth and fifth rows in Table 4, we observe that the image feature raises the detection results by 2.34%, 0.75%, and 0.8% 3D AP respectively in terms of easy, moderate, and hard. We carefully analyze the effect of the cut-and-paste augmentation

(CPA) at different stages in Table 11. We find that the refinement stage is hardly affected by CPA. Thus, we can conveniently train the LiDAR branch and the image branch end-to-end without the help of CPA. We also provide the study of different image features, i.e., the RGB of the input image, the segmentation scores, and the output features of the 2D detector. We find that using the 2D features achieves the best results.

5   Conclusions

We present an accurate and efficient 3D object detector Graph R-CNN that can be applied to existing 3D detectors. Our framework can handle the unevenly distributed and sparse point clouds by utilizing the dynamic point aggregation and the semantic-decorated local graph.

Acknowledgments.. This work was supported in part by The National Key Research and Development Program of China (Grant Nos: 2018AAA0101400), in part by The National Nature Science Foundation of China (Grant Nos: 62036009, U1909203, 61936006, 62133013), in part by Innovation Capability Support Program of Shaanxi (Program No. 2021TD-05).

References

1. Bewley, A., Sun, P., Mensink, T., Anguelov, D., Sminchisescu, C.: Range conditioned dilated convolutions for scale invariant 3D object detection. In: Conference on Robot Learning (2020)
2. Chai, Y., et al.: To the point: efficient 3D object detection in the range image with graph convolution kernels (2021)
3. Chen, C., Chen, Z., Zhang, J., Tao, D.: SASA: semantics-augmented set abstraction for point-based 3D object detection. In: Proceedings of the AAAI Conference on Artificial Intelligence (2022)
4. Chen, X., Ma, H., Wan, J., Li, B., Xia, T.: Multi-view 3D object detection network for autonomous driving. In: Proceedings of the IEEE Conference on Computer Vision and Pattern Recognition (2017)
5. Chen, Y., Liu, S., Shen, X., Jia, J.: Fast point R-CNN. In: Proceedings of the IEEE International Conference on Computer Vision (2019)
6. Cheng, B., Sheng, L., Shi, S., Yang, M., Xu, D.: Back-tracing representative points for voting-based 3D object detection in point clouds (2021)
7. Deng, J., Shi, S., Li, P., Zhou, W., Zhang, Y., Li, H.: Voxel R-CNN: towards high performance voxel-based 3D object detection. In: Proceedings of the AAAI Conference on Artificial Intelligence (2021)
8. Geiger, A., Lenz, P., Urtasun, R.: Are we ready for autonomous driving? The KITTI vision benchmark suite. In: Proceedings of the IEEE Conference on Computer Vision and Pattern Recognition (2012)
9. Gori, M., Monfardini, G., Scarselli, F.: A new model for learning in graph domains. In: Proceedings of the IEEE International Joint Conference on Neural Networks (2005)

10. He, C., Zeng, H., Huang, J., Hua, X.S., Zhang, L.: Structure aware single-stage 3D object detection from point cloud. In: Proceedings of the IEEE Conference on Computer Vision and Pattern Recognition (2020)

11. Huang, T., Liu, Z., Chen, X., Bai, X.: EPNet: enhancing point features with image semantics for 3D object detection. In: Proceedings of the European Conference on Computer Vision (2020)

12. Lang, A.H., Vora, S., Caesar, H., Zhou, L., Yang, J., Beijbom, O.: Pointpillars: fast encoders for object detection from point clouds. In: Proceedings of the IEEE Conference on Computer Vision and Pattern Recognition (2019)

13. Lee, J., Lee, Y., Kim, J., Kosiorek, A.R., Choi, S., Teh, Y.W.: Set transformer: a framework for attention-based permutation-invariant neural networks. In: Proceedings of the International Conference on Machine Learning (2019)

14. Li, Z., Wang, F., Wang, N.: Lidar R-CNN: an efficient and universal 3D object detector. In: Proceedings of the IEEE Conference on Computer Vision and Pattern Recognition (2021)

15. Liang, M., Yang, B., Chen, Y., Hu, R., Urtasun, R.: Multi-task multi-sensor fusion for 3D object detection. In: Proceedings of the IEEE Conference on Computer Vision and Pattern Recognition (2019)

16. Liu, Z., Xu, G., Yang, H., Liu, H., Cai, D.: SparsePoint: fully end-to-end sparse 3D object detector. CoRR abs/2103.10042 (2021)

17. Mao, J., Niu, M., Bai, H., Liang, X., Xu, H., Xu, C.: Pyramid R-CNN: towards better performance and adaptability for 3D object detection. In: Proceedings of the IEEE International Conference on Computer Vision (2021)

18. Mao, J., et al.: Voxel transformer for 3D object detection. In: Proceedings of the IEEE International Conference on Computer Vision (2021)

19. Najibi, M., et al.: DOPS: learning to detect 3D objects and predict their 3D shapes. In: Proceedings of the IEEE Conference on Computer Vision and Pattern Recognition (2020)

20. Pang, S., Morris, D.D., Radha, H.: CloCS: camera-lidar object candidates fusion for 3D object detection. In: International Conference on Intelligent Robots and Systems (2020)

21. Qi, C.R., Su, H., Mo, K., Guibas, L.J.: PointNet: deep learning on point sets for 3D classification and segmentation. In: Proceedings of the IEEE Conference on Computer Vision and Pattern Recognition (2017)

22. Qi, C.R., Yi, L., Su, H., Guibas, L.J.: Pointnet++: deep hierarchical feature learning on point sets in a metric space. In: Advances in Neural Information Processing Systems (2017)

23. Sheng, H., et al.: Improving 3D object detection with channel-wise transformer. In: Proceedings of the IEEE International Conference on Computer Vision (2021)

24. Shi, S., Guo, C., Jiang, L., Wang, Z., Shi, J., Wang, X., Li, H.: PV-RCNN: point-voxel feature set abstraction for 3D object detection. In: Proceedings of the IEEE Conference on Computer Vision and Pattern Recognition (2020)

25. Shi, S., Wang, X., Li, H.: PointRCNN: 3D object proposal generation and detection from point cloud. In: Proceedings of the IEEE Conference on Computer Vision and Pattern Recognition (2019)

26. Shi, S., Wang, Z., Shi, J., Wang, X., Li, H.: From points to parts: 3D object detection from point cloud with part-aware and part-aggregation network. IEEE Trans. Pattern Anal. Mach. Intell. (2020)

27. Shi, W., Rajkumar, R.: Point-GNN: graph neural network for 3D object detection in a point cloud. In: Proceedings of the IEEE Conference on Computer Vision and Pattern Recognition (2020)

28. Sun, P., et al.: Scalability in perception for autonomous driving: Waymo open dataset. In: Proceedings of the IEEE Conference on Computer Vision and Pattern Recognition (2020)
29. Vora, S., Lang, A.H., Helou, B., Beijbom, O.: PointPainting: sequential fusion for 3D object detection. In: Proceedings of the IEEE Conference on Computer Vision and Pattern Recognition (2020)
30. Wang, C., Ma, C., Zhu, M., Yang, X.: PointAugmenting: cross-modal augmentation for 3D object detection. In: Proceedings of the IEEE Conference on Computer Vision and Pattern Recognition (2021)
31. Wang, J., Lan, S., Gao, M., Davis, L.S.: InfoFocus: 3D object detection for autonomous driving with dynamic information modeling. In: Vedaldi, A., Bischof, H., Brox, T., Frahm, J.-M. (eds.) ECCV 2020. LNCS, vol. 12355, pp. 405–420. Springer, Cham (2020). https://doi.org/10.1007/978-3-030-58607-2_24
32. Wang, Y., et al.: Pillar-based object detection for autonomous driving. In: Vedaldi, A., Bischof, H., Brox, T., Frahm, J.-M. (eds.) ECCV 2020. LNCS, vol. 12367, pp. 18–34. Springer, Cham (2020). https://doi.org/10.1007/978-3-030-58542-6_2
33. Wang, Y., Solomon, J.: Object DGCNN: 3D object detection using dynamic graphs. In: Advances in Neural Information Processing Systems (2021)
34. Wang, Y., Sun, Y., Liu, Z., Sarma, S.E., Bronstein, M.M., Solomon, J.M.: Dynamic graph CNN for learning on point clouds. ACM Trans. Graph. (2019)
35. Wu, X., et al.: Sparse fuse dense: towards high quality 3D detection with depth completion. In: Proceedings of the IEEE Conference on Computer Vision and Pattern Recognition (2022)
36. Xie, L., et al.: PI-RCNN: an efficient multi-sensor 3D object detector with point-based attentive cont-conv fusion module. In: Proceedings of the AAAI Conference on Artificial Intelligence (2020)
37. Xu, Q., Zhou, Y., Wang, W., Qi, C.R., Anguelov, D.: SPG: unsupervised domain adaptation for 3D object detection via semantic point generation (2021)
38. Yan, Y., Mao, Y., Li, B.: Second: sparsely embedded convolutional detection. Sensors 18(10) (2018)
39. Yang, Z., Sun, Y., Liu, S., Jia, J.: 3DSSD: point-based 3D single stage object detector. In: Proceedings of the IEEE Conference on Computer Vision and Pattern Recognition (2020)
40. Yang, Z., Sun, Y., Liu, S., Shen, X., Jia, J.: STD: sparse-to-dense 3D object detector for point cloud. In: Proceedings of the IEEE International Conference on Computer Vision (2019)
41. Yin, J., Shen, J., Guan, C., Zhou, D., Yang, R.: Lidar-based online 3D video object detection with graph-based message passing and spatiotemporal transformer attention. In: Proceedings of the IEEE Conference on Computer Vision and Pattern Recognition (2020)
42. Yin, T., Zhou, X., Krähenbühl, P.: Center-based 3D object detection and tracking. In: Proceedings of the IEEE Conference on Computer Vision and Pattern Recognition (2021)
43. Yoo, J.H., Kim, Y., Kim, J.S., Choi, J.W.: 3D-CVF: generating joint camera and lidar features using cross-view spatial feature fusion for 3D object detection. In: Proceedings of the European Conference on Computer Vision (2020)
44. Yu, F., Wang, D., Shelhamer, E., Darrell, T.: Deep layer aggregation. In: Proceedings of the IEEE Conference on Computer Vision and Pattern Recognition (2018)
45. Zhang, W., Wang, Z., Loy, C.C.: Multi-modality cut and paste for 3D object detection. CoRR abs/2012.12741 (2020)

46. Zheng, W., Tang, W., Chen, S., Jiang, L., Fu, C.W.: CIA-SSD: Confident IoU-aware single-stage object detector from point cloud. In: Proceedings of the AAAI Conference on Artificial Intelligence (2021)
47. Zheng, W., Tang, W., Jiang, L., Fu, C.W.: SE-SSD: self-ensembling single-stage object detector from point cloud. In: Proceedings of the IEEE Conference on Computer Vision and Pattern Recognition (2021)
48. Zhou, X., Wang, D., Krähenbühl, P.: Objects as points. CoRR abs/1904.07850 (2019)
49. Zhou, Y., et al.: End-to-end multi-view fusion for 3D object detection in lidar point clouds. In: Conference on Robot Learning (2019)
50. Zhou, Y., Tuzel, O.: VoxelNet: end-to-end learning for point cloud based 3D object detection. In: Proceedings of the IEEE Conference on Computer Vision and Pattern Recognition (2018)

MPPNet: Multi-frame Feature Intertwining with Proxy Points for 3D Temporal Object Detection

Xuesong Chen[1,4], Shaoshuai Shi[2(✉)], Benjin Zhu[1], Ka Chun Cheung[3], Hang Xu[4], and Hongsheng Li[1(✉)]

[1] MMLab, CUHK, Shatin, Hong Kong
chenxuesong@link.cuhk.edu.hk, hsli@ee.cuhk.edu.hk
[2] MPI-INF, Saarbrücken, Germany
shaoshuaics@gmail.com
[3] HKBU, Kowloon Tong, Hong Kong
[4] Huawei Noah's Ark Lab, Beijing, China

Abstract. Accurate and reliable 3D detection is vital for many applications including autonomous driving vehicles and service robots. In this paper, we present a flexible and high-performance 3D detection framework, named MPPNet, for 3D temporal object detection with point cloud sequences. We propose a novel three-hierarchy framework with proxy points for multi-frame feature encoding and interactions to achieve better detection. The three hierarchies conduct per-frame feature encoding, short-clip feature fusion, and whole-sequence feature aggregation, respectively. To enable processing long-sequence point clouds with reasonable computational resources, intra-group feature mixing and inter-group feature attention are proposed to form the second and third feature encoding hierarchies, which are recurrently applied for aggregating multi-frame trajectory features. The proxy points not only act as consistent object representations for each frame, but also serve as the courier to facilitate feature interaction between frames. The experiments on large Waymo Open dataset show that our approach outperforms state-of-the-art methods with large margins when applied to both short (*e.g.*, 4-frame) and long (*e.g.*, 16-frame) point cloud sequences. Code will be publicly available at https://github.com/open-mmlab/OpenPCDet.

Keywords: 3d object detection · Point cloud sequence · LiDAR

1 Introduction

3D object detection from point clouds is an important task for 3D scene perception, which aims to output the 3D bounding boxes and semantic labels of the

---

X. Chen and S. Shi—Equal contribution

Supplementary Information The online version contains supplementary material available at https://doi.org/10.1007/978-3-031-20074-8_39.

Table 1. Pilot experiments of CenterPoint [40] on Waymo validation set in terms of mAPH (LEVEL 2) of the vehicle class by taking concatenated point clouds as input.

Frames	1-frame	4-frame	8-frame	12-frame	16-frame
mAPH@L2	64.50	**65.77**	65.69	65.33	64.69

objects in the given scenes. The accurate and reliable 3D detection algorithms are essential for many applications such as the service robots and autonomous driving vehicles, which need accurate detection results for behaviour planning.

However, as one of the most widely adopted depth sensors, LiDAR sensors can only produce point clouds to capture one partial view of the scene at a time. This characteristic leads to incomplete point distributions of objects in driving scenes, posing difficulties for detection methods to accurately estimate the states of the objects. In real-world scenarios, the sensors continuously generate point clouds over time as the vehicle moves, and the point cloud sequence naturally provides multiple views of objects, which makes it possible to detect challenging objects more accurately by utilizing the sequence.

Recently, several approaches [8,28,40] have demonstrated that a simple concatenation of multi-frame point clouds can significantly improve the performance over single-frame detection. However, this strategy is only suitable for handling very short sequences (*e.g.*, 2–4 frames), and its performance might even drop when used to process more frames, since the fused point clouds of long sequences might show "tails" (see Fig. 2 (a)) of different visual patterns from different moving objects, posing additional challenges to the detectors. As shown in Table 1, our pilot study demonstrates that CenterPoint [40] detector achieves the best performance with 4-frame sequences while it fails on handling longer sequences. Hence, how to consistently improve the performance of 3D detection with multi-frame point clouds is the main challenge we aim to address in this paper.

We propose a novel two-stage 3D detection framework, named MPPNet, to effectively integrate features from **M**ulti-frame point clouds via **P**roxy **P**oints for achieving more accurate 3D detection results. The first stage adopts existing single-stage 3D detectors to generate 3D proposal trajectories, and we mainly focus on the second stage that takes a 3D proposal trajectory as input to aggregate multi-frame features in an object-centric manner for estimating more accurate 3D bounding boxes. The key idea of our approach is a series of inherently aligned proxy points to encode consistent representations of an object over time and a three-hierarchy paradigm for better fusing long-term feature sequences.

Specifically, in the first stage, we adopt existing 3D detectors [12,40] to generate high-quality 3D proposal boxes, and these boxes of all the frames are associated to generate the proposal trajectory for each object, where the box association is based on the predicted speeds of the object. The proposal trajectories and their associated object points serve as the input to our second stage.

However, it is challenging to directly aggregate the object features from the multi-frame object points, as the object points at different frames may have significantly different spatial distributions. To address this challenge, we propose to adopt a set of inherently aligned proxy points at each frame, which are placed at fixed and consistent relative positions in the proposal box of each frame. These proxy points make the aggregation of the multi-frame features easier by providing consistent representations at different frames. Based on the proxy points, our approach can more effectively aggregate the multi-frame features with a three-hierarchy model for 3D temporal object detection. The first hierarchy learns to encode per-frame features, the second hierarchy conducts feature interaction within each short clip (group), and the final hierarchy propagates the whole-sequence information among all the frames and effectively enhances single-frame representations to achieve more accurate detection.

Specifically, in the first hierarchy, to encode per-frame proposal features, we adopt set abstraction [21] to aggregate the object point features to a series of relatively consistent proxy points, which encode the object geometry of each frame. However, encoding in each frame's local coordinate system inevitably loses the motion information of the proposal trajectory, which is vital for the temporal detection task. To properly encode the motion features of per-frame proposals, we propose to separately encode the relative positions between the per-frame proxy points and the latest proposal box, which effectively encodes the motion state of per-frame proposal boxes. This decoupling strategy for encoding object geometry and motion features at each frame has been experimentally evidenced to benefit the performance of the multi-frame 3D object detection.

The small number of proxy points are also used for feature interaction between multiple frames. However, it is still unaffordable to build connections among all the proxy points as it might incur large costs to computational resources, especially when dealing with long (e.g., 16-frame) trajectories. Therefore, we adopt a short-clip grouping strategy to temporally divide each proposal trajectory into a small number of groups, where each group contains a short clip of sub-trajectory. By utilizing the per-frame proxy points as the intermediary, our second hierarchy conducts intra-group feature mixing with a novel 3D MLP Mixer module and the third hierarchy further utilizes cross-attention for inter-group feature interactions. Through this multi-frame feature propagation with our three-hierarchy model, it captures richer trajectory features by aggregating object information from different perspectives of the trajectory, which are used to predict a high-quality 3D bounding box by a detection head.

In a nutshell, our contributions are three-fold: 1) We propose a two-stage 3D detection framework MPPNet, which adopts a series of novel proxy points for multi-frame feature encoding and aggregation. Such inherently aligned proxy points not only effectively encode the geometry and motion features of the proposal trajectory in a decoupled manner, but also serve as the courier to facilitate multi-frame feature interaction. 2) We present a novel three-hierarchy model to better fuse the multi-frame features of long trajectories, which consists of per-frame encoding, intra-group feature mixing, and inter-group feature attention. 3) Our framework can process long point cloud sequences to consistently improve the performance of 3D object detection. Experiments demonstrate that our approach outperforms state-of-the-art methods by large margins when applied to both short (e.g., 4-frame) and long (e.g., 16-frame) sequences.

2   Related Work

3D Object Detection with Single-Frame Point Cloud. The current single-frame 3D detection algorithms can be roughly divided into three categories: point-based, voxel-based, and jointly employing both of them. First, the point-based methods [18,25,38] directly extracts information from the original point clouds. Through some well-designed operations, like set abstraction [21], the network can perceive the spatial position features of the irregular 3D point clouds to perform 3D object detection. Different from the point-based method, the voxel-based strategy first converts the irregular points into a number of fixed-size spatial voxels. Some high-efficiency methods [5,12,33,37] employ the bird-eye view (BEV) representation, integrating the height information, to encode the voxel features, and then utilize 2D CNN for efficient 3D detection. On the other hand, some works [36,40,42] exploit 3D CNN to directly extract feature of each voxel in 3D space. Besides, some recent works [13,23,24] exploit a voxel-based backbone to obtain 3D proposals, and then use point-based strategies [19,21] for box refinement, achieving state-of-the-art detection results.

2D Object Detection with Image Videos. Different from the scale-invariant 3D bounding boxes, 2D bounding boxes are highly affected by the relative positions of objects and the camera. Therefore, some 2D video detection approaches [6,9–11,32,43] mainly focus on using the appearance and motion features of the previous frame to align the objects in the current frame. Previous 2D multi-frame object detection methods mainly use optical flow [7,43,44], motion [1,4], LSTM [35] to align and aggregate information from different frames. Recently, many methods [2,3,34] employ the popular self-attention layer [30] as the relation modules to align the features of the previous frame to the current frame, achieving more robust multi-frame detection results.

3D Object Detection with Point Cloud Sequences. The earlier multi-frame 3D detectors generally adopt a feature-based strategy to gradually aggregate temporal features with 2D CNN [15] or transformer [31,41]. Besides that, some state-of-the-art 3D detectors [8,28,40] have demonstrated that a simple multi-frame point concatenation strategy can already outperform the single-frame setting with remarkable margins by taking a short point cloud sequence. But when it comes to longer sequences, this simple strategy might fail due to the challenge of handling various moving patterns of objects. 3D-MAN [39] employs attention mechanism to align different views from 3D object in point cloud and exploits a memory bank to store and aggregate the temporal information to process long point cloud sequence. SimTrack [14] presents an end-to-end trainable

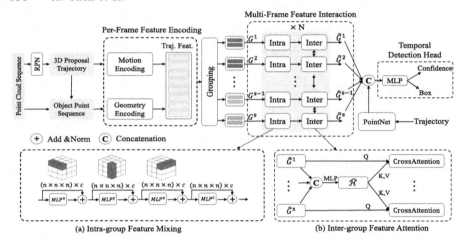

Fig. 1. The overall architecture of our proposed MPPNet. Our approach takes a point cloud sequence as input for temporal 3D object detection, where a three-hierarchy model is proposed for the multi-frame feature encoding and interaction.

model for joint detection and tracking from raw point clouds by feature alignment. Recently, Offboard3D [20] proposes an offboard 3D detector that greatly improves the detection performance by taking the whole point cloud sequence as input, but it depends on both past and future frames for generating accurate 3D bounding boxes. In this paper, we propose a two-stage 3D detector, MPP-Net, where we carefully design the multi-frame feature encoding and interaction modules.

3   Methodology

Most state-of-the-art 3D detection approaches adopt a simple concatenation strategy [23,40] to take multi-frame point clouds as input for improving 3D temporal detection, which are generally effective at handling short point cloud sequences but fail to deal with long sequences due to the challenge of point-cloud trajectories with different moving patterns. 3D-MAN [39] utilizes the attention networks to aggregate multi-frame features, which, however, may attend to mismatched proposals due to the dense connections among all proposals.

We propose MPPNet, a two-stage 3D detection framework, which takes the point cloud sequences as input to greatly improve the detection results. In the first stage, we adopt existing single-stage 3D detectors to generate 3D proposal trajectories. Our main innovation focuses on the second stage that takes a 3D proposal trajectory as input and effectively aggregates the multi-frame object features for predicting more accurate 3D bounding boxes. In Sect. 3.1, we briefly introduce the 1st-stage single-frame proposal generation network and the strategy to generate 3D proposal trajectories. In Sect. 3.2, we present the 2nd-stage trajectory proposal feature encoding that adopts the proxy point strategy and a three-hierarchy model for multi-frame feature encoding and interaction. Finally, in Sect. 3.3, we introduce the 3D detection head to generate 3D boxes from the summarized temporal features and also discuss the optimization of our approach.

3.1 Single-Frame Proposal Network and 3D Proposal Trajectories

In this section, we briefly introduce the 1st-stage of our approach that aims to generate the 3D proposal trajectories. Given a point cloud sequence, we create consecutive 4-frame clips and extend the single-stage 3D detectors [12,40] as [8, 28] to generate per-frame 3D detection boxes. The choice of 4-frame clips is determined according to the results of Table 1.

To associate the 3D detection boxes as 3D proposal trajectories, we add an extra speed prediction head for estimating the speeds of the detected objects, where the speeds are utilized to associate the 3D proposal boxes with a predefined Intersection-over-Union (IoU) threshold as in [40].

After associating per-frame 3D proposal boxes to create a 3D proposal trajectory, let $\{\mathcal{B}^1,\ldots,\mathcal{B}^T\}$ denote the T-frame 3D proposal trajectory and $\mathcal{K}^t = \{l_1^t,\ldots,l_m^t\}_{t=1,\cdots,T}$ denote object points region pooled [25] from each frame t. They are input into the second stage of our framework for multi-frame feature encoding and interaction to generate more accurate a 3D bounding box.

3.2 Three-Hierarchy Feature Aggregation with Proxy Points

The proposal trajectory and its contained object points capture an object candidate from multiple views, which provide richer information to estimate its 3D bounding box more accurately. However, it is challenging to aggregate useful information from a long sequence of object points, as the number of object points is large and they also have very different spatial distributions over time.

To address the challenge, we propose to adopt a set of inherently aligned proxy points at each frame, which not only provide consistent per-frame representations for the object points, but also facilitate multi-frame feature interaction by serving as the courier for cross-time propagation. With the proxy points, we further present a three-hierarchy model to effectively aggregate multi-frame features from the object point sequence for improve the performance of 3D detection, where the first hierarchy encodes the per-frame object geometry and motion features in a decoupled manner, the second hierarchy performs the feature mixing within each short clip (group) and the third hierarchy propagates whole-sequence information among all clips. By alternatively stacking the intra-group and inter-group feature interactions, the multi-frame features can be well summarized to achieve more accurate detection.

Proxy Points.   The proxy points are placed at fixed and consistent relative positions in each 3D proposal box of the proposal trajectory. Specifically, at each time t, $N = n \times n \times n$ proxy points are uniformly sampled within the

3D proposal box and are denoted as $P^t = \{p_1^t, p_2^t, \ldots, p_N^t\}$. These proxy points maintain the temporal order as the order of the trajectory boxes. As they are uniformly sampled in the same way across time, they naturally align the same spatial parts of the object proposals over time.

Decoupled Per-frame Feature Encoding. Our first hierarchy performs per-frame feature encoding. The object geometry and motion features are separately encoded based on the proxy points as illustrated in Fig. 2 (b).

For encoding geometry features with proxy points, the relative differences between each object point $l_i^t \in \mathcal{K}^t$ and the 8 corner + 1 center points of the proposal box $\mathcal{B}^t = \{b_j^t\}_{j=1}^9$ are first calculated as

$$\triangle l_i^t = \text{Concat}\left(\{l_i^t - b_j^t\}_{j=1}^9\right). \tag{1}$$

Hence, the object points' geometry representations are first enhanced as $F^t = \{(l_i^t, \Delta_i^t)\}_{i=1}^m$. To encode the object geometry features via the proxy points, the set abstraction [21] is adopted to aggregate the neighboring object points to every proxy point p_k^t as

$$g_k^t = \text{SetAbstraction}(p_k^t, F^t), \text{ for } k = 1, \ldots, N. \tag{2}$$

However, the above geometry feature encoding conducted in the local coordinate of $\{\mathcal{B}^t\}_{t=1}^T$, which inevitably loses the object points' motion information.

The per-frame motion information is also important for the object points and also needs to be properly encoded. We propose to separately calculate the relative positions between the per-frame proxy points P^t and the latest proposal box's 8 corner + 1 center points $\{b_j^T\}_{j=1}^9$ as Eq. (1):

$$\Delta p_k^t = \text{Concat}\left(\{p_k^t - b_j^T\}_{j=1}^9\right). \tag{3}$$

Here, note that the per-frame proxy point p_k^t and the box point b_j^T are all transformed to the same world coordinate system to correctly capture the global motion information. This strategy effectively encodes the motion state of each proposal box $\mathcal{B}^t$ with respect to the latest box $\mathcal{B}^T$, as the proxy points at each time t have fixed relative positions in the proposal boxes.

With an extra one-dimensional time offset embedding e^t, the final motion encoding of each proxy point is formulated as

$$f_k^t = \text{MLP}(\text{Concat}(\Delta p_k^t, e^t)), \text{ for } k = 1, \ldots, N. \tag{4}$$

By adding the per-frame object geometry features and the motion features, the features of the each proxy point is calculated as

$$r_k^t = g_k^t + f_k^t, \text{ for } k = 1, \ldots, N, \tag{5}$$

which forms the final per-frame object features $R^t = \{r_1^t, \ldots, r_N^t\}$ at time t.

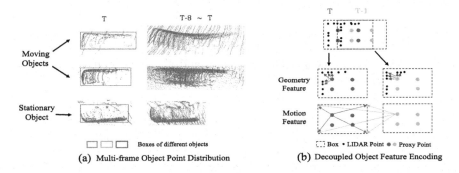

(a) Multi-frame Object Point Distribution   **(b)** Decoupled Object Feature Encoding

Fig. 2. Illustration of point distribution of different objects (a) and the decoupled feature encoding for object geometry and motion state (b).

Grouping for Multi-frame Feature Interaction. The above per-frame encoding aggregates per-frame information to the proxy points, which serve as the representations of each frame to facilitate the multi-frame feature interaction. However, naively establishing dense connections among all frames' proxy points is still unaffordable and unscaleable in consideration of the tremendous computational costs and GPU memory. Therefore, we adopt a grouping strategy to temporally divide the long proposal trajectory into a small number of non-overlapping groups, where each group contains a short sub-trajectory.

Specifically, the trajectory's per-frame features $\{R^1, \ldots, R^T\}$ are evenly divided into S groups and each group has T' frames (we assume that $T = T' \times S$). The proposed grouping strategy enables the following multi-frame feature interaction to be more efficiently conducted with the proposed intra-group feature mixing and inter-group cross-attention.

Intra-group Feature Mixing. The second hierarchy aims to encode group-wise temporal features of the proposal trajectory by conducting the feature interactions within each group. We first collect the features of the inherently aligned per-frame proxy points within each group i as $G^i = \{r_1^t, \ldots, r_N^t\}_{t \in \mathcal{G}_i}$, where $\mathcal{G}_i$ is the temporal index set indicating which frames are included in the i-th group (e.g., $\mathcal{G}_1 = \{1, 2, 3, 4\}$ or $\{1, 5, 9, 13\}$ when $S = 4$). The group feature G^i can be represented as a three-dimensional feature matrix that has $G^i \in \mathbb{R}^{T' \times N \times D}$, where D is the feature dimension of each proxy point. This feature matrix G^i can be considered as an $N \times (T' \times D)$ matrix and input to an MLP to obtain group-level proxy points as $\hat{G}^i = \mathrm{MLP}\left(G^i\right)$, where $\hat{G}^i \in \mathbb{R}^{N \times D}$, and the $\mathrm{MLP}(\cdot)$ fuses each group's representation from $(T' \times D)$ to D dimensions.

To further conduct the feature interaction among all proxy points within each group, inspired by [29], we propose the 3D MLP Mixer module to mix each group i's features in the x, y, z and channel dimensions separately and sequentially. As illustrated in Fig. 1 (a), we conduct the feature interaction for each $\hat{G}^i$ as

$$\hat{G}^i = \text{MLP}^{4d}(\hat{G}^i), \text{ for } s = 1, \dots, S, \tag{6}$$

where $\text{MLP}^{4d}(\cdot)$ indicates an MLP with four axis-aligned projection layers for feature mixing along the spatial x, y, z axes and along the channel axis (c) on the proxy points, respectively.

Inter-Group Feature Attention. After the intra-group feature mixing, our third hierarchy aims to propagate information of the group-level proxy points across different groups to capture richer whole-sequence information. We exploit the cross-attention per-group feature representations by querying from the features of the all-group summarization of the whole sequence.

Specifically, the all-group features $\{\hat{G}^1, \dots, \hat{G}^S\}$ can be represented as a three-dimensional feature matrix denoted as $\mathcal{H} \in \mathbb{R}^{S \times N \times D}$. It can be considered as an $N \times (S \times D)$ matrix and input to an MLP to obtain the all-group summarization as $\hat{\mathcal{H}} = \text{MLP}(\mathcal{H})$, where $\hat{\mathcal{H}} \in \mathbb{R}^{N \times D}$ and the MLP$(\cdot)$ fuses the all-group summarization from $(S \times D)$ to D dimensions.

Using the all-group summarization as a intermediary, we conduct the inter-group cross-attention for each group $\hat{G}^i$ to aggregate features from $\hat{\mathcal{H}}$ as

$$\hat{G}^i = \text{MultiHeadAttn}(Q(\hat{G}^i + \text{PE}), K(\hat{\mathcal{H}} + \text{PE}), V(\hat{\mathcal{H}})), \text{ for } i = 1, \dots, S, \tag{7}$$

where $Q(\cdot), K(\cdot), V(\cdot)$ are linear projection layers to generate query, key, value features for the multi-head cross-attention [30], and 'PE' represents a learnable index-based 3D positional embedding for each proxy point, obtained by projecting proxy points' indices (i, j, k) via a MLP.

The above intra-group feature mixing and inter-group cross-attention are recurrently stacked for multiple times so that the trajectory's representations gradually become aware of both global and local contexts for predicting a more accurate 3D bounding box from the trajectory proposal.

3.3 Temporal 3D Detection Head and Optimization

Through the proposed three-hierarchy feature aggregation, our model obtains richer and more reliable feature representation from input point cloud sequences. A 3D detection head to generate final bounding boxes is introduced on top of the above trajectory temporal features, which is supervised by the training losses.

3D Temporal Detection Head with Transformer. Given the aforementioned group feature $\hat{G}^i$, we propose to adopt a simple transformer layer to obtain a single feature vector from each group. Specifically, we create a learnable feature embedding $E \in \mathbb{R}^{1 \times D}$ as the query, to aggregate features from each group feature $\hat{G}^i$ with a multi-head attention as

$$E^i = \text{MultiHeadAttn}(Q(E), K(\hat{G}^i + \text{PE}), V(\hat{G}^i)), \text{ for } i = 1, \dots, S, \tag{8}$$

where 'PE' is similarly defined as that in Eq. (7). In addition to group features extracted from the raw point clouds, following [20], we also exploit a Point-Net [19] that takes $\{\mathcal{B}_1, \ldots, \mathcal{B}_T\}$ as input to extract the boxes' embedding, where each box is treated as a point with 7-dim geometry and 1-dim time encoding.

Our detection head therefore integrates group-wise features $\{E^1, \ldots, E^S\}$ from both the object points and the boxes' embedding via feature concatenation, for the final confidence prediction and box regression.

Training Losses. The overall training loss is the summation of the confidence prediction loss $\mathcal{L}_{\text{conf}}$, the box regression loss $\mathcal{L}_{\text{reg}}$ as:

$$\mathcal{L} = \mathcal{L}_{\text{conf}} + \alpha \mathcal{L}_{\text{reg}}, \tag{9}$$

where α is the hyper-parameter for balancing different losses. We adopt the same binary cross entropy loss and box regression loss, employed in CT3D [22], as our $\mathcal{L}_{\text{conf}}$ and $\mathcal{L}_{\text{reg}}$. At training stage, we use the intermediate supervision by adding loss to the intra-group output of each iteration and sum all the intermediate losses to train the model. At test time, we only use the bounding boxes and confidences results predicted from the last intra-group output feature.

4   Experiments

4.1   Dataset and Implementation Details

Waymo Open Dataset. The Waymo dataset [27] is a large-scale 3D detection dataset in autonomous driving scenarios, which contains 1150 sequences divided into 798 training, 202 validation, and 150 testing sequences. All frames of each sequence are well-calibrated so the 3D temporal detection can be performed. Our models are trained on the training set and evaluated on both the validation set and testing set. The official evaluation metrics are standard 3D mean Average Precision (mAP) and mAP weighted by heading accuracy (mAPH). Meanwhile, according to the number of inside points for each object, the data is split into two difficulty levels: LELVEL 1 where objects include more than 5 points and LELVEL 2 where objects include at least 1 points.

Implementation Details. The two stages of our MPPNet are trained separately. We follow the official training strategy for our adopted 1st-stage sub-network (RPN) [12,40], while the 2nd-stage sub-network is trained with the ADAM optimizer for 6 epochs with an initial learning rate of 0.003 and a batch size of 16. We set the IoU matching threshold to 0.5 for generating the propose trajectories in the 1st stage. During training, we conduct the proposal-centric box jitter augmentation as PointRCNN [25] on the per-frame 3D proposal box. We randomly sample 128 raw LiDAR points and set $N = 64$ for the proxy points of each proposal in a trajectory. The feature dimension D of each proxy point is set as 256. For the multi-frame feature interaction, we set the number of groups as $S = 4$ for different lengths of trajectories (*e.g.*, for 4-frame input, each frame forms a group; for 16-frame input, every 4 frames forms a group). We alternately conduct the intra-group feature mixing and inter-group feature attention module for 2 times, followed by an extra intra-group module to attach our proposed 3D detection head for predicting the confidence and 3D bounding box. We set $\alpha = 2$ for balancing the terms in the overall loss. During inference, we can store objects' feature of past frames in a memory bank to speed up.

4.2   Main Results of MPPNet on Waymo Open Dataset

Waymo Validation Set. Table 2 shows the result of published state-of-the-art single-frame and multi-frame methods. Firstly, when compared with state-of-the-art single-frame method PV-RCNN++ [24], our MPPNet, using CenterPoint [40] with 4-frame input as 1st-stage, improves the overall 3D mAPH (LEVEL 2) significantly by 5.05%, 8.76%, 4.9% on vehicle, pedestrian and cyclist, respectively, by exploiting 16-frame point cloud sequences as input. Secondly, compared with multi-frame methods, MPPNet improves the overall 3D mAPH (LEVEL 2) of the vehicle class by 7.82% for 3D-MAN [39] and 4.12% for CT3D-MF, where we extend the open-sourced codes of CT3D [22] to a multi-frame version CT3D-MF by using the point concatenation strategy. Considering that CT3D is a high-performance method, where both the features of raw LiDAR point and proposals from region proposal network are employed, we think it is suitable as a baseline to evaluate the temporal impact from multi-frame points and 3D proposals.

As demonstrated in Table 2, MPPNet can effectively integrate temporal information in point cloud sequences to improve detection accuracy. Specifically, MPPNet achieves significantly gains compared to single-frame detectors, which verifies that our approach successfully exploits temporal information for more

Table 2. Performance comparison on the validation set of Waymo Open Dataset. † indicates the method implemented by us. The Centerpoint with 4-frame input is adopted as MPPNet's 1st-stage.

Method	Frames	ALL (3D APH)		VEH (3D AP/APH)		PED(3D AP/APH)		CYC(3D AP/APH)	
		L1	L2	L1	L2	L1	L2	L1	L2
SECOND [36]	1	63.05	57.23	72.27/71.69	63.85/63.33	68.70/58.18	60.72/51.31	60.62/59.28	58.34/57.05
PointPillar [12]	1	63.33	57.53	71.60/71.00	63.10/62.50	70.60/56.70	62.90/50.20	64.40/62.30	61.90/59.90
LiDAR R-CNN [13]	1	66.20	60.10	73.50/73.00	64.70/64.20	71.20/58.70	63.10/51.70	68.60/66.90	66.10/64.40
RSN [28]	1	-	-	75.10/74.60	66.00/65.50	77.80/72.70	68.30/63.70	-	-
Pyramid [16]	1	-	-	76.30/75.68	67.23/66.68	-	-	-	-
PV-RCNN [23]	1	69.63	63.33	77.51/76.89	68.98/68.41	75.01/65.65	66.04/57.61	67.81/66.35	65.39/63.98
Part-A2 [26]	1	70.25	63.84	77.05/76.51	68.47/67.97	75.24/66.87	66.18/58.62	68.60/67.36	66.13/64.93
Centerpoint [40]	1	-	65.50	-	-/66.20	-	-/62.60	-	-/67.60
CT3D [22]	1	-	-	-	69.04/-	-	-	-	-
PV-RCNN++ [24]	1	75.21	68.61	79.10/78.63	70.34/69.91	80.62/74.62	71.86/66.30	73.49/72.38	70.70/69.62
3D-MAN [39]	16	-	-	74.53/74.03	67.61/67.14	-	-	-	-
† Centerpoint [40]	4	74.88	69.38	76.71/76.17	69.13/68.63	78.88/75.55	71.73/68.61	73.73/72.96	71.63/70.89
† CT3D-MF [22]	12	-	-	79.30/78.82	71.82/70.84	-	-	-	-
† CT3D-MF [22]	16	-	-	79.04/78.55	71.14/70.68	-	-	-	-
MPPNet (Ours)	4	79.83	74.22	81.54/81.06	74.07/73.61	84.56/81.94	77.20/74.67	77.15/76.50	75.01/74.38
MPPNet (Ours)	16	**80.40**	**74.85**	**82.74/82.28**	**75.41/74.96**	**84.69/82.25**	**77.43/75.06**	**77.28/76.66**	**75.13/74.52**

accurately estimating the 3D bounding boxes of some difficult cases in single-frame setting. Moreover, MPPNet still performs much better than state-of-the-art multi-frame 3D detector 3D-MAN [39] when utilizing the same input length of point cloud sequences, indicating that our three-hierarchy design can aggregate spatial-temporal information more thoroughly to benefit 3D detection.

In addition, we also provide the performance of MPPNet with short sequence input. It can be seen that even with 4-frame input, our method still has advantages over both single-frame and multi-frame methods, improving 3.7% over PV-RCNN++ [24] and 2.77% over CT3D-MF [22] in terms of 3D mAPH (LEVEL 2) of the vehicle class. Note that 3D-MAN [39], a representative detection algorithm that can handle long sequence inputs, uses a low-performance PointPillar [12] as their 1st-stage single-frame detection model. For fair comparison with 3D-MAN, we also adopt a 1st-stage model that has similar performance with theirs then we extend the model with 4-frame input to get the speed for trajectory generation. Table 4 demonstrates that MPPNet achieves better results than 3D-MAN. Our proposed MPPNet greatly improves the L2 mAPH of single-frame RPN by 16.26%, which indicates that our MPPNet can extract useful information to benefit the detection even with the noisy input trajectories. Moreover, when employing a higher-performance single-frame detection model, the performance of our MPPNet can be further improved.

Waymo Testing Set. We also evaluate our method on the testing set of Waymo dataset to further validate the generalization of our approach. As shown in Table 3, our approach achieves much better performance than both the state-of-the-art single-frame method [24] and multi-frame methods [39,40] by large margins. Note that we do not use test-time augmentations and model ensemble.

4.3 Ablation Studies

We conduct comprehensive ablation studies to verify the effectiveness of each component of MPPNet. To save the training cost, unless otherwise mentioned, all ablation experiments of MPPNet are trained on the vehicle category for 3

Table 3. Performance comparison on the testing set of Waymo Open Dataset.

Method	Frames	ALL (3D APH)		VEH (3D AP/APH)		PED(3D AP/APH)		CYC(3D AP/APH)	
		L1	L2	L1	L2	L1	L2	L1	L2
StarNet [17]	1	-	-	61.50/61.00	54.90/54.50	67.80/59.90	61.10/54.00	-	-
PointPillar [12]	1	-	-	68.60/68.10	60.50/60.10	68.00/55.50	61.40/50.10	-	-
CenterPoint [40]	1	-	-	80.20/79.70	72.20/71.80	78.30/72.10	72.20/66.40	-	-
PV-RCNN++ [24]	1	75.65	70.21	81.62/73.86	81.20/73.47	80.41/74.12	74.99/69.00	71.93/69.28	70.76/68.15
RSN [28]	3	-	-	80.70/80.30	71.90/71.60	78.90/75.60	70.70/67.80	-	-
Centerpoint [40]	2	77.18	71.93	81.05/80.59	73.42/72.99	80.47/77.28	74.56/71.52	74.60/73.68	72.17/71.28
PV-RCNN Ens [23]	2	76.90	71.52	81.06/80.57	73.69/73.23	80.31/76.28	73.98/70.16	75.10/73.84	72.38/71.16
Pyramid [16]	2	-	-	81.77/81.32	74.87/74.43	-	-	-	-
3D-MAN [39]	16	-	-	78.71/78.28	70.37/69.98	69.97/65.98	63.98/60.26	-	-
MPPNet (Ours)	16	**80.59**	**75.67**	**84.27/83.88**	**77.29/76.91**	**84.12/81.52**	**78.44/75.93**	**77.11/76.36**	**74.91/74.18**

Table 4. Performance comparison with 3D-MAN [39], where ES and FT indicate early-stop and fully-trained models.

Method	Frames	mAPH@L2
PointPillar	1	54.69
PointPillar-ES	1	55.13
PointPillar-FT	1	64.37
3D-MAN w/ PointPillar	16	67.14 (+12.45)
Ours w/ PointPillar-ES	16	71.39 (+16.26)
Ours w/ PointPillar-FT	16	72.90 (+8.53)

Table 5. Effects of the input trajectory length. All experiments adopt the CenterPoint [40] as RPN by training with 6 epochs for saving the training cost.

Method	CT3D-MF	MPPNet
4-frame	70.19	72.63
8-frame	70.71 (+0.52)	73.22 (+0.59)
12-frame	70.84 (+0.65)	73.55 (+0.92)
16-frame	70.68 (+0.49)	73.81 (+1.18)

epochs by taking four-frame point cloud as input. We take the mAPH (LEVEL 2) as the default metric for comparison. The results are shown in Table 6.

Effects of the Input Length of Trajectory and Boxes' Embedding. Table 5 verifies the ability of MPPNet to aggregate multi-frame temporal information from the trajectories with different lengths. We observe that CT3D-MF [22] achieves the best performance when processing 12-frame sequences, demonstrating that it has relatively better temporal modeling capabilities than CenterPoint [40] but still struggles at handling longer sequences (*e.g.* 16 frames). In contrast, our MPPNet can constantly improve the performance by taking longer sequences (*i.e.*, from 4 to 16 frames) as input, which demonstrates the effectiveness of our proxy point based three-hierarchy model for multi-frame feature encoding and interaction. In addition, removing the boxes' embedding leads to a slight performance drop of -0.1% (see the last row of Table 6).

Effects of Proxy Points. We investigate the importance of the proposed proxy points by comparing with a baseline that directly use raw LiDAR points. Considering that the raw LiDAR points are unordered, we first replace 3D MLP Mixer with a self-attention module for intra-group feature fusion, and then we employ 128 LiDAR points' feature as the representation of each proposal for the multi-frame feature interaction. The 2rd and 3th rows of Table 6 show that removing the proxy point substantially decreases the performance by 1.95%. It demonstrates that our proposed proxy points can provide consistent representations for different frames and greatly benefit feature propagation among all the frames, while directly aggregating temporal features from the unordered point clouds is very less effective. Moreover, we explore the effects of different numbers of proxy points in Table 7. Here we observe that a smaller number of proxy points (*i.e.*, $27 = 3^3$) degrades the performance by -0.54% since the too few proxy points cannot finely represent the geometric details of objects, while adopting more proxy points (*i.e.*, 64 and 125) achieves similar performance but more proxy points lead to more computations. Hence our MPPNet adopts $64 = 4 \times 4 \times 4$ proxy points as a trade-off.

Table 6. Effects of different components in our proposed framework, where the first row is our MPPNet with 4-frame sequences and default settings for comparison.

Proxy Point	Boxes's Embedding	Per-frame Feature Encoding	Multi-frame Feature Fusion Intra	Multi-frame Feature Fusion Inter	mAPH@L2
✓	✓	Geometry+Motion	3D MLP Mixer	Cross-Attn	73.08
×	✓	Geometry+Motion	Self-Attn	Cross-Attn	71.13 (-1.95)
✓	✓	Geometry+Motion	Self-Attn	Cross-Attn	72.71 (-0.37)
✓	✓	Geometry	3D MLP Mixer	Cross-Attn	72.78 (-0.30)
✓	✓	Integrated	3D MLP Mixer	Cross-Attn	72.89 (-0.19)
✓	✓	Geometry+Motion	3D MLP Mixer	×	72.36 (-0.72)
✓	✓	Geometry+Motion	3D MLP Mixer	Cross-Attn w/o PE	72.97 (-0.11)
✓	✓	Geometry+Motion	3D MLP Mixer	Cross-Attn w/o Sum.	72.95 (-0.13)
✓	×	Geometry+Motion	3D MLP Mixer	Cross-Attn	72.98 (-0.10)

Effects of Intra-Group Feature mmixing. We adopt different designs to investigate the effectiveness of our proposed 3D MLP Mixer for intra-group feature mixing. As shown in the 3rd row of Table 6, we replace the proposed 3D MLP Mixer by a standard self-attention module [30], which results in a 0.37% performance drop compared with the 1st row. It demonstrates that the information propagation manner in 3D MLP Mixer is better for intra-group feature fusion.

Effects of Inter-Group Feature Interaction. By comparing 1st and 6th rows of Table 6, we observe that the performance drops a lot (-0.72%) after removing the inter-group feature attention module. It demonstrates that the interactions among different groups are essential for achieving accurate detection, since the model can better integrate multi-view information from the whole 3D trajectory. Moreover, we also provide two variants of the proposed cross-attention module to verify the effectiveness of our design. For the first variant, we remove our proposed index-based position embedding in the cross attention, and by comparing 1st and 7th rows of Table 6 we observe that the proposed index-based position embedding brings 0.11% performance gain. Meanwhile, in another variant of inter-group cross-attention, we use each group's features as query ($N \times D$) to aggregate features from the concatenation of all other groups' features ($((S-1) \times N) \times D$), rather than using the all-group summarization, and the 1st and 8th rows of Table 6 show that the performance drops a bit (-0.13%).

Effects of Decoupled Encoding for Geometry and Motion Feature. As shown in the 4th and 5th rows of Table 6, without motion encoding, MPPNet suffers from a performance drop by -0.3%, suggesting that motion information is beneficial for state estimation of objects from point cloud sequences. Meanwhile, compared with our proposed decoupled encoding strategy, the integrated encoding manner by attaching a per-frame time encoding to each LiDAR point will

Table 7. Effects of different numbers of proxy points in our MPPNet. $n \times n \times n$ proxy points are uniformly sampled within each proposal box.

# (Proxy Point)	mAPH@L2
$3 \times 3 \times 3$	72.54
$4 \times 4 \times 4$	73.08
$5 \times 5 \times 5$	72.98

Table 8. Effects of trajectory augmentation, intermediate supervision and grouping strategy. The upper part investigates the training strategy with 4-frame input, while the lower part explores the grouping strategy with 16-frame input.

Training	MPPNet	w/o Traj. Aug	w/o Int. Loss
Strategy	73.08	72.62 (-0.46)	72.47 (-0.61)
Grouping	Stride 4	Stride 1	-
Strategy	74.21	74.06	-

degrade the performance by -0.19%, which proves that the decoupled feature encoding strategy is beneficial for the network's feature learning.

Effects of Trajectory Augmentation and Intermediate Supervision. The top part of Table 8 shows that the performance drops by -0.46% without data augmentation, and drops by -0.61% without the intermediate supervisions. We consider that the intermediate loss can help the network to gradually optimize and refine the features by supervising them after each block.

Effects of Clip Grouping Strategy. We investigate different grouping strategies' impact with 16-frame input. As shown in the bottom part of Table 7, when setting stride to 4 to form the groups, *e.g.*, $\{1, 5, 9, 13\}$ (denoted as 'stride 4'), the network achieves better results than using temporal stride 1 to form every group, *e.g.*, $\{1, 2, 3, 4\}$ (denoted as 'stride 1').

5 Conclusions

In this work, we present a two-stage 3D detection framework MPPNet, adopting a series of novel proxy points to integrate multi-frame features for 3D object detection. With the inherently aligned proxy points, MPPNet encodes the per-frame object geometry and motion features in an decoupled manner then they are deeply interacted through our proposed intra-group feature mixing and inter-group feature attention, which effectively propagate the features among the per-frame proxy points in the whole trajectory to perform more accurate 3D detection. The experiments on large-scale Waymo Open dataset demonstrate that our approach captures better multi-view features from the point cloud sequences and outperforms state-of-the-art methods with remarkable margins.

Acknowledgement. This work is supported in part by NVIDIA, in part by Centre for Perceptual and Interactive Intelligence Limited, in part by the General Research Fund through the Research Grants Council of Hong Kong under Grants (Nos. 14204021, 14207319), in part by CUHK Strategic Fund. Hongsheng Li is also a PI at Centre for Perceptual and Interactive Intelligence Limited.

References

1. Bertasius, G., Torresani, L., Shi, J.: Object detection in video with spatiotemporal sampling networks. In: Ferrari, V., Hebert, M., Sminchisescu, C., Weiss, Y. (eds.) ECCV 2018. LNCS, vol. 11216, pp. 342–357. Springer, Cham (2018). https://doi.org/10.1007/978-3-030-01258-8_21
2. Chen, Y., Cao, Y., Hu, H., Wang, L.: Memory enhanced global-local aggregation for video object detection. In: Proceedings of the IEEE/CVF Conference on Computer Vision and Pattern Recognition, pp. 10337–10346 (2020)
3. Deng, J., Pan, Y., Yao, T., Zhou, W., Li, H., Mei, T.: Relation distillation networks for video object detection. In: Proceedings of the IEEE/CVF International Conference on Computer Vision, pp. 7023–7032 (2019)
4. Feichtenhofer, C., Pinz, A., Zisserman, A.: Detect to track and track to detect. In: Proceedings of the IEEE International Conference on Computer Vision, pp. 3038–3046 (2017)
5. Ge, R., Ding, Z., Hu, Y., Wang, Y., Chen, S., Huang, L., Li, Y.: AFDet: anchor free one stage 3D object detection. arXiv preprint arXiv:2006.12671 (2020)
6. Han, M., Wang, Y., Chang, X., Qiao, Yu.: Mining inter-video proposal relations for video object detection. In: Vedaldi, A., Bischof, H., Brox, T., Frahm, J.-M. (eds.) ECCV 2020. LNCS, vol. 12366, pp. 431–446. Springer, Cham (2020). https://doi.org/10.1007/978-3-030-58589-1_26
7. Hetang, C., Qin, H., Liu, S., Yan, J.: Impression network for video object detection. arXiv preprint arXiv:1712.05896 (2017)
8. Hu, Y., et al.: AFDetV2: rethinking the necessity of the second stage for object detection from point clouds. arXiv preprint arXiv:2112.09205 (2021)
9. Jiao, L., Zhang, R., Liu, F., Yang, S., Hou, B., Li, L., Tang, X.: New generation deep learning for video object detection: a survey. IEEE Trans. Neural Netw. Learn. Syst. **33**(8), 3195–3215 (2021)
10. Kang, K., et al.: Object detection in videos with tubelet proposal networks. In: Proceedings of the IEEE Conference on Computer Vision and Pattern Recognition, pp. 727–735 (2017)
11. Kang, K., et al.: T-CNN: tubelets with convolutional neural networks for object detection from videos. IEEE Trans. Circuits Syst. Video Technol. **28**(10), 2896–2907 (2017)
12. Lang, A.H., Vora, S., Caesar, H., Zhou, L., Yang, J., Beijbom, O.: PointPillars: fast encoders for object detection from point clouds. In: Proceedings of the IEEE/CVF Conference on Computer Vision and Pattern Recognition, pp. 12697–12705 (2019)
13. Li, Z., Wang, F., Wang, N.: LiDAR R-CNN: an efficient and universal 3D object detector. In: Proceedings of the IEEE/CVF Conference on Computer Vision and Pattern Recognition, pp. 7546–7555 (2021)
14. Luo, C., Yang, X., Yuille, A.: Exploring simple 3D multi-object tracking for autonomous driving. In: Proceedings of the IEEE/CVF International Conference on Computer Vision, pp. 10488–10497 (2021)
15. Luo, W., Yang, B., Urtasun, R.: Fast and furious: real time end-to-end 3D detection, tracking and motion forecasting with a single convolutional net. In: Proceedings of the IEEE Conference on Computer Vision and Pattern Recognition, pp. 3569–3577 (2018)
16. Mao, J., Niu, M., Bai, H., Liang, X., Xu, H., Xu, C.: Pyramid R-CNN: towards better performance and adaptability for 3D object detection. In: Proceedings of the IEEE/CVF International Conference on Computer Vision, pp. 2723–2732 (2021)

17. Ngiam, J., et al.: StarNet: targeted computation for object detection in point clouds. arXiv preprint arXiv:1908.11069 (2019)
18. Qi, C.R., Litany, O., He, K., Guibas, L.J.: Deep hough voting for 3D object detection in point clouds. In: Proceedings of the IEEE/CVF International Conference on Computer Vision, pp. 9277–9286 (2019)
19. Qi, C.R., Su, H., Mo, K., Guibas, L.J.: PointNet: deep learning on point sets for 3D classification and segmentation. In: Proceedings of the IEEE Conference on Computer Vision and Pattern Recognition, pp. 652–660 (2017)
20. Qi, C.R., Zhou, Y., Najibi, M., Sun, P., Vo, K., Deng, B., Anguelov, D.: Offboard 3D object detection from point cloud sequences. In: Proceedings of the IEEE/CVF Conference on Computer Vision and Pattern Recognition, pp. 6134–6144 (2021)
21. Qi, C.R., Yi, L., Su, H., Guibas, L.J.: PointNet++: deep hierarchical feature learning on point sets in a metric space. In: Advances in Neural Information Processing Systems, vol. 30 (2017)
22. Sheng, H., et al.: Improving 3D object detection with channel-wise transformer. In: Proceedings of the IEEE/CVF International Conference on Computer Vision, pp. 2743–2752 (2021)
23. Shi, S., Guo, C., Yang, J., Li, H.: PV-RCNN: the top-performing lidar-only solutions for 3D detection/3D tracking/domain adaptation of Waymo open dataset challenges. arXiv preprint arXiv:2008.12599 (2020)
24. Shi, S., et al.: PV-RCNN++: point-voxel feature set abstraction with local vector representation for 3D object detection. arXiv preprint arXiv:2102.00463 (2021)
25. Shi, S., Wang, X., Li, H.: PointRCNN: 3D object proposal generation and detection from point cloud. In: Proceedings of the IEEE/CVF Conference on Computer Vision and Pattern Recognition, pp. 770–779 (2019)
26. Shi, S., Wang, Z., Shi, J., Wang, X., Li, H.: From points to parts: 3D object detection from point cloud with part-aware and part-aggregation network. IEEE Trans. Pattern Anal. Mach. Intell. **43**(8), 2647–2664 (2020)
27. Sun, P., et al.: Scalability in perception for autonomous driving: Waymo open dataset. In: Proceedings of the IEEE/CVF Conference on Computer Vision and Pattern Recognition, pp. 2446–2454 (2020)
28. Sun, P., et al.: RSN: range sparse net for efficient, accurate lidar 3D object detection. In: Proceedings of the IEEE/CVF Conference on Computer Vision and Pattern Recognition, pp. 5725–5734 (2021)
29. Tolstikhin, I.O., et al.: MLP-Mixer: an all-MLP architecture for vision. In: Advances in Neural Information Processing Systems, vol. 34 (2021)
30. Vaswani, A., et al.: Attention is all you need. In: Advances in Neural Information Processing Systems, vol. 30 (2017)
31. Wang, J., Chakraborty, R., Yu, S.X.: Spatial transformer for 3D point clouds. IEEE Trans. Pattern Anal. Mach. Intell. 1 (2021). https://doi.org/10.1109/TPAMI.2021.3070341
32. Wang, S., Zhou, Y., Yan, J., Deng, Z.: Fully motion-aware network for video object detection. In: Ferrari, V., Hebert, M., Sminchisescu, C., Weiss, Y. (eds.) ECCV 2018. LNCS, vol. 11217, pp. 557–573. Springer, Cham (2018). https://doi.org/10.1007/978-3-030-01261-8_33
33. Wang, Y., et al.: Pillar-based object detection for autonomous driving. In: Vedaldi, A., Bischof, H., Brox, T., Frahm, J.-M. (eds.) ECCV 2020. LNCS, vol. 12367, pp. 18–34. Springer, Cham (2020). https://doi.org/10.1007/978-3-030-58542-6_2
34. Wu, H., Chen, Y., Wang, N., Zhang, Z.: Sequence level semantics aggregation for video object detection. In: Proceedings of the IEEE/CVF International Conference on Computer Vision, pp. 9217–9225 (2019)

35. Xiao, F., Lee, Y.J.: Video object detection with an aligned spatial-temporal memory. In: Ferrari, V., Hebert, M., Sminchisescu, C., Weiss, Y. (eds.) ECCV 2018. LNCS, vol. 11212, pp. 494–510. Springer, Cham (2018). https://doi.org/10.1007/978-3-030-01237-3_30

36. Yan, Y., Mao, Y., Li, B.: Second: sparsely embedded convolutional detection. Sensors 18(10), 3337 (2018)

37. Yang, B., Luo, W., Urtasun, R.: PIXOR: real-time 3D object detection from point clouds. In: Proceedings of the IEEE Conference on Computer Vision and Pattern Recognition, pp. 7652–7660 (2018)

38. Yang, Z., Sun, Y., Liu, S., Shen, X., Jia, J.: STD: sparse-to-dense 3D object detector for point cloud. In: Proceedings of the IEEE/CVF International Conference on Computer Vision, pp. 1951–1960 (2019)

39. Yang, Z., Zhou, Y., Chen, Z., Ngiam, J.: 3D-MAN: 3D multi-frame attention network for object detection. In: Proceedings of the IEEE/CVF Conference on Computer Vision and Pattern Recognition, pp. 1863–1872 (2021)

40. Yin, T., Zhou, X., Krahenbuhl, P.: Center-based 3D object detection and tracking. In: Proceedings of the IEEE/CVF Conference on Computer Vision and Pattern Recognition, pp. 11784–11793 (2021)

41. Yuan, Z., Song, X., Bai, L., Wang, Z., Ouyang, W.: Temporal-channel transformer for 3D lidar-based video object detection for autonomous driving. IEEE Trans. Circ. Syst. Video Technol. 1 (2021). https://doi.org/10.1109/TCSVT.2021.3082763

42. Zhou, Y., Tuzel, O.: VoxeLNet: end-to-end learning for point cloud based 3D object detection. In: Proceedings of the IEEE Conference on Computer Vision and Pattern Recognition, pp. 4490–4499 (2018)

43. Zhu, X., Wang, Y., Dai, J., Yuan, L., Wei, Y.: Flow-guided feature aggregation for video object detection. In: Proceedings of the IEEE International Conference on Computer Vision, pp. 408–417 (2017)

44. Zhu, X., Xiong, Y., Dai, J., Yuan, L., Wei, Y.: Deep feature flow for video recognition. In: Proceedings of the IEEE Conference on Computer Vision and Pattern Recognition, pp. 2349–2358 (2017)

Long-tail Detection with Effective Class-Margins

Jang Hyun Cho$^{(\boxtimes)}$ and Philipp Krähenbühl

The University of Texas at Austin, Austin, TX 78712, USA
janghyuncho7@utexas.edu, philkr@cs.utexas.edu
https://github.com/janghyuncho/ECM-Loss

Abstract. Large-scale object detection and instance segmentation face a severe data imbalance. The finer-grained object classes become, the less frequent they appear in our datasets. However, at test-time, we expect a detector that performs well for all classes and not just the most frequent ones. In this paper, we provide a theoretical understanding of the long-trail detection problem. We show how the commonly used mean average precision evaluation metric on an unknown test set is bound by a margin-based binary classification error on a long-tailed object detection training set. We optimize margin-based binary classification error with a novel surrogate objective called **Effective Class-Margin Loss** (ECM). The ECM loss is simple, theoretically well-motivated, and outperforms other heuristic counterparts on LVIS v1 benchmark over a wide range of architecture and detectors. Code is available at https://github.com/janghyuncho/ECM-Loss.

Keywords: Object detection · Long-tail object detection · Long-tail instance segmentation · Margin bound · Loss function

1 Introduction

The state-of-the-art performance of common object detectors has more than tripled over the past 5 years. However, much of this progress is measured on just 80 common object categories [26]. These categories cover only a small portion of our visual experiences. They are nicely balanced and hide much of the complexities of large-scale object detection. In a natural setting, objects follow a long-tail distribution, and artificially balancing them is hard [15]. Many recent large-scale detection approaches instead balance the training loss [38,43,50] or its gradient [23,39] to emulate a balanced training setup. Despite the steady progress over the past few years, these methods largely rely on heuristics or experimental discovery. Consequently, they are often based on intuition, require extensive hyper-parameter tuning, and include a large bag-of-tricks.

Supplementary Information The online version contains supplementary material available at https://doi.org/10.1007/978-3-031-20074-8_40.

S. Avidan et al. (Eds.): ECCV 2022, LNCS 13668, pp. 698–714, 2022.
https://doi.org/10.1007/978-3-031-20074-8_40

In this paper, we take a statistical approach to the problem. The core issue in long-tail recognition is that training and evaluation metrics do not line up, see Fig. 1. At test time, we expect the detector to do well on all classes, not just a select few. This is reflected in the common evaluation metric: mean-average-precision (mAP) [11,15,21,26,37]. At training time, we ideally learn from all available data using a cross-entropy [5,16,35] or related loss [22,25,32,48]. Here, we draw a theoretical connection between the balanced evaluation metric, mAP, and margin-based binary classification. We show that mAP is bound from above and below by a pairwise ranking error, which in turn reduces to binary classification. We address the class imbalance through the theory of margin-bounds [1,4,18,20], and reduce detector training to a margin-based binary classification problem.

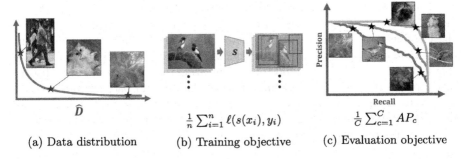

(a) Data distribution   (b) Training objective   (c) Evaluation objective

Fig. 1. In long-trail detection, training objectives (b) do not align with evaluation objectives (c). During training, we optimize an empirical objective on a long-tail data distribution (a). However at test time, we expect a detector that performs well on all classes. In this paper, we connect the detection objective (c) on an unknown test set to an empirical training objective (b) on a long-tail real-world data distribution (a) through the margin-bound theory [1,4,18,20].

Putting it all together, margin-based binary classification provides a closed-form solution for the ideal margin for each object category. This margin depends only on the number of positive and negative annotations for each object category. At training time, we relax the margin-based binary classification problem to binary cross entropy on a surrogate objective. We call this surrogate loss **Effective Class-Margin Loss** (ECM). This relaxation converts margins into weights on the loss function. Our ECM loss is completely *hyperparameter-free* and applicable to a large number of detectors and backbones.

We evaluate the ECM loss on LVIS v1 and OpenImages. It outperforms state-of-the-art large-scale detection approaches across various frameworks and backbones. The ECM loss naturally extends to one-stage detectors [41,48,49,53].

2   Related Works

Object detection is largely divided into one-stage and two-stage pipelines. In one-stage object detection [25,32–34,53], classification and localization are simultaneously predicted densely on each coordinate of feature map representation. Hence, one-stage detection faces extreme foreground-background imbalance aside from cross-category imbalance. These issues are addressed either by carefully engineered loss function such as the Focal Loss [25,53], or sampling heuristics like ATSS [49]. Two-stage object detection [3,14,35] mitigates the foreground-background imbalance using a category-agnostic classifier in the first-stage. However, neither type of detection pipelines handles cross-category imbalance. We show that our ECM loss trains well with both types of detectors.

Long-Tail Detection. Learning under severely long-tailed distribution is challenging. There are two broad categories of approaches: data-based and loss-based. Data-based approaches include external datasets [47], extensive data augmentation with larger backbones [13], or optimized data-sampling strategies [15,44,45]. Loss-based approaches [23,38–40,43,50,51] modify or re-weights the classification loss used to train detectors. They perform this re-weighting either *implicitly* or *explicitly*. The Equalization Loss [39] ignores the negative gradient for rare classes. It builds on the intuition that rare classes are "discouraged" by all the negative gradients of other classes (and background samples). Balanced Group Softmax (BaGS) [23] divides classes into several groups according to their frequency in the training set. BaGS then applies a cross-entropy with softmax only within each group. This implicitly controls the negative gradient to the rare classes from frequent classes and backgrounds. The federated loss [51] only provides negative gradients to classes that appear in an image. This implicitly reduces the impact of the negative gradient to the rare classes. The Equalization Loss v2 [38] directly balances the ratio of cumulative positive and negative gradients per class. The Seesaw Loss [43] similarly uses the class frequency to directly reduce the weight of negative gradients for rare classes. In addition, it compensates for the diminished gradient from misclassifications by scaling up by the ratio of the predicted probability of a class and that of the ground truth class. These methods share the common premise that overwhelming negative gradients will influence the training dynamics of the detector and result in a biased classifier. While this makes intuitive sense, there is little analytical or theoretical justification for particular re-weighting schemes. This paper provides a theoretical link between commonly used mean average precision on a test set and a **weighted binary cross entropy** loss on an unbalanced training set. We provide an optimal weighting scheme that bounds the expected test mAP.

Learning with Class-Margins. Margin-based learning has been widely used in face recognition [10,27,42] and classification under imbalanced data [4]. In fact, assigning proper margins has a long history in bounds to generalization error [1,2,18,20]. Cao et al. [4] showed the effectiveness of analytically derived margins in imbalanced classification. In *separable* two-class setting (i.e., training error can converge to 0), closed form class-margins follow from a simple constrained optimization. Many recent heuristics in long-tail detection use this setting as the basis of re-weighted losses [23,39,43]. We take a slightly different approach. We show that the margin-based classification theory applies to detection by first establishing a connection between mean average precision (mAP) and a pairwise ranking error. This ranking error is bound from above by a margin-based classification loss. This theoretical connection then provides us with a set of weights for a surrogate loss on a *training set* that optimizes the mAP on an *unknown test set*.

Optimizing Average Precision. Several works optimize the average precision metric directly. Rolínek et al. [36] address non-differentiability and introduced black-box differentiation. Chen et al. [7] propose an AP Loss which applies an error-driven update mechanism for the non-differentiable part of the computation graph. Oksuz et al. [30] took a similar approach to optimize for Localization-Recall-Precision (LRP) [29]. In contrast, we reduce average precision to ranking and then margin-based binary classification, which allows us to use tools from learning theory to bound and minimize the generalization error of our detector.

3 Preliminary

Test Error Bound. Classical learning theory bounds the test error in terms of training error and some complexity measures. Much work builds on the Lipschitz bound of Bartlett and Mendelson [2]. For any Lipschitz continuous loss function ℓ, it relates the expected error $\mathcal{L}(f) = E[\ell(f(x), y)]$ and empirical error $\hat{\mathcal{L}}(f) = \frac{1}{n} \sum_{i=1}^{n} \ell(f(x_i), y_i)$ over a dataset of size n with inputs x_i and labels y_i. In detection, we commonly refer to the expected error as a test error over an unknown test set or distribution, and empirical error as a training error. Training and testing data usually follow the same underlying distribution, but different samples.

Theorem 1 (Class-margin bound [4,18]). *Suppose $\ell(x) = 1_{[x<0]}$ a zero-one error and $\ell_\gamma = 1_{[x<\gamma]}$ a margin error with a non-negative margin γ. Similarly, $\mathcal{L}_y(f) = E[\ell(f(x)_y)]$ and $\mathcal{L}_{\gamma,y}(f) = E[\ell_\gamma(f(x)_y)]$. Then, for each class-conditional data distribution $P(X|Y = c)$, for all $f \in \mathcal{F}$ and class-margin $\gamma_c > 0$, with probability $1 - \delta_c$, the class-conditional test error for class $c \in C$ can be bounded from above as following:*

$$\mathcal{L}_c(f) \leq \hat{\mathcal{L}}_{\gamma_c,c}(f) + \frac{4}{\gamma_c} \mathcal{R}_n(\mathcal{F}) + \sqrt{\frac{\log(2/\delta_c)}{n_c}} + \epsilon(n_c, \gamma_c, \delta_c)$$

where $\mathcal{R}_n(\mathcal{F})$ is the Rademacher complexity of a function class $\mathcal{F}$ which is typically bounded by $\sqrt{\frac{C(\mathcal{F})}{n}}$ for some complexity measure of C [1,4,18].

Kakade et al. [18] prove the above theorem for binary classification, and Cao et al. [4] extend it to multi-class classification under a long-tail. Their proof follows Lipschitz bounds of Bartlett and Mendelson [2]. Theorem 1 will be our main tool to bound the generalization error of a detector.

Detection Metrics. Object detection measures the performance of a model through average precision along with different recall values. Let $\mathrm{TP}(t)$, $\mathrm{FP}(t)$, and $\mathrm{FN}(t)$ be the true positive, false positive, and false negative detections for a score threshold t. Let $\mathrm{Pc}(t)$ be the precision and $\mathrm{Rc}(t)$ be the recall. Average precision AP then integrates precision over equally spaced recall thresholds $t \in T$:

$$\mathrm{Pc}(t) = \frac{\mathrm{TP}(t)}{\mathrm{TP}(t) + \mathrm{FP}(t)} \quad \mathrm{Rc}(t) = \frac{\mathrm{TP}(t)}{\mathrm{TP}(t) + \mathrm{FN}(t)} \quad \mathrm{AP} = \frac{1}{|T|} \sum_{t \in T} \mathrm{Pc}(t). \quad (1)$$

Generally, true positives, false positives, and false negatives follow an assignment procedure that enumerates all annotated objects. If a ground truth object has a close-by prediction with a score $s > t$, it counts as a positive. Here closeness is measured by overlap. If there is no close-by prediction, it is a false negative. Any remaining predictions with score $s > t$ count towards false positives. All above metrics are defined on finite sets and do not directly extend general distributions.

In this paper, we base our derivations on a probabilistic version of average precision. For every class $c \in C$, let D_c be the distribution of positive samples, and $D_{\neg c}$ be the distribution of negative samples. These positives and negatives may use an overlap metric to ground truth annotations. Let $P(c)$ and $P(\neg c)$ be the prior probabilities on labels of class c or not c. $P(c)$ is proportional to the number of annotated examples of class c at training time. Let $s_c(x) \in [0,1]$ be the score of a detector for input x. The probability of a detector s_c to produce a true positive of class c with threshold t is $tp_c(t) = P(c)P_{x \sim D_c}(s_c(x) > t)$, false positive $fp_c(t) = P(\neg c)P_{x \sim D_{\neg c}}(s_c(x) > t)$, and false negative $fn_c(t) = P(c)P_{x \sim D_c}(s_c(x) \leq t)$. This leads to a probabilistic recall and precision

$$r_c(t) = \frac{tp_c(t)}{tp_c(t) + fn_c(t)} = \frac{tp_c(t)}{P(c)} = P_{x \sim D_c}(s_c(x) > t), \quad (2)$$

$$p_c(t) = \frac{tp_c(t)}{tp_c(t) + fp_c(t)} = \frac{r_c(t)}{r_c(t) + \alpha_c P_{x \sim D_{\neg c}}(s_c(x) > t)}. \quad (3)$$

Here, $\alpha_c = \frac{P(\neg c)}{P(c)}$ corrects for the different frequency of foreground and background samples for class c. By definition $1 - r_c(t)$ is a cumulative distribution function $r_c(1) = 0$, $r_c(0) = 1$ and $r_c(t) \geq r_c(t + \delta)$ for $\delta > 0$. Without loss of generality, we assume that the recall is strictly monotonous $r_c(t) > r_c(t + \delta)$[1]. For a strictly monotonous recall $r_c(t)$, the quantile function is the inverse $r_c^{-1}(\beta)$. Average precision then integrates over these quantiles.

Definition 1 (Probabilistic average precision).

$$ap_c = \int_0^1 p_c(r_c^{-1}(\beta))d\beta = \int_0^1 \frac{\beta}{\beta + \alpha P_{x \sim D_{\neg c}}(s_c(x) > r_c^{-1}(\beta))} d\beta$$

---

[1] For any detector s_c with a non-strict monotonous recall, there is a nearly identical detector s_c' with strictly monotonous recall: $s_c'(x) = s_c(x)$ with chance $1 - \varepsilon$ and uniform at random $s_c'(x) \in U[0,1]$ with chance ε for any small value $\varepsilon > 0$.

There are two core differences between regular AP and probabilistic AP: 1) The probabilistic formulation scores a nearly exhaustive list of candidate objects, similar to one-stage detectors or the second stage of two-stage detectors. It does not consider bounding box regression. 2) Regular AP penalizes duplicate detections as false positives, probabilistic AP does not. This means that at training time, positives and negatives are strictly defined for probabilistic AP, which makes a proper analysis possible. At test time, non-maxima-suppression removes most duplicate detections without major issues.

In the next section, we show how this probabilistic AP relates to a pairwise ranking error on detections.

Definition 2 (Pairwise Ranking Error).

$$R_c = P_{x,x' \sim D_c \times D_{\neg c}}\big(s_c(x) < s_c(x')\big) = E_{x' \sim D_{\neg c}}\left[1 - r_c(s_c(x'))\right]$$

The pairwise ranking error measures how frequently negative samples x' rank above positives x. The second equality is derived in supplement.

While it is possible to optimize the ranking error empirically, it is hard to bound the empirical error. We instead bound R_c by a margin-based 0–1 classification problem and use Theorem 1.

4   Effective Class-Margins

We aim to train an object detector that performs well for all object classes. This is best expressed by maximizing mean average precision over all classes equally: $mAP = \frac{1}{|C|} \sum_{c \in C} ap_c$. Equivalently, we aim to minimize the detection error

$$\mathcal{L}^{\text{Det}} = 1 - mAP = \frac{1}{|C|} \sum_{c \in C} \underbrace{(1 - ap_c)}_{\mathcal{L}_c^{\text{Det}}} \tag{4}$$

Optimizing the detection error or mAP directly is hard [7,30,31,36]. First, ap_c involves a computation over the entire distribution of detections and does not easily factorize over individual samples. Second, our goal is to optimize the expected detection error. However, at training time, we only have access to an empirical estimate over our training set $\hat{D}$.

Despite these complexities, it is possible to optimize the expected detection error. The core idea follows a series of bounds for each training class c:

$$\mathcal{L}_c^{\text{Det}} \lesssim m_c R_c \lesssim m_c \hat{\mathcal{L}}_{\gamma_c^{\pm},c},$$

where $\lesssim$ refers to inequalities up to a constant. In Sect. 4.1, we bound the detection error $\mathcal{L}_c^{\text{Det}}$ by a weighted version of the ranking error R_c. In Sect. 4.2, we directly optimize an empirical upper bound $\hat{\mathcal{L}}_{\gamma_c^{\pm},c}$ to the weighted ranking error using class-margin-bounds in Theorem 1. Finally, in Sect. 4.3 we present a differentiable loss function to optimize the class-margin-bound.

4.1 Detection Error Bound

There is a strong correlation between the detection error $\mathcal{L}_c^{\mathrm{Det}}$ and the ranking objective R_c. For example, a perfect detector, that scores all positives above negatives, achieves both a ranking and detection error of zero. A detector that scores all negatives higher than positives has a ranking error of 1 and a detection error close to 1. For other error values the the ranking error R_c bounds the ap_c from both above and below, as shown in Fig. 2 and Theorem 2.

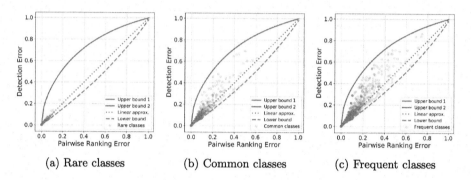

(a) Rare classes   (b) Common classes   (c) Frequent classes

Fig. 2. Visualization of the upper and lower bound of Detection Error with respect to Pairwise Ranking Error. The solid and dotted lines are the theoretical bounds discussed in Theorem 2. We show that **actual detection errors** strictly follow the derived bounds. We evaluate multiple checkpoints of the same detector on rare, common, and frequent classes of lvis v1. Each point represents a checkpoint's performance on one class. We compute AP and ranking errors over the training set which has low errors especially for rare classes. In practice the upper and lower bounds are tight and the linear approximation fits well.

Theorem 2 *(AP - Pairwise Ranking Bound). For a class c with negative-to-positive ratio* $\alpha_c = \frac{P(\neg c)}{P(c)}$, *the ranking error* R_c *bounds the probabilistic average precision* ap_c *from above and below:*

$$\alpha_c \log\left(\frac{1+\alpha_c}{1+\alpha_c - R_c}\right) \leq \mathcal{L}_c^{\mathrm{Det}} \leq \min\left(\sqrt{\frac{2}{3}\alpha_c R_c}, 1 - \frac{8}{9}\frac{1}{1+2\alpha_c R_c}\right).$$

We provide a full proof in supplement and sketch out the proof strategy here. We derive both bounds using a constrained variational problem. For any detector s_c, data distributions D_c and $D_{\neg c}$, the average precision has the form

$$ap_c = \int_0^1 \frac{\beta}{\beta + \alpha g(\beta)} d\beta, \tag{5}$$

where $g(\beta) = P_{x'\sim D_{\neg c}}\left(s_c(x') > r_c^{-1}(\beta)\right) = P_{x'\sim D_{\neg c}}\left(r_c(s_c(x')) < \beta\right)$, since the recall is a strictly monotonously decreasing function. At the same time the ranking loss reduces to

$$R_c = \int_0^1 g(\beta)d\beta = E_{x'\sim D_{\neg c}}\left[1 - r_c(s_c(x'))\right]. \tag{6}$$

For a fixed ranking error $R_c = \kappa$, we find a function $0 \leq g(\beta) \leq 1$ that minimizes or maximizes the detection error $\mathcal{L}_c^{\mathrm{Det}}$ though variational optimization. See supplement for more details. See Fig. 2 for a visualization of the bounds.

Theorem 2 clearly establishes the connection between the ranking and detection. Unfortunately, the exact upper bound is hard to further simplify. We instead chose a linear approximation $\mathcal{L}_c^{\mathrm{Det}} \approx m_c R_c$, for $\alpha_c \log \left(\frac{1+\alpha_c}{\alpha_c} \right) \leq m_c \leq \frac{\frac{1}{2}+2\alpha_c}{1+2\alpha_c}$. Figure 2 visualizes this linear approximation. The linear approximation even bounds the detection error from above $\mathcal{L}_c^{\mathrm{Det}} \leq m_c R_c + o$ with an appropriate offset o. We denote this as $\mathcal{L}_c^{\mathrm{Det}} \lesssim m_c R_c$.

In the next section, we show how this ranking loss is bound from above with a margin-based classification problem, which we minimize in 4.3.

4.2   Ranking Bounds

To connect the ranking loss to the generalization error, we first reduce ranking to binary classification.

Theorem 3 (Binary error bound). *The ranking loss is bound from above by*

$$R_c \leq P_{x \sim D_c}\big(s_c(x) \leq t\big) + P_{x \sim D_{\neg c}}\big(t < s_c(x)\big),$$

for an arbitrary threshold t.

Proof. For any indicator $1_{[a<b]} \leq 1_{[a<t]} + 1_{[t \leq b]}$. Let's first rewrite ranking as expectations over indicator functions:

$$\begin{aligned}
R_c &= E_{x \sim D_c}\left[E_{x' \sim D_{\neg c}}\left[1_{[s_c(x) < s_c(x')]} \right] \right] \\
&\leq E_{x \sim D_c}\left[E_{x' \sim D_{\neg c}}\left[1_{[s_c(x) \leq t]} + 1_{[t < s_c(x')]} \right] \right] \\
&= E_{x \sim D_c}\left[1_{[s_c(x) \leq t]} \right] + E_{x' \sim D_{\neg c}}\left[1_{[t < s_c(x')]} \right].
\end{aligned}$$

The last line uses the linearity of expectation. $\qquad\square$

Figure 3 visualizes this upper bound. While any threshold t leads to an upper bound to ranking. We would like to optimize for the tightest upper bound t. We do this by folding t into the optimization. In a deep network, this simply means optimizing for a bias term of the detector score $s_c(x)$. For the remainder of the exposition, we assume t is part of s_c and use a detection threshold of $\frac{1}{2}$.

Next, lets us use Theorem 1 to bound the classification error, and thus the detection objective, by an empirical bound

$$\mathcal{L}_c^{\mathrm{Det}} \lesssim m_c \left(\hat{\mathcal{L}}_{\gamma_c^+, c} + \hat{\mathcal{L}}_{\gamma_c^-, \neg c} + \frac{2}{\gamma_c^+}\sqrt{\frac{C(\mathcal{F})}{n_c}} + \frac{2}{\gamma_c^-}\sqrt{\frac{C(\mathcal{F})}{n_{\neg c}}} + \epsilon(n_c) + \epsilon(n_{\neg c}) \right), \quad (7)$$

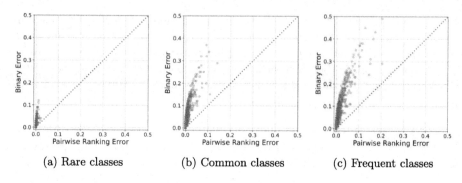

(a) Rare classes   (b) Common classes   (c) Frequent classes

Fig. 3. Visualization of the upper bound of Pairwise Ranking Error with respect to a binary classification error under an optimal threshold t. The blue dots correspond to actual binary errors of a detector. We evaluate multiple checkpoints of the same detector on rare, common, and frequent classes of lvis v1. Each point represents a checkpoint's performance in one class. We compute classification and ranking errors over the training set which has low errors, especially for rare classes. (Color figure online)

where ϵ is a small constant that depends on the number of training samples n_c and $n_{\neg c}$. Here, we use empirical foreground $\hat{\mathcal{L}}_{\gamma_c^+,c} = \frac{1}{n}\sum_{i=1}^{n} 1_{[y_i=c]} 1_{[s_c(\hat{x}_i) \leq \gamma_c^+]}$ and background $\hat{\mathcal{L}}_{\gamma_c^-,\neg c} = \frac{1}{n}\sum_{i=1}^{n} 1_{[y_i \neq c]} 1_{[s_{\neg c}(\hat{x}_i) \leq \gamma_c^-]}$ classification errors for detector s_c. γ_c^+ and γ_c^- are positive and negative margins respectively.

Under a separability assumption, the tightest margins take the form

$$\gamma_c^+ = \frac{n_{\neg c}^{1/4}}{n_c^{1/4} + n_{\neg c}^{1/4}} \qquad \gamma_c^- = \frac{n_c^{1/4}}{n_c^{1/4} + n_{\neg c}^{1/4}}. \tag{8}$$

See Cao et al. [4] or the supplement for a derivation of these margins.

We have now arrived at an upper bound of the detection error $\mathcal{L}^{\text{Det}} = \frac{1}{|C|}\sum_{c \in C} \mathcal{L}_c^{\text{Det}}$ using an empirical margin-based classifier for each class c. This margin-based objective takes the generalization error and any potential class imbalance into account.

In the next section, we derive a continuous loss function for this binary objective and optimize it in a deep-network-based object detection system. Note that standard detector training is already classification-based, and our objective only introduces a margin and weight for each class.

4.3 Effective Class-Margin Loss

Our goal is to minimize the empirical margin-based error

$$\hat{\mathcal{L}}_{\gamma_c^{\pm},c} = \hat{\mathcal{L}}_{\gamma_c^+,c} + \hat{\mathcal{L}}_{\gamma_c^-,\neg c} = \frac{1}{n}\sum_{i=1}^{n}\left(1_{[y_i=c]} 1_{[s_c(\hat{x}_i) \leq \gamma_c^+]} + 1_{[y_i \neq c]} 1_{[s_{\neg c}(\hat{x}_i) \leq \gamma_c^-]}\right) \tag{9}$$

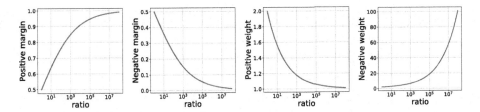

Fig. 4. Visualization of the positive and negative margins and weights as a function of the negative-to-positive ratio α_c.

for a scoring function $s_c(x) \in [0, 1]$. A natural choice of scoring function is a sigmoid $s_c(x) = \frac{\exp(f(x))}{\exp(f(x)) + \exp(-f(x))}$.

However, there is no natural equivalent to a margin-based binary cross-entropy (BCE) loss. Regular binary cross-entropy optimizes a margin $s_c(x) = s_{\neg c}(x) = \frac{1}{2}$ at $f(x) = 0$, which does not conform to our margin-based loss. We instead want to move this decision boundary to $s_c(x) = \gamma_c^+$ and $s_{\neg c}(x) = \gamma_c^-$.

We achieve this with a surrogate **Effective Class-Margin Loss**:

$$\mathcal{L}_c^{\mathrm{ECM}} = -\frac{1}{n} \sum_{i=1}^{n} m_c \left(1_{[y=c]} \log(\hat{s}_c(x)) + 1_{[y \neq c]} \log(1 - \hat{s}_c(x)) \right). \quad (10)$$

The ECM loss optimizes a binary cross entropy on a surrogate scoring function

$$\hat{s}_c(x) = \frac{w_c^+ e^{f(x)_c}}{w_c^+ e^{f(x)_c} + w_c^- e^{-f(x)_c}}, \qquad w_c^\pm = (\gamma_c^\pm)^{-1}. \quad (11)$$

This surrogate scoring function has the same properties as a sigmoid $\hat{s}_c \in [0, 1]$ and $\hat{s}_{\neg c}(x) = 1 - \hat{s}_c(x)$. However, its decision boundary $\hat{s}_c(x) = \hat{s}_{\neg c}(x)$ lies at $f(x) = \frac{1}{2}(\log w_c^- - \log w_c^+)$. In the original sigmoid scoring function s, this decision boundary corresponds to $s_c(x) = \gamma_c^+$ and $s_{\neg c}(x) = \gamma_c^-$. Hence, the **Effective Class-Margin Loss** minimizes the binary classification error under the margins specified by our empirical objective (9). In Fig. 4, we visualize the relationship between the negative-to-positive ratio α_c and the positive and negative class margins/weights.

We use this ECM loss as a plug-in replacement to the standard binary cross entropy or softmax cross entropy used in object detection.

5   Experiments

5.1   Experimental Settings

Datasets. Our method is tested mainly on LVIS v1.0 [15] dataset. LVIS v1.0 is a large-scale object detection and instance segmentation dataset, with includes 1203 object categories which follows extreme long-tail distribution. Object categories in LVIS dataset are divided into three groups by frequency: *frequent,*

Table 1. LVIS v1 validation set results. We compare different methods on various frameworks and backbones on 2× schedule. For Swin-B backbones [28], we use ImageNet-21k pretrained weight as initialization. We used the results of the original papers if available, and reproduced them from the official code otherwise.

Framework	Backbone	Method	mAP$_{segm}$	AP$_r$	AP$_c$	AP$_f$	mAP$_{bbox}$
Mask R-CNN	ResNet-50	CE Loss	22.7	10.6	21.8	29.1	23.3
		Federated Loss [51]	26.0	18.7	24.8	30.6	26.7
		Seesaw Loss [43]	26.7	18.0	26.5	**32.4**	27.3
		LOCE [12]	26.6	18.5	26.2	30.7	27.4
		ECM Loss	**27.4**	**19.7**	**27.0**	31.1	**27.9**
Mask R-CNN	ResNet-101	CE Loss	25.5	16.6	24.5	30.6	26.6
		EQL v1 [39]	26.2	17.0	26.2	30.2	27.6
		BAGS [23]	25.8	16.5	25.7	30.1	26.5
		EQL v2 [38]	27.2	20.6	25.9	31.4	27.9
		Federated Loss [51]	27.9	20.9	26.8	32.3	28.8
		Seesaw Loss [43]	28.1	20.0	**28.0**	31.8	28.9
		LOCE [12]	28.0	19.5	27.8	32.0	29.0
		ECM Loss	**28.7**	21.9	27.9	**32.3**	**29.4**
Cascade Mask R-CNN	ResNet-101	CE Loss	27.0	16.6	26.7	32.0	30.3
		EQL v1 [39]	27.1	17.0	27.2	31.4	30.4
		De-confound TDE [40]	27.1	16.0	26.9	32.1	30.0
		BAGS [23]	27.0	16.9	26.9	31.7	30.2
		Federated Loss [23]	28.6	20.3	27.5	33.4	31.8
		DisAlign [50]	28.9	18.0	29.3	33.3	32.7
		Seesaw Loss [43]	30.1	**21.4**	30.0	33.9	32.8
		ECM Loss	**30.6**	19.7	**30.7**	**35.0**	**33.4**
Cascade Mask R-CNN	Swin-B	Seesaw Loss [43]	38.7	**34.3**	39.6	39.6	42.8
		ECM Loss	**39.7**	33.5	**40.6**	**41.4**	**43.6**

common, and *rare*. Categories that appear on less than 10 images is considered rare, more than 10 but less than 100 is common, and frequent otherwise. There are about 1.3 M instances in the dataset over 120k images (100k train, 20k validation split). Additionally, we test our method on OpenImages Object Detection dataset, another large-scale dataset with 500 object categories over 1.7 M images, with similar degree of long-tail nature.

Evaluation. We test the models trained with ECM Loss and other methods on both the conventional evaluation metric (mAP) as well as the newly proposed metric (mAP$_{fixed}$ [9]). mAP measures the mean average precision over IoU thresholds from 0.5 to 0.95 similar to [26], but for each image the number of detection is extended to 300. mAP$_{fixed}$ [9] improves the original metric by setting no limit for per-image detection but instead setting 10k per-*class* detection predictions over the entire dataset. Please note that due to exploding memory consumption of mask prediction, we limit per-image detection to 800 instead of ∞. We also evaluate based on the boundary IoU (mAP$_{boundary}$ [8]), which is also the new evaluation metric in this year's LVIS Challenge. For OpenImages, we follow evaluation protocol of [52] and measure mAP@0.5.

Table 2. Comparison on LVIS v1 validation set. Models are trained with Mask R-CNN with ResNet-50 backbone on 1x schedule. Numbers with * use a different implementation [9]. $mAP^{fixed}_{boundary}$ and mAP^{fixed}_{bbox} refer to the new LVIS Challenge evaluation metrics [8,9].

Method	mAP_{segm}	AP_r	AP_c	AP_f	mAP_{bbox}	$mAP^{fixed}_{boundary}$	mAP^{fixed}_{bbox}
RFS+CE Loss	21.7	9.5	21.1	27.7	22.2	18.3	25.7
LWS [19]	17.0	2.0	13.5	27.4	17.5	–	–
cRT [19]	22.1	11.9	20.2	29.0	22.2	–	–
BAGS [23]	23.1	13.1	22.5	28.2	23.7	–	26.2*
EQL v2 [38]	23.9	12.5	22.7	30.4	24.0	20.3	25.9
Federated Loss [51]	23.9	15.8	23.3	30.7	24.9	–	26.3*
Seesaw Loss [43]	25.2	16.4	24.4	**30.8**	25.4	19.8	26.5
ECM Loss	**26.3**	**19.5**	**26.0**	29.8	**26.7**	**21.4**	**27.4**

5.2 Implementation Details

Our implementation is based on Detectron2 [46] and MMDetection [6], two most popular open-source libraries for object detection tasks. We train both Mask R-CNN [16] and Cascade Mask R-CNN [3] with various backbones: ResNet-50 and ResNet-101 [17] with Feature Pyramid Network [24], and the Swin Transformer [28]. We use a number of popular one-stage detectors: FCOS [41], ATSS [49] and VarifocalNet [48]. We largely follow the standard COCO and LVIS setup and hyperparameters for all models. For OpenImages, we follow the setup of Zhou et al. [52]. More details are in the supplementary material.

ECM Loss. Our ECM Loss is a plug-in replacement to the sigmoid function used in most detectors. Notably, ECM Loss does not require any hyperparameter. We use the training set from each dataset to measure $\alpha_c, n_c, n_{\neg c}$ of each class.

5.3 Experimental Results

Table 1 compares our approach on frameworks and backbones using a standard 2× training schedule. We compare different long-tail loss functions under different experimental setups. With Mask R-CNN on a ResNet-50 backbone, our ECM Loss outperforms all alternative losses by 0.7 mAP_{segm} and 0.5 mAP_{bbox}. With Mask R-CNN on a ResNet-101 backbone, our ECM loss outperforms alternatives with a 0.6 mAP_{segm} and 0.4 mAP_{bbox}. The results also hold up in the more advanced Cascade R-CNN framework [3] with ResNet-101 and Swin-B backends. Here the gains are 0.5 mAP_{segm} and 0.6 mAP_{bbox} for ResNet-101, and 1 mAP_{segm} and 0.8 mAP_{bbox} for Swin-B. The overall gains over a simple cross-entropy baseline are 3–5 mAP throughout all settings. The consistent improvement in accuracy throughout all settings highlights the empirical efficacy of our method, in addition to the grounding in learning theory.

710   J. Hyun Cho and P. Krähenbühl

Table 3. One-stage object detection results on LVIS v1 validation set. We compare popular one-stage detectors with ResNet-50 and ResNet-101 backbones, on 1x schedule.

Framework	Backbone	Method	AP_r	AP_c	AP_f	mAP_{bbox}
FCOS	ResNet-50	Focal Loss [25]	11.2	21.0	**27.8**	22.0
		ECM Loss	**14.5**	**22.7**	27.6	**23.2**
FCOS	ResNet-101	Focal Loss [25]	14.1	22.6	**29.8**	24.0
		ECM Loss	**17.2**	**24.2**	29.6	**25.1**
ATSS	ResNet-50	Focal Loss [25]	8.6	20.5	**29.8**	22.1
		ECM Loss	**15.8**	**23.5**	29.5	**24.5**
ATSS	ResNet-101	Focal Loss [25]	12.9	24.0	**31.9**	25.2
		ECM Loss	**17.7**	**25.6**	31.5	**26.5**
VarifocalNet	ResNet-50	Varifocal Loss [48]	14.2	23.6	**30.7**	24.8
		ECM Loss	**17.1**	**25.5**	29.7	**25.7**

For reference, Table 2 compares our method on Mask R-CNN with ResNet-50 backbone on 1× schedule. Our ECM Loss outperforms all prior approaches by 1.1 mAP_{segm} and 1.3 mAP_{bbox}. Our method achieves a 10 mAP gain over cross-entropy loss baseline, and 3.1 AP_r gain over the state-of-the-art. Our method shows similar gains on the new evaluation metrics $mAP_{boundary}^{fixed}$ and mAP_{bbox}^{fixed} whereas prior methods tend show a more moderate improvement on new metrics. This improvement is particularly noteworthy, as our approach uses no additional hyperparameters, and is competitive out of the box.

Table 3 compares our ECM Loss with baseline losses on FCOS, ATSS and VarifocalNet, trained with ResNet-50 and ResNet-101 backbones on 1x schedule. The ECM Loss shows consistent gains over Focal Loss and its variants. With FCOS, ECM improves box mAP 1.2 and 1.1 points, respectively, for ResNet-50 and ResNet-101 backbones. With ATSS, ECM Loss improves Focal Loss 7.2 and 4.8 points on AP_r, and 2.4 and 1.3 points mAP, respectively. We further test on VarifocalNet, a recently proposed one-stage detector, and show similar advantage using the ResNet-50 backbone. Our ECM loss consistently improves the overall performance of a one-stage detector, especially in rare classes. It thus serves as a true plug-in replacement to the standard cross-entropy or focal losses.

Table 4 further analyze our ECM Loss with Focal Loss on FCOS and ATSS trained with ResNet-50 backbone on 2x schedule. Our ECM maintains improvement of 0.9 point mAP for FCOS, and 0.5 point mAP for ATSS. For AP_r, both methods consistently improve 2.7 and 2.1 points, respectively.

In Table 5, we compare ECM Loss with a variant of Equalization Loss on the class hierarchy of Zhou et al. [52]. Although OpenImages have a long-tail distribution of classes, the number of classes and the associated prior probabilities are very different. Nevertheless, ECM Loss improves over the baseline for 1.2 mAP. This result confirms the generality of our method.

Table 4. One-stage object detection results on LVIS v1 validation set. We compare different methods with ResNet-50 backbone on 2x schedule.

Framework	Backbone	Method	AP_r	AP_c	AP_f	mAP_{bbox}
FCOS	ResNet-50	Focal Loss	12.0	22.9	**29.5**	23.5
		ECM Loss	**14.7**	**23.0**	**29.5**	**24.4**
ATSS	ResNet-50	Focal Loss	14.5	24.3	**31.8**	25.6
		ECM Loss	**16.6**	**25.2**	31.3	**26.1**

Table 5. Comparisons of ECM Loss on OpenImages dataset following the evaluation protocol of Zhou *et al.* [52]. We compare using a Cascade R-CNN with ResNet-50 backbone.

Framework	Backbone	Method	Schedule	mAP
Cascade R-CNN	ResNet-50	EQL + Hier. [39,52]	2x	64.6
		ECM Loss	2x	**65.8**

For all our experiments, the class frequencies were measured directly from the annotation set of LVIS v1 training dataset. Note that for each class, the negative sample not only includes other foreground classes but also the background class. However, the prior probability for background class is not defined apriori from the dataset itself since it solely depends on the particular detection framework of choice. Hence, we measure the background frequency for each detector of choice and factor it into the final derivation of overall class frequencies. This can be done within the first few iterations during training. We then compute the effective class-margins with the derived optimal solution in Eq. (8) and finally define the surrogate scoring function (11).

6   Conclusion

In this paper, we tackle the long-tail object detection problem using a statistical approach. We connect the training objective and the detection evaluation objective in the form of margin theory. We show how a probabilistic version of average precision is optimized using a ranking and then margin-based binary classification problem. We present a novel loss function, called Effective Class-Margin (ECM) Loss, to optimize the margin-based classification problem. This ECM loss serves as a plug-in replacement to standard cross-entropy-based losses across various detection frameworks, backbones, and detector designs. The ECM loss consistently improves the performance of the detector in a long-tail setting. The loss is simple and hyperparameter-free.

Acknowledgments. This material is in part based upon work supported by the National Science Foundation under Grant No. IIS-1845485 and IIS-2006820.

References

1. Bartlett, P., Foster, D.J., Telgarsky, M.: Spectrally-normalized margin bounds for neural networks. arXiv preprint arXiv:1706.08498 (2017)
2. Bartlett, P.L., Mendelson, S.: Rademacher and gaussian complexities: risk bounds and structural results. J. Mach. Learn. Res. **3**, 463–482 (2003)
3. Cai, Z., Vasconcelos, N.: Cascade R-CNN: delving into high quality object detection. In: Proceedings of the IEEE Conference on Computer Vision and Pattern Recognition, pp. 6154–6162 (2018)
4. Cao, K., Wei, C., Gaidon, A., Arechiga, N., Ma, T.: Learning imbalanced datasets with label-distribution-aware margin loss. arXiv preprint arXiv:1906.07413 (2019)
5. Carion, N., Massa, F., Synnaeve, G., Usunier, N., Kirillov, A., Zagoruyko, S.: End-to-end object detection with transformers. In: Vedaldi, A., Bischof, H., Brox, T., Frahm, J.-M. (eds.) ECCV 2020. LNCS, vol. 12346, pp. 213–229. Springer, Cham (2020). https://doi.org/10.1007/978-3-030-58452-8_13
6. Chen, K., et al.: MMDetection: open MMLab detection toolbox and benchmark. arXiv preprint arXiv:1906.07155 (2019)
7. Chen, K., Lin, W., Li, J., See, J., Wang, J., Zou, J.: AP-loss for accurate one-stage object detection. IEEE Trans. Pattern Anal. Mach. Intell. **43**(11), 3782–3798 (2020)
8. Cheng, B., Girshick, R., Dollár, P., Berg, A.C., Kirillov, A.: Boundary IoU: improving object-centric image segmentation evaluation. In: Proceedings of the IEEE/CVF Conference on Computer Vision and Pattern Recognition, pp. 15334–15342 (2021)
9. Dave, A., Dollár, P., Ramanan, D., Kirillov, A., Girshick, R.: Evaluating large-vocabulary object detectors: the devil is in the details. arXiv preprint arXiv:2102.01066 (2021)
10. Deng, J., Guo, J., Xue, N., Zafeiriou, S.: ArcFace: additive angular margin loss for deep face recognition. In: Proceedings of the IEEE/CVF Conference on Computer Vision and Pattern Recognition, pp. 4690–4699 (2019)
11. Everingham, M., Van Gool, L., Williams, C.K.I., Winn, J., Zisserman, A.: The pascal visual object classes (VOC) challenge. Int. J. Comput. Vision **88**(2), 303–338 (2010)
12. Feng, C., Zhong, Y., Huang, W.: Exploring classification equilibrium in long-tailed object detection. In: ICCV (2021)
13. Ghiasi, G., et al.: Simple copy-paste is a strong data augmentation method for instance segmentation. In: Proceedings of the IEEE/CVF Conference on Computer Vision and Pattern Recognition, pp. 2918–2928 (2021)
14. Girshick, R.: Fast R-CNN. In: Proceedings of the IEEE International Conference on Computer Vision, pp. 1440–1448 (2015)
15. Gupta, A., Dollar, P., Girshick, R.: LVIS: a dataset for large vocabulary instance segmentation. In: Proceedings of the IEEE/CVF Conference on Computer Vision and Pattern Recognition, pp. 5356–5364 (2019)
16. He, K., Gkioxari, G., Dollár, P., Girshick, R.: Mask R-CNN. In: Proceedings of the IEEE International Conference on Computer Vision, pp. 2961–2969 (2017)
17. He, K., Zhang, X., Ren, S., Sun, J.: Deep residual learning for image recognition. In: Proceedings of the IEEE Conference on Computer Vision and Pattern Recognition, pp. 770–778 (2016)
18. Kakade, S.M., Sridharan, K., Tewari, A.: On the complexity of linear prediction: risk bounds, margin bounds, and regularization. In: Proceedings of the 21st International Conference on Neural Information Processing Systems, NIPS'08, Curran Associates Inc., Red Hook, NY, USA, pp. 793–800 (2008)

19. Kang, B., et al.: Decoupling representation and classifier for long-tailed recognition. In: International Conference on Learning Representations (2020). https://openreview.net/forum?id=r1gRTCVFvB
20. Koltchinskii, V., Panchenko, D.: Empirical margin distributions and bounding the generalization error of combined classifiers. Ann. Stat. **30**(1), 1–50 (2002)
21. Kuznetsova, A., et al.: The open images dataset v4. Int. J. Comput. Vision **128**(7), 1956–1981 (2020)
22. Li, X., et al.: Generalized focal loss: learning qualified and distributed bounding boxes for dense object detection. In: Advances in Neural Information Processing Systems, vol. 33, pp. 21002–21012 (2020)
23. Li, Y., et al.: Overcoming classifier imbalance for long-tail object detection with balanced group softmax. In: Proceedings of the IEEE/CVF Conference on Computer Vision and Pattern Recognition, pp. 10991–11000 (2020)
24. Lin, T.Y., Dollár, P., Girshick, R., He, K., Hariharan, B., Belongie, S.: Feature pyramid networks for object detection. In: Proceedings of the IEEE Conference on Computer Vision and Pattern Recognition, pp. 2117–2125 (2017)
25. Lin, T.Y., Goyal, P., Girshick, R., He, K., Dollár, P.: Focal loss for dense object detection. In: Proceedings of the IEEE International Conference on Computer Vision, pp. 2980–2988 (2017)
26. Lin, T.-Y., et al.: Microsoft COCO: common objects in context. In: Fleet, D., Pajdla, T., Schiele, B., Tuytelaars, T. (eds.) ECCV 2014. LNCS, vol. 8693, pp. 740–755. Springer, Cham (2014). https://doi.org/10.1007/978-3-319-10602-1_48
27. Liu, W., Wen, Y., Yu, Z., Yang, M.: Large-margin softmax loss for convolutional neural networks. In: International Conference on Machin Learning, vol. 2, p. 7 (2016)
28. Liu, Z., et al.: Swin transformer: hierarchical vision transformer using shifted windows. In: International Conference on Computer Vision (ICCV) (2021)
29. Oksuz, K., Cam, B.C., Akbas, E., Kalkan, S.: Localization recall precision (LRP): a new performance metric for object detection. In: Ferrari, V., Hebert, M., Sminchisescu, C., Weiss, Y. (eds.) ECCV 2018. LNCS, vol. 11211, pp. 521–537. Springer, Cham (2018). https://doi.org/10.1007/978-3-030-01234-2_31
30. Oksuz, K., Cam, B.C., Akbas, E., Kalkan, S.: A ranking-based, balanced loss function unifying classification and localisation in object detection. In: Advances in Neural Information Processing Systems (NeurIPS) (2020)
31. Oksuz, K., Cam, B.C., Akbas, E., Kalkan, S.: Rank & sort loss for object detection and instance segmentation. In: International Conference on Computer Vision (ICCV) (2021)
32. Redmon, J., Divvala, S., Girshick, R., Farhadi, A.: You only look once: unified, real-time object detection. In: Proceedings of the IEEE Conference on Computer Vision and Pattern Recognition, pp. 779–788 (2016)
33. Redmon, J., Farhadi, A.: YOLO9000: better, faster, stronger. In: Proceedings of the IEEE Conference on Computer Vision and Pattern Recognition, pp. 7263–7271 (2017)
34. Redmon, J., Farhadi, A.: YOLOv3: an incremental improvement. arXiv preprint arXiv:1804.02767 (2018)
35. Ren, S., He, K., Girshick, R., Sun, J.: Faster R-CNN: towards real-time object detection with region proposal networks. In: Advances in Neural Information Processing Systems, vol. 28, pp. 91–99 (2015)

36. Rolinek, M., Musil, V., Paulus, A., Vlastelica, M., Michaelis, C., Martius, G.: Optimizing rank-based metrics with blackbox differentiation. In: Proceedings of the IEEE/CVF Conference on Computer Vision and Pattern Recognition (CVPR) (2020)
37. Shao, S., et al.: Objects365: a large-scale, high-quality dataset for object detection. In: Proceedings of the IEEE/CVF International Conference on Computer Vision (ICCV) (2019)
38. Tan, J., Lu, X., Zhang, G., Yin, C., Li, Q.: Equalization loss v2: a new gradient balance approach for long-tailed object detection. In: Proceedings of the IEEE/CVF Conference on Computer Vision and Pattern Recognition, pp. 1685–1694 (2021)
39. Tan, J., et al.: Equalization loss for long-tailed object recognition. In: Proceedings of the IEEE/CVF Conference on Computer Vision and Pattern Recognition, pp. 11662–11671 (2020)
40. Tang, K., Huang, J., Zhang, H.: Long-tailed classification by keeping the good and removing the bad momentum causal effect. In: Conference on Neural Information Processing Systems (2020)
41. Tian, Z., Shen, C., Chen, H., He, T.: FCOS: fully convolutional one-stage object detection. In: Proceedings of the IEEE/CVF International Conference on Computer Vision, pp. 9627–9636 (2019)
42. Wang, F., Cheng, J., Liu, W., Liu, H.: Additive margin softmax for face verification. IEEE Signal Process. Lett. **25**(7), 926–930 (2018)
43. Wang, J., Zhang, et al.: Seesaw loss for long-tailed instance segmentation. In: Proceedings of the IEEE/CVF Conference on Computer Vision and Pattern Recognition, pp. 9695–9704 (2021)
44. Wang, T., et al.: The devil is in classification: a simple framework for long-tail instance segmentation. arXiv preprint arXiv:2007.11978 (2020)
45. Wu, J., Song, L., Wang, T., Zhang, Q., Yuan, J.: Forest R-CNN: large-vocabulary long-tailed object detection and instance segmentation. In: Proceedings of the 28th ACM International Conference on Multimedia, pp. 1570–1578 (2020)
46. Wu, Y., Kirillov, A., Massa, F., Lo, W.Y., Girshick, R.: Detectron2 (2019). https://github.com/facebookresearch/detectron2
47. Zhang, C., et al.: MosaicOS: a simple and effective use of object-centric images for long-tailed object detection. In: Proceedings of the IEEE/CVF International Conference on Computer Vision, pp. 417–427 (2021)
48. Zhang, H., Wang, Y., Dayoub, F., Sunderhauf, N.: VarifocalNet: an IoU-aware dense object detector. In: Proceedings of the IEEE/CVF Conference on Computer Vision and Pattern Recognition, pp. 8514–8523 (2021)
49. Zhang, S., Chi, C., Yao, Y., Lei, Z., Li, S.Z.: Bridging the gap between anchor-based and anchor-free detection via adaptive training sample selection. In: Proceedings of the IEEE/CVF Conference on Computer Vision and Pattern Recognition, pp. 9759–9768 (2020)
50. Zhang, S., Li, Z., Yan, S., He, X., Sun, J.: Distribution alignment: a unified framework for long-tail visual recognition. In: Proceedings of the IEEE/CVF Conference on Computer Vision and Pattern Recognition, pp. 2361–2370 (2021)
51. Zhou, X., Koltun, V., Krähenbühl, P.: Probabilistic two-stage detection. arXiv preprint arXiv:2103.07461 (2021)
52. Zhou, X., Koltun, V., Krähenbühl, P.: Simple multi-dataset detection. In: arXiv preprint arXiv:2102.13086 (2021)
53. Zhou, X., Wang, D., Krähenbühl, P.: Objects as points. arXiv preprint arXiv:1904.07850 (2019)

Semi-supervised Monocular 3D Object Detection by Multi-view Consistency

Qing Lian[1], Yanbo Xu[1], Weilong Yao[3], Yingcong Chen[1,2],
and Tong Zhang[1,4(✉)]

[1] The Hong Kong University of Science and Technology, Hong Kong, China
{qlianab,yxubu}@connect.ust.hk, {yingcongchen,tongzhang}@ust.hk
[2] The Hong Kong University of Science and Technology, Guangzhou, China
[3] Autowise.AI, Shanghai, China
yaoweilong@autowise.ai
[4] Google Research, San Francisco, USA

Abstract. The success of monocular 3D object detection highly relies on considerable labeled data, which is costly to obtain. To alleviate the annotation effort, we propose MVC-MonoDet, the first semi-supervised training framework that improves **Mono**cular 3D object **det**ection by enforcing **multi-view** consistency. In particular, a box-level regularization and an object-level regularization are designed to enforce the consistency of 3D bounding box predictions of the detection model across unlabeled multi-view data (stereo or video). The box-level regularizer requires the model to consistently estimate 3D boxes in different views so that the model can learn cross-view invariant features for 3D detection. The object-level regularizer employs an object-wise photometric consistency loss that mitigates 3D box estimation error through structure-from-motion (SFM). A key innovation in our approach to effectively utilize these consistency losses from multi-view data is a novel relative depth module that replaces the standard depth module in vanilla SFM. This technique allows the depth estimation to be coupled with the estimated 3D bounding boxes, so that the derivative of consistency regularization can be used to directly optimize the estimated 3D bounding boxes using unlabeled data. We show that the proposed semi-supervised learning techniques effectively improve the performance of 3D detection on the KITTI and nuScenes datasets. We also demonstrate that the framework is flexible and can be adapted to both stereo and video data.

Keywords: Monocular 3D object detection · Semi-supervised training · Structure from motion

1 Introduction

Localizing objects in 3D space is an essential task in autonomous driving, which enables systems to perceive and understand surrounding environments. Motivated

---

Supplementary Information The online version contains supplementary material available at https://doi.org/10.1007/978-3-031-20074-8_41.

S. Avidan et al. (Eds.): ECCV 2022, LNCS 13668, pp. 715–731, 2022.
https://doi.org/10.1007/978-3-031-20074-8_41

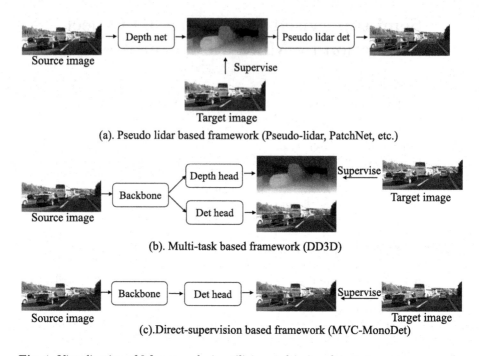

Fig. 1. Visualization of 3 frameworks in utilizing multi-view data to improve monocular 3D detection. (a) The pseudo-lidar based framework [27,44] can use multi-view images to improve depth estimation model, leading to better image to lidar data conversion. (b) The multi-task framework (*e.g.,* DD3D [30]) builds a shared backbone for 3D detection and depth estimation. The multi-view data can be leveraged to train a stronger backbone by depth estimation. (c) Our MVC-MonoDet provides *direct* supervision signals for the detection model and no latent depth estimation module is required.

by the cheap and easy-to-deploy properties, academia and industry have been made a great effort to tackle monocular-based 3D object detection. Recently, deep learning based approaches [2,5,6,20,29,50,54] have achieved great success, leading to sophisticated deep neural networks as the main solution. The training of such neural networks often requires a large amount of high-quality labeled data. However, labeling 3D annotation is very tedious and expensive, as even humans can not directly annotate the ground-truth from a single image perfectly [4,13].

Typically, semi-supervised learning is a promising direction to relieve the annotation burden. Existing approaches [23,39,41,49,51] have primarily focused on 2D tasks. However, recent work [29] identifies that the 3D detection performance is dominated by accurately regressing the 3D attributes (3D location, dimension and orientation). To improve the performance of the 3D attributes regression, we consider utilizing unlabeled multi-view data (stereo or video) to provide external 3D supervision. Meanwhile, the unlabeled multi-view data in autonomous driving scenarios is abundant and cheap to collect.

Existing monocular 3D detectors can utilize the multi-view data from two perspectives: data conversion in pseudo-lidar [44,48] and shared representation in multi-task [30] frameworks. As visualized in Fig. 1, these two frameworks require intermediate pixel-level depth representation to bridge the 3d detection with multi-view data. However, the objectives of these two tasks are different, where depth estimation focuses on background and object surface, but 3D detection only considers the object center. This difference may cause the supervision bias to the background regions and ignore the object-level 3D attributes. Furthermore, it is also demonstrated [11,22] that neural networks learn different visual cues for these two tasks.

To better utilize the multi-view data, we design two kinds of multi-view consistency regularization that provide *direct* supervision signals on the foreground objects. (1) From the box space, we enforce the model to estimate consistent 3D bounding boxes in different views. This regularizes the model to learn robust features for different view angles and positions, leading to better generalization on the unlabeled and unseen data.

(2) From the object space, we design an object-wise photometric consistency module that utilizes structure-from-motion (SFM) to directly optimize 3D box. The vanilla SFM learner [14,52] is tailored for depth estimation that leverages the photometric error between the source and projected views to represent and mitigate depth error. However, the standard depth estimation module in vanilla SFM is not coupled with 3D bounding boxes, and the corresponding SFM module can not be directly used to optimize 3D box positions. Inspired by Stereo R-CNN [19], we design a relative depth module that couples pixel-level depth with 3D boxes, so that the cross-view photometric consistency can be used to directly optimize the detection error. Based on this technique, we can directly mitigate the bounding boxes error by regularizing the cross-view photometric consistency.

We validate the effectiveness of our MVC-MonoDet on two standard 3D detection benchmarks: KITTI [13] and nuScenes [4] datasets. On the KITTI dataset, we show that the proposed approach can leverage stereo or video data to improve the state-of-the-art fully-supervised approaches with 22% and 11%. On the nuScenes dataset, we witness a relative 18% and 5% improvement with 10% and 100% of labeled data.

Our main contributions are as follows:

- We provide the first multi-view semi-supervised training framework for monocular 3D object detection. The framework leverages abundant and cheap unlabeled multi-view data to alleviate 3D annotation burden.
- Based on the multi-view framework, a box-level and an object-level consistency regularization are proposed to improve the 3D detector, and a relative depth module is proposed to allow effective coupling of 3D box error with the consistency losses.
- Experimental results on the KITTI and nuScenes datasets demonstrate the effectiveness of our semi-supervised learning framework with different types of multi-view data.

2   Related Work

We briefly review the recent work on monocular 3D object detection, semi-supervised object detection and self-supervised learning with multi-view data.

2.1   Monocular 3D Object Detection

Traditional monocular 3D object detection methods [2, 6, 7, 35, 38, 54] recover the 3D bounding boxes by using the shape priors, semantic information, ground plane assumption, *etc.*. To alleviate the challenging depth recovery, later work [8, 25, 38] pays more attention to the design of training pipelines [25, 29] and loss function [38]. Except for directly adopting neural networks to estimate depth, several studies [5, 20, 21, 24] propose to reason depth by solving the geometric constraints between 2D and 3D coordinates.

In addition, some approaches adopt pixel-level depth estimation models to assist the 3D detection. Pseudo-lidar based approaches [27, 28, 44] project the image and depth data into pseudo point cloud and adopt point cloud detectors [17, 33, 34] to localize objects. Except for projecting the input modality, D4LCN and it's follow-up [12, 42] leverage depth map to build dynamic convolution or graph propagation modules for better extracting 3D features in 2D space. DD3D [30] proposes a multi-task framework that leverages depth estimation to pre-train a strong feature representation for 3D object detection. By connecting depth estimation with 3D object detection, the large-scale unlabeled multi-view images can be utilized to improve the performance of 3D detection.

2.2   Semi-supervised Object Detection

Due to the heavy annotation burden in object detection, great efforts have been made to leverage unlabeled or weakly annotated data to improve performance. Inspired by the success of confidence regularization in semi-supervised classification, one line of approaches [15, 31, 40] focus on designing consistency regularization methods with different kinds of image perturbation. Another line of approaches [23, 39, 41, 49, 51] leverage neural networks to annotate pseudo labels for self-training. Despite the fast development in semi-supervised object detection, there is only one semi-supervised approach [21] for monocular 3D object detection. Li et al. [21] propose a consistency regularization method on a keypoint-constraint based approach [20], where the consistency regularization is employed on the intermediate keypoint detection task. However, due to the intermediate regularization, KM3D [21] only can be adopted to the keypoint-based approaches, while they are less effective compared to other end-to-end detectors [25, 32, 50]. By contrast, our work provides supervision signals on the final output, which is flexible and can be applied to arbitrary monocular 3D object detectors.

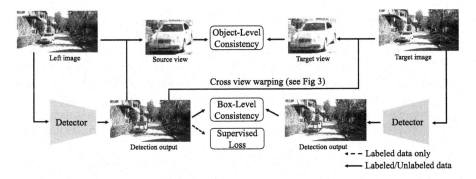

Fig. 2. Visualization of our multi-view semi-supervised training pipeline for monocular 3D object detection.

2.3 Self-supervised Learning with Multi-view Data

It is a popular topic that trains a model to recover 3D information (*e.g.*, depth, ego-motion, flow, *etc.*) by unlabeled multi-view data. One group of methods take the multi-view consistency by structure from motion (SFM) to train neural networks for 3D reconstruction. Specifically, the supervision signal is obtained by pursuing photometric consistency between the origin frame and the reconstructed nearby frame, where the reconstructed nearby frame is warped by using the estimated depth and camera intrinsic [1,14,47,52]. Traditional work [47] first takes the calibrated stereo camera to achieve the unsupervised depth training. Except for stereo data, video data is another cheap and easy-to-collect alternative for providing multi-view observations. However, the video data is unstructured, requiring further to estimate the ego and object poses. Zhou et al. [52] first design a unified framework that jointly trains a depth estimation and a camera motion model by minimizing the photometric error between the source and projected target frames. To address the scale inconsistent problem, Bian et al. [1] propose a geometric consistency loss to regularize the inconsistency prediction between adjacent views. Later studies further estimate object masks [14] or predict the object motion [18] to handle the occluded regions or dynamic objects.

However, little attention was paid to leveraging the multi-view information for monocular 3D object detection. One potential reason is that the cross-view warping in SFM requires the depth for each pixel surface, however, 3D detection only estimates the depth of object center. To mitigate this mismatch, we propose a relative depth module that recovers the per-pixel depth by object shape and estimated bounding boxes.

3   Background

Given an input image, the objectives of monocular 3D object detection are to recognize the interested objects and localize the corresponding 3D boxes. In our semi-supervised learning setting, we have a labeled split $\{I_s^i, I_t^i, T_{s \to t}^i, y^i\}_{i=1}^{N_l}$

with N_l labeled samples and unlabeled split $\{I_s^i, I_t^i, T_{s \to t}^i\}_{i=1}^{N_u}$ with N_u unlabeled samples, where I_s and I_t denote the multi-view image, and $T_{s \to t} \in R^{4 \times 4}$ denotes the ego-pose matrix for cross-view projection. In this paper, we use $u \in R^{1 \times 2}$ and $p \in R^{1 \times 3}$ to denote a point in 2D and 3D coordinates, respectively. $K \in R^{3 \times 3}$ denotes the camera intrinsic, and $I(p, K)$ represents the corresponding pixel indexed by point p. The label y comprises a set of 3D bounding boxes, which are represented by the eight corner points in the box: $b \in \mathcal{R}^{8 \times 3}$. In autonomous driving, the 3D bounding box can be further decomposed to object 3D location, dimension, and yaw angle.

The multi-view images can come from a stereo camera or a monocular camera with different time stamps (video). Our baseline model is the modified version of the one-stage detector CenterNet [53,54] and adds several parallel heads for estimating the 3D attributes.

4   Approach

With unlabeled multi-view data, traditional approaches [14,52] leverage multi-view consistency to train a per-pixel depth estimation network. However, as aforementioned, the supervision through the intermediate depth representation is not specialized for 3D detection, which may lead to sub-optimal utilization. Our framework provides two direct consistency regularization terms tailored for monocular 3D object detection. Figure 2 describes the overview of our multi-view semi-supervised training framework. Specifically, we introduce a box-level and an object-level consistency regularization techniques to a monocular 3D object detection model. From the box-level one, we regularize the model to estimate consistent 3D box attributes for the images taken from different views. This regularizes the model to be robust to variant view angles and positions. From the object-level one, we design an object-level photometric consistency loss to identify and mitigate bounding boxes error. It is worthy to note that during inference, only a single image is required to predict 3D bounding boxes.

4.1   Box-Level Consistency

Given input images from different views, Box-Level Consistency (BLC) regularization enforces the estimated 3D boxes to be consistent in a rectified coordinate. This means that after converting the estimated 3D box to the target image, its attributes should match with the box estimated in the target image. Given the cross-view ego pose $T_{s \to t}$, the consistency loss is represented as:

$$\mathcal{L}_{output} = \frac{1}{N_b} \sum_{i=1}^{N_b} \|[\hat{b}_s^i, 1]T_{s \to t}^T - \hat{b}_t^i\|, \tag{1}$$

where $\hat{b}_s$ and $\hat{b}_t$ denote the boxes estimated in the source and target images, and N_b denotes the number of selected candidate boxes. In the video data, we further model the object motion [9] in the source to target conversion process.

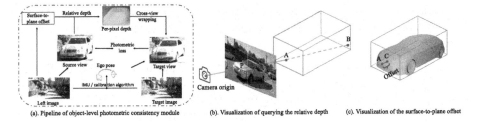

(a). Pipeline of object-level photometric consistency module   (b). Visualization of querying the relative depth   (c). Visualization of the surface-to-plane offset

Fig. 3. (a). Visualization of the pipeline in computing the object-level photometric loss. The ego pose comes from pre-calibration (stereo) or the external hardware device and calibration algorithm (video). (b). A ray emitted from the camera origin to the pixel P in the image. It intersects with bounding box planes at points A and B. Point B is occluded by A (c). Points A and C lie on the bounding box planes and object surface, respectively.

In practice, one image may contain multiple objects. Therefore, matching the 3D boxes across images is necessary. In this paper, we propose a simple yet effective solution to achieve this. Popular 3D detection methods like MonoDLE [29] and CenterNet [54] produce 2D boxes in parallel with a 3D ones. The estimated 2D boxes are more accurate than the 3D boxes even with limited training data (See Appendix for illustration). Hence, we utilize the pixels in the region spanned by the 2D boxes to match 3D boxes. For each source box b_s^i, we calculate the SSIM [45] similarity scores with all the boxes in the target image and select the box that achieves the minimum SSIM scores as the paired target box b_t^i. To filter the background region, we filter out the bounding boxes that the estimated class confidence is smaller than 0.5.

4.2   Object-Level Consistency

Note the box-level consistency regularization does not directly mitigate the prediction error but improves the performance through enhancing the model robustness. Furthermore, it can only provide sparse supervision. In this section, we propose an Object-Level Consistency (OLC) regularization to further leverage multi-view information for dense supervision.

The proposed OLC regularizes the photometric consistency between two views within bounding boxes. Specifically, OLC first utilizes SFM to reconstruct the source view of the objects by projecting the target views. Then we utilize the per-pixel photometric consistency to identify the bounding box prediction error. Note that the estimated bounding boxes are coupled with the depth used in the cross-view projection so that the consistency loss can reflect the localization error. Through enhancing the per-pixel photometric consistency, OLC provides much denser supervision than BLC regularization. The training procedure of one iteration is summarized as follows.

Step 1. We generate the source view by 3D boxes. On the labeled image, we directly take the ground truth. On the unlabeled images, we leverage the detector to predict the 3D boxes. We refer the source image area spanned by the 3D box as the source view. See the image patch of the source view as an example in Fig. 3.

Step 2. We project the source view to the target view by the 3D boxes. Specifically, for each point in the source view, we calculate its projected location in the target view. The target image area spanned by the set of projected points is referred as the target view. Note that a source-to-target projection can not be done without knowing each pixel's depth in the source view. To this end, we design a *relative depth* with a *surface-to-cube offset head* to infer each pixel's depth through the 3D box. See details in Sect. 4.2.1.

Step 3. An object-level photometric loss is computed to measure the misalignment between the source and target views. To filter the noise in the view projection process, we also model the shape uncertainty to get an accurate photometric loss. See details in Sect. 4.2.2.

4.2.1   Target View Projection by Relative Depth

This section presents the relative depth module used in Step 2, which infers each pixel's depth of the object's surface through a 3D box. To achieve this, we first start from a cube-shaped assumption that models all the objects as cube-shaped [19], and progressively learn the shape during training.

With a cube-shaped assumption, we can infer the depth of each pixel by a ray forwarding process [19] in a pinhole camera. Specifically, we first emit a ray from the camera origin o to the pixel in the source view p with vector op (see the solid red line in Fig. 3.b for an example). Under the cube-shaped assumption, the pixel would be the perspective projection of a certain 3D point on the 3D box plane. In other words, the 3D point is the intersection between the ray and the 3D box planes. The intersections can be represented with $\{op \times bb^{ij}\}_{j=1}^{6}$, where b^{ij} denotes the jth direction vector of the bounding box i. Invalid intersections can be filtered out by checking if they are inside the 3D box. Finally, only the closest intersection j^* to the camera is selected when occlusion occurs:

$$j^* = \arg\min_{j}\{op \times bb^{ij}|_z\}_{j=1}^{6}, \tag{2}$$

where $|_z$ denotes the depth in of the intersection. Figure 3.b provides an example for the occlusion. Since the direction vector is based on the estimated 3D box, the gradient from the photometric loss can be directly back-propagated to the estimated 3D boxes. We present the details of generating the direction vector in the Appendix.

Surface-to-Plane Offset. As visualized in Fig. 3.c, most of the pixels satisfy the cube-shaped assumption, especially for the side and bottom parts of the car. However, we found that this assumption does not always hold for variant regions (*e.g.,* car's corners, windshield, etc.). This observation motivates us to design a regression head to model the object shape. Specifically, the regression head leans an offset ΔZ that fills the gap between the depth computed from the cube-shaped assumption with the actual depth. See an offset example in Fig. 3.c. Through modeling this offset, the projection process is robust to variant shapes, leading to accurate supervision signals for object localization. Finally, given a point u_s in the 2D coordinate of the source image, its corresponding 3D point can be acquired by $p_s = \pi(b, u, K, \Delta Z)$, where b, u, K, ΔZ represent the 3D box, 2D point, camera intrinsic, and the estimated offset, respectively. Note that the box b can be selected from the ground truth and the estimated bounding boxes. In the labeled data, we adopt the ground truth boxes to let the network learn the offset. In the unlabeled data, we adopt the estimated 3D boxes and jointly optimize the box and offset.

4.2.2 Object-Level Photometric Loss

After the view projection, we can acquire the pixels in the source view with $I_s(p_s, K)$ and $I_t(T_{s \rightarrow t}p_s, K)$, and compute their photometric consistency loss.

It should be noted that in practice, some pixels in the objects are less informative, and matching them makes learning unstable. We propose an uncertainty-aware model to deal with this problem. Specifically, we model the uncertainty of the surface-to-plane offset and treat it as a re-weighting factor when computing the object-level photometric loss. In particular, we model the distribution of the offset as a Laplacian distribution based on ℓ_1 error [16,29]. And the loss for one object is represented as follows:

$$\mathcal{L}_{photo}(p_s, \hat{p}_{s \rightarrow t}) = \frac{1}{N_p} \sum_{i=1}^{N_p} \frac{\sqrt{2}}{\sigma_i} \|I_s(p_s^i, K), I_t([p_s^i, 1]T_{s \rightarrow t}^T, K)\| + \log \sigma_i, \qquad (3)$$

where N_p is the number of points and σ_i is the standard deviation of the offset. Intuitively, this uncertainty reweighting is similar to the curriculum learning in pseudo labeling for object classification: iteratively enlarges the training set from easy to complex data.

4.3 Overall Loss

The overall loss function in our semi-supervised training framework is represented as follows:

$$\mathcal{L}_{sup} = \mathcal{L}_{det} + \lambda_1 \cdot \mathcal{L}_{output} + \lambda_2 \cdot \mathcal{L}_{photo}, \qquad (4)$$

where $\mathcal{L}_{det}$ is from the detection loss with ground truth bounding boxes, λ_1 and λ_2 are the manually tuned hyper-parameters.

5 Experiments

To validate the effectiveness of our semi-supervised framework, we conduct experiments on the KITTI [13] and nuScenes [4] datasets.

Table 1. Experimental results of 3D detection accuracy (Car) with different numbers of labeled data on the KITTI validation set. The metrics of $AP|_{R40}$ with IoU threshold $= 0.7$ on three difficulties (easy, moderate and hard) are reported. We randomly sample 10%, 50%, and 100% data from the KITTI training set as the labeled split and select all the data in "Eigen Clean" as the unlabeled split. The models are trained with different types of multi-view data and evaluated with a single image.

Multi-view	Method	10%			50%			100%		
		Easy	Mod	Hard	Easy	Mod	Hard	Easy	Mod	Hard
–	Baseline	10.13	7.25	6.24	18.52	14.56	12.53	21.99	16.32	14.48
Lidar	Multi-task	**13.89**	8.86	7.53	20.91	15.70	13.58	23.98	18.01	15.33
Stereo	Multi-task	12.56	8.93	5.45	20.12	15.14	12.48	23.21	17.21	15.03
	MVC-MonoDet	13.34	**9.14**	**7.75**	**21.52**	**16.40**	**14.83**	**26.85**	**18.63**	**15.37**
Video	Multi-task	10.49	6.87	5.15	19.14	14.67	12.56	22.36	16.71	14.56
	MVC-MonoDet	12.13	7.96	7.02	21.15	16.01	13.37	24.45	17.34	15.15

5.1   Datasets

In this section, we first introduce the datasets we used and then describe the related evaluation metrics for 3D object detection.

KITTI is a popular dataset to benchmark multiple autonomous driving tasks. The 3D detection split consists of 14,999 annotated key frames with 7,481 for training and 7,518 for testing. Each key frame contains calibrated images from the left and right cameras with annotated 3D bounding boxes. Each labeled key frame is also accompanied with three adjacent unlabeled frames for providing temporal information. For a fair comparison, we follow recent work [6,7] and split the training set into training and validation subsets with 3,712 and 3,769 frames, respectively. For the unlabeled split, we follow the recent pseudo lidar based approach [37] and adopt the "Eigen clean" subset that does not have overlap with the detection validation set. The "Eigen clean" subset selects 14,490 unlabeled video frames from 45,200 frames in the "Eigen" set.

nuScenes is a large scale autonomous driving dataset, which contains 1,000 video sequences. The official protocol splits the video sequences into 700 for the training subset, 150 for the validation subset, and 150 for the test subset. nuScenes annotated the 3D bounding box on each key frames with up to annotated 40k images from 6 cameras. We utilize the annotated key frames as the labeled split for supervised training and the other frames as the unlabeled split for semi-supervised training.

Evaluation Metrics. For the KITTI dataset, we adopt the official $AP|_{R40}$ metric that averages the precision number over 40 recall points. The IoU threshold is set as 0.7 for "Car" and 0.5 for both "Pedestrian" and "Cyclist", respectively. Following the benchmark [13], we classify the instances into three kinds of difficulty (easy, moderate, and hard) based on their 2D bounding box height, the occlusion and truncation levels. For the nuScenes dataset, we adopt the official

Table 2. Experimental results of Pedestrian and Cyclist on the KITTI validation set. (100% of labeled data is used.) The metrics of $AP|_{R40}$ with IoU threshold $= 0.7$ on three difficulties (easy, moderate and hard) are reported.

Method	Pedestrian			Cyclist		
	Easy	Moderate	Hard	Easy	Moderate	Hard
Baseline	7.02	5.53	5.86	5.37	2.95	2.87
Multi-task	**8.44**	**6.89**	5.83	6.13	**4.10**	**3.96**
MVC-MonoDet	8.04	6.26	**6.94**	**6.94**	4.04	3.94

AP (average precision with threshold of 0.5m, 1.0m, 2m, and 4m) and ATE (average translation error) to evaluate the localization accuracy of the trained detectors.

5.2 Experimental Setup

For a fair comparison, we initialize the network backbone (a modified version of DLA-34) with ImageNet [10] pre-trained weights and optimize the network by AdamW optimizer. The learning rate is set as $3e-4$ and $1e-4$ on the KITTI and nuScenes datasets, respectively. To select the foreground pixels for computing the photometric loss, we adopt a pre-trained segmentation model [46] to filter out the background pixel. In the semi-supervised training stage, we first pre-train the detector on the labeled subset with 70 epochs and 10 epochs for the KITTI and nuScenes dataset, respectively. Then we fine-tune the detector with the proposed semi-supervised framework on both the labeled and unlabeled subsets with extra 70 epochs for the KITTI dataset and 10 epochs for the nuScenes dataset. We set the training batch size as 8 and train the model on one NVIDIA 2080Ti GPU. Regarding the input data, we pad the images to the size of 1280×384 on the KITTI dataset and downsample the images to half of the resolution (800×450) on the nuScenes dataset. During inference, only a single image is fed to the detector and the image resolution is kept as in training.

For the ego pose, we directly adopt the calibrated ego pose provided in the dataset for training. In the video framework, we utilize the calibrated ego pose provided in the dataset for training. If the ego motion is unavailable, one also can adopt a motion network to estimate the object motion. To tackle dynamic objects in the video data, we follow [9,18] previous work that models the corresponding object motion across frames. We repeat the experiments with three different random seeds and record their average value on the validation set.

5.3 Experimental Results on the KITTI Validation Set

In Table 1, we represent the experimental results of our framework and the other competitors on the KITTI validation set. We conduct experiments with different numbers of labeled data, including 10%, 50%, and 100% of data sampled from the training subset. To the best of our knowledge, there is no other

Table 3. Experimental results of 3D detection accuracy ($AP|_{R40}$ with IoU threshold = 0.7) on the KITTI test benchmark. The best and second best results are marked with **bold** and blue color, respectively. "–" denotes that the method does not report the related statistics. EC denotes the clean subset of Eigen split. DDAD denotes the 15M private driving dataset in [30].

Setting	Extra	Method	Easy	Moderate	Hard	FPS
Vanilla	MonoFlex [50]	None	19.94	13.89	12.07	30
	Mono R-CNN [36]	None	18.36	12.65	10.03	70
	AutoShape [24]	None	22.47	14.17	11.36	50
	MonoRun [5]	None	19.65	12.30	10.58	70
	M3DSSD [26]	None	17.51	11.46	8.98	–
	Kinemantic [3]	None	19.07	12.72	9.17	–
	MonoDLE [29]	None	17.23	12.26	10.29	40
	GUP-Net [25]	None	20.11	14.20	11.77	30
	MonoEF [55]	Eigen	21.29	13.87	11.71	30
Pseudo-lidar	PatchNet [27]	Eigen	15.68	11.12	10.17	488
	PCT [43]	Eigen	21.00	13.37	11.31	487
	Demystifying [37]	EC	22.40	12.53	10.64	488
Multi-task	DD3D [30]	EC+DDAD	23.22	13.64	14.20	148
Direct-based	Baseline	None	20.63	13.21	11.05	30
	MVC-MonoDet	EC	**25.05**	**16.89**	**14.83**	30

semi-supervised monocular 3D object detection approach sharing the same setting with us. Hence, except for fully supervised training and our approach, we further provide a "multi-task" framework [30] for comparison. The multi-task framework adds a parallel head on the modified CenterNet for depth estimation. In the multi-task framework, the supervision signal of depth estimation from either lidar, stereo or video can be used to update the joint feature representation. When using the stereo unlabeled data, our method outperforms the baseline approach with different numbers of labeled data, with ratios of 31.63%, 16.20%, and 22.10% on the easy split for three kinds of settings, respectively. The improvements validate the effectiveness of our approach in leveraging unlabeled data to improve the performance of the baseline. Given 50% labeled data, our approach even achieves comparable results with the baseline module that uses 100% labeled data.

When the number of labeled data is scarce, our approach still can improve the baseline module and the multi-task method. We also observe that the improvement is limited in the scarce data, and the potential reason is that the consistency modules need few labeled data to control the training. Furthermore, the large margin improvement on the 50% and 100% of labeled data also demonstrates the effectiveness of our approach providing direct supervision signals on the estimated bounding boxes. Compared between different modalities, the video version is not as effective as the stereo version, but still yields consistent improvements over the baseline approach. The performance gap between the stereo and video versions may come from the noise of ego and object motions in the video data.

To evaluate the effectiveness of our proposed approach in the non-rigid class, we also display the results of the pedestrian and cyclist classes in Table 2. Although the improvement is less ineffective than the car class, our approach yields consistent improvements over the baseline and multi-task framework, illustrating the flexibility of our framework in handling different kinds of objects. Note that the number of annotated instances in the pedestrian and cyclist is small (Pedestrian: 4,487, Cyclist: 1,627, and Car: 28,742). This may introduce performance fluctuations.

Table 4. Experimental results of different numbers of training data on the nuScenes validation set.

Setting	10%		100%	
	mAP ↑	ATE ↓	mAP ↑	ATE ↓
Baseline	15.9	0.87	33.2	0.68
Multi-task	17.2	0.86	33.6	0.67
MVC-MonoDet	18.8	0.82	34.9	0.64

5.4 Comparison with State-of-the-Art Detectors on the KITTI Test Set

Table 3 displays the comparison between our approach with state-of-the-art monocular detection methods on the KITTI test set. As illustrated, our framework outperforms the fully supervised detectors by a large margin and against the second-best approach with 14.02%, 14.29%, and 20.22% on the "Easy", "Moderate" and "Hard" settings.

Compared to the pseudo-lidar based approaches, our method uses cheaper and less training data, in which pseudo-lidar based approaches utilize the full Eigen set (23,488) with lidar sensor while we use the Eigen clean subset (14,490). Although using less training data, our approach still achieves much better performance. Compared with the multi-task framework, our framework does not utilize the extra private pre-trained dataset but still achieves better performance. This also demonstrates the effectiveness of the designed direct-based module for improving detection. Regarding the runtime efficiency, we follow previous work [50,55] and evaluate the frame per second (FPS) on the RTX-2080Ti. Benefits from the semi-supervised training framework, the detector is improved and keeps high efficiency.

5.5 Experimental Results on the nuScenes Dataset

Except for the KITTI dataset, we also provide the experimental results of MVC-MonoDet on the nuScenes dataset. Since the nuScenes dataset only uses the monocular camera to collect image data, we provide the experimental results with our video framework. Table 4 displays the results of detectors trained with 10% and 100% of labeled data in the training subset. Similar to the observation on the KITTI dataset, our approach consistently improves the fully-supervised baseline and multi-task semi-supervised framework in both the mAP and ATE metrics.

5.6 Ablation Study

In Table 5, we present the ablation study for different consistency regularization modules in our semi-supervised training framework. The ablation study is conducted on the KITTI dataset and 100% of labeled data is used in semi-supervised training. As shown in Table 5, both the box-level and object-level can effectively improve the baseline method. Meanwhile, these two kinds of regularization improve the detector from a different perspective, box-level is through enhancing model robustness and object-level is by latent appearance-based localization supervision. As a result, their combination can better improve the baseline method in different multi-view data.

Table 5. Ablation study of different components in our MVC-MonoDet framework. The mAP of Car category on the KITTI validation set is reported.

Multi-view	Box-level	Object-level	Easy	Moderate	Hard
–	–	–	21.99	16.32	14.48
Stereo	✓		24.93	17.56	14.71
		✓	24.16	17.85	14.92
	✓	✓	**26.85**	**18.63**	**15.37**
Video	✓		23.14	17.01	15.02
		✓	23.21	16.75	14.71
	✓	✓	**24.45**	**17.34**	**15.15**

6   Conclusion

In this paper, we proposed a semi-supervised monocular 3D object detection framework that leverages the unlabeled multi-view data (stereo or video) to improve performance. In the framework, we provide a box-level and an object-level consistency regularization to improve the performance of 3D detection. The box-level regularization provides sparse supervision to enhance the model's cross-view generalization on the unlabeled and unseen data. The object-level regularization utilizes dense supervision to explicitly identify and mitigate the bounding box prediction error. We showed that the designed regularization modules are effective in different types of multi-view data, leading to superior improvement over state-of-the-art results on the KITTI and nuScenes datasets.

References

1. Bian, J.W., et al.: Unsupervised scale-consistent depth learning from video. In: IJCV (2021)
2. Brazil, G., Liu, X.: M3D-RPN: monocular 3D region proposal network for object detection. In: ICCV (2019)
3. Brazil, G., Pons-Moll, G., Liu, X., Schiele, B.: Kinematic 3D object detection in monocular video. In: Vedaldi, A., Bischof, H., Brox, T., Frahm, J.-M. (eds.) ECCV 2020. LNCS, vol. 12368, pp. 135–152. Springer, Cham (2020). https://doi.org/10.1007/978-3-030-58592-1_9
4. Caesar, H., et al.: nuScenes: a multimodal dataset for autonomous driving. In: CVPR (2020)
5. Chen, H., Huang, Y., Tian, W., Gao, Z., Xiong, L.: Monorun: monocular 3D object detection by reconstruction and uncertainty propagation. In: CVPR (2021)
6. Chen, X., Kundu, K., Zhang, Z., Ma, H., Fidler, S., Urtasun, R.: Monocular 3D object detection for autonomous driving. In: CVPR (2016)
7. Chen, X., et al.: 3D object proposals for accurate object class detection. In: NeurIPS (2015)
8. Chen, Y., Tai, L., Sun, K., Li, M.: Monopair: monocular 3D object detection using pairwise spatial relationships. In: CVPR (2020)
9. Dai, Q., Patil, V., Hecker, S., Dai, D., Van Gool, L., Schindler, K.: Self-supervised object motion and depth estimation from video. In: CVPRW (2020)
10. Deng, J., Dong, W., Socher, R., Li, L.J., Li, K., Fei-Fei, L.: Imagenet: a large-scale hierarchical image database. In: CVPR (2009)
11. van Dijk, T., de Croon, G.: How do neural networks see depth in single images? In: ICCV (2019)
12. Ding, M., et al.: Learning depth-guided convolutions for monocular 3D object detection. In: CVPR (2020)
13. Geiger, A., Lenz, P., Urtasun, R.: Are we ready for autonomous driving? The KITTI vision benchmark suite. In: CVPR (2012)
14. Godard, C., Mac Aodha, O., Firman, M., Brostow, G.J.: Digging into self-supervised monocular depth prediction. In: ICCV (2019)
15. Jeong, J., Lee, S., Kim, J., Kwak, N.: Consistency-based semi-supervised learning for object detection. In: NeurIPS (2019)
16. Kendall, A., Gal, Y.: What uncertainties do we need in Bayesian deep learning for computer vision? In: NeurIPS. Curran Associates, Inc. (2017)
17. Lang, A.H., Vora, S., Caesar, H., Zhou, L., Yang, J., Beijbom, O.: Pointpillars: fast encoders for object detection from point clouds. In: CVPR (2019)
18. Li, H., Gordon, A., Zhao, H., Casser, V., Angelova, A.: Unsupervised monocular depth learning in dynamic scenes. arXiv preprint arXiv:2010.16404 (2020)
19. Li, P., Chen, X., Shen, S.: Stereo R-CNN based 3D object detection for autonomous driving. In: CVPR (2019)
20. Li, P., Zhao, H., Liu, P., Cao, F.: RTM3D: real-time monocular 3d detection from object keypoints for autonomous driving. In: Vedaldi, A., Bischof, H., Brox, T., Frahm, J.-M. (eds.) ECCV 2020. LNCS, vol. 12348, pp. 644–660. Springer, Cham (2020). https://doi.org/10.1007/978-3-030-58580-8_38
21. Li, P., Zhao, H., Liu, P., Cao, F.: RTM3D: real-time monocular 3D detection from object keypoints for autonomous driving. arXiv preprint arXiv:2001.03343 (2020)
22. Lian, Q., Ye, B., Xu, R., Yao, W., Zhang, T.: Geometry-aware data augmentation for monocular 3D object detection. arXiv preprint arXiv:2104.05858 (2021)

23. Liu, Y.C., et al.: Unbiased teacher for semi-supervised object detection. In: ICLR (2021)
24. Liu, Z., Zhou, D., Lu, F., Fang, J., Zhang, L.: Autoshape: real-time shape-aware monocular 3D object detection. In: ICCV (2021)
25. Lu, Y., et al.: Geometry uncertainty projection network for monocular 3D object detection. In: ICCV (2021)
26. Luo, S., Dai, H., Shao, L., Ding, Y.: M3DSSD: monocular 3D single stage object detector. In: CVPR (2021)
27. Ma, X., Liu, S., Xia, Z., Zhang, H., Zeng, X., Ouyang, W.: Rethinking pseudo-LiDAR representation. In: Vedaldi, A., Bischof, H., Brox, T., Frahm, J.-M. (eds.) ECCV 2020. LNCS, vol. 12358, pp. 311–327. Springer, Cham (2020). https://doi.org/10.1007/978-3-030-58601-0_19
28. Ma, X., Wang, Z., Li, H., Zhang, P., Ouyang, W., Fan, X.: Accurate monocular 3D object detection via color-embedded 3D reconstruction for autonomous driving. In: ICCV (2019)
29. Ma, X., et al.: Delving into localization errors for monocular 3D object detection. In: CVPR (2021)
30. Park, D., Ambrus, R., Guizilini, V., Li, J., Gaidon, A.: Is pseudo-lidar needed for monocular 3D object detection? In: ICCV (2021)
31. Qian, S., Sun, K., Wu, W., Qian, C., Jia, J.: Aggregation via separation: boosting facial landmark detector with semi-supervised style translation. In: ICCV (2019)
32. Reading, C., Harakeh, A., Chae, J., Waslander, S.L.: Categorical depth distribution network for monocular 3D object detection. In: CVPR (2021)
33. Shi, S., et al.: PV-RCNN: point-voxel feature set abstraction for 3D object detection. In: CVPR (2020)
34. Shi, S., Wang, X., Li, H.: PointRCNN: 3D object proposal generation and detection from point cloud. In: CVPR (2019)
35. Shi, X., Chen, Z., Kim, T.-K.: Distance-normalized unified representation for monocular 3D object detection. In: Vedaldi, A., Bischof, H., Brox, T., Frahm, J.-M. (eds.) ECCV 2020. LNCS, vol. 12374, pp. 91–107. Springer, Cham (2020). https://doi.org/10.1007/978-3-030-58526-6_6
36. Shi, X., et al.: Geometry-based distance decomposition for monocular 3D object detection. In: ICCV (2021)
37. Simonelli, A., Bulò, S.R., Porzi, L., Kontschieder, P., Ricci, E.: Are we missing confidence in pseudo-lidar methods for monocular 3D object detection? In: ICCV (2021)
38. Simonelli, A., Bulò, S.R.R., Porzi, L., López-Antequera, M., Kontschieder, P.: Disentangling monocular 3D object detection. arXiv preprint arXiv:1905.12365 (2019)
39. Sohn, K., Zhang, Z., Li, C.L., Zhang, H., Lee, C.Y., Pfister, T.: A simple semi-supervised learning framework for object detection. arXiv preprint arXiv:2005.04757 (2020)
40. Tang, P., Ramaiah, C., Wang, Y., Xu, R., Xiong, C.: Proposal learning for semi-supervised object detection. In: WACV (2021)
41. Wang, H., Cong, Y., Litany, O., Gao, Y., Guibas, L.J.: 3DIoUMatch: leveraging IoU prediction for semi-supervised 3D object detection. In: CVPR (2021)
42. Wang, L., et al.: Depth-conditioned dynamic message propagation for monocular 3D object detection. In: CVPR (2021)
43. Wang, L., et al.: Progressive coordinate transforms for monocular 3D object detection. In: NeurIPS (2021)

44. Wang, Y., Chao, W.L., Garg, D., Hariharan, B., Campbell, M., Weinberger, K.Q.: Pseudo-lidar from visual depth estimation: bridging the gap in 3D object detection for autonomous driving. In: CVPR (2019)
45. Wang, Z., Bovik, A., Sheikh, H., Simoncelli, E.: Image quality assessment: from error visibility to structural similarity. TIP **13**(4), 600–612 (2004)
46. Wu, Y., Kirillov, A., Massa, F., Lo, W.Y., Girshick, R.: Detectron2. https://github.com/facebookresearch/detectron2 (2019)
47. Xie, J., Girshick, R., Farhadi, A.: Deep3D: fully automatic 2D-to-3D video conversion with deep convolutional neural networks. In: Leibe, B., Matas, J., Sebe, N., Welling, M. (eds.) ECCV 2016. LNCS, vol. 9908, pp. 842–857. Springer, Cham (2016). https://doi.org/10.1007/978-3-319-46493-0_51
48. You, Y., et al.: Pseudo-lidar++: accurate depth for 3D object detection in autonomous driving. arXiv preprint arXiv:1906.06310 (2019)
49. Zhang, F., Pan, T., Wang, B.: Semi-supervised object detection with adaptive class-rebalancing self-training. arXiv preprint arXiv:2107.05031 (2021)
50. Zhang, Y., Lu, J., Zhou, J.: Objects are different: flexible monocular 3D object detection. In: CVPR (2021)
51. Zhao, N., Chua, T.S., Lee, G.H.: SESS: self-ensembling semi-supervised 3D object detection. In: CVPR (2020)
52. Zhou, T., Brown, M., Snavely, N., Lowe, D.G.: Unsupervised learning of depth and ego-motion from video. In: CVPR (2017)
53. Zhou, X., Koltun, V., Krähenbühl, P.: Tracking objects as points. In: Vedaldi, A., Bischof, H., Brox, T., Frahm, J.-M. (eds.) ECCV 2020. LNCS, vol. 12349, pp. 474–490. Springer, Cham (2020). https://doi.org/10.1007/978-3-030-58548-8_28
54. Zhou, X., Wang, D., Krähenbühl, P.: Objects as points. In: arXiv preprint arXiv:1904.07850 (2019)
55. Zhou, Y., He, Y., Zhu, H., Wang, C., Li, H., Jiang, Q.: Monocular 3D object detection: an extrinsic parameter free approach. In: CVPR (2021)

PTSEFormer: Progressive Temporal-Spatial Enhanced TransFormer Towards Video Object Detection

Han Wang[1], Jun Tang[2], Xiaodong Liu[2], Shanyan Guan[3], Rong Xie[1], and Li Song[1,3(✉)]

[1] Institute of Image Communication and Network Engineering, Shanghai Jiao Tong University, Shanghai, China
`song_li@sjtu.edu.cn`
[2] HIKVISION Inc., Hangzhou, China
[3] MoE Key Lab of Artificial Intelligence, AI Institute, Shanghai Jiao Tong University, Shanghai, China

Abstract. Recent years have witnessed a trend of applying context frames to boost the performance of object detection as video object detection. Existing methods usually aggregate features at one stroke to enhance the feature. These methods, however, usually lack spatial information from neighboring frames and suffer from insufficient feature aggregation. To address the issues, we perform a progressive way to introduce both temporal information and spatial information for an integrated enhancement. The temporal information is introduced by the temporal feature aggregation model (TFAM), by conducting an attention mechanism between the context frames and the target frame (*i.e.*, the frame to be detected). Meanwhile, we employ a Spatial Transition Awareness Model (STAM) to convey the location transition information between each context frame and target frame. Built upon a transformer-based detector DETR, our PTSEFormer also follows an end-to-end fashion to avoid heavy post-processing procedures while achieving 88.1% mAP on the ImageNet VID dataset. Codes are available at https://github.com/Hon-Wong/PTSEFormer.

Keywords: Video object detection · Transformer

1 Introduction

Video Object Detection (VOD) [4,29,32,33,35] has emerged as a hot topic in computer vision. Given a target frame and its context frames, VOD aims to detect objects in the target frame, with the compensation of observation from context frames. By observing the same instance in different poses from context frames, many hard cases, such as blurry appearance and background occlusion, are possible to be tackled (Fig. 1).

Previous works [4,11,13,32] usually aggregate features at one stroke, suffering from insufficient utilization of temporal information. In particular, they employ

© The Author(s), under exclusive license to Springer Nature Switzerland AG 2022
S. Avidan et al. (Eds.): ECCV 2022, LNCS 13668, pp. 732–747, 2022.
https://doi.org/10.1007/978-3-031-20074-8_42

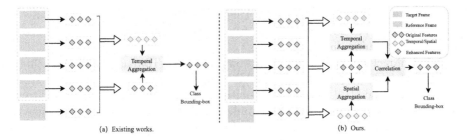

Fig. 1. The differences between existing works and ours. Previous works usually conduct temporal feature aggregation at one stroke, lacking in spatial information and suffering from insufficient feature aggregation. In contrast, our PTSEFormer utilizes both spatial and temporal information and performs feature aggregation in a progressive way.

isolated box-level associations [4,11,13] to enhance the instance feature of the target frame only using the extracted features of proposals, ignoring the spatial relations between frames. To diversify context frame features, those works put effort into how to excavate information from long-range context frames. However, as a common sense of human vision, information from a nearby time window is enough for detection in most scenarios. Specifically, when distinguishing a blurry object from the target frame, we often refer to the frame sliding near the target frame temporally, instead of observing the whole video. In this way, how to fully utilize the information from context frames, rather than enlarging the range of context frames, should be valued in the first place.

In this paper, we propose PTSEFormer to tackle the problems mentioned above. Motivated by DETR [2,34], PTSEFormer uses Transformer [27] as the basic structure to avoid complicated post-processing (*e.g.,* Seq-NMS [14], Tublet-Linking [17], Viterbi [10], Tublet-Rescore [3]). In contrast to aggregating features of the target frame and context frames at one stroke by attention layers [4,13,32] and conducting box-level associations upon extracted proposals [4,11,13], PTSE-Former conducts a progressive way to focus on both the temporal information and the spatial transition relations between frames. Specifically, **Temporal Feature Aggregation Module** is designed to introduce the temporal information to enhance the feature of the target frame with different perspectives towards the same objects in all the context frames. **Spatial Transition Awareness Module** is designed for estimating the position transition of the objects between the target frame and each context frame, enhancing the target feature with frame-to-frame spatial information. To build a balanced correlation model upon transformer decoder, we further propose the Gated Correlation model, which considers the imbalance caused by the residual connection layer and adds a gate to fix it.

Furthermore, as an important design of DETR, object queries contain inherent object position distribution learned from training data, and are fixed during inferring. We propose the Query Assembling Module (QAM) to regress object queries directly from context frames. Due to the fact that it is more reasonable to infer position from adjacent context frames, rather than from fixed parameters decided by training data.

We conduct extensive experiments on ImageNet VID dataset [24] and achieve a **4.9%** absolute improvement on mAP compared to previous end-to-end state-of-the-art method [13] and **3.3%** absolute improvement on mAP compared to its variant with post-processing when applied on a ResNet-101 backbone, showing the effectiveness of our method.

2   Related Works

2.1   Vision Transformer

Recent years have witnessed great progress on vision transformers. ViT [8] first introduces a transformer architecture to the image classification and draws much attention. DETR [2,34] builds a transformer-based architecture for object detection, with delicately designed object queries to learn the position distribution of objects. After successful applications, transformers have achieved leading performance in many downstream tasks of computer vision. For instance, in visual object tracking (VOT), TrDimp/TrSiam [28] modifies the transformer decoder for correlation between features from images, as a replacement of classical correlation model (*i.e.*, depth-wise cross correlation [19]) in VOT. HiFT [1] also utilizes the transformer decoder for correlation on hierarchical features extracted from images via a CNN backbone. The multi-head attentions in the decoder seems naturally suitable for feature correlation. However, we cast doubt on the direct usage of the decoder as a feature fusion model for features in the same feature space.

2.2   Video Object Detection

Object detection suffers from image deterioration problems, such as motion blur, background occlusion, deformation, etc. To tackle this problem, many works [4,11, 13,25] explored to use temporal context frames to provide compensation guidance (*i.e.*, the object at context frames with different viewpoints). Built upon a two-stage detector (*e.g.*, Faster-RCNN [22], R-FCN [6], FPN [20]), Early works [4,11, 13,30] conduct box-level associations and achieve remarkable success. However, these methods highly rely on the features of proposals extracted by the two-stage detector, lacking spatial information. In recent years, the rapid progress of anchor-free object detectors obtain remarkable performance. We observe several attempts to introduce anchor-free methods to video object detection and boost the performance by spatial information. CHP [31] uses an anchor-free detector CenterNet [9] as a base detector and propagates its heat map by post-processing to deliver the spatial information. Apparently, it ignores the support from the temporal features. TransVOD [32] is the first to apply transformer architecture [27] into VOD and builds upon DETR. However, suffering from insufficient feature aggregation and

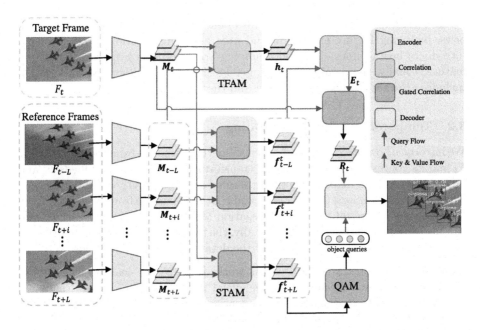

Fig. 2. Overview of the proposed PTSEFormer. First, image features M are extracted by a transformer-based encoder. The image features are further input to TFAM and STAM to obtain temporal feature h_t and spatial features $\{f_t^i\}_{i=-L:L}$, and then are progressively aggregated. Finally, the aggregated feature, together with regressed object queries from QAM, is decoded for final detection result

lacking spatial information, its performance is inferior to those with box-level associations when applied on the same backbone. To address the limitations mentioned above, we propose an end-to-end framework with temporal-spatial feature aggregation design to better employ context frames information.

3   PTSEFormer

3.1   Overview

The overview of PTSEFormer is shown in Fig. 2. Given a target frame F_t and its context frames $F_t^c = \{F_{t+i}\}_{i=-L:L}$, PTSEFormer detects the class and bounding-box of objects at F_t. To better explore the context information from F_t^c, PTSEFormer extracts both temporal features (representing the motion of objects) and spatial features (representing position and transformations of objects). Next, the temporal and spatial features are progressively aggregated. Then a decoder learns to infer the class and bounding boxes from the aggregated feature and the object query. Particularly, our object query is conditioned on F_t^c, and thus leads to more accurate object position distribution.

In Sect. 3.2, we introduce the details of encoding temporal and spatial memories, including feature extraction and progressive aggregation. Next, Sect. 3.3 introduces how to infer class and bounding-box of objects from the aggregated feature. Finally, the details of learning PTSEFormer are described in Sect. 3.4, including the total objective function and the network details.

3.2   Temporal and Spatial Encoding

We introduce how to extract temporal and spatial memories from the target frame F_t and its context frames F_t^c. First, a transformer-based encoder embeds F_t and F_t^c to latent feature maps respectively, termed as M_t and $M_t^c = \{M_{t+i}\}_{i=-L:L}$. Then our model obtains the temporal and spatial memories from M_t and M_t^c by two modules: Temporal Feature Aggregation Module (TFAM) and Spatial Transition Awareness Module (STAM). Finally, the temporal and spatial memories are progressively aggregated. We describe the details of each module below.

TFAM. As demonstrated in previous works [4,13,25,32], learning the temporal relation between F_t and F_t^c is beneficial for detecting objects with blurry appearance or distorted shape. Consequently, we propose TFAM to extract this temporal memory h_t, which is formulated as:

$$h_t = \mathcal{C}(M_t, M_t^c), \tag{1}$$

where $\mathcal{C}(\cdot, \cdot)$ is the correlation operator:

$$\mathcal{C}(Q, V) = \text{softmax}(\frac{QK^T}{\sqrt{d_k}})V + Q, \tag{2}$$

where $Q \in \mathbb{R}^{N_Q \times d_k}$, $K, V \in \mathbb{R}^{N_V \times d_k}$, and '+' represents the residual connection.

STAM. STAM is proposed to learn relative positional transition of objects from a context frame F_{t+i} to the target frame F_t. Since the object identity annotation is unavailable in the VOD task, unsupervised learning of the relations of the objects at F_{t+i} and F_t is non-trivial.

A straightforward idea is to employ the correlation operator $\mathcal{C}(\cdot)$ to model the relative transitions between F_{t+i} and F_t. However, the imbalance weight on Q and V in Eq. 2 makes it infeasible to match the objects at two frames. Specifically, the weights before Q and V are 1 and $\text{softmax}(\frac{QK^T}{\sqrt{d_k}})$, respectively. The average value of $\text{softmax}(\frac{QK^T}{\sqrt{d_k}})$ is decided by the size of Q and K. When the size goes large, the weight is far less than 1, leading to severer imbalance attention on Q and V. Commonly, this architecture is used for correlation between features from different space and dimensions, which naturally need biased attention. However, in some recent researches [1,28,32], it is also used for correlation between features in the same spaces without any modification. We believe the imbalanced attention could do harm to the performance.

To address the limitation mentioned above and inspired by the gate control design by GRU [5], we design a **Gated Correlation operation**, denoted as

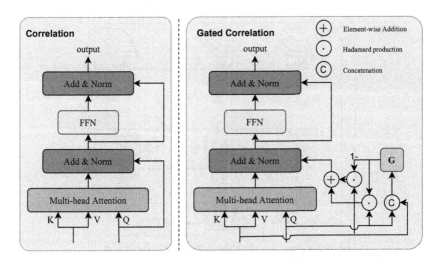

Fig. 3. Illustration of correlation (left) and gated correlation (right).

$\mathcal{C}^g$. By adding a gate control to the residual connection of the decoder, we can change the weight before Q. Furthermore, to get the gate control awareness of the input Q and V, the control weight must be decided by Q and K. Thus, we pass Q and K through a fully connected gate layer for the weight. The process can be changed into:

$$\mathcal{C}^g = \text{softmax}(\frac{QK^T}{\sqrt{d_k}})V + M \odot Q + (1 - M) \odot V, \tag{3}$$

$$M = \sigma(\mathcal{G}([Q, V])), \tag{4}$$

where $\mathcal{G}(\cdot)$ refers to the gated function, consisting of a fully connected function. $\sigma(\cdot)$ is the Sigmoid function. $[\cdot, \cdot]$ is the concatenation operation, and $\odot$ refers to the Hadamard production. Note that Q, K, V and M must be of the same size. When initializing, the Sigmoid function in gate can project the output to $(0, 1)$ with a primal value of 0.5, conducting fair attention on both Q and V.

The final STAM can be formulated as:

$$f_i^t = \mathcal{C}^g(M_t, M_{t+i}), \tag{5}$$

where $i = -L : L$, and f_i^t is the extracted spatial memory (Fig. 3).

Progressive Aggregation. We aggregate the h_t and f_i^t in a progressive way. First, h_t and f_i^t are combined with the Correlation operation $\mathcal{C}(\cdot)$ to generate a temporal-spatial memory E_t. The formulation is written as:

$$E_t = \mathcal{C}(h_t, \{f_i^t\}_{i=-L:L}). \tag{6}$$

By aggregating features from context frames, E_t contains both long-term temporal and spatial transition information. However, in some scenes, the context

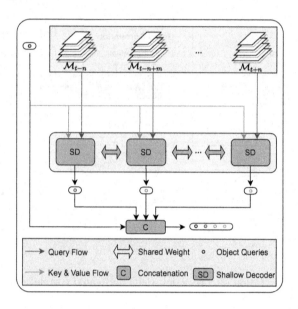

Fig. 4. Illustration of the Query Assembling Model (QAM). We apply a shared shallow decoder to combine the primal object queries and each context frame. All the output from shallow decoders are concatenated to form the final object queries.

frames are likely to be low-quality and the spatial-temporal memory may be useless and even misleading. In this situation, we should take more information of the current frame instead of context frame. Thus, we use a Gated Correlation between the feature of current frame and the temporal-spatial memory to obtain the final enhanced memory R_t. The operation is denoted as Residual Gated Correlation, which can be written as:

$$R_t = \mathcal{C}^g(E_t, M_t), \tag{7}$$

3.3 Enhanced Memory Decoding

In original DETR, a group of learned embeddings is designed to learn the position distribution of different objects. With each object query, the decoder decodes one bounding box and its class on the memory. Following the same protocols, we decode our enhanced memory R_t with a transformer decoder. However, there remains a question that the original object queries are fixed through time, cannot benefit from the context frames. Thus, we propose a Query Assembling Model to diversify the object query and convey the position distribution information through time (Fig. 4).

Query Assembling Model. Query Assembling Model aims at propagating implicit position distribution information via object queries through time. As primal object queries in DETR are fixed embeddings in the inference stage and have no difference across frames, we apply a shallow correlation model to inherit location information of the primal object queries and diversify information from features. The final object queries can be described as:

$$Q = [Q_p, \{\text{SD}(Q_p, \boldsymbol{M}_{t+i}), i = -L : L\}], \tag{8}$$

where Q_p is the primal object query, and SD is a shallow transformer decoder with 2 layers. $[\cdot, \cdot]$ is the concatenation operation.

3.4 Learning PTSEFormer

Following DETR, we adopt a Hungarian algorithm [26] to calculate the matching cost between the ground truths and predictions. The objective function is formulated as follows:

$$\mathcal{L} = \lambda_{cls}\mathcal{L}_{cls} + \lambda_{box}\mathcal{L}_{box}, \tag{9}$$

$$\mathcal{L}_{box} = \lambda_{L1}\mathcal{L}_{L1} + \lambda_{giou}\mathcal{L}_{giou}, \tag{10}$$

where $\mathcal{L}_{cls}$ is focal loss [21] for classification. $\mathcal{L}_{L1}$, $\mathcal{L}_{giou}$ represent the L1 loss and GIoU loss [23] for bounding box regression, respectively. λ_{cls}, λ_{box}, λ_{L1}, λ_{giou} are hyper-parameters to balance the multi-task losses.

Network Details. PTSEFormer is built upon the DETR with several modifications. The number of layers in the encoder and decoder is decreased to 2 for a trade-off between speed and precision. Notice that our method also adopts multi-scale features to boost the performance for detecting small objects. We adopt the ResNet models as our backbones. In particular, we adopt ResNet-101 [15] for a fair comparison with previous works. All the components (*i.e.*, TFAM, STAM, Correlation and Gated correlation) also have a two-layer structure. The number of heads in multi-head attention is fixed as 6 and the number of primal object queries is set to be 100, the same as the original DETR.

4 Experiments

4.1 Implement Details

Dataset and Metric. For a fair and convincing comparison, we conduct our experiments on ImageNet VID dataset [24] which is a large-scale public dataset for video object detection and contains more than 1M frames for training and more than 100k frames for validation. In particular, we train our model on the training split of ImageNet VID and DET dataset [24] following common protocols. Same as previous works [4,32], we adopt mean average precision (mAP) as our metric.

Training Details. We train our PTSEFormer on 8 GPUs of Tesla V100 with Adam [18], and each GPU holds one target frame and its reference frames. The whole training procedure lasts for 50 epochs, each taking almost 1.5 h. The initial learning rate is 1e−4, with a drop in the 40th epoch to 1e−5. For each target

Table 1. End-to-end methods comparisons (with ResNet-50 backbone).

Methods	Base detector	Stages	Backbone	mAP (%)
DFF [36]	R-FCN	2	ResNet-50	70.4
FGFA [35]	R-FCN	2	ResNet-50	74.0
RDN [7]	Faster-RCNN	2	ResNet-50	76.7
MEGA [4]	Faster-RCNN	2	ResNet-50	77.3
TransVOD [32]	Deformable DETR	1	ResNet-50	79.9
OURS	Deformable DETR	1	ResNet-50	**87.4**

Table 2. End-to-end methods comparisons (with ResNet-101 backbone).

Methods	Base detector	Stages	Backbone	mAP (%)
LLTR [25]	FPN	2	ResNet-101	81.0
DFF [36]	R-FCN	2	ResNet-101	73.0
D&T [10]	R-FCN	2	ResNet-101	75.8
LSTS [16]	R-FCN	2	ResNet-101	77.2
FGFA [35]	R-FCN	2	ResNet-101	76.3
SELSA [30]	Faster-RCNN	2	ResNet-101	80.3
TROI [11] + SELSA [30]	Faster-RCNN	2	ResNet-101	82.0
MEGA [4]	Faster-RCNN	2	ResNet-101	82.9
HVRNet [13]	Faster-RCNN	2	ResNet-101	83.2
CHP [31]	CenterNet	1	ResNet-101	76.7
TransVOD [32]	Deformable DETR	1	ResNet-101	81.9
OURS	Deformable DETR	1	ResNet-101	**88.1**

frame, we randomly sample 2 frames from a sliding window with a length of 25 as the reference frames. The input images are all resized to hold a shorter size of 800 pixels without any other extra data augmentation applied. All the networks including the single frame baseline are trained from the very beginning with a pre-trained backbone.

4.2 State-of-the-Art Comparison

We first compare our PTSEFomer with several state-of-the-art methods in an end-to-end fashion. As shown in Table 1 and Table 2, we group these methods into two categories by their backbones. Previous end-to-end methods are also mostly built upon a two-stage detector without a post-processing procedure for VOD. The existing one-stage based VOD approaches, however, fall behind. Built upon a one-stage detector, we achieve much higher performance on mAP than existing methods with a magnificent margin. Reasonably, the larger backbone boosts the performance of all the methods, including ours. As illustrated in Table 1 and Table 2, Our PTSEFomer leads the performance with ResNet-50 and ResNet-101 [15].

We also compare our PTSEFormer with several state-of-the-art methods with post-processing procedures in Table 3. Post-processing proves useful in many

Table 3. State-of-the-art methods comparisons (with Post-processing).

Methods	Base detector	Stages	Backbone	Post-processing	mAP (%)
PSLA [12]	R-FCN	2	ResNet-101	Seq-NMS	81.4
D&T [10]	R-FCN	2	ResNet-101	Viterbi	79.8
MANet [29]	R-FCN	2	ResNet-101	Seq-NMS	80.3
Scale-Time Lattice [3]	R-FCN	2	ResNet-101	Tublet-Rescore	79.6
FGFA [35]	R-FCN	2	ResNet-101	Seq-NMS	78.4
SELSA [30]	Faster-RCNN	2	ResNet-101	Seq-NMS	82.5
MEGA [4]	Faster-RCNN	2	ResNet-101	Seq-NMS	84.5
HVRNet [13]	Faster-RCNN	2	ResNet-101	Seq-NMS	84.8
CHP [30]	CenterNet	1	ResNet-101	Seq-NMS	78.4
TransVOD [32]	Deformable DETR	1	ResNet-101	-	81.9
OURS	Deformable DETR	1	ResNet-101	-	**88.1**

Table 4. Ablation studies of STAM and TFAM.

Method	STAM	TFAM	mAP (%)
Single frame baseline [34]	✗	✗	81.2
PTSEFormer	✓	✗	84.5
PTSEFormer	✓	✓	**87.4**

VOD methods, especially in those built upon an anchor-based detector. Indeed, most existing methods have their versions with post-processing to boost the performance. For instance, the most widely used post-processing, Seq-NMS, conducts an NMS operation through a sequence, boosting the mAP by 1%–2%. However, those post-processing procedures, though prove effective, demand extra computations. Thus, our PTSEFormer obtains an end-to-end structure. We declare that even we do not adopt post-processing, our method still obtains the best score on mAP.

4.3   Ablation Studies

Considering the speed, we adopt the ResNet-50 model as our backbone for ablation study. The effectiveness of each component of PTSEFormer is verified independently.

TFAM and STAM. To verify the effectiveness of the TFAM and STAM, we conduct ablation studies on both, respectively. As shown in Table 4, we add our STAM model and TFAM model step by step to verify the effectiveness of both. The use of STAM improves the mAP by 3.3%, performing spatial relations between the target frame and each reference frame and offering spatial transferring information. As mentioned above, TFAM conducts a temporal feature aggregation, providing the temporal memory of the target frame. The TFAM leads to an increase of 2.9% compared with only applying STAM.

Table 5. Ablation studies on QAM, Gated Correlation, RGC and Multi-scale.

QAM	GatedCorr	RGC	Multi-scale	mAP (%)
✗	✓	✓	✓	86.1
✓	✗	✓	✓	86.7
✓	✓	✗	✓	86.3
✓	✓	✓	✗	86.4
✓	✓	✓	✓	**87.4**

Query Assembling Model. Query Assembling Model carries the spatial information through time, offering implicit track information. The original object queries in DETR are fixed embeddings, expected to learn the position distribution of the objects in the dataset. We compare QAM with the original object queries in DETR in our experiment by replacing the QAM with original object queries. By comparing line 1 and line 5 in Table 5, results have shown the assistance from the specially designed QAM by an improvement of 1.3% on mAP.

Gated Correlation. To alleviate the imbalanced attention on Key and Value of the transformer decoder as a correlation model, we propose Gated Correlation to carry out a relation between temporal memory and spatial memories. To prove it useful, we replace it with the original transformer decoder. The results show a little drop in mAP which is illustrated in line 2 and line 5 in Table 5.

Residual Gated Correlation. The Residual Gated Correlation model is designed for gating out the memories from low-quality reference frames and boosts the performance of our method. We also investigate it in our experiment and the results from line 3 and line 5 in Table 5 show its positive influence on the performance. In particular, application of Residual Gated Correlation leads to a 1.1% increasement on mAP.

Multi-scale. Similar to the original DETR, the designs of our methods also benefit from the multi-scale features. We obtain 1% increment on mAP with a multi-scale architecture by comparing line 4 and line 5 in Table 5.

4.4 Visualization

Feature Visualization. We first visualize the feature maps of our network to figure out how our TFAM and STAM work. As depicted in Fig. 5, we demonstrate three target frames and their corresponding reference frames and feature maps, respectively. The first column shows the original input frames (*i.e.*, target frame and its two reference frames, from top to bottom), and the second column shows the original memories after a shared backbone and encoder, referred to as M_t and M_{t+i}. Obviously, it is hard to distinguish the object from the background on these feature maps. The third column shows the temporal memory T_t and the spatial memories S_{t+i}. Compared with the original memory M_t, it is clear

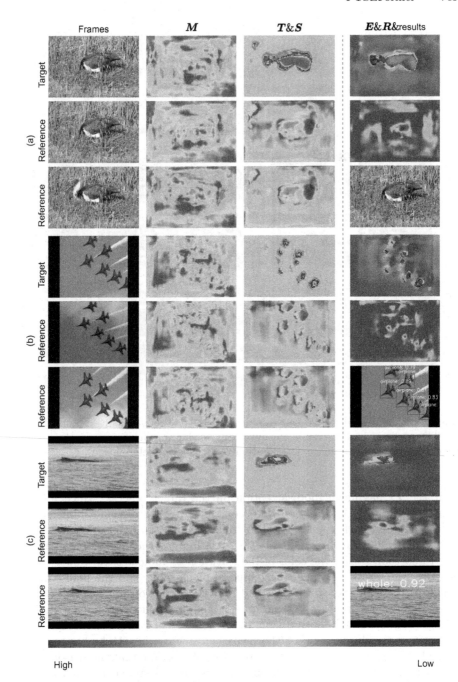

Fig. 5. The feature maps of our models. We select three target frames to figure out what the network learns.

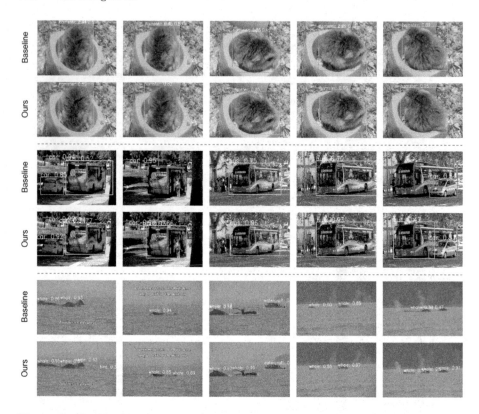

Fig. 6. Results Visualization. Our results are in the odd row, and single frame detector DETR results as baseline are in the even row. As shown in figure, our method is more robust against various image deterioration(*e.g.*,occlusion, deformation).

that the T_t has much more attention on the target objects, which indicates that the temporal information does contribute to the distinguishing between foreground and background. The last column shows the temporal-spatial memory E_t, R_t after the Residual Gated Correlation and the detection results from top to bottom. Notice the color of the feature map indicates the value. Observing the original memory M_t the temporal memory T_t and the final enhanced memory R_t, it is easy to find a trend that the values of foreground and background become more easy to separate. The temporal information contributes to recognizing a object by introducing different poses of it. Furthermore, the spatial information helps our PTSEFormer to locate objects with higher confidence score by using spatial transition information. We declare that the reason of such excellent results is the contribution of temporal and spatial information from our TFAM and STAM.

Results Visualization. We present the results of both the single frame baseline method and our PTSEFormer in Fig. 6. In particular, the detection results are exhibited in the time order. Compared with the single frame baseline method

DETR, Our method shows the priority towards the image deterioration problems. By exploiting the temporal and spatial information, we get a higher confidence score in normal situations and behave much better dealing with occlusion and posture deformation. For example, when the face of a hamster gets occluded by the background, the baseline single frame detector is confused about the category, and easily fooled to predict it as a domestic cat. However, its appearances in context frames are clear and easy to recognize, so our method succeeds in predicting the right category by introducing temporal information. In the second video, the detector is expected to detect several cars and a bus. Interfered by the background and occluded by a car, the baseline method fails at detection in some frames. In contrast, with the help of spatial information, our method can sense the motion of the bus and cars and produce the correct results. In the third video, when two whales get too close, it is hard for the baseline detector to recognize both, causing false detection. In this situation, our PTSEFormer behaves much better according to the temporal-spatial enhancement. It is necessary to introduce temporal-spatial information in this situation to better distinguish one object from another. Consequently, our PTSEFormer achieves much better performance than the single frame baseline method thanks to the temporal-spatial information.

5 Conclusion

In this work, we propose a progressive temporal-spatial enhanced transformer towards video object detection. Based on a one-stage object detector DETR, we boost the performance with proper design of introducing progressive feature aggregation. Temporal information and spatial information are proved useful to improve the robustness of detector against image deterioration. We also conduct extensive experiments on the public dataset ImageNet VID to verify the effectiveness of our method. We hope our work can shed light on the research on VOD applying anchor-free approaches.

Acknowledgements. This work was partly supported by MoE-China Mobile Research Fund Project (MCM20180702), the 111 Project (B07022 and Sheitc No. 150633) and the Shanghai Key Laboratory of Digital Media Processing and Transmissions. And part of this work was done while Han Wang performed as an intern at HIKVISION.

References

1. Cao, Z., Fu, C., Ye, J., Li, B., Li, Y.: HIFT: hierarchical feature transformer for aerial tracking. In: ICCV, pp. 15457–15466 (2021)
2. Carion, N., Massa, F., Synnaeve, G., Usunier, N., Kirillov, A., Zagoruyko, S.: End-to-end object detection with transformers. In: Vedaldi, A., Bischof, H., Brox, T., Frahm, J.-M. (eds.) ECCV 2020. LNCS, vol. 12346, pp. 213–229. Springer, Cham (2020). https://doi.org/10.1007/978-3-030-58452-8_13

3. Chen, K., et al.: Optimizing video object detection via a scale-time lattice. In: CVPR, pp. 7814–7823 (2018)
4. Chen, Y., Cao, Y., Hu, H., Wang, L.: Memory enhanced global-local aggregation for video object detection. In: CVPR, pp. 10337–10346 (2020)
5. Cho, K., et al.: Learning phrase representations using RNN encoder-decoder for statistical machine translation. arXiv preprint arXiv:1406.1078 (2014)
6. Dai, J., Li, Y., He, K., Sun, J.: R-FCN: object detection via region-based fully convolutional networks. In: Advances in Neural Information Processing Systems, vol. 29 (2016)
7. Deng, J., Pan, Y., Yao, T., Zhou, W., Li, H., Mei, T.: Relation distillation networks for video object detection. In: ICCV, pp. 7023–7032 (2019)
8. Dosovitskiy, A., et al.: An image is worth 16x16 words: transformers for image recognition at scale. arXiv preprint arXiv:2010.11929 (2020)
9. Duan, K., Bai, S., Xie, L., Qi, H., Huang, Q., Tian, Q.: CenterNet: keypoint triplets for object detection. In: ICCV, pp. 6569–6578 (2019)
10. Feichtenhofer, C., Pinz, A., Zisserman, A.: Detect to track and track to detect. In: ICCV, pp. 3038–3046 (2017)
11. Gong, T., et al.: Temporal ROI align for video object recognition. In: AAAI, pp. 1442–1450 (2021)
12. Guo, C., et al.: Progressive sparse local attention for video object detection. In: ICCV, pp. 3909–3918 (2019)
13. Han, M., Wang, Y., Chang, X., Qiao, Yu.: Mining inter-video proposal relations for video object detection. In: Vedaldi, A., Bischof, H., Brox, T., Frahm, J.-M. (eds.) ECCV 2020. LNCS, vol. 12366, pp. 431–446. Springer, Cham (2020). https://doi.org/10.1007/978-3-030-58589-1_26
14. Han, W., et al.: Seq-NMS for video object detection. arXiv preprint arXiv:1602.08465 (2016)
15. He, K., Zhang, X., Ren, S., Sun, J.: Deep residual learning for image recognition. In: Proceedings of the IEEE Conference on Computer Vision and Pattern Recognition, pp. 770–778 (2016)
16. Jiang, Z., et al.: Learning where to focus for efficient video object detection. In: Vedaldi, A., Bischof, H., Brox, T., Frahm, J.-M. (eds.) ECCV 2020. LNCS, vol. 12361, pp. 18–34. Springer, Cham (2020). https://doi.org/10.1007/978-3-030-58517-4_2
17. Kang, K., et al.: T-CNN: tubelets with convolutional neural networks for object detection from videos. TCSVT 28(10), 2896–2907 (2017)
18. Kingma, D.P., Ba, J.: Adam: a method for stochastic optimization. arXiv preprint arXiv:1412.6980 (2014)
19. Li, B., Wu, W., Wang, Q., Zhang, F., Xing, J., Yan, J.: SiamRPN++: evolution of Siamese visual tracking with very deep networks. In: CVPR, pp. 4282–4291 (2019)
20. Lin, T.Y., Dollár, P., Girshick, R., He, K., Hariharan, B., Belongie, S.: Feature pyramid networks for object detection. In: Proceedings of the IEEE Conference on Computer Vision and Pattern Recognition, pp. 2117–2125 (2017)
21. Lin, T.Y., Goyal, P., Girshick, R., He, K., Dollár, P.: Focal loss for dense object detection. In: ICCV, pp. 2980–2988 (2017)
22. Ren, S., He, K., Girshick, R., Sun, J.: Faster R-CNN: towards real-time object detection with region proposal networks. In: NeurIPS, vol. 28 (2015)
23. Rezatofighi, H., Tsoi, N., Gwak, J., Sadeghian, A., Reid, I., Savarese, S.: Generalized intersection over union: a metric and a loss for bounding box regression. In: CVPR, pp. 658–666 (2019)

24. Russakovsky, O., et al.: Imagenet large scale visual recognition challenge. Int. J. Comput. Vision **115**(3), 211–252 (2015)
25. Shvets, M., Liu, W., Berg, A.C.: Leveraging long-range temporal relationships between proposals for video object detection. In: ICCV, pp. 9756–9764 (2019)
26. Stewart, R., Andriluka, M., Ng, A.Y.: End-to-end people detection in crowded scenes. In: Proceedings of the IEEE Conference on Computer Vision and Pattern Recognition, pp. 2325–2333 (2016)
27. Vaswani, A., et al.: Attention is all you need. In: NeurIPS, vol. 30 (2017)
28. Wang, N., Zhou, W., Wang, J., Li, H.: Transformer meets tracker: exploiting temporal context for robust visual tracking. In: CVPR, pp. 1571–1580 (2021)
29. Wang, S., Zhou, Y., Yan, J., Deng, Z.: Fully motion-aware network for video object detection. In: Ferrari, V., Hebert, M., Sminchisescu, C., Weiss, Y. (eds.) ECCV 2018. LNCS, vol. 11217, pp. 557–573. Springer, Cham (2018). https://doi.org/10.1007/978-3-030-01261-8_33
30. Wu, H., Chen, Y., Wang, N., Zhang, Z.: Sequence level semantics aggregation for video object detection. In: ICCV, pp. 9217–9225 (2019)
31. Xu, Z., Hrustic, E., Vivet, D.: CenterNet heatmap propagation for real-time video object detection. In: Vedaldi, A., Bischof, H., Brox, T., Frahm, J.-M. (eds.) ECCV 2020. LNCS, vol. 12370, pp. 220–234. Springer, Cham (2020). https://doi.org/10.1007/978-3-030-58595-2_14
32. Zhou, Q., et al.: TransVOD: end-to-end video object detection with spatial-temporal transformers. arXiv preprint arXiv:2201.05047 (2022)
33. Zhu, H., Wei, H., Li, B., Yuan, X., Kehtarnavaz, N.: A review of video object detection: datasets, metrics and methods. Appl. Sci. **10**(21), 7834 (2020)
34. Zhu, X., Su, W., Lu, L., Li, B., Wang, X., Dai, J.: Deformable DeTR: deformable transformers for end-to-end object detection. arXiv preprint arXiv:2010.04159 (2020)
35. Zhu, X., Wang, Y., Dai, J., Yuan, L., Wei, Y.: Flow-guided feature aggregation for video object detection. In: ICCV, pp. 408–417 (2017)
36. Zhu, X., Xiong, Y., Dai, J., Yuan, L., Wei, Y.: Deep feature flow for video recognition. In: CVPR, pp. 2349–2358 (2017)

Author Index

Abdelreheem, Ahmed   110
Adam, Hartwig   271
Aggarwal, Pranav   219
Agrawal, Sanjna   312
Argaw, Dawit Mureja   201
Arsan, Deniz   312

Bao, Linchao   74
Beery, Sara   290
Bell, Alexander   575
Belongie, Serge   271
Bergamo, Alessandro   504
Berneshawi, Andrew   504
Bhandari, Keshav   557
Bhunia, Ayan Kumar   253
Boden, Alyssa   504
Briggs, Jo   219
Büchler, Uta   504
Burns, Andrea   312
Busam, Benjamin   645

Cai, Deng   662
Cesari, Fabio   345
Chadwicke Jenkins, Odest   381
Chai, Zenghao   74
Chandraker, Manmohan   592
Chang, Minsuk   1
Chen, Jie-Neng   128
Chen, Wei   522
Chen, Xiaotong   381
Chen, Xuesong   680
Chen, Yingcong   715
Chen, Zehui   628
Cheng, Shiyang   467
Cheung, Ka Chun   680
Choe, Jaesung   181
Choo, Jaegul   414
Chowdhury, Pinaki Nath   253
Chrysos, Grigorios   467
Chun, Sanghyuk   1
Chung, Sunghyo   414
Clark, Christopher   146

Collomosse, John   219
Cornia, Marcella   345
Cucchiara, Rita   345

Dai, Bo   329
Dai, Feng   237
Dendorfer, Patrick   20
Deng, Jiankang   467
Deng, Siqi   290
Dokania, Shubham   592
Duan, Bin   557

Elhoseiny, Mohamed   110

Faieta, Baldo   219
Fang, Liangji   628
Feng, Bailan   237
Ferrari, Vittorio   540
Filipkowski, Alex   219
Fincato, Matteo   345
Fotiadou, Eftychia   467

Ge, Songwei   431
Gecer, Baris   467
Gedeon, Tom   38
Gilbert, Andrew   219
Gou, Minghao   56
Gryaditskaya, Yulia   253
Guan, Shanyan   732
Guo, Weizhi   522
Gurari, Danna   575

Ha, Hyowon   181
Haurum, Joakim Bruslund   20
Hayes, Thomas   431
He, Ju   128, 163
He, Xiaofei   662
Heilbron, Fabian Caba   201
Hofmann, Jessica   609
Hu, Qiyuan   431
Hu, Siqi   56
Hu, Yue   93
Huang, Hui   93

Hutter, Andreas   645
Hyun Cho, Jang   698

Ilic, Slobodan   645
Im, Sunghoon   181

Jawahar, C. V.   592
Jeon, Hae-Gon   181
Jiang, Qinhong   628
Jin, Hailin   219

Kale, Ajinkya   219
Kampouris, Christos   467
Kang, Di   74
Kang, Minjun   181
Kay, Justin   290
Khandelwal, Apoorv   146
Kiko, Rainer   363
Kim, Kangyeol   414
Kim, Wonjae   1
Koch, Reinhard   363
Kollias, Dimitrios   467
Kortylewski, Adam   128, 163
Krähenbühl, Philipp   698
Kulits, Peter   290
Kumar, Ranjitha   312
Kweon, In So   181, 201

Landi, Federico   345
Latapie, Hugo   557
Lee, Jaeseong   414
Lee, Joon-Young   201
Lee, Junsoo   414
Li, Hongsheng   680
Li, Xiaodong   237
Li, Yuchen   110
Li, Zhenyu   628
Lian, Qing   715
Lin, Liqiang   93
Lin, Zhe   219
Liu, Gaowen   557
Liu, Shuai   128
Liu, Xiaodong   732
Liu, Yilin   93
Liu, Yuchi   38
Liu, Zili   662
Liu, Ziyuan   56
Loy, Chen Change   329
Lupp, Nicolas   397
Lv, Pei   522

Ma, Wufei   163
Ma, Yike   237
Mac Aodha, Oisin   271
Manocha, Dinesh   522
Marino, Kenneth   146
Marri, Naveen   219
Maucher, Johannes   609
Mei, Shenxiao   163
Mensink, Thomas   540
Moeslund, Thomas B.   20
Moltisanti, Davide   329
Morelli, Davide   345
Moschoglou, Stylianos   467
Mottaghi, Roozbeh   146
Mundt, Martin   397

Niu, Ransen   450

Oh, Seong Joon   1
Opipari, Anthony   381

Pang, Guan   431
Papaioannou, Athanasios   467
Parikh, Devi   431
Park, Song   1
Park, Sunghyun   414
Pedersen, Malte   20
Perona, Pietro   290
Pliushch, Iuliia   397
Ploumpis, Stylianos   467
Plummer, Bryan A.   312
Ponniah, Allan   467
Pothigara, Suhail   110
Prajapati, Arpit   110

Qian, Rui   271
Qian, Wei   662
Qiu, Yu   485

Ramesh, Visvanathan   397
Ren, Jing   74
Roussos, Anastasios   467
Ruta, Dan   219

Saenko, Kate   312
Sain, Aneeshan   253
Santarossa, Monty   363
Schilling, Andreas   609
Schmarje, Lars   363
Schröder, Simon-Martin   363
Schwenk, Dustin   146
Sheng, Sasha   431

Shi, Shaoshuai   680
Shrestha, Rakesh   56
Shuai, Bing   504
Shugurov, Ivan   645
Slim, Habib   110
Song, Li   732
Song, Yi-Zhe   253
Songsri-In, Kritaphat   467
Speed, Chris   219
Stathatos, Suzanne   290
Stracke, Jenny   363
Subramanian, Anbumani   592

Tan, Ping   56
Tang, Jun   732
Theodoridis, Johannes   609
Tighe, Joseph   504
Trigeorgis, George   467
Tseng, Yu-Yun   575
Tzirakis, Panagiotis   467

Uijlings, Jasper   540
Upadhyay, Ujjwal   110
Upchurch, Paul   450

Van Horn, Grant   271, 290
Ververas, Evangelos   467
Volkmann, Nina   363
Vutukur, Shishir Reddy   645

Wang, Angtian   163
Wang, Han   732
Wang, Wentong   522
Wang, Wenxiao   662
Wang, Zhongdao   38
Wilber, Kimberly   271
Wonka, Peter   110
Woodson, Markus   201
Wu, Jinyi   329
Wu, Xiaopei   662

Xiang, Tao   253
Xie, Ke   93
Xie, Rong   732

Xu, Hang   237, 680
Xu, Jing   485
Xu, Mingliang   522
Xu, Yanbo   715
Xu, Zhengzhuo   74

Yan, Chenggang   237
Yan, Xingguang   93
Yan, Yan   557
Yang, Cheng   128
Yang, Harry   431
Yang, Honghui   662
Yang, Shaokang   128
Yang, Shuo   128
Yao, Weilong   715
Yin, Xi   431
Yoon, Kuk-Jin   181
Young, Erik   290
Yu, Mingxin   163
Yu, Qihang   128
Yu, Shaozuo   163
Yu, Zeren   381
Yuan, Chun   74
Yuan, Peng   237
Yuan, Xiaoding   128
Yuille, Alan   128, 163

Zafeiriou, Stefanos   467
Zelenka, Claudius   363
Zhang, Haoxian   74
Zhang, Huijie   381
Zhang, Shiquan   628
Zhang, Songyang   431
Zhang, Tong   715
Zhang, Yuzhen   522
Zhao, Bingchen   163
Zhao, Feng   628
Zhao, Qiang   237
Zhe, Xuefei   74
Zheng, Liang   38
Zhou, Yuxiang   467
Zhu, Benjin   680
Zong, Ziliang   557

Printed in the United States
by Baker & Taylor Publisher Services